D1631672

Yearbook
of Tourism Statistics

Data 2009–2013

2015 Edition

World Tourism Organization (UNWTO)
Calle Capitán Haya 42 · 28020 Madrid · Spain

Yearbook of Tourism Statistics, Data 2009 – 2013, 2015 Edition
ISBN (printed version):   978-92-844-1635-6
ISBN (electronic version): 978-92-844-1636-3

Published by the World Tourism Organization (UNWTO), Madrid, Spain.
First printing: 2015
All rights reserved.

Printed in Spain.

The designations employed and the presentation of material in this publication do not imply the expression of any opinions whatsoever on the part of the Secretariat of the World Tourism Organization concerning the legal status of any country, territory, city or area, or of its authorities or concerning the delimitation of its frontiers or boundaries.

World Tourism Organization (UNWTO)   Tel.: (+34) 915 678 100
Calle Capitán Haya, 42   Fax: (+34) 915 713 733
28020 Madrid   Website: www.unwto.org
Spain   E-mail: omt@unwto.org

Citation:

English:
World Tourism Organization (2015), *Yearbook of Tourism Statistics, Data 2009 – 2013, 2015 Edition*, UNWTO, Madrid.

Español:
Organización Mundial del Turismo (2015), *Anuario de estadísticas de turismo, 2009 – 2013, Edición 2015*, OMT, Madrid.

Français:
Organisation mondiale du tourisme (2015), *Annuaire des statistiques du tourisme, 2009 – 2013, édition 2015*, OMT, Madrid.

Foreword

Decision making requires reliable information to guide adequate policies and development strategies. To support countries monitor and better understand the impact and evolution of tourism across their economies, the World Tourism Organization (UNWTO) systematically gathers tourism statistics from countries and territories around the world into a vast database that, each year, gives way to two key statistical publications: the *Compendium of Tourism Statistics* and the *Yearbook of Tourism Statistics*. Together, these two publications constitute the most comprehensive statistical information available on the tourism sector.

The UNWTO *Compendium of Tourism Statistics* provides data and indicators on inbound, outbound and domestic tourism, as well as on the number and types of tourism industries, the number of employees by tourism industries, and macroeconomic indicators related to international tourism. This data is complemented by the *Yearbook of Tourism Statistics* which focuses specifically on inbound tourism related data (total arrivals and overnight stays), broken down by country of origin.

The statistics presented in the 2015 Editions of the *Compendium* and the *Yearbook* give an insight into tourism's multiple facets and its ever growing importance and are an indispensible reference guide for all tourism stakeholders. Above all, they provide decision makers with the evidence for more informed policy-making and, as a result, more sustainable tourism development.

Taleb Rifai
Secretary-General

Avant-propos

La prise de décision doit pouvoir s'appuyer sur des informations fiables permettant de définir des politiques et des stratégies de développement adéquates. Pour aider les pays à assurer le suivi de l'impact et de l'évolution du tourisme dans leurs économies et à en avoir une meilleure compréhension, l'Organisation mondiale du tourisme (OMT) procède à une collecte systématique de statistiques du tourisme auprès de pays et de territoires du monde entier. Ces statistiques sont rassemblées dans une vaste base de données qui permet, chaque année, de faire paraître deux publications statistiques clés : le *Compendium des statistiques du tourisme* et l'*Annuaire des statistiques du tourisme*. À elles deux, ces publications offrent les informations statistiques les plus complètes sur le secteur touristique.

Le *Compendium des statistiques du tourisme* préparé par l'OMT contient des données et des indicateurs sur le tourisme récepteur, émetteur et interne, sur le nombre et les types d'industries touristiques et le nombre de salariés par industrie touristique, ainsi que des indicateurs macroéconomiques liés au tourisme international. Ces données sont complétées par l'*Annuaire des statistiques du tourisme* qui se concentre spécifiquement sur les données liées au tourisme récepteur (nombre total d'arrivées et de nuitées), avec une ventilation par pays d'origine.

Les statistiques présentées dans les éditions 2015 du *Compendium* et de l'*Annuaire* apportent un éclairage sur les multiples facettes du tourisme et sur son importance croissante. Elles constituent un guide de référence incontournable pour toutes les parties prenantes du secteur touristique. Et par-dessus tout, elles fournissent aux décideurs les éléments d'appréciation dont ils ont besoin pour formuler des politiques en connaissance de cause et, partant, assurer un développement plus durable du tourisme.

Taleb Rifai
Secrétaire général

Prólogo

La adopción de decisiones requiere información fiable que permita orientar adecuadamente las políticas y las estrategias de desarrollo. Con el fin de ayudar a los países a supervisar y entender mejor la incidencia y la evolución del turismo en su economía, la Organización Mundial del Turismo (OMT) compila sistemáticamente estadísticas de turismo de países y territorios de todo el mundo en una extensa base de datos que cada año da lugar a dos publicaciones estadísticas clave: el *Compendio de estadísticas de turismo* y el *Anuario de estadísticas de turismo*. Juntas, estas dos publicaciones constituyen la más completa información estadística disponible sobre el sector turístico.

El *Compendio de estadísticas de turismo* de la OMT proporciona datos e indicadores sobre turismo receptor, emisor e interno, sobre el número y los tipos de industrias turísticas, sobre el número de asalariados por industria turística y sobre aspectos macroeconómicos relacionados con el turismo internacional. Estos datos se complementan con el *Anuario de estadísticas de turismo* que se centra específicamente en los datos relacionados con el turismo receptor (totales de llegadas y de pernoctaciones) desglosados por país de origen.

Las estadísticas presentadas en las ediciones de 2015 del *Compendio* y del *Anuario* permiten explorar las múltiples facetas del turismo y su creciente importancia y son una guía de referencia indispensable para todos los agentes del turismo. Sobre todo, proporcionan datos fehacientes a los responsables públicos para que sus políticas tengan mayor fundamento y, como resultado, promuevan el desarrollo de un turismo más sostenible.

Taleb Rifai
Secretario General

TABLE OF CONTENTS

TABLE OF CONTENTS

Pages

Pages

viii

TABLE OF CONTENTS

COUNTRY TABLES BY GEOGRAPHICAL ORDER

AFRICA – AFRIQUE – ÁFRICA

East Africa – Afrique orientale – África Oriental

Central Africa – Afrique centrale – África Central

North Africa – Afrique du Nord – África del Norte

Southern Africa – Afrique australe – África Austral

West Africa – Afrique occidentale – África Occidental

AMERICAS – AMÉRIQUES – AMÉRICAS

Caribbean – Caraïbes – El Caribe

Yearbook of Tourism Statistics, Data 2009 – 2013, 2015 Edition

TABLE OF CONTENTS

TABLE OF CONTENTS

Pages

Pages

n.a. Not available

INTRODUCTION

The United Nations recognizes the World Tourism Organization (UNWTO) as the appropriate organization to collect, analyse, publish, standardise and improve the statistics of tourism and to promote the integration of these statistics within the sphere of the United Nations' system.

The *Yearbook of Tourism Statistics 2015 Edition* presents inbound tourism data for 198 countries and territories, broken down by country of origin. It is the 67th edition in a series initiated in 1947. It constitutes, together with the *Compendium of Tourism Statistics*, the World Tourism Organization's (UNWTO) main dataset and publications on annual tourism statistics, both under the responsibility of the Statistics and Tourism Satellite Account Programme.

The *Yearbook* contains data on total arrivals and overnight stays of international inbound tourism, broken down by country of origin for both arrivals and overnight stays.

> **Arrivals**

    A.   Border statistics
- Table 1.   Arrivals of non-resident tourists at national borders
- Table 2.   Arrivals of non-resident visitors at national borders

    B.   Statistics on accommodation establishments
- Table 3.   Arrivals of non-resident tourists in hotels and similar establishments
- Table 4.   Arrivals of non-resident tourists in all types of accommodation establishments.

When a person visits the same country several times a year, each visit is counted as one arrival. If a person visits several countries during the course of a single trip, his/her arrival in each country is also recorded separately. Consequently, *arrivals* are not necessarily equal to the number of persons travelling, as one person can generate several arrivals.

Arrivals data correspond to international visitors to the economic territory of the country of reference and include both tourists and same-day, non-resident visitors.

Data may be obtained from different sources: border statistics derived from administrative records (police, immigration, traffic counts, and other types of controls), border surveys and registrations at accommodation establishments.

> **Overnight stays**

- Table 5.   Overnight stays of non-resident tourists in hotels and similar establishments
- Table 6.   Overnight stays of non-resident tourists in all types of accommodation establishments.

Overnight stays refers to the number of nights spent by non-resident tourists in accommodation establishments (*guests*). If one person travels to a country and spends five nights there, that makes five tourist overnight stays (or person-nights).

In the 2015 hardcover edition of the *Yearbook*, the titles of the tables, names of countries, regions and sub-regions as well as the classification included in the tables are provided in English only, with notes in English, French and Spanish. Countries are classified according to the English alphabetical order. Data published originates from official sources and has undergone various checks by UNWTO's Statistics and Tourism Satellite Account Programme, which consults the reporting entity in the event that discrepancies are detected.

The 2015 Edition of the *Yearbook* reflects official data as entered in the UNWTO database as of 31 December 2014. Any corrections or changes in the tables received after this date will be included in the next edition of the *Yearbook*. Due to the rounding in the partial figures, the totals shown in the different tables of the *Yearbook* may not coincide with the totals shown in the basic indicators of the *Compendium of Tourism Statistics*.

INTRODUCTION

UNWTO wishes to express its gratitude to the national tourism administrations and national statistical offices for their valuable support, recognizing especially the crucial role of all contributing countries and territories for their continued commitment to the development and improvement of tourism statistics.

Madrid, January 2015

INTRODUCTION

L'Organisation des Nations Unies reconnaît en l'Organisation mondiale du tourisme (OMT) l'organisme approprié pour recueillir, analyser, publier, unifier et améliorer les statistiques touristiques et promouvoir l'intégration de ces statistiques à l'échelle du système des Nations Unies.

L'édition 2015 de l'*Annuaire des statistiques du tourisme* présente des données sur le tourisme récepteur de 198 pays et territoires, ventilées par pays d'origine. C'est la 67ème édition d'une série lancée en 1947. L'Annuaire et le *Compendium des statistiques du tourisme* constituent à eux deux les principales réalisations de l'Organisation mondiale du tourisme (OMT) en termes de bases de données et de publications sur les statistiques annuelles du tourisme. Tous deux sont préparés sous la direction du programme Statistiques et compte satellite du tourisme.

L'*Annuaire* contient des données sur le nombre total d'arrivées et de nuitées du tourisme récepteur international, ventilées par pays d'origine pour les arrivées comme pour les nuitées.

> **Arrivées**

    A.   Statistiques aux frontières
- Tableau 1. Arrivées de touristes non résidents aux frontières nationales
- Tableau 2. Arrivées de visiteurs non résidents aux frontières nationales

    B.   Statistiques sur les établissements d'hébergement
- Tableau 3. Nuitées de touristes non résidents dans les hôtels et établissements assimilés
- Tableau 4. Nuitées de touristes non résidents dans tous les types d'établissements d'hébergement.

Lorsqu'une personne visite le même pays plusieurs fois dans l'année, chacune de ses visites est comptée séparément comme une arrivée. Si une personne visite plusieurs pays au cours d'un seul et même voyage, son arrivée dans chaque pays est elle aussi enregistrée séparément. Par conséquent, le nombre d'*arrivées* n'est pas forcément égal au nombre de personnes qui voyagent, étant donné qu'une personne peut donner lieu à plusieurs arrivées.

Les données des arrivées correspondent aux visiteurs internationaux sur le territoire économique du pays dont il s'agit, visiteurs qui comprennent à la fois les touristes et les visiteurs de la journée (excursionnistes) non résidents.

Ces données peuvent être obtenues de différentes sources : statistiques aux frontières tirées des registres administratifs (police, immigration, comptages de véhicules et autres types de contrôle), enquêtes aux frontières et registres des établissements d'hébergement.

> **Nuitées**

- Tableau 5.   Nuitées de touristes non résidents dans les hôtels et établissements assimilés
- Tableau 6.   Nuitées de touristes non résidents dans tous les types d'établissements d'hébergement.

Les *nuitées* correspondent au nombre de nuits que les touristes non résidents ont passées dans les établissements d'hébergement (en qualité de *clients*). Si une personne se rend dans un pays et y passe cinq nuits, on enregistre cinq nuitées de touriste (ou nuits-personne).

Dans l'édition 2015 reliée de l'*Annuaire*, les titres des tableaux, les noms des pays, des régions et des sous-régions ainsi que la classification incluse dans les tableaux apparaissent uniquement en anglais, tandis que les notes sont en anglais, espagnol et français. Les pays sont classés selon l'ordre alphabétique anglais. Les données publiées proviennent de sources officielles et ont fait l'objet de différentes vérifications de la part du programme de l'OMT Statistiques et compte satellite du tourisme, qui contacte l'entité déclarante si elle repère des divergences.

L'édition 2015 de l'*Annuaire* reflète les données officielles telles qu'elles ont été saisies dans la base de données de l'OMT au 31 décembre 2014. Toutes les corrections ou modifications ayant été

INTRODUCTION

reçues après cette date apparaîtront dans l'édition suivante de l'*Annuaire*. En raison de l'arrondissement des données partielles, les totaux figurant dans les différents tableaux de l'*Annuaire* peuvent ne pas correspondre aux totaux des indicateurs de base du *Compendium des statistiques du tourisme*.

L'OMT exprime sa gratitude, pour leur aide précieuse, aux administrations nationales du tourisme et aux bureaux nationaux de statistique. Elle tient à saluer plus spécialement le rôle crucial joué par tous les pays et territoires ayant apporté leur contribution, témoignant de leur engagement constant à l'appui du développement et de l'amélioration des statistiques du tourisme.

Madrid, janvier 2015

INTRODUCCIÓN

Las Naciones Unidas reconocen que la Organización Mundial del Turismo es la organización competente para recoger, analizar, publicar, uniformar y mejorar las estadísticas de turismo y promover la integración de esas estadísticas en el marco del sistema de las Naciones Unidas.

La edición de 2015 del Anuario de estadísticas de turismo presenta datos sobre turismo receptor para 198 países y territorios, desglosados por país de origen. Constituye la 67ª edición de una serie que comenzó en 1947. El Anuario y el Compendio de estadísticas de turismo son los conjuntos de datos y publicaciones más importantes de la Organización Mundial del Turismo (OMT) sobre estadísticas anuales de turismo, siendo ambos responsabilidad del Programa de Estadísticas y Cuenta Satélite del Turismo.

El Anuario contiene datos sobre totales de llegadas y pernoctaciones del turismo receptor internacional, desglosados en ambos casos por país de origen.

> **Llegadas**

    A.   Estadísticas de fronteras
- Tabla 1.   Llegadas de turistas no residentes a las fronteras nacionales
- Tabla 2.   Llegadas de visitantes no residentes a las fronteras nacionales

    B.   Estadísticas en establecimientos de alojamiento
- Tabla 3.   Llegadas de turistas no residentes a los hoteles y establecimientos asimilados
- Tabla 4.   Llegadas de turistas no residentes a todo tipo de establecimientos de alojamiento

Cuando una persona visita un mismo país varias veces en un año, cada una de esas visitas se cuenta como una llegada. Si una persona visita varios países en el transcurso de un mismo viaje, cada llegada a uno de esos países se registra también por separado. Por lo tanto, el número de *llegadas* no coincide necesariamente con el número de personas que viajan, ya que una persona puede generar varias llegadas.

Los datos de llegadas se refieren a los visitantes internacionales que llegan al territorio económico del país de referencia, sean turistas o visitantes del día no residentes.

Los datos pueden proceder de diversas fuentes: estadísticas de fronteras basadas en registros administrativos (policía, inmigración, recuentos de circulación y otros tipos de controles), encuestas en las fronteras y registros en establecimientos de alojamiento.

> **Pernoctaciones**

- Tabla 5.   Pernoctaciones de turistas no residentes en hoteles y establecimientos asimilados
- Tabla 6.   Pernoctaciones de turistas no residentes en todo tipo de establecimientos de alojamiento

Las *pernoctaciones* se refieren al número de noches que pasan los turistas no residentes en establecimientos de alojamiento (*huéspedes*). Si una persona viaja a un país y pasa en él cinco noches, se contarán cinco pernoctaciones turísticas (o pernoctaciones/persona).

En la edición impresa de 2015 del *Anuario,* los títulos de las tablas, los nombres de los países, las regiones y las subregiones, así como la clasificación incluida en las tablas, figuran únicamente en inglés, mientras que las notas aparecen en español, francés e inglés. Los países aparecen siguiendo el orden alfabético en inglés. Los datos publicados proceden de fuentes oficiales y han sido comprobados por el Programa de Estadísticas y Cuenta Satélite de Turismo de la OMT, que consulta a la entidad en caso de que se detecten discrepancias.

La edición de 2015 del *Anuario* muestra los datos oficiales introducidos en la base de datos estadística de la OMT a 31 de diciembre de 2014. Por lo tanto, cualquier corrección o cambio en las tablas recibido después de esta fecha aparecerá en la siguiente edición del *Anuario*. Debido al redondeo de las cifras parciales, los totales que figuran en las distintas tablas del *Anuario* pueden no coincidir con los totales que aparecen en los indicadores básicos del *Compendio de estadísticas de turismo*.

La Organización Mundial del Turismo desea expresar su agradecimiento por su valioso apoyo a las administraciones nacionales de turismo y a las oficinas nacionales de estadística, y reconocer especialmente el papel crucial de todos los países y territorios que contribuyen con sus datos y mantienen su compromiso de desarrollar y mejorar las estadísticas de turismo.

Madrid, enero de 2015

Country tables
2009-2013

➤ <u>Arrivals</u>

    A.   Border statistics

- Table 1.   Arrivals of non-resident tourists at national borders

- Table 2.   Arrivals of non-resident visitors at national borders

    B.   Statistics on accommodation establishments

- Table 3.   Arrivals of non-resident tourists in hotels and similar establishments

- Table 4.   Arrivals of non-resident tourists in all types of accommodation establishments

➤ <u>Overnight stays</u>

- Table 5.   Overnight stays of non-resident tourists in hotels and similar establishments

- Table 6.   Overnight stays of non-resident tourists in all types of accommodation establishments

ALBANIA

2. Arrivals of non-resident visitors at national borders, by nationality

	2009	2010	2011	2012	2013	Market share 2013	% Change 2013-2012
TOTAL (*)	1,855,634	2,417,337	2,932,132	3,513,666	3,255,988	100.00	-7.33
AFRICA	211	3,193	432	1,057	919	0.03	-13.06
CENTRAL AFRICA	23	12	12	175	162	0.00	-7.43
Democratic Republic of the Congo	23	12	12	175	162	0.00	-7.43
NORTH AFRICA	164	3,041	252	535	446	0.01	-16.64
Morocco	78	2,924	139	184	40	0.00	-78.26
Sudan	33	54	39	266	246	0.01	-7.52
Tunisia	53	63	74	85	160	0.00	88.24
SOUTHERN AFRICA	24	140	168	347	311	0.01	-10.37
South Africa	24	140	168	347	311	0.01	-10.37
AMERICAS	59,945	61,878	70,291	73,810	73,291	2.25	-0.70
CARIBBEAN	50	782	263	627	142	0.00	-77.35
Dominican Republic	18	59	20	28	117	0.00	317.86
Saint Lucia	32	723	243	599	25	0.00	-95.83
CENTRAL AMERICA	60	25	59	78	87	0.00	11.54
El Salvador	26	11	18	20	46	0.00	130.00
Honduras	24	13	32	52	25	0.00	-51.92
Nicaragua	10	1	9	6	16	0.00	166.67
NORTH AMERICA	57,875	59,941	67,529	71,454	70,247	2.16	-1.69
Canada	9,243	10,301	11,468	12,761	12,430	0.38	-2.59
Mexico	33	103	111	72	207	0.01	187.50
United States of America	48,599	49,537	55,950	58,621	57,610	1.77	-1.72
SOUTH AMERICA	1,960	1,130	2,440	1,651	2,815	0.09	70.50
Argentina	140	294	293	310	462	0.01	49.03
Brazil	1,660	609	1,871	1,084	1,956	0.06	80.44
Colombia	66	60	97	100	173	0.01	73.00
Peru	51	101	108	84	146	0.00	73.81
Uruguay	11	22	22	23	19	0.00	-17.39
Venezuela	32	44	49	50	59	0.00	18.00
EAST ASIA AND THE PACIFIC	28,433	11,361	17,418	19,689	23,628	0.73	20.01
NORTH-EAST ASIA	19,991	4,303	7,170	9,126	11,153	0.34	22.21
China	1,346	1,718	1,967	3,129	3,961	0.12	26.59
Japan	1,116	1,529	2,713	2,475	3,126	0.10	26.30
Korea, Republic of	17,529	1,056	2,490	3,522	4,066	0.12	15.45
SOUTH-EAST ASIA	835	759	2,220	923	1,640	0.05	77.68
Malaysia	238	243	1,423	286	769	0.02	168.88
Philippines	439	397	547	443	576	0.02	30.02
Singapore	115	62	110	126	236	0.01	87.30
Thailand	43	57	140	68	59	0.00	-13.24
AUSTRALASIA	7,607	6,299	8,028	9,640	10,835	0.33	12.40
Australia	6,435	5,429	6,753	8,337	9,416	0.29	12.94
New Zealand	1,172	870	1,275	1,303	1,419	0.04	8.90
EUROPE	1,512,734	2,238,958	2,738,846	3,214,111	2,963,583	91.02	-7.79
CENTRAL/EASTERN EUROPE	60,880	63,722	82,418	90,643	112,333	3.45	23.93
Bulgaria	14,327	13,760	16,117	18,759	20,802	0.64	10.89
Czech Republic	7,000	7,006	8,165	9,350	8,402	0.26	-10.14
Estonia	1,143	510	640	1,068	1,125	0.03	5.34
Hungary	4,697	5,939	6,319	6,580	6,661	0.20	1.23
Lithuania	984	889	1,312	1,733	3,312	0.10	91.11
Poland	17,037	17,350	23,869	26,528	35,751	1.10	34.77
Republic of Moldova	243	365	491	454	635	0.02	39.87
Romania	7,242	8,705	10,399	10,278	10,707	0.33	4.17
Russian Federation	4,555	5,657	9,752	10,074	16,194	0.50	60.75
Slovakia	2,456	2,133	2,861	2,928	4,190	0.13	43.10
Ukraine	1,196	1,408	2,493	2,891	4,554	0.14	57.52
NORTHERN EUROPE	79,931	85,463	109,924	117,434	119,016	3.66	1.35
Denmark	2,831	3,186	4,068	4,893	4,886	0.15	-0.14
Finland	3,094	3,299	4,671	4,154	5,087	0.16	22.46
Iceland	233	383	236	317	239	0.01	-24.61

3

ALBANIA

2. Arrivals of non-resident visitors at national borders, by nationality

	2009	2010	2011	2012	2013	Market share 2013	% Change 2013-2012
Ireland	2,910	2,425	2,701	2,677	3,231	0.10	20.69
Norway	3,654	5,315	7,556	9,519	10,554	0.32	10.87
Sweden	6,073	8,604	14,673	17,335	14,646	0.45	-15.51
United Kingdom	61,136	62,251	76,019	78,539	80,373	2.47	2.34
SOUTHERN EUROPE	**1,220,254**	**1,912,383**	**2,320,746**	**2,759,374**	**2,467,195**	**75.77**	**-10.59**
Bosnia and Herzegovina	3,833	8,646	9,094	11,334	14,192	0.44	25.22
Croatia	11,824	26,438	20,734	22,524	23,554	0.72	4.57
Greece	106,227	113,008	155,086	225,175	269,201	8.27	19.55
Holy See	8	14		14	16	0.00	14.29
Italy	109,702	125,036	135,389	147,018	170,370	5.23	15.88
Malta	781	1,586	735	3,852	1,987	0.06	-48.42
Montenegro	128,547	123,833	159,838	186,536	174,519	5.36	-6.44
Portugal	780	640	1,167	2,003	1,344	0.04	-32.90
Serbia	40,873	43,940	48,029	38,156	40,790	1.25	6.90
Slovenia	9,745	9,834	11,283	10,554	9,237	0.28	-12.48
Spain	3,573	3,813	4,288	4,184	4,734	0.15	13.15
TFYR of Macedonia	330,939	276,268	335,380	399,281	432,646	13.29	8.36
Other countries of Southern Europe	473,422	1,179,327	1,439,723	1,708,743	1,324,605	40.68	-22.48
WESTERN EUROPE	**116,030**	**141,187**	**186,531**	**200,462**	**210,845**	**6.48**	**5.18**
Austria	11,809	15,659	21,149	22,562	21,467	0.66	-4.85
Belgium	9,609	11,094	14,973	16,189	16,259	0.50	0.43
France	20,165	25,651	30,410	30,128	36,677	1.13	21.74
Germany	48,408	55,919	73,102	70,060	79,925	2.45	14.08
Luxembourg	388	540	690	798	954	0.03	19.55
Netherlands	9,691	10,055	15,333	18,179	19,800	0.61	8.92
Switzerland	15,960	22,269	30,874	42,546	35,763	1.10	-15.94
EAST MEDITERRANEAN EUROPE	**35,639**	**36,203**	**39,227**	**46,198**	**54,194**	**1.66**	**17.31**
Cyprus	733	850	890	1,082	953	0.03	-11.92
Israel	4,337	1,809	2,121	2,292	3,032	0.09	32.29
Turkey	30,569	33,544	36,216	42,824	50,209	1.54	17.25
MIDDLE EAST	**1,313**	**1,247**	**1,178**	**1,524**	**3,944**	**0.12**	**158.79**
Egypt	675	724	616	567	79	0.00	-86.07
Iraq	26	24	17	31	68	0.00	119.35
Jordan	82	72	83	154	152	0.00	-1.30
Kuwait	94	41	29	195	1,500	0.05	669.23
Libya	37	65	36	62	153	0.00	146.77
Palestine	26	32	39	55	844	0.03	1,434.55
Saudi Arabia	202	151	206	318	380	0.01	19.50
Syrian Arab Republic	171	138	152	142	768	0.02	440.85
SOUTH ASIA	**661**	**764**	**909**	**1,135**	**961**	**0.03**	**-15.33**
Bangladesh	30	31	42	45	48	0.00	6.67
India	393	423	514	565	527	0.02	-6.73
Iran, Islamic Republic of	150	196	265	408	256	0.01	-37.25
Nepal	7	10	7	2	7	0.00	250.00
Pakistan	81	104	81	115	123	0.00	6.96
NOT SPECIFIED	**252,337**	**99,936**	**103,058**	**202,340**	**189,662**	**5.83**	**-6.27**
Other countries of the World	252,337	99,936	103,058	202,340	189,662	5.83	-6.27

Yearbook of Tourism Statistics, Data 2009 – 2013, 2015 Edition

ALGERIA

2. Arrivals of non-resident visitors at national borders, by nationality

	2009	2010	2011	2012	2013	Market share 2013	% Change 2013-2012
TOTAL (*)	1,911,506	2,070,496	2,394,887	2,634,056			
AFRICA	257,936	310,684	554,380	635,237			
NORTH AFRICA	215,211	262,337	502,251	552,721			
Morocco	17,300	17,115	17,218	21,125			
Tunisia	197,911	245,222	485,033	531,596			
WEST AFRICA	29,277	35,429	38,991	42,387			
Mali	23,907	30,648	34,478	35,752			
Mauritania	4,450	4,318	3,445	4,435			
Niger	920	463	1,068	2,200			
OTHER AFRICA	13,448	12,918	13,138	40,129			
Other countries of Africa	13,448	12,918	13,138	40,129			
AMERICAS	13,120	10,495	12,265	11,844			
NORTH AMERICA	10,085	7,442	9,155	9,383			
Canada	5,010	3,151	4,063	3,844			
Mexico	380	370	393	525			
United States of America	4,695	3,921	4,699	5,014			
SOUTH AMERICA	857	898	733	708			
Argentina	273	376	275	256			
Brazil	584	522	458	452			
OTHER AMERICAS	2,178	2,155	2,377	1,753			
Other countries of the Americas	2,178	2,155	2,377	1,753			
EAST ASIA AND THE PACIFIC	46,613	42,171	55,246	54,978			
NORTH-EAST ASIA	4,468	3,325	23,725	28,951			
China			20,153	25,383			
Japan	4,468	3,325	3,572	3,568			
AUSTRALASIA	662	775	832	571			
Australia	560	667	687	474			
New Zealand	102	108	145	97			
OTHER EAST ASIA AND THE PACIFIC	41,483	38,071	30,689	25,456			
Other countries of Asia	41,483	38,071	30,689	25,456			
EUROPE	283,843	241,637	218,629	239,578			
NORTHERN EUROPE	12,968	10,688	11,023	10,207			
Denmark	668	441	450	462			
Finland	461	336	389	361			
Norway	884	660	935	687			
Sweden	1,580	1,227	1,257	1,285			
United Kingdom	9,375	8,024	7,992	7,412			
SOUTHERN EUROPE	49,634	49,183	53,310	64,336			
Greece	581	525	548	960			
Italy	18,824	16,886	19,127	23,070			
Portugal	6,483	6,139	5,584	7,257			
Spain	23,746	25,633	28,051	33,049			
WESTERN EUROPE	197,546	161,654	133,199	141,767			
Austria	1,253	1,037	1,121	1,292			
Belgium	6,843	6,414	5,889	6,319			
France	171,314	140,129	112,241	119,518			
Germany	12,148	9,244	9,492	9,937			
Luxembourg	176	193	93	136			
Netherlands	2,217	1,764	1,541	1,490			
Switzerland	3,595	2,873	2,822	3,075			
EAST MEDITERRANEAN EUROPE	12,140	9,783	9,653	10,369			
Turkey	12,140	9,783	9,653	10,369			
OTHER EUROPE	11,555	10,329	11,444	12,899			
Other countries of Europe	11,555	10,329	11,444	12,899			
MIDDLE EAST	54,298	50,000	61,122	40,318			
Libya	16,359	19,313	28,615	25,850			
Syrian Arab Republic			12,444				
Other countries of Middle East	37,939	30,687	20,063	14,468			
NOT SPECIFIED	1,255,696	1,415,509	1,493,245	1,652,101			
Nationals Residing Abroad	1,255,696	1,415,509	1,493,245	1,652,101			

5

AMERICAN SAMOA

1. Arrivals of non-resident tourists at national borders, by nationality

	2009	2010	2011	2012	2013	Market share 2013	% Change 2013-2012
TOTAL	23,544	22,629	21,929	21,612			
AFRICA	25	15	9	40			
SOUTHERN AFRICA				10			
South Africa				10			
OTHER AFRICA	25	15	9	30			
Other countries of Africa				30			
All countries of Africa	25	15	9				
AMERICAS	7,876	7,727	6,717	6,618			
CENTRAL AMERICA	20	28	19	238			
All countries of Central America	20	28	19	238			
NORTH AMERICA	7,819	7,672	6,662	6,311			
Canada	85	132	97	128			
Mexico	10	17	17	24			
United States of America	7,724	7,523	6,548	6,159			
SOUTH AMERICA	37	27	36	69			
All countries of South America	37	27	36	69			
EAST ASIA AND THE PACIFIC	15,165	14,465	14,751	14,487			
NORTH-EAST ASIA	570	430	577	649			
China	325	257	401	400			
Japan	74	40	58	64			
Korea, Republic of	69	83	55	116			
Taiwan, Province of China	102	50	63	69			
SOUTH-EAST ASIA	408	342	377	509			
Indonesia	61	38	43	68			
Malaysia	5	3	10	14			
Philippines	323	289	307	383			
Singapore	15	10	15	27			
Thailand	4	2	2	3			
Viet Nam				13			
Other countries of South-East Asia				1			
AUSTRALASIA	4,116	3,565	3,717	3,636			
Australia	933	812	910	892			
New Zealand	3,183	2,753	2,807	2,744			
MELANESIA	415	387	367	462			
Fiji	312	355	332	352			
Papua New Guinea	19	15	9	32			
Solomon Islands	24	9	18	56			
Vanuatu	60	8	8	22			
MICRONESIA	30	28	24	29			
Kiribati	11	8	6	11			
Micronesia, Federated States of	19	20	18	12			
Palau				6			
POLYNESIA	9,572	9,669	9,646	9,157			
Samoa	9,244	9,301	9,439	8,909			
Tonga	328	368	207	248			
OTHER EAST ASIA AND THE PACIFIC	54	44	43	45			
Other countries of Oceania	54	44	43	45			
EUROPE	410	367	380	373			
CENTRAL/EASTERN EUROPE	3	3	7	12			
Russian Federation	3	3	7	12			
NORTHERN EUROPE	205	165	143	163			
Denmark	7	6	7	4			
Finland	4	5	3	1			
Norway	26	8	5	16			
Sweden	11	5	7	15			
United Kingdom	157	141	121	127			
SOUTHERN EUROPE	68	45	50	74			
Italy	34	9	19	29			
Portugal	16	18	14	27			

Yearbook of Tourism Statistics, Data 2009 – 2013, 2015 Edition

AMERICAN SAMOA

1. Arrivals of non-resident tourists at national borders, by nationality

	2009	2010	2011	2012	2013	Market share 2013	% Change 2013-2012
Spain	18	18	17	18			
WESTERN EUROPE	**113**	**131**	**126**	**110**			
Austria	6	3	4	4			
Belgium	2	4	1	1			
France	38	36	53	40			
Germany	40	63	39	41			
Netherlands	20	18	18	20			
Switzerland	7	7	11	4			
OTHER EUROPE	**21**	**23**	**54**	**14**			
Other countries of Europe	21	23	54	14			
MIDDLE EAST	**2**	**2**	**5**	**1**			
All countries of Middle East	2	2	5	1			
SOUTH ASIA	**35**	**26**	**44**	**70**			
Bangladesh				5			
India	32	18	18	50			
Nepal				7			
Pakistan		1	1	1			
Sri Lanka	3	7	25	7			
NOT SPECIFIED	**31**	**27**	**23**	**23**			
Other countries of the World	31	27	23	23			

Yearbook of Tourism Statistics, Data 2009 – 2013, 2015 Edition

ANDORRA

1. Arrivals of non-resident tourists at national borders, by country of residence

		2009	2010	2011	2012	2013	Market share 2013	% Change 2013-2012
TOTAL	(*)	1,829,869	1,808,001	2,241,559	2,237,939	2,335,314	100.00	4.35
EUROPE		1,829,869	1,808,001	2,241,559	2,237,939	2,335,314	100.00	4.35
SOUTHERN EUROPE		1,409,868	1,414,298	1,588,907	1,570,604	1,643,417	70.37	4.64
Spain		1,409,868	1,414,298	1,588,907	1,570,604	1,643,417	70.37	4.64
WESTERN EUROPE		332,783	310,800	341,484	345,898	392,750	16.82	13.55
France		332,783	310,800	341,484	345,898	392,750	16.82	13.55
OTHER EUROPE		87,218	82,903	311,168	321,437	299,147	12.81	-6.93
Other countries of Europe		87,218	82,903	311,168	321,437	299,147	12.81	-6.93

Yearbook of Tourism Statistics, Data 2009 – 2013, 2015 Edition

ANGOLA

1. Arrivals of non-resident tourists at national borders, by country of residence

	2009	2010	2011	2012	2013	Market share 2013	% Change 2013-2012
TOTAL	365,784	424,919	481,207	528,133	650,033	100.00	23.08
AFRICA	46,476	72,519	147,903	173,297	222,830	34.28	28.58
EAST AFRICA	4,271	7,418	15,740	16,847	24,625	3.79	46.17
Burundi	21	34	37	40	33	0.01	-17.50
Comoros	5						
Djibouti	1	6	6	2			
Eritrea	366	351	467	645	644	0.10	-0.16
Ethiopia	252	383	300	345	190	0.03	-44.93
Kenya	326	411	516	465	274	0.04	-41.08
Madagascar	48	91	77	138	10	0.00	-92.75
Malawi	98	96	113	92	52	0.01	-43.48
Mauritius	104	43	63	214	20	0.00	-90.65
Mozambique	1,550	3,089	1,577	1,720	2,311	0.36	34.36
Rwanda	75	71	60	71	107	0.02	50.70
Seychelles	9	7	3	17			
Somalia	10	16	120	254	67	0.01	-73.62
Uganda	67	70	157	84	160	0.02	90.48
United Republic of Tanzania	140	120	174	380	212	0.03	-44.21
Zambia	601	1,313	10,894	10,976	19,575	3.01	78.34
Zimbabwe	598	1,317	1,176	1,404	970	0.15	-30.91
CENTRAL AFRICA	5,414	9,387	23,203	11,202	19,727	3.03	76.10
Cameroon	633	3,405	556	470	622	0.10	32.34
Central African Republic	22	21	18	161	13	0.00	-91.93
Chad	79	69	61	104	67	0.01	-35.58
Congo	728	568	9,436	660	5,185	0.80	685.61
Democratic Republic of the Congo	890	446	10,241	6,958	9,528	1.47	36.94
Equatorial Guinea	72	85	101	91	107	0.02	17.58
Gabon	294	956	142	229	171	0.03	-25.33
Sao Tome and Principe	2,696	3,837	2,648	2,529	4,034	0.62	59.51
NORTH AFRICA	2,956	9,364	967	998	872	0.13	-12.63
Algeria	2,589	3,460	327	406	449	0.07	10.59
Morocco	115	2,762	295	150	177	0.03	18.00
Sudan	72	30	96	46	53	0.01	15.22
Tunisia	180	3,112	249	396	193	0.03	-51.26
SOUTHERN AFRICA	27,238	32,872	100,467	136,504	167,925	25.83	23.02
Botswana	130	88	145	179	100	0.02	-44.13
Lesotho	19	20	40	27	17	0.00	-37.04
Namibia	1,225	3,506	37,834	54,219	73,614	11.32	35.77
South Africa	25,803	29,217	62,380	82,021	94,177	14.49	14.82
Swaziland	61	41	68	58	17	0.00	-70.69
WEST AFRICA	6,597	13,478	6,321	7,746	8,166	1.26	5.42
Benin	90	1,134	47	58	41	0.01	-29.31
Burkina Faso	68	101	46	49	49	0.01	
Cabo Verde	1,085	821	957	1,070	1,294	0.20	20.93
Côte d'Ivoire	571	1,495	309	228			
Gambia	327	230	303	393	479	0.07	21.88
Ghana	289	1,483	325	321	266	0.04	-17.13
Guinea	280	32	27	128	27	0.00	-78.91
Guinea-Bissau	353	974	495	452	394	0.06	-12.83
Liberia	31	39	18	29	138	0.02	375.86
Mali	532	1,839	392	736	551	0.08	-25.14
Mauritania	426	449	471	1,425	1,208	0.19	-15.23
Niger	18	131	48	112	1,763	0.27	1,474.11
Nigeria	2,038	2,996	2,528	2,337	1,600	0.25	-31.54
Senegal	341	1,635	215	254	222	0.03	-12.60
Sierra Leone	91	56	70	111	123	0.02	10.81
Togo	57	63	70	43	11	0.00	-74.42
OTHER AFRICA			1,205		1,515	0.23	
Other countries of Africa			1,205		1,515	0.23	

9

Yearbook of Tourism Statistics, Data 2009 – 2013, 2015 Edition

ANGOLA

1. Arrivals of non-resident tourists at national borders, by country of residence

	2009	2010	2011	2012	2013	Market share 2013	% Change 2013-2012
AMERICAS	**76,321**	**82,835**	**58,233**	**67,639**	**74,216**	**11.42**	**9.72**
CARIBBEAN	**5,674**	**4,811**	**4,454**	**5,309**	**5,481**	**0.84**	**3.24**
Antigua and Barbuda		1		20			
Aruba	4	1					
Bahamas	7	4		2			
Barbados		8					
Cuba	5,045	4,113	4,058	4,563	5,351	0.82	17.27
Dominica			6	46			
Dominican Republic	40	167	7	2	80	0.01	3,900.00
Grenada	2						
Guadeloupe	1						
Haiti	8	3	2	16	8	0.00	-50.00
Jamaica	8	12		43	39	0.01	-9.30
Martinique		1		103			
Puerto Rico	3	4			3	0.00	
Trinidad and Tobago	556	497	381	514			
CENTRAL AMERICA	**407**	**554**	**273**	**4,888**	**194**	**0.03**	**-96.03**
Belize	5	4	7	15			
Costa Rica	30	77	30	34	4	0.00	-88.24
El Salvador	33	15	9	5			
Guatemala	22	27	49	167	3	0.00	-98.20
Honduras	225	154	162	206	141	0.02	-31.55
Nicaragua	15	181	3	13	19	0.00	46.15
Panama	77	96	13	4,448	27	0.00	-99.39
NORTH AMERICA	**18,055**	**25,826**	**19,782**	**22,492**	**19,696**	**3.03**	**-12.43**
Canada	2,583	3,024	2,223	2,434	1,917	0.29	-21.24
Mexico	332	2,489	389	1,825	355	0.05	-80.55
United States of America	15,140	20,313	17,170	18,233	17,424	2.68	-4.44
SOUTH AMERICA	**52,185**	**51,644**	**33,683**	**34,950**	**48,845**	**7.51**	**39.76**
Argentina	1,492	1,849	789	1,870	823	0.13	-55.99
Bolivia	126	133	134	140	137	0.02	-2.14
Brazil	46,866	45,848	29,738	29,336	43,615	6.71	48.67
Chile	326	471	167	184	163	0.03	-11.41
Colombia	665	779	602	621	521	0.08	-16.10
Ecuador	230	498	144	144	152	0.02	5.56
Guyana	688	818	843	1,175	2,128	0.33	81.11
Paraguay	118	66	50	130	53	0.01	-59.23
Peru	595	353	388	437	403	0.06	-7.78
Uruguay	193	149	141	116	125	0.02	7.76
Venezuela	886	680	687	797	725	0.11	-9.03
OTHER AMERICAS				**41**			
Other countries of the Americas				41			
EAST ASIA AND THE PACIFIC	**66,492**	**80,515**	**87,626**	**94,326**	**105,747**	**16.27**	**12.11**
NORTH-EAST ASIA	**54,056**	**62,336**	**71,241**	**71,079**	**85,696**	**13.18**	**20.56**
China	51,900	60,577	69,907	69,334	84,300	12.97	21.59
Japan	759	904	800	856	633	0.10	-26.05
Korea, Dem. People's Republic of	461	246	135	175	157	0.02	-10.29
Korea, Republic of	821	504	279	531	371	0.06	-30.13
Macao, China	11	7	1	6	3	0.00	-50.00
Mongolia	1				176	0.03	
Taiwan, Province of China	103	98	119	177	56	0.01	-68.36
SOUTH-EAST ASIA	**11,021**	**15,538**	**15,210**	**22,021**	**17,987**	**2.77**	**-18.32**
Cambodia	2	5	1	2			
Indonesia	1,536	1,336	948	1,155	1,400	0.22	21.21
Malaysia	844	836	789	737	536	0.08	-27.27
Myanmar	3			44			
Philippines	6,096	8,414	7,452	8,553	7,516	1.16	-12.12
Singapore	295	299	225	1,617	225	0.03	-86.09
Thailand	180	288	313	157	142	0.02	-9.55

10

ANGOLA

1. Arrivals of non-resident tourists at national borders, by country of residence

	2009	2010	2011	2012	2013	Market share 2013	% Change 2013-2012
Timor-Leste	3	9	33	17	4	0.00	-76.47
Viet Nam	2,062	4,351	5,449	9,739	8,164	1.26	-16.17
AUSTRALASIA	**1,415**	**2,638**	**1,175**	**1,226**	**2,064**	**0.32**	**68.35**
Australia	1,197	1,473	944	913	1,728	0.27	89.27
New Zealand	218	1,165	231	313	336	0.05	7.35
MELANESIA		**3**					
Solomon Islands		3					
EUROPE	**161,169**	**170,381**	**170,488**	**176,663**	**231,266**	**35.58**	**30.91**
CENTRAL/EASTERN EUROPE	**9,545**	**10,412**	**7,837**	**12,091**	**9,227**	**1.42**	**-23.69**
Armenia	57	22	36	22	26	0.00	18.18
Azerbaijan	167	144	152	217	243	0.04	11.98
Belarus	251	165	242	1,895	191	0.03	-89.92
Bulgaria	322	229	262	396	629	0.10	58.84
Czech Republic	168	846	127	110	62	0.01	-43.64
Estonia	21	28	14	30	24	0.00	-20.00
Georgia	20	23	28	72	16	0.00	-77.78
Hungary	146	77	56	88			
Kazakhstan	129	95	86	230	78	0.01	-66.09
Kyrgyzstan	31	2					
Latvia	46	36	85	75	92	0.01	22.67
Lithuania	242	186	249	295	267	0.04	-9.49
Poland	1,395	1,949	1,803	2,033	1,953	0.30	-3.94
Republic of Moldova	837	1,381		1,101	1,019	0.16	-7.45
Romania	814	1,934	975	1,154	1,250	0.19	8.32
Russian Federation	2,694	1,484	1,737	1,849	1,589	0.24	-14.06
Slovakia	51	53	62	50	37	0.01	-26.00
Tajikistan	14	2	4		91	0.01	
Turkmenistan	20	6	18	87	90	0.01	3.45
Ukraine	1,994	1,670	1,794	2,264	1,445	0.22	-36.17
Uzbekistan	126	80	107	123	125	0.02	1.63
NORTHERN EUROPE	**20,613**	**22,586**	**36,398**	**34,687**	**35,895**	**5.52**	**3.48**
Denmark	1,332	957	939	1,150	1,309	0.20	13.83
Finland	71	90	712	106	105	0.02	-0.94
Iceland	14	24	10	51	407	0.06	698.04
Ireland	544	485	555	911	542	0.08	-40.50
Norway	2,269	1,728	1,836	1,953	1,593	0.25	-18.43
Sweden	513	536	414	480	191	0.03	-60.21
United Kingdom	15,870	18,766	31,932	30,036	31,748	4.88	5.70
SOUTHERN EUROPE	**97,328**	**109,916**	**94,454**	**102,906**	**154,872**	**23.83**	**50.50**
Albania	11	8	7	7			
Andorra	180	4	2				
Bosnia and Herzegovina	24	34	23	28			
Croatia	1,119	947	1,147	1,237	1,104	0.17	-10.75
Greece	105	116	109	122	766	0.12	527.87
Italy	4,259	3,854	4,133	4,137	4,409	0.68	6.57
Malta	77	69	54	85	77	0.01	-9.41
Portugal	86,330	100,645	84,755	92,204	141,351	21.75	53.30
Serbia	12	40	16				
Serbia and Montenegro	68	13					
Slovenia	115	88	70	429	70	0.01	-83.68
Spain	5,007	4,052	4,138	4,657	7,054	1.09	51.47
TFYR of Macedonia	21	46			41	0.01	
WESTERN EUROPE	**30,343**	**25,003**	**27,801**	**24,257**	**27,097**	**4.17**	**11.71**
Austria	246	234	201	231	282	0.04	22.08
Belgium	1,650	1,472	1,458	1,258	1,281	0.20	1.83
France	21,760	18,243	20,884	17,297	19,491	3.00	12.68
Germany	3,361	2,334	2,254	2,486	3,864	0.59	55.43
Luxembourg	9	17	5	81			
Monaco		1					

11

ANGOLA

1. Arrivals of non-resident tourists at national borders, by country of residence

	2009	2010	2011	2012	2013	Market share 2013	% Change 2013-2012
Netherlands	2,910	2,098	2,324	2,219	1,766	0.27	-20.41
Switzerland	407	604	675	685	413	0.06	-39.71
EAST MEDITERRANEAN EUROPE	**3,340**	**2,464**	**2,454**	**2,722**	**1,787**	**0.27**	**-34.35**
Cyprus	8	7	15	30	17	0.00	-43.33
Israel	3,081	2,183	2,036	2,190	1,655	0.25	-24.43
Turkey	251	274	403	502	115	0.02	-77.09
OTHER EUROPE			1,544		2,388	0.37	
Other countries of Europe			1,544		2,388	0.37	
MIDDLE EAST	**4,404**	**8,639**	**2,946**	**5,681**	**7,533**	**1.16**	**32.60**
Egypt	1,634	3,177	1,181	1,506	1,270	0.20	-15.67
Iraq	8	138	7	235	774	0.12	229.36
Jordan	129	147	152	147	129	0.02	-12.24
Kuwait	6	6	2				
Lebanon	2,291	2,701	1,315	2,342	4,273	0.66	82.45
Libya	17	972	24	38	245	0.04	544.74
Oman	19			1	2	0.00	100.00
Palestine	40	43	31	207	615	0.09	197.10
Qatar	17	3	1				
Saudi Arabia	8	274	2	11	9	0.00	-18.18
Syrian Arab Republic	168	1,147	184	19	216	0.03	1,036.84
United Arab Emirates	49	2	10	11			
Yemen	15	14	37	746			
Other countries of Middle East	3	15		418			
SOUTH ASIA	**10,922**	**10,030**	**14,011**	**10,527**	**8,441**	**1.30**	**-19.82**
Afghanistan	13	3	9	4			
Bangladesh	308	211	231	271	277	0.04	2.21
India	9,517	8,831	12,741	9,231	6,923	1.07	-25.00
Iran, Islamic Republic of	70	51	38	94	174	0.03	85.11
Maldives		12	8	36	253	0.04	602.78
Nepal	125	224	84	101	66	0.01	-34.65
Pakistan	814	628	827	696	682	0.10	-2.01
Sri Lanka	75	70	73	94	66	0.01	-29.79

Yearbook of Tourism Statistics, Data 2009 – 2013, 2015 Edition

ANGUILLA

1. Arrivals of non-resident tourists at national borders, by country of residence

	2009	2010	2011	2012	2013	Market share 2013	% Change 2013-2012
TOTAL (*)	57,891	61,998	65,783	64,698	69,068	100.00	6.75
AMERICAS	49,029	53,136	56,606	55,267	59,539	86.20	7.73
CARIBBEAN	12,924	11,851	10,954	10,181	10,454	15.14	2.68
Puerto Rico	724	346	286	484	243	0.35	-49.79
Other countries of the Caribbean	12,200	11,505	10,668	9,697	10,211	14.78	5.30
NORTH AMERICA	36,105	41,285	45,652	45,086	49,085	71.07	8.87
Canada	2,032	2,403	2,823	3,291	3,575	5.18	8.63
United States of America	34,073	38,882	42,829	41,795	45,510	65.89	8.89
EUROPE	7,457	7,544	7,523	7,223	7,434	10.76	2.92
NORTHERN EUROPE	2,947	2,914	3,118	2,599	2,796	4.05	7.58
United Kingdom	2,947	2,914	3,118	2,599	2,796	4.05	7.58
SOUTHERN EUROPE	1,312	1,449	1,226	1,065	1,037	1.50	-2.63
Italy	1,312	1,449	1,226	1,065	1,037	1.50	-2.63
WESTERN EUROPE	2,083	2,215	1,994	2,303	2,332	3.38	1.26
Austria	69	82	105	109	97	0.14	-11.01
Belgium	83	86	71	139	72	0.10	-48.20
France	1,404	1,425	1,321	1,507	1,705	2.47	13.14
Germany	425	478	372	419	354	0.51	-15.51
Luxembourg	1	2		6	1	0.00	-83.33
Switzerland	101	142	125	123	103	0.15	-16.26
OTHER EUROPE	1,115	966	1,185	1,256	1,269	1.84	1.04
Other countries of Europe	1,115	966	1,185	1,256	1,269	1.84	1.04
NOT SPECIFIED	1,405	1,318	1,654	2,208	2,095	3.03	-5.12
Other countries of the World	1,405	1,318	1,654	2,208	2,095	3.03	-5.12

13

ANGUILLA

2. Arrivals of non-resident visitors at national borders, by country of residence

	2009	2010	2011	2012	2013	Market share 2013	% Change 2013-2012
TOTAL	112,115	118,411	123,558	129,391	151,303	100.00	16.93
AMERICAS	88,459	93,584	97,166	101,803	119,104	78.72	16.99
CARIBBEAN	25,976	25,103	23,626	23,619	23,758	15.70	0.59
Puerto Rico	909	559	403	655	428	0.28	-34.66
Other countries of the Caribbean	25,067	24,544	23,223	22,964	23,330	15.42	1.59
NORTH AMERICA	62,483	68,481	73,540	78,184	95,346	63.02	21.95
Canada	5,110	5,982	7,141	7,994	9,931	6.56	24.23
United States of America	57,373	62,499	66,399	70,190	85,415	56.45	21.69
EUROPE	20,412	20,260	20,451	21,417	24,673	16.31	15.20
NORTHERN EUROPE	4,667	4,471	4,557	4,251	5,382	3.56	26.61
United Kingdom	4,667	4,471	4,557	4,251	5,382	3.56	26.61
SOUTHERN EUROPE	2,385	2,278	2,139	2,431	2,049	1.35	-15.71
Italy	2,385	2,278	2,139	2,431	2,049	1.35	-15.71
WESTERN EUROPE	9,831	10,369	10,267	10,758	12,077	7.98	12.26
Austria	157	213	205	232	288	0.19	24.14
Belgium	195	381	373	426	509	0.34	19.48
France	8,220	8,148	8,336	8,665	9,453	6.25	9.09
Germany	931	1,239	1,024	1,091	1,465	0.97	34.28
Luxembourg	13	22	11	14	24	0.02	71.43
Switzerland	315	366	318	330	338	0.22	2.42
OTHER EUROPE	3,529	3,142	3,488	3,977	5,165	3.41	29.87
Other countries of Europe	3,529	3,142	3,488	3,977	5,165	3.41	29.87
NOT SPECIFIED	3,244	4,567	5,941	6,171	7,526	4.97	21.96
Other countries of the World	3,244	4,567	5,941	6,171	7,526	4.97	21.96

14

ANTIGUA AND BARBUDA

1. Arrivals of non-resident tourists at national borders, by country of residence

		2009	2010	2011	2012	2013	Market share 2013	% Change 2013-2012
TOTAL	(*)	**234,410**	**229,943**	**241,331**	**246,926**	**243,932**	**100.00**	**-1.21**
AMERICAS		**138,489**	**138,455**	**146,638**	**154,297**	**152,619**	**62.57**	**-1.09**
CARIBBEAN		**38,848**	**35,181**	**35,256**	**32,657**	**29,850**	**12.24**	**-8.60**
Anguilla		856	841	669	589	648	0.27	10.02
Bahamas		155	189	205	194	167	0.07	-13.92
Barbados		3,515	3,363	3,138	3,255	2,921	1.20	-10.26
Bermuda		200	207	183	205	108	0.04	-47.32
British Virgin Islands		1,872	1,662	1,547	1,297	1,371	0.56	5.71
Cayman Islands		125	108	97	124	88	0.04	-29.03
Cuba		175	158	148	202	277	0.11	37.13
Curaçao		129	110	117	159	100	0.04	-37.11
Dominica		4,989	4,120	3,856	3,277	2,960	1.21	-9.67
Dominican Republic		820	552	764	687	758	0.31	10.33
Grenada		811	679	751	645	719	0.29	11.47
Guadeloupe		772	743	925	879	710	0.29	-19.23
Haiti		105	105	95	107	173	0.07	61.68
Jamaica		4,476	4,133	4,281	4,355	3,319	1.36	-23.79
Martinique		386	236	632	908	332	0.14	-63.44
Montserrat		2,788	2,269	1,925	1,859	1,577	0.65	-15.17
Puerto Rico		1,070	1,140	838	803	709	0.29	-11.71
Saint Kitts and Nevis		3,306	3,022	3,605	2,746	2,753	1.13	0.25
Saint Lucia		2,142	2,027	2,170	1,899	1,984	0.81	4.48
Saint Vincent and the Grenadines		1,082	854	1,070	866	887	0.36	2.42
Sint Maarten		1,280	1,220	1,038	822	908	0.37	10.46
Trinidad and Tobago		4,386	4,258	4,267	4,125	3,751	1.54	-9.07
Turks and Caicos Islands		52	49	41	54	37	0.02	-31.48
United States Virgin Islands		3,160	2,911	2,731	2,428	2,452	1.01	0.99
Other countries of the Caribbean		196	225	163	172	141	0.06	-18.02
CENTRAL AMERICA		**594**	**416**	**391**	**402**	**280**	**0.11**	**-30.35**
Belize		106	83	114	100	68	0.03	-32.00
Costa Rica				55	75	49	0.02	-34.67
El Salvador				28	22	18	0.01	-18.18
Guatemala				48	55	21	0.01	-61.82
Honduras				13	9	2	0.00	-77.78
Nicaragua				7	18	7	0.00	-61.11
Panama				126	123	115	0.05	-6.50
Other countries of Central America		488	333					
NORTH AMERICA		**95,015**	**99,416**	**107,392**	**117,569**	**119,393**	**48.95**	**1.55**
Canada		12,947	17,818	22,403	24,185	30,442	12.48	25.87
Mexico				157	170	133	0.05	-21.76
United States of America		82,068	81,598	84,832	93,214	88,818	36.41	-4.72
SOUTH AMERICA		**4,032**	**3,442**	**3,599**	**3,669**	**3,096**	**1.27**	**-15.62**
Argentina		261	248	215	205	311	0.13	51.71
Bolivia				3	8	1	0.00	-87.50
Brazil		255	291	275	270	289	0.12	7.04
Chile				60	80	92	0.04	15.00
Colombia		199	152	94	57	100	0.04	75.44
Ecuador				9	26	19	0.01	-26.92
Falkland Islands, Malvinas				1	5	3	0.00	-40.00
French Guiana				2		3	0.00	
Guyana		2,466	2,130	2,395	2,367	1,795	0.74	-24.17
Paraguay				5	7	10	0.00	42.86
Peru				30	67	71	0.03	5.97
Suriname		126	111	122	125	88	0.04	-29.60
Uruguay				12	25	19	0.01	-24.00
Venezuela		481	341	376	427	295	0.12	-30.91
Other countries of South America		244	169					

ANTIGUA AND BARBUDA

1. Arrivals of non-resident tourists at national borders, by country of residence

	2009	2010	2011	2012	2013	Market share 2013	% Change 2013-2012
EAST ASIA AND THE PACIFIC	150	122	1,268	1,440	1,549	0.64	7.57
NORTH-EAST ASIA	150	122	485	576	658	0.27	14.24
China			342	450	540	0.22	20.00
Japan	150	122	143	126	118	0.05	-6.35
AUSTRALASIA			783	864	891	0.37	3.13
Australia			568	609	718	0.29	17.90
New Zealand			215	255	173	0.07	-32.16
EUROPE	93,442	88,945	92,097	89,909	88,468	36.27	-1.60
CENTRAL/EASTERN EUROPE			550	913	763	0.31	-16.43
Russian Federation			550	913	763	0.31	-16.43
NORTHERN EUROPE	75,886	69,089	71,763	71,009	71,162	29.17	0.22
Denmark	248	271	297	232	243	0.10	4.74
Ireland	1,368	1,050	985	920	853	0.35	-7.28
Norway	456	442	487	451	431	0.18	-4.43
Sweden	563	703	810	729	701	0.29	-3.84
United Kingdom	73,251	66,623	69,184	68,677	68,934	28.26	0.37
SOUTHERN EUROPE	8,411	10,869	11,754	9,735	8,678	3.56	-10.86
Greece	85	98	58	65	58	0.02	-10.77
Italy	7,726	10,180	11,048	9,041	7,960	3.26	-11.96
Portugal	87	64	94	79	113	0.05	43.04
Spain	513	527	554	550	547	0.22	-0.55
WESTERN EUROPE	7,546	7,192	6,881	6,793	6,289	2.58	-7.42
Austria	493	410	485	459	366	0.15	-20.26
Belgium	286	254	248	266	223	0.09	-16.17
France	1,567	1,661	1,747	1,783	1,738	0.71	-2.52
Germany	3,752	3,339	2,899	2,768	2,446	1.00	-11.63
Luxembourg	14	15	25	72	66	0.03	-8.33
Netherlands	466	542	373	331	291	0.12	-12.08
Switzerland	968	971	1,104	1,114	1,159	0.48	4.04
OTHER EUROPE	1,599	1,795	1,149	1,459	1,576	0.65	8.02
Other countries of Europe	1,599	1,795	1,149	1,459	1,576	0.65	8.02
NOT SPECIFIED	2,329	2,421	1,328	1,280	1,296	0.53	1.25
Other countries of the World	2,329	2,421	1,328	1,280	1,296	0.53	1.25

Yearbook of Tourism Statistics, Data 2009 – 2013, 2015 Edition

ARGENTINA

1. Arrivals of non-resident tourists at national borders, by nationality

	2009	2010	2011	2012	2013	Market share 2013	% Change 2013-2012
TOTAL	**4,307,666**	**5,325,130**	**5,704,650**	**5,586,903**	**5,570,970**	**100.00**	**-0.29**
AMERICAS	**3,392,017**	**4,367,985**	**4,760,388**	**4,670,990**	**4,700,684**	**84.38**	**0.64**
NORTH AMERICA	**395,376**	**404,770**	**360,616**	**355,839**	**321,160**	**5.76**	**-9.75**
Canada, United States	395,376	404,770	360,616	355,839	321,160	5.76	-9.75
SOUTH AMERICA	**2,580,176**	**3,544,037**	**3,898,602**	**3,812,889**	**3,836,164**	**68.86**	**0.61**
Bolivia	164,406	184,697	231,636	251,535	268,792	4.82	6.86
Brazil	718,203	1,196,832	1,282,374	1,217,374	1,083,250	19.44	-11.02
Chile	820,128	1,076,372	1,101,337	1,133,846	1,098,302	19.71	-3.13
Paraguay	389,619	432,200	627,620	602,667	642,355	11.53	6.59
Uruguay	487,820	653,936	655,635	607,467	743,465	13.35	22.39
OTHER AMERICAS	**416,465**	**419,178**	**501,170**	**502,262**	**543,360**	**9.75**	**8.18**
Other countries of the Americas	416,465	419,178	501,170	502,262	543,360	9.75	8.18
EUROPE	**721,622**	**751,331**	**738,778**	**707,666**	**668,512**	**12.00**	**-5.53**
OTHER EUROPE	**721,622**	**751,331**	**738,778**	**707,666**	**668,512**	**12.00**	**-5.53**
All countries of Europe	721,622	751,331	738,778	707,666	668,512	12.00	-5.53
NOT SPECIFIED	**194,027**	**205,814**	**205,484**	**208,247**	**201,774**	**3.62**	**-3.11**
Other countries of the World	194,027	205,814	205,484	208,247	201,774	3.62	-3.11

Yearbook of Tourism Statistics, Data 2009 – 2013, 2015 Edition

ARMENIA

1. Arrivals of non-resident tourists at national borders, by country of residence

	2009	2010	2011	2012	2013	Market share 2013	% Change 2013-2012
TOTAL	575,284	683,979	757,935	963,035	1,084,188	100.00	12.58
AFRICA	443	215	603	686	666	0.06	-2.92
EAST AFRICA	83		19	31	27	0.00	-12.90
Ethiopia	65		14	21	22	0.00	4.76
Zambia			2	6	3	0.00	-50.00
Zimbabwe	18		3	4	2	0.00	-50.00
CENTRAL AFRICA	30		29	13	9	0.00	-30.77
Cameroon	30		29	13	9	0.00	-30.77
NORTH AFRICA	330	215	365	384	382	0.04	-0.52
Algeria	180	215	211	215	209	0.02	-2.79
Morocco	150		154	169	173	0.02	2.37
SOUTHERN AFRICA			182	223	247	0.02	10.76
All countries of Southern Africa			182	223	247	0.02	10.76
WEST AFRICA			8	35	1	0.00	-97.14
Liberia			8	35	1	0.00	-97.14
AMERICAS	134,940	135,673	144,632	128,871	147,189	13.58	14.21
CARIBBEAN		31	22	43	39	0.00	-9.30
Cuba		30	22	43	39	0.00	-9.30
Puerto Rico		1					
CENTRAL AMERICA		60	70	22	33	0.00	50.00
El Salvador		4	3	3	4	0.00	33.33
Guatemala		1	9	12	9	0.00	-25.00
Honduras			2	2	3	0.00	50.00
Nicaragua		55	56	5	17	0.00	240.00
NORTH AMERICA	95,000	97,760	103,715	88,530	105,253	9.71	18.89
Canada	30,200	30,350	32,807	16,034	29,625	2.73	84.76
Mexico	1,700	1,650	1,992	90	107	0.01	18.89
United States of America	63,100	65,760	68,916	72,406	75,521	6.97	4.30
SOUTH AMERICA	39,940	37,822	40,825	40,276	41,864	3.86	3.94
Argentina	26,600	24,350	26,414	25,673	26,035	2.40	1.41
Brazil	10,500	10,490	11,203	11,394	12,967	1.20	13.81
Chile		180	178	139	47	0.00	-66.19
Colombia		25	27	25	48	0.00	92.00
Ecuador		18	10	20	11	0.00	-45.00
Guyana		2	2	1			
Peru	200	217	218	219	22	0.00	-89.95
Uruguay	2,240	2,170	2,411	2,460	2,397	0.22	-2.56
Venezuela	400	370	362	345	337	0.03	-2.32
EAST ASIA AND THE PACIFIC	24,600	25,584	29,222	29,814	30,716	2.83	3.03
NORTH-EAST ASIA	20,300	21,008	23,510	23,680	24,015	2.22	1.41
China	8,400	8,450	9,713	9,867	9,924	0.92	0.58
Japan	11,900	11,730	12,973	12,968	13,011	1.20	0.33
Korea, Republic of		733	591	706	905	0.08	28.19
Mongolia		41	42	37	22	0.00	-40.54
Taiwan, Province of China		54	191	102	153	0.01	50.00
SOUTH-EAST ASIA		236	357	538	791	0.07	47.03
Cambodia			13	6			
Indonesia		21	49	126	137	0.01	8.73
Malaysia		50	98	77	111	0.01	44.16
Philippines		127	128	227	371	0.03	63.44
Thailand		36	55	94	149	0.01	58.51
Viet Nam		2	14	8	23	0.00	187.50
AUSTRALASIA	4,300	4,340	5,355	5,596	5,910	0.55	5.61
Australia	4,300	4,340	5,224	5,414	5,737	0.53	5.97
New Zealand			131	182	173	0.02	-4.95
EUROPE	311,268	350,926	375,195	605,731	702,183	64.77	15.92
CENTRAL/EASTERN EUROPE	215,198	240,223	253,639	478,914	574,922	53.03	20.05
Bulgaria	3,950	3,915	4,506	4,506	5,127	0.47	13.78
Czech Republic	1,720	1,745	1,825	3,015	3,119	0.29	3.45

18

ARMENIA

1. Arrivals of non-resident tourists at national borders, by country of residence

	2009	2010	2011	2012	2013	Market share 2013	% Change 2013-2012
Estonia				585	1,152	0.11	96.92
Hungary		489	572	515	531	0.05	3.11
Latvia		761	970	985	1,216	0.11	23.45
Lithuania		750	919	1,506	1,178	0.11	-21.78
Poland	1,200	2,350	3,351	3,758	7,295	0.67	94.12
Romania		890	899	815	922	0.09	13.13
Slovakia		513	619	588	668	0.06	13.61
Commonwealth Independent States	208,328	228,810	239,978	462,641	553,714	51.07	19.69
NORTHERN EUROPE	**11,900**	**14,013**	**14,308**	**15,012**	**15,690**	**1.45**	**4.52**
Denmark	990	1,071	1,263	1,417	1,562	0.14	10.23
Finland	710	826	826	1,108	835	0.08	-24.64
Iceland		16	31	39	57	0.01	46.15
Ireland	250	765	416	473	467	0.04	-1.27
Norway	940	975	917	712	846	0.08	18.82
Sweden	910	1,640	1,727	1,919	2,177	0.20	13.44
United Kingdom	8,100	8,720	9,128	9,344	9,746	0.90	4.30
SOUTHERN EUROPE	**20,600**	**21,415**	**25,151**	**26,683**	**27,916**	**2.57**	**4.62**
Albania		55	48	80	71	0.01	-11.25
Bosnia and Herzegovina	950	985	1,034	160	157	0.01	-1.88
Croatia		235	270	211	350	0.03	65.88
Greece	8,700	8,930	11,765	12,092	13,115	1.21	8.46
Italy	7,900	7,945	8,722	9,604	9,084	0.84	-5.41
Malta		95	48	30	129	0.01	330.00
Portugal		730	729	395	393	0.04	-0.51
Serbia				355	449	0.04	26.48
Serbia and Montenegro	700			411	76	0.01	-81.51
Slovenia	700	760	762	315	419	0.04	33.02
Spain	1,650	1,680	1,773	3,030	3,673	0.34	21.22
WESTERN EUROPE	**57,070**	**58,854**	**65,013**	**69,573**	**69,056**	**6.37**	**-0.74**
Austria	5,200	5,270	6,137	6,336	6,412	0.59	1.20
Belgium	4,800	4,830	5,122	5,974	6,086	0.56	1.87
France	24,100	24,250	24,735	26,312	26,537	2.45	0.86
Germany	18,970	19,120	22,193	23,785	22,310	2.06	-6.20
Netherlands	2,300	3,604	4,814	5,260	5,557	0.51	5.65
Switzerland	1,700	1,780	2,012	1,906	2,154	0.20	13.01
EAST MEDITERRANEAN EUROPE	**6,500**	**16,421**	**17,084**	**15,549**	**14,599**	**1.35**	**-6.11**
Cyprus	1,800	1,930	2,143	283	282	0.03	-0.35
Israel	2,500	2,834	3,124	5,637	4,345	0.40	-22.92
Turkey	2,200	11,657	11,817	9,629	9,972	0.92	3.56
MIDDLE EAST	**44,690**	**46,470**	**49,598**	**49,700**	**52,134**	**4.81**	**4.90**
Egypt	590	615	597	500	400	0.04	-20.00
Iraq		398	911	1,062	1,490	0.14	40.30
Jordan		358	363	329	332	0.03	0.91
Kuwait		44	97	174	352	0.03	102.30
Lebanon	23,100	23,330	24,171	24,119	24,793	2.29	2.79
Libya			18	3	8	0.00	166.67
Qatar		120	121	16	26	0.00	62.50
Saudi Arabia		80	73	22	16	0.00	-27.27
Syrian Arab Republic	21,000	21,340	23,001	23,198	24,314	2.24	4.81
United Arab Emirates		185	246	277	403	0.04	45.49
SOUTH ASIA	**59,343**	**125,111**	**158,685**	**148,233**	**151,300**	**13.96**	**2.07**
Afghanistan			4	33	10	0.00	-69.70
Bangladesh			6	14	6	0.00	-57.14
India	4,100	4,180	4,311	4,881	5,013	0.46	2.70
Iran, Islamic Republic of	55,243	120,863	154,278	143,208	146,184	13.48	2.08
Nepal		15	23	24	18	0.00	-25.00
Pakistan		38	36	34	27	0.00	-20.59
Sri Lanka		15	27	39	42	0.00	7.69

19

ARUBA

1. Arrivals of non-resident tourists at national borders, by country of residence

	2009	2010	2011	2012	2013	Market share 2013	% Change 2013-2012
TOTAL	812,623	824,330	868,973	903,934	979,254	100.00	8.33
AMERICAS	735,339	745,723	784,980	820,484	898,419	91.75	9.50
CARIBBEAN	24,554	26,457	29,481	32,126	30,865	3.15	-3.93
Dominican Republic	839	1,028	1,161	1,497	1,685	0.17	12.56
Netherlands Antilles	21,536	23,363	25,773	27,361	26,682	2.72	-2.48
Puerto Rico	119	86	19	74	32	0.00	-56.76
Trinidad and Tobago	873	953	1,268	1,817	1,193	0.12	-34.34
Other countries of the Caribbean	1,187	1,027	1,260	1,377	1,273	0.13	-7.55
NORTH AMERICA	563,308	574,533	572,891	578,090	602,340	61.51	4.19
Canada	33,856	37,643	40,487	45,887	44,338	4.53	-3.38
Mexico	1,348	1,223	1,293	1,328	1,744	0.18	31.33
United States of America	528,104	535,667	531,111	530,875	556,258	56.80	4.78
SOUTH AMERICA	147,477	144,733	182,608	210,268	265,214	27.08	26.13
Argentina	5,486	6,365	10,326	12,865	15,574	1.59	21.06
Brazil	10,594	20,235	22,413	21,070	23,293	2.38	10.55
Chile	1,345	1,840	2,431	3,163	5,505	0.56	74.04
Colombia	15,685	15,004	16,703	18,127	19,485	1.99	7.49
Ecuador	1,186	2,532	3,520	1,659	1,272	0.13	-23.33
Peru	1,092	1,372	1,377	1,007	1,213	0.12	20.46
Suriname	3,651	3,556	4,220	5,117	6,253	0.64	22.20
Venezuela	105,063	90,709	117,838	143,201	188,020	19.20	31.30
Other countries of South America	3,375	3,120	3,780	4,059	4,599	0.47	13.30
EAST ASIA AND THE PACIFIC	158	152	118	176	186	0.02	5.68
NORTH-EAST ASIA	158	152	118	176	186	0.02	5.68
Japan	158	152	118	176	186	0.02	5.68
EUROPE	75,000	76,077	80,874	79,570	77,006	7.86	-3.22
CENTRAL/EASTERN EUROPE	272	285	444	441	568	0.06	28.80
Russian Federation	272	285	444	441	568	0.06	28.80
NORTHERN EUROPE	16,018	21,477	21,836	22,168	20,216	2.06	-8.81
Denmark	305	166	350	293	532	0.05	81.57
Finland	826	766	963	648	810	0.08	25.00
Norway	613	617	808	1,230	2,449	0.25	99.11
Sweden	2,762	5,398	5,845	6,285	7,110	0.73	13.13
United Kingdom	11,512	14,530	13,870	13,712	9,315	0.95	-32.07
SOUTHERN EUROPE	8,148	4,065	7,911	5,333	6,822	0.70	27.92
Italy	6,369	2,869	6,514	3,963	5,008	0.51	26.37
Portugal	200	165	244	181	256	0.03	41.44
Spain	1,579	1,031	1,153	1,189	1,558	0.16	31.03
WESTERN EUROPE	47,885	47,573	47,441	48,376	45,839	4.68	-5.24
Austria	347	407	368	351	268	0.03	-23.65
Belgium	2,161	2,377	2,424	2,803	2,533	0.26	-9.63
Germany	3,357	3,568	3,493	4,054	3,841	0.39	-5.25
Netherlands	41,211	40,294	40,068	39,973	37,788	3.86	-5.47
Switzerland	809	927	1,088	1,195	1,409	0.14	17.91
OTHER EUROPE	2,677	2,677	3,242	3,252	3,561	0.36	9.50
Other countries of Europe	2,677	2,677	3,242	3,252	3,561	0.36	9.50
NOT SPECIFIED	2,126	2,378	3,001	3,704	3,643	0.37	-1.65
Other countries of the World	2,126	2,378	3,001	3,704	3,643	0.37	-1.65

ARUBA

3. Arrivals of non-resident tourists in hotels and similar establishments, by country of residence

	2009	2010	2011	2012	2013	Market share 2013	% Change 2013-2012
TOTAL	719,347	727,590	735,677	764,104	797,398	100.00	4.36
AMERICAS	664,735	672,653	679,373	709,269	747,255	93.71	5.36
CARIBBEAN	13,273	15,068	12,707	14,320	14,820	1.86	3.49
Dominican Republic	328	387	266	402	387	0.05	-3.73
Netherlands Antilles	11,502	13,284	10,966	11,840	12,910	1.62	9.04
Trinidad and Tobago	642	748	954	1,476	991	0.12	-32.86
Other countries of the Caribbean	801	649	521	602	532	0.07	-11.63
NORTH AMERICA	534,620	542,173	529,139	534,708	557,626	69.93	4.29
Canada	31,274	34,496	36,224	40,678	38,503	4.83	-5.35
Mexico	1,050	1,026	953	1,001	1,251	0.16	24.98
United States of America	502,296	506,651	491,962	493,029	517,872	64.95	5.04
SOUTH AMERICA	116,842	115,412	137,527	160,241	174,809	21.92	9.09
Argentina	5,283	6,167	9,820	12,209	14,856	1.86	21.68
Brazil	10,115	19,558	21,027	19,513	21,277	2.67	9.04
Chile	1,288	1,778	2,317	3,039	5,271	0.66	73.45
Colombia	11,470	11,804	12,569	13,748	14,337	1.80	4.28
Ecuador	805	2,236	3,171	1,279	905	0.11	-29.24
Peru	797	1,086	1,103	795	976	0.12	22.77
Suriname	1,627	1,728	1,443	1,902	2,528	0.32	32.91
Venezuela	81,467	67,455	81,943	103,437	110,902	13.91	7.22
Other countries of South America	3,990	3,600	4,134	4,319	3,757	0.47	-13.01
EAST ASIA AND THE PACIFIC	126	108	95	93	140	0.02	50.54
NORTH-EAST ASIA	126	108	95	93	140	0.02	50.54
Japan	126	108	95	93	140	0.02	50.54
EUROPE	52,819	54,415	55,841	53,757	48,150	6.04	-10.43
CENTRAL/EASTERN EUROPE	140	187	230	299	251	0.03	-16.05
Russian Federation	140	187	230	299	251	0.03	-16.05
NORTHERN EUROPE	14,895	20,381	19,910	20,378	16,878	2.12	-17.18
Denmark	215	126	218	202	397	0.05	96.53
Finland	756	699	781	543	594	0.07	9.39
Norway	495	483	672	997	2,054	0.26	106.02
Sweden	2,641	5,172	5,463	5,773	5,531	0.69	-4.19
United Kingdom	10,788	13,901	12,776	12,863	8,302	1.04	-35.46
SOUTHERN EUROPE	7,236	3,252	6,705	4,168	5,190	0.65	24.52
Italy	5,972	2,383	5,721	3,238	4,030	0.51	24.46
Portugal	158	134	186	146	183	0.02	25.34
Spain	1,106	735	798	784	977	0.12	24.62
WESTERN EUROPE	28,493	28,583	26,855	26,783	22,853	2.87	-14.67
Austria	294	321	274	298	179	0.02	-39.93
Belgium	1,641	1,869	1,841	2,123	1,737	0.22	-18.18
Germany	2,877	2,952	2,673	3,059	2,648	0.33	-13.44
Netherlands	23,017	22,718	21,266	20,374	17,327	2.17	-14.96
Switzerland	664	723	801	929	962	0.12	3.55
OTHER EUROPE	2,055	2,012	2,141	2,129	2,978	0.37	39.88
Other countries of Europe	2,055	2,012	2,141	2,129	2,978	0.37	39.88
NOT SPECIFIED	1,667	414	368	985	1,853	0.23	88.12
Other countries of the World	1,667	414	368	985	1,853	0.23	88.12

21

ARUBA

5. Overnight stays of non-resident tourists in hotels and similar establishments, by country of residence

	2009	2010	2011	2012	2013	Market share 2013	% Change 2013-2012
TOTAL	5,138,557	5,272,565	5,254,913	5,433,271	5,504,058	100.00	1.30
AMERICAS	4,595,415	4,697,020	4,695,165	4,880,490	5,022,162	91.24	2.90
CARIBBEAN	51,214	56,565	46,313	53,664	52,955	0.96	-1.32
Dominican Republic	1,538	1,785	1,376	2,109	1,910	0.03	-9.44
Netherlands Antilles	41,718	47,684	38,499	41,514	44,259	0.80	6.61
Trinidad and Tobago	3,588	3,794	4,078	7,026	4,361	0.08	-37.93
Other countries of the Caribbean	4,370	3,302	2,360	3,015	2,425	0.04	-19.57
NORTH AMERICA	3,894,317	3,956,611	3,863,749	3,900,405	3,973,229	72.19	1.87
Canada	261,918	285,358	294,698	327,457	308,775	5.61	-5.71
United States of America	3,632,399	3,671,253	3,569,051	3,572,948	3,664,454	66.58	2.56
SOUTH AMERICA	649,884	683,844	785,103	926,421	995,978	18.10	7.51
Argentina	43,811	50,572	80,994	104,302	123,807	2.25	18.70
Brazil	63,805	120,697	131,284	122,155	140,154	2.55	14.73
Chile	8,842	12,752	16,176	21,734	39,057	0.71	79.70
Colombia	72,056	73,261	72,547	78,147	80,685	1.47	3.25
Ecuador	5,329	11,778	14,851	7,435	4,256	0.08	-42.76
Peru	6,354	7,556	6,663	5,577	6,630	0.12	18.88
Suriname	8,090	7,658	7,036	9,437	11,382	0.21	20.61
Venezuela	421,498	378,816	432,287	553,592	563,121	10.23	1.72
Other countries of South America	20,099	20,754	23,265	24,042	26,886	0.49	11.83
EAST ASIA AND THE PACIFIC	586	381	329	396	665	0.01	67.93
NORTH-EAST ASIA	586	381	329	396	665	0.01	67.93
Japan	586	381	329	396	665	0.01	67.93
EUROPE	533,300	567,032	550,733	539,457	469,660	8.53	-12.94
CENTRAL/EASTERN EUROPE	1,327	1,983	2,174	2,940	2,499	0.05	-15.00
Russian Federation	1,327	1,983	2,174	2,940	2,499	0.05	-15.00
NORTHERN EUROPE	180,769	251,231	233,408	239,047	206,052	3.74	-13.80
Denmark	2,063	952	1,654	1,473	3,855	0.07	161.71
Finland	7,325	7,410	7,976	5,299	5,205	0.09	-1.77
Norway	5,108	4,863	6,876	11,169	23,932	0.43	114.27
Sweden	30,218	63,992	66,937	70,568	76,483	1.39	8.38
United Kingdom	136,055	174,014	149,965	150,538	96,577	1.75	-35.85
SOUTHERN EUROPE	57,499	25,447	54,250	33,291	37,249	0.68	11.89
Italy	47,652	19,028	47,313	25,895	29,449	0.54	13.72
Portugal	1,335	855	1,281	917	1,440	0.03	57.03
Spain	8,512	5,564	5,656	6,479	6,360	0.12	-1.84
WESTERN EUROPE	275,891	270,810	243,460	245,373	205,580	3.74	-16.22
Austria	3,033	3,471	2,971	3,084	1,698	0.03	-44.94
Belgium	15,785	17,094	15,542	18,730	14,787	0.27	-21.05
Germany	32,206	29,323	28,161	30,733	24,084	0.44	-21.63
Netherlands	218,619	214,323	189,557	184,378	156,236	2.84	-15.26
Switzerland	6,248	6,599	7,229	8,448	8,775	0.16	3.87
OTHER EUROPE	17,814	17,561	17,441	18,806	18,280	0.33	-2.80
Other countries of Europe	17,814	17,561	17,441	18,806	18,280	0.33	-2.80
NOT SPECIFIED	9,256	8,132	8,686	12,928	11,571	0.21	-10.50
Other countries of the World	9,256	8,132	8,686	12,928	11,571	0.21	-10.50

ARUBA

6. Overnight stays of non-resident tourists in all types of accommodation establishments, by country of residence

	2009	2010	2011	2012	2013	Market share 2013	% Change 2013-2012
TOTAL	6,172,913	6,466,217	6,685,807	6,907,143	7,126,771	100.00	3.18
AMERICAS	5,270,446	5,539,453	5,742,183	5,954,445	6,219,899	87.28	4.46
CARIBBEAN	141,274	157,940	184,875	203,436	176,847	2.48	-13.07
Dominican Republic	9,363	18,508	29,922	31,938	27,764	0.39	-13.07
Netherlands Antilles	113,347	120,034	125,284	139,658	125,838	1.77	-9.90
Puerto Rico	609	617	95	345	150	0.00	-56.52
Trinidad and Tobago	6,876	6,883	8,545	11,379	6,670	0.09	-41.38
Other countries of the Caribbean	11,079	11,898	21,029	20,116	16,425	0.23	-18.35
NORTH AMERICA	4,191,931	4,286,388	4,274,388	4,314,691	4,394,447	61.66	1.85
Canada	295,177	325,361	345,578	390,284	376,897	5.29	-3.43
Mexico	8,498	9,058	8,776	9,415	11,915	0.17	26.55
United States of America	3,888,256	3,951,969	3,920,034	3,914,992	4,005,635	56.21	2.32
SOUTH AMERICA	937,241	1,095,125	1,282,920	1,436,318	1,648,605	23.13	14.78
Argentina	46,072	53,291	86,820	111,984	131,884	1.85	17.77
Brazil	67,939	127,293	141,571	133,560	154,011	2.16	15.31
Chile	9,341	13,530	17,240	22,911	41,194	0.58	79.80
Colombia	128,743	145,143	169,478	172,653	171,911	2.41	-0.43
Ecuador	10,236	18,022	21,632	14,902	9,479	0.13	-36.39
Peru	11,348	14,233	13,499	10,807	11,011	0.15	1.89
Suriname	32,114	29,295	36,174	39,558	43,031	0.60	8.78
Venezuela	612,030	670,662	772,863	903,545	1,056,837	14.83	16.97
Other countries of South America	19,418	23,656	23,643	26,398	29,247	0.41	10.79
EAST ASIA AND THE PACIFIC	739	562	540	640	1,075	0.02	67.97
NORTH-EAST ASIA	739	562	540	640	1,075	0.02	67.97
Japan	739	562	540	640	1,075	0.02	67.97
EUROPE	884,079	906,628	909,099	914,934	877,462	12.31	-4.10
CENTRAL/EASTERN EUROPE	2,282	2,654	3,093	4,172	4,945	0.07	18.53
Russian Federation	2,282	2,654	3,093	4,172	4,945	0.07	18.53
NORTHERN EUROPE	195,808	267,813	258,940	261,432	235,270	3.30	-10.01
Denmark	2,987	1,343	2,682	1,998	5,058	0.07	153.15
Finland	8,320	8,487	12,502	6,375	6,896	0.10	8.17
Norway	7,377	6,906	8,941	14,497	29,377	0.41	102.64
Sweden	31,780	67,185	72,012	76,991	85,246	1.20	10.72
United Kingdom	145,344	183,892	162,803	161,571	108,693	1.53	-32.73
SOUTHERN EUROPE	68,960	38,159	69,172	49,238	56,434	0.79	14.61
Italy	52,893	25,680	56,166	34,580	39,819	0.56	15.15
Portugal	1,997	1,259	1,772	1,242	2,223	0.03	78.99
Spain	14,070	11,220	11,234	13,416	14,392	0.20	7.27
WESTERN EUROPE	591,452	571,025	546,676	567,249	547,440	7.68	-3.49
Austria	3,922	4,242	3,719	3,480	3,080	0.04	-11.49
Belgium	23,548	25,045	23,199	27,649	24,765	0.35	-10.43
Germany	39,523	37,778	37,818	41,489	37,160	0.52	-10.43
Netherlands	515,662	494,926	472,198	482,881	468,814	6.58	-2.91
Switzerland	8,797	9,034	9,742	11,750	13,621	0.19	15.92
OTHER EUROPE	25,577	26,977	31,218	32,843	33,373	0.47	1.61
Other countries of Europe	25,577	26,977	31,218	32,843	33,373	0.47	1.61
NOT SPECIFIED	17,649	19,574	33,985	37,124	28,335	0.40	-23.67
Other countries of the World	17,649	19,574	33,985	37,124	28,335	0.40	-23.67

Yearbook of Tourism Statistics, Data 2009 – 2013, 2015 Edition

AUSTRALIA

2. Arrivals of non-resident visitors at national borders, by country of residence

		2009	2010	2011	2012	2013	Market share 2013	% Change 2013-2012
TOTAL	(*)	5,490,180	5,790,230	5,770,980	6,032,420	6,382,370	100.00	5.80
AFRICA		81,660	86,560	89,080	82,440	80,160	1.26	-2.77
EAST AFRICA		18,650	21,070	21,050	19,820	19,280	0.30	-2.72
Burundi		50	10	40	40	70	0.00	75.00
Comoros				10	10	10	0.00	
Djibouti				20	20	20	0.00	
Eritrea		40	30	30	20	60	0.00	200.00
Ethiopia		260	300	280	270	460	0.01	70.37
Kenya		2,700	2,860	2,960	2,930	3,250	0.05	10.92
Madagascar		150	170	110	200	210	0.00	5.00
Malawi		180	170	250	280	280	0.00	
Mauritius		5,750	6,710	6,720	6,470	6,250	0.10	-3.40
Mozambique		250	370	410	300	540	0.01	80.00
Reunion		3,960	4,950	3,960	3,300	1,770	0.03	-46.36
Rwanda		50	100	150	170	90	0.00	-47.06
Seychelles		430	510	400	310	320	0.01	3.23
Somalia		20	80	110	110	100	0.00	-9.09
Uganda		340	530	650	590	790	0.01	33.90
United Republic of Tanzania		920	770	1,050	820	1,160	0.02	41.46
Zambia		950	1,000	1,380	1,230	1,210	0.02	-1.63
Zimbabwe		2,600	2,510	2,520	2,750	2,690	0.04	-2.18
CENTRAL AFRICA		430	550	700	900	760	0.01	-15.56
Angola		130	390	170	280	220	0.00	-21.43
Cameroon		110	30	120	80	190	0.00	137.50
Central African Republic					10	20	0.00	100.00
Chad		60	20	150	160	90	0.00	-43.75
Congo		70	70	110	110	150	0.00	36.36
Democratic Republic of the Congo		10	20	20	40	40	0.00	
Equatorial Guinea		40			60			
Gabon		10	20	120	160	40	0.00	-75.00
Sao Tome and Principe				10		10	0.00	
NORTH AFRICA		690	1,110	1,070	940	1,250	0.02	32.98
Algeria		210	280	390	260	340	0.01	30.77
Morocco		260	360	320	290	390	0.01	34.48
Sudan		160	270	120	230	190	0.00	-17.39
Tunisia		60	200	240	160	330	0.01	106.25
SOUTHERN AFRICA		59,300	61,400	63,470	57,490	55,820	0.87	-2.90
Botswana		660	810	780	850	960	0.02	12.94
Lesotho		50	90	50	70	70	0.00	
Namibia		480	580	600	710	630	0.01	-11.27
South Africa		57,930	59,770	61,900	55,710	53,920	0.84	-3.21
Swaziland		180	150	140	150	240	0.00	60.00
WEST AFRICA		2,470	2,320	2,690	3,170	3,000	0.05	-5.36
Benin		10	10	10	30	10	0.00	-66.67
Burkina Faso		10	20	30	50	30	0.00	-40.00
Cabo Verde					10	20	0.00	100.00
Côte d'Ivoire		60	70	30	50	30	0.00	-40.00
Gambia		10	10	20	30	50	0.00	66.67
Ghana		510	530	520	780	710	0.01	-8.97
Guinea		20	180	150	160	180	0.00	12.50
Liberia		50	50	80	140	190	0.00	35.71
Mali		170	30	50	60	120	0.00	100.00
Mauritania		290	230	90	100	80	0.00	-20.00
Niger		80	50	180	30	90	0.00	200.00
Nigeria		1,160	1,020	1,280	1,560	1,160	0.02	-25.64
Senegal		60	80	80	80	90	0.00	12.50
Sierra Leone		30	30	140	70	190	0.00	171.43
Togo		10	10	30	20	50	0.00	150.00

24

AUSTRALIA

2. Arrivals of non-resident visitors at national borders, by country of residence

	2009	2010	2011	2012	2013	Market share 2013	% Change 2013-2012
OTHER AFRICA	**120**	**110**	**100**	**120**	**50**	**0.00**	**-58.33**
Other countries of Africa	120	110	100	120	50	0.00	-58.33
AMERICAS	**670,980**	**661,060**	**644,830**	**682,820**	**726,040**	**11.38**	**6.33**
CARIBBEAN	**3,130**	**3,380**	**2,730**	**2,950**	**2,930**	**0.05**	**-0.68**
Anguilla	20				30	0.00	
Antigua and Barbuda	10	10	20	10	50	0.00	400.00
Aruba	60		40	40	10	0.00	-75.00
Bahamas	330	160	240	220	350	0.01	59.09
Barbados	230	300	140	170	130	0.00	-23.53
Bermuda	660	530	580	300	420	0.01	40.00
British Virgin Islands		40		150			
Cayman Islands	430	690	390	440	390	0.01	-11.36
Cuba	160	240	230	110	230	0.00	109.09
Dominica	50	20	50	240	90	0.00	-62.50
Dominican Republic	60	90	50	130	60	0.00	-53.85
Grenada	60	60	130	160	70	0.00	-56.25
Guadeloupe	70	20	10	10	20	0.00	100.00
Haiti	10	60	70	10	10	0.00	
Jamaica	340	310	270	230	380	0.01	65.22
Martinique	50	90	10		10	0.00	
Montserrat	10	30					
Netherlands Antilles	10			20	30	0.00	50.00
Puerto Rico	190	300	50	220	70	0.00	-68.18
Saint Kitts and Nevis	10	10	20	10	20	0.00	100.00
Saint Lucia	20	30	30	30	70	0.00	133.33
Saint Vincent and the Grenadines	10	10	20	30	20	0.00	-33.33
Trinidad and Tobago	340	380	340	420	470	0.01	11.90
Turks and Caicos Islands			40				
CENTRAL AMERICA	**1,240**	**1,180**	**990**	**1,330**	**1,480**	**0.02**	**11.28**
Belize	30	20	20	50	50	0.00	
Costa Rica	460	380	310	320	390	0.01	21.88
El Salvador	170	190	110	250	260	0.00	4.00
Guatemala	140	250	140	170	220	0.00	29.41
Honduras	70	100	90	70	110	0.00	57.14
Nicaragua	30	30	130	140	90	0.00	-35.71
Panama	340	210	190	330	360	0.01	9.09
NORTH AMERICA	**610,410**	**599,470**	**578,570**	**603,760**	**636,990**	**9.98**	**5.50**
Canada	131,360	129,950	124,990	126,650	128,670	2.02	1.59
Mexico	6,810	6,580	6,430	6,250	7,270	0.11	16.32
Saint Pierre and Miquelon	10						
United States of America	472,230	462,940	447,150	470,860	501,050	7.85	6.41
SOUTH AMERICA	**56,200**	**57,030**	**62,540**	**74,780**	**84,640**	**1.33**	**13.19**
Argentina	7,840	7,900	8,790	13,190	14,930	0.23	13.19
Bolivia	240	270	220	330	370	0.01	12.12
Brazil	26,320	27,510	29,980	31,640	35,670	0.56	12.74
Chile	9,940	9,300	10,240	13,290	15,450	0.24	16.25
Colombia	6,390	6,270	6,730	8,280	9,920	0.16	19.81
Ecuador	500	510	900	810	1,150	0.02	41.98
Falkland Islands, Malvinas		30		20			
French Guiana	20				10	0.00	
Guyana	50	60	70	40	70	0.00	75.00
Paraguay	140	230	190	230	240	0.00	4.35
Peru	2,400	2,280	2,650	2,730	2,780	0.04	1.83
Suriname	30	20	40	70	30	0.00	-57.14
Uruguay	920	1,050	1,130	2,070	1,400	0.02	-32.37
Venezuela	1,410	1,600	1,600	2,080	2,620	0.04	25.96

Yearbook of Tourism Statistics, Data 2009 – 2013, 2015 Edition

AUSTRALIA

2. Arrivals of non-resident visitors at national borders, by country of residence

	2009	2010	2011	2012	2013	Market share 2013	% Change 2013-2012
EAST ASIA AND THE PACIFIC	3,120,240	3,404,190	3,447,240	3,649,470	3,847,700	60.29	5.43
NORTH-EAST ASIA	1,141,010	1,301,560	1,310,890	1,436,560	1,529,770	23.97	6.49
China	356,240	445,860	533,370	618,820	708,770	11.11	14.54
Hong Kong, China	144,480	151,650	153,850	162,460	183,460	2.87	12.93
Japan	348,460	390,550	325,740	348,050	324,320	5.08	-6.82
Korea, Dem. People's Republic of	50			10	20	0.00	100.00
Korea, Republic of	186,510	220,170	205,220	203,360	197,520	3.09	-2.87
Macao, China	4,320	3,910	4,430	4,660	5,510	0.09	18.24
Mongolia	1,100	1,500	2,010	2,300	2,490	0.04	8.26
Taiwan, Province of China	99,850	87,920	86,270	96,900	107,680	1.69	11.12
SOUTH-EAST ASIA	727,790	792,750	815,880	865,490	962,320	15.08	11.19
Brunei Darussalam	6,730	6,670	6,700	6,240	6,360	0.10	1.92
Cambodia	5,480	5,500	5,140	5,010	4,920	0.08	-1.80
Indonesia	104,670	119,880	133,770	137,530	141,610	2.22	2.97
Lao People's Democratic Republic	2,060	1,760	1,770	1,750	1,900	0.03	8.57
Malaysia	201,670	223,370	225,110	245,540	278,140	4.36	13.28
Myanmar	1,640	1,600	2,120	2,060	3,540	0.06	71.84
Philippines	47,720	52,150	56,820	59,220	66,760	1.05	12.73
Singapore	250,020	270,830	274,300	297,700	339,760	5.32	14.13
Thailand	72,030	72,720	74,170	70,670	75,300	1.18	6.55
Timor-Leste	3,140	4,000	4,440	4,660	4,180	0.07	-10.30
Viet Nam	32,630	34,270	31,540	35,110	39,850	0.62	13.50
AUSTRALASIA	1,094,420	1,145,960	1,156,310	1,184,660	1,192,810	18.69	0.69
New Zealand	1,094,420	1,145,960	1,156,310	1,184,660	1,192,810	18.69	0.69
MELANESIA	135,900	142,080	140,590	139,840	140,350	2.20	0.36
Fiji	29,190	29,650	28,150	27,990	29,840	0.47	6.61
New Caledonia	45,840	45,780	41,970	38,620	38,230	0.60	-1.01
Norfolk Island	2,420	2,370	2,710	1,700	1,840	0.03	8.24
Papua New Guinea	42,000	47,220	50,070	55,450	56,020	0.88	1.03
Solomon Islands	7,300	7,630	7,760	7,080	5,080	0.08	-28.25
Vanuatu	9,150	9,430	9,930	9,000	9,340	0.15	3.78
MICRONESIA	5,550	4,290	4,960	5,390	5,740	0.09	6.49
Guam	1,690	1,410	1,170	860	1,220	0.02	41.86
Kiribati	1,380	960	1,150	1,280	1,030	0.02	-19.53
Marshall Islands	240	190	190	310	230	0.00	-25.81
Micronesia, Federated States of	290	260	320	410	310	0.00	-24.39
Nauru	1,620	1,270	1,790	2,290	2,860	0.04	24.89
Northern Mariana Islands	20	10					
Palau	310	190	340	240	90	0.00	-62.50
POLYNESIA	15,570	17,550	18,610	17,360	16,700	0.26	-3.80
American Samoa	120	110	60	40	10	0.00	-75.00
Cook Islands	1,550	2,130	1,930	1,890	2,560	0.04	35.45
French Polynesia	4,480	3,930	3,850	3,020	2,600	0.04	-13.91
Niue	250	220	60	300	170	0.00	-43.33
Samoa	4,130	4,910	4,770	5,220	5,590	0.09	7.09
Tokelau	90			180			
Tonga	4,470	5,910	7,490	6,350	5,400	0.08	-14.96
Tuvalu	130	80	40	70	40	0.00	-42.86
Wallis and Futuna Islands	350	260	410	290	330	0.01	13.79
OTHER EAST ASIA AND THE PACIFIC				170	10	0.00	-94.12
Other countries of Oceania				170	10	0.00	-94.12
EUROPE	1,401,400	1,389,820	1,335,470	1,345,940	1,434,450	22.48	6.58
CENTRAL/EASTERN EUROPE	47,190	48,210	48,300	56,220	60,330	0.95	7.31
Armenia	90	110	140	190	170	0.00	-10.53
Azerbaijan	110	120	160	150	290	0.00	93.33
Belarus	320	380	280	430	570	0.01	32.56
Bulgaria	1,250	1,050	950	1,300	1,490	0.02	14.62
Czech Republic	6,690	6,410	6,050	7,350	6,980	0.11	-5.03
Estonia	2,470	2,380	2,480	3,020	3,500	0.05	15.89

26

Yearbook of Tourism Statistics, Data 2009 – 2013, 2015 Edition

AUSTRALIA

2. Arrivals of non-resident visitors at national borders, by country of residence

	2009	2010	2011	2012	2013	Market share 2013	% Change 2013-2012
Georgia	100	60	90	100	120	0.00	20.00
Hungary	4,160	3,810	3,730	4,400	4,470	0.07	1.59
Kazakhstan	660	920	930	1,020	1,220	0.02	19.61
Kyrgyzstan	110	100	60	130	100	0.00	-23.08
Latvia	1,080	870	870	1,070	1,050	0.02	-1.87
Lithuania	1,110	1,220	1,200	1,550	1,520	0.02	-1.94
Poland	8,740	8,880	8,690	9,720	11,370	0.18	16.98
Republic of Moldova	90	150	120	150	260	0.00	73.33
Romania	1,450	1,420	1,100	1,600	1,510	0.02	-5.63
Russian Federation	12,940	14,200	14,930	17,570	18,920	0.30	7.68
Slovakia	2,850	3,060	3,110	2,870	3,020	0.05	5.23
Tajikistan	40	50	20	30	20	0.00	-33.33
Turkmenistan	20		10	10	10	0.00	
Ukraine	2,640	2,730	3,160	3,260	3,450	0.05	5.83
Uzbekistan	270	290	220	300	290	0.00	-3.33
NORTHERN EUROPE	**832,270**	**807,900**	**773,600**	**766,670**	**819,230**	**12.84**	**6.86**
Channel Islands	1,530	1,100	960	1,370	1,290	0.02	-5.84
Denmark	24,980	23,960	22,920	23,720	23,950	0.38	0.97
Faeroe Islands	40	90	20	20	20	0.00	
Finland	12,240	12,290	12,370	13,610	13,360	0.21	-1.84
Iceland	750	490	560	480	500	0.01	4.17
Ireland	64,480	54,780	60,060	62,170	63,280	0.99	1.79
Isle of Man	830	430	450	650	490	0.01	-24.62
Norway	18,550	20,110	19,050	20,000	20,220	0.32	1.10
Sweden	34,420	35,850	36,350	38,360	40,310	0.63	5.08
United Kingdom	674,450	658,800	620,860	606,290	655,810	10.28	8.17
SOUTHERN EUROPE	**102,800**	**106,440**	**104,560**	**114,110**	**123,220**	**1.93**	**7.98**
Albania	350	180	170	220	250	0.00	13.64
Andorra	160	140	100	170	60	0.00	-64.71
Bosnia and Herzegovina	680	730	690	670	760	0.01	13.43
Croatia	2,200	2,150	2,110	2,300	2,970	0.05	29.13
Gibraltar	100	220	150	110	210	0.00	90.91
Greece	7,170	8,150	7,760	8,910	8,890	0.14	-0.22
Italy	56,980	58,070	57,070	63,910	70,830	1.11	10.83
Malta	2,840	2,790	2,880	2,310	2,400	0.04	3.90
Portugal	3,820	3,900	3,690	4,360	4,560	0.07	4.59
San Marino	30	60	20	10	50	0.00	400.00
Serbia and Montenegro	2,190	2,480	2,770	2,780	3,010	0.05	8.27
Slovenia	2,380	2,480	2,420	2,270	2,390	0.04	5.29
Spain	22,560	23,680	23,480	24,550	25,030	0.39	1.96
TFYR of Macedonia	1,340	1,410	1,250	1,540	1,810	0.03	17.53
WESTERN EUROPE	**397,480**	**403,750**	**387,960**	**390,070**	**410,910**	**6.44**	**5.34**
Austria	17,220	16,980	14,740	14,820	15,790	0.25	6.55
Belgium	15,420	17,310	16,390	16,700	17,810	0.28	6.65
France	97,750	102,780	99,630	103,680	110,330	1.73	6.41
Germany	165,430	164,860	159,870	159,860	170,250	2.67	6.50
Liechtenstein	90	90	30	60	100	0.00	66.67
Luxembourg	1,320	1,130	990	910	1,350	0.02	48.35
Monaco	570	530	600	740	500	0.01	-32.43
Netherlands	54,050	52,730	49,870	46,720	45,580	0.71	-2.44
Switzerland	45,630	47,340	45,840	46,580	49,200	0.77	5.62
EAST MEDITERRANEAN EUROPE	**21,570**	**23,380**	**20,940**	**18,760**	**20,650**	**0.32**	**10.07**
Cyprus	2,060	2,190	2,220	2,090	2,180	0.03	4.31
Israel	14,370	14,950	12,530	10,660	11,490	0.18	7.79
Turkey	5,140	6,240	6,190	6,010	6,980	0.11	16.14
OTHER EUROPE	**90**	**140**	**110**	**110**	**110**	**0.00**	
Other countries of Europe	90	140	110	110	110	0.00	

27

AUSTRALIA

2. Arrivals of non-resident visitors at national borders, by country of residence

	2009	2010	2011	2012	2013	Market share 2013	% Change 2013-2012
MIDDLE EAST	**64,640**	**70,270**	**62,350**	**63,040**	**70,750**	**1.11**	**12.23**
Bahrain	2,570	2,560	1,720	1,460	1,280	0.02	-12.33
Egypt	2,450	2,850	2,570	2,690	3,170	0.05	17.84
Iraq	810	1,110	1,150	1,010	970	0.02	-3.96
Jordan	1,270	1,100	1,230	1,310	1,530	0.02	16.79
Kuwait	2,280	3,030	3,080	3,470	3,990	0.06	14.99
Lebanon	5,740	5,240	5,010	5,160	4,910	0.08	-4.84
Libya	300	500	210	190	180	0.00	-5.26
Oman	2,290	2,790	2,550	2,230	2,960	0.05	32.74
Qatar	3,730	3,730	4,160	3,650	5,410	0.08	48.22
Saudi Arabia	12,160	13,040	13,040	13,440	13,210	0.21	-1.71
Syrian Arab Republic	710	550	400	170	180	0.00	5.88
United Arab Emirates	30,160	33,530	27,080	28,170	32,900	0.52	16.79
Yemen	130	190	40	20	20	0.00	
Other countries of Middle East	40	50	110	70	40	0.00	-42.86
SOUTH ASIA	**151,230**	**178,190**	**191,980**	**208,550**	**223,210**	**3.50**	**7.03**
Afghanistan	330	300	240	580	290	0.00	-50.00
Bangladesh	5,040	6,530	7,200	7,210	8,520	0.13	18.17
Bhutan	320	350	390	730	560	0.01	-23.29
India	116,110	133,710	143,960	154,740	168,800	2.64	9.09
Iran, Islamic Republic of	4,550	7,150	8,430	9,000	7,260	0.11	-19.33
Maldives	470	640	460	470	550	0.01	17.02
Nepal	4,470	5,000	4,740	6,030	6,580	0.10	9.12
Pakistan	6,120	7,740	8,820	9,870	9,930	0.16	0.61
Sri Lanka	13,820	16,770	17,740	19,920	20,720	0.32	4.02
NOT SPECIFIED	**30**	**140**	**30**	**160**	**60**	**0.00**	**-62.50**
Other countries of the World	30	140	30	160	60	0.00	-62.50

AUSTRIA

3. Arrivals of non-resident tourists in hotels and similar establishments, by country of residence

	2009	2010	2011	2012	2013	Market share 2013	% Change 2013-2012
TOTAL (*)	15,520,385	16,169,935	16,972,001	17,727,876	18,163,665	100.00	2.46
AFRICA	34,631	40,676	47,141	51,561	53,533	0.29	3.82
SOUTHERN AFRICA	12,764	17,099	17,533	18,528	16,948	0.09	-8.53
South Africa	12,764	17,099	17,533	18,528	16,948	0.09	-8.53
OTHER AFRICA	21,867	23,577	29,608	33,033	36,585	0.20	10.75
Other countries of Africa	21,867	23,577	29,608	33,033	36,585	0.20	10.75
AMERICAS	546,539	638,867	664,935	717,953	768,093	4.23	6.98
NORTH AMERICA	468,770	543,442	536,997	566,318	610,569	3.36	7.81
Canada	69,227	77,923	84,364	84,154	81,890	0.45	-2.69
United States of America	399,543	465,519	452,633	482,164	528,679	2.91	9.65
SOUTH AMERICA		3,407	43,453	57,897	61,781	0.34	6.71
Brazil		3,407	43,453	57,897	61,781	0.34	6.71
OTHER AMERICAS	77,769	92,018	84,485	93,738	95,743	0.53	2.14
Other countries of the Americas	77,769	92,018	84,485	93,738	95,743	0.53	2.14
EAST ASIA AND THE PACIFIC	582,651	668,022	820,794	1,004,065	1,120,789	6.17	11.63
NORTH-EAST ASIA	418,173	477,455	603,608	756,265	853,783	4.70	12.89
China	147,417	173,116	245,340	338,064	391,509	2.16	15.81
Japan	191,321	206,217	220,691	253,019	251,108	1.38	-0.76
Korea, Republic of	50,103	62,534	83,011	108,458	150,733	0.83	38.98
Taiwan, Province of China	29,332	35,588	54,566	56,724	60,433	0.33	6.54
SOUTH-EAST ASIA	39,072	47,799	67,930	83,706	95,787	0.53	14.43
All countries of South-East Asia	39,072	47,799	67,930	83,706	95,787	0.53	14.43
AUSTRALASIA	89,781	99,269	107,836	117,214	123,914	0.68	5.72
Australia	78,521	87,742	96,316	104,646	110,134	0.61	5.24
New Zealand	11,260	11,527	11,520	12,568	13,780	0.08	9.64
OTHER EAST ASIA AND THE PACIFIC	35,625	43,499	41,420	46,880	47,305	0.26	0.91
Other countries of Asia	35,625	43,499	41,420	46,880	47,305	0.26	0.91
EUROPE	13,964,009	14,405,592	15,009,616	15,446,474	15,691,772	86.39	1.59
CENTRAL/EASTERN EUROPE	1,516,356	1,635,813	1,832,305	1,918,559	1,980,630	10.90	3.24
Bulgaria	50,093	50,052	56,949	59,797	61,722	0.34	3.22
Czech Republic	318,086	332,214	360,611	366,885	372,684	2.05	1.58
Estonia	12,805	15,805	13,293	15,291	15,531	0.09	1.57
Hungary	283,542	291,622	310,792	319,381	323,211	1.78	1.20
Latvia	11,640	11,322	12,844	14,890	14,462	0.08	-2.87
Lithuania	13,937	14,383	15,722	16,675	16,581	0.09	-0.56
Poland	206,416	228,861	247,051	239,135	254,702	1.40	6.51
Romania	238,325	223,919	236,469	224,779	214,835	1.18	-4.42
Russian Federation	208,613	275,932	359,348	422,243	449,568	2.48	6.47
Slovakia	89,048	97,499	106,142	108,670	114,228	0.63	5.11
Ukraine	56,623	60,041	75,288	90,152	97,331	0.54	7.96
Other countries Central/East Europe	27,228	34,163	37,796	40,661	45,775	0.25	12.58
NORTHERN EUROPE	1,117,272	1,182,644	1,152,609	1,184,028	1,223,206	6.73	3.31
Denmark	199,532	205,901	200,370	201,446	205,236	1.13	1.88
Finland	68,630	68,690	73,418	74,046	73,515	0.40	-0.72
Iceland	5,441	6,525	6,823	6,927	7,503	0.04	8.32
Ireland	52,473	48,052	42,994	43,115	43,971	0.24	1.99
Norway	57,437	68,649	73,605	75,079	77,047	0.42	2.62
Sweden	139,883	164,721	158,229	165,285	167,807	0.92	1.53
United Kingdom	593,876	620,106	597,170	618,130	648,127	3.57	4.85
SOUTHERN EUROPE	1,434,049	1,483,900	1,561,455	1,500,368	1,456,920	8.02	-2.90
Croatia	83,348	79,825	80,470	81,092	81,701	0.45	0.75
Greece	83,145	73,029	59,856	49,980	47,104	0.26	-5.75
Italy	895,285	907,257	918,414	880,136	839,291	4.62	-4.64
Malta	3,632	5,048	5,172	5,391	6,157	0.03	14.21
Portugal	26,231	28,212	30,014	25,580	26,147	0.14	2.22
Serbia and Montenegro	49,721	70,662	92,072	93,490	103,159	0.57	10.34
Slovenia	70,358	73,650	81,001	82,522	85,837	0.47	4.02
Spain	222,329	246,217	294,456	282,177	267,524	1.47	-5.19

29

Yearbook of Tourism Statistics, Data 2009 – 2013, 2015 Edition

AUSTRIA

3. Arrivals of non-resident tourists in hotels and similar establishments, by country of residence

	2009	2010	2011	2012	2013	Market share 2013	% Change 2013-2012
WESTERN EUROPE	9,792,268	9,978,470	10,315,335	10,672,792	10,849,614	59.73	1.66
Belgium	353,483	353,391	373,709	372,756	374,924	2.06	0.58
France	397,979	414,677	434,953	431,308	423,782	2.33	-1.74
Germany	7,258,959	7,394,154	7,547,259	7,826,949	8,041,954	44.27	2.75
Luxembourg	44,468	46,863	49,262	50,143	53,987	0.30	7.67
Netherlands	875,811	853,187	864,401	886,240	852,632	4.69	-3.79
Switzerland	861,568	916,198	1,045,751	1,105,396	1,102,335	6.07	-0.28
EAST MEDITERRANEAN EUROPE	104,064	124,765	147,912	170,727	181,402	1.00	6.25
Cyprus	8,310	9,029	7,677	7,635	7,093	0.04	-7.10
Israel	58,826	65,551	73,296	84,939	93,716	0.52	10.33
Turkey	36,928	50,185	66,939	78,153	80,593	0.44	3.12
MIDDLE EAST	89,519	109,523	142,173	189,193	224,150	1.23	18.48
All countries of Middle East	89,519	109,523	142,173	189,193	224,150	1.23	18.48
SOUTH ASIA	45,482	57,368	79,891	84,574	84,101	0.46	-0.56
All countries of South Asia	45,482	57,368	79,891	84,574	84,101	0.46	-0.56
NOT SPECIFIED	257,554	249,887	207,451	234,056	221,227	1.22	-5.48
Other countries of the World	257,554	249,887	207,451	234,056	221,227	1.22	-5.48

Yearbook of Tourism Statistics, Data 2009 – 2013, 2015 Edition

AUSTRIA

4. Arrivals of non-resident tourists in all types of accommodation establishments, by country of residence

	2009	2010	2011	2012	2013	Market share 2013	% Change 2013-2012
TOTAL (*)	21,355,439	22,004,266	23,011,956	24,150,776	24,813,128	100.00	2.74
AFRICA	38,794	44,965	52,345	58,087	60,827	0.25	4.72
SOUTHERN AFRICA	15,699	19,874	20,479	21,737	20,282	0.08	-6.69
South Africa	15,699	19,874	20,479	21,737	20,282	0.08	-6.69
OTHER AFRICA	23,095	25,091	31,866	36,350	40,545	0.16	11.54
Other countries of Africa	23,095	25,091	31,866	36,350	40,545	0.16	11.54
AMERICAS	616,730	708,515	742,821	805,619	860,311	3.47	6.79
NORTH AMERICA	523,314	596,125	594,679	629,280	676,055	2.72	7.43
Canada	81,466	90,684	98,545	97,807	96,042	0.39	-1.80
United States of America	441,848	505,441	496,134	531,473	580,013	2.34	9.13
SOUTH AMERICA		3,918	50,796	68,257	72,504	0.29	6.22
Brazil		3,918	50,796	68,257	72,504	0.29	6.22
OTHER AMERICAS	93,416	108,472	97,346	108,082	111,752	0.45	3.40
Other countries of the Americas	93,416	108,472	97,346	108,082	111,752	0.45	3.40
EAST ASIA AND THE PACIFIC	645,203	741,244	914,840	1,105,297	1,227,438	4.95	11.05
NORTH-EAST ASIA	445,635	512,054	654,442	812,653	915,601	3.69	12.67
China	155,179	182,282	259,944	354,657	408,509	1.65	15.18
Japan	198,751	213,581	228,559	261,261	259,184	1.04	-0.79
Korea, Republic of	59,351	77,560	106,359	134,856	182,442	0.74	35.29
Taiwan, Province of China	32,354	38,631	59,580	61,879	65,466	0.26	5.80
SOUTH-EAST ASIA	43,269	53,425	74,242	90,866	103,467	0.42	13.87
All countries of South-East Asia	43,269	53,425	74,242	90,866	103,467	0.42	13.87
AUSTRALASIA	118,112	129,818	142,258	151,922	157,318	0.63	3.55
Australia	103,063	114,457	126,169	134,800	138,742	0.56	2.92
New Zealand	15,049	15,361	16,089	17,122	18,576	0.07	8.49
OTHER EAST ASIA AND THE PACIFIC	38,187	45,947	43,898	49,856	51,052	0.21	2.40
Other countries of Asia	38,187	45,947	43,898	49,856	51,052	0.21	2.40
EUROPE	19,613,283	20,042,806	20,818,964	21,599,410	22,043,146	88.84	2.05
CENTRAL/EASTERN EUROPE	2,131,821	2,279,602	2,519,532	2,633,952	2,727,708	10.99	3.56
Bulgaria	56,305	55,947	63,992	68,238	71,326	0.29	4.53
Czech Republic	556,073	569,279	603,581	619,287	630,398	2.54	1.79
Estonia	16,551	19,670	16,759	21,179	20,797	0.08	-1.80
Hungary	426,498	442,245	466,860	472,793	479,083	1.93	1.33
Latvia	15,634	15,766	18,371	21,058	20,771	0.08	-1.36
Lithuania	23,766	23,007	25,417	26,757	27,410	0.11	2.44
Poland	317,222	346,582	372,924	362,870	381,875	1.54	5.24
Romania	273,225	261,439	275,722	265,774	257,211	1.04	-3.22
Russian Federation	230,598	305,714	400,399	476,397	513,460	2.07	7.78
Slovakia	123,164	135,332	148,080	152,960	161,691	0.65	5.71
Ukraine	63,929	68,264	86,649	102,720	113,829	0.46	10.81
Other countries Central/East Europe	28,856	36,357	40,778	43,919	49,857	0.20	13.52
NORTHERN EUROPE	1,403,027	1,478,706	1,447,011	1,500,402	1,551,914	6.25	3.43
Denmark	312,734	321,642	313,013	316,890	323,037	1.30	1.94
Finland	79,189	80,922	87,105	91,363	93,451	0.38	2.29
Iceland	6,198	7,613	7,912	8,440	9,197	0.04	8.97
Ireland	64,110	59,152	53,416	53,210	54,558	0.22	2.53
Norway	67,775	79,838	84,951	87,230	90,720	0.37	4.00
Sweden	171,774	198,122	191,405	202,297	206,834	0.83	2.24
United Kingdom	701,247	731,417	709,209	740,972	774,117	3.12	4.47
SOUTHERN EUROPE	1,694,882	1,748,616	1,842,030	1,794,186	1,759,077	7.09	-1.96
Croatia	109,903	105,712	105,184	106,129	104,470	0.42	-1.56
Greece	88,208	77,587	64,210	53,689	51,447	0.21	-4.18
Italy	1,056,491	1,067,721	1,086,957	1,060,105	1,023,530	4.12	-3.45
Malta	4,086	5,424	5,877	5,884	6,758	0.03	14.85
Portugal	30,082	32,051	33,846	29,617	30,519	0.12	3.05
Serbia and Montenegro	54,602	78,950	102,125	104,145	115,491	0.47	10.89
Slovenia	102,126	106,520	117,740	122,677	129,662	0.52	5.69
Spain	249,384	274,651	326,091	311,940	297,200	1.20	-4.73

Yearbook of Tourism Statistics, Data 2009 – 2013, 2015 Edition

AUSTRIA

4. Arrivals of non-resident tourists in all types of accommodation establishments, by country of residence

	2009	2010	2011	2012	2013	Market share 2013	% Change 2013-2012
WESTERN EUROPE	14,263,593	14,392,893	14,841,017	15,473,410	15,792,292	63.64	2.06
Belgium	461,299	461,784	488,810	494,014	501,365	2.02	1.49
France	478,747	499,894	521,955	519,519	514,524	2.07	-0.96
Germany	10,622,835	10,706,153	10,929,670	11,411,557	11,758,193	47.39	3.04
Luxembourg	51,164	53,804	57,004	58,229	62,999	0.25	8.19
Netherlands	1,654,959	1,617,692	1,644,620	1,714,513	1,673,536	6.74	-2.39
Switzerland	994,589	1,053,566	1,198,958	1,275,578	1,281,675	5.17	0.48
EAST MEDITERRANEAN EUROPE	119,960	142,989	169,374	197,460	212,155	0.86	7.44
Cyprus	8,951	9,624	8,218	8,244	7,684	0.03	-6.79
Israel	71,678	80,296	89,834	105,317	117,053	0.47	11.14
Turkey	39,331	53,069	71,322	83,899	87,418	0.35	4.19
MIDDLE EAST	97,053	120,055	160,005	218,070	268,476	1.08	23.11
All countries of Middle East	97,053	120,055	160,005	218,070	268,476	1.08	23.11
SOUTH ASIA	47,604	59,780	83,911	88,864	87,916	0.35	-1.07
All countries of South Asia	47,604	59,780	83,911	88,864	87,916	0.35	-1.07
NOT SPECIFIED	296,772	286,901	239,070	275,429	265,014	1.07	-3.78
Other countries of the World	296,772	286,901	239,070	275,429	265,014	1.07	-3.78

Yearbook of Tourism Statistics, Data 2009 – 2013, 2015 Edition

AUSTRIA

5. Overnight stays of non-resident tourists in hotels and similar establishments, by country of residence

	2009	2010	2011	2012	2013	Market share 2013	% Change 2013-2012
TOTAL (*)	57,798,255	58,314,787	59,146,607	61,359,896	62,137,088	100.00	1.27
AFRICA	108,776	128,883	149,633	160,143	169,937	0.27	6.12
SOUTHERN AFRICA	50,416	59,254	62,914	64,044	61,388	0.10	-4.15
South Africa	50,416	59,254	62,914	64,044	61,388	0.10	-4.15
OTHER AFRICA	58,360	69,629	86,719	96,099	108,549	0.17	12.96
Other countries of Africa	58,360	69,629	86,719	96,099	108,549	0.17	12.96
AMERICAS	1,342,812	1,524,758	1,568,231	1,680,026	1,755,364	2.82	4.48
NORTH AMERICA	1,159,958	1,313,600	1,283,178	1,334,351	1,406,106	2.26	5.38
Canada	170,513	190,823	205,616	202,047	199,062	0.32	-1.48
United States of America	989,445	1,122,777	1,077,562	1,132,304	1,207,044	1.94	6.60
SOUTH AMERICA		7,924	96,380	131,874	136,645	0.22	3.62
Brazil		7,924	96,380	131,874	136,645	0.22	3.62
OTHER AMERICAS	182,854	203,234	188,673	213,801	212,613	0.34	-0.56
Other countries of the Americas	182,854	203,234	188,673	213,801	212,613	0.34	-0.56
EAST ASIA AND THE PACIFIC	1,096,782	1,214,144	1,418,535	1,718,206	1,882,107	3.03	9.54
NORTH-EAST ASIA	727,575	795,424	955,351	1,193,440	1,314,504	2.12	10.14
China	206,576	249,334	340,655	471,430	543,537	0.87	15.30
Japan	387,987	393,431	417,538	484,679	480,129	0.77	-0.94
Korea, Republic of	82,138	91,387	116,888	154,567	204,293	0.33	32.17
Taiwan, Province of China	50,874	61,272	80,270	82,764	86,545	0.14	4.57
SOUTH-EAST ASIA	74,191	89,710	122,214	145,245	166,905	0.27	14.91
All countries of South-East Asia	74,191	89,710	122,214	145,245	166,905	0.27	14.91
AUSTRALASIA	212,390	235,320	251,823	282,412	297,669	0.48	5.40
Australia	187,649	208,685	225,447	252,215	266,398	0.43	5.62
New Zealand	24,741	26,635	26,376	30,197	31,271	0.05	3.56
OTHER EAST ASIA AND THE PACIFIC	82,626	93,690	89,147	97,109	103,029	0.17	6.10
Other countries of Asia	82,626	93,690	89,147	97,109	103,029	0.17	6.10
EUROPE	54,267,191	54,438,114	54,939,775	56,512,270	56,964,184	91.68	0.80
CENTRAL/EASTERN EUROPE	4,817,482	5,050,336	5,547,838	5,811,896	5,926,990	9.54	1.98
Bulgaria	119,747	123,252	137,444	147,078	153,845	0.25	4.60
Czech Republic	970,092	992,854	1,066,545	1,085,607	1,086,811	1.75	0.11
Estonia	43,394	51,130	42,431	45,658	44,070	0.07	-3.48
Hungary	878,544	873,197	918,744	941,573	918,603	1.48	-2.44
Latvia	37,803	34,040	37,172	42,946	45,210	0.07	5.27
Lithuania	51,068	45,664	47,798	52,933	53,545	0.09	1.16
Poland	729,691	752,794	801,360	774,235	779,703	1.25	0.71
Romania	662,774	627,184	645,438	615,389	582,792	0.94	-5.30
Russian Federation	802,394	981,242	1,217,496	1,420,315	1,537,380	2.47	8.24
Slovakia	281,003	295,712	313,888	322,289	330,877	0.53	2.66
Ukraine	166,819	178,530	217,819	253,422	271,944	0.44	7.31
Other countries Central/East Europe	74,153	94,737	101,703	110,451	122,210	0.20	10.65
NORTHERN EUROPE	4,772,415	4,803,177	4,615,983	4,688,301	4,814,500	7.75	2.69
Denmark	884,510	888,454	849,192	832,941	823,336	1.33	-1.15
Finland	233,717	225,430	241,533	246,732	242,042	0.39	-1.90
Iceland	19,335	21,327	24,939	25,179	26,718	0.04	6.11
Ireland	250,742	211,253	182,739	183,218	181,893	0.29	-0.72
Norway	191,839	223,083	234,757	254,205	254,960	0.41	0.30
Sweden	523,827	584,509	579,911	606,415	613,637	0.99	1.19
United Kingdom	2,668,445	2,649,121	2,502,912	2,539,611	2,671,914	4.30	5.21
SOUTHERN EUROPE	3,751,722	3,805,545	3,867,234	3,681,034	3,513,923	5.66	-4.54
Croatia	241,935	219,400	209,847	210,857	203,786	0.33	-3.35
Greece	231,312	201,413	163,446	134,926	126,923	0.20	-5.93
Italy	2,367,675	2,372,913	2,352,970	2,224,264	2,084,154	3.35	-6.30
Malta	15,008	19,697	18,590	20,265	21,702	0.03	7.09
Portugal	73,430	74,792	76,836	69,508	69,559	0.11	0.07
Serbia and Montenegro	116,137	161,867	202,324	201,663	216,314	0.35	7.27
Slovenia	177,879	182,082	201,087	206,430	213,462	0.34	3.41
Spain	528,346	573,381	642,134	613,121	578,023	0.93	-5.72

33

AUSTRIA

5. Overnight stays of non-resident tourists in hotels and similar establishments, by country of residence

	2009	2010	2011	2012	2013	Market share 2013	% Change 2013-2012
WESTERN EUROPE	40,605,574	40,398,966	40,466,734	41,853,848	42,193,761	67.90	0.81
Belgium	1,848,562	1,793,325	1,860,265	1,847,697	1,845,325	2.97	-0.13
France	1,414,698	1,445,896	1,484,696	1,470,441	1,456,302	2.34	-0.96
Germany	29,851,032	29,701,628	29,328,739	30,460,997	31,010,037	49.91	1.80
Luxembourg	232,605	240,851	254,089	246,205	264,356	0.43	7.37
Netherlands	4,276,323	4,091,901	3,999,146	4,088,591	3,892,512	6.26	-4.80
Switzerland	2,982,354	3,125,365	3,539,799	3,739,917	3,725,229	6.00	-0.39
EAST MEDITERRANEAN EUROPE	319,998	380,090	441,986	477,191	515,010	0.83	7.93
Cyprus	24,770	27,261	22,238	21,135	19,892	0.03	-5.88
Israel	199,474	227,075	256,823	268,538	297,199	0.48	10.67
Turkey	95,754	125,754	162,925	187,518	197,919	0.32	5.55
MIDDLE EAST	270,280	327,847	409,365	538,580	622,829	1.00	15.64
All countries of Middle East	270,280	327,847	409,365	538,580	622,829	1.00	15.64
SOUTH ASIA	90,103	103,892	145,647	148,667	148,117	0.24	-0.37
All countries of South Asia	90,103	103,892	145,647	148,667	148,117	0.24	-0.37
NOT SPECIFIED	622,311	577,149	515,421	602,004	594,550	0.96	-1.24
Other countries of the World	622,311	577,149	515,421	602,004	594,550	0.96	-1.24

Yearbook of Tourism Statistics, Data 2009 – 2013, 2015 Edition

AUSTRIA

6. Overnight stays of non-resident tourists in all types of accommodation establishments, by country of residence

		2009	2010	2011	2012	2013	Market share 2013	% Change 2013-2012
TOTAL	(*)	89,864,164	89,857,167	90,705,554	95,051,917	96,874,372	100.00	1.92
AFRICA		130,413	152,378	177,467	194,232	211,484	0.22	8.88
SOUTHERN AFRICA		66,412	74,114	79,954	81,604	80,332	0.08	-1.56
South Africa		66,412	74,114	79,954	81,604	80,332	0.08	-1.56
OTHER AFRICA		64,001	78,264	97,513	112,628	131,152	0.14	16.45
Other countries of Africa		64,001	78,264	97,513	112,628	131,152	0.14	16.45
AMERICAS		1,531,406	1,723,910	1,788,074	1,940,897	2,021,425	2.09	4.15
NORTH AMERICA		1,317,648	1,472,085	1,449,928	1,530,172	1,608,066	1.66	5.09
Canada		207,190	229,015	246,821	244,467	240,823	0.25	-1.49
United States of America		1,110,458	1,243,070	1,203,107	1,285,705	1,367,243	1.41	6.34
SOUTH AMERICA			9,371	113,007	156,943	162,359	0.17	3.45
Brazil			9,371	113,007	156,943	162,359	0.17	3.45
OTHER AMERICAS		213,758	242,454	225,139	253,782	251,000	0.26	-1.10
Other countries of the Americas		213,758	242,454	225,139	253,782	251,000	0.26	-1.10
EAST ASIA AND THE PACIFIC		1,244,356	1,382,262	1,634,091	1,961,328	2,137,417	2.21	8.98
NORTH-EAST ASIA		784,816	863,947	1,057,035	1,314,322	1,444,617	1.49	9.91
China		222,225	267,483	369,718	506,618	579,155	0.60	14.32
Japan		407,112	412,494	437,949	508,292	502,063	0.52	-1.23
Korea, Republic of		97,859	116,720	158,835	205,918	266,239	0.27	29.29
Taiwan, Province of China		57,620	67,250	90,533	93,494	97,160	0.10	3.92
SOUTH-EAST ASIA		84,200	101,781	136,251	161,903	183,886	0.19	13.58
All countries of South-East Asia		84,200	101,781	136,251	161,903	183,886	0.19	13.58
AUSTRALASIA		285,489	315,130	343,338	379,139	394,377	0.41	4.02
Australia		250,998	279,417	304,430	335,554	349,751	0.36	4.23
New Zealand		34,491	35,713	38,908	43,585	44,626	0.05	2.39
OTHER EAST ASIA AND THE PACIFIC		89,851	101,404	97,467	105,964	114,537	0.12	8.09
Other countries of Asia		89,851	101,404	97,467	105,964	114,537	0.12	8.09
EUROPE		85,776,665	85,388,146	85,806,605	89,290,120	90,710,573	93.64	1.59
CENTRAL/EASTERN EUROPE		7,745,592	8,091,969	8,838,267	9,265,872	9,543,773	9.85	3.00
Bulgaria		145,774	150,509	168,678	185,793	199,175	0.21	7.20
Czech Republic		1,955,027	1,972,457	2,078,822	2,123,891	2,150,183	2.22	1.24
Estonia		60,901	68,219	59,150	70,231	67,545	0.07	-3.82
Hungary		1,499,474	1,510,379	1,597,850	1,624,206	1,622,437	1.67	-0.11
Latvia		59,085	55,052	62,767	73,406	74,943	0.08	2.09
Lithuania		105,013	93,384	97,039	110,189	114,266	0.12	3.70
Poland		1,385,970	1,422,764	1,518,525	1,478,694	1,495,559	1.54	1.14
Romania		841,457	822,928	853,549	831,278	802,875	0.83	-3.42
Russian Federation		969,166	1,195,360	1,501,355	1,785,754	1,954,599	2.02	9.46
Slovakia		424,182	464,825	499,057	525,192	556,815	0.57	6.02
Ukraine		209,856	226,260	282,264	326,274	360,952	0.37	10.63
Other countries Central/East Europe		89,687	109,832	119,211	130,964	144,424	0.15	10.28
NORTHERN EUROPE		6,306,276	6,369,751	6,166,919	6,325,512	6,531,747	6.74	3.26
Denmark		1,501,450	1,514,888	1,464,303	1,447,258	1,448,608	1.50	0.09
Finland		279,429	280,480	303,829	336,601	351,996	0.36	4.57
Iceland		23,427	26,001	30,121	32,657	35,277	0.04	8.02
Ireland		308,291	269,442	235,490	234,778	234,112	0.24	-0.28
Norway		240,005	271,184	282,148	307,116	310,552	0.32	1.12
Sweden		689,808	754,680	746,684	786,586	806,569	0.83	2.54
United Kingdom		3,263,866	3,253,076	3,104,344	3,180,516	3,344,633	3.45	5.16
SOUTHERN EUROPE		4,837,856	4,903,684	4,995,293	4,853,145	4,713,370	4.87	-2.88
Croatia		387,895	351,491	333,806	334,594	314,681	0.32	-5.95
Greece		255,116	221,551	183,410	151,809	148,099	0.15	-2.44
Italy		3,015,873	3,020,992	3,013,847	2,917,854	2,777,844	2.87	-4.80
Malta		17,177	21,815	21,891	22,418	24,588	0.03	9.68
Portugal		90,141	94,320	90,226	86,515	91,435	0.09	5.69
Serbia and Montenegro		144,902	210,582	256,448	257,491	282,035	0.29	9.53
Slovenia		310,055	317,008	354,656	374,446	403,136	0.42	7.66
Spain		616,697	665,925	741,009	708,018	671,552	0.69	-5.15

35

AUSTRIA

6. Overnight stays of non-resident tourists in all types of accommodation establishments, by country of residence

	2009	2010	2011	2012	2013	Market share 2013	% Change 2013-2012
WESTERN EUROPE	66,494,567	65,559,316	65,267,644	68,250,456	69,271,558	71.51	1.50
Belgium	2,530,232	2,464,985	2,565,423	2,583,143	2,605,997	2.69	0.88
France	1,739,002	1,785,956	1,834,629	1,818,852	1,808,491	1.87	-0.57
Germany	48,856,862	48,155,743	47,389,531	49,606,383	50,822,726	52.46	2.45
Luxembourg	274,864	284,358	301,951	295,170	317,477	0.33	7.56
Netherlands	9,451,747	9,071,437	8,899,263	9,389,082	9,139,675	9.43	-2.66
Switzerland	3,641,860	3,796,837	4,276,847	4,557,826	4,577,192	4.72	0.42
EAST MEDITERRANEAN EUROPE	392,374	463,426	538,482	595,135	650,125	0.67	9.24
Cyprus	28,388	30,235	24,764	24,458	22,085	0.02	-9.70
Israel	257,619	295,279	337,004	364,306	409,095	0.42	12.29
Turkey	106,367	137,912	176,714	206,371	218,945	0.23	6.09
MIDDLE EAST	331,139	410,128	527,108	712,514	872,571	0.90	22.46
All countries of Middle East	331,139	410,128	527,108	712,514	872,571	0.90	22.46
SOUTH ASIA	96,857	110,442	158,686	164,226	160,295	0.17	-2.39
All countries of South Asia	96,857	110,442	158,686	164,226	160,295	0.17	-2.39
NOT SPECIFIED	753,328	689,901	613,523	788,600	760,607	0.79	-3.55
Other countries of the World	753,328	689,901	613,523	788,600	760,607	0.79	-3.55

Yearbook of Tourism Statistics, Data 2009 – 2013, 2015 Edition

AZERBAIJAN

2. Arrivals of non-resident visitors at national borders, by country of residence

	2009	2010	2011	2012	2013	Market share 2013	% Change 2013-2012
TOTAL	1,830,367	1,962,906	2,239,141	2,484,048	2,508,904	100.00	1.00
AFRICA	1,732	2,056	1,781	2,361	2,723	0.11	15.33
EAST AFRICA	140	165	189	241	270	0.01	12.03
British Indian Ocean Territory	2						
Burundi	3	2	5	2	16	0.00	700.00
Comoros	1	9	12	8	16	0.00	100.00
Djibouti	2	6	4		15	0.00	
Eritrea	2	1	4	4	9	0.00	125.00
Ethiopia	36	30	22	30	29	0.00	-3.33
Kenya	12	37	22	52	54	0.00	3.85
Madagascar	3	1	4	7	2	0.00	-71.43
Malawi	3	3	4	2	6	0.00	200.00
Mauritius	19	15	32	20	20	0.00	
Mozambique	6	7	6	11	8	0.00	-27.27
Reunion	15				1	0.00	
Rwanda	2	6	15	1	8	0.00	700.00
Seychelles				4			
Somalia	1	3	1	3	5	0.00	66.67
Uganda	12	13	21	21	24	0.00	14.29
United Republic of Tanzania	8	15	13	16	22	0.00	37.50
Zambia		9	7	31	20	0.00	-35.48
Zimbabwe	13	8	17	29	15	0.00	-48.28
CENTRAL AFRICA	142	63	109	101	205	0.01	102.97
Angola	24	9	14	20	12	0.00	-40.00
Cameroon	47	40	55	40	119	0.00	197.50
Central African Republic			1	1			
Chad				4	8	0.00	100.00
Congo	6	1	11	5	25	0.00	400.00
Democratic Republic of the Congo	5	9	9	13	18	0.00	38.46
Equatorial Guinea				4	3	0.00	-25.00
Gabon	28	4	19	12	14	0.00	16.67
Sao Tome and Principe	32			2	6	0.00	200.00
NORTH AFRICA	557	634	506	458	682	0.03	48.91
Algeria	213	229	180	135	197	0.01	45.93
Morocco	196	155	183	158	250	0.01	58.23
Sudan	50	98	47	62	104	0.00	67.74
Tunisia	98	152	96	103	130	0.01	26.21
Western Sahara					1	0.00	
SOUTHERN AFRICA	553	728	567	905	927	0.04	2.43
Botswana	2	9	4	5	5	0.00	
Lesotho			4	1			
Namibia		2	8	19	5	0.00	-73.68
South Africa	549	716	550	878	916	0.04	4.33
Swaziland	2	1	1	2	1	0.00	-50.00
WEST AFRICA	340	466	410	656	639	0.03	-2.59
Benin	2	6	7	7	10	0.00	42.86
Burkina Faso	7	6	7	1	18	0.00	1,700.00
Côte d'Ivoire	10	12	29	28	75	0.00	167.86
Gambia	3	17	9	94	11	0.00	-88.30
Ghana	37	38	64	119	44	0.00	-63.03
Guinea	7	16	7	7	42	0.00	500.00
Guinea-Bissau	4	3	1		3	0.00	
Liberia	7	7		4	19	0.00	375.00
Mali	3	12	19	19	60	0.00	215.79
Mauritania	9	53	4	5	17	0.00	240.00
Niger	6	5	7	15	13	0.00	-13.33
Nigeria	218	223	178	263	249	0.01	-5.32
Senegal	25	45	43	52	50	0.00	-3.85
Sierra Leone	1	12	33	36	23	0.00	-36.11

37

Yearbook of Tourism Statistics, Data 2009 – 2013, 2015 Edition

AZERBAIJAN

2. Arrivals of non-resident visitors at national borders, by country of residence

	2009	2010	2011	2012	2013	Market share 2013	% Change 2013-2012
Togo	1	11	2	6	5	0.00	-16.67
AMERICAS	**15,445**	**15,789**	**15,532**	**18,825**	**20,825**	**0.83**	**10.62**
CARIBBEAN	**346**	**386**	**484**	**416**	**512**	**0.02**	**23.08**
Aruba	13				6	0.00	
Bahamas	2	3	4				
Barbados	3	3	4	9	4	0.00	-55.56
Cayman Islands			2				
Cuba	32	88	81	74	98	0.00	32.43
Dominica	2	2	8				
Dominican Republic	12	13	33	24	39	0.00	62.50
Grenada	9	1	3	1			
Haiti	1		1				
Jamaica	3	2	8	7	4	0.00	-42.86
Netherlands Antilles				18	9	0.00	-50.00
Puerto Rico				1			
Saint Kitts and Nevis				2	12	0.00	500.00
Saint Vincent and the Grenadines				3			
Trinidad and Tobago	253	274	336	276	340	0.01	23.19
Turks and Caicos Islands	16		4	1			
CENTRAL AMERICA	**25**	**56**	**92**	**131**	**85**	**0.00**	**-35.11**
Belize	1	6	3	1	2	0.00	100.00
Costa Rica	6	11	18	47	13	0.00	-72.34
El Salvador	2	4	7	13	12	0.00	-7.69
Guatemala	7	6	15	22	25	0.00	13.64
Honduras	5	15	20	23	19	0.00	-17.39
Nicaragua	1	7	14	11	10	0.00	-9.09
Panama	3	7	15	14	4	0.00	-71.43
NORTH AMERICA	**13,833**	**14,134**	**13,465**	**16,474**	**18,191**	**0.73**	**10.42**
Canada	2,036	2,050	1,851	2,566	2,411	0.10	-6.04
Mexico	134	98	171	221	168	0.01	-23.98
United States of America	11,663	11,986	11,443	13,687	15,612	0.62	14.06
SOUTH AMERICA	**1,241**	**1,213**	**1,491**	**1,804**	**2,037**	**0.08**	**12.92**
Argentina	97	71	159	484	258	0.01	-46.69
Bolivia	27	53	36	34	55	0.00	61.76
Brazil	399	434	500	516	817	0.03	58.33
Chile	13	28	35	66	96	0.00	45.45
Colombia	349	332	417	427	437	0.02	2.34
Ecuador	44	37	89	30	52	0.00	73.33
Guyana	1	1	2	1	2	0.00	100.00
Paraguay	12	11	7	27	27	0.00	
Peru	43	31	54	28	40	0.00	42.86
Suriname		2		1			
Uruguay	47	26	18	65	50	0.00	-23.08
Venezuela	209	187	174	125	203	0.01	62.40
EAST ASIA AND THE PACIFIC	**13,839**	**14,730**	**15,092**	**15,757**	**19,607**	**0.78**	**24.43**
NORTH-EAST ASIA	**9,680**	**10,405**	**11,060**	**10,239**	**12,178**	**0.49**	**18.94**
China	6,322	5,846	6,224	5,060	6,465	0.26	27.77
Hong Kong, China	1						
Japan	1,076	1,809	2,098	2,230	2,471	0.10	10.81
Korea, Dem. People's Republic of	4	15	3	42	3	0.00	-92.86
Korea, Republic of	2,082	2,647	2,461	2,829	3,134	0.12	10.78
Macao, China	3		1				
Mongolia	84	59	87	64	93	0.00	45.31
Taiwan, Province of China	108	29	186	14	12	0.00	-14.29
SOUTH-EAST ASIA	**2,763**	**2,898**	**2,539**	**3,759**	**5,410**	**0.22**	**43.92**
Brunei Darussalam	6	9	4	3	19	0.00	533.33
Cambodia	14		7	19	11	0.00	-42.11
Indonesia	314	353	440	577	706	0.03	22.36
Lao People's Democratic Republic		2	8	7	7	0.00	

38

AZERBAIJAN

2. Arrivals of non-resident visitors at national borders, by country of residence

	2009	2010	2011	2012	2013	Market share 2013	% Change 2013-2012
Malaysia	603	550	402	805	2,058	0.08	155.65
Myanmar	24	39	13	16	51	0.00	218.75
Philippines	1,216	1,153	1,003	1,322	1,445	0.06	9.30
Singapore	246	316	203	315	429	0.02	36.19
Thailand	245	298	207	386	481	0.02	24.61
Viet Nam	95	178	252	309	203	0.01	-34.30
AUSTRALASIA	**1,390**	**1,419**	**1,485**	**1,745**	**2,010**	**0.08**	**15.19**
Australia	1,109	1,122	1,129	1,296	1,518	0.06	17.13
New Zealand	281	297	356	449	492	0.02	9.58
MELANESIA	**1**		**1**	**6**	**6**	**0.00**	
Fiji	1		1	4	4	0.00	
Papua New Guinea				2			
Vanuatu					2	0.00	
MICRONESIA	**2**	**1**	**1**				
Kiribati		1					
Palau	2		1				
POLYNESIA	**3**	**7**	**6**	**8**	**3**	**0.00**	**-62.50**
American Samoa				2			
French Polynesia				1			
Samoa	1	3	2		1	0.00	
Tuvalu	2	4	4	5	1	0.00	-80.00
Wallis and Futuna Islands					1	0.00	
EUROPE	**1,454,046**	**1,568,063**	**1,786,769**	**2,147,613**	**2,306,463**	**91.93**	**7.40**
CENTRAL/EASTERN EUROPE	**1,205,273**	**1,282,747**	**1,470,964**	**1,760,165**	**1,849,954**	**73.74**	**5.10**
Armenia				16			
Belarus	5,308	5,479	5,724	7,038	8,251	0.33	17.24
Bulgaria	1,351	1,638	1,984	2,231	2,028	0.08	-9.10
Czech Republic	948	1,013	1,025	1,279	1,497	0.06	17.04
Estonia	606	566	559	791	787	0.03	-0.51
Georgia	529,613	491,942	573,063	763,251	810,390	32.30	6.18
Hungary	597	737	910	950	1,825	0.07	92.11
Kazakhstan	16,048	19,209	28,225	25,295	28,226	1.13	11.59
Kyrgyzstan	1,921	2,279	2,337	2,905	2,594	0.10	-10.71
Latvia	1,281	1,295	1,536	1,875	1,731	0.07	-7.68
Lithuania	1,133	1,372	1,557	1,698	1,797	0.07	5.83
Poland	1,699	2,455	2,224	3,168	3,716	0.15	17.30
Republic of Moldova	4,289	3,645	3,753	4,375	4,448	0.18	1.67
Romania	1,039	1,296	1,417	1,678	2,053	0.08	22.35
Russian Federation	598,894	701,110	786,684	876,013	903,242	36.00	3.11
Slovakia	511	518	445	622	659	0.03	5.95
Tajikistan	675	742	1,009	1,264	1,515	0.06	19.86
Turkmenistan	3,687	4,072	3,969	4,906	4,766	0.19	-2.85
Ukraine	28,606	31,500	40,030	42,393	51,802	2.06	22.19
Uzbekistan	7,067	11,879	14,513	18,417	18,627	0.74	1.14
NORTHERN EUROPE	**31,508**	**30,488**	**30,666**	**36,739**	**40,512**	**1.61**	**10.27**
Denmark	688	745	870	1,099	1,087	0.04	-1.09
Finland	1,098	1,041	699	902	935	0.04	3.66
Iceland	219	170	384	651	700	0.03	7.53
Ireland	757	961	919	969	1,068	0.04	10.22
Norway	1,921	2,054	1,874	1,981	2,024	0.08	2.17
Sweden	1,126	1,357	1,274	2,012	1,857	0.07	-7.70
United Kingdom	25,699	24,160	24,646	29,125	32,841	1.31	12.76
SOUTHERN EUROPE	**9,851**	**10,025**	**10,072**	**14,352**	**17,216**	**0.69**	**19.96**
Albania	159	136	177	164	208	0.01	26.83
Andorra	1	6	5	26	32	0.00	23.08
Bosnia and Herzegovina	1,301	276	179	278	254	0.01	-8.63
Croatia	415	497	730	1,092	1,126	0.04	3.11
Greece	736	729	832	1,213	1,320	0.05	8.82
Holy See	14	17	13	10	7	0.00	-30.00

Yearbook of Tourism Statistics, Data 2009 – 2013, 2015 Edition

AZERBAIJAN

2. Arrivals of non-resident visitors at national borders, by country of residence

	2009	2010	2011	2012	2013	Market share 2013	% Change 2013-2012
Italy	4,066	4,732	4,857	6,767	8,566	0.34	26.58
Malta	30	61	68	84	114	0.00	35.71
Montenegro				124	112	0.00	-9.68
Portugal	976	948	414	512	773	0.03	50.98
San Marino	3	1	2	13	3	0.00	-76.92
Serbia		655	907	1,589	1,407	0.06	-11.45
Slovenia	254	237	265	491	675	0.03	37.47
Spain	936	1,074	1,388	1,685	2,321	0.09	37.74
TFYR of Macedonia	175	292	221	301	298	0.01	-1.00
Other countries of Southern Europe	785	364	14	3			
WESTERN EUROPE	**23,431**	**23,781**	**26,643**	**34,218**	**30,281**	**1.21**	**-11.51**
Austria	1,801	2,513	3,021	3,499	2,567	0.10	-26.64
Belgium	2,389	2,233	2,299	2,255	1,725	0.07	-23.50
France	3,994	4,128	4,799	5,870	5,919	0.24	0.83
Germany	10,695	10,602	11,927	16,445	13,920	0.55	-15.35
Liechtenstein	1	3	4	8	3	0.00	-62.50
Luxembourg	527	378	316	460	498	0.02	8.26
Monaco		8	5	4	13	0.00	225.00
Netherlands	2,595	2,689	3,026	3,970	4,036	0.16	1.66
Switzerland	1,429	1,227	1,246	1,707	1,600	0.06	-6.27
EAST MEDITERRANEAN EUROPE	**183,983**	**221,022**	**248,424**	**302,139**	**368,500**	**14.69**	**21.96**
Cyprus	159	82	147	221	98	0.00	-55.66
Israel	6,516	6,346	5,671	6,369	6,989	0.28	9.73
Turkey	177,308	214,594	242,606	295,549	361,413	14.41	22.29
MIDDLE EAST	**3,095**	**3,581**	**3,932**	**4,985**	**5,611**	**0.22**	**12.56**
Bahrain	80	87	97	107	188	0.01	75.70
Egypt	407	559	663	955	963	0.04	0.84
Iraq	476	549	679	917	991	0.04	8.07
Jordan	299	392	379	387	442	0.02	14.21
Kuwait	149	322	324	233	392	0.02	68.24
Lebanon	282	270	308	363	382	0.02	5.23
Libya	38	36	27	54	163	0.01	201.85
Oman	67	63	26	33	150	0.01	354.55
Palestine	42	25	68	53	69	0.00	30.19
Qatar	131	83	123	470	309	0.01	-34.26
Saudi Arabia	290	312	284	380	479	0.02	26.05
Syrian Arab Republic	492	390	426	414	375	0.01	-9.42
United Arab Emirates	270	412	469	551	638	0.03	15.79
Yemen	72	81	59	68	70	0.00	2.94
SOUTH ASIA	**339,949**	**356,590**	**414,045**	**292,519**	**151,731**	**6.05**	**-48.13**
Afghanistan	303	194	270	393	636	0.03	61.83
Bangladesh	453	576	439	1,151	581	0.02	-49.52
Bhutan			3	1	1	0.00	
India	3,721	3,755	3,715	5,048	4,791	0.19	-5.09
Iran, Islamic Republic of	329,913	349,960	407,576	283,739	143,579	5.72	-49.40
Maldives	5	4	5	6	7	0.00	16.67
Nepal	52	56	79	282	120	0.00	-57.45
Pakistan	5,416	1,949	1,743	1,675	1,767	0.07	5.49
Sri Lanka	86	96	215	224	249	0.01	11.16
NOT SPECIFIED	**2,261**	**2,097**	**1,990**	**1,988**	**1,944**	**0.08**	**-2.21**
Other countries of the World	2,261	2,097	1,990	1,988	1,944	0.08	-2.21

AZERBAIJAN

3. Arrivals of non-resident tourists in hotels and similar establishments, by country of residence

	2009	2010	2011	2012	2013	Market share 2013	% Change 2013-2012
TOTAL	208,868	212,356	257,987	372,117	395,461	100.00	6.27
AMERICAS	11,622	15,013	7,947	22,807	31,109	7.87	36.40
NORTH AMERICA	11,622	15,013	7,947	22,807	31,109	7.87	36.40
Canada	272	548	630	3,229	3,711	0.94	14.93
United States of America	11,350	14,465	7,317	19,578	27,398	6.93	39.94
EAST ASIA AND THE PACIFIC	5,087	6,913	4,448	5,648	6,540	1.65	15.79
NORTH-EAST ASIA	4,499	6,167	4,448	5,648	6,540	1.65	15.79
China	3,545	5,037	3,671	4,329	5,240	1.33	21.04
Japan	950	782	777	1,319	1,300	0.33	-1.44
Korea, Dem. People's Republic of	4	348					
SOUTH-EAST ASIA	275	431					
Malaysia	56	269					
Philippines	219	162					
AUSTRALASIA	313	315					
Australia	313	315					
EUROPE	138,817	139,139	167,342	243,784	247,772	62.65	1.64
CENTRAL/EASTERN EUROPE	39,420	43,052	54,662	71,400	86,951	21.99	21.78
Belarus	523	1,181					
Georgia	8,210	2,435	3,701	6,516	11,370	2.88	74.49
Kazakhstan	1,841	2,070	3,856	5,464	6,929	1.75	26.81
Latvia	108	394	424	792	896	0.23	13.13
Poland	80	500	946	1,220	1,699	0.43	39.26
Romania	67	195	495	700	1,051	0.27	50.14
Russian Federation	23,261	29,570	36,503	45,404	52,845	13.36	16.39
Ukraine	5,330	6,707	8,737	11,304	12,161	3.08	7.58
NORTHERN EUROPE	26,823	17,077	29,904	68,793	58,741	14.85	-14.61
Finland	123	227	225	591	561	0.14	-5.08
Norway	1,451	2,209	3,285	4,304	4,480	1.13	4.09
Sweden	522	448	880	2,270	2,856	0.72	25.81
United Kingdom	24,727	14,193	25,514	61,628	50,844	12.86	-17.50
SOUTHERN EUROPE	4,534	4,914	5,248	9,075	10,029	2.54	10.51
Greece	87	161					
Italy	4,021	4,005	3,706	7,390	8,183	2.07	10.73
Spain	426	748	1,542	1,685	1,846	0.47	9.55
WESTERN EUROPE	11,729	12,508	16,229	37,494	34,904	8.83	-6.91
Austria	1,195	912					
Belgium	269	840	651	1,613	1,608	0.41	-0.31
France	3,512	3,696	4,767	7,320	8,980	2.27	22.68
Germany	5,903	6,115	9,903	20,358	16,058	4.06	-21.12
Netherlands	850	945	908	8,203	8,258	2.09	0.67
EAST MEDITERRANEAN EUROPE	56,311	61,588	61,299	57,022	57,147	14.45	0.22
Israel	2,935	3,305	1,431	7,438	7,429	1.88	-0.12
Turkey	53,376	58,283	59,868	49,584	49,718	12.57	0.27
MIDDLE EAST	2	387					
United Arab Emirates	2	387					
SOUTH ASIA	31,255	19,423	23,158	25,250	28,667	7.25	13.53
India	1,162	485	743	4,713	7,007	1.77	48.67
Iran, Islamic Republic of	29,798	18,775	21,779	20,009	20,616	5.21	3.03
Pakistan	295	163	636	528	1,044	0.26	97.73
NOT SPECIFIED	22,085	31,481	55,092	74,628	81,373	20.58	9.04
Other countries of the World	22,085	31,481	55,092	74,628	81,373	20.58	9.04

    Yearbook of Tourism Statistics, Data 2009 – 2013, 2015 Edition

AZERBAIJAN

5. Overnight stays of non-resident tourists in hotels and similar establishments, by country of residence

	2009	2010	2011	2012	2013	Market share 2013	% Change 2013-2012
TOTAL	561,343	568,056	673,811	803,089	821,552	100.00	2.30
AMERICAS	25,071	25,627	15,560	51,978	66,784	8.13	28.49
NORTH AMERICA	25,071	25,627	15,560	51,978	66,784	8.13	28.49
Canada	458	937	1,148	4,165	5,409	0.66	29.87
United States of America	24,613	24,690	14,412	47,813	61,375	7.47	28.36
EAST ASIA AND THE PACIFIC	12,013	16,198	9,085	11,420	20,684	2.52	81.12
NORTH-EAST ASIA	10,388	12,457	9,085	11,420	20,684	2.52	81.12
China	8,424	10,205	6,694	9,300	17,793	2.17	91.32
Japan	1,952	1,874	2,391	2,120	2,891	0.35	36.37
Korea, Dem. People's Republic of	12	378					
SOUTH-EAST ASIA	1,172	3,263					
Malaysia	104	2,833					
Philippines	1,068	430					
AUSTRALASIA	453	478					
Australia	453	478					
EUROPE	292,247	421,195	489,685	555,199	493,692	60.09	-11.08
CENTRAL/EASTERN EUROPE	87,195	94,923	133,824	157,586	182,120	22.17	15.57
Georgia	13,301	4,748	6,465	9,875	19,886	2.42	101.38
Kazakhstan	8,726	5,787	12,719	12,381	15,128	1.84	22.19
Latvia	380	745	597	1,405	1,614	0.20	14.88
Poland	794	763	1,685	1,775	3,922	0.48	120.96
Romania	302	786	605	891	1,568	0.19	75.98
Russian Federation	51,411	66,894	84,323	102,399	113,205	13.78	10.55
Ukraine	12,281	15,200	27,430	28,860	26,797	3.26	-7.15
NORTHERN EUROPE	69,477	43,292	72,962	148,264	119,250	14.52	-19.57
Finland	781	374	270	691	825	0.10	19.39
Norway	2,649	2,624	3,736	4,857	5,032	0.61	3.60
Sweden	686	588	2,144	2,737	8,022	0.98	193.09
United Kingdom	65,361	39,706	66,812	139,979	105,371	12.83	-24.72
SOUTHERN EUROPE	6,683	8,310	9,172	11,417	13,207	1.61	15.68
Greece	287	332					
Italy	5,770	6,639	6,798	9,115	10,453	1.27	14.68
Spain	626	1,339	2,374	2,302	2,754	0.34	19.64
WESTERN EUROPE	24,145	21,645	25,200	62,592	62,782	7.64	0.30
Austria	1,499	1,508					
Belgium	479	1,084	800	2,697	2,068	0.25	-23.32
France	7,253	5,808	6,218	9,968	17,294	2.11	73.50
Germany	12,496	11,959	16,906	41,054	34,070	4.15	-17.01
Netherlands	2,418	1,286	1,276	8,873	9,350	1.14	5.38
EAST MEDITERRANEAN EUROPE	104,747	253,025	248,527	175,340	116,333	14.16	-33.65
Israel	3,622	4,133	1,969	8,209	8,593	1.05	4.68
Turkey	101,125	248,892	246,558	167,131	107,740	13.11	-35.54
MIDDLE EAST	22	535					
United Arab Emirates	22	535					
SOUTH ASIA	52,079	48,079	49,322	40,176	49,814	6.06	23.99
India	1,767	1,289	2,960	6,169	8,177	1.00	32.55
Iran, Islamic Republic of	49,733	46,509	44,819	33,384	39,942	4.86	19.64
Pakistan	579	281	1,543	623	1,695	0.21	172.07
NOT SPECIFIED	179,911	56,422	110,159	144,316	190,578	23.20	32.06
Other countries of the World	179,911	56,422	110,159	144,316	190,578	23.20	32.06

Yearbook of Tourism Statistics, Data 2009 – 2013, 2015 Edition

BAHAMAS

1. Arrivals of non-resident tourists at national borders, by country of residence

	2009	2010	2011	2012	2013	Market share 2013	% Change 2013-2012
TOTAL	1,327,007	1,370,174	1,346,372	1,421,753	1,364,153	100.00	-4.05
AFRICA	1,778	1,654	1,733	2,245	2,173	0.16	-3.21
EAST AFRICA	179	145	136	187	175	0.01	-6.42
Burundi	1	1					
Comoros	2						
Djibouti	1	1		1			
Eritrea	3	2		1			
Ethiopia	14	16	14	9	9	0.00	
Kenya	19	36	27	40	47	0.00	17.50
Madagascar	11	1	1	5			
Malawi	6	2	1	10	4	0.00	-60.00
Mauritius	25	12	20	25	22	0.00	-12.00
Mozambique	9	3	4	14	9	0.00	-35.71
Rwanda	3	2					
Seychelles	8	8	4	1	1	0.00	
Somalia	2						
Uganda	22	21	8	21	11	0.00	-47.62
United Republic of Tanzania	23	8	9	6	12	0.00	100.00
Zambia	17	7	22	20	15	0.00	-25.00
Zimbabwe	13	25	26	34	45	0.00	32.35
CENTRAL AFRICA	57	35	88	104	89	0.01	-14.42
Angola	16	6	31	27	19	0.00	-29.63
Cameroon	17	1	6	7	1	0.00	-85.71
Central African Republic	2		2				
Chad	7	13	15	21	43	0.00	104.76
Congo	13	7	9	23	14	0.00	-39.13
Equatorial Guinea			13	4	1	0.00	-75.00
Gabon	2	8	12	22	11	0.00	-50.00
NORTH AFRICA	138	82	76	101	81	0.01	-19.80
Algeria	1	2	10	5	13	0.00	160.00
Morocco	58	68	42	80	61	0.00	-23.75
Sudan	5		2	1	2	0.00	100.00
Tunisia	74	12	22	15	5	0.00	-66.67
SOUTHERN AFRICA	1,175	1,226	1,222	1,629	1,607	0.12	-1.35
Botswana	23	36	24	27	15	0.00	-44.44
Lesotho	7	8	1				
Namibia	21	16	11	19	7	0.00	-63.16
South Africa	1,090	1,127	1,169	1,561	1,501	0.11	-3.84
Swaziland	34	39	17	22	84	0.01	281.82
WEST AFRICA	229	166	211	224	221	0.02	-1.34
Benin	1				1	0.00	
Burkina Faso	2	1	4	1	1	0.00	
Cabo Verde	3	1	7	1	1	0.00	
Côte d'Ivoire	6	8	18	10	19	0.00	90.00
Gambia	8	1	1	2	2	0.00	
Ghana	38	27	30	37	38	0.00	2.70
Guinea	10	3	7	1	2	0.00	100.00
Liberia	3	1	2	2			
Mali	1	5	1				
Mauritania	3	2	1	1	3	0.00	200.00
Niger	4		1		4	0.00	
Nigeria	128	95	121	133	132	0.01	-0.75
Senegal	15	18	12	20	6	0.00	-70.00
Sierra Leone	6	3	6	9	10	0.00	11.11
Togo	1	1		7	2	0.00	-71.43
AMERICAS	1,213,309	1,255,741	1,230,533	1,302,864	1,240,738	90.95	-4.77
CARIBBEAN	18,463	18,049	17,458	16,768	18,086	1.33	7.86
Anguilla	29	50	23	28	34	0.00	21.43
Antigua and Barbuda	122	131	169	158	163	0.01	3.16
Aruba	106	78	117	142	98	0.01	-30.99
Barbados	852	1,052	943	977	1,004	0.07	2.76

43

BAHAMAS

1. Arrivals of non-resident tourists at national borders, by country of residence

	2009	2010	2011	2012	2013	Market share 2013	% Change 2013-2012
Bermuda	1,009	857	805	987	926	0.07	-6.18
British Virgin Islands	99	119	91	125	149	0.01	19.20
Cayman Islands	1,964	1,699	1,458	1,393	1,417	0.10	1.72
Cuba	365	365	455	412	451	0.03	9.47
Curaçao	137	153	164	209	189	0.01	-9.57
Dominica	166	117	138	117	102	0.01	-12.82
Dominican Republic	578	493	540	548	521	0.04	-4.93
Grenada	76	55	74	80	97	0.01	21.25
Haiti	1,318	556	491	343	1,545	0.11	350.44
Jamaica	6,207	6,831	6,888	6,441	6,291	0.46	-2.33
Martinique	57	41	50	70	47	0.00	-32.86
Montserrat	19	16	9	8	7	0.00	-12.50
Netherlands Antilles	23	33	22	5	495	0.04	9,800.00
Puerto Rico	226	252	270	283	208	0.02	-26.50
Saint Kitts and Nevis	144	127	100	73	76	0.01	4.11
Saint Lucia	197	199	199	209	196	0.01	-6.22
Saint Vincent and the Grenadines	74	72	85	71	81	0.01	14.08
Sint Eustatius	4	4	6	3	7	0.00	133.33
Sint Maarten	75	68	114	112	142	0.01	26.79
Trinidad and Tobago	1,453	1,693	1,759	1,725	1,754	0.13	1.68
Turks and Caicos Islands	3,080	2,946	2,433	2,178	2,028	0.15	-6.89
United States Virgin Islands	30	23	16	26	18	0.00	-30.77
Other countries of the Caribbean	53	19	39	45	40	0.00	-11.11
CENTRAL AMERICA	**1,987**	**1,851**	**2,819**	**3,599**	**3,403**	**0.25**	**-5.45**
Belize	123	117	122	122	125	0.01	2.46
Costa Rica	372	334	490	579	558	0.04	-3.63
El Salvador	257	126	209	127	271	0.02	113.39
Guatemala	312	295	356	603	469	0.03	-22.22
Honduras	194	196	254	188	207	0.02	10.11
Nicaragua	90	97	79	133	78	0.01	-41.35
Panama	639	686	1,309	1,847	1,695	0.12	-8.23
NORTH AMERICA	**1,179,664**	**1,220,032**	**1,187,547**	**1,256,538**	**1,194,168**	**87.54**	**-4.96**
Canada	107,041	119,321	124,166	131,064	123,720	9.07	-5.60
Greenland	2	3	1	4			
Mexico	3,895	3,524	4,698	3,873	4,384	0.32	13.19
United States of America	1,068,726	1,097,184	1,058,682	1,121,597	1,066,064	78.15	-4.95
SOUTH AMERICA	**13,195**	**15,809**	**22,709**	**25,959**	**25,081**	**1.84**	**-3.38**
Argentina	2,579	3,167	4,992	5,339	5,045	0.37	-5.51
Bolivia	158	113	141	228	149	0.01	-34.65
Brazil	4,309	5,310	6,595	7,476	8,878	0.65	18.75
Chile	548	637	1,106	1,113	1,118	0.08	0.45
Colombia	1,281	1,720	4,155	4,822	3,707	0.27	-23.12
Ecuador	487	529	547	1,163	990	0.07	-14.88
Guyana	306	373	433	378	397	0.03	5.03
Paraguay	250	620	838	922	903	0.07	-2.06
Peru	807	879	1,027	1,189	1,057	0.08	-11.10
Suriname	87	97	88	81	120	0.01	48.15
Uruguay	230	323	405	509	596	0.04	17.09
Venezuela	2,153	2,041	2,382	2,739	2,121	0.16	-22.56
EAST ASIA AND THE PACIFIC	**6,232**	**7,143**	**6,707**	**8,127**	**7,868**	**0.58**	**-3.19**
NORTH-EAST ASIA	**2,081**	**2,527**	**2,045**	**2,877**	**2,389**	**0.18**	**-16.96**
China	486	384	682	890	782	0.06	-12.13
Hong Kong, China	205	283	277	369	365	0.03	-1.08
Japan	1,018	874	776	1,012	841	0.06	-16.90
Korea, Dem. People's Republic of		1	2	5	4	0.00	-20.00
Korea, Republic of	298	514	228	426	321	0.02	-24.65
Mongolia	8	1	2	4	3	0.00	-25.00
Taiwan, Province of China	66	470	78	171	73	0.01	-57.31
SOUTH-EAST ASIA	**760**	**947**	**764**	**892**	**810**	**0.06**	**-9.19**
Brunei Darussalam	2	5	2	3	3	0.00	
Cambodia	4	3	6	5	7	0.00	40.00

44

BAHAMAS

1. Arrivals of non-resident tourists at national borders, by country of residence

	2009	2010	2011	2012	2013	Market share 2013	% Change 2013-2012
Indonesia	65	73	58	103	89	0.01	-13.59
Lao People's Democratic Republic	3			2	1	0.00	-50.00
Malaysia	59	165	99	106	125	0.01	17.92
Myanmar	4	2	3	10	15	0.00	50.00
Philippines	315	297	232	235	253	0.02	7.66
Singapore	201	293	280	292	209	0.02	-28.42
Thailand	86	84	67	122	86	0.01	-29.51
Viet Nam	21	25	17	14	22	0.00	57.14
AUSTRALASIA	**3,328**	**3,634**	**3,871**	**4,308**	**4,616**	**0.34**	**7.15**
Australia	2,758	3,075	3,267	3,609	3,858	0.28	6.90
New Zealand	570	559	604	699	758	0.06	8.44
MELANESIA	**30**	**12**	**16**	**29**	**20**	**0.00**	**-31.03**
Fiji	17	7	8	12	12	0.00	
Papua New Guinea	4	2	4	13	5	0.00	-61.54
Solomon Islands	3	2	3	2	2	0.00	
Vanuatu	6	1	1	2	1	0.00	-50.00
MICRONESIA	**11**	**5**	**3**	**6**	**10**	**0.00**	**66.67**
Kiribati	5		1				
Marshall Islands	2	1			2	0.00	
Micronesia, Federated States of	4	4	2	4	8	0.00	100.00
Palau				2			
POLYNESIA	**22**	**18**	**8**	**15**	**23**	**0.00**	**53.33**
French Polynesia	13	13	5	8	18	0.00	125.00
Samoa	6	5	3	5	5	0.00	
Tonga	3			2			
EUROPE	**79,648**	**78,900**	**78,929**	**79,539**	**81,266**	**5.96**	**2.17**
CENTRAL/EASTERN EUROPE	**2,934**	**4,156**	**4,347**	**4,733**	**4,728**	**0.35**	**-0.11**
Armenia	11	7	3	5	18	0.00	260.00
Azerbaijan	15	4	19	23	20	0.00	-13.04
Belarus	11	15	13	28	39	0.00	39.29
Bulgaria	113	166	144	131	129	0.01	-1.53
Czech Republic	303	407	330	354	308	0.02	-12.99
Estonia	120	96	85	145	185	0.01	27.59
Georgia	19	21	21	39	27	0.00	-30.77
Hungary	289	369	334	325	338	0.02	4.00
Kazakhstan	12	52	18	92	18	0.00	-80.43
Kyrgyzstan	6	8			1	0.00	
Latvia	55	76	59	70	68	0.00	-2.86
Lithuania	33	74	85	105	80	0.01	-23.81
Poland	574	785	924	863	861	0.06	-0.23
Republic of Moldova	5	19	7	21	18	0.00	-14.29
Romania	253	398	334	297	269	0.02	-9.43
Russian Federation	822	1,203	1,582	1,893	1,958	0.14	3.43
Slovakia	166	276	235	190	216	0.02	13.68
Tajikistan	3			5	4	0.00	-20.00
Turkmenistan	3	4		5	3	0.00	-40.00
Ukraine	112	173	149	139	165	0.01	18.71
Uzbekistan	9	3	5	3	3	0.00	
NORTHERN EUROPE	**32,057**	**28,791**	**28,679**	**30,028**	**29,495**	**2.16**	**-1.78**
Denmark	1,007	933	921	938	866	0.06	-7.68
Faeroe Islands	4	2	14	9	19	0.00	111.11
Finland	751	696	584	650	661	0.05	1.69
Iceland	70	75	100	61	75	0.01	22.95
Ireland	1,184	970	638	684	720	0.05	5.26
Norway	1,088	1,337	1,228	1,182	1,304	0.10	10.32
Sweden	1,552	1,599	1,698	1,789	1,861	0.14	4.02
United Kingdom	26,401	23,179	23,496	24,715	23,989	1.76	-2.94
SOUTHERN EUROPE	**12,421**	**13,899**	**13,589**	**12,180**	**13,366**	**0.98**	**9.74**
Albania	16	10	10	11	17	0.00	54.55
Andorra	30	20	9	40	30	0.00	-25.00
Bosnia and Herzegovina	8	18	6	23	13	0.00	-43.48

45

BAHAMAS

1. Arrivals of non-resident tourists at national borders, by country of residence

	2009	2010	2011	2012	2013	Market share 2013	% Change 2013-2012
Croatia	98	124	119	113	97	0.01	-14.16
Greece	392	450	472	368	331	0.02	-10.05
Italy	9,269	10,228	9,853	8,710	8,362	0.61	-4.00
Malta	55	52	77	57	59	0.00	3.51
Montenegro	5	3	6	3	17	0.00	466.67
Portugal	402	629	505	468	541	0.04	15.60
San Marino	15	7	21	1	1	0.00	
Serbia	66	61	80	88	127	0.01	44.32
Serbia and Montenegro	2	1					
Slovenia	67	99	111	96	82	0.01	-14.58
Spain	1,979	2,180	2,295	2,175	3,669	0.27	68.69
TFYR of Macedonia	17	17	25	27	20	0.00	-25.93
WESTERN EUROPE	**31,033**	**30,747**	**31,158**	**31,252**	**32,521**	**2.38**	**4.06**
Austria	1,533	1,461	1,439	1,555	1,614	0.12	3.79
Belgium	1,436	1,466	1,355	1,216	1,406	0.10	15.63
France	13,667	12,495	13,190	12,857	14,001	1.03	8.90
Germany	8,236	8,632	7,973	8,556	8,934	0.65	4.42
Liechtenstein	40	22	54	41	43	0.00	4.88
Luxembourg	202	207	178	206	210	0.02	1.94
Monaco	184	133	154	132	167	0.01	26.52
Netherlands	1,924	2,075	1,835	1,677	1,106	0.08	-34.05
Switzerland	3,811	4,256	4,980	5,012	5,040	0.37	0.56
EAST MEDITERRANEAN EUROPE	**1,203**	**1,307**	**1,153**	**1,346**	**1,156**	**0.08**	**-14.12**
Cyprus	109	93	114	97	70	0.01	-27.84
Israel	774	742	684	771	640	0.05	-16.99
Turkey	320	472	355	478	446	0.03	-6.69
OTHER EUROPE			3				
Other countries of Europe			3				
MIDDLE EAST	**708**	**593**	**708**	**833**	**770**	**0.06**	**-7.56**
Bahrain	31	52	22	31	30	0.00	-3.23
Egypt	74	76	66	71	45	0.00	-36.62
Iraq	3	4		2	3	0.00	50.00
Jordan	28	15	16	16	16	0.00	
Kuwait	77	65	93	122	131	0.01	7.38
Lebanon	28	22	37	32	33	0.00	3.13
Libya		2					
Oman	13	8	9	14	14	0.00	
Palestine	2	2					
Qatar	38	25	31	30	67	0.00	123.33
Saudi Arabia	155	113	214	226	192	0.01	-15.04
Syrian Arab Republic	10	7	6	2	2	0.00	
United Arab Emirates	249	202	211	287	237	0.02	-17.42
Yemen			3				
SOUTH ASIA	**526**	**666**	**494**	**715**	**541**	**0.04**	**-24.34**
Afghanistan	5	2	2	3	3	0.00	
Bangladesh	6	18	15	13	12	0.00	-7.69
Bhutan	3	2	1		2	0.00	
India	435	561	398	596	421	0.03	-29.36
Iran, Islamic Republic of	7	9	6	15	21	0.00	40.00
Maldives	3		1	4	1	0.00	-75.00
Nepal	16	15	13	11	15	0.00	36.36
Pakistan	12	20	17	25	25	0.00	
Sri Lanka	39	39	41	48	41	0.00	-14.58
NOT SPECIFIED	**24,806**	**25,477**	**27,268**	**27,430**	**30,797**	**2.26**	**12.27**
Other countries of the World	24,806	25,477	27,268	27,430	30,797	2.26	12.27

46

BAHAMAS

6. Overnight stays of non-resident tourists in all types of accommodation establishments, by country of residence

	2009	2010	2011	2012	2013	Market share 2013	% Change 2013-2012
TOTAL (*)	9,039,234	9,128,113	9,123,171	9,628,795	9,335,695	100.00	-3.04
AFRICA	21,000	22,515	22,988	36,207	36,696	0.39	1.35
EAST AFRICA	2,124	1,444	1,182	2,716	2,919	0.03	7.47
Burundi	4	30					
Comoros	9						
Djibouti	5	3		2			
Eritrea	12	16		6			
Ethiopia	114	122	147	95	122	0.00	28.42
Kenya	123	362	145	397	690	0.01	73.80
Madagascar	54	3	7	20			
Malawi	36	10	5	59	14	0.00	-76.27
Mauritius	652	124	332	525	504	0.01	-4.00
Mozambique	31	15	22	58	53	0.00	-8.62
Rwanda	12	6					
Seychelles	104	87	45	7	2	0.00	-71.43
Somalia	7						
Uganda	397	317	71	168	138	0.00	-17.86
United Republic of Tanzania	286	128	71	57	189	0.00	231.58
Zambia	184	37	138	202	143	0.00	-29.21
Zimbabwe	94	184	199	1,120	1,064	0.01	-5.00
CENTRAL AFRICA	277	213	580	612	736	0.01	20.26
Angola	44	44	105	156	137	0.00	-12.18
Cameroon	81	5	193	58	7	0.00	-87.93
Central African Republic	10		15				
Chad	34	91	111	147	347	0.00	136.05
Congo	96	20	28	127	105	0.00	-17.32
Equatorial Guinea			56	15	3	0.00	-80.00
Gabon	12	53	72	109	137	0.00	25.69
NORTH AFRICA	817	513	671	543	543	0.01	
Algeria	2	4	132	37	56	0.00	51.35
Morocco	297	469	335	442	342	0.00	-22.62
Sudan	21		6	10	7	0.00	-30.00
Tunisia	497	40	198	54	138	0.00	155.56
SOUTHERN AFRICA	16,192	19,163	18,327	30,365	30,640	0.33	0.91
Botswana	530	237	286	205	160	0.00	-21.95
Lesotho	39	29	7				
Namibia	185	122	66	245	18	0.00	-92.65
South Africa	15,183	18,587	17,706	29,760	29,774	0.32	0.05
Swaziland	255	188	262	155	688	0.01	343.87
WEST AFRICA	1,590	1,182	2,228	1,971	1,858	0.02	-5.73
Benin	4				7	0.00	
Burkina Faso	8	25	18	22	3	0.00	-86.36
Cabo Verde	34	14	102	1	9	0.00	800.00
Côte d'Ivoire	29	46	95	59	164	0.00	177.97
Gambia	43	4	2	29	35	0.00	20.69
Ghana	421	268	688	463	525	0.01	13.39
Guinea	67	13	39	5	9	0.00	80.00
Liberia	13	2	14	7			
Mali	4	25	7				
Mauritania	37	4	28	5			
Niger	22		3		21	0.00	
Nigeria	804	631	1,115	975	902	0.01	-7.49
Saint Helena				3			
Senegal	70	127	89	175	40	0.00	-77.14
Sierra Leone	31	21	28	145	104	0.00	-28.28
Togo	3	2		82	39	0.00	-52.44
AMERICAS	7,900,946	8,027,668	8,011,185	8,480,506	8,143,827	87.23	-3.97
CARIBBEAN	158,798	152,196	152,018	154,858	180,228	1.93	16.38
Anguilla	171	252	106	145	167	0.00	15.17
Antigua and Barbuda	1,283	865	1,393	1,341	1,663	0.02	24.01
Aruba	586	404	940	798	687	0.01	-13.91

47

BAHAMAS

6. Overnight stays of non-resident tourists in all types of accommodation establishments, by country of residence

	2009	2010	2011	2012	2013	Market share 2013	% Change 2013-2012
Barbados	4,956	6,811	5,620	5,938	5,688	0.06	-4.21
Bermuda	8,069	6,170	5,306	7,227	6,830	0.07	-5.49
British Virgin Islands	1,123	1,288	765	1,093	887	0.01	-18.85
Cayman Islands	8,774	8,244	7,005	6,920	6,204	0.07	-10.35
Cuba	5,695	6,109	7,572	8,674	8,186	0.09	-5.63
Curaçao	798	837	798	1,017	1,132	0.01	11.31
Dominica	1,063	657	1,291	842	668	0.01	-20.67
Dominican Republic	4,958	3,078	3,519	3,725	4,094	0.04	9.91
Grenada	565	386	728	410	968	0.01	136.10
Haiti	20,919	7,817	5,670	4,599	29,091	0.31	532.55
Jamaica	66,985	75,673	79,694	80,296	80,344	0.86	0.06
Martinique	288	212	370	412	230	0.00	-44.17
Montserrat	153	179	64	36	37	0.00	2.78
Netherlands Antilles	194	166	303	28	4,589	0.05	16,289.29
Puerto Rico	982	1,207	1,263	1,316	963	0.01	-26.82
Saint Kitts and Nevis	981	976	903	434	501	0.01	15.44
Saint Lucia	1,534	1,771	1,845	2,637	1,452	0.02	-44.94
Saint Vincent and the Grenadines	973	606	847	548	517	0.01	-5.66
Sint Eustatius	11	23	55	68	40	0.00	-41.18
Sint Maarten	562	374	697	778	2,615	0.03	236.12
Trinidad and Tobago	10,684	12,101	11,750	11,808	10,995	0.12	-6.89
Turks and Caicos Islands	15,758	15,725	12,887	13,313	11,537	0.12	-13.34
United States Virgin Islands	262	157	170	183	143	0.00	-21.86
Other countries of the Caribbean	471	108	457	272			
CENTRAL AMERICA	**13,297**	**14,136**	**19,125**	**24,260**	**23,010**	**0.25**	**-5.15**
Belize	759	741	891	889	936	0.01	5.29
Costa Rica	2,373	2,983	3,058	3,975	3,901	0.04	-1.86
El Salvador	2,123	1,247	1,726	1,234	1,576	0.02	27.71
Guatemala	1,928	2,509	2,921	4,854	4,062	0.04	-16.32
Honduras	1,336	1,592	2,466	1,812	1,996	0.02	10.15
Nicaragua	761	489	401	798	676	0.01	-15.29
Panama	4,017	4,575	7,662	10,698	9,863	0.11	-7.81
NORTH AMERICA	**7,650,947**	**7,770,613**	**7,706,085**	**8,138,807**	**7,786,893**	**83.41**	**-4.32**
Canada	897,050	957,193	980,819	1,031,408	996,240	10.67	-3.41
Greenland	6	27	4	44			
Mexico	26,254	21,607	27,329	32,425	33,250	0.36	2.54
United States of America	6,727,637	6,791,786	6,697,933	7,074,930	6,757,403	72.38	-4.49
SOUTH AMERICA	**77,904**	**90,723**	**133,957**	**162,581**	**153,696**	**1.65**	**-5.46**
Argentina	14,351	17,534	30,298	34,381	31,498	0.34	-8.39
Bolivia	793	637	866	1,167	738	0.01	-36.76
Brazil	22,125	27,723	36,658	44,743	52,139	0.56	16.53
Chile	3,787	3,683	7,262	7,478	7,219	0.08	-3.46
Colombia	8,547	10,242	23,209	29,240	23,077	0.25	-21.08
Ecuador	3,265	3,589	3,819	6,195	6,036	0.06	-2.57
Guyana	4,904	4,953	5,664	6,255	4,490	0.05	-28.22
Paraguay	860	2,082	2,690	3,009	3,258	0.03	8.28
Peru	4,716	6,441	7,049	9,247	7,797	0.08	-15.68
Suriname	1,374	452	491	494	772	0.01	56.28
Uruguay	1,805	2,596	3,173	4,129	4,831	0.05	17.00
Venezuela	11,377	10,791	12,778	16,243	11,841	0.13	-27.10
EAST ASIA AND THE PACIFIC	**67,705**	**68,944**	**67,681**	**77,328**	**82,018**	**0.88**	**6.07**
NORTH-EAST ASIA	**11,890**	**13,645**	**11,882**	**16,165**	**15,090**	**0.16**	**-6.65**
China	3,207	2,881	4,364	5,506	5,586	0.06	1.45
Hong Kong, China	1,045	1,698	1,606	2,296	2,436	0.03	6.10
Japan	5,895	4,406	4,165	5,730	5,166	0.06	-9.84
Korea, Dem. People's Republic of		6	38	22	32	0.00	45.45
Korea, Republic of	1,354	2,448	1,256	2,017	1,436	0.02	-28.81
Mongolia	35	7	92	32	12	0.00	-62.50
Taiwan, Province of China	354	2,199	361	562	422	0.00	-24.91
SOUTH-EAST ASIA	**7,965**	**10,822**	**8,705**	**8,738**	**10,668**	**0.11**	**22.09**
Brunei Darussalam	8	17	14	15	15	0.00	

48

BAHAMAS

6. Overnight stays of non-resident tourists in all types of accommodation establishments, by country of residence

	2009	2010	2011	2012	2013	Market share 2013	% Change 2013-2012
Cambodia	14	21	23	13	42	0.00	223.08
Indonesia	568	485	321	533	1,156	0.01	116.89
Lao People's Democratic Republic	12			13	45	0.00	246.15
Malaysia	414	975	731	548	738	0.01	34.67
Myanmar	13	5	14	125	367	0.00	193.60
Philippines	4,514	6,102	3,899	4,652	5,733	0.06	23.24
Singapore	1,138	2,261	2,626	1,685	1,306	0.01	-22.49
Thailand	1,076	737	897	1,000	1,130	0.01	13.00
Viet Nam	208	219	180	154	136	0.00	-11.69
AUSTRALASIA	**47,292**	**44,069**	**46,933**	**51,979**	**55,761**	**0.60**	**7.28**
Australia	36,009	33,712	35,512	37,259	40,535	0.43	8.79
New Zealand	11,283	10,357	11,421	14,720	15,226	0.16	3.44
MELANESIA	**259**	**138**	**55**	**223**	**149**	**0.00**	**-33.18**
Fiji	198	67	42	116	85	0.00	-26.72
Papua New Guinea	22	33	8	90	46	0.00	-48.89
Solomon Islands	15	22	3	13	14	0.00	7.69
Vanuatu	24	16	2	4	4	0.00	
MICRONESIA	**161**	**116**	**15**	**55**	**70**	**0.00**	**27.27**
Kiribati	26		5				
Marshall Islands	120	90			8	0.00	
Micronesia, Federated States of	15	26	10	49	62	0.00	26.53
Palau				6			
POLYNESIA	**138**	**154**	**91**	**168**	**280**	**0.00**	**66.67**
French Polynesia	100	113	74	124	210	0.00	69.35
Samoa	26	41	17	27	70	0.00	159.26
Tonga	12			17			
EUROPE	**811,786**	**776,920**	**773,421**	**784,190**	**785,634**	**8.42**	**0.18**
CENTRAL/EASTERN EUROPE	**27,387**	**33,442**	**38,564**	**42,317**	**43,928**	**0.47**	**3.81**
Armenia	83	28	7	46	226	0.00	391.30
Azerbaijan	85	13	140	132	131	0.00	-0.76
Belarus	60	98	142	355	326	0.00	-8.17
Bulgaria	1,168	1,813	1,530	1,727	1,163	0.01	-32.66
Czech Republic	2,535	2,295	2,737	3,173	3,534	0.04	11.38
Estonia	1,504	908	1,599	2,180	2,856	0.03	31.01
Georgia	129	138	222	239	416	0.00	74.06
Hungary	1,949	2,525	3,090	2,838	2,947	0.03	3.84
Kazakhstan	189	377	144	683	120	0.00	-82.43
Kyrgyzstan	199	42			10	0.00	
Latvia	385	439	442	618	497	0.01	-19.58
Lithuania	339	562	672	978	909	0.01	-7.06
Poland	5,823	7,226	8,257	7,421	9,231	0.10	24.39
Republic of Moldova	20	119	31	165	262	0.00	58.79
Romania	2,566	3,863	3,763	4,794	2,737	0.03	-42.91
Russian Federation	6,756	8,805	12,330	14,645	14,974	0.16	2.25
Slovakia	1,766	2,250	1,705	1,196	1,791	0.02	49.75
Tajikistan	15			22	23	0.00	4.55
Turkmenistan	12	14		15	7	0.00	-53.33
Ukraine	1,768	1,911	1,735	1,080	1,763	0.02	63.24
Uzbekistan	36	16	18	10	5	0.00	-50.00
NORTHERN EUROPE	**381,216**	**342,081**	**337,559**	**345,889**	**341,258**	**3.66**	**-1.34**
Denmark	10,017	8,099	8,836	9,352	8,116	0.09	-13.22
Faeroe Islands	13	28	230	115	231	0.00	100.87
Finland	5,439	4,534	4,965	5,303	5,596	0.06	5.53
Iceland	1,474	1,114	1,503	838	610	0.01	-27.21
Ireland	12,679	9,641	7,619	6,863	7,378	0.08	7.50
Norway	9,685	12,561	11,939	11,049	11,724	0.13	6.11
Sweden	15,051	14,620	14,772	16,758	16,468	0.18	-1.73
United Kingdom	326,858	291,484	287,695	295,611	291,135	3.12	-1.51
SOUTHERN EUROPE	**98,237**	**102,583**	**103,360**	**96,225**	**99,230**	**1.06**	**3.12**
Albania	192	63	71	78	135	0.00	73.08
Andorra	708	301	59	731	511	0.01	-30.10

49

BAHAMAS

6. Overnight stays of non-resident tourists in all types of accommodation establishments, by country of residence

	2009	2010	2011	2012	2013	Market share 2013	% Change 2013-2012
Bosnia and Herzegovina	46	105	65	250	179	0.00	-28.40
Croatia	969	1,051	1,387	1,144	1,129	0.01	-1.31
Greece	2,789	3,467	3,860	3,089	3,087	0.03	-0.06
Italy	72,381	73,854	73,297	67,198	63,770	0.68	-5.10
Malta	487	541	643	673	793	0.01	17.83
Montenegro	95	33	28	43	310	0.00	620.93
Portugal	3,375	5,524	4,608	4,202	4,801	0.05	14.26
San Marino	66	42	189	6	5	0.00	-16.67
Serbia	802	1,042	1,425	2,042	3,036	0.03	48.68
Serbia and Montenegro	35	14					
Slovenia	438	788	813	761	915	0.01	20.24
Spain	15,745	15,439	16,573	15,775	20,318	0.22	28.80
TFYR of Macedonia	109	319	342	233	241	0.00	3.43
WESTERN EUROPE	**296,150**	**289,175**	**285,620**	**289,454**	**293,565**	**3.14**	**1.42**
Austria	17,033	15,378	14,033	14,554	15,648	0.17	7.52
Belgium	12,957	13,883	13,482	10,680	14,618	0.16	36.87
France	118,382	106,397	110,396	110,220	118,376	1.27	7.40
Germany	90,467	90,165	81,903	89,793	87,178	0.93	-2.91
Liechtenstein	230	251	412	227	291	0.00	28.19
Luxembourg	1,869	1,761	2,267	2,062	2,018	0.02	-2.13
Monaco	2,141	1,487	1,376	1,431	1,551	0.02	8.39
Netherlands	17,599	18,206	16,899	15,064	9,817	0.11	-34.83
Switzerland	35,472	41,647	44,852	45,423	44,068	0.47	-2.98
EAST MEDITERRANEAN EUROPE	**8,796**	**9,639**	**8,318**	**10,305**	**7,653**	**0.08**	**-25.74**
Cyprus	625	463	582	970	533	0.01	-45.05
Israel	6,538	6,636	6,057	7,021	4,875	0.05	-30.57
Turkey	1,633	2,540	1,679	2,314	2,245	0.02	-2.98
MIDDLE EAST	**4,562**	**4,098**	**5,676**	**5,107**	**4,544**	**0.05**	**-11.02**
Bahrain	188	314	147	164	192	0.00	17.07
Egypt	461	513	366	538	296	0.00	-44.98
Iraq	15	28		16	9	0.00	-43.75
Jordan	127	110	99	92	65	0.00	-29.35
Kuwait	441	452	463	643	536	0.01	-16.64
Lebanon	167	119	243	169	244	0.00	44.38
Libya	8	12					
Oman	81	75	51	58	66	0.00	13.79
Palestine	7	11					
Qatar	223	112	183	156	310	0.00	98.72
Saudi Arabia	1,310	865	2,871	1,374	1,560	0.02	13.54
Syrian Arab Republic	50	56	67	15	5	0.00	-66.67
United Arab Emirates	1,484	1,431	1,172	1,882	1,261	0.01	-33.00
Yemen			14				
SOUTH ASIA	**5,302**	**4,532**	**4,957**	**5,907**	**6,760**	**0.07**	**14.44**
Afghanistan	23	12	18	21	24	0.00	14.29
Bangladesh	25	57	128	43	86	0.00	100.00
Bhutan	9	5	5		42	0.00	
India	4,367	3,771	3,691	4,277	4,629	0.05	8.23
Iran, Islamic Republic of	126	79	43	102	150	0.00	47.06
Maldives	22		4	26	30	0.00	15.38
Nepal	432	164	175	55	171	0.00	210.91
Pakistan	49	74	188	117	123	0.00	5.13
Sri Lanka	249	370	705	1,266	1,505	0.02	18.88
NOT SPECIFIED	**227,933**	**223,436**	**237,263**	**239,550**	**276,216**	**2.96**	**15.31**
Other countries of the World	227,933	223,436	237,263	239,550	276,216	2.96	15.31

Yearbook of Tourism Statistics, Data 2009 – 2013, 2015 Edition

BAHRAIN

2. Arrivals of non-resident visitors at national borders, by nationality

	2009	2010	2011	2012	2013	Market share 2013	% Change 2013-2012
TOTAL	(*)		6,731,974	8,062,359	9,162,738	100.00	13.65
AFRICA			99,545	113,960	124,128	1.35	8.92
EAST AFRICA			15,626	18,214	22,033	0.24	20.97
Burundi			1	3	12	0.00	300.00
Comoros			18	29	79	0.00	172.41
Djibouti			132	154	154	0.00	
Eritrea			2,155	1,963	1,928	0.02	-1.78
Ethiopia			7,017	8,779	13,666	0.15	55.67
Kenya			2,824	3,552	3,130	0.03	-11.88
Madagascar			20	35	63	0.00	80.00
Malawi			60	53	64	0.00	20.75
Mauritius			268	209			
Mozambique			13	55	92	0.00	67.27
Seychelles			478	530	483	0.01	-8.87
Somalia			1,505	1,777	1,918	0.02	7.93
Uganda			139	199	133	0.00	-33.17
United Republic of Tanzania			330	326			
Zambia			27	27	25	0.00	-7.41
Zimbabwe			639	523	286	0.00	-45.32
CENTRAL AFRICA			604	665	761	0.01	14.44
Angola			9	5	18	0.00	260.00
Cameroon			171	261	221	0.00	-15.33
Chad			173	257	342	0.00	33.07
Congo			213	124	98	0.00	-20.97
Equatorial Guinea			2		77	0.00	
Gabon			35	18	4	0.00	-77.78
Sao Tome and Principe			1		1	0.00	
NORTH AFRICA			57,013	66,962	71,207	0.78	6.34
Algeria			4,392	5,376	5,792	0.06	7.74
Morocco			8,657	13,974	16,259	0.18	16.35
Sudan			38,733	41,088	42,531	0.46	3.51
Tunisia			5,231	6,524	6,625	0.07	1.55
SOUTHERN AFRICA			22,026	22,723	24,289	0.27	6.89
Botswana			27	9	22	0.00	144.44
Namibia			20	18	19	0.00	5.56
South Africa			21,976	22,681	24,248	0.26	6.91
Swaziland			3	15			
WEST AFRICA			4,215	5,396	5,838	0.06	8.19
Benin			123	107	275	0.00	157.01
Burkina Faso			29	86	49	0.00	-43.02
Cabo Verde			1	1	1	0.00	
Côte d'Ivoire			64	143	128	0.00	-10.49
Gambia			12	21	32	0.00	52.38
Ghana			786	973	1,051	0.01	8.02
Guinea			61	110	77	0.00	-30.00
Guinea-Bissau			13	13	10	0.00	-23.08
Liberia			5	9	3	0.00	-66.67
Mali			101	336	779	0.01	131.85
Mauritania			103	147	199	0.00	35.37
Niger			99	148	181	0.00	22.30
Nigeria			2,674	3,081	2,900	0.03	-5.87
Senegal			123	182	119	0.00	-34.62
Sierra Leone			17	32	24	0.00	-25.00
Togo			4	7	10	0.00	42.86
OTHER AFRICA			61				
Other countries of Africa			61				
AMERICAS			291,253	326,111	334,803	3.65	2.67
CARIBBEAN			2,340	2,264	2,782	0.03	22.88
Antigua and Barbuda			6				

Yearbook of Tourism Statistics, Data 2009 – 2013, 2015 Edition

BAHRAIN

2. Arrivals of non-resident visitors at national borders, by nationality

	2009	2010	2011	2012	2013	Market share 2013	% Change 2013-2012
Bahamas			44	49	25	0.00	-48.98
Barbados			9	19	6	0.00	-68.42
Cayman Islands			3				
Cuba			58	26	106	0.00	307.69
Dominica			16	14	41	0.00	192.86
Dominican Republic			29	33			
Grenada			4	5	5	0.00	
Jamaica			84	102	113	0.00	10.78
Netherlands Antilles			4				
Saint Lucia			2	12	11	0.00	-8.33
Saint Vincent and the Grenadines			12	7	9	0.00	28.57
Trinidad and Tobago			2,069	1,997	2,466	0.03	23.49
CENTRAL AMERICA			**612**	**720**	**495**	**0.01**	**-31.25**
Belize			29	52			
Costa Rica			141	116	92	0.00	-20.69
El Salvador			37	17	22	0.00	29.41
Guatemala			69	84			
Honduras			26	46	69	0.00	50.00
Nicaragua			37	49	37	0.00	-24.49
Panama			273	356	275	0.00	-22.75
NORTH AMERICA			**272,186**	**307,142**	**315,634**	**3.44**	**2.76**
Canada			64,019	66,321	69,137	0.75	4.25
Mexico			1,546	1,598	1,896	0.02	18.65
United States of America			206,354	238,844	244,575	2.67	2.40
Other countries of North America			267	379	26	0.00	-93.14
SOUTH AMERICA			**16,115**	**15,985**	**15,892**	**0.17**	**-0.58**
Argentina			1,633	1,525	1,592	0.02	4.39
Bolivia			234	189	151	0.00	-20.11
Brazil			2,252	2,366	2,947	0.03	24.56
Chile			167	184	163	0.00	-11.41
Colombia			3,701	3,541	3,191	0.03	-9.88
Ecuador			243	263	189	0.00	-28.14
Guyana			6	24			
Paraguay			2	5	4	0.00	-20.00
Peru			564	447	343	0.00	-23.27
Uruguay			90	109	58	0.00	-46.79
Venezuela			7,223	7,332	7,254	0.08	-1.06
EAST ASIA AND THE PACIFIC			**338,724**	**366,700**	**334,705**	**3.65**	**-8.73**
NORTH-EAST ASIA			**69,352**	**78,706**	**60,052**	**0.66**	**-23.70**
China			22,418	22,805	1,211	0.01	-94.69
Hong Kong, China			3,711	562	719	0.01	27.94
Japan			17,129	21,543	22,050	0.24	2.35
Korea, Dem. People's Republic of			107	43	27	0.00	-37.21
Korea, Republic of			25,908	33,686	36,004	0.39	6.88
Macao, China			1	2			
Mongolia			78	65	41	0.00	-36.92
SOUTH-EAST ASIA			**234,081**	**251,683**	**238,646**	**2.60**	**-5.18**
Brunei Darussalam			88	95	131	0.00	37.89
Cambodia			14	6	33	0.00	450.00
Indonesia			25,597	27,730	24,424	0.27	-11.92
Lao People's Democratic Republic			18	17			
Malaysia			20,218	12,832	10,902	0.12	-15.04
Myanmar			730	722			
Philippines			175,775	196,797	186,084	2.03	-5.44
Singapore			3,915	3,638	3,031	0.03	-16.68
Thailand			7,247	9,406	13,111	0.14	39.39
Viet Nam			479	440	930	0.01	111.36
AUSTRALASIA			**35,220**	**36,240**	**35,972**	**0.39**	**-0.74**
Australia			27,315	28,429	28,716	0.31	1.01

BAHRAIN

2. Arrivals of non-resident visitors at national borders, by nationality

	2009	2010	2011	2012	2013	Market share 2013	% Change 2013-2012
New Zealand			7,905	7,811	7,256	0.08	-7.11
MELANESIA			**46**	**52**	**32**	**0.00**	**-38.46**
Fiji			42	48	31	0.00	-35.42
Papua New Guinea			4	4	1	0.00	-75.00
MICRONESIA			**3**	**10**	**3**	**0.00**	**-70.00**
Marshall Islands			1	1	3	0.00	200.00
Nauru			1	8			
Palau			1	1			
POLYNESIA			**22**	**9**			
Tonga			10	9			
Tuvalu			12				
EUROPE			**513,232**	**541,071**	**552,338**	**6.03**	**2.08**
CENTRAL/EASTERN EUROPE			**27,396**	**29,475**	**33,380**	**0.36**	**13.25**
Armenia			79	104	109	0.00	4.81
Azerbaijan			992	883	1,059	0.01	19.93
Belarus			805	880	1,018	0.01	15.68
Bulgaria			1,064	1,068	1,317	0.01	23.31
Czech Republic			1,552	1,625	1,552	0.02	-4.49
Czech Republic/Slovakia			8	7			
Estonia			198	197	294	0.00	49.24
Georgia			213	162	103	0.00	-36.42
Hungary			1,062	1,294	1,343	0.01	3.79
Kazakhstan			498	576	666	0.01	15.63
Kyrgyzstan			108	135	430	0.00	218.52
Latvia			234	257	230	0.00	-10.51
Lithuania			123	157	179	0.00	14.01
Poland			1,866	2,987	3,726	0.04	24.74
Republic of Moldova			154	58	208	0.00	258.62
Romania			5,102	5,278	5,060	0.06	-4.13
Russian Federation			10,630	11,170	12,850	0.14	15.04
Slovakia			633	660	588	0.01	-10.91
Tajikistan			26	18	99	0.00	450.00
Turkmenistan			272	215			
Ukraine			1,322	1,223	2,015	0.02	64.76
Uzbekistan			455	521	534	0.01	2.50
NORTHERN EUROPE			**281,029**	**296,541**	**293,571**	**3.20**	**-1.00**
Denmark			4,507	5,417	3,723	0.04	-31.27
Finland			2,447	2,278	1,893	0.02	-16.90
Iceland			147	223	248	0.00	11.21
Ireland			17,190	19,675	21,024	0.23	6.86
Norway			2,697	2,477	2,428	0.03	-1.98
Sweden			3,490	3,880	3,717	0.04	-4.20
United Kingdom			250,551	262,591	260,538	2.84	-0.78
SOUTHERN EUROPE			**48,638**	**46,616**	**50,633**	**0.55**	**8.62**
Albania			34	53	50	0.00	-5.66
Bosnia and Herzegovina			345	330	425	0.00	28.79
Croatia			877	1,328	1,880	0.02	41.57
Greece			6,320	5,880	6,259	0.07	6.45
Italy			28,197	24,177	25,014	0.27	3.46
Malta			235	274	350	0.00	27.74
Montenegro			10	17			
Portugal			1,897	2,711	4,086	0.04	50.72
San Marino			7	3	2	0.00	-33.33
Serbia			645	723	909	0.01	25.73
Serbia and Montenegro			688				
Slovenia			101	184			
Spain			9,205	10,878	11,530	0.13	5.99
TFYR of Macedonia			77	58	128	0.00	120.69
WESTERN EUROPE			**128,733**	**145,856**	**152,635**	**1.67**	**4.65**

Yearbook of Tourism Statistics, Data 2009 – 2013, 2015 Edition

BAHRAIN

2. Arrivals of non-resident visitors at national borders, by nationality

	2009	2010	2011	2012	2013	Market share 2013	% Change 2013-2012
Austria			6,196	6,125	6,610	0.07	7.92
Belgium			7,079	7,930	7,825	0.09	-1.32
France			38,742	36,812	35,069	0.38	-4.73
Germany			55,329	70,895	80,141	0.87	13.04
Liechtenstein			11	9	15	0.00	66.67
Luxembourg			150	227	353	0.00	55.51
Monaco			7	7			
Netherlands			17,715	19,746	18,678	0.20	-5.41
Switzerland			3,504	4,105	3,944	0.04	-3.92
EAST MEDITERRANEAN EUROPE			**27,436**	**22,583**	**22,119**	**0.24**	**-2.05**
Cyprus			2,917	2,327	2,411	0.03	3.61
Turkey			24,519	20,256	19,708	0.22	-2.71
MIDDLE EAST			**4,276,021**	**5,333,158**	**6,422,870**	**70.10**	**20.43**
Egypt			130,916	159,770	186,454	2.03	16.70
Iraq			7,122	7,868	10,870	0.12	38.15
Jordan			132,041	159,581	178,308	1.95	11.74
Kuwait			275,897	282,396	356,284	3.89	26.16
Lebanon			61,128	78,482	90,796	0.99	15.69
Libya			1,100	1,487	1,846	0.02	24.14
Oman			39,452	47,292	58,879	0.64	24.50
Palestine			34,004	44,937	51,052	0.56	13.61
Qatar			96,214	115,823	122,351	1.34	5.64
Saudi Arabia			3,320,188	4,213,412	5,062,463	55.25	20.15
Syrian Arab Republic			74,078	95,514	116,432	1.27	21.90
United Arab Emirates			42,789	46,978	89,564	0.98	90.65
Yemen			61,092	79,618	97,571	1.06	22.55
SOUTH ASIA			**1,213,199**	**1,381,359**	**1,393,894**	**15.21**	**0.91**
Afghanistan			1,649	1,859	1,651	0.02	-11.19
Bangladesh			70,858	80,261	88,946	0.97	10.82
Bhutan			16	5	15	0.00	200.00
India			837,514	963,194	966,306	10.55	0.32
Iran, Islamic Republic of			3,158	2,792	2,884	0.03	3.30
Maldives			54	67	79	0.00	17.91
Nepal			51,985	49,199	37,322	0.41	-24.14
Pakistan			214,952	250,523	263,217	2.87	5.07
Sri Lanka			33,013	33,459	33,474	0.37	0.04

Yearbook of Tourism Statistics, Data 2009 – 2013, 2015 Edition

BANGLADESH

1. Arrivals of non-resident tourists at national borders, by nationality

	2009	2010	2011	2012	2013	Market share 2013	% Change 2013-2012
TOTAL			154,617	124,943	148,327	100.00	18.72
AMERICAS			7,160	1,203	4,815	3.25	300.25
NORTH AMERICA			7,160	1,203	4,815	3.25	300.25
Canada			1,410	1,203	933	0.63	-22.44
United States of America			5,750		3,882	2.62	
EAST ASIA AND THE PACIFIC			8,096	8,623	6,452	4.35	-25.18
NORTH-EAST ASIA			5,675	5,773	4,456	3.00	-22.81
Japan			5,675	5,773	4,456	3.00	-22.81
SOUTH-EAST ASIA			853	1,455	974	0.66	-33.06
Singapore				811	469	0.32	-42.17
Thailand			853	644	505	0.34	-21.58
AUSTRALASIA			1,568	1,395	1,022	0.69	-26.74
Australia			1,381	1,395	862	0.58	-38.21
New Zealand			187		160	0.11	
EUROPE			9,619	8,480	6,947	4.68	-18.08
CENTRAL/EASTERN EUROPE			149	195	235	0.16	20.51
USSR (former)			149	195	235	0.16	20.51
NORTHERN EUROPE			5,126	4,145	3,226	2.17	-22.17
Norway			262	227	284	0.19	25.11
Sweden			693	686	517	0.35	-24.64
United Kingdom			4,171	3,232	2,425	1.63	-24.97
SOUTHERN EUROPE			1,018	975	908	0.61	-6.87
Greece			60	54	49	0.03	-9.26
Italy			958	921	859	0.58	-6.73
WESTERN EUROPE			3,326	3,165	2,578	1.74	-18.55
France			986	911	698	0.47	-23.38
Germany			1,227	1,158	935	0.63	-19.26
Netherlands			791	752	671	0.45	-10.77
Switzerland			322	344	274	0.18	-20.35
SOUTH ASIA			105,522	78,119	78,975	53.24	1.10
India			105,522	78,119	78,975	53.24	1.10
NOT SPECIFIED			24,220	28,518	51,138	34.48	79.32
Other countries of the World			24,220	28,518	51,138	34.48	79.32

Yearbook of Tourism Statistics, Data 2009 – 2013, 2015 Edition

BARBADOS

1. Arrivals of non-resident tourists at national borders, by country of residence

	2009	2010	2011	2012	2013	Market share 2013	% Change 2013-2012
TOTAL	518,564	532,180	567,724	536,303	508,520	100.00	-5.18
AFRICA	954	1,284	1,175	1,011	1,334	0.26	31.95
EAST AFRICA	108	175	193	171	229	0.05	33.92
Ethiopia	4	2	4	5	5	0.00	
Kenya	38	72	61	63	57	0.01	-9.52
Malawi	2	1	3	8	4	0.00	-50.00
Mauritius	10	9	22	12	25	0.00	108.33
Rwanda	1	3	4	2	2	0.00	
Seychelles		2	10	5	9	0.00	80.00
Uganda	13	16	16	19	22	0.00	15.79
United Republic of Tanzania	17	15	13	15	12	0.00	-20.00
Zambia	8	11	32	16	31	0.01	93.75
Zimbabwe	15	44	28	26	62	0.01	138.46
CENTRAL AFRICA	4	19	15	20	25	0.00	25.00
Angola	2	3	6	4	4	0.00	
Cameroon	2	9	5	7	20	0.00	185.71
Congo		7	4	9	1	0.00	-88.89
NORTH AFRICA	20	24	31	46	76	0.01	65.22
Morocco	13	9	14	13	26	0.01	100.00
Sudan	1	3		5	8	0.00	60.00
Tunisia	6	12	17	28	42	0.01	50.00
SOUTHERN AFRICA	446	690	420	416	482	0.09	15.87
Botswana	13	18	22	9	10	0.00	11.11
Lesotho	5	2	1	4	2	0.00	-50.00
Namibia	7	11	8	6	13	0.00	116.67
South Africa	413	652	366	393	452	0.09	15.01
Swaziland	8	7	23	4	5	0.00	25.00
WEST AFRICA	376	376	516	358	522	0.10	45.81
Gambia		5	2	6	3	0.00	-50.00
Ghana	35	34	41	26	42	0.01	61.54
Guinea	1	4	2	1	1	0.00	
Liberia			3	1	2	0.00	100.00
Mali	6	1	1		3	0.00	
Nigeria	329	326	462	324	455	0.09	40.43
Sierra Leone	5	6	5		16	0.00	
AMERICAS	292,435	312,551	336,920	318,381	291,615	57.35	-8.41
CARIBBEAN	88,302	85,573	94,722	90,562	81,975	16.12	-9.48
Anguilla	797	658	498	456	401	0.08	-12.06
Antigua and Barbuda	5,345	4,518	4,287	4,004	3,918	0.77	-2.15
Aruba	76	98	118	84	31	0.01	-63.10
Bahamas	916	921	971	807	1,053	0.21	30.48
Bermuda	1,482	1,424	1,220	990	777	0.15	-21.52
British Virgin Islands	2,132	1,800	1,630	1,410	1,242	0.24	-11.91
Cayman Islands	886	769	727	514	435	0.09	-15.37
Cuba	185	160	143	123	143	0.03	16.26
Curaçao	206	212	228	178	127	0.02	-28.65
Dominica	5,251	5,185	5,146	4,472	4,529	0.89	1.27
Dominican Republic	322	360	391	412	296	0.06	-28.16
Grenada	5,231	4,941	5,035	4,413	4,442	0.87	0.66
Guadeloupe	846	1,168	1,010	982	754	0.15	-23.22
Haiti	202	194	212	213	166	0.03	-22.07
Jamaica	8,078	7,948	8,862	8,423	7,951	1.56	-5.60
Martinique	2,692	2,975	2,844	2,462	1,900	0.37	-22.83
Montserrat	279	244	250	181	226	0.04	24.86
Netherlands Antilles	1,489	1,317	915	856	514	0.10	-39.95
Puerto Rico	898	742	683	587	446	0.09	-24.02
Saint Kitts and Nevis	3,928	3,589	3,000	2,714	2,624	0.52	-3.32
Saint Lucia	9,421	8,451	8,199	7,479	7,535	1.48	0.75
Saint Vincent and the Grenadines	10,410	9,900	10,596	10,344	10,402	2.05	0.56

56

BARBADOS

1. Arrivals of non-resident tourists at national borders, by country of residence

	2009	2010	2011	2012	2013	Market share 2013	% Change 2013-2012
Sint Maarten			238	1	55	0.01	5,400.00
Trinidad and Tobago	26,510	27,292	36,825	38,005	31,614	6.22	-16.82
Turks and Caicos Islands	200	243	238	130	116	0.02	-10.77
United States Virgin Islands	520	464	456	322	278	0.05	-13.66
CENTRAL AMERICA	**1,270**	**1,461**	**1,535**	**1,562**	**1,272**	**0.25**	**-18.57**
Belize	502	508	573	540	515	0.10	-4.63
Costa Rica	224	318	259	272	175	0.03	-35.66
El Salvador	35	41	45	62	48	0.01	-22.58
Guatemala	86	136	131	141	102	0.02	-27.66
Honduras	31	36	46	68	56	0.01	-17.65
Nicaragua	22	17	32	48	29	0.01	-39.58
Panama	370	405	449	431	347	0.07	-19.49
NORTH AMERICA	**186,965**	**208,368**	**214,975**	**203,442**	**188,489**	**37.07**	**-7.35**
Canada	63,826	72,434	71,953	72,020	67,295	13.23	-6.56
Greenland		1	1		1	0.00	
Mexico	434	444	607	660	609	0.12	-7.73
United States of America	122,705	135,489	142,414	130,762	120,584	23.71	-7.78
SOUTH AMERICA	**15,898**	**17,149**	**25,688**	**22,815**	**19,879**	**3.91**	**-12.87**
Argentina	375	317	656	522	412	0.08	-21.07
Bolivia	45	26	30	85	25	0.00	-70.59
Brazil	504	2,354	4,842	4,633	4,700	0.92	1.45
Chile	116	86	131	116	171	0.03	47.41
Colombia	333	373	399	509	474	0.09	-6.88
Ecuador	35	46	39	65	41	0.01	-36.92
French Guiana	58	96	97	126	50	0.01	-60.32
Guyana	12,010	11,673	16,524	14,167	11,626	2.29	-17.94
Paraguay	3	2	15	41	10	0.00	-75.61
Peru	103	131	92	263	141	0.03	-46.39
Suriname	532	518	681	557	543	0.11	-2.51
Uruguay	16	20	49	47	39	0.01	-17.02
Venezuela	1,768	1,507	2,133	1,684	1,647	0.32	-2.20
EAST ASIA AND THE PACIFIC	**3,325**	**4,107**	**3,723**	**4,498**	**3,616**	**0.71**	**-19.61**
NORTH-EAST ASIA	**891**	**728**	**799**	**923**	**836**	**0.16**	**-9.43**
China	531	397	403	499	485	0.10	-2.81
Hong Kong, China	103	82	71	92	40	0.01	-56.52
Japan	231	214	310	315	287	0.06	-8.89
Korea, Republic of	5	15	6	7	5	0.00	-28.57
Taiwan, Province of China	21	20	9	10	19	0.00	90.00
SOUTH-EAST ASIA	**990**	**970**	**768**	**671**	**603**	**0.12**	**-10.13**
Brunei Darussalam		3	5	2			
Indonesia	65	69	76	36	51	0.01	41.67
Malaysia	91	85	58	89	37	0.01	-58.43
Philippines	644	633	506	403	404	0.08	0.25
Singapore	117	112	86	99	70	0.01	-29.29
Thailand	64	61	34	39	33	0.01	-15.38
Viet Nam	9	7	3	3	8	0.00	166.67
AUSTRALASIA	**1,431**	**2,390**	**2,139**	**2,874**	**2,139**	**0.42**	**-25.57**
Australia	1,169	1,971	1,765	2,512	1,757	0.35	-30.06
New Zealand	262	419	374	362	382	0.08	5.52
MELANESIA	**12**	**13**	**13**	**14**	**25**	**0.00**	**78.57**
Fiji	4	8	11	14	20	0.00	42.86
Papua New Guinea	7	4	2		4	0.00	
Vanuatu	1	1			1	0.00	
POLYNESIA	**1**	**6**	**4**	**16**	**13**	**0.00**	**-18.75**
Cook Islands			2	2			
Samoa	1	2	1	8	11	0.00	37.50
Tonga		4	1	6	2	0.00	-66.67

Yearbook of Tourism Statistics, Data 2009 – 2013, 2015 Edition

BARBADOS

1. Arrivals of non-resident tourists at national borders, by country of residence

	2009	2010	2011	2012	2013	Market share 2013	% Change 2013-2012
EUROPE	218,770	210,726	223,964	209,604	208,503	41.00	-0.53
CENTRAL/EASTERN EUROPE	2,497	3,094	4,204	3,768	4,430	0.87	17.57
Azerbaijan	1	8	2	15	3	0.00	-80.00
Belarus	15	30	41	41	37	0.01	-9.76
Bulgaria	84	59	126	59	151	0.03	155.93
Czech Republic	278	257	345	318	375	0.07	17.92
Czech Republic/Slovakia		2	2				
Estonia	98	168	514	70	153	0.03	118.57
Georgia	3	6	11	12	5	0.00	-58.33
Hungary	163	195	196	187	212	0.04	13.37
Kazakhstan	12	49	41	59	71	0.01	20.34
Latvia	31	52	71	66	90	0.02	36.36
Lithuania	14	47	68	87	82	0.02	-5.75
Poland	343	407	491	405	587	0.12	44.94
Romania	128	149	144	140	184	0.04	31.43
Russian Federation	1,024	1,217	1,718	1,844	1,884	0.37	2.17
Slovakia	97	133	161	179	262	0.05	46.37
Ukraine	206	315	273	286	334	0.07	16.78
NORTHERN EUROPE	196,987	188,079	197,814	183,767	180,810	35.56	-1.61
Denmark	806	947	938	844	692	0.14	-18.01
Finland	381	426	612	1,353	2,650	0.52	95.86
Iceland	18	22	21	33	33	0.01	
Ireland	4,105	3,852	3,738	3,519	3,638	0.72	3.38
Norway	694	1,016	1,056	1,218	1,175	0.23	-3.53
Sweden	1,270	1,526	2,299	3,281	3,889	0.76	18.53
United Kingdom	189,713	180,290	189,150	173,519	168,733	33.18	-2.76
SOUTHERN EUROPE	5,940	5,507	5,972	5,204	4,981	0.98	-4.29
Albania	6	8	8	14	7	0.00	-50.00
Andorra	7	1	5	1			
Bosnia and Herzegovina	1	4	5	6	4	0.00	-33.33
Croatia	92	63	72	149	85	0.02	-42.95
Gibraltar	39	49	29	38	40	0.01	5.26
Greece	72	168	149	136	157	0.03	15.44
Italy	4,421	3,944	4,426	3,710	3,418	0.67	-7.87
Malta	60	54	37	46	57	0.01	23.91
Montenegro	4	1	3	2	3	0.00	50.00
Portugal	157	222	161	187	178	0.04	-4.81
San Marino	7	12	25	4	15	0.00	275.00
Serbia	39	36	33	37	27	0.01	-27.03
Serbia and Montenegro	4						
Slovenia	78	82	95	61	81	0.02	32.79
Spain	953	863	924	813	909	0.18	11.81
WESTERN EUROPE	13,045	13,725	15,676	16,566	18,026	3.54	8.81
Austria	710	857	916	994	961	0.19	-3.32
Belgium	647	624	550	593	553	0.11	-6.75
France	2,416	2,524	3,167	3,252	3,953	0.78	21.56
Germany	7,038	7,300	8,401	9,182	10,300	2.03	12.18
Liechtenstein	12	26	22	10	13	0.00	30.00
Luxembourg	105	155	172	137	113	0.02	-17.52
Monaco	108	108	97	138	120	0.02	-13.04
Netherlands	412	310	357	281	123	0.02	-56.23
Switzerland	1,597	1,821	1,994	1,979	1,890	0.37	-4.50
EAST MEDITERRANEAN EUROPE	301	321	298	299	256	0.05	-14.38
Cyprus	92	54	57	35	40	0.01	14.29
Israel	141	172	179	209	162	0.03	-22.49
Turkey	68	95	62	55	54	0.01	-1.82

Yearbook of Tourism Statistics, Data 2009 – 2013, 2015 Edition

BARBADOS

1. Arrivals of non-resident tourists at national borders, by country of residence

	2009	2010	2011	2012	2013	Market share 2013	% Change 2013-2012
MIDDLE EAST	**299**	**344**	**305**	**233**	**290**	**0.06**	**24.46**
Bahrain	15	14	13	7	16	0.00	128.57
Egypt	13	24	19	14	14	0.00	
Jordan	9	6	19	16	13	0.00	-18.75
Kuwait	9	6	11	2	24	0.00	1,100.00
Lebanon	10	9	28	10	15	0.00	50.00
Oman	12	4	7	5	8	0.00	60.00
Saudi Arabia	35	18	55	20	33	0.01	65.00
Syrian Arab Republic	6	3					
United Arab Emirates	188	260	152	158	167	0.03	5.70
Yemen	2		1	1			
SOUTH ASIA	**1,082**	**1,634**	**1,440**	**886**	**1,093**	**0.21**	**23.36**
Afghanistan	2	26			2	0.00	
Bangladesh	30	58	8	3	12	0.00	300.00
India	959	1,317	1,230	758	965	0.19	27.31
Iran, Islamic Republic of	2	3	6	5	5	0.00	
Maldives		1		2	3	0.00	50.00
Nepal	9	8	16	13	14	0.00	7.69
Pakistan	50	122	119	62	72	0.01	16.13
Sri Lanka	30	99	61	43	20	0.00	-53.49
NOT SPECIFIED	**1,699**	**1,534**	**197**	**1,690**	**2,069**	**0.41**	**22.43**
Other countries of the World	1,699	1,534	197	1,690	2,069	0.41	22.43

BELARUS

1. Arrivals of non-resident tourists at national borders, by nationality

	2009	2010	2011	2012	2013	Market share 2013	% Change 2013-2012
TOTAL (*)	94,719	119,370	116,049	118,749	136,810	100.00	15.21
AFRICA	138	101	44	16	127	0.09	693.75
EAST AFRICA	2	8					
Ethiopia		8					
Zimbabwe	2						
CENTRAL AFRICA	3	4	1		15	0.01	
Angola	2	4			15	0.01	
Cameroon			1				
Congo	1						
NORTH AFRICA	11	11	8	1			
Algeria	3	7	3	1			
Morocco	5	1	5				
Sudan		3					
Tunisia	3						
SOUTHERN AFRICA	67	24	21	8	110	0.08	1,275.00
Lesotho			2				
Namibia	5	4	2				
South Africa	62	20	17	8	110	0.08	1,275.00
WEST AFRICA	55	54	14	7	2	0.00	-71.43
Côte d'Ivoire			2				
Ghana	26	1		3	1	0.00	-66.67
Nigeria	28	52	12	4	1	0.00	-75.00
Sierra Leone		1					
Togo	1						
AMERICAS	1,075	974	657	1,179	1,442	1.05	22.31
CARIBBEAN	4	1	35		10	0.01	
Anguilla			4				
Cayman Islands			9				
Cuba	4				10	0.01	
Dominican Republic			2				
Jamaica		1					
Saint Lucia			20				
CENTRAL AMERICA		2	1	1			
Costa Rica				1			
Guatemala			1				
Nicaragua		2					
NORTH AMERICA	963	820	567	1,114	1,390	1.02	24.78
Canada	79	129	33	74	245	0.18	231.08
Mexico	20	8	7	23	75	0.05	226.09
United States of America	864	683	527	1,017	1,070	0.78	5.21
SOUTH AMERICA	108	151	54	64	42	0.03	-34.38
Argentina	13	10	11	5	4	0.00	-20.00
Bolivia	4						
Brazil	22	43	29	31	19	0.01	-38.71
Chile	12	5	3	4	3	0.00	-25.00
Colombia	6		1	4	12	0.01	200.00
Ecuador			2		1	0.00	
Paraguay		1					
Peru	14	9	5	4	2	0.00	-50.00
Uruguay		1			1	0.00	
Venezuela	37	82	3	16			
EAST ASIA AND THE PACIFIC	963	1,040	4,251	1,015	2,488	1.82	145.12
NORTH-EAST ASIA	811	839	1,053	870	1,461	1.07	67.93
China	391	603	364	314	682	0.50	117.20
Hong Kong, China		1	37	105	175	0.13	66.67
Japan	235	197	269	385	571	0.42	48.31
Korea, Dem. People's Republic of	34	1	2		3	0.00	
Korea, Republic of	55	14	50	43	2	0.00	-95.35
Mongolia	10	3	79	1	28	0.02	2,700.00

Yearbook of Tourism Statistics, Data 2009 – 2013, 2015 Edition

BELARUS

1. Arrivals of non-resident tourists at national borders, by nationality

	2009	2010	2011	2012	2013	Market share 2013	% Change 2013-2012
Taiwan, Province of China	86	20	252	22			
SOUTH-EAST ASIA	**57**	**52**	**48**	**11**	**92**	**0.07**	**736.36**
Indonesia	3	4	4		2	0.00	
Malaysia	7	5		4	11	0.01	175.00
Myanmar			2				
Philippines	21	5		1	22	0.02	2,100.00
Singapore	5	1		1	25	0.02	2,400.00
Thailand	1	8		3			
Viet Nam	20	29	42	2	32	0.02	1,500.00
AUSTRALASIA	**95**	**149**	**3,150**	**134**	**935**	**0.68**	**597.76**
Australia	57	132	65	124	858	0.63	591.94
New Zealand	38	17	3,085	10	77	0.06	670.00
EUROPE	**91,778**	**116,342**	**110,232**	**116,001**	**132,217**	**96.64**	**13.98**
CENTRAL/EASTERN EUROPE	**69,271**	**94,218**	**95,054**	**102,307**	**121,782**	**89.02**	**19.04**
Armenia			30	23	69	0.05	200.00
Azerbaijan	290	194	251	64	176	0.13	175.00
Bulgaria	143	50	63	24	71	0.05	195.83
Czech Republic	421	350	334	198	402	0.29	103.03
Estonia	690	595	464	738	670	0.49	-9.21
Georgia			36	149	106	0.08	-28.86
Hungary	119	136	105	62	50	0.04	-19.35
Kazakhstan			165	180	464	0.34	157.78
Kyrgyzstan	29	8	12	8	42	0.03	425.00
Latvia	1,550	1,409	1,550	1,107	1,031	0.75	-6.87
Lithuania	2,979	4,357	3,170	1,688	2,093	1.53	23.99
Poland	3,729	4,006	2,983	2,027	3,126	2.28	54.22
Republic of Moldova	158	104	40	87	79	0.06	-9.20
Romania	69	91	99	160	25	0.02	-84.38
Russian Federation	56,547	80,881	83,843	94,187	111,286	81.34	18.15
Slovakia	124	118	144	108	25	0.02	-76.85
Tajikistan			5	5	20	0.01	300.00
Turkmenistan			26	31	49	0.04	58.06
Ukraine	2,423	1,919	1,693	1,441	1,979	1.45	37.34
Uzbekistan			41	20	19	0.01	-5.00
NORTHERN EUROPE	**6,701**	**8,172**	**4,233**	**3,832**	**2,414**	**1.76**	**-37.00**
Denmark	185	230	267	100	76	0.06	-24.00
Finland	610	770	560	358	341	0.25	-4.75
Iceland	6	59	476	20	10	0.01	-50.00
Ireland	178	57	39	50	43	0.03	-14.00
Norway	156	192	133	51	83	0.06	62.75
Sweden	604	644	346	220	204	0.15	-7.27
United Kingdom	4,962	6,220	2,412	3,033	1,657	1.21	-45.37
SOUTHERN EUROPE	**3,868**	**3,428**	**2,627**	**2,421**	**1,613**	**1.18**	**-33.37**
Albania	1	49					
Bosnia and Herzegovina	5	20	137	12	2	0.00	-83.33
Croatia	195	89	108	97	112	0.08	15.46
Greece	162	83	49	46	76	0.06	65.22
Italy	2,531	2,275	1,816	1,535	952	0.70	-37.98
Malta	8		5	2	37	0.03	1,750.00
Montenegro	32		17		55	0.04	
Portugal	118	72	16	78	10	0.01	-87.18
Serbia	277	63	44	162	115	0.08	-29.01
Slovenia	238	136	38	23	58	0.04	152.17
Spain	274	582	349	366	160	0.12	-56.28
TFYR of Macedonia	27	59	48	100	36	0.03	-64.00
WESTERN EUROPE	**5,988**	**4,432**	**4,111**	**3,948**	**3,895**	**2.85**	**-1.34**
Austria	471	295	250	220	182	0.13	-17.27
Belgium	155	249	120	247	358	0.26	44.94
France	1,114	808	754	749	729	0.53	-2.67

61

BELARUS

1. Arrivals of non-resident tourists at national borders, by nationality

	2009	2010	2011	2012	2013	Market share 2013	% Change 2013-2012
Germany	2,568	2,245	2,191	2,071	1,931	1.41	-6.76
Liechtenstein		2					
Luxembourg	19	12	53	2	6	0.00	200.00
Netherlands	475	552	327	229	402	0.29	75.55
Switzerland	1,186	269	416	430	287	0.21	-33.26
EAST MEDITERRANEAN EUROPE	**5,950**	**6,092**	**4,207**	**3,493**	**2,513**	**1.84**	**-28.06**
Cyprus	314	460	272	141	60	0.04	-57.45
Israel	956	925	339	584	465	0.34	-20.38
Turkey	4,680	4,707	3,596	2,768	1,988	1.45	-28.18
MIDDLE EAST	**331**	**522**	**395**	**270**	**486**	**0.36**	**80.00**
Bahrain			37	8	58	0.04	625.00
Egypt	26	53	30	47	17	0.01	-63.83
Iraq	16	16	22	25	68	0.05	172.00
Jordan	15	14	6	1	22	0.02	2,100.00
Kuwait	6	10		2	20	0.01	900.00
Lebanon	83	225	245	117	70	0.05	-40.17
Libya	11	2	6	22	114	0.08	418.18
Oman			8	13	31	0.02	138.46
Palestine				13			
Qatar			6				
Saudi Arabia	19	50	9	7	52	0.04	642.86
Syrian Arab Republic	21	8	3	11	4	0.00	-63.64
United Arab Emirates	130	137	23	2	22	0.02	1,000.00
Yemen	4	7		2	8	0.01	300.00
SOUTH ASIA	**434**	**391**	**470**	**268**	**50**	**0.04**	**-81.34**
Afghanistan	1	7	2		1	0.00	
Bangladesh	1	1		3	22	0.02	633.33
India	154	73	97	18	18	0.01	
Iran, Islamic Republic of	255	298	368	235	8	0.01	-96.60
Maldives			1				
Nepal	5	5		5			
Pakistan	7		1	1	1	0.00	
Sri Lanka	11	7	1	6			

BELGIUM

3. Arrivals of non-resident tourists in hotels and similar establishments, by country of residence

	2009	2010	2011	2012	2013	Market share 2013	% Change 2013-2012
TOTAL	5,451,600	5,771,650	6,076,926	6,145,699	6,227,649	100.00	1.33
AFRICA	59,410	57,194	57,570	56,915	59,981	0.96	5.39
EAST AFRICA	9,575	8,734	8,573	6,479	6,926	0.11	6.90
Burundi	430	450	530	718	640	0.01	-10.86
Comoros	14	58	28	32	45	0.00	40.63
Djibouti	148	138	93	118	140	0.00	18.64
Eritrea	38	66	92	100	86	0.00	-14.00
Ethiopia	4,474	3,717	3,439	1,077	1,616	0.03	50.05
Kenya	931	799	874	1,050	1,036	0.02	-1.33
Madagascar	323	313	283	334	288	0.00	-13.77
Malawi	63	69	76	87	88	0.00	1.15
Mauritius	251	227	314	364	427	0.01	17.31
Mozambique	158	132	186	169	140	0.00	-17.16
Rwanda	687	819	735	830	833	0.01	0.36
Seychelles	245	219	337	242	97	0.00	-59.92
Somalia	166	111	175	87	148	0.00	70.11
Uganda	555	424	358	314	404	0.01	28.66
United Republic of Tanzania	530	483	417	285	374	0.01	31.23
Zambia	111	136	127	136	169	0.00	24.26
Zimbabwe	451	573	509	536	395	0.01	-26.31
CENTRAL AFRICA	10,953	10,231	10,443	11,005	11,477	0.18	4.29
Angola	1,144	1,070	1,096	1,240	1,335	0.02	7.66
Cameroon	2,590	2,236	2,078	2,020	2,336	0.04	15.64
Central African Republic	234	303	326	438	581	0.01	32.65
Chad	190	171	158	83	217	0.00	161.45
Congo	2,730	2,713	2,494	3,055	2,817	0.05	-7.79
Democratic Republic of the Congo	2,975	2,795	3,220	3,340	3,473	0.06	3.98
Equatorial Guinea	29	126	79	91	70	0.00	-23.08
Gabon	1,012	775	950	683	619	0.01	-9.37
Sao Tome and Principe	49	42	42	55	29	0.00	-47.27
NORTH AFRICA	19,620	18,602	18,006	17,644	19,126	0.31	8.40
Algeria	3,225	3,032	3,116	2,891	3,780	0.06	30.75
Morocco	13,295	12,218	11,239	11,401	11,640	0.19	2.10
South Sudan				30	10	0.00	-66.67
Sudan	282	389	396	270	281	0.00	4.07
Tunisia	2,818	2,963	3,255	3,052	3,415	0.05	11.89
SOUTHERN AFRICA	7,441	7,735	8,481	8,784	8,739	0.14	-0.51
Botswana	94	125	145	421	169	0.00	-59.86
Lesotho	44	56	47	75	111	0.00	48.00
Namibia	736	561	402	292	241	0.00	-17.47
South Africa	5,657	6,036	7,090	7,159	7,546	0.12	5.41
Swaziland	910	957	797	837	672	0.01	-19.71
WEST AFRICA	11,821	11,892	12,067	13,003	13,713	0.22	5.46
Benin	380	322	489	439	634	0.01	44.42
Burkina Faso	498	470	678	653	667	0.01	2.14
Cabo Verde	71	152	213	152	125	0.00	-17.76
Côte d'Ivoire	1,107	1,155	1,186	1,465	1,275	0.02	-12.97
Gambia	235	265	250	167	217	0.00	29.94
Ghana	493	648	674	664	568	0.01	-14.46
Guinea	729	694	769	1,205	1,352	0.02	12.20
Guinea-Bissau	38	85	98	74	94	0.00	27.03
Liberia	232	257	221	153	238	0.00	55.56
Mali	628	702	622	912	897	0.01	-1.64
Mauritania	423	597	384	412	466	0.01	13.11
Niger	2,213	1,198	1,269	1,438	1,650	0.03	14.74
Nigeria	1,841	1,870	2,041	2,182	2,263	0.04	3.71
Senegal	1,338	1,662	1,402	1,603	1,535	0.02	-4.24
Sierra Leone	1,339	1,573	1,481	1,197	1,376	0.02	14.95

63

BELGIUM

3. Arrivals of non-resident tourists in hotels and similar establishments, by country of residence

	2009	2010	2011	2012	2013	Market share 2013	% Change 2013-2012
Togo	256	242	290	287	356	0.01	24.04
AMERICAS	**333,104**	**388,039**	**442,620**	**457,836**	**463,071**	**7.44**	**1.14**
CARIBBEAN	**2,620**	**2,665**	**2,543**	**2,422**	**2,073**	**0.03**	**-14.41**
Antigua and Barbuda	249	317	233	173	131	0.00	-24.28
Bahamas	105	374	131	101	102	0.00	0.99
Barbados	579	242	201	133	183	0.00	37.59
Cuba	240	298	276	399	290	0.00	-27.32
Dominica	159	113	175	91	70	0.00	-23.08
Dominican Republic	306	429	418	560	464	0.01	-17.14
Grenada	208	108	109	48	61	0.00	27.08
Haiti	130	180	173	268	204	0.00	-23.88
Jamaica	308	369	569	411	325	0.01	-20.92
Saint Kitts and Nevis	35	20	33	71	45	0.00	-36.62
Saint Lucia	17	33	24	21	24	0.00	14.29
Saint Vincent and the Grenadines	70	20	84	23	10	0.00	-56.52
Trinidad and Tobago	214	162	117	123	164	0.00	33.33
CENTRAL AMERICA	**3,127**	**3,860**	**4,529**	**4,176**	**4,355**	**0.07**	**4.29**
Belize	167	255	303	522	575	0.01	10.15
Costa Rica	1,215	1,475	1,330	1,349	1,482	0.02	9.86
El Salvador	476	551	849	743	445	0.01	-40.11
Guatemala	342	437	511	419	526	0.01	25.54
Honduras	247	230	475	300	302	0.00	0.67
Nicaragua	295	374	398	268	381	0.01	42.16
Panama	385	538	663	575	644	0.01	12.00
NORTH AMERICA	**289,411**	**330,889**	**369,894**	**375,958**	**375,781**	**6.03**	**-0.05**
Canada	33,353	40,746	47,127	48,853	47,675	0.77	-2.41
Mexico	10,449	13,807	15,978	18,586	21,611	0.35	16.28
United States of America	245,609	276,336	306,789	308,519	306,495	4.92	-0.66
SOUTH AMERICA	**37,946**	**50,625**	**65,654**	**75,280**	**80,862**	**1.30**	**7.41**
Argentina	6,768	8,968	11,944	15,163	17,244	0.28	13.72
Bolivia	488	353	445	351	449	0.01	27.92
Brazil	19,681	29,135	38,511	42,915	43,453	0.70	1.25
Chile	2,373	2,638	3,566	4,436	4,769	0.08	7.51
Colombia	3,007	3,732	3,865	4,263	5,335	0.09	25.15
Ecuador	1,052	891	1,083	1,189	1,456	0.02	22.46
Guyana	64	65	76	67	68	0.00	1.49
Paraguay	143	182	315	319	327	0.01	2.51
Peru	1,100	1,312	1,446	1,710	1,949	0.03	13.98
Suriname	209	285	450	430	537	0.01	24.88
Uruguay	1,100	1,317	1,668	1,253	1,332	0.02	6.30
Venezuela	1,961	1,747	2,285	3,184	3,943	0.06	23.84
EAST ASIA AND THE PACIFIC	**208,563**	**226,179**	**275,432**	**334,893**	**364,057**	**5.85**	**8.71**
NORTH-EAST ASIA	**160,141**	**168,188**	**208,499**	**254,902**	**279,499**	**4.49**	**9.65**
China	71,547	75,201	95,880	115,909	142,770	2.29	23.17
Japan	74,509	75,976	86,778	107,252	107,027	1.72	-0.21
Korea, Dem. People's Republic of	1,540	1,687	2,167	2,114	2,119	0.03	0.24
Korea, Republic of	6,272	10,094	11,930	13,196	12,944	0.21	-1.91
Mongolia	181	137	275	338	266	0.00	-21.30
Taiwan, Province of China	6,092	5,093	11,469	16,093	14,373	0.23	-10.69
SOUTH-EAST ASIA	**18,317**	**22,282**	**27,101**	**37,783**	**40,429**	**0.65**	**7.00**
Brunei Darussalam	90	171	182	208	121	0.00	-41.83
Cambodia	134	122	123	176	120	0.00	-31.82
Indonesia	2,353	2,699	3,250	5,096	5,840	0.09	14.60
Lao People's Democratic Republic	151	247	252	254	142	0.00	-44.09
Malaysia	2,565	3,232	4,289	5,079	7,357	0.12	44.85
Myanmar	104	123	123	104	222	0.00	113.46
Philippines	4,614	4,537	5,330	5,006	5,072	0.08	1.32
Singapore	3,488	4,333	4,941	6,142	6,803	0.11	10.76
Thailand	3,406	4,909	6,639	13,301	12,019	0.19	-9.64

Yearbook of Tourism Statistics, Data 2009 – 2013, 2015 Edition

BELGIUM

3. Arrivals of non-resident tourists in hotels and similar establishments, by country of residence

	2009	2010	2011	2012	2013	Market share 2013	% Change 2013-2012
Timor-Leste	5	26	16	18	13	0.00	-27.78
Viet Nam	1,407	1,883	1,956	2,399	2,720	0.04	13.38
AUSTRALASIA	**29,307**	**34,778**	**38,805**	**41,398**	**43,275**	**0.69**	**4.53**
Australia	25,458	30,250	34,238	36,179	37,916	0.61	4.80
New Zealand	3,849	4,528	4,567	5,219	5,359	0.09	2.68
MELANESIA	**316**	**374**	**439**	**374**	**368**	**0.01**	**-1.60**
Fiji	102	150	171	117	92	0.00	-21.37
Papua New Guinea	83	73	75	75	57	0.00	-24.00
Solomon Islands	93	128	114	94	80	0.00	-14.89
Vanuatu	38	23	79	88	139	0.00	57.95
MICRONESIA	**263**	**454**	**355**	**336**	**335**	**0.01**	**-0.30**
Kiribati	27	48	48	26	50	0.00	92.31
Marshall Islands	2	7	4	9	13	0.00	44.44
Micronesia, Federated States of	54	161	78	151	76	0.00	-49.67
Nauru	129	197	191	111	148	0.00	33.33
Palau	51	41	34	39	48	0.00	23.08
POLYNESIA	**219**	**103**	**233**	**100**	**151**	**0.00**	**51.00**
Samoa	28	13	135	48	60	0.00	25.00
Tonga	86	79	72	34	65	0.00	91.18
Tuvalu	105	11	26	18	26	0.00	44.44
EUROPE	**4,675,581**	**4,974,321**	**5,192,869**	**5,180,659**	**5,204,144**	**83.57**	**0.45**
CENTRAL/EASTERN EUROPE	**265,228**	**301,414**	**340,657**	**358,892**	**367,882**	**5.91**	**2.50**
Armenia	1,040	1,028	1,192	970	1,155	0.02	19.07
Azerbaijan	527	655	1,018	1,167	1,297	0.02	11.14
Belarus	2,490	2,373	2,629	3,098	4,022	0.06	29.83
Bulgaria	14,063	15,205	15,905	16,112	15,781	0.25	-2.05
Czech Republic	26,154	28,363	28,356	29,771	29,418	0.47	-1.19
Estonia	5,221	6,291	6,791	7,343	7,525	0.12	2.48
Georgia	3,060	2,744	2,245	2,251	2,264	0.04	0.58
Hungary	23,071	24,221	27,746	30,356	29,849	0.48	-1.67
Kazakhstan	835	940	1,147	1,406	1,289	0.02	-8.32
Kyrgyzstan	137	133	212	166	193	0.00	16.27
Latvia	5,529	8,297	9,487	9,930	9,436	0.15	-4.97
Lithuania	10,967	13,938	14,805	14,875	16,856	0.27	13.32
Poland	70,407	74,955	78,955	78,259	79,492	1.28	1.58
Republic of Moldova	527	590	666	752	757	0.01	0.66
Romania	30,999	35,709	39,726	37,863	40,412	0.65	6.73
Russian Federation	50,435	66,511	87,055	99,449	100,664	1.62	1.22
Slovakia	9,816	10,314	11,539	12,036	11,975	0.19	-0.51
Tajikistan	103	74	152	150	211	0.00	40.67
Turkmenistan	107	72	117	85	119	0.00	40.00
Ukraine	9,391	8,716	10,555	12,624	14,933	0.24	18.29
Uzbekistan	349	285	359	229	234	0.00	2.18
NORTHERN EUROPE	**997,273**	**1,026,628**	**1,034,371**	**1,062,209**	**1,093,605**	**17.56**	**2.96**
Denmark	49,684	51,261	54,763	55,504	54,627	0.88	-1.58
Finland	29,445	32,290	34,801	35,599	33,054	0.53	-7.15
Iceland	3,678	6,311	5,715	5,474	4,879	0.08	-10.87
Ireland	38,497	38,810	40,749	44,956	49,477	0.79	10.06
Norway	29,322	33,407	36,869	37,676	38,259	0.61	1.55
Sweden	62,365	68,827	68,451	69,615	65,539	1.05	-5.86
United Kingdom	784,282	795,722	793,023	813,385	847,770	13.61	4.23
SOUTHERN EUROPE	**575,843**	**646,412**	**703,119**	**672,990**	**683,921**	**10.98**	**1.62**
Albania	3,547	3,021	4,249	4,588	6,511	0.10	41.91
Andorra	476	479	509	545	1,673	0.03	206.97
Bosnia and Herzegovina	1,903	1,675	1,971	1,489	1,801	0.03	20.95
Croatia	5,393	5,972	6,455	7,710	9,252	0.15	20.00
Greece	28,622	28,367	30,952	26,110	27,244	0.44	4.34
Holy See	74	89	45	118	85	0.00	-27.97
Italy	220,777	242,079	262,177	256,170	259,112	4.16	1.15

Yearbook of Tourism Statistics, Data 2009 – 2013, 2015 Edition

BELGIUM

3. Arrivals of non-resident tourists in hotels and similar establishments, by country of residence

	2009	2010	2011	2012	2013	Market share 2013	% Change 2013-2012
Malta	5,030	5,605	6,062	6,019	5,797	0.09	-3.69
Montenegro	478	594	1,031	1,400	1,580	0.03	12.86
Portugal	35,810	37,418	36,588	38,575	39,972	0.64	3.62
San Marino	179	68	128	703	1,110	0.02	57.89
Serbia	5,906	3,936	6,020	5,265	6,240	0.10	18.52
Slovenia	7,031	7,992	8,235	7,630	8,334	0.13	9.23
Spain	259,442	307,875	337,147	315,222	313,681	5.04	-0.49
TFYR of Macedonia	1,175	1,242	1,550	1,446	1,529	0.02	5.74
WESTERN EUROPE	**2,787,372**	**2,942,795**	**3,046,946**	**3,007,800**	**2,974,313**	**47.76**	**-1.11**
Austria	32,368	34,259	36,789	39,659	38,715	0.62	-2.38
France	921,253	963,845	1,008,316	984,966	1,008,373	16.19	2.38
Germany	607,863	640,451	664,550	636,728	657,785	10.56	3.31
Liechtenstein	2,302	2,000	1,236	777	594	0.01	-23.55
Luxembourg	68,150	72,813	80,702	80,864	83,252	1.34	2.95
Monaco	934	945	1,041	1,325	1,449	0.02	9.36
Netherlands	1,089,867	1,154,451	1,170,608	1,174,775	1,093,336	17.56	-6.93
Switzerland	64,635	74,031	83,704	88,706	90,809	1.46	2.37
EAST MEDITERRANEAN EUROPE	**49,865**	**57,072**	**67,776**	**78,768**	**84,423**	**1.36**	**7.18**
Cyprus	4,739	5,284	6,722	8,557	5,712	0.09	-33.25
Israel	22,224	25,603	28,224	34,263	36,393	0.58	6.22
Turkey	22,902	26,185	32,830	35,948	42,318	0.68	17.72
MIDDLE EAST	**19,519**	**24,981**	**30,100**	**35,635**	**39,165**	**0.63**	**9.91**
Bahrain	382	393	529	548	703	0.01	28.28
Egypt	4,155	5,536	5,444	6,157	6,051	0.10	-1.72
Iraq	494	577	654	501	709	0.01	41.52
Jordan	1,673	1,441	1,364	1,165	1,175	0.02	0.86
Kuwait	1,186	1,201	1,835	2,257	3,546	0.06	57.11
Lebanon	2,081	2,066	2,918	3,491	3,715	0.06	6.42
Libya	616	811	420	1,169	1,485	0.02	27.03
Oman	324	447	559	727	743	0.01	2.20
Palestine	47	63	108	95	123	0.00	29.47
Qatar	535	780	1,042	1,742	2,012	0.03	15.50
Saudi Arabia	2,827	3,997	4,057	5,471	6,667	0.11	21.86
Syrian Arab Republic	814	739	632	523	468	0.01	-10.52
United Arab Emirates	4,180	6,823	10,299	11,624	11,599	0.19	-0.22
Yemen	205	107	239	165	169	0.00	2.42
SOUTH ASIA	**45,221**	**49,912**	**52,356**	**50,235**	**52,765**	**0.85**	**5.04**
Afghanistan	2,111	1,078	1,001	1,335	912	0.01	-31.69
Bangladesh	396	566	525	538	391	0.01	-27.32
Bhutan	80	22	61	159	49	0.00	-69.18
India	34,711	40,447	42,709	41,316	44,843	0.72	8.54
Iran, Islamic Republic of	6,029	5,506	5,683	4,762	4,252	0.07	-10.71
Maldives	49	28	58	33	81	0.00	145.45
Nepal	196	214	261	249	347	0.01	39.36
Pakistan	1,415	1,764	1,708	1,471	1,449	0.02	-1.50
Sri Lanka	234	287	350	372	441	0.01	18.55
NOT SPECIFIED	**110,202**	**51,024**	**25,979**	**29,526**	**44,466**	**0.71**	**50.60**
Other countries of the World	110,202	51,024	25,979	29,526	44,466	0.71	50.60

Yearbook of Tourism Statistics, Data 2009 – 2013, 2015 Edition

BELGIUM

4. Arrivals of non-resident tourists in all types of accommodation establishments, by country of residence

	2009	2010	2011	2012	2013	Market share 2013	% Change 2013-2012
TOTAL (*)	6,815,141	7,186,419	7,494,141	7,559,995	7,684,275	100.00	1.64
AFRICA	63,444	61,332	61,949	60,608	64,246	0.84	6.00
EAST AFRICA	9,778	9,171	8,912	6,915	7,350	0.10	6.29
Burundi	456	469	545	735	661	0.01	-10.07
Comoros	14	60	30	32	45	0.00	40.63
Djibouti	149	142	116	118	152	0.00	28.81
Eritrea	43	76	97	109	96	0.00	-11.93
Ethiopia	4,491	3,737	3,484	1,101	1,663	0.02	51.04
Kenya	946	813	890	1,108	1,062	0.01	-4.15
Madagascar	328	338	315	356	329	0.00	-7.58
Malawi	63	75	84	96	91	0.00	-5.21
Mauritius	265	257	331	385	435	0.01	12.99
Mozambique	173	132	186	176	144	0.00	-18.18
Rwanda	700	942	762	939	863	0.01	-8.09
Seychelles	268	237	341	262	107	0.00	-59.16
Somalia	172	123	178	100	156	0.00	56.00
Uganda	560	437	372	333	441	0.01	32.43
United Republic of Tanzania	533	498	458	311	396	0.01	27.33
Zambia	118	137	130	141	170	0.00	20.57
Zimbabwe	499	698	593	613	539	0.01	-12.07
CENTRAL AFRICA	11,377	10,569	10,944	11,397	11,923	0.16	4.62
Angola	1,162	1,130	1,326	1,266	1,369	0.02	8.14
Cameroon	2,664	2,306	2,175	2,088	2,419	0.03	15.85
Central African Republic	240	304	328	441	582	0.01	31.97
Chad	193	175	161	85	220	0.00	158.82
Congo	2,763	2,747	2,533	3,079	2,864	0.04	-6.98
Democratic Republic of the Congo	3,245	2,940	3,323	3,589	3,662	0.05	2.03
Equatorial Guinea	29	135	84	93	82	0.00	-11.83
Gabon	1,022	789	970	693	693	0.01	
Sao Tome and Principe	59	43	44	63	32	0.00	-49.21
NORTH AFRICA	21,058	19,512	19,261	18,661	20,371	0.27	9.16
Algeria	3,789	3,272	3,543	3,142	4,066	0.05	29.41
Morocco	13,993	12,780	11,944	12,034	12,451	0.16	3.47
Sudan	292	398	407	275	288	0.00	4.73
Tunisia	2,984	3,062	3,367	3,210	3,566	0.05	11.09
SOUTHERN AFRICA	8,790	9,267	9,786	9,584	9,830	0.13	2.57
Botswana	96	125	145	423	177	0.00	-58.16
Lesotho	44	56	47	76	111	0.00	46.05
Namibia	755	599	411	312	253	0.00	-18.91
South Africa	6,951	7,508	8,344	7,932	8,599	0.11	8.41
Swaziland	944	979	839	841	690	0.01	-17.95
WEST AFRICA	12,441	12,813	13,046	14,051	14,772	0.19	5.13
Benin	394	326	500	480	659	0.01	37.29
Burkina Faso	508	479	746	697	710	0.01	1.87
Cabo Verde	72	152	214	157	141	0.00	-10.19
Côte d'Ivoire	1,134	1,205	1,224	1,497	1,307	0.02	-12.69
Gambia	236	265	255	170	230	0.00	35.29
Ghana	502	708	737	709	635	0.01	-10.44
Guinea	740	700	785	1,222	1,366	0.02	11.78
Guinea-Bissau	41	87	98	76	98	0.00	28.95
Liberia	233	269	228	162	238	0.00	46.91
Mali	803	939	773	1,055	980	0.01	-7.11
Mauritania	428	598	391	418	491	0.01	17.46
Niger	2,327	1,506	1,605	1,795	1,911	0.02	6.46
Nigeria	1,928	1,949	2,152	2,258	2,432	0.03	7.71
Senegal	1,374	1,711	1,480	1,701	1,597	0.02	-6.11
Sierra Leone	1,448	1,674	1,553	1,352	1,598	0.02	18.20
Togo	273	245	305	302	379	0.00	25.50

Yearbook of Tourism Statistics, Data 2009 – 2013, 2015 Edition

BELGIUM

4. Arrivals of non-resident tourists in all types of accommodation establishments, by country of residence

	2009	2010	2011	2012	2013	Market share 2013	% Change 2013-2012
AMERICAS	374,791	429,439	488,577	505,109	517,322	6.73	2.42
CARIBBEAN	2,840	2,898	2,833	2,598	2,312	0.03	-11.01
Antigua and Barbuda	310	368	335	188	152	0.00	-19.15
Bahamas	124	429	204	104	110	0.00	5.77
Barbados	638	274	228	140	222	0.00	58.57
Cuba	255	306	282	426	319	0.00	-25.12
Dominica	165	122	180	109	89	0.00	-18.35
Dominican Republic	340	462	470	615	519	0.01	-15.61
Grenada	209	109	109	60	77	0.00	28.33
Haiti	136	186	179	283	226	0.00	-20.14
Jamaica	327	399	582	422	352	0.00	-16.59
Saint Kitts and Nevis	35	20	33	80	45	0.00	-43.75
Saint Lucia	17	34	26	21	24	0.00	14.29
Saint Vincent and the Grenadines	70	20	84	23	10	0.00	-56.52
Trinidad and Tobago	214	169	121	127	167	0.00	31.50
CENTRAL AMERICA	3,479	4,329	5,008	4,683	4,792	0.06	2.33
Belize	210	262	310	573	593	0.01	3.49
Costa Rica	1,344	1,664	1,567	1,562	1,679	0.02	7.49
El Salvador	489	632	911	803	484	0.01	-39.73
Guatemala	425	536	600	493	584	0.01	18.46
Honduras	273	250	501	342	346	0.00	1.17
Nicaragua	327	389	417	296	425	0.01	43.58
Panama	411	596	702	614	681	0.01	10.91
NORTH AMERICA	320,035	359,199	401,180	408,017	412,627	5.37	1.13
Canada	41,905	48,517	55,159	56,833	56,237	0.73	-1.05
Mexico	13,965	17,679	20,781	23,197	26,480	0.34	14.15
United States of America	264,165	293,003	325,240	327,987	329,910	4.29	0.59
SOUTH AMERICA	48,437	63,013	79,556	89,811	97,591	1.27	8.66
Argentina	9,334	12,106	15,259	18,882	21,027	0.27	11.36
Bolivia	556	424	565	429	509	0.01	18.65
Brazil	24,770	35,052	45,160	49,726	52,033	0.68	4.64
Chile	3,038	3,467	4,669	5,514	6,050	0.08	9.72
Colombia	3,932	4,855	5,181	5,608	6,611	0.09	17.89
Ecuador	1,255	1,160	1,394	1,459	1,713	0.02	17.41
Guyana	84	77	81	70	73	0.00	4.29
Paraguay	164	214	362	372	405	0.01	8.87
Peru	1,415	1,714	1,780	2,035	2,295	0.03	12.78
Suriname	226	310	510	513	647	0.01	26.12
Uruguay	1,334	1,601	2,091	1,724	1,816	0.02	5.34
Venezuela	2,329	2,033	2,504	3,479	4,412	0.06	26.82
EAST ASIA AND THE PACIFIC	237,535	255,712	307,495	366,859	397,651	5.17	8.39
NORTH-EAST ASIA	173,728	183,800	225,765	272,394	298,777	3.89	9.69
China	75,219	79,908	101,448	122,054	149,399	1.94	22.40
Japan	80,093	81,026	91,414	111,962	112,278	1.46	0.28
Korea, Dem. People's Republic of	3,441	4,009	5,363	4,006	4,204	0.05	4.94
Korea, Republic of	7,853	12,788	14,658	16,572	16,813	0.22	1.45
Mongolia	183	147	325	349	297	0.00	-14.90
Taiwan, Province of China	6,939	5,922	12,557	17,451	15,786	0.21	-9.54
SOUTH-EAST ASIA	20,633	24,436	29,397	40,371	43,338	0.56	7.35
Brunei Darussalam	102	227	198	238	146	0.00	-38.66
Cambodia	136	132	136	197	133	0.00	-32.49
Indonesia	2,483	2,928	3,493	5,360	6,059	0.08	13.04
Lao People's Democratic Republic	159	251	256	268	143	0.00	-46.64
Malaysia	2,982	3,712	4,732	5,597	7,921	0.10	41.52
Myanmar	105	130	127	105	228	0.00	117.14
Philippines	4,731	4,643	5,481	5,156	5,219	0.07	1.22
Singapore	3,924	4,824	5,488	6,801	7,533	0.10	10.76
Thailand	4,370	5,478	7,254	13,922	12,963	0.17	-6.89
Timor-Leste	6	27	25	18	13	0.00	-27.78

68

BELGIUM

4. Arrivals of non-resident tourists in all types of accommodation establishments, by country of residence

	2009	2010	2011	2012	2013	Market share 2013	% Change 2013-2012
Viet Nam	1,635	2,084	2,207	2,709	2,980	0.04	10.00
AUSTRALASIA	**42,352**	**46,502**	**51,217**	**53,164**	**54,624**	**0.71**	**2.75**
Australia	36,684	40,480	45,026	46,223	47,714	0.62	3.23
New Zealand	5,668	6,022	6,191	6,941	6,910	0.09	-0.45
MELANESIA	**321**	**381**	**456**	**408**	**392**	**0.01**	**-3.92**
Fiji	105	154	178	122	99	0.00	-18.85
Papua New Guinea	84	74	76	75	57	0.00	-24.00
Solomon Islands	94	130	122	123	96	0.00	-21.95
Vanuatu	38	23	80	88	140	0.00	59.09
MICRONESIA	**280**	**487**	**374**	**374**	**360**	**0.00**	**-3.74**
Kiribati	27	48	49	27	54	0.00	100.00
Marshall Islands	2	12	4	12	13	0.00	8.33
Micronesia, Federated States of	54	161	79	151	76	0.00	-49.67
Nauru	132	225	208	145	169	0.00	16.55
Palau	65	41	34	39	48	0.00	23.08
POLYNESIA	**221**	**106**	**286**	**148**	**160**	**0.00**	**8.11**
Samoa	28	13	171	94	67	0.00	-28.72
Tonga	87	81	77	34	65	0.00	91.18
Tuvalu	106	12	38	20	28	0.00	40.00
EUROPE	**5,956,385**	**6,310,386**	**6,522,652**	**6,507,995**	**6,560,457**	**85.38**	**0.81**
CENTRAL/EASTERN EUROPE	**285,636**	**323,683**	**363,437**	**386,425**	**395,416**	**5.15**	**2.33**
Armenia	1,138	1,172	1,299	1,023	1,229	0.02	20.14
Azerbaijan	547	694	1,068	1,203	1,351	0.02	12.30
Belarus	2,584	2,505	2,774	3,277	4,185	0.05	27.71
Bulgaria	14,623	15,874	16,221	16,804	16,727	0.22	-0.46
Czech Republic	29,339	31,311	31,368	33,430	32,570	0.42	-2.57
Estonia	5,461	6,566	7,041	7,755	7,994	0.10	3.08
Georgia	3,158	2,803	2,261	2,350	2,382	0.03	1.36
Hungary	24,985	26,633	30,643	32,465	31,959	0.42	-1.56
Kazakhstan	866	961	1,197	1,441	1,362	0.02	-5.48
Kyrgyzstan	143	147	218	176	203	0.00	15.34
Latvia	5,854	8,762	10,104	10,533	9,895	0.13	-6.06
Lithuania	11,946	14,834	15,429	15,567	17,754	0.23	14.05
Poland	78,976	84,115	87,733	88,632	89,268	1.16	0.72
Republic of Moldova	539	601	684	789	825	0.01	4.56
Romania	32,291	37,186	41,399	40,448	42,990	0.56	6.28
Russian Federation	52,031	68,609	89,942	103,606	105,462	1.37	1.79
Slovakia	10,957	11,197	12,500	13,246	13,041	0.17	-1.55
Tajikistan	106	82	174	185	235	0.00	27.03
Turkmenistan	115	108	118	89	122	0.00	37.08
Ukraine	9,605	9,234	10,879	13,167	15,614	0.20	18.58
Uzbekistan	372	289	385	239	248	0.00	3.77
NORTHERN EUROPE	**1,089,227**	**1,117,879**	**1,135,286**	**1,197,512**	**1,235,801**	**16.08**	**3.20**
Denmark	57,206	58,283	62,073	63,059	62,513	0.81	-0.87
Finland	31,312	34,238	36,665	38,320	35,480	0.46	-7.41
Iceland	3,897	6,489	6,021	5,884	5,287	0.07	-10.15
Ireland	41,648	41,581	44,072	48,824	53,043	0.69	8.64
Norway	30,745	35,122	38,463	39,624	40,686	0.53	2.68
Sweden	65,776	72,647	72,161	73,988	70,345	0.92	-4.92
United Kingdom	858,643	869,519	875,831	927,813	968,447	12.60	4.38
SOUTHERN EUROPE	**633,603**	**702,088**	**756,201**	**724,604**	**739,887**	**9.63**	**2.11**
Albania	3,696	3,245	4,624	4,911	6,955	0.09	41.62
Andorra	546	523	637	634	1,711	0.02	169.87
Bosnia and Herzegovina	2,009	1,729	2,048	1,597	1,881	0.02	17.78
Croatia	5,729	6,830	6,787	8,469	9,878	0.13	16.64
Greece	29,848	29,176	31,851	27,188	28,375	0.37	4.37
Holy See	81	91	46	118	106	0.00	-10.17
Italy	236,806	258,163	278,908	274,874	280,252	3.65	1.96
Malta	5,120	5,642	6,246	6,120	5,953	0.08	-2.73

69

BELGIUM

4. Arrivals of non-resident tourists in all types of accommodation establishments, by country of residence

	2009	2010	2011	2012	2013	Market share 2013	% Change 2013-2012
Montenegro	484	611	1,047	1,428	1,636	0.02	14.57
Portugal	38,170	39,429	39,065	41,068	44,218	0.58	7.67
San Marino	185	68	129	709	1,112	0.01	56.84
Serbia	6,034	4,071	6,269	5,481	6,518	0.08	18.92
Slovenia	7,922	9,177	9,719	9,174	9,559	0.12	4.20
Spain	295,764	342,025	367,236	341,267	340,154	4.43	-0.33
TFYR of Macedonia	1,209	1,308	1,589	1,566	1,579	0.02	0.83
WESTERN EUROPE	**3,895,618**	**4,107,209**	**4,197,026**	**4,116,880**	**4,100,151**	**53.36**	**-0.41**
Austria	36,272	37,623	40,897	44,253	42,891	0.56	-3.08
France	1,096,341	1,153,949	1,211,281	1,211,080	1,258,878	16.38	3.95
Germany	770,258	814,684	838,287	814,775	838,320	10.91	2.89
Liechtenstein	2,321	2,025	1,270	847	638	0.01	-24.68
Luxembourg	80,116	83,906	93,689	94,551	96,268	1.25	1.82
Monaco	948	954	1,068	1,375	1,479	0.02	7.56
Netherlands	1,838,549	1,933,579	1,920,003	1,852,656	1,760,620	22.91	-4.97
Switzerland	70,813	80,489	90,531	97,343	101,057	1.32	3.82
EAST MEDITERRANEAN EUROPE	**52,301**	**59,527**	**70,702**	**82,574**	**89,202**	**1.16**	**8.03**
Cyprus	4,848	5,358	6,797	8,712	5,870	0.08	-32.62
Israel	23,389	26,507	29,410	35,940	38,413	0.50	6.88
Turkey	24,064	27,662	34,495	37,922	44,919	0.58	18.45
MIDDLE EAST	**19,976**	**25,599**	**30,602**	**36,399**	**40,305**	**0.52**	**10.73**
Bahrain	389	422	565	548	715	0.01	30.47
Egypt	4,296	5,611	5,553	6,342	6,224	0.08	-1.86
Iraq	561	669	753	565	820	0.01	45.13
Jordan	1,695	1,518	1,388	1,200	1,233	0.02	2.75
Kuwait	1,211	1,232	1,850	2,304	3,621	0.05	57.16
Lebanon	2,116	2,148	2,962	3,538	3,830	0.05	8.25
Libya	628	818	432	1,187	1,512	0.02	27.38
Oman	328	449	569	728	745	0.01	2.34
Palestine	68	108	116	149	151	0.00	1.34
Qatar	539	780	1,052	1,795	2,161	0.03	20.39
Saudi Arabia	2,857	4,047	4,111	5,618	6,886	0.09	22.57
Syrian Arab Republic	841	780	659	531	498	0.01	-6.21
United Arab Emirates	4,240	6,910	10,350	11,729	11,737	0.15	0.07
Yemen	207	107	242	165	172	0.00	4.24
SOUTH ASIA	**46,950**	**51,726**	**54,726**	**52,508**	**55,515**	**0.72**	**5.73**
Afghanistan	2,184	1,337	1,417	1,437	940	0.01	-34.59
Bangladesh	412	614	570	573	489	0.01	-14.66
Bhutan	80	23	79	167	51	0.00	-69.46
India	35,730	41,554	44,195	42,825	46,783	0.61	9.24
Iran, Islamic Republic of	6,560	5,780	5,941	5,204	4,716	0.06	-9.38
Maldives	51	28	71	52	87	0.00	67.31
Nepal	206	238	285	282	397	0.01	40.78
Pakistan	1,473	1,844	1,803	1,584	1,585	0.02	0.06
Sri Lanka	254	308	365	384	467	0.01	21.61
NOT SPECIFIED	**116,060**	**52,225**	**28,140**	**30,517**	**48,779**	**0.63**	**59.84**
Other countries of the World	116,060	52,225	28,140	30,517	48,779	0.63	59.84

Yearbook of Tourism Statistics, Data 2009 – 2013, 2015 Edition

BELGIUM

5. Overnight stays of non-resident tourists in hotels and similar establishments, by country of residence

	2009	2010	2011	2012	2013	Market share 2013	% Change 2013-2012
TOTAL	10,336,598	10,854,245	11,436,408	11,546,367	11,624,465	100.00	0.68
AFRICA	134,559	140,428	137,706	138,665	146,899	1.26	5.94
EAST AFRICA	21,708	20,959	20,423	18,262	19,111	0.16	4.65
Burundi	1,598	1,348	1,773	1,919	2,166	0.02	12.87
Comoros	35	99	55	70	97	0.00	38.57
Djibouti	460	274	199	304	284	0.00	-6.58
Eritrea	73	172	206	172	162	0.00	-5.81
Ethiopia	6,413	6,651	5,349	2,357	3,246	0.03	37.72
Kenya	2,665	2,528	2,337	3,145	3,329	0.03	5.85
Madagascar	824	685	672	745	740	0.01	-0.67
Malawi	201	218	205	308	314	0.00	1.95
Mauritius	648	593	1,885	2,027	1,771	0.02	-12.63
Mozambique	544	524	480	470	399	0.00	-15.11
Rwanda	1,768	2,331	2,127	2,472	2,169	0.02	-12.26
Seychelles	730	403	891	522	313	0.00	-40.04
Somalia	482	425	297	153	299	0.00	95.42
Uganda	1,595	1,270	898	893	1,146	0.01	28.33
United Republic of Tanzania	2,317	1,628	1,303	910	1,183	0.01	30.00
Zambia	346	479	446	595	566	0.00	-4.87
Zimbabwe	1,009	1,331	1,300	1,200	927	0.01	-22.75
CENTRAL AFRICA	23,486	25,971	26,088	26,104	27,272	0.23	4.47
Angola	2,391	2,911	3,038	3,358	3,659	0.03	8.96
Cameroon	4,679	5,228	4,841	4,312	4,692	0.04	8.81
Central African Republic	680	1,040	785	976	1,228	0.01	25.82
Chad	625	412	340	224	666	0.01	197.32
Congo	6,378	6,772	6,171	7,040	6,635	0.06	-5.75
Democratic Republic of the Congo	6,500	7,616	8,562	8,150	8,632	0.07	5.91
Equatorial Guinea	92	264	156	209	161	0.00	-22.97
Gabon	2,030	1,626	2,099	1,706	1,539	0.01	-9.79
Sao Tome and Principe	111	102	96	129	60	0.00	-53.49
NORTH AFRICA	43,688	39,269	39,280	40,343	43,863	0.38	8.73
Algeria	9,904	8,473	7,711	7,194	11,277	0.10	56.76
Morocco	25,863	22,978	23,036	25,096	23,245	0.20	-7.38
Sudan	788	1,065	909	740	785	0.01	6.08
Tunisia	7,133	6,753	7,624	7,313	8,556	0.07	17.00
SOUTHERN AFRICA	18,431	20,259	21,955	23,707	22,786	0.20	-3.88
Botswana	232	412	352	708	560	0.00	-20.90
Lesotho	116	126	104	219	270	0.00	23.29
Namibia	1,212	1,472	698	1,121	582	0.01	-48.08
South Africa	15,010	16,397	19,226	19,934	20,075	0.17	0.71
Swaziland	1,861	1,852	1,575	1,725	1,299	0.01	-24.70
WEST AFRICA	27,246	33,970	29,960	30,249	33,867	0.29	11.96
Benin	1,180	1,095	1,324	1,436	1,654	0.01	15.18
Burkina Faso	1,301	1,743	2,270	2,033	1,971	0.02	-3.05
Cabo Verde	189	376	468	252	319	0.00	26.59
Côte d'Ivoire	2,579	2,847	2,786	3,252	2,680	0.02	-17.59
Gambia	703	1,125	653	335	526	0.00	57.01
Ghana	1,231	2,237	1,958	1,708	1,591	0.01	-6.85
Guinea	2,619	2,675	1,682	2,270	2,917	0.03	28.50
Guinea-Bissau	67	283	236	328	205	0.00	-37.50
Liberia	427	573	514	302	699	0.01	131.46
Mali	1,437	1,756	1,695	1,768	2,235	0.02	26.41
Mauritania	1,044	1,486	934	1,038	1,132	0.01	9.06
Niger	3,870	2,316	2,416	3,754	3,627	0.03	-3.38
Nigeria	3,909	5,456	5,414	4,835	6,443	0.06	33.26
Senegal	3,347	4,753	3,430	3,729	4,167	0.04	11.75
Sierra Leone	2,676	3,552	3,464	2,457	2,847	0.02	15.87
Togo	667	1,697	716	752	854	0.01	13.56

71

Yearbook of Tourism Statistics, Data 2009 – 2013, 2015 Edition

BELGIUM

5. Overnight stays of non-resident tourists in hotels and similar establishments, by country of residence

	2009	2010	2011	2012	2013	Market share 2013	% Change 2013-2012
AMERICAS	727,655	840,134	955,148	975,924	992,840	8.54	1.73
CARIBBEAN	5,388	5,857	5,649	5,395	4,628	0.04	-14.22
Antigua and Barbuda	469	634	505	454	228	0.00	-49.78
Bahamas	188	552	265	175	284	0.00	62.29
Barbados	938	589	442	304	324	0.00	6.58
Cuba	613	556	722	869	660	0.01	-24.05
Dominica	378	291	342	164	216	0.00	31.71
Dominican Republic	771	1,127	957	1,150	888	0.01	-22.78
Grenada	281	356	219	108	96	0.00	-11.11
Haiti	334	537	423	655	600	0.01	-8.40
Jamaica	658	648	1,075	929	736	0.01	-20.78
Saint Kitts and Nevis	66	53	143	197	111	0.00	-43.65
Saint Lucia	83	174	109	41	72	0.00	75.61
Saint Vincent and the Grenadines	145	37	146	39	17	0.00	-56.41
Trinidad and Tobago	464	303	301	310	396	0.00	27.74
CENTRAL AMERICA	7,511	8,800	9,244	8,913	9,242	0.08	3.69
Belize	291	449	507	1,018	1,085	0.01	6.58
Costa Rica	2,934	3,260	2,766	2,662	3,213	0.03	20.70
El Salvador	1,098	1,214	1,607	1,533	977	0.01	-36.27
Guatemala	870	1,118	1,037	1,028	1,098	0.01	6.81
Honduras	703	675	1,048	649	609	0.01	-6.16
Nicaragua	759	962	747	655	778	0.01	18.78
Panama	856	1,122	1,532	1,368	1,482	0.01	8.33
NORTH AMERICA	638,070	724,173	805,749	813,080	812,904	6.99	-0.02
Canada	79,201	95,307	110,521	113,600	110,987	0.95	-2.30
Mexico	18,833	25,267	29,144	32,357	37,554	0.32	16.06
United States of America	540,036	603,599	666,084	667,123	664,363	5.72	-0.41
SOUTH AMERICA	76,686	101,304	134,506	148,536	166,066	1.43	11.80
Argentina	12,771	17,415	23,443	28,357	32,517	0.28	14.67
Bolivia	1,258	920	1,080	682	981	0.01	43.84
Brazil	39,403	57,118	79,664	85,677	90,943	0.78	6.15
Chile	4,893	5,580	7,493	9,455	10,032	0.09	6.10
Colombia	5,832	7,647	6,768	7,565	11,272	0.10	49.00
Ecuador	2,395	1,851	2,148	2,482	3,202	0.03	29.01
Guyana	189	184	273	173	250	0.00	44.51
Paraguay	401	487	793	618	691	0.01	11.81
Peru	2,437	2,759	3,149	3,593	3,687	0.03	2.62
Suriname	774	706	1,409	1,042	1,108	0.01	6.33
Uruguay	2,401	3,037	3,382	2,553	2,660	0.02	4.19
Venezuela	3,932	3,600	4,904	6,339	8,723	0.08	37.61
EAST ASIA AND THE PACIFIC	382,073	416,187	499,647	589,596	630,113	5.42	6.87
NORTH-EAST ASIA	282,435	296,213	357,350	426,681	452,808	3.90	6.12
China	112,941	115,428	141,839	167,240	198,589	1.71	18.74
Japan	144,168	150,866	172,833	210,001	207,426	1.78	-1.23
Korea, Dem. People's Republic of	3,023	3,801	5,192	4,212	3,887	0.03	-7.72
Korea, Republic of	12,768	17,813	21,782	22,817	23,054	0.20	1.04
Mongolia	285	283	573	511	557	0.00	9.00
Taiwan, Province of China	9,250	8,022	15,131	21,900	19,295	0.17	-11.89
SOUTH-EAST ASIA	36,588	46,355	55,553	71,082	76,711	0.66	7.92
Brunei Darussalam	180	381	515	524	231	0.00	-55.92
Cambodia	329	367	379	422	397	0.00	-5.92
Indonesia	4,736	6,554	6,546	8,731	10,346	0.09	18.50
Lao People's Democratic Republic	295	459	504	430	309	0.00	-28.14
Malaysia	5,380	6,436	8,500	10,211	12,835	0.11	25.70
Myanmar	144	261	194	239	393	0.00	64.44
Philippines	6,965	7,359	9,716	8,195	8,942	0.08	9.12
Singapore	8,451	10,797	12,165	13,846	15,618	0.13	12.80
Thailand	7,475	9,538	12,699	23,746	22,557	0.19	-5.01
Timor-Leste	11	89	20	62	46	0.00	-25.81

BELGIUM

5. Overnight stays of non-resident tourists in hotels and similar establishments, by country of residence

	2009	2010	2011	2012	2013	Market share 2013	% Change 2013-2012
Viet Nam	2,622	4,114	4,315	4,676	5,037	0.04	7.72
AUSTRALASIA	**61,278**	**71,725**	**84,466**	**89,858**	**98,190**	**0.84**	**9.27**
Australia	53,178	62,640	73,046	78,260	85,334	0.73	9.04
New Zealand	8,100	9,085	11,420	11,598	12,856	0.11	10.85
MELANESIA	**826**	**849**	**1,135**	**1,058**	**1,266**	**0.01**	**19.66**
Fiji	253	294	414	397	509	0.00	28.21
Papua New Guinea	332	227	213	209	231	0.00	10.53
Solomon Islands	167	265	316	274	231	0.00	-15.69
Vanuatu	74	63	192	178	295	0.00	65.73
MICRONESIA	**459**	**852**	**670**	**641**	**727**	**0.01**	**13.42**
Kiribati	42	122	101	69	132	0.00	91.30
Marshall Islands	4	7	8	20	58	0.00	190.00
Micronesia, Federated States of	68	334	120	223	115	0.00	-48.43
Nauru	221	307	371	190	259	0.00	36.32
Palau	124	82	70	139	163	0.00	17.27
POLYNESIA	**487**	**193**	**473**	**276**	**411**	**0.00**	**48.91**
Samoa	54	19	255	127	132	0.00	3.94
Tonga	240	156	168	105	226	0.00	115.24
Tuvalu	193	18	50	44	53	0.00	20.45
EUROPE	**8,728,486**	**9,182,019**	**9,593,960**	**9,572,664**	**9,546,164**	**82.12**	**-0.28**
CENTRAL/EASTERN EUROPE	**558,868**	**631,326**	**737,367**	**755,776**	**768,669**	**6.61**	**1.71**
Armenia	2,545	4,768	2,786	2,339	2,940	0.03	25.69
Azerbaijan	1,713	1,847	2,761	3,115	3,100	0.03	-0.48
Belarus	4,238	3,853	4,918	5,246	7,445	0.06	41.92
Bulgaria	29,080	32,118	35,099	33,062	32,542	0.28	-1.57
Czech Republic	52,577	58,653	61,253	61,455	57,103	0.49	-7.08
Estonia	9,919	11,334	12,026	13,196	12,520	0.11	-5.12
Georgia	6,446	5,775	4,670	5,004	5,474	0.05	9.39
Hungary	53,123	50,629	58,694	69,434	64,780	0.56	-6.70
Kazakhstan	2,401	2,476	3,233	3,724	3,266	0.03	-12.30
Kyrgyzstan	258	326	399	381	410	0.00	7.61
Latvia	9,534	14,080	15,971	16,364	15,857	0.14	-3.10
Lithuania	21,231	25,782	27,571	28,104	32,456	0.28	15.49
Poland	149,135	162,008	183,088	173,310	180,045	1.55	3.89
Republic of Moldova	1,461	1,640	1,823	2,207	2,277	0.02	3.17
Romania	71,879	81,096	100,182	85,598	85,419	0.73	-0.21
Russian Federation	102,914	133,000	172,752	198,386	207,468	1.78	4.58
Slovakia	21,453	22,510	26,688	27,667	25,159	0.22	-9.06
Tajikistan	312	196	371	441	790	0.01	79.14
Turkmenistan	263	266	187	193	378	0.00	95.85
Ukraine	17,425	18,140	21,994	25,912	28,682	0.25	10.69
Uzbekistan	961	829	901	638	558	0.00	-12.54
NORTHERN EUROPE	**1,962,570**	**1,992,823**	**2,003,730**	**2,053,502**	**2,122,913**	**18.26**	**3.38**
Denmark	92,088	95,219	101,083	102,534	101,334	0.87	-1.17
Finland	54,459	61,678	68,671	67,909	62,641	0.54	-7.76
Iceland	8,496	13,885	13,609	13,055	11,626	0.10	-10.95
Ireland	77,600	72,457	77,673	88,437	96,459	0.83	9.07
Norway	57,588	65,957	74,393	75,377	78,475	0.68	4.11
Sweden	113,129	127,844	127,462	130,559	121,308	1.04	-7.09
United Kingdom	1,559,210	1,555,783	1,540,839	1,575,631	1,651,070	14.20	4.79
SOUTHERN EUROPE	**1,194,579**	**1,309,535**	**1,423,395**	**1,414,174**	**1,403,011**	**12.07**	**-0.79**
Albania	13,770	7,244	8,139	8,449	11,888	0.10	40.70
Andorra	2,292	925	1,084	1,000	2,948	0.03	194.80
Bosnia and Herzegovina	3,698	3,773	4,147	3,056	3,602	0.03	17.87
Croatia	13,019	13,540	13,416	15,311	18,895	0.16	23.41
Greece	65,140	62,938	66,501	55,717	57,636	0.50	3.44
Holy See	155	166	104	280	163	0.00	-41.79
Italy	447,082	486,592	522,022	519,079	518,263	4.46	-0.16
Malta	10,954	11,669	12,982	13,214	12,418	0.11	-6.02

73

BELGIUM

5. Overnight stays of non-resident tourists in hotels and similar establishments, by country of residence

	2009	2010	2011	2012	2013	Market share 2013	% Change 2013-2012
Montenegro	1,404	1,361	2,368	3,667	3,971	0.03	8.29
Portugal	76,679	79,399	77,053	122,789	96,297	0.83	-21.58
San Marino	508	141	219	1,578	2,097	0.02	32.89
Serbia	13,660	10,403	14,438	13,090	14,164	0.12	8.20
Slovenia	15,314	16,236	16,951	16,673	17,981	0.15	7.85
Spain	528,284	612,194	680,499	636,882	638,733	5.49	0.29
TFYR of Macedonia	2,620	2,954	3,472	3,389	3,955	0.03	16.70
WESTERN EUROPE	**4,902,867**	**5,126,293**	**5,285,997**	**5,186,593**	**5,080,496**	**43.71**	**-2.05**
Austria	68,778	72,122	80,125	87,330	81,049	0.70	-7.19
France	1,511,377	1,566,510	1,652,525	1,622,311	1,639,514	14.10	1.06
Germany	1,219,512	1,285,781	1,316,049	1,262,318	1,282,371	11.03	1.59
Liechtenstein	4,979	3,884	2,407	1,531	1,109	0.01	-27.56
Luxembourg	132,001	139,409	149,036	145,733	147,255	1.27	1.04
Monaco	1,810	1,895	1,951	2,509	2,819	0.02	12.36
Netherlands	1,838,111	1,919,062	1,924,846	1,894,585	1,749,216	15.05	-7.67
Switzerland	126,299	137,630	159,058	170,276	177,163	1.52	4.04
EAST MEDITERRANEAN EUROPE	**109,602**	**122,042**	**143,471**	**162,619**	**171,075**	**1.47**	**5.20**
Cyprus	11,633	12,397	15,458	19,918	13,707	0.12	-31.18
Israel	46,341	51,490	58,242	66,123	70,829	0.61	7.12
Turkey	51,628	58,155	69,771	76,578	86,539	0.74	13.01
MIDDLE EAST	**58,297**	**74,513**	**84,545**	**109,221**	**120,621**	**1.04**	**10.44**
Bahrain	1,081	1,202	1,684	1,470	2,013	0.02	36.94
Egypt	10,919	13,274	12,505	13,967	14,124	0.12	1.12
Iraq	1,771	2,077	1,713	1,427	2,380	0.02	66.78
Jordan	4,084	3,752	3,535	3,205	3,311	0.03	3.31
Kuwait	3,878	3,999	6,080	7,479	12,339	0.11	64.98
Lebanon	5,516	5,571	6,932	8,434	8,805	0.08	4.40
Libya	1,474	1,799	1,144	5,776	4,563	0.04	-21.00
Oman	1,057	1,587	1,980	2,443	2,539	0.02	3.93
Palestine	101	152	233	273	335	0.00	22.71
Qatar	1,927	2,965	3,294	6,429	8,025	0.07	24.83
Saudi Arabia	8,731	11,118	12,755	17,603	18,325	0.16	4.10
Syrian Arab Republic	2,695	1,973	1,646	1,343	1,027	0.01	-23.53
United Arab Emirates	14,518	24,723	30,508	38,658	42,408	0.36	9.70
Yemen	545	321	536	714	427	0.00	-40.20
SOUTH ASIA	**94,671**	**104,830**	**116,850**	**108,168**	**109,100**	**0.94**	**0.86**
Afghanistan	4,037	3,237	3,137	3,373	1,963	0.02	-41.80
Bangladesh	870	1,240	1,377	1,253	850	0.01	-32.16
Bhutan	263	44	96	226	73	0.00	-67.70
India	71,101	82,881	94,665	88,663	92,462	0.80	4.28
Iran, Islamic Republic of	14,087	12,287	12,434	10,024	8,525	0.07	-14.95
Maldives	89	80	109	68	215	0.00	216.18
Nepal	401	401	519	604	705	0.01	16.72
Pakistan	3,200	3,970	3,582	3,095	3,129	0.03	1.10
Sri Lanka	623	690	931	862	1,178	0.01	36.66
NOT SPECIFIED	**210,857**	**96,134**	**48,552**	**52,129**	**78,728**	**0.68**	**51.03**
Other countries of the World	210,857	96,134	48,552	52,129	78,728	0.68	51.03

Yearbook of Tourism Statistics, Data 2009 – 2013, 2015 Edition

BELGIUM

6. Overnight stays of non-resident tourists in all types of accommodation establishments, by country of residence

		2009	2010	2011	2012	2013	Market share 2013	% Change 2013-2012
TOTAL	(*)	15,452,987	16,169,676	16,723,867	16,432,600	16,511,689	100.00	0.48
AFRICA		144,605	151,982	150,181	150,402	159,648	0.97	6.15
EAST AFRICA		22,257	22,281	21,175	19,337	20,551	0.12	6.28
Burundi		1,686	1,401	1,798	2,002	2,253	0.01	12.54
Comoros		35	103	59	70	97	0.00	38.57
Djibouti		461	278	258	304	305	0.00	0.33
Eritrea		83	191	212	183	218	0.00	19.13
Ethiopia		6,457	6,696	5,476	2,423	3,345	0.02	38.05
Kenya		2,701	2,564	2,368	3,285	3,393	0.02	3.29
Madagascar		832	730	758	834	901	0.01	8.03
Malawi		201	228	215	321	324	0.00	0.93
Mauritius		673	646	1,909	2,125	1,782	0.01	-16.14
Mozambique		619	524	480	500	408	0.00	-18.40
Rwanda		1,803	2,808	2,165	2,606	2,246	0.01	-13.81
Seychelles		770	437	904	554	329	0.00	-40.61
Somalia		500	458	317	186	311	0.00	67.20
Uganda		1,608	1,338	934	926	1,235	0.01	33.37
United Republic of Tanzania		2,348	1,667	1,409	958	1,239	0.01	29.33
Zambia		358	480	449	604	570	0.00	-5.63
Zimbabwe		1,122	1,732	1,464	1,456	1,595	0.01	9.55
CENTRAL AFRICA		25,049	27,000	27,333	27,605	28,771	0.17	4.22
Angola		2,453	2,989	3,327	3,406	3,886	0.02	14.09
Cameroon		5,217	5,446	5,041	4,497	4,968	0.03	10.47
Central African Republic		694	1,041	788	986	1,230	0.01	24.75
Chad		637	427	349	226	674	0.00	198.23
Congo		6,481	6,864	6,294	7,178	6,739	0.04	-6.12
Democratic Republic of the Congo		7,290	8,203	9,137	9,219	9,315	0.06	1.04
Equatorial Guinea		92	275	161	213	181	0.00	-15.02
Gabon		2,044	1,648	2,138	1,737	1,713	0.01	-1.38
Sao Tome and Principe		141	107	98	143	65	0.00	-54.55
NORTH AFRICA		47,528	41,706	42,375	43,089	47,423	0.29	10.06
Algeria		10,942	8,929	8,519	7,909	12,232	0.07	54.66
Morocco		27,927	24,688	24,737	26,648	25,168	0.15	-5.55
Sudan		824	1,096	923	748	800	0.00	6.95
Tunisia		7,835	6,993	8,196	7,784	9,223	0.06	18.49
SOUTHERN AFRICA		21,181	24,338	26,624	26,014	26,069	0.16	0.21
Botswana		234	412	352	713	612	0.00	-14.17
Lesotho		116	126	104	221	270	0.00	22.17
Namibia		1,290	1,580	710	1,234	644	0.00	-47.81
South Africa		17,636	20,280	23,563	22,115	23,206	0.14	4.93
Swaziland		1,905	1,940	1,895	1,731	1,337	0.01	-22.76
WEST AFRICA		28,590	36,657	32,674	34,357	36,834	0.22	7.21
Benin		1,228	1,120	1,386	1,665	1,755	0.01	5.41
Burkina Faso		1,333	1,772	2,765	2,162	2,314	0.01	7.03
Cabo Verde		190	376	470	257	360	0.00	40.08
Côte d'Ivoire		2,618	2,972	2,872	3,427	2,777	0.02	-18.97
Gambia		705	1,125	662	339	548	0.00	61.65
Ghana		1,266	2,485	2,123	1,872	1,754	0.01	-6.30
Guinea		2,640	2,683	1,712	2,301	2,977	0.02	29.38
Guinea-Bissau		72	286	236	330	234	0.00	-29.09
Liberia		429	593	522	313	699	0.00	123.32
Mali		1,648	2,060	1,927	1,985	2,342	0.01	17.98
Mauritania		1,049	1,487	946	1,053	1,175	0.01	11.59
Niger		4,157	3,488	3,288	5,708	4,207	0.03	-26.30
Nigeria		4,249	5,835	5,760	5,077	6,802	0.04	33.98
Senegal		3,414	4,886	3,636	4,058	4,385	0.03	8.06
Sierra Leone		2,852	3,789	3,598	3,023	3,573	0.02	18.19
Togo		740	1,700	771	787	932	0.01	18.42

Yearbook of Tourism Statistics, Data 2009 – 2013, 2015 Edition

BELGIUM

6. Overnight stays of non-resident tourists in all types of accommodation establishments, by country of residence

	2009	2010	2011	2012	2013	Market share 2013	% Change 2013-2012
AMERICAS	791,281	907,808	1,031,301	1,062,818	1,093,890	6.62	2.92
CARIBBEAN	5,786	6,318	6,152	5,706	5,293	0.03	-7.24
Antigua and Barbuda	597	712	633	471	276	0.00	-41.40
Bahamas	207	689	414	179	302	0.00	68.72
Barbados	1,029	626	478	326	446	0.00	36.81
Cuba	659	566	734	921	808	0.00	-12.27
Dominica	392	302	351	184	268	0.00	45.65
Dominican Republic	823	1,178	1,042	1,236	1,011	0.01	-18.20
Grenada	283	359	219	122	114	0.00	-6.56
Haiti	344	560	460	700	649	0.00	-7.29
Jamaica	694	728	1,111	945	820	0.00	-13.23
Saint Kitts and Nevis	66	53	143	210	111	0.00	-47.14
Saint Lucia	83	178	111	41	72	0.00	75.61
Saint Vincent and the Grenadines	145	37	146	39	17	0.00	-56.41
Trinidad and Tobago	464	330	310	332	399	0.00	20.18
CENTRAL AMERICA	8,271	9,581	10,095	9,693	10,102	0.06	4.22
Belize	380	466	531	1,118	1,130	0.01	1.07
Costa Rica	3,243	3,588	3,138	2,972	3,581	0.02	20.49
El Salvador	1,115	1,368	1,727	1,624	1,045	0.01	-35.65
Guatemala	996	1,244	1,195	1,140	1,218	0.01	6.84
Honduras	777	710	1,102	714	697	0.00	-2.38
Nicaragua	868	990	809	700	885	0.01	26.43
Panama	892	1,215	1,593	1,425	1,546	0.01	8.49
NORTH AMERICA	685,622	771,286	858,657	874,491	883,531	5.35	1.03
Canada	92,726	108,803	125,031	129,336	128,463	0.78	-0.67
Mexico	23,473	30,545	35,751	39,031	45,028	0.27	15.36
United States of America	569,423	631,938	697,875	706,124	710,040	4.30	0.55
SOUTH AMERICA	91,602	120,623	156,397	172,928	194,964	1.18	12.74
Argentina	16,303	22,270	28,268	33,766	38,471	0.23	13.93
Bolivia	1,359	1,042	1,250	843	1,105	0.01	31.08
Brazil	46,531	66,453	90,458	97,939	105,873	0.64	8.10
Chile	5,812	6,797	9,468	11,141	12,197	0.07	9.48
Colombia	7,075	9,213	8,692	9,843	13,723	0.08	39.42
Ecuador	2,741	2,371	2,581	2,937	3,636	0.02	23.80
Guyana	269	196	278	176	261	0.00	48.30
Paraguay	457	541	855	757	816	0.00	7.79
Peru	2,884	3,379	3,649	4,195	4,647	0.03	10.77
Suriname	812	754	1,575	1,196	1,263	0.01	5.60
Uruguay	2,732	3,480	4,020	3,280	3,438	0.02	4.82
Venezuela	4,627	4,127	5,303	6,855	9,534	0.06	39.08
EAST ASIA AND THE PACIFIC	425,803	462,634	552,824	647,145	692,918	4.20	7.07
NORTH-EAST ASIA	302,506	318,948	383,230	454,799	485,942	2.94	6.85
China	118,001	122,462	150,047	177,158	211,047	1.28	19.13
Japan	152,694	158,383	180,330	218,278	216,835	1.31	-0.66
Korea, Dem. People's Republic of	5,737	7,057	9,671	7,146	7,003	0.04	-2.00
Korea, Republic of	15,135	21,393	25,411	27,603	28,753	0.17	4.17
Mongolia	288	295	780	531	601	0.00	13.18
Taiwan, Province of China	10,651	9,358	16,991	24,083	21,703	0.13	-9.88
SOUTH-EAST ASIA	41,388	49,866	59,317	76,042	83,446	0.51	9.74
Brunei Darussalam	208	455	537	575	275	0.00	-52.17
Cambodia	338	383	396	460	419	0.00	-8.91
Indonesia	4,974	6,979	6,863	9,134	10,754	0.07	17.74
Lao People's Democratic Republic	308	463	508	453	312	0.00	-31.13
Malaysia	6,028	7,215	9,096	10,961	13,731	0.08	25.27
Myanmar	146	274	202	240	419	0.00	74.58
Philippines	7,112	7,601	10,162	8,812	9,414	0.06	6.83
Singapore	9,098	11,518	13,092	15,161	16,919	0.10	11.60
Thailand	10,199	10,456	13,760	24,968	25,708	0.16	2.96
Timor-Leste	12	90	34	62	46	0.00	-25.81

BELGIUM

6. Overnight stays of non-resident tourists in all types of accommodation establishments, by country of residence

	2009	2010	2011	2012	2013	Market share 2013	% Change 2013-2012
Viet Nam	2,965	4,432	4,667	5,216	5,449	0.03	4.47
AUSTRALASIA	**80,027**	**91,847**	**107,831**	**114,122**	**121,018**	**0.73**	**6.04**
Australia	69,087	80,066	93,539	98,798	104,765	0.63	6.04
New Zealand	10,940	11,781	14,292	15,324	16,253	0.10	6.06
MELANESIA	**844**	**861**	**1,176**	**1,144**	**1,325**	**0.01**	**15.82**
Fiji	267	301	434	411	516	0.00	25.55
Papua New Guinea	334	230	218	209	231	0.00	10.53
Solomon Islands	169	267	330	346	281	0.00	-18.79
Vanuatu	74	63	194	178	297	0.00	66.85
MICRONESIA	**549**	**915**	**706**	**719**	**757**	**0.00**	**5.29**
Kiribati	42	122	106	70	136	0.00	94.29
Marshall Islands	4	14	8	26	58	0.00	123.08
Micronesia, Federated States of	68	334	121	223	115	0.00	-48.43
Nauru	284	363	401	261	285	0.00	9.20
Palau	151	82	70	139	163	0.00	17.27
POLYNESIA	**489**	**197**	**564**	**319**	**430**	**0.00**	**34.80**
Samoa	54	19	327	166	148	0.00	-10.84
Tonga	241	158	174	105	226	0.00	115.24
Tuvalu	194	20	63	48	56	0.00	16.67
EUROPE	**13,703,740**	**14,362,734**	**14,728,013**	**14,289,844**	**14,228,390**	**86.17**	**-0.43**
CENTRAL/EASTERN EUROPE	**639,908**	**746,507**	**868,655**	**913,182**	**884,413**	**5.36**	**-3.15**
Armenia	2,854	5,243	3,004	2,435	3,278	0.02	34.62
Azerbaijan	1,749	1,969	2,825	3,230	3,207	0.02	-0.71
Belarus	4,487	4,130	5,155	5,533	7,803	0.05	41.03
Bulgaria	30,578	33,550	35,785	35,917	35,152	0.21	-2.13
Czech Republic	59,920	65,544	70,373	75,065	68,620	0.42	-8.59
Estonia	10,401	11,953	12,490	14,288	13,518	0.08	-5.39
Georgia	6,658	5,870	4,697	5,177	5,697	0.03	10.04
Hungary	59,506	58,050	67,498	77,652	73,724	0.45	-5.06
Kazakhstan	2,496	2,536	3,368	3,811	3,395	0.02	-10.92
Kyrgyzstan	265	343	409	403	421	0.00	4.47
Latvia	10,122	15,004	17,328	19,105	17,169	0.10	-10.13
Lithuania	23,512	27,420	29,032	30,069	34,670	0.21	15.30
Poland	197,467	238,986	272,693	260,711	240,332	1.46	-7.82
Republic of Moldova	1,502	1,663	1,859	2,299	2,411	0.01	4.87
Romania	76,319	87,254	107,076	103,862	95,761	0.58	-7.80
Russian Federation	107,530	138,376	179,392	206,803	217,880	1.32	5.36
Slovakia	25,032	28,062	31,420	38,303	29,518	0.18	-22.94
Tajikistan	315	205	393	538	838	0.01	55.76
Turkmenistan	273	357	188	197	381	0.00	93.40
Ukraine	17,894	19,158	22,615	27,123	30,056	0.18	10.81
Uzbekistan	1,028	834	1,055	661	582	0.00	-11.95
NORTHERN EUROPE	**2,217,800**	**2,247,665**	**2,286,958**	**2,420,794**	**2,493,893**	**15.10**	**3.02**
Denmark	114,196	116,335	123,655	122,780	124,233	0.75	1.18
Finland	59,134	66,162	73,064	75,233	69,476	0.42	-7.65
Iceland	9,370	14,536	14,488	14,398	12,917	0.08	-10.29
Ireland	87,497	78,751	87,665	109,081	108,866	0.66	-0.20
Norway	61,051	69,907	78,252	82,220	85,609	0.52	4.12
Sweden	121,646	138,103	138,595	142,900	134,266	0.81	-6.04
United Kingdom	1,764,906	1,763,871	1,771,239	1,874,182	1,958,526	11.86	4.50
SOUTHERN EUROPE	**1,315,923**	**1,425,684**	**1,537,009**	**1,535,375**	**1,562,500**	**9.46**	**1.77**
Albania	14,131	7,683	8,889	9,261	12,870	0.08	38.97
Andorra	2,424	979	1,307	1,142	3,025	0.02	164.89
Bosnia and Herzegovina	3,869	4,067	5,195	3,509	4,082	0.02	16.33
Croatia	13,691	23,165	14,384	16,850	20,947	0.13	24.31
Greece	82,302	65,158	69,084	61,145	60,226	0.36	-1.50
Holy See	169	170	105	280	219	0.00	-21.79
Italy	477,343	517,006	555,628	559,955	564,864	3.42	0.88
Malta	11,183	11,774	13,536	13,470	12,787	0.08	-5.07

77

Yearbook of Tourism Statistics, Data 2009 – 2013, 2015 Edition

BELGIUM

6. Overnight stays of non-resident tourists in all types of accommodation establishments, by country of residence

	2009	2010	2011	2012	2013	Market share 2013	% Change 2013-2012
Montenegro	1,417	1,404	2,422	3,722	4,065	0.02	9.22
Portugal	85,378	83,964	84,060	131,121	140,903	0.85	7.46
San Marino	534	141	222	1,590	2,100	0.01	32.08
Serbia	13,816	10,731	14,994	13,655	14,992	0.09	9.79
Slovenia	17,336	20,768	27,785	23,421	21,866	0.13	-6.64
Spain	589,606	675,582	735,857	692,654	695,494	4.21	0.41
TFYR of Macedonia	2,724	3,092	3,541	3,600	4,060	0.02	12.78
WESTERN EUROPE	**9,414,937**	**9,814,878**	**9,884,862**	**9,248,118**	**9,104,256**	**55.14**	**-1.56**
Austria	77,851	80,752	90,910	99,785	92,062	0.56	-7.74
France	2,089,571	2,173,874	2,301,498	2,306,015	2,404,823	14.56	4.28
Germany	1,879,846	1,992,544	2,027,052	1,933,828	1,913,843	11.59	-1.03
Liechtenstein	5,012	3,924	2,536	1,639	1,194	0.01	-27.15
Luxembourg	184,544	189,479	203,259	200,362	197,238	1.19	-1.56
Monaco	1,933	1,910	2,039	2,604	2,887	0.02	10.87
Netherlands	5,035,124	5,220,042	5,081,035	4,509,683	4,285,281	25.95	-4.98
Switzerland	141,056	152,353	176,533	194,202	206,928	1.25	6.55
EAST MEDITERRANEAN EUROPE	**115,172**	**128,000**	**150,529**	**172,375**	**183,328**	**1.11**	**6.35**
Cyprus	11,888	12,580	15,788	20,712	15,279	0.09	-26.23
Israel	49,272	54,224	62,349	70,981	77,115	0.47	8.64
Turkey	54,012	61,196	72,392	80,682	90,934	0.55	12.71
MIDDLE EAST	**59,874**	**77,266**	**85,920**	**113,116**	**124,167**	**0.75**	**9.77**
Bahrain	1,107	1,243	1,771	1,470	2,041	0.01	38.84
Egypt	11,207	13,553	12,730	15,530	14,465	0.09	-6.86
Iraq	1,987	2,451	1,972	1,753	2,887	0.02	64.69
Jordan	4,176	4,283	3,617	3,341	3,440	0.02	2.96
Kuwait	4,024	4,177	6,118	7,711	12,682	0.08	64.47
Lebanon	5,573	5,724	7,034	8,558	9,034	0.05	5.56
Libya	1,508	1,817	1,163	5,881	4,632	0.03	-21.24
Oman	1,085	1,589	2,008	2,446	2,543	0.02	3.97
Palestine	242	696	246	388	379	0.00	-2.32
Qatar	1,971	2,965	3,306	6,679	8,845	0.05	32.43
Saudi Arabia	8,812	11,291	12,966	17,969	18,932	0.11	5.36
Syrian Arab Republic	2,922	2,064	1,693	1,360	1,101	0.01	-19.04
United Arab Emirates	14,713	25,092	30,757	39,316	42,755	0.26	8.75
Yemen	547	321	539	714	431	0.00	-39.64
SOUTH ASIA	**98,108**	**108,265**	**121,261**	**113,476**	**116,186**	**0.70**	**2.39**
Afghanistan	4,150	3,625	4,020	3,493	2,025	0.01	-42.03
Bangladesh	908	1,303	1,441	1,299	1,121	0.01	-13.70
Bhutan	263	46	118	234	75	0.00	-67.95
India	72,852	85,089	97,323	91,683	97,606	0.59	6.46
Iran, Islamic Republic of	15,502	12,859	12,983	11,755	9,781	0.06	-16.79
Maldives	91	80	122	114	233	0.00	104.39
Nepal	417	447	564	649	782	0.00	20.49
Pakistan	3,281	4,095	3,733	3,362	3,335	0.02	-0.80
Sri Lanka	644	721	957	887	1,228	0.01	38.44
NOT SPECIFIED	**229,576**	**98,987**	**54,367**	**55,799**	**96,490**	**0.58**	**72.92**
Other countries of the World	229,576	98,987	54,367	55,799	96,490	0.58	72.92

Yearbook of Tourism Statistics, Data 2009 – 2013, 2015 Edition

BELIZE

1. Arrivals of non-resident tourists at national borders, by nationality

	2009	2010	2011	2012	2013	Market share 2013	% Change 2013-2012
TOTAL	232,249	241,919	250,263	277,135	294,177	100.00	6.15
AFRICA	668	577	472	453	403	0.14	-11.04
OTHER AFRICA	668	577	472	453	403	0.14	-11.04
All countries of Africa	668	577	472	453	403	0.14	-11.04
AMERICAS	188,240	195,568	203,128	226,961	240,347	81.70	5.90
CARIBBEAN	2,388	2,505	2,049	2,288	2,180	0.74	-4.72
Jamaica	669	663	599	644	591	0.20	-8.23
Other countries of the Caribbean	1,719	1,842	1,451	1,644	1,589	0.54	-3.35
CENTRAL AMERICA	22,208	21,908	16,834	16,112	19,064	6.48	18.32
Guatemala	12,957	12,448	7,423	7,048	8,860	3.01	25.71
Honduras	3,506	3,680	3,731	3,892	4,553	1.55	16.98
Other countries of Central America	5,745	5,780	5,679	5,172	5,651	1.92	9.26
NORTH AMERICA	161,555	168,958	181,984	206,029	216,068	73.45	4.87
Canada	17,211	18,246	20,093	24,223	26,713	9.08	10.28
Mexico	4,783	4,840	5,598	5,164	5,842	1.99	13.13
United States of America	139,561	145,872	156,293	176,642	183,513	62.38	3.89
SOUTH AMERICA	2,089	2,197	2,261	2,532	3,035	1.03	19.87
All countries of South America	2,089	2,197	2,261	2,532	3,035	1.03	19.87
EAST ASIA AND THE PACIFIC	4,973	6,069	5,737	6,933	7,862	2.67	13.40
OTHER EAST ASIA AND THE PACIFIC	4,973	6,069	5,737	6,933	7,862	2.67	13.40
All countries of Asia	2,459	2,937	2,995	3,443	3,430	1.17	-0.38
All countries of Oceania	2,514	3,133	2,741	3,490	4,432	1.51	26.99
EUROPE	29,603	30,025	30,142	29,362	32,191	10.94	9.63
NORTHERN EUROPE	9,334	10,142	9,046	8,999	10,163	3.45	12.93
Sweden	800	841	847	1,018	1,093	0.37	7.37
United Kingdom	8,534	9,301	8,199	7,981	9,070	3.08	13.64
SOUTHERN EUROPE	3,151	3,412	3,657	3,018	3,085	1.05	2.22
Italy	1,679	1,877	2,218	1,774	1,694	0.58	-4.51
Spain	1,472	1,535	1,440	1,244	1,391	0.47	11.82
WESTERN EUROPE	9,994	9,856	10,254	10,122	10,592	3.60	4.64
France	3,269	2,916	3,101	3,308	3,070	1.04	-7.19
Germany	3,376	3,438	3,262	3,525	3,961	1.35	12.37
Netherlands	2,607	2,461	2,869	2,384	2,520	0.86	5.70
Switzerland	742	1,041	1,021	905	1,041	0.35	15.03
OTHER EUROPE	7,124	6,615	7,184	7,223	8,351	2.84	15.62
Other countries of Europe	7,124	6,615	7,184	7,223	8,351	2.84	15.62
MIDDLE EAST	400	863	628	1,324	1,885	0.64	42.37
All countries of Middle East	400	863	628	1,324	1,885	0.64	42.37
NOT SPECIFIED	8,365	8,817	10,157	12,102	11,489	3.91	-5.07
Nationals Residing Abroad	8,365	8,817	10,157	12,102	11,489	3.91	-5.07

79

BELIZE

2. Arrivals of non-resident visitors at national borders, by nationality

	2009	2010	2011	2012	2013	Market share 2013	% Change 2013-2012
TOTAL (*)	1,091,406	1,197,326	1,177,462	1,051,907	1,112,908	100.00	5.80
AMERICAS	989,821	1,105,499	1,077,276	958,330	1,017,177	91.40	6.14
CARIBBEAN	9,067	7,823	7,646	7,617	6,076	0.55	-20.23
Cuba	1,170	1,165	1,121	1,081	735	0.07	-32.01
Jamaica	1,292	1,213	1,184	1,266	1,071	0.10	-15.40
Other countries of the Caribbean	6,605	5,445	5,341	5,270	4,270	0.38	-18.98
CENTRAL AMERICA	129,308	154,968	168,044	171,256	129,032	11.59	-24.66
Costa Rica	1,230	1,235	1,056	1,350	1,470	0.13	8.89
El Salvador	4,792	5,182	5,069	5,961	6,091	0.55	2.18
Guatemala	116,123	141,083	154,954	155,745	113,771	10.22	-26.95
Honduras	4,824	5,283	5,070	6,068	6,183	0.56	1.90
Other countries of Central America	2,339	2,185	1,895	2,132	1,517	0.14	-28.85
NORTH AMERICA	840,771	933,035	892,230	769,176	870,512	78.22	13.17
Canada	60,503	63,971	67,257	68,331	71,214	6.40	4.22
Mexico	26,259	26,101	33,864	36,652	32,593	2.93	-11.07
United States of America	754,009	842,963	791,109	664,193	766,705	68.89	15.43
SOUTH AMERICA	10,675	9,673	9,356	10,281	11,557	1.04	12.41
All countries of South America	10,675	9,673	9,356	10,281	11,557	1.04	12.41
EAST ASIA AND THE PACIFIC	5,925	6,424	7,862	10,361	8,902	0.80	-14.08
OTHER EAST ASIA AND THE PACIFIC	5,925	6,424	7,862	10,361	8,902	0.80	-14.08
All countries of Asia	5,925	6,424	7,862	10,361	8,902	0.80	-14.08
EUROPE	86,247	75,690	84,038	73,446	76,335	6.86	3.93
NORTHERN EUROPE	19,885	18,500	20,474	16,263	16,387	1.47	0.76
United Kingdom	19,885	18,500	20,474	16,263	16,387	1.47	0.76
OTHER EUROPE	66,362	57,190	63,564	57,183	59,948	5.39	4.84
Other countries of Europe	66,362	57,190	63,564	57,183	59,948	5.39	4.84
NOT SPECIFIED	9,413	9,713	8,286	9,770	10,494	0.94	7.41
Other countries of the World	9,413	9,713	8,286	9,770	10,494	0.94	7.41

Yearbook of Tourism Statistics, Data 2009 – 2013, 2015 Edition

BENIN

1. Arrivals of non-resident tourists at national borders, by country of residence

	2009	2010	2011	2012	2013	Market share 2013	% Change 2013-2012
TOTAL	190,000	199,491	209,475	219,949	230,946	100.00	5.00
AFRICA	90,757	138,000	125,685	135,347	133,987	58.02	-1.00
EAST AFRICA	2,634	5,914	5,027	5,397	3,592	1.56	-33.44
Burundi	31	1,035	611	512	345	0.15	-32.62
Comoros	106	515	498	566	214	0.09	-62.19
Djibouti	30	120	200	105	92	0.04	-12.38
Eritrea		9		11	15	0.01	36.36
Ethiopia	47	110	118	88	88	0.04	
Kenya	142	76	120	315	120	0.05	-61.90
Madagascar	239	980	612	714	458	0.20	-35.85
Malawi	35	1,100	940	669	492	0.21	-26.46
Mauritius	1	33		15	21	0.01	40.00
Mozambique	26	500	610	380	441	0.19	16.05
Rwanda	1,061	845	900	810	580	0.25	-28.40
Seychelles	20	11	5	21	17	0.01	-19.05
Somalia	717	300	187	481	249	0.11	-48.23
Uganda	60	54	47	200	118	0.05	-41.00
United Republic of Tanzania	78	88	150	33	38	0.02	15.15
Zambia	11	121	18	300	225	0.10	-25.00
Zimbabwe	30	17	11	177	79	0.03	-55.37
CENTRAL AFRICA	24,163	58,494	50,263	33,762	28,398	12.30	-15.89
Angola	609	11,410	9,872	473	625	0.27	32.14
Cameroon	5,357	10,620	12,500	13,879	8,690	3.76	-37.39
Central African Republic	840	800	700	600	855	0.37	42.50
Chad	1,900	2,007	1,800	2,200	1,687	0.73	-23.32
Congo	6,839	25,953	22,897	9,633	9,233	4.00	-4.15
Democratic Republic of the Congo	47	915	600	456	540	0.23	18.42
Equatorial Guinea	253	200	87	820	625	0.27	-23.78
Gabon	8,313	6,589	1,807	5,699	6,138	2.66	7.70
Sao Tome and Principe	5			2	5	0.00	150.00
NORTH AFRICA	2,526	2,697	2,500	6,534	5,613	2.43	-14.10
Algeria	966	850	740	1,600	1,153	0.50	-27.94
Morocco	416	600	700	1,053	910	0.39	-13.58
Sudan	227	320	350	600	653	0.28	8.83
Tunisia	917	927	710	3,281	2,897	1.25	-11.70
SOUTHERN AFRICA	1,160	977	512	983	1,016	0.44	3.36
Botswana	135	200	99	80	55	0.02	-31.25
Lesotho	47	55	36	60	75	0.03	25.00
Namibia	63	57	20	55	35	0.02	-36.36
South Africa	915	663	346	780	844	0.37	8.21
Swaziland		2	11	8	7	0.00	-12.50
WEST AFRICA	60,274	69,918	67,383	88,671	95,368	41.29	7.55
Burkina Faso	9,700	9,122	6,980	9,891	12,077	5.23	22.10
Cabo Verde	700	540	410	610	480	0.21	-21.31
Côte d'Ivoire	7,550	18,937	15,813	19,500	11,692	5.06	-40.04
Gambia	545	180	200	858	587	0.25	-31.59
Ghana	5,126	4,400	5,500	6,008	6,899	2.99	14.83
Guinea	422	1,800	918	1,799	1,560	0.68	-13.29
Guinea-Bissau	116	200	325	500	620	0.27	24.00
Liberia	178	300	340	660	654	0.28	-0.91
Mali	1,273	1,945	2,600	3,012	2,347	1.02	-22.08
Mauritania	445	333	260	366	299	0.13	-18.31
Niger	5,900	6,000	5,500	8,100	13,997	6.06	72.80
Nigeria	13,184	15,975	17,614	20,200	24,652	10.67	22.04
Senegal	3,059	4,600	3,100	5,877	4,328	1.87	-26.36
Sierra Leone	525	186	223	300	285	0.12	-5.00
Togo	11,551	5,400	7,600	10,990	14,891	6.45	35.50

Yearbook of Tourism Statistics, Data 2009 – 2013, 2015 Edition

BENIN

1. Arrivals of non-resident tourists at national borders, by country of residence

	2009	2010	2011	2012	2013	Market share 2013	% Change 2013-2012
AMERICAS	5,104	3,173	3,066	4,558	8,041	3.48	76.42
CARIBBEAN	336	266	189	92	244	0.11	165.22
Cuba	117	57	28	12	44	0.02	266.67
Dominican Republic	91	19	11	15	21	0.01	40.00
Guadeloupe		7	10	4	9	0.00	125.00
Haiti	120	152	129	33	89	0.04	169.70
Jamaica	8	11	6	21	55	0.02	161.90
Netherlands Antilles		20	5	7	26	0.01	271.43
CENTRAL AMERICA			11	25	31	0.01	24.00
Honduras			3	7	11	0.00	57.14
Nicaragua			8	18	20	0.01	11.11
NORTH AMERICA	3,756	1,974	2,150	3,439	6,992	3.03	103.31
Canada	952	612	840	1,093	3,430	1.49	213.82
Mexico	120	375	420	350	546	0.24	56.00
United States of America	2,684	987	890	1,996	3,016	1.31	51.10
SOUTH AMERICA	1,012	933	716	1,002	774	0.34	-22.75
Argentina	604	500	422	577	457	0.20	-20.80
Bolivia		9	12	20			
Brazil	360	407	120	360	220	0.10	-38.89
Chile		2	20	7			
Colombia	48	11	89	11	29	0.01	163.64
Uruguay		3	13	4	13	0.01	225.00
Venezuela		1	40	23	55	0.02	139.13
EAST ASIA AND THE PACIFIC	860	800	1,126	2,726	6,187	2.68	126.96
NORTH-EAST ASIA	603	679	972	2,533	5,843	2.53	130.68
China	410	371	580	1,877	3,870	1.68	106.18
Japan	174	200	240	557	1,756	0.76	215.26
Korea, Dem. People's Republic of	19	108	152	99	217	0.09	119.19
SOUTH-EAST ASIA	113	88	97	157	288	0.12	83.44
Indonesia	45	13	25	99	155	0.07	56.57
Malaysia	19	6	2	12	9	0.00	-25.00
Philippines	12	7	5	7	3	0.00	-57.14
Singapore	1	12	12	9	54	0.02	500.00
Thailand	22	41	34	19	20	0.01	5.26
Viet Nam	14	9	19	11	47	0.02	327.27
AUSTRALASIA	144	33	55	36	47	0.02	30.56
Australia	144	30	19	21	40	0.02	90.48
New Zealand		3	36	15	7	0.00	-53.33
MELANESIA			2		9	0.00	
Fiji			2		9	0.00	
EUROPE	35,448	32,886	57,081	54,339	50,360	21.81	-7.32
NORTHERN EUROPE	3,856	610	2,903	1,482	2,147	0.93	44.87
Denmark	1,538	291	300	445	91	0.04	-79.55
Finland	578	22	30	13	66	0.03	407.69
Ireland	34	33	987	87	100	0.04	14.94
Norway	358	45	800	360	210	0.09	-41.67
Sweden	1,348	219	786	577	1,680	0.73	191.16
SOUTHERN EUROPE	6,224	2,897	4,855	4,646	3,784	1.64	-18.55
Bosnia and Herzegovina			2		7	0.00	
Greece	314	300	206	100	157	0.07	57.00
Italy	3,237	1,438	3,074	2,996	1,840	0.80	-38.58
Montenegro		1	7		2	0.00	
Portugal	466	346	600	500	547	0.24	9.40
Serbia and Montenegro			1				
Slovenia		5	15		20	0.01	
Spain	2,207	807	950	1,050	1,211	0.52	15.33

Yearbook of Tourism Statistics, Data 2009 – 2013, 2015 Edition

BENIN

1. Arrivals of non-resident tourists at national borders, by country of residence

	2009	2010	2011	2012	2013	Market share 2013	% Change 2013-2012
WESTERN EUROPE	17,616	22,641	41,132	41,011	34,203	14.81	-16.60
Austria	222	600	200	180	149	0.06	-17.22
Belgium	2,162	4,670	3,600	4,000	3,788	1.64	-5.30
France	2,519	13,206	20,386	19,783	12,116	5.25	-38.76
Germany	1,992	1,950	2,317	2,210	2,020	0.87	-8.60
Luxembourg	30	81	229	144	300	0.13	108.33
Netherlands	4,120	900	8,900	7,056	9,600	4.16	36.05
Switzerland	6,571	1,234	5,500	7,638	6,230	2.70	-18.43
EAST MEDITERRANEAN EUROPE	142	108	202	120	236	0.10	96.67
Israel	142	88	135	99	203	0.09	105.05
Turkey		20	67	21	33	0.01	57.14
OTHER EUROPE	7,610	6,630	7,989	7,080	9,990	4.33	41.10
Other countries of Europe	7,610	6,630	7,989	7,080	9,990	4.33	41.10
MIDDLE EAST	367	2,388	2,670	2,916	3,661	1.59	25.55
Egypt		45	41	33	130	0.06	293.94
Iraq	30	19	11	7	21	0.01	200.00
Jordan	20	33	7		40	0.02	
Kuwait		15	25	19	51	0.02	168.42
Lebanon	290	1,300	1,659	1,897	2,050	0.89	8.07
Libya		940	889	797	1,210	0.52	51.82
Palestine		20	17	10	15	0.01	50.00
Qatar	18	11	12	144	99	0.04	-31.25
Saudi Arabia	9	3	5		33	0.01	
Syrian Arab Republic		2	4	9	12	0.01	33.33
SOUTH ASIA	453	845	1,147	1,063	1,710	0.74	60.87
Afghanistan	181	81	58	100	89	0.04	-11.00
Bangladesh			2		3	0.00	
India	212	707	1,037	900	1,540	0.67	71.11
Iran, Islamic Republic of	9	22	19	45	48	0.02	6.67
Nepal	1	5	11	6	3	0.00	-50.00
Pakistan	50	30	15	12	21	0.01	75.00
Sri Lanka			5		6	0.00	
NOT SPECIFIED	57,011	21,399	18,700	19,000	27,000	11.69	42.11
Other countries of the World	57,011	21,399	18,700	19,000	27,000	11.69	42.11

Yearbook of Tourism Statistics, Data 2009 – 2013, 2015 Edition

BERMUDA

1. Arrivals of non-resident tourists at national borders, by country of residence

	2009	2010	2011	2012	2013	Market share 2013	% Change 2013-2012
TOTAL (*)	**235,860**	**232,262**	**236,038**	**232,063**	**236,343**	**100.00**	**1.84**
AMERICAS	**197,515**	**196,418**	**202,107**	**198,743**	**198,828**	**84.13**	**0.04**
NORTH AMERICA	**197,515**	**196,418**	**202,107**	**198,743**	**198,828**	**84.13**	**0.04**
Canada	24,867	30,402	29,217	30,565	27,613	11.68	-9.66
United States of America	172,648	166,016	172,890	168,178	171,215	72.44	1.81
EAST ASIA AND THE PACIFIC	**811**	**1,088**	**1,058**	**868**			
NORTH-EAST ASIA	**336**	**385**	**367**	**331**			
Japan	336	385	367	331			
AUSTRALASIA	**475**	**703**	**691**	**537**			
Australia	475	703	691	537			
EUROPE	**28,949**	**28,498**	**26,940**	**25,766**	**28,760**	**12.17**	**11.62**
NORTHERN EUROPE	**24,218**	**23,501**	**21,797**	**21,226**	**23,904**	**10.11**	**12.62**
Sweden	313	261	273	197	294	0.12	49.24
United Kingdom	23,905	23,240	21,524	21,029	23,610	9.99	12.27
SOUTHERN EUROPE	**1,253**	**1,244**	**1,184**	**906**	**888**	**0.38**	**-1.99**
Italy	1,253	1,244	1,184	906	888	0.38	-1.99
WESTERN EUROPE	**2,516**	**2,760**	**2,870**	**2,532**	**2,779**	**1.18**	**9.76**
Austria	135	168	176	122	144	0.06	18.03
France	754	711	698	572	637	0.27	11.36
Germany	1,032	994	1,116	990	1,172	0.50	18.38
Switzerland	595	887	880	848	826	0.35	-2.59
OTHER EUROPE	**962**	**993**	**1,089**	**1,102**	**1,189**	**0.50**	**7.89**
Other countries of Europe	962	993	1,089	1,102	1,189	0.50	7.89
NOT SPECIFIED	**8,585**	**6,258**	**5,933**	**6,686**	**8,755**	**3.70**	**30.95**
Other countries of the World	8,585	6,258	5,933	6,686	8,755	3.70	30.95

BHUTAN

1. Arrivals of non-resident tourists at national borders, by nationality

		2009	2010	2011	2012	2013	Market share 2013	% Change 2013-2012
TOTAL	(*)	23,480	27,210	37,479	43,931	44,252	100.00	0.73
AFRICA		48	102	92	93	92	0.21	-1.08
EAST AFRICA		7	6	21	4	15	0.03	275.00
Ethiopia						1	0.00	
Kenya		2	4	6	2	5	0.01	150.00
Madagascar						1	0.00	
Mauritius		5	1	14		4	0.01	
Mozambique						1	0.00	
Seychelles					1	1	0.00	
Uganda			1			1	0.00	
United Republic of Tanzania				1				
Zambia					1			
Zimbabwe						1	0.00	
CENTRAL AFRICA				3	2			
Chad				3	2			
NORTH AFRICA		5		1	1	6	0.01	500.00
Algeria						1	0.00	
Morocco		4			1	1	0.00	
Sudan				1				
Tunisia		1				4	0.01	
SOUTHERN AFRICA		36	74	63	82	65	0.15	-20.73
Namibia			1	1	5	6	0.01	20.00
South Africa		32	70	62	77	59	0.13	-23.38
Swaziland		4	3					
WEST AFRICA				4	4	6	0.01	50.00
Benin				1				
Côte d'Ivoire						2	0.00	
Ghana						1	0.00	
Mauritania						1	0.00	
Nigeria				3	4	2	0.00	-50.00
OTHER AFRICA			22					
Other countries of Africa			22					
AMERICAS		5,743	6,506	8,056	7,879	9,085	20.53	15.31
CARIBBEAN				8	3	11	0.02	266.67
Antigua and Barbuda				1				
Bahamas						1	0.00	
Cuba				1				
Dominican Republic					2	5	0.01	150.00
Grenada				1				
Haiti				1				
Jamaica				1		4	0.01	
Saint Kitts and Nevis						1	0.00	
Trinidad and Tobago				3	1			
CENTRAL AMERICA		2	13	17	13	18	0.04	38.46
Belize			1	1				
Costa Rica			10	1	5	2	0.00	-60.00
El Salvador				2		1	0.00	
Guatemala		2		11		10	0.02	
Honduras			2			1	0.00	
Nicaragua						1	0.00	
Panama				2	8	3	0.01	-62.50
NORTH AMERICA		5,467	6,141	7,511	7,199	8,219	18.57	14.17
Canada		556	786	1,061	999	1,055	2.38	5.61
Mexico		125	166	224	193	237	0.54	22.80
United States of America		4,786	5,189	6,226	6,007	6,927	15.65	15.32
SOUTH AMERICA		274	338	520	664	837	1.89	26.05
Argentina		59	40	80	88	113	0.26	28.41
Bolivia					2	2	0.00	
Brazil		178	229	304	462	556	1.26	20.35

Yearbook of Tourism Statistics, Data 2009 – 2013, 2015 Edition

BHUTAN

1. Arrivals of non-resident tourists at national borders, by nationality

	2009	2010	2011	2012	2013	Market share 2013	% Change 2013-2012
Chile	8	18	45	40	89	0.20	122.50
Colombia	14	27	45	40	41	0.09	2.50
Ecuador		1		4	5	0.01	25.00
Guyana					2	0.00	
Peru	6	19	12	6	6	0.01	
Suriname					1	0.00	
Uruguay	1	1		7	1	0.00	-85.71
Venezuela	8	3	34	15	21	0.05	40.00
OTHER AMERICAS		**14**					
Other countries of the Americas		14					
EAST ASIA AND THE PACIFIC	**7,743**	**8,599**	**14,949**	**21,329**	**21,238**	**47.99**	**-0.43**
NORTH-EAST ASIA	**4,412**	**4,827**	**8,147**	**12,178**	**10,479**	**23.68**	**-13.95**
China	1,143	1,494	2,896	3,766	4,764	10.77	26.50
Japan	3,136	2,963	3,943	6,967	4,015	9.07	-42.37
Korea, Dem. People's Republic of			3	11	2	0.00	-81.82
Korea, Republic of	49	182	407	630	596	1.35	-5.40
Macao, China	1	3					
Mongolia		1	7	3			
Taiwan, Province of China	83	184	891	801	1,102	2.49	37.58
SOUTH-EAST ASIA	**2,239**	**2,277**	**4,885**	**7,033**	**8,499**	**19.21**	**20.84**
Brunei Darussalam			3	1	8	0.02	700.00
Cambodia	2			3	3	0.01	
Indonesia	98	110	295	202	579	1.31	186.63
Lao People's Democratic Republic			4	2	11	0.02	450.00
Malaysia	367	356	788	1,307	2,029	4.59	55.24
Myanmar	5	1	3	12	5	0.01	-58.33
Philippines	59	119	128	243	238	0.54	-2.06
Singapore	708	785	1,349	1,605	2,037	4.60	26.92
Thailand	975	875	2,235	3,573	3,494	7.90	-2.21
Viet Nam	25	31	80	85	95	0.21	11.76
AUSTRALASIA	**1,092**	**1,423**	**1,917**	**2,118**	**2,254**	**5.09**	**6.42**
Australia	970	1,318	1,773	1,926	2,043	4.62	6.07
New Zealand	122	105	144	192	211	0.48	9.90
MELANESIA					**6**	**0.01**	
Fiji					6	0.01	
OTHER EAST ASIA AND THE PACIFIC		**72**					
Other countries of Asia		72					
EUROPE	**9,861**	**11,883**	**14,181**	**14,412**	**13,621**	**30.78**	**-5.49**
CENTRAL/EASTERN EUROPE	**720**	**857**	**1,065**	**1,007**	**1,151**	**2.60**	**14.30**
Armenia			10	1	4	0.01	300.00
Azerbaijan			1				
Belarus	2	2	1	11	12	0.03	9.09
Bulgaria	12	11	11	14	24	0.05	71.43
Czech Republic	77	71	135	148	160	0.36	8.11
Estonia	14	31	2	12	16	0.04	33.33
Georgia				5	1	0.00	-80.00
Hungary	49	65	45	69	108	0.24	56.52
Kazakhstan	5		15	3	5	0.01	66.67
Kyrgyzstan			1	1	1	0.00	
Latvia	3	9	44	32	17	0.04	-46.88
Lithuania	4	13	44	3	18	0.04	500.00
Poland	184	268	311	240	289	0.65	20.42
Republic of Moldova				2			
Romania	19	52	35	19	34	0.08	78.95
Russian Federation	270	275	291	365	392	0.89	7.40
Slovakia	53	32	38	36	37	0.08	2.78
Ukraine	28	27	81	44	33	0.07	-25.00
Uzbekistan		1		2			

Yearbook of Tourism Statistics, Data 2009 – 2013, 2015 Edition

BHUTAN

1. Arrivals of non-resident tourists at national borders, by nationality

	2009	2010	2011	2012	2013	Market share 2013	% Change 2013-2012
NORTHERN EUROPE	**2,521**	**2,690**	**4,025**	**3,370**	**3,188**	**7.20**	**-5.40**
Denmark	153	412	430	332	202	0.46	-39.16
Finland	161	174	245	112	144	0.33	28.57
Iceland			7	5	1	0.00	-80.00
Ireland	59	59	78	72	64	0.14	-11.11
Norway	92	136	214	142	219	0.49	54.23
Sweden	88	137	256	241	267	0.60	10.79
United Kingdom	1,968	1,772	2,795	2,466	2,291	5.18	-7.10
SOUTHERN EUROPE	**1,506**	**1,826**	**2,054**	**1,831**	**1,555**	**3.51**	**-15.07**
Albania			2				
Andorra	3	1	1	6	2	0.00	-66.67
Bosnia and Herzegovina	1		2	1			
Croatia	4	1	6	15	14	0.03	-6.67
Greece	107	88	70	60	48	0.11	-20.00
Italy	759	1,028	1,014	786	750	1.69	-4.58
Malta			4	9			
Montenegro			1	1			
Portugal	116	116	214	118	223	0.50	88.98
Serbia			2	5	2	0.00	-60.00
Slovenia	30	64	11	41	28	0.06	-31.71
Spain	485	528	727	789	488	1.10	-38.15
Yugoslavia, SFR (former)	1						
WESTERN EUROPE	**4,899**	**6,272**	**6,689**	**7,817**	**7,389**	**16.70**	**-5.48**
Austria	420	505	528	611	653	1.48	6.87
Belgium	364	404	539	505	514	1.16	1.78
France	1,189	1,454	1,585	1,847	1,561	3.53	-15.48
Germany	1,587	2,250	2,287	2,880	2,753	6.22	-4.41
Liechtenstein			3	5	3	0.01	-40.00
Luxembourg	16	23	33	38	54	0.12	42.11
Monaco				6	1	0.00	-83.33
Netherlands	780	847	933	993	785	1.77	-20.95
Switzerland	543	789	781	932	1,065	2.41	14.27
EAST MEDITERRANEAN EUROPE	**215**	**232**	**348**	**387**	**338**	**0.76**	**-12.66**
Cyprus	5	5	4	7	3	0.01	-57.14
Israel	159	127	278	172	168	0.38	-2.33
Turkey	51	100	66	208	167	0.38	-19.71
OTHER EUROPE			**6**				
Other countries of Europe			6				
MIDDLE EAST	**31**	**27**	**44**	**36**	**23**	**0.05**	**-36.11**
Bahrain			1		3	0.01	
Egypt	18	10					
Jordan		1	21	3	4	0.01	33.33
Kuwait		2	8	8			
Lebanon		5	4	5	6	0.01	20.00
Oman		1	2	5	1	0.00	-80.00
Qatar					2	0.00	
Saudi Arabia			2	12	6	0.01	-50.00
United Arab Emirates		8	5	3	1	0.00	-66.67
Yemen			1				
Other countries of Middle East	13						
SOUTH ASIA	**52**	**93**	**157**	**182**	**193**	**0.44**	**6.04**
Afghanistan				2			
Iran, Islamic Republic of		1	4	1	4	0.01	300.00
Nepal	41	60	145	150	168	0.38	12.00
Pakistan	5	2	2	12	6	0.01	-50.00
Sri Lanka	6	30	6	17	15	0.03	-11.76
NOT SPECIFIED	**2**						
Other countries of the World	2						

87

BHUTAN

5. Overnight stays of non-resident tourists in hotels and similar establishments, by nationality

	2009	2010	2011	2012	2013	Market share 2013	% Change 2013-2012
TOTAL			276,880	303,319	302,965	100.00	-0.12
AFRICA				687	777	0.26	13.10
EAST AFRICA				25	102	0.03	308.00
Ethiopia					6	0.00	
Kenya				12	35	0.01	191.67
Madagascar					4	0.00	
Mauritius					15	0.00	
Mozambique					14	0.00	
Seychelles				10	16	0.01	60.00
Uganda					5	0.00	
Zambia				3			
Zimbabwe					7	0.00	
CENTRAL AFRICA				8			
Chad				8			
NORTH AFRICA				8	24	0.01	200.00
Algeria					5	0.00	
Morocco				8	2	0.00	-75.00
Tunisia					17	0.01	
SOUTHERN AFRICA				610	539	0.18	-11.64
Namibia				30	27	0.01	-10.00
South Africa				580	512	0.17	-11.72
WEST AFRICA				36	112	0.04	211.11
Côte d'Ivoire					14	0.00	
Ghana					17	0.01	
Mauritania					6	0.00	
Nigeria				36	75	0.02	108.33
AMERICAS			59,791	60,999	66,886	22.08	9.65
CARIBBEAN				12	57	0.02	375.00
Bahamas					10	0.00	
Dominican Republic				6	20	0.01	233.33
Jamaica					23	0.01	
Saint Kitts and Nevis					4	0.00	
Trinidad and Tobago				6			
CENTRAL AMERICA				72	113	0.04	56.94
Costa Rica				20	21	0.01	5.00
El Salvador					6	0.00	
Guatemala					64	0.02	
Honduras					3	0.00	
Nicaragua					7	0.00	
Panama				52	12	0.00	-76.92
NORTH AMERICA			59,791	57,268	62,381	20.59	8.93
Canada			9,503	8,118	8,743	2.89	7.70
Mexico				1,113	1,198	0.40	7.64
United States of America			50,288	48,037	52,440	17.31	9.17
SOUTH AMERICA				3,647	4,335	1.43	18.86
Argentina				476	485	0.16	1.89
Bolivia				8	13	0.00	62.50
Brazil				2,487	2,814	0.93	13.15
Chile				327	613	0.20	87.46
Colombia				195	202	0.07	3.59
Ecuador				27	22	0.01	-18.52
Guyana					10	0.00	
Peru				27	26	0.01	-3.70
Suriname					5	0.00	
Uruguay				27	9	0.00	-66.67
Venezuela				73	136	0.04	86.30
EAST ASIA AND THE PACIFIC			71,882	116,845	116,871	38.58	0.02
NORTH-EAST ASIA			35,991	60,587	51,811	17.10	-14.48

88

BHUTAN

5. Overnight stays of non-resident tourists in hotels and similar establishments, by nationality

	2009	2010	2011	2012	2013	Market share 2013	% Change 2013-2012
China			14,694	18,666	23,425	7.73	25.50
Japan			21,297	34,013	19,133	6.32	-43.75
Korea, Dem. People's Republic of				44	9	0.00	-79.55
Korea, Republic of				2,880	2,888	0.95	0.28
Mongolia				13			
Taiwan, Province of China				4,971	6,356	2.10	27.86
SOUTH-EAST ASIA			**19,364**	**36,727**	**44,731**	**14.76**	**21.79**
Brunei Darussalam				3	53	0.02	1,666.67
Cambodia				9	31	0.01	244.44
Indonesia				1,237	2,775	0.92	124.33
Lao People's Democratic Republic				13	45	0.01	246.15
Malaysia				7,215	10,508	3.47	45.64
Myanmar				50	34	0.01	-32.00
Philippines				1,500	1,171	0.39	-21.93
Singapore			9,591	11,101	14,739	4.86	32.77
Thailand			9,773	15,059	14,810	4.89	-1.65
Viet Nam				540	565	0.19	4.63
AUSTRALASIA			**16,527**	**19,531**	**20,286**	**6.70**	**3.87**
Australia			16,527	17,666	18,418	6.08	4.26
New Zealand				1,865	1,868	0.62	0.16
MELANESIA					**43**	**0.01**	
Fiji					43	0.01	
EUROPE			**59,888**	**123,585**	**117,341**	**38.73**	**-5.05**
CENTRAL/EASTERN EUROPE				**6,236**	**7,518**	**2.48**	**20.56**
Armenia				4	21	0.01	425.00
Belarus				71	78	0.03	9.86
Bulgaria				66	92	0.03	39.39
Czech Republic				1,208	1,554	0.51	28.64
Estonia				76	73	0.02	-3.95
Georgia				29	3	0.00	-89.66
Hungary				328	504	0.17	53.66
Kazakhstan				16	46	0.02	187.50
Kyrgyzstan				7	5	0.00	-28.57
Latvia				266	155	0.05	-41.73
Lithuania				28	157	0.05	460.71
Poland				1,243	1,757	0.58	41.35
Republic of Moldova				12			
Romania				103	189	0.06	83.50
Russian Federation				2,217	2,370	0.78	6.90
Slovakia				280	345	0.11	23.21
Ukraine				268	169	0.06	-36.94
Uzbekistan				14			
NORTHERN EUROPE			**24,549**	**27,886**	**26,919**	**8.89**	**-3.47**
Denmark				3,015	1,890	0.62	-37.31
Finland				797	1,106	0.37	38.77
Iceland				42	7	0.00	-83.33
Ireland				511	459	0.15	-10.18
Norway				985	1,568	0.52	59.19
Sweden				1,607	1,725	0.57	7.34
United Kingdom			24,549	20,929	20,164	6.66	-3.66
SOUTHERN EUROPE				**12,996**	**10,994**	**3.63**	**-15.40**
Andorra				48	18	0.01	-62.50
Bosnia and Herzegovina				8			
Croatia				97	97	0.03	
Greece				367	327	0.11	-10.90
Italy				6,162	5,900	1.95	-4.25
Malta				100			
Montenegro				4			
Portugal				702	1,148	0.38	63.53

89

BHUTAN

5. Overnight stays of non-resident tourists in hotels and similar establishments, by nationality

	2009	2010	2011	2012	2013	Market share 2013	% Change 2013-2012
Serbia				29	10	0.00	-65.52
Slovenia				287	149	0.05	-48.08
Spain				5,192	3,345	1.10	-35.57
WESTERN EUROPE			**35,339**	**74,069**	**69,813**	**23.04**	**-5.75**
Austria				5,378	5,586	1.84	3.87
Belgium				4,656	4,477	1.48	-3.84
France			14,065	16,946	14,872	4.91	-12.24
Germany			21,274	26,350	25,539	8.43	-3.08
Liechtenstein				54	24	0.01	-55.56
Luxembourg				313	459	0.15	46.65
Monaco				54	16	0.01	-70.37
Netherlands				10,154	7,386	2.44	-27.26
Switzerland				10,164	11,454	3.78	12.69
EAST MEDITERRANEAN EUROPE				**2,398**	**2,097**	**0.69**	**-12.55**
Cyprus				41	19	0.01	-53.66
Israel				1,229	1,350	0.45	9.85
Turkey				1,128	728	0.24	-35.46
MIDDLE EAST				**227**	**118**	**0.04**	**-48.02**
Bahrain					15	0.00	
Jordan				32	22	0.01	-31.25
Kuwait				43			
Lebanon				30	39	0.01	30.00
Oman				15	4	0.00	-73.33
Qatar					7	0.00	
Saudi Arabia				97	27	0.01	-72.16
United Arab Emirates				10	4	0.00	-60.00
SOUTH ASIA				**976**	**972**	**0.32**	**-0.41**
Afghanistan				14			
Iran, Islamic Republic of				10	23	0.01	130.00
Nepal				859	825	0.27	-3.96
Pakistan				33	52	0.02	57.58
Sri Lanka				60	72	0.02	20.00
NOT SPECIFIED			**85,319**				
Other countries of the World			85,319				

Yearbook of Tourism Statistics, Data 2009 – 2013, 2015 Edition

BOLIVIA

1. Arrivals of non-resident tourists at national borders, by nationality

	2009	2010	2011	2012	2013	Market share 2013	% Change 2013-2012
TOTAL	**599,264**	**678,592**	**711,340**	**797,912**	**798,272**	**100.00**	**0.05**
AFRICA	**988**	**1,124**	**1,005**	**3,180**	**1,251**	**0.16**	**-60.66**
OTHER AFRICA	**988**	**1,124**	**1,005**	**3,180**	**1,251**	**0.16**	**-60.66**
All countries of Africa	988	1,124	1,005	3,180	1,251	0.16	-60.66
AMERICAS	**421,326**	**505,981**	**499,803**	**579,987**	**584,134**	**73.17**	**0.72**
NORTH AMERICA	**46,674**	**54,788**	**62,148**	**60,647**	**62,951**	**7.89**	**3.80**
Canada	10,764	12,237	14,258	12,948	14,642	1.83	13.08
Mexico	8,531	8,905	10,363	11,200	12,027	1.51	7.38
United States of America	27,379	33,646	37,527	36,499	36,282	4.55	-0.59
SOUTH AMERICA	**358,756**	**433,180**	**416,551**	**497,626**	**498,337**	**62.43**	**0.14**
Argentina	99,739	125,488	127,390	155,397	154,582	19.36	-0.52
Brazil	48,553	50,171	60,767	60,419	73,062	9.15	20.93
Chile	45,240	53,160	56,344	78,547	76,554	9.59	-2.54
Colombia	12,910	14,579	17,125	23,247	25,711	3.22	10.60
Ecuador	5,989	9,020	7,526	9,936	9,652	1.21	-2.86
Paraguay	17,632	15,713	17,492	18,449	17,544	2.20	-4.91
Peru	116,910	148,180	111,538	134,839	122,964	15.40	-8.81
Uruguay	4,945	7,226	8,253	8,665	7,652	0.96	-11.69
Venezuela	6,838	9,643	10,116	8,127	10,616	1.33	30.63
OTHER AMERICAS	**15,896**	**18,013**	**21,104**	**21,714**	**22,846**	**2.86**	**5.21**
Other countries of the Americas	15,896	18,013	21,104	21,714	22,846	2.86	5.21
EAST ASIA AND THE PACIFIC	**36,194**	**37,436**	**42,504**	**48,975**	**55,845**	**7.00**	**14.03**
NORTH-EAST ASIA	**7,170**	**5,464**	**7,809**	**11,909**	**15,486**	**1.94**	**30.04**
Japan	7,170	5,464	7,809	11,909	15,486	1.94	30.04
OTHER EAST ASIA AND THE PACIFIC	**29,024**	**31,972**	**34,695**	**37,066**	**40,359**	**5.06**	**8.88**
Other countries of Asia	12,478	14,166	16,995	19,177	19,248	2.41	0.37
All countries of Oceania	16,546	17,806	17,700	17,889	21,111	2.64	18.01
EUROPE	**140,756**	**134,051**	**168,028**	**165,770**	**157,042**	**19.67**	**-5.27**
NORTHERN EUROPE	**22,694**	**20,218**	**22,959**	**22,670**	**22,366**	**2.80**	**-1.34**
Sweden	4,022	4,160	6,447	4,652	5,373	0.67	15.50
United Kingdom	18,672	16,058	16,512	18,018	16,993	2.13	-5.69
SOUTHERN EUROPE	**27,378**	**22,625**	**38,601**	**39,027**	**33,707**	**4.22**	**-13.63**
Italy	9,314	9,017	14,489	11,933	12,117	1.52	1.54
Spain	18,064	13,608	24,112	27,094	21,590	2.70	-20.31
WESTERN EUROPE	**62,139**	**58,066**	**74,424**	**74,141**	**70,490**	**8.83**	**-4.92**
France	25,161	26,113	29,767	30,003	28,766	3.60	-4.12
Germany	23,196	19,903	27,532	28,463	27,746	3.48	-2.52
Netherlands	6,762	5,730	6,780	6,775	5,240	0.66	-22.66
Switzerland	7,020	6,320	10,345	8,900	8,738	1.09	-1.82
OTHER EUROPE	**28,545**	**33,142**	**32,044**	**29,932**	**30,479**	**3.82**	**1.83**
Other countries of Europe	28,545	33,142	32,044	29,932	30,479	3.82	1.83

Yearbook of Tourism Statistics, Data 2009 – 2013, 2015 Edition

BOLIVIA

3. Arrivals of non-resident tourists in hotels and similar establishments, by nationality

	2009	2010	2011	2012	2013	Market share 2013	% Change 2013-2012
TOTAL (*)	499,811	527,200	560,325	563,486	579,208	100.00	2.79
AFRICA	1,501	1,583	1,635	1,644	1,690	0.29	2.80
OTHER AFRICA	1,501	1,583	1,635	1,644	1,690	0.29	2.80
All countries of Africa	1,501	1,583	1,635	1,644	1,690	0.29	2.80
AMERICAS	303,935	320,592	348,185	350,149	359,920	62.14	2.79
NORTH AMERICA	59,500	62,762	70,448	70,845	72,821	12.57	2.79
Canada	10,634	11,217	12,951	13,024	13,387	2.31	2.79
Mexico	6,621	6,984	7,335	7,376	7,582	1.31	2.79
United States of America	42,245	44,561	50,162	50,445	51,852	8.95	2.79
SOUTH AMERICA	234,337	247,179	268,185	269,698	277,225	47.86	2.79
Argentina	55,316	58,347	62,816	63,170	64,933	11.21	2.79
Brazil	35,748	37,707	40,908	41,139	42,287	7.30	2.79
Chile	25,647	27,052	30,947	31,122	31,990	5.52	2.79
Colombia	10,651	11,235	12,813	12,885	13,245	2.29	2.79
Ecuador	6,335	6,682	7,021	7,061	7,258	1.25	2.79
Paraguay	5,418	5,715	5,934	5,967	6,133	1.06	2.78
Peru	85,639	90,332	96,582	97,127	99,839	17.24	2.79
Uruguay	3,815	4,024	4,078	4,101	4,215	0.73	2.78
Venezuela	5,768	6,085	7,086	7,126	7,325	1.26	2.79
OTHER AMERICAS	10,098	10,651	9,552	9,606	9,874	1.70	2.79
Other countries of the Americas	10,098	10,651	9,552	9,606	9,874	1.70	2.79
EAST ASIA AND THE PACIFIC	27,071	28,554	27,978	28,136	28,920	4.99	2.79
NORTH-EAST ASIA	7,435	7,842	7,536	7,579	7,790	1.34	2.78
Japan	7,435	7,842	7,536	7,579	7,790	1.34	2.78
OTHER EAST ASIA AND THE PACIFIC	19,636	20,712	20,442	20,557	21,130	3.65	2.79
Other countries of Asia	7,121	7,511	7,067	7,107	7,305	1.26	2.79
All countries of Oceania	12,515	13,201	13,375	13,450	13,825	2.39	2.79
EUROPE	167,304	176,471	182,527	183,557	188,678	32.58	2.79
NORTHERN EUROPE	25,506	26,903	28,082	28,241	29,029	5.01	2.79
Sweden	3,437	3,625	3,657	3,678	3,781	0.65	2.80
United Kingdom	22,069	23,278	24,425	24,563	25,248	4.36	2.79
SOUTHERN EUROPE	27,181	28,670	29,936	30,105	30,945	5.34	2.79
Italy	9,325	9,836	10,935	10,997	11,304	1.95	2.79
Spain	17,856	18,834	19,001	19,108	19,641	3.39	2.79
WESTERN EUROPE	70,637	74,508	79,650	80,099	82,334	14.21	2.79
France	27,011	28,491	30,697	30,870	31,731	5.48	2.79
Germany	23,847	25,154	26,406	26,555	27,296	4.71	2.79
Netherlands	9,630	10,158	11,924	11,991	12,326	2.13	2.79
Switzerland	10,149	10,705	10,623	10,683	10,981	1.90	2.79
EAST MEDITERRANEAN EUROPE	12,387	13,066	12,847	12,919	13,279	2.29	2.79
Israel	12,387	13,066	12,847	12,919	13,279	2.29	2.79
OTHER EUROPE	31,593	33,324	32,012	32,193	33,091	5.71	2.79
Other countries of Europe	31,593	33,324	32,012	32,193	33,091	5.71	2.79

Yearbook of Tourism Statistics, Data 2009 – 2013, 2015 Edition

BOLIVIA

5. Overnight stays of non-resident tourists in hotels and similar establishments, by nationality

	2009	2010	2011	2012	2013	Market share 2013	% Change 2013-2012
TOTAL (*)	850,351	864,868	896,294	852,445	887,120	100.00	4.07
AFRICA	4,079	4,152	4,175	3,971	4,133	0.47	4.08
OTHER AFRICA	4,079	4,152	4,175	3,971	4,133	0.47	4.08
All countries of Africa	4,079	4,152	4,175	3,971	4,133	0.47	4.08
AMERICAS	533,163	542,263	564,443	536,829	558,665	62.98	4.07
NORTH AMERICA	104,432	106,213	112,502	106,998	111,350	12.55	4.07
Canada	16,521	16,802	19,420	18,470	19,221	2.17	4.07
Mexico	11,842	12,044	13,876	13,197	13,734	1.55	4.07
United States of America	76,069	77,367	79,206	75,331	78,395	8.84	4.07
SOUTH AMERICA	394,018	400,744	415,728	395,390	411,473	46.38	4.07
Argentina	94,464	96,101	98,214	93,409	97,209	10.96	4.07
Brazil	71,037	72,349	74,727	71,071	73,962	8.34	4.07
Chile	36,867	37,496	39,042	37,132	38,642	4.36	4.07
Colombia	27,460	27,829	28,351	26,964	28,061	3.16	4.07
Ecuador	12,985	13,207	14,785	14,062	14,634	1.65	4.07
Paraguay	12,826	13,023	15,956	15,175	15,792	1.78	4.07
Peru	114,868	116,827	119,423	113,581	118,201	13.32	4.07
Uruguay	7,096	7,217	7,692	7,316	7,614	0.86	4.07
Venezuela	16,415	16,695	17,538	16,680	17,358	1.96	4.06
OTHER AMERICAS	34,713	35,306	36,213	34,441	35,842	4.04	4.07
Other countries of the Americas	34,713	35,306	36,213	34,441	35,842	4.04	4.07
EAST ASIA AND THE PACIFIC	45,356	46,130	48,539	46,165	48,043	5.42	4.07
NORTH-EAST ASIA	16,245	16,522	17,211	16,369	17,035	1.92	4.07
Japan	16,245	16,522	17,211	16,369	17,035	1.92	4.07
OTHER EAST ASIA AND THE PACIFIC	29,111	29,608	31,328	29,796	31,008	3.50	4.07
Other countries of Asia	12,016	12,221	13,701	13,031	13,561	1.53	4.07
All countries of Oceania	17,095	17,387	17,627	16,765	17,447	1.97	4.07
EUROPE	267,753	272,323	279,137	265,480	276,279	31.14	4.07
NORTHERN EUROPE	39,081	39,748	41,553	39,519	41,126	4.64	4.07
Sweden	6,735	6,850	7,967	7,576	7,884	0.89	4.07
United Kingdom	32,346	32,898	33,586	31,943	33,242	3.75	4.07
SOUTHERN EUROPE	50,630	51,494	53,010	50,417	52,468	5.91	4.07
Italy	16,478	16,759	17,298	16,452	17,121	1.93	4.07
Spain	34,152	34,735	35,712	33,965	35,347	3.98	4.07
WESTERN EUROPE	99,740	101,443	104,762	99,637	103,690	11.69	4.07
France	36,065	36,681	38,005	36,146	37,616	4.24	4.07
Germany	33,153	33,719	34,576	32,884	34,222	3.86	4.07
Netherlands	14,335	14,580	15,967	15,186	15,804	1.78	4.07
Switzerland	16,187	16,463	16,214	15,421	16,048	1.81	4.07
EAST MEDITERRANEAN EUROPE	29,424	29,926	30,529	29,035	30,216	3.41	4.07
Israel	29,424	29,926	30,529	29,035	30,216	3.41	4.07
OTHER EUROPE	48,878	49,712	49,283	46,872	48,779	5.50	4.07
Other countries of Europe	48,878	49,712	49,283	46,872	48,779	5.50	4.07

Yearbook of Tourism Statistics, Data 2009 – 2013, 2015 Edition

BOSNIA AND HERZEGOVINA

4. Arrivals of non-resident tourists in all types of accommodation establishments, by country of residence

	2009	2010	2011	2012	2013	Market share 2013	% Change 2013-2012
TOTAL	310,942	365,454	391,945	438,585	528,579	100.00	20.52
AFRICA					997	0.19	
SOUTHERN AFRICA					147	0.03	
South Africa					147	0.03	
OTHER AFRICA					850	0.16	
Other countries of Africa					850	0.16	
AMERICAS	8,126	10,389	10,411	11,947	18,548	3.51	55.25
NORTH AMERICA	8,126	10,389	10,411	11,947	13,862	2.62	16.03
Canada	1,462	2,150	1,874	2,204	3,019	0.57	36.98
United States of America	6,664	8,239	8,537	9,743	10,336	1.96	6.09
Other countries of North America					507	0.10	
SOUTH AMERICA					2,703	0.51	
Brazil					2,703	0.51	
OTHER AMERICAS					1,983	0.38	
Other countries of the Americas					1,983	0.38	
EAST ASIA AND THE PACIFIC	4,496	7,092	9,464	11,549	35,088	6.64	203.82
NORTH-EAST ASIA	2,379	3,741	5,445	6,795	20,630	3.90	203.61
China	478	770	2,244	3,369	5,642	1.07	67.47
Japan	1,901	2,971	3,201	3,426	3,396	0.64	-0.88
Korea, Republic of					11,592	2.19	
AUSTRALASIA	2,117	3,351	4,019	4,754	5,515	1.04	16.01
Australia	1,853	2,951	3,601	4,165	4,866	0.92	16.83
New Zealand	264	400	418	589	649	0.12	10.19
OTHER EAST ASIA AND THE PACIFIC					8,943	1.69	
Other countries of Asia					8,623	1.63	
Other countries of Oceania					320	0.06	
EUROPE	291,903	338,500	355,718	384,067	461,845	87.37	20.25
CENTRAL/EASTERN EUROPE	27,370	34,236	41,324	48,113	62,243	11.78	29.37
Bulgaria	1,654	1,632	2,133	2,573	4,377	0.83	70.11
Czech Republic	3,171	3,366	3,557	3,913	4,549	0.86	16.25
Estonia					356	0.07	
Hungary	5,124	4,906	5,415	5,920	6,498	1.23	9.76
Latvia					448	0.08	
Lithuania					1,208	0.23	
Poland	12,616	17,888	22,633	27,017	33,754	6.39	24.94
Romania	1,830	2,748	3,048	3,641	3,346	0.63	-8.10
Russian Federation	1,526	2,140	2,567	3,061	4,242	0.80	38.58
Slovakia	1,449	1,556	1,971	1,988	2,457	0.46	23.59
Ukraine					1,008	0.19	
NORTHERN EUROPE	14,406	17,318	17,456	18,056	24,154	4.57	33.77
Denmark	1,637	1,776	1,507	1,611	2,402	0.45	49.10
Finland	873	1,030	1,027	981	1,342	0.25	36.80
Iceland	155	97	82	188	176	0.03	-6.38
Ireland	983	2,638	1,897	1,428	1,604	0.30	12.32
Norway	2,332	2,493	2,438	2,259	3,917	0.74	73.40
Sweden	3,349	3,608	4,551	4,940	6,434	1.22	30.24
United Kingdom	5,077	5,676	5,954	6,649	8,279	1.57	24.51
SOUTHERN EUROPE	179,763	202,443	210,812	220,001	248,448	47.00	12.93
Albania	1,916	3,996	1,732	2,064	2,970	0.56	43.90
Croatia	50,838	56,100	64,028	72,587	82,176	15.55	13.21
Greece	2,214	2,824	3,623	3,190	4,952	0.94	55.24
Italy	15,443	23,749	26,379	26,137	29,319	5.55	12.17
Malta					737	0.14	
Montenegro	7,848	8,392	7,679	7,474	9,513	1.80	27.28
Portugal	840	961	1,119	795	927	0.18	16.60
Serbia	56,221	56,370	54,169	57,380	62,731	11.87	9.33
Slovenia	34,580	40,246	41,267	39,949	42,019	7.95	5.18
Spain	5,053	5,155	5,662	5,656	7,199	1.36	27.28
TFYR of Macedonia	4,810	4,650	5,154	4,769	5,905	1.12	23.82

94

BOSNIA AND HERZEGOVINA

4. Arrivals of non-resident tourists in all types of accommodation establishments, by country of residence

	2009	2010	2011	2012	2013	Market share 2013	% Change 2013-2012
WESTERN EUROPE	**50,840**	**53,532**	**53,830**	**57,473**	**65,814**	**12.45**	**14.51**
Austria	13,005	14,344	14,786	15,990	17,270	3.27	8.01
Belgium	2,401	2,110	1,835	2,138	3,077	0.58	43.92
France	9,291	10,734	9,609	10,141	11,434	2.16	12.75
Germany	17,813	17,281	18,220	19,581	21,226	4.02	8.40
Luxembourg	343	192	254	224	300	0.06	33.93
Netherlands	5,124	5,567	5,465	5,141	6,990	1.32	35.97
Switzerland	2,863	3,304	3,661	4,258	5,517	1.04	29.57
EAST MEDITERRANEAN EUROPE	**15,397**	**25,834**	**27,724**	**35,397**	**58,885**	**11.14**	**66.36**
Cyprus					317	0.06	
Israel	1,737	1,810	1,831	2,895	2,872	0.54	-0.79
Turkey	13,660	24,024	25,893	32,502	55,696	10.54	71.36
OTHER EUROPE	**4,127**	**5,137**	**4,572**	**5,027**	**2,301**	**0.44**	**-54.23**
Other countries of Europe	4,127	5,137	4,572	5,027	2,301	0.44	-54.23
MIDDLE EAST	**313**	**624**	**937**	**1,754**	**11,479**	**2.17**	**554.45**
Egypt	134	160	286	324	424	0.08	30.86
Kuwait					8,051	1.52	
Saudi Arabia	179	464	651	1,430	3,004	0.57	110.07
SOUTH ASIA	**206**	**253**	**167**	**163**	**622**	**0.12**	**281.60**
India					304	0.06	
Iran, Islamic Republic of	206	253	167	163	318	0.06	95.09
NOT SPECIFIED	**5,898**	**8,596**	**15,248**	**29,105**			
Other countries of the World	5,898	8,596	15,248	29,105			

Yearbook of Tourism Statistics, Data 2009 – 2013, 2015 Edition

BOSNIA AND HERZEGOVINA

6. Overnight stays of non-resident tourists in all types of accommodation establishments, by country of residence

	2009	2010	2011	2012	2013	Market share 2013	% Change 2013-2012
TOTAL	671,128	772,754	836,005	931,081	1,108,905	100.00	19.10
AFRICA					4,728	0.43	
SOUTHERN AFRICA					357	0.03	
South Africa					357	0.03	
OTHER AFRICA					4,371	0.39	
Other countries of Africa					4,371	0.39	
AMERICAS	23,040	26,540	24,145	25,425	38,931	3.51	53.12
NORTH AMERICA	23,040	26,540	24,145	25,425	29,958	2.70	17.83
Canada	3,496	4,159	3,599	4,538	5,882	0.53	29.62
United States of America	19,544	22,381	20,546	20,887	22,895	2.06	9.61
Other countries of North America					1,181	0.11	
SOUTH AMERICA					4,945	0.45	
Brazil					4,945	0.45	
OTHER AMERICAS					4,028	0.36	
Other countries of the Americas					4,028	0.36	
EAST ASIA AND THE PACIFIC	7,817	10,869	14,789	17,755	56,636	5.11	218.99
NORTH-EAST ASIA	4,210	5,523	8,438	10,000	25,153	2.27	151.53
China	934	1,255	3,874	4,880	7,221	0.65	47.97
Japan	3,276	4,268	4,564	5,120	5,181	0.47	1.19
Korea, Republic of					12,751	1.15	
AUSTRALASIA	3,607	5,346	6,351	7,755	9,560	0.86	23.28
Australia	3,143	4,815	5,744	6,918	8,604	0.78	24.37
New Zealand	464	531	607	837	956	0.09	14.22
OTHER EAST ASIA AND THE PACIFIC					21,923	1.98	
Other countries of Asia					21,454	1.93	
Other countries of Oceania					469	0.04	
EUROPE	620,832	708,598	758,494	807,045	962,661	86.81	19.28
CENTRAL/EASTERN EUROPE	71,731	95,613	116,052	127,820	146,630	13.22	14.72
Bulgaria	4,077	3,845	4,591	5,146	8,289	0.75	61.08
Czech Republic	9,744	10,387	11,015	9,757	11,488	1.04	17.74
Estonia					1,273	0.11	
Hungary	11,404	9,996	12,833	11,310	12,670	1.14	12.02
Latvia					698	0.06	
Lithuania					2,284	0.21	
Poland	33,467	54,989	65,853	75,009	80,796	7.29	7.72
Romania	4,576	6,545	9,253	9,709	7,315	0.66	-24.66
Russian Federation	4,889	6,300	7,699	12,549	14,662	1.32	16.84
Slovakia	3,574	3,551	4,808	4,340	4,712	0.42	8.57
Ukraine					2,443	0.22	
NORTHERN EUROPE	34,974	45,787	42,146	41,632	56,146	5.06	34.86
Denmark	4,117	4,359	3,670	3,692	6,649	0.60	80.09
Finland	1,984	2,046	2,428	1,872	2,762	0.25	47.54
Iceland	774	208	351	544	411	0.04	-24.45
Ireland	2,667	13,440	8,296	5,152	5,032	0.45	-2.33
Norway	4,612	5,125	5,278	5,238	8,404	0.76	60.44
Sweden	8,943	9,185	9,939	12,221	15,369	1.39	25.76
United Kingdom	11,877	11,424	12,184	12,913	17,519	1.58	35.67
SOUTHERN EUROPE	358,304	392,490	421,745	447,594	506,660	45.69	13.20
Albania	3,183	7,236	3,201	3,926	5,133	0.46	30.74
Croatia	93,601	104,863	130,326	150,814	169,940	15.33	12.68
Greece	4,718	8,128	6,625	6,094	8,886	0.80	45.82
Italy	32,685	49,113	54,485	56,001	62,659	5.65	11.89
Malta					5,049	0.46	
Montenegro	19,506	22,830	19,174	18,384	22,286	2.01	21.22
Portugal	2,129	2,132	2,325	1,885	2,062	0.19	9.39
Serbia	120,850	113,840	114,424	121,639	131,579	11.87	8.17
Slovenia	60,762	64,959	69,960	69,183	75,595	6.82	9.27
Spain	11,337	10,398	10,429	9,497	12,248	1.10	28.97
TFYR of Macedonia	9,533	8,991	10,796	10,171	11,223	1.01	10.34

Yearbook of Tourism Statistics, Data 2009 – 2013, 2015 Edition

BOSNIA AND HERZEGOVINA

6. Overnight stays of non-resident tourists in all types of accommodation establishments, by country of residence

	2009	2010	2011	2012	2013	Market share 2013	% Change 2013-2012
WESTERN EUROPE	**112,843**	**115,270**	**115,108**	**115,325**	**137,342**	**12.39**	**19.09**
Austria	22,734	25,229	27,885	28,620	30,940	2.79	8.11
Belgium	5,751	5,180	4,426	4,377	7,481	0.67	70.92
France	24,835	28,476	24,882	22,399	26,904	2.43	20.11
Germany	40,944	36,925	37,627	38,968	44,710	4.03	14.74
Luxembourg	693	396	810	610	731	0.07	19.84
Netherlands	11,840	12,531	12,142	11,190	15,309	1.38	36.81
Switzerland	6,046	6,533	7,336	9,161	11,267	1.02	22.99
EAST MEDITERRANEAN EUROPE	**34,837**	**48,795**	**53,893**	**63,791**	**110,589**	**9.97**	**73.36**
Cyprus					586	0.05	
Israel	2,900	3,446	3,483	4,823	4,651	0.42	-3.57
Turkey	31,937	45,349	50,410	58,968	105,352	9.50	78.66
OTHER EUROPE	**8,143**	**10,643**	**9,550**	**10,883**	**5,294**	**0.48**	**-51.36**
Other countries of Europe	8,143	10,643	9,550	10,883	5,294	0.48	-51.36
MIDDLE EAST	**1,048**	**1,689**	**2,762**	**5,081**	**44,333**	**4.00**	**772.53**
Egypt	381	545	763	986	1,517	0.14	53.85
Kuwait					34,120	3.08	
Saudi Arabia	667	1,144	1,999	4,095	8,696	0.78	112.36
SOUTH ASIA	**580**	**577**	**526**	**514**	**1,616**	**0.15**	**214.40**
India					770	0.07	
Iran, Islamic Republic of	580	577	526	514	846	0.08	64.59
NOT SPECIFIED	**17,811**	**24,481**	**35,289**	**75,261**			
Other countries of the World	17,811	24,481	35,289	75,261			

Yearbook of Tourism Statistics, Data 2009 – 2013, 2015 Edition

BRAZIL

1. Arrivals of non-resident tourists at national borders, by country of residence

	2009	2010	2011	2012	2013	Market share 2013	% Change 2013-2012
TOTAL	4,802,217	5,161,379	5,433,354	5,676,843	5,813,342	100.00	2.40
AFRICA	78,110	83,688	86,511	92,349	94,832	1.63	2.69
CENTRAL AFRICA	36,123	38,051	37,221	37,779	38,587	0.66	2.14
Angola	36,123	38,051	37,221	37,779	38,587	0.66	2.14
SOUTHERN AFRICA	23,132	21,311	22,754	23,047	21,212	0.36	-7.96
South Africa	23,132	21,311	22,754	23,047	21,212	0.36	-7.96
WEST AFRICA	6,108	5,391	5,993	6,898	7,076	0.12	2.58
Cabo Verde	4,233	2,664	2,736	3,235	3,158	0.05	-2.38
Nigeria	1,875	2,727	3,257	3,663	3,918	0.07	6.96
OTHER AFRICA	12,747	18,935	20,543	24,625	27,957	0.48	13.53
Other countries of Africa	12,747	18,935	20,543	24,625	27,957	0.48	13.53
AMERICAS	2,862,171	3,196,300	3,401,592	3,582,256	3,726,448	64.10	4.03
CARIBBEAN	3,550	4,004	4,246	4,292	4,940	0.08	15.10
Cuba	3,550	4,004	4,246	4,292	4,940	0.08	15.10
CENTRAL AMERICA	28,271	34,929	38,633	38,862	47,580	0.82	22.43
Costa Rica	8,539	9,792	10,125	10,284	11,771	0.20	14.46
Guatemala	3,725	5,136	5,453	5,294	6,497	0.11	22.72
Panama	5,153	6,424	7,344	7,496	8,512	0.15	13.55
Other countries of Central America	10,854	13,577	15,711	15,788	20,800	0.36	31.75
NORTH AMERICA	734,998	773,181	729,756	716,583	737,175	12.68	2.87
Canada	63,296	64,188	70,358	68,462	67,610	1.16	-1.24
Mexico	68,028	67,616	64,451	61,658	76,738	1.32	24.46
United States of America	603,674	641,377	594,947	586,463	592,827	10.20	1.09
SOUTH AMERICA	2,095,352	2,384,186	2,628,957	2,822,519	2,936,753	50.52	4.05
Argentina	1,211,159	1,399,592	1,593,775	1,671,604	1,711,491	29.44	2.39
Bolivia	83,454	99,359	85,429	112,639	95,028	1.63	-15.63
Chile	170,491	200,724	217,200	250,586	268,203	4.61	7.03
Colombia	78,010	85,567	91,345	100,324	116,461	2.00	16.08
Ecuador	26,220	23,095	25,495	26,462	29,324	0.50	10.82
French Guiana	15,152	12,592	9,457	9,278	10,175	0.18	9.67
Guyana	4,594	5,236	4,314	3,400	4,286	0.07	26.06
Paraguay	180,373	194,340	192,730	246,401	268,932	4.63	9.14
Peru	78,975	81,020	86,795	91,996	98,602	1.70	7.18
Suriname	3,626	2,930	3,952	4,859	3,430	0.06	-29.41
Uruguay	189,412	228,545	261,204	253,864	262,512	4.52	3.41
Venezuela	53,886	51,186	57,261	51,106	68,309	1.18	33.66
EAST ASIA AND THE PACIFIC	208,379	210,582	260,642	294,228	299,432	5.15	1.77
NORTH-EAST ASIA	119,025	128,450	163,855	189,036	191,704	3.30	1.41
China	28,230	37,849	55,978	65,945	60,140	1.03	-8.80
Japan	66,655	59,742	63,247	73,102	87,225	1.50	19.32
Korea, Republic of	24,140	30,859	44,630	49,989	44,339	0.76	-11.30
AUSTRALASIA	48,186	45,982	44,451	52,503	53,952	0.93	2.76
Australia	38,756	36,846	35,642	43,161	45,079	0.78	4.44
New Zealand	9,430	9,136	8,809	9,342	8,873	0.15	-5.02
OTHER EAST ASIA AND THE PACIFIC	41,168	36,150	52,336	52,689	53,776	0.93	2.06
Other countries of Asia	41,059	35,830	52,130	52,377	53,447	0.92	2.04
Other countries of Oceania	109	320	206	312	329	0.01	5.45
EUROPE	1,642,070	1,651,840	1,662,829	1,685,728	1,669,697	28.72	-0.95
CENTRAL/EASTERN EUROPE	35,913	40,224	50,601	56,170	62,044	1.07	10.46
Czech Republic	5,258	5,732	6,774	7,657	8,066	0.14	5.34
Hungary	5,525	4,854	5,045	5,240	5,713	0.10	9.03
Poland	15,092	13,775	16,427	18,132	22,727	0.39	25.34
Russian Federation	10,038	15,863	22,355	25,141	25,538	0.44	1.58
NORTHERN EUROPE	297,534	280,480	267,938	274,391	284,133	4.89	3.55
Denmark	25,645	21,460	22,208	22,780	21,261	0.37	-6.67
Finland	15,873	13,251	13,049	11,994	12,258	0.21	2.20
Ireland	17,620	16,475	16,871	18,457	19,352	0.33	4.85
Norway	29,339	27,793	30,462	30,319	28,069	0.48	-7.42
Sweden	36,414	34,146	35,784	35,293	33,461	0.58	-5.19

Yearbook of Tourism Statistics, Data 2009 – 2013, 2015 Edition

BRAZIL

1. Arrivals of non-resident tourists at national borders, by country of residence

	2009	2010	2011	2012	2013	Market share 2013	% Change 2013-2012
United Kingdom	172,643	167,355	149,564	155,548	169,732	2.92	9.12
SOUTHERN EUROPE	**619,318**	**621,433**	**610,027**	**585,512**	**577,548**	**9.93**	**-1.36**
Greece	7,550	7,537	6,423	6,343	6,304	0.11	-0.61
Italy	253,545	245,491	229,484	230,114	233,243	4.01	1.36
Portugal	183,697	189,065	183,728	168,649	168,250	2.89	-0.24
Spain	174,526	179,340	190,392	180,406	169,751	2.92	-5.91
WESTERN EUROPE	**625,420**	**633,388**	**647,075**	**681,971**	**657,445**	**11.31**	**-3.60**
Austria	24,185	26,603	26,560	28,035	25,929	0.45	-7.51
Belgium	31,526	34,030	32,773	34,169	33,356	0.57	-2.38
France	205,860	199,719	207,890	218,626	224,078	3.85	2.49
Germany	215,595	226,630	241,739	258,437	236,505	4.07	-8.49
Netherlands	75,518	76,411	72,162	73,133	69,187	1.19	-5.40
Switzerland	72,736	69,995	65,951	69,571	68,390	1.18	-1.70
EAST MEDITERRANEAN EUROPE	**29,405**	**36,976**	**41,646**	**33,523**	**33,128**	**0.57**	**-1.18**
Israel	29,405	36,976	41,646	33,523	33,128	0.57	-1.18
OTHER EUROPE	**34,480**	**39,339**	**45,542**	**54,161**	**55,399**	**0.95**	**2.29**
Other countries of Europe	34,480	39,339	45,542	54,161	55,399	0.95	2.29
SOUTH ASIA	**11,361**	**18,829**	**21,530**	**22,096**	**22,719**	**0.39**	**2.82**
India	11,361	18,829	21,530	22,096	22,719	0.39	2.82
NOT SPECIFIED	**126**	**140**	**250**	**186**	**214**	**0.00**	**15.05**
Other countries of the World	126	140	250	186	214	0.00	15.05

 Yearbook of Tourism Statistics, Data 2009 – 2013, 2015 Edition

BRITISH VIRGIN ISLANDS

1. Arrivals of non-resident tourists at national borders, by country of residence

	2009	2010	2011	2012	2013	Market share 2013	% Change 2013-2012
TOTAL	308,793	330,343	337,773	351,404	366,108	100.00	4.18
AFRICA	982	1,235	1,445	1,002	1,202	0.33	19.96
EAST AFRICA	27	31	41	18	31	0.01	72.22
British Indian Ocean Territory			2		2	0.00	
Comoros	5	7	6		4	0.00	
Ethiopia			3	1	3	0.00	200.00
Kenya	4	2	4		4	0.00	
Seychelles				1			
Uganda	4	4	6	4	4	0.00	
Zimbabwe	14	18	20	12	14	0.00	16.67
CENTRAL AFRICA	11	24	18	3	6	0.00	100.00
Cameroon	11	24	12	3	6	0.00	100.00
Congo			6				
NORTH AFRICA	1	1	9	14	10	0.00	-28.57
Algeria			6	8	4	0.00	-50.00
Morocco	1	1	3	5	4	0.00	-20.00
Tunisia				1	2	0.00	100.00
SOUTHERN AFRICA	931	1,162	1,339	940	1,102	0.30	17.23
Botswana		2	4		2	0.00	
Namibia	2		3	5	3	0.00	-40.00
South Africa	891	1,077	1,263	856	1,006	0.27	17.52
Swaziland	38	83	69	79	91	0.02	15.19
WEST AFRICA	12	17	38	27	53	0.01	96.30
Benin	8	10	14		14	0.00	
Côte d'Ivoire	2		5		6	0.00	
Gambia				1			
Ghana	2	4	4		8	0.00	
Liberia			6	4	8	0.00	100.00
Nigeria			3	18	16	0.00	-11.11
Senegal				4	1	0.00	-75.00
Togo		3	6				
AMERICAS	280,607	299,399	300,507	315,693	321,426	87.80	1.82
CARIBBEAN	55,073	59,550	58,766	77,149	80,249	21.92	4.02
Anguilla	125	207	99	405	413	0.11	1.98
Antigua and Barbuda	1,375	1,440	955	1,818	921	0.25	-49.34
Aruba	22	58	14	50	38	0.01	-24.00
Bahamas	14	30	58	130	56	0.02	-56.92
Barbados	923	971	198	927	989	0.27	6.69
Bermuda	32	56	76	120	138	0.04	15.00
Bonaire	27	32	22	17	37	0.01	117.65
British Virgin Islands	128	117	178	239	154	0.04	-35.56
Cayman Islands	98	154	210	266	298	0.08	12.03
Cuba	8	10	6	4	14	0.00	250.00
Curaçao	52	62	28	118	152	0.04	28.81
Dominica	434	502	362	1,294	1,061	0.29	-18.01
Dominican Republic	232	403	255	584	732	0.20	25.34
Grenada	503	532	232	452	648	0.18	43.36
Guadeloupe	119	144	107	170	182	0.05	7.06
Haiti	80	64	14	28	42	0.01	50.00
Jamaica	448	379	167	713	947	0.26	32.82
Martinique	38	53	98	43	98	0.03	127.91
Montserrat	47	19	9	37	22	0.01	-40.54
Netherlands Antilles	681	785	576	471	891	0.24	89.17
Puerto Rico	5,890	6,628	5,363	13,126	14,827	4.05	12.96
Saint Kitts and Nevis	295	307	334	1,787	1,788	0.49	0.06
Saint Lucia	715	764	174	713	695	0.19	-2.52
Saint Vincent and the Grenadines	1,758	1,884	529		819	0.22	

Yearbook of Tourism Statistics, Data 2009 – 2013, 2015 Edition

BRITISH VIRGIN ISLANDS

1. Arrivals of non-resident tourists at national borders, by country of residence

	2009	2010	2011	2012	2013	Market share 2013	% Change 2013-2012
Sint Maarten	257	241	235	481	503	0.14	4.57
Trinidad and Tobago	1,420	1,484	307	1,040	1,352	0.37	30.00
Turks and Caicos Islands	12	8	6	24	30	0.01	25.00
United States Virgin Islands	39,340	42,216	48,154	52,092	52,402	14.31	0.60
CENTRAL AMERICA	**300**	**387**	**472**	**621**	**642**	**0.18**	**3.38**
Belize	12	13	14	25	30	0.01	20.00
Costa Rica	56	60	70	50	53	0.01	6.00
El Salvador	26	23	28	21	42	0.01	100.00
Guatemala	39	49	54	59	49	0.01	-16.95
Honduras	49	72	82	159	149	0.04	-6.29
Nicaragua	6	5	6	36	24	0.01	-33.33
Panama	112	165	218	271	295	0.08	8.86
NORTH AMERICA	**221,913**	**235,866**	**238,552**	**233,962**	**236,388**	**64.57**	**1.04**
Canada	9,725	11,599	15,844	16,030	17,522	4.79	9.31
Greenland		8		7	14	0.00	100.00
Mexico	419	446	433	420	485	0.13	15.48
United States of America	211,769	223,813	222,263	217,476	218,345	59.64	0.40
Other countries of North America			12	29	22	0.01	-24.14
SOUTH AMERICA	**3,321**	**3,596**	**2,717**	**3,961**	**4,147**	**1.13**	**4.70**
Argentina	818	832	960	874	906	0.25	3.66
Bolivia	8	14		13	8	0.00	-38.46
Brazil	903	951	947	795	819	0.22	3.02
Chile	176	218	224	526	582	0.16	10.65
Colombia	16	17	34	139	176	0.05	26.62
Ecuador	12	21	30	39	12	0.00	-69.23
Guyana	824	858	104	618	690	0.19	11.65
Paraguay	94	40	14	68	83	0.02	22.06
Peru	174	212	112	274	212	0.06	-22.63
Suriname	22	10		8	8	0.00	
Uruguay	106	173	60	293	319	0.09	8.87
Venezuela	168	250	232	314	332	0.09	5.73
EAST ASIA AND THE PACIFIC	**3,193**	**3,457**	**3,495**	**2,760**	**3,752**	**1.02**	**35.94**
NORTH-EAST ASIA	**130**	**165**	**204**	**245**	**315**	**0.09**	**28.57**
China	28	24	22	20	30	0.01	50.00
Hong Kong, China	12	32	20	72	83	0.02	15.28
Japan	78	92	136	122	164	0.04	34.43
Korea, Dem. People's Republic of			2	5			
Korea, Republic of				9			
Mongolia			6	3	12	0.00	300.00
Taiwan, Province of China	12	17	18	14	26	0.01	85.71
SOUTH-EAST ASIA	**183**	**285**	**346**	**272**	**390**	**0.11**	**43.38**
Indonesia	6	6	10	7	16	0.00	128.57
Malaysia	2		2	11	16	0.00	45.45
Philippines	139	251	304	213	295	0.08	38.50
Singapore	18	8	6	20	36	0.01	80.00
Thailand	18	20	24	21	27	0.01	28.57
AUSTRALASIA	**2,863**	**2,989**	**2,909**	**2,228**	**3,027**	**0.83**	**35.86**
Australia	1,936	2,054	1,972	1,890	2,054	0.56	8.68
New Zealand	927	935	937	338	973	0.27	187.87
MELANESIA	**10**	**12**	**15**	**15**	**12**	**0.00**	**-20.00**
Fiji	10	12	13	12	8	0.00	-33.33
Vanuatu			2	3	4	0.00	33.33
MICRONESIA				**10**			
Christmas Island, Australia				6			
Kiribati				4			
POLYNESIA	**7**	**6**	**11**		**8**	**0.00**	
French Polynesia	1		3		2	0.00	
Wallis and Futuna Islands	6	6	8		6	0.00	

Yearbook of Tourism Statistics, Data 2009 – 2013, 2015 Edition

BRITISH VIRGIN ISLANDS

1. Arrivals of non-resident tourists at national borders, by country of residence

	2009	2010	2011	2012	2013	Market share 2013	% Change 2013-2012
EUROPE	**23,329**	**25,840**	**31,797**	**31,730**	**39,445**	**10.77**	**24.31**
CENTRAL/EASTERN EUROPE	**779**	**790**	**1,421**	**743**	**1,011**	**0.28**	**36.07**
Bulgaria	29	81	67	29	105	0.03	262.07
Czech Republic/Slovakia	115	136	174	133	115	0.03	-13.53
Estonia	20	16		22	18	0.00	-18.18
Hungary	109	127	133	139	128	0.03	-7.91
Latvia	1			1			
Lithuania	2	6	8	8	12	0.00	50.00
Poland	282	258	746	234	282	0.08	20.51
Romania	42	47	52	57	62	0.02	8.77
Russian Federation	159	103	199	99	247	0.07	149.49
Ukraine	20	16	42	21	42	0.01	100.00
NORTHERN EUROPE	**10,349**	**12,353**	**15,786**	**16,311**	**20,994**	**5.73**	**28.71**
Denmark	972	870	968	866	1,070	0.29	23.56
Faeroe Islands	12	20	29		31	0.01	
Finland	142	147	337	132	237	0.06	79.55
Iceland	39	26	52	25	33	0.01	32.00
Ireland	280	268	240	400	411	0.11	2.75
Norway	897	947	1,397	847	1,447	0.40	70.84
Sweden	589	632	1,180	548	1,761	0.48	221.35
United Kingdom	7,418	9,443	11,468	13,493	16,004	4.37	18.61
United Kingdom/Ireland			115				
SOUTHERN EUROPE	**1,846**	**2,103**	**2,314**	**2,367**	**2,874**	**0.79**	**21.42**
Andorra	4			4			
Croatia	17	24	30	25	17	0.00	-32.00
Greece	50	64	78	85	78	0.02	-8.24
Italy	895	1,056	1,378	1,539	1,713	0.47	11.31
Malta	18	28	39	50	57	0.02	14.00
Portugal	19	10	39	68	77	0.02	13.24
San Marino				3			
Spain	820	921	706	593	932	0.25	57.17
Yugoslavia, SFR (former)	23		44				
WESTERN EUROPE	**10,281**	**10,506**	**11,969**	**12,182**	**14,430**	**3.94**	**18.45**
Austria	195	188	271	454	461	0.13	1.54
Belgium	358	370	482	538	524	0.14	-2.60
France	5,347	5,901	6,486	7,009	7,503	2.05	7.05
Germany	2,834	2,275	2,747	2,159	3,398	0.93	57.39
Liechtenstein	20	29		30	53	0.01	76.67
Luxembourg	48	40	44	57	64	0.02	12.28
Monaco	24	55	66	37	31	0.01	-16.22
Netherlands	576	733	890	1,047	1,413	0.39	34.96
Switzerland	879	915	983	851	983	0.27	15.51
EAST MEDITERRANEAN EUROPE	**74**	**88**	**307**	**127**	**136**	**0.04**	**7.09**
Cyprus	4		6	22	16	0.00	-27.27
Israel	42	56	257	63	57	0.02	-9.52
Turkey	28	32	44	42	63	0.02	50.00
MIDDLE EAST	**77**	**94**	**102**	**82**	**90**	**0.02**	**9.76**
Bahrain		2	2		2	0.00	
Egypt	8	4	6	5	10	0.00	100.00
Jordan		1	2	1	5	0.00	400.00
Kuwait	6	2	2	4			
Lebanon	16	20		30	24	0.01	-20.00
Qatar	29	52	60	37	41	0.01	10.81
Saudi Arabia	18	13	24	5			
United Arab Emirates			6		8	0.00	

Yearbook of Tourism Statistics, Data 2009 – 2013, 2015 Edition

BRITISH VIRGIN ISLANDS

1. Arrivals of non-resident tourists at national borders, by country of residence

	2009	2010	2011	2012	2013	Market share 2013	% Change 2013-2012
SOUTH ASIA	**140**	**178**	**187**	**137**	**193**	**0.05**	**40.88**
Bangladesh	10	19	16		12	0.00	
India	74	82	89	84	94	0.03	11.90
Maldives			1				
Nepal	46	62	78	36	63	0.02	75.00
Pakistan	4			5			
Sri Lanka	6	15	3	12	24	0.01	100.00
NOT SPECIFIED	**465**	**140**	**240**				
Other countries of the World	465	140	240				

Yearbook of Tourism Statistics, Data 2009 – 2013, 2015 Edition

BRITISH VIRGIN ISLANDS

2. Arrivals of non-resident visitors at national borders, by country of residence

	2009	2010	2011	2012	2013	Market share 2013	% Change 2013-2012
TOTAL	856,864	842,497	831,435	753,148	741,847	100.00	-1.50
AFRICA	2,725	3,150	3,557	2,148	2,435	0.33	13.36
EAST AFRICA	75	79	101	39	63	0.01	61.54
All countries of East Africa	75	79	101	39	63	0.01	61.54
CENTRAL AFRICA	31	61	44	6	12	0.00	100.00
All countries of Central Africa	31	61	44	6	12	0.00	100.00
NORTH AFRICA	3	3	22	30	20	0.00	-33.33
All countries of North Africa	3	3	22	30	20	0.00	-33.33
SOUTHERN AFRICA	2,583	2,964	3,296	2,015	2,233	0.30	10.82
All countries of Southern Africa	2,583	2,964	3,296	2,015	2,233	0.30	10.82
WEST AFRICA	33	43	94	58	107	0.01	84.48
All countries of West Africa	33	43	94	58	107	0.01	84.48
AMERICAS	778,652	763,578	739,703	676,610	651,308	87.80	-3.74
CARIBBEAN	152,822	151,875	144,654	165,350	162,609	21.92	-1.66
All countries of the Caribbean	152,822	151,875	144,654	165,350	162,609	21.92	-1.66
CENTRAL AMERICA	832	987	1,162	1,331	1,301	0.18	-2.25
All countries of Central America	832	987	1,162	1,331	1,301	0.18	-2.25
NORTH AMERICA	615,783	601,545	587,199	501,440	478,995	64.57	-4.48
Canada	26,986	29,582	39,000	34,356	35,505	4.79	3.34
United States of America	587,634	570,806	547,104	466,106	442,434	59.64	-5.08
Other countries of North America	1,163	1,157	1,095	978	1,056	0.14	7.98
SOUTH AMERICA	9,215	9,171	6,688	8,489	8,403	1.13	-1.01
All countries of South America	9,215	9,171	6,688	8,489	8,403	1.13	-1.01
EAST ASIA AND THE PACIFIC	8,860	8,817	8,604	5,915	7,603	1.02	28.54
NORTH-EAST ASIA	361	421	502	525	638	0.09	21.52
All north-east Asia	361	421	502	525	638	0.09	21.52
SOUTH-EAST ASIA	508	727	852	583	790	0.11	35.51
All countries of South-East Asia	508	727	852	583	790	0.11	35.51
AUSTRALASIA	7,944	7,623	7,161	4,775	6,134	0.83	28.46
Australia, New Zealand	7,944	7,623	7,161	4,775	6,134	0.83	28.46
MELANESIA	28	31	37	32	24	0.00	-25.00
All countries of Melanesia	28	31	37	32	24	0.00	-25.00
MICRONESIA				25			
All countries of Micronesia				25			
POLYNESIA	19	15	27		17	0.00	
All countries of Polynesia	19	15	27		17	0.00	
EUROPE	64,735	65,901	78,269	68,005	79,928	10.77	17.53
CENTRAL/EASTERN EUROPE	2,162	2,015	3,498	1,592	2,048	0.28	28.64
All countries Central/East Europe	2,162	2,015	3,498	1,592	2,048	0.28	28.64
NORTHERN EUROPE	28,717	31,505	38,857	34,959	42,540	5.73	21.69
All countries of Northern Europe	28,717	31,505	38,857	34,959	42,540	5.73	21.69
SOUTHERN EUROPE	5,122	5,363	5,696	5,073	5,824	0.79	14.80
All countries of Southern Europe	5,122	5,363	5,696	5,073	5,824	0.79	14.80
WESTERN EUROPE	28,529	26,794	29,462	26,109	29,240	3.94	11.99
All countries of Western Europe	28,529	26,794	29,462	26,109	29,240	3.94	11.99
OTHER EUROPE	205	224	756	272	276	0.04	1.47
Other countries of Europe	205	224	756	272	276	0.04	1.47
MIDDLE EAST	214	240	251	176	182	0.02	3.41
All countries of Middle East	214	240	251	176	182	0.02	3.41
SOUTH ASIA	388	454	460	294	391	0.05	32.99
All countries of South Asia	388	454	460	294	391	0.05	32.99
NOT SPECIFIED	1,290	357	591				
Other countries of the World	1,290	357	591				

Yearbook of Tourism Statistics, Data 2009 – 2013, 2015 Edition

BRUNEI DARUSSALAM

1. Arrivals of non-resident tourists at national borders, by nationality

	2009	2010	2011	2012	2013	Market share 2013	% Change 2013-2012
TOTAL (*)	157,474	214,290	242,061	209,108	224,904	100.00	7.55
AMERICAS	5,108	5,940	6,611	6,304	7,605	3.38	20.64
NORTH AMERICA	5,108	5,940	6,611	6,304	7,605	3.38	20.64
Canada	1,940	2,199	2,411	2,237	2,443	1.09	9.21
United States of America	3,168	3,741	4,200	4,067	5,162	2.30	26.92
EAST ASIA AND THE PACIFIC	121,652	170,555	194,809	169,641	180,547	80.28	6.43
NORTH-EAST ASIA	23,637	33,055	41,397	40,227	42,331	18.82	5.23
China	15,800	24,579	32,853	27,490	30,481	13.55	10.88
Hong Kong, China	1,197	1,210	1,270	1,601	1,869	0.83	16.74
Japan	3,549	3,637	4,140	4,310	5,747	2.56	33.34
Korea, Republic of	1,604	1,712	1,696	4,277	2,344	1.04	-45.20
Taiwan, Province of China	1,487	1,917	1,438	2,549	1,890	0.84	-25.85
SOUTH-EAST ASIA	75,955	109,939	124,186	115,902	122,722	54.57	5.88
Cambodia	133	251	227	216	774	0.34	258.33
Indonesia	8,576	16,343	20,350	18,245	18,109	8.05	-0.75
Lao People's Democratic Republic	44	106	123	165	664	0.30	302.42
Malaysia	38,193	54,127	61,470	56,214	57,476	25.56	2.24
Myanmar	300	529	522	570	1,050	0.47	84.21
Philippines	11,013	14,720	17,446	19,189	18,868	8.39	-1.67
Singapore	14,221	15,973	16,221	15,933	17,819	7.92	11.84
Thailand	3,390	4,589	4,809	3,997	6,063	2.70	51.69
Viet Nam	85	3,301	3,018	1,373	1,899	0.84	38.31
AUSTRALASIA	22,060	27,561	29,226	13,512	15,494	6.89	14.67
Australia	13,824	17,237	18,845	11,877	13,823	6.15	16.38
New Zealand	8,236	10,324	10,381	1,635	1,671	0.74	2.20
EUROPE	21,553	26,199	28,581	20,837	22,899	10.18	9.90
CENTRAL/EASTERN EUROPE	705	989	1,009	934	1,409	0.63	50.86
Czech Republic	355	305	228	104	167	0.07	60.58
Poland	155	297	352	351	462	0.21	31.62
Russian Federation	195	387	429	479	780	0.35	62.84
NORTHERN EUROPE	15,687	18,834	20,203	12,960	14,121	6.28	8.96
Denmark	276	343	363	256	268	0.12	4.69
Finland	129	145	151	234	190	0.08	-18.80
Ireland	322	379	699	376	352	0.16	-6.38
Norway	261	250	400	339	810	0.36	138.94
Sweden	313	301	368	354	339	0.15	-4.24
United Kingdom	14,386	17,416	18,222	11,401	12,162	5.41	6.67
SOUTHERN EUROPE	847	1,162	1,293	1,080	1,100	0.49	1.85
Greece	40	91	81	91	50	0.02	-45.05
Italy	467	524	676	561	603	0.27	7.49
Portugal	107	184	218	128	122	0.05	-4.69
Spain	233	363	318	300	325	0.14	8.33
WESTERN EUROPE	4,314	5,214	6,076	5,863	6,269	2.79	6.92
Austria	89	88	86	128	120	0.05	-6.25
Belgium	192	219	219	197	170	0.08	-13.71
France	1,195	1,315	2,301	1,780	2,172	0.97	22.02
Germany	1,520	1,713	1,819	1,706	1,890	0.84	10.79
Netherlands	1,081	1,127	1,332	1,437	1,599	0.71	11.27
Switzerland	237	752	319	615	318	0.14	-48.29
MIDDLE EAST	711	1,571	1,527	819	670	0.30	-18.19
Bahrain	42	51	34	36	21	0.01	-41.67
Kuwait	48	58	53	67	66	0.03	-1.49
Oman	160	174	266	242	243	0.11	0.41
Qatar	14	19	20	94	15	0.01	-84.04
Saudi Arabia	261	1,021	837	180	177	0.08	-1.67
United Arab Emirates	186	248	317	200	148	0.07	-26.00

105

BRUNEI DARUSSALAM

1. Arrivals of non-resident tourists at national borders, by nationality

	2009	2010	2011	2012	2013	Market share 2013	% Change 2013-2012
SOUTH ASIA	**4,451**	**7,241**	**7,573**	**7,782**	**9,558**	**4.25**	**22.82**
Bangladesh	387	844	1,004	996	1,365	0.61	37.05
India	2,879	4,904	4,616	5,104	6,281	2.79	23.06
Nepal	483	597	986	677	878	0.39	29.69
Pakistan	474	607	579	509	537	0.24	5.50
Sri Lanka	228	289	388	496	497	0.22	0.20
NOT SPECIFIED	**3,999**	**2,784**	**2,960**	**3,725**	**3,625**	**1.61**	**-2.68**
Other countries of the World	3,999	2,784	2,960	3,725	3,625	1.61	-2.68

Yearbook of Tourism Statistics, Data 2009 – 2013, 2015 Edition

BRUNEI DARUSSALAM

2. Arrivals of non-resident visitors at national borders, by nationality

	2009	2010	2011	2012	2013	Market share 2013	% Change 2013-2012
TOTAL (*)					3,279,160	100.00	
AMERICAS					17,377	0.53	
NORTH AMERICA					17,377	0.53	
Canada					7,971	0.24	
United States of America					9,406	0.29	
EAST ASIA AND THE PACIFIC					3,142,513	95.83	
NORTH-EAST ASIA					60,458	1.84	
China					39,860	1.22	
Hong Kong, China					2,311	0.07	
Japan					9,039	0.28	
Korea, Republic of					4,836	0.15	
Taiwan, Province of China					4,412	0.13	
SOUTH-EAST ASIA					3,053,529	93.12	
Cambodia					991	0.03	
Indonesia					237,194	7.23	
Lao People's Democratic Republic					928	0.03	
Malaysia					2,623,621	80.01	
Myanmar					2,144	0.07	
Philippines					130,127	3.97	
Singapore					32,943	1.00	
Thailand					19,861	0.61	
Viet Nam					5,720	0.17	
AUSTRALASIA					28,526	0.87	
Australia					22,628	0.69	
New Zealand					5,898	0.18	
EUROPE					68,233	2.08	
CENTRAL/EASTERN EUROPE					2,456	0.07	
Czech Republic					370	0.01	
Poland					941	0.03	
Russian Federation					1,145	0.03	
NORTHERN EUROPE					35,007	1.07	
Denmark					509	0.02	
Finland					344	0.01	
Ireland					787	0.02	
Norway					2,732	0.08	
Sweden					763	0.02	
United Kingdom					29,872	0.91	
SOUTHERN EUROPE					2,076	0.06	
Greece					121	0.00	
Italy					1,106	0.03	
Portugal					241	0.01	
Spain					608	0.02	
WESTERN EUROPE					28,694	0.88	
Austria					863	0.03	
Belgium					417	0.01	
France					3,867	0.12	
Germany					17,811	0.54	
Netherlands					4,937	0.15	
Switzerland					799	0.02	
MIDDLE EAST					1,685	0.05	
Bahrain					24	0.00	
Kuwait					110	0.00	
Oman					1,077	0.03	
Qatar					19	0.00	
Saudi Arabia					270	0.01	
United Arab Emirates					185	0.01	

Yearbook of Tourism Statistics, Data 2009 – 2013, 2015 Edition

BRUNEI DARUSSALAM

2. Arrivals of non-resident visitors at national borders, by nationality

	2009	2010	2011	2012	2013	Market share 2013	% Change 2013-2012
SOUTH ASIA					**40,531**	**1.24**	
Bangladesh					2,534	0.08	
India					30,321	0.92	
Nepal					4,006	0.12	
Pakistan					2,760	0.08	
Sri Lanka					910	0.03	
NOT SPECIFIED					**8,821**	**0.27**	
Other countries of the World					8,821	0.27	

Yearbook of Tourism Statistics, Data 2009 – 2013, 2015 Edition

BULGARIA

2. Arrivals of non-resident visitors at national borders, by country of residence

	2009	2010	2011	2012	2013	Market share 2013	% Change 2013-2012
TOTAL	7,872,805	8,374,034	8,712,821	8,866,552	9,191,782	100.00	3.67
AFRICA	2,242	2,452	2,323	2,608	5,922	0.06	127.07
EAST AFRICA	25	54	39	80	376	0.00	370.00
Ethiopia	25	54	39	80	57	0.00	-28.75
Kenya					159	0.00	
Mozambique					32	0.00	
Uganda					24	0.00	
United Republic of Tanzania					35	0.00	
Zimbabwe					69	0.00	
CENTRAL AFRICA					275	0.00	
Angola					50	0.00	
Cameroon					128	0.00	
Congo					17	0.00	
Democratic Republic of the Congo					51	0.00	
Equatorial Guinea					29	0.00	
NORTH AFRICA	1,695	1,921	1,876	1,931	2,663	0.03	37.91
Algeria	425	499	457	506	742	0.01	46.64
Morocco	686	617	614	841	1,064	0.01	26.52
Sudan	126	130	346	147	124	0.00	-15.65
Tunisia	458	675	459	437	733	0.01	67.73
SOUTHERN AFRICA					1,592	0.02	
South Africa					1,592	0.02	
WEST AFRICA	522	477	408	597	1,016	0.01	70.18
Benin					23	0.00	
Ghana	107	116	66	83	101	0.00	21.69
Mali					11	0.00	
Nigeria	415	361	342	514	881	0.01	71.40
AMERICAS	82,101	83,617	87,722	93,603	101,895	1.11	8.86
CARIBBEAN	402	334	279	357	338	0.00	-5.32
Cuba	402	334	279	357	338	0.00	-5.32
CENTRAL AMERICA					549	0.01	
Belize					4	0.00	
Costa Rica					219	0.00	
Honduras					165	0.00	
Nicaragua					58	0.00	
Panama					103	0.00	
NORTH AMERICA	77,406	78,787	82,095	87,596	92,083	1.00	5.12
Canada	13,262	14,260	14,849	16,061	17,082	0.19	6.36
Mexico	1,438	1,745	1,763	2,212	2,392	0.03	8.14
United States of America	62,706	62,782	65,483	69,323	72,609	0.79	4.74
SOUTH AMERICA	4,293	4,496	5,348	5,650	8,925	0.10	57.96
Argentina	1,155	980	995	1,216	1,467	0.02	20.64
Bolivia					87	0.00	
Brazil	2,666	2,954	3,744	3,849	3,948	0.04	2.57
Chile					829	0.01	
Colombia					1,018	0.01	
Ecuador					198	0.00	
Paraguay					51	0.00	
Peru					342	0.00	
Uruguay					174	0.00	
Venezuela	472	562	609	585	811	0.01	38.63
EAST ASIA AND THE PACIFIC	41,773	43,772	51,145	56,053	77,631	0.84	38.50
NORTH-EAST ASIA	22,571	25,604	30,257	33,858	41,781	0.45	23.40
China	6,165	6,438	6,638	8,685	11,570	0.13	33.22
Hong Kong, China					1,033	0.01	
Japan	8,458	9,969	10,236	11,148	11,268	0.12	1.08
Korea, Dem. People's Republic of					184	0.00	
Korea, Republic of	7,582	8,834	12,940	13,508	15,129	0.16	12.00

109

BULGARIA

2. Arrivals of non-resident visitors at national borders, by country of residence

	2009	2010	2011	2012	2013	Market share 2013	% Change 2013-2012
Macao, China					25	0.00	
Mongolia	366	363	443	517	442	0.00	-14.51
Taiwan, Province of China					2,130	0.02	
SOUTH-EAST ASIA	**4,593**	**4,116**	**3,869**	**5,207**	**18,491**	**0.20**	**255.12**
Indonesia	2,034	1,674	1,667	2,438	2,221	0.02	-8.90
Malaysia					1,514	0.02	
Philippines					10,564	0.11	
Singapore					885	0.01	
Thailand					740	0.01	
Viet Nam	2,559	2,442	2,202	2,769	2,567	0.03	-7.30
AUSTRALASIA	**14,609**	**14,052**	**17,019**	**16,988**	**17,359**	**0.19**	**2.18**
Australia	11,941	11,461	14,267	14,207	14,516	0.16	2.17
New Zealand	2,668	2,591	2,752	2,781	2,843	0.03	2.23
EUROPE	**7,602,264**	**8,080,924**	**8,389,436**	**8,525,443**	**8,888,765**	**96.70**	**4.26**
CENTRAL/EASTERN EUROPE	**2,705,690**	**2,875,306**	**3,058,269**	**3,273,290**	**3,505,818**	**38.14**	**7.10**
Azerbaijan					8,050	0.09	
Belarus	36,882	49,163	43,450	84,684	131,465	1.43	55.24
Czech Republic	197,863	184,440	176,135	173,739	171,315	1.86	-1.40
Estonia					6,386	0.07	
Georgia					29,621	0.32	
Hungary	137,195	124,438	123,735	120,883	115,205	1.25	-4.70
Kazakhstan					9,128	0.10	
Latvia					5,183	0.06	
Lithuania					11,756	0.13	
Poland	304,659	294,131	289,742	286,267	283,498	3.08	-0.97
Republic of Moldova	75,740	93,468	109,862	113,888	111,826	1.22	-1.81
Romania	1,398,694	1,445,342	1,499,415	1,468,179	1,465,600	15.94	-0.18
Russian Federation	295,713	389,864	469,772	609,630	695,853	7.57	14.14
Slovakia	104,243	95,380	94,355	90,076	81,488	0.89	-9.53
Ukraine	154,701	199,080	251,803	325,944	379,444	4.13	16.41
NORTHERN EUROPE	**639,799**	**578,807**	**562,614**	**494,720**	**471,031**	**5.12**	**-4.79**
Denmark	90,672	84,172	81,860	72,216	70,915	0.77	-1.80
Finland	57,057	45,527	43,620	38,926	37,812	0.41	-2.86
Iceland	4,294	2,131	2,055	1,845	1,228	0.01	-33.44
Ireland	46,102	33,089	29,941	26,722	18,405	0.20	-31.12
Norway	59,598	55,414	48,707	28,993	30,768	0.33	6.12
Sweden	65,148	48,992	49,492	43,942	42,247	0.46	-3.86
United Kingdom	316,928	309,482	306,939	282,076	269,656	2.93	-4.40
SOUTHERN EUROPE	**1,732,575**	**2,022,288**	**2,257,849**	**2,237,346**	**2,290,626**	**24.92**	**2.38**
Albania	12,993	14,241	26,512	27,966	29,768	0.32	6.44
Bosnia and Herzegovina	18,626	16,972	38,551	41,882	40,383	0.44	-3.58
Croatia	22,802	21,355	26,520	23,781	23,137	0.25	-2.71
Greece	924,220	1,017,914	1,120,640	1,087,260	1,105,437	12.03	1.67
Italy	126,108	125,683	130,259	128,851	129,115	1.40	0.20
Malta	7,479	6,370	4,178	4,369	2,988	0.03	-31.61
Montenegro	5,237	11,515	14,401	13,501	13,261	0.14	-1.78
Portugal	9,339	9,381	9,099	7,325	6,944	0.08	-5.20
San Marino					29	0.00	
Serbia	217,940	307,838	365,644	396,448	428,582	4.66	8.11
Slovenia	22,871	22,550	22,340	22,459	22,002	0.24	-2.03
Spain	54,847	58,499	60,026	59,322	59,972	0.65	1.10
TFYR of Macedonia	310,113	409,970	439,679	424,182	429,008	4.67	1.14
WESTERN EUROPE	**1,578,158**	**1,508,192**	**1,489,738**	**1,421,600**	**1,449,237**	**15.77**	**1.94**
Austria	182,075	181,577	186,438	185,242	192,298	2.09	3.81
Belgium	96,334	91,183	91,947	95,678	94,735	1.03	-0.99
France	196,174	181,317	182,407	180,060	180,114	1.96	0.03
Germany	898,352	853,430	836,845	784,678	812,189	8.84	3.51
Liechtenstein					5	0.00	

Yearbook of Tourism Statistics, Data 2009 – 2013, 2015 Edition

BULGARIA

2. Arrivals of non-resident visitors at national borders, by country of residence

	2009	2010	2011	2012	2013	Market share 2013	% Change 2013-2012
Luxembourg	6,408	4,681	4,432	4,232	4,332	0.05	2.36
Netherlands	157,485	156,436	149,193	144,382	134,683	1.47	-6.72
Switzerland	41,330	39,568	38,476	27,328	30,881	0.34	13.00
EAST MEDITERRANEAN EUROPE	**946,042**	**1,096,331**	**1,020,966**	**1,098,487**	**1,172,053**	**12.75**	**6.70**
Cyprus	22,557	22,050	21,361	18,689	17,785	0.19	-4.84
Israel	106,825	131,144	138,951	95,586	101,222	1.10	5.90
Turkey	816,660	943,137	860,654	984,212	1,053,046	11.46	6.99
MIDDLE EAST	**21,352**	**25,413**	**23,972**	**29,646**	**43,966**	**0.48**	**48.30**
Bahrain					90	0.00	
Egypt	1,848	1,633	1,902	2,545	2,810	0.03	10.41
Iraq	2,551	2,849	2,633	4,300	5,229	0.06	21.60
Jordan	1,606	1,941	1,573	1,376	1,237	0.01	-10.10
Kuwait	998	1,685	2,977	3,412	4,040	0.04	18.41
Lebanon	4,794	5,543	4,997	5,776	6,093	0.07	5.49
Libya	390	390	169	372	727	0.01	95.43
Qatar					232	0.00	
Saudi Arabia	156	214	217	233	362	0.00	55.36
Syrian Arab Republic	8,837	10,962	9,368	11,375	22,760	0.25	100.09
United Arab Emirates	172	196	136	257	255	0.00	-0.78
Yemen					131	0.00	
SOUTH ASIA	**23,025**	**24,105**	**27,129**	**25,911**	**23,533**	**0.26**	**-9.18**
Afghanistan	441	353	424	620	666	0.01	7.42
Bangladesh	178	180	128	162	200	0.00	23.46
India	4,106	3,696	3,849	4,722	5,402	0.06	14.40
Iran, Islamic Republic of	17,782	19,299	22,026	19,459	16,248	0.18	-16.50
Pakistan	518	577	702	948	1,017	0.01	7.28
NOT SPECIFIED	**100,048**	**113,751**	**131,094**	**133,288**	**50,070**	**0.54**	**-62.43**
Other countries of the World	100,048	113,751	131,094	133,288	50,070	0.54	-62.43

Yearbook of Tourism Statistics, Data 2009 – 2013, 2015 Edition

BULGARIA

3. Arrivals of non-resident tourists in hotels and similar establishments, by country of residence

	2009	2010	2011	2012	2013	Market share 2013	% Change 2013-2012
TOTAL	1,931,258	2,064,167	2,387,427	2,579,134	2,754,493	100.00	6.80
AFRICA	796	674	808	3,841	2,668	0.10	-30.54
SOUTHERN AFRICA	796	674	808	1,445	1,191	0.04	-17.58
South Africa	796	674	808	1,445	1,191	0.04	-17.58
OTHER AFRICA				2,396	1,477	0.05	-38.36
Other countries of Africa				2,396	1,477	0.05	-38.36
AMERICAS	37,648	41,281	42,687	51,018	53,553	1.94	4.97
NORTH AMERICA	30,668	34,935	39,646	46,541	48,587	1.76	4.40
Canada	4,197	5,076	5,936	6,754	7,407	0.27	9.67
United States of America	26,471	29,859	33,710	38,595	39,726	1.44	2.93
Other countries of North America				1,192	1,454	0.05	21.98
SOUTH AMERICA	6,980	6,346	3,041	3,079	3,443	0.12	11.82
Brazil	6,980	6,346	3,041	3,079	3,443	0.12	11.82
OTHER AMERICAS				1,398	1,523	0.06	8.94
Other countries of the Americas				1,398	1,523	0.06	8.94
EAST ASIA AND THE PACIFIC	20,666	26,802	32,774	38,021	45,276	1.64	19.08
NORTH-EAST ASIA	16,007	21,335	24,928	29,352	36,906	1.34	25.74
China	3,851	3,847	5,439	9,095	10,641	0.39	17.00
Japan	9,942	13,332	12,749	13,501	17,136	0.62	26.92
Korea, Republic of	2,214	4,156	6,740	6,756	9,129	0.33	35.12
AUSTRALASIA	4,659	5,467	7,846	8,669	8,370	0.30	-3.45
Australia	4,659	5,467	7,846	8,669	8,370	0.30	-3.45
EUROPE	1,783,311	1,873,839	2,171,568	2,321,070	2,442,868	88.69	5.25
CENTRAL/EASTERN EUROPE	589,654	667,050	872,086	1,022,723	1,110,344	40.31	8.57
Czech Republic	34,565	36,261	44,259	58,249	54,481	1.98	-6.47
Estonia	5,193	5,004	6,172	7,684	12,819	0.47	66.83
Hungary	20,661	24,991	31,994	31,239	35,594	1.29	13.94
Latvia	4,423	3,677	4,868	7,080	9,754	0.35	37.77
Lithuania	4,890	4,044	7,014	11,180	14,980	0.54	33.99
Poland	61,427	83,997	110,661	127,214	132,401	4.81	4.08
Romania	243,253	259,225	332,740	332,022	349,895	12.70	5.38
Russian Federation	175,695	196,211	246,464	323,731	354,571	12.87	9.53
Slovakia	15,276	17,186	28,032	31,203	33,196	1.21	6.39
Ukraine	24,271	36,454	59,882	93,121	112,653	4.09	20.97
NORTHERN EUROPE	281,152	274,242	283,446	288,708	316,445	11.49	9.61
Denmark	30,706	31,701	28,976	27,601	28,790	1.05	4.31
Finland	26,434	25,262	25,463	20,280	22,452	0.82	10.71
Iceland	3,141	1,153	1,647	1,014	921	0.03	-9.17
Ireland	15,386	11,349	11,527	9,922	11,502	0.42	15.92
Norway	31,011	31,602	40,778	40,859	47,409	1.72	16.03
Sweden	30,425	25,828	26,789	24,644	25,835	0.94	4.83
United Kingdom	144,049	147,347	148,266	164,388	179,536	6.52	9.21
SOUTHERN EUROPE	226,491	234,003	225,396	206,895	205,088	7.45	-0.87
Greece	123,084	139,868	126,586	108,371	112,861	4.10	4.14
Italy	52,337	48,282	54,312	55,524	51,349	1.86	-7.52
Malta	4,196	1,516	1,999	2,893	1,613	0.06	-44.24
Portugal	6,889	7,870	5,903	5,587	5,022	0.18	-10.11
Slovenia	11,698	9,727	11,390	10,767	11,546	0.42	7.24
Spain	28,287	26,740	25,206	23,753	22,697	0.82	-4.45
WESTERN EUROPE	495,853	484,213	544,773	569,262	542,349	19.69	-4.73
Austria	28,912	30,900	35,206	39,078	42,059	1.53	7.63
Belgium	34,394	33,096	35,482	34,728	35,632	1.29	2.60
France	83,457	68,062	70,223	72,855	71,729	2.60	-1.55
Germany	299,031	305,048	352,518	370,588	344,876	12.52	-6.94
Luxembourg	2,902	1,975	2,655	2,389	2,135	0.08	-10.63
Netherlands	35,658	34,110	34,259	33,925	30,189	1.10	-11.01
Switzerland	11,499	11,022	14,430	15,699	15,729	0.57	0.19
EAST MEDITERRANEAN EUROPE	146,089	157,465	173,667	149,514	174,499	6.34	16.71

112

BULGARIA

3. Arrivals of non-resident tourists in hotels and similar establishments, by country of residence

	2009	2010	2011	2012	2013	Market share 2013	% Change 2013-2012
Cyprus	8,198	6,486	6,484	5,553	4,311	0.16	-22.37
Israel	97,286	103,317	117,452	77,094	80,785	2.93	4.79
Turkey	40,605	47,662	49,731	66,867	89,403	3.25	33.70
OTHER EUROPE	**44,072**	**56,866**	**72,200**	**83,968**	**94,143**	**3.42**	**12.12**
Other countries of Europe	44,072	56,866	72,200	83,968	94,143	3.42	12.12
NOT SPECIFIED	**88,837**	**121,571**	**139,590**	**165,184**	**210,128**	**7.63**	**27.21**
Other countries of the World	88,837	121,571	139,590	165,184	210,128	7.63	27.21

113

BULGARIA

4. Arrivals of non-resident tourists in all types of accommodation establishments, by country of residence

	2009	2010	2011	2012	2013	Market share 2013	% Change 2013-2012
TOTAL	1,944,368	2,078,747	2,409,269	2,632,062	2,820,673	100.00	7.17
AFRICA		678	809	3,889	2,708	0.10	-30.37
SOUTHERN AFRICA		678	809	1,472	1,223	0.04	-16.92
South Africa		678	809	1,472	1,223	0.04	-16.92
OTHER AFRICA				2,417	1,485	0.05	-38.56
Other countries of Africa				2,417	1,485	0.05	-38.56
AMERICAS	37,959	41,524	42,899	52,410	55,453	1.97	5.81
NORTH AMERICA	30,888	35,169	39,825	47,806	50,271	1.78	5.16
Canada	4,222	5,117	5,972	7,020	7,763	0.28	10.58
United States of America	26,666	30,052	33,853	39,581	41,034	1.45	3.67
Other countries of North America				1,205	1,474	0.05	22.32
SOUTH AMERICA	7,071	6,355	3,074	3,166	3,589	0.13	13.36
Brazil	7,071	6,355	3,074	3,166	3,589	0.13	13.36
OTHER AMERICAS				1,438	1,593	0.06	10.78
Other countries of the Americas				1,438	1,593	0.06	10.78
EAST ASIA AND THE PACIFIC	18,493	26,867	32,821	39,501	46,991	1.67	18.96
NORTH-EAST ASIA	13,814	21,375	24,948	30,216	37,862	1.34	25.30
China	3,865	3,873	5,446	9,235	10,784	0.38	16.77
Japan	9,949	13,344	12,759	13,969	17,641	0.63	26.29
Korea, Republic of		4,158	6,743	7,012	9,437	0.33	34.58
AUSTRALASIA	4,679	5,492	7,873	9,285	9,129	0.32	-1.68
Australia	4,679	5,492	7,873	9,285	9,129	0.32	-1.68
EUROPE	1,795,231	1,886,522	2,190,901	2,356,580	2,496,230	88.50	5.93
CENTRAL/EASTERN EUROPE	594,228	672,444	882,458	1,048,139	1,142,639	40.51	9.02
Czech Republic	34,908	36,751	44,773	59,772	55,440	1.97	-7.25
Estonia	5,202	5,008	6,186	7,758	12,937	0.46	66.76
Hungary	20,932	25,208	32,353	31,950	36,158	1.28	13.17
Latvia	4,433	3,683	4,888	7,234	9,981	0.35	37.97
Lithuania	4,898	4,078	7,039	11,355	15,125	0.54	33.20
Poland	61,823	84,565	111,166	129,411	134,675	4.77	4.07
Romania	243,771	260,318	333,974	336,135	354,508	12.57	5.47
Russian Federation	177,852	198,609	252,404	336,326	372,637	13.21	10.80
Slovakia	15,609	17,355	28,154	31,421	33,565	1.19	6.82
Ukraine	24,800	36,869	61,521	96,777	117,613	4.17	21.53
NORTHERN EUROPE	283,327	276,153	286,093	292,255	320,809	11.37	9.77
Denmark	30,758	31,773	29,053	27,861	29,064	1.03	4.32
Finland	26,466	25,278	25,681	20,418	22,766	0.81	11.50
Iceland	3,145	1,154	1,648	1,046	966	0.03	-7.65
Ireland	15,561	11,407	11,551	10,051	11,742	0.42	16.82
Norway	31,159	31,805	40,942	41,196	47,722	1.69	15.84
Sweden	30,727	25,945	26,982	24,839	26,090	0.92	5.04
United Kingdom	145,511	148,791	150,236	166,844	182,459	6.47	9.36
SOUTHERN EUROPE	227,631	235,091	226,538	287,170	304,792	10.81	6.14
Greece	123,677	140,273	127,079	109,539	114,167	4.05	4.22
Italy	52,505	48,560	54,539	56,329	52,347	1.86	-7.07
Malta	4,223	1,527	2,004	2,905	1,636	0.06	-43.68
Portugal	6,944	7,981	5,972	5,729	5,113	0.18	-10.75
Serbia				27,360	31,448	1.11	14.94
Slovenia	11,754	9,769	11,467	10,937	11,860	0.42	8.44
Spain	28,528	26,981	25,477	24,663	23,730	0.84	-3.78
TFYR of Macedonia				49,708	64,491	2.29	29.74
WESTERN EUROPE	498,720	486,966	548,431	577,555	551,330	19.55	-4.54
Austria	29,094	31,023	35,356	39,521	42,463	1.51	7.44
Belgium	34,535	33,295	35,704	35,327	36,371	1.29	2.96
France	84,112	68,757	71,111	75,492	74,673	2.65	-1.08
Germany	300,060	306,360	354,052	373,133	347,667	12.33	-6.82
Luxembourg	2,933	1,978	2,657	2,442	2,145	0.08	-12.16
Netherlands	36,440	34,489	35,059	35,692	31,903	1.13	-10.62

114

BULGARIA

4. Arrivals of non-resident tourists in all types of accommodation establishments, by country of residence

	2009	2010	2011	2012	2013	Market share 2013	% Change 2013-2012
Switzerland	11,546	11,064	14,492	15,948	16,108	0.57	1.00
EAST MEDITERRANEAN EUROPE	**146,449**	**158,085**	**174,296**	**151,461**	**176,660**	**6.26**	**16.64**
Cyprus	8,206	6,506	6,511	5,617	4,357	0.15	-22.43
Israel	97,422	103,634	117,668	77,934	81,357	2.88	4.39
Turkey	40,821	47,945	50,117	67,910	90,946	3.22	33.92
OTHER EUROPE	**44,876**	**57,783**	**73,085**				
Other countries of Europe	44,876	57,783	73,085				
NOT SPECIFIED	**92,685**	**123,156**	**141,839**	**179,682**	**219,291**	**7.77**	**22.04**
Other countries of the World	92,685	123,156	141,839	179,682	219,291	7.77	22.04

115

BULGARIA

5. Overnight stays of non-resident tourists in hotels and similar establishments, by country of residence

	2009	2010	2011	2012	2013	Market share 2013	% Change 2013-2012
TOTAL	9,377,995	10,454,674	12,286,819	13,151,707	13,987,515	100.00	6.36
AFRICA	2,240	1,899	2,927	13,688	7,894	0.06	-42.33
SOUTHERN AFRICA	2,240	1,899	2,927	7,176	3,862	0.03	-46.18
South Africa	2,240	1,899	2,927	7,176	3,862	0.03	-46.18
OTHER AFRICA				6,512	4,032	0.03	-38.08
Other countries of Africa				6,512	4,032	0.03	-38.08
AMERICAS	146,207	142,309	110,531	136,357	126,258	0.90	-7.41
NORTH AMERICA	95,580	96,701	99,095	121,021	113,444	0.81	-6.26
Canada	10,157	13,462	14,338	15,738	17,047	0.12	8.32
United States of America	85,423	83,239	84,757	101,816	93,386	0.67	-8.28
Other countries of North America				3,467	3,011	0.02	-13.15
SOUTH AMERICA	50,627	45,608	11,436	11,029	8,958	0.06	-18.78
Brazil	50,627	45,608	11,436	11,029	8,958	0.06	-18.78
OTHER AMERICAS				4,307	3,856	0.03	-10.47
Other countries of the Americas				4,307	3,856	0.03	-10.47
EAST ASIA AND THE PACIFIC	41,903	48,889	64,030	77,039	86,349	0.62	12.08
NORTH-EAST ASIA	30,141	37,105	45,360	55,459	67,366	0.48	21.47
China	7,719	8,205	13,582	20,562	22,378	0.16	8.83
Japan	18,757	21,953	20,644	23,538	30,188	0.22	28.25
Korea, Republic of	3,665	6,947	11,134	11,359	14,800	0.11	30.29
AUSTRALASIA	11,762	11,784	18,670	21,580	18,983	0.14	-12.03
Australia	11,762	11,784	18,670	21,580	18,983	0.14	-12.03
EUROPE	8,805,328	9,712,792	11,486,671	12,101,170	12,687,343	90.70	4.84
CENTRAL/EASTERN EUROPE	3,058,719	4,001,282	5,220,334	5,968,116	6,514,380	46.57	9.15
Czech Republic	194,018	206,265	271,504	338,316	307,602	2.20	-9.08
Estonia	29,559	29,930	35,373	42,794	72,028	0.51	68.31
Hungary	92,049	102,379	153,830	139,896	165,873	1.19	18.57
Latvia	26,241	18,112	27,151	37,627	52,442	0.37	39.37
Lithuania	40,233	23,196	39,481	61,315	94,313	0.67	53.82
Poland	422,449	552,650	738,158	785,551	824,809	5.90	5.00
Romania	814,994	1,024,323	1,344,116	1,336,926	1,440,755	10.30	7.77
Russian Federation	1,182,012	1,689,907	2,021,541	2,430,560	2,643,324	18.90	8.75
Slovakia	109,154	122,474	197,160	208,857	219,554	1.57	5.12
Ukraine	148,010	232,046	392,020	586,274	693,680	4.96	18.32
NORTHERN EUROPE	1,679,111	1,636,183	1,725,908	1,666,401	1,852,019	13.24	11.14
Denmark	187,559	190,379	180,737	167,529	164,515	1.18	-1.80
Finland	166,021	151,093	157,388	112,015	122,208	0.87	9.10
Iceland	5,991	2,273	5,669	2,892	2,718	0.02	-6.02
Ireland	74,184	54,060	59,664	44,600	56,269	0.40	26.16
Norway	218,108	221,828	300,114	282,728	333,970	2.39	18.12
Sweden	185,943	143,934	157,623	133,213	140,392	1.00	5.39
United Kingdom	841,305	872,616	864,713	923,424	1,031,947	7.38	11.75
SOUTHERN EUROPE	508,133	519,154	496,042	476,058	459,296	3.28	-3.52
Greece	227,528	272,585	241,627	210,235	222,896	1.59	6.02
Italy	122,537	113,966	129,987	141,744	127,583	0.91	-9.99
Malta	25,812	4,372	6,192	8,409	4,203	0.03	-50.02
Portugal	26,635	26,188	18,740	18,093	13,504	0.10	-25.36
Slovenia	41,025	39,732	47,811	47,214	43,631	0.31	-7.59
Spain	64,596	62,311	51,685	50,363	47,479	0.34	-5.73
WESTERN EUROPE	2,986,215	2,905,168	3,289,394	3,292,096	3,075,592	21.99	-6.58
Austria	88,377	99,926	116,028	133,636	167,064	1.19	25.01
Belgium	183,207	177,382	186,123	165,979	175,829	1.26	5.93
France	296,842	231,324	219,726	237,470	251,762	1.80	6.02
Germany	2,158,649	2,161,331	2,512,804	2,507,244	2,276,695	16.28	-9.20
Luxembourg	16,994	10,795	15,222	13,349	12,026	0.09	-9.91
Netherlands	200,092	187,193	191,668	179,958	141,022	1.01	-21.64
Switzerland	42,054	37,217	47,823	54,460	51,194	0.37	-6.00
EAST MEDITERRANEAN EUROPE	429,142	474,545	532,993	443,511	498,581	3.56	12.42

116

BULGARIA

5. Overnight stays of non-resident tourists in hotels and similar establishments, by country of residence

	2009	2010	2011	2012	2013	Market share 2013	% Change 2013-2012
Cyprus	20,557	16,886	16,566	14,677	12,124	0.09	-17.39
Israel	322,539	367,271	414,753	301,176	316,836	2.27	5.20
Turkey	86,046	90,388	101,674	127,658	169,621	1.21	32.87
OTHER EUROPE	**144,008**	**176,460**	**222,000**	**254,988**	**287,475**	**2.06**	**12.74**
Other countries of Europe	144,008	176,460	222,000	254,988	287,475	2.06	12.74
NOT SPECIFIED	**382,317**	**548,785**	**622,660**	**823,453**	**1,079,671**	**7.72**	**31.12**
Other countries of the World	382,317	548,785	622,660	823,453	1,079,671	7.72	31.12

Yearbook of Tourism Statistics, Data 2009 – 2013, 2015 Edition

BULGARIA

6. Overnight stays of non-resident tourists in all types of accommodation establishments, by country of residence

	2009	2010	2011	2012	2013	Market share 2013	% Change 2013-2012
TOTAL	9,460,922	10,627,547	12,426,723	13,451,440	14,370,426	100.00	6.83
AFRICA		1,921	2,932	13,834	7,993	0.06	-42.22
SOUTHERN AFRICA		1,921	2,932	7,242	3,947	0.03	-45.50
South Africa		1,921	2,932	7,242	3,947	0.03	-45.50
OTHER AFRICA				6,592	4,046	0.03	-38.62
Other countries of Africa				6,592	4,046	0.03	-38.62
AMERICAS	148,212	142,748	110,989	139,461	130,366	0.91	-6.52
NORTH AMERICA	96,514	97,118	99,461	123,901	117,143	0.82	-5.45
Canada	10,197	13,547	14,438	16,289	17,817	0.12	9.38
United States of America	86,317	83,571	85,023	104,127	96,279	0.67	-7.54
Other countries of North America				3,485	3,047	0.02	-12.57
SOUTH AMERICA	51,698	45,630	11,528	11,184	9,274	0.06	-17.08
Brazil	51,698	45,630	11,528	11,184	9,274	0.06	-17.08
OTHER AMERICAS				4,376	3,949	0.03	-9.76
Other countries of the Americas				4,376	3,949	0.03	-9.76
EAST ASIA AND THE PACIFIC	38,329	49,049	64,179	80,180	89,817	0.63	12.02
NORTH-EAST ASIA	26,507	37,165	45,430	57,296	69,369	0.48	21.07
China	7,743	8,246	13,626	20,837	22,633	0.16	8.62
Japan	18,764	21,970	20,662	24,493	31,269	0.22	27.67
Korea, Republic of		6,949	11,142	11,966	15,467	0.11	29.26
AUSTRALASIA	11,822	11,884	18,749	22,884	20,448	0.14	-10.64
Australia	11,822	11,884	18,749	22,884	20,448	0.14	-10.64
EUROPE	8,881,833	9,792,606	11,612,025	12,354,301	13,001,131	90.47	5.24
CENTRAL/EASTERN EUROPE	3,094,094	4,042,469	5,300,643	6,160,384	6,760,361	47.04	9.74
Czech Republic	195,362	207,716	273,614	343,170	312,840	2.18	-8.84
Estonia	29,570	29,960	35,430	43,249	72,667	0.51	68.02
Hungary	92,781	103,066	155,116	142,886	168,056	1.17	17.62
Latvia	26,283	18,121	27,298	38,302	53,484	0.37	39.64
Lithuania	40,248	23,499	39,532	62,027	94,953	0.66	53.08
Poland	423,627	554,269	740,126	796,880	837,196	5.83	5.06
Romania	817,442	1,029,468	1,348,630	1,349,832	1,454,411	10.12	7.75
Russian Federation	1,204,938	1,717,026	2,078,704	2,564,743	2,823,295	19.65	10.08
Slovakia	111,285	123,692	197,790	210,004	222,026	1.55	5.72
Ukraine	152,558	235,652	404,403	609,291	721,433	5.02	18.41
NORTHERN EUROPE	1,695,193	1,653,628	1,741,925	1,679,807	1,867,885	13.00	11.20
Denmark	187,728	190,815	181,063	168,452	165,581	1.15	-1.70
Finland	166,155	151,201	158,224	112,451	123,609	0.86	9.92
Iceland	6,002	2,274	5,671	2,970	2,777	0.02	-6.50
Ireland	75,247	54,519	59,747	44,971	56,899	0.40	26.52
Norway	219,171	223,246	301,442	284,142	335,719	2.34	18.15
Sweden	187,643	144,561	158,409	133,664	141,273	0.98	5.69
United Kingdom	853,247	887,012	877,369	933,157	1,042,027	7.25	11.67
SOUTHERN EUROPE	511,620	522,116	499,352	726,597	762,705	5.31	4.97
Greece	229,070	273,561	242,525	212,745	225,925	1.57	6.20
Italy	122,923	114,443	130,388	144,100	130,237	0.91	-9.62
Malta	26,123	4,443	6,202	8,425	4,258	0.03	-49.46
Portugal	26,857	26,564	19,160	18,870	13,663	0.10	-27.59
Serbia				99,352	108,705	0.76	9.41
Slovenia	41,107	39,798	48,080	47,862	45,296	0.32	-5.36
Spain	65,540	63,307	52,997	52,058	49,924	0.35	-4.10
TFYR of Macedonia				143,185	184,697	1.29	28.99
WESTERN EUROPE	3,004,712	2,918,020	3,310,407	3,321,979	3,106,590	21.62	-6.48
Austria	88,901	100,543	116,801	134,874	167,999	1.17	24.56
Belgium	183,473	177,805	186,756	167,228	177,567	1.24	6.18
France	298,147	232,571	221,939	244,828	259,255	1.80	5.89
Germany	2,165,932	2,169,804	2,524,149	2,516,335	2,286,613	15.91	-9.13
Luxembourg	17,189	10,798	15,224	13,463	12,040	0.08	-10.57
Netherlands	208,948	189,193	197,443	190,147	151,084	1.05	-20.54

118

BULGARIA

6. Overnight stays of non-resident tourists in all types of accommodation establishments, by country of residence

	2009	2010	2011	2012	2013	Market share 2013	% Change 2013-2012
Switzerland	42,122	37,306	48,095	55,104	52,032	0.36	-5.57
EAST MEDITERRANEAN EUROPE	**429,874**	**475,732**	**534,546**	**447,634**	**503,590**	**3.50**	**12.50**
Cyprus	20,589	16,960	16,623	14,808	12,202	0.08	-17.60
Israel	322,772	367,813	415,242	302,855	318,596	2.22	5.20
Turkey	86,513	90,959	102,681	129,971	172,792	1.20	32.95
OTHER EUROPE	**146,340**	**180,641**	**225,152**	**17,900**			
Other countries of Europe	146,340	180,641	225,152	17,900			
NOT SPECIFIED	**392,548**	**641,223**	**636,598**	**863,664**	**1,141,119**	**7.94**	**32.13**
Other countries of the World	392,548	641,223	636,598	863,664	1,141,119	7.94	32.13

Yearbook of Tourism Statistics, Data 2009 – 2013, 2015 Edition

BURKINA FASO

3. Arrivals of non-resident tourists in hotels and similar establishments, by nationality

	2009	2010	2011	2012	2013	Market share 2013	% Change 2013-2012
TOTAL	269,227	274,330	237,725	237,457	217,988	100.00	-8.20
AFRICA	119,243	128,237	117,337	117,992	107,708	49.41	-8.72
WEST AFRICA	98,238	102,591	96,848	95,886	89,268	40.95	-6.90
Benin	11,138	11,754	10,032	9,211	8,622	3.96	-6.39
Côte d'Ivoire	18,090	19,251	18,276	19,004	18,852	8.65	-0.80
Ghana	8,412	8,402	10,152	8,787	7,090	3.25	-19.31
Guinea	4,747	4,922	5,103	4,904	3,849	1.77	-21.51
Mali	14,474	15,643	14,846	16,949	16,065	7.37	-5.22
Mauritania	1,943	2,217	2,501	1,860	1,909	0.88	2.63
Niger	14,888	14,342	12,486	11,917	11,265	5.17	-5.47
Nigeria	5,561	4,297	4,045	3,494	3,446	1.58	-1.37
Senegal	9,875	10,638	9,570	10,174	9,566	4.39	-5.98
Togo	9,110	11,125	9,837	9,586	8,604	3.95	-10.24
OTHER AFRICA	21,005	25,646	20,489	22,106	18,440	8.46	-16.58
Other countries of Africa	21,005	25,646	20,489	22,106	18,440	8.46	-16.58
AMERICAS	17,509	20,154	17,333	19,151	20,208	9.27	5.52
NORTH AMERICA	15,026	17,927	14,697	16,683	17,225	7.90	3.25
Canada	6,434	8,833	7,442	8,136	9,477	4.35	16.48
United States of America	8,592	9,094	7,255	8,547	7,748	3.55	-9.35
OTHER AMERICAS	2,483	2,227	2,636	2,468	2,983	1.37	20.87
Other countries of the Americas	2,483	2,227	2,636	2,468	2,983	1.37	20.87
EAST ASIA AND THE PACIFIC	7,253	7,313	8,180	9,313	9,335	4.28	0.24
NORTH-EAST ASIA	1,591	1,898	1,587	2,262	2,492	1.14	10.17
China	1,591	1,898	1,587	2,262	2,492	1.14	10.17
OTHER EAST ASIA AND THE PACIFIC	5,662	5,415	6,593	7,051	6,843	3.14	-2.95
Other countries of Asia	5,662	5,415	6,593	7,051	6,843	3.14	-2.95
EUROPE	116,180	107,098	85,535	78,670	67,926	31.16	-13.66
NORTHERN EUROPE	4,712	4,523	4,749	3,893	2,367	1.09	-39.20
United Kingdom	4,712	4,523	4,749	3,893	2,367	1.09	-39.20
SOUTHERN EUROPE	6,726	5,892	4,875	5,015	4,590	2.11	-8.47
Italy	6,726	5,892	4,875	5,015	4,590	2.11	-8.47
WESTERN EUROPE	92,592	85,784	64,898	59,329	52,542	24.10	-11.44
Belgium	7,806	7,344	6,491	6,507	5,982	2.74	-8.07
France	67,866	63,715	42,296	40,570	35,715	16.38	-11.97
Germany	7,193	6,855	6,420	6,000	5,088	2.33	-15.20
Netherlands	4,536	3,645	5,545	3,061	3,009	1.38	-1.70
Switzerland	5,191	4,225	4,146	3,191	2,748	1.26	-13.88
OTHER EUROPE	12,150	10,899	11,013	10,433	8,427	3.87	-19.23
Other countries of Europe	12,150	10,899	11,013	10,433	8,427	3.87	-19.23
MIDDLE EAST	1,572	1,355	1,795	1,535	1,777	0.82	15.77
Lebanon	1,572	1,355	1,795	1,535	1,777	0.82	15.77
NOT SPECIFIED	7,470	10,173	7,545	10,796	11,034	5.06	2.20
Nationals Residing Abroad	7,470	10,173	7,545	10,796	11,034	5.06	2.20

Yearbook of Tourism Statistics, Data 2009 – 2013, 2015 Edition

BURKINA FASO

5. Overnight stays of non-resident tourists in hotels and similar establishments, by nationality

	2009	2010	2011	2012	2013	Market share 2013	% Change 2013-2012
TOTAL	792,843	815,196	707,944	710,017	697,183	100.00	-1.81
AFRICA	375,082	392,274	334,706	336,097	338,122	48.50	0.60
WEST AFRICA	293,719	305,845	269,016	266,949	273,287	39.20	2.37
Benin	34,132	36,638	29,374	29,727	29,302	4.20	-1.43
Côte d'Ivoire	57,028	58,043	55,124	55,779	56,355	8.08	1.03
Ghana	21,263	21,589	23,036	18,743	18,000	2.58	-3.96
Guinea	14,229	15,755	12,467	11,895	11,882	1.70	-0.11
Mali	44,645	46,189	40,983	45,600	50,313	7.22	10.34
Mauritania	5,231	6,801	5,824	4,755	5,472	0.78	15.08
Niger	42,360	38,899	31,823	33,585	33,962	4.87	1.12
Nigeria	14,887	13,187	10,450	8,905	9,486	1.36	6.52
Senegal	32,468	38,229	33,137	33,200	31,868	4.57	-4.01
Togo	27,476	30,515	26,798	24,760	26,647	3.82	7.62
OTHER AFRICA	81,363	86,429	65,690	69,148	64,835	9.30	-6.24
Other countries of Africa	81,363	86,429	65,690	69,148	64,835	9.30	-6.24
AMERICAS	58,773	74,409	57,519	66,092	64,169	9.20	-2.91
NORTH AMERICA	52,178	67,600	49,563	57,519	54,870	7.87	-4.61
Canada	20,890	29,056	24,562	26,339	27,092	3.89	2.86
United States of America	31,288	38,544	25,001	31,180	27,778	3.98	-10.91
OTHER AMERICAS	6,595	6,809	7,956	8,573	9,299	1.33	8.47
Other countries of the Americas	6,595	6,809	7,956	8,573	9,299	1.33	8.47
EAST ASIA AND THE PACIFIC	24,640	28,062	30,555	32,020	39,696	5.69	23.97
NORTH-EAST ASIA	4,978	8,001	6,391	6,560	9,725	1.39	48.25
China	4,978	8,001	6,391	6,560	9,725	1.39	48.25
OTHER EAST ASIA AND THE PACIFIC	19,662	20,061	24,164	25,460	29,971	4.30	17.72
Other countries of Asia	19,662	20,061	24,164	25,460	29,971	4.30	17.72
EUROPE	312,750	293,932	266,094	249,618	224,939	32.26	-9.89
NORTHERN EUROPE	12,476	11,020	10,988	9,670	7,270	1.04	-24.82
United Kingdom	12,476	11,020	10,988	9,670	7,270	1.04	-24.82
SOUTHERN EUROPE	20,810	16,702	15,447	14,653	16,452	2.36	12.28
Italy	20,810	16,702	15,447	14,653	16,452	2.36	12.28
WESTERN EUROPE	244,159	234,284	204,979	183,575	173,280	24.85	-5.61
Belgium	22,330	22,515	20,794	18,718	18,912	2.71	1.04
France	176,285	169,317	141,106	126,032	121,978	17.50	-3.22
Germany	20,374	19,612	20,619	19,223	15,087	2.16	-21.52
Netherlands	11,032	10,064	9,875	10,101	8,476	1.22	-16.09
Switzerland	14,138	12,776	12,585	9,501	8,827	1.27	-7.09
OTHER EUROPE	35,305	31,926	34,680	41,720	27,937	4.01	-33.04
Other countries of Europe	35,305	31,926	34,680	41,720	27,937	4.01	-33.04
MIDDLE EAST	3,623	3,596	4,449	4,955	5,277	0.76	6.50
Lebanon	3,623	3,596	4,449	4,955	5,277	0.76	6.50
NOT SPECIFIED	17,975	22,923	14,621	21,235	24,980	3.58	17.64
Nationals Residing Abroad	17,975	22,923	14,621	21,235	24,980	3.58	17.64

Yearbook of Tourism Statistics, Data 2009 – 2013, 2015 Edition

CABO VERDE

3. Arrivals of non-resident tourists in hotels and similar establishments, by country of residence

		2009	2010	2011	2012	2013	Market share 2013	% Change 2013-2012
TOTAL		287,183	336,086	428,273	482,267	502,874	100.00	4.27
AFRICA		175	218	2,819	278	1,321	0.26	375.18
SOUTHERN AFRICA		175	218	2,819	278	1,321	0.26	375.18
South Africa		175	218	2,819	278	1,321	0.26	375.18
AMERICAS		3,935	3,188	3,711	4,906	4,209	0.84	-14.21
NORTH AMERICA		3,935	3,188	3,711	4,906	4,209	0.84	-14.21
United States of America		3,935	3,188	3,711	4,906	4,209	0.84	-14.21
EUROPE		244,060	297,614	385,424	402,932	394,436	78.44	-2.11
NORTHERN EUROPE		57,011	72,019	90,481	115,238	94,709	18.83	-17.81
United Kingdom		57,011	72,019	90,481	115,238	94,709	18.83	-17.81
SOUTHERN EUROPE		98,891	108,508	135,858	110,849	98,580	19.60	-11.07
Italy		42,628	40,717	56,378	30,345	30,769	6.12	1.40
Portugal		50,617	60,277	65,693	67,790	58,070	11.55	-14.34
Spain		5,646	7,514	13,787	12,714	9,741	1.94	-23.38
WESTERN EUROPE		88,158	117,087	159,085	176,845	201,147	40.00	13.74
Austria		977	962	1,772	1,571	1,980	0.39	26.03
Belgium	(*)	22,091	21,655	24,169	34,608	46,556	9.26	34.52
France		22,675	43,496	66,641	69,593	74,239	14.76	6.68
Germany		40,138	48,920	60,495	67,306	74,238	14.76	10.30
Switzerland		2,277	2,054	6,008	3,767	4,134	0.82	9.74
NOT SPECIFIED		39,013	35,066	36,319	74,151	102,908	20.46	38.78
Other countries of the World		39,013	35,066	36,319	74,151	102,908	20.46	38.78

122

CABO VERDE

5. Overnight stays of non-resident tourists in hotels and similar establishments, by country of residence

		2009	2010	2011	2012	2013	Market share 2013	% Change 2013-2012
TOTAL		1,897,573	2,217,563	2,703,909	3,184,524	3,279,928	100.00	3.00
AFRICA		606	663	14,540	851	3,796	0.12	346.06
SOUTHERN AFRICA		606	663	14,540	851	3,796	0.12	346.06
South Africa		606	663	14,540	851	3,796	0.12	346.06
AMERICAS		10,632	10,162	12,988	12,286	12,837	0.39	4.48
NORTH AMERICA		10,632	10,162	12,988	12,286	12,837	0.39	4.48
United States of America		10,632	10,162	12,988	12,286	12,837	0.39	4.48
EUROPE		1,663,042	2,006,352	2,507,979	2,723,056	2,637,656	80.42	-3.14
NORTHERN EUROPE		517,655	610,465	766,740	1,057,852	836,425	25.50	-20.93
United Kingdom		517,655	610,465	766,740	1,057,852	836,425	25.50	-20.93
SOUTHERN EUROPE		556,055	609,939	794,378	596,085	587,740	17.92	-1.40
Italy		290,662	278,261	397,473	215,113	218,026	6.65	1.35
Portugal		242,905	299,228	335,688	318,099	323,956	9.88	1.84
Spain		22,488	32,450	61,217	62,873	45,758	1.40	-27.22
WESTERN EUROPE		589,332	785,948	946,861	1,069,119	1,213,491	37.00	13.50
Austria		5,541	5,397	13,208	9,282	10,877	0.33	17.18
Belgium	(*)	161,667	159,061	171,851	245,814	326,580	9.96	32.86
France		102,015	241,527	293,334	300,622	317,955	9.69	5.77
Germany		307,861	370,359	426,532	495,341	528,136	16.10	6.62
Switzerland		12,248	9,604	41,936	18,060	29,943	0.91	65.80
NOT SPECIFIED		223,293	200,386	168,402	448,331	625,639	19.07	39.55
Other countries of the World		223,293	200,386	168,402	448,331	625,639	19.07	39.55

Yearbook of Tourism Statistics, Data 2009 – 2013, 2015 Edition

CAMBODIA

1. Arrivals of non-resident tourists at national borders, by country of residence

	2009	2010	2011	2012	2013	Market share 2013	% Change 2013-2012
TOTAL	2,161,577	2,508,289	2,881,862	3,584,307	4,210,165	100.00	17.46
AFRICA	5,403	4,627	5,993	5,626	5,902	0.14	4.91
EAST AFRICA			582	346	364	0.01	5.20
Kenya			283	266	298	0.01	12.03
Uganda			299	80	66	0.00	-17.50
CENTRAL AFRICA	1,051	493	545	291	205	0.00	-29.55
Cameroon	1,051	493	388	225	147	0.00	-34.67
Congo			157	66	58	0.00	-12.12
NORTH AFRICA	32	37	48	52	60	0.00	15.38
Sudan	32	37	48	52	60	0.00	15.38
SOUTHERN AFRICA	2,104	2,459	3,216	3,530	4,043	0.10	14.53
South Africa	2,104	2,459	3,216	3,530	4,043	0.10	14.53
WEST AFRICA	1,724	1,272	1,278	813	791	0.02	-2.71
Ghana	624	503	415	149	134	0.00	-10.07
Liberia			335	94	52	0.00	-44.68
Nigeria	1,100	769	528	570	605	0.01	6.14
OTHER AFRICA	492	366	324	594	439	0.01	-26.09
Other countries of Africa	492	366	324	594	439	0.01	-26.09
AMERICAS	201,130	199,089	217,500	244,291	263,175	6.25	7.73
CENTRAL AMERICA			201	245	305	0.01	24.49
Costa Rica			201	245	305	0.01	24.49
NORTH AMERICA	187,544	187,880	199,901	225,069	240,797	5.72	6.99
Canada	36,340	38,718	42,462	47,829	50,867	1.21	6.35
Mexico	2,722	3,157	3,486	4,164	4,966	0.12	19.26
United States of America	148,482	146,005	153,953	173,076	184,964	4.39	6.87
SOUTH AMERICA	7,541	8,803	14,711	15,351	19,973	0.47	30.11
Argentina	1,717	2,212	5,223	4,500	5,763	0.14	28.07
Brazil	2,204	2,490	3,616	5,110	6,860	0.16	34.25
Chile	1,943	2,240	2,633	2,973	3,969	0.09	33.50
Colombia	942	1,060	2,060	1,497	1,803	0.04	20.44
Ecuador			184	191	283	0.01	48.17
Peru	422	468	483	576	677	0.02	17.53
Uruguay	313	333	512	504	618	0.01	22.62
OTHER AMERICAS	6,045	2,406	2,687	3,626	2,100	0.05	-42.08
Other countries of the Americas	6,045	2,406	2,687	3,626	2,100	0.05	-42.08
EAST ASIA AND THE PACIFIC	1,467,406	1,788,814	2,084,540	2,685,192	3,198,857	75.98	19.13
NORTH-EAST ASIA	548,422	715,045	855,697	1,026,152	1,211,004	28.76	18.01
China	128,210	177,636	247,197	333,894	463,123	11.00	38.70
Hong Kong, China	3,888	4,378	5,266	8,282	8,576	0.20	3.55
Japan	146,286	151,795	161,804	179,327	206,932	4.92	15.39
Korea, Republic of	197,725	289,702	342,810	411,491	435,009	10.33	5.72
Mongolia	194	305	257	347	372	0.01	7.20
Taiwan, Province of China	72,119	91,229	98,363	92,811	96,992	2.30	4.50
SOUTH-EAST ASIA	808,661	962,570	1,101,111	1,514,267	1,831,507	43.50	20.95
Brunei Darussalam	406	460	481	964	814	0.02	-15.56
Indonesia	9,585	12,636	15,817	22,544	28,199	0.67	25.08
Lao People's Democratic Republic	102,313	92,276	128,525	254,022	414,531	9.85	63.19
Malaysia	77,759	89,952	102,929	116,764	130,704	3.10	11.94
Myanmar	2,316	2,614	4,199	4,744	5,089	0.12	7.27
Philippines	49,079	56,156	70,718	97,487	118,999	2.83	22.07
Singapore	41,273	45,079	47,594	53,184	57,808	1.37	8.69
Thailand	159,036	149,108	116,758	201,422	221,259	5.26	9.85
Viet Nam	366,894	514,289	614,090	763,136	854,104	20.29	11.92
AUSTRALASIA	98,678	107,306	121,485	136,773	152,605	3.62	11.58
Australia	84,581	93,598	105,010	117,729	132,028	3.14	12.15
New Zealand	14,097	13,708	16,475	19,044	20,577	0.49	8.05
MELANESIA			117	106	107	0.00	0.94
Fiji			117	106	107	0.00	0.94

124

CAMBODIA

1. Arrivals of non-resident tourists at national borders, by country of residence

	2009	2010	2011	2012	2013	Market share 2013	% Change 2013-2012
OTHER EAST ASIA AND THE PACIFIC	11,645	3,893	6,130	7,894	3,634	0.09	-53.97
Other countries East Asia/Pacific	11,645	3,893	6,130	7,894	3,634	0.09	-53.97
EUROPE	470,181	495,586	551,452	621,700	708,966	16.84	14.04
CENTRAL/EASTERN EUROPE	34,457	54,401	93,538	129,591	168,577	4.00	30.08
Bulgaria	384	445	470	696	961	0.02	38.07
Czech Republic	2,649	3,113	3,310	4,064	4,845	0.12	19.22
Estonia			954	1,022	1,366	0.03	33.66
Hungary	2,184	2,740	2,585	2,537	2,947	0.07	16.16
Kazakhstan			1,224	1,842	2,511	0.06	36.32
Lithuania			1,238	1,089	1,608	0.04	47.66
Poland	6,319	8,712	9,151	9,994	12,507	0.30	25.15
Romania	774	1,171	1,081	1,327	1,526	0.04	15.00
Russian Federation	19,395	34,170	67,747	99,750	131,675	3.13	32.01
Slovakia	895	1,286	1,269	1,693	2,098	0.05	23.92
Ukraine	1,857	2,764	3,788	4,999	5,919	0.14	18.40
Uzbekistan			721	578	614	0.01	6.23
NORTHERN EUROPE	153,311	145,767	151,600	160,447	178,063	4.23	10.98
Denmark	8,937	7,810	9,352	10,013	10,485	0.25	4.71
Finland	6,559	5,244	6,410	6,343	6,731	0.16	6.12
Iceland	183	229	355	578	788	0.02	36.33
Ireland	9,037	8,567	8,541	8,865	10,245	0.24	15.57
Norway	7,017	7,774	8,128	8,251	9,482	0.23	14.92
Sweden	14,741	13,076	14,762	16,215	16,413	0.39	1.22
United Kingdom	106,837	103,067	104,052	110,182	123,919	2.94	12.47
SOUTHERN EUROPE	38,405	44,082	49,023	54,163	59,422	1.41	9.71
Croatia	313	470	532	705	798	0.02	13.19
Greece	1,406	1,395	1,168	1,073	1,135	0.03	5.78
Italy	17,154	19,808	20,837	22,625	25,196	0.60	11.36
Portugal	2,481	2,554	3,081	3,061	4,087	0.10	33.52
Serbia			408	411	613	0.01	49.15
Slovenia	740	692	874	939	1,221	0.03	30.03
Spain	16,311	19,163	22,123	25,349	26,372	0.63	4.04
WESTERN EUROPE	226,057	238,812	242,011	259,499	287,434	6.83	10.76
Austria	8,681	8,547	7,601	8,148	9,091	0.22	11.57
Belgium	12,980	14,295	13,905	14,762	16,171	0.38	9.54
France	105,437	113,285	117,408	121,175	131,486	3.12	8.51
Germany	59,916	62,864	63,398	72,537	81,565	1.94	12.45
Luxembourg	472	639	497	474	571	0.01	20.46
Monaco			82	55	103	0.00	87.27
Netherlands	22,058	23,537	22,725	24,559	28,076	0.67	14.32
Switzerland	16,513	15,645	16,395	17,789	20,371	0.48	14.51
EAST MEDITERRANEAN EUROPE	7,179	9,238	9,929	11,329	12,355	0.29	9.06
Israel	5,439	6,186	6,644	7,921	7,684	0.18	-2.99
Turkey	1,740	3,052	3,285	3,408	4,671	0.11	37.06
OTHER EUROPE	10,772	3,286	5,351	6,671	3,115	0.07	-53.31
Other countries of Europe	10,772	3,286	5,351	6,671	3,115	0.07	-53.31
MIDDLE EAST	1,144	1,071	1,565	2,148	2,700	0.06	25.70
Egypt	173	220	196	219	329	0.01	50.23
Iraq			91	83	134	0.00	61.45
Kuwait	633	543	530	712	1,121	0.03	57.44
Oman			107	150	199	0.00	32.67
Palestine			34	51	94	0.00	84.31
Qatar			62	70	95	0.00	35.71
Saudi Arabia	48	64	78	87	150	0.00	72.41
United Arab Emirates			155	243	146	0.00	-39.92
Yemen			98	156	144	0.00	-7.69
Other countries of Middle East	290	244	214	377	288	0.01	-23.61

Yearbook of Tourism Statistics, Data 2009 – 2013, 2015 Edition

CAMBODIA

1. Arrivals of non-resident tourists at national borders, by country of residence

	2009	2010	2011	2012	2013	Market share 2013	% Change 2013-2012
SOUTH ASIA	**16,313**	**19,102**	**20,812**	**25,350**	**30,565**	**0.73**	**20.57**
Afghanistan	126	180	113	154	273	0.01	77.27
Bangladesh	925	1,658	1,316	1,367	1,611	0.04	17.85
Bhutan			81	134	101	0.00	-24.63
India	12,461	13,542	15,240	18,999	23,610	0.56	24.27
Iran, Islamic Republic of	338	518	696	646	655	0.02	1.39
Nepal	908	1,081	1,156	1,478	1,475	0.04	-0.20
Pakistan	798	1,092	1,113	1,168	1,180	0.03	1.03
Sri Lanka	757	1,031	1,097	1,404	1,660	0.04	18.23

Yearbook of Tourism Statistics, Data 2009 – 2013, 2015 Edition

CANADA

1. Arrivals of non-resident tourists at national borders, by country of residence

		2009	2010	2011	2012	2013	Market share 2013	% Change 2013-2012
TOTAL	(*)	15,737,150	16,219,399	16,014,405	16,344,011	16,589,694	100.00	1.50
AFRICA		75,717	81,277	85,902	91,858	97,971	0.59	6.65
EAST AFRICA		14,219	14,956	15,137	17,530	17,792	0.11	1.49
Burundi		254	269	318	441	357	0.00	-19.05
Comoros		54	61	110	74	66	0.00	-10.81
Djibouti		66	195	112	151	180	0.00	19.21
Eritrea		198	241	218	248	230	0.00	-7.26
Ethiopia		1,182	1,296	1,284	2,019	2,123	0.01	5.15
Kenya		3,430	3,441	3,509	3,788	4,060	0.02	7.18
Madagascar		600	662	693	657	594	0.00	-9.59
Malawi		228	304	319	255	246	0.00	-3.53
Mauritius		1,738	2,103	1,953	2,066	2,241	0.01	8.47
Mozambique		255	265	330	327	303	0.00	-7.34
Reunion		1,257	1,226	1,523	1,753	1,694	0.01	-3.37
Rwanda		386	451	436	560	748	0.00	33.57
Seychelles		63	70	42	62	90	0.00	45.16
Somalia		195	215	217	210	267	0.00	27.14
Uganda		1,120	1,375	1,228	1,620	1,671	0.01	3.15
United Republic of Tanzania		1,742	1,542	1,450	1,799	1,537	0.01	-14.56
Zambia		701	502	583	660	592	0.00	-10.30
Zimbabwe		750	738	812	840	793	0.00	-5.60
CENTRAL AFRICA		3,695	3,888	3,798	4,508	5,126	0.03	13.71
Angola		307	395	382	355	423	0.00	19.15
Cameroon		1,711	1,758	1,743	2,178	2,372	0.01	8.91
Central African Republic		22	16	28	30	16	0.00	-46.67
Chad		163	111	111	193	154	0.00	-20.21
Congo		85	84	176	155	180	0.00	16.13
Democratic Republic of the Congo		897	1,003	859	1,175	1,407	0.01	19.74
Equatorial Guinea		37	22	11	7	14	0.00	100.00
Gabon		473	495	488	413	560	0.00	35.59
Sao Tome and Principe			4		2			
NORTH AFRICA		21,666	22,909	24,919	27,330	29,134	0.18	6.60
Algeria		6,446	6,954	8,216	9,707	10,295	0.06	6.06
Morocco		10,832	11,471	11,760	12,676	13,470	0.08	6.26
Sudan		390	550	519	489	494	0.00	1.02
Tunisia		3,998	3,932	4,424	4,458	4,870	0.03	9.24
Western Sahara			2			5	0.00	
SOUTHERN AFRICA		19,957	20,473	22,791	22,032	20,912	0.13	-5.08
Botswana		571	598	558	619	393	0.00	-36.51
Lesotho		114	71	87	71	90	0.00	26.76
Namibia		420	707	1,193	415	404	0.00	-2.65
South Africa		18,715	18,916	20,826	20,706	19,881	0.12	-3.98
Swaziland		137	181	127	221	144	0.00	-34.84
WEST AFRICA		16,111	19,003	19,240	20,454	24,997	0.15	22.21
Benin		795	735	795	601	647	0.00	7.65
Burkina Faso		698	758	772	1,048	1,007	0.01	-3.91
Cabo Verde		10	21	13	16	21	0.00	31.25
Côte d'Ivoire		1,087	1,093	715	1,286	1,382	0.01	7.47
Gambia		164	138	148	128	124	0.00	-3.13
Ghana		2,008	2,138	2,264	2,581	2,744	0.02	6.32
Guinea		495	540	657	757	724	0.00	-4.36
Guinea-Bissau		10	27	2		14	0.00	
Liberia		107	137	202	143	126	0.00	-11.89
Mali		883	744	953	847	751	0.00	-11.33
Mauritania		199	158	236	244	240	0.00	-1.64
Niger		243	195	233	237	209	0.00	-11.81
Nigeria		7,371	10,195	9,821	10,239	14,719	0.09	43.75
Saint Helena				13		4	0.00	
Senegal		1,667	1,711	1,896	1,861	1,821	0.01	-2.15

127

Yearbook of Tourism Statistics, Data 2009 – 2013, 2015 Edition

CANADA

1. Arrivals of non-resident tourists at national borders, by country of residence

	2009	2010	2011	2012	2013	Market share 2013	% Change 2013-2012
Sierra Leone	117	142	142	140	101	0.00	-27.86
Togo	257	271	378	326	363	0.00	11.35
OTHER AFRICA	**69**	**48**	**17**	**4**	**10**	**0.00**	**150.00**
Other countries of Africa	69	48	17	4	10	0.00	150.00
AMERICAS	**12,150,425**	**12,336,321**	**12,079,843**	**12,395,137**	**12,532,694**	**75.55**	**1.11**
CARIBBEAN	**128,036**	**134,944**	**134,975**	**133,385**	**136,821**	**0.82**	**2.58**
Anguilla	140	213	159	216	280	0.00	29.63
Antigua and Barbuda	1,373	1,408	1,605	1,771	1,722	0.01	-2.77
Bahamas	9,284	9,139	8,932	9,040	9,194	0.06	1.70
Barbados	10,822	11,897	11,462	11,448	11,301	0.07	-1.28
Bermuda	19,234	21,604	20,800	19,077	17,288	0.10	-9.38
British Virgin Islands	570	476	504	477	465	0.00	-2.52
Cayman Islands	5,636	5,379	6,281	5,883	6,220	0.04	5.73
Cuba	5,554	5,281	5,172	5,512	8,773	0.05	59.16
Dominica	513	641	706	518	669	0.00	29.15
Dominican Republic	4,114	5,330	5,087	5,478	5,852	0.04	6.83
Grenada	965	944	894	1,053	1,006	0.01	-4.46
Guadeloupe	3,152	3,984	4,264	3,696	4,028	0.02	8.98
Haiti	6,659	6,230	6,725	7,377	6,808	0.04	-7.71
Jamaica	24,323	26,077	25,147	25,197	27,583	0.17	9.47
Martinique	2,394	2,806	2,921	3,215	3,121	0.02	-2.92
Montserrat	33	59	19	26	47	0.00	80.77
Netherlands Antilles	1,269	1,503	1,838	1,832	1,880	0.01	2.62
Puerto Rico	1,103	995	1,005	939	1,242	0.01	32.27
Saint Kitts and Nevis	863	832	872	811	960	0.01	18.37
Saint Lucia	2,934	3,668	3,937	3,130	1,307	0.01	-58.24
Saint Vincent and the Grenadines	2,898	3,351	3,257	2,398	917	0.01	-61.76
Trinidad and Tobago	22,779	21,778	22,004	22,815	24,713	0.15	8.32
Turks and Caicos Islands	1,349	1,281	1,337	1,418	1,384	0.01	-2.40
United States Virgin Islands	75	68	47	58	61	0.00	5.17
CENTRAL AMERICA	**19,045**	**19,926**	**19,448**	**21,439**	**22,302**	**0.13**	**4.03**
Belize	825	946	1,017	1,246	1,195	0.01	-4.09
Costa Rica	4,647	4,682	4,438	4,868	5,220	0.03	7.23
El Salvador	2,326	2,160	1,770	2,019	2,021	0.01	0.10
Guatemala	6,598	6,938	6,443	7,266	7,574	0.05	4.24
Honduras	1,167	1,248	1,487	1,463	1,546	0.01	5.67
Nicaragua	894	949	896	960	932	0.01	-2.92
Panama	2,588	3,003	3,397	3,617	3,810	0.02	5.34
Other countries of Central America					4	0.00	
NORTH AMERICA	**11,856,529**	**12,009,757**	**11,743,918**	**12,046,445**	**12,175,673**	**73.39**	**1.07**
Greenland	213	406	267	247	278	0.00	12.55
Mexico	168,724	120,499	132,217	141,921	150,896	0.91	6.32
Saint Pierre and Miquelon	20,359	18,008	16,071	17,327	16,523	0.10	-4.64
United States of America	11,667,233	11,870,844	11,595,363	11,886,950	12,007,976	72.38	1.02
SOUTH AMERICA	**146,815**	**171,694**	**181,502**	**193,868**	**197,898**	**1.19**	**2.08**
Argentina	15,013	16,744	17,737	16,619	17,435	0.11	4.91
Bolivia	831	853	976	1,078	1,080	0.01	0.19
Brazil	61,829	80,188	87,904	93,570	93,757	0.57	0.20
Chile	13,602	18,255	17,336	20,399	20,296	0.12	-0.50
Colombia	16,568	16,267	18,762	20,074	21,424	0.13	6.73
Ecuador	3,716	3,792	3,633	3,558	4,006	0.02	12.59
Falkland Islands, Malvinas	12	8	5	23	16	0.00	-30.43
French Guiana	182	185	238	259	257	0.00	-0.77
Guyana	3,947	3,267	3,803	4,484	4,793	0.03	6.89
Paraguay	1,074	1,202	1,312	1,207	1,492	0.01	23.61
Peru	8,016	10,119	9,470	10,577	11,010	0.07	4.09
Suriname	262	283	262	357	349	0.00	-2.24
Uruguay	1,638	1,921	2,180	1,930	2,359	0.01	22.23
Venezuela	20,125	18,610	17,884	19,733	19,624	0.12	-0.55

128

CANADA

1. Arrivals of non-resident tourists at national borders, by country of residence

	2009	2010	2011	2012	2013	Market share 2013	% Change 2013-2012
EAST ASIA AND THE PACIFIC	**1,025,526**	**1,170,281**	**1,222,621**	**1,285,606**	**1,389,437**	**8.38**	**8.08**
NORTH-EAST ASIA	**654,969**	**763,735**	**787,524**	**828,960**	**914,458**	**5.51**	**10.31**
China	160,833	194,979	243,692	288,279	352,597	2.13	22.31
Hong Kong, China	107,410	114,973	123,060	120,022	129,068	0.78	7.54
Japan	197,752	235,510	211,062	226,215	224,858	1.36	-0.60
Korea, Dem. People's Republic of	2	8			2	0.00	
Korea, Republic of	138,150	164,282	151,101	139,999	144,583	0.87	3.27
Macao, China	151	181	157	301	318	0.00	5.65
Mongolia	671	989	769	969	994	0.01	2.58
Taiwan, Province of China	50,000	52,813	57,683	53,175	62,038	0.37	16.67
SOUTH-EAST ASIA	**121,165**	**124,704**	**146,489**	**149,227**	**157,835**	**0.95**	**5.77**
Brunei Darussalam	450	527	548	509	533	0.00	4.72
Cambodia	566	502	762	837	816	0.00	-2.51
Indonesia	11,117	12,428	15,142	16,864	18,487	0.11	9.62
Lao People's Democratic Republic	180	176	223	268	204	0.00	-23.88
Malaysia	8,754	11,255	11,867	12,077	11,937	0.07	-1.16
Myanmar	487	318	262	179	289	0.00	61.45
Philippines	61,473	54,946	59,674	63,141	65,373	0.39	3.53
Singapore	21,043	24,770	29,254	30,492	33,494	0.20	9.85
Thailand	11,419	13,197	21,449	16,952	17,663	0.11	4.19
Viet Nam	5,676	6,585	7,308	7,908	9,039	0.05	14.30
AUSTRALASIA	**245,971**	**278,280**	**285,114**	**303,818**	**313,300**	**1.89**	**3.12**
Australia	204,383	232,855	242,430	258,115	264,207	1.59	2.36
New Zealand	41,588	45,425	42,684	45,703	49,093	0.30	7.42
MELANESIA	**2,122**	**2,122**	**1,940**	**2,295**	**2,457**	**0.01**	**7.06**
Fiji	1,216	1,091	903	879	1,123	0.01	27.76
New Caledonia	690	749	819	1,072	1,074	0.01	0.19
Papua New Guinea	140	185	138	269	199	0.00	-26.02
Solomon Islands	24	28	31	18	18	0.00	
Vanuatu	52	69	49	57	43	0.00	-24.56
MICRONESIA	**150**	**112**	**109**	**90**	**106**	**0.00**	**17.78**
Guam	35	22	18	13	30	0.00	130.77
Kiribati	13	18	26	14	19	0.00	35.71
Marshall Islands	36	9	14	12	12	0.00	
Micronesia, Federated States of	62	47	41	47	39	0.00	-17.02
Nauru		12	4	4	4	0.00	
Northern Mariana Islands	4	4	6		2	0.00	
POLYNESIA	**1,135**	**1,312**	**1,437**	**1,210**	**1,265**	**0.01**	**4.55**
American Samoa	28	53	23	18	21	0.00	16.67
Cook Islands	12	26	6	20	37	0.00	85.00
French Polynesia	1,046	1,201	1,371	1,139	1,141	0.01	0.18
Samoa	10	14	12	18	20	0.00	11.11
Tonga	31	12	22	15	32	0.00	113.33
Tuvalu		2	3				
Wallis and Futuna Islands	8	4			14	0.00	
OTHER EAST ASIA AND THE PACIFIC	**14**	**16**	**8**	**6**	**16**	**0.00**	**166.67**
Other countries East Asia/Pacific	10	2		2			
Other countries of Oceania	4	14	8	4	16	0.00	300.00
EUROPE	**2,262,129**	**2,375,518**	**2,355,777**	**2,298,886**	**2,286,167**	**13.78**	**-0.55**
CENTRAL/EASTERN EUROPE	**122,740**	**128,378**	**127,616**	**129,873**	**131,361**	**0.79**	**1.15**
Armenia	341	480	604	477	429	0.00	-10.06
Azerbaijan	408	455	476	627	470	0.00	-25.04
Belarus	1,537	1,461	1,245	1,312	1,335	0.01	1.75
Bulgaria	3,278	3,210	3,128	2,999	3,070	0.02	2.37
Czech Republic	16,068	11,864	11,112	11,492	12,005	0.07	4.46
Estonia	1,675	1,540	1,577	1,723	1,742	0.01	1.10
Georgia	214	378	283	282	194	0.00	-31.21
Hungary	11,752	12,284	12,878	11,228	10,718	0.06	-4.54
Kazakhstan	2,004	2,116	2,158	2,382	2,398	0.01	0.67

129

CANADA

1. Arrivals of non-resident tourists at national borders, by country of residence

	2009	2010	2011	2012	2013	Market share 2013	% Change 2013-2012
Kyrgyzstan	283	245	261	304	266	0.00	-12.50
Latvia	2,398	2,488	2,027	2,281	2,204	0.01	-3.38
Lithuania	1,461	1,715	1,871	2,154	2,058	0.01	-4.46
Poland	28,352	29,295	29,536	31,677	33,182	0.20	4.75
Republic of Moldova	1,480	1,783	1,910	2,130	2,035	0.01	-4.46
Romania	15,408	15,633	15,416	13,832	13,660	0.08	-1.24
Russian Federation	19,389	25,027	23,796	25,220	25,083	0.15	-0.54
Slovakia	6,516	7,567	7,320	7,107	7,157	0.04	0.70
Tajikistan	65	80	64	50	94	0.00	88.00
Turkmenistan	78	75	70	70	54	0.00	-22.86
Ukraine	9,755	10,406	11,675	12,214	12,937	0.08	5.92
Uzbekistan	278	276	209	312	270	0.00	-13.46
NORTHERN EUROPE	**850,301**	**874,143**	**846,280**	**818,070**	**809,120**	**4.88**	**-1.09**
Denmark	26,654	33,085	38,179	37,656	35,941	0.22	-4.55
Faeroe Islands	83	151	97	108	106	0.00	-1.85
Finland	14,742	16,791	14,706	14,215	14,490	0.09	1.93
Iceland	3,450	4,244	5,087	3,449	3,986	0.02	15.57
Ireland	43,664	46,273	42,638	43,382	44,202	0.27	1.89
Norway	20,329	24,723	24,691	25,657	24,449	0.15	-4.71
Sweden	30,866	37,187	41,054	39,682	40,249	0.24	1.43
United Kingdom	710,513	711,689	679,828	653,921	645,697	3.89	-1.26
SOUTHERN EUROPE	**208,326**	**219,305**	**215,140**	**200,227**	**200,819**	**1.21**	**0.30**
Albania	1,349	1,330	1,156	1,174	1,210	0.01	3.07
Andorra	327	364	281	224	200	0.00	-10.71
Bosnia and Herzegovina	1,487	1,529	1,389	1,127	1,263	0.01	12.07
Croatia	4,569	5,248	5,273	5,851	6,016	0.04	2.82
Gibraltar	238	261	324	211	305	0.00	44.55
Greece	12,058	12,799	12,482	12,795	12,380	0.07	-3.24
Holy See	1	4	6	19	6	0.00	-68.42
Italy	92,393	101,738	98,191	93,127	92,691	0.56	-0.47
Malta	2,090	1,892	1,875	1,742	1,881	0.01	7.98
Portugal	18,108	19,556	20,879	21,019	23,376	0.14	11.21
San Marino	30	64	48	24	43	0.00	79.17
Serbia and Montenegro	4,949	5,467	5,270	4,863	4,711	0.03	-3.13
Slovenia	2,979	3,702	3,212	2,881	3,027	0.02	5.07
Spain	66,733	64,383	63,858	54,413	52,953	0.32	-2.68
TFYR of Macedonia	1,015	968	896	757	757	0.00	
WESTERN EUROPE	**1,012,096**	**1,078,818**	**1,089,427**	**1,073,600**	**1,070,035**	**6.45**	**-0.33**
Austria	32,949	38,086	36,925	35,646	34,854	0.21	-2.22
Belgium	48,057	52,600	54,848	54,174	52,039	0.31	-3.94
France	407,653	435,465	459,140	455,300	459,475	2.77	0.92
Germany	309,684	332,086	315,901	311,692	311,379	1.88	-0.10
Liechtenstein	462	483	473	395	423	0.00	7.09
Luxembourg	3,497	4,179	4,260	4,599	4,207	0.03	-8.52
Monaco	1,204	1,286	1,315	1,199	1,399	0.01	16.68
Netherlands	109,133	109,208	105,842	100,644	97,689	0.59	-2.94
Switzerland	99,457	105,425	110,723	109,951	108,570	0.65	-1.26
EAST MEDITERRANEAN EUROPE	**68,666**	**74,874**	**77,314**	**77,116**	**74,832**	**0.45**	**-2.96**
Cyprus	1,535	1,853	1,712	1,845	1,525	0.01	-17.34
Israel	57,704	60,681	63,322	62,935	60,464	0.36	-3.93
Turkey	9,427	12,340	12,280	12,336	12,843	0.08	4.11
MIDDLE EAST	**77,602**	**83,668**	**85,069**	**85,464**	**91,327**	**0.55**	**6.86**
Bahrain	1,553	1,671	1,696	1,397	1,426	0.01	2.08
Egypt	9,009	10,434	8,942	9,852	10,901	0.07	10.65
Iraq	1,190	1,576	1,554	1,343	1,247	0.01	-7.15
Jordan	3,443	3,422	3,787	3,662	3,748	0.02	2.35
Kuwait	3,197	3,385	3,615	3,872	3,793	0.02	-2.04
Lebanon	8,300	8,372	9,925	9,245	9,987	0.06	8.03
Libya	1,504	1,558	441	1,091	2,088	0.01	91.38

130

CANADA

1. Arrivals of non-resident tourists at national borders, by country of residence

	2009	2010	2011	2012	2013	Market share 2013	% Change 2013-2012
Oman	1,300	1,536	1,387	1,423	1,659	0.01	16.58
Qatar	3,740	4,072	4,803	4,896	5,602	0.03	14.42
Saudi Arabia	17,799	20,124	18,756	19,603	21,143	0.13	7.86
Syrian Arab Republic	2,277	2,209	2,506	1,830	1,183	0.01	-35.36
United Arab Emirates	23,904	25,000	27,378	27,026	28,284	0.17	4.65
Yemen	386	309	279	224	266	0.00	18.75
SOUTH ASIA	**145,751**	**172,334**	**185,193**	**187,060**	**192,098**	**1.16**	**2.69**
Afghanistan	656	680	812	1,077	742	0.00	-31.10
Bangladesh	4,120	5,455	5,138	4,886	5,578	0.03	14.16
Bhutan	97	299	372	392	171	0.00	-56.38
India	107,959	127,619	139,213	146,652	147,099	0.89	0.30
Iran, Islamic Republic of	11,830	15,616	14,329	11,962	13,822	0.08	15.55
Maldives	53	44	73	63	75	0.00	19.05
Nepal	1,164	1,435	1,445	1,485	1,422	0.01	-4.24
Pakistan	16,804	17,574	19,685	16,298	19,466	0.12	19.44
Sri Lanka	3,068	3,612	4,126	4,245	3,723	0.02	-12.30

Yearbook of Tourism Statistics, Data 2009 – 2013, 2015 Edition

CANADA

2. Arrivals of non-resident visitors at national borders, by country of residence

		2009	2010	2011	2012	2013	Market share 2013	% Change 2013-2012
TOTAL	(*)	24,695,500	25,621,300	25,066,500	25,300,800	25,163,170	100.00	-0.54
AFRICA		76,300	81,800	86,500	76,600	98,473	0.39	28.55
SOUTHERN AFRICA		19,100	19,200	21,100	21,200	20,208	0.08	-4.68
South Africa		19,100	19,200	21,100	21,200	20,208	0.08	-4.68
OTHER AFRICA		57,200	62,600	65,400	55,400	78,265	0.31	41.27
Other countries of Africa		57,200	62,600	65,400	55,400	78,265	0.31	41.27
AMERICAS		21,014,000	21,636,800	21,035,300	21,236,600	20,967,202	83.32	-1.27
CARIBBEAN		128,700	135,700	135,900	134,400	135,841	0.54	1.07
Bermuda		19,200	21,600	20,800	19,100	17,317	0.07	-9.34
Jamaica		24,500	26,200	25,400	25,600	27,805	0.11	8.61
Trinidad and Tobago		22,900	21,900	22,100	22,900	24,809	0.10	8.34
Other countries of the Caribbean		62,100	66,000	67,600	66,800	65,910	0.26	-1.33
NORTH AMERICA		20,718,200	21,307,800	20,696,800	20,884,400	20,608,990	81.90	-1.32
Greenland		200	400	300	300	282	0.00	-6.00
Mexico		172,000	123,800	136,900	147,700	156,856	0.62	6.20
Saint Pierre and Miquelon		20,400	18,000	16,100	17,300	16,523	0.07	-4.49
United States of America		20,525,600	21,165,600	20,543,500	20,719,100	20,435,329	81.21	-1.37
SOUTH AMERICA		147,900	173,200	182,900	196,000	199,733	0.79	1.90
Argentina		15,100	16,800	17,900	16,800	17,619	0.07	4.88
Brazil		62,200	80,800	88,500	94,600	94,555	0.38	-0.05
Colombia		16,800	16,500	19,000	20,400	21,750	0.09	6.62
Venezuela		20,300	18,800	18,000	19,900	19,752	0.08	-0.74
Other countries of South America		33,500	40,300	39,500	44,300	46,057	0.18	3.97
OTHER AMERICAS		19,200	20,100	19,700	21,800	22,638	0.09	3.84
Other countries of the Americas		19,200	20,100	19,700	21,800	22,638	0.09	3.84
EAST ASIA AND THE PACIFIC		1,064,200	1,211,300	1,262,300	1,346,800	1,460,571	5.80	8.45
NORTH-EAST ASIA		680,000	787,800	809,500	867,500	960,797	3.82	10.75
China	(*)	166,900	201,000	249,700	299,000	366,311	1.46	22.51
Hong Kong, China		111,800	119,400	126,800	123,900	133,453	0.53	7.71
Japan		205,600	243,000	218,800	240,000	238,474	0.95	-0.64
Korea, Republic of		144,100	170,000	155,700	150,600	158,523	0.63	5.26
Taiwan, Province of China		51,600	54,400	58,500	54,000	64,036	0.25	18.59
SOUTH-EAST ASIA		116,800	120,100	142,700	145,900	154,265	0.61	5.73
Indonesia		11,500	12,900	15,800	17,800	19,687	0.08	10.60
Malaysia		9,000	11,500	12,200	12,700	12,681	0.05	-0.15
Philippines		62,700	56,600	61,200	64,700	67,401	0.27	4.17
Singapore		21,900	25,600	30,800	32,800	35,689	0.14	8.81
Thailand		11,700	13,500	22,700	17,900	18,807	0.07	5.07
AUSTRALASIA		256,400	291,400	297,300	319,700	330,745	1.31	3.45
Australia		213,700	244,200	253,300	272,200	279,936	1.11	2.84
New Zealand		42,700	47,200	44,000	47,500	50,809	0.20	6.97
OTHER EAST ASIA AND THE PACIFIC		11,000	12,000	12,800	13,700	14,764	0.06	7.77
Other countries of Asia		7,600	8,400	9,300	10,100	10,900	0.04	7.92
Other countries of Oceania		3,400	3,600	3,500	3,600	3,864	0.02	7.33
EUROPE		2,310,900	2,427,400	2,403,400	2,359,400	2,344,348	9.32	-0.64
CENTRAL/EASTERN EUROPE		127,000	133,300	132,200	134,300	135,868	0.54	1.17
Czech Republic/Slovakia		23,000	19,600	18,700	18,800	19,435	0.08	3.38
Estonia	(*)	5,600	5,800	5,500	6,300	6,035	0.02	-4.21
Hungary	(*)	33,800	35,200	35,100	31,300	30,868	0.12	-1.38
Poland		28,600	29,600	29,800	32,200	33,577	0.13	4.28
Commonwealth Independent States		36,000	43,100	43,100	45,700	45,953	0.18	0.55
NORTHERN EUROPE		867,400	893,900	864,400	839,100	829,689	3.30	-1.12
Denmark	(*)	27,400	33,900	38,900	38,600	36,703	0.15	-4.91
Finland		15,000	17,000	15,000	14,500	14,826	0.06	2.25
Iceland		3,500	4,300	5,200	3,500	4,007	0.02	14.49
Ireland		44,600	48,000	43,900	44,600	45,140	0.18	1.21
Norway		20,600	25,200	25,000	26,000	24,810	0.10	-4.58
Sweden		31,600	37,700	41,500	40,200	40,679	0.16	1.19
United Kingdom	(*)	724,700	727,800	694,900	671,700	663,524	2.64	-1.22

132

CANADA

2. Arrivals of non-resident visitors at national borders, by country of residence

		2009	2010	2011	2012	2013	Market share 2013	% Change 2013-2012
SOUTHERN EUROPE		**218,700**	**226,700**	**223,000**	**211,800**	**210,335**	**0.84**	**-0.69**
Greece		12,300	13,100	12,800	13,300	12,783	0.05	-3.89
Italy	(*)	101,500	110,400	106,500	103,800	102,767	0.41	-1.00
Portugal		18,500	19,900	21,300	21,500	23,750	0.09	10.47
Spain		72,900	68,600	68,100	59,100	56,657	0.23	-4.13
Yugoslavia, SFR (former)	(*)	13,500	14,700	14,300	14,100	14,378	0.06	1.97
WESTERN EUROPE		**1,029,500**	**1,099,300**	**1,106,900**	**1,096,700**	**1,092,693**	**4.34**	**-0.37**
Austria		33,400	38,800	37,300	36,200	35,471	0.14	-2.01
France	(*)	413,300	442,400	466,200	463,300	467,157	1.86	0.83
Germany		318,800	342,000	324,000	322,400	322,419	1.28	0.01
Netherlands		110,700	111,000	107,100	102,900	100,233	0.40	-2.59
Switzerland	(*)	101,200	107,700	112,700	112,200	110,728	0.44	-1.31
Belgium / Luxembourg		52,100	57,400	59,600	59,700	56,685	0.23	-5.05
EAST MEDITERRANEAN EUROPE		**68,300**	**74,200**	**76,900**	**77,500**	**75,763**	**0.30**	**-2.24**
Israel		58,800	61,800	64,400	65,000	62,806	0.25	-3.38
Turkey		9,500	12,400	12,500	12,500	12,957	0.05	3.66
MIDDLE EAST		**92,100**	**102,200**	**102,400**	**99,800**	**91,783**	**0.36**	**-8.03**
All countries of Middle East		92,100	102,200	102,400	99,800	91,783	0.36	-8.03
SOUTH ASIA		**138,000**	**161,800**	**176,600**	**181,600**	**200,793**	**0.80**	**10.57**
All countries of South Asia		138,000	161,800	176,600	181,600	200,793	0.80	10.57

Yearbook of Tourism Statistics, Data 2009 – 2013, 2015 Edition

CANADA

6. Overnight stays of non-resident tourists in all types of accommodation establishments, by country of residence

		2009	2010	2011	2012	2013	Market share 2013	% Change 2013-2012
TOTAL	(*)	114,888,500	120,102,200	124,395,700	129,164,700			
AFRICA		1,689,300	1,952,400	2,489,000	2,295,000			
SOUTHERN AFRICA		331,100	352,100	405,900	300,000			
South Africa		331,100	352,100	405,900	300,000			
OTHER AFRICA		1,358,200	1,600,300	2,083,100	1,995,000			
Other countries of Africa		1,358,200	1,600,300	2,083,100	1,995,000			
AMERICAS		55,439,100	55,583,800	56,223,100	60,472,400			
CARIBBEAN		1,610,500	2,167,400	2,206,000	2,786,900			
Bermuda		156,200	207,600	197,700	276,900			
Jamaica		357,000	603,600	651,800	763,400			
Trinidad and Tobago		370,000	462,800	466,200	657,100			
Other countries of the Caribbean		727,300	893,400	890,300	1,089,500			
NORTH AMERICA		51,071,600	50,263,600	50,417,100	54,167,200			
Greenland		2,200	2,900	2,000	2,300			
Mexico		3,622,000	2,584,400	2,907,700	3,195,600			
Saint Pierre and Miquelon		82,500	71,900	81,200	120,400			
United States of America		47,364,900	47,604,400	47,426,200	50,848,900			
SOUTH AMERICA		2,397,400	2,911,000	3,325,800	3,240,200			
Argentina		200,500	250,600	302,100	210,100			
Brazil		979,600	1,381,800	1,464,400	1,530,700			
Colombia		313,900	415,200	541,000	526,000			
Venezuela		350,600	275,400	319,100	296,400			
Other countries of South America		552,800	588,000	699,200	677,000			
OTHER AMERICAS		359,600	241,800	274,200	278,100			
Other countries of the Americas		359,600	241,800	274,200	278,100			
EAST ASIA AND THE PACIFIC		19,924,400	22,529,200	25,110,400	26,469,100			
NORTH-EAST ASIA		13,027,800	15,588,000	17,026,200	18,127,100			
China	(*)	4,470,800	5,401,000	6,903,700	8,136,200			
Hong Kong, China		1,780,000	1,958,100	2,131,700	2,237,400			
Japan		2,468,500	3,045,800	2,754,300	2,800,000			
Korea, Republic of		3,450,500	4,232,400	4,007,600	4,012,100			
Taiwan, Province of China		858,000	950,700	1,228,900	941,400			
SOUTH-EAST ASIA		3,189,400	3,108,700	4,082,800	3,936,700			
Indonesia		180,200	128,000	216,800	214,400			
Malaysia		185,200	234,500	122,100	123,700			
Philippines		2,384,800	2,043,400	3,098,400	3,018,700			
Singapore		234,700	293,700	347,700	336,600			
Thailand		204,500	409,100	297,800	243,300			
AUSTRALASIA		3,546,600	3,606,400	3,808,800	4,168,700			
Australia		2,644,200	3,023,600	3,293,300	3,424,500			
New Zealand		902,400	582,800	515,500	744,200			
OTHER EAST ASIA AND THE PACIFIC		160,600	226,100	192,600	236,600			
Other countries of Asia		103,200	162,200	133,500	172,700			
Other countries of Oceania		57,400	63,900	59,100	63,900			
EUROPE		33,197,600	34,504,500	34,400,300	33,552,600			
CENTRAL/EASTERN EUROPE		2,304,100	3,124,200	3,510,300	3,048,400			
Czech Republic/Slovakia		425,200	377,100	619,800	374,800			
Estonia	(*)	63,500	111,200	49,900	61,700			
Hungary	(*)	680,900	782,500	976,800	747,600			
Poland		502,200	594,600	792,500	728,000			
Commonwealth Independent States		632,300	1,258,800	1,071,300	1,136,300			
NORTHERN EUROPE		11,085,100	10,796,400	10,564,700	10,611,200			
Denmark	(*)	332,700	363,800	381,600	484,000			
Finland		215,500	262,200	152,800	152,100			
Iceland		28,700	40,700	46,500	45,800			
Ireland		453,400	559,900	636,100	780,500			
Norway		230,800	280,700	358,500	336,900			
Sweden		463,800	379,800	537,800	488,400			
United Kingdom	(*)	9,360,200	8,909,300	8,451,400	8,323,500			

CANADA

6. Overnight stays of non-resident tourists in all types of accommodation establishments, by country of residence

		2009	2010	2011	2012	2013	Market share 2013	% Change 2013-2012
SOUTHERN EUROPE		3,112,900	2,926,800	2,814,900	2,643,700			
Greece		188,400	185,600	122,500	226,500			
Italy	(*)	1,196,600	1,270,800	1,213,300	1,264,200			
Portugal		347,600	243,800	223,000	312,700			
Spain		898,500	821,100	750,500	529,300			
Yugoslavia, SFR (former)	(*)	481,800	405,500	505,600	311,000			
WESTERN EUROPE		15,845,000	16,872,700	16,554,700	16,203,900			
Austria		530,000	601,400	397,000	376,300			
France	(*)	6,351,000	6,657,200	6,939,200	7,026,200			
Germany		5,160,900	5,515,100	5,082,700	4,804,600			
Netherlands		1,579,400	1,565,500	1,497,800	1,499,500			
Switzerland	(*)	1,562,300	1,608,400	1,779,800	1,826,200			
Belgium / Luxembourg		661,400	925,100	858,200	671,100			
EAST MEDITERRANEAN EUROPE		850,500	784,400	955,700	1,045,400			
Israel		604,300	646,200	757,700	818,000			
Turkey		246,200	138,200	198,000	227,400			
MIDDLE EAST		1,961,100	2,282,300	2,427,000	2,383,800			
All countries of Middle East		1,961,100	2,282,300	2,427,000	2,383,800			
SOUTH ASIA		2,677,000	3,250,000	3,745,900	3,991,800			
All countries of South Asia		2,677,000	3,250,000	3,745,900	3,991,800			

Yearbook of Tourism Statistics, Data 2009 – 2013, 2015 Edition

CAYMAN ISLANDS

1. Arrivals of non-resident tourists at national borders, by country of residence

	2009	2010	2011	2012	2013	Market share 2013	% Change 2013-2012
TOTAL (*)	271,949	288,193	309,092	321,650			
AFRICA	518	673	615	665			
EAST AFRICA	48	76	67	41			
Comoros	3	2	1				
Eritrea			1				
Ethiopia		5					
Kenya	26	34	31	12			
Madagascar	1	1	1	4			
Malawi	3	1		4			
Mauritius	1	7	4	3			
Reunion			1				
Rwanda		3					
Seychelles			1	2			
Somalia			1				
Uganda	1		2				
United Republic of Tanzania		1	5	1			
Zambia	5	4	7	2			
Zimbabwe	8	18	12	13			
CENTRAL AFRICA	9	20	28	29			
Angola				4			
Cameroon	2			1			
Chad		1		1			
Congo		1					
Gabon		1					
Sao Tome and Principe	7	17	28	23			
NORTH AFRICA	2	6	6	10			
Algeria	1		1				
Morocco		4	4	9			
Sudan	1	2	1	1			
SOUTHERN AFRICA	420	547	464	549			
Botswana	7	8	10	5			
Lesotho				1			
Namibia	5		1	2			
South Africa	364	487	386	478			
Swaziland	44	52	67	63			
WEST AFRICA	39	24	50	36			
Cabo Verde	3	1					
Côte d'Ivoire				1			
Gambia		1	1				
Ghana	8	6	6	3			
Liberia	1	1	1	1			
Mauritania	1		1				
Nigeria	19	10	35	28			
Saint Helena	3						
Senegal		1	1	2			
Sierra Leone		1	2				
Togo	4	3	3	1			
AMERICAS	249,692	264,999	284,543	296,355			
CARIBBEAN	12,985	13,000	12,531	14,071			
Anguilla	10	37	16	12			
Antigua and Barbuda	27	72	64	66			
Bahamas	717	1,048	830	772			
Barbados	446	478	460	636			
Bermuda	570	788	526	553			
British Virgin Islands	72	97	98	97			
Cuba	340	1,328	1,815	2,451			
Dominica	14	23	19	28			
Dominican Republic	243	247	292	254			
Grenada	24	37	22	30			

136

CAYMAN ISLANDS

1. Arrivals of non-resident tourists at national borders, by country of residence

	2009	2010	2011	2012	2013	Market share 2013	% Change 2013-2012
Guadeloupe	1	10	9	1			
Haiti	26	13	15	16			
Jamaica	9,527	7,609	7,378	8,070			
Martinique		17	2				
Montserrat	6	11	7	9			
Netherlands Antilles	8	12	9	3			
Puerto Rico	67	76	58	72			
Saint Kitts and Nevis	26	47	39	45			
Saint Lucia	80	81	73	71			
Saint Vincent and the Grenadines	35	47	38	48			
Sint Maarten	10	9	10	5			
Trinidad and Tobago	609	758	632	700			
Turks and Caicos Islands	96	111	66	62			
United States Virgin Islands	31	44	53	70			
CENTRAL AMERICA	**2,200**	**1,839**	**1,910**	**2,354**			
Belize	107	99	107	108			
Costa Rica	170	131	118	90			
El Salvador	18	21	55	19			
Guatemala	56	66	48	73			
Honduras	1,418	1,277	1,310	1,621			
Nicaragua	284	118	106	133			
Panama	147	127	166	310			
NORTH AMERICA	**232,705**	**248,343**	**268,035**	**277,759**			
Canada	17,254	19,499	24,629	24,092			
Mexico	409	383	477	458			
United States of America	215,042	228,461	242,929	253,209			
SOUTH AMERICA	**1,802**	**1,817**	**2,067**	**2,171**			
Argentina	274	296	377	515			
Bolivia	1	11	4	3			
Brazil	438	536	681	662			
Chile	100	97	117	116			
Colombia	421	355	286	307			
Ecuador	67	57	68	69			
Falkland Islands, Malvinas	1	1					
French Guiana	1		1				
Guyana	244	194	194	170			
Paraguay		2	4	1			
Peru	84	80	109	125			
Suriname	6	6	36	40			
Uruguay	19	28	19	14			
Venezuela	146	154	171	149			
EAST ASIA AND THE PACIFIC	**1,816**	**1,872**	**1,981**	**2,288**			
NORTH-EAST ASIA	**312**	**280**	**490**	**540**			
China	51	47	119	193			
Hong Kong, China	50	51	81	70			
Japan	193	153	261	225			
Korea, Republic of	9	25	24	34			
Mongolia				2			
Taiwan, Province of China	9	4	5	16			
SOUTH-EAST ASIA	**276**	**212**	**154**	**119**			
Brunei Darussalam	4	1	2				
Cambodia	2	2	1	4			
Indonesia	16	19	15	10			
Malaysia	42	35	34	26			
Myanmar	3						
Philippines	147	85	32				
Singapore	46	66	61	66			
Thailand	10	4	7	12			
Timor-Leste			1				

Yearbook of Tourism Statistics, Data 2009 – 2013, 2015 Edition

CAYMAN ISLANDS

1. Arrivals of non-resident tourists at national borders, by country of residence

	2009	2010	2011	2012	2013	Market share 2013	% Change 2013-2012
Viet Nam	6		1	1			
AUSTRALASIA	**1,223**	**1,369**	**1,332**	**1,620**			
Australia	942	1,118	1,069	1,267			
New Zealand	281	251	263	353			
MELANESIA		**5**	**1**	**1**			
Fiji		1	1				
New Caledonia		1					
Norfolk Island				1			
Papua New Guinea		1					
Solomon Islands		2					
MICRONESIA	**5**	**5**	**3**	**6**			
Cocos (Keeling) Islands		1	1	2			
Guam	2		1	3			
Kiribati		2		1			
Marshall Islands		1					
Micronesia, Federated States of	2						
Nauru	1	1					
Palau			1				
POLYNESIA		**1**	**1**	**2**			
Niue		1		2			
Samoa			1				
EUROPE	**19,262**	**20,002**	**21,314**	**21,585**			
CENTRAL/EASTERN EUROPE	**470**	**467**	**665**	**641**			
Armenia			2				
Belarus		3	1	3			
Bulgaria	24	27	43	23			
Czech Republic	129	79	120	98			
Estonia	13	6	31	8			
Georgia	1		1				
Hungary	82	95	95	100			
Kazakhstan	1		4	3			
Latvia	7	6	11	12			
Lithuania	1	18	17	6			
Poland	70	71	136	121			
Republic of Moldova			1	1			
Romania	63	65	88	89			
Russian Federation	45	81	85	92			
Slovakia	21		22	50			
Ukraine	13	16	8	34			
Uzbekistan				1			
NORTHERN EUROPE	**14,605**	**14,215**	**14,539**	**14,321**			
Denmark	124	138	200	172			
Finland	48	69	113	106			
Iceland	2	9	13	10			
Ireland	965	946	1,085	956			
Isle of Man	7	8	7	7			
Norway	137	243	224	255			
Svalbard and Jan Mayen Islands			1				
Sweden	222	299	362	381			
United Kingdom	13,100	12,503	12,534	12,434			
SOUTHERN EUROPE	**1,514**	**2,152**	**2,688**	**3,098**			
Albania	1	1		1			
Andorra	61	82	67	31			
Bosnia and Herzegovina	4	1	3				
Croatia	12	11	12	6			
Gibraltar	20	10	4	8			
Greece	53	73	67	58			
Holy See		1					
Italy	960	935	1,104	1,143			

138

CAYMAN ISLANDS

1. Arrivals of non-resident tourists at national borders, by country of residence

	2009	2010	2011	2012	2013	Market share 2013	% Change 2013-2012
Malta	3	2	7	2			
Portugal	62	115	114	160			
San Marino	2	1		3			
Serbia	15	13	11	7			
Serbia and Montenegro	4						
Slovenia	19	36	32	48			
Spain	298	870	1,264	1,631			
TFYR of Macedonia		1	3				
WESTERN EUROPE	**2,577**	**3,038**	**3,290**	**3,397**			
Austria	187	248	245	237			
Belgium	106	131	155	138			
France	501	603	639	739			
Germany	913	1,106	1,174	1,219			
Liechtenstein	2	1	7	6			
Luxembourg	9	13	21	9			
Monaco	5	5	13	8			
Netherlands	404	440	490	441			
Switzerland	450	491	546	600			
EAST MEDITERRANEAN EUROPE	**96**	**130**	**132**	**128**			
Cyprus	9	15	8	9			
Israel	60	99	105	100			
Turkey	27	16	19	19			
MIDDLE EAST	**88**	**98**	**118**	**136**			
Bahrain	3	2	8	6			
Egypt	12	5	13	13			
Iraq	1						
Jordan		4	2	1			
Kuwait	6	4	4	6			
Lebanon	4	4	2	6			
Libya				1			
Oman	3	8	1	3			
Qatar		16	31	35			
Saudi Arabia	44	41	42	39			
Syrian Arab Republic			1				
United Arab Emirates	14	13	14	26			
Yemen	1	1					
SOUTH ASIA	**202**	**187**	**179**	**198**			
Afghanistan	1	1					
Bangladesh	1	1	1	1			
India	171	157	149	161			
Iran, Islamic Republic of		5	2	3			
Nepal	11	7	4	14			
Pakistan	2	5	5	2			
Sri Lanka	16	11	18	17			
NOT SPECIFIED	**371**	**362**	**342**	**423**			
Other countries of the World	371	362	342	423			

Yearbook of Tourism Statistics, Data 2009 – 2013, 2015 Edition

CENTRAL AFRICAN REPUBLIC

1. Arrivals of non-resident tourists at national borders, by nationality

	2009	2010	2011	2012	2013	Market share 2013	% Change 2013-2012
TOTAL (*)	52,429	53,821	65,435	70,816			
AFRICA	26,984	26,684	32,681	35,915			
EAST AFRICA	2,052	2,284	2,437	2,641			
Rwanda	566	674	722	815			
Other countries of East Africa	1,486	1,610	1,715	1,826			
CENTRAL AFRICA	9,964	10,926	14,228	15,292			
Cameroon	4,125	2,861	3,967	4,265			
Chad	3,221	2,732	2,125	1,998			
Congo	734	1,845	818	886			
Democratic Republic of the Congo	588	1,124	1,898	2,369			
Gabon	695	762	3,720	3,954			
Other countries of Central Africa	601	1,602	1,700	1,820			
NORTH AFRICA	1,884	2,184	2,831	3,373			
Sudan	886	577	715	798			
Other countries of North Africa	998	1,607	2,116	2,575			
SOUTHERN AFRICA	2,898	1,587	1,957	2,195			
South Africa	1,553	709	937	998			
Other countries of Southern Africa	1,345	878	1,020	1,197			
WEST AFRICA	8,795	8,737	10,298	11,435			
Benin	1,386	1,088	1,816	2,124			
Côte d'Ivoire	1,116	1,236	1,624	1,834			
Mali	1,052	924	975	1,126			
Nigeria	1,133	1,350	1,500	1,678			
Senegal	1,662	1,577	1,485	1,578			
Togo	1,124	736	798	820			
Other countries of West Africa	1,322	1,826	2,100	2,275			
OTHER AFRICA	1,391	966	930	979			
Other countries of Africa	1,391	966	930	979			
AMERICAS	3,171	5,074	5,062	5,188			
NORTH AMERICA	2,443	3,287	2,965	3,000			
Canada	1,076	1,130	1,250	1,306			
United States of America	1,367	2,157	1,715	1,694			
OTHER AMERICAS	728	1,787	2,097	2,188			
Other countries of the Americas	728	1,787	2,097	2,188			
EAST ASIA AND THE PACIFIC	3,888	5,035	5,813	5,877			
NORTH-EAST ASIA	2,656	3,319	3,815	3,454			
China	1,748	1,997	2,300	2,125			
Japan	908	1,322	1,515	1,329			
OTHER EAST ASIA AND THE PACIFIC	1,232	1,716	1,998	2,423			
Other countries of Asia	1,232	1,716	1,998	2,423			
EUROPE	16,612	13,141	16,600	17,573			
NORTHERN EUROPE	2,028	868	979	1,176			
United Kingdom	2,028	868	979	1,176			
SOUTHERN EUROPE	2,017	1,229	1,385	1,512			
Italy	2,017	1,229	1,385	1,512			
WESTERN EUROPE	8,263	9,899	11,411	11,908			
Belgium	1,407	803	912	924			
France	4,431	7,661	8,924	9,200			
Germany	1,276	672	860	986			
Switzerland	1,149	763	715	798			
OTHER EUROPE	4,304	1,145	2,825	2,977			
Other countries of Europe	4,304	1,145	2,825	2,977			
MIDDLE EAST	1,257	2,747	3,779	4,645			
Lebanon	712	1,484	1,879	2,430			
Other countries of Middle East	545	1,263	1,900	2,215			
NOT SPECIFIED	517	1,140	1,500	1,618			
Other countries of the World	517	1,140	1,500	1,618			

Yearbook of Tourism Statistics, Data 2009 – 2013, 2015 Edition

CHAD

1. Arrivals of non-resident tourists at national borders, by nationality

	2009	2010	2011	2012	2013	Market share 2013	% Change 2013-2012
TOTAL	69,779	71,155	76,920	85,521	99,702	100.00	16.58
AFRICA	15,615	34,218	51,024	60,084	67,568	67.77	12.46
OTHER AFRICA	15,615	34,218	51,024	60,084	67,568	67.77	12.46
All countries of Africa	15,615	34,218	51,024	60,084	67,568	67.77	12.46
AMERICAS	11,453	6,096	3,540	3,256	4,433	4.45	36.15
OTHER AMERICAS	11,453	6,096	3,540	3,256	4,433	4.45	36.15
All countries of the Americas	11,453	6,096	3,540	3,256	4,433	4.45	36.15
EAST ASIA AND THE PACIFIC	8,849	2,720	9,516	9,070	9,762	9.79	7.63
OTHER EAST ASIA AND THE PACIFIC	8,849	2,720	9,516	9,070	9,762	9.79	7.63
All countries East Asia/Pacific	8,849	2,720	9,516	9,070	9,762	9.79	7.63
EUROPE	23,883	25,316	11,370	12,501	14,344	14.39	14.74
OTHER EUROPE	23,883	25,316	11,370	12,501	14,344	14.39	14.74
All countries of Europe	23,883	25,316	11,370	12,501	14,344	14.39	14.74
MIDDLE EAST	9,979	2,067	1,205	610	2,594	2.60	325.25
All countries of Middle East	9,979	2,067	1,205	610	2,594	2.60	325.25
SOUTH ASIA		738	265		1,001	1.00	
All countries of South Asia		738	265		1,001	1.00	

CHAD

3. Arrivals of non-resident tourists in hotels and similar establishments, by nationality

	2009	2010	2011	2012	2013	Market share 2013	% Change 2013-2012
TOTAL (*)	31,169	14,298	25,381	30,054	32,126	100.00	6.89
AFRICA	7,890	4,007	9,165	13,239	10,865	33.82	-17.93
EAST AFRICA	74	146	711	1,031	579	1.80	-43.84
All countries of East Africa	74	146	711	1,031	579	1.80	-43.84
CENTRAL AFRICA	2,389	990	3,185	2,853	2,615	8.14	-8.34
All countries of Central Africa	2,389	990	3,185	2,853	2,615	8.14	-8.34
NORTH AFRICA	1,174	208	451	940	728	2.27	-22.55
All countries of North Africa	1,174	208	451	940	728	2.27	-22.55
WEST AFRICA	3,112	657	2,198	2,393	2,848	8.87	19.01
All countries of West Africa	3,112	657	2,198	2,393	2,848	8.87	19.01
OTHER AFRICA	1,141	2,006	2,620	6,022	4,095	12.75	-32.00
Other countries of Africa	1,141	2,006	2,620	6,022	4,095	12.75	-32.00
AMERICAS	3,553	1,440	3,243	3,919	3,108	9.67	-20.69
NORTH AMERICA	3,091	1,311	2,900	3,473	2,789	8.68	-19.69
Canada	512	230	440	537	1,115	3.47	107.64
United States of America	2,579	1,081	2,460	2,936	1,674	5.21	-42.98
OTHER AMERICAS	462	129	343	446	319	0.99	-28.48
Other countries of the Americas	462	129	343	446	319	0.99	-28.48
EAST ASIA AND THE PACIFIC	1,124	457	1,837	1,620	1,424	4.43	-12.10
NORTH-EAST ASIA	536	113	658	654	604	1.88	-7.65
China	536	57	544	535	393	1.22	-26.54
Japan		21	112	90	139	0.43	54.44
Korea, Republic of		35	2	29	72	0.22	148.28
OTHER EAST ASIA AND THE PACIFIC	588	344	1,179	966	820	2.55	-15.11
Other countries East Asia/Pacific	588	344	1,179	966	820	2.55	-15.11
EUROPE	16,348	8,170	10,064	11,067	11,033	34.34	-0.31
NORTHERN EUROPE	518	281	430	358	677	2.11	89.11
United Kingdom	518	281	427	355	668	2.08	88.17
Scandinavia			3	3	9	0.03	200.00
SOUTHERN EUROPE	484	224	419	563	516	1.61	-8.35
Italy	484	224	419	563	516	1.61	-8.35
WESTERN EUROPE	7,253	6,435	7,602	8,282	8,182	25.47	-1.21
Belgium	335	198	352	496	593	1.85	19.56
France	6,564	5,843	6,644	6,865	7,066	21.99	2.93
Germany	285	243	407	625	302	0.94	-51.68
Netherlands	33	52	22	151	135	0.42	-10.60
Switzerland	36	99	177	145	86	0.27	-40.69
OTHER EUROPE	8,093	1,230	1,613	1,864	1,658	5.16	-11.05
Other countries of Europe	8,093	1,230	1,613	1,864	1,658	5.16	-11.05
MIDDLE EAST	2,254	224	1,072	209	475	1.48	127.27
Egypt	190	30	185				
Lebanon	136	20	304	12	12	0.04	
Libya	827	7	159				
Saudi Arabia		22	13	3	61	0.19	1,933.33
Syrian Arab Republic		4	6		16	0.05	
Other countries of Middle East	1,101	141	405	194	386	1.20	98.97
NOT SPECIFIED					5,221	16.25	
Other countries of the World					5,221	16.25	

142

CHAD

5. Overnight stays of non-resident tourists in hotels and similar establishments, by nationality

	2009	2010	2011	2012	2013	Market share 2013	% Change 2013-2012
TOTAL (*)		36,915	59,239	70,170	85,962	100.00	22.51
AFRICA		13,913	21,588	28,989	27,691	32.21	-4.48
EAST AFRICA		251	1,558	2,920	2,108	2.45	-27.81
All countries of East Africa		251	1,558	2,920	2,108	2.45	-27.81
CENTRAL AFRICA		3,214	6,834	7,083	8,388	9.76	18.42
All countries of Central Africa		3,214	6,834	7,083	8,388	9.76	18.42
NORTH AFRICA		866	1,466	2,146	2,961	3.44	37.98
All countries of North Africa		866	1,466	2,146	2,961	3.44	37.98
WEST AFRICA		2,184	5,083	7,748	6,433	7.48	-16.97
All countries of West Africa		2,184	5,083	7,748	6,433	7.48	-16.97
OTHER AFRICA		7,398	6,647	9,092	7,801	9.07	-14.20
Other countries of Africa		7,398	6,647	9,092	7,801	9.07	-14.20
AMERICAS		3,494	7,462	8,218	14,035	16.33	70.78
NORTH AMERICA		2,895	6,490	7,350	12,938	15.05	76.03
Canada		670	969	1,571	7,704	8.96	390.39
United States of America		2,225	5,521	5,779	5,234	6.09	-9.43
OTHER AMERICAS		599	972	868	1,097	1.28	26.38
Other countries of the Americas		599	972	868	1,097	1.28	26.38
EAST ASIA AND THE PACIFIC		1,119	4,817	4,129	3,686	4.29	-10.73
NORTH-EAST ASIA		233	2,104	1,981	1,962	2.28	-0.96
China		183	1,502	1,833	1,587	1.85	-13.42
Japan		41	599	117	269	0.31	129.91
Korea, Republic of		9	3	31	106	0.12	241.94
OTHER EAST ASIA AND THE PACIFIC		886	2,713	2,148	1,724	2.01	-19.74
Other countries East Asia/Pacific		886	2,713	2,148	1,724	2.01	-19.74
EUROPE		17,781	21,989	27,846	26,153	30.42	-6.08
NORTHERN EUROPE		702	1,069	1,013	1,366	1.59	34.85
United Kingdom		702	1,069	1,010	1,360	1.58	34.65
Scandinavia				3	6	0.01	100.00
SOUTHERN EUROPE		527	878	1,489	1,561	1.82	4.84
Italy		527	878	1,489	1,561	1.82	4.84
WESTERN EUROPE		13,158	16,680	20,329	19,091	22.21	-6.09
Belgium		493	752	896	1,141	1.33	27.34
France		11,433	13,989	15,604	16,156	18.79	3.54
Germany		845	1,476	1,961	915	1.06	-53.34
Netherlands		111	64	1,559	622	0.72	-60.10
Switzerland		276	399	309	257	0.30	-16.83
OTHER EUROPE		3,394	3,362	5,015	4,135	4.81	-17.55
Other countries of Europe		3,394	3,362	5,015	4,135	4.81	-17.55
MIDDLE EAST		608	3,383	988	2,154	2.51	118.02
Egypt		29	236	28			
Lebanon		38	1,310	99	280	0.33	182.83
Libya		100	581	4			
Saudi Arabia		1	41	9	112	0.13	1,144.44
Syrian Arab Republic		12	6		466	0.54	
Other countries of Middle East		428	1,209	848	1,296	1.51	52.83
NOT SPECIFIED					12,243	14.24	
Other countries of the World					12,243	14.24	

143

CHILE

1. Arrivals of non-resident tourists at national borders, by nationality

	2009	2010	2011	2012	2013	Market share 2013	% Change 2013-2012
TOTAL (*)	**2,759,695**	**2,800,637**	**3,137,285**	**3,554,279**	**3,576,204**	**100.00**	**0.62**
AFRICA	**3,894**	**3,967**	**4,127**	**4,293**	**4,047**	**0.11**	**-5.73**
EAST AFRICA	**132**	**121**	**81**	**80**	**119**	**0.00**	**48.75**
Kenya	63	53	50	54	64	0.00	18.52
Somalia			1				
Zimbabwe	69	68	30	26	55	0.00	111.54
CENTRAL AFRICA	**59**	**28**	**52**	**44**	**96**	**0.00**	**118.18**
Angola	59	28	52	44	96	0.00	118.18
NORTH AFRICA	**299**	**246**	**198**	**483**	**220**	**0.01**	**-54.45**
Algeria	151	76	55	262	53	0.00	-79.77
Morocco	121	145	118	149	118	0.00	-20.81
Tunisia	27	25	25	72	49	0.00	-31.94
SOUTHERN AFRICA	**2,996**	**3,016**	**3,392**	**3,192**	**3,005**	**0.08**	**-5.86**
South Africa	2,996	3,016	3,392	3,192	3,005	0.08	-5.86
WEST AFRICA	**75**	**144**	**97**	**143**	**85**	**0.00**	**-40.56**
Cabo Verde	18	8	9	12	7	0.00	-41.67
Ghana	17	47	24	39	41	0.00	5.13
Nigeria	40	89	64	92	37	0.00	-59.78
OTHER AFRICA	**333**	**412**	**307**	**351**	**522**	**0.01**	**48.72**
Other countries of Africa	333	412	307	351	522	0.01	48.72
AMERICAS	**2,174,166**	**2,222,002**	**2,532,750**	**2,899,056**	**2,900,564**	**81.11**	**0.05**
CARIBBEAN	**5,680**	**6,193**	**8,023**	**8,232**	**6,963**	**0.19**	**-15.42**
Bahamas	52	19	59	44	66	0.00	50.00
Barbados	57	48	75	84	67	0.00	-20.24
Cuba	1,230	1,277	1,066	1,074	1,590	0.04	48.04
Dominica	26	18	49	67	30	0.00	-55.22
Dominican Republic	3,260	3,491	4,683	4,878	2,449	0.07	-49.79
Grenada	23	15	32	59	17	0.00	-71.19
Haiti	477	820	1,389	1,215	2,025	0.06	66.67
Jamaica	166	124	159	184	164	0.00	-10.87
Puerto Rico	22	10	110	192	102	0.00	-46.88
Saint Lucia	13	10	20	28	38	0.00	35.71
Saint Vincent and the Grenadines	27	7	18	30	32	0.00	6.67
Trinidad and Tobago	253	272	253	222	251	0.01	13.06
Other countries of the Caribbean	74	82	110	155	132	0.00	-14.84
CENTRAL AMERICA	**12,677**	**12,175**	**13,577**	**15,530**	**16,140**	**0.45**	**3.93**
Belize	59	37	49	79	54	0.00	-31.65
Costa Rica	4,121	4,081	4,882	5,635	5,912	0.17	4.92
El Salvador	1,720	1,540	1,715	1,809	1,959	0.05	8.29
Guatemala	2,140	1,952	2,158	2,420	2,484	0.07	2.64
Honduras	841	926	1,096	1,272	1,339	0.04	5.27
Nicaragua	707	696	641	731	727	0.02	-0.55
Panama	3,089	2,943	3,036	3,584	3,665	0.10	2.26
NORTH AMERICA	**226,002**	**204,346**	**221,706**	**229,948**	**223,439**	**6.25**	**-2.83**
Canada	34,574	32,389	34,297	35,250	30,734	0.86	-12.81
Mexico	28,711	29,007	34,947	36,196	38,501	1.08	6.37
United States of America	162,693	142,937	152,446	158,493	154,204	4.31	-2.71
Other countries of North America	24	13	16	9			
SOUTH AMERICA	**1,929,807**	**1,999,288**	**2,289,444**	**2,645,346**	**2,654,022**	**74.21**	**0.33**
Argentina	996,813	1,001,125	1,118,767	1,377,645	1,362,752	38.11	-1.08
Bolivia	309,401	307,475	321,488	355,758	383,765	10.73	7.87
Brazil	209,485	229,337	324,594	373,840	362,162	10.13	-3.12
Colombia	47,768	52,477	67,834	81,884	85,614	2.39	4.56
Ecuador	23,097	23,591	27,888	28,596	28,230	0.79	-1.28
Guyana	28	22	29	36	27	0.00	-25.00
Paraguay	22,349	28,267	30,024	28,979	29,418	0.82	1.51
Peru	269,534	308,759	338,916	338,026	331,274	9.26	-2.00
Suriname	68	16	36	62	46	0.00	-25.81
Uruguay	29,804	30,614	36,888	35,624	36,291	1.01	1.87
Venezuela	21,460	17,602	22,980	24,790	34,443	0.96	38.94
Other countries of South America		3		106			

144

CHILE

1. Arrivals of non-resident tourists at national borders, by nationality

	2009	2010	2011	2012	2013	Market share 2013	% Change 2013-2012
EAST ASIA AND THE PACIFIC	**73,370**	**71,888**	**77,715**	**97,820**	**99,527**	**2.78**	**1.75**
NORTH-EAST ASIA	**27,399**	**29,052**	**34,215**	**40,272**	**39,023**	**1.09**	**-3.10**
China	6,256	6,787	10,076	12,088	11,289	0.32	-6.61
Japan	13,129	14,261	12,693	15,059	14,704	0.41	-2.36
Korea, Dem. People's Republic of	345	333	358	450	319	0.01	-29.11
Korea, Republic of	6,582	6,541	9,808	11,030	10,796	0.30	-2.12
Mongolia	20	27	23	19	19	0.00	
Taiwan, Province of China	1,067	1,103	1,257	1,626	1,896	0.05	16.61
SOUTH-EAST ASIA	**3,015**	**3,360**	**3,740**	**4,422**	**4,452**	**0.12**	**0.68**
Brunei Darussalam	4	2	20	6	11	0.00	83.33
Cambodia		9	3	5	9	0.00	80.00
Indonesia	406	627	607	635	723	0.02	13.86
Lao People's Democratic Republic	2	13		4	9	0.00	125.00
Malaysia	645	625	743	861	980	0.03	13.82
Myanmar	9	16	18	18	17	0.00	-5.56
Philippines	869	891	1,036	1,280	838	0.02	-34.53
Singapore	493	770	810	915	1,011	0.03	10.49
Thailand	296	304	379	573	649	0.02	13.26
Viet Nam	291	103	124	125	205	0.01	64.00
AUSTRALASIA	**42,335**	**39,014**	**38,900**	**52,003**	**54,793**	**1.53**	**5.37**
Australia	33,601	30,694	31,105	43,341	44,943	1.26	3.70
New Zealand	8,734	8,320	7,795	8,662	9,850	0.28	13.72
POLYNESIA	**1**	**5**		**5**	**2**	**0.00**	**-60.00**
Samoa	1	5		5	2	0.00	-60.00
OTHER EAST ASIA AND THE PACIFIC	**620**	**457**	**860**	**1,118**	**1,257**	**0.04**	**12.43**
Other countries of Asia	386	381	806	1,033	1,175	0.03	13.75
Other countries of Oceania	234	76	54	85	82	0.00	-3.53
EUROPE	**383,168**	**363,117**	**375,857**	**388,474**	**396,419**	**11.08**	**2.05**
CENTRAL/EASTERN EUROPE	**11,585**	**10,742**	**13,161**	**15,596**	**16,808**	**0.47**	**7.77**
Armenia	18	23	15	22	21	0.00	-4.55
Azerbaijan	6	9	16	12	14	0.00	16.67
Belarus					156	0.00	
Bulgaria	475	505	548	752	639	0.02	-15.03
Estonia	242	187	254	411	303	0.01	-26.28
Georgia	8	13	33	22	142	0.00	545.45
Hungary	959	759	749	1,005	1,071	0.03	6.57
Kazakhstan	34	40	31	43	52	0.00	20.93
Kyrgyzstan	8	10	5	4	6	0.00	50.00
Latvia	241	222	202	309	234	0.01	-24.27
Lithuania	410	243	312	327	450	0.01	37.61
Poland	4,291	3,967	3,987	4,030	4,346	0.12	7.84
Republic of Moldova	8	14	26	19	17	0.00	-10.53
Romania	893	867	1,111	1,088	1,270	0.04	16.73
Russian Federation	2,582	2,629	4,344	5,792	6,298	0.18	8.74
Slovakia	908	682	830	901	1,129	0.03	25.31
Tajikistan		4		2			
Turkmenistan			7		3	0.00	
Ukraine	489	560	683	848	643	0.02	-24.17
Uzbekistan	13	8	8	9	14	0.00	55.56
NORTHERN EUROPE	**78,609**	**71,015**	**73,724**	**73,427**	**72,638**	**2.03**	**-1.07**
Denmark	5,010	4,667	4,802	4,976	4,896	0.14	-1.61
Finland	3,035	2,831	3,104	3,071	3,292	0.09	7.20
Iceland	230	209	342	354	283	0.01	-20.06
Ireland	4,879	4,135	3,782	3,556	4,257	0.12	19.71
Norway	5,561	5,665	5,793	6,176	5,717	0.16	-7.43
Sweden	12,289	11,981	12,355	12,873	13,003	0.36	1.01
United Kingdom	47,605	41,527	43,546	42,421	41,190	1.15	-2.90
SOUTHERN EUROPE	**88,953**	**85,372**	**90,648**	**99,126**	**109,645**	**3.07**	**10.61**
Albania	26	51	60	57	51	0.00	-10.53
Andorra	134	89	100	129	111	0.00	-13.95
Bosnia and Herzegovina	13	40	41	60	44	0.00	-26.67

145

Yearbook of Tourism Statistics, Data 2009 – 2013, 2015 Edition

CHILE

1. Arrivals of non-resident tourists at national borders, by nationality

	2009	2010	2011	2012	2013	Market share 2013	% Change 2013-2012
Croatia	553	653	642	610	557	0.02	-8.69
Greece	1,314	1,185	1,198	961	960	0.03	-0.10
Holy See	3	4	2	6	4	0.00	-33.33
Italy	27,477	26,603	27,164	28,540	30,134	0.84	5.59
Malta	137	97	103	162	166	0.00	2.47
Portugal	3,566	3,820	4,630	4,913	5,535	0.15	12.66
San Marino	16	15	13	16	12	0.00	-25.00
Serbia	313	264	324	359	320	0.01	-10.86
Slovenia	880	646	696	639	545	0.02	-14.71
Spain	54,504	51,874	55,643	62,646	71,143	1.99	13.56
TFYR of Macedonia	17	31	32	28	63	0.00	125.00
WESTERN EUROPE	**174,976**	**167,979**	**170,470**	**174,409**	**174,635**	**4.88**	**0.13**
Austria	7,508	6,894	6,809	7,180	7,178	0.20	-0.03
Belgium	8,748	8,804	9,268	9,659	9,379	0.26	-2.90
France	61,130	60,091	60,993	60,220	60,873	1.70	1.08
Germany	62,006	57,899	58,202	62,891	63,674	1.78	1.25
Liechtenstein	35	51	40	33	40	0.00	21.21
Luxembourg	295	288	276	333	292	0.01	-12.31
Monaco	36	13	22	20	23	0.00	15.00
Netherlands	18,430	17,072	17,374	16,402	15,433	0.43	-5.91
Switzerland	16,788	16,867	17,486	17,671	17,743	0.50	0.41
EAST MEDITERRANEAN EUROPE	**23,583**	**23,049**	**24,432**	**22,283**	**20,019**	**0.56**	**-10.16**
Cyprus	58	80	86	66	84	0.00	27.27
Israel	22,235	21,543	22,777	20,435	18,408	0.51	-9.92
Turkey	1,290	1,426	1,569	1,782	1,527	0.04	-14.31
OTHER EUROPE	**5,462**	**4,960**	**3,422**	**3,633**	**2,674**	**0.07**	**-26.40**
Other countries of Europe	5,462	4,960	3,422	3,633	2,674	0.07	-26.40
MIDDLE EAST	**517**	**506**	**478**	**651**	**682**	**0.02**	**4.76**
Bahrain	5	4	2	11	8	0.00	-27.27
Egypt	70	83	117	132	127	0.00	-3.79
Iraq	66	8	7	17	16	0.00	-5.88
Jordan	61	55	69	76	82	0.00	7.89
Kuwait	2	57	24	16	37	0.00	131.25
Lebanon	96	76	89	119	92	0.00	-22.69
Libya	5	4	3	12	1	0.00	-91.67
Oman	6	2	3	24	29	0.00	20.83
Qatar		28	5	2	22	0.00	1,000.00
Saudi Arabia	30	27	60	62	75	0.00	20.97
Syrian Arab Republic	36	32	35	49	49	0.00	
United Arab Emirates	58	104	13	62	75	0.00	20.97
Yemen	4	1	6	3	11	0.00	266.67
Other countries of Middle East	78	25	45	66	58	0.00	-12.12
SOUTH ASIA	**2,821**	**2,794**	**3,155**	**3,379**	**3,359**	**0.09**	**-0.59**
Afghanistan	23	11	12	102	103	0.00	0.98
Bangladesh	28	55	25	14	28	0.00	100.00
Bhutan	1	2	2	4	3	0.00	-25.00
India	2,339	2,206	2,671	2,871	2,900	0.08	1.01
Iran, Islamic Republic of	58	83	83	88	88	0.00	
Maldives		7					
Nepal	36	26	27	49	24	0.00	-51.02
Pakistan	307	377	295	212	164	0.00	-22.64
Sri Lanka	29	27	40	39	49	0.00	25.64
NOT SPECIFIED	**121,759**	**136,363**	**143,203**	**160,606**	**171,606**	**4.80**	**6.85**
Other countries of the World	65	57	140	200	212	0.01	6.00
Nationals Residing Abroad	121,694	136,306	143,063	160,406	171,394	4.79	6.85

Yearbook of Tourism Statistics, Data 2009 – 2013, 2015 Edition

CHINA

2. Arrivals of non-resident visitors at national borders, by nationality

	2009	2010	2011	2012	2013	Market share 2013	% Change 2013-2012
TOTAL	126,475,923	133,762,239	135,423,453	132,405,325	129,077,758	100.00	-2.51
AFRICA	340,443	391,475	424,482	439,619	461,450	0.36	4.97
EAST AFRICA	77,544	96,882	111,792	120,435	131,299	0.10	9.02
Burundi	727	934	1,298	1,241	1,290	0.00	3.95
Comoros	443	733	781	870	882	0.00	1.38
Djibouti					716	0.00	
Eritrea					857	0.00	
Ethiopia	11,952	14,776	18,561	23,086	24,534	0.02	6.27
Kenya	11,169	13,051	15,158	15,696	18,429	0.01	17.41
Madagascar	6,308	8,377	9,392	9,931	9,804	0.01	-1.28
Malawi					1,760	0.00	
Mauritius	15,084	17,465	18,289	17,454	17,745	0.01	1.67
Mozambique	1,732	2,280	3,195	3,751	3,915	0.00	4.37
Rwanda					2,078	0.00	
Seychelles	1,145	1,346	1,385	1,467	1,682	0.00	14.66
Somalia	564	709	951	1,300	1,173	0.00	-9.77
Uganda	7,742	10,821	14,456	14,878	14,064	0.01	-5.47
United Republic of Tanzania	13,429	15,246	16,441	18,572	19,678	0.02	5.96
Zambia	2,888	4,256	4,813	5,659	6,620	0.01	16.98
Zimbabwe	4,361	6,888	7,072	6,530	6,071	0.00	-7.03
Other countries of East Africa					1	0.00	
CENTRAL AFRICA	19,971	24,087	26,540	30,203	56,463	0.04	86.95
Angola					24,998	0.02	
Cameroon	6,886	6,871	7,052	7,873	7,191	0.01	-8.66
Central African Republic	327	375	426	572	216	0.00	-62.24
Chad	685	824	808	945	964	0.00	2.01
Congo	4,409	4,408	5,111	5,584	5,602	0.00	0.32
Democratic Republic of the Congo	6,853	10,491	12,080	14,001	14,960	0.01	6.85
Equatorial Guinea					1,072	0.00	
Gabon	811	1,118	1,063	1,228	1,365	0.00	11.16
Sao Tome and Principe					95	0.00	
NORTH AFRICA	55,396	61,910	62,376	63,499	68,266	0.05	7.51
Algeria	24,893	25,776	27,982	27,627	29,565	0.02	7.01
Morocco	12,434	14,034	13,810	13,973	14,407	0.01	3.11
South Sudan					838	0.00	
Sudan	9,928	11,475	11,944	11,766	12,719	0.01	8.10
Tunisia	8,141	10,625	8,640	10,133	10,737	0.01	5.96
SOUTHERN AFRICA	53,847	68,899	72,201	76,506	73,104	0.06	-4.45
Botswana	1,643	2,367	2,545	2,436	1,913	0.00	-21.47
Lesotho	343	474	555	595	463	0.00	-22.18
Namibia	892	1,327	1,438	1,722	1,891	0.00	9.81
South Africa	50,783	64,477	67,354	71,529	68,613	0.05	-4.08
Swaziland	186	254	309	224	224	0.00	
WEST AFRICA	108,684	110,067	119,111	111,797	132,318	0.10	18.36
Benin	3,887	4,694	4,993	4,819	5,260	0.00	9.15
Burkina Faso					3,270	0.00	
Cabo Verde					565	0.00	
Côte d'Ivoire	2,445	2,886	2,301	3,697	3,924	0.00	6.14
Gambia	1,874	2,167	2,100	2,169	2,030	0.00	-6.41
Ghana	14,657	17,152	19,767	16,918	16,564	0.01	-2.09
Guinea	8,005	9,068	9,868	9,987	9,481	0.01	-5.07
Guinea-Bissau					983	0.00	
Liberia					1,576	0.00	
Mali	12,230	14,389	15,038	13,806	16,037	0.01	16.16
Mauritania					1,895	0.00	
Niger	5,457	6,465	6,890	7,945	10,619	0.01	33.66
Nigeria	50,567	41,372	45,440	38,852	45,582	0.04	17.32
Senegal	5,625	7,484	8,026	8,492	8,987	0.01	5.83

147

CHINA

2. Arrivals of non-resident visitors at national borders, by nationality

	2009	2010	2011	2012	2013	Market share 2013	% Change 2013-2012
Sierra Leone	1,172	1,279	1,585	1,871	2,092	0.00	11.81
Togo	2,765	3,111	3,103	3,241	3,453	0.00	6.54
OTHER AFRICA	**25,001**	**29,630**	**32,462**	**37,179**			
Other countries of Africa	25,001	29,630	32,462	37,179			
AMERICAS	**2,491,190**	**2,995,397**	**3,201,031**	**3,179,516**	**3,123,834**	**2.42**	**-1.75**
CARIBBEAN	**12,548**	**13,805**	**13,857**	**15,798**	**19,954**	**0.02**	**26.31**
Anguilla					2	0.00	
Antigua and Barbuda	201	268	223	277	253	0.00	-8.66
Aruba					3	0.00	
Bahamas	401	586	623	669	636	0.00	-4.93
Barbados					440	0.00	
Bermuda					37	0.00	
British Virgin Islands					5	0.00	
Cayman Islands					12	0.00	
Cuba	2,391	2,705	2,433	2,644	3,566	0.00	34.87
Dominica	890	661	578	701	747	0.00	6.56
Dominican Republic	2,593	3,036	2,943	3,301	3,381	0.00	2.42
Grenada					187	0.00	
Haiti	203	270	336	378	574	0.00	51.85
Jamaica	3,627	3,978	4,612	5,330	6,028	0.00	13.10
Netherlands Antilles	3	4	1	3	8	0.00	166.67
Puerto Rico	14	11	8	7	11	0.00	57.14
Saint Kitts and Nevis					738	0.00	
Saint Lucia					171	0.00	
Saint Vincent and the Grenadines					734	0.00	
Trinidad and Tobago	2,225	2,286	2,100	2,488	2,418	0.00	-2.81
Turks and Caicos Islands					3	0.00	
CENTRAL AMERICA	**18,371**	**21,827**	**22,661**	**23,339**	**24,055**	**0.02**	**3.07**
Belize	3,474	3,186	3,225	3,053	3,291	0.00	7.80
Costa Rica	4,111	5,084	5,451	5,748	5,627	0.00	-2.11
El Salvador	860	987	1,120	1,218	1,233	0.00	1.23
Guatemala	1,637	2,135	2,350	2,538	2,561	0.00	0.91
Honduras	2,459	2,780	2,709	2,943	3,151	0.00	7.07
Nicaragua					660	0.00	
Panama	5,830	7,655	7,806	7,839	7,532	0.01	-3.92
NORTH AMERICA	**2,292,444**	**2,744,250**	**2,917,845**	**2,884,069**	**2,829,614**	**2.19**	**-1.89**
Canada	550,333	685,304	747,981	708,294	684,216	0.53	-3.40
Greenland					1	0.00	
Mexico	32,298	49,351	53,720	57,716	60,144	0.05	4.21
United States of America	1,709,813	2,009,595	2,116,144	2,118,059	2,085,253	1.62	-1.55
SOUTH AMERICA	**166,294**	**213,441**	**244,915**	**253,872**	**250,211**	**0.19**	**-1.44**
Argentina	16,767	23,084	25,656	24,883	26,488	0.02	6.45
Bolivia	4,083	5,252	6,470	6,454	6,198	0.00	-3.97
Brazil	63,676	85,050	97,912	99,445	95,754	0.07	-3.71
Chile	12,245	15,927	17,763	19,661	20,310	0.02	3.30
Colombia	20,441	26,870	31,792	34,315	34,636	0.03	0.94
Ecuador	4,893	6,271	7,211	7,965	8,257	0.01	3.67
Guyana	782	761	837	1,072	943	0.00	-12.03
Paraguay	1,119	1,673	1,535	1,444	1,352	0.00	-6.37
Peru	10,910	12,798	14,190	15,043	15,646	0.01	4.01
Suriname	2,658	2,637	2,944	3,056	3,236	0.00	5.89
Uruguay	2,641	3,540	3,784	3,886	4,291	0.00	10.42
Venezuela	26,079	29,578	34,821	36,648	33,100	0.03	-9.68
OTHER AMERICAS	**1,533**	**2,074**	**1,753**	**2,438**			
Other countries of the Americas	1,533	2,074	1,753	2,438			
EAST ASIA AND THE PACIFIC	**117,588,819**	**122,889,279**	**123,828,043**	**120,801,853**	**117,744,092**	**91.22**	**-2.53**
NORTH-EAST ASIA	**111,734,016**	**116,353,704**	**117,301,530**	**113,992,778**	**110,890,609**	**85.91**	**-2.72**
Hong Kong, China	77,335,996	79,321,851	79,357,701	78,712,983	76,884,622	59.56	-2.32
Japan	3,317,459	3,731,200	3,658,169	3,518,153	2,877,533	2.23	-18.21

Yearbook of Tourism Statistics, Data 2009 – 2013, 2015 Edition

CHINA

2. Arrivals of non-resident visitors at national borders, by nationality

	2009	2010	2011	2012	2013	Market share 2013	% Change 2013-2012
Korea, Dem. People's Republic of	103,880	116,382	152,300	180,573	206,617	0.16	14.42
Korea, Republic of	3,197,538	4,076,392	4,185,398	4,069,868	3,968,998	3.07	-2.48
Macao, China	22,718,406	23,172,939	23,690,767	21,160,557	20,740,333	16.07	-1.99
Mongolia	576,696	794,386	994,181	1,010,450	1,049,997	0.81	3.91
Taiwan, Province of China	4,484,041	5,140,554	5,263,014	5,340,194	5,162,509	4.00	-3.33
SOUTH-EAST ASIA	**5,182,042**	**5,745,684**	**5,666,788**	**5,893,827**	**5,990,088**	**4.64**	**1.63**
Brunei Darussalam	7,538	10,051	9,449	9,409	8,809	0.01	-6.38
Cambodia	20,104	24,265	26,534	29,803	34,578	0.03	16.02
Indonesia	469,044	573,409	608,675	621,970	605,321	0.47	-2.68
Lao People's Democratic Republic	9,674	11,927	14,186	16,764	19,399	0.02	15.72
Malaysia	1,059,004	1,245,160	1,245,092	1,235,463	1,206,535	0.93	-2.34
Myanmar	607,737	493,400	191,038	205,936	134,671	0.10	-34.61
Philippines	748,943	828,284	894,309	961,975	996,672	0.77	3.61
Singapore	889,538	1,003,658	1,062,993	1,027,745	966,605	0.75	-5.95
Thailand	541,830	635,539	608,044	647,597	651,654	0.50	0.63
Timor-Leste					442	0.00	
Viet Nam	828,630	919,991	1,006,468	1,137,165	1,365,402	1.06	20.07
AUSTRALASIA	**661,980**	**777,394**	**847,082**	**902,579**	**851,660**	**0.66**	**-5.64**
Australia	561,542	661,342	726,184	774,328	723,088	0.56	-6.62
New Zealand	100,438	116,052	120,898	128,251	128,572	0.10	0.25
MELANESIA	**2,788**	**3,805**	**3,710**	**3,988**	**6,193**	**0.00**	**55.29**
Fiji	2,398	3,342	3,207	3,462	3,766	0.00	8.78
Papua New Guinea					1,366	0.00	
Solomon Islands					642	0.00	
Vanuatu	390	463	503	526	419	0.00	-20.34
MICRONESIA	**1,988**	**2,289**	**2,652**	**2,590**	**2,838**	**0.00**	**9.58**
Christmas Island, Australia					1	0.00	
Kiribati	1,988	2,289	2,652	2,590	1,935	0.00	-25.29
Marshall Islands					349	0.00	
Micronesia, Federated States of					104	0.00	
Nauru					415	0.00	
Palau					33	0.00	
Wake Island					1	0.00	
POLYNESIA	**1,183**	**1,139**	**1,379**	**1,355**	**2,703**	**0.00**	**99.48**
Pitcairn					1	0.00	
Samoa					1,019	0.00	
Tonga	1,183	1,139	1,379	1,355	1,306	0.00	-3.62
Tuvalu					377	0.00	
OTHER EAST ASIA AND THE PACIFIC	**4,822**	**5,264**	**4,902**	**4,736**	**1**	**0.00**	**-99.98**
Other countries of Asia	329	560	412	350			
Other countries of Oceania	4,493	4,704	4,490	4,386	1	0.00	-99.98
EUROPE	**5,131,487**	**6,365,849**	**6,771,977**	**6,769,946**	**6,422,382**	**4.98**	**-5.13**
CENTRAL/EASTERN EUROPE	**2,392,709**	**3,180,919**	**3,528,537**	**3,415,649**	**3,102,664**	**2.40**	**-9.16**
Armenia	3,528	4,684	5,347	5,492	5,797	0.00	5.55
Azerbaijan	15,122	18,605	18,202	17,757	18,089	0.01	1.87
Belarus	7,458	10,914	10,939	14,121	14,347	0.01	1.60
Bulgaria	13,846	16,421	17,556	16,847	17,582	0.01	4.36
Czech Republic	15,768	19,483	20,285	21,229	20,640	0.02	-2.77
Estonia					5,739	0.00	
Georgia	5,178	5,355	6,719	6,458	7,232	0.01	11.99
Hungary	13,626	15,791	16,289	16,905	18,674	0.01	10.46
Kazakhstan	279,875	380,312	506,215	491,381	393,530	0.30	-19.91
Kyrgyzstan	32,787	35,444	47,633	48,105	49,936	0.04	3.81
Latvia	5,066	5,708	5,747	7,341	7,061	0.01	-3.81
Lithuania	5,821	7,000	7,508	8,730	8,774	0.01	0.50
Poland	53,718	62,109	67,986	68,605	71,598	0.06	4.36
Republic of Moldova					2,886	0.00	
Romania	27,760	33,232	36,290	35,262	37,950	0.03	7.62

149

Yearbook of Tourism Statistics, Data 2009 – 2013, 2015 Edition

CHINA

2. Arrivals of non-resident visitors at national borders, by nationality

	2009	2010	2011	2012	2013	Market share 2013	% Change 2013-2012
Russian Federation	1,742,973	2,370,313	2,536,321	2,426,161	2,186,281	1.69	-9.89
Slovakia	4,969	9,028	9,183	10,508	10,415	0.01	-0.89
Tajikistan	17,480	23,398	26,441	28,739	31,916	0.02	11.05
Turkmenistan	11,647	14,836	15,590	15,629	14,562	0.01	-6.83
Ukraine	86,553	105,711	120,248	120,214	121,938	0.09	1.43
Uzbekistan	49,534	42,575	54,038	56,165	57,717	0.04	2.76
NORTHERN EUROPE	**874,363**	**978,140**	**1,007,792**	**1,041,094**	**1,027,029**	**0.80**	**-1.35**
Denmark	77,340	86,718	84,637	84,330	81,385	0.06	-3.49
Faeroe Islands					1	0.00	
Finland	60,906	69,226	65,288	67,811	65,662	0.05	-3.17
Iceland	2,686	3,056	3,009	3,370	3,407	0.00	1.10
Ireland	31,221	36,164	37,596	42,166	41,229	0.03	-2.22
Norway	47,653	53,500	51,428	53,478	51,439	0.04	-3.81
Sweden	125,771	154,513	170,137	171,588	158,951	0.12	-7.36
United Kingdom	528,786	574,963	595,697	618,351	624,955	0.48	1.07
SOUTHERN EUROPE	**415,259**	**485,354**	**491,243**	**508,936**	**516,030**	**0.40**	**1.39**
Albania	2,586	2,740	2,638	2,478	2,461	0.00	-0.69
Andorra					130	0.00	
Bosnia and Herzegovina					1,490	0.00	
Croatia	16,072	16,159	16,355	16,918	16,807	0.01	-0.66
Gibraltar					1	0.00	
Greece	32,060	34,690	32,652	32,490	34,460	0.03	6.06
Italy	191,357	229,233	235,041	251,991	251,162	0.19	-0.33
Malta	1,563	1,934	1,833	2,015	1,717	0.00	-14.79
Montenegro	4,431	6,038	6,584	6,959	6,905	0.01	-0.78
Portugal	43,634	47,678	47,033	48,577	49,395	0.04	1.68
San Marino					179	0.00	
Serbia	6,236	8,448	9,231	10,593	11,441	0.01	8.01
Serbia and Montenegro	2,835	179			4	0.00	
Slovenia					5,583	0.00	
Spain	114,485	138,255	139,876	136,915	132,378	0.10	-3.31
TFYR of Macedonia					1,917	0.00	
WESTERN EUROPE	**1,292,574**	**1,533,403**	**1,543,373**	**1,603,610**	**1,590,082**	**1.23**	**-0.84**
Austria	56,223	67,289	66,922	66,079	65,711	0.05	-0.56
Belgium	60,770	76,249	70,400	71,103	68,404	0.05	-3.80
France	424,770	512,734	493,132	524,837	533,538	0.41	1.66
Germany	518,533	608,621	637,015	659,627	649,298	0.50	-1.57
Liechtenstein	251	378	300	310	344	0.00	10.97
Luxembourg	2,446	4,471	2,692	3,276	3,558	0.00	8.61
Monaco	118	237	88	118	110	0.00	-6.78
Netherlands	166,884	189,128	197,530	195,474	188,562	0.15	-3.54
Switzerland	62,579	74,296	75,294	82,786	80,557	0.06	-2.69
EAST MEDITERRANEAN EUROPE	**140,254**	**171,413**	**184,250**	**181,749**	**186,577**	**0.14**	**2.66**
Cyprus	2,884	3,569	3,229	3,148	2,931	0.00	-6.89
Israel	73,008	83,384	82,234	82,548	79,699	0.06	-3.45
Turkey	64,362	84,460	98,787	96,053	103,947	0.08	8.22
OTHER EUROPE	**16,328**	**16,620**	**16,782**	**18,908**			
Other countries of Europe	16,328	16,620	16,782	18,908			
MIDDLE EAST	**207,488**	**246,794**	**239,427**	**264,171**	**269,131**	**0.21**	**1.88**
Bahrain	3,792	3,839	3,222	3,085	3,374	0.00	9.37
Egypt	49,665	59,119	60,880	72,662	74,443	0.06	2.45
Iraq	19,234	22,246	19,289	20,746	23,497	0.02	13.26
Jordan	22,661	25,343	27,568	27,553	28,151	0.02	2.17
Kuwait	6,948	7,746	8,303	9,042	8,952	0.01	-1.00
Lebanon	20,186	22,251	22,854	22,607	21,298	0.02	-5.79
Libya	11,051	12,956	3,414	12,605	16,778	0.01	33.11
Oman	3,619	4,739	4,630	5,006	4,773	0.00	-4.65
Palestine	5,050	6,886	6,336	6,874	6,283	0.00	-8.60

150

CHINA

2. Arrivals of non-resident visitors at national borders, by nationality

	2009	2010	2011	2012	2013	Market share 2013	% Change 2013-2012
Qatar	1,876	2,940	2,431	2,499	2,507	0.00	0.32
Saudi Arabia	19,030	27,223	34,635	35,424	36,531	0.03	3.13
Syrian Arab Republic	19,745	21,029	18,473	15,773	12,802	0.01	-18.84
United Arab Emirates	5,256	8,816	9,041	8,274	7,904	0.01	-4.47
Yemen	19,375	21,661	18,351	22,021	21,838	0.02	-0.83
SOUTH ASIA	**714,327**	**871,339**	**956,602**	**948,300**	**1,054,714**	**0.82**	**11.22**
Afghanistan	15,519	11,809	11,695	11,651	10,674	0.01	-8.39
Bangladesh	32,281	41,648	47,661	50,855	58,872	0.05	15.76
Bhutan	282	569	597	619	623	0.00	0.65
India	448,942	549,321	606,474	610,194	676,682	0.52	10.90
Iran, Islamic Republic of	87,636	116,999	125,077	90,991	88,895	0.07	-2.30
Maldives	1,330	2,025	2,623	3,589	4,115	0.00	14.66
Nepal	23,272	30,796	31,944	40,949	58,817	0.05	43.63
Pakistan	81,491	87,320	92,518	96,707	106,548	0.08	10.18
Sri Lanka	23,574	30,852	38,013	42,745	49,488	0.04	15.77
NOT SPECIFIED	**2,169**	**2,106**	**1,891**	**1,920**	**2,155**	**0.00**	**12.24**
Other countries of the World	2,169	2,106	1,891	1,920	2,155	0.00	12.24

Yearbook of Tourism Statistics, Data 2009 – 2013, 2015 Edition

COLOMBIA

1. Arrivals of non-resident tourists at national borders, by country of residence

		2009	2010	2011	2012	2013	Market share 2013	% Change 2013-2012
TOTAL	(*)	1,353,700	1,404,641	2,042,425	2,174,681	2,288,003	100.00	5.21
AFRICA		2,014	2,252	2,833	2,561	2,976	0.13	16.20
EAST AFRICA		374	292	332	413	496	0.02	20.10
British Indian Ocean Territory			8	7	1			
Burundi		7	7	4	5	12	0.00	140.00
Djibouti		3	5	9		2	0.00	
Eritrea		33	8	12	19	7	0.00	-63.16
Ethiopia		51	25	30	43	53	0.00	23.26
Kenya		113	73	124	181	163	0.01	-9.94
Madagascar		5	13	9	13	14	0.00	7.69
Malawi		5	8	6	6	13	0.00	116.67
Mauritius		11	15	9	9	13	0.00	44.44
Mozambique		26	11	33	26	31	0.00	19.23
Reunion			6	7		2	0.00	
Rwanda		14	12	5	9	9	0.00	
Seychelles			1	2		1	0.00	
Somalia					1	1	0.00	
Uganda		40	37	21	35	79	0.00	125.71
United Republic of Tanzania		27	21	13	16	26	0.00	62.50
Zambia		13	15	16	12	24	0.00	100.00
Zimbabwe		26	27	25	37	46	0.00	24.32
CENTRAL AFRICA		198	213	274	224	264	0.01	17.86
Angola		78	53	21	27	71	0.00	162.96
Cameroon		52	42	91	57	40	0.00	-29.82
Central African Republic		10	47	65	31	40	0.00	29.03
Chad		8	10	5	11	6	0.00	-45.45
Congo		37	36	61	82	76	0.00	-7.32
Democratic Republic of the Congo		3						
Equatorial Guinea		6	12	9	5	10	0.00	100.00
Gabon		4	11	18	11	20	0.00	81.82
Sao Tome and Principe			2	4		1	0.00	
NORTH AFRICA		186	583	575	562	366	0.02	-34.88
Algeria		49	371	362	413	159	0.01	-61.50
Morocco		101	89	118	70	118	0.01	68.57
Sudan		16	7	16	17	27	0.00	58.82
Tunisia		20	115	78	62	62	0.00	
Western Sahara			1	1				
SOUTHERN AFRICA		979	897	1,241	1,114	1,486	0.06	33.39
Botswana		5	6	14	5	16	0.00	220.00
Lesotho			1	16	4	9	0.00	125.00
Namibia		5	8	2	17	20	0.00	17.65
South Africa		969	882	1,207	1,088	1,435	0.06	31.89
Swaziland				2		6	0.00	
WEST AFRICA		277	267	411	248	364	0.02	46.77
Benin		12	10	6	17	15	0.00	-11.76
Burkina Faso		10	19	12	3	18	0.00	500.00
Cabo Verde		6	13	32	23	12	0.00	-47.83
Côte d'Ivoire		17	18	26	20	38	0.00	90.00
Gambia		6	3	5	3	3	0.00	
Ghana		50	47	32	55	37	0.00	-32.73
Guinea		6	11	16	5	10	0.00	100.00
Guinea-Bissau		4	5	4	3	6	0.00	100.00
Liberia		5	8	2	8	7	0.00	-12.50
Mali		7	2	46	1	8	0.00	700.00
Mauritania		2	4	14	5	10	0.00	100.00
Niger		5	12	21	5	7	0.00	40.00
Nigeria		101	76	116	83	141	0.01	69.88
Saint Helena			2	6	8	6	0.00	-25.00
Senegal		23	23	62		32	0.00	

152

COLOMBIA

1. Arrivals of non-resident tourists at national borders, by country of residence

	2009	2010	2011	2012	2013	Market share 2013	% Change 2013-2012
Sierra Leone	7	7	4	6	6	0.00	
Togo	16	7	7	3	8	0.00	166.67
AMERICAS	**1,063,828**	**1,140,118**	**1,192,891**	**1,277,572**	**1,388,720**	**60.70**	**8.70**
CARIBBEAN	**15,802**	**28,704**	**32,047**	**35,123**	**33,854**	**1.48**	**-3.61**
Anguilla	251	3	1	2	2	0.00	
Antigua and Barbuda		39	31	47	65	0.00	38.30
Aruba	498	5,270	5,272	5,454	4,244	0.19	-22.19
Bahamas	17	170	188	228	241	0.01	5.70
Barbados	2	100	135	126	210	0.01	66.67
Bermuda	78	57	47	178	138	0.01	-22.47
British Virgin Islands	150	3	3	3	5	0.00	66.67
Cayman Islands	122	120	102	145	170	0.01	17.24
Cuba	25	2,427	2,325	2,410	2,977	0.13	23.53
Curaçao		5,705	6,859	7,442	6,458	0.28	-13.22
Dominica	4,074	150	203	198	116	0.01	-41.41
Dominican Republic	50	8,682	8,641	9,322	10,084	0.44	8.17
Grenada	44	25	87		38	0.00	
Guadeloupe	51	96	67	44	6	0.00	-86.36
Haiti		243	227	360	330	0.01	-8.33
Jamaica	233	426	502	502	615	0.03	22.51
Martinique	149	78	21	25	10	0.00	-60.00
Montserrat	2			2			
Netherlands Antilles	3						
Puerto Rico		3,951	6,141	6,885	6,555	0.29	-4.79
Saint Kitts and Nevis		17	26		48	0.00	
Saint Lucia	8,820	41	51	103	82	0.00	-20.39
Saint Vincent and the Grenadines	13	30	37	27	33	0.00	22.22
Trinidad and Tobago	48	1,064	1,081	1,581	1,345	0.06	-14.93
Turks and Caicos Islands	35	3			7	0.00	
Other countries of the Caribbean	1,137	4		39	75	0.00	92.31
CENTRAL AMERICA	**68,785**	**80,083**	**85,602**	**88,295**	**103,136**	**4.51**	**16.81**
Belize	156	170	176	146	227	0.01	55.48
Costa Rica	20,184	22,589	23,394	24,068	27,567	1.20	14.54
El Salvador	4,512	6,300	9,465	11,965	16,358	0.71	36.72
Guatemala	7,693	7,795	9,823	9,422	11,696	0.51	24.14
Honduras	3,657	4,078	4,121	4,533	5,460	0.24	20.45
Nicaragua	1,627	1,329	1,457	1,573	1,782	0.08	13.29
Panama	30,956	37,822	37,166	36,588	40,046	1.75	9.45
NORTH AMERICA	**400,489**	**452,739**	**439,522**	**451,692**	**477,419**	**20.87**	**5.70**
Canada	28,157	30,389	35,848	41,878	39,257	1.72	-6.26
Mexico	57,474	64,886	75,011	80,865	94,271	4.12	16.58
United States of America	314,858	357,464	328,663	328,949	343,891	15.03	4.54
SOUTH AMERICA	**578,752**	**578,592**	**635,720**	**702,462**	**774,311**	**33.84**	**10.23**
Argentina	61,358	77,499	86,365	103,370	120,757	5.28	16.82
Bolivia	6,293	6,119	6,280	9,081	11,596	0.51	27.70
Brazil	47,493	63,794	90,646	83,112	89,757	3.92	8.00
Chile	36,168	42,976	53,732	73,869	88,490	3.87	19.79
Ecuador	101,820	116,359	101,512	107,452	114,135	4.99	6.22
French Guiana	25						
Guyana	130	112	150	210	258	0.01	22.86
Paraguay	1,634	2,102	2,544	2,951	3,702	0.16	25.45
Peru	77,733	74,093	71,488	82,797	96,502	4.22	16.55
Suriname	409	361	410	404	558	0.02	38.12
Uruguay	7,611	7,558	7,586	9,004	9,272	0.41	2.98
Venezuela	238,078	187,619	215,007	230,212	239,284	10.46	3.94
EAST ASIA AND THE PACIFIC	**25,784**	**25,217**	**28,802**	**33,526**	**35,562**	**1.55**	**6.07**
NORTH-EAST ASIA	**14,619**	**12,367**	**14,166**	**17,749**	**19,053**	**0.83**	**7.35**
China	4,264	3,378	4,196	5,604	6,125	0.27	9.30
Hong Kong, China	14	157	211	294	298	0.01	1.36

153

COLOMBIA

1. Arrivals of non-resident tourists at national borders, by country of residence

	2009	2010	2011	2012	2013	Market share 2013	% Change 2013-2012
Japan	4,987	4,312	4,769	5,578	5,805	0.25	4.07
Korea, Dem. People's Republic of	3	203	178	34	20	0.00	-41.18
Korea, Republic of	4,015	3,510	3,973	5,228	5,382	0.24	2.95
Mongolia	10	13	3		53	0.00	
Taiwan, Province of China	1,326	794	836	1,011	1,370	0.06	35.51
SOUTH-EAST ASIA	**2,704**	**2,974**	**3,395**	**3,654**	**4,269**	**0.19**	**16.83**
Brunei Darussalam	8	12	7	12	9	0.00	-25.00
Cambodia	9	12	4	16	14	0.00	-12.50
Indonesia	363	494	485	515	483	0.02	-6.21
Lao People's Democratic Republic	209	93	42	6	6	0.00	
Malaysia	4	281	333	437	476	0.02	8.92
Myanmar	20	3	8	8	72	0.00	800.00
Philippines	1,728	1,591	1,994	2,062	2,312	0.10	12.12
Singapore	210	306	317	363	570	0.02	57.02
Thailand	41	122	118	144	208	0.01	44.44
Viet Nam	112	60	87	91	119	0.01	30.77
AUSTRALASIA	**8,440**	**9,694**	**11,042**	**12,013**	**12,133**	**0.53**	**1.00**
Australia	7,104	8,401	9,569	10,439	10,443	0.46	0.04
New Zealand	1,336	1,293	1,473	1,574	1,690	0.07	7.37
MELANESIA	**7**	**101**	**131**	**87**	**72**	**0.00**	**-17.24**
Fiji	2	5	18	2	13	0.00	550.00
New Caledonia	1	76	87	70	45	0.00	-35.71
Papua New Guinea	2	8	2	8	2	0.00	-75.00
Solomon Islands	1		3	1			
Vanuatu	1	12	21	6	12	0.00	100.00
MICRONESIA	**9**	**15**	**9**	**2**	**4**	**0.00**	**100.00**
Cocos (Keeling) Islands		2					
Guam		3	4		1	0.00	
Kiribati	1	4	2		1	0.00	
Micronesia, Federated States of	1						
Midway Islands	1	3	2				
Nauru		1					
Northern Mariana Islands	1		1		1	0.00	
Palau	4	2					
Wake Island	1			2	1	0.00	-50.00
POLYNESIA	**5**	**66**	**57**	**16**	**21**	**0.00**	**31.25**
French Polynesia	1	59	55	16	12	0.00	-25.00
Tonga	4	6	1		5	0.00	
Tuvalu					4	0.00	
Wallis and Futuna Islands		1	1				
OTHER EAST ASIA AND THE PACIFIC			**2**	**5**	**10**	**0.00**	**100.00**
Other countries of Asia			1	1	8	0.00	700.00
Other countries of Oceania			1	4	2	0.00	-50.00
EUROPE	**257,649**	**232,367**	**267,182**	**272,311**	**293,605**	**12.83**	**7.82**
CENTRAL/EASTERN EUROPE	**8,023**	**7,318**	**10,608**	**9,658**	**11,621**	**0.51**	**20.33**
Armenia	20	8	18	22	25	0.00	13.64
Azerbaijan	7	28	20	44	47	0.00	6.82
Belarus	214	189	229	94	205	0.01	118.09
Bulgaria	51	120	125	160	219	0.01	36.88
Czech Republic	609	1,111	814	346	948	0.04	173.99
Estonia	2,471	116	369	202	214	0.01	5.94
Georgia	10	28	54	46	38	0.00	-17.39
Hungary	483	420	406	505	738	0.03	46.14
Kazakhstan	43	31	32	42	52	0.00	23.81
Kyrgyzstan	3	6	3	5	18	0.00	260.00
Latvia	104	104	158	182	240	0.01	31.87
Lithuania	216	168	325	200	313	0.01	56.50
Poland	1,067	1,499	2,728	2,198	2,248	0.10	2.27
Republic of Moldova	1,668	19	38	32	33	0.00	3.13

154

COLOMBIA

1. Arrivals of non-resident tourists at national borders, by country of residence

	2009	2010	2011	2012	2013	Market share 2013	% Change 2013-2012
Romania		591	884	897	991	0.04	10.48
Russian Federation	10	2,079	3,577	3,877	4,171	0.18	7.58
Slovakia	624	396	490	401	445	0.02	10.97
Turkmenistan	2	93	30	3	4	0.00	33.33
Ukraine	396	304	297	399	667	0.03	67.17
Uzbekistan	25	8	11	3	5	0.00	66.67
NORTHERN EUROPE	**35,927**	**33,384**	**37,108**	**37,254**	**40,149**	**1.75**	**7.77**
Denmark	2,032	1,761	2,080	2,115	2,274	0.10	7.52
Finland	1,251	1,286	1,720	2,122	1,314	0.06	-38.08
Iceland	189	133	156	226	193	0.01	-14.60
Ireland	2,166	1,754	1,654	2,150	2,510	0.11	16.74
Isle of Man	4,351	1,628	1,052	1,033	637	0.03	-38.33
Norway	2,161	2,395	2,603	2,713	2,870	0.13	5.79
Sweden	4,830	4,372	4,741	4,778	5,161	0.23	8.02
United Kingdom	18,947	20,055	23,102	22,117	25,190	1.10	13.89
SOUTHERN EUROPE	**108,281**	**102,636**	**111,049**	**114,240**	**119,241**	**5.21**	**4.38**
Albania	34	44	29	26	21	0.00	-19.23
Andorra	87	40	62	51	62	0.00	21.57
Bosnia and Herzegovina	21	18	10	16	32	0.00	100.00
Croatia	343	286	410	433	430	0.02	-0.69
Gibraltar					1	0.00	
Greece	827	731	869	763	878	0.04	15.07
Holy See	6	8	4	7	5	0.00	-28.57
Italy	26,054	22,706	22,699	22,098	22,749	0.99	2.95
Malta	67	40	70	40	63	0.00	57.50
Montenegro	4						
Portugal	2,381	1,825	2,585	3,147	4,769	0.21	51.54
San Marino	4	11	8	13	10	0.00	-23.08
Serbia and Montenegro	80	107	117	159	214	0.01	34.59
Slovenia	406	324	420	432	472	0.02	9.26
Spain	77,913	76,485	83,761	87,052	89,535	3.91	2.85
TFYR of Macedonia	54	11	5	3			
WESTERN EUROPE	**96,551**	**81,284**	**100,422**	**103,259**	**114,211**	**4.99**	**10.61**
Austria	2,849	2,443	3,006	3,469	3,551	0.16	2.36
Belgium	4,115	3,500	4,101	4,708	5,445	0.24	15.65
France	30,366	29,898	33,105	32,948	34,385	1.50	4.36
Germany	26,138	24,134	36,010	36,568	39,521	1.73	8.08
Liechtenstein	27	20	22	47	30	0.00	-36.17
Luxembourg	154	144	180	202	205	0.01	1.49
Monaco	15	26	39	32	45	0.00	40.63
Netherlands	23,621	12,064	13,721	14,285	18,837	0.82	31.87
Switzerland	9,266	9,055	10,238	11,000	12,192	0.53	10.84
EAST MEDITERRANEAN EUROPE	**8,867**	**7,706**	**7,949**	**7,852**	**8,317**	**0.36**	**5.92**
Cyprus	82	67	45	61	68	0.00	11.48
Israel	8,036	6,808	6,729	6,631	6,807	0.30	2.65
Turkey	749	831	1,175	1,160	1,442	0.06	24.31
OTHER EUROPE		**39**	**46**	**48**	**66**	**0.00**	**37.50**
Other countries of Europe		39	46	48	66	0.00	37.50
MIDDLE EAST	**1,311**	**896**	**1,096**	**1,163**	**1,467**	**0.06**	**26.14**
Bahrain	6	20	16	20	22	0.00	10.00
Egypt	179	200	241	227	242	0.01	6.61
Iraq	7	9	26		66	0.00	
Jordan	63	55	69	32	54	0.00	68.75
Kuwait	27	21	35	31	53	0.00	70.97
Lebanon	808	359	300	334	346	0.02	3.59
Libya	6						
Oman	5	1	14	13	19	0.00	46.15
Palestine	27	26	52	100	52	0.00	-48.00
Qatar	16	9	12	30	180	0.01	500.00

155

COLOMBIA

1. Arrivals of non-resident tourists at national borders, by country of residence

	2009	2010	2011	2012	2013	Market share 2013	% Change 2013-2012
Saudi Arabia	48	69	165	134	173	0.01	29.10
Syrian Arab Republic	34	23	13	9	19	0.00	111.11
United Arab Emirates	81	98	151	229	235	0.01	2.62
Yemen	4	6	2	4	6	0.00	50.00
SOUTH ASIA	**2,924**	**3,375**	**3,309**	**3,144**	**3,541**	**0.15**	**12.63**
Afghanistan	21	507	378	32	25	0.00	-21.88
Bangladesh	30	29	51	18	55	0.00	205.56
Bhutan	5	1	4	5	6	0.00	20.00
India	2,483	2,533	2,516	2,899	3,064	0.13	5.69
Iran, Islamic Republic of	206	167	174		199	0.01	
Maldives		2	2		1	0.00	
Nepal	41	30	57	30	35	0.00	16.67
Pakistan	102	79	96	138	113	0.00	-18.12
Sri Lanka	36	27	31	22	43	0.00	95.45
NOT SPECIFIED	**190**	**416**	**546,312**	**584,404**	**562,132**	**24.57**	**-3.81**
Other countries of the World	190	416	288	843	429	0.02	-49.11
Nationals Residing Abroad			546,024	583,561	561,703	24.55	-3.75

Yearbook of Tourism Statistics, Data 2009 – 2013, 2015 Edition

COMOROS

1. Arrivals of non-resident tourists at national borders, by nationality

		2009	2010	2011	2012	2013	Market share 2013	% Change 2013-2012
TOTAL	(*)	**11,306**	**15,251**	**18,765**				
AFRICA		**2,889**	**1,800**	**1,428**				
EAST AFRICA		**1,113**		**1,393**				
Madagascar		206		112				
Mauritius				21				
Reunion		907		480				
Other countries of East Africa				780				
OTHER AFRICA		**1,776**	**1,800**	**35**				
Other countries of Africa		1,776		35				
All countries of Africa			1,800					
AMERICAS		**137**	**213**	**846**				
OTHER AMERICAS		**137**	**213**	**846**				
All countries of the Americas		137	213	846				
EAST ASIA AND THE PACIFIC		**272**	**167**	**613**				
OTHER EAST ASIA AND THE PACIFIC		**272**	**167**	**613**				
All countries of Asia		183	167	613				
All countries of Oceania		89						
EUROPE		**7,484**	**12,498**	**14,543**				
NORTHERN EUROPE		**146**	**1,046**	**1,708**				
United Kingdom		146	1,046	1,708				
WESTERN EUROPE		**7,074**	**10,720**	**11,535**				
France		6,957	10,720	11,535				
Germany		117						
OTHER EUROPE		**264**	**732**	**1,300**				
Other countries of Europe		264	732	1,300				
NOT SPECIFIED		**524**	**573**	**1,335**				
Other countries of the World		524	573	1,335				

Yearbook of Tourism Statistics, Data 2009 – 2013, 2015 Edition

CONGO

2. Arrivals of non-resident visitors at national borders, by country of residence

		2009	2010	2011	2012	2013	Market share 2013	% Change 2013-2012
TOTAL	(*)			224,267	259,574	305,077	100.00	17.53
AFRICA				153,356	147,969	151,706	49.73	2.53
EAST AFRICA				5,970	3,611	6,613	2.17	83.13
Burundi				443	332	452	0.15	36.14
Comoros					350	370	0.12	5.71
Ethiopia				774	444	790	0.26	77.93
Kenya				2,453	857	2,352	0.77	174.45
Madagascar				889	378	745	0.24	97.09
Malawi					35	52	0.02	48.57
Mauritius					35	60	0.02	71.43
Rwanda				425	698	953	0.31	36.53
Uganda				387	162	252	0.08	55.56
United Republic of Tanzania				406	127	352	0.12	177.17
Zambia					12	32	0.01	166.67
Zimbabwe				193	181	203	0.07	12.15
CENTRAL AFRICA				110,296	108,116	95,611	31.34	-11.57
Angola				9,661	7,896	8,451	2.77	7.03
Cameroon				10,242	12,531	14,758	4.84	17.77
Central African Republic				2,492	3,786	4,986	1.63	31.70
Chad				1,682	847	1,562	0.51	84.42
Democratic Republic of the Congo				80,170	78,331	60,542	19.84	-22.71
Equatorial Guinea					320	335	0.11	4.69
Gabon				5,991	4,336	4,895	1.60	12.89
Sao Tome and Principe				58	69	82	0.03	18.84
NORTH AFRICA				2,167	7,329	9,230	3.03	25.94
Algeria				58	2,895	3,654	1.20	26.22
Morocco				1,181	2,681	3,486	1.14	30.03
Sudan				58	216	345	0.11	59.72
Tunisia				870	1,537	1,745	0.57	13.53
SOUTHERN AFRICA				4,058	2,616	4,076	1.34	55.81
Botswana					12	25	0.01	108.33
Namibia					127	254	0.08	100.00
South Africa				4,058	2,477	3,797	1.24	53.29
WEST AFRICA				30,865	26,297	36,176	11.86	37.57
Benin				6,397	4,134	5,256	1.72	27.14
Burkina Faso				1,372	1,404	1,560	0.51	11.11
Cabo Verde					35	37	0.01	5.71
Côte d'Ivoire				3,730	4,290	4,865	1.59	13.40
Gambia				56	177	187	0.06	5.65
Ghana				251	1,383	1,980	0.65	43.17
Guinea				2,165	320	2,223	0.73	594.69
Guinea-Bissau					424	520	0.17	22.64
Liberia				58	165	174	0.06	5.45
Mali				7,171	5,615	7,280	2.39	29.65
Mauritania				1,026	1,819	2,100	0.69	15.45
Niger				541	316	586	0.19	85.44
Nigeria				2,183	2,142	2,549	0.84	19.00
Senegal				5,064	3,067	5,260	1.72	71.50
Sierra Leone					23	32	0.01	39.13
Togo				851	983	1,567	0.51	59.41
AMERICAS				3,767	9,743	10,602	3.48	8.82
CARIBBEAN					112	117	0.04	4.46
Cuba					77	75	0.02	-2.60
Haiti					35	42	0.01	20.00
CENTRAL AMERICA					23	25	0.01	8.70
El Salvador					23	25	0.01	8.70
NORTH AMERICA				3,574	8,845	9,460	3.10	6.95
Canada				1,024	1,367	1,450	0.48	6.07
Mexico				193	2,126	2,356	0.77	10.82

158

CONGO

2. Arrivals of non-resident visitors at national borders, by country of residence

	2009	2010	2011	2012	2013	Market share 2013	% Change 2013-2012
United States of America			2,357	5,352	5,654	1.85	5.64
SOUTH AMERICA			**193**	**763**	**1,000**	**0.33**	**31.06**
Brazil				662	752	0.25	13.60
Chile				54	62	0.02	14.81
Colombia			193	23	153	0.05	565.22
Guyana				12	15	0.00	25.00
Peru				12	18	0.01	50.00
EAST ASIA AND THE PACIFIC			**8,814**	**19,666**	**25,309**	**8.30**	**28.69**
NORTH-EAST ASIA			**7,093**	**12,156**	**15,093**	**4.95**	**24.16**
China			6,919	9,641	12,350	4.05	28.10
Japan			116	2,376	2,568	0.84	8.08
Korea, Republic of			58	139	175	0.06	25.90
SOUTH-EAST ASIA			**967**	**7,287**	**9,446**	**3.10**	**29.63**
Cambodia				12	18	0.01	50.00
Indonesia				185	368	0.12	98.92
Malaysia			387	3,856	4,859	1.59	26.01
Philippines			387	3,165	3,971	1.30	25.47
Singapore			193	69	230	0.08	233.33
AUSTRALASIA			**754**	**223**	**770**	**0.25**	**245.29**
Australia			696	69	530	0.17	668.12
New Zealand			58	154	240	0.08	55.84
EUROPE			**51,524**	**75,725**	**103,302**	**33.86**	**36.42**
CENTRAL/EASTERN EUROPE			**1,525**	**7,301**	**10,018**	**3.28**	**37.21**
Bulgaria			56	309	378	0.12	22.33
Hungary				12	29	0.01	141.67
Lithuania				58	65	0.02	12.07
Poland			58	1,541	2,154	0.71	39.78
Republic of Moldova				12	19	0.01	58.33
Romania			367	1,311	1,980	0.65	51.03
Russian Federation			986	4,023	5,267	1.73	30.92
Slovakia			58	23	62	0.02	169.57
Ukraine				12	64	0.02	433.33
NORTHERN EUROPE			**2,223**	**6,463**	**7,407**	**2.43**	**14.61**
Denmark				12	25	0.01	108.33
Finland				35	42	0.01	20.00
Ireland			541	35	45	0.01	28.57
Norway			387	35	469	0.15	1,240.00
Sweden			174	231	364	0.12	57.58
United Kingdom			1,121	6,115	6,462	2.12	5.67
SOUTHERN EUROPE			**3,517**	**11,115**	**12,432**	**4.08**	**11.85**
Bosnia and Herzegovina				12	30	0.01	150.00
Croatia				12	24	0.01	100.00
Italy			2,357	5,984	6,456	2.12	7.89
Portugal			425	748	957	0.31	27.94
Spain			735	4,359	4,965	1.63	13.90
WESTERN EUROPE			**44,066**	**50,484**	**72,924**	**23.90**	**44.45**
Austria				35	47	0.02	34.29
Belgium			3,729	4,958	5,752	1.89	16.01
France			37,998	40,744	60,240	19.75	47.85
Germany			1,875	2,177	2,976	0.98	36.70
Luxembourg				23	39	0.01	69.57
Netherlands			116	1,334	1,850	0.61	38.68
Switzerland			348	1,213	2,020	0.66	66.53
EAST MEDITERRANEAN EUROPE			**193**	**362**	**521**	**0.17**	**43.92**
Cyprus				54	67	0.02	24.07
Israel			193	285	379	0.12	32.98
Turkey				23	75	0.02	226.09

159

CONGO

2. Arrivals of non-resident visitors at national borders, by country of residence

	2009	2010	2011	2012	2013	Market share 2013	% Change 2013-2012
MIDDLE EAST			4,524	3,214	8,769	2.87	172.84
Egypt			696	656	896	0.29	36.59
Lebanon			1,702	2,007	4,658	1.53	132.09
Palestine				12	80	0.03	566.67
Qatar				46	68	0.02	47.83
Saudi Arabia				23	35	0.01	52.17
Syrian Arab Republic			1,933	23	2,458	0.81	10,586.96
United Arab Emirates			193	424	529	0.17	24.76
Yemen				23	45	0.01	95.65
SOUTH ASIA			2,282	3,257	5,389	1.77	65.46
Bangladesh			425	548	657	0.22	19.89
India			1,410	2,373	3,654	1.20	53.98
Iran, Islamic Republic of			60	66	98	0.03	48.48
Pakistan			387	270	980	0.32	262.96

Yearbook of Tourism Statistics, Data 2009 – 2013, 2015 Edition

CONGO

3. Arrivals of non-resident tourists in hotels and similar establishments, by country of residence

	2009	2010	2011	2012	2013	Market share 2013	% Change 2013-2012
TOTAL (*)	94,337	101,111	168,037	205,140	285,336	100.00	39.09
AFRICA	38,867	41,542	73,272	95,527	142,369	49.90	49.04
CENTRAL AFRICA	17,113	20,420	37,893	50,609	81,035	28.40	60.12
Angola	3,193	3,352	13,386	7,577	10,857	3.80	43.29
Cameroon	3,182	3,954	6,936	14,288	20,548	7.20	43.81
Central African Republic	1,114	1,482	1,579	2,037	30,471	10.68	1,395.88
Chad	630	625	774	1,044	2,004	0.70	91.95
Democratic Republic of the Congo	7,052	8,712	9,567	10,495	1,250	0.44	-88.09
Gabon	1,763	2,116	5,099	14,714	15,300	5.36	3.98
Other countries of Central Africa	179	179	552	454	605	0.21	33.26
NORTH AFRICA	9,406	6,332	7,960	10,422	14,523	5.09	39.35
All countries of North Africa	9,406	6,332	7,960	10,422	14,523	5.09	39.35
WEST AFRICA	9,047	10,623	20,048	26,798	35,931	12.59	34.08
Benin	60	76	104	250	452	0.16	80.80
Côte d'Ivoire	1,873	1,974	3,532	5,253	6,900	2.42	31.35
Mali	1,265	1,505	2,213	2,362	3,254	1.14	37.76
Mauritania	540	420	390	580	810	0.28	39.66
Senegal	1,092	1,421	2,034	2,837	3,759	1.32	32.50
Togo	941	938	1,057	1,293	1,856	0.65	43.54
Other countries of West Africa	3,276	4,289	10,718	14,223	18,900	6.62	32.88
OTHER AFRICA	3,301	4,167	7,371	7,698	10,880	3.81	41.34
Other countries of Africa	3,301	4,167	7,371	7,698	10,880	3.81	41.34
AMERICAS	4,976	4,899	10,572	11,250	16,240	5.69	44.36
NORTH AMERICA	2,948	2,882	4,671	6,312	9,290	3.26	47.18
Canada	792	733	1,018	2,417	3,400	1.19	40.67
United States of America	2,156	2,149	3,653	3,895	5,890	2.06	51.22
OTHER AMERICAS	2,028	2,017	5,901	4,938	6,950	2.44	40.75
Other countries of the Americas	2,028	2,017	5,901	4,938	6,950	2.44	40.75
EAST ASIA AND THE PACIFIC	2,974	3,442	12,140	11,318	13,723	4.81	21.25
NORTH-EAST ASIA	1,307	1,574	3,011	3,846	6,160	2.16	60.17
China	994	1,351	2,592	3,452	5,750	2.02	66.57
Japan	313	223	419	394	410	0.14	4.06
OTHER EAST ASIA AND THE PACIFIC	1,667	1,868	9,129	7,472	7,563	2.65	1.22
Other countries of Asia	1,667	1,868	9,129	7,472	7,563	2.65	1.22
EUROPE	43,885	46,154	68,300	82,427	104,904	36.77	27.27
CENTRAL/EASTERN EUROPE	953	1,269	2,328	1,937	2,452	0.86	26.59
Russian Federation	953	1,269	2,328	1,937	2,452	0.86	26.59
NORTHERN EUROPE	2,565	3,607	6,159	12,375	14,580	5.11	17.82
United Kingdom	2,565	3,607	6,159	12,375	14,580	5.11	17.82
SOUTHERN EUROPE	3,097	2,945	4,570	3,674	5,869	2.06	59.74
Italy	3,097	2,945	4,570	3,674	5,869	2.06	59.74
WESTERN EUROPE	33,374	33,213	46,026	52,117	67,650	23.71	29.80
Belgium	1,149	1,518	2,425	2,572	2,745	0.96	6.73
France	30,343	30,181	40,888	46,915	60,845	21.32	29.69
Germany	831	762	1,666	1,258	2,500	0.88	98.73
Switzerland	1,051	752	1,047	1,372	1,560	0.55	13.70
OTHER EUROPE	3,896	5,120	9,217	12,324	14,353	5.03	16.46
Other countries of Europe	3,896	5,120	9,217	12,324	14,353	5.03	16.46
MIDDLE EAST			233	332	2,034	0.71	512.65
Lebanon			163	250	1,856	0.65	642.40
Other countries of Middle East			70	82	178	0.06	117.07
SOUTH ASIA			447	186	325	0.11	74.73
India			447	186	325	0.11	74.73
NOT SPECIFIED	3,635	5,074	3,073	4,100	5,741	2.01	40.02
Other countries of the World	3,635	5,074	3,073	4,100	5,741	2.01	40.02

Yearbook of Tourism Statistics, Data 2009 – 2013, 2015 Edition

CONGO

5. Overnight stays of non-resident tourists in hotels and similar establishments, by country of residence

	2009	2010	2011	2012	2013	Market share 2013	% Change 2013-2012
TOTAL (*)	192,945	218,910	365,121	555,010	639,225	100.00	15.17
AFRICA	75,485	94,291	160,621	259,003	279,914	43.79	8.07
CENTRAL AFRICA	35,272	46,652	80,898	137,775	140,370	21.96	1.88
Angola	6,000	9,641	25,361	24,605	26,354	4.12	7.11
Cameroon	7,439	10,072	18,391	42,395	60,745	9.50	43.28
Central African Republic	2,334	3,353	3,530	4,780	5,640	0.88	17.99
Chad	1,078	1,116	1,453	2,029	2,846	0.45	40.27
Democratic Republic of the Congo	14,286	16,615	18,454	25,564	1,875	0.29	-92.67
Gabon	3,703	5,217	12,211	36,890	40,126	6.28	8.77
Other countries of Central Africa	432	638	1,498	1,512	2,784	0.44	84.13
NORTH AFRICA	13,506	10,019	13,137	20,208	25,327	3.96	25.33
All countries of North Africa	13,506	10,019	13,137	20,208	25,327	3.96	25.33
WEST AFRICA	17,668	25,609	47,724	79,011	89,187	13.95	12.88
Benin	236	388	440	589	750	0.12	27.33
Côte d'Ivoire	3,606	4,087	7,974	11,919	13,567	2.12	13.83
Mali	2,390	3,163	4,873	5,242	5,490	0.86	4.73
Mauritania	59	65	71	82	98	0.02	19.51
Senegal	1,750	3,040	4,366	4,474	5,902	0.92	31.92
Togo	1,625	1,675	1,860	2,209	2,578	0.40	16.70
Other countries of West Africa	8,002	13,191	28,140	54,496	60,802	9.51	11.57
OTHER AFRICA	9,039	12,011	18,862	22,009	25,030	3.92	13.73
Other countries of Africa	9,039	12,011	18,862	22,009	25,030	3.92	13.73
AMERICAS	12,345	12,154	26,339	43,632	53,096	8.31	21.69
NORTH AMERICA	7,086	6,865	11,163	17,618	22,240	3.48	26.23
Canada	1,717	1,627	2,120	7,005	9,546	1.49	36.27
United States of America	5,369	5,238	9,043	10,613	12,694	1.99	19.61
OTHER AMERICAS	5,259	5,289	15,176	26,014	30,856	4.83	18.61
Other countries of the Americas	5,259	5,289	15,176	26,014	30,856	4.83	18.61
EAST ASIA AND THE PACIFIC	6,889	6,998	27,600	35,188	43,465	6.80	23.52
NORTH-EAST ASIA	3,361	3,352	7,894	12,272	17,161	2.68	39.84
China	2,547	2,917	6,735	10,067	13,598	2.13	35.07
Japan	814	435	1,159	2,205	3,563	0.56	61.59
OTHER EAST ASIA AND THE PACIFIC	3,528	3,646	19,706	22,916	26,304	4.11	14.78
Other countries of Asia	3,528	3,646	19,706	22,916	26,304	4.11	14.78
EUROPE	90,923	94,172	143,911	207,160	246,299	38.53	18.89
CENTRAL/EASTERN EUROPE	1,830	2,484	4,780	5,691	7,500	1.17	31.79
Russian Federation	1,830	2,484	4,780	5,691	7,500	1.17	31.79
NORTHERN EUROPE	7,948	11,785	20,573	45,608	48,423	7.58	6.17
United Kingdom	7,948	11,785	20,573	45,608	48,423	7.58	6.17
SOUTHERN EUROPE	10,287	9,599	13,490	12,703	15,309	2.39	20.51
Italy	10,287	9,599	13,490	12,703	15,309	2.39	20.51
WESTERN EUROPE	60,755	59,272	84,400	115,327	138,667	21.69	20.24
Belgium	2,761	3,999	5,867	6,882	7,904	1.24	14.85
France	54,777	52,536	73,020	102,998	120,560	18.86	17.05
Germany	1,684	1,520	3,697	3,372	6,550	1.02	94.25
Switzerland	1,533	1,217	1,816	2,075	3,653	0.57	76.05
OTHER EUROPE	10,103	11,032	20,668	27,831	36,400	5.69	30.79
Other countries of Europe	10,103	11,032	20,668	27,831	36,400	5.69	30.79
MIDDLE EAST			593	1,420	3,549	0.56	149.93
Lebanon			344	890	1,556	0.24	74.83
Other countries of Middle East			249	530	1,993	0.31	276.04
SOUTH ASIA			1,506	1,870	2,452	0.38	31.12
India			1,506	1,870	2,452	0.38	31.12
NOT SPECIFIED	7,303	11,295	4,551	6,737	10,450	1.63	55.11
Other countries of the World	7,303	11,295	4,551	6,737	10,450	1.63	55.11

Yearbook of Tourism Statistics, Data 2009 – 2013, 2015 Edition

COOK ISLANDS

1. Arrivals of non-resident tourists at national borders, by country of residence

		2009	2010	2011	2012	2013	Market share 2013	% Change 2013-2012
TOTAL	(*)	**101,229**	**104,265**	**113,114**	**122,384**	**121,158**	**100.00**	**-1.00**
AMERICAS		**6,066**	**6,995**	**6,915**	**6,672**	**6,849**	**5.65**	**2.65**
NORTH AMERICA		**6,066**	**6,590**	**6,499**	**6,672**	**6,849**	**5.65**	**2.65**
Canada		2,069	2,262	2,044	2,082	2,160	1.78	3.75
United States of America		3,997	4,328	4,455	4,590	4,689	3.87	2.16
OTHER AMERICAS			**405**	**416**				
Other countries of the Americas			405	416				
EAST ASIA AND THE PACIFIC		**82,066**	**86,713**	**95,905**	**104,696**	**103,411**	**85.35**	**-1.23**
NORTH-EAST ASIA					**449**	**602**	**0.50**	**34.08**
China					167	171	0.14	2.40
Hong Kong, China					43	57	0.05	32.56
Japan					239	374	0.31	56.49
SOUTH-EAST ASIA					**156**	**216**	**0.18**	**38.46**
Indonesia					45	54	0.04	20.00
Philippines					68	100	0.08	47.06
Singapore					43	62	0.05	44.19
AUSTRALASIA		**78,331**	**84,328**	**93,724**	**103,283**	**101,927**	**84.13**	**-1.31**
Australia		14,795	16,841	18,538	20,921	22,802	18.82	8.99
New Zealand		63,536	67,487	75,186	82,362	79,125	65.31	-3.93
POLYNESIA		**1,120**	**838**	**643**	**622**	**513**	**0.42**	**-17.52**
French Polynesia		1,120	838	643	622	513	0.42	-17.52
OTHER EAST ASIA AND THE PACIFIC		**2,615**	**1,547**	**1,538**	**186**	**153**	**0.13**	**-17.74**
Other countries of Asia					186	153	0.13	-17.74
All countries of Asia		676	780	687				
Other countries of Oceania		1,939	767	851				
EUROPE		**12,448**	**10,547**	**10,290**	**9,466**	**9,401**	**7.76**	**-0.69**
CENTRAL/EASTERN EUROPE					**23**	**51**	**0.04**	**121.74**
Poland					23	51	0.04	121.74
NORTHERN EUROPE		**7,040**	**5,126**	**4,800**	**3,962**	**4,044**	**3.34**	**2.07**
Denmark		214	174	157	128	101	0.08	-21.09
Finland		107	169	382	263	125	0.10	-52.47
Ireland					33	57	0.05	72.73
Norway		303	287	253	205	277	0.23	35.12
Sweden		518	498	534	528	525	0.43	-0.57
United Kingdom		5,898	3,998	3,474	2,805	2,959	2.44	5.49
SOUTHERN EUROPE		**894**	**1,088**	**1,201**	**1,055**	**1,014**	**0.84**	**-3.89**
Italy		533	711	697	612	773	0.64	26.31
Slovenia		132	153	286	156	39	0.03	-75.00
Spain		229	224	218	287	202	0.17	-29.62
WESTERN EUROPE		**3,821**	**3,663**	**3,721**	**4,021**	**3,895**	**3.21**	**-3.13**
Austria		389	324	353	305	211	0.17	-30.82
Belgium		80	74	105	91	63	0.05	-30.77
France		236	213	125	257	322	0.27	25.29
Germany		2,466	2,296	2,293	2,444	2,226	1.84	-8.92
Netherlands		79	160	105	211	354	0.29	67.77
Switzerland		571	596	740	713	719	0.59	0.84
EAST MEDITERRANEAN EUROPE					**10**	**22**	**0.02**	**120.00**
Israel					10	22	0.02	120.00
OTHER EUROPE		**693**	**670**	**568**	**395**	**375**	**0.31**	**-5.06**
Other countries of Europe		693	670	568	395	375	0.31	-5.06
SOUTH ASIA					**32**	**24**	**0.02**	**-25.00**
India					32	24	0.02	-25.00
NOT SPECIFIED		**649**	**10**	**4**	**1,518**	**1,473**	**1.22**	**-2.96**
Other countries of the World		649	10	4	1,518	1,473	1.22	-2.96

Yearbook of Tourism Statistics, Data 2009 – 2013, 2015 Edition

COSTA RICA

1. Arrivals of non-resident tourists at national borders, by nationality

	2009	2010	2011	2012	2013	Market share 2013	% Change 2013-2012
TOTAL	1,922,579	2,099,829	2,192,059	2,343,213	2,427,941	100.00	3.62
AFRICA	1,631	1,823	1,898	1,971	2,167	0.09	9.94
OTHER AFRICA	1,631	1,823	1,898	1,971	2,167	0.09	9.94
All countries of Africa	1,631	1,823	1,898	1,971	2,167	0.09	9.94
AMERICAS	1,634,866	1,781,572	1,856,794	2,009,211	2,075,146	85.47	3.28
CARIBBEAN	16,184	14,579	13,043	12,052	12,393	0.51	2.83
Cuba	7,043	5,882	4,399	3,583	3,372	0.14	-5.89
Dominican Republic	5,836	5,094	5,199	4,893	5,155	0.21	5.35
Jamaica	725	752	719	698	891	0.04	27.65
Puerto Rico	47	95	25	35	12	0.00	-65.71
Trinidad and Tobago	846	972	976	985	1,071	0.04	8.73
Other countries of the Caribbean	1,687	1,784	1,725	1,858	1,892	0.08	1.83
CENTRAL AMERICA	588,739	642,517	670,271	721,049	736,161	30.32	2.10
Belize	975	843	838	846	1,060	0.04	25.30
El Salvador	44,185	53,669	61,257	64,923	64,552	2.66	-0.57
Guatemala	40,340	48,682	54,759	55,334	56,756	2.34	2.57
Honduras	31,324	34,043	35,598	35,036	38,840	1.60	10.86
Nicaragua	413,713	427,362	432,766	474,011	476,678	19.63	0.56
Panama	58,202	77,918	85,053	90,899	98,275	4.05	8.11
NORTH AMERICA	920,371	1,005,309	1,044,569	1,139,624	1,162,368	47.87	2.00
Canada	102,471	119,654	133,033	151,568	160,398	6.61	5.83
Mexico	47,771	54,662	52,707	66,959	72,568	2.99	8.38
United States of America	770,129	830,993	858,829	921,097	929,402	38.28	0.90
SOUTH AMERICA	109,572	119,167	128,911	136,486	164,224	6.76	20.32
Argentina	18,987	20,080	22,186	24,545	23,856	0.98	-2.81
Bolivia	1,788	2,025	2,071	1,826	2,072	0.09	13.47
Brazil	11,617	13,121	14,449	15,071	15,934	0.66	5.73
Chile	7,682	8,504	9,129	10,000	11,406	0.47	14.06
Colombia	32,014	32,999	33,121	33,712	36,202	1.49	7.39
Ecuador	4,431	5,039	5,637	5,674	5,734	0.24	1.06
Paraguay	657	786	975	912	872	0.04	-4.39
Peru	8,167	9,122	10,076	10,164	9,390	0.39	-7.62
Uruguay	3,091	2,905	3,030	3,150	3,354	0.14	6.48
Venezuela	21,138	24,586	28,237	31,432	55,404	2.28	76.27
EAST ASIA AND THE PACIFIC	26,900	29,479	31,432	35,891	38,885	1.60	8.34
NORTH-EAST ASIA	13,256	14,411	14,591	17,178	18,008	0.74	4.83
China	3,346	3,589	4,525	6,573	7,791	0.32	18.53
Japan	4,746	5,026	4,758	5,117	4,932	0.20	-3.62
Korea, Republic of	2,724	3,236	3,311	3,437	3,482	0.14	1.31
Taiwan, Province of China	2,440	2,560	1,997	2,051	1,803	0.07	-12.09
AUSTRALASIA	7,995	8,597	9,613	10,277	11,817	0.49	14.98
Australia, New Zealand	7,995	8,597	9,613	10,277	11,817	0.49	14.98
OTHER EAST ASIA AND THE PACIFIC	5,649	6,471	7,228	8,436	9,060	0.37	7.40
Other countries of Asia	5,649	6,471	7,228	8,436	9,060	0.37	7.40
EUROPE	259,126	286,923	301,929	296,091	311,706	12.84	5.27
CENTRAL/EASTERN EUROPE	5,826	6,832	7,342	7,567	8,874	0.37	17.27
Czech Republic	1,466	2,184	1,639	1,618	2,028	0.08	25.34
Poland	1,926	2,085	2,425	2,405	2,700	0.11	12.27
Russian Federation	2,434	2,563	3,278	3,544	4,146	0.17	16.99
NORTHERN EUROPE	47,640	53,744	55,841	51,619	54,848	2.26	6.26
Denmark	3,823	3,834	4,269	4,002	3,961	0.16	-1.02
Finland	1,930	1,930	1,775	1,667	1,885	0.08	13.08
Ireland	2,730	2,828	2,557	2,554	2,794	0.12	9.40
Norway	3,336	3,455	3,709	3,635	3,501	0.14	-3.69
Sweden	6,939	6,952	7,842	7,831	7,509	0.31	-4.11
United Kingdom	28,882	34,745	35,689	31,930	35,198	1.45	10.23
SOUTHERN EUROPE	66,761	70,513	70,141	69,856	77,878	3.21	11.48
Italy	18,497	19,658	20,225	20,335	22,802	0.94	12.13
Portugal	1,807	2,363	2,134	2,016	2,126	0.09	5.46

Yearbook of Tourism Statistics, Data 2009 – 2013, 2015 Edition

COSTA RICA

1. Arrivals of non-resident tourists at national borders, by nationality

	2009	2010	2011	2012	2013	Market share 2013	% Change 2013-2012
Spain	46,457	48,492	47,782	47,505	52,950	2.18	11.46
WESTERN EUROPE	**124,017**	**139,683**	**150,311**	**148,089**	**150,702**	**6.21**	**1.76**
Austria	5,504	5,863	6,348	6,150	6,858	0.28	11.51
Belgium	9,509	13,306	12,508	10,235	9,177	0.38	-10.34
France	30,737	35,266	38,290	38,139	39,728	1.64	4.17
Germany	40,918	44,539	49,225	50,938	54,754	2.26	7.49
Netherlands	25,006	26,373	27,731	25,758	23,121	0.95	-10.24
Switzerland	12,343	14,336	16,209	16,869	17,064	0.70	1.16
EAST MEDITERRANEAN EUROPE	**8,972**	**9,511**	**11,210**	**11,095**	**10,764**	**0.44**	**-2.98**
Israel	8,972	9,511	11,210	11,095	10,764	0.44	-2.98
OTHER EUROPE	**5,910**	**6,640**	**7,084**	**7,865**	**8,640**	**0.36**	**9.85**
Other countries of Europe	5,910	6,640	7,084	7,865	8,640	0.36	9.85
NOT SPECIFIED	**56**	**32**	**6**	**49**	**37**	**0.00**	**-24.49**
Other countries of the World	56	32	6	49	37	0.00	-24.49

CROATIA

3. Arrivals of non-resident tourists in hotels and similar establishments, by country of residence

	2009	2010	2011	2012	2013	Market share 2013	% Change 2013-2012
TOTAL	3,684,215	3,955,433	4,308,270	4,521,803	4,672,944	100.00	3.34
AMERICAS	115,723	133,053	145,742	165,720	191,671	4.10	15.66
NORTH AMERICA	115,723	133,053	145,742	165,720	191,671	4.10	15.66
Canada	22,484	27,998	31,663	35,821	38,240	0.82	6.75
United States of America	93,239	105,055	114,079	129,899	153,431	3.28	18.12
EAST ASIA AND THE PACIFIC	180,905	180,589	183,799	211,491	217,049	4.64	2.63
NORTH-EAST ASIA	143,868	132,315	125,263	148,515	147,775	3.16	-0.50
Japan	143,868	132,315	125,263	148,515	147,775	3.16	-0.50
AUSTRALASIA	37,037	48,274	58,536	62,976	69,274	1.48	10.00
Australia	31,510	41,439	51,889	53,843	60,181	1.29	11.77
New Zealand	5,527	6,835	6,647	9,133	9,093	0.19	-0.44
EUROPE	3,321,698	3,542,954	3,813,900	3,898,870	3,963,233	84.81	1.65
CENTRAL/EASTERN EUROPE	611,022	671,586	741,519	781,957	753,876	16.13	-3.59
Belarus	1,672	1,524	1,928	2,720	3,690	0.08	35.66
Bulgaria	29,535	25,655	30,098	30,412	35,753	0.77	17.56
Czech Republic	128,366	132,801	143,765	149,281	142,711	3.05	-4.40
Estonia	3,731	2,038	2,845	4,525	5,578	0.12	23.27
Hungary	95,719	94,728	103,733	105,071	114,314	2.45	8.80
Latvia	3,995	4,006	4,821	5,798	8,425	0.18	45.31
Lithuania	10,526	8,709	7,874	8,751	8,611	0.18	-1.60
Poland	108,591	129,645	144,994	155,353	168,588	3.61	8.52
Romania	33,056	29,946	33,355	33,199	33,564	0.72	1.10
Russian Federation	95,660	128,827	138,529	141,939	103,194	2.21	-27.30
Slovakia	74,309	78,210	90,587	96,161	97,305	2.08	1.19
Ukraine	25,862	35,497	38,990	48,747	32,143	0.69	-34.06
NORTHERN EUROPE	304,474	325,678	344,210	395,081	463,586	9.92	17.34
Denmark	20,992	22,441	21,476	24,558	26,545	0.57	8.09
Finland	14,016	15,218	21,644	24,480	29,603	0.63	20.93
Iceland	1,232	1,134	1,507	1,337	2,104	0.05	57.37
Ireland	18,338	17,839	17,194	17,326	19,536	0.42	12.76
Norway	38,662	48,956	52,202	56,480	68,363	1.46	21.04
Sweden	59,186	62,838	67,079	73,668	88,978	1.90	20.78
United Kingdom	152,048	157,252	163,108	197,232	228,457	4.89	15.83
SOUTHERN EUROPE	938,117	997,684	1,062,707	934,417	937,231	20.06	0.30
Bosnia and Herzegovina	86,799	89,328	94,267	91,502	94,998	2.03	3.82
Greece	16,241	30,065	30,491	19,103	27,988	0.60	46.51
Italy	427,513	417,452	421,637	376,391	362,114	7.75	-3.79
Portugal	20,333	20,986	23,658	18,404	17,467	0.37	-5.09
Slovenia	238,973	267,917	308,612	295,493	311,701	6.67	5.49
Spain	132,133	158,288	168,357	120,767	107,770	2.31	-10.76
TFYR of Macedonia	16,125	13,648	15,685	12,757	15,193	0.33	19.10
WESTERN EUROPE	1,359,383	1,415,957	1,517,096	1,637,402	1,668,216	35.70	1.88
Austria	416,271	440,930	486,521	522,960	529,991	11.34	1.34
Belgium	44,650	50,022	55,812	63,094	73,372	1.57	16.29
France	242,739	231,098	232,885	239,209	238,466	5.10	-0.31
Germany	510,558	538,617	583,473	638,838	647,169	13.85	1.30
Luxembourg	2,244	2,353	2,453	2,392	2,608	0.06	9.03
Netherlands	82,965	82,109	79,597	90,391	91,715	1.96	1.46
Switzerland	59,956	70,828	76,355	80,518	84,895	1.82	5.44
EAST MEDITERRANEAN EUROPE	38,093	58,292	65,299	67,711	52,070	1.11	-23.10
Israel	21,140	25,437	26,539	26,392	26,380	0.56	-0.05
Turkey	16,953	32,855	38,760	41,319	25,690	0.55	-37.83
OTHER EUROPE	70,609	73,757	83,069	82,302	88,254	1.89	7.23
Other countries of Europe	70,609	73,757	83,069	82,302	88,254	1.89	7.23
NOT SPECIFIED	65,889	98,837	164,829	245,722	300,991	6.44	22.49
Other countries of the World	65,889	98,837	164,829	245,722	300,991	6.44	22.49

CROATIA

4. Arrivals of non-resident tourists in all types of accommodation establishments, by country of residence

		2009	2010	2011	2012	2013	Market share 2013	% Change 2013-2012
TOTAL	(*)	8,693,796	9,110,742	9,926,674	10,369,226	10,955,168	100.00	5.65
AFRICA		9,904	11,293	13,399	16,935	19,853	0.18	17.23
SOUTHERN AFRICA		4,790	5,578	6,908	8,460	9,686	0.09	14.49
South Africa		4,790	5,578	6,908	8,460	9,686	0.09	14.49
OTHER AFRICA		5,114	5,715	6,491	8,475	10,167	0.09	19.96
Other countries of Africa		5,114	5,715	6,491	8,475	10,167	0.09	19.96
AMERICAS		179,685	208,417	250,418	291,988	381,626	3.48	30.70
NORTH AMERICA		155,178	176,614	201,135	230,052	287,444	2.62	24.95
Canada		34,763	41,483	48,877	55,090	65,700	0.60	19.26
United States of America		118,996	132,751	150,831	173,501	220,043	2.01	26.83
Other countries of North America		1,419	2,380	1,427	1,461	1,701	0.02	16.43
SOUTH AMERICA		9,836	14,015	22,083	30,913	56,546	0.52	82.92
Brazil		9,836	14,015	22,083	30,913	56,546	0.52	82.92
OTHER AMERICAS		14,671	17,788	27,200	31,023	37,636	0.34	21.32
Other countries of the Americas		14,671	17,788	27,200	31,023	37,636	0.34	21.32
EAST ASIA AND THE PACIFIC		271,067	298,789	360,124	468,856	546,766	4.99	16.62
NORTH-EAST ASIA		181,114	178,797	187,260	245,097	275,326	2.51	12.33
China		7,534	13,195	22,459	43,249	41,129	0.38	-4.90
Japan		163,173	147,119	131,630	155,088	160,025	1.46	3.18
Korea, Republic of		10,407	18,483	33,171	46,760	74,172	0.68	58.62
AUSTRALASIA		62,137	76,690	95,561	104,258	125,055	1.14	19.95
Australia		51,452	64,526	82,729	87,735	106,402	0.97	21.28
New Zealand		10,685	12,164	12,832	16,523	18,653	0.17	12.89
OTHER EAST ASIA AND THE PACIFIC		27,816	43,302	77,303	119,501	146,385	1.34	22.50
Other countries of Asia		24,906	39,916	74,286	116,732	142,404	1.30	21.99
Other countries of Oceania		2,910	3,386	3,017	2,769	3,981	0.04	43.77
EUROPE		8,233,140	8,592,243	9,302,733	9,591,447	10,006,923	91.34	4.33
CENTRAL/EASTERN EUROPE		1,886,151	2,005,719	2,173,622	2,249,141	2,324,920	21.22	3.37
Belarus		3,547	2,605	3,231	4,819	7,431	0.07	54.20
Bulgaria		34,678	29,586	36,699	36,538	45,052	0.41	23.30
Czech Republic		578,517	605,732	638,036	647,211	652,216	5.95	0.77
Estonia		7,352	5,464	6,128	8,610	12,487	0.11	45.03
Hungary		298,359	297,667	328,106	307,912	326,504	2.98	6.04
Latvia		7,658	7,142	8,813	10,640	15,404	0.14	44.77
Lithuania		23,514	20,029	20,674	23,684	25,715	0.23	8.58
Poland		417,849	454,445	494,702	544,134	635,593	5.80	16.81
Romania		64,536	57,761	63,526	61,272	64,695	0.59	5.59
Russian Federation		121,971	164,999	182,203	196,308	151,131	1.38	-23.01
Slovakia		292,450	310,031	335,021	337,429	337,099	3.08	-0.10
Ukraine		35,720	50,258	56,483	70,584	51,593	0.47	-26.91
NORTHERN EUROPE		539,520	580,086	610,153	699,148	887,122	8.10	26.89
Denmark		76,068	77,412	73,975	85,854	89,630	0.82	4.40
Finland		24,612	27,145	34,583	38,806	54,283	0.50	39.88
Iceland		1,638	1,562	2,317	1,913	2,843	0.03	48.61
Ireland		29,252	28,933	28,284	28,166	38,258	0.35	35.83
Norway		66,269	85,135	92,276	102,090	134,474	1.23	31.72
Sweden		112,613	118,682	122,454	135,363	178,399	1.63	31.79
United Kingdom		229,068	241,217	256,264	306,956	389,235	3.55	26.80
SOUTHERN EUROPE		2,583,878	2,645,066	2,882,202	2,655,965	2,641,170	24.11	-0.56
Bosnia and Herzegovina		212,505	217,051	222,978	220,375	211,805	1.93	-3.89
Greece		18,570	32,567	33,068	21,283	31,599	0.29	48.47
Italy		1,057,893	1,018,375	1,150,311	1,050,514	1,017,407	9.29	-3.15
Malta		1,485	1,265	1,358	1,474	1,931	0.02	31.00
Montenegro		9,089	9,798	12,361	12,353	13,479	0.12	9.12
Portugal		26,087	28,171	29,319	23,470	25,899	0.24	10.35
Serbia		85,211	86,797	86,582	85,768	89,991	0.82	4.92
Slovenia		962,604	1,016,572	1,099,919	1,053,553	1,066,808	9.74	1.26
Spain		180,013	211,094	220,957	166,176	158,275	1.44	-4.75
TFYR of Macedonia		30,421	23,376	25,349	20,999	23,976	0.22	14.18

167

CROATIA

4. Arrivals of non-resident tourists in all types of accommodation establishments, by country of residence

	2009	2010	2011	2012	2013	Market share 2013	% Change 2013-2012
WESTERN EUROPE	**3,156,404**	**3,265,719**	**3,521,052**	**3,869,890**	**4,043,336**	**36.91**	**4.48**
Austria	776,450	810,340	892,467	945,578	968,490	8.84	2.42
Belgium	93,913	103,341	119,916	137,261	159,995	1.46	16.56
France	393,192	388,320	394,482	418,412	449,280	4.10	7.38
Germany	1,463,281	1,525,133	1,661,346	1,852,731	1,932,846	17.64	4.32
Luxembourg	3,745	4,152	4,344	4,579	5,374	0.05	17.36
Netherlands	296,086	285,257	286,986	335,266	336,271	3.07	0.30
Switzerland	129,737	149,176	161,511	176,063	191,080	1.74	8.53
EAST MEDITERRANEAN EUROPE	**50,209**	**71,539**	**79,945**	**85,537**	**70,648**	**0.64**	**-17.41**
Cyprus	1,194	1,292	1,505	1,299	1,579	0.01	21.56
Israel	28,421	32,657	34,162	35,541	36,871	0.34	3.74
Turkey	20,594	37,590	44,278	48,697	32,198	0.29	-33.88
OTHER EUROPE	**16,978**	**24,114**	**35,759**	**31,766**	**39,727**	**0.36**	**25.06**
Other countries of Europe	16,978	24,114	35,759	31,766	39,727	0.36	25.06

CROATIA

5. Overnight stays of non-resident tourists in hotels and similar establishments, by country of residence

	2009	2010	2011	2012	2013	Market share 2013	% Change 2013-2012
TOTAL	16,085,143	17,011,494	18,054,427	18,879,352	18,900,602	100.00	0.11
AMERICAS	270,297	300,442	339,156	376,508	428,661	2.27	13.85
NORTH AMERICA	270,297	300,442	339,156	376,508	428,661	2.27	13.85
Canada	54,242	65,110	73,497	85,968	89,678	0.47	4.32
United States of America	216,055	235,332	265,659	290,540	338,983	1.79	16.67
EAST ASIA AND THE PACIFIC	274,120	285,356	293,168	342,636	341,478	1.81	-0.34
NORTH-EAST ASIA	195,926	183,752	172,514	206,548	196,948	1.04	-4.65
Japan	195,926	183,752	172,514	206,548	196,948	1.04	-4.65
AUSTRALASIA	78,194	101,604	120,654	136,088	144,530	0.76	6.20
Australia	66,355	88,128	106,993	117,084	126,038	0.67	7.65
New Zealand	11,839	13,476	13,661	19,004	18,492	0.10	-2.69
EUROPE	15,400,318	16,225,867	17,131,890	17,733,233	17,641,675	93.34	-0.52
CENTRAL/EASTERN EUROPE	3,493,424	3,879,788	4,186,799	4,360,817	4,023,394	21.29	-7.74
Belarus	8,339	9,819	10,005	15,380	19,169	0.10	24.64
Bulgaria	55,451	46,181	53,035	50,553	60,449	0.32	19.58
Czech Republic	825,402	840,197	909,239	949,286	897,612	4.75	-5.44
Estonia	10,985	7,046	10,865	17,019	21,693	0.11	27.46
Hungary	440,346	427,483	465,975	464,386	513,224	2.72	10.52
Latvia	11,627	11,741	16,915	15,808	21,540	0.11	36.26
Lithuania	30,544	24,425	22,512	25,172	27,853	0.15	10.65
Poland	530,160	612,847	650,808	681,650	743,035	3.93	9.01
Romania	128,222	113,154	122,011	115,103	112,870	0.60	-1.94
Russian Federation	804,646	1,048,374	1,097,479	1,098,621	785,586	4.16	-28.49
Slovakia	473,104	496,353	561,659	599,534	594,750	3.15	-0.80
Ukraine	174,598	242,168	266,296	328,305	225,613	1.19	-31.28
NORTHERN EUROPE	1,591,319	1,614,129	1,707,353	1,986,602	2,340,679	12.38	17.82
Denmark	111,402	120,757	113,135	132,082	129,366	0.68	-2.06
Finland	49,955	58,124	94,675	106,418	124,013	0.66	16.53
Iceland	3,190	2,762	4,584	4,354	5,815	0.03	33.56
Ireland	78,599	75,534	74,018	79,628	87,316	0.46	9.65
Norway	210,419	266,199	285,399	312,163	371,861	1.97	19.12
Sweden	319,897	317,539	330,658	363,085	450,243	2.38	24.00
United Kingdom	817,857	773,214	804,884	988,872	1,172,065	6.20	18.53
SOUTHERN EUROPE	3,315,224	3,413,491	3,561,161	3,152,708	3,062,218	16.20	-2.87
Bosnia and Herzegovina	292,519	288,596	309,914	312,777	324,055	1.71	3.61
Greece	34,463	62,625	55,248	34,864	46,787	0.25	34.20
Italy	1,603,643	1,507,672	1,472,506	1,263,444	1,172,815	6.21	-7.17
Portugal	41,399	40,586	45,365	37,597	37,044	0.20	-1.47
Slovenia	1,043,760	1,176,469	1,324,916	1,244,806	1,248,769	6.61	0.32
Spain	255,892	304,662	317,822	227,553	197,207	1.04	-13.34
TFYR of Macedonia	43,548	32,881	35,390	31,667	35,541	0.19	12.23
WESTERN EUROPE	6,689,689	6,945,842	7,279,935	7,858,864	7,870,962	41.64	0.15
Austria	1,897,595	1,993,975	2,148,567	2,301,769	2,303,143	12.19	0.06
Belgium	205,373	233,560	249,681	268,480	302,019	1.60	12.49
France	969,855	892,091	887,044	894,038	897,734	4.75	0.41
Germany	2,954,812	3,142,763	3,313,031	3,640,139	3,635,704	19.24	-0.12
Luxembourg	7,822	8,935	9,469	9,507	11,457	0.06	20.51
Netherlands	425,941	414,685	396,548	448,030	416,636	2.20	-7.01
Switzerland	228,291	259,833	275,595	296,901	304,269	1.61	2.48
EAST MEDITERRANEAN EUROPE	97,484	162,721	177,974	153,627	114,118	0.60	-25.72
Israel	50,704	63,702	68,351	56,847	62,807	0.33	10.48
Turkey	46,780	99,019	109,623	96,780	51,311	0.27	-46.98
OTHER EUROPE	213,178	209,896	218,668	220,615	230,304	1.22	4.39
Other countries of Europe	213,178	209,896	218,668	220,615	230,304	1.22	4.39
NOT SPECIFIED	140,408	199,829	290,213	426,975	488,788	2.59	14.48
Other countries of the World	140,408	199,829	290,213	426,975	488,788	2.59	14.48

Yearbook of Tourism Statistics, Data 2009 – 2013, 2015 Edition

CROATIA

6. Overnight stays of non-resident tourists in all types of accommodation establishments, by country of residence

	2009	2010	2011	2012	2013	Market share 2013	% Change 2013-2012
TOTAL (*)	49,229,508	50,992,321	54,751,305	57,522,137	59,688,187	100.00	3.77
AFRICA	36,754	37,341	42,304	57,723	71,132	0.12	23.23
SOUTHERN AFRICA	13,938	14,056	16,306	20,298	23,173	0.04	14.16
South Africa	13,938	14,056	16,306	20,298	23,173	0.04	14.16
OTHER AFRICA	22,816	23,285	25,998	37,425	47,959	0.08	28.15
Other countries of Africa	22,816	23,285	25,998	37,425	47,959	0.08	28.15
AMERICAS	480,807	545,362	652,142	735,252	939,040	1.57	27.72
NORTH AMERICA	417,470	463,931	534,071	588,014	729,500	1.22	24.06
Canada	98,933	114,692	134,288	149,828	176,007	0.29	17.47
United States of America	314,442	341,398	395,084	433,227	548,727	0.92	26.66
Other countries of North America	4,095	7,841	4,699	4,959	4,766	0.01	-3.89
SOUTH AMERICA	25,323	35,740	54,003	70,386	117,642	0.20	67.14
Brazil	25,323	35,740	54,003	70,386	117,642	0.20	67.14
OTHER AMERICAS	38,014	45,691	64,068	76,852	91,898	0.15	19.58
Other countries of the Americas	38,014	45,691	64,068	76,852	91,898	0.15	19.58
EAST ASIA AND THE PACIFIC	475,070	547,070	643,828	834,331	941,247	1.58	12.81
NORTH-EAST ASIA	251,305	253,351	263,618	347,038	382,158	0.64	10.12
China	15,479	23,143	34,578	64,092	62,026	0.10	-3.22
Japan	221,002	204,422	185,740	220,499	221,526	0.37	0.47
Korea, Republic of	14,824	25,786	43,300	62,447	98,606	0.17	57.90
AUSTRALASIA	155,878	186,405	225,283	257,600	304,625	0.51	18.26
Australia	128,472	157,872	194,777	218,164	259,635	0.43	19.01
New Zealand	27,406	28,533	30,506	39,436	44,990	0.08	14.08
OTHER EAST ASIA AND THE PACIFIC	67,887	107,314	154,927	229,693	254,464	0.43	10.78
Other countries of Asia	61,726	99,967	149,079	223,212	245,159	0.41	9.83
Other countries of Oceania	6,161	7,347	5,848	6,481	9,305	0.02	43.57
EUROPE	48,236,877	49,862,548	53,413,031	55,894,831	57,736,768	96.73	3.30
CENTRAL/EASTERN EUROPE	12,031,352	12,920,632	13,936,471	14,427,977	14,773,980	24.75	2.40
Belarus	20,001	17,986	19,210	29,988	42,103	0.07	40.40
Bulgaria	70,899	58,791	75,977	68,210	85,540	0.14	25.41
Czech Republic	3,961,828	4,170,084	4,388,696	4,519,489	4,539,151	7.60	0.44
Estonia	24,159	19,860	24,141	34,847	49,378	0.08	41.70
Hungary	1,594,794	1,604,753	1,746,138	1,629,552	1,727,969	2.89	6.04
Latvia	24,460	23,749	31,368	34,379	48,490	0.08	41.05
Lithuania	82,665	70,692	73,438	90,907	98,533	0.17	8.39
Poland	2,685,037	2,895,162	3,134,012	3,407,685	4,079,179	6.83	19.71
Romania	294,486	253,556	270,523	251,242	254,862	0.43	1.44
Russian Federation	1,051,991	1,375,981	1,497,761	1,577,872	1,221,660	2.05	-22.58
Slovakia	1,974,402	2,084,013	2,282,066	2,294,100	2,258,368	3.78	-1.56
Ukraine	246,630	346,005	393,141	489,706	368,747	0.62	-24.70
NORTHERN EUROPE	2,997,092	3,104,617	3,251,431	3,774,899	4,784,321	8.02	26.74
Denmark	562,683	567,053	537,679	625,723	688,464	1.15	10.03
Finland	95,110	108,557	151,599	172,298	237,744	0.40	37.98
Iceland	5,245	4,825	7,751	6,971	8,847	0.01	26.91
Ireland	126,881	124,131	119,384	127,510	165,269	0.28	29.61
Norway	387,475	489,923	545,800	606,801	804,854	1.35	32.64
Sweden	628,127	637,408	652,363	730,219	971,888	1.63	33.10
United Kingdom	1,191,571	1,172,720	1,236,855	1,505,377	1,907,255	3.20	26.70
SOUTHERN EUROPE	12,587,745	12,783,262	13,582,233	12,807,391	12,544,497	21.02	-2.05
Bosnia and Herzegovina	1,077,624	1,047,909	1,061,467	1,066,036	1,001,711	1.68	-6.03
Greece	42,522	70,697	63,877	43,232	58,314	0.10	34.89
Italy	4,925,252	4,731,832	4,994,547	4,534,564	4,396,530	7.37	-3.04
Malta	6,490	5,544	5,702	6,369	7,411	0.01	16.36
Montenegro	31,960	29,917	31,352	31,662	33,309	0.06	5.20
Portugal	58,214	70,060	61,541	54,408	60,893	0.10	11.92
Serbia	433,445	419,553	433,048	415,313	426,018	0.71	2.58
Slovenia	5,512,808	5,885,315	6,389,183	6,239,493	6,159,280	10.32	-1.29
Spain	360,003	423,468	437,258	333,766	315,399	0.53	-5.50
TFYR of Macedonia	139,427	98,967	104,258	82,548	85,632	0.14	3.74

170

CROATIA

6. Overnight stays of non-resident tourists in all types of accommodation establishments, by country of residence

	2009	2010	2011	2012	2013	Market share 2013	% Change 2013-2012
WESTERN EUROPE	20,435,860	20,781,204	22,314,522	24,593,589	25,352,246	42.47	3.08
Austria	4,258,338	4,420,058	4,836,232	5,103,762	5,207,945	8.73	2.04
Belgium	509,980	545,342	604,678	687,426	763,294	1.28	11.04
France	1,510,894	1,464,114	1,483,546	1,538,457	1,644,294	2.75	6.88
Germany	11,166,827	11,476,383	12,487,389	13,946,703	14,436,295	24.19	3.51
Luxembourg	15,630	17,345	18,941	21,156	24,929	0.04	17.83
Netherlands	2,424,071	2,244,521	2,223,874	2,565,712	2,491,680	4.17	-2.89
Switzerland	550,120	613,441	659,862	730,373	783,809	1.31	7.32
EAST MEDITERRANEAN EUROPE	131,065	199,690	219,204	201,135	163,609	0.27	-18.66
Cyprus	3,692	3,738	4,471	3,734	3,871	0.01	3.67
Israel	66,167	80,293	86,284	76,327	85,322	0.14	11.78
Turkey	61,206	115,659	128,449	121,074	74,416	0.12	-38.54
OTHER EUROPE	53,763	73,143	109,170	89,840	118,115	0.20	31.47
Other countries of Europe	53,763	73,143	109,170	89,840	118,115	0.20	31.47

Yearbook of Tourism Statistics, Data 2009 – 2013, 2015 Edition

CUBA

2. Arrivals of non-resident visitors at national borders, by country of residence

	2009	2010	2011	2012	2013	Market share 2013	% Change 2013-2012
TOTAL	2,429,809	2,531,745	2,716,317	2,838,607	2,852,572	100.00	0.49
AFRICA	8,691	8,698	8,202	10,975	12,573	0.44	14.56
EAST AFRICA	1,370	1,050	646	675	691	0.02	2.37
All countries of East Africa	1,370	1,050	646	675	691	0.02	2.37
CENTRAL AFRICA	1,757	2,558	3,180	4,196	6,413	0.22	52.84
Angola	1,440	2,307	2,838	3,793	5,380	0.19	41.84
Other countries of Central Africa	317	251	342	403	1,033	0.04	156.33
NORTH AFRICA	1,935	1,882	1,789	1,994	2,412	0.08	20.96
All countries of North Africa	1,935	1,882	1,789	1,994	2,412	0.08	20.96
SOUTHERN AFRICA	1,385	1,223	1,355	2,300	1,555	0.05	-32.39
All countries of Southern Africa	1,385	1,223	1,355	2,300	1,555	0.05	-32.39
WEST AFRICA	2,244	1,985	1,232	1,810	1,502	0.05	-17.02
All countries of West Africa	2,244	1,985	1,232	1,810	1,502	0.05	-17.02
AMERICAS	1,535,853	1,664,043	1,799,074	1,926,601	1,964,113	68.85	1.95
CARIBBEAN	315,039	389,766	413,409	399,756	390,342	13.68	-2.35
Antigua and Barbuda	201	54	76	89	90	0.00	1.12
Bahamas	3,456	3,122	2,966	3,007	2,644	0.09	-12.07
Barbados	695	209	165	172	149	0.01	-13.37
Bermuda	210	143	99	114	123	0.00	7.89
Cayman Islands	562	480	583	637	723	0.03	13.50
Dominica	521	138	112	91	103	0.00	13.19
Dominican Republic	5,022	4,735	4,969	4,807	4,652	0.16	-3.22
Grenada	110	93	81	84	80	0.00	-4.76
Guadeloupe	6	8					
Haiti	4,691	2,549	3,839	3,836	5,351	0.19	39.49
Jamaica	2,173	1,512	1,285	1,309	1,636	0.06	24.98
Martinique	5	5	3				
Netherlands Antilles	49	51	86	37			
Puerto Rico	64	19	10	4	10	0.00	150.00
Saint Lucia	188	148	179	104	108	0.00	3.85
Saint Vincent and the Grenadines	94	141	102	120	88	0.00	-26.67
Trinidad and Tobago	811	855	892	1,097	955	0.03	-12.94
Other countries of the Caribbean	296,181	375,504	397,962	384,248	373,630	13.10	-2.76
CENTRAL AMERICA	29,801	26,695	29,075	33,425	28,922	1.01	-13.47
Belize	800	211	230	300	299	0.01	-0.33
Costa Rica	7,855	7,319	8,071	8,119	5,783	0.20	-28.77
El Salvador	3,496	2,368	2,700	3,817	3,659	0.13	-4.14
Guatemala	3,874	3,268	3,689	3,712	3,144	0.11	-15.30
Honduras	1,819	1,686	1,950	2,806	1,106	0.04	-60.58
Nicaragua	2,280	2,187	2,088	2,373	2,166	0.08	-8.72
Panama	9,677	9,656	10,347	12,298	12,765	0.45	3.80
NORTH AMERICA	1,028,826	1,074,944	1,152,210	1,248,035	1,282,781	44.97	2.78
Canada	914,884	945,248	1,002,318	1,071,696	1,105,729	38.76	3.18
Mexico	61,487	66,650	76,326	78,289	84,704	2.97	8.19
United States of America	52,455	63,046	73,566	98,050	92,348	3.24	-5.82
SOUTH AMERICA	162,187	172,638	204,380	245,385	262,068	9.19	6.80
Argentina	48,543	58,612	75,968	94,691	90,084	3.16	-4.87
Bolivia	2,002	1,600	1,286	2,204	2,440	0.09	10.71
Brazil	13,498	14,367	14,507	16,174	17,573	0.62	8.65
Chile	18,205	17,521	23,527	27,551	35,952	1.26	30.49
Colombia	21,287	20,624	24,873	33,343	34,828	1.22	4.45
Ecuador	9,473	7,011	6,964	6,281	7,369	0.26	17.32
French Guiana	5	5		1	1	0.00	
Guyana	617	238	297	294	282	0.01	-4.08
Paraguay	492	412	559	677	661	0.02	-2.36
Peru	14,708	16,049	15,188	19,737	18,528	0.65	-6.13
Suriname	114	106	106	149	100	0.00	-32.89
Uruguay	4,585	5,128	7,009	7,910	8,294	0.29	4.85
Venezuela	28,657	30,965	34,096	36,373	45,943	1.61	26.31

172

CUBA

2. Arrivals of non-resident visitors at national borders, by country of residence

	2009	2010	2011	2012	2013	Market share 2013	% Change 2013-2012
Other countries of South America	1				13	0.00	
EAST ASIA AND THE PACIFIC	**40,558**	**41,349**	**48,498**	**53,158**	**56,229**	**1.97**	**5.78**
NORTH-EAST ASIA	**20,887**	**21,811**	**25,403**	**31,790**	**33,991**	**1.19**	**6.92**
China	12,352	11,247	14,749	18,836	22,218	0.78	17.95
Hong Kong, China	10	6	10	15	2	0.00	-86.67
Japan	5,460	6,372	5,420	7,348	5,896	0.21	-19.76
Korea, Dem. People's Republic of	338	202	318	234	149	0.01	-36.32
Korea, Republic of	2,382	3,481	4,352	4,568	4,996	0.18	9.37
Mongolia	36	46	78	98	87	0.00	-11.22
Taiwan, Province of China	305	449	468	688	640	0.02	-6.98
Other countries of North-East Asia	4	8	8	3	3	0.00	
SOUTH-EAST ASIA	**11,812**	**11,419**	**14,611**	**11,061**	**10,676**	**0.37**	**-3.48**
Cambodia	19	17	19	25	25	0.00	
Indonesia	562	990	1,277	854	621	0.02	-27.28
Lao People's Democratic Republic	15	14	3	8	9	0.00	12.50
Malaysia	253	387	299	404	346	0.01	-14.36
Philippines	9,478	8,721	11,561	8,289	8,461	0.30	2.08
Singapore	233	239	255	261	285	0.01	9.20
Thailand	204	157	159	241	229	0.01	-4.98
Viet Nam	1,000	867	1,031	960	672	0.02	-30.00
Other countries of South-East Asia	48	27	7	19	28	0.00	47.37
AUSTRALASIA	**7,763**	**8,076**	**8,423**	**10,253**	**11,518**	**0.40**	**12.34**
Australia	6,410	6,797	7,115	8,719	9,792	0.34	12.31
New Zealand	1,353	1,279	1,308	1,534	1,726	0.06	12.52
MELANESIA	**19**	**18**	**41**	**40**	**33**	**0.00**	**-17.50**
Fiji	7	16	15	25	22	0.00	-12.00
New Caledonia	1	1	20	1			
Papua New Guinea	11	1	1	4	2	0.00	-50.00
Vanuatu			5	10	9	0.00	-10.00
MICRONESIA	**30**	**18**	**13**	**8**	**7**	**0.00**	**-12.50**
All countries of Micronesia	30	18	13	8	7	0.00	-12.50
POLYNESIA	**20**	**7**	**7**	**6**	**4**	**0.00**	**-33.33**
All countries of Polynesia	20	7	7	6	4	0.00	-33.33
OTHER EAST ASIA AND THE PACIFIC	**27**						
Other countries of Oceania	27						
EUROPE	**838,340**	**809,515**	**852,065**	**839,258**	**810,381**	**28.41**	**-3.44**
CENTRAL/EASTERN EUROPE	**85,081**	**100,070**	**127,179**	**136,926**	**123,144**	**4.32**	**-10.07**
Bulgaria	1,663	1,517	1,832	1,885	2,041	0.07	8.28
Czech Republic	11,516	8,855	8,927	8,723	9,145	0.32	4.84
Estonia	494	383	527	592	651	0.02	9.97
Hungary	3,439	3,028	3,512	3,064	3,361	0.12	9.69
Latvia	529	607	691	954	900	0.03	-5.66
Lithuania	866	1,180	1,279	1,185	1,366	0.05	15.27
Poland	13,501	12,793	13,972	13,035	13,395	0.47	2.76
Romania	2,693	2,705	3,023	3,336	3,252	0.11	-2.52
Russian Federation	37,391	56,245	78,472	86,944	70,401	2.47	-19.03
Slovakia	4,387	4,115	4,324	4,679	4,749	0.17	1.50
Ukraine	6,353	5,686	6,771	7,519	8,250	0.29	9.72
Uzbekistan	49	86	68	117	225	0.01	92.31
Other countries Central/East Europe	2,200	2,870	3,781	4,893	5,408	0.19	10.53
NORTHERN EUROPE	**206,188**	**207,119**	**210,758**	**193,677**	**191,363**	**6.71**	**-1.19**
Denmark	8,782	8,476	8,009	8,031	8,419	0.30	4.83
Finland	5,265	4,935	5,756	6,381	7,932	0.28	24.31
Iceland	190	154	188	242	209	0.01	-13.64
Ireland	6,592	5,638	5,171	4,972	5,231	0.18	5.21
Norway	7,202	7,441	8,754	10,743	9,697	0.34	-9.74
Sweden	5,837	6,131	7,055	9,571	10,357	0.36	8.21
United Kingdom	172,318	174,343	175,822	153,737	149,515	5.24	-2.75
Other countries of Northern Europe	2	1	3		3	0.00	

Yearbook of Tourism Statistics, Data 2009 – 2013, 2015 Edition

CUBA

2. Arrivals of non-resident visitors at national borders, by country of residence

	2009	2010	2011	2012	2013	Market share 2013	% Change 2013-2012
SOUTHERN EUROPE	285,845	247,098	235,698	203,233	187,755	6.58	-7.62
Albania	376	404	351	378	408	0.01	7.94
Andorra	124	113	113	81	84	0.00	3.70
Bosnia and Herzegovina	307	299	288	304	340	0.01	11.84
Croatia	1,442	1,344	1,383	1,578	1,581	0.06	0.19
Greece	4,769	4,263	3,427	2,551	2,676	0.09	4.90
Italy	118,347	112,298	110,432	103,290	95,542	3.35	-7.50
Malta	140	117	125	117	104	0.00	-11.11
Montenegro	96	142	151	165	161	0.01	-2.42
Portugal	26,055	18,762	13,733	9,148	9,440	0.33	3.19
San Marino	145	119	111	94	249	0.01	164.89
Serbia		1,683	1,669	2,022	2,317	0.08	14.59
Serbia and Montenegro	1,430						
Slovenia	2,358	2,130	1,941	1,853	1,491	0.05	-19.54
Spain	129,224	104,948	101,631	81,354	73,056	2.56	-10.20
Other countries of Southern Europe	1,032	476	343	298	306	0.01	2.68
WESTERN EUROPE	253,812	246,704	266,923	294,292	295,895	10.37	0.54
Austria	12,004	11,486	11,803	13,250	15,201	0.53	14.72
Belgium	15,722	13,049	14,266	14,414	14,098	0.49	-2.19
France	83,478	80,470	94,370	101,522	96,640	3.39	-4.81
Germany	93,437	93,136	95,124	108,712	115,984	4.07	6.69
Liechtenstein	62	64	85	87	92	0.00	5.75
Luxembourg	613	598	693	724	677	0.02	-6.49
Monaco	34	19	37	45	46	0.00	2.22
Netherlands	33,123	31,787	32,402	35,284	32,165	1.13	-8.84
Switzerland	15,339	16,095	18,143	20,254	20,992	0.74	3.64
EAST MEDITERRANEAN EUROPE	7,414	8,524	11,507	11,130	12,224	0.43	9.83
Cyprus	367	282	344	240	217	0.01	-9.58
Israel	3,306	3,926	5,327	4,857	5,549	0.19	14.25
Turkey	3,741	4,316	5,836	6,033	6,458	0.23	7.04
MIDDLE EAST	1,810	2,053	1,814	2,191	2,321	0.08	5.93
Bahrain	17	22	22	22	22	0.00	
Egypt	240	271	292	23	458	0.02	1,891.30
Iraq	54	67	78	103	156	0.01	51.46
Jordan	211	172	162	173	218	0.01	26.01
Kuwait	23	153	52	47	38	0.00	-19.15
Lebanon	533	522	574	616	593	0.02	-3.73
Libya	80	73	29	12	16	0.00	33.33
Oman	56	27	19	50	24	0.00	-52.00
Palestine	96	71	56	60	67	0.00	11.67
Qatar	17	34	7	36	15	0.00	-58.33
Saudi Arabia	115	185	210	300	387	0.01	29.00
Syrian Arab Republic	215	368	266	388	263	0.01	-32.22
Yemen	76	52	32	36	45	0.00	25.00
Other countries of Middle East	77	36	15	325	19	0.00	-94.15
SOUTH ASIA	4,467	5,832	5,841	5,901	6,728	0.24	14.01
Afghanistan	49	42	48	61	76	0.00	24.59
Bangladesh	80	118	91	108	107	0.00	-0.93
India	2,551	3,614	3,574	3,480	3,870	0.14	11.21
Iran, Islamic Republic of	940	1,092	1,075	1,048	1,239	0.04	18.23
Maldives	55	81	1	3	3	0.00	
Pakistan	179	208	185	212	233	0.01	9.91
Sri Lanka	483	487	362	466	570	0.02	22.32
Other countries of South Asia	130	190	505	523	630	0.02	20.46
NOT SPECIFIED	90	255	823	523	227	0.01	-56.60
Other countries of the World	90	255	823	523	227	0.01	-56.60

Yearbook of Tourism Statistics, Data 2009 – 2013, 2015 Edition

CURAÇAO

1. Arrivals of non-resident tourists at national borders, by country of residence

		2009	2010	2011	2012	2013	Market share 2013	% Change 2013-2012
TOTAL	(*)	**366,703**	**341,651**	**390,111**	**420,868**	**440,714**	**100.00**	**4.72**
AMERICAS		**210,790**	**170,818**	**210,093**	**234,479**	**244,673**	**55.52**	**4.35**
CARIBBEAN		**36,637**	**39,107**	**41,573**	**40,079**	**38,969**	**8.84**	**-2.77**
Aruba		16,756	18,817	20,453	21,670	20,048	4.55	-7.49
Barbados		862	1,144	929	709	588	0.13	-17.07
Dominican Republic		2,644	2,927	4,098	4,132	4,875	1.11	17.98
Haiti		1,811	1,914	2,273	2,331	2,515	0.57	7.89
Jamaica		7,064	5,109	5,155	3,898	3,615	0.82	-7.26
Puerto Rico		756	711	442	362	206	0.05	-43.09
Trinidad and Tobago		5,318	6,852	6,438	5,404	5,653	1.28	4.61
Other countries of the Caribbean		1,426	1,633	1,785	1,573	1,469	0.33	-6.61
CENTRAL AMERICA		**634**	**734**	**841**	**1,137**	**1,519**	**0.34**	**33.60**
Panama		634	734	841	1,137	1,519	0.34	33.60
NORTH AMERICA		**42,560**	**56,449**	**71,655**	**71,933**	**71,317**	**16.18**	**-0.86**
Canada		6,513	7,628	8,769	9,822	9,608	2.18	-2.18
United States of America		36,047	48,821	62,886	62,111	61,709	14.00	-0.65
SOUTH AMERICA		**130,959**	**74,528**	**96,024**	**121,330**	**132,868**	**30.15**	**9.51**
Argentina		709	929	1,289	1,848	2,294	0.52	24.13
Brazil		4,466	8,096	8,825	9,270	10,840	2.46	16.94
Chile		338	357	534	597	784	0.18	31.32
Colombia		6,260	6,280	8,181	10,444	9,989	2.27	-4.36
Ecuador		1,744	2,319	2,629	2,888	2,079	0.47	-28.01
Guyana		917	1,029	990	1,022	1,442	0.33	41.10
Peru		288	266	179	214	257	0.06	20.09
Suriname		9,218	9,440	9,978	10,799	12,395	2.81	14.78
Venezuela		105,932	44,350	61,567	83,324	92,395	20.96	10.89
Other countries of South America		1,087	1,462	1,852	924	393	0.09	-57.47
EUROPE		**149,538**	**163,831**	**169,142**	**175,161**	**175,843**	**39.90**	**0.39**
NORTHERN EUROPE		**5,316**	**5,448**	**5,730**	**5,023**	**7,058**	**1.60**	**40.51**
Denmark		446	299	464	305	526	0.12	72.46
Finland		887	747	667	585	1,255	0.28	114.53
Norway		659	742	835	743	945	0.21	27.19
Sweden		1,236	1,480	1,224	1,253	1,925	0.44	53.63
United Kingdom		2,088	2,180	2,540	2,137	2,407	0.55	12.63
SOUTHERN EUROPE		**1,819**	**2,332**	**2,992**	**2,745**	**2,919**	**0.66**	**6.34**
Italy		730	1,131	1,851	1,297	1,299	0.29	0.15
Portugal		248	249	229	296	269	0.06	-9.12
Spain		841	952	912	1,152	1,351	0.31	17.27
WESTERN EUROPE		**140,178**	**153,931**	**157,863**	**164,333**	**161,925**	**36.74**	**-1.47**
Austria		340	367	474	1,163	1,281	0.29	10.15
Belgium		3,744	4,429	5,114	5,081	6,017	1.37	18.42
France		1,123	1,192	1,405	1,958	2,646	0.60	35.14
Germany		6,842	6,652	8,065	15,677	17,627	4.00	12.44
Netherlands		127,175	140,161	141,529	138,555	132,176	29.99	-4.60
Switzerland		954	1,130	1,276	1,899	2,178	0.49	14.69
OTHER EUROPE		**2,225**	**2,120**	**2,557**	**3,060**	**3,941**	**0.89**	**28.79**
Other countries of Europe		2,225	2,120	2,557	3,060	3,941	0.89	28.79
NOT SPECIFIED		**6,375**	**7,002**	**10,876**	**11,228**	**20,198**	**4.58**	**79.89**
Other countries of the World		6,375	7,002	10,876	11,228	20,198	4.58	79.89

175

CURAÇAO

3. Arrivals of non-resident tourists in hotels and similar establishments, by country of residence

	2009	2010	2011	2012	2013	Market share 2013	% Change 2013-2012
TOTAL (*)	234,070	223,044	248,884	230,499	291,117	100.00	26.30
AMERICAS	140,072	117,250	144,713	139,416	169,198	58.12	21.36
CARIBBEAN	18,313	23,834	22,673	19,086	20,889	7.18	9.45
Aruba	7,072	10,763	11,163	10,535	11,341	3.90	7.65
Barbados	672	793	663	453	455	0.16	0.44
Dominican Republic	816	875	953	926	1,151	0.40	24.30
Haiti	844	893	1,093	889	1,015	0.35	14.17
Jamaica	3,344	3,369	2,099	1,353	1,128	0.39	-16.63
Puerto Rico	469	558	320	238	154	0.05	-35.29
Trinidad and Tobago	4,263	5,586	5,140	3,866	4,517	1.55	16.84
Other countries of the Caribbean	833	997	1,242	826	1,128	0.39	36.56
NORTH AMERICA	32,781	46,925	57,240	48,155	57,380	19.71	19.16
Canada	5,436	6,567	7,185	6,731	7,812	2.68	16.06
United States of America	27,345	40,358	50,055	41,424	49,568	17.03	19.66
SOUTH AMERICA	88,978	46,491	64,800	72,175	90,929	31.23	25.98
Argentina	547	797	1,014	1,232	1,917	0.66	55.60
Brazil	3,704	7,413	7,423	6,271	9,487	3.26	51.28
Colombia	2,685	3,473	4,920	5,595	6,545	2.25	16.98
Ecuador	1,439	2,100	2,404	1,841	1,813	0.62	-1.52
Guyana	461	581	587	557	884	0.30	58.71
Peru	142		82	79	129	0.04	63.29
Suriname	3,325	843	4,362	4,095	6,115	2.10	49.33
Venezuela	75,154	29,349	42,163	50,557	62,452	21.45	23.53
Other countries of South America	1,521	1,935	1,845	1,948	1,587	0.55	-18.53
EUROPE	92,603	104,420	102,017	89,158	119,474	41.04	34.00
NORTHERN EUROPE	3,739	3,836	3,691	3,021	5,319	1.83	76.07
Denmark	317	193	333	130	366	0.13	181.54
Finland	808	676	541	467	1,045	0.36	123.77
Norway	462	489	555	467	736	0.25	57.60
Sweden	962	1,181	977	784	1,640	0.56	109.18
United Kingdom	1,190	1,297	1,285	1,173	1,532	0.53	30.61
SOUTHERN EUROPE	1,029	1,401	1,974	1,303	1,690	0.58	29.70
Italy	476	795	1,427	656	796	0.27	21.34
Portugal	147	150	95	98	150	0.05	53.06
Spain	406	456	452	549	744	0.26	35.52
WESTERN EUROPE	86,277	97,525	94,417	83,163	109,305	37.55	31.43
Austria	246	266	338	737	989	0.34	34.19
Belgium	2,389	3,094	3,285	2,978	4,471	1.54	50.13
Germany	4,588	4,443	5,211	9,194	13,733	4.72	49.37
Netherlands	78,385	88,885	84,674	69,097	88,381	30.36	27.91
Switzerland	669	837	909	1,157	1,731	0.59	49.61
OTHER EUROPE	1,558	1,658	1,935	1,671	3,160	1.09	89.11
Other countries of Europe	1,558	1,658	1,935	1,671	3,160	1.09	89.11
NOT SPECIFIED	1,395	1,374	2,154	1,925	2,445	0.84	27.01
Other countries of the World	1,395	1,374	2,154	1,925	2,445	0.84	27.01

Yearbook of Tourism Statistics, Data 2009 – 2013, 2015 Edition

CURAÇAO

6. Overnight stays of non-resident tourists in all types of accommodation establishments, by country of residence

	2009	2010	2011	2012	2013	Market share 2013	% Change 2013-2012
TOTAL	**2,696,798**	**2,907,435**	**3,200,356**	**3,687,240**	**3,750,629**	**100.00**	**1.72**
AMERICAS	**1,028,550**	**1,063,734**	**1,303,411**	**1,634,898**	**1,677,621**	**44.73**	**2.61**
CARIBBEAN	**180,228**	**213,512**	**251,473**	**264,790**	**255,642**	**6.82**	**-3.45**
Aruba	72,310	83,351	90,905	114,270	104,409	2.78	-8.63
Barbados	2,982	5,237	4,042	3,497	2,651	0.07	-24.19
Dominican Republic	24,222	34,200	62,157	59,615	67,129	1.79	12.60
Haiti	13,383	16,621	20,005	22,566	21,473	0.57	-4.84
Jamaica	37,292	32,190	36,021	28,620	26,138	0.70	-8.67
Puerto Rico	3,187	2,930	1,902	2,060	1,285	0.03	-37.62
Trinidad and Tobago	19,120	27,823	26,221	23,444	23,695	0.63	1.07
Other countries of the Caribbean	7,732	11,160	10,220	10,718	8,862	0.24	-17.32
CENTRAL AMERICA	**2,680**	**3,612**	**3,955**	**6,171**	**8,213**	**0.22**	**33.09**
Panama	2,680	3,612	3,955	6,171	8,213	0.22	33.09
NORTH AMERICA	**300,174**	**375,576**	**469,450**	**506,983**	**486,773**	**12.98**	**-3.99**
Canada	53,342	62,825	75,057	84,359	83,548	2.23	-0.96
United States of America	246,832	312,751	394,393	422,624	403,225	10.75	-4.59
SOUTH AMERICA	**545,468**	**471,034**	**578,533**	**856,954**	**926,993**	**24.72**	**8.17**
Argentina	3,923	5,730	7,569	12,381	16,387	0.44	32.36
Brazil	22,602	40,540	45,886	57,032	65,818	1.75	15.41
Chile	2,743	2,320	2,170	4,261	6,143	0.16	44.17
Colombia	81,107	87,177	108,327	102,654	109,149	2.91	6.33
Ecuador	7,589	12,179	12,244	16,136	14,087	0.38	-12.70
Guyana	4,713	5,385	6,182	7,028	8,237	0.22	17.20
Peru	1,927	1,695	1,501	1,935	2,817	0.08	45.58
Suriname	60,472	60,660	61,025	72,667	77,855	2.08	7.14
Venezuela	353,292	242,654	318,410	569,067	610,705	16.28	7.32
Other countries of South America	7,100	12,694	15,219	13,793	15,795	0.42	14.51
EUROPE	**1,634,474**	**1,805,450**	**1,850,752**	**1,980,735**	**1,943,886**	**51.83**	**-1.86**
NORTHERN EUROPE	**52,081**	**54,611**	**51,459**	**50,047**	**68,482**	**1.83**	**36.84**
Denmark	4,113	2,999	4,213	3,127	5,848	0.16	87.02
Finland	8,037	6,910	5,153	4,956	10,758	0.29	117.07
Norway	6,528	6,900	7,781	6,972	8,455	0.23	21.27
Sweden	11,899	15,023	11,661	11,988	17,762	0.47	48.16
United Kingdom	21,504	22,779	22,651	23,004	25,659	0.68	11.54
SOUTHERN EUROPE	**16,812**	**19,570**	**25,566**	**27,175**	**27,003**	**0.72**	**-0.63**
Italy	5,730	9,103	14,549	10,724	11,660	0.31	8.73
Portugal	2,886	1,659	2,127	4,030	2,640	0.07	-34.49
Spain	8,196	8,808	8,890	12,421	12,703	0.34	2.27
WESTERN EUROPE	**1,550,079**	**1,713,843**	**1,749,567**	**1,876,092**	**1,815,763**	**48.41**	**-3.22**
Austria	3,769	3,940	5,004	11,589	13,498	0.36	16.47
Belgium	40,101	45,585	50,378	52,640	61,636	1.64	17.09
France	9,982	8,883	11,146	16,407	18,646	0.50	13.65
Germany	81,164	78,149	94,222	168,872	195,136	5.20	15.55
Netherlands	1,406,180	1,566,903	1,576,224	1,608,899	1,504,899	40.12	-6.46
Switzerland	8,883	10,383	12,593	17,685	21,948	0.59	24.11
OTHER EUROPE	**15,502**	**17,426**	**24,160**	**27,421**	**32,638**	**0.87**	**19.03**
Other countries of Europe	15,502	17,426	24,160	27,421	32,638	0.87	19.03
NOT SPECIFIED	**33,774**	**38,251**	**46,193**	**71,607**	**129,122**	**3.44**	**80.32**
Other countries of the World	33,774	38,251	46,193	71,607	129,122	3.44	80.32

CYPRUS

1. Arrivals of non-resident tourists at national borders, by country of residence

	2009	2010	2011	2012	2013	Market share 2013	% Change 2013-2012
TOTAL	**2,141,193**	**2,172,998**	**2,392,228**	**2,464,908**	**2,405,387**	**100.00**	**-2.41**
AFRICA	**6,833**	**6,481**	**6,615**	**5,617**	**6,177**	**0.26**	**9.97**
SOUTHERN AFRICA	**5,623**	**4,816**	**5,793**	**4,708**	**4,947**	**0.21**	**5.08**
South Africa	5,623	4,816	5,793	4,708	4,947	0.21	5.08
OTHER AFRICA	**1,210**	**1,665**	**822**	**909**	**1,230**	**0.05**	**35.31**
Other countries of Africa	1,210	1,665	822	909	1,230	0.05	35.31
AMERICAS	**23,737**	**31,357**	**32,080**	**25,084**	**27,731**	**1.15**	**10.55**
NORTH AMERICA	**22,619**	**29,541**	**31,012**	**24,292**	**26,769**	**1.11**	**10.20**
Canada	4,698	6,822	5,180	3,830	4,841	0.20	26.40
United States of America	17,921	22,719	25,832	20,462	21,928	0.91	7.16
OTHER AMERICAS	**1,118**	**1,816**	**1,068**	**792**	**962**	**0.04**	**21.46**
Other countries of the Americas	1,118	1,816	1,068	792	962	0.04	21.46
EAST ASIA AND THE PACIFIC	**15,060**	**19,093**	**16,535**	**15,746**	**16,163**	**0.67**	**2.65**
NORTH-EAST ASIA	**1,520**	**2,377**	**2,049**	**2,475**	**2,203**	**0.09**	**-10.99**
China	441	655	651	735	1,171	0.05	59.32
Japan	560	1,194	694	1,249	689	0.03	-44.84
Korea, Republic of	60	144	292	81			
Other countries of North-East Asia	459	384	412	410	343	0.01	-16.34
AUSTRALASIA	**10,996**	**14,139**	**13,110**	**12,218**	**12,997**	**0.54**	**6.38**
Australia	10,523	13,282	12,455	11,681	12,497	0.52	6.99
New Zealand	473	857	655	537	500	0.02	-6.89
OTHER EAST ASIA AND THE PACIFIC	**2,544**	**2,577**	**1,376**	**1,053**	**963**	**0.04**	**-8.55**
Other countries of Asia	2,511	2,534	1,294	1,025	939	0.04	-8.39
Other countries of Oceania	33	43	82	28	24	0.00	-14.29
EUROPE	**2,039,961**	**2,055,439**	**2,278,934**	**2,356,234**	**2,291,471**	**95.26**	**-2.75**
CENTRAL/EASTERN EUROPE	**245,429**	**325,061**	**463,583**	**604,337**	**732,104**	**30.44**	**21.14**
Belarus	2,186	3,507	3,371	5,221	6,342	0.26	21.47
Bulgaria	8,922	8,905	10,247	10,443	6,632	0.28	-36.49
Czech Republic	20,477	15,458	20,576	14,741	11,487	0.48	-22.07
Estonia	2,077	970	2,074	1,591	2,200	0.09	38.28
Georgia	195	146	141	194	244	0.01	25.77
Hungary	9,700	10,721	11,334	12,376	11,129	0.46	-10.08
Latvia	1,538	1,825	1,934	2,088	2,184	0.09	4.60
Lithuania	1,423	2,546	2,182	6,766	4,210	0.18	-37.78
Poland	17,186	18,439	24,236	30,981	24,875	1.03	-19.71
Romania	19,931	19,980	30,601	20,557	14,805	0.62	-27.98
Russian Federation	148,740	223,861	334,083	474,426	608,576	25.30	28.28
Slovakia	3,719	5,061	5,030	3,608	3,853	0.16	6.79
Ukraine	7,496	11,766	14,274	19,482	34,022	1.41	74.63
Other countries Central/East Europe	1,839	1,876	3,500	1,863	1,545	0.06	-17.07
NORTHERN EUROPE	**1,318,879**	**1,243,031**	**1,277,048**	**1,215,250**	**1,139,350**	**47.37**	**-6.25**
Denmark	29,667	30,335	34,064	31,763	30,011	1.25	-5.52
Finland	32,758	32,886	36,289	29,216	28,381	1.18	-2.86
Iceland	223	144	88	280			
Ireland	18,537	10,527	9,662	7,832	6,035	0.25	-22.94
Norway	60,245	63,347	64,024	69,410	65,736	2.73	-5.29
Sweden	108,253	109,746	112,212	117,286	117,958	4.90	0.57
United Kingdom	1,069,196	996,046	1,020,709	959,463	891,229	37.05	-7.11
SOUTHERN EUROPE	**162,546**	**154,782**	**172,168**	**183,784**	**140,747**	**5.85**	**-23.42**
Croatia					604	0.03	
Greece	131,875	127,667	138,721	132,990	104,949	4.36	-21.09
Italy	15,604	12,992	16,828	34,415	23,481	0.98	-31.77
Malta	6,154	4,358	4,511	4,866	3,333	0.14	-31.50
Montenegro	104	168	86				
Portugal	1,106	1,161	1,034	925	741	0.03	-19.89
Serbia	3,678	3,431	3,986	3,960	2,432	0.10	-38.59
Slovenia	953	1,046	2,245	1,124	824	0.03	-26.69
Spain	3,072	3,959	4,757	5,504	4,383	0.18	-20.37
WESTERN EUROPE	**280,455**	**292,856**	**333,038**	**311,926**	**233,626**	**9.71**	**-25.10**

Yearbook of Tourism Statistics, Data 2009 – 2013, 2015 Edition

CYPRUS

1. Arrivals of non-resident tourists at national borders, by country of residence

	2009	2010	2011	2012	2013	Market share 2013	% Change 2013-2012
Austria	27,463	21,559	23,341	23,166	16,800	0.70	-27.48
Belgium	22,966	24,125	27,346	25,930	28,810	1.20	11.11
France	26,187	28,749	34,363	35,955	27,154	1.13	-24.48
Germany	131,161	139,190	157,890	144,407	98,930	4.11	-31.49
Luxembourg	3,020	3,374	3,154	2,591	524	0.02	-79.78
Netherlands	30,996	34,212	41,631	33,024	20,241	0.84	-38.71
Switzerland	38,662	41,647	45,313	46,853	41,167	1.71	-12.14
EAST MEDITERRANEAN EUROPE	**31,480**	**38,197**	**32,174**	**39,473**	**43,808**	**1.82**	**10.98**
Israel	31,364	37,876	31,910	39,420	43,653	1.81	10.74
Turkey	116	321	264	53	155	0.01	192.45
OTHER EUROPE	**1,172**	**1,512**	**923**	**1,464**	**1,836**	**0.08**	**25.41**
Other countries of Europe	1,172	1,512	923	1,464	1,836	0.08	25.41
MIDDLE EAST	**49,947**	**51,110**	**50,799**	**56,402**	**58,634**	**2.44**	**3.96**
Bahrain	2,970	2,184	1,766	1,862	1,588	0.07	-14.72
Egypt	5,067	4,324	4,940	5,338	6,214	0.26	16.41
Iraq	89	358	1,409	2,757	372	0.02	-86.51
Jordan	4,040	3,575	4,184	3,490	3,924	0.16	12.44
Kuwait	2,544	1,480	1,268	1,698	1,287	0.05	-24.20
Lebanon	15,431	20,664	21,202	25,658	25,833	1.07	0.68
Libya	408	298	145	169	574	0.02	239.64
Saudi Arabia	2,071	2,463	1,445	1,537	1,483	0.06	-3.51
Syrian Arab Republic	1,455	1,626	983	1,272	371	0.02	-70.83
United Arab Emirates	14,197	11,832	11,433	10,664	14,603	0.61	36.94
Other countries of Middle East	1,675	2,306	2,024	1,957	2,385	0.10	21.87
SOUTH ASIA	**5,020**	**8,406**	**6,963**	**5,666**	**4,813**	**0.20**	**-15.05**
Iran, Islamic Republic of	3,627	4,336	5,742	4,402	3,407	0.14	-22.60
Other countries of South Asia	1,393	4,070	1,221	1,264	1,406	0.06	11.23
NOT SPECIFIED	**635**	**1,112**	**302**	**159**	**398**	**0.02**	**150.31**
Other countries of the World	635	1,112	302	159	398	0.02	150.31

Yearbook of Tourism Statistics, Data 2009 – 2013, 2015 Edition

CYPRUS

3. Arrivals of non-resident tourists in hotels and similar establishments, by country of residence

	2009	2010	2011	2012	2013	Market share 2013	% Change 2013-2012
TOTAL	1,646,564	1,788,372	1,921,951	1,996,168	1,922,928	100.00	-3.67
AFRICA	1,529	2,201	2,090	1,793	1,719	0.09	-4.13
SOUTHERN AFRICA	1,529	2,201	2,090	1,793	1,719	0.09	-4.13
South Africa	1,529	2,201	2,090	1,793	1,719	0.09	-4.13
AMERICAS	19,706	23,951	23,828	18,827	17,038	0.89	-9.50
NORTH AMERICA	19,706	23,951	23,828	18,827	17,038	0.89	-9.50
Canada	9,155	10,709	9,917	5,846	5,405	0.28	-7.54
United States of America	10,551	13,242	13,911	12,981	11,633	0.60	-10.38
EAST ASIA AND THE PACIFIC	8,535	9,616	8,247	10,529	12,176	0.63	15.64
NORTH-EAST ASIA	3,585	4,339	4,199	6,342	7,703	0.40	21.46
China	1,405	1,631	1,533	3,442	4,679	0.24	35.94
Japan	2,180	2,708	2,666	2,900	3,024	0.16	4.28
AUSTRALASIA	4,950	5,277	4,048	4,187	4,473	0.23	6.83
Australia	4,950	5,277	4,048	4,187	4,473	0.23	6.83
EUROPE	1,517,681	1,642,363	1,768,517	1,842,889	1,773,462	92.23	-3.77
CENTRAL/EASTERN EUROPE	187,270	268,914	379,716	485,021	588,736	30.62	21.38
Bulgaria	3,726	3,971	4,357	3,275	3,176	0.17	-3.02
Czech Republic	15,396	16,037	18,965	14,211	12,292	0.64	-13.50
Estonia	1,985	1,381	1,579	1,730	1,788	0.09	3.35
Hungary	6,162	7,934	7,425	7,470	7,425	0.39	-0.60
Latvia	1,016	1,273	953	1,515	1,601	0.08	5.68
Lithuania	2,043	3,051	1,176	3,521	2,207	0.11	-37.32
Poland	15,517	19,388	24,404	23,571	18,117	0.94	-23.14
Romania	9,511	10,109	14,551	9,846	8,442	0.44	-14.26
Russian Federation	128,174	201,250	302,423	415,598	529,532	27.54	27.41
Slovakia	3,740	4,520	3,883	4,284	4,156	0.22	-2.99
NORTHERN EUROPE	943,525	941,827	946,180	937,568	865,372	45.00	-7.70
Denmark	22,626	25,714	25,307	26,269	25,599	1.33	-2.55
Finland	28,168	30,466	33,941	25,793	31,077	1.62	20.49
Iceland	4,314	2,583	4,903	4,122	4,461	0.23	8.22
Ireland	14,293	12,076	10,106	9,983	6,600	0.34	-33.89
Norway	57,228	63,207	69,191	65,107	60,627	3.15	-6.88
Sweden	101,245	104,324	108,476	109,094	119,502	6.21	9.54
United Kingdom	715,651	703,457	694,256	697,200	617,506	32.11	-11.43
SOUTHERN EUROPE	100,933	108,677	114,691	109,916	81,611	4.24	-25.75
Greece	68,394	74,281	74,791	60,956	47,092	2.45	-22.74
Italy	18,170	19,472	22,121	32,996	23,474	1.22	-28.86
Malta	5,543	4,299	5,013	3,968	3,033	0.16	-23.56
Portugal	2,523	2,514	2,921	3,245	1,605	0.08	-50.54
Slovenia	1,533	1,595	2,411	1,938	1,465	0.08	-24.41
Spain	4,770	6,516	7,434	6,813	4,942	0.26	-27.46
WESTERN EUROPE	285,953	322,945	327,930	310,384	237,743	12.36	-23.40
Austria	20,036	21,459	19,477	18,652	16,581	0.86	-11.10
Belgium	20,850	24,017	25,434	24,522	19,497	1.01	-20.49
France	36,571	47,785	50,169	48,952	37,900	1.97	-22.58
Germany	147,826	159,998	155,843	144,239	101,689	5.29	-29.50
Luxembourg	3,625	3,248	2,654	2,929	1,187	0.06	-59.47
Netherlands	27,573	33,077	40,683	31,824	19,114	0.99	-39.94
Switzerland	29,472	33,361	33,670	39,266	41,775	2.17	6.39
NOT SPECIFIED	99,113	110,241	119,269	122,130	118,533	6.16	-2.95
Other countries of the World	99,113	110,241	119,269	122,130	118,533	6.16	-2.95

Yearbook of Tourism Statistics, Data 2009 – 2013, 2015 Edition

CYPRUS

4. Arrivals of non-resident tourists in all types of accommodation establishments, by country of residence

	2009	2010	2011	2012	2013	Market share 2013	% Change 2013-2012
TOTAL	1,671,864	1,814,328	1,947,446	2,021,180	1,947,836	100.00	-3.63
AFRICA	1,655	2,347	2,220	1,901	1,842	0.09	-3.10
SOUTHERN AFRICA	1,655	2,347	2,220	1,901	1,842	0.09	-3.10
South Africa	1,655	2,347	2,220	1,901	1,842	0.09	-3.10
AMERICAS	20,054	24,394	24,223	19,202	17,444	0.90	-9.16
NORTH AMERICA	20,054	24,394	24,223	19,202	17,444	0.90	-9.16
Canada	9,289	10,872	10,077	5,976	5,555	0.29	-7.04
United States of America	10,765	13,522	14,146	13,226	11,889	0.61	-10.11
EAST ASIA AND THE PACIFIC	8,900	10,055	8,681	10,960	12,704	0.65	15.91
NORTH-EAST ASIA	3,804	4,616	4,469	6,628	8,058	0.41	21.58
China	1,508	1,760	1,656	3,601	4,864	0.25	35.07
Japan	2,296	2,856	2,813	3,027	3,194	0.16	5.52
AUSTRALASIA	5,096	5,439	4,212	4,332	4,646	0.24	7.25
Australia	5,096	5,439	4,212	4,332	4,646	0.24	7.25
EUROPE	1,540,209	1,665,018	1,791,403	1,864,734	1,794,832	92.14	-3.75
CENTRAL/EASTERN EUROPE	189,726	272,261	383,165	488,791	593,440	30.47	21.41
Bulgaria	3,877	4,162	4,533	3,463	3,340	0.17	-3.55
Czech Republic	15,637	16,330	19,240	14,421	12,515	0.64	-13.22
Estonia	2,099	1,500	1,714	1,832	1,914	0.10	4.48
Hungary	6,332	8,139	7,613	7,627	7,622	0.39	-0.07
Latvia	1,117	1,381	1,054	1,613	1,731	0.09	7.32
Lithuania	2,144	3,179	1,279	3,658	2,343	0.12	-35.95
Poland	15,733	19,654	24,667	23,855	18,423	0.95	-22.77
Romania	9,733	10,375	14,857	10,094	8,670	0.45	-14.11
Russian Federation	129,186	202,889	304,189	417,827	532,594	27.34	27.47
Slovakia	3,868	4,652	4,019	4,401	4,288	0.22	-2.57
NORTHERN EUROPE	958,753	955,346	959,568	950,389	876,926	45.02	-7.73
Denmark	22,908	26,262	25,739	26,594	25,872	1.33	-2.71
Finland	28,524	30,849	34,320	26,148	31,425	1.61	20.18
Iceland	4,489	2,713	5,066	4,221	4,635	0.24	9.81
Ireland	14,481	12,276	10,353	10,208	6,807	0.35	-33.32
Norway	57,889	63,828	70,261	66,069	61,671	3.17	-6.66
Sweden	105,194	107,581	111,753	112,104	122,338	6.28	9.13
United Kingdom	725,268	711,837	702,076	705,045	624,178	32.04	-11.47
SOUTHERN EUROPE	102,381	110,235	116,239	111,491	83,032	4.26	-25.53
Greece	68,936	74,873	75,314	61,466	47,538	2.44	-22.66
Italy	18,449	19,850	22,487	33,486	23,898	1.23	-28.63
Malta	5,709	4,477	5,219	4,117	3,173	0.16	-22.93
Portugal	2,729	2,633	3,057	3,356	1,716	0.09	-48.87
Slovenia	1,628	1,706	2,529	2,047	1,571	0.08	-23.25
Spain	4,930	6,696	7,633	7,019	5,136	0.26	-26.83
WESTERN EUROPE	289,349	327,176	332,431	314,063	241,434	12.39	-23.13
Austria	20,317	21,777	19,806	18,941	16,903	0.87	-10.76
Belgium	21,168	24,351	25,789	24,846	19,838	1.02	-20.16
France	37,104	48,519	50,806	49,644	38,473	1.98	-22.50
Germany	149,064	161,708	157,835	145,490	102,864	5.28	-29.30
Luxembourg	3,786	3,415	2,816	3,051	1,300	0.07	-57.39
Netherlands	28,042	33,621	41,286	32,395	19,535	1.00	-39.70
Switzerland	29,868	33,785	34,093	39,696	42,521	2.18	7.12
NOT SPECIFIED	101,046	112,514	120,919	124,383	121,014	6.21	-2.71
Other countries of the World	101,046	112,514	120,919	124,383	121,014	6.21	-2.71

Yearbook of Tourism Statistics, Data 2009 – 2013, 2015 Edition

CYPRUS

5. Overnight stays of non-resident tourists in hotels and similar establishments, by country of residence

	2009	2010	2011	2012	2013	Market share 2013	% Change 2013-2012
TOTAL	11,488,361	12,267,921	12,933,024	13,333,840	12,994,887	100.00	-2.54
AFRICA	5,355	7,581	8,262	6,354	6,656	0.05	4.75
SOUTHERN AFRICA	5,355	7,581	8,262	6,354	6,656	0.05	4.75
South Africa	5,355	7,581	8,262	6,354	6,656	0.05	4.75
AMERICAS	87,796	92,594	99,121	77,523	67,244	0.52	-13.26
NORTH AMERICA	87,796	92,594	99,121	77,523	67,244	0.52	-13.26
Canada	47,940	46,115	54,906	29,918	22,823	0.18	-23.71
United States of America	39,856	46,479	44,215	47,605	44,421	0.34	-6.69
EAST ASIA AND THE PACIFIC	32,763	31,498	24,997	34,652	39,375	0.30	13.63
NORTH-EAST ASIA	9,652	11,079	10,421	18,097	22,101	0.17	22.13
China	4,388	4,974	4,764	11,165	15,520	0.12	39.01
Japan	5,264	6,105	5,657	6,932	6,581	0.05	-5.06
AUSTRALASIA	23,111	20,419	14,576	16,555	17,274	0.13	4.34
Australia	23,111	20,419	14,576	16,555	17,274	0.13	4.34
EUROPE	10,968,124	11,725,629	12,322,509	12,704,386	12,401,964	95.44	-2.38
CENTRAL/EASTERN EUROPE	1,389,566	2,023,462	2,708,095	3,650,713	4,361,808	33.57	19.48
Bulgaria	21,800	23,259	21,767	13,096	14,985	0.12	14.42
Czech Republic	115,004	110,833	126,912	99,858	82,499	0.63	-17.38
Estonia	11,952	7,592	8,054	8,474	9,027	0.07	6.53
Hungary	34,447	40,934	39,560	37,587	37,642	0.29	0.15
Latvia	4,182	6,302	3,555	6,026	6,047	0.05	0.35
Lithuania	11,251	18,392	4,501	17,905	10,725	0.08	-40.10
Poland	114,197	141,083	164,444	143,160	116,816	0.90	-18.40
Romania	42,316	51,588	70,293	47,557	39,647	0.31	-16.63
Russian Federation	1,009,963	1,594,304	2,244,688	3,250,651	4,016,223	30.91	23.55
Slovakia	24,454	29,175	24,321	26,399	28,197	0.22	6.81
NORTHERN EUROPE	7,145,584	7,033,697	6,894,782	6,585,354	6,133,145	47.20	-6.87
Denmark	166,314	184,340	177,212	188,571	170,001	1.31	-9.85
Finland	191,165	215,030	223,188	166,146	181,369	1.40	9.16
Iceland	33,531	15,771	40,591	18,861	28,574	0.22	51.50
Ireland	94,174	76,487	51,280	48,603	35,274	0.27	-27.42
Norway	430,975	519,232	530,107	523,524	482,638	3.71	-7.81
Sweden	754,013	803,474	775,120	791,063	855,172	6.58	8.10
United Kingdom	5,475,412	5,219,363	5,097,284	4,848,586	4,380,117	33.71	-9.66
SOUTHERN EUROPE	382,878	395,405	394,850	363,526	277,712	2.14	-23.61
Greece	237,930	234,997	232,519	166,006	137,428	1.06	-17.22
Italy	87,210	91,616	90,120	134,035	95,486	0.73	-28.76
Malta	22,334	21,081	22,393	16,680	13,989	0.11	-16.13
Portugal	10,543	13,182	11,605	14,292	6,370	0.05	-55.43
Slovenia	8,672	9,115	12,613	9,268	6,726	0.05	-27.43
Spain	16,189	25,414	25,600	23,245	17,713	0.14	-23.80
WESTERN EUROPE	2,050,096	2,273,065	2,324,782	2,104,793	1,629,299	12.54	-22.59
Austria	142,865	155,367	142,150	122,974	111,718	0.86	-9.15
Belgium	147,207	171,904	166,798	143,024	122,989	0.95	-14.01
France	171,133	218,898	245,568	220,257	160,485	1.23	-27.14
Germany	1,149,174	1,219,945	1,216,119	1,093,426	784,280	6.04	-28.27
Luxembourg	23,852	23,025	19,346	18,306	4,681	0.04	-74.43
Netherlands	182,201	221,999	275,127	211,518	128,222	0.99	-39.38
Switzerland	233,664	261,927	259,674	295,288	316,924	2.44	7.33
NOT SPECIFIED	394,323	410,619	478,135	510,925	479,648	3.69	-6.12
Other countries of the World	394,323	410,619	478,135	510,925	479,648	3.69	-6.12

Yearbook of Tourism Statistics, Data 2009 – 2013, 2015 Edition

CYPRUS

6. Overnight stays of non-resident tourists in all types of accommodation establishments, by country of residence

	2009	2010	2011	2012	2013	Market share 2013	% Change 2013-2012
TOTAL	11,666,663	12,448,159	13,112,597	13,488,127	13,152,589	100.00	-2.49
AFRICA	5,827	8,163	8,790	6,693	7,122	0.05	6.41
SOUTHERN AFRICA	5,827	8,163	8,790	6,693	7,122	0.05	6.41
South Africa	5,827	8,163	8,790	6,693	7,122	0.05	6.41
AMERICAS	89,289	94,657	100,766	78,785	68,746	0.52	-12.74
NORTH AMERICA	89,289	94,657	100,766	78,785	68,746	0.52	-12.74
Canada	48,525	46,820	55,546	30,354	23,389	0.18	-22.95
United States of America	40,764	47,837	45,220	48,431	45,357	0.34	-6.35
EAST ASIA AND THE PACIFIC	34,465	33,151	26,656	35,982	41,224	0.31	14.57
NORTH-EAST ASIA	10,748	12,038	11,369	18,917	23,234	0.18	22.82
China	4,766	5,486	5,262	11,656	16,175	0.12	38.77
Japan	5,982	6,552	6,107	7,261	7,059	0.05	-2.78
AUSTRALASIA	23,717	21,113	15,287	17,065	17,990	0.14	5.42
Australia	23,717	21,113	15,287	17,065	17,990	0.14	5.42
EUROPE	11,134,307	11,890,914	12,487,513	12,847,344	12,545,743	95.39	-2.35
CENTRAL/EASTERN EUROPE	1,405,506	2,046,319	2,729,730	3,670,439	4,389,584	33.37	19.59
Bulgaria	22,507	24,184	22,549	13,620	15,566	0.12	14.29
Czech Republic	116,430	112,649	128,604	100,735	83,536	0.64	-17.07
Estonia	12,519	8,199	8,699	8,849	9,573	0.07	8.18
Hungary	35,277	42,361	40,592	38,207	38,524	0.29	0.83
Latvia	4,592	6,820	3,978	6,357	6,565	0.05	3.27
Lithuania	11,731	18,999	4,908	18,487	11,299	0.09	-38.88
Poland	115,410	142,645	165,858	144,369	118,453	0.90	-17.95
Romania	43,424	53,018	71,825	48,508	40,558	0.31	-16.39
Russian Federation	1,018,545	1,607,554	2,257,729	3,264,465	4,036,722	30.69	23.66
Slovakia	25,071	29,890	24,988	26,842	28,788	0.22	7.25
NORTHERN EUROPE	7,268,409	7,141,690	7,000,579	6,685,854	6,222,641	47.31	-6.93
Denmark	167,784	187,791	179,754	190,022	171,243	1.30	-9.88
Finland	193,340	217,471	225,410	167,746	183,259	1.39	9.25
Iceland	34,385	16,338	41,247	19,718	29,297	0.22	48.58
Ireland	95,163	77,765	52,862	49,867	36,362	0.28	-27.08
Norway	435,388	523,564	539,137	531,709	491,138	3.73	-7.63
Sweden	786,829	831,000	797,679	818,324	877,414	6.67	7.22
United Kingdom	5,555,520	5,287,761	5,164,490	4,908,468	4,433,928	33.71	-9.67
SOUTHERN EUROPE	389,138	402,525	402,342	368,505	283,087	2.15	-23.18
Greece	240,230	237,444	234,764	167,520	138,894	1.06	-17.09
Italy	88,416	93,534	92,264	135,624	97,287	0.74	-28.27
Malta	23,036	21,963	23,309	17,187	14,545	0.11	-15.37
Portugal	11,532	13,747	12,384	14,642	6,793	0.05	-53.61
Slovenia	9,126	9,683	13,137	9,606	7,194	0.05	-25.11
Spain	16,798	26,154	26,484	23,926	18,374	0.14	-23.20
WESTERN EUROPE	2,071,254	2,300,380	2,354,862	2,122,546	1,650,431	12.55	-22.24
Austria	144,525	157,408	144,218	124,448	113,408	0.86	-8.87
Belgium	149,130	173,863	168,537	144,399	124,518	0.95	-13.77
France	173,554	222,107	248,492	222,853	162,999	1.24	-26.86
Germany	1,158,271	1,232,561	1,231,935	1,100,343	791,691	6.02	-28.05
Luxembourg	24,734	24,138	20,466	18,784	5,092	0.04	-72.89
Netherlands	184,973	225,595	279,000	214,291	130,586	0.99	-39.06
Switzerland	236,067	264,708	262,214	297,428	322,137	2.45	8.31
NOT SPECIFIED	402,775	421,274	488,872	519,323	489,754	3.72	-5.69
Other countries of the World	402,775	421,274	488,872	519,323	489,754	3.72	-5.69

Yearbook of Tourism Statistics, Data 2009 – 2013, 2015 Edition

CZECH REPUBLIC

3. Arrivals of non-resident tourists in hotels and similar establishments, by nationality

	2009	2010	2011	2012	2013	Market share 2013	% Change 2013-2012
TOTAL	5,609,025	5,974,227	6,376,697	7,166,917	7,326,692	100.00	2.23
AFRICA	18,592	24,290	28,423	34,774	36,008	0.49	3.55
SOUTHERN AFRICA	4,068	5,163	6,039	9,362	8,220	0.11	-12.20
South Africa	4,068	5,163	6,039	9,362	8,220	0.11	-12.20
OTHER AFRICA	14,524	19,127	22,384	25,412	27,788	0.38	9.35
Other countries of Africa	14,524	19,127	22,384	25,412	27,788	0.38	9.35
AMERICAS	379,615	440,387	465,364	582,764	609,278	8.32	4.55
NORTH AMERICA	317,828	367,084	380,253	461,641	482,837	6.59	4.59
Canada	42,793	50,930	54,163	63,846	65,642	0.90	2.81
Mexico	12,806	16,215	20,811	26,202	27,803	0.38	6.11
United States of America	262,229	299,939	305,279	371,593	389,392	5.31	4.79
SOUTH AMERICA	28,590	36,781	42,360	57,175	59,012	0.81	3.21
Brazil	28,590	36,781	42,360	57,175	59,012	0.81	3.21
OTHER AMERICAS	33,197	36,522	42,751	63,948	67,429	0.92	5.44
Other countries of the Americas	33,197	36,522	42,751	63,948	67,429	0.92	5.44
EAST ASIA AND THE PACIFIC	465,479	568,741	657,245	754,358	796,323	10.87	5.56
NORTH-EAST ASIA	225,361	283,759	320,947	419,064	450,325	6.15	7.46
China	59,429	76,809	105,878	147,690	166,476	2.27	12.72
Japan	112,814	131,223	119,914	138,347	133,096	1.82	-3.80
Korea, Republic of	53,118	75,727	95,155	133,027	150,753	2.06	13.33
AUSTRALASIA	49,562	62,352	70,335	81,189	84,965	1.16	4.65
Australia	43,906	56,021	63,076	72,211	75,254	1.03	4.21
New Zealand	5,656	6,331	7,259	8,978	9,711	0.13	8.16
OTHER EAST ASIA AND THE PACIFIC	190,556	222,630	265,963	254,105	261,033	3.56	2.73
Other countries of Asia	185,660	217,234	260,872	248,360	255,733	3.49	2.97
Other countries of Oceania	4,896	5,396	5,091	5,745	5,300	0.07	-7.75
EUROPE	4,745,339	4,940,809	5,225,665	5,770,522	5,857,965	79.95	1.52
CENTRAL/EASTERN EUROPE	1,137,156	1,304,962	1,535,280	1,837,222	1,956,962	26.71	6.52
Bulgaria	17,365	19,836	21,551	25,084	25,800	0.35	2.85
Estonia	12,665	11,431	15,523	17,119	19,490	0.27	13.85
Hungary	82,669	96,623	102,198	112,997	107,105	1.46	-5.21
Latvia	9,488	8,100	9,383	13,336	15,451	0.21	15.86
Lithuania	41,511	40,552	45,460	43,139	46,868	0.64	8.64
Poland	299,525	313,918	338,014	359,631	381,577	5.21	6.10
Romania	46,185	49,199	56,227	60,464	62,480	0.85	3.33
Russian Federation	310,294	398,438	537,268	701,260	767,103	10.47	9.39
Slovakia	244,896	266,218	303,921	376,825	392,201	5.35	4.08
Ukraine	72,558	100,647	105,735	127,367	138,887	1.90	9.04
NORTHERN EUROPE	688,439	688,224	626,261	684,210	717,398	9.79	4.85
Denmark	89,481	101,251	89,329	102,270	97,788	1.33	-4.38
Finland	40,005	39,078	43,167	48,109	56,425	0.77	17.29
Iceland	3,455	3,398	3,466	3,697	3,717	0.05	0.54
Ireland	32,023	26,738	21,432	26,717	30,651	0.42	14.72
Norway	83,501	75,919	69,917	61,528	67,566	0.92	9.81
Sweden	77,632	82,417	78,400	89,285	101,134	1.38	13.27
United Kingdom	362,342	359,423	320,550	352,604	360,117	4.92	2.13
SOUTHERN EUROPE	700,884	673,630	717,798	727,675	679,587	9.28	-6.61
Croatia	36,500	39,580	46,977	43,524	35,323	0.48	-18.84
Greece	65,694	50,063	43,496	35,018	33,221	0.45	-5.13
Italy	344,667	323,854	328,612	360,238	344,434	4.70	-4.39
Malta	1,766	1,869	2,346	3,008	3,164	0.04	5.19
Portugal	26,419	26,016	23,362	26,778	25,859	0.35	-3.43
Serbia and Montenegro	13,371	18,962	27,749	27,754	29,846	0.41	7.54
Slovenia	24,037	23,007	24,318	27,721	28,227	0.39	1.83
Spain	188,430	190,279	220,938	203,634	179,513	2.45	-11.85
WESTERN EUROPE	1,955,883	1,990,148	2,070,982	2,237,133	2,204,693	30.09	-1.45
Austria	169,803	183,098	177,819	209,581	218,074	2.98	4.05
Belgium	80,144	78,195	80,078	82,917	84,914	1.16	2.41
France	209,956	240,675	272,209	276,622	274,569	3.75	-0.74

184

CZECH REPUBLIC

3. Arrivals of non-resident tourists in hotels and similar establishments, by nationality

	2009	2010	2011	2012	2013	Market share 2013	% Change 2013-2012
Germany	1,278,621	1,258,852	1,303,329	1,415,454	1,382,292	18.87	-2.34
Liechtenstein	811	896	901	1,033	937	0.01	-9.29
Luxembourg	5,332	5,038	4,952	3,944	3,312	0.05	-16.02
Netherlands	146,862	151,359	159,089	164,229	152,624	2.08	-7.07
Switzerland	64,354	72,035	72,605	83,353	87,971	1.20	5.54
EAST MEDITERRANEAN EUROPE	**119,407**	**135,419**	**136,255**	**151,994**	**167,302**	**2.28**	**10.07**
Cyprus	7,811	8,154	7,510	4,280	2,927	0.04	-31.61
Israel	78,561	81,980	80,716	90,895	101,525	1.39	11.69
Turkey	33,035	45,285	48,029	56,819	62,850	0.86	10.61
OTHER EUROPE	**143,570**	**148,426**	**139,089**	**132,288**	**132,023**	**1.80**	**-0.20**
Other countries of Europe	143,570	148,426	139,089	132,288	132,023	1.80	-0.20
SOUTH ASIA				**24,499**	**27,118**	**0.37**	**10.69**
India				24,499	27,118	0.37	10.69

Yearbook of Tourism Statistics, Data 2009 – 2013, 2015 Edition

CZECH REPUBLIC

4. Arrivals of non-resident tourists in all types of accommodation establishments, by nationality

	2009	2010	2011	2012	2013	Market share 2013	% Change 2013-2012
TOTAL	6,032,370	6,333,996	6,715,067	7,647,044	7,851,865	100.00	2.68
AFRICA	20,191	25,981	29,759	37,179	38,915	0.50	4.67
SOUTHERN AFRICA	4,445	5,365	6,184	9,906	8,858	0.11	-10.58
South Africa	4,445	5,365	6,184	9,906	8,858	0.11	-10.58
OTHER AFRICA	15,746	20,616	23,575	27,273	30,057	0.38	10.21
Other countries of Africa	15,746	20,616	23,575	27,273	30,057	0.38	10.21
AMERICAS	397,586	460,259	480,668	613,183	650,323	8.28	6.06
NORTH AMERICA	333,235	384,163	393,061	486,724	515,046	6.56	5.82
Canada	45,549	54,004	56,615	68,129	71,053	0.90	4.29
Mexico	13,375	17,276	21,496	27,960	30,908	0.39	10.54
United States of America	274,311	312,883	314,950	390,635	413,085	5.26	5.75
SOUTH AMERICA	29,634	37,811	43,248	59,782	63,916	0.81	6.92
Brazil	29,634	37,811	43,248	59,782	63,916	0.81	6.92
OTHER AMERICAS	34,717	38,285	44,359	66,677	71,361	0.91	7.02
Other countries of the Americas	34,717	38,285	44,359	66,677	71,361	0.91	7.02
EAST ASIA AND THE PACIFIC	484,815	586,903	673,850	781,472	836,762	10.66	7.08
NORTH-EAST ASIA	232,015	289,925	326,897	431,882	467,960	5.96	8.35
China	61,798	79,186	108,629	152,866	174,263	2.22	14.00
Japan	114,777	133,052	121,663	141,596	137,844	1.76	-2.65
Korea, Republic of	55,440	77,687	96,605	137,420	155,853	1.98	13.41
AUSTRALASIA	55,669	67,676	74,787	86,948	94,336	1.20	8.50
Australia	48,715	60,240	66,783	76,837	82,841	1.06	7.81
New Zealand	6,954	7,436	8,004	10,111	11,495	0.15	13.69
OTHER EAST ASIA AND THE PACIFIC	197,131	229,302	272,166	262,642	274,466	3.50	4.50
Other countries of Asia	192,021	223,236	266,790	256,728	268,947	3.43	4.76
Other countries of Oceania	5,110	6,066	5,376	5,914	5,519	0.07	-6.68
EUROPE	5,129,778	5,260,853	5,530,790	6,190,138	6,297,069	80.20	1.73
CENTRAL/EASTERN EUROPE	1,258,082	1,417,334	1,646,597	1,991,898	2,120,017	27.00	6.43
Bulgaria	18,713	20,970	22,613	26,569	27,450	0.35	3.32
Estonia	13,480	12,505	16,288	18,216	20,431	0.26	12.16
Hungary	90,096	103,485	107,689	120,957	114,858	1.46	-5.04
Latvia	9,998	8,502	10,098	14,133	16,076	0.20	13.75
Lithuania	45,168	44,550	48,737	46,909	50,571	0.64	7.81
Poland	341,136	350,637	371,127	401,997	424,402	5.41	5.57
Romania	48,367	50,762	57,484	62,321	66,216	0.84	6.25
Russian Federation	326,895	414,671	559,021	731,835	803,152	10.23	9.74
Slovakia	287,810	307,192	344,101	435,595	452,421	5.76	3.86
Ukraine	76,419	104,060	109,439	133,366	144,440	1.84	8.30
NORTHERN EUROPE	716,102	712,788	646,218	715,510	759,649	9.67	6.17
Denmark	99,563	109,292	96,311	109,750	105,325	1.34	-4.03
Finland	42,537	40,690	44,599	50,116	59,400	0.76	18.53
Iceland	3,535	3,509	3,518	3,794	3,795	0.05	0.03
Ireland	33,159	28,152	22,366	28,291	33,254	0.42	17.54
Norway	85,001	77,343	70,948	62,936	72,794	0.93	15.66
Sweden	80,961	85,159	80,525	92,618	105,708	1.35	14.13
United Kingdom	371,346	368,643	327,951	368,005	379,373	4.83	3.09
SOUTHERN EUROPE	726,129	693,609	736,824	758,728	711,012	9.06	-6.29
Croatia	38,268	40,889	48,192	45,586	37,373	0.48	-18.02
Greece	66,648	51,002	44,054	36,044	34,018	0.43	-5.62
Italy	357,492	332,551	337,645	374,651	357,099	4.55	-4.68
Malta	1,803	1,916	2,407	3,180	5,196	0.07	63.40
Portugal	27,482	27,088	24,416	28,291	27,804	0.35	-1.72
Serbia and Montenegro	14,021	19,672	28,287	28,944	31,263	0.40	8.01
Slovenia	26,009	24,480	26,045	30,262	30,835	0.39	1.89
Spain	194,406	196,011	225,778	211,770	187,424	2.39	-11.50
WESTERN EUROPE	2,160,024	2,148,046	2,220,718	2,430,600	2,397,646	30.54	-1.36
Austria	177,715	189,886	185,719	220,404	229,729	2.93	4.23
Belgium	87,851	83,404	85,316	88,953	93,560	1.19	5.18
France	223,901	251,468	283,480	296,298	292,623	3.73	-1.24

186

CZECH REPUBLIC

4. Arrivals of non-resident tourists in all types of accommodation establishments, by nationality

	2009	2010	2011	2012	2013	Market share 2013	% Change 2013-2012
Germany	1,393,112	1,348,482	1,386,976	1,521,246	1,484,169	18.90	-2.44
Liechtenstein	911	915	924	1,084	1,013	0.01	-6.55
Luxembourg	5,415	5,323	5,054	4,057	3,405	0.04	-16.07
Netherlands	203,764	194,138	197,975	210,742	198,728	2.53	-5.70
Switzerland	67,355	74,430	75,274	87,816	94,419	1.20	7.52
EAST MEDITERRANEAN EUROPE	**122,784**	**138,512**	**139,223**	**156,589**	**172,754**	**2.20**	**10.32**
Cyprus	7,987	8,278	7,643	4,554	3,030	0.04	-33.47
Israel	80,634	83,997	82,346	93,510	104,542	1.33	11.80
Turkey	34,163	46,237	49,234	58,525	65,182	0.83	11.37
OTHER EUROPE	**146,657**	**150,564**	**141,210**	**136,813**	**135,991**	**1.73**	**-0.60**
Other countries of Europe	146,657	150,564	141,210	136,813	135,991	1.73	-0.60
SOUTH ASIA				**25,072**	**28,796**	**0.37**	**14.85**
India				25,072	28,796	0.37	14.85

Yearbook of Tourism Statistics, Data 2009 – 2013, 2015 Edition

CZECH REPUBLIC

5. Overnight stays of non-resident tourists in hotels and similar establishments, by nationality

	2009	2010	2011	2012	2013	Market share 2013	% Change 2013-2012
TOTAL	16,013,046	16,880,869	18,027,007	19,936,405	20,071,692	100.00	0.68
AFRICA	56,814	71,152	78,046	90,169	95,297	0.47	5.69
SOUTHERN AFRICA	11,496	13,241	15,061	21,964	20,120	0.10	-8.40
South Africa	11,496	13,241	15,061	21,964	20,120	0.10	-8.40
OTHER AFRICA	45,318	57,911	62,985	68,205	75,177	0.37	10.22
Other countries of Africa	45,318	57,911	62,985	68,205	75,177	0.37	10.22
AMERICAS	1,010,235	1,155,862	1,216,515	1,463,430	1,497,730	7.46	2.34
NORTH AMERICA	846,664	964,078	992,152	1,155,674	1,180,077	5.88	2.11
Canada	120,114	143,566	149,447	172,436	169,178	0.84	-1.89
Mexico	30,065	39,002	50,339	63,189	64,797	0.32	2.54
United States of America	696,485	781,510	792,366	920,049	946,102	4.71	2.83
SOUTH AMERICA	74,753	98,668	115,350	149,163	154,143	0.77	3.34
Brazil	74,753	98,668	115,350	149,163	154,143	0.77	3.34
OTHER AMERICAS	88,818	93,116	109,013	158,593	163,510	0.81	3.10
Other countries of the Americas	88,818	93,116	109,013	158,593	163,510	0.81	3.10
EAST ASIA AND THE PACIFIC	966,083	1,161,176	1,316,457	1,500,607	1,566,804	7.81	4.41
NORTH-EAST ASIA	407,374	494,443	555,377	698,030	748,084	3.73	7.17
China	106,193	132,195	182,071	238,696	262,201	1.31	9.85
Japan	219,406	247,050	230,877	255,621	254,490	1.27	-0.44
Korea, Republic of	81,775	115,198	142,429	203,713	231,393	1.15	13.59
AUSTRALASIA	124,008	155,166	172,989	193,795	202,900	1.01	4.70
Australia	109,769	138,896	154,612	173,042	180,131	0.90	4.10
New Zealand	14,239	16,270	18,377	20,753	22,769	0.11	9.71
OTHER EAST ASIA AND THE PACIFIC	434,701	511,567	588,091	608,782	615,820	3.07	1.16
Other countries of Asia	422,923	499,778	576,267	596,761	603,708	3.01	1.16
Other countries of Oceania	11,778	11,789	11,824	12,021	12,112	0.06	0.76
EUROPE	13,979,914	14,492,679	15,415,989	16,819,876	16,840,991	83.90	0.13
CENTRAL/EASTERN EUROPE	3,313,849	3,879,450	4,806,764	5,767,170	6,127,561	30.53	6.25
Bulgaria	39,862	43,634	49,264	58,331	60,345	0.30	3.45
Estonia	29,788	22,053	31,360	32,988	35,204	0.18	6.72
Hungary	174,756	213,690	223,134	233,407	214,423	1.07	-8.13
Latvia	18,286	15,558	19,164	26,923	31,658	0.16	17.59
Lithuania	65,956	64,702	71,018	72,390	77,826	0.39	7.51
Poland	618,352	649,343	693,354	741,367	772,830	3.85	4.24
Romania	115,283	127,306	143,815	142,616	149,510	0.74	4.83
Russian Federation	1,542,449	1,948,142	2,667,596	3,351,637	3,633,739	18.10	8.42
Slovakia	473,299	517,688	586,675	723,265	741,943	3.70	2.58
Ukraine	235,818	277,334	321,384	384,246	410,083	2.04	6.72
NORTHERN EUROPE	1,896,006	1,868,866	1,662,426	1,783,606	1,859,632	9.26	4.26
Denmark	284,961	333,323	278,625	322,108	300,520	1.50	-6.70
Finland	120,218	112,361	125,401	134,697	159,826	0.80	18.66
Iceland	8,694	9,062	10,354	9,895	9,386	0.05	-5.14
Ireland	88,341	71,965	55,391	68,748	76,975	0.38	11.97
Norway	250,016	222,229	201,504	165,447	182,612	0.91	10.37
Sweden	207,307	213,811	203,369	232,573	267,637	1.33	15.08
United Kingdom	936,469	906,115	787,782	850,138	862,676	4.30	1.47
SOUTHERN EUROPE	2,026,641	1,935,317	2,034,797	2,004,893	1,804,490	8.99	-10.00
Croatia	104,003	111,694	131,050	119,832	92,220	0.46	-23.04
Greece	199,346	152,926	125,987	102,938	91,999	0.46	-10.63
Italy	983,227	926,051	922,535	998,683	926,189	4.61	-7.26
Malta	5,219	5,971	8,123	11,206	10,175	0.05	-9.20
Portugal	75,679	74,952	70,418	71,818	67,436	0.34	-6.10
Serbia and Montenegro	38,954	55,015	78,396	74,511	76,884	0.38	3.18
Slovenia	44,993	42,515	48,739	55,287	54,101	0.27	-2.15
Spain	575,220	566,193	649,549	570,618	485,486	2.42	-14.92
WESTERN EUROPE	5,928,794	5,944,796	6,074,507	6,405,987	6,176,659	30.77	-3.58
Austria	345,584	373,309	361,679	415,434	419,620	2.09	1.01
Belgium	220,146	210,497	210,354	214,997	223,032	1.11	3.74
France	538,260	624,549	709,314	712,007	694,198	3.46	-2.50

Yearbook of Tourism Statistics, Data 2009 – 2013, 2015 Edition

CZECH REPUBLIC

5. Overnight stays of non-resident tourists in hotels and similar establishments, by nationality

	2009	2010	2011	2012	2013	Market share 2013	% Change 2013-2012
Germany	4,194,151	4,090,860	4,134,975	4,377,626	4,193,446	20.89	-4.21
Liechtenstein	1,537	1,881	1,857	2,004	2,033	0.01	1.45
Luxembourg	13,853	12,654	12,941	10,552	8,898	0.04	-15.67
Netherlands	454,876	452,529	467,587	469,233	424,512	2.11	-9.53
Switzerland	160,387	178,517	175,800	204,134	210,920	1.05	3.32
EAST MEDITERRANEAN EUROPE	**399,090**	**452,152**	**457,672**	**485,786**	**518,986**	**2.59**	**6.83**
Cyprus	22,980	23,028	22,644	13,549	8,942	0.04	-34.00
Israel	288,901	308,411	306,303	324,265	355,045	1.77	9.49
Turkey	87,209	120,713	128,725	147,972	154,999	0.77	4.75
OTHER EUROPE	**415,534**	**412,098**	**379,823**	**372,434**	**353,663**	**1.76**	**-5.04**
Other countries of Europe	415,534	412,098	379,823	372,434	353,663	1.76	-5.04
SOUTH ASIA				**62,323**	**70,870**	**0.35**	**13.71**
India				62,323	70,870	0.35	13.71

Yearbook of Tourism Statistics, Data 2009 – 2013, 2015 Edition

CZECH REPUBLIC

6. Overnight stays of non-resident tourists in all types of accommodation establishments, by nationality

	2009	2010	2011	2012	2013	Market share 2013	% Change 2013-2012
TOTAL	17,746,893	18,365,947	19,424,839	21,793,985	22,144,896	100.00	1.61
AFRICA	64,047	77,616	87,561	101,290	114,515	0.52	13.06
SOUTHERN AFRICA	13,570	13,880	15,564	23,712	22,109	0.10	-6.76
South Africa	13,570	13,880	15,564	23,712	22,109	0.10	-6.76
OTHER AFRICA	50,477	63,736	71,997	77,578	92,406	0.42	19.11
Other countries of Africa	50,477	63,736	71,997	77,578	92,406	0.42	19.11
AMERICAS	1,071,563	1,218,499	1,268,806	1,550,861	1,609,942	7.27	3.81
NORTH AMERICA	901,250	1,019,997	1,037,527	1,230,956	1,271,403	5.74	3.29
Canada	127,476	151,646	156,000	184,631	183,982	0.83	-0.35
Mexico	31,460	41,762	52,131	67,764	71,701	0.32	5.81
United States of America	742,314	826,589	829,396	978,561	1,015,720	4.59	3.80
SOUTH AMERICA	77,968	101,183	117,483	155,019	165,953	0.75	7.05
Brazil	77,968	101,183	117,483	155,019	165,953	0.75	7.05
OTHER AMERICAS	92,345	97,319	113,796	164,886	172,586	0.78	4.67
Other countries of the Americas	92,345	97,319	113,796	164,886	172,586	0.78	4.67
EAST ASIA AND THE PACIFIC	1,057,706	1,240,989	1,387,785	1,612,225	1,734,221	7.83	7.57
NORTH-EAST ASIA	423,022	507,766	568,386	726,225	785,349	3.55	8.14
China	111,120	136,742	187,380	248,911	278,117	1.26	11.73
Japan	225,308	251,422	234,651	264,336	264,747	1.20	0.16
Korea, Republic of	86,594	119,602	146,355	212,978	242,485	1.09	13.85
AUSTRALASIA	137,152	166,472	181,900	206,551	227,928	1.03	10.35
Australia	120,030	147,661	161,942	182,988	200,857	0.91	9.77
New Zealand	17,122	18,811	19,958	23,563	27,071	0.12	14.89
OTHER EAST ASIA AND THE PACIFIC	497,532	566,751	637,499	679,449	720,944	3.26	6.11
Other countries of Asia	485,242	553,635	625,233	666,934	708,223	3.20	6.19
Other countries of Oceania	12,290	13,116	12,266	12,515	12,721	0.06	1.65
EUROPE	15,553,577	15,828,843	16,680,687	18,465,497	18,611,194	84.04	0.79
CENTRAL/EASTERN EUROPE	3,697,146	4,274,339	5,236,276	6,360,305	6,805,570	30.73	7.00
Bulgaria	42,744	46,409	52,372	62,565	65,277	0.29	4.33
Estonia	31,590	24,903	32,956	36,351	37,608	0.17	3.46
Hungary	192,150	229,777	237,938	254,029	235,702	1.06	-7.21
Latvia	20,483	17,381	21,128	28,593	33,545	0.15	17.32
Lithuania	73,039	76,616	78,413	80,764	86,090	0.39	6.59
Poland	718,423	739,425	777,019	845,605	877,767	3.96	3.80
Romania	120,276	131,105	147,744	147,957	158,737	0.72	7.29
Russian Federation	1,662,497	2,092,320	2,864,815	3,618,450	3,979,347	17.97	9.97
Slovakia	582,305	620,723	683,159	874,133	894,311	4.04	2.31
Ukraine	253,639	295,680	340,732	411,858	437,186	1.97	6.15
NORTHERN EUROPE	1,971,360	1,939,815	1,719,639	1,869,070	1,976,876	8.93	5.77
Denmark	316,392	361,741	301,254	346,255	327,419	1.48	-5.44
Finland	125,916	116,376	129,864	140,870	167,693	0.76	19.04
Iceland	8,906	9,339	10,475	10,116	9,651	0.04	-4.60
Ireland	91,087	75,449	58,009	72,492	82,915	0.37	14.38
Norway	253,652	225,457	204,004	169,037	195,432	0.88	15.61
Sweden	215,927	220,996	208,897	240,918	280,072	1.26	16.25
United Kingdom	959,480	930,457	807,136	889,382	913,694	4.13	2.73
SOUTHERN EUROPE	2,087,408	1,986,789	2,087,523	2,085,140	1,888,605	8.53	-9.43
Croatia	109,733	116,052	134,320	124,923	96,897	0.44	-22.43
Greece	202,184	156,070	128,466	106,134	95,011	0.43	-10.48
Italy	1,013,057	947,233	946,206	1,033,501	956,712	4.32	-7.43
Malta	5,360	6,094	8,298	11,748	15,748	0.07	34.05
Portugal	79,484	78,510	73,830	76,176	73,310	0.33	-3.76
Serbia and Montenegro	41,093	57,484	80,647	78,371	80,595	0.36	2.84
Slovenia	49,304	45,675	52,767	61,190	60,109	0.27	-1.77
Spain	587,193	579,671	662,989	593,097	510,223	2.30	-13.97
WESTERN EUROPE	6,945,606	6,729,373	6,768,995	7,245,079	7,022,911	31.71	-3.07
Austria	364,287	391,722	380,184	440,442	448,446	2.03	1.82
Belgium	241,499	226,078	228,509	234,717	259,812	1.17	10.69
France	568,151	649,458	739,150	758,086	742,815	3.35	-2.01

190

CZECH REPUBLIC

6. Overnight stays of non-resident tourists in all types of accommodation establishments, by nationality

	2009	2010	2011	2012	2013	Market share 2013	% Change 2013-2012
Germany	4,851,927	4,609,595	4,578,249	4,873,331	4,663,406	21.06	-4.31
Liechtenstein	1,656	1,927	1,907	2,134	2,305	0.01	8.01
Luxembourg	14,152	13,356	13,351	10,964	9,302	0.04	-15.16
Netherlands	736,412	652,844	644,627	708,410	669,508	3.02	-5.49
Switzerland	167,522	184,393	183,018	216,995	227,317	1.03	4.76
EAST MEDITERRANEAN EUROPE	**428,188**	**479,140**	**481,548**	**518,257**	**551,189**	**2.49**	**6.35**
Cyprus	23,486	23,752	23,171	14,511	9,207	0.04	-36.55
Israel	314,341	332,110	325,646	349,303	378,989	1.71	8.50
Turkey	90,361	123,278	132,731	154,443	162,993	0.74	5.54
OTHER EUROPE	**423,869**	**419,387**	**386,706**	**387,646**	**366,043**	**1.65**	**-5.57**
Other countries of Europe	423,869	419,387	386,706	387,646	366,043	1.65	-5.57
SOUTH ASIA				**64,112**	**75,024**	**0.34**	**17.02**
India				64,112	75,024	0.34	17.02

Yearbook of Tourism Statistics, Data 2009 – 2013, 2015 Edition

DEMOCRATIC REPUBLIC OF THE CONGO

1. Arrivals of non-resident tourists at national borders, by nationality

		2009	2010	2011	2012	2013	Market share 2013	% Change 2013-2012
TOTAL	(*)	**53,402**	**81,117**	**186,000**	**167,220**	**191,414**	**100.00**	**14.47**
AFRICA		**31,328**	**20,301**	**43,765**	**66,020**	**72,701**	**37.98**	**10.12**
EAST AFRICA				**11,926**		**14,313**	**7.48**	
Burundi				2,107		3,526	1.84	
Kenya				2,668		3,716	1.94	
Rwanda				2,665				
Uganda						3,171	1.66	
United Republic of Tanzania				2,593		2,100	1.10	
Zambia				1,893		1,800	0.94	
CENTRAL AFRICA		**1,916**	**10,219**	**10,955**	**11,100**	**10,667**	**5.57**	**-3.90**
Angola				5,529	5,600	5,600	2.93	
Congo		805	3,995	5,426	5,500	3,017	1.58	-45.15
Other countries of Central Africa		1,111	6,224			2,050	1.07	
NORTH AFRICA				**6,906**		**3,041**	**1.59**	
Morocco				1,698				
Tunisia				1,850		3,041	1.59	
Other countries of North Africa				3,358				
SOUTHERN AFRICA				**4,962**		**4,970**	**2.60**	
South Africa				4,962		4,970	2.60	
OTHER AFRICA		**29,412**	**10,082**	**9,016**	**54,920**	**39,710**	**20.75**	**-27.69**
Other countries of Africa		29,412	10,082	9,016	54,920	39,710	20.75	-27.69
AMERICAS		**3,433**	**7,184**	**20,507**	**18,009**	**20,372**	**10.64**	**13.12**
CENTRAL AMERICA				**2,585**				
Panama				89				
Other countries of Central America				2,496				
NORTH AMERICA				**12,386**		**11,003**	**5.75**	
Canada				6,694		4,273	2.23	
Mexico				1,540				
Other countries of North America				4,152		6,730	3.52	
SOUTH AMERICA				**5,536**		**6,286**	**3.28**	
Brazil				1,708		3,169	1.66	
Paraguay				1,131				
Other countries of South America				2,697		3,117	1.63	
OTHER AMERICAS		**3,433**	**7,184**		**18,009**	**3,083**	**1.61**	**-82.88**
Other countries of the Americas						3,083	1.61	
All countries of the Americas		3,433	7,184		18,009			
EAST ASIA AND THE PACIFIC		**5,540**	**3,884**	**14,272**	**21,580**	**13,617**	**7.11**	**-36.90**
NORTH-EAST ASIA						**7,508**	**3.92**	
China						4,219	2.20	
Japan						3,289	1.72	
SOUTH-EAST ASIA			**85**	**1,670**				
Thailand			85	1,670				
AUSTRALASIA			**178**	**2,489**		**6,109**	**3.19**	
Australia						3,018	1.58	
New Zealand						3,091	1.61	
Australia, New Zealand			178	2,489				
OTHER EAST ASIA AND THE PACIFIC		**5,540**	**3,621**	**10,113**	**21,580**			
Other countries of Asia			3,621	10,113				
All countries of Asia		5,244			21,580			
All countries of Oceania		296						
EUROPE		**13,101**	**35,012**	**67,895**	**50,755**	**49,061**	**25.63**	**-3.34**
CENTRAL/EASTERN EUROPE				**7,322**		**3,167**	**1.65**	
Russian Federation				1,980		3,167	1.65	
Ukraine				1,872				
Other countries Central/East Europe				3,470				
NORTHERN EUROPE				**10,925**		**5,777**	**3.02**	
Norway				1,826				
United Kingdom				5,997		5,777	3.02	
Other countries of Northern Europe				3,102				

192

DEMOCRATIC REPUBLIC OF THE CONGO

1. Arrivals of non-resident tourists at national borders, by nationality

	2009	2010	2011	2012	2013	Market share 2013	% Change 2013-2012
SOUTHERN EUROPE	1,182	4,153	10,975		11,118	5.81	
Italy	1,182	2,012	4,053		4,410	2.30	
Portugal			2,244		3,267	1.71	
Spain			2,657		3,441	1.80	
Other countries of Southern Europe		2,141	2,021				
WESTERN EUROPE	8,165	25,036	36,068	28,997	25,841	13.50	-10.88
Belgium	4,087	12,047	15,631	15,597	10,952	5.72	-29.78
France	2,654	10,038	14,734	13,400	10,841	5.66	-19.10
Germany	1,424	1,595	3,081		4,048	2.11	
Other countries of Western Europe		1,356	2,622				
EAST MEDITERRANEAN EUROPE		353	2,605		3,158	1.65	
Israel		353	2,605		3,158	1.65	
OTHER EUROPE	3,754	5,470		21,758			
Other countries of Europe	3,754	5,470		21,758			
MIDDLE EAST		1,650	6,060	10,856	3,182	1.66	-70.69
Lebanon		1,243	3,560		3,182	1.66	
Other countries of Middle East		407	2,500				
All countries of Middle East				10,856			
SOUTH ASIA		2,767	5,668		4,951	2.59	
India		2,767	5,668		4,951	2.59	
NOT SPECIFIED		10,319	27,833		27,530	14.38	
Other countries of the World			27,833		24,064	12.57	
Nationals Residing Abroad		10,319			3,466	1.81	

Yearbook of Tourism Statistics, Data 2009 – 2013, 2015 Edition

DENMARK

3. Arrivals of non-resident tourists in hotels and similar establishments, by country of residence

	2009	2010	2011	2012	2013	Market share 2013	% Change 2013-2012
TOTAL (*)	1,892,468	2,157,344	1,498,610	1,587,821	1,653,234	100.00	4.12
AMERICAS	142,854	154,726	120,507	128,575	137,551	8.32	6.98
NORTH AMERICA	127,827	136,337	104,894	109,456	117,234	7.09	7.11
Canada	13,665	14,561	11,422	11,779	13,261	0.80	12.58
United States of America	114,162	121,776	93,472	97,677	103,973	6.29	6.45
SOUTH AMERICA				7,515	7,931	0.48	5.54
Brazil				7,515	7,931	0.48	5.54
OTHER AMERICAS	15,027	18,389	15,613	11,604	12,386	0.75	6.74
Other countries of the Americas	15,027	18,389	15,613	11,604	12,386	0.75	6.74
EAST ASIA AND THE PACIFIC	66,150	73,319	50,637	100,112	118,341	7.16	18.21
NORTH-EAST ASIA	29,584	32,625	19,778	51,713	60,549	3.66	17.09
China				28,023	37,157	2.25	32.59
Japan	29,584	32,625	19,778	19,959	19,206	1.16	-3.77
Korea, Republic of				3,731	4,186	0.25	12.20
AUSTRALASIA				15,330	16,276	0.98	6.17
Australia				15,330	16,276	0.98	6.17
OTHER EAST ASIA AND THE PACIFIC	36,566	40,694	30,859	33,069	41,516	2.51	25.54
Other countries of Asia	36,566	40,694	30,859	33,069	41,516	2.51	25.54
EUROPE	1,631,994	1,866,553	1,279,511	1,343,210	1,378,861	83.40	2.65
CENTRAL/EASTERN EUROPE	16,418	17,858	17,072	37,379	43,647	2.64	16.77
Poland	16,418	17,858	17,072	16,751	19,665	1.19	17.40
Russian Federation				20,628	23,982	1.45	16.26
NORTHERN EUROPE	1,010,917	1,153,621	764,803	795,087	812,813	49.17	2.23
Finland	45,284	52,872	49,862	60,624	55,932	3.38	-7.74
Ireland				6,869	7,760	0.47	12.97
Norway	361,167	394,494	253,400	260,536	257,344	15.57	-1.23
Sweden	425,779	509,385	337,455	341,340	355,754	21.52	4.22
United Kingdom	178,687	196,870	124,086	125,718	136,023	8.23	8.20
SOUTHERN EUROPE	103,179	113,243	74,683	83,737	88,099	5.33	5.21
Greece				4,368	4,316	0.26	-1.19
Italy	49,141	53,314	47,678	50,863	56,211	3.40	10.51
Portugal				4,926	4,762	0.29	-3.33
Spain	54,038	59,929	27,005	23,580	22,810	1.38	-3.27
WESTERN EUROPE	377,299	431,231	305,597	318,240	316,179	19.12	-0.65
Austria	7,960	13,054	8,864	10,777	12,135	0.73	12.60
France	45,773	51,792	43,833	45,545	45,884	2.78	0.74
Germany	204,221	232,219	146,131	151,690	147,643	8.93	-2.67
Netherlands	69,469	78,183	55,365	55,201	55,371	3.35	0.31
Switzerland	27,255	29,948	31,580	33,899	32,941	1.99	-2.83
Belgium / Luxembourg	22,621	26,035	19,824	21,128	22,205	1.34	5.10
OTHER EUROPE	124,181	150,600	117,356	108,767	118,123	7.14	8.60
Other countries of Europe	124,181	150,600	117,356	108,767	118,123	7.14	8.60
NOT SPECIFIED	51,470	62,746	47,955	15,924	18,481	1.12	16.06
Other countries of the World	51,470	62,746	47,955	15,924	18,481	1.12	16.06

Yearbook of Tourism Statistics, Data 2009 – 2013, 2015 Edition

DENMARK

4. Arrivals of non-resident tourists in all types of accommodation establishments, by country of residence

		2009	2010	2011	2012	2013	Market share 2013	% Change 2013-2012
TOTAL	(*)	**9,264,870**	**9,425,096**	**8,471,236**	**8,443,454**	**8,557,093**	**100.00**	**1.35**
AMERICAS		**647,752**	**645,508**	**683,949**	**589,196**	**598,701**	**7.00**	**1.61**
NORTH AMERICA		**589,593**	**583,730**	**618,952**	**522,213**	**530,196**	**6.20**	**1.53**
Canada		77,559	77,925	87,697	77,232	78,600	0.92	1.77
United States of America		512,034	505,805	531,255	444,981	451,596	5.28	1.49
SOUTH AMERICA					**12,152**	**12,646**	**0.15**	**4.07**
Brazil					12,152	12,646	0.15	4.07
OTHER AMERICAS		**58,159**	**61,778**	**64,997**	**54,831**	**55,859**	**0.65**	**1.87**
Other countries of the Americas		58,159	61,778	64,997	54,831	55,859	0.65	1.87
EAST ASIA AND THE PACIFIC		**182,297**	**190,452**	**166,176**	**231,046**	**249,161**	**2.91**	**7.84**
NORTH-EAST ASIA		**30,726**	**33,837**	**20,687**	**57,512**	**66,264**	**0.77**	**15.22**
China					30,228	39,638	0.46	31.13
Japan		30,726	33,837	20,687	22,670	21,667	0.25	-4.42
Korea, Republic of					4,614	4,959	0.06	7.48
AUSTRALASIA					**26,322**	**27,461**	**0.32**	**4.33**
Australia					26,322	27,461	0.32	4.33
OTHER EAST ASIA AND THE PACIFIC		**151,571**	**156,615**	**145,489**	**147,212**	**155,436**	**1.82**	**5.59**
Other countries of Asia		151,571	156,615	145,489	147,212	155,436	1.82	5.59
EUROPE		**7,988,695**	**8,128,384**	**7,173,932**	**7,249,758**	**7,291,659**	**85.21**	**0.58**
CENTRAL/EASTERN EUROPE		**91,520**	**92,107**	**88,417**	**115,382**	**124,007**	**1.45**	**7.48**
Poland		91,520	92,107	88,417	87,089	92,100	1.08	5.75
Russian Federation					28,293	31,907	0.37	12.77
NORTHERN EUROPE		**3,639,024**	**3,789,674**	**3,372,219**	**3,310,754**	**3,385,647**	**39.57**	**2.26**
Finland		57,483	65,521	62,594	72,949	68,816	0.80	-5.67
Ireland					9,347	10,075	0.12	7.79
Norway		1,628,381	1,665,429	1,481,565	1,481,173	1,486,052	17.37	0.33
Sweden		1,241,798	1,336,600	1,176,408	1,145,888	1,207,795	14.11	5.40
United Kingdom		711,362	722,124	651,652	601,397	612,909	7.16	1.91
SOUTHERN EUROPE		**316,881**	**327,122**	**341,657**	**385,743**	**390,797**	**4.57**	**1.31**
Greece					4,982	5,012	0.06	0.60
Italy		169,588	173,964	194,519	210,577	216,640	2.53	2.88
Portugal					8,561	8,255	0.10	-3.57
Spain		147,293	153,158	147,138	161,623	160,890	1.88	-0.45
WESTERN EUROPE		**3,337,909**	**3,349,660**	**2,946,599**	**3,027,743**	**3,011,312**	**35.19**	**-0.54**
Austria		42,971	48,442	48,827	54,193	55,760	0.65	2.89
France		234,620	241,755	243,304	255,232	255,781	2.99	0.22
Germany		2,538,209	2,526,299	2,165,225	2,232,870	2,209,981	25.83	-1.03
Netherlands		319,267	323,513	280,182	265,976	268,392	3.14	0.91
Switzerland		92,594	95,897	102,098	107,591	107,819	1.26	0.21
Belgium / Luxembourg		110,248	113,754	106,963	111,881	113,579	1.33	1.52
OTHER EUROPE		**603,361**	**569,821**	**425,040**	**410,136**	**379,896**	**4.44**	**-7.37**
Other countries of Europe		603,361	569,821	425,040	410,136	379,896	4.44	-7.37
NOT SPECIFIED		**446,126**	**460,752**	**447,179**	**373,454**	**417,572**	**4.88**	**11.81**
Other countries of the World		446,126	460,752	447,179	373,454	417,572	4.88	11.81

 Yearbook of Tourism Statistics, Data 2009 – 2013, 2015 Edition

DENMARK

5. Overnight stays of non-resident tourists in hotels and similar establishments, by country of residence

	2009	2010	2011	2012	2013	Market share 2013	% Change 2013-2012
TOTAL (*)	**4,434,605**	**5,074,913**	**5,590,430**	**5,945,550**	**6,241,182**	**100.00**	**4.97**
AMERICAS	**431,758**	**467,686**	**601,770**	**552,550**	**591,808**	**9.48**	**7.10**
NORTH AMERICA	**391,009**	**416,958**	**450,350**	**468,890**	**502,842**	**8.06**	**7.24**
Canada	37,152	40,126	52,960	54,820	61,623	0.99	12.41
United States of America	353,857	376,832	397,390	414,070	441,219	7.07	6.56
SOUTH AMERICA				**32,750**	**34,613**	**0.55**	**5.69**
Brazil				32,750	34,613	0.55	5.69
OTHER AMERICAS	**40,749**	**50,728**	**151,420**	**50,910**	**54,353**	**0.87**	**6.76**
Other countries of the Americas	40,749	50,728	151,420	50,910	54,353	0.87	6.76
EAST ASIA AND THE PACIFIC	**193,646**	**214,596**	**145,150**	**429,300**	**505,277**	**8.10**	**17.70**
NORTH-EAST ASIA	**81,651**	**89,357**	**89,630**	**218,560**	**253,605**	**4.06**	**16.03**
China				111,820	148,809	2.38	33.08
Japan	81,651	89,357	89,630	90,460	86,584	1.39	-4.28
Korea, Republic of				16,280	18,212	0.29	11.87
AUSTRALASIA				**61,940**	**65,877**	**1.06**	**6.36**
Australia				61,940	65,877	1.06	6.36
OTHER EAST ASIA AND THE PACIFIC	**111,995**	**125,239**	**55,520**	**148,800**	**185,795**	**2.98**	**24.86**
Other countries of Asia	111,995	125,239	55,520	148,800	185,795	2.98	24.86
EUROPE	**3,649,142**	**4,197,280**	**4,643,770**	**4,891,700**	**5,060,662**	**81.08**	**3.45**
CENTRAL/EASTERN EUROPE	**46,443**	**50,516**	**63,820**	**155,170**	**180,446**	**2.89**	**16.29**
Poland	46,443	50,516	63,820	62,690	73,397	1.18	17.08
Russian Federation				92,480	107,049	1.72	15.75
NORTHERN EUROPE	**2,080,994**	**2,384,952**	**2,656,930**	**2,761,550**	**2,848,143**	**45.63**	**3.14**
Finland	105,718	122,099	151,220	184,330	170,018	2.72	-7.76
Ireland				23,670	26,760	0.43	13.05
Norway	795,048	879,665	962,900	988,630	978,226	15.67	-1.05
Sweden	751,752	907,694	1,011,340	1,022,950	1,066,987	17.10	4.30
United Kingdom	428,476	475,494	531,470	541,970	606,152	9.71	11.84
SOUTHERN EUROPE	**293,227**	**327,276**	**321,710**	**354,070**	**372,090**	**5.96**	**5.09**
Greece				17,460	17,244	0.28	-1.24
Italy	166,386	184,397	180,240	192,440	213,726	3.42	11.06
Portugal				19,680	19,025	0.30	-3.33
Spain	126,841	142,879	141,470	124,490	122,095	1.96	-1.92
WESTERN EUROPE	**875,918**	**1,006,870**	**1,112,520**	**1,162,820**	**1,158,165**	**18.56**	**-0.40**
Austria	22,658	37,151	38,470	47,270	53,530	0.86	13.24
France	113,184	129,445	148,630	156,290	157,535	2.52	0.80
Germany	439,583	501,766	533,910	553,820	541,082	8.67	-2.30
Netherlands	173,471	195,282	198,780	197,830	198,986	3.19	0.58
Switzerland	77,577	85,226	122,570	132,870	128,214	2.05	-3.50
Belgium / Luxembourg	49,445	58,000	70,160	74,740	78,818	1.26	5.46
OTHER EUROPE	**352,560**	**427,666**	**488,790**	**458,090**	**501,818**	**8.04**	**9.55**
Other countries of Europe	352,560	427,666	488,790	458,090	501,818	8.04	9.55
NOT SPECIFIED	**160,059**	**195,351**	**199,740**	**72,000**	**83,435**	**1.34**	**15.88**
Other countries of the World	160,059	195,351	199,740	72,000	83,435	1.34	15.88

Yearbook of Tourism Statistics, Data 2009 – 2013, 2015 Edition

DENMARK

6. Overnight stays of non-resident tourists in all types of accommodation establishments, by country of residence

	2009	2010	2011	2012	2013	Market share 2013	% Change 2013-2012
TOTAL (*)	**43,984,095**	**44,361,815**	**45,921,450**	**46,038,510**	**45,746,268**	**100.00**	**-0.63**
AMERICAS	**2,673,126**	**2,696,883**	**3,039,300**	**2,761,420**	**2,802,958**	**6.13**	**1.50**
NORTH AMERICA	**2,245,932**	**2,258,517**	**2,366,170**	**2,283,650**	**2,317,299**	**5.07**	**1.47**
Canada	376,110	379,119	405,660	396,240	402,264	0.88	1.52
United States of America	1,869,822	1,879,398	1,960,510	1,887,410	1,915,035	4.19	1.46
SOUTH AMERICA				39,790	42,642	0.09	7.17
Brazil				39,790	42,642	0.09	7.17
OTHER AMERICAS	**427,194**	**438,366**	**673,130**	**437,980**	**443,017**	**0.97**	**1.15**
Other countries of the Americas	427,194	438,366	673,130	437,980	443,017	0.97	1.15
EAST ASIA AND THE PACIFIC	**712,777**	**738,729**	**541,320**	**978,530**	**1,054,590**	**2.31**	**7.77**
NORTH-EAST ASIA	**86,256**	**94,329**	**94,570**	**233,650**	**268,554**	**0.59**	**14.94**
China				117,880	156,690	0.34	32.92
Japan	86,256	94,329	94,570	97,010	91,624	0.20	-5.55
Korea, Republic of				18,760	20,240	0.04	7.89
AUSTRALASIA				79,900	85,323	0.19	6.79
Australia				79,900	85,323	0.19	6.79
OTHER EAST ASIA AND THE PACIFIC	**626,521**	**644,400**	**446,750**	**664,980**	**700,713**	**1.53**	**5.37**
Other countries of Asia	626,521	644,400	446,750	664,980	700,713	1.53	5.37
EUROPE	**38,086,453**	**38,346,505**	**40,004,500**	**40,138,250**	**39,340,611**	**86.00**	**-1.99**
CENTRAL/EASTERN EUROPE	**1,020,454**	**1,016,069**	**1,015,060**	**1,115,770**	**1,145,750**	**2.50**	**2.69**
Poland	1,020,454	1,016,069	1,015,060	1,010,480	1,024,194	2.24	1.36
Russian Federation				105,290	121,556	0.27	15.45
NORTHERN EUROPE	**12,559,044**	**12,927,175**	**13,417,230**	**13,478,070**	**13,627,199**	**29.79**	**1.11**
Finland	176,606	197,533	227,250	261,240	247,560	0.54	-5.24
Ireland				30,070	31,956	0.07	6.27
Norway	6,193,991	6,306,417	6,505,840	6,507,540	6,524,531	14.26	0.26
Sweden	3,734,035	3,925,394	4,117,910	4,144,730	4,227,443	9.24	2.00
United Kingdom	2,454,412	2,497,831	2,566,230	2,534,490	2,595,709	5.67	2.42
SOUTHERN EUROPE	**1,543,969**	**1,577,749**	**1,626,530**	**1,695,960**	**1,718,811**	**3.76**	**1.35**
Greece				19,350	19,404	0.04	0.28
Italy	897,200	914,919	938,210	959,710	985,261	2.15	2.66
Portugal				29,550	28,020	0.06	-5.18
Spain	646,769	662,830	688,320	687,350	686,126	1.50	-0.18
WESTERN EUROPE	**20,152,466**	**19,940,571**	**20,824,840**	**20,764,570**	**20,093,025**	**43.92**	**-3.23**
Austria	203,081	219,006	227,340	239,390	245,493	0.54	2.55
France	1,306,349	1,329,176	1,365,050	1,383,040	1,384,015	3.03	0.07
Germany	16,237,180	15,976,463	16,798,930	16,816,300	16,142,746	35.29	-4.01
Netherlands	1,676,310	1,664,214	1,614,690	1,491,820	1,484,129	3.24	-0.52
Switzerland	344,740	356,263	404,510	416,200	416,478	0.91	0.07
Belgium / Luxembourg	384,806	395,449	414,320	417,820	420,164	0.92	0.56
OTHER EUROPE	**2,810,520**	**2,884,941**	**3,120,840**	**3,083,880**	**2,755,826**	**6.02**	**-10.64**
Other countries of Europe	2,810,520	2,884,941	3,120,840	3,083,880	2,755,826	6.02	-10.64
NOT SPECIFIED	**2,511,739**	**2,579,698**	**2,336,330**	**2,160,310**	**2,548,109**	**5.57**	**17.95**
Other countries of the World	2,511,739	2,579,698	2,336,330	2,160,310	2,548,109	5.57	17.95

Yearbook of Tourism Statistics, Data 2009 – 2013, 2015 Edition

DOMINICA

1. Arrivals of non-resident tourists at national borders, by country of residence

	2009	2010	2011	2012	2013	Market share 2013	% Change 2013-2012
TOTAL	74,924	76,518	75,546	78,965	78,277	100.00	-0.87
AFRICA	119	179	200	251	355	0.45	41.43
EAST AFRICA	12	26	43	23	55	0.07	139.13
Burundi	1						
Comoros			1				
Ethiopia	2	4		2			
Kenya	1	6	10	5	6	0.01	20.00
Madagascar		1			2	0.00	
Malawi			1	1	3	0.00	200.00
Mauritius		1	1		2	0.00	
Reunion		2	14	9	7	0.01	-22.22
Rwanda	2						
Seychelles			1	1	3	0.00	200.00
Uganda	2	2	2	1	1	0.00	
United Republic of Tanzania	1	1	8	2	4	0.01	100.00
Zambia	1	3			2	0.00	
Zimbabwe	2	6	5	2	25	0.03	1,150.00
CENTRAL AFRICA	4	8	1	7	5	0.01	-28.57
Cameroon	3	3	1	7	3	0.00	-57.14
Congo	1	4			2	0.00	
Equatorial Guinea		1					
NORTH AFRICA		10	26	37	46	0.06	24.32
Algeria		1	1				
Morocco		9	24	36	45	0.06	25.00
Tunisia			1	1			
Western Sahara					1	0.00	
SOUTHERN AFRICA	41	73	28	41	51	0.07	24.39
Botswana	2	4		3			
Lesotho	1						
Namibia	2	1	1	2	5	0.01	150.00
South Africa	36	66	26	35	46	0.06	31.43
Swaziland		2	1	1			
WEST AFRICA	62	62	102	143	198	0.25	38.46
Benin					1	0.00	
Burkina Faso			2				
Cabo Verde				1			
Côte d'Ivoire	1	1	1				
Gambia		2		1			
Ghana	5	2	3	6	2	0.00	-66.67
Guinea	1	7		1	1	0.00	
Liberia	1			2			
Mauritania	1	1		1			
Niger	1						
Nigeria	51	47	92	128	190	0.24	48.44
Senegal	1	1	4	3	2	0.00	-33.33
Sierra Leone					2	0.00	
Togo		1					
AMERICAS	62,533	64,789	62,901	64,762	63,426	81.03	-2.06
CARIBBEAN	40,180	41,536	40,820	41,623	41,254	52.70	-0.89
Anguilla	443	418	334	309	294	0.38	-4.85
Antigua and Barbuda	3,763	3,670	3,479	3,454	2,793	3.57	-19.14
Aruba	34	73	42	44	35	0.04	-20.45
Bahamas	106	126	134	107	132	0.17	23.36
Barbados	1,935	1,961	1,897	2,208	2,244	2.87	1.63
Bermuda	58	48	60	45	44	0.06	-2.22
Bonaire	12	9	3	7	12	0.02	71.43
British Virgin Islands	1,085	1,089	1,079	968	1,075	1.37	11.05
Cayman Islands	19	10	22	19	21	0.03	10.53

198

Yearbook of Tourism Statistics, Data 2009 – 2013, 2015 Edition

DOMINICA

1. Arrivals of non-resident tourists at national borders, by country of residence

	2009	2010	2011	2012	2013	Market share 2013	% Change 2013-2012
Cuba	76	88	73	77	171	0.22	122.08
Curaçao	102	117	107	60	69	0.09	15.00
Dominican Republic	183	300	224	273	277	0.35	1.47
Grenada	397	325	419	289	317	0.40	9.69
Guadeloupe	15,053	15,707	15,089	16,009	15,676	20.03	-2.08
Haiti	974	831	705	880	1,408	1.80	60.00
Jamaica	592	526	555	428	431	0.55	0.70
Martinique	5,409	6,096	6,428	7,002	6,687	8.54	-4.50
Montserrat	114	98	131	95	120	0.15	26.32
Puerto Rico	360	296	246	267	301	0.38	12.73
Saint Kitts and Nevis	478	579	494	463	426	0.54	-7.99
Saint Lucia	1,952	1,914	2,080	1,980	1,918	2.45	-3.13
Saint Vincent and the Grenadines	536	469	548	492	413	0.53	-16.06
Sint Maarten	1,993	2,089	1,898	1,869	2,099	2.68	12.31
Trinidad and Tobago	1,335	1,356	1,621	1,323	1,424	1.82	7.63
Turks and Caicos Islands	37	26	24	14	7	0.01	-50.00
United States Virgin Islands	3,066	3,230	3,103	2,913	2,821	3.60	-3.16
Other countries of the Caribbean	68	85	25	28	39	0.05	39.29
CENTRAL AMERICA	**91**	**99**	**200**	**97**	**116**	**0.15**	**19.59**
Belize	36	38	45	31	49	0.06	58.06
Costa Rica	19	16	14	12	16	0.02	33.33
El Salvador	5	4	4	5	9	0.01	80.00
Guatemala	8	6	4	6	6	0.01	
Honduras	3	5	3	3	9	0.01	200.00
Nicaragua	3	11	34	6	9	0.01	50.00
Panama	17	19	96	34	18	0.02	-47.06
NORTH AMERICA	**20,847**	**22,150**	**20,855**	**22,097**	**21,089**	**26.94**	**-4.56**
Canada	2,618	2,859	2,986	3,063	3,018	3.86	-1.47
Mexico	36	25	49	32	22	0.03	-31.25
United States of America	18,193	19,266	17,820	19,002	18,049	23.06	-5.02
SOUTH AMERICA	**1,415**	**1,004**	**1,026**	**945**	**967**	**1.24**	**2.33**
Argentina	21	24	16	24	32	0.04	33.33
Bolivia	10	4	2	3	1	0.00	-66.67
Brazil	17	27	48	45	65	0.08	44.44
Chile	7	6	7	18	25	0.03	38.89
Colombia	40	36	48	54	59	0.08	9.26
Ecuador	3	8	9	4	15	0.02	275.00
Falkland Islands, Malvinas					3	0.00	
French Guiana	81	53	136	126	149	0.19	18.25
Guyana	279	293	295	276	210	0.27	-23.91
Paraguay		2	1	6	4	0.01	-33.33
Peru	17	17	4	15	13	0.02	-13.33
Suriname	30	32	50	28	27	0.03	-3.57
Uruguay	1	1		1	5	0.01	400.00
Venezuela	909	501	410	345	359	0.46	4.06
EAST ASIA AND THE PACIFIC	**431**	**551**	**651**	**909**	**717**	**0.92**	**-21.12**
NORTH-EAST ASIA	**323**	**384**	**483**	**622**	**464**	**0.59**	**-25.40**
China	178	227	341	360	286	0.37	-20.56
Hong Kong, China	10	8	9	7	10	0.01	42.86
Japan	111	115	91	107	114	0.15	6.54
Korea, Dem. People's Republic of	1	4	10	36	3	0.00	-91.67
Korea, Republic of	3	4	1	4	3	0.00	-25.00
Mongolia			1	1			
Taiwan, Province of China	20	26	30	107	48	0.06	-55.14
SOUTH-EAST ASIA	**35**	**40**	**46**	**33**	**51**	**0.07**	**54.55**
Cambodia				2	1	0.00	-50.00
Indonesia		8	9	2	6	0.01	200.00
Malaysia	1		4	7	10	0.01	42.86

199

Yearbook of Tourism Statistics, Data 2009 – 2013, 2015 Edition

DOMINICA

1. Arrivals of non-resident tourists at national borders, by country of residence

	2009	2010	2011	2012	2013	Market share 2013	% Change 2013-2012
Myanmar			1				
Philippines	17	20	16	15	15	0.02	
Singapore	10	4	13	4	11	0.01	175.00
Thailand	5	6	2	1	7	0.01	600.00
Viet Nam	2	2	1	2	1	0.00	-50.00
AUSTRALASIA	**72**	**125**	**116**	**252**	**199**	**0.25**	**-21.03**
Australia	51	107	95	231	170	0.22	-26.41
New Zealand	21	18	21	21	29	0.04	38.10
MELANESIA	**1**	**2**	**6**	**2**	**1**	**0.00**	**-50.00**
Fiji	1						
New Caledonia		2	5	1			
Papua New Guinea			1				
Solomon Islands				1			
Vanuatu					1	0.00	
MICRONESIA					**2**	**0.00**	
Kiribati					1	0.00	
Micronesia, Federated States of					1	0.00	
EUROPE	**11,607**	**10,748**	**11,568**	**12,833**	**13,578**	**17.35**	**5.81**
CENTRAL/EASTERN EUROPE	**188**	**195**	**240**	**302**	**500**	**0.64**	**65.56**
Belarus					2	0.00	
Bulgaria	11	4	2	4	13	0.02	225.00
Czech Republic/Slovakia	32	26	50	107	155	0.20	44.86
Estonia					15	0.02	
Hungary	44	30	49	42	46	0.06	9.52
Kazakhstan					1	0.00	
Lithuania					9	0.01	
Poland	42	50	66	71	121	0.15	70.42
Romania	11	3	8	9	13	0.02	44.44
Russian Federation	48	82	65	69	111	0.14	60.87
Ukraine					14	0.02	
NORTHERN EUROPE	**4,908**	**5,127**	**5,238**	**5,431**	**5,450**	**6.96**	**0.35**
Denmark	106	81	78	100	108	0.14	8.00
Finland	35	44	47	99	110	0.14	11.11
Iceland	9	3	52	88	84	0.11	-4.55
Ireland	61	58	63	73	68	0.09	-6.85
Norway	39	44	55	78	109	0.14	39.74
Svalbard and Jan Mayen Islands			1				
Sweden	304	296	320	327	343	0.44	4.89
United Kingdom	4,354	4,601	4,622	4,666	4,628	5.91	-0.81
SOUTHERN EUROPE	**272**	**251**	**269**	**293**	**347**	**0.44**	**18.43**
Albania			1				
Andorra	1	1	1	2	1	0.00	-50.00
Bosnia and Herzegovina					1	0.00	
Gibraltar		3					
Greece	20	10	11	23	26	0.03	13.04
Italy	124	107	135	139	149	0.19	7.19
Malta	2	5	8	8	5	0.01	-37.50
Montenegro					1	0.00	
Portugal	28	12	9	15	21	0.03	40.00
San Marino		1					
Serbia					1	0.00	
Slovenia					28	0.04	
Spain	97	112	104	106	114	0.15	7.55
WESTERN EUROPE	**6,175**	**5,093**	**5,703**	**6,728**	**7,205**	**9.20**	**7.09**
Austria	127	129	147	176	178	0.23	1.14
Belgium	165	163	187	193	206	0.26	6.74
France	4,469	3,323	3,680	4,188	4,584	5.86	9.46
Germany	966	898	1,011	1,397	1,499	1.91	7.30

200

DOMINICA

1. Arrivals of non-resident tourists at national borders, by country of residence

	2009	2010	2011	2012	2013	Market share 2013	% Change 2013-2012
Liechtenstein	1		2				
Luxembourg	3	8	11	16	13	0.02	-18.75
Monaco	2	1	2	1			
Netherlands	172	182	185	162	191	0.24	17.90
Switzerland	270	389	478	595	534	0.68	-10.25
EAST MEDITERRANEAN EUROPE	**24**	**34**	**44**	**17**	**38**	**0.05**	**123.53**
Cyprus	3	3	6		1	0.00	
Israel	19	23	29	17	26	0.03	52.94
Turkey	2	8	9		11	0.01	
OTHER EUROPE	**40**	**48**	**74**	**62**	**38**	**0.05**	**-38.71**
Other countries of Europe	40	48	74	62	38	0.05	-38.71
MIDDLE EAST	**16**	**40**	**48**	**43**	**73**	**0.09**	**69.77**
Bahrain		1					
Egypt	3	5	3	7	2	0.00	-71.43
Iraq	1	3	1	2	6	0.01	200.00
Jordan		2			4	0.01	
Kuwait	1	2		1	2	0.00	100.00
Lebanon		4	3	4	2	0.00	-50.00
Libya	3	5					
Oman					1	0.00	
Palestine			1	1			
Qatar		6	3	3	3	0.00	
Saudi Arabia	4	6	14	9	10	0.01	11.11
Syrian Arab Republic	1	5	3	4	11	0.01	175.00
United Arab Emirates	3	1	20	12	32	0.04	166.67
SOUTH ASIA	**167**	**155**	**137**	**157**	**127**	**0.16**	**-19.11**
Afghanistan	3	6	2	5	5	0.01	
Bangladesh	25	1		2	3	0.00	50.00
India	112	123	106	122	85	0.11	-30.33
Iran, Islamic Republic of	7	14	16	14	23	0.03	64.29
Nepal		2	6	6	1	0.00	-83.33
Pakistan	14	3	4	4	5	0.01	25.00
Sri Lanka	6	6	3	4	5	0.01	25.00
NOT SPECIFIED	**51**	**56**	**41**	**10**	**1**	**0.00**	**-90.00**
Other countries of the World	51	56	41	10	1	0.00	-90.00

Yearbook of Tourism Statistics, Data 2009 – 2013, 2015 Edition

DOMINICAN REPUBLIC

1. Arrivals of non-resident tourists at national borders, by country of residence

	2009	2010	2011	2012	2013	Market share 2013	% Change 2013-2012
TOTAL (*)	3,992,303	4,124,543	4,306,431	4,562,606	4,689,770	100.00	2.79
AMERICAS	2,202,697	2,367,965	2,559,180	2,818,384	2,972,635	63.39	5.47
CARIBBEAN	138,236	154,201	143,254	151,566	145,278	3.10	-4.15
Aruba	1,910	1,873	1,888	1,505	2,284	0.05	51.76
Cuba	3,295	3,818	3,838	3,996	7,121	0.15	78.20
Curaçao	4,366	4,407	4,382	5,311	4,494	0.10	-15.38
Guadeloupe	5,334	5,188	3,436	6,077	7,306	0.16	20.22
Haiti	5,456	9,518	9,717	9,431	7,261	0.15	-23.01
Jamaica	882	1,124	1,027	1,046	913	0.02	-12.72
Martinique	3,386	4,252	3,833	4,618	4,264	0.09	-7.67
Puerto Rico	107,610	118,201	109,505	112,593	103,822	2.21	-7.79
Sint Maarten	2,944	2,520	2,654	3,411	3,571	0.08	4.69
Trinidad and Tobago	943	1,438	1,207	1,272	1,991	0.04	56.53
Turks and Caicos Islands	1,041	1,036	918	1,241	1,347	0.03	8.54
United States Virgin Islands	1,069	826	849	1,065	904	0.02	-15.12
CENTRAL AMERICA	30,083	29,124	35,033	36,363	36,131	0.77	-0.64
Costa Rica	8,110	8,411	9,618	9,879	10,948	0.23	10.82
El Salvador	3,462	3,710	3,870	3,922	2,984	0.06	-23.92
Guatemala	5,783	5,420	6,708	6,259	5,757	0.12	-8.02
Honduras	1,759	2,177	2,458	1,997	2,780	0.06	39.21
Panama	10,969	9,406	12,379	14,306	13,662	0.29	-4.50
NORTH AMERICA	1,819,294	1,902,316	1,988,935	2,195,068	2,334,437	49.78	6.35
Canada	650,111	662,058	668,290	689,543	687,891	14.67	-0.24
Mexico	18,308	20,695	23,467	26,610	23,708	0.51	-10.91
United States of America	1,150,875	1,219,563	1,297,178	1,478,915	1,622,838	34.60	9.73
SOUTH AMERICA	208,580	276,016	383,450	429,778	451,398	9.63	5.03
Argentina	43,130	69,182	97,462	101,321	105,701	2.25	4.32
Bolivia	3,053	5,106	7,621	7,401	8,959	0.19	21.05
Brazil	19,570	37,153	76,625	79,937	91,314	1.95	14.23
Chile	29,495	40,729	49,862	60,804	73,924	1.58	21.58
Colombia	29,156	31,263	40,982	44,955	43,596	0.93	-3.02
Ecuador	15,797	16,597	18,786	13,889	10,974	0.23	-20.99
Peru	19,825	24,636	30,646	38,953	35,150	0.75	-9.76
Uruguay	3,865	4,454	5,626	5,870	5,734	0.12	-2.32
Venezuela	42,635	45,196	53,079	72,680	70,404	1.50	-3.13
Other countries of South America	2,054	1,700	2,761	3,968	5,642	0.12	42.19
OTHER AMERICAS	6,504	6,308	8,508	5,609	5,391	0.11	-3.89
Other countries of the Americas	6,504	6,308	8,508	5,609	5,391	0.11	-3.89
EAST ASIA AND THE PACIFIC	6,753	8,345	9,773	8,557	8,642	0.18	0.99
NORTH-EAST ASIA	3,831	4,738	4,989	4,702	5,173	0.11	10.02
China	381	646	901	963	1,205	0.03	25.13
Japan	2,036	2,231	2,270	2,036	1,643	0.04	-19.30
Korea, Republic of	937	1,406	1,300	1,216	1,455	0.03	19.65
Taiwan, Province of China	477	455	518	487	870	0.02	78.64
AUSTRALASIA	1,397	1,676	1,361	1,658	1,585	0.03	-4.40
Australia	1,397	1,676	1,361	1,658	1,585	0.03	-4.40
OTHER EAST ASIA AND THE PACIFIC	1,525	1,931	3,423	2,197	1,884	0.04	-14.25
Other countries of Asia	1,525	1,931	3,423	2,197	1,884	0.04	-14.25
EUROPE	1,204,701	1,142,666	1,132,009	1,094,841	1,081,667	23.06	-1.20
CENTRAL/EASTERN EUROPE	63,195	92,670	139,462	180,134	202,198	4.31	12.25
Bulgaria	499	582	555	613	511	0.01	-16.64
Czech Republic	5,526	6,112	5,996	5,522	5,979	0.13	8.28
Hungary	704	803	780	546	771	0.02	41.21
Poland	3,795	4,934	6,906	6,587	5,870	0.13	-10.89
Romania	592	748	971	567	654	0.01	15.34
Russian Federation	49,752	76,059	120,752	163,157	183,965	3.92	12.75
Ukraine	2,327	3,432	3,502	3,142	4,448	0.09	41.57
NORTHERN EUROPE	198,892	185,826	149,997	106,755	126,292	2.69	18.30
Denmark	2,061	2,145	1,709	2,299	3,147	0.07	36.89

Yearbook of Tourism Statistics, Data 2009 – 2013, 2015 Edition

DOMINICAN REPUBLIC

1. Arrivals of non-resident tourists at national borders, by country of residence

	2009	2010	2011	2012	2013	Market share 2013	% Change 2013-2012
Finland	4,445	4,245	2,383	2,785	3,411	0.07	22.48
Ireland	1,767	1,564	1,096	840	678	0.01	-19.29
Norway	2,575	1,891	1,527	1,617	2,506	0.05	54.98
Sweden	6,153	7,760	5,339	3,603	10,610	0.23	194.48
United Kingdom	181,891	168,221	137,943	95,611	105,940	2.26	10.80
SOUTHERN EUROPE	**390,347**	**321,994**	**299,872**	**271,826**	**231,073**	**4.93**	**-14.99**
Greece	567	495	454	342	337	0.01	-1.46
Italy	115,775	94,952	99,822	89,767	74,176	1.58	-17.37
Portugal	42,730	36,941	29,403	25,525	16,574	0.35	-35.07
Spain	231,275	189,606	170,193	156,192	139,986	2.98	-10.38
WESTERN EUROPE	**545,410**	**530,292**	**540,275**	**533,201**	**519,523**	**11.08**	**-2.57**
Austria	10,049	9,640	8,239	7,914	7,449	0.16	-5.88
Belgium	38,129	38,187	36,955	34,111	28,065	0.60	-17.72
France	247,038	230,975	246,416	245,033	218,399	4.66	-10.87
Germany	178,533	181,318	183,847	183,533	213,233	4.55	16.18
Luxembourg	473	495	435	570	466	0.01	-18.25
Netherlands	41,605	40,100	37,861	34,225	25,416	0.54	-25.74
Switzerland	29,583	29,577	26,522	27,815	26,495	0.56	-4.75
EAST MEDITERRANEAN EUROPE	**1,445**	**1,476**	**1,204**	**1,077**	**1,223**	**0.03**	**13.56**
Israel	1,445	1,476	1,204	1,077	1,223	0.03	13.56
OTHER EUROPE	**5,412**	**10,408**	**1,199**	**1,848**	**1,358**	**0.03**	**-26.52**
Other countries of Europe	5,412	10,408	1,199	1,848	1,358	0.03	-26.52
SOUTH ASIA	**806**	**848**	**964**	**941**	**889**	**0.02**	**-5.53**
India	806	848	964	941	889	0.02	-5.53
NOT SPECIFIED	**577,346**	**604,719**	**604,505**	**639,883**	**625,937**	**13.35**	**-2.18**
Other countries of the World	659	1,286	1,071	970	921	0.02	-5.05
Nationals Residing Abroad	576,687	603,433	603,434	638,913	625,016	13.33	-2.18

Yearbook of Tourism Statistics, Data 2009 – 2013, 2015 Edition

ECUADOR

2. Arrivals of non-resident visitors at national borders, by nationality

	2009	2010	2011	2012	2013	Market share 2013	% Change 2013-2012
TOTAL (*)	968,499	1,047,098	1,141,037	1,271,901	1,364,057	100.00	7.25
AFRICA	3,113	3,051	2,352	2,557	4,531	0.33	77.20
EAST AFRICA	836	932	199	272	309	0.02	13.60
Burundi	2	3	1	3	5	0.00	66.67
Comoros	1	5	6	12	3	0.00	-75.00
Djibouti	4	3	2	4	5	0.00	25.00
Eritrea	256	411	4	4	2	0.00	-50.00
Ethiopia	175	188	14	21	20	0.00	-4.76
Kenya	267	164	58	66	41	0.00	-37.88
Madagascar	10	17	12	23	16	0.00	-30.43
Malawi	2	1	2		3	0.00	
Mauritius	1	7	9	13	12	0.00	-7.69
Mozambique	13	18	16	23	76	0.01	230.43
Reunion	17	5	3	12	7	0.00	-41.67
Rwanda	1	5	3	2	8	0.00	300.00
Seychelles	1		1	2	2	0.00	
Somalia	17	55	3	1	4	0.00	300.00
Uganda	16	14	23	27	42	0.00	55.56
United Republic of Tanzania	29	13	26	41	7	0.00	-82.93
Zambia	12	3	2	6	17	0.00	183.33
Zimbabwe	12	20	14	12	39	0.00	225.00
CENTRAL AFRICA	181	175	153	162	436	0.03	169.14
Angola	30	27	9	26	258	0.02	892.31
Cameroon	85	73	70	65	76	0.01	16.92
Central African Republic	15	15	10	13	7	0.00	-46.15
Chad	6	13	19	18	20	0.00	11.11
Congo	32	38	37	35	44	0.00	25.71
Democratic Republic of the Congo	1	1					
Equatorial Guinea	2	2	4	4	6	0.00	50.00
Gabon	4	2	4	1	18	0.00	1,700.00
Sao Tome and Principe	6	4			7	0.00	
NORTH AFRICA	534	513	499	395	445	0.03	12.66
Algeria	173	129	183	183	198	0.01	8.20
Morocco	90	82	93	96	151	0.01	57.29
Sudan	10	33	33	11	12	0.00	9.09
Tunisia	28	29	30	44	50	0.00	13.64
Western Sahara	233	240	160	61	34	0.00	-44.26
SOUTHERN AFRICA	606	627	989	967	998	0.07	3.21
Botswana	15	13	1	12	9	0.00	-25.00
Lesotho	4	3	5	7	7	0.00	
Namibia	25	13	4	17	254	0.02	1,394.12
South Africa	556	594	976	931	728	0.05	-21.80
Swaziland	6	4	3				
WEST AFRICA	870	706	390	609	1,821	0.13	199.01
Benin	27	30	24	24	24	0.00	
Burkina Faso	4	7	8	10	14	0.00	40.00
Cabo Verde	15	37	36	40	44	0.00	10.00
Côte d'Ivoire	17	18	15	40	22	0.00	-45.00
Gambia	9	7	2	10	6	0.00	-40.00
Ghana	66	49	70	57	74	0.01	29.82
Guinea	79	67	43	26	35	0.00	34.62
Guinea-Bissau	2	4	1	2	2	0.00	
Liberia	9	7	9	6	5	0.00	-16.67
Mali	3	8	11	14	10	0.00	-28.57
Mauritania	31	24	27	13	5	0.00	-61.54
Nigeria	545	359	80	77	145	0.01	88.31
Saint Helena		1		1			
Senegal	30	32	22	247	1,383	0.10	459.92
Sierra Leone	29	48	40	38	45	0.00	18.42

204

Yearbook of Tourism Statistics, Data 2009 – 2013, 2015 Edition

ECUADOR

2. Arrivals of non-resident visitors at national borders, by nationality

	2009	2010	2011	2012	2013	Market share 2013	% Change 2013-2012
Togo	4	8	2	4	7	0.00	75.00
OTHER AFRICA	**86**	**98**	**122**	**152**	**522**	**0.04**	**243.42**
Other countries of Africa	86	98	122	152	522	0.04	243.42
AMERICAS	**734,527**	**810,281**	**885,383**	**996,023**	**1,085,737**	**79.60**	**9.01**
CARIBBEAN	**31,428**	**31,958**	**29,897**	**28,049**	**42,749**	**3.13**	**52.41**
Anguilla	1	1		1			
Antigua and Barbuda	6	7	5	6	12	0.00	100.00
Aruba	1	4	1	2	6	0.00	200.00
Bahamas	47	61	60	68	96	0.01	41.18
Barbados	55	33	43	44	30	0.00	-31.82
Bermuda	24	10	10	16	30	0.00	87.50
British Virgin Islands		9	6		9	0.00	
Cayman Islands	4	3	4	1	4	0.00	300.00
Cuba	27,065	27,001	24,064	21,480	24,380	1.79	13.50
Curaçao	13	8	8	6	24	0.00	300.00
Dominica	44	64	38	42	31	0.00	-26.19
Dominican Republic	2,480	2,619	2,446	2,811	3,425	0.25	21.84
Grenada	16	20	11	19	14	0.00	-26.32
Guadeloupe	12	15	14	26	12	0.00	-53.85
Haiti	1,257	1,681	2,546	3,023	14,099	1.03	366.39
Jamaica	137	119	161	170	176	0.01	3.53
Montserrat		1	6				
Netherlands Antilles	2	3					
Puerto Rico	26	31	39	57	124	0.01	117.54
Saint Kitts and Nevis	4	5	2	7	7	0.00	
Saint Lucia	15	8	28	13	12	0.00	-7.69
Saint Vincent and the Grenadines		4	7	5	9	0.00	80.00
Trinidad and Tobago	219	251	398	252	249	0.02	-1.19
CENTRAL AMERICA	**13,652**	**15,772**	**21,021**	**24,836**	**28,914**	**2.12**	**16.42**
Belize	57	41	37	51	54	0.00	5.88
Costa Rica	3,921	4,560	4,833	5,060	7,550	0.55	49.21
El Salvador	1,419	1,994	2,655	3,700	3,625	0.27	-2.03
Guatemala	2,048	2,296	2,230	3,101	3,176	0.23	2.42
Honduras	1,072	1,256	1,391	1,581	1,593	0.12	0.76
Nicaragua	856	985	984	1,253	1,189	0.09	-5.11
Panama	4,279	4,640	8,891	10,090	11,727	0.86	16.22
NORTH AMERICA	**278,284**	**288,705**	**285,896**	**294,685**	**297,872**	**21.84**	**1.08**
Canada	22,489	23,867	24,834	26,979	27,922	2.05	3.50
Greenland	4						
Mexico	13,695	15,757	19,457	19,642	21,098	1.55	7.41
United States of America	242,096	249,081	241,605	248,064	248,852	18.24	0.32
SOUTH AMERICA	**411,162**	**473,846**	**548,569**	**648,452**	**716,201**	**52.51**	**10.45**
Argentina	22,675	30,653	37,465	46,199	49,231	3.61	6.56
Bolivia	4,487	5,522	4,964	5,360	6,249	0.46	16.59
Brazil	14,395	15,083	17,543	18,174	19,230	1.41	5.81
Chile	25,195	28,478	34,864	41,645	40,649	2.98	-2.39
Colombia	160,116	203,916	265,557	349,455	343,004	25.15	-1.85
French Guiana	5	12	5	5	14	0.00	180.00
Guyana	51	54	45	60	71	0.01	18.33
Paraguay	1,233	1,115	1,375	1,219	1,333	0.10	9.35
Peru	150,548	154,216	144,905	137,084	150,427	11.03	9.73
Suriname	74	87	80	57	87	0.01	52.63
Uruguay	2,967	3,152	3,458	3,493	4,263	0.31	22.04
Venezuela	29,416	31,558	38,308	45,701	101,643	7.45	122.41
OTHER AMERICAS	**1**			**1**	**1**	**0.00**	
Other countries of the Americas	1			1	1	0.00	
EAST ASIA AND THE PACIFIC	**29,472**	**31,172**	**41,317**	**49,254**	**44,383**	**3.25**	**-9.89**
NORTH-EAST ASIA	**16,578**	**16,720**	**19,706**	**23,416**	**26,025**	**1.91**	**11.14**
China	7,844	6,879	9,296	12,245	14,613	1.07	19.34

205

Yearbook of Tourism Statistics, Data 2009 – 2013, 2015 Edition

ECUADOR

2. Arrivals of non-resident visitors at national borders, by nationality

	2009	2010	2011	2012	2013	Market share 2013	% Change 2013-2012
Hong Kong, China	143	158	217	259	256	0.02	-1.16
Japan	4,951	5,106	5,114	5,342	5,576	0.41	4.38
Korea, Dem. People's Republic of	1,294	1,810	1,664	1,914	1,688	0.12	-11.81
Korea, Republic of	1,688	2,044	2,621	2,818	3,064	0.22	8.73
Macao, China	2	2	5	3	3	0.00	
Mongolia	2	3	12	6	15	0.00	150.00
Taiwan, Province of China	654	718	777	829	810	0.06	-2.29
SOUTH-EAST ASIA	**2,941**	**3,499**	**9,629**	**11,940**	**4,617**	**0.34**	**-61.33**
Brunei Darussalam	2	1		8	4	0.00	-50.00
Cambodia	4	2	3	10	13	0.00	30.00
Indonesia	194	262	382	761	446	0.03	-41.39
Malaysia	192	251	257	314	240	0.02	-23.57
Myanmar	130	158	352	300	81	0.01	-73.00
Philippines	2,060	2,330	7,990	9,704	2,809	0.21	-71.05
Singapore	201	292	368	401	526	0.04	31.17
Thailand	72	148	193	335	224	0.02	-33.13
Timor-Leste	2		2		12	0.00	
Viet Nam	84	55	82	107	262	0.02	144.86
AUSTRALASIA	**9,876**	**10,820**	**11,882**	**13,664**	**13,613**	**1.00**	**-0.37**
Australia	8,241	9,167	10,238	11,782	11,875	0.87	0.79
New Zealand	1,635	1,653	1,644	1,882	1,738	0.13	-7.65
MELANESIA	**53**	**73**	**37**	**77**	**28**	**0.00**	**-63.64**
Fiji	4	3	5	26	5	0.00	-80.77
New Caledonia	45	62	26	38	18	0.00	-52.63
Norfolk Island	3	6	4	4	2	0.00	-50.00
Papua New Guinea			2	2	2	0.00	
Vanuatu	1	2		7	1	0.00	-85.71
MICRONESIA	**7**	**40**	**32**	**128**	**88**	**0.01**	**-31.25**
Cocos (Keeling) Islands	1						
Johnston Island	1				1	0.00	
Kiribati	4	34	30	121	82	0.01	-32.23
Marshall Islands		2		1	1	0.00	
Micronesia, Federated States of	1	2	1	3	4	0.00	33.33
Nauru		2		1			
Palau				2			
Wake Island			1				
POLYNESIA	**16**	**20**	**31**	**29**	**12**	**0.00**	**-58.62**
French Polynesia	9	17	18	10	4	0.00	-60.00
Samoa	4	1	7	11	6	0.00	-45.45
Tonga	1	2		5			
Tuvalu	2		6	3	2	0.00	-33.33
OTHER EAST ASIA AND THE PACIFIC	**1**						
Other countries of Oceania	1						
EUROPE	**197,543**	**198,115**	**207,215**	**218,375**	**217,550**	**15.95**	**-0.38**
CENTRAL/EASTERN EUROPE	**9,445**	**9,483**	**13,281**	**14,918**	**13,185**	**0.97**	**-11.62**
Armenia	11	26	18	15	20	0.00	33.33
Azerbaijan	32	40	37	52	73	0.01	40.38
Belarus	113	113	170	242	260	0.02	7.44
Bulgaria	225	268	277	435	377	0.03	-13.33
Czech Republic	919	846	900	1,040	1,138	0.08	9.42
Estonia	109	103	115	151	145	0.01	-3.97
Georgia	23	35	103	70	54	0.00	-22.86
Hungary	398	360	363	387	347	0.03	-10.34
Kazakhstan	60	67	119	109	148	0.01	35.78
Kyrgyzstan	6	6	8	5	8	0.00	60.00
Latvia	186	132	279	451	237	0.02	-47.45
Lithuania	284	185	324	436	439	0.03	0.69
Poland	2,144	1,903	2,458	2,479	2,036	0.15	-17.87

206

ECUADOR

2. Arrivals of non-resident visitors at national borders, by nationality

	2009	2010	2011	2012	2013	Market share 2013	% Change 2013-2012
Republic of Moldova	24	32	47	33	43	0.00	30.30
Romania	567	617	939	1,062	808	0.06	-23.92
Russian Federation	3,033	3,350	4,445	4,985	5,105	0.37	2.41
Slovakia	461	381	315	320	325	0.02	1.56
Tajikistan	1	1	5	10	8	0.00	-20.00
Turkmenistan	1	2	2	2	6	0.00	200.00
Ukraine	840	998	2,348	2,623	1,594	0.12	-39.23
Uzbekistan	8	18	9	11	14	0.00	27.27
NORTHERN EUROPE	**37,536**	**34,880**	**35,165**	**33,965**	**35,653**	**2.61**	**4.97**
Denmark	2,867	2,867	2,795	2,525	2,652	0.19	5.03
Faeroe Islands					1	0.00	
Finland	1,047	1,116	1,233	1,163	1,151	0.08	-1.03
Iceland	104	99	163	192	120	0.01	-37.50
Ireland	2,871	2,398	2,388	2,919	2,756	0.20	-5.58
Norway	1,993	2,026	1,942	1,988	1,876	0.14	-5.63
Sweden	3,624	3,777	3,646	4,036	3,734	0.27	-7.48
United Kingdom	25,030	22,597	22,998	21,142	23,363	1.71	10.51
SOUTHERN EUROPE	**74,060**	**76,902**	**78,628**	**84,003**	**82,746**	**6.07**	**-1.50**
Albania	56	71	100	142	147	0.01	3.52
Andorra	15	23	36	33	30	0.00	-9.09
Bosnia and Herzegovina	9	9	11	13	26	0.00	100.00
Croatia	218	248	421	548	394	0.03	-28.10
Gibraltar				1	1	0.00	
Greece	544	562	486	596	532	0.04	-10.74
Holy See	2	4	1		2	0.00	
Italy	14,759	15,076	14,645	14,774	14,626	1.07	-1.00
Malta	49	51	23	49	36	0.00	-26.53
Portugal	1,520	1,404	1,781	1,626	1,902	0.14	16.97
San Marino	3	4	8	12	9	0.00	-25.00
Slovenia	294	245	284	248	144	0.01	-41.94
Spain	56,400	59,030	60,666	65,764	64,726	4.75	-1.58
TFYR of Macedonia	11	8	12	19	11	0.00	-42.11
Yugoslavia, SFR (former)	180	167	154	178	160	0.01	-10.11
WESTERN EUROPE	**71,823**	**72,156**	**75,193**	**80,055**	**81,287**	**5.96**	**1.54**
Austria	2,456	2,522	2,786	3,095	3,025	0.22	-2.26
Belgium	5,021	4,945	5,129	5,341	5,404	0.40	1.18
France	19,810	20,272	20,431	19,547	20,222	1.48	3.45
Germany	24,841	25,011	26,669	29,582	28,292	2.07	-4.36
Liechtenstein	18	23	22	23	21	0.00	-8.70
Luxembourg	197	137	154	168	185	0.01	10.12
Monaco	4	8	2	4	8	0.00	100.00
Netherlands	10,690	10,354	10,546	12,392	13,769	1.01	11.11
Switzerland	8,786	8,884	9,454	9,903	10,361	0.76	4.62
EAST MEDITERRANEAN EUROPE	**4,678**	**4,693**	**4,948**	**5,431**	**4,679**	**0.34**	**-13.85**
Cyprus	22	19	28	38	37	0.00	-2.63
Israel	4,335	4,300	4,246	4,599	4,046	0.30	-12.02
Turkey	321	374	674	794	596	0.04	-24.94
OTHER EUROPE	**1**	**1**		**3**			
Other countries of Europe	1	1		3			
MIDDLE EAST	**626**	**696**	**575**	**916**	**1,217**	**0.09**	**32.86**
Bahrain	4	6	3	10	9	0.00	-10.00
Egypt	115	133	122	175	266	0.02	52.00
Iraq	13	8	12	17	28	0.00	64.71
Jordan	67	66	70	68	81	0.01	19.12
Kuwait	13	30	21	19	74	0.01	289.47
Lebanon	222	228	202	453	299	0.02	-34.00
Libya	26	41	13	15	5	0.00	-66.67
Oman	5	4		11	14	0.00	27.27
Qatar	10	11	6	5	114	0.01	2,180.00

207

ECUADOR

2. Arrivals of non-resident visitors at national borders, by nationality

	2009	2010	2011	2012	2013	Market share 2013	% Change 2013-2012
Saudi Arabia	27	52	49	39	116	0.01	197.44
Syrian Arab Republic	68	69	37	66	147	0.01	122.73
United Arab Emirates	11	13	16	15	31	0.00	106.67
Yemen	45	35	24	23	33	0.00	43.48
SOUTH ASIA	**3,149**	**3,653**	**4,082**	**4,672**	**3,964**	**0.29**	**-15.15**
Afghanistan	70	62	13	11	25	0.00	127.27
Bangladesh	321	362	115	36	36	0.00	
Bhutan	2		4		1	0.00	
India	1,570	2,060	3,073	3,770	3,364	0.25	-10.77
Iran, Islamic Republic of	269	232	374	342	212	0.02	-38.01
Maldives	8	5	6	5	12	0.00	140.00
Nepal	234	159	25	35	20	0.00	-42.86
Pakistan	497	518	128	144	138	0.01	-4.17
Sri Lanka	178	255	344	329	156	0.01	-52.58
NOT SPECIFIED	**69**	**130**	**113**	**104**	**6,675**	**0.49**	**6,318.27**
Other countries of the World	69	130	113	104	6,675	0.49	6,318.27

Yearbook of Tourism Statistics, Data 2009 – 2013, 2015 Edition

EGYPT

2. Arrivals of non-resident visitors at national borders, by nationality

	2009	2010	2011	2012	2013	Market share 2013	% Change 2013-2012
TOTAL (*)	12,535,885	14,730,813	9,845,066	11,531,858	9,464,349	100.00	-17.93
AFRICA	455,262	491,416	434,867	428,168	399,010	4.22	-6.81
EAST AFRICA	42,019	48,167	34,970	38,872	40,244	0.43	3.53
Burundi	574	467	304	312	243	0.00	-22.12
Comoros	850	877	447	234			
Djibouti	2,131	2,545	1,781	2,000	1,758	0.02	-12.10
Eritrea	5,323	6,661	4,743	5,881	9,107	0.10	54.85
Ethiopia	6,409	6,668	4,879	6,880	6,434	0.07	-6.48
Kenya	8,233	9,613	8,301	8,123	7,711	0.08	-5.07
Malawi	429	445	258	267	218	0.00	-18.35
Mauritius	1,004	999	529	525	486	0.01	-7.43
Mozambique	343	405	235	255	212	0.00	-16.86
Rwanda	510	419	385	411	341	0.00	-17.03
Seychelles	85	126	110	82	106	0.00	29.27
Somalia	6,781	6,350	4,414	4,332	3,398	0.04	-21.56
Uganda	2,495	2,533	3,138	3,208	3,455	0.04	7.70
United Republic of Tanzania	4,709	7,567	4,310	5,193	5,135	0.05	-1.12
Zambia	1,097	1,120	509	528	562	0.01	6.44
Zimbabwe	1,046	1,372	627	641	1,078	0.01	68.17
CENTRAL AFRICA	5,940	6,030	23,187	4,841	4,534	0.05	-6.34
Angola	678	547	303	354	209	0.00	-40.96
Cameroon	1,264	1,185	936	934	893	0.01	-4.39
Central African Republic	116	188	67	113	68	0.00	-39.82
Chad	2,292	2,620	20,758	2,314	2,017	0.02	-12.83
Congo	1,035	686	443	341	447	0.00	31.09
Democratic Republic of the Congo	242	532	464	633	719	0.01	13.59
Gabon	301	262	216	152	181	0.00	19.08
Sao Tome and Principe	12	10					
NORTH AFRICA	296,555	319,137	282,187	296,964	260,668	2.75	-12.22
Algeria	44,585	22,782	20,982	26,955	25,127	0.27	-6.78
Morocco	53,663	57,591	37,274	39,417	31,287	0.33	-20.63
Sudan	159,588	189,731	200,376	198,018	178,971	1.89	-9.62
Tunisia	38,719	49,033	23,555	32,574	25,283	0.27	-22.38
SOUTHERN AFRICA	32,981	38,260	19,604	22,638	21,381	0.23	-5.55
Botswana	166		103				
Lesotho	147	107	79	71	46	0.00	-35.21
Namibia	416	389	181	233	278	0.00	19.31
South Africa	31,930	37,635	19,164	22,205	20,885	0.22	-5.94
Swaziland	322	129	77	129	172	0.00	33.33
WEST AFRICA	76,006	77,846	74,271	63,850	71,039	0.75	11.26
Benin	543	387	253	376	332	0.00	-11.70
Côte d'Ivoire	1,056	1,262	702	842	1,166	0.01	38.48
Gambia	308	348	155	181	185	0.00	2.21
Ghana	8,291	10,018	8,366	8,502	10,021	0.11	17.87
Guinea	1,679	1,491	1,520	1,267	925	0.01	-26.99
Guinea-Bissau	62	36	73	16	62	0.00	287.50
Liberia	185	276	178	259	203	0.00	-21.62
Mali	729	739	1,612	643	615	0.01	-4.35
Mauritania	1,781	2,008	1,396	1,263	1,225	0.01	-3.01
Niger	1,156	1,343	10,670	2,915	4,986	0.05	71.05
Nigeria	57,967	57,731	47,889	46,182	49,822	0.53	7.88
Senegal	1,425	1,432	999	895	891	0.01	-0.45
Sierra Leone	297	248	149	222	179	0.00	-19.37
Togo	527	527	309	287	427	0.00	48.78
OTHER AFRICA	1,761	1,976	648	1,003	1,144	0.01	14.06
Other countries of Africa	1,761	1,976	648	1,003	1,144	0.01	14.06
AMERICAS	488,785	563,365	287,187	285,280	239,885	2.53	-15.91
CARIBBEAN	3,259	3,393	1,715	1,682	1,033	0.01	-38.59
Bahamas	83	63	22	39	25	0.00	-35.90

209

EGYPT

2. Arrivals of non-resident visitors at national borders, by nationality

	2009	2010	2011	2012	2013	Market share 2013	% Change 2013-2012
Barbados	58	60	32	71	36	0.00	-49.30
Cuba	823	742	437	493	363	0.00	-26.37
Dominica	801	941	382	413	387	0.00	-6.30
Haiti	104	125	67	86	64	0.00	-25.58
Jamaica	742	645	192	219	158	0.00	-27.85
Trinidad and Tobago	648	817	583	361			
CENTRAL AMERICA	**7,497**	**9,082**	**4,083**	**3,189**	**1,649**	**0.02**	**-48.29**
Costa Rica	1,360	2,333	663	1,176	536	0.01	-54.42
El Salvador	1,425	1,125	788	507	298	0.00	-41.22
Guatemala	1,326	1,796	494	615	359	0.00	-41.63
Honduras	2,577	2,907	387	438	190	0.00	-56.62
Nicaragua	448	387	191	296	118	0.00	-60.14
Panama	361	534	1,560	157	148	0.00	-5.73
NORTH AMERICA	**421,593**	**476,314**	**240,990**	**238,143**	**204,099**	**2.16**	**-14.30**
Canada	88,591	96,418	50,687	51,623	51,020	0.54	-1.17
Mexico	11,720	18,373	5,695	6,886	5,455	0.06	-20.78
United States of America	321,282	361,523	184,608	179,634	147,624	1.56	-17.82
SOUTH AMERICA	**55,869**	**74,027**	**40,184**	**41,916**	**32,717**	**0.35**	**-21.95**
Argentina	9,949	14,341	6,397	7,019	6,617	0.07	-5.73
Bolivia	536	770	422	385	343	0.00	-10.91
Brazil	19,695	30,384	17,249	15,554	12,117	0.13	-22.10
Chile	4,263	4,847	2,370	2,764	2,421	0.03	-12.41
Colombia	9,731	11,073	7,218	8,529	5,171	0.05	-39.37
Ecuador	2,618	3,529	2,124	2,477	1,423	0.02	-42.55
Guyana	33	39	17	20	5	0.00	-75.00
Paraguay	226	260	122	197	494	0.01	150.76
Peru	3,362	3,691	1,806	2,312	1,780	0.02	-23.01
Suriname	70	85	47	167	48	0.00	-71.26
Uruguay	1,295	1,549	930	823	785	0.01	-4.62
Venezuela	4,091	3,459	1,482	1,669	1,513	0.02	-9.35
OTHER AMERICAS	**567**	**549**	**215**	**350**	**387**	**0.00**	**10.57**
Other countries of the Americas	567	549	215	350	387	0.00	10.57
EAST ASIA AND THE PACIFIC	**448,416**	**559,018**	**277,866**	**304,926**	**245,196**	**2.59**	**-19.59**
NORTH-EAST ASIA	**208,812**	**288,997**	**109,687**	**135,056**	**109,367**	**1.16**	**-19.02**
China	80,933	106,227	48,620	61,155	55,453	0.59	-9.32
Japan	92,409	126,393	27,635	39,008	31,181	0.33	-20.07
Korea, Republic of	27,585	45,024	26,437	27,414	22,558	0.24	-17.71
Mongolia	471	311	252	237	175	0.00	-26.16
Taiwan, Province of China	7,414	11,042	6,743	7,242			
SOUTH-EAST ASIA	**154,479**	**176,156**	**121,454**	**127,126**	**98,092**	**1.04**	**-22.84**
Cambodia	107	77	77	88	77	0.00	-12.50
Indonesia	35,377	44,841	31,236	32,651	25,885	0.27	-20.72
Malaysia	29,592	32,564	25,681	30,409	32,809	0.35	7.89
Philippines	62,358	67,477	44,332	45,668	25,297	0.27	-44.61
Singapore	6,707	8,889	4,189	4,180	2,527	0.03	-39.55
Thailand	18,578	20,075	13,997	13,171	10,528	0.11	-20.07
Viet Nam	1,760	2,233	1,942	959	969	0.01	1.04
AUSTRALASIA	**74,772**	**84,007**	**43,573**	**39,984**	**31,720**	**0.34**	**-20.67**
Australia	63,029	71,723	36,676	33,280	26,809	0.28	-19.44
New Zealand	11,743	12,284	6,897	6,704	4,911	0.05	-26.75
POLYNESIA	**51**	**54**	**5**	**5**	**5**	**0.00**	
Samoa	51	54	5	5	5	0.00	
OTHER EAST ASIA AND THE PACIFIC	**10,302**	**9,804**	**3,147**	**2,755**	**6,012**	**0.06**	**118.22**
Other countries of Asia	10,302	9,804	3,147	2,755	6,012	0.06	118.22
EUROPE	**9,416,206**	**11,176,923**	**7,211,060**	**8,415,612**	**6,976,333**	**73.71**	**-17.10**
CENTRAL/EASTERN EUROPE	**2,879,908**	**3,943,193**	**2,480,873**	**3,239,061**	**2,792,007**	**29.50**	**-13.80**
Armenia	5,834	8,725	3,381	4,618	4,801	0.05	3.96
Azerbaijan	2,870	2,927	1,146	1,539	1,463	0.02	-4.94
Bulgaria	15,562	15,513	5,896	5,143	4,320	0.05	-16.00

Yearbook of Tourism Statistics, Data 2009 – 2013, 2015 Edition

EGYPT

2. Arrivals of non-resident visitors at national borders, by nationality

	2009	2010	2011	2012	2013	Market share 2013	% Change 2013-2012
Czech Republic/Slovakia	216,798	287,617	158,674	134,940	33,001	0.35	-75.54
Estonia	35,353	29,405	18,638	24,095	21,764	0.23	-9.67
Georgia	3,049	5,726	3,883	7,023	7,670	0.08	9.21
Hungary	58,528	68,428	48,381	43,001	27,063	0.29	-37.06
Kazakhstan	13,114	17,950	5,512	9,266	9,229	0.10	-0.40
Poland	454,567	593,596	378,134	462,721	271,429	2.87	-41.34
Romania	38,903	55,649	23,864	27,276	16,229	0.17	-40.50
Russian Federation	2,035,330	2,855,723	1,832,388	2,518,275	2,393,908	25.29	-4.94
Uzbekistan		1,934	976	1,164	1,130	0.01	-2.92
NORTHERN EUROPE	**1,801,029**	**2,023,857**	**1,371,079**	**1,407,458**	**1,219,244**	**12.88**	**-13.37**
Denmark	100,349	135,051	93,347	126,062	95,946	1.01	-23.89
Finland	65,227	93,865	42,191	41,133	25,347	0.27	-38.38
Iceland	624	879	614	1,360	512	0.01	-62.35
Ireland	62,458	30,733	18,976	18,375	17,865	0.19	-2.78
Norway	66,948	97,431	64,716	74,483	38,344	0.41	-48.52
Sweden	158,699	209,992	116,822	134,270	85,886	0.91	-36.03
United Kingdom	1,346,724	1,455,906	1,034,413	1,011,775	955,344	10.09	-5.58
SOUTHERN EUROPE	**1,309,096**	**1,450,553**	**671,699**	**834,608**	**581,801**	**6.15**	**-30.29**
Albania	5,127	4,034	3,115	2,467	1,478	0.02	-40.09
Croatia	9,407	11,891	5,248	6,068	4,110	0.04	-32.27
Greece	45,849	53,236	18,678	19,464	14,935	0.16	-23.27
Italy	1,047,997	1,144,384	555,246	718,703	504,110	5.33	-29.86
Malta	2,081	2,821	4,524	1,739	1,409	0.01	-18.98
Portugal	17,182	20,451	8,607	8,688	6,230	0.07	-28.29
Serbia and Montenegro	22,247	37,404	27,100	24,970	12,363	0.13	-50.49
Slovenia	22,979	26,930	14,272	18,317	13,586	0.14	-25.83
Spain	136,227	149,402	34,909	34,192	23,580	0.25	-31.04
WESTERN EUROPE	**2,603,121**	**2,860,729**	**1,985,465**	**2,212,684**	**1,270,224**	**13.42**	**-42.59**
Austria	214,298	240,516	168,298	179,279	135,142	1.43	-24.62
Belgium	189,475	195,919	155,793	150,401	109,657	1.16	-27.09
France	551,694	599,363	344,949	318,449	191,689	2.03	-39.81
Germany	1,202,339	1,328,960	964,599	1,164,556	558,479	5.90	-52.04
Luxembourg	9,056	7,920	4,933	4,917	3,614	0.04	-26.50
Monaco	182	183	61		24	0.00	
Netherlands	249,017	291,154	206,684	239,237	170,017	1.80	-28.93
Switzerland	187,060	196,714	140,148	155,845	101,602	1.07	-34.81
EAST MEDITERRANEAN EUROPE	**258,767**	**299,024**	**215,329**	**194,405**	**188,317**	**1.99**	**-3.13**
Cyprus	9,411	9,195	3,566	3,980	3,037	0.03	-23.69
Israel	203,275	226,456	177,808	132,217	133,620	1.41	1.06
Turkey	46,081	63,373	33,955	58,208	51,660	0.55	-11.25
OTHER EUROPE	**564,285**	**599,567**	**486,615**	**527,396**	**924,740**	**9.77**	**75.34**
Other countries of Europe	564,285	599,567	486,615	527,396	924,740	9.77	75.34
MIDDLE EAST	**1,571,212**	**1,761,245**	**1,511,401**	**1,965,492**	**1,493,854**	**15.78**	**-24.00**
Bahrain	19,098	20,290	12,587	14,831	12,777	0.14	-13.85
Iraq	32,437	38,432	35,137	38,950	36,959	0.39	-5.11
Jordan	164,247	171,217	151,835	179,344	155,352	1.64	-13.38
Kuwait	138,376	145,402	76,512	95,696	81,655	0.86	-14.67
Lebanon	74,822	75,475	52,340	56,958	49,275	0.52	-13.49
Libya	410,222	451,068	524,544	583,044	307,056	3.24	-47.34
Oman	19,037	20,435	12,391	13,554	10,666	0.11	-21.31
Palestine	104,712	177,333	229,844	326,815	246,583	2.61	-24.55
Qatar	21,123	24,787	16,129	24,765	20,083	0.21	-18.91
Saudi Arabia	347,971	374,946	198,320	241,635	207,620	2.19	-14.08
Syrian Arab Republic	106,864	115,657	102,367	259,639	255,820	2.70	-1.47
United Arab Emirates	49,578	53,815	24,661	27,034	20,707	0.22	-23.40
Yemen	82,725	92,388	74,734	103,227	89,301	0.94	-13.49
SOUTH ASIA	**118,004**	**144,192**	**101,718**	**107,602**	**87,519**	**0.92**	**-18.66**
Afghanistan	894	1,126	732	1,420	2,004	0.02	41.13
Bangladesh	6,965	6,252	12,023	9,073	3,195	0.03	-64.79

Yearbook of Tourism Statistics, Data 2009 – 2013, 2015 Edition

EGYPT

2. Arrivals of non-resident visitors at national borders, by nationality

	2009	2010	2011	2012	2013	Market share 2013	% Change 2013-2012
India	86,698	114,248	73,443	82,698	67,401	0.71	-18.50
Iran, Islamic Republic of	3,503	849	542	754	749	0.01	-0.66
Maldives	230	258	218	153	3,475	0.04	2,171.24
Nepal	1,413	1,589	1,558	1,008	692	0.01	-31.35
Pakistan	12,887	14,203	10,745	9,090	7,525	0.08	-17.22
Sri Lanka	5,414	5,667	2,457	3,406	2,478	0.03	-27.25
NOT SPECIFIED	**38,000**	**34,654**	**20,967**	**24,778**	**22,552**	**0.24**	**-8.98**
Other countries of the World	38,000	34,654	20,967	24,778	22,552	0.24	-8.98

Yearbook of Tourism Statistics, Data 2009 – 2013, 2015 Edition

EGYPT

5. Overnight stays of non-resident tourists in hotels and similar establishments, by nationality

	2009	2010	2011	2012	2013	Market share 2013	% Change 2013-2012
TOTAL	126,533,535	147,385,089	114,213,521	137,818,456	94,410,172	100.00	-31.50
AFRICA	5,357,057	5,956,672	6,100,700	5,898,513	3,528,306	3.74	-40.18
EAST AFRICA	450,945	468,586	377,237	398,295	219,552	0.23	-44.88
Burundi	7,443	6,302	3,824	4,715	870	0.00	-81.55
Comoros	22,437	11,993	9,950	2,820			
Djibouti	31,778	34,214	26,808	21,856	8,338	0.01	-61.85
Eritrea	37,741	35,698	38,814	38,497	24,707	0.03	-35.82
Ethiopia	144,588	154,521	114,463	126,755	57,970	0.06	-54.27
Kenya	78,238	93,421	90,525	88,825	47,233	0.05	-46.82
Malawi	4,468	6,326	3,131	3,335	2,024	0.00	-39.31
Mauritius	6,812	9,787	6,227	6,124	3,390	0.00	-44.64
Mozambique	4,703	4,090	2,943	1,863	797	0.00	-57.22
Rwanda	6,977	6,641	4,256	4,413	1,092	0.00	-75.25
Seychelles	628	1,560	873	589	854	0.00	44.99
Somalia	45,404	41,305	19,461	37,949	34,382	0.04	-9.40
Uganda	20,981	16,995	21,878	30,876	19,695	0.02	-36.21
United Republic of Tanzania	23,913	27,674	23,436	17,641	10,500	0.01	-40.48
Zambia	7,724	10,284	5,956	5,949	4,395	0.00	-26.12
Zimbabwe	7,110	7,775	4,692	6,088	3,305	0.00	-45.71
CENTRAL AFRICA	108,539	119,606	426,590	108,223	47,296	0.05	-56.30
Angola	9,769	7,539	5,174	3,442	2,655	0.00	-22.86
Cameroon	18,014	14,996	11,708	21,799	5,178	0.01	-76.25
Central African Republic		626	246	2,298	10,318	0.01	349.00
Chad	60,846	65,681	391,786	55,620	25,537	0.03	-54.09
Congo	15,847	18,236	4,510	12,837	1,235	0.00	-90.38
Democratic Republic of the Congo		8,797	10,065	8,374	1,235	0.00	-85.25
Gabon	4,063	3,731	3,101	3,853	1,138	0.00	-70.46
NORTH AFRICA	4,094,967	4,706,765	4,607,119	4,856,867	2,946,613	3.12	-39.33
Algeria	447,637	198,863	140,645	220,149	187,833	0.20	-14.68
Morocco	419,087	459,692	385,108	322,276	192,359	0.20	-40.31
Sudan	2,939,349	3,676,806	3,909,918	3,923,017	2,381,584	2.52	-39.29
Tunisia	288,894	371,404	171,448	391,425	184,837	0.20	-52.78
SOUTHERN AFRICA	205,790	227,142	159,839	150,939	97,530	0.10	-35.38
Lesotho	1,174	1,311	669	121	34	0.00	-71.90
Namibia	5,617	4,016	2,198	2,875	1,432	0.00	-50.19
South Africa	196,939	220,803	156,679	147,498	95,923	0.10	-34.97
Swaziland	2,060	1,012	293	445	141	0.00	-68.31
WEST AFRICA	467,852	428,039	516,223	355,521	206,814	0.22	-41.83
Côte d'Ivoire	12,313	13,540	9,018	15,545	7,169	0.01	-53.88
Ghana	29,868	34,278	44,467	22,787	16,564	0.02	-27.31
Guinea	19,692	14,898	13,074	8,478	6,322	0.01	-25.43
Liberia	2,022	2,756	1,664	2,097	970	0.00	-53.74
Mali	10,482	5,916	14,381	13,867	7,739	0.01	-44.19
Mauritania	17,655	14,735	15,121	11,389	8,163	0.01	-28.33
Niger	15,221	7,269	58,604	11,717	4,156	0.00	-64.53
Nigeria	337,594	316,364	344,069	257,036	146,462	0.16	-43.02
Senegal	16,001	12,304	12,439	10,937	7,027	0.01	-35.75
Sierra Leone	3,604	2,487	1,832	338	713	0.00	110.95
Togo	3,400	3,492	1,554	1,330	1,529	0.00	14.96
OTHER AFRICA	28,964	6,534	13,692	28,668	10,501	0.01	-63.37
Other countries of Africa	28,964	6,534	13,692	28,668	10,501	0.01	-63.37
AMERICAS	5,813,541	6,621,105	4,351,353	4,109,006	2,429,528	2.57	-40.87
CARIBBEAN	26,897	23,784	17,809	18,863	7,105	0.01	-62.33
Bahamas	742	203	165	114	12	0.00	-89.47
Barbados	534	381	53	340	37	0.00	-89.12
Cuba	9,139	5,738	4,702	4,080	1,811	0.00	-55.61
Dominica	4,597	4,016	4,197	3,813	3,758	0.00	-1.44
Haiti	1,267	471	171	133	60	0.00	-54.89
Jamaica	2,272	2,773	2,203	1,185	1,427	0.00	20.42

213

EGYPT

5. Overnight stays of non-resident tourists in hotels and similar establishments, by nationality

	2009	2010	2011	2012	2013	Market share 2013	% Change 2013-2012
Trinidad and Tobago	8,346	10,202	6,318	9,198			
CENTRAL AMERICA	**49,037**	**53,795**	**26,650**	**55,229**	**7,249**	**0.01**	**-86.87**
Costa Rica	11,457	13,939	7,405	31,645	2,772	0.00	-91.24
El Salvador	16,800	10,811	5,281	13,009	906	0.00	-93.04
Guatemala	10,198	17,022	6,145	7,790	1,930	0.00	-75.22
Honduras	5,644	5,642	5,218	1,129	361	0.00	-68.02
Nicaragua	1,574	1,789	726	590	271	0.00	-54.07
Panama	3,364	4,592	1,875	1,066	1,009	0.00	-5.35
NORTH AMERICA	**5,201,244**	**5,869,144**	**3,824,276**	**3,503,882**	**2,190,051**	**2.32**	**-37.50**
Canada	1,133,889	1,255,121	858,008	809,422	530,210	0.56	-34.50
Mexico	110,542	144,387	63,865	89,460	34,917	0.04	-60.97
United States of America	3,956,813	4,469,636	2,902,403	2,605,000	1,624,924	1.72	-37.62
SOUTH AMERICA	**533,105**	**670,634**	**480,695**	**530,352**	**222,419**	**0.24**	**-58.06**
Argentina	102,793	134,008	76,337	77,403	51,874	0.05	-32.98
Bolivia	5,222	6,350	5,692	3,963	2,615	0.00	-34.01
Brazil	175,243	257,884	186,480	189,994	83,824	0.09	-55.88
Chile	42,883	49,486	29,718	34,778	18,075	0.02	-48.03
Colombia	99,401	105,020	89,722	109,460	30,908	0.03	-71.76
Ecuador	23,561	36,417	26,976	42,221	8,379	0.01	-80.15
Paraguay	3,500	2,869	1,744	1,933	1,238	0.00	-35.95
Peru	22,449	25,477	19,147	26,415	9,389	0.01	-64.46
Suriname	871	249	81	191	58	0.00	-69.63
Uruguay	16,524	15,206	14,008	13,915	3,353	0.00	-75.90
Venezuela	40,658	37,668	30,790	30,079	12,706	0.01	-57.76
OTHER AMERICAS	**3,258**	**3,748**	**1,923**	**680**	**2,704**	**0.00**	**297.65**
Other countries of the Americas	3,258	3,748	1,923	680	2,704	0.00	297.65
EAST ASIA AND THE PACIFIC	**3,818,962**	**5,861,271**	**2,921,263**	**2,951,172**	**1,866,210**	**1.98**	**-36.76**
NORTH-EAST ASIA	**1,652,441**	**2,288,906**	**1,228,574**	**1,348,519**	**875,143**	**0.93**	**-35.10**
China	642,331	880,756	555,323	643,130	431,866	0.46	-32.85
Japan	707,721	877,508	332,490	308,791	249,109	0.26	-19.33
Korea, Republic of	227,518	347,497	270,570	313,999	193,328	0.20	-38.43
Mongolia	8,697	4,008	3,949	2,224	840	0.00	-62.23
Taiwan, Province of China	66,174	179,137	66,242	80,375			
SOUTH-EAST ASIA	**1,025,127**	**1,161,642**	**946,086**	**944,254**	**542,529**	**0.57**	**-42.54**
Cambodia	530	646	204	279	71	0.00	-74.55
Indonesia	331,638	327,675	259,983	408,271	151,621	0.16	-62.86
Malaysia	206,536	245,785	223,029	199,038	216,332	0.23	8.69
Philippines	324,148	410,095	296,380	231,009	125,985	0.13	-45.46
Singapore	86,415	97,862	69,880	54,169	18,927	0.02	-65.06
Thailand	75,860	79,579	96,610	51,488	29,593	0.03	-42.52
AUSTRALASIA	**1,056,791**	**1,122,553**	**702,092**	**621,416**	**379,428**	**0.40**	**-38.94**
Australia	919,436	977,937	604,408	527,127	327,457	0.35	-37.88
New Zealand	137,355	144,616	97,684	94,289	51,971	0.06	-44.88
POLYNESIA	**45**	**56**	**4**	**4**	**5**	**0.00**	**25.00**
Samoa	45	56	4	4	5	0.00	25.00
OTHER EAST ASIA AND THE PACIFIC	**84,558**	**1,288,114**	**44,507**	**36,979**	**69,105**	**0.07**	**86.88**
Other countries of Asia	84,558	1,288,114	44,507	36,979	69,105	0.07	86.88
EUROPE	**89,331,393**	**102,969,099**	**73,976,481**	**92,091,887**	**66,178,474**	**70.10**	**-28.14**
CENTRAL/EASTERN EUROPE	**24,974,882**	**33,738,278**	**20,299,965**	**31,264,097**	**26,496,576**	**28.07**	**-15.25**
Armenia	64,241	71,008	27,741	45,880	43,909	0.05	-4.30
Azerbaijan	27,527	25,061	21,582	19,471	15,814	0.02	-18.78
Bulgaria	138,967	129,931	70,745	56,546	32,895	0.03	-41.83
Czech Republic/Slovakia	1,843,756	2,441,086	1,435,309	1,270,117	204,177	0.22	-83.92
Estonia	263,617	223,861	157,134	377,449	200,873	0.21	-46.78
Georgia	27,762	58,858	35,334	78,229	45,818	0.05	-41.43
Hungary	523,747	557,788	477,576	494,559	226,441	0.24	-54.21
Kazakhstan	125,919	169,429	65,082	94,170	83,042	0.09	-11.82
Poland	3,721,789	4,546,312	3,248,698	4,415,632	1,751,208	1.85	-60.34
Romania	319,827	477,899	327,330	380,451	164,525	0.17	-56.76

Yearbook of Tourism Statistics, Data 2009 – 2013, 2015 Edition

EGYPT

5. Overnight stays of non-resident tourists in hotels and similar establishments, by nationality

	2009	2010	2011	2012	2013	Market share 2013	% Change 2013-2012
Russian Federation	17,917,730	25,037,045	14,433,434	24,031,593	23,727,874	25.13	-1.26
NORTHERN EUROPE	**18,306,200**	**21,001,596**	**16,302,687**	**17,645,754**	**12,727,270**	**13.48**	**-27.87**
Denmark	1,129,413	1,469,239	1,266,824	1,586,174	1,083,005	1.15	-31.72
Finland	558,535	914,589	564,362	525,726	336,596	0.36	-35.98
Iceland	6,781	9,396	6,719	5,257	4,265	0.00	-18.87
Ireland	337,774	332,812	258,976	232,368	158,314	0.17	-31.87
Norway	733,639	1,062,004	939,160	1,015,542	484,111	0.51	-52.33
Sweden	1,746,785	2,315,656	1,809,540	1,733,804	1,182,476	1.25	-31.80
United Kingdom	13,793,273	14,897,900	11,457,106	12,546,883	9,478,503	10.04	-24.46
SOUTHERN EUROPE	**11,778,286**	**12,945,224**	**7,393,784**	**9,166,151**	**5,399,800**	**5.72**	**-41.09**
Albania	58,796	49,028	43,332	27,301	9,826	0.01	-64.01
Croatia	127,828	117,065	83,720	103,152	50,416	0.05	-51.12
Greece	345,479	400,846	228,658	238,808	138,966	0.15	-41.81
Italy	9,307,804	9,972,492	6,007,113	7,757,406	4,708,426	4.99	-39.30
Malta	21,774	31,145	16,257	21,325	9,942	0.01	-53.38
Portugal	172,143	196,867	112,236	114,527	47,480	0.05	-58.54
Serbia and Montenegro	212,665	401,660	310,538	235,324	86,116	0.09	-63.41
Slovenia	202,543	229,338	118,547	228,279	137,733	0.15	-39.66
Spain	1,329,254	1,546,783	473,383	440,029	210,895	0.22	-52.07
WESTERN EUROPE	**28,474,255**	**30,490,671**	**24,299,933**	**27,822,806**	**16,097,934**	**17.05**	**-42.14**
Austria	2,451,865	2,778,529	2,545,486	2,163,113	1,401,678	1.48	-35.20
Belgium	1,951,145	2,005,681	1,665,382	1,788,216	938,226	0.99	-47.53
France	5,603,877	5,253,060	3,484,272	3,110,938	1,571,799	1.66	-49.48
Germany	13,578,690	14,920,653	11,982,252	15,443,700	9,200,052	9.74	-40.43
Luxembourg	90,078	88,874	44,246	64,211	28,240	0.03	-56.02
Monaco	963	1,486	322		35	0.00	
Netherlands	2,930,926	3,471,090	2,921,817	3,422,938	1,864,277	1.97	-45.54
Switzerland	1,866,711	1,971,298	1,656,156	1,829,690	1,093,627	1.16	-40.23
EAST MEDITERRANEAN EUROPE	**1,564,214**	**1,862,701**	**1,554,914**	**1,720,688**	**1,367,004**	**1.45**	**-20.55**
Cyprus	72,403	77,869	55,205	47,350	24,671	0.03	-47.90
Israel	1,068,808	1,168,750	1,069,937	1,178,908	870,087	0.92	-26.20
Turkey	423,003	616,082	429,772	494,430	472,246	0.50	-4.49
OTHER EUROPE	**4,233,556**	**2,930,629**	**4,125,198**	**4,472,391**	**4,089,890**	**4.33**	**-8.55**
Other countries of Europe	4,233,556	2,930,629	4,125,198	4,472,391	4,089,890	4.33	-8.55
MIDDLE EAST	**20,833,755**	**24,313,983**	**25,593,272**	**31,293,260**	**19,801,469**	**20.97**	**-36.72**
Bahrain	308,319	310,250	191,067	245,897	175,867	0.19	-28.48
Iraq	490,934	538,607	750,661	594,621	430,015	0.46	-27.68
Jordan	1,669,592	1,936,773	2,535,977	2,693,269	1,831,201	1.94	-32.01
Kuwait	2,158,996	2,126,279	1,111,225	1,926,926	1,177,409	1.25	-38.90
Lebanon	685,059	722,037	735,614	1,051,545	560,878	0.59	-46.66
Libya	5,194,416	6,151,782	8,351,661	8,259,890	4,362,609	4.62	-47.18
Oman	306,367	320,584	251,165	244,457	170,335	0.18	-30.32
Palestine	1,254,741	2,555,718	3,685,800	3,794,361	2,626,519	2.78	-30.78
Qatar	329,682	369,349	270,589	592,592	444,548	0.47	-24.98
Saudi Arabia	4,846,004	5,236,041	3,901,955	5,404,566	3,068,322	3.25	-43.23
Syrian Arab Republic	1,180,034	1,384,272	1,602,653	3,468,166	3,087,310	3.27	-10.98
United Arab Emirates	751,068	778,397	321,717	377,160	244,541	0.26	-35.16
Yemen	1,658,543	1,883,894	1,883,188	2,639,810	1,621,915	1.72	-38.56
SOUTH ASIA	**1,006,483**	**1,248,102**	**1,056,534**	**1,177,490**	**499,973**	**0.53**	**-57.54**
Afghanistan	12,784	14,414	7,718	24,358	10,784	0.01	-55.73
Bangladesh	53,998	41,861	128,775	58,214	17,243	0.02	-70.38
India	698,893	929,390	711,653	892,304	375,221	0.40	-57.95
Iran, Islamic Republic of	12,631	14,620	5,672	22,646	6,637	0.01	-70.69
Maldives	1,864	1,885	2,033	173	392	0.00	126.59
Nepal	16,489	21,112	17,423	9,953	5,911	0.01	-40.61
Pakistan	145,826	152,900	139,212	126,841	65,475	0.07	-48.38
Sri Lanka	63,998	71,920	44,048	43,001	18,310	0.02	-57.42
NOT SPECIFIED	**372,344**	**414,857**	**213,918**	**297,128**	**106,212**	**0.11**	**-64.25**
Other countries of the World	372,344	414,857	213,918	297,128	106,212	0.11	-64.25

215

EL SALVADOR

1. Arrivals of non-resident tourists at national borders, by nationality

	2009	2010	2011	2012	2013	Market share 2013	% Change 2013-2012
TOTAL	1,090,926	1,149,562	1,184,497	1,254,724	1,282,793	100.00	2.24
AFRICA	91	172	488	883	731	0.06	-17.21
SOUTHERN AFRICA	11	156	120	46	55	0.00	19.57
South Africa	11	156	120	46	55	0.00	19.57
OTHER AFRICA	80	16	368	837	676	0.05	-19.24
Other countries of Africa	80	16	368	837	676	0.05	-19.24
AMERICAS	1,066,917	1,122,757	1,139,772	1,219,748	1,241,681	96.80	1.80
CARIBBEAN	2,452	2,602	3,086	3,078	4,590	0.36	49.12
Cuba	596	861	580	594	1,101	0.09	85.35
Dominican Republic	1,321	1,292	1,847	1,475	2,689	0.21	82.31
Haiti	95	95	110	87	133	0.01	52.87
Jamaica	162	119	154	162	236	0.02	45.68
Trinidad and Tobago	66	156	152	239	146	0.01	-38.91
Other countries of the Caribbean	212	79	243	521	285	0.02	-45.30
CENTRAL AMERICA	673,324	739,843	734,796	740,698	708,542	55.23	-4.34
Belize	1,611	2,508	1,317	2,284	1,374	0.11	-39.84
Costa Rica	17,714	18,443	20,300	20,306	25,150	1.96	23.86
Guatemala	462,944	518,957	535,245	537,612	465,055	36.25	-13.50
Honduras	138,104	145,868	126,446	136,451	171,763	13.39	25.88
Nicaragua	42,844	43,488	40,755	32,566	32,937	2.57	1.14
Panama	10,107	10,579	10,733	11,479	12,263	0.96	6.83
NORTH AMERICA	371,280	356,608	368,641	443,075	482,211	37.59	8.83
Canada	26,333	20,432	28,205	30,216	31,911	2.49	5.61
Mexico	17,633	17,607	19,699	15,950	27,489	2.14	72.34
United States of America	327,314	318,569	320,737	396,909	422,811	32.96	6.53
SOUTH AMERICA	19,861	23,704	33,249	32,897	46,338	3.61	40.86
Argentina	2,673	2,501	3,727	2,524	2,950	0.23	16.88
Bolivia	409	401	562	473	986	0.08	108.46
Brazil	3,613	4,180	4,816	4,099	4,974	0.39	21.35
Chile	1,511	2,090	2,194	1,717	1,816	0.14	5.77
Colombia	5,957	7,698	12,062	14,913	17,428	1.36	16.86
Ecuador	1,016	1,108	1,706	2,056	4,135	0.32	101.12
Paraguay	243	322	458	278	326	0.03	17.27
Peru	1,914	2,269	4,334	4,149	8,758	0.68	111.09
Uruguay	69	1,183	680	588	589	0.05	0.17
Venezuela	501	1,871	2,656	2,085	4,324	0.34	107.39
Other countries of South America	1,955	81	54	15	52	0.00	246.67
EAST ASIA AND THE PACIFIC	5,068	6,750	9,858	8,001	7,988	0.62	-0.16
NORTH-EAST ASIA	1,845	4,011	5,823	4,380	4,036	0.31	-7.85
China	704	2,276	1,527	1,452	2,226	0.17	53.31
Japan	863	839	3,184	2,354	1,183	0.09	-49.75
Korea, Republic of	278	896	1,112	574	627	0.05	9.23
AUSTRALASIA	1,803	1,784	2,764	2,337	2,180	0.17	-6.72
Australia	1,706	1,745	2,508	1,989	1,885	0.15	-5.23
New Zealand	97	39	256	348	295	0.02	-15.23
OTHER EAST ASIA AND THE PACIFIC	1,420	955	1,271	1,284	1,772	0.14	38.01
Other countries of Asia	1,323	916	1,221	1,144	1,662	0.13	45.28
Other countries of Oceania	97	39	50	140	110	0.01	-21.43
EUROPE	18,842	19,879	34,351	26,068	32,345	2.52	24.08
CENTRAL/EASTERN EUROPE	900	1,004	347	133	623	0.05	368.42
Czech Republic/Slovakia	677	877	250	72	491	0.04	581.94
Poland	223	127	97	61	132	0.01	116.39
NORTHERN EUROPE	3,145	2,238	3,921	3,498	3,959	0.31	13.18
Denmark	286	284	275	267	287	0.02	7.49
Finland	105	68	145	139	154	0.01	10.79
Iceland	539	22	91	18	21	0.00	16.67
Ireland	421	407	341	274	232	0.02	-15.33
Norway	135	161	197	257	321	0.03	24.90
Sweden	632	537	953	904	974	0.08	7.74

Yearbook of Tourism Statistics, Data 2009 – 2013, 2015 Edition

EL SALVADOR

1. Arrivals of non-resident tourists at national borders, by nationality

	2009	2010	2011	2012	2013	Market share 2013	% Change 2013-2012
United Kingdom	1,027	759	1,919	1,639	1,970	0.15	20.20
SOUTHERN EUROPE	**8,575**	**8,462**	**16,174**	**12,525**	**11,891**	**0.93**	**-5.06**
Greece	109	46	61	52	83	0.01	59.62
Italy	2,843	2,475	5,228	3,611	3,582	0.28	-0.80
Portugal	85	86	265	238	438	0.03	84.03
Spain	5,496	5,843	10,620	8,624	7,788	0.61	-9.69
Yugoslavia, SFR (former)	42	12					
WESTERN EUROPE	**5,401**	**5,233**	**11,129**	**7,961**	**11,585**	**0.90**	**45.52**
Austria	185	146	365	207	206	0.02	-0.48
Belgium	260	365	471	392	456	0.04	16.33
France	1,780	1,332	3,023	2,239	3,456	0.27	54.35
Germany	1,968	2,020	4,993	3,265	5,440	0.42	66.62
Netherlands	419	589	1,368	1,051	827	0.06	-21.31
Switzerland	789	781	909	807	1,200	0.09	48.70
EAST MEDITERRANEAN EUROPE	**376**	**477**	**460**	**324**	**429**	**0.03**	**32.41**
Israel	376	477	460	324	429	0.03	32.41
OTHER EUROPE	**445**	**2,465**	**2,320**	**1,627**	**3,858**	**0.30**	**137.12**
Other countries of Europe	445	2,465	2,320	1,627	3,858	0.30	137.12
MIDDLE EAST	**8**	**4**	**28**	**24**	**48**	**0.00**	**100.00**
Egypt	8	4	28	24	48	0.00	100.00

Yearbook of Tourism Statistics, Data 2009 – 2013, 2015 Edition

EL SALVADOR

3. Arrivals of non-resident tourists in hotels and similar establishments, by nationality

	2009	2010	2011	2012	2013	Market share 2013	% Change 2013-2012
TOTAL	461,436	595,281	642,280	599,559	615,754	100.00	2.70
AFRICA	48	70	202	371	540	0.09	45.55
SOUTHERN AFRICA	48	70	47	20	41	0.01	105.00
South Africa	48	70	47	20	41	0.01	105.00
OTHER AFRICA			155	351	499	0.08	42.17
Other countries of Africa			155	351	499	0.08	42.17
AMERICAS	451,021	586,178	624,801	585,268	585,441	95.08	0.03
CARIBBEAN	1,299	1,057	1,691	1,188	1,248	0.20	5.05
Cuba	316	350	318	229	299	0.05	30.57
Dominican Republic	700	525	1,013	569	731	0.12	28.47
Jamaica	50	39	84	63	64	0.01	1.59
Trinidad and Tobago	86	48	83	92	40	0.01	-56.52
Other countries of the Caribbean	147	95	193	235	114	0.02	-51.49
CENTRAL AMERICA	316,414	457,164	504,219	492,983	428,922	69.66	-12.99
Belize	596	676	722	881	374	0.06	-57.55
Costa Rica	6,554	4,970	11,132	7,835	6,838	1.11	-12.72
Guatemala	241,194	372,871	416,082	414,588	351,162	57.03	-15.30
Honduras	44,193	48,064	41,991	44,752	47,242	7.67	5.56
Nicaragua	20,137	27,732	28,406	20,498	19,972	3.24	-2.57
Panama	3,740	2,851	5,886	4,429	3,334	0.54	-24.72
NORTH AMERICA	119,173	115,975	99,466	70,153	129,277	20.99	84.28
Canada	8,690	6,835	11,022	12,285	4,180	0.68	-65.97
Mexico	2,469	2,579	11,403	4,609	12,512	2.03	171.47
United States of America	108,014	106,561	77,041	53,259	112,585	18.28	111.39
SOUTH AMERICA	7,861	7,248	13,308	15,072	18,770	3.05	24.54
Argentina	1,902	1,264	2,177	1,608	1,655	0.27	2.92
Colombia	4,240	3,891	7,047	9,494	9,776	1.59	2.97
Peru	1,362	1,147	2,532	2,642	4,913	0.80	85.96
Venezuela	357	946	1,552	1,328	2,426	0.39	82.68
OTHER AMERICAS	6,274	4,734	6,117	5,872	7,224	1.17	23.02
Other countries of the Americas	6,274	4,734	6,117	5,872	7,224	1.17	23.02
EAST ASIA AND THE PACIFIC	2,537	2,379	3,852	3,276	5,574	0.91	70.15
NORTH-EAST ASIA	830	1,266	1,841	1,549	2,514	0.41	62.30
China	373	925	597	591	1,642	0.27	177.83
Japan	457	341	1,244	958	872	0.14	-8.98
AUSTRALASIA	955	725	1,080	951	1,607	0.26	68.98
Australia	904	709	980	809	1,390	0.23	71.82
New Zealand	51	16	100	142	217	0.04	52.82
OTHER EAST ASIA AND THE PACIFIC	752	388	931	776	1,453	0.24	87.24
Other countries of Asia	701	372	911	716	1,372	0.22	91.62
Other countries of Oceania	51	16	20	60	81	0.01	35.00
EUROPE	7,830	6,652	13,423	10,633	24,164	3.92	127.25
NORTHERN EUROPE	767	474	883	779	1,623	0.26	108.34
Ireland	223	165	133	112	171	0.03	52.68
United Kingdom	544	309	750	667	1,452	0.24	117.69
SOUTHERN EUROPE	4,420	3,381	6,193	4,977	8,384	1.36	68.45
Italy	1,507	1,006	2,043	1,469	2,641	0.43	79.78
Spain	2,913	2,375	4,150	3,508	5,743	0.93	63.71
WESTERN EUROPE	2,208	1,601	3,667	2,667	7,169	1.16	168.80
France	943	541	1,181	911	2,548	0.41	179.69
Germany	1,043	821	1,951	1,328	4,011	0.65	202.03
Netherlands	222	239	535	428	610	0.10	42.52
EAST MEDITERRANEAN EUROPE	199	194	180	133	316	0.05	137.59
Israel	199	194	180	133	316	0.05	137.59
OTHER EUROPE	236	1,002	2,500	2,077	6,672	1.08	221.23
Other countries of Europe	236	1,002	2,500	2,077	6,672	1.08	221.23
MIDDLE EAST		2	2	11	35	0.01	218.18
Egypt		2	2	11	35	0.01	218.18

218

EL SALVADOR

5. Overnight stays of non-resident tourists in hotels and similar establishments, by nationality

	2009	2010	2011	2012	2013	Market share 2013	% Change 2013-2012
TOTAL	2,741,223	2,815,521	2,694,470	2,367,753	2,864,233	100.00	20.97
AFRICA			1,803	3,650	5,573	0.19	52.68
OTHER AFRICA			1,803	3,650	5,573	0.19	52.68
All countries of Africa			1,803	3,650	5,573	0.19	52.68
AMERICAS	2,667,294	2,767,057	2,538,226	2,231,342	2,570,182	89.73	15.19
CARIBBEAN	6,130	6,505	14,046	12,377	12,854	0.45	3.85
All countries of the Caribbean	6,130	6,505	14,046	12,377	12,854	0.45	3.85
CENTRAL AMERICA	1,683,310	1,809,771	1,390,387	1,276,372	1,071,128	37.40	-16.08
Belize	4,029	6,270	5,994	9,183	3,847	0.13	-58.11
Costa Rica	44,285	26,448	92,393	81,637	70,429	2.46	-13.73
Guatemala	1,157,361	1,297,393	954,245	892,586	737,440	25.75	-17.38
Honduras	345,260	364,670	152,449	139,962	151,175	5.28	8.01
Nicaragua	107,110	108,720	136,456	106,853	73,897	2.58	-30.84
Panama	25,265	6,270	48,850	46,151	34,340	1.20	-25.59
NORTH AMERICA	928,202	891,521	932,237	734,811	1,231,463	42.99	67.59
Canada	65,834	51,080	98,532	117,258	40,546	1.42	-65.42
Mexico	44,084	44,018	98,421	43,859	87,587	3.06	99.70
United States of America	818,284	796,423	735,284	573,694	1,103,330	38.52	92.32
SOUTH AMERICA	49,652	59,260	201,556	207,782	254,737	8.89	22.60
All countries of South America	49,652	59,260	201,556	207,782	254,737	8.89	22.60
EAST ASIA AND THE PACIFIC	8,163	10,579	36,045	32,540	57,141	1.99	75.60
OTHER EAST ASIA AND THE PACIFIC	8,163	10,579	36,045	32,540	57,141	1.99	75.60
All countries East Asia/Pacific	8,163	10,579	36,045	32,540	57,141	1.99	75.60
EUROPE	65,766	37,885	118,396	100,221	231,337	8.08	130.83
SOUTHERN EUROPE	13,740	26,294	37,100	33,482	55,703	1.94	66.37
Spain	13,740	26,294	37,100	33,482	55,703	1.94	66.37
WESTERN EUROPE	4,921	9,090	17,443	12,679	38,910	1.36	206.89
Germany	4,921	9,090	17,443	12,679	38,910	1.36	206.89
OTHER EUROPE	47,105	2,501	63,853	54,060	136,724	4.77	152.91
Other countries of Europe	47,105	2,501	63,853	54,060	136,724	4.77	152.91

Yearbook of Tourism Statistics, Data 2009 – 2013, 2015 Edition

EL SALVADOR

6. Overnight stays of non-resident tourists in all types of accommodation establishments, by nationality

	2009	2010	2011	2012	2013	Market share 2013	% Change 2013-2012
TOTAL	5,844,349	6,045,433	6,404,634	7,516,856	7,593,299	100.00	1.02
AFRICA	683	1,118	4,613	8,651	7,558	0.10	-12.63
OTHER AFRICA	683	1,118	4,613	8,651	7,558	0.10	-12.63
All countries of Africa	683	1,118	4,613	8,651	7,558	0.10	-12.63
AMERICAS	5,712,853	5,932,413	6,004,796	7,183,025	7,194,511	94.75	0.16
CARIBBEAN	18,390	16,913	25,614	32,078	47,278	0.62	47.38
All countries of the Caribbean	18,390	16,913	25,614	32,078	47,278	0.62	47.38
CENTRAL AMERICA	2,760,903	3,443,471	2,150,875	2,108,974	2,047,620	26.97	-2.91
Belize	12,086	16,302	10,931	23,801	14,151	0.19	-40.54
Costa Rica	132,856	119,880	168,490	211,588	259,041	3.41	22.43
Guatemala	1,481,422	2,335,307	1,227,534	1,157,452	976,616	12.86	-15.62
Honduras	925,889	656,406	459,061	426,756	549,641	7.24	28.80
Nicaragua	132,856	195,696	195,775	169,763	121,866	1.60	-28.21
Panama	75,794	119,880	89,084	119,614	126,305	1.66	5.59
NORTH AMERICA	2,784,604	2,317,953	3,483,323	4,715,615	4,645,508	61.18	-1.49
Canada	197,501	132,808	252,150	288,407	309,539	4.08	7.33
Mexico	132,251	114,446	170,025	151,775	192,423	2.53	26.78
United States of America	2,454,852	2,070,699	3,061,148	4,275,433	4,143,546	54.57	-3.08
SOUTH AMERICA	148,956	154,076	344,984	326,358	454,105	5.98	39.14
All countries of South America	148,956	154,076	344,984	326,358	454,105	5.98	39.14
EAST ASIA AND THE PACIFIC	62,038	32,026	92,242	79,461	77,493	1.02	-2.48
OTHER EAST ASIA AND THE PACIFIC	62,038	32,026	92,242	79,461	77,493	1.02	-2.48
All countries East Asia/Pacific	62,038	32,026	92,242	79,461	77,493	1.02	-2.48
EUROPE	68,775	79,876	302,983	245,719	313,737	4.13	27.68
SOUTHERN EUROPE	41,219	37,980	94,942	82,319	75,544	0.99	-8.23
Spain	41,219	37,980	94,942	82,319	75,544	0.99	-8.23
WESTERN EUROPE	14,763	30,300	44,637	31,167	52,769	0.69	69.31
Germany	14,763	30,300	44,637	31,167	52,769	0.69	69.31
OTHER EUROPE	12,793	11,596	163,404	132,233	185,424	2.44	40.23
Other countries of Europe	12,793	11,596	163,404	132,233	185,424	2.44	40.23

Yearbook of Tourism Statistics, Data 2009 – 2013, 2015 Edition

ERITREA

2. Arrivals of non-resident visitors at national borders, by nationality

	2009	2010	2011	2012	2013	Market share 2013	% Change 2013-2012
TOTAL	**79,334**	**83,947**	**107,090**				
AFRICA	**6,825**	**7,854**	**21,319**				
EAST AFRICA	**466**	**804**	**662**				
Ethiopia	32	68	49				
Kenya	234	247	343				
Malawi	11	15	7				
Mozambique	3	3	8				
Somalia	44	75	30				
Uganda	22	67	35				
United Republic of Tanzania	14	14	15				
Zambia	68	214	102				
Zimbabwe	38	101	73				
NORTH AFRICA	**5,866**	**6,220**	**19,653**				
Sudan	5,866	6,220	19,653				
SOUTHERN AFRICA	**157**	**460**	**471**				
Botswana	2	6	3				
Namibia	2	4	16				
South Africa	153	450	452				
OTHER AFRICA	**336**	**370**	**533**				
Other countries of Africa	336	370	533				
AMERICAS	**775**	**1,149**	**1,314**				
NORTH AMERICA	**710**	**1,085**	**1,269**				
Canada	199	347	438				
United States of America	511	738	831				
OTHER AMERICAS	**65**	**64**	**45**				
Other countries of the Americas	65	64	45				
EAST ASIA AND THE PACIFIC	**1,403**	**1,436**	**1,698**				
NORTH-EAST ASIA	**858**	**659**	**1,010**				
China	671	594	871				
Japan	151	60	78				
Korea, Republic of	36	5	61				
SOUTH-EAST ASIA	**211**	**272**	**179**				
Indonesia	27	34	48				
Malaysia	2	5	12				
Philippines	182	233	117				
Singapore			2				
AUSTRALASIA	**196**	**215**	**322**				
Australia	183	186	291				
New Zealand	13	29	31				
OTHER EAST ASIA AND THE PACIFIC	**138**	**290**	**187**				
Other countries of Asia	138	290	187				
EUROPE	**5,064**	**4,869**	**5,169**				
NORTHERN EUROPE	**1,249**	**1,143**	**1,324**				
United Kingdom	843	703	968				
Scandinavia	406	440	356				
SOUTHERN EUROPE	**1,944**	**1,754**	**1,694**				
Italy	1,944	1,754	1,694				
WESTERN EUROPE	**1,373**	**1,609**	**1,610**				
France	372	381	260				
Germany	775	880	1,004				
Netherlands	78	151	159				
Switzerland	75	104	138				
Benelux	49	41	47				
Other countries of Western Europe	24	52	2				
EAST MEDITERRANEAN EUROPE	**25**	**19**	**35**				
Israel	25	19	35				
OTHER EUROPE	**473**	**344**	**506**				
Other countries of Europe	473	344	506				

Yearbook of Tourism Statistics, Data 2009 – 2013, 2015 Edition

ERITREA

2. Arrivals of non-resident visitors at national borders, by nationality

	2009	2010	2011	2012	2013	Market share 2013	% Change 2013-2012
MIDDLE EAST	**1,343**	**1,326**	**1,224**				
Egypt	262	282	304				
Saudi Arabia	423	261	392				
Yemen	275	473	299				
Other countries of Middle East	383	310	229				
SOUTH ASIA	**718**	**730**	**577**				
India	718	730	577				
NOT SPECIFIED	**63,206**	**66,583**	**75,789**				
Other countries of the World	41						
Nationals Residing Abroad	63,165	66,583	75,789				

Yearbook of Tourism Statistics, Data 2009 – 2013, 2015 Edition

ESTONIA

3. Arrivals of non-resident tourists in hotels and similar establishments, by country of residence

	2009	2010	2011	2012	2013	Market share 2013	% Change 2013-2012
TOTAL	1,307,548	1,487,497	1,702,592	1,746,733	1,798,392	100.00	2.96
AFRICA	880	1,155	1,946	1,881	1,462	0.08	-22.28
SOUTHERN AFRICA	219	230	404	411	351	0.02	-14.60
South Africa	219	230	404	411	351	0.02	-14.60
OTHER AFRICA	661	925	1,542	1,470	1,111	0.06	-24.42
Other countries of Africa	661	925	1,542	1,470	1,111	0.06	-24.42
AMERICAS	20,387	24,996	29,728	35,682	33,117	1.84	-7.19
NORTH AMERICA	18,509	21,748	25,918	31,101	28,277	1.57	-9.08
Canada	3,876	2,807	3,725	3,801	3,178	0.18	-16.39
United States of America	14,633	18,941	22,193	27,300	25,099	1.40	-8.06
SOUTH AMERICA	1,034	1,833	1,700	2,640	2,545	0.14	-3.60
Brazil	1,034	1,833	1,700	2,640	2,545	0.14	-3.60
OTHER AMERICAS	844	1,415	2,110	1,941	2,295	0.13	18.24
Other countries of the Americas	844	1,415	2,110	1,941	2,295	0.13	18.24
EAST ASIA AND THE PACIFIC	18,164	19,943	26,416	32,121	39,173	2.18	21.95
NORTH-EAST ASIA	10,016	11,464	15,534	17,552	23,221	1.29	32.30
China	1,888	2,642	5,185	5,426	6,893	0.38	27.04
Japan	6,973	6,988	8,263	8,138	9,843	0.55	20.95
Korea, Republic of	1,155	1,834	2,086	3,988	6,485	0.36	62.61
AUSTRALASIA	3,046	3,127	4,383	3,917	4,376	0.24	11.72
Australia	3,046	3,127	4,383	3,917	4,376	0.24	11.72
OTHER EAST ASIA AND THE PACIFIC	5,102	5,352	6,499	10,652	11,576	0.64	8.67
Other countries of Asia	4,487	4,708	5,696	9,837	10,694	0.59	8.71
Other countries of Oceania	615	644	803	815	882	0.05	8.22
EUROPE	1,264,256	1,429,858	1,632,102	1,663,515	1,717,231	95.49	3.23
CENTRAL/EASTERN EUROPE	206,269	261,785	353,824	422,271	460,940	25.63	9.16
Bulgaria	916	1,501	1,559	1,522	1,346	0.07	-11.56
Czech Republic	4,385	3,855	4,588	5,385	4,927	0.27	-8.51
Hungary	2,015	2,447	3,318	3,073	3,331	0.19	8.40
Latvia	59,849	63,625	74,751	86,502	89,651	4.99	3.64
Lithuania	29,077	29,848	41,543	41,699	44,726	2.49	7.26
Poland	15,001	17,491	24,807	22,921	23,055	1.28	0.58
Romania	1,128	1,257	2,213	2,140	2,325	0.13	8.64
Russian Federation	89,429	135,665	192,456	247,975	280,297	15.59	13.03
Slovakia	860	1,393	1,469	2,441	1,774	0.10	-27.32
Ukraine	3,609	4,703	7,120	8,613	9,508	0.53	10.39
NORTHERN EUROPE	889,818	975,315	1,030,368	986,663	1,019,201	56.67	3.30
Denmark	11,354	10,341	12,821	13,395	11,187	0.62	-16.48
Finland	730,011	810,711	812,998	796,851	858,802	47.75	7.77
Iceland	546	717	947	825	1,166	0.06	41.33
Ireland	2,297	1,986	7,185	4,585	2,734	0.15	-40.37
Norway	39,318	39,258	49,984	47,128	35,735	1.99	-24.17
Sweden	74,833	78,696	82,839	75,454	71,112	3.95	-5.75
United Kingdom	31,459	33,606	63,594	48,425	38,465	2.14	-20.57
SOUTHERN EUROPE	37,391	42,780	61,287	56,480	49,846	2.77	-11.75
Greece	2,240	3,319	2,613	2,425	1,931	0.11	-20.37
Italy	17,673	20,851	30,262	27,140	23,415	1.30	-13.73
Malta	212	258	247	345	373	0.02	8.12
Portugal	2,358	2,100	2,703	2,612	2,521	0.14	-3.48
Slovenia	787	1,149	1,126	1,475	1,384	0.08	-6.17
Spain	14,121	15,103	24,336	22,483	20,222	1.12	-10.06
WESTERN EUROPE	110,386	122,082	152,872	160,393	143,870	8.00	-10.30
Austria	6,078	4,819	7,131	7,472	5,408	0.30	-27.62
Belgium	5,460	5,760	8,502	7,424	6,797	0.38	-8.45
France	14,776	16,694	19,008	20,406	19,097	1.06	-6.41
Germany	68,236	77,447	94,082	99,395	90,521	5.03	-8.93
Luxembourg	814	878	964	1,369	950	0.05	-30.61
Netherlands	9,863	10,100	15,063	15,111	13,155	0.73	-12.94
Switzerland	5,159	6,384	8,122	9,216	7,942	0.44	-13.82

...nization (UNWTO)

Yearbook of Tourism Statistics, Data 2009 – 2013, 2015 Edition

ESTONIA

3. Arrivals of non-resident tourists in hotels and similar establishments, by country of residence

	2009	2010	2011	2012	2013	Market share 2013	% Change 2013-2012
EAST MEDITERRANEAN EUROPE	**2,834**	**3,567**	**4,861**	**5,420**	**5,605**	**0.31**	**3.41**
Cyprus	286	380	470	637	341	0.02	-46.47
Turkey	2,548	3,187	4,391	4,783	5,264	0.29	10.06
OTHER EUROPE	**17,558**	**24,329**	**28,890**	**32,288**	**37,769**	**2.10**	**16.98**
Other countries of Europe	17,558	24,329	28,890	32,288	37,769	2.10	16.98
NOT SPECIFIED	**3,861**	**11,545**	**12,400**	**13,534**	**7,409**	**0.41**	**-45.26**
Other countries of the World	3,861	11,545	12,400	13,534	7,409	0.41	-45.26

Yearbook of Tourism

ESTONIA

4. Arrivals of non-resident tourists in all types of accommodation establishments, by country of residence

	2009	2010	2011	2012	2013	Market share 2013	% Change 2013-2012
TOTAL	1,380,540	1,563,952	1,807,919	1,873,519	1,940,130	100.00	3.56
AFRICA	1,031	1,221	2,057	2,039	1,636	0.08	-19.76
SOUTHERN AFRICA	258	259	433	460	410	0.02	-10.87
South Africa	258	259	433	460	410	0.02	-10.87
OTHER AFRICA	773	962	1,624	1,579	1,226	0.06	-22.36
Other countries of Africa	773	962	1,624	1,579	1,226	0.06	-22.36
AMERICAS	23,023	27,213	32,454	39,608	36,980	1.91	-6.64
NORTH AMERICA	20,864	23,742	28,095	34,114	31,265	1.61	-8.35
Canada	4,580	3,239	4,271	4,513	3,823	0.20	-15.29
United States of America	16,284	20,503	23,824	29,601	27,442	1.41	-7.29
SOUTH AMERICA	1,162	1,899	1,985	3,167	2,975	0.15	-6.06
Brazil	1,162	1,899	1,985	3,167	2,975	0.15	-6.06
OTHER AMERICAS	997	1,572	2,374	2,327	2,740	0.14	17.75
Other countries of the Americas	997	1,572	2,374	2,327	2,740	0.14	17.75
EAST ASIA AND THE PACIFIC	20,210	21,687	29,348	36,364	44,166	2.28	21.46
NORTH-EAST ASIA	10,663	12,063	16,692	19,030	25,499	1.31	33.99
China	2,058	2,823	5,549	5,934	7,806	0.40	31.55
Japan	7,253	7,235	8,732	8,778	10,768	0.56	22.67
Korea, Republic of	1,352	2,005	2,411	4,318	6,925	0.36	60.38
AUSTRALASIA	3,849	3,695	5,472	5,516	5,981	0.31	8.43
Australia	3,849	3,695	5,472	5,516	5,981	0.31	8.43
OTHER EAST ASIA AND THE PACIFIC	5,698	5,929	7,184	11,818	12,686	0.65	7.34
Other countries of Asia	4,753	5,063	6,216	10,619	11,462	0.59	7.94
Other countries of Oceania	945	866	968	1,199	1,224	0.06	2.09
EUROPE	1,332,335	1,502,008	1,731,493	1,781,861	1,849,635	95.34	3.80
CENTRAL/EASTERN EUROPE	227,474	285,508	385,521	465,921	515,926	26.59	10.73
Bulgaria	1,005	1,625	1,668	1,640	1,499	0.08	-8.60
Czech Republic	5,232	4,550	5,669	6,474	6,184	0.32	-4.48
Hungary	2,306	2,800	3,694	3,540	3,871	0.20	9.35
Latvia	68,320	72,684	85,229	100,638	105,480	5.44	4.81
Lithuania	33,441	34,107	47,003	47,397	52,201	2.69	10.14
Poland	17,062	19,522	27,093	25,513	26,001	1.34	1.91
Romania	1,167	1,343	2,295	2,326	2,717	0.14	16.81
Russian Federation	93,947	141,964	203,204	266,192	304,644	15.70	14.45
Slovakia	978	1,643	1,860	2,812	2,148	0.11	-23.61
Ukraine	4,016	5,270	7,806	9,389	11,181	0.58	19.09
NORTHERN EUROPE	917,900	1,004,269	1,071,562	1,030,761	1,065,284	54.91	3.35
Denmark	12,036	11,140	13,902	14,091	11,900	0.61	-15.55
Finland	750,984	832,874	840,714	829,225	894,504	46.11	7.87
Iceland	588	761	994	890	1,222	0.06	37.30
Ireland	2,512	2,192	8,243	5,359	3,318	0.17	-38.09
Norway	40,915	40,414	51,510	48,479	36,918	1.90	-23.85
Sweden	77,470	81,196	86,287	78,412	74,313	3.83	-5.23
United Kingdom	33,395	35,692	69,912	54,305	43,109	2.22	-20.62
SOUTHERN EUROPE	42,462	48,332	69,540	64,727	57,422	2.96	-11.29
Albania	94	173	198	303	162	0.01	-46.53
Croatia	526	719	1,232	1,124	727	0.04	-35.32
Greece	2,337	3,447	2,711	2,586	2,082	0.11	-19.49
Italy	19,959	23,017	33,618	30,574	26,506	1.37	-13.31
Malta	248	315	314	403	417	0.02	3.47
Portugal	2,617	2,471	3,026	3,010	2,990	0.15	-0.66
Slovenia	974	1,330	1,335	1,724	1,612	0.08	-6.50
Spain	15,707	16,860	27,106	25,003	22,926	1.18	-8.31
WESTERN EUROPE	124,060	135,403	170,941	182,058	165,141	8.51	-9.29
Austria	6,859	5,473	7,841	8,293	6,297	0.32	-24.07
Belgium	6,077	6,418	9,197	8,312	7,855	0.40	-5.50
France	16,864	19,319	22,301	24,089	22,780	1.17	-5.43
Germany	75,966	84,454	103,559	111,251	101,596	5.24	-8.68
Luxembourg	890	902	992	1,469	1,042	0.05	-29.07

225

Yearbook of Tourism Statistics, Data 2009 – 2013, 2015 Edition

ESTONIA

4. Arrivals of non-resident tourists in all types of accommodation establishments, by country of residence

	2009	2010	2011	2012	2013	Market share 2013	% Change 2013-2012
Netherlands	11,595	11,713	17,968	18,279	16,358	0.84	-10.51
Switzerland	5,809	7,124	9,083	10,365	9,213	0.47	-11.11
EAST MEDITERRANEAN EUROPE	**3,071**	**3,974**	**5,208**	**5,820**	**6,174**	**0.32**	**6.08**
Cyprus	326	414	479	661	363	0.02	-45.08
Turkey	2,745	3,560	4,729	5,159	5,811	0.30	12.64
OTHER EUROPE	**17,368**	**24,522**	**28,721**	**32,574**	**39,688**	**2.05**	**21.84**
Other countries of Europe	17,368	24,522	28,721	32,574	39,688	2.05	21.84
NOT SPECIFIED	**3,941**	**11,823**	**12,567**	**13,647**	**7,713**	**0.40**	**-43.48**
Other countries of the World	3,941	11,823	12,567	13,647	7,713	0.40	-43.48

Yearbook of Tourism Statistics, Data 2009 – 2013, 2015 Edition

ESTONIA

5. Overnight stays of non-resident tourists in hotels and similar establishments, by country of residence

	2009	2010	2011	2012	2013	Market share 2013	% Change 2013-2012
TOTAL	2,555,011	3,002,781	3,478,042	3,498,683	3,536,875	100.00	1.09
AFRICA	1,944	2,787	3,816	3,732	3,515	0.10	-5.81
SOUTHERN AFRICA	455	539	657	762	701	0.02	-8.01
South Africa	455	539	657	762	701	0.02	-8.01
OTHER AFRICA	1,489	2,248	3,159	2,970	2,814	0.08	-5.25
Other countries of Africa	1,489	2,248	3,159	2,970	2,814	0.08	-5.25
AMERICAS	46,958	53,996	64,839	77,584	73,313	2.07	-5.51
NORTH AMERICA	43,039	46,752	56,528	68,670	63,570	1.80	-7.43
Canada	9,409	6,110	8,747	8,616	7,328	0.21	-14.95
United States of America	33,630	40,642	47,781	60,054	56,242	1.59	-6.35
SOUTH AMERICA	2,148	3,996	3,797	4,977	5,214	0.15	4.76
Brazil	2,148	3,996	3,797	4,977	5,214	0.15	4.76
OTHER AMERICAS	1,771	3,248	4,514	3,937	4,529	0.13	15.04
Other countries of the Americas	1,771	3,248	4,514	3,937	4,529	0.13	15.04
EAST ASIA AND THE PACIFIC	33,695	38,152	48,752	55,430	65,822	1.86	18.75
NORTH-EAST ASIA	17,464	20,238	26,527	27,823	36,152	1.02	29.94
China	3,548	4,665	8,469	8,694	11,354	0.32	30.60
Japan	12,363	12,677	14,855	14,169	17,045	0.48	20.30
Korea, Republic of	1,553	2,896	3,203	4,960	7,753	0.22	56.31
AUSTRALASIA	6,310	6,962	9,277	8,282	9,425	0.27	13.80
Australia	6,310	6,962	9,277	8,282	9,425	0.27	13.80
OTHER EAST ASIA AND THE PACIFIC	9,921	10,952	12,948	19,325	20,245	0.57	4.76
Other countries of Asia	8,682	9,276	11,136	17,708	18,280	0.52	3.23
Other countries of Oceania	1,239	1,676	1,812	1,617	1,965	0.06	21.52
EUROPE	2,464,562	2,888,022	3,335,568	3,335,327	3,380,843	95.59	1.36
CENTRAL/EASTERN EUROPE	394,986	522,252	715,840	832,558	921,812	26.06	10.72
Bulgaria	3,658	5,449	4,710	3,810	3,593	0.10	-5.70
Czech Republic	7,774	7,610	9,696	10,545	8,886	0.25	-15.73
Hungary	4,605	6,864	8,762	6,182	7,280	0.21	17.76
Latvia	88,626	97,436	111,767	126,751	130,555	3.69	3.00
Lithuania	45,612	45,987	65,522	66,625	72,873	2.06	9.38
Poland	26,625	30,640	43,913	42,329	48,862	1.38	15.43
Romania	2,496	3,484	4,934	5,065	6,189	0.17	22.19
Russian Federation	205,037	310,840	446,742	547,408	620,577	17.55	13.37
Slovakia	2,014	3,089	3,277	5,394	3,927	0.11	-27.20
Ukraine	8,539	10,853	16,517	18,449	19,070	0.54	3.37
NORTHERN EUROPE	1,727,616	1,978,864	2,107,122	1,997,289	1,974,404	55.82	-1.15
Denmark	23,626	21,523	25,159	25,620	22,098	0.62	-13.75
Finland	1,367,795	1,612,483	1,617,598	1,584,126	1,615,893	45.69	2.01
Iceland	1,355	1,985	2,357	1,942	2,957	0.08	52.27
Ireland	5,565	5,332	17,440	11,220	6,688	0.19	-40.39
Norway	104,416	99,161	118,550	107,236	88,276	2.50	-17.68
Sweden	152,235	162,442	171,475	153,484	151,069	4.27	-1.57
United Kingdom	72,624	75,938	154,543	113,661	87,423	2.47	-23.08
SOUTHERN EUROPE	80,023	95,793	134,896	119,365	114,389	3.23	-4.17
Greece	4,955	7,424	5,511	5,197	4,748	0.13	-8.64
Italy	39,458	47,414	68,573	58,965	52,989	1.50	-10.13
Malta	570	491	591	734	885	0.03	20.57
Portugal	5,269	5,809	5,631	5,568	4,965	0.14	-10.83
Slovenia	2,137	2,277	2,473	3,136	3,599	0.10	14.76
Spain	27,634	32,378	52,117	45,765	47,203	1.33	3.14
WESTERN EUROPE	221,861	240,615	313,537	315,767	283,000	8.00	-10.38
Austria	12,980	9,954	14,880	14,947	11,389	0.32	-23.80
Belgium	12,224	12,619	18,650	15,908	14,286	0.40	-10.20
France	30,104	34,230	37,789	39,885	39,189	1.11	-1.75
Germany	133,783	148,813	191,846	193,904	174,702	4.94	-9.90
Luxembourg	1,533	1,703	1,868	2,631	1,723	0.05	-34.51
Netherlands	21,130	21,167	32,482	31,359	26,552	0.75	-15.33
Switzerland	10,107	12,129	16,022	17,133	15,159	0.43	-11.52

227

Yearbook of Tourism Statistics, Data 2009 – 2013, 2015 Edition

ESTONIA

5. Overnight stays of non-resident tourists in hotels and similar establishments, by country of residence

	2009	2010	2011	2012	2013	Market share 2013	% Change 2013-2012
EAST MEDITERRANEAN EUROPE	**5,834**	**8,294**	**10,154**	**11,079**	**12,777**	**0.36**	**15.33**
Cyprus	602	1,064	1,338	1,384	873	0.02	-36.92
Turkey	5,232	7,230	8,816	9,695	11,904	0.34	22.78
OTHER EUROPE	**34,242**	**42,204**	**54,019**	**59,269**	**74,461**	**2.11**	**25.63**
Other countries of Europe	34,242	42,204	54,019	59,269	74,461	2.11	25.63
NOT SPECIFIED	**7,852**	**19,824**	**25,067**	**26,610**	**13,382**	**0.38**	**-49.71**
Other countries of the World	7,852	19,824	25,067	26,610	13,382	0.38	-49.71

Yearbook of Tourism Statistics, Data 2009 – 2013, 2015 E ...

ESTONIA

6. Overnight stays of non-resident tourists in all types of accommodation establishments, by country of residence

	2009	2010	2011	2012	2013	Market share 2013	% Change 2013-2012
TOTAL	2,740,696	3,203,721	3,748,865	3,823,039	3,909,326	100.00	2.26
AFRICA	2,309	2,910	4,214	4,622	4,361	0.11	-5.65
SOUTHERN AFRICA	544	596	761	946	942	0.02	-0.42
South Africa	544	596	761	946	942	0.02	-0.42
OTHER AFRICA	1,765	2,314	3,453	3,676	3,419	0.09	-6.99
Other countries of Africa	1,765	2,314	3,453	3,676	3,419	0.09	-6.99
AMERICAS	55,624	61,255	72,277	87,711	84,256	2.16	-3.94
NORTH AMERICA	51,103	53,582	62,703	77,177	72,625	1.86	-5.90
Canada	11,493	7,277	10,316	10,452	8,935	0.23	-14.51
United States of America	39,610	46,305	52,387	66,725	63,690	1.63	-4.55
SOUTH AMERICA	2,495	4,122	4,326	5,924	6,267	0.16	5.79
Brazil	2,495	4,122	4,326	5,924	6,267	0.16	5.79
OTHER AMERICAS	2,026	3,551	5,248	4,610	5,364	0.14	16.36
Other countries of the Americas	2,026	3,551	5,248	4,610	5,364	0.14	16.36
EAST ASIA AND THE PACIFIC	39,571	43,893	57,269	66,701	80,126	2.05	20.13
NORTH-EAST ASIA	19,174	21,520	29,129	31,870	43,437	1.11	36.29
China	4,268	5,057	9,429	10,337	15,339	0.39	48.39
Japan	12,998	13,303	15,967	15,723	19,272	0.49	22.57
Korea, Republic of	1,908	3,160	3,733	5,810	8,826	0.23	51.91
AUSTRALASIA	8,643	8,390	11,982	12,100	13,133	0.34	8.54
Australia	8,643	8,390	11,982	12,100	13,133	0.34	8.54
OTHER EAST ASIA AND THE PACIFIC	11,754	13,983	16,158	22,731	23,556	0.60	3.63
Other countries of Asia	9,620	11,886	13,969	20,343	20,882	0.53	2.65
Other countries of Oceania	2,134	2,097	2,189	2,388	2,674	0.07	11.98
EUROPE	2,634,927	3,074,832	3,589,403	3,637,093	3,726,680	95.33	2.46
CENTRAL/EASTERN EUROPE	446,534	578,495	793,482	942,192	1,066,510	27.28	13.19
Bulgaria	4,578	5,856	5,470	4,552	3,981	0.10	-12.54
Czech Republic	10,008	9,768	12,488	20,886	16,890	0.43	-19.13
Hungary	5,426	8,079	10,136	8,429	10,280	0.26	21.96
Latvia	103,091	112,122	130,154	152,491	158,031	4.04	3.63
Lithuania	55,465	55,535	77,428	77,585	93,784	2.40	20.88
Poland	31,878	36,442	52,153	50,351	60,788	1.55	20.73
Romania	2,700	3,719	5,304	5,633	10,841	0.28	92.46
Russian Federation	220,945	330,276	475,905	593,783	679,343	17.38	14.41
Slovakia	2,499	4,143	5,172	6,985	6,150	0.16	-11.95
Ukraine	9,944	12,555	19,272	21,497	26,422	0.68	22.91
NORTHERN EUROPE	1,794,481	2,047,552	2,201,059	2,095,755	2,077,693	53.15	-0.86
Denmark	25,725	23,489	27,928	27,887	24,174	0.62	-13.31
Finland	1,416,113	1,664,139	1,677,119	1,651,965	1,691,035	43.26	2.37
Iceland	1,452	2,056	2,478	2,166	3,178	0.08	46.72
Ireland	6,170	5,893	19,820	13,177	8,300	0.21	-37.01
Norway	108,207	102,019	122,443	111,131	91,451	2.34	-17.71
Sweden	158,492	168,165	179,523	161,460	159,813	4.09	-1.02
United Kingdom	78,322	81,791	171,748	127,969	99,742	2.55	-22.06
SOUTHERN EUROPE	94,629	112,817	159,106	144,082	138,416	3.54	-3.93
Albania	299	370	666	578	447	0.01	-22.66
Croatia	1,420	1,667	2,346	2,140	2,509	0.06	17.24
Greece	5,293	7,876	5,761	6,081	5,928	0.15	-2.52
Italy	46,856	54,451	79,455	70,070	62,700	1.60	-10.52
Malta	637	621	710	853	962	0.02	12.78
Portugal	6,549	7,610	7,408	7,254	6,965	0.18	-3.98
Slovenia	2,486	2,853	3,233	3,962	4,272	0.11	7.82
Spain	31,089	37,369	59,527	53,144	54,633	1.40	2.80
WESTERN EUROPE	257,020	278,869	366,843	379,876	348,788	8.92	-8.18
Austria	14,684	12,862	17,612	17,672	15,306	0.39	-13.39
Belgium	14,258	14,678	20,445	18,162	16,539	0.42	-8.94
France	35,908	44,236	51,223	54,790	52,368	1.34	-4.42
Germany	154,260	167,508	218,698	227,959	210,955	5.40	-7.46
Luxembourg	1,680	1,758	1,923	2,897	1,844	0.05	-36.35

Yearbook of Tourism Statistics, Data 2009 – 2013, 2015 Edition

ESTONIA

6. Overnight stays of non-resident tourists in all types of accommodation establishments, by country of residence

	2009	2010	2011	2012	2013	Market share 2013	% Change 2013-2012
Netherlands	24,876	24,227	38,930	38,906	34,117	0.87	-12.31
Switzerland	11,354	13,600	18,012	19,490	17,659	0.45	-9.39
EAST MEDITERRANEAN EUROPE	**7,233**	**11,599**	**11,986**	**13,144**	**14,879**	**0.38**	**13.20**
Cyprus	901	1,331	1,384	1,648	931	0.02	-43.51
Turkey	6,332	10,268	10,602	11,496	13,948	0.36	21.33
OTHER EUROPE	**35,030**	**45,500**	**56,927**	**62,044**	**80,394**	**2.06**	**29.58**
Other countries of Europe	35,030	45,500	56,927	62,044	80,394	2.06	29.58
NOT SPECIFIED	**8,265**	**20,831**	**25,702**	**26,912**	**13,903**	**0.36**	**-48.34**
Other countries of the World	8,265	20,831	25,702	26,912	13,903	0.36	-48.34

230

ETHIOPIA

1. Arrivals of non-resident tourists at national borders, by country of residence

		2009	2010	2011	2012	2013	Market share 2013	% Change 2013-2012
TOTAL	(*)	427,286	468,305	523,438	596,641	681,249	100.00	14.18
AFRICA		150,102	140,076	160,311	168,909	216,786	31.82	28.34
EAST AFRICA		49,143	53,291	52,087	57,540	74,020	10.87	28.64
Djibouti		7,276	8,140	5,962	8,944	10,359	1.52	15.82
Eritrea		628	686	340	601	775	0.11	28.95
Kenya		15,532	15,322	19,904	20,279	23,521	3.45	15.99
Malawi		2,657	3,878	3,625	4,175	4,667	0.69	11.78
Rwanda		3,306	4,123	2,542	3,581	4,969	0.73	38.76
Somalia		4,020	4,543	1,842	2,388	6,218	0.91	160.39
Uganda		6,330	7,151	7,148	7,154	9,461	1.39	32.25
United Republic of Tanzania		5,797	5,756	5,464	5,965	8,118	1.19	36.09
Zimbabwe		3,597	3,692	5,260	4,453	5,932	0.87	33.21
CENTRAL AFRICA		5,423	5,190	3,966	3,587	7,069	1.04	97.07
Chad		5,423	5,190	3,966	3,587	7,069	1.04	97.07
NORTH AFRICA		12,515	12,979	17,922	16,814	20,313	2.98	20.81
Sudan		12,515	12,979	17,922	16,814	20,313	2.98	20.81
SOUTHERN AFRICA		8,427	10,541	13,433	11,470	14,512	2.13	26.52
South Africa		8,427	10,541	13,433	11,470	14,512	2.13	26.52
WEST AFRICA		18,811	17,938	23,034	23,859	29,692	4.36	24.45
Ghana		3,255	4,407	4,764	5,129	6,270	0.92	22.25
Mali		3,651	3,097	1,833	2,029	4,477	0.66	120.65
Nigeria		11,905	10,434	16,437	16,701	18,945	2.78	13.44
OTHER AFRICA		55,783	40,137	49,869	55,639	71,180	10.45	27.93
Other countries of Africa		55,783	40,137	49,869	55,639	71,180	10.45	27.93
AMERICAS		77,826	95,203	96,246	121,210	129,694	19.04	7.00
NORTH AMERICA		76,647	88,601	93,933	114,648	124,889	18.33	8.93
Canada		9,490	11,871	12,889	15,007	16,800	2.47	11.95
United States of America		67,157	76,730	81,044	99,641	108,089	15.87	8.48
OTHER AMERICAS		1,179	6,602	2,313	6,562	4,805	0.71	-26.78
Other countries of the Americas		1,179	6,602	2,313	6,562	4,805	0.71	-26.78
EAST ASIA AND THE PACIFIC		30,837	38,669	35,768	52,392	51,909	7.62	-0.92
NORTH-EAST ASIA		23,210	27,892	26,424	40,219	38,589	5.66	-4.05
China		18,968	22,722	20,197	35,383	31,688	4.65	-10.44
Japan		2,770	3,377	3,283	2,986	4,233	0.62	41.76
Korea, Republic of		1,472	1,793	2,944	1,850	2,668	0.39	44.22
SOUTH-EAST ASIA		1,213	2,045	1,406	1,553	2,047	0.30	31.81
Philippines		1,213	2,045	1,406	1,553	2,047	0.30	31.81
AUSTRALASIA		4,340	5,221	5,874	5,252	7,144	1.05	36.02
Australia		3,835	4,655	4,914	4,479	6,167	0.91	37.69
New Zealand		505	566	960	773	977	0.14	26.39
OTHER EAST ASIA AND THE PACIFIC		2,074	3,511	2,064	5,368	4,129	0.61	-23.08
Other countries of Asia		2,065	3,456	1,054	4,174	3,575	0.52	-14.35
Other countries of Oceania		9	55	1,010	1,194	554	0.08	-53.60
EUROPE		118,689	136,690	162,784	181,309	200,745	29.47	10.72
CENTRAL/EASTERN EUROPE		1,296	1,269	1,740	1,849	2,043	0.30	10.49
Russian Federation		1,296	1,269	1,740	1,849	2,043	0.30	10.49
NORTHERN EUROPE		37,504	43,295	49,252	52,841	61,576	9.04	16.53
Denmark		2,121	2,313	2,622	2,805	3,279	0.48	16.90
Finland		1,346	2,028	2,213	2,567	2,620	0.38	2.06
Norway		3,307	4,521	5,068	5,248	6,053	0.89	15.34
Sweden		7,576	9,343	10,404	10,616	12,644	1.86	19.10
United Kingdom		23,154	25,090	28,945	31,605	36,980	5.43	17.01
SOUTHERN EUROPE		15,393	17,641	20,129	23,696	25,737	3.78	8.61
Greece		925	1,113	965	1,075	1,524	0.22	41.77
Italy		14,468	16,528	19,164	22,621	24,213	3.55	7.04
WESTERN EUROPE		46,580	51,377	69,490	78,376	80,294	11.79	2.45
Austria		2,194	2,172	3,772	2,859	3,574	0.52	25.01
Belgium		4,073	4,506	6,998	5,366	6,814	1.00	26.98
France		12,000	12,635	16,517	20,970	20,290	2.98	-3.24

231

ETHIOPIA

1. Arrivals of non-resident tourists at national borders, by country of residence

	2009	2010	2011	2012	2013	Market share 2013	% Change 2013-2012
Germany	16,695	18,777	24,780	29,917	29,286	4.30	-2.11
Netherlands	7,864	8,863	9,052	10,613	12,496	1.83	17.74
Switzerland	3,754	4,424	8,371	8,651	7,834	1.15	-9.44
EAST MEDITERRANEAN EUROPE	**8,885**	**10,448**	**9,165**	**10,732**	**14,323**	**2.10**	**33.46**
Israel	6,608	7,484	6,369	7,754	10,705	1.57	38.06
Turkey	2,277	2,964	2,796	2,978	3,618	0.53	21.49
OTHER EUROPE	**9,031**	**12,660**	**13,008**	**13,815**	**16,772**	**2.46**	**21.40**
Other countries of Europe	9,031	12,660	13,008	13,815	16,772	2.46	21.40
MIDDLE EAST	**37,428**	**42,301**	**47,583**	**51,282**	**58,750**	**8.62**	**14.56**
Egypt	4,123	3,671	2,956	2,983	4,833	0.71	62.02
Kuwait	1,854	1,194	2,158	1,977	2,406	0.35	21.70
Saudi Arabia	10,456	14,019	18,891	18,435	19,495	2.86	5.75
United Arab Emirates	9,271	11,077	8,255	9,368	13,211	1.94	41.02
Yemen	6,918	6,847	5,340	6,172	9,326	1.37	51.10
Other countries of Middle East	4,806	5,493	9,983	12,347	9,479	1.39	-23.23
SOUTH ASIA	**12,404**	**15,366**	**20,746**	**21,539**	**23,365**	**3.43**	**8.48**
India	11,525	14,607	19,667	19,211	21,789	3.20	13.42
Pakistan	879	759	1,079	2,328	1,576	0.23	-32.30

Yearbook of Tourism Statistics, Data 2009 – 2013, 2015 Edition

FIJI

1. Arrivals of non-resident tourists at national borders, by country of residence

	2009	2010	2011	2012	2013	Market share 2013	% Change 2013-2012
TOTAL (*)	**542,186**	**631,868**	**675,050**	**660,590**	**657,706**	**100.00**	**-0.44**
AMERICAS	**65,044**	**66,092**	**69,188**	**69,904**	**68,437**	**10.41**	**-2.10**
NORTH AMERICA	**65,044**	**66,092**	**69,188**	**69,904**	**68,437**	**10.41**	**-2.10**
Canada	13,452	12,970	14,099	13,426	13,052	1.98	-2.79
United States of America	51,592	53,122	55,089	56,478	55,385	8.42	-1.94
EAST ASIA AND THE PACIFIC	**415,414**	**503,660**	**542,354**	**535,252**	**532,574**	**80.97**	**-0.50**
NORTH-EAST ASIA	**25,052**	**38,233**	**40,812**	**39,377**	**35,742**	**5.43**	**-9.23**
China	4,087	18,147	24,389	26,395	23,423	3.56	-11.26
Hong Kong, China		1,748	1,706	1,509	780	0.12	-48.31
Japan	14,975	12,011	9,616	7,069	7,314	1.11	3.47
Korea, Republic of	4,904	6,327	5,101	4,404	4,225	0.64	-4.06
Taiwan, Province of China	1,086						
AUSTRALASIA	**339,487**	**416,042**	**448,010**	**443,413**	**448,390**	**68.17**	**1.12**
Australia	248,589	318,185	344,829	337,291	340,151	51.72	0.85
New Zealand	90,898	97,857	103,181	106,122	108,239	16.46	1.99
OTHER EAST ASIA AND THE PACIFIC	**50,875**	**49,385**	**53,532**	**52,462**	**48,442**	**7.37**	**-7.66**
Other countries of Asia	15,797	10,187	14,709	13,576	8,992	1.37	-33.77
Other countries East Asia/Pacific	35,078	39,198	38,823	38,886	39,450	6.00	1.45
EUROPE	**55,139**	**53,901**	**56,408**	**46,403**	**46,114**	**7.01**	**-0.62**
NORTHERN EUROPE	**31,055**	**27,995**	**29,333**	**21,585**	**17,209**	**2.62**	**-20.27**
Denmark	1,345	1,025	1,139	1,065			
Finland	523	498	629	579			
Norway	1,509	1,126	1,599	1,442			
Sweden	1,465	1,533	1,912	1,423			
United Kingdom	26,213	23,813	24,054	17,076	17,209	2.62	0.78
SOUTHERN EUROPE	**4,374**	**4,834**	**4,600**	**4,315**			
Italy	3,255	3,582	3,252	2,994			
Spain	1,119	1,252	1,348	1,321			
WESTERN EUROPE	**17,188**	**18,014**	**18,736**	**16,715**			
Austria	1,012	1,102	1,065	1,031			
Belgium	343	403					
France	4,683	4,603	4,995	4,375			
Germany	7,223	7,710	8,319	7,841			
Netherlands	2,077	2,010	2,017	1,590			
Switzerland	1,850	2,186	2,340	1,878			
OTHER EUROPE	**2,522**	**3,058**	**3,739**	**3,788**	**28,905**	**4.39**	**663.07**
Other countries of Europe	2,522	3,058	3,739	3,788	28,905	4.39	663.07
SOUTH ASIA		**1,836**	**2,188**	**2,507**	**2,826**	**0.43**	**12.72**
India		1,836	2,188	2,507	2,826	0.43	12.72
NOT SPECIFIED	**6,589**	**6,379**	**4,912**	**6,524**	**7,755**	**1.18**	**18.87**
Other countries of the World	6,589	6,379	4,912	6,524	7,755	1.18	18.87

Yearbook of Tourism Statistics, Data 2009 – 2013, 2015 Edition

FIJI

5. Overnight stays of non-resident tourists in hotels and similar establishments, by country of residence

	2009	2010	2011	2012	2013	Market share 2013	% Change 2013-2012
TOTAL	2,356,903	2,889,509	3,102,536	3,120,849	3,172,156	100.00	1.64
AMERICAS	240,957	264,710	271,405	278,266	268,826	8.47	-3.39
NORTH AMERICA	240,957	264,710	271,405	278,266	268,826	8.47	-3.39
Canada	34,132	37,961	39,296	37,937	35,992	1.13	-5.13
United States of America	206,825	226,749	232,109	240,329	232,834	7.34	-3.12
EAST ASIA AND THE PACIFIC	1,732,209	2,171,475	2,324,761	2,329,811	2,344,623	73.91	0.64
NORTH-EAST ASIA	65,078	50,842	40,851	32,424	31,433	0.99	-3.06
Japan	65,078	50,842	40,851	32,424	31,433	0.99	-3.06
AUSTRALASIA	1,604,548	2,050,037	2,198,908	2,192,304	2,221,879	70.04	1.35
Australia	1,264,015	1,698,625	1,835,563	1,816,899	1,809,905	57.06	-0.38
New Zealand	340,533	351,412	363,345	375,405	411,974	12.99	9.74
OTHER EAST ASIA AND THE PACIFIC	62,583	70,596	85,002	105,083	91,311	2.88	-13.11
Other countries of Oceania	62,583	70,596	85,002	105,083	91,311	2.88	-13.11
EUROPE	237,444	253,374	258,621	225,941	220,966	6.97	-2.20
NORTHERN EUROPE	143,592	134,985	124,693	104,433	97,977	3.09	-6.18
United Kingdom	143,592	134,985	124,693	104,433	97,977	3.09	-6.18
OTHER EUROPE	93,852	118,389	133,928	121,508	122,989	3.88	1.22
Other countries of Europe	93,852	118,389	133,928	121,508	122,989	3.88	1.22
NOT SPECIFIED	146,293	199,950	247,749	286,831	337,741	10.65	17.75
Other countries of the World	146,293	199,950	247,749	286,831	337,741	10.65	17.75

Yearbook of Tourism Statistics, Data 2009 – 2013, 2015 Edition

FINLAND

2. Arrivals of non-resident visitors at national borders, by country of residence

		2009	2010	2011	2012	2013	Market share 2013	% Change 2013-2012
TOTAL	(*)	5,695,000	6,182,000	7,260,000	7,636,000			
AFRICA		7,000	14,000	11,000	16,000			
OTHER AFRICA		7,000	14,000	11,000	16,000			
All countries of Africa		7,000	14,000	11,000	16,000			
AMERICAS		151,000	150,000	181,000	223,000			
NORTH AMERICA		127,000	121,000	145,000	199,000			
Canada		23,000	32,000	24,000	25,000			
United States of America		104,000	89,000	121,000	174,000			
SOUTH AMERICA		24,000	29,000	35,000	24,000			
All countries of South America		24,000	29,000	35,000	24,000			
OTHER AMERICAS				1,000				
Other countries of the Americas				1,000				
EAST ASIA AND THE PACIFIC		310,000	347,000	427,000	474,000			
NORTH-EAST ASIA		203,000	220,000	270,000	307,000			
China		61,000	73,000	74,000	116,000			
Japan		142,000	109,000	150,000	143,000			
Korea, Republic of			38,000	46,000	48,000			
AUSTRALASIA			43,000	23,000	33,000			
Australia			43,000	23,000	33,000			
OTHER EAST ASIA AND THE PACIFIC		107,000	84,000	134,000	134,000			
Other countries of Asia		107,000	84,000	132,000	131,000			
Other countries of Oceania				2,000	3,000			
EUROPE		5,182,000	5,646,000	6,641,000	6,923,000			
CENTRAL/EASTERN EUROPE		2,889,000	3,302,000	4,134,000	4,562,000			
Czech Republic			22,000	26,000	31,000			
Estonia		583,000	561,000	708,000	758,000			
Hungary			20,000		13,000			
Latvia		54,000	37,000	39,000	36,000			
Lithuania		16,000	29,000	38,000	41,000			
Poland		44,000	55,000	62,000	77,000			
Romania					12,000			
Russian Federation		2,192,000	2,561,000	3,261,000	3,578,000			
Ukraine			17,000		16,000			
NORTHERN EUROPE		1,278,000	1,272,000	1,291,000	1,324,000			
Denmark		98,000	102,000	116,000	114,000			
Norway		160,000	195,000	216,000	235,000			
Sweden		753,000	712,000	681,000	702,000			
United Kingdom		267,000	263,000	278,000	273,000			
SOUTHERN EUROPE		202,000	213,000	228,000	183,000			
Italy		79,000	85,000	108,000	94,000			
Portugal			18,000					
Spain		123,000	110,000	120,000	89,000			
WESTERN EUROPE		667,000	747,000	821,000	752,000			
Austria		44,000	47,000	35,000	48,000			
Belgium		64,000	57,000	48,000	53,000			
France		94,000	132,000	145,000	127,000			
Germany		332,000	363,000	399,000	342,000			
Netherlands		80,000	86,000	101,000	92,000			
Switzerland		53,000	62,000	93,000	90,000			
OTHER EUROPE		146,000	112,000	167,000	102,000			
Other countries of Europe		146,000	112,000	167,000	102,000			
MIDDLE EAST		9,000						
All countries of Middle East		9,000						
SOUTH ASIA		23,000	25,000					
India		23,000	25,000					
NOT SPECIFIED		13,000						
Other countries of the World		13,000						

235

FINLAND

4. Arrivals of non-resident tourists in all types of accommodation establishments, by country of residence

	2009	2010	2011	2012	2013	Market share 2013	% Change 2013-2012
TOTAL	2,220,267	2,318,712	2,622,586	2,778,464	2,796,839	100.00	0.66
AFRICA	5,904	6,666	7,233	7,884	7,385	0.26	-6.33
EAST AFRICA	1,002	1,446	1,506	1,657	1,595	0.06	-3.74
British Indian Ocean Territory		5	2	30	18	0.00	-40.00
Burundi		13	7	5	14	0.00	180.00
Comoros					4	0.00	
Djibouti		9	27	11	6	0.00	-45.45
Eritrea	10	23	31	11	13	0.00	18.18
Ethiopia	125	190	209	215	178	0.01	-17.21
Kenya	276	435	388	425	484	0.02	13.88
Madagascar	4	9	2	7	8	0.00	14.29
Malawi	8	33	16	58	37	0.00	-36.21
Mauritius	15	39	25	72	49	0.00	-31.94
Mozambique	46	26	90	73	36	0.00	-50.68
Reunion	3	16	34	39	13	0.00	-66.67
Rwanda	11	26	32	63	36	0.00	-42.86
Seychelles	43	18	29	48	16	0.00	-66.67
Somalia	54	72	84	37	64	0.00	72.97
Uganda	51	49	102	112	86	0.00	-23.21
United Republic of Tanzania	252	330	296	259	340	0.01	31.27
Zambia	76	99	77	147	142	0.01	-3.40
Zimbabwe	28	54	55	45	51	0.00	13.33
CENTRAL AFRICA	221	597	458	523	429	0.02	-17.97
Angola	27	430	159	277	196	0.01	-29.24
Cameroon	56	72	62	63	83	0.00	31.75
Central African Republic	22	7	18	24	8	0.00	-66.67
Chad		5	4	6	8	0.00	33.33
Congo	45	33	116	103	85	0.00	-17.48
Democratic Republic of the Congo	59	24	67	24	9	0.00	-62.50
Equatorial Guinea					1	0.00	
Gabon	12	23	32	24	28	0.00	16.67
Sao Tome and Principe		3		2	11	0.00	450.00
NORTH AFRICA	994	796	785	965	958	0.03	-0.73
Algeria	362	259	200	266	250	0.01	-6.02
Morocco	310	259	334	381	373	0.01	-2.10
Sudan	90	94	65	62	79	0.00	27.42
Tunisia	232	184	186	255	255	0.01	
Western Sahara				1	1	0.00	
SOUTHERN AFRICA	2,198	2,264	2,686	2,898	2,927	0.10	1.00
Botswana	10	102	43	36	25	0.00	-30.56
Lesotho				2	7	0.00	250.00
Namibia	112	77	119	198	217	0.01	9.60
South Africa	2,022	1,975	2,389	2,532	2,530	0.09	-0.08
Swaziland	54	110	135	130	148	0.01	13.85
WEST AFRICA	1,489	1,563	1,798	1,841	1,476	0.05	-19.83
Benin	25	26	22	17	18	0.00	5.88
Burkina Faso	5	4	4	11	14	0.00	27.27
Cabo Verde				10	21	0.00	110.00
Côte d'Ivoire	8	24	47	56	64	0.00	14.29
Gambia	43	30	43	76	35	0.00	-53.95
Ghana	139	115	256	246	197	0.01	-19.92
Guinea		30	30	12	15	0.00	25.00
Guinea-Bissau			7				
Liberia	17	22	8	9	14	0.00	55.56
Mali	42	42	89	101	50	0.00	-50.50
Mauritania	9	12	14	20	28	0.00	40.00
Niger	151	206	184	196	157	0.01	-19.90
Nigeria	470	505	651	621	516	0.02	-16.91
Saint Helena	47	42	3	7	13	0.00	85.71

Yearbook of Tourism Statistics, Data 2009 – 2013, 2015 Edition

FINLAND

4. Arrivals of non-resident tourists in all types of accommodation establishments, by country of residence

	2009	2010	2011	2012	2013	Market share 2013	% Change 2013-2012
Senegal	111	150	94	101	71	0.00	-29.70
Sierra Leone	417	346	326	347	262	0.01	-24.50
Togo	5	9	20	11	1	0.00	-90.91
AMERICAS	**90,882**	**97,324**	**119,984**	**123,211**	**121,014**	**4.33**	**-1.78**
CARIBBEAN	**841**	**531**	**730**	**851**	**790**	**0.03**	**-7.17**
Anguilla	10	17	11	12	11	0.00	-8.33
Antigua and Barbuda	8	12	13	5	40	0.00	700.00
Aruba				11	3	0.00	-72.73
Bahamas	243	16	14	44	36	0.00	-18.18
Barbados	10	5	22	13	14	0.00	7.69
Bermuda	122	11	16	19	17	0.00	-10.53
British Virgin Islands				16	7	0.00	-56.25
Cayman Islands	28	6	7	10	2	0.00	-80.00
Cuba	145	99	261	289	281	0.01	-2.77
Dominica	7	31	20	23	4	0.00	-82.61
Dominican Republic	22	30	43	70	61	0.00	-12.86
Grenada	9	30	9	18	7	0.00	-61.11
Guadeloupe	4	16	30	1	15	0.00	1,400.00
Haiti	10	44	27	35	20	0.00	-42.86
Jamaica	63	86	103	112	57	0.00	-49.11
Martinique				5	10	0.00	100.00
Montserrat				2			
Netherlands Antilles	38	30	26	40	50	0.00	25.00
Puerto Rico	71	57	50	29	39	0.00	34.48
Saint Kitts and Nevis		10	1	4	4	0.00	
Saint Lucia				38	11	0.00	-71.05
Saint Vincent and the Grenadines	8	6	2	2			
Trinidad and Tobago	19	18	21	28	46	0.00	64.29
Turks and Caicos Islands	14		11	19	9	0.00	-52.63
United States Virgin Islands	10	7	43	6	46	0.00	666.67
CENTRAL AMERICA	**422**	**658**	**737**	**555**	**852**	**0.03**	**53.51**
Belize	30	24	27	7	27	0.00	285.71
Costa Rica	177	185	271	179	233	0.01	30.17
El Salvador	31	206	239	205	378	0.01	84.39
Guatemala	59	99	27	65	34	0.00	-47.69
Honduras	18	37	44	28	93	0.00	232.14
Nicaragua	55	40	60	47	45	0.00	-4.26
Panama	52	67	69	24	42	0.00	75.00
NORTH AMERICA	**82,478**	**87,500**	**106,724**	**108,679**	**106,396**	**3.80**	**-2.10**
Canada	11,805	11,308	14,291	15,075	14,724	0.53	-2.33
Greenland	55	39	71	66	43	0.00	-34.85
Mexico	1,765	1,983	2,634	2,356	2,564	0.09	8.83
Saint Pierre and Miquelon				1			
United States of America	68,853	74,170	89,728	91,181	89,065	3.18	-2.32
SOUTH AMERICA	**7,141**	**8,635**	**11,793**	**13,126**	**12,976**	**0.46**	**-1.14**
Argentina	820	1,061	1,514	1,444	2,033	0.07	40.79
Bolivia	34	60	85	50	47	0.00	-6.00
Brazil	4,239	5,277	6,563	8,123	7,397	0.26	-8.94
Chile	540	834	1,002	1,218	1,175	0.04	-3.53
Colombia	495	485	566	798	908	0.03	13.78
Ecuador	71	132	147	228	190	0.01	-16.67
Falkland Islands, Malvinas	8	14	17	8	10	0.00	25.00
French Guiana		7		11	5	0.00	-54.55
Guyana		16	11	2	7	0.00	250.00
Paraguay	12	11	24	6	19	0.00	216.67
Peru	211	195	307	307	348	0.01	13.36
Suriname	24	26	29	31	31	0.00	
Uruguay	398	272	1,140	509	530	0.02	4.13

Yearbook of Tourism Statistics, Data 2009 – 2013, 2015 Edition

FINLAND

4. Arrivals of non-resident tourists in all types of accommodation establishments, by country of residence

	2009	2010	2011	2012	2013	Market share 2013	% Change 2013-2012
Venezuela	289	245	388	391	276	0.01	-29.41
EAST ASIA AND THE PACIFIC	**144,300**	**159,050**	**192,810**	**228,510**	**272,582**	**9.75**	**19.29**
NORTH-EAST ASIA	**114,836**	**126,618**	**152,385**	**182,810**	**221,970**	**7.94**	**21.42**
China	32,603	39,217	50,280	59,491	79,379	2.84	33.43
Hong Kong, China	3,610	3,285	6,107	8,202	10,291	0.37	25.47
Japan	65,949	68,747	75,680	91,783	106,769	3.82	16.33
Korea, Dem. People's Republic of	1,123	1,358	850	1,927	1,271	0.05	-34.04
Korea, Republic of	7,450	9,578	12,446	13,609	15,855	0.57	16.50
Macao, China	22	60	63	92	117	0.00	27.17
Mongolia	58	137	96	128	106	0.00	-17.19
Taiwan, Province of China	4,021	4,236	6,863	7,578	8,182	0.29	7.97
SOUTH-EAST ASIA	**10,186**	**13,184**	**19,016**	**21,942**	**25,098**	**0.90**	**14.38**
Brunei Darussalam	13	2	8	17	13	0.00	-23.53
Cambodia	14	8	14	7	23	0.00	228.57
Indonesia	869	1,293	2,276	2,721	3,450	0.12	26.79
Lao People's Democratic Republic	75	62	69	45	72	0.00	60.00
Malaysia	1,143	1,168	1,420	2,054	2,018	0.07	-1.75
Myanmar	34	87	43	72	136	0.00	88.89
Philippines	967	1,221	1,327	1,202	1,151	0.04	-4.24
Singapore	2,427	2,356	5,244	6,729	8,631	0.31	28.27
Thailand	4,139	6,486	8,095	8,387	8,926	0.32	6.43
Timor-Leste					3	0.00	
Viet Nam	505	501	520	708	675	0.02	-4.66
AUSTRALASIA	**19,135**	**18,988**	**20,984**	**23,417**	**25,123**	**0.90**	**7.29**
Australia	17,684	17,547	19,337	21,553	23,153	0.83	7.42
New Zealand	1,451	1,441	1,647	1,864	1,970	0.07	5.69
MELANESIA	**56**	**143**	**134**	**100**	**138**	**0.00**	**38.00**
Fiji		92	64	32	30	0.00	-6.25
New Caledonia	31	23	34	44	84	0.00	90.91
Papua New Guinea	10	8	26	10	12	0.00	20.00
Solomon Islands	15	20	10	11	11	0.00	
Vanuatu				3	1	0.00	-66.67
MICRONESIA	**14**	**36**	**33**	**20**	**43**	**0.00**	**115.00**
Christmas Island, Australia				1			
Cocos (Keeling) Islands					3	0.00	
Guam	14	17	14	2	1	0.00	-50.00
Kiribati		19	17	11	12	0.00	9.09
Micronesia, Federated States of				2	14	0.00	600.00
Nauru			2	1	11	0.00	1,000.00
Northern Mariana Islands					2	0.00	
Palau				3			
POLYNESIA	**73**	**81**	**258**	**221**	**210**	**0.01**	**-4.98**
American Samoa	55	27	207	145	115	0.00	-20.69
Cook Islands			11	2	7	0.00	250.00
French Polynesia		7	20	16	9	0.00	-43.75
Niue				2	3	0.00	50.00
Pitcairn				2	4	0.00	100.00
Samoa				4	7	0.00	75.00
Tokelau	18	42	13	35	53	0.00	51.43
Tonga		5	5		5	0.00	
Tuvalu			2	10	7	0.00	-30.00
Wallis and Futuna Islands				5			
EUROPE	**1,846,249**	**1,921,558**	**2,150,835**	**2,238,356**	**2,218,427**	**79.32**	**-0.89**
CENTRAL/EASTERN EUROPE	**623,189**	**691,669**	**831,157**	**937,617**	**965,899**	**34.54**	**3.02**
Armenia	203	143	203	256	247	0.01	-3.52
Azerbaijan	218	153	234	399	342	0.01	-14.29
Belarus	1,280	2,097	2,040	2,359	2,324	0.08	-1.48
Bulgaria	2,586	2,099	2,633	1,979	1,858	0.07	-6.11

238

Yearbook of Tourism Statistics, Data 2009 – 2013, 2015 Edition

FINLAND

4. Arrivals of non-resident tourists in all types of accommodation establishments, by country of residence

	2009	2010	2011	2012	2013	Market share 2013	% Change 2013-2012
Czech Republic	11,748	11,999	13,924	14,262	13,105	0.47	-8.11
Estonia	73,071	82,448	91,814	94,800	80,409	2.87	-15.18
Georgia	976	924	1,176	1,385	1,246	0.04	-10.04
Hungary	9,731	9,408	10,612	8,224	7,904	0.28	-3.89
Kazakhstan	775	776	704	1,416	2,176	0.08	53.67
Kyrgyzstan	34	48	36	207	49	0.00	-76.33
Latvia	17,227	20,163	21,189	20,256	20,542	0.73	1.41
Lithuania	10,931	11,337	12,091	13,697	11,986	0.43	-12.49
Poland	24,418	26,331	28,395	28,451	26,293	0.94	-7.58
Republic of Moldova	114	94	204	263	176	0.01	-33.08
Romania	6,306	5,983	6,042	6,396	6,249	0.22	-2.30
Russian Federation	456,388	509,237	630,064	731,261	778,574	27.84	6.47
Slovakia	2,914	3,707	3,768	4,570	3,973	0.14	-13.06
Tajikistan		28	22	75	41	0.00	-45.33
Turkmenistan	7	6	17	32	27	0.00	-15.63
Ukraine	4,179	4,606	5,895	7,246	8,251	0.30	13.87
Uzbekistan	83	82	94	83	127	0.00	53.01
NORTHERN EUROPE	**574,800**	**584,252**	**617,437**	**617,828**	**618,984**	**22.13**	**0.19**
Denmark	48,591	48,569	55,968	50,618	48,071	1.72	-5.03
Faeroe Islands	378	139	195	275	162	0.01	-41.09
Iceland	3,266	3,384	4,332	4,197	3,339	0.12	-20.44
Ireland	7,754	6,894	7,235	7,610	7,795	0.28	2.43
Isle of Man					2	0.00	
Norway	74,967	80,403	87,851	92,478	90,627	3.24	-2.00
Sweden	278,169	290,922	307,045	301,651	291,405	10.42	-3.40
United Kingdom	161,675	153,941	154,811	160,999	177,583	6.35	10.30
SOUTHERN EUROPE	**137,558**	**133,855**	**153,120**	**124,883**	**113,372**	**4.05**	**-9.22**
Albania	505	360	268	332	184	0.01	-44.58
Andorra	116	157	82	141	145	0.01	2.84
Bosnia and Herzegovina	227	210	287	237	170	0.01	-28.27
Croatia	1,418	1,450	2,001	1,503	1,858	0.07	23.62
Gibraltar		50	40	48	61	0.00	27.08
Greece	9,088	7,588	7,825	5,828	5,022	0.18	-13.83
Holy See		5	1	6	139	0.00	2,216.67
Italy	65,270	61,656	72,412	60,000	54,455	1.95	-9.24
Malta	380	377	413	390	274	0.01	-29.74
Montenegro	9	50	7	22	37	0.00	68.18
Portugal	7,365	8,212	7,330	7,027	5,493	0.20	-21.83
San Marino	64	39	58	103	26	0.00	-74.76
Serbia	369	623	759	828	703	0.03	-15.10
Slovenia	2,511	3,055	3,071	2,995	3,241	0.12	8.21
Spain	50,077	50,023	58,320	45,206	41,379	1.48	-8.47
TFYR of Macedonia	159		246	217	185	0.01	-14.75
WESTERN EUROPE	**498,518**	**495,406**	**534,613**	**542,197**	**500,114**	**17.88**	**-7.76**
Austria	23,572	24,892	29,413	30,705	23,116	0.83	-24.72
Belgium	21,181	21,713	23,112	24,927	23,376	0.84	-6.22
France	79,877	82,813	83,460	83,217	79,595	2.85	-4.35
Germany	249,277	246,137	270,897	268,810	245,350	8.77	-8.73
Liechtenstein	605	195	273	240	223	0.01	-7.08
Luxembourg	1,721	1,675	1,892	2,136	2,390	0.09	11.89
Monaco	226	178	199	293	260	0.01	-11.26
Netherlands	74,867	68,907	71,922	72,961	69,163	2.47	-5.21
Switzerland	47,192	48,896	53,445	58,908	56,641	2.03	-3.85
EAST MEDITERRANEAN EUROPE	**12,184**	**16,376**	**14,508**	**15,831**	**20,058**	**0.72**	**26.70**
Cyprus	754	687	619	666	476	0.02	-28.53
Israel	5,364	8,023	6,294	6,830	10,402	0.37	52.30
Turkey	6,066	7,666	7,595	8,335	9,180	0.33	10.14

Yearbook of Tourism Statistics, Data 2009 – 2013, 2015 Edition

FINLAND

4. Arrivals of non-resident tourists in all types of accommodation establishments, by country of residence

	2009	2010	2011	2012	2013	Market share 2013	% Change 2013-2012
MIDDLE EAST	4,008	3,793	4,278	4,706	5,371	0.19	14.13
Bahrain	230	99	107	97	80	0.00	-17.53
Egypt	690	720	1,016	839	998	0.04	18.95
Iraq	164	167	161	158	232	0.01	46.84
Jordan	121	128	167	155	214	0.01	38.06
Kuwait	178	168	226	196	341	0.01	73.98
Lebanon	296	214	168	275	279	0.01	1.45
Libya	64	68	25	66	75	0.00	13.64
Oman	101	232	119	146	173	0.01	18.49
Palestine				19	14	0.00	-26.32
Qatar	119	157	136	170	291	0.01	71.18
Saudi Arabia	1,184	811	761	983	1,035	0.04	5.29
Syrian Arab Republic	81	85	112	102	97	0.00	-4.90
United Arab Emirates	726	912	1,260	1,476	1,524	0.05	3.25
Yemen	54	32	20	24	18	0.00	-25.00
SOUTH ASIA	15,625	16,849	18,604	17,152	18,534	0.66	8.06
Afghanistan	948	781	538	323	350	0.01	8.36
Bangladesh	132	97	125	180	141	0.01	-21.67
Bhutan	6		7	4	20	0.00	400.00
India	12,941	14,100	15,827	14,432	16,083	0.58	11.44
Iran, Islamic Republic of	913	1,165	1,249	1,260	1,037	0.04	-17.70
Maldives	5	9	7	2			
Nepal	155	170	185	271	302	0.01	11.44
Pakistan	436	473	542	528	512	0.02	-3.03
Sri Lanka	89	54	124	152	89	0.00	-41.45
NOT SPECIFIED	113,299	113,472	128,842	158,645	153,526	5.49	-3.23
Other countries of the World	113,299	113,472	128,842	158,645	153,526	5.49	-3.23

Yearbook of Tourism Statistics, Data 2009 – 2013, 2015 Edition

FINLAND

5. Overnight stays of non-resident tourists in hotels and similar establishments, by country of residence

	2009	2010	2011	2012	2013	Market share 2013	% Change 2013-2012
TOTAL	4,197,575	4,296,915	4,711,041	4,948,446	4,906,135	100.00	-0.86
AFRICA	19,267	18,612	18,790	21,406	18,876	0.38	-11.82
EAST AFRICA	3,479	3,639	4,115	4,741	4,450	0.09	-6.14
British Indian Ocean Territory		8	4	36	22	0.00	-38.89
Burundi		26	18	27	34	0.00	25.93
Comoros					1	0.00	
Djibouti		28	33	15	37	0.00	146.67
Eritrea	15	41	43	13	18	0.00	38.46
Ethiopia	439	547	487	522	542	0.01	3.83
Kenya	1,243	1,087	1,070	1,366	1,175	0.02	-13.98
Madagascar	17	21	3	19	44	0.00	131.58
Malawi	40	113	39	144	122	0.00	-15.28
Mauritius	54	54	82	248	157	0.00	-36.69
Mozambique	184	76	211	273	156	0.00	-42.86
Reunion	9	40	31	62	32	0.00	-48.39
Rwanda	33	47	42	121	166	0.00	37.19
Seychelles	90	58	68	98	46	0.00	-53.06
Somalia	69	108	82	54	64	0.00	18.52
Uganda	220	126	346	271	310	0.01	14.39
United Republic of Tanzania	710	802	1,038	700	826	0.02	18.00
Zambia	299	391	382	604	507	0.01	-16.06
Zimbabwe	57	66	136	168	191	0.00	13.69
CENTRAL AFRICA	410	1,448	839	1,272	761	0.02	-40.17
Angola	41	1,090	259	747	342	0.01	-54.22
Cameroon	110	189	121	178	178	0.00	
Central African Republic	51	18	23	39	19	0.00	-51.28
Chad		12	6	25	16	0.00	-36.00
Congo	67	47	188	200	127	0.00	-36.50
Democratic Republic of the Congo	104	26	149	29	17	0.00	-41.38
Equatorial Guinea					6	0.00	
Gabon	37	60	86	49	36	0.00	-26.53
Sao Tome and Principe		6	7	5	20	0.00	300.00
NORTH AFRICA	2,672	2,449	1,764	2,141	2,111	0.04	-1.40
Algeria	842	901	424	776	672	0.01	-13.40
Morocco	731	593	735	743	663	0.01	-10.77
Sudan	358	369	153	118	214	0.00	81.36
Tunisia	741	586	452	503	560	0.01	11.33
Western Sahara				1	2	0.00	100.00
SOUTHERN AFRICA	6,270	6,624	8,114	8,947	7,924	0.16	-11.43
Botswana	40	128	107	205	128	0.00	-37.56
Lesotho				32	92	0.00	187.50
Namibia	325	271	328	681	598	0.01	-12.19
South Africa	5,756	5,983	7,357	7,616	6,866	0.14	-9.85
Swaziland	149	242	322	413	240	0.00	-41.89
WEST AFRICA	4,003	4,447	3,958	4,305	3,630	0.07	-15.68
Benin	85	86	36	39	36	0.00	-7.69
Burkina Faso	40	24	8	59	81	0.00	37.29
Cabo Verde				21	25	0.00	19.05
Côte d'Ivoire	22	88	101	144	80	0.00	-44.44
Gambia	55	82	53	92	50	0.00	-45.65
Ghana	725	564	1,128	674	511	0.01	-24.18
Guinea		84	52	25	36	0.00	44.00
Guinea-Bissau			24				
Liberia	43	42	13	87	23	0.00	-73.56
Mali	78	100	131	267	107	0.00	-59.93
Mauritania	56	54	51	51	50	0.00	-1.96
Niger	295	483	357	388	360	0.01	-7.22
Nigeria	1,256	1,339	1,104	1,140	1,011	0.02	-11.32
Saint Helena	198	207	5	18	46	0.00	155.56

241

FINLAND

5. Overnight stays of non-resident tourists in hotels and similar establishments, by country of residence

	2009	2010	2011	2012	2013	Market share 2013	% Change 2013-2012
Senegal	281	357	207	339	276	0.01	-18.58
Sierra Leone	857	901	654	907	937	0.02	3.31
Togo	12	36	34	54	1	0.00	-98.15
OTHER AFRICA	**2,433**	**5**					
Other countries of Africa	2,433	5					
AMERICAS	**220,461**	**231,342**	**263,612**	**265,509**	**248,491**	**5.06**	**-6.41**
CARIBBEAN	**3,124**	**1,382**	**1,576**	**2,182**	**1,920**	**0.04**	**-12.01**
Anguilla	86	57	27	12	18	0.00	50.00
Antigua and Barbuda	17	23	21	10	83	0.00	730.00
Aruba			41	23	4	0.00	-82.61
Bahamas	371	24	39	269	138	0.00	-48.70
Barbados	22	22	66	62	23	0.00	-62.90
Bermuda	903	39	23	32	51	0.00	59.38
British Virgin Islands				51	12	0.00	-76.47
Cayman Islands	267	7	28	23	10	0.00	-56.52
Cuba	312	165	472	714	510	0.01	-28.57
Dominica	11	92	34	47	14	0.00	-70.21
Dominican Republic	34	68	156	181	117	0.00	-35.36
Grenada	11	72	12	30	9	0.00	-70.00
Guadeloupe	9	53	74	1	30	0.00	2,900.00
Haiti	34	83	50	56	39	0.00	-30.36
Jamaica	187	243	161	291	124	0.00	-57.39
Martinique				5	44	0.00	780.00
Montserrat				2			
Netherlands Antilles	105	69	46	24	48	0.00	100.00
Puerto Rico	444	148	86	74	64	0.00	-13.51
Saint Kitts and Nevis		38	1	10	27	0.00	170.00
Saint Lucia				69	45	0.00	-34.78
Saint Vincent and the Grenadines	88	76	3	2			
Trinidad and Tobago	153	78	60	108	390	0.01	261.11
Turks and Caicos Islands	47	8	18	71	27	0.00	-61.97
United States Virgin Islands	23	17	158	15	93	0.00	520.00
CENTRAL AMERICA	**1,343**	**1,433**	**1,354**	**1,275**	**1,533**	**0.03**	**20.24**
Belize	95	71	48	7	50	0.00	614.29
Costa Rica	530	514	538	395	494	0.01	25.06
El Salvador	63	292	358	457	622	0.01	36.11
Guatemala	153	192	47	159	77	0.00	-51.57
Honduras	48	63	47	55	129	0.00	134.55
Nicaragua	246	141	145	120	93	0.00	-22.50
Panama	208	160	171	82	68	0.00	-17.07
NORTH AMERICA	**198,154**	**207,918**	**234,361**	**232,653**	**218,495**	**4.45**	**-6.09**
Canada	30,326	29,277	32,595	34,318	31,768	0.65	-7.43
Greenland	307	95	169	111	146	0.00	31.53
Mexico	4,603	4,959	5,118	4,857	5,233	0.11	7.74
Saint Pierre and Miquelon				1			
United States of America	162,918	173,587	196,479	193,366	181,348	3.70	-6.22
SOUTH AMERICA	**17,812**	**20,601**	**26,321**	**29,399**	**26,543**	**0.54**	**-9.71**
Argentina	2,265	2,405	3,433	2,860	3,677	0.07	28.57
Bolivia	70	83	165	129	123	0.00	-4.65
Brazil	11,365	13,039	15,605	19,411	15,949	0.33	-17.84
Chile	1,237	1,791	2,002	2,446	2,344	0.05	-4.17
Colombia	1,236	1,263	1,183	1,590	1,907	0.04	19.94
Ecuador	146	262	302	474	522	0.01	10.13
Falkland Islands, Malvinas	56	20	29	10	17	0.00	70.00
French Guiana				24	5	0.00	-79.17
Guyana	10	44	16	8	29	0.00	262.50
Paraguay	19	16	113	43	47	0.00	9.30
Peru	479	377	758	583	722	0.01	23.84

242

FINLAND

5. Overnight stays of non-resident tourists in hotels and similar establishments, by country of residence

	2009	2010	2011	2012	2013	Market share 2013	% Change 2013-2012
Suriname	75	58	135	147	82	0.00	-44.22
Uruguay	205	598	1,773	729	453	0.01	-37.86
Venezuela	649	645	807	945	666	0.01	-29.52
OTHER AMERICAS	**28**	**8**					
Other countries of the Americas	28	8					
EAST ASIA AND THE PACIFIC	**290,970**	**310,617**	**352,656**	**407,026**	**473,516**	**9.65**	**16.34**
NORTH-EAST ASIA	**228,043**	**243,179**	**274,949**	**320,477**	**379,294**	**7.73**	**18.35**
China	65,950	75,332	89,244	96,781	122,855	2.50	26.94
Hong Kong, China	6,015	5,303	9,385	11,932	15,660	0.32	31.24
Japan	130,171	132,540	141,527	171,590	199,786	4.07	16.43
Korea, Dem. People's Republic of	2,827	2,722	1,531	4,722	2,239	0.05	-52.58
Korea, Republic of	16,074	18,931	22,236	24,115	26,688	0.54	10.67
Macao, China	78	141	123	174	218	0.00	25.29
Mongolia	149	334	334	342	346	0.01	1.17
Taiwan, Province of China	6,779	7,876	10,569	10,821	11,502	0.23	6.29
SOUTH-EAST ASIA	**23,211**	**27,736**	**32,118**	**37,178**	**42,155**	**0.86**	**13.39**
Brunei Darussalam	31	10	16	24	22	0.00	-8.33
Cambodia	106	14	29	101	73	0.00	-27.72
Indonesia	1,814	2,374	3,588	4,462	5,085	0.10	13.96
Lao People's Democratic Republic	123	109	156	98	223	0.00	127.55
Malaysia	3,083	3,235	3,079	3,984	3,990	0.08	0.15
Myanmar	36	175	82	80	321	0.01	301.25
Philippines	3,356	3,364	2,237	2,527	2,293	0.05	-9.26
Singapore	6,496	5,763	12,310	12,543	15,771	0.32	25.74
Thailand	7,054	11,608	9,500	11,865	13,133	0.27	10.69
Timor-Leste					2	0.00	
Viet Nam	1,112	1,084	1,121	1,494	1,242	0.03	-16.87
AUSTRALASIA	**39,448**	**39,147**	**44,828**	**48,777**	**51,343**	**1.05**	**5.26**
Australia	36,309	36,410	41,371	44,904	47,747	0.97	6.33
New Zealand	3,139	2,737	3,457	3,873	3,596	0.07	-7.15
MELANESIA	**195**	**279**	**279**	**171**	**284**	**0.01**	**66.08**
Fiji		156	114	47	54	0.00	14.89
New Caledonia	57	40	70	88	154	0.00	75.00
Papua New Guinea	36	16	61	17	42	0.00	147.06
Solomon Islands	71	46	34	16	29	0.00	81.25
Vanuatu	31	21		3	5	0.00	66.67
MICRONESIA	**33**	**87**	**70**	**46**	**56**	**0.00**	**21.74**
Christmas Island, Australia				3			
Cocos (Keeling) Islands					4	0.00	
Guam	33	32	35	3	1	0.00	-66.67
Kiribati		48	32	21	18	0.00	-14.29
Micronesia, Federated States of		7		11	19	0.00	72.73
Nauru			3	1	11	0.00	1,000.00
Northern Mariana Islands					3	0.00	
Palau				7			
POLYNESIA	**40**	**189**	**412**	**377**	**384**	**0.01**	**1.86**
American Samoa		34	286	185	160	0.00	-13.51
Cook Islands				3	14	0.00	366.67
French Polynesia	8	15	72	17	17	0.00	
Niue				2	3	0.00	50.00
Pitcairn				20	5	0.00	-75.00
Samoa				10	29	0.00	190.00
Tokelau	32	124	43	68	119	0.00	75.00
Tonga		16	6		11	0.00	
Tuvalu				58	26	0.00	-55.17
Wallis and Futuna Islands			5	14			

Yearbook of Tourism Statistics, Data 2009 – 2013, 2015 Edition

FINLAND

5. Overnight stays of non-resident tourists in hotels and similar establishments, by country of residence

	2009	2010	2011	2012	2013	Market share 2013	% Change 2013-2012
EUROPE	**3,415,728**	**3,484,840**	**3,810,834**	**3,957,343**	**3,870,248**	**78.89**	**-2.20**
CENTRAL/EASTERN EUROPE	**1,160,003**	**1,268,560**	**1,502,726**	**1,671,194**	**1,638,510**	**33.40**	**-1.96**
Armenia	699	577	406	702	650	0.01	-7.41
Azerbaijan	517	372	606	993	811	0.02	-18.33
Belarus	3,502	8,040	6,484	6,613	6,155	0.13	-6.93
Bulgaria	6,449	5,931	5,914	4,806	3,959	0.08	-17.62
Czech Republic	23,304	23,373	26,909	29,421	25,112	0.51	-14.65
Estonia	125,169	152,605	171,737	179,349	142,688	2.91	-20.44
Georgia	2,015	1,793	2,319	2,960	2,396	0.05	-19.05
Hungary	20,572	19,432	22,448	18,021	16,981	0.35	-5.77
Kazakhstan	3,634	3,142	2,338	5,659	8,686	0.18	53.49
Kyrgyzstan	95	187	123	385	122	0.00	-68.31
Latvia	25,131	30,237	28,712	31,974	30,354	0.62	-5.07
Lithuania	16,588	17,526	19,427	24,048	20,151	0.41	-16.21
Poland	52,615	56,075	61,322	65,585	55,951	1.14	-14.69
Republic of Moldova	371	276	412	762	477	0.01	-37.40
Romania	14,082	14,553	15,573	14,703	12,438	0.25	-15.41
Russian Federation	843,842	909,186	1,110,551	1,251,335	1,277,117	26.03	2.06
Slovakia	6,750	10,190	9,417	11,336	9,636	0.20	-15.00
Tajikistan	11	52	46	234	88	0.00	-62.39
Turkmenistan		10	52	104	85	0.00	-18.27
Ukraine	14,422	14,786	17,748	21,925	24,344	0.50	11.03
Uzbekistan	235	217	182	279	309	0.01	10.75
NORTHERN EUROPE	**1,008,357**	**988,580**	**1,014,509**	**1,031,452**	**1,050,454**	**21.41**	**1.84**
Denmark	79,848	79,708	88,542	80,257	77,174	1.57	-3.84
Faeroe Islands	1,758	454	309	542	407	0.01	-24.91
Iceland	7,387	7,984	10,129	8,952	7,275	0.15	-18.73
Ireland	16,974	15,567	14,145	14,885	16,483	0.34	10.74
Isle of Man					2	0.00	
Norway	112,556	119,062	130,089	143,211	135,735	2.77	-5.22
Sweden	384,158	404,164	427,838	419,890	408,863	8.33	-2.63
United Kingdom	405,676	361,641	343,457	363,715	404,515	8.25	11.22
SOUTHERN EUROPE	**291,042**	**281,281**	**304,738**	**248,670**	**225,760**	**4.60**	**-9.21**
Albania	1,364	912	647	688	310	0.01	-54.94
Andorra	214	295	145	491	277	0.01	-43.58
Bosnia and Herzegovina	623	664	776	528	517	0.01	-2.08
Croatia	3,774	3,609	4,950	4,728	3,997	0.08	-15.46
Gibraltar	1,379	105	89	87	92	0.00	5.75
Greece	23,054	18,015	17,077	13,201	10,997	0.22	-16.70
Holy See		10	2	8	306	0.01	3,725.00
Italy	137,134	127,207	138,225	116,293	101,751	2.07	-12.50
Malta	1,086	946	1,033	912	792	0.02	-13.16
Montenegro	25	107	16	81	114	0.00	40.74
Portugal	18,148	19,129	16,711	16,423	13,513	0.28	-17.72
San Marino	122	89	161	354	46	0.00	-87.01
Serbia	844	1,908	1,870	1,772	1,606	0.03	-9.37
Slovenia	5,524	6,167	5,821	6,670	6,997	0.14	4.90
Spain	97,363	101,576	116,727	85,865	83,853	1.71	-2.34
TFYR of Macedonia	388	542	488	569	592	0.01	4.04
WESTERN EUROPE	**925,766**	**910,614**	**955,502**	**970,587**	**914,235**	**18.63**	**-5.81**
Austria	41,249	42,519	49,857	49,864	43,005	0.88	-13.76
Belgium	41,836	42,319	44,824	47,901	44,657	0.91	-6.77
France	184,659	185,221	186,464	190,892	187,040	3.81	-2.02
Germany	437,459	424,910	450,681	444,459	411,672	8.39	-7.38
Liechtenstein	1,378	497	407	434	443	0.01	2.07
Luxembourg	3,801	3,662	3,517	4,034	4,352	0.09	7.88
Monaco	441	355	323	568	525	0.01	-7.57
Netherlands	132,727	129,637	130,465	130,037	125,466	2.56	-3.52
Switzerland	82,216	81,494	88,964	102,398	97,075	1.98	-5.20

244

FINLAND

5. Overnight stays of non-resident tourists in hotels and similar establishments, by country of residence

	2009	2010	2011	2012	2013	Market share 2013	% Change 2013-2012
EAST MEDITERRANEAN EUROPE	**30,560**	**35,805**	**33,359**	**35,440**	**41,289**	**0.84**	**16.50**
Cyprus	1,843	1,841	1,952	1,704	1,105	0.02	-35.15
Israel	14,210	17,345	15,321	16,430	22,815	0.47	38.86
Turkey	14,507	16,619	16,086	17,306	17,369	0.35	0.36
MIDDLE EAST	**13,008**	**11,266**	**11,410**	**12,492**	**14,698**	**0.30**	**17.66**
Bahrain	623	220	227	266	204	0.00	-23.31
Egypt	2,238	2,169	2,603	2,051	2,323	0.05	13.26
Iraq	326	425	722	416	524	0.01	25.96
Jordan	427	131	419	340	1,114	0.02	227.65
Kuwait	510	653	568	559	783	0.02	40.07
Lebanon	726	729	429	610	798	0.02	30.82
Libya	143	195	65	195	249	0.01	27.69
Oman	312	400	301	854	1,522	0.03	78.22
Palestine				45	28	0.00	-37.78
Qatar	603	569	273	541	652	0.01	20.52
Saudi Arabia	4,704	3,038	2,344	2,950	2,785	0.06	-5.59
Syrian Arab Republic	201	323	285	450	225	0.00	-50.00
United Arab Emirates	1,807	2,283	3,103	3,111	3,472	0.07	11.60
Yemen	388	131	71	104	19	0.00	-81.73
SOUTH ASIA	**60,290**	**66,698**	**58,961**	**48,230**	**47,819**	**0.97**	**-0.85**
Afghanistan	2,393	2,242	1,576	545	652	0.01	19.63
Bangladesh	294	222	351	601	287	0.01	-52.25
Bhutan	20		10	13	103	0.00	692.31
India	51,406	57,589	52,196	42,128	42,645	0.87	1.23
Iran, Islamic Republic of	2,418	2,767	2,866	2,739	2,059	0.04	-24.83
Maldives	26	33	35	2			
Nepal	546	474	410	586	582	0.01	-0.68
Pakistan	2,892	3,224	1,267	1,086	1,262	0.03	16.21
Sri Lanka	295	147	250	530	229	0.00	-56.79
NOT SPECIFIED	**177,851**	**173,540**	**194,778**	**236,440**	**232,487**	**4.74**	**-1.67**
Other countries of the World	177,851	173,540	194,778	236,440	232,487	4.74	-1.67

FINLAND

6. Overnight stays of non-resident tourists in all types of accommodation establishments, by country of residence

	2009	2010	2011	2012	2013	Market share 2013	% Change 2013-2012
TOTAL	4,890,006	5,005,068	5,507,468	5,802,959	5,860,447	100.00	0.99
AFRICA	17,475	19,572	20,115	22,631	20,512	0.35	-9.36
EAST AFRICA	3,569	3,900	4,435	4,937	4,990	0.09	1.07
British Indian Ocean Territory		8	4	36	22	0.00	-38.89
Burundi		27	18	29	65	0.00	124.14
Comoros					4	0.00	
Djibouti		28	33	15	38	0.00	153.33
Eritrea	19	41	51	18	18	0.00	
Ethiopia	445	565	509	564	601	0.01	6.56
Kenya	1,266	1,131	1,092	1,405	1,464	0.02	4.20
Madagascar	18	25	3	19	45	0.00	136.84
Malawi	40	125	39	144	122	0.00	-15.28
Mauritius	54	132	82	256	158	0.00	-38.28
Mozambique	188	76	211	273	156	0.00	-42.86
Reunion	9	40	49	63	32	0.00	-49.21
Rwanda	33	52	46	121	175	0.00	44.63
Seychelles	90	62	70	98	47	0.00	-52.04
Somalia	87	128	251	57	93	0.00	63.16
Uganda	220	135	371	293	322	0.01	9.90
United Republic of Tanzania	733	842	1,083	741	895	0.02	20.78
Zambia	302	391	382	619	540	0.01	-12.76
Zimbabwe	65	92	141	186	193	0.00	3.76
CENTRAL AFRICA	384	1,525	869	1,353	903	0.02	-33.26
Angola	41	1,091	259	765	357	0.01	-53.33
Cameroon		236	134	191	240	0.00	25.65
Central African Republic	69	18	33	41	19	0.00	-53.66
Chad		16	6	27	21	0.00	-22.22
Congo	91	47	191	211	162	0.00	-23.22
Democratic Republic of the Congo	140	51	153	59	28	0.00	-52.54
Equatorial Guinea					6	0.00	
Gabon	43	60	86	54	36	0.00	-33.33
Sao Tome and Principe		6	7	5	34	0.00	580.00
NORTH AFRICA	2,872	2,568	1,939	2,310	2,301	0.04	-0.39
Algeria	909	922	465	794	701	0.01	-11.71
Morocco	832	667	841	857	800	0.01	-6.65
Sudan	363	370	158	121	222	0.00	83.47
Tunisia	768	609	475	537	576	0.01	7.26
Western Sahara				1	2	0.00	100.00
SOUTHERN AFRICA	6,379	6,861	8,498	9,117	8,208	0.14	-9.97
Botswana	44	128	107	205	136	0.00	-33.66
Lesotho		9	22	32	92	0.00	187.50
Namibia	327	273	367	709	623	0.01	-12.13
South Africa	6,008	6,209	7,644	7,743	7,106	0.12	-8.23
Swaziland		242	358	428	251	0.00	-41.36
WEST AFRICA	4,271	4,718	4,374	4,914	4,110	0.07	-16.36
Benin	103	39	40	50	55	0.00	10.00
Burkina Faso	43	24	9	59	81	0.00	37.29
Cabo Verde				21	82	0.00	290.48
Côte d'Ivoire	24	109	105	144	82	0.00	-43.06
Gambia	77	82	79	165	65	0.00	-60.61
Ghana	781	582	1,179	738	530	0.01	-28.18
Guinea		110	59	27	42	0.00	55.56
Guinea-Bissau			24				
Liberia	56	45	13	87	24	0.00	-72.41
Mali	79	102	131	267	108	0.00	-59.55
Mauritania	57	56	51	51	50	0.00	-1.96
Niger	305	556	374	400	363	0.01	-9.25
Nigeria	1,349	1,500	1,353	1,558	1,343	0.02	-13.80
Saint Helena	207	207	5	18	46	0.00	155.56

246

FINLAND

6. Overnight stays of non-resident tourists in all types of accommodation establishments, by country of residence

	2009	2010	2011	2012	2013	Market share 2013	% Change 2013-2012
Senegal	315	360	257	361	301	0.01	-16.62
Sierra Leone	860	910	658	911	937	0.02	2.85
Togo	15	36	37	57	1	0.00	-98.25
AMERICAS	**228,274**	**239,089**	**276,012**	**275,908**	**259,675**	**4.43**	**-5.88**
CARIBBEAN	**3,170**	**1,335**	**1,590**	**2,248**	**2,025**	**0.03**	**-9.92**
Anguilla	86	57	27	12	18	0.00	50.00
Antigua and Barbuda	17	23	21	10	83	0.00	730.00
Aruba				23	4	0.00	-82.61
Bahamas	371	30	39	269	139	0.00	-48.33
Barbados	22	22	66	63	23	0.00	-63.49
Bermuda	991	39	23	32	51	0.00	59.38
British Virgin Islands				51	12	0.00	-76.47
Cayman Islands	267	7	28	23	10	0.00	-56.52
Cuba	334	175	509	725	520	0.01	-28.28
Dominica	11	92	34	49	14	0.00	-71.43
Dominican Republic	38	68	156	183	130	0.00	-28.96
Grenada	11	72	13	30	9	0.00	-70.00
Guadeloupe	9	53	74	1	30	0.00	2,900.00
Haiti	34	85	50	59	41	0.00	-30.51
Jamaica	199	243	161	291	135	0.00	-53.61
Martinique				5	44	0.00	780.00
Montserrat				2			
Netherlands Antilles	105	69	46	69	100	0.00	44.93
Puerto Rico	442	149	86	74	80	0.00	8.11
Saint Kitts and Nevis		38	1	10	27	0.00	170.00
Saint Lucia		10	20	69	45	0.00	-34.78
Saint Vincent and the Grenadines				2			
Trinidad and Tobago	163	78	60	108	390	0.01	261.11
Turks and Caicos Islands	47	8	18	73	27	0.00	-63.01
United States Virgin Islands	23	17	158	15	93	0.00	520.00
CENTRAL AMERICA	**1,374**	**1,524**	**1,444**	**1,335**	**1,661**	**0.03**	**24.42**
Belize	95	71	48	7	50	0.00	614.29
Costa Rica	533	546	576	424	537	0.01	26.65
El Salvador	63	304	358	470	666	0.01	41.70
Guatemala	165	200	47	163	83	0.00	-49.08
Honduras	49	63	63	61	138	0.00	126.23
Nicaragua	254	151	178	126	101	0.00	-19.84
Panama	215	189	174	84	86	0.00	2.38
NORTH AMERICA	**204,630**	**214,566**	**242,508**	**241,118**	**226,867**	**3.87**	**-5.91**
Canada	32,295	30,455	34,754	36,792	33,604	0.57	-8.66
Greenland	307	95	169	111	146	0.00	31.53
Mexico	5,134	5,534	5,731	5,489	5,872	0.10	6.98
Saint Pierre and Miquelon				1			
United States of America	166,894	178,482	201,854	198,725	187,245	3.20	-5.78
SOUTH AMERICA	**19,100**	**21,664**	**30,470**	**31,207**	**29,122**	**0.50**	**-6.68**
Argentina	2,368	2,538	3,660	3,121	3,917	0.07	25.50
Bolivia	79	104	175	136	130	0.00	-4.41
Brazil	11,877	13,489	16,339	20,207	17,266	0.29	-14.55
Chile	1,326	1,925	2,180	2,564	2,516	0.04	-1.87
Colombia	1,257	1,324	1,618	1,763	2,136	0.04	21.16
Ecuador	151	267	341	538	555	0.01	3.16
Falkland Islands, Malvinas	56	21	29	10	17	0.00	70.00
French Guiana		16		24	5	0.00	-79.17
Guyana	10	44	16	8	29	0.00	262.50
Paraguay	20	16	116	44	48	0.00	9.09
Peru	519	446	851	638	778	0.01	21.94
Suriname	75	58	135	147	82	0.00	-44.22
Uruguay	612	672	4,129	1,054	942	0.02	-10.63

Yearbook of Tourism Statistics, Data 2009 – 2013, 2015 Edition

FINLAND

6. Overnight stays of non-resident tourists in all types of accommodation establishments, by country of residence

	2009	2010	2011	2012	2013	Market share 2013	% Change 2013-2012
Venezuela	750	744	881	953	701	0.01	-26.44
EAST ASIA AND THE PACIFIC	**306,455**	**327,557**	**396,783**	**447,156**	**519,505**	**8.86**	**16.18**
NORTH-EAST ASIA	**235,910**	**252,112**	**285,874**	**332,109**	**393,123**	**6.71**	**18.37**
China	67,542	77,540	92,099	100,057	126,495	2.16	26.42
Hong Kong, China	6,159	5,497	9,792	12,534	16,307	0.28	30.10
Japan	134,363	136,804	146,433	176,919	205,988	3.51	16.43
Korea, Dem. People's Republic of	2,921	2,777	1,541	4,786	2,263	0.04	-52.72
Korea, Republic of	17,419	20,730	24,385	26,013	29,296	0.50	12.62
Macao, China	78	141	123	177	240	0.00	35.59
Mongolia	160	351	365	342	361	0.01	5.56
Taiwan, Province of China	7,268	8,272	11,136	11,281	12,173	0.21	7.91
SOUTH-EAST ASIA	**26,904**	**31,932**	**61,397**	**62,129**	**70,030**	**1.19**	**12.72**
Brunei Darussalam	31	10	18	41	38	0.00	-7.32
Cambodia	106	14	30	108	79	0.00	-26.85
Indonesia	1,837	2,421	3,668	4,900	5,213	0.09	6.39
Lao People's Democratic Republic	123	113	156	98	317	0.01	223.47
Malaysia	3,151	3,470	3,214	4,130	4,146	0.07	0.39
Myanmar	49	176	84	96	325	0.01	238.54
Philippines	3,357	3,453	2,289	2,562	2,716	0.05	6.01
Singapore	6,652	6,028	12,757	13,047	16,502	0.28	26.48
Thailand	10,162	15,120	37,922	35,575	39,318	0.67	10.52
Timor-Leste					3	0.00	
Viet Nam	1,436	1,127	1,259	1,572	1,373	0.02	-12.66
AUSTRALASIA	**43,265**	**42,957**	**48,752**	**52,317**	**55,617**	**0.95**	**6.31**
Australia	39,767	39,677	44,875	48,035	51,652	0.88	7.53
New Zealand	3,498	3,280	3,877	4,282	3,965	0.07	-7.40
MELANESIA	**172**	**280**	**279**	**178**	**292**	**0.00**	**64.04**
Fiji		157	114	48	54	0.00	12.50
New Caledonia	62	40	70	94	162	0.00	72.34
Papua New Guinea	39	16	61	17	42	0.00	147.06
Solomon Islands	71	46	34	16	29	0.00	81.25
Vanuatu				3	5	0.00	66.67
All countries of Melanesia		21					
MICRONESIA	**33**	**87**	**71**	**46**	**59**	**0.00**	**28.26**
Christmas Island, Australia				3			
Cocos (Keeling) Islands					4	0.00	
Guam	33	32	35	3	1	0.00	-66.67
Kiribati		48	33	21	18	0.00	-14.29
Micronesia, Federated States of		7		11	19	0.00	72.73
Nauru			3	1	14	0.00	1,300.00
Northern Mariana Islands					3	0.00	
Palau					7		
POLYNESIA	**171**	**189**	**410**	**377**	**384**	**0.01**	**1.86**
American Samoa	129	34	286	185	160	0.00	-13.51
Cook Islands				3	14	0.00	366.67
French Polynesia	12	15	72	17	17	0.00	
Niue				2	3	0.00	50.00
Pitcairn				20	5	0.00	-75.00
Samoa				10	29	0.00	190.00
Tokelau	30	124	43	68	119	0.00	75.00
Tonga		16	6		11	0.00	
Tuvalu			3	58	26	0.00	-55.17
Wallis and Futuna Islands				14			
EUROPE	**4,074,071**	**4,157,709**	**4,543,390**	**4,753,805**	**4,757,941**	**81.19**	**0.09**
CENTRAL/EASTERN EUROPE	**1,380,370**	**1,512,867**	**1,782,115**	**2,032,730**	**2,071,870**	**35.35**	**1.93**
Armenia	709	587	432	716	670	0.01	-6.42
Azerbaijan	527	439	642	1,053	839	0.01	-20.32
Belarus	6,753	10,683	9,621	10,688	7,021	0.12	-34.31

Yearbook of Tourism Statistics, Data 2009 – 2013, 2015 Edition

FINLAND

6. Overnight stays of non-resident tourists in all types of accommodation establishments, by country of residence

	2009	2010	2011	2012	2013	Market share 2013	% Change 2013-2012
Bulgaria	6,836	6,400	6,207	5,166	4,417	0.08	-14.50
Czech Republic	28,175	27,936	32,474	35,273	31,215	0.53	-11.50
Estonia	167,816	205,429	228,187	235,482	187,295	3.20	-20.46
Georgia	2,090	1,856	2,369	3,046	2,530	0.04	-16.94
Hungary	22,719	22,214	25,388	20,157	19,307	0.33	-4.22
Kazakhstan	3,760	3,295	2,391	5,980	9,090	0.16	52.01
Kyrgyzstan	99	191	134	385	140	0.00	-63.64
Latvia	33,446	39,002	38,528	42,368	42,858	0.73	1.16
Lithuania	21,747	24,037	25,277	31,998	26,012	0.44	-18.71
Poland	63,935	67,902	74,860	76,385	66,158	1.13	-13.39
Republic of Moldova	432	293	434	785	481	0.01	-38.73
Romania	16,758	18,204	17,360	17,391	14,561	0.25	-16.27
Russian Federation	979,526	1,056,424	1,286,598	1,506,900	1,620,419	27.65	7.53
Slovakia	8,866	11,424	10,934	12,391	10,949	0.19	-11.64
Tajikistan	9	56	47	238	103	0.00	-56.72
Turkmenistan	6	17	53	104	85	0.00	-18.27
Ukraine	15,903	16,255	19,893	25,920	27,405	0.47	5.73
Uzbekistan	258	223	286	304	315	0.01	3.62
NORTHERN EUROPE	**1,223,492**	**1,194,777**	**1,236,933**	**1,238,948**	**1,270,217**	**21.67**	**2.52**
Denmark	87,449	85,609	94,823	86,676	83,141	1.42	-4.08
Faeroe Islands	1,841	483	346	666	488	0.01	-26.73
Iceland	7,707	8,360	10,572	9,485	7,784	0.13	-17.93
Ireland	18,922	16,827	16,772	16,939	18,676	0.32	10.25
Isle of Man					2	0.00	
Norway	149,279	159,377	173,254	182,639	174,147	2.97	-4.65
Sweden	494,002	517,849	552,129	537,002	531,375	9.07	-1.05
United Kingdom	464,292	406,272	389,037	405,541	454,604	7.76	12.10
SOUTHERN EUROPE	**320,967**	**311,941**	**340,072**	**277,532**	**257,387**	**4.39**	**-7.26**
Albania	1,409	952	748	751	434	0.01	-42.21
Andorra	221	295	153	495	277	0.00	-44.04
Bosnia and Herzegovina	634	671	798	535	564	0.01	5.42
Croatia	3,911	3,838	5,152	4,858	4,862	0.08	0.08
Gibraltar	1,379	105	89	87	92	0.00	5.75
Greece	24,277	18,924	17,810	13,879	12,004	0.20	-13.51
Holy See	5	10	2	26	339	0.01	1,203.85
Italy	151,658	142,389	156,509	130,847	115,681	1.97	-11.59
Malta	1,172	989	1,118	962	815	0.01	-15.28
Montenegro	26	107	16	81	114	0.00	40.74
Portugal	18,912	19,875	17,606	17,411	14,674	0.25	-15.72
San Marino	122	109	173	391	61	0.00	-84.40
Serbia	971	2,063	2,131	1,894	1,766	0.03	-6.76
Slovenia	6,590	7,248	7,191	7,923	8,213	0.14	3.66
Spain	109,240	113,804	130,046	96,820	96,876	1.65	0.06
TFYR of Macedonia	440	562	530	572	615	0.01	7.52
WESTERN EUROPE	**1,116,337**	**1,099,502**	**1,148,255**	**1,166,539**	**1,113,266**	**19.00**	**-4.57**
Austria	48,921	50,836	57,325	57,494	52,725	0.90	-8.29
Belgium	45,909	46,521	49,021	53,449	49,334	0.84	-7.70
France	212,887	213,414	213,588	217,886	214,248	3.66	-1.67
Germany	525,880	510,280	541,031	534,239	501,650	8.56	-6.10
Liechtenstein	1,410	524	471	470	503	0.01	7.02
Luxembourg	4,046	3,934	3,891	4,575	6,814	0.12	48.94
Monaco	450	355	326	608	553	0.01	-9.05
Netherlands	169,213	165,779	164,593	164,918	158,668	2.71	-3.79
Switzerland	107,621	107,859	118,009	132,900	128,771	2.20	-3.11
EAST MEDITERRANEAN EUROPE	**32,905**	**38,622**	**36,015**	**38,056**	**45,201**	**0.77**	**18.77**
Cyprus	1,889	1,875	1,992	1,747	1,154	0.02	-33.94
Israel	15,701	19,370	17,320	18,317	25,712	0.44	40.37
Turkey	15,315	17,377	16,703	17,992	18,335	0.31	1.91

Yearbook of Tourism Statistics, Data 2009 – 2013, 2015 Edition

FINLAND

6. Overnight stays of non-resident tourists in all types of accommodation establishments, by country of residence

	2009	2010	2011	2012	2013	Market share 2013	% Change 2013-2012
MIDDLE EAST	**13,231**	**11,749**	**11,647**	**12,710**	**14,925**	**0.25**	**17.43**
Bahrain	629	220	227	266	206	0.00	-22.56
Egypt	2,312	2,297	2,687	2,094	2,361	0.04	12.75
Iraq	376	444	752	446	551	0.01	23.54
Jordan	434	345	435	364	1,118	0.02	207.14
Kuwait	511	664	571	560	783	0.01	39.82
Lebanon	767	745	462	620	814	0.01	31.29
Libya	146	215	69	196	260	0.00	32.65
Oman	313	400	301	854	1,522	0.03	78.22
Palestine				52	47	0.00	-9.62
Qatar	607	581	273	543	661	0.01	21.73
Saudi Arabia	4,714	3,064	2,376	2,954	2,818	0.05	-4.60
Syrian Arab Republic	204	325	306	450	231	0.00	-48.67
United Arab Emirates	1,830	2,304	3,105	3,207	3,527	0.06	9.98
Yemen	388	145	83	104	26	0.00	-75.00
SOUTH ASIA	**61,207**	**68,094**	**60,849**	**49,788**	**50,238**	**0.86**	**0.90**
Afghanistan	2,404	2,266	1,616	576	680	0.01	18.06
Bangladesh	328	259	364	631	563	0.01	-10.78
Bhutan	20		10	13	103	0.00	692.31
India	52,138	58,657	53,672	42,756	44,330	0.76	3.68
Iran, Islamic Republic of	2,484	2,924	3,032	2,862	2,238	0.04	-21.80
Maldives	26	33	35	2			
Nepal	556	523	470	651	670	0.01	2.92
Pakistan	2,927	3,285	1,386	1,722	1,409	0.02	-18.18
Sri Lanka	324	147	264	575	245	0.00	-57.39
NOT SPECIFIED	**189,293**	**181,298**	**198,672**	**240,961**	**237,651**	**4.06**	**-1.37**
Other countries of the World	189,293	181,298	198,672	240,961	237,651	4.06	-1.37

Yearbook of Tourism Statistics, Data 2009 – 2013, 2015 Edition

FRANCE

1. Arrivals of non-resident tourists at national borders, by country of residence

		2009	2010	2011	2012	2013	Market share 2013	% Change 2013-2012
TOTAL	(*)	**76,766,000**	**77,648,325**	**81,550,308**	**83,050,687**	**84,726,270**	**100.00**	**2.02**
AFRICA		**1,823,000**	**1,720,086**	**2,129,199**	**2,052,894**	**2,132,265**	**2.52**	**3.87**
NORTH AFRICA		**1,268,000**	**1,191,148**	**1,387,011**	**1,382,621**	**1,435,594**	**1.69**	**3.83**
All countries of North Africa	(*)	1,268,000	1,191,148	1,387,011	1,382,621	1,435,594	1.69	3.83
OTHER AFRICA		**555,000**	**528,938**	**742,188**	**670,273**	**696,671**	**0.82**	**3.94**
Other countries of Africa		555,000	528,938	742,188	670,273	696,671	0.82	3.94
AMERICAS		**5,491,000**	**5,679,079**	**6,674,810**	**6,455,650**	**6,564,888**	**7.75**	**1.69**
NORTH AMERICA		**4,288,000**	**4,192,314**	**4,796,433**	**4,314,122**	**4,490,360**	**5.30**	**4.09**
Canada		873,000	961,804	937,963	932,845	1,079,984	1.27	15.77
Mexico		354,000	321,363	506,553	360,355	308,011	0.36	-14.53
United States of America		3,061,000	2,909,147	3,351,917	3,020,922	3,102,365	3.66	2.70
OTHER AMERICAS		**1,203,000**	**1,486,765**	**1,878,377**	**2,141,528**	**2,074,528**	**2.45**	**-3.13**
Other countries of the Americas		1,203,000	1,486,765	1,878,377	2,141,528	2,074,528	2.45	-3.13
EAST ASIA AND THE PACIFIC		**3,371,000**	**3,583,594**	**4,120,568**	**4,396,826**	**4,925,963**	**5.81**	**12.03**
NORTH-EAST ASIA		**1,437,000**	**1,505,608**	**1,742,131**	**2,125,534**	**2,402,788**	**2.84**	**13.04**
China	(*)	740,000	909,631	1,129,872	1,394,165	1,720,404	2.03	23.40
Japan		697,000	595,977	612,259	731,369	682,384	0.81	-6.70
OTHER EAST ASIA AND THE PACIFIC		**1,934,000**	**2,077,986**	**2,378,437**	**2,271,292**	**2,523,175**	**2.98**	**11.09**
Other countries of Asia		842,000	909,414	1,107,263	978,095	1,004,677	1.19	2.72
All countries of Oceania		1,092,000	1,168,572	1,271,174	1,293,197	1,518,498	1.79	17.42
EUROPE		**65,246,000**	**65,776,196**	**67,846,133**	**69,330,687**	**70,133,550**	**82.78**	**1.16**
CENTRAL/EASTERN EUROPE		**1,278,000**	**1,187,584**	**1,561,971**	**2,082,109**	**2,208,459**	**2.61**	**6.07**
Poland		365,000	370,308	433,714	434,068	512,216	0.60	18.00
Other countries Central/East Europe		913,000	817,276	1,128,257	1,648,041	1,696,243	2.00	2.92
NORTHERN EUROPE		**14,362,000**	**14,411,002**	**14,433,476**	**14,107,323**	**14,740,417**	**17.40**	**4.49**
Denmark		696,000	614,136	654,986	534,972	678,649	0.80	26.86
Finland		182,000	285,953	262,485	235,455	212,301	0.25	-9.83
Sweden		603,000	614,269	682,859	623,212	691,576	0.82	10.97
United Kingdom/Ireland		12,881,000	12,896,644	12,833,146	12,713,684	13,157,891	15.53	3.49
SOUTHERN EUROPE		**13,447,000**	**13,359,596**	**14,676,259**	**15,330,417**	**14,718,176**	**17.37**	**-3.99**
Greece		357,000	244,151	169,005	167,928	201,221	0.24	19.83
Italy		7,250,000	7,178,166	8,067,905	8,057,231	7,814,990	9.22	-3.01
Portugal		966,000	998,223	1,005,365	1,057,866	1,384,489	1.63	30.88
Spain		4,874,000	4,939,056	5,433,984	6,047,392	5,317,476	6.28	-12.07
WESTERN EUROPE		**34,900,000**	**35,368,819**	**35,537,734**	**36,840,998**	**37,288,103**	**44.01**	**1.21**
Austria		646,000	765,220	992,343	1,053,676	772,689	0.91	-26.67
Germany		10,692,000	11,409,526	11,622,256	12,232,111	13,031,567	15.38	6.54
Netherlands		7,224,000	7,002,184	6,493,126	6,349,825	6,547,240	7.73	3.11
Switzerland	(*)	5,438,000	5,450,197	5,661,117	6,072,602	6,474,172	7.64	6.61
Belgium / Luxembourg		10,900,000	10,741,692	10,768,892	11,132,784	10,462,435	12.35	-6.02
OTHER EUROPE		**1,259,000**	**1,449,195**	**1,636,693**	**969,840**	**1,178,395**	**1.39**	**21.50**
Other countries of Europe		1,259,000	1,449,195	1,636,693	969,840	1,178,395	1.39	21.50
MIDDLE EAST		**835,000**	**889,370**	**779,598**	**814,630**	**969,604**	**1.14**	**19.02**
All countries of Middle East		835,000	889,370	779,598	814,630	969,604	1.14	19.02

Yearbook of Tourism Statistics, Data 2009 – 2013, 2015 Edition

FRANCE

3. Arrivals of non-resident tourists in hotels and similar establishments, by country of residence

	2009	2010	2011	2012	2013	Market share 2013	% Change 2013-2012
TOTAL (*)	28,765,875	29,844,582	30,487,350	30,966,072	33,347,665	100.00	7.69
AFRICA	416,147	435,753	458,644	500,957	571,780	1.71	14.14
NORTH AFRICA	182,986	206,480	204,999	216,755	234,957	0.70	8.40
All countries of North Africa	182,986	206,480	204,999	216,755	234,957	0.70	8.40
OTHER AFRICA	233,161	229,273	253,645	284,202	336,823	1.01	18.52
Other countries of Africa	233,161	229,273	253,645	284,202	336,823	1.01	18.52
AMERICAS	3,297,733	3,616,455	3,856,643	4,165,952	4,751,065	14.25	14.05
NORTH AMERICA	2,644,740	2,798,977	2,908,434	3,178,749	3,665,907	10.99	15.33
Canada	371,351	401,734	427,677	454,791	475,215	1.43	4.49
United States of America	2,273,389	2,397,243	2,480,757	2,723,958	3,190,692	9.57	17.13
OTHER AMERICAS	652,993	817,478	948,209	987,203	1,085,158	3.25	9.92
Other countries of the Americas	652,993	817,478	948,209	987,203	1,085,158	3.25	9.92
EAST ASIA AND THE PACIFIC	2,459,439	2,849,378	3,215,012	3,470,545	4,127,916	12.38	18.94
NORTH-EAST ASIA	1,507,798	1,724,553	1,876,476	2,001,191	2,394,287	7.18	19.64
China	395,210	581,205	752,750	836,392	1,230,616	3.69	47.13
Japan	1,112,588	1,143,348	1,123,726	1,164,799	1,163,671	3.49	-0.10
AUSTRALASIA	253,192	319,357	373,508	427,802	486,544	1.46	13.73
Australia	253,192	319,357	373,508	427,802	486,544	1.46	13.73
OTHER EAST ASIA AND THE PACIFIC	698,449	805,468	965,028	1,041,552	1,247,085	3.74	19.73
Other countries East Asia/Pacific	698,449	805,468	965,028	1,041,552	1,247,085	3.74	19.73
EUROPE	22,203,552	22,442,153	22,423,107	22,217,261	23,160,284	69.45	4.24
CENTRAL/EASTERN EUROPE	932,590	1,113,527	1,309,521	1,470,933	1,611,615	4.83	9.56
Bulgaria	23,876	26,106	26,124	28,760	33,370	0.10	16.03
Czech Republic	66,121	90,688	106,697	116,874	126,758	0.38	8.46
Estonia	5,709	6,640	10,044	13,498	13,646	0.04	1.10
Hungary	56,438	54,039	66,128	70,671	67,170	0.20	-4.95
Latvia	5,643	7,972	9,531	10,752	12,192	0.04	13.39
Lithuania	12,407	17,898	20,157	31,763	29,678	0.09	-6.56
Poland	194,398	198,750	224,665	243,819	277,034	0.83	13.62
Romania	88,998	102,603	127,534	130,786	149,397	0.45	14.23
Russian Federation	452,463	580,880	688,744	789,738	864,765	2.59	9.50
Slovakia	26,537	27,951	29,897	34,272	37,605	0.11	9.73
NORTHERN EUROPE	6,423,132	6,325,320	6,104,204	6,183,987	6,479,408	19.43	4.78
Denmark	202,401	218,081	216,164	222,010	214,673	0.64	-3.30
Finland	95,532	105,145	115,624	107,173	117,250	0.35	9.40
Iceland	14,393	14,522	21,419	18,036	16,643	0.05	-7.72
Ireland	230,997	221,727	212,218	200,566	197,839	0.59	-1.36
Norway	136,376	159,214	167,350	189,644	207,632	0.62	9.49
Sweden	200,340	227,112	260,080	263,971	307,836	0.92	16.62
United Kingdom	5,543,093	5,379,519	5,111,349	5,182,587	5,417,535	16.25	4.53
SOUTHERN EUROPE	5,338,970	5,430,643	5,147,989	4,609,954	4,672,904	14.01	1.37
Croatia	18,274	15,749	19,283	19,585	21,448	0.06	9.51
Greece	146,790	133,663	111,100	96,492	93,532	0.28	-3.07
Italy	2,790,805	2,782,927	2,555,858	2,326,038	2,346,025	7.04	0.86
Malta	7,584	12,448	11,405	15,279	14,352	0.04	-6.07
Portugal	258,253	286,097	270,535	268,488	303,496	0.91	13.04
Slovenia	18,267	17,646	18,438	16,343	18,391	0.06	12.53
Spain	2,098,997	2,182,113	2,161,370	1,867,729	1,875,660	5.62	0.42
WESTERN EUROPE	8,989,714	8,950,576	9,241,839	9,304,323	9,637,840	28.90	3.58
Austria	168,817	180,412	180,324	190,822	208,257	0.62	9.14
Belgium	2,780,830	2,729,200	2,789,309	2,757,343	2,855,428	8.56	3.56
Germany	2,915,293	2,986,584	3,057,730	3,063,432	3,203,378	9.61	4.57
Luxembourg	109,364	124,136	132,626	146,977	165,420	0.50	12.55
Netherlands	1,845,505	1,742,887	1,755,582	1,719,490	1,677,361	5.03	-2.45
Switzerland	1,169,905	1,187,357	1,326,268	1,426,259	1,527,996	4.58	7.13
EAST MEDITERRANEAN EUROPE	78,054	111,666	131,323	130,900	156,563	0.47	19.61
Cyprus	9,822	13,900	14,570	13,183	10,672	0.03	-19.05
Turkey	68,232	97,766	116,753	117,717	145,891	0.44	23.93

Yearbook of Tourism Statistics, Data 2009 – 2013, 2015 Edition

FRANCE

3. Arrivals of non-resident tourists in hotels and similar establishments, by country of residence

	2009	2010	2011	2012	2013	Market share 2013	% Change 2013-2012
OTHER EUROPE	**441,092**	**510,421**	**488,231**	**517,164**	**601,954**	**1.81**	**16.40**
Other countries of Europe	441,092	510,421	488,231	517,164	601,954	1.81	16.40
MIDDLE EAST	**389,004**	**500,843**	**533,944**	**611,357**	**736,620**	**2.21**	**20.49**
All countries of Middle East	389,004	500,843	533,944	611,357	736,620	2.21	20.49

253

FRANCE

5. Overnight stays of non-resident tourists in hotels and similar establishments, by country of residence

	2009	2010	2011	2012	2013	Market share 2013	% Change 2013-2012
TOTAL (*)	63,203,046	65,860,952	67,175,802	68,426,020	71,991,583	100.00	5.21
AFRICA	1,014,682	1,089,878	1,138,509	1,241,054	1,382,093	1.92	11.36
NORTH AFRICA	433,374	494,543	498,203	523,290	550,859	0.77	5.27
All countries of North Africa	433,374	494,543	498,203	523,290	550,859	0.77	5.27
OTHER AFRICA	581,308	595,335	640,306	717,764	831,234	1.15	15.81
Other countries of Africa	581,308	595,335	640,306	717,764	831,234	1.15	15.81
AMERICAS	8,177,377	9,051,871	9,677,880	10,534,506	11,738,542	16.31	11.43
NORTH AMERICA	6,428,335	6,805,654	7,079,977	7,787,743	8,845,107	12.29	13.58
Canada	912,536	970,835	1,037,915	1,091,373	1,127,694	1.57	3.33
United States of America	5,515,799	5,834,819	6,042,062	6,696,370	7,717,413	10.72	15.25
OTHER AMERICAS	1,749,042	2,246,217	2,597,903	2,746,763	2,893,435	4.02	5.34
Other countries of the Americas	1,749,042	2,246,217	2,597,903	2,746,763	2,893,435	4.02	5.34
EAST ASIA AND THE PACIFIC	5,311,596	6,170,662	6,876,290	7,473,708	8,614,501	11.97	15.26
NORTH-EAST ASIA	3,185,836	3,666,195	3,917,854	4,196,217	4,830,842	6.71	15.12
China	787,259	1,167,534	1,474,536	1,631,236	2,349,236	3.26	44.02
Japan	2,398,577	2,498,661	2,443,318	2,564,981	2,481,606	3.45	-3.25
AUSTRALASIA	620,935	777,171	917,515	1,063,416	1,202,509	1.67	13.08
Australia	620,935	777,171	917,515	1,063,416	1,202,509	1.67	13.08
OTHER EAST ASIA AND THE PACIFIC	1,504,825	1,727,296	2,040,921	2,214,075	2,581,150	3.59	16.58
Other countries East Asia/Pacific	1,504,825	1,727,296	2,040,921	2,214,075	2,581,150	3.59	16.58
EUROPE	47,584,765	48,154,362	48,026,775	47,518,789	48,312,729	67.11	1.67
CENTRAL/EASTERN EUROPE	2,306,107	2,790,852	3,333,890	3,682,417	3,870,719	5.38	5.11
Bulgaria	56,735	62,537	63,062	68,404	74,005	0.10	8.19
Czech Republic	137,018	183,510	219,658	246,760	256,994	0.36	4.15
Estonia	14,096	16,324	25,074	33,271	31,813	0.04	-4.38
Hungary	122,960	118,653	145,601	155,812	140,750	0.20	-9.67
Latvia	13,357	19,971	22,917	26,026	29,335	0.04	12.71
Lithuania	27,637	38,923	43,826	63,357	58,753	0.08	-7.27
Poland	394,792	419,662	492,394	521,552	560,543	0.78	7.48
Romania	215,504	250,987	305,420	303,974	326,228	0.45	7.32
Russian Federation	1,264,371	1,620,175	1,946,863	2,184,501	2,308,554	3.21	5.68
Slovakia	59,637	60,110	69,075	78,760	83,744	0.12	6.33
NORTHERN EUROPE	13,784,180	13,378,296	13,086,881	13,340,030	13,858,564	19.25	3.89
Denmark	480,447	516,515	515,749	520,761	486,648	0.68	-6.55
Finland	237,551	262,036	289,879	265,324	284,584	0.40	7.26
Iceland	37,553	32,362	46,284	40,611	38,365	0.05	-5.53
Ireland	640,646	602,576	556,237	532,256	500,976	0.70	-5.88
Norway	334,715	402,069	420,596	474,622	512,674	0.71	8.02
Sweden	491,988	553,436	645,642	639,588	744,446	1.03	16.39
United Kingdom	11,561,280	11,009,302	10,612,494	10,866,868	11,290,871	15.68	3.90
SOUTHERN EUROPE	12,510,498	12,680,240	11,841,049	10,565,332	10,299,894	14.31	-2.51
Croatia	43,236	36,295	44,458	44,918	49,105	0.07	9.32
Greece	422,277	372,082	300,338	251,017	232,776	0.32	-7.27
Italy	6,479,711	6,457,675	5,862,752	5,361,065	5,176,438	7.19	-3.44
Malta	25,150	41,244	34,872	46,178	38,066	0.05	-17.57
Portugal	582,836	650,347	591,369	576,419	634,049	0.88	10.00
Slovenia	36,386	39,330	40,438	35,582	38,459	0.05	8.09
Spain	4,920,902	5,083,267	4,966,822	4,250,153	4,131,001	5.74	-2.80
WESTERN EUROPE	17,767,289	17,831,194	18,291,124	18,467,221	18,609,067	25.85	0.77
Austria	386,168	419,769	413,250	439,561	469,113	0.65	6.72
Belgium	5,347,716	5,310,980	5,363,668	5,275,606	5,300,251	7.36	0.47
Germany	5,914,513	6,087,922	6,220,744	6,275,501	6,379,712	8.86	1.66
Luxembourg	222,704	255,655	265,418	289,812	321,534	0.45	10.95
Netherlands	3,483,710	3,323,004	3,322,693	3,244,884	3,064,653	4.26	-5.55
Switzerland	2,412,478	2,433,864	2,705,351	2,941,857	3,073,804	4.27	4.49
EAST MEDITERRANEAN EUROPE	209,409	302,164	342,368	336,585	386,707	0.54	14.89
Cyprus	28,988	41,949	40,730	35,723	27,283	0.04	-23.63
Turkey	180,421	260,215	301,638	300,862	359,424	0.50	19.46

254

FRANCE

5. Overnight stays of non-resident tourists in hotels and similar establishments, by country of residence

	2009	2010	2011	2012	2013	Market share 2013	% Change 2013-2012
OTHER EUROPE	**1,007,282**	**1,171,616**	**1,131,463**	**1,127,204**	**1,287,778**	**1.79**	**14.25**
Other countries of Europe	1,007,282	1,171,616	1,131,463	1,127,204	1,287,778	1.79	14.25
MIDDLE EAST	**1,114,626**	**1,394,179**	**1,451,566**	**1,657,963**	**1,943,718**	**2.70**	**17.24**
All countries of Middle East	1,114,626	1,394,179	1,451,566	1,657,963	1,943,718	2.70	17.24
NOT SPECIFIED			**4,782**				
Other countries of the World			4,782				

Yearbook of Tourism Statistics, Data 2009 – 2013, 2015 Edition

FRANCE

6. Overnight stays of non-resident tourists in all types of accommodation establishments, by country of residence

		2009	2010	2011	2012	2013	Market share 2013	% Change 2013-2012
TOTAL	(*)	515,234,000	525,290,750	564,312,198	573,250,158	599,688,936	100.00	4.61
AFRICA		25,232,000	25,281,135	30,215,144	29,752,631	30,776,551	5.13	3.44
NORTH AFRICA		17,852,000	18,129,051	20,159,578	19,872,121	20,448,496	3.41	2.90
All countries of North Africa	(*)	17,852,000	18,129,051	20,159,578	19,872,121	20,448,496	3.41	2.90
OTHER AFRICA		7,380,000	7,152,084	10,055,566	9,880,510	10,328,055	1.72	4.53
Other countries of Africa		7,380,000	7,152,084	10,055,566	9,880,510	10,328,055	1.72	4.53
AMERICAS		48,277,000	50,257,940	58,829,765	56,879,122	57,034,319	9.51	0.27
NORTH AMERICA		37,506,000	38,059,369	43,780,507	39,634,831	40,228,180	6.71	1.50
Canada		8,676,000	9,877,596	9,925,792	10,038,713	11,466,218	1.91	14.22
Mexico		2,929,000	2,582,545	3,514,368	2,843,395	2,238,675	0.37	-21.27
United States of America		25,901,000	25,599,228	30,340,347	26,752,723	26,523,287	4.42	-0.86
OTHER AMERICAS		10,771,000	12,198,571	15,049,258	17,244,291	16,806,139	2.80	-2.54
Other countries of the Americas		10,771,000	12,198,571	15,049,258	17,244,291	16,806,139	2.80	-2.54
EAST ASIA AND THE PACIFIC		25,742,000	27,596,504	31,431,319	34,254,831	36,649,412	6.11	6.99
NORTH-EAST ASIA		9,555,000	10,171,242	11,999,862	15,094,938	15,429,516	2.57	2.22
China	(*)	5,383,000	6,567,036	8,101,469	10,534,997	11,021,424	1.84	4.62
Japan		4,172,000	3,604,206	3,898,393	4,559,941	4,408,092	0.74	-3.33
OTHER EAST ASIA AND THE PACIFIC		16,187,000	17,425,262	19,431,457	19,159,893	21,219,896	3.54	10.75
Other countries of Asia		7,233,000	7,760,752	9,168,629	9,102,277	9,295,616	1.55	2.12
All countries of Oceania		8,954,000	9,664,510	10,262,828	10,057,616	11,924,280	1.99	18.56
EUROPE		408,167,000	413,342,999	436,080,000	444,428,831	465,234,722	77.58	4.68
CENTRAL/EASTERN EUROPE		13,822,000	16,036,426	21,236,125	18,142,871	20,406,762	3.40	12.48
Poland		3,060,000	3,289,252	3,729,750	3,285,157	4,399,396	0.73	33.92
Other countries Central/East Europe		10,762,000	12,747,174	17,506,375	14,857,714	16,007,366	2.67	7.74
NORTHERN EUROPE		91,146,000	93,648,852	98,065,797	97,175,477	105,228,818	17.55	8.29
Denmark		4,652,000	4,080,089	4,758,150	3,886,454	5,313,310	0.89	36.71
Finland		1,269,000	1,706,775	1,763,746	1,449,272	1,352,014	0.23	-6.71
Sweden		3,469,000	3,623,595	4,456,088	4,202,096	4,955,521	0.83	17.93
United Kingdom/Ireland		81,756,000	84,238,393	87,087,813	87,637,655	93,607,973	15.61	6.81
SOUTHERN EUROPE		74,855,000	72,619,935	80,861,842	85,048,299	87,393,523	14.57	2.76
Greece		2,512,000	1,736,860	1,191,442	1,226,894	1,944,219	0.32	58.47
Italy		40,657,000	40,487,586	45,189,492	44,830,388	43,310,175	7.22	-3.39
Portugal		6,948,000	6,716,569	6,965,789	8,501,864	12,719,680	2.12	49.61
Spain		24,738,000	23,678,920	27,515,119	30,489,153	29,419,449	4.91	-3.51
WESTERN EUROPE		218,447,000	224,807,827	228,144,158	237,174,010	243,563,543	40.61	2.69
Austria		5,471,000	7,044,550	9,743,991	9,382,859	6,595,043	1.10	-29.71
Germany		70,768,000	76,798,195	80,290,768	83,651,501	89,661,927	14.95	7.19
Netherlands		54,196,000	54,288,511	49,606,579	49,084,343	50,928,592	8.49	3.76
Switzerland	(*)	28,506,000	28,078,131	29,081,675	32,435,782	34,649,615	5.78	6.83
Belgium / Luxembourg		59,506,000	58,598,440	59,421,145	62,619,525	61,728,366	10.29	-1.42
OTHER EUROPE		9,897,000	6,229,959	7,772,078	6,888,174	8,642,076	1.44	25.46
Other countries of Europe		9,897,000	6,229,959	7,772,078	6,888,174	8,642,076	1.44	25.46
MIDDLE EAST		7,816,000	8,812,172	7,755,970	7,934,743	9,993,932	1.67	25.95
All countries of Middle East		7,816,000	8,812,172	7,755,970	7,934,743	9,993,932	1.67	25.95

Yearbook of Tourism Statistics, Data 2009 – 2013, 2015 Edition

FRENCH POLYNESIA

1. Arrivals of non-resident tourists at national borders, by country of residence

		2009	2010	2011	2012	2013	Market share 2013	% Change 2013-2012
TOTAL	(*)	**160,447**	**153,919**	**162,776**	**168,978**	**164,393**	**100.00**	**-2.71**
AFRICA		**278**	**275**	**272**	**288**	**309**	**0.19**	**7.29**
OTHER AFRICA		**278**	**275**	**272**	**288**	**309**	**0.19**	**7.29**
All countries of Africa		278	275	272	288	309	0.19	7.29
AMERICAS		**51,716**	**53,338**	**63,547**	**67,212**	**68,331**	**41.57**	**1.66**
CENTRAL AMERICA		**135**	**134**	**137**	**175**	**94**	**0.06**	**-46.29**
All countries of Central America		135	134	137	175	94	0.06	-46.29
NORTH AMERICA		**45,790**	**47,302**	**57,876**	**60,959**	**61,746**	**37.56**	**1.29**
Canada		4,265	5,468	7,458	7,034	7,206	4.38	2.45
Mexico		745	814	1,033	1,067	884	0.54	-17.15
United States of America		40,403	40,735	49,097	52,527	53,480	32.53	1.81
Hawaii, USA		377	285	288	331	176	0.11	-46.83
SOUTH AMERICA		**5,791**	**5,902**	**5,534**	**6,078**	**6,491**	**3.95**	**6.79**
Argentina		1,433	1,253	1,098	1,264	1,087	0.66	-14.00
Brazil		2,047	2,360	2,530	2,787	3,064	1.86	9.94
Chile		1,706	1,849	1,328	1,328	1,624	0.99	22.29
Other countries of South America		605	440	578	699	716	0.44	2.43
EAST ASIA AND THE PACIFIC		**35,106**	**33,196**	**34,052**	**38,089**	**36,911**	**22.45**	**-3.09**
NORTH-EAST ASIA		**17,948**	**15,682**	**14,846**	**15,394**	**16,119**	**9.81**	**4.71**
China		543	1,143	978	1,183	1,876	1.14	58.58
Hong Kong, China		99	1	214	301	240	0.15	-20.27
Japan		16,353	13,761	12,990	12,989	13,175	8.01	1.43
Korea, Republic of		765	686	506	682	568	0.35	-16.72
Taiwan, Province of China		188	91	158	239	260	0.16	8.79
SOUTH-EAST ASIA		**674**	**659**	**616**	**614**	**687**	**0.42**	**11.89**
Indonesia		128	98	86	65	98	0.06	50.77
Malaysia		62	104	72	134	120	0.07	-10.45
Philippines		187	176	121	91	131	0.08	43.96
Singapore		191	200	200	244	257	0.16	5.33
Thailand		106	81	137	80	81	0.05	1.25
AUSTRALASIA		**11,471**	**12,073**	**13,720**	**17,390**	**15,644**	**9.52**	**-10.04**
Australia		6,557	6,945	8,236	10,224	9,167	5.58	-10.34
New Zealand		4,914	5,128	5,484	7,166	6,477	3.94	-9.61
MELANESIA		**4,006**	**4,048**	**4,085**	**4,114**	**3,914**	**2.38**	**-4.86**
Fiji		131	108	139	92	88	0.05	-4.35
New Caledonia		3,875	3,940	3,946	4,022	3,826	2.33	-4.87
POLYNESIA		**379**	**342**	**361**	**251**	**272**	**0.17**	**8.37**
Cook Islands		268	265	284	215	212	0.13	-1.40
Samoa	(*)	75	72	54	24	39	0.02	62.50
Tonga		36	5	23	12	21	0.01	75.00
OTHER EAST ASIA AND THE PACIFIC		**628**	**392**	**424**	**326**	**275**	**0.17**	**-15.64**
Other countries of Asia		79	56	77	37	57	0.03	54.05
Other countries of Oceania		549	336	347	289	218	0.13	-24.57
EUROPE		**72,857**	**66,561**	**64,272**	**62,661**	**58,045**	**35.31**	**-7.37**
CENTRAL/EASTERN EUROPE		**601**	**519**	**699**	**587**	**847**	**0.52**	**44.29**
Russian Federation		601	519	699	587	847	0.52	44.29
NORTHERN EUROPE		**4,523**	**3,790**	**3,522**	**3,538**	**4,069**	**2.48**	**15.01**
Denmark		228	236	162	197	156	0.09	-20.81
Finland		234	232	205	194	89	0.05	-54.12
Norway		168	158	201	244	296	0.18	21.31
Sweden		411	324	283	286	273	0.17	-4.55
United Kingdom		3,482	2,840	2,671	2,617	3,255	1.98	24.38
SOUTHERN EUROPE		**16,835**	**15,623**	**14,320**	**12,664**	**10,753**	**6.54**	**-15.09**
Italy		11,944	11,208	10,471	9,409	8,103	4.93	-13.88
Portugal		337	311	374	251	224	0.14	-10.76
Spain		4,554	4,104	3,475	3,004	2,426	1.48	-19.24
WESTERN EUROPE		**48,551**	**44,976**	**43,817**	**44,077**	**41,035**	**24.96**	**-6.90**
Austria		999	757	688	619	577	0.35	-6.79
Belgium		995	796	852	882	858	0.52	-2.72

257

Yearbook of Tourism Statistics, Data 2009 – 2013, 2015 Edition

FRENCH POLYNESIA

1. Arrivals of non-resident tourists at national borders, by country of residence

	2009	2010	2011	2012	2013	Market share 2013	% Change 2013-2012
France	39,256	36,544	35,835	35,898	32,946	20.04	-8.22
Germany	4,346	4,256	3,604	3,552	3,477	2.12	-2.11
Luxembourg	143	198	109	135	60	0.04	-55.56
Netherlands	676	565	487	432	454	0.28	5.09
Switzerland	2,136	1,860	2,242	2,559	2,663	1.62	4.06
OTHER EUROPE	**2,347**	**1,653**	**1,914**	**1,795**	**1,341**	**0.82**	**-25.29**
Other countries of Europe	2,347	1,653	1,914	1,795	1,341	0.82	-25.29
MIDDLE EAST	**201**	**231**	**201**	**268**	**276**	**0.17**	**2.99**
All countries of Middle East	201	231	201	268	276	0.17	2.99
SOUTH ASIA	**289**	**318**	**432**	**460**	**521**	**0.32**	**13.26**
India	289	318	432	460	521	0.32	13.26

Yearbook of Tourism Statistics, Data 2009 – 2013, 2015 Edition

FRENCH POLYNESIA

3. Arrivals of non-resident tourists in hotels and similar establishments, by country of residence

	2009	2010	2011	2012	2013	Market share 2013	% Change 2013-2012
TOTAL	138,151	133,032	142,056	148,443	146,304	100.00	-1.44
AFRICA	213	219	206	237	260	0.18	9.70
OTHER AFRICA	213	219	206	237	260	0.18	9.70
All countries of Africa	213	219	206	237	260	0.18	9.70
AMERICAS	48,539	50,606	60,773	64,156	65,517	44.78	2.12
CENTRAL AMERICA	128	129	126	171	89	0.06	-47.95
All countries of Central America	128	129	126	171	89	0.06	-47.95
NORTH AMERICA	43,089	45,015	55,422	58,359	59,254	40.50	1.53
Canada	4,067	5,303	7,241	6,771	6,992	4.78	3.26
Mexico	710	783	1,005	1,014	863	0.59	-14.89
United States of America	38,175	38,807	47,049	50,426	51,334	35.09	1.80
Hawaii, USA	137	122	127	148	65	0.04	-56.08
SOUTH AMERICA	5,322	5,462	5,225	5,626	6,174	4.22	9.74
Argentina	1,402	1,213	1,088	1,206	1,079	0.74	-10.53
Brazil	1,966	2,252	2,469	2,678	3,007	2.06	12.29
Chile	1,387	1,581	1,111	1,077	1,397	0.95	29.71
Other countries of South America	567	416	557	665	691	0.47	3.91
EAST ASIA AND THE PACIFIC	31,156	29,146	29,949	34,019	33,048	22.59	-2.85
NORTH-EAST ASIA	17,740	15,496	14,610	15,207	15,897	10.87	4.54
China	503	1,081	923	1,159	1,812	1.24	56.34
Hong Kong, China	97	1	197	274	226	0.15	-17.52
Japan	16,209	13,657	12,859	12,892	13,078	8.94	1.44
Korea, Republic of	756	672	491	669	552	0.38	-17.49
Taiwan, Province of China	175	85	140	213	229	0.16	7.51
SOUTH-EAST ASIA	584	566	544	524	598	0.41	14.12
Indonesia	108	71	71	47	81	0.06	72.34
Malaysia	50	88	64	122	101	0.07	-17.21
Philippines	168	165	114	78	122	0.08	56.41
Singapore	174	176	185	223	235	0.16	5.38
Thailand	84	66	110	54	59	0.04	9.26
AUSTRALASIA	10,113	10,832	12,489	16,034	14,395	9.84	-10.22
Australia	6,055	6,483	7,680	9,699	8,694	5.94	-10.36
New Zealand	4,058	4,349	4,809	6,335	5,701	3.90	-10.01
MELANESIA	2,117	1,913	1,949	1,991	1,877	1.28	-5.73
Fiji	123	75	100	66	74	0.05	12.12
New Caledonia	1,994	1,838	1,849	1,925	1,803	1.23	-6.34
POLYNESIA	185	133	130	109	109	0.07	
Cook Islands	81	99	70	81	78	0.05	-3.70
Samoa	70	31	42	18	17	0.01	-5.56
Tonga	34	3	18	10	14	0.01	40.00
OTHER EAST ASIA AND THE PACIFIC	417	206	227	154	172	0.12	11.69
Other countries of Asia	63	45	64	24	45	0.03	87.50
Other countries of Oceania	354	161	163	130	127	0.09	-2.31
EUROPE	57,781	52,551	50,518	49,335	46,719	31.93	-5.30
CENTRAL/EASTERN EUROPE	581	515	689	581	825	0.56	42.00
Russian Federation	581	515	689	581	825	0.56	42.00
NORTHERN EUROPE	4,344	3,641	3,388	3,395	3,950	2.70	16.35
Denmark	217	221	155	188	153	0.10	-18.62
Finland	230	225	198	192	86	0.06	-55.21
Norway	154	144	192	232	291	0.20	25.43
Sweden	388	310	269	277	259	0.18	-6.50
United Kingdom	3,355	2,741	2,574	2,506	3,161	2.16	26.14
SOUTHERN EUROPE	16,543	15,409	14,062	12,469	10,567	7.22	-15.25
Italy	11,828	11,083	10,332	9,322	8,011	5.48	-14.06
Portugal	328	307	361	241	210	0.14	-12.86
Spain	4,387	4,019	3,369	2,906	2,346	1.60	-19.27
WESTERN EUROPE	34,033	31,398	30,552	31,180	30,091	20.57	-3.49
Austria	982	740	683	598	565	0.39	-5.52
Belgium	873	693	725	756	774	0.53	2.38

259

FRENCH POLYNESIA

3. Arrivals of non-resident tourists in hotels and similar establishments, by country of residence

	2009	2010	2011	2012	2013	Market share 2013	% Change 2013-2012
France	25,187	23,364	22,958	23,489	22,415	15.32	-4.57
Germany	4,230	4,148	3,514	3,420	3,380	2.31	-1.17
Luxembourg	130	191	101	130	55	0.04	-57.69
Netherlands	655	540	475	420	425	0.29	1.19
Switzerland	1,976	1,722	2,096	2,367	2,477	1.69	4.65
OTHER EUROPE	**2,280**	**1,588**	**1,827**	**1,710**	**1,286**	**0.88**	**-24.80**
Other countries of Europe	2,280	1,588	1,827	1,710	1,286	0.88	-24.80
MIDDLE EAST	**185**	**202**	**180**	**242**	**249**	**0.17**	**2.89**
All countries of Middle East	185	202	180	242	249	0.17	2.89
SOUTH ASIA	**277**	**308**	**430**	**454**	**511**	**0.35**	**12.56**
India	277	308	430	454	511	0.35	12.56

FRENCH POLYNESIA

5. Overnight stays of non-resident tourists in hotels and similar establishments, by country of residence

	2009	2010	2011	2012	2013	Market share 2013	% Change 2013-2012
TOTAL	1,601,188	1,569,826	1,657,407	1,733,039	1,753,608	100.00	1.19
AFRICA	2,911	2,833	2,833	3,430	3,464	0.20	0.99
OTHER AFRICA	2,911	2,833	2,833	3,430	3,464	0.20	0.99
All countries of Africa	2,911	2,833	2,833	3,430	3,464	0.20	0.99
AMERICAS	482,246	506,164	590,195	630,817	659,744	37.62	4.59
CENTRAL AMERICA	1,364	1,498	1,122	1,875	805	0.05	-57.07
All countries of Central America	1,364	1,498	1,122	1,875	805	0.05	-57.07
NORTH AMERICA	425,814	445,653	534,201	567,611	590,493	33.67	4.03
Canada	48,205	62,979	82,105	77,126	84,356	4.81	9.37
Mexico	6,711	7,383	8,459	9,185	8,432	0.48	-8.20
United States of America	369,538	373,683	442,229	479,717	496,874	28.33	3.58
Hawaii, USA	1,360	1,608	1,408	1,583	831	0.05	-47.50
SOUTH AMERICA	55,068	59,013	54,872	61,331	68,446	3.90	11.60
Argentina	16,434	14,010	13,529	15,518	14,342	0.82	-7.58
Brazil	21,016	24,908	24,896	27,820	31,394	1.79	12.85
Chile	12,101	15,410	10,828	10,931	15,158	0.86	38.67
Other countries of South America	5,517	4,685	5,619	7,062	7,552	0.43	6.94
EAST ASIA AND THE PACIFIC	238,941	231,803	251,157	291,060	288,827	16.47	-0.77
NORTH-EAST ASIA	111,427	98,496	98,263	104,957	108,546	6.19	3.42
China	4,356	9,465	8,052	10,461	16,401	0.94	56.78
Hong Kong, China	865	1	1,891	2,740	2,408	0.14	-12.12
Japan	100,200	84,081	83,243	84,871	84,140	4.80	-0.86
Korea, Republic of	4,587	4,245	3,755	4,932	3,698	0.21	-25.02
Taiwan, Province of China	1,419	704	1,322	1,953	1,899	0.11	-2.76
SOUTH-EAST ASIA	6,923	5,561	5,234	6,654	7,247	0.41	8.91
Indonesia	1,315	853	721	1,505	868	0.05	-42.33
Malaysia	605	937	821	1,629	1,516	0.09	-6.94
Philippines	1,709	1,227	984	795	1,285	0.07	61.64
Singapore	1,765	1,839	1,491	2,123	2,880	0.16	35.66
Thailand	1,529	705	1,217	602	698	0.04	15.95
AUSTRALASIA	90,083	102,763	119,934	152,149	144,798	8.26	-4.83
Australia	56,383	65,594	77,965	97,926	92,019	5.25	-6.03
New Zealand	33,700	37,169	41,969	54,223	52,779	3.01	-2.66
MELANESIA	24,425	21,392	24,071	24,036	24,626	1.40	2.45
Fiji	1,138	709	1,010	522	704	0.04	34.87
New Caledonia	23,287	20,683	23,061	23,514	23,922	1.36	1.74
POLYNESIA	1,629	1,242	1,377	1,172	1,062	0.06	-9.39
Cook Islands	659	913	601	906	764	0.04	-15.67
Samoa	288	307	645	156	209	0.01	33.97
Tonga	682	22	131	110	89	0.01	-19.09
OTHER EAST ASIA AND THE PACIFIC	4,454	2,349	2,278	2,092	2,548	0.15	21.80
Other countries of Asia	736	764	626	515	994	0.06	93.01
Other countries of Oceania	3,718	1,585	1,652	1,577	1,554	0.09	-1.46
EUROPE	873,019	824,401	808,104	801,656	793,742	45.26	-0.99
CENTRAL/EASTERN EUROPE	7,250	6,008	8,607	7,329	11,253	0.64	53.54
Russian Federation	7,250	6,008	8,607	7,329	11,253	0.64	53.54
NORTHERN EUROPE	45,831	40,233	35,964	38,613	47,226	2.69	22.31
Denmark	3,338	3,416	2,215	3,238	2,274	0.13	-29.77
Finland	2,201	2,684	2,167	1,839	1,417	0.08	-22.95
Norway	1,895	1,976	2,319	3,880	3,551	0.20	-8.48
Sweden	4,262	3,885	3,513	3,371	4,141	0.24	22.84
United Kingdom	34,135	28,272	25,750	26,285	35,843	2.04	36.36
SOUTHERN EUROPE	178,393	162,466	148,594	130,506	118,514	6.76	-9.19
Italy	135,168	123,124	113,602	101,171	91,854	5.24	-9.21
Portugal	3,171	3,053	3,797	2,937	3,078	0.18	4.80
Spain	40,054	36,289	31,195	26,398	23,582	1.34	-10.67
WESTERN EUROPE	615,218	596,736	593,303	605,400	601,158	34.28	-0.70
Austria	12,471	10,600	9,440	8,849	8,285	0.47	-6.37
Belgium	14,739	11,837	12,265	13,315	13,078	0.75	-1.78

261

FRENCH POLYNESIA

5. Overnight stays of non-resident tourists in hotels and similar establishments, by country of residence

	2009	2010	2011	2012	2013	Market share 2013	% Change 2013-2012
France	488,396	481,901	482,488	484,981	483,426	27.57	-0.32
Germany	57,548	53,935	46,516	49,156	48,227	2.75	-1.89
Luxembourg	1,835	2,915	1,718	1,985	794	0.05	-60.00
Netherlands	7,704	6,964	6,060	5,812	5,312	0.30	-8.60
Switzerland	32,525	28,584	34,816	41,302	42,036	2.40	1.78
OTHER EUROPE	**26,327**	**18,958**	**21,636**	**19,808**	**15,591**	**0.89**	**-21.29**
Other countries of Europe	26,327	18,958	21,636	19,808	15,591	0.89	-21.29
MIDDLE EAST	**1,978**	**2,347**	**2,037**	**2,636**	**2,711**	**0.15**	**2.85**
All countries of Middle East	1,978	2,347	2,037	2,636	2,711	0.15	2.85
SOUTH ASIA	**2,093**	**2,278**	**3,081**	**3,440**	**5,120**	**0.29**	**48.84**
India	2,093	2,278	3,081	3,440	5,120	0.29	48.84

Yearbook of Tourism Statistics, Data 2009 – 2013, 2015 Edition

FRENCH POLYNESIA

6. Overnight stays of non-resident tourists in all types of accommodation establishments, by country of residence

	2009	2010	2011	2012	2013	Market share 2013	% Change 2013-2012
TOTAL	2,204,955	2,166,994	2,281,874	2,379,851	2,311,123	100.00	-2.89
AFRICA	4,321	5,868	5,171	5,238	4,715	0.20	-9.98
OTHER AFRICA	4,321	5,868	5,171	5,238	4,715	0.20	-9.98
All countries of Africa	4,321	5,868	5,171	5,238	4,715	0.20	-9.98
AMERICAS	539,282	559,071	640,922	692,322	713,663	30.88	3.08
CENTRAL AMERICA	1,650	1,582	1,385	1,920	983	0.04	-48.80
All countries of Central America	1,650	1,582	1,385	1,920	983	0.04	-48.80
NORTH AMERICA	474,378	491,536	578,347	620,961	637,048	27.56	2.59
Canada	52,840	67,846	88,141	86,936	89,888	3.89	3.40
Mexico	7,439	8,992	9,206	10,642	9,202	0.40	-13.53
United States of America	409,241	410,715	476,477	518,455	535,200	23.16	3.23
Hawaii, USA	4,858	3,983	4,523	4,928	2,758	0.12	-44.03
SOUTH AMERICA	63,254	65,953	61,190	69,441	75,632	3.27	8.92
Argentina	16,997	14,430	13,683	16,649	14,930	0.65	-10.32
Brazil	23,186	27,606	26,337	30,054	32,673	1.41	8.71
Chile	16,704	18,556	14,967	14,937	19,288	0.83	29.13
Other countries of South America	6,367	5,361	6,203	7,801	8,741	0.38	12.05
EAST ASIA AND THE PACIFIC	311,768	306,380	330,019	370,639	366,124	15.84	-1.22
NORTH-EAST ASIA	114,526	102,025	103,762	109,219	112,701	4.88	3.19
China	5,021	10,923	9,164	10,978	17,737	0.77	61.57
Hong Kong, China	881	1	2,451	3,478	2,646	0.11	-23.92
Japan	102,346	85,818	85,537	86,552	85,883	3.72	-0.77
Korea, Republic of	4,680	4,459	4,667	5,696	4,101	0.18	-28.00
Taiwan, Province of China	1,598	824	1,943	2,515	2,334	0.10	-7.20
SOUTH-EAST ASIA	11,067	7,879	7,662	9,712	10,550	0.46	8.63
Indonesia	2,450	1,696	1,171	2,171	1,418	0.06	-34.68
Malaysia	1,005	1,180	1,083	2,030	1,888	0.08	-7.00
Philippines	2,029	1,414	1,206	1,293	1,450	0.06	12.14
Singapore	2,121	2,320	1,898	2,468	4,369	0.19	77.03
Thailand	3,462	1,269	2,304	1,750	1,425	0.06	-18.57
AUSTRALASIA	113,636	123,910	142,081	176,519	167,472	7.25	-5.13
Australia	66,511	74,142	88,400	108,364	100,828	4.36	-6.95
New Zealand	47,125	49,768	53,681	68,155	66,644	2.88	-2.22
MELANESIA	58,579	61,370	64,715	65,400	65,711	2.84	0.48
Fiji	1,220	1,312	1,777	1,005	1,015	0.04	1.00
New Caledonia	57,359	60,058	62,938	64,395	64,696	2.80	0.47
POLYNESIA	3,891	4,555	4,402	3,181	4,774	0.21	50.08
Cook Islands	2,741	2,999	3,183	2,715	2,783	0.12	2.50
Samoa	802	1,503	1,029	326	1,853	0.08	468.40
Tonga	348	53	190	140	138	0.01	-1.43
OTHER EAST ASIA AND THE PACIFIC	10,069	6,641	7,397	6,608	4,916	0.21	-25.61
Other countries of Asia	1,200	1,169	2,019	971	1,641	0.07	69.00
Other countries of Oceania	8,869	5,472	5,378	5,637	3,275	0.14	-41.90
EUROPE	1,344,929	1,289,821	1,299,966	1,304,206	1,217,519	52.68	-6.65
CENTRAL/EASTERN EUROPE	7,811	6,133	8,762	7,499	12,268	0.53	63.60
Russian Federation	7,811	6,133	8,762	7,499	12,268	0.53	63.60
NORTHERN EUROPE	49,853	44,092	39,706	43,315	51,146	2.21	18.08
Denmark	3,955	3,748	2,314	3,449	2,323	0.10	-32.65
Finland	2,245	2,807	2,341	1,850	1,690	0.07	-8.65
Norway	2,159	2,308	2,779	4,155	3,819	0.17	-8.09
Sweden	4,863	4,195	3,854	3,573	4,529	0.20	26.76
United Kingdom	36,631	31,034	28,418	30,288	38,785	1.68	28.05
SOUTHERN EUROPE	185,035	169,435	156,422	136,455	125,075	5.41	-8.34
Italy	137,994	126,849	117,760	103,466	94,934	4.11	-8.25
Portugal	3.292	3,139	4,164	3,120	3,599	0.16	15.35
Spain	43,749	39,447	34,498	29,869	26,542	1.15	-11.14
WESTERN EUROPE	1,074,293	1,048,989	1,070,680	1,094,502	1,011,785	43.78	-7.56
Austria	12,730	10,872	9,604	9,294	8,588	0.37	-7.60
Belgium	17,870	15,682	15,898	17,845	16,405	0.71	-8.07

263

Yearbook of Tourism Statistics, Data 2009 – 2013, 2015 Edition

FRENCH POLYNESIA

6. Overnight stays of non-resident tourists in all types of accommodation establishments, by country of residence

	2009	2010	2011	2012	2013	Market share 2013	% Change 2013-2012
France	936,340	921,390	948,470	959,467	880,944	38.12	-8.18
Germany	60,118	57,119	49,204	52,577	51,078	2.21	-2.85
Luxembourg	2,065	3,071	1,958	2,060	924	0.04	-55.15
Netherlands	8,127	7,656	6,340	6,159	5,849	0.25	-5.03
Switzerland	37,043	33,199	39,206	47,100	47,997	2.08	1.90
OTHER EUROPE	**27,937**	**21,172**	**24,396**	**22,435**	**17,245**	**0.75**	**-23.13**
Other countries of Europe	27,937	21,172	24,396	22,435	17,245	0.75	-23.13
MIDDLE EAST	**2,364**	**3,353**	**2,691**	**3,477**	**3,654**	**0.16**	**5.09**
All countries of Middle East	2,364	3,353	2,691	3,477	3,654	0.16	5.09
SOUTH ASIA	**2,291**	**2,501**	**3,105**	**3,969**	**5,448**	**0.24**	**37.26**
India	2,291	2,501	3,105	3,969	5,448	0.24	37.26

Yearbook of Tourism Statistics, Data 2009 – 2013, 2015 Edition

GAMBIA

1. Arrivals of non-resident tourists at national borders, by nationality

	2009	2010	2011	2012	2013	Market share 2013	% Change 2013-2012
TOTAL (*)	**141,569**	**91,099**	**106,393**	**157,323**	**171,200**	**100.00**	**8.82**
AFRICA	**3,111**	**2,274**	**15,306**	**16,191**	**22,808**	**13.32**	**40.87**
OTHER AFRICA	**3,111**	**2,274**	**15,306**	**16,191**	**22,808**	**13.32**	**40.87**
All countries of Africa	3,111	2,274	15,306	16,191	22,808	13.32	40.87
AMERICAS	**2,342**	**1,504**	**2,236**	**3,149**	**3,104**	**1.81**	**-1.43**
NORTH AMERICA	**2,342**	**1,504**	**2,236**	**3,149**	**3,104**	**1.81**	**-1.43**
Canada	412	241	200				
United States of America	1,930	1,263	2,036	3,149	3,104	1.81	-1.43
EAST ASIA AND THE PACIFIC	**151**	**77**	**66**				
NORTH-EAST ASIA	**151**	**77**	**66**				
Taiwan, Province of China	151	77	66				
EUROPE	**115,260**	**72,984**	**86,692**	**108,633**	**108,956**	**63.64**	**0.30**
CENTRAL/EASTERN EUROPE	**425**	**489**	**261**	**465**	**2,093**	**1.22**	**350.11**
Czech Republic	71	219	27	193	113	0.07	-41.45
Estonia	56	43	11				
Poland	298	227	223	272	1,980	1.16	627.94
NORTHERN EUROPE	**85,814**	**53,891**	**61,571**	**73,266**	**61,308**	**35.81**	**-16.32**
Denmark	4,547	2,627	1,316	1,660	1,448	0.85	-12.77
Finland	3,586	1,598	2,904	1,896	2,624	1.53	38.40
Iceland	42	23	67				
Ireland	1,277	1,530	2,662	2,084	1,539	0.90	-26.15
Norway	4,123	1,370	1,253	1,540	1,878	1.10	21.95
Sweden	8,302	6,493	6,387	8,057	7,953	4.65	-1.29
United Kingdom	63,937	40,250	46,982	58,029	45,866	26.79	-20.96
SOUTHERN EUROPE	**6,211**	**4,147**	**5,206**	**3,982**	**6,242**	**3.65**	**56.76**
Greece	43	24	9				
Italy	1,200	245	234	412	562	0.33	36.41
Spain	4,968	3,878	4,963	3,570	5,680	3.32	59.10
WESTERN EUROPE	**22,810**	**14,457**	**19,654**	**30,920**	**39,313**	**22.96**	**27.14**
Austria	351	254	489	402	910	0.53	126.37
Belgium	3,118	1,983	2,234	5,322	5,068	2.96	-4.77
France	1,130	834	812	1,147	1,568	0.92	36.70
Germany	3,539	2,290	3,020	5,350	6,250	3.65	16.82
Netherlands	14,246	8,870	12,906	18,699	25,517	14.90	36.46
Switzerland	426	226	193				
NOT SPECIFIED	**20,705**	**14,260**	**2,093**	**29,350**	**36,332**	**21.22**	**23.79**
Other countries of the World	3,757	3,079	2,093	6,098	7,157	4.18	17.37
Nationals Residing Abroad	16,948	11,181		23,252	29,175	17.04	25.47

Yearbook of Tourism Statistics, Data 2009 – 2013, 2015 Edition

GEORGIA

2. Arrivals of non-resident visitors at national borders, by country of residence

	2009	2010	2011	2012	2013	Market share 2013	% Change 2013-2012
TOTAL	1,500,049	2,031,717	2,822,363	4,428,221	5,392,303	100.00	21.77
AFRICA	1,090	3,397	4,229	7,110	5,024	0.09	-29.34
EAST AFRICA	210	2,242	1,878	3,789	2,591	0.05	-31.62
Burundi	3			5	7	0.00	40.00
Comoros			2	8	34	0.00	325.00
Djibouti		2	1	7	4	0.00	-42.86
Eritrea	4		1	9	9	0.00	
Ethiopia	17	32	17	36	33	0.00	-8.33
Kenya	16	26	18	53	72	0.00	35.85
Madagascar	16	41	18	36	39	0.00	8.33
Malawi	2	4	6	7	8	0.00	14.29
Mauritius	14	19	4	28	35	0.00	25.00
Mozambique	4	1		8	8	0.00	
Reunion	12	55	18	15	23	0.00	53.33
Rwanda	14	9	9	17	13	0.00	-23.53
Seychelles	2	445	403	546	244	0.00	-55.31
Somalia	15	56	47	48	79	0.00	64.58
Uganda	12	21	25	31	18	0.00	-41.94
United Republic of Tanzania	7	12	13	13	11	0.00	-15.38
Zambia	8	252	173	274	176	0.00	-35.77
Zimbabwe	61	1,263	1,122	2,647	1,778	0.03	-32.83
Other countries of East Africa	3	4	1	1			
CENTRAL AFRICA	175	70	89	89	61	0.00	-31.46
Angola	2	4	1	4	7	0.00	75.00
Cameroon	130	38	63	60	34	0.00	-43.33
Central African Republic	1	4	2	3	5	0.00	66.67
Chad		1	1	2	4	0.00	100.00
Congo	12	8	13	14	7	0.00	-50.00
Gabon	19	15	9	6	4	0.00	-33.33
Sao Tome and Principe	11						
NORTH AFRICA	114	213	358	582	655	0.01	12.54
Algeria	13	44	34	58	61	0.00	5.17
Morocco	46	96	262	342	387	0.01	13.16
Sudan	28	37	28	49	47	0.00	-4.08
Tunisia	27	36	34	133	160	0.00	20.30
SOUTHERN AFRICA	197	248	536	990	1,044	0.02	5.45
Botswana	6	4		2	23	0.00	1,050.00
Lesotho			1				
Namibia	1	16	7	15	4	0.00	-73.33
South Africa	179	228	525	973	1,015	0.02	4.32
Swaziland	11		3		2	0.00	
WEST AFRICA	394	624	1,368	1,660	673	0.01	-59.46
Benin		4	2	15	5	0.00	-66.67
Burkina Faso	8	1	2	3	3	0.00	
Cabo Verde	7	80	23	10	7	0.00	-30.00
Côte d'Ivoire	200	87	49	68	39	0.00	-42.65
Gambia	7	1		13	11	0.00	-15.38
Ghana	68	17	62	84	25	0.00	-70.24
Guinea	16	1	11	11	8	0.00	-27.27
Guinea-Bissau			1	5	3	0.00	-40.00
Liberia	9	295	822	389	32	0.00	-91.77
Mali	9	1	10	11	14	0.00	27.27
Mauritania			4	6	1	0.00	-83.33
Niger		2	5	11	9	0.00	-18.18
Nigeria	60	67	325	958	468	0.01	-51.15
Senegal	4	59	43	63	36	0.00	-42.86
Sierra Leone	4	3	7	10	9	0.00	-10.00
Togo	2	6	2	3	3	0.00	

Yearbook of Tourism Statistics, Data 2009 – 2013, 2015 Edition

GEORGIA

2. Arrivals of non-resident visitors at national borders, by country of residence

	2009	2010	2011	2012	2013	Market share 2013	% Change 2013-2012
AMERICAS	19,659	24,656	29,286	33,898	32,593	0.60	-3.85
CARIBBEAN	177	1,291	1,028	497	568	0.01	14.29
Anguilla			1	1			
Antigua and Barbuda	67	1,046	682	173	159	0.00	-8.09
Bahamas	31	44	147	24	40	0.00	66.67
Barbados	2	1	1	4			
Bermuda	1						
British Virgin Islands		22	26	26	20	0.00	-23.08
Cuba	15	30	37	57	51	0.00	-10.53
Dominica		2		6	12	0.00	100.00
Dominican Republic	9	1	11	15	26	0.00	73.33
Grenada	1			2			
Guadeloupe	1	1					
Haiti	1	11	3	6	1	0.00	-83.33
Jamaica	7	26	6	30	16	0.00	-46.67
Netherlands Antilles				1	1	0.00	
Puerto Rico	2	2	9	1			
Saint Kitts and Nevis	1	2	6	52	103	0.00	98.08
Saint Lucia		1		9	1	0.00	-88.89
Saint Vincent and the Grenadines		9	12	11	63	0.00	472.73
Trinidad and Tobago	39	56	58	44	43	0.00	-2.27
Turks and Caicos Islands		18	15	21	20	0.00	-4.76
United States Virgin Islands		19	14	14	12	0.00	-14.29
CENTRAL AMERICA	48	284	321	314	193	0.00	-38.54
Belize	2	5	4	4	1	0.00	-75.00
Costa Rica	5	8	21	58	42	0.00	-27.59
El Salvador	7	26	9	36	46	0.00	27.78
Guatemala	6	2	22	30	11	0.00	-63.33
Honduras	15	34	27	37	21	0.00	-43.24
Nicaragua	1	2	3	5	3	0.00	-40.00
Panama	12	207	235	144	69	0.00	-52.08
NORTH AMERICA	18,924	22,232	26,716	31,697	30,214	0.56	-4.68
Canada	1,913	2,052	2,345	2,951	3,290	0.06	11.49
Mexico	77	99	135	233	211	0.00	-9.44
United States of America	16,934	20,081	24,236	28,513	26,713	0.50	-6.31
SOUTH AMERICA	510	849	1,221	1,390	1,618	0.03	16.40
Argentina	158	97	164	203	278	0.01	36.95
Bolivia	9	15	10	35	36	0.00	2.86
Brazil	169	257	311	428	604	0.01	41.12
Chile	13	31	48	70	71	0.00	1.43
Colombia	37	72	70	103	163	0.00	58.25
Ecuador	50	33	135	62	78	0.00	25.81
French Guiana		155	332	305	182	0.00	-40.33
Guyana	2		3	2	5	0.00	150.00
Paraguay	1	13	12	14	10	0.00	-28.57
Peru	29	72	65	71	66	0.00	-7.04
Suriname		2		13	12	0.00	-7.69
Uruguay	7	9	40	18	46	0.00	155.56
Venezuela	35	93	31	66	67	0.00	1.52
EAST ASIA AND THE PACIFIC	11,373	14,492	19,613	26,062	28,606	0.53	9.76
NORTH-EAST ASIA	4,152	5,807	10,862	15,929	16,632	0.31	4.41
China	2,013	2,725	6,522	9,995	8,830	0.16	-11.66
Hong Kong, China	5	21	14	34	19	0.00	-44.12
Japan	919	1,798	2,419	3,447	4,513	0.08	30.93
Korea, Dem. People's Republic of		8	1	3	9	0.00	200.00
Korea, Republic of	662	935	1,419	1,763	2,433	0.05	38.00
Mongolia	106	86	128	167	154	0.00	-7.78
Taiwan, Province of China	447	234	359	520	674	0.01	29.62

Yearbook of Tourism Statistics, Data 2009 – 2013, 2015 Edition

GEORGIA

2. Arrivals of non-resident visitors at national borders, by country of residence

	2009	2010	2011	2012	2013	Market share 2013	% Change 2013-2012
SOUTH-EAST ASIA	**6,024**	**7,334**	**6,894**	**7,904**	**9,136**	**0.17**	**15.59**
Brunei Darussalam		3	6				
Cambodia	6	7	11	8	4	0.00	-50.00
Indonesia	188	600	311	389	539	0.01	38.56
Lao People's Democratic Republic	4	5	1	7	7	0.00	
Malaysia	58	67	112	281	263	0.00	-6.41
Myanmar	202	92	84	74	99	0.00	33.78
Philippines	5,386	6,342	6,114	6,310	7,255	0.13	14.98
Singapore	53	115	84	237	190	0.00	-19.83
Thailand	92	45	110	252	723	0.01	186.90
Viet Nam	35	58	61	346	56	0.00	-83.82
AUSTRALASIA	**1,153**	**1,193**	**1,618**	**2,094**	**2,722**	**0.05**	**29.99**
Australia	949	956	1,319	1,658	2,176	0.04	31.24
New Zealand	204	237	299	436	546	0.01	25.23
MELANESIA	**8**	**62**	**23**	**54**	**31**	**0.00**	**-42.59**
Fiji	3	2		41	11	0.00	-73.17
Papua New Guinea		1	4	1	1	0.00	
Solomon Islands	3	9	8	5	12	0.00	140.00
Vanuatu	2	50	11	7	7	0.00	
MICRONESIA	**1**	**71**	**164**	**50**	**52**	**0.00**	**4.00**
Kiribati		1					
Marshall Islands	1	68	164	48	52	0.00	8.33
Nauru		2					
Palau				2			
POLYNESIA	**35**	**25**	**52**	**31**	**33**	**0.00**	**6.45**
American Samoa	7	9	6	9	7	0.00	-22.22
French Polynesia			3	2	1	0.00	-50.00
Samoa	1	5	31	5	16	0.00	220.00
Tonga	5	1	2	1	1	0.00	
Tuvalu	21	2	10	3	2	0.00	-33.33
Wallis and Futuna Islands	1	8		11	6	0.00	-45.45
EUROPE	**1,447,516**	**1,956,552**	**2,695,235**	**4,225,635**	**5,168,046**	**95.84**	**22.30**
CENTRAL/EASTERN EUROPE	**974,871**	**1,317,444**	**1,830,148**	**2,541,032**	**3,390,455**	**62.88**	**33.43**
Armenia	351,049	547,510	699,382	921,929	1,291,838	23.96	40.12
Azerbaijan	418,992	497,969	714,418	931,933	1,075,857	19.95	15.44
Belarus	2,503	5,016	5,344	7,972	12,915	0.24	62.00
Bulgaria	7,123	8,738	10,309	10,668	10,878	0.20	1.97
Czech Republic	2,290	3,060	3,897	4,984	6,562	0.12	31.66
Estonia	1,754	2,207	2,749	4,366	3,721	0.07	-14.77
Hungary	808	836	1,130	1,337	1,880	0.03	40.61
Kazakhstan	5,531	8,411	18,565	15,115	21,148	0.39	39.91
Kyrgyzstan	1,107	2,222	3,183	2,626	2,672	0.05	1.75
Latvia	2,588	3,525	4,802	5,693	6,336	0.12	11.29
Lithuania	2,448	2,916	4,081	5,319	5,647	0.10	6.17
Poland	4,634	7,105	12,082	20,563	36,946	0.69	79.67
Republic of Moldova	1,880	2,390	2,737	4,001	5,442	0.10	36.02
Romania	1,614	1,933	2,347	3,597	3,524	0.07	-2.03
Russian Federation	127,937	170,584	278,458	513,930	767,396	14.23	49.32
Slovakia	861	976	1,085	1,300	1,836	0.03	41.23
Tajikistan	237	333	540	687	816	0.02	18.78
Turkmenistan	375	1,287	1,126	2,550	2,506	0.05	-1.73
Ukraine	39,339	47,596	58,966	76,610	126,797	2.35	65.51
Uzbekistan	1,801	2,830	4,947	5,852	5,738	0.11	-1.95
NORTHERN EUROPE	**16,523**	**18,168**	**21,130**	**26,211**	**30,167**	**0.56**	**15.09**
Denmark	1,036	1,370	1,452	2,130	2,501	0.05	17.42
Finland	944	1,227	1,460	2,236	3,331	0.06	48.97
Iceland	45	47	161	102	92	0.00	-9.80
Ireland	804	884	970	1,330	1,381	0.03	3.83
Norway	894	1,184	1,483	1,894	2,008	0.04	6.02

Yearbook of Tourism Statistics, Data 2009 – 2013, 2015 Edition

GEORGIA

2. Arrivals of non-resident visitors at national borders, by country of residence

	2009	2010	2011	2012	2013	Market share 2013	% Change 2013-2012
Sweden	2,167	2,471	2,991	3,714	4,182	0.08	12.60
United Kingdom	10,633	10,985	12,613	14,805	16,672	0.31	12.61
SOUTHERN EUROPE	**23,190**	**27,710**	**32,188**	**37,286**	**42,853**	**0.79**	**14.93**
Albania	161	329	258	403	315	0.01	-21.84
Andorra	2	6	9	13	6	0.00	-53.85
Bosnia and Herzegovina	203	206	340	503	473	0.01	-5.96
Croatia	533	623	1,307	839	1,329	0.02	58.40
Greece	14,300	16,424	17,664	19,777	22,024	0.41	11.36
Holy See	35	36	35	38	23	0.00	-39.47
Italy	4,994	5,886	6,873	8,438	9,677	0.18	14.68
Malta	86	167	91	102	88	0.00	-13.73
Montenegro	406	574	194	136	124	0.00	-8.82
Portugal	283	448	559	863	1,098	0.02	27.23
San Marino	15	74	35	41	77	0.00	87.80
Serbia	12	3	593	1,223	1,485	0.03	21.42
Slovenia	410	528	833	777	937	0.02	20.59
Spain	1,585	2,229	3,156	3,758	4,723	0.09	25.68
TFYR of Macedonia	165	177	241	375	474	0.01	26.40
WESTERN EUROPE	**31,491**	**37,878**	**47,839**	**56,617**	**66,661**	**1.24**	**17.74**
Austria	1,794	2,488	3,144	4,737	5,758	0.11	21.55
Belgium	1,622	1,991	2,391	2,795	3,763	0.07	34.63
France	6,941	8,486	10,695	12,004	14,239	0.26	18.62
Germany	15,351	17,619	22,204	26,448	30,815	0.57	16.51
Liechtenstein	9	7	11	21	31	0.00	47.62
Luxembourg	65	111	126	165	175	0.00	6.06
Monaco	6	2	7	1	4	0.00	300.00
Netherlands	4,145	5,198	6,883	7,437	8,181	0.15	10.00
Switzerland	1,558	1,976	2,378	3,009	3,695	0.07	22.80
EAST MEDITERRANEAN EUROPE	**401,441**	**555,352**	**763,930**	**1,564,489**	**1,637,910**	**30.37**	**4.69**
Cyprus	202	312	407	402	550	0.01	36.82
Israel	16,757	19,447	25,438	30,851	39,922	0.74	29.40
Turkey	384,482	535,593	738,085	1,533,236	1,597,438	29.62	4.19
MIDDLE EAST	**3,308**	**3,427**	**5,663**	**17,141**	**63,063**	**1.17**	**267.91**
Bahrain	8	5	19	110	497	0.01	351.82
Egypt	391	431	733	2,596	9,103	0.17	250.65
Iraq	157	126	599	6,947	41,239	0.76	493.62
Jordan	155	172	216	318	566	0.01	77.99
Kuwait	46	59	110	374	1,511	0.03	304.01
Lebanon	249	272	481	742	956	0.02	28.84
Libya	13	24	26	70	88	0.00	25.71
Oman	13	21	14	154	398	0.01	158.44
Palestine	10	14	7	18	44	0.00	144.44
Qatar	4	22	21	72	152	0.00	111.11
Saudi Arabia	19	189	166	1,169	3,780	0.07	223.35
Syrian Arab Republic	2,135	2,021	3,115	4,020	3,291	0.06	-18.13
United Arab Emirates	72	60	147	498	1,339	0.02	168.88
Yemen	36	11	9	53	99	0.00	86.79
SOUTH ASIA	**14,572**	**27,810**	**66,073**	**97,925**	**93,043**	**1.73**	**-4.99**
Afghanistan	55	45	63	111	97	0.00	-12.61
Bangladesh	130	77	495	135	124	0.00	-8.15
Bhutan				1	1	0.00	
India	3,674	5,653	4,578	6,833	6,195	0.11	-9.34
Iran, Islamic Republic of	9,848	21,313	60,191	89,697	85,598	1.59	-4.57
Maldives	10	9	5	12	16	0.00	33.33
Nepal	244	284	145	178	152	0.00	-14.61
Pakistan	329	220	316	401	382	0.01	-4.74
Sri Lanka	282	209	280	557	478	0.01	-14.18
NOT SPECIFIED	**2,531**	**1,383**	**2,264**	**20,450**	**1,928**	**0.04**	**-90.57**
Other countries of the World	2,531	1,383	2,264	20,450	1,928	0.04	-90.57

Yearbook of Tourism Statistics, Data 2009 – 2013, 2015 Edition

GEORGIA

3. Arrivals of non-resident tourists in hotels and similar establishments, by country of residence

	2009	2010	2011	2012	2013	Market share 2013	% Change 2013-2012
TOTAL	150,898	306,547	438,477	625,558	773,816	100.00	23.70
AFRICA	434	337	1,436	4,433	2,425	0.31	-45.30
OTHER AFRICA	434	337	1,436	4,433	2,425	0.31	-45.30
All countries of Africa	434	337	1,436	4,433	2,425	0.31	-45.30
AMERICAS	21,500	29,338	27,340	39,297	15,773	2.04	-59.86
NORTH AMERICA	21,049	28,942	26,444	38,097	14,743	1.91	-61.30
Canada	504	3,414	543	1,746	1,491	0.19	-14.60
Mexico	14	6	6	51	35	0.00	-31.37
United States of America	20,531	25,522	25,895	36,300	13,217	1.71	-63.59
SOUTH AMERICA	431	366	495	991	348	0.04	-64.88
Argentina	80	138	340	564	256	0.03	-54.61
Brazil	63	227	125	410	69	0.01	-83.17
Chile	131	1	12	13	22	0.00	69.23
Uruguay	157		18	4	1	0.00	-75.00
OTHER AMERICAS	20	30	401	209	682	0.09	226.32
Other countries of the Americas	20	30	401	209	682	0.09	226.32
EAST ASIA AND THE PACIFIC	2,881	4,787	9,627	15,475	25,722	3.32	66.22
NORTH-EAST ASIA	1,598	2,309	5,398	6,245	7,321	0.95	17.23
China	920	582	4,099	4,439	5,040	0.65	13.54
Japan	678	1,727	1,299	1,806	2,281	0.29	26.30
AUSTRALASIA	301	954	356	933	1,580	0.20	69.35
Australia	301	954	356	933	1,580	0.20	69.35
OTHER EAST ASIA AND THE PACIFIC	982	1,524	3,873	8,297	16,821	2.17	102.74
Other countries of Asia	982	1,524	3,873	8,297	16,821	2.17	102.74
EUROPE	124,849	250,977	347,543	498,471	582,530	75.28	16.86
CENTRAL/EASTERN EUROPE	63,079	124,288	171,029	253,041	322,034	41.62	27.27
Armenia	16,239	27,715	32,947	42,630	48,316	6.24	13.34
Azerbaijan	14,465	30,501	48,124	67,064	60,631	7.84	-9.59
Belarus	445	1,374	1,528	4,674	5,087	0.66	8.84
Bulgaria	1,581	1,269	1,254	2,489	2,348	0.30	-5.66
Czech Republic	856	1,619	3,926	4,519	2,775	0.36	-38.59
Hungary	339	1,002	692	1,372	1,083	0.14	-21.06
Kazakhstan	1,496	3,481	6,383	7,155	10,628	1.37	48.54
Kyrgyzstan	1,203	602	787	839	700	0.09	-16.57
Poland	3,026	4,671	6,549	17,075	29,692	3.84	73.89
Republic of Moldova	264	740	1,035	1,480	978	0.13	-33.92
Romania	550	1,568	1,133	1,993	2,243	0.29	12.54
Russian Federation	7,479	11,436	17,379	40,683	51,960	6.71	27.72
Slovakia	370	560	528	576	1,670	0.22	189.93
Tajikistan	285	735	668	631	117	0.02	-81.46
Turkmenistan	970	8,336	10,191	975	1,641	0.21	68.31
Ukraine	9,096	18,537	25,542	45,288	62,830	8.12	38.73
Uzbekistan	453	1,046	1,489	1,564	1,463	0.19	-6.46
Other countries Central/East Europe	3,962	9,096	10,874	12,034	37,872	4.89	214.71
NORTHERN EUROPE	10,625	16,342	25,409	27,217	14,627	1.89	-46.26
Denmark	561	1,084	1,720	2,034	1,891	0.24	-7.03
Finland	488	762	1,006	1,436	826	0.11	-42.48
Iceland	50	81	516	262	144	0.02	-45.04
Ireland	87	662	834	1,367	1,171	0.15	-14.34
Norway	390	329	520	1,355	1,102	0.14	-18.67
Sweden	939	1,835	2,349	3,305	2,623	0.34	-20.64
United Kingdom	8,110	11,589	18,464	17,458	6,870	0.89	-60.65
SOUTHERN EUROPE	6,090	9,424	17,149	17,749	18,124	2.34	2.11
Greece	1,324	2,598	5,164	5,339	5,809	0.75	8.80
Italy	3,145	4,167	6,519	7,052	7,306	0.94	3.60
Portugal	125	280	818	765	277	0.04	-63.79
Serbia and Montenegro	84	233	50	131	45	0.01	-65.65
Spain	1,412	2,146	4,598	4,462	4,687	0.61	5.04

Yearbook of Tourism Statistics, Data 2009 – 2013, 2015 Edition

GEORGIA

3. Arrivals of non-resident tourists in hotels and similar establishments, by country of residence

	2009	2010	2011	2012	2013	Market share 2013	% Change 2013-2012
WESTERN EUROPE	16,055	27,823	38,079	46,076	46,184	5.97	0.23
Austria	1,159	2,438	3,081	3,777	1,602	0.21	-57.59
Belgium	819	1,115	1,643	2,372	1,559	0.20	-34.27
France	3,537	6,520	8,275	10,763	11,874	1.53	10.32
Germany	8,348	11,837	18,571	20,893	24,034	3.11	15.03
Luxembourg	157	1,113	229	223	130	0.02	-41.70
Netherlands	1,920	4,327	5,400	6,110	4,687	0.61	-23.29
Switzerland	115	473	880	1,938	2,298	0.30	18.58
EAST MEDITERRANEAN EUROPE	28,599	72,087	95,419	151,528	168,389	21.76	11.13
Israel	10,667	26,367	27,359	32,765	51,772	6.69	58.01
Turkey	17,932	45,720	68,060	118,763	116,617	15.07	-1.81
OTHER EUROPE	401	1,013	458	2,860	13,172	1.70	360.56
Other countries of Europe	401	1,013	458	2,860	13,172	1.70	360.56
SOUTH ASIA	1,234	17,413	23,990	41,678	39,565	5.11	-5.07
India	688	1,355	1,415	2,681	2,300	0.30	-14.21
Iran, Islamic Republic of	546	16,058	22,575	38,997	37,265	4.82	-4.44
NOT SPECIFIED		3,695	28,541	26,204	107,801	13.93	311.39
Other countries of the World		3,695	28,541	26,204	107,801	13.93	311.39

Yearbook of Tourism Statistics, Data 2009 – 2013, 2015 Edition

GERMANY

3. Arrivals of non-resident tourists in hotels and similar establishments, by country of residence

		2009	2010	2011	2012	2013	Market share 2013	% Change 2013-2012
TOTAL		21,467,043	23,896,638	25,310,793	27,076,452	28,122,653	100.00	3.86
AFRICA		144,609	180,743	181,422	212,239	222,146	0.79	4.67
SOUTHERN AFRICA		46,865	61,996	64,399	70,126	67,360	0.24	-3.94
South Africa		46,865	61,996	64,399	70,126	67,360	0.24	-3.94
OTHER AFRICA		97,744	118,747	117,023	142,113	154,786	0.55	8.92
Other countries of Africa		97,744	118,747	117,023	142,113	154,786	0.55	8.92
AMERICAS		2,322,295	2,720,333	2,754,473	2,972,331	3,003,543	10.68	1.05
NORTH AMERICA		2,098,850	2,421,642	2,400,339	2,555,439	2,557,010	9.09	0.06
Canada		208,940	251,173	259,836	271,944	269,988	0.96	-0.72
Mexico		43,720	59,394	64,206	71,881	81,282	0.29	13.08
United States of America		1,846,190	2,111,075	2,076,297	2,211,614	2,205,740	7.84	-0.27
SOUTH AMERICA		121,725	176,576	216,933	255,679	267,329	0.95	4.56
Brazil		121,725	176,576	216,933	255,679	267,329	0.95	4.56
OTHER AMERICAS		101,720	122,115	137,201	161,213	179,204	0.64	11.16
Other countries of the Americas		101,720	122,115	137,201	161,213	179,204	0.64	11.16
EAST ASIA AND THE PACIFIC		1,656,636	2,037,023	2,312,695	2,663,265	2,817,675	10.02	5.80
NORTH-EAST ASIA		1,059,437	1,278,733	1,493,324	1,744,687	1,842,361	6.55	5.60
China	(*)	367,819	491,112	615,346	729,438	837,489	2.98	14.81
Japan		517,842	586,012	624,970	714,938	692,730	2.46	-3.11
Korea, Republic of		111,194	130,590	158,848	194,582	203,903	0.73	4.79
Taiwan, Province of China		62,582	71,019	94,160	105,729	108,239	0.38	2.37
AUSTRALASIA		197,796	252,881	267,027	289,316	297,910	1.06	2.97
Australia, New Zealand		197,796	252,881	267,027	289,316	297,910	1.06	2.97
OTHER EAST ASIA AND THE PACIFIC		399,403	505,409	552,344	629,262	677,404	2.41	7.65
Other countries East Asia/Pacific	(*)	399,403	505,409	552,344	629,262	677,404	2.41	7.65
EUROPE		16,363,802	17,995,732	19,163,324	20,215,986	20,938,310	74.45	3.57
CENTRAL/EASTERN EUROPE		1,412,665	1,697,777	1,978,456	2,249,185	2,465,157	8.77	9.60
Czech Republic		246,627	283,448	320,627	345,274	365,242	1.30	5.78
Hungary		163,796	187,158	206,567	215,338	223,744	0.80	3.90
Poland		453,899	536,123	602,766	650,150	714,769	2.54	9.94
Russian Federation		434,314	558,700	698,679	873,020	987,433	3.51	13.11
Baltic countries		114,029	132,348	149,817	165,403	173,969	0.62	5.18
NORTHERN EUROPE		3,895,275	4,347,998	4,447,148	4,690,113	4,873,223	17.33	3.90
Denmark		955,600	1,021,525	1,048,335	1,147,029	1,196,904	4.26	4.35
Finland		220,830	250,488	265,213	263,784	262,901	0.93	-0.33
Iceland		33,278	30,926	33,560	30,055	29,115	0.10	-3.13
Ireland		120,070	123,081	119,797	117,375	117,502	0.42	0.11
Norway		296,674	349,394	349,537	374,112	380,758	1.35	1.78
Sweden		696,742	784,273	775,409	815,093	838,368	2.98	2.86
United Kingdom		1,572,081	1,788,311	1,855,297	1,942,665	2,047,675	7.28	5.41
SOUTHERN EUROPE		2,284,089	2,429,673	2,493,084	2,497,597	2,476,943	8.81	-0.83
Greece		179,664	157,339	152,300	119,296	118,692	0.42	-0.51
Italy		1,311,616	1,392,917	1,411,844	1,447,877	1,444,241	5.14	-0.25
Portugal		102,422	111,561	113,138	108,543	109,273	0.39	0.67
Spain		690,387	767,856	815,802	821,881	804,737	2.86	-2.09
WESTERN EUROPE		7,862,667	8,472,059	9,069,147	9,482,412	9,685,347	34.44	2.14
Austria		1,156,134	1,284,219	1,393,422	1,454,911	1,518,429	5.40	4.37
Belgium		956,360	1,006,397	1,057,611	1,094,003	1,123,592	4.00	2.70
France		1,107,476	1,207,179	1,299,743	1,356,161	1,391,921	4.95	2.64
Luxembourg		186,184	198,047	202,295	213,252	221,925	0.79	4.07
Netherlands		2,793,164	2,960,893	3,055,443	3,140,309	3,113,984	11.07	-0.84
Switzerland		1,663,349	1,815,324	2,060,633	2,223,776	2,315,496	8.23	4.12
EAST MEDITERRANEAN EUROPE		298,532	357,075	400,916	454,145	483,770	1.72	6.52
Israel		142,953	171,942	185,951	219,360	235,325	0.84	7.28
Turkey		155,579	185,133	214,965	234,785	248,445	0.88	5.82
OTHER EUROPE		610,574	691,150	774,573	842,534	953,870	3.39	13.21
Other countries of Europe		610,574	691,150	774,573	842,534	953,870	3.39	13.21

Yearbook of Tourism Statistics, Data 2009 – 2013, 2015 Edition

GERMANY

3. Arrivals of non-resident tourists in hotels and similar establishments, by country of residence

	2009	2010	2011	2012	2013	Market share 2013	% Change 2013-2012
MIDDLE EAST	**254,820**	**331,426**	**337,139**	**439,607**	**506,878**	**1.80**	**15.30**
All countries of Middle East	254,820	331,426	337,139	439,607	506,878	1.80	15.30
NOT SPECIFIED	**724,881**	**631,381**	**561,740**	**573,024**	**634,101**	**2.25**	**10.66**
Other countries of the World	724,881	631,381	561,740	573,024	634,101	2.25	10.66

Yearbook of Tourism Statistics, Data 2009 – 2013, 2015 Edition

GERMANY

4. Arrivals of non-resident tourists in all types of accommodation establishments, by country of residence

		2009	2010	2011	2012	2013	Market share 2013	% Change 2013-2012
TOTAL		24,219,634	26,875,288	28,374,101	30,410,491	31,545,132	100.00	3.73
AFRICA		158,458	192,895	193,193	226,767	245,620	0.78	8.31
SOUTHERN AFRICA		50,675	66,512	68,100	74,459	71,323	0.23	-4.21
South Africa		50,675	66,512	68,100	74,459	71,323	0.23	-4.21
OTHER AFRICA		107,783	126,383	125,093	152,308	174,297	0.55	14.44
Other countries of Africa		107,783	126,383	125,093	152,308	174,297	0.55	14.44
AMERICAS		2,475,506	2,882,982	2,914,184	3,155,152	3,191,546	10.12	1.15
NORTH AMERICA		2,221,644	2,547,859	2,517,136	2,689,183	2,693,276	8.54	0.15
Canada		233,526	275,413	281,876	295,234	292,642	0.93	-0.88
Mexico		49,280	66,107	71,501	79,996	90,749	0.29	13.44
United States of America		1,938,838	2,206,339	2,163,759	2,313,953	2,309,885	7.32	-0.18
SOUTH AMERICA		136,274	194,960	237,125	279,092	292,152	0.93	4.68
Brazil		136,274	194,960	237,125	279,092	292,152	0.93	4.68
OTHER AMERICAS		117,588	140,163	159,923	186,877	206,118	0.65	10.30
Other countries of the Americas		117,588	140,163	159,923	186,877	206,118	0.65	10.30
EAST ASIA AND THE PACIFIC		1,790,469	2,046,055	2,296,515	2,665,861	2,805,217	8.89	5.23
NORTH-EAST ASIA		1,113,479	1,336,237	1,552,033	1,815,214	1,920,923	6.09	5.82
China	(*)	384,576	510,611	637,362	757,290	870,748	2.76	14.98
Japan		537,984	605,231	642,542	734,475	711,529	2.26	-3.12
Korea, Republic of		123,937	144,306	172,839	210,983	223,782	0.71	6.07
Taiwan, Province of China		66,982	76,089	99,290	112,466	114,864	0.36	2.13
AUSTRALASIA		255,069	276,097	282,278	313,123	306,001	0.97	-2.27
Australia			276,097	282,278	313,123	306,001	0.97	-2.27
Australia, New Zealand		255,069						
OTHER EAST ASIA AND THE PACIFIC		421,921	433,721	462,204	537,524	578,293	1.83	7.58
Other countries of Asia			389,075	420,164	489,743	527,798	1.67	7.77
Other countries East Asia/Pacific	(*)	421,921						
Other countries of Oceania			44,646	42,040	47,781	50,495	0.16	5.68
EUROPE		18,781,861	20,609,923	21,860,790	23,121,212	23,899,697	75.76	3.37
CENTRAL/EASTERN EUROPE		1,565,423	2,229,922	2,589,652	2,936,102	3,225,530	10.23	9.86
Bulgaria			56,077	68,444	71,995	79,353	0.25	10.22
Czech Republic		281,313	320,868	358,908	391,964	414,439	1.31	5.73
Estonia			37,503	42,326	46,142	48,461	0.15	5.03
Hungary		180,562	203,445	224,933	235,645	243,649	0.77	3.40
Latvia			42,191	50,044	55,318	58,168	0.18	5.15
Lithuania			68,474	73,470	82,775	84,006	0.27	1.49
Poland		514,561	604,274	684,193	737,327	814,467	2.58	10.46
Romania			153,693	170,581	188,517	210,595	0.67	11.71
Russian Federation		459,849	590,092	737,105	918,226	1,038,826	3.29	13.13
Slovakia			78,113	86,773	95,712	104,191	0.33	8.86
Ukraine			75,192	92,875	112,481	129,375	0.41	15.02
Baltic countries		129,138						
NORTHERN EUROPE		4,403,474	4,906,426	4,999,834	5,294,118	5,496,484	17.42	3.82
Denmark		1,138,910	1,214,319	1,242,806	1,356,666	1,400,534	4.44	3.23
Finland		249,252	281,263	293,948	291,788	290,496	0.92	-0.44
Iceland		36,862	36,488	37,910	34,261	32,230	0.10	-5.93
Ireland		137,629	140,736	134,820	135,039	135,553	0.43	0.38
Norway		328,479	387,468	388,896	416,842	423,246	1.34	1.54
Sweden		762,679	859,261	846,615	897,033	920,308	2.92	2.59
United Kingdom		1,749,663	1,986,891	2,054,839	2,162,489	2,294,117	7.27	6.09
SOUTHERN EUROPE		2,502,734	2,735,986	2,796,957	2,809,878	2,848,341	9.03	1.37
Croatia						54,423	0.17	
Greece		188,030	166,319	160,856	126,920	126,240	0.40	-0.54
Italy		1,444,144	1,524,134	1,538,369	1,581,041	1,580,753	5.01	-0.02
Malta			11,697	11,871	13,650	14,513	0.05	6.32
Portugal		109,462	120,824	120,859	118,063	118,405	0.38	0.29
Slovenia			70,227	75,496	80,549	79,633	0.25	-1.14
Spain		761,098	842,785	889,506	889,655	874,374	2.77	-1.72

Yearbook of Tourism Statistics, Data 2009 – 2013, 2015 Edition

GERMANY

4. Arrivals of non-resident tourists in all types of accommodation establishments, by country of residence

	2009	2010	2011	2012	2013	Market share 2013	% Change 2013-2012
WESTERN EUROPE	9,321,918	10,047,229	10,706,647	11,231,799	11,436,568	36.25	1.82
Austria	1,252,439	1,387,683	1,494,688	1,567,483	1,631,436	5.17	4.08
Belgium	1,070,316	1,131,887	1,192,592	1,238,094	1,272,710	4.03	2.80
France	1,249,522	1,366,153	1,462,096	1,535,077	1,572,518	4.98	2.44
Luxembourg	200,690	215,443	220,006	232,117	241,582	0.77	4.08
Netherlands	3,692,084	3,917,640	4,035,783	4,169,435	4,124,308	13.07	-1.08
Switzerland	1,856,867	2,028,423	2,301,482	2,489,593	2,594,014	8.22	4.19
EAST MEDITERRANEAN EUROPE	317,864	395,106	442,339	500,423	533,209	1.69	6.55
Cyprus		13,891	14,434	17,837	17,824	0.06	-0.07
Israel	155,231	187,818	203,595	237,822	254,975	0.81	7.21
Turkey	162,633	193,397	224,310	244,764	260,410	0.83	6.39
OTHER EUROPE	670,448	295,254	325,361	348,892	359,565	1.14	3.06
Other countries of Europe	670,448	295,254	325,361	348,892	359,565	1.14	3.06
MIDDLE EAST	258,883	336,193	343,263	449,249	517,104	1.64	15.10
All countries of Middle East	258,883	336,193	343,263	449,249	517,104	1.64	15.10
SOUTH ASIA		141,524	160,599	171,738	189,534	0.60	10.36
India		141,524	160,599	171,738	189,534	0.60	10.36
NOT SPECIFIED	754,457	665,716	605,557	620,512	696,414	2.21	12.23
Other countries of the World	754,457	665,716	605,557	620,512	696,414	2.21	12.23

Yearbook of Tourism Statistics, Data 2009 – 2013, 2015 Edition

GERMANY

5. Overnight stays of non-resident tourists in hotels and similar establishments, by country of residence

		2009	2010	2011	2012	2013	Market share 2013	% Change 2013-2012
TOTAL		45,843,407	50,772,948	53,792,524	58,095,898	60,803,581	100.00	4.66
AFRICA		376,662	453,711	443,677	543,734	612,642	1.01	12.67
SOUTHERN AFRICA		108,501	134,544	144,314	160,232	165,109	0.27	3.04
South Africa		108,501	134,544	144,314	160,232	165,109	0.27	3.04
OTHER AFRICA		268,161	319,167	299,363	383,502	447,533	0.74	16.70
Other countries of Africa		268,161	319,167	299,363	383,502	447,533	0.74	16.70
AMERICAS		5,090,630	5,863,967	5,923,716	6,271,629	6,443,318	10.60	2.74
NORTH AMERICA		4,548,764	5,142,578	5,067,656	5,261,067	5,359,403	8.81	1.87
Canada		432,096	512,524	530,166	550,539	566,151	0.93	2.84
Mexico		107,071	141,119	153,911	170,805	188,812	0.31	10.54
United States of America		4,009,597	4,488,935	4,383,579	4,539,723	4,604,440	7.57	1.43
SOUTH AMERICA		296,142	429,256	525,484	623,076	656,365	1.08	5.34
Brazil		296,142	429,256	525,484	623,076	656,365	1.08	5.34
OTHER AMERICAS		245,724	292,133	330,576	387,486	427,550	0.70	10.34
Other countries of the Americas		245,724	292,133	330,576	387,486	427,550	0.70	10.34
EAST ASIA AND THE PACIFIC		3,462,566	4,310,627	4,878,163	5,610,292	5,916,160	9.73	5.45
NORTH-EAST ASIA		2,030,661	2,481,330	2,870,391	3,337,189	3,484,459	5.73	4.41
China	(*)	766,508	1,032,983	1,241,960	1,475,819	1,629,784	2.68	10.43
Japan		906,759	1,036,699	1,138,115	1,270,967	1,249,473	2.05	-1.69
Korea, Republic of		233,316	262,273	315,924	385,548	404,870	0.67	5.01
Taiwan, Province of China		124,078	149,375	174,392	204,855	200,332	0.33	-2.21
AUSTRALASIA		423,949	546,152	577,128	631,090	672,728	1.11	6.60
Australia, New Zealand		423,949	546,152	577,128	631,090	672,728	1.11	6.60
OTHER EAST ASIA AND THE PACIFIC		1,007,956	1,283,145	1,430,644	1,642,013	1,758,973	2.89	7.12
Other countries East Asia/Pacific	(*)	1,007,956	1,283,145	1,430,644	1,642,013	1,758,973	2.89	7.12
EUROPE		34,783,705	38,033,826	40,519,845	43,373,658	45,173,667	74.29	4.15
CENTRAL/EASTERN EUROPE		3,110,431	3,707,247	4,457,679	5,322,121	5,815,235	9.56	9.27
Czech Republic		499,256	565,906	651,421	718,082	760,563	1.25	5.92
Hungary		377,999	440,823	535,195	598,861	606,320	1.00	1.25
Poland		956,111	1,118,897	1,356,513	1,618,221	1,727,807	2.84	6.77
Russian Federation		1,072,476	1,343,599	1,639,107	2,069,849	2,388,262	3.93	15.38
Baltic countries		204,589	238,022	275,443	317,108	332,283	0.55	4.79
NORTHERN EUROPE		7,650,809	8,503,790	8,698,831	9,330,906	9,844,459	16.19	5.50
Denmark		1,895,593	2,027,862	2,062,665	2,306,836	2,416,117	3.97	4.74
Finland		438,008	499,570	533,981	546,510	562,254	0.92	2.88
Iceland		74,762	73,615	76,905	69,975	75,896	0.12	8.46
Ireland		270,026	276,716	266,560	255,655	259,391	0.43	1.46
Norway		551,187	645,967	656,572	733,928	759,589	1.25	3.50
Sweden		1,216,781	1,357,009	1,367,349	1,477,351	1,537,015	2.53	4.04
United Kingdom		3,204,452	3,623,051	3,734,799	3,940,651	4,234,197	6.96	7.45
SOUTHERN EUROPE		4,975,509	5,309,414	5,386,074	5,471,023	5,463,067	8.98	-0.15
Greece		459,479	402,810	380,303	297,418	305,852	0.50	2.84
Italy		2,747,124	2,947,684	2,931,157	3,107,427	3,111,521	5.12	0.13
Portugal		233,117	256,445	262,877	252,969	259,174	0.43	2.45
Spain		1,535,789	1,702,475	1,811,737	1,813,209	1,786,520	2.94	-1.47
WESTERN EUROPE		16,920,139	18,027,338	19,152,028	20,062,636	20,448,020	33.63	1.92
Austria		2,277,439	2,527,378	2,732,558	2,896,779	3,042,341	5.00	5.02
Belgium		2,174,456	2,251,265	2,341,702	2,435,610	2,454,543	4.04	0.78
France		2,094,192	2,295,164	2,475,242	2,560,627	2,640,189	4.34	3.11
Luxembourg		411,155	430,286	435,570	453,163	475,270	0.78	4.88
Netherlands		6,701,012	6,977,366	7,122,264	7,305,258	7,181,674	11.81	-1.69
Switzerland		3,261,885	3,545,879	4,044,692	4,411,199	4,654,003	7.65	5.50
EAST MEDITERRANEAN EUROPE		709,786	872,018	970,018	1,115,737	1,243,669	2.05	11.47
Israel		368,306	444,757	485,488	578,518	672,468	1.11	16.24
Turkey		341,480	427,261	484,530	537,219	571,201	0.94	6.33
OTHER EUROPE		1,417,031	1,614,019	1,855,215	2,071,235	2,359,217	3.88	13.90
Other countries of Europe		1,417,031	1,614,019	1,855,215	2,071,235	2,359,217	3.88	13.90

276

GERMANY

5. Overnight stays of non-resident tourists in hotels and similar establishments, by country of residence

	2009	2010	2011	2012	2013	Market share 2013	% Change 2013-2012
MIDDLE EAST	**734,450**	**926,413**	**960,767**	**1,218,746**	**1,462,731**	**2.41**	**20.02**
All countries of Middle East	734,450	926,413	960,767	1,218,746	1,462,731	2.41	20.02
NOT SPECIFIED	**1,395,394**	**1,184,404**	**1,066,356**	**1,077,839**	**1,195,063**	**1.97**	**10.88**
Other countries of the World	1,395,394	1,184,404	1,066,356	1,077,839	1,195,063	1.97	10.88

Yearbook of Tourism Statistics, Data 2009 – 2013, 2015 Edition

GERMANY

6. Overnight stays of non-resident tourists in all types of accommodation establishments, by country of residence

		2009	2010	2011	2012	2013	Market share 2013	% Change 2013-2012
TOTAL		54,823,716	60,310,448	63,746,372	68,827,658	71,919,385	100.00	4.49
AFRICA		448,260	513,985	504,517	621,727	706,295	0.98	13.60
SOUTHERN AFRICA		123,220	149,026	156,752	174,892	178,748	0.25	2.20
South Africa		123,220	149,026	156,752	174,892	178,748	0.25	2.20
OTHER AFRICA		325,040	364,959	347,765	446,835	527,547	0.73	18.06
Other countries of Africa		325,040	364,959	347,765	446,835	527,547	0.73	18.06
AMERICAS		5,562,598	6,350,191	6,429,114	6,842,839	7,013,938	9.75	2.50
NORTH AMERICA		4,918,084	5,515,227	5,439,369	5,676,268	5,736,809	7.98	1.07
Canada		499,531	579,401	597,579	623,867	634,559	0.88	1.71
Mexico		127,248	166,453	180,193	197,625	185,750	0.26	-6.01
United States of America		4,291,305	4,769,373	4,661,597	4,854,776	4,916,500	6.84	1.27
SOUTH AMERICA		339,588	482,310	586,590	694,440	732,888	1.02	5.54
Brazil		339,588	482,310	586,590	694,440	732,888	1.02	5.54
OTHER AMERICAS		304,926	352,654	403,155	472,131	544,241	0.76	15.27
Other countries of the Americas		304,926	352,654	403,155	472,131	544,241	0.76	15.27
EAST ASIA AND THE PACIFIC		3,851,425	4,267,183	4,770,515	5,519,403	5,821,176	8.09	5.47
NORTH-EAST ASIA		2,182,324	2,632,462	3,041,171	3,532,984	3,707,910	5.16	4.95
China	(*)	820,187	1,092,470	1,322,564	1,563,298	1,734,693	2.41	10.96
Japan		959,969	1,084,285	1,185,279	1,325,544	1,307,950	1.82	-1.33
Korea, Republic of		267,428	294,829	346,856	423,530	449,235	0.62	6.07
Taiwan, Province of China		134,740	160,878	186,472	220,612	216,032	0.30	-2.08
AUSTRALASIA		562,589	613,212	637,644	701,601	714,634	0.99	1.86
Australia			613,212	637,644	701,601	714,634	0.99	1.86
Australia, New Zealand		562,589						
OTHER EAST ASIA AND THE PACIFIC		1,106,512	1,021,509	1,091,700	1,284,818	1,398,632	1.94	8.86
Other countries of Asia			923,769	997,508	1,179,009	1,284,715	1.79	8.97
Other countries East Asia/Pacific	(*)	1,106,512						
Other countries of Oceania			97,740	94,192	105,809	113,917	0.16	7.66
EUROPE		42,624,382	46,456,990	49,268,358	52,746,984	54,831,024	76.24	3.95
CENTRAL/EASTERN EUROPE		3,683,872	5,269,138	6,320,231	7,520,207	8,279,842	11.51	10.10
Bulgaria			142,014	173,845	196,009	226,535	0.31	15.57
Czech Republic		606,507	672,257	765,879	858,798	906,064	1.26	5.50
Estonia			68,751	80,347	89,411	93,934	0.13	5.06
Hungary		445,567	510,219	618,408	714,635	712,173	0.99	-0.34
Latvia			84,129	99,889	116,914	121,218	0.17	3.68
Lithuania			125,968	139,190	164,942	168,089	0.23	1.91
Poland		1,192,951	1,380,549	1,716,479	2,013,267	2,201,369	3.06	9.34
Romania			401,726	465,393	557,124	637,882	0.89	14.50
Russian Federation		1,199,072	1,486,471	1,786,603	2,247,281	2,595,270	3.61	15.48
Slovakia			220,444	267,996	301,061	318,085	0.44	5.65
Ukraine			176,610	206,202	260,765	299,223	0.42	14.75
Baltic countries		239,775						
NORTHERN EUROPE		8,963,273	9,952,349	10,155,974	10,892,993	11,469,270	15.95	5.29
Denmark		2,360,550	2,528,220	2,583,749	2,855,677	2,962,136	4.12	3.73
Finland		502,844	574,818	600,392	612,339	627,638	0.87	2.50
Iceland		87,199	89,025	88,452	82,401	83,985	0.12	1.92
Ireland		329,938	331,405	312,169	302,591	315,206	0.44	4.17
Norway		623,853	733,407	749,284	843,686	864,081	1.20	2.42
Sweden		1,359,645	1,514,850	1,525,431	1,659,463	1,712,503	2.38	3.20
United Kingdom		3,699,244	4,180,624	4,296,497	4,536,836	4,903,721	6.82	8.09
SOUTHERN EUROPE		5,607,912	6,145,142	6,226,372	6,371,819	6,532,490	9.08	2.52
Croatia						149,480	0.21	
Greece		499,064	438,501	414,230	329,824	336,721	0.47	2.09
Italy		3,101,720	3,295,849	3,262,617	3,468,347	3,485,300	4.85	0.49
Malta			29,642	30,830	35,038	39,281	0.05	12.11
Portugal		256,603	292,773	290,202	289,827	296,721	0.41	2.38
Slovenia			158,871	183,319	220,981	208,439	0.29	-5.68
Spain		1,750,525	1,929,506	2,045,174	2,027,802	2,016,548	2.80	-0.55

Yearbook of Tourism Statistics, Data 2009 – 2013, 2015 Edition

GERMANY

6. Overnight stays of non-resident tourists in all types of accommodation establishments, by country of residence

	2009	2010	2011	2012	2013	Market share 2013	% Change 2013-2012
WESTERN EUROPE	21,927,960	23,391,115	24,655,304	25,847,274	26,275,212	36.53	1.66
Austria	2,573,826	2,838,779	3,030,904	3,221,467	3,368,594	4.68	4.57
Belgium	2,540,634	2,639,425	2,755,820	2,870,823	2,897,300	4.03	0.92
France	2,509,231	2,735,869	2,933,315	3,064,548	3,142,370	4.37	2.54
Luxembourg	486,020	507,506	517,564	539,748	558,703	0.78	3.51
Netherlands	9,962,061	10,483,114	10,653,148	10,939,882	10,824,588	15.05	-1.05
Switzerland	3,856,188	4,186,422	4,764,553	5,210,806	5,483,657	7.62	5.24
EAST MEDITERRANEAN EUROPE	786,909	998,998	1,111,834	1,282,607	1,421,745	1.98	10.85
Cyprus		35,692	36,982	45,690	45,222	0.06	-1.02
Israel	416,107	505,206	554,795	660,936	762,707	1.06	15.40
Turkey	370,802	458,100	520,057	575,981	613,816	0.85	6.57
OTHER EUROPE	1,654,456	700,248	798,643	832,084	852,465	1.19	2.45
Other countries of Europe	1,654,456	700,248	798,643	832,084	852,465	1.19	2.45
MIDDLE EAST	770,980	968,336	1,006,856	1,284,583	1,543,717	2.15	20.17
All countries of Middle East	770,980	968,336	1,006,856	1,284,583	1,543,717	2.15	20.17
SOUTH ASIA		455,655	547,480	584,508	615,617	0.86	5.32
India		455,655	547,480	584,508	615,617	0.86	5.32
NOT SPECIFIED	1,566,071	1,298,108	1,219,532	1,227,614	1,387,618	1.93	13.03
Other countries of the World	1,566,071	1,298,108	1,219,532	1,227,614	1,387,618	1.93	13.03

Yearbook of Tourism Statistics, Data 2009 – 2013, 2015 Edition

GREECE

1. Arrivals of non-resident tourists at national borders, by country of residence

	2009	2010	2011	2012	2013	Market share 2013	% Change 2013-2012
TOTAL (*)	14,914,534	15,007,490	16,427,248	15,517,625	17,919,578	100.00	15.48
AFRICA	25,576	28,314	33,775	32,688	26,867	0.15	-17.81
SOUTHERN AFRICA	20,539	19,985	21,981	19,686	17,644	0.10	-10.37
South Africa	20,539	19,985	21,981	19,686	17,644	0.10	-10.37
OTHER AFRICA	5,037	8,329	11,794	13,002	9,223	0.05	-29.06
Other countries of Africa	5,037	8,329	11,794	13,002	9,223	0.05	-29.06
AMERICAS	729,446	691,379	719,661	558,729	754,487	4.21	35.04
NORTH AMERICA	675,168	622,129	632,527	484,592	673,084	3.76	38.90
Canada	134,983	113,358	142,287	102,694	186,701	1.04	81.80
Mexico	8,909	10,470	5,532	8,067	19,863	0.11	146.23
United States of America	531,276	498,301	484,708	373,831	466,520	2.60	24.79
SOUTH AMERICA	38,418	51,787	65,952	51,332	52,843	0.29	2.94
Argentina	13,878	17,772	13,834	20,207	25,488	0.14	26.13
Brazil	24,540	34,015	52,118	31,125	27,355	0.15	-12.11
OTHER AMERICAS	15,860	17,463	21,182	22,805	28,560	0.16	25.24
Other countries of the Americas	15,860	17,463	21,182	22,805	28,560	0.16	25.24
EAST ASIA AND THE PACIFIC	206,209	199,452	207,360	215,864	238,157	1.33	10.33
NORTH-EAST ASIA	19,681	31,264	27,809	27,145	48,776	0.27	79.69
China	7,793	13,620	15,838	12,203	28,328	0.16	132.14
Japan	6,765	10,021	10,125	8,841	13,141	0.07	48.64
Korea, Republic of	5,123	7,623	1,846	6,101	7,307	0.04	19.77
AUSTRALASIA	133,869	108,088	115,902	117,852	129,112	0.72	9.55
Australia	133,869	108,088	115,902	117,852	129,112	0.72	9.55
OTHER EAST ASIA AND THE PACIFIC	52,659	60,100	63,649	70,867	60,269	0.34	-14.95
Other countries of Asia	25,016	42,015	44,572	55,351	46,739	0.26	-15.56
Other countries of Oceania	27,643	18,085	19,077	15,516	13,530	0.08	-12.80
EUROPE	13,884,208	14,034,319	15,429,714	14,661,081	16,821,975	93.87	14.74
CENTRAL/EASTERN EUROPE	1,902,280	2,281,324	2,551,433	2,404,238	3,183,230	17.76	32.40
Bulgaria	657,130	664,389	686,209	599,110	691,874	3.86	15.48
Czech Republic	267,833	294,936	309,062	289,034	286,974	1.60	-0.71
Estonia	21,242	13,842	9,862	4,757	8,094	0.05	70.15
Hungary	70,894	109,160	69,756	69,789	80,623	0.45	15.52
Latvia	12,027	21,948	7,846	15,300	20,283	0.11	32.57
Lithuania	37,501	16,295	13,666	21,601	31,874	0.18	47.56
Poland	203,487	402,170	450,618	254,682	385,474	2.15	51.36
Romania	307,596	257,939	223,699	230,396	278,873	1.56	21.04
Russian Federation	276,021	451,239	738,927	874,787	1,352,901	7.55	54.65
Slovakia	48,549	49,406	41,788	44,782	46,260	0.26	3.30
NORTHERN EUROPE	3,294,786	2,782,059	2,790,183	2,928,408	2,865,954	15.99	-2.13
Denmark	264,040	240,563	244,986	205,194	202,477	1.13	-1.32
Finland	170,341	205,282	167,632	154,134	139,341	0.78	-9.60
Iceland	3,340			2,059	1,578	0.01	-23.36
Ireland	73,167	65,623	58,939	32,357	42,575	0.24	31.58
Norway	315,595	187,319	226,627	294,114	264,816	1.48	-9.96
Sweden	356,154	281,069	333,906	319,756	368,834	2.06	15.35
United Kingdom	2,112,149	1,802,203	1,758,093	1,920,794	1,846,333	10.30	-3.88
SOUTHERN EUROPE	1,895,695	2,016,863	2,263,450	2,151,868	2,373,363	13.24	10.29
Albania	234,276	242,083	411,245	469,213	504,809	2.82	7.59
Italy	935,011	843,613	938,232	848,073	964,314	5.38	13.71
Malta	4,367	9,651	1,368	2,206	1,494	0.01	-32.28
Portugal	13,300	19,497	34,642	20,483	13,304	0.07	-35.05
Serbia	498,356	706,635	692,059	620,450	778,765	4.35	25.52
Slovenia	45,924	40,082	31,130	35,721	18,689	0.10	-47.68
Spain	164,461	155,302	154,774	155,722	91,988	0.51	-40.93
WESTERN EUROPE	5,040,130	4,406,588	5,083,455	4,442,810	4,948,676	27.62	11.39
Austria	352,223	338,367	310,358	236,416	236,476	1.32	0.03
Belgium	334,240	339,836	432,625	326,937	344,554	1.92	5.39
France	962,435	868,346	1,149,388	977,376	1,152,217	6.43	17.89
Germany	2,364,486	2,038,871	2,240,481	2,108,787	2,267,546	12.65	7.53

280

GREECE

1. Arrivals of non-resident tourists at national borders, by country of residence

		2009	2010	2011	2012	2013	Market share 2013	% Change 2013-2012
Luxembourg		22,792	18,593	28,475	15,192	20,498	0.11	34.93
Netherlands		651,440	528,157	560,723	478,483	580,867	3.24	21.40
Switzerland		352,514	274,418	361,405	299,619	346,518	1.93	15.65
EAST MEDITERRANEAN EUROPE		**717,537**	**1,333,121**	**1,217,957**	**1,234,844**	**1,442,587**	**8.05**	**16.82**
Cyprus		434,746	574,764	439,757	424,827	399,008	2.23	-6.08
Israel		82,443	197,159	226,110	207,711	212,466	1.19	2.29
Turkey		200,348	561,198	552,090	602,306	831,113	4.64	37.99
OTHER EUROPE		**1,033,780**	**1,214,364**	**1,523,236**	**1,498,913**	**2,008,165**	**11.21**	**33.97**
Other countries of Europe		1,033,780	1,214,364	1,523,236	1,498,913	2,008,165	11.21	33.97
MIDDLE EAST		**55,844**	**44,837**	**27,990**	**35,632**	**72,849**	**0.41**	**104.45**
Egypt	(*)	12,610	15,925	4,675	4,724	4,038	0.02	-14.52
Lebanon	(*)	14,753	4,639	4,916	12,846	36,591	0.20	184.84
Other countries of Middle East		28,481	24,273	18,399	18,062	32,220	0.18	78.39
SOUTH ASIA		**1,647**	**9,189**	**8,748**	**13,631**	**5,243**	**0.03**	**-61.54**
Iran, Islamic Republic of		1,647	9,189	8,748	13,631	5,243	0.03	-61.54
NOT SPECIFIED		**11,604**						
Other countries of the World		11,604						

Yearbook of Tourism Statistics, Data 2009 – 2013, 2015 Edition

GREECE

3. Arrivals of non-resident tourists in hotels and similar establishments, by country of residence

	2009	2010	2011	2012	2013	Market share 2013	% Change 2013-2012
TOTAL	8,542,307	8,964,224	10,041,765	9,243,951	10,490,963	100.00	13.49
AFRICA	37,283	45,813	55,596	90,691	66,229	0.63	-26.97
SOUTHERN AFRICA	1,516	1,615	1,901	1,784			
South Africa	1,516	1,615	1,901	1,784			
OTHER AFRICA	35,767	44,198	53,695	88,907	66,229	0.63	-25.51
Other countries of Africa	35,767	44,198	53,695	88,907			
All countries of Africa					66,229	0.63	
AMERICAS	784,527	811,559	847,173	639,022	728,899	6.95	14.06
NORTH AMERICA	698,606	713,437	725,429	536,429	600,679	5.73	11.98
Canada	110,149	110,993	119,584	85,464	105,984	1.01	24.01
United States of America	588,457	602,444	605,845	450,965	494,695	4.72	9.70
SOUTH AMERICA	34,549	41,974	57,899	43,878			
Brazil	34,549	41,974	57,899	43,878			
OTHER AMERICAS	51,372	56,148	63,845	58,715	128,220	1.22	118.38
Other countries of the Americas	51,372	56,148	63,845	58,715	128,220	1.22	118.38
EAST ASIA AND THE PACIFIC	496,523	622,797	722,597	661,398	828,760	7.90	25.30
NORTH-EAST ASIA	145,023	139,789	165,597	137,077	195,706	1.87	42.77
China	48,033	59,268	87,323	88,450	134,901	1.29	52.52
Japan	96,075	79,228	74,971	45,711	60,805	0.58	33.02
Korea, Republic of	915	1,293	3,303	2,916			
AUSTRALASIA	114,951	149,887	167,884	152,210	177,771	1.69	16.79
Australia	114,951	149,887	167,884	152,210	177,771	1.69	16.79
OTHER EAST ASIA AND THE PACIFIC	236,549	333,121	389,116	372,111	455,283	4.34	22.35
Other countries of Asia	229,008	324,059	377,419	362,471	444,844	4.24	22.73
Other countries of Oceania	7,541	9,062	11,697	9,640	10,439	0.10	8.29
EUROPE	7,219,060	7,476,544	8,409,601	7,847,644	8,861,033	84.46	12.91
CENTRAL/EASTERN EUROPE	1,264,196	1,322,434	1,644,773	1,744,185	2,136,897	20.37	22.52
Bulgaria	152,479	126,122	146,586	145,347	172,066	1.64	18.38
Czech Republic	164,347	151,759	164,349	155,605	170,799	1.63	9.76
Estonia	14,294	15,353	14,063	13,644	11,689	0.11	-14.33
Hungary	47,746	43,399	45,950	41,161	45,298	0.43	10.05
Latvia	11,208	9,080	10,585	10,094	11,267	0.11	11.62
Lithuania	17,461	15,703	18,618	17,341	20,609	0.20	18.85
Poland	231,087	234,075	288,028	245,554	290,301	2.77	18.22
Romania	181,291	153,496	172,575	185,920	239,644	2.28	28.90
Russian Federation	376,138	494,020	686,717	820,618	1,141,085	10.88	39.05
Slovakia	39,336	35,849	40,370	32,551	34,139	0.33	4.88
Ukraine	28,809	43,578	56,932	76,350			
NORTHERN EUROPE	1,822,281	1,938,724	2,158,294	2,102,141	2,258,605	21.53	7.44
Denmark	158,482	164,095	183,434	171,736	177,776	1.69	3.52
Finland	126,025	129,759	160,140	144,970	151,384	1.44	4.42
Iceland	3,970	3,082	4,419	4,668	5,911	0.06	26.63
Ireland	42,870	40,344	40,411	30,984	31,893	0.30	2.93
Norway	181,891	207,069	236,119	245,972	264,436	2.52	7.51
Sweden	242,262	284,355	322,286	316,719	345,611	3.29	9.12
United Kingdom	1,066,781	1,110,020	1,211,485	1,187,092	1,281,594	12.22	7.96
SOUTHERN EUROPE	844,945	867,639	934,303	733,694	759,266	7.24	3.49
Croatia					11,454	0.11	
Italy	600,955	656,834	701,056	564,754	576,038	5.49	2.00
Malta	5,131	4,017	4,375	3,729	4,286	0.04	14.94
Portugal	21,765	20,153	18,784	13,853	17,388	0.17	25.52
Slovenia	35,465	30,576	30,612	25,361	28,575	0.27	12.67
Spain	181,629	156,059	179,476	125,997	121,525	1.16	-3.55
WESTERN EUROPE	2,822,129	2,824,398	3,079,658	2,670,366	2,901,872	27.66	8.67
Austria	191,743	175,593	171,512	149,786	162,971	1.55	8.80
Belgium	225,718	232,627	265,696	229,144	245,012	2.34	6.92
France	749,442	737,178	826,929	714,749	779,926	7.43	9.12
Germany	1,136,774	1,163,238	1,244,474	1,082,024	1,156,193	11.02	6.85
Luxembourg	12,814	11,229	13,282	12,066	13,845	0.13	14.74

282

GREECE

3. Arrivals of non-resident tourists in hotels and similar establishments, by country of residence

	2009	2010	2011	2012	2013	Market share 2013	% Change 2013-2012
Netherlands	360,959	360,747	395,221	333,474	377,445	3.60	13.19
Switzerland	144,679	143,786	162,544	149,123	166,480	1.59	11.64
EAST MEDITERRANEAN EUROPE	**230,711**	**253,482**	**274,331**	**293,118**	**349,366**	**3.33**	**19.19**
Cyprus	169,978	177,129	168,104	164,877	151,674	1.45	-8.01
Turkey	60,733	76,353	106,227	128,241	197,692	1.88	54.16
OTHER EUROPE	**234,798**	**269,867**	**318,242**	**304,140**	**455,027**	**4.34**	**49.61**
Other countries of Europe	234,798	269,867	318,242	304,140	455,027	4.34	49.61
NOT SPECIFIED	**4,914**	**7,511**	**6,798**	**5,196**	**6,042**	**0.06**	**16.28**
Other countries of the World	4,914	7,511	6,798	5,196	6,042	0.06	16.28

Yearbook of Tourism Statistics, Data 2009 – 2013, 2015 Edition

GREECE

4. Arrivals of non-resident tourists in all types of accommodation establishments, by country of residence

	2009	2010	2011	2012	2013	Market share 2013	% Change 2013-2012
TOTAL	8,781,095	9,196,924	10,266,462	9,396,050	10,667,573	100.00	13.53
AFRICA	37,504	46,093	55,790	90,888	66,430	0.62	-26.91
SOUTHERN AFRICA	1,550	1,663	1,960	1,840			
South Africa	1,550	1,663	1,960	1,840			
OTHER AFRICA	35,954	44,430	53,830	89,048	66,430	0.62	-25.40
Other countries of Africa	35,954	44,430	53,830	89,048			
All countries of Africa					66,430	0.62	
AMERICAS	787,843	815,038	850,413	641,478	732,010	6.86	14.11
NORTH AMERICA	701,449	716,216	728,131	538,290	602,919	5.65	12.01
Canada	111,296	112,313	120,967	86,431	107,125	1.00	23.94
United States of America	590,153	603,903	607,164	451,859	495,794	4.65	9.72
SOUTH AMERICA	34,749	42,140	58,097	44,041			
Brazil	34,749	42,140	58,097	44,041			
OTHER AMERICAS	51,645	56,682	64,185	59,147	129,091	1.21	118.25
Other countries of the Americas	51,645	56,682	64,185	59,147	129,091	1.21	118.25
EAST ASIA AND THE PACIFIC	503,190	630,840	730,454	667,916	835,672	7.83	25.12
NORTH-EAST ASIA	145,123	139,913	165,745	137,232	195,911	1.84	42.76
China	48,096	59,342	87,390	88,541	135,028	1.27	52.50
Japan	96,106	79,270	75,036	45,769	60,883	0.57	33.02
Korea, Republic of	921	1,301	3,319	2,922			
AUSTRALASIA	120,243	155,742	173,662	157,092	182,990	1.72	16.49
Australia	120,243	155,742	173,662	157,092	182,990	1.72	16.49
OTHER EAST ASIA AND THE PACIFIC	237,824	335,185	391,047	373,592	456,771	4.28	22.26
Other countries of Asia	229,498	324,825	378,168	362,954	445,326	4.17	22.69
Other countries of Oceania	8,326	10,360	12,879	10,638	11,445	0.11	7.59
EUROPE	7,447,642	7,697,419	8,622,981	7,990,560	9,027,398	84.62	12.98
CENTRAL/EASTERN EUROPE	1,285,292	1,342,227	1,665,235	1,763,699	2,161,959	20.27	22.58
Bulgaria	157,747	132,129	153,847	154,836	184,375	1.73	19.08
Czech Republic	167,117	154,061	166,828	157,108	172,969	1.62	10.10
Estonia	14,491	15,540	14,175	13,769	11,843	0.11	-13.99
Hungary	50,562	45,989	48,158	42,565	47,247	0.44	11.00
Latvia	11,310	9,183	10,669	10,153	11,317	0.11	11.46
Lithuania	17,653	15,813	18,798	17,475	20,759	0.19	18.79
Poland	237,055	239,536	293,197	249,491	294,961	2.77	18.23
Romania	183,934	155,393	174,554	187,799	242,074	2.27	28.90
Russian Federation	376,589	494,555	687,161	821,159	1,141,927	10.70	39.06
Slovakia	39,898	36,317	40,780	32,844	34,487	0.32	5.00
Ukraine	28,936	43,711	57,068	76,500			
NORTHERN EUROPE	1,832,848	1,948,282	2,167,087	2,108,634	2,266,097	21.24	7.47
Denmark	160,463	166,271	185,139	172,904	179,527	1.68	3.83
Finland	126,309	129,971	160,329	145,094	151,561	1.42	4.46
Iceland	3,984	3,096	4,442	4,685	5,930	0.06	26.57
Ireland	43,501	40,842	40,905	31,348	32,295	0.30	3.02
Norway	182,179	207,416	236,425	246,173	264,642	2.48	7.50
Sweden	242,848	284,998	322,822	317,114	346,060	3.24	9.13
United Kingdom	1,073,564	1,115,688	1,217,025	1,191,316	1,286,082	12.06	7.95
SOUTHERN EUROPE	889,395	909,213	973,552	757,838	786,541	7.37	3.79
Croatia					11,612	0.11	
Italy	639,105	692,595	734,806	585,384	599,006	5.62	2.33
Malta	5,451	4,049	4,404	3,742	4,309	0.04	15.15
Portugal	22,170	20,444	19,049	14,028	17,582	0.16	25.34
Slovenia	38,150	33,079	33,083	26,860	30,744	0.29	14.46
Spain	184,519	159,046	182,210	127,824	123,288	1.16	-3.55
WESTERN EUROPE	2,970,561	2,968,753	3,218,628	2,757,597	3,001,634	28.14	8.85
Austria	203,996	187,287	182,204	156,808	171,744	1.61	9.53
Belgium	230,155	236,960	270,132	231,770	247,799	2.32	6.92
France	790,787	777,158	867,489	741,803	811,089	7.60	9.34
Germany	1,195,325	1,217,220	1,295,676	1,113,695	1,193,212	11.19	7.14
Luxembourg	12,880	11,289	13,347	12,100	13,890	0.13	14.79

GREECE

4. Arrivals of non-resident tourists in all types of accommodation establishments, by country of residence

	2009	2010	2011	2012	2013	Market share 2013	% Change 2013-2012
Netherlands	385,918	387,692	420,422	348,238	392,223	3.68	12.63
Switzerland	151,500	151,147	169,358	153,183	171,677	1.61	12.07
EAST MEDITERRANEAN EUROPE	**231,367**	**254,288**	**275,060**	**293,832**	**350,308**	**3.28**	**19.22**
Cyprus	170,404	177,493	168,433	165,145	151,939	1.42	-8.00
Turkey	60,963	76,795	106,627	128,687	198,369	1.86	54.15
OTHER EUROPE	**238,179**	**274,656**	**323,419**	**308,960**	**460,859**	**4.32**	**49.16**
Other countries of Europe	238,179	274,656	323,419	308,960	460,859	4.32	49.16
NOT SPECIFIED	**4,916**	**7,534**	**6,824**	**5,208**	**6,063**	**0.06**	**16.42**
Other countries of the World	4,916	7,534	6,824	5,208	6,063	0.06	16.42

Yearbook of Tourism Statistics, Data 2009 – 2013, 2015 Edition

GREECE

5. Overnight stays of non-resident tourists in hotels and similar establishments, by country of residence

	2009	2010	2011	2012	2013	Market share 2013	% Change 2013-2012
TOTAL	45,925,585	48,243,634	53,768,033	50,539,507	57,061,724	100.00	12.91
AFRICA	113,352	120,683	170,882	474,658	228,770	0.40	-51.80
SOUTHERN AFRICA	5,004	5,054	6,147	6,172			
South Africa	5,004	5,054	6,147	6,172			
OTHER AFRICA	108,348	115,629	164,735	468,486	228,770	0.40	-51.17
Other countries of Africa	108,348	115,629	164,735	468,486			
All countries of Africa					228,770	0.40	
AMERICAS	1,664,877	1,715,269	1,894,781	1,442,993	1,674,077	2.93	16.01
NORTH AMERICA	1,460,114	1,487,159	1,617,227	1,207,869	1,375,214	2.41	13.85
Canada	253,912	253,154	278,404	203,704	256,078	0.45	25.71
United States of America	1,206,202	1,234,005	1,338,823	1,004,165	1,119,136	1.96	11.45
SOUTH AMERICA	81,156	98,118	132,134	101,161			
Brazil	81,156	98,118	132,134	101,161			
OTHER AMERICAS	123,607	129,992	145,420	133,963	298,863	0.52	123.09
Other countries of the Americas	123,607	129,992	145,420	133,963	298,863	0.52	123.09
EAST ASIA AND THE PACIFIC	1,215,251	1,580,516	1,847,533	1,736,058	2,159,187	3.78	24.37
NORTH-EAST ASIA	249,525	241,942	297,335	243,473	339,471	0.59	39.43
China	92,937	108,841	160,404	153,842	225,640	0.40	46.67
Japan	155,058	131,185	132,566	85,575	113,831	0.20	33.02
Korea, Republic of	1,530	1,916	4,365	4,056			
AUSTRALASIA	271,811	346,096	392,709	348,541	412,731	0.72	18.42
Australia	271,811	346,096	392,709	348,541	412,731	0.72	18.42
OTHER EAST ASIA AND THE PACIFIC	693,915	992,478	1,157,489	1,144,044	1,406,985	2.47	22.98
Other countries of Asia	676,359	971,473	1,127,023	1,119,859	1,381,414	2.42	23.36
Other countries of Oceania	17,556	21,005	30,466	24,185	25,571	0.04	5.73
EUROPE	42,915,120	44,805,322	49,830,236	46,869,216	52,980,797	92.85	13.04
CENTRAL/EASTERN EUROPE	7,733,283	8,514,530	10,510,562	11,225,713	13,644,056	23.91	21.54
Bulgaria	453,389	391,898	476,494	490,415	557,864	0.98	13.75
Czech Republic	1,296,205	1,200,054	1,294,741	1,187,063	1,311,746	2.30	10.50
Estonia	86,759	89,982	85,492	78,018	64,455	0.11	-17.38
Hungary	278,030	261,180	279,339	249,198	270,469	0.47	8.54
Latvia	67,982	53,634	63,135	60,664	61,887	0.11	2.02
Lithuania	120,061	102,320	114,394	102,825	123,678	0.22	20.28
Poland	1,466,042	1,497,626	1,834,435	1,572,684	1,821,079	3.19	15.79
Romania	806,581	711,191	808,992	866,293	1,050,414	1.84	21.25
Russian Federation	2,713,015	3,655,568	4,905,157	5,924,494	8,130,478	14.25	37.23
Slovakia	290,110	282,382	317,825	242,788	251,986	0.44	3.79
Ukraine	155,109	268,695	330,558	451,271			
NORTHERN EUROPE	12,025,104	12,927,181	14,035,613	13,718,669	14,732,176	25.82	7.39
Denmark	1,031,557	1,091,539	1,195,555	1,129,231	1,166,745	2.04	3.32
Finland	851,657	881,678	1,036,516	942,607	995,784	1.75	5.64
Iceland	19,612	13,119	18,871	18,802	25,425	0.04	35.22
Ireland	236,494	212,770	197,548	147,334	145,363	0.25	-1.34
Norway	1,310,086	1,517,015	1,626,310	1,681,017	1,808,964	3.17	7.61
Sweden	1,570,400	1,851,611	2,072,624	2,023,370	2,261,003	3.96	11.74
United Kingdom	7,005,298	7,359,449	7,888,189	7,776,308	8,328,892	14.60	7.11
SOUTHERN EUROPE	3,515,676	3,405,767	3,729,433	2,977,536	3,091,731	5.42	3.84
Croatia					37,391	0.07	
Italy	2,806,170	2,789,213	3,062,246	2,473,306	2,535,968	4.44	2.53
Malta	22,252	17,271	17,736	16,214	17,410	0.03	7.38
Portugal	69,801	66,021	60,984	44,209	56,434	0.10	27.65
Slovenia	208,494	177,661	174,292	145,917	157,766	0.28	8.12
Spain	408,959	355,601	414,175	297,890	286,762	0.50	-3.74
WESTERN EUROPE	17,987,125	18,014,357	19,324,593	16,699,675	18,318,079	32.10	9.69
Austria	1,211,417	1,175,892	1,139,149	986,998	1,071,323	1.88	8.54
Belgium	1,452,533	1,471,804	1,597,661	1,371,449	1,524,353	2.67	11.15
France	3,480,867	3,404,558	3,833,788	3,334,773	3,614,408	6.33	8.39
Germany	8,332,465	8,509,308	9,073,654	7,793,880	8,469,670	14.84	8.67
Luxembourg	90,724	81,101	85,895	70,660	85,799	0.15	21.43

Yearbook of Tourism Statistics, Data 2009 – 2013, 2015 Edition

GREECE

5. Overnight stays of non-resident tourists in hotels and similar establishments, by country of residence

	2009	2010	2011	2012	2013	Market share 2013	% Change 2013-2012
Netherlands	2,552,027	2,513,056	2,623,056	2,256,129	2,577,136	4.52	14.23
Switzerland	867,092	858,638	971,390	885,786	975,390	1.71	10.12
EAST MEDITERRANEAN EUROPE	**614,701**	**677,384**	**703,330**	**728,451**	**794,118**	**1.39**	**9.01**
Cyprus	495,477	525,704	502,203	482,861	429,325	0.75	-11.09
Turkey	119,224	151,680	201,127	245,590	364,793	0.64	48.54
OTHER EUROPE	**1,039,231**	**1,266,103**	**1,526,705**	**1,519,172**	**2,400,637**	**4.21**	**58.02**
Other countries of Europe	1,039,231	1,266,103	1,526,705	1,519,172	2,400,637	4.21	58.02
NOT SPECIFIED	**16,985**	**21,844**	**24,601**	**16,582**	**18,893**	**0.03**	**13.94**
Other countries of the World	16,985	21,844	24,601	16,582	18,893	0.03	13.94

Yearbook of Tourism Statistics, Data 2009 – 2013, 2015 Edition

GREECE

6. Overnight stays of non-resident tourists in all types of accommodation establishments, by country of residence

	2009	2010	2011	2012	2013	Market share 2013	% Change 2013-2012
TOTAL	46,676,987	48,986,136	54,518,196	51,094,912	57,747,993	100.00	13.02
AFRICA	114,011	121,483	171,446	475,116	229,298	0.40	-51.74
SOUTHERN AFRICA	5,083	5,203	6,277	6,315			
South Africa	5,083	5,203	6,277	6,315			
OTHER AFRICA	108,928	116,280	165,169	468,801	229,298	0.40	-51.09
Other countries of Africa	108,928	116,280	165,169	468,801			
All countries of Africa					229,298	0.40	
AMERICAS	1,672,432	1,723,589	1,902,383	1,449,437	1,682,571	2.91	16.08
NORTH AMERICA	1,466,392	1,493,714	1,623,500	1,212,905	1,381,070	2.39	13.86
Canada	256,506	256,299	281,707	206,282	259,049	0.45	25.58
United States of America	1,209,886	1,237,415	1,341,793	1,006,623	1,122,021	1.94	11.46
SOUTH AMERICA	81,628	98,540	132,597	101,556			
Brazil	81,628	98,540	132,597	101,556			
OTHER AMERICAS	124,412	131,335	146,286	134,976	301,501	0.52	123.37
Other countries of the Americas	124,412	131,335	146,286	134,976	301,501	0.52	123.37
EAST ASIA AND THE PACIFIC	1,230,135	1,600,396	1,866,523	1,752,426	2,177,864	3.77	24.28
NORTH-EAST ASIA	249,763	242,152	297,557	243,700	339,861	0.59	39.46
China	93,087	108,966	160,512	153,976	225,891	0.39	46.71
Japan	155,139	131,261	132,663	85,660	113,970	0.20	33.05
Korea, Republic of	1,537	1,925	4,382	4,064			
AUSTRALASIA	283,840	361,433	407,396	360,919	426,928	0.74	18.29
Australia	283,840	361,433	407,396	360,919	426,928	0.74	18.29
OTHER EAST ASIA AND THE PACIFIC	696,532	996,811	1,161,570	1,147,807	1,411,075	2.44	22.94
Other countries of Asia	677,278	972,699	1,128,399	1,120,961	1,382,606	2.39	23.34
Other countries of Oceania	19,254	24,112	33,171	26,846	28,469	0.05	6.05
EUROPE	43,643,422	45,518,776	50,553,177	47,401,312	53,639,292	92.89	13.16
CENTRAL/EASTERN EUROPE	7,803,121	8,583,404	10,590,489	11,304,573	13,757,656	23.82	21.70
Bulgaria	472,060	415,843	509,675	532,055	623,982	1.08	17.28
Czech Republic	1,304,435	1,207,537	1,303,131	1,192,853	1,319,315	2.28	10.60
Estonia	87,233	90,412	85,711	78,379	64,947	0.11	-17.14
Hungary	286,772	268,718	286,207	255,011	277,688	0.48	8.89
Latvia	68,168	53,813	63,266	60,754	62,012	0.11	2.07
Lithuania	120,520	102,656	114,743	103,212	124,120	0.21	20.26
Poland	1,483,854	1,515,522	1,853,481	1,586,156	1,838,843	3.18	15.93
Romania	817,749	718,749	817,306	873,509	1,060,040	1.84	21.35
Russian Federation	2,714,642	3,656,772	4,906,374	5,926,291	8,132,786	14.08	37.23
Slovakia	292,305	284,424	319,732	244,563	253,923	0.44	3.83
Ukraine	155,383	268,958	330,863	451,790			
NORTHERN EUROPE	12,058,253	12,960,034	14,067,363	13,743,930	14,763,491	25.57	7.42
Denmark	1,040,490	1,101,202	1,203,989	1,136,131	1,178,295	2.04	3.71
Finland	852,338	882,435	1,037,072	942,947	996,415	1.73	5.67
Iceland	19,645	13,170	18,910	18,855	25,467	0.04	35.07
Ireland	238,108	214,181	199,068	148,394	146,627	0.25	-1.19
Norway	1,310,892	1,518,004	1,627,143	1,681,747	1,809,715	3.13	7.61
Sweden	1,573,083	1,854,258	2,075,562	2,025,199	2,262,990	3.92	11.74
United Kingdom	7,023,697	7,376,784	7,905,619	7,790,657	8,343,982	14.45	7.10
SOUTHERN EUROPE	3,642,299	3,528,191	3,851,303	3,063,284	3,189,343	5.52	4.12
Croatia					37,651	0.07	
Italy	2,918,214	2,897,992	3,171,276	2,549,977	2,621,057	4.54	2.79
Malta	23,237	17,325	17,796	16,256	17,475	0.03	7.50
Portugal	70,628	66,687	61,553	44,602	56,891	0.10	27.55
Slovenia	215,373	184,148	181,300	150,566	165,049	0.29	9.62
Spain	414,847	362,039	419,378	301,883	291,220	0.50	-3.53
WESTERN EUROPE	18,456,065	18,460,432	19,768,501	16,996,499	18,681,931	32.35	9.92
Austria	1,257,525	1,222,500	1,185,220	1,021,473	1,116,659	1.93	9.32
Belgium	1,464,392	1,484,285	1,610,084	1,380,285	1,533,814	2.66	11.12
France	3,574,165	3,497,512	3,926,078	3,400,597	3,693,042	6.40	8.60
Germany	8,554,859	8,702,157	9,272,121	7,923,166	8,633,993	14.95	8.97
Luxembourg	90,907	81,305	86,102	70,795	85,960	0.15	21.42

288

GREECE

6. Overnight stays of non-resident tourists in all types of accommodation establishments, by country of residence

	2009	2010	2011	2012	2013	Market share 2013	% Change 2013-2012
Netherlands	2,626,203	2,592,614	2,697,669	2,302,199	2,626,300	4.55	14.08
Switzerland	888,014	880,059	991,227	897,984	992,163	1.72	10.49
EAST MEDITERRANEAN EUROPE	**616,451**	**678,925**	**704,890**	**730,233**	**796,452**	**1.38**	**9.07**
Cyprus	496,687	526,562	503,119	483,739	430,231	0.75	-11.06
Turkey	119,764	152,363	201,771	246,494	366,221	0.63	48.57
OTHER EUROPE	**1,067,233**	**1,307,790**	**1,570,631**	**1,562,793**	**2,450,419**	**4.24**	**56.80**
Other countries of Europe	1,067,233	1,307,790	1,570,631	1,562,793	2,450,419	4.24	56.80
NOT SPECIFIED	**16,987**	**21,892**	**24,667**	**16,621**	**18,968**	**0.03**	**14.12**
Other countries of the World	16,987	21,892	24,667	16,621	18,968	0.03	14.12

Yearbook of Tourism Statistics, Data 2009 – 2013, 2015 Edition

GRENADA

1. Arrivals of non-resident tourists at national borders, by nationality

	2009	2010	2011	2012	2013	Market share 2013	% Change 2013-2012
TOTAL	113,894	110,419	118,295	116,242			
AFRICA	725	667	617	517			
EAST AFRICA	103	83	62	59			
Ethiopia		1		2			
Kenya	42	20	19	28			
Mauritius	7	12	5	4			
Uganda	12	11	9	14			
Zambia	13	8	21	8			
Zimbabwe	29	31	8	3			
CENTRAL AFRICA	6	6	4	1			
Cameroon	6	6	3	1			
Democratic Republic of the Congo			1				
NORTH AFRICA	3	7	4	11			
Algeria	1	2	1	1			
Morocco	2	4	3	2			
Sudan		1		8			
SOUTHERN AFRICA	288	223	286	207			
Botswana	107	64	110	50			
South Africa	181	159	176	157			
WEST AFRICA	307	314	243	221			
Ghana	18	24	26	20			
Liberia	2	1		1			
Nigeria	286	287	217	199			
Senegal	1	2		1			
OTHER AFRICA	18	34	18	18			
Other countries of Africa	18	34	18	18			
AMERICAS	61,648	59,175	64,855	66,828			
CARIBBEAN	25,205	22,784	25,877	24,188			
Anguilla	71	41	44	58			
Antigua and Barbuda	831	534	510	383			
Bahamas	124	109	94	61			
Barbados	4,027	3,579	3,526	3,124			
Cayman Islands	39	44	38	28			
Cuba	119	89	71	82			
Dominica	425	476	472	581			
Dominican Republic	64	35	29	44			
Guadeloupe	26	100	64	29			
Haiti	27	26	26	39			
Jamaica	1,212	966	987	955			
Montserrat	52	50	35	39			
Saint Kitts and Nevis	333	305	300	226			
Saint Lucia	1,485	1,505	1,275	1,328			
Saint Vincent and the Grenadines	1,930	1,712	1,922	1,452			
Sint Maarten	103	123	95	108			
Trinidad and Tobago	13,277	12,283	15,715	15,086			
Other countries of the Caribbean	1,060	807	674	565			
CENTRAL AMERICA	201	187	172	114			
Belize	65	69	60	43			
Costa Rica	32	20	18	12			
Honduras	6	6	6	4			
Nicaragua	13	10	8	8			
Panama	52	48	34	35			
Other countries of Central America	33	34	46	12			
NORTH AMERICA	33,268	33,446	36,240	39,773			
Canada	7,194	7,322	7,490	8,065			
Mexico	91	69	36	47			
United States of America	25,983	26,055	28,714	31,661			
SOUTH AMERICA	2,974	2,758	2,566	2,753			
Argentina	120	120	116	89			

290

Yearbook of Tourism Statistics, Data 2009 – 2013, 2015 Edition

GRENADA

1. Arrivals of non-resident tourists at national borders, by nationality

	2009	2010	2011	2012	2013	Market share 2013	% Change 2013-2012
Bolivia	12	28	9	36			
Brazil	284	365	354	385			
Chile	73	39	37	51			
Colombia	97	64	50	73			
Ecuador	10	8	9	14			
Guyana	1,122	1,113	1,073	1,176			
Paraguay		21	30	31			
Peru	28	21	36	22			
Suriname	82	114	103	78			
Uruguay	13	10	13	14			
Venezuela	1,131	850	736	776			
Other countries of South America	2	5		8			
EAST ASIA AND THE PACIFIC	**1,442**	**1,527**	**1,432**	**849**			
NORTH-EAST ASIA	**81**	**94**	**101**	**84**			
Japan	81	94	101	84			
AUSTRALASIA	**304**	**355**	**361**	**325**			
Australia	248	313	306	251			
New Zealand	56	42	55	74			
MELANESIA	**4**	**3**	**2**	**1**			
Fiji	4	3	2	1			
OTHER EAST ASIA AND THE PACIFIC	**1,053**	**1,075**	**968**	**439**			
Other countries of Asia	1,053	1,075	968	439			
EUROPE	**36,096**	**35,361**	**36,277**	**32,826**			
CENTRAL/EASTERN EUROPE	**384**	**547**	**490**	**416**			
Bulgaria	25	7	11	7			
Czech Republic/Slovakia	67	144	141	111			
Hungary	5	38	50	21			
Poland	87	97	115	88			
Romania	26	16	26	17			
Ukraine	4	34	2	6			
USSR (former)	170	211	145	162			
Other countries Central/East Europe				4			
NORTHERN EUROPE	**29,335**	**28,073**	**29,489**	**26,239**			
Denmark	282	231	188	143			
Finland	85	56	129	94			
Ireland	502	370	367	220			
Norway	365	344	339	286			
Sweden	386	481	638	538			
United Kingdom	27,715	26,591	27,828	24,958			
SOUTHERN EUROPE	**825**	**986**	**754**	**717**			
Greece	28	52	44	36			
Italy	578	697	512	533			
Malta	7	3	3	4			
Portugal	44	38	41	24			
Serbia and Montenegro	3	1					
Spain	165	195	154	120			
WESTERN EUROPE	**5,457**	**5,686**	**5,429**	**3,783**			
Austria	545	512	500	255			
Belgium	134	175	171	134			
France	1,105	1,229	1,332	1,110			
Germany	2,698	2,613	2,347	1,497			
Liechtenstein		2		1			
Luxembourg	18	24	17	9			
Netherlands	340	486	357	186			
Switzerland	617	645	705	591			
EAST MEDITERRANEAN EUROPE	**69**	**50**	**59**	**31**			
Cyprus	1	8	5	4			
Israel	25	33	42	19			
Turkey	43	9	12	8			

291

GRENADA

1. Arrivals of non-resident tourists at national borders, by nationality

	2009	2010	2011	2012	2013	Market share 2013	% Change 2013-2012
OTHER EUROPE	**26**	**19**	**56**	**1,640**			
Other countries of Europe	26	19	56	1,640			
MIDDLE EAST	**64**	**59**	**52**	**45**			
Egypt	2	4	4	4			
Jordan	2	1	3	2			
Lebanon	32	11	7	8			
Saudi Arabia		6	5	2			
Syrian Arab Republic	23	21	26	9			
Other countries of Middle East	5	16	7	20			
NOT SPECIFIED	**13,919**	**13,630**	**15,062**	**15,177**			
Other countries of the World	34	133	171	403			
Nationals Residing Abroad	13,885	13,497	14,891	14,774			

Yearbook of Tourism Statistics, Data 2009 – 2013, 2015 Edition

GRENADA

3. Arrivals of non-resident tourists in hotels and similar establishments, by nationality

	2009	2010	2011	2012	2013	Market share 2013	% Change 2013-2012
TOTAL	**51,098**	**49,530**	**58,077**	**60,063**			
AMERICAS	**26,914**	**25,419**	**32,612**	**35,685**			
CARIBBEAN	**13,356**	**11,437**	**14,006**	**14,185**			
All countries of the Caribbean	13,356	11,437	14,006	14,185			
NORTH AMERICA	**12,931**	**13,542**	**18,220**	**21,017**			
Canada	2,974	3,152	3,671	4,247			
United States of America	9,957	10,390	14,549	16,770			
SOUTH AMERICA	**627**	**440**	**386**	**483**			
Venezuela	627	440	386	483			
EUROPE	**22,182**	**21,626**	**23,222**	**21,886**			
NORTHERN EUROPE	**18,352**	**17,518**	**19,158**	**18,162**			
Sweden	229	256	337	334			
United Kingdom	18,123	17,262	18,821	17,828			
SOUTHERN EUROPE	**271**	**319**	**280**	**207**			
Italy	271	319	280	207			
WESTERN EUROPE	**2,091**	**2,200**	**2,276**	**1,627**			
France	305	373	497	459			
Germany	1,537	1,485	1,405	911			
Switzerland	249	342	374	257			
OTHER EUROPE	**1,468**	**1,589**	**1,508**	**1,890**			
Other countries of Europe	1,468	1,589	1,508	1,890			
NOT SPECIFIED	**2,002**	**2,485**	**2,243**	**2,492**			
Other countries of the World	1,408	2,105	1,984	2,230			
Nationals Residing Abroad	594	380	259	262			

293

GRENADA

4. Arrivals of non-resident tourists in all types of accommodation establishments, by nationality

	2009	2010	2011	2012	2013	Market share 2013	% Change 2013-2012
TOTAL	**113,894**	**110,419**	**118,295**	**116,242**			
AMERICAS	**60,782**	**57,129**	**64,224**	**64,690**			
CARIBBEAN	**26,474**	**22,902**	**27,284**	**24,188**			
All countries of the Caribbean	26,474	22,902	27,284	24,188			
NORTH AMERICA	**33,177**	**33,377**	**36,204**	**39,726**			
Canada	7,194	7,322	7,490	8,065			
United States of America	25,983	26,055	28,714	31,661			
SOUTH AMERICA	**1,131**	**850**	**736**	**776**			
Venezuela	1,131	850	736	776			
EUROPE	**36,086**	**35,350**	**36,235**	**32,826**			
NORTHERN EUROPE	**28,101**	**27,072**	**28,466**	**25,496**			
Sweden	386	481	638	538			
United Kingdom	27,715	26,591	27,828	24,958			
SOUTHERN EUROPE	**578**	**697**	**512**	**533**			
Italy	578	697	512	533			
WESTERN EUROPE	**4,420**	**4,487**	**4,384**	**3,198**			
France	1,105	1,229	1,332	1,110			
Germany	2,698	2,613	2,347	1,497			
Switzerland	617	645	705	591			
OTHER EUROPE	**2,987**	**3,094**	**2,873**	**3,599**			
Other countries of Europe	2,987	3,094	2,873	3,599			
NOT SPECIFIED	**17,026**	**17,940**	**17,836**	**18,726**			
Other countries of the World	3,141	4,443	2,945	3,952			
Nationals Residing Abroad	13,885	13,497	14,891	14,774			

Yearbook of Tourism Statistics, Data 2009 – 2013, 2015 Edition

GUADELOUPE

1. Arrivals of non-resident tourists at national borders, by country of residence

		2009	2010	2011	2012	2013	Market share 2013	% Change 2013-2012
TOTAL	(*)	**346,507**	**392,282**			**487,416**	**100.00**	
AFRICA		**187**				**208**	**0.04**	
NORTH AFRICA		**187**				**208**	**0.04**	
Morocco		187				208	0.04	
AMERICAS		**1,919**	**1,354**			**57,160**	**11.73**	
CARIBBEAN		**1,170**	**709**			**19,069**	**3.91**	
Dominica		94				6,389	1.31	
Haiti		140				12,680	2.60	
Martinique		936	709					
NORTH AMERICA		**281**				**14,128**	**2.90**	
United States of America		281				14,128	2.90	
SOUTH AMERICA		**468**	**645**			**23,963**	**4.92**	
Guyana		468	645			23,963	4.92	
EUROPE		**343,465**	**384,801**			**374,191**	**76.77**	
NORTHERN EUROPE		**842**				**2,063**	**0.42**	
Denmark						401	0.08	
Norway		281				98	0.02	
Sweden						947	0.19	
United Kingdom		561				617	0.13	
SOUTHERN EUROPE		**2,666**				**4,238**	**0.87**	
Italy		2,105				2,787	0.57	
Spain		561				1,451	0.30	
WESTERN EUROPE		**337,291**	**370,482**			**367,890**	**75.48**	
Austria		281				243	0.05	
Belgium		4,631				21	0.00	
France		329,011	370,482			360,000	73.86	
Germany		1,403				2,744	0.56	
Luxembourg		187				65	0.01	
Switzerland		1,778				4,817	0.99	
OTHER EUROPE		**2,666**	**14,319**					
Other countries of Europe		2,666	14,319					
NOT SPECIFIED		**936**	**6,127**			**55,857**	**11.46**	
Other countries of the World		936	6,127			55,857	11.46	

Yearbook of Tourism Statistics, Data 2009 – 2013, 2015 Edition

GUAM

1. Arrivals of non-resident tourists at national borders, by country of residence

	2009	2010	2011	2012	2013	Market share 2013	% Change 2013-2012
TOTAL	1,052,871	1,196,295	1,159,778	1,308,035	1,334,497	100.00	2.02
AMERICAS	56,192	61,887	62,102	63,432	59,678	4.47	-5.92
NORTH AMERICA	56,192	61,887	62,102	63,432	59,678	4.47	-5.92
Canada	667	661	757	814	1,096	0.08	34.64
United States of America	55,525	61,226	61,345	62,618	58,582	4.39	-6.45
EAST ASIA AND THE PACIFIC	982,625	1,119,681	1,081,873	1,224,851	1,252,074	93.82	2.22
NORTH-EAST ASIA	936,353	1,071,331	1,034,138	1,178,750	1,207,508	90.48	2.44
China	3,286	4,765	7,068	8,939	11,225	0.84	25.57
Hong Kong, China	2,872	6,890	8,903	8,609	8,857	0.66	2.88
Japan	825,129	893,667	824,005	929,229	893,118	66.93	-3.89
Korea, Republic of	82,978	134,689	149,076	182,829	245,655	18.41	34.36
Taiwan, Province of China	22,088	31,320	45,086	49,144	48,653	3.65	-1.00
SOUTH-EAST ASIA	11,927	12,736	10,681	10,981	11,417	0.86	3.97
Philippines	11,581	12,340	10,097	10,483	10,920	0.82	4.17
Thailand	293	318	488	383	396	0.03	3.39
Viet Nam	53	78	96	115	101	0.01	-12.17
AUSTRALASIA	2,418	3,093	3,867	3,763	3,339	0.25	-11.27
Australia	2,418	3,093	3,867	3,763	3,339	0.25	-11.27
MICRONESIA	31,927	32,521	33,187	31,357	29,810	2.23	-4.93
Marshall Islands	1,022	1,247	1,192	1,152	879	0.07	-23.70
Micronesia, Federated States of	9,683	9,537	10,222	10,069	9,842	0.74	-2.25
Northern Mariana Islands	17,811	18,301	18,062	16,717	16,154	1.21	-3.37
Palau	3,411	3,436	3,711	3,419	2,935	0.22	-14.16
EUROPE	2,005	1,948	2,117	5,723	10,215	0.77	78.49
CENTRAL/EASTERN EUROPE	339	422	632	4,040	8,084	0.61	100.10
Russian Federation	339	422	632	4,040	8,084	0.61	100.10
OTHER EUROPE	1,666	1,526	1,485	1,683	2,131	0.16	26.62
Other countries of Europe	1,666	1,526	1,485	1,683	2,131	0.16	26.62
NOT SPECIFIED	12,049	12,779	13,686	14,029	12,530	0.94	-10.69
Other countries of the World	12,049	12,779	13,686	14,029	12,530	0.94	-10.69

Yearbook of Tourism Statistics, Data 2009 – 2013, 2015 Edition

GUATEMALA

2. Arrivals of non-resident visitors at national borders, by country of residence

	2009	2010	2011	2012	2013	Market share 2013	% Change 2013-2012
TOTAL	**1,776,868**	**1,875,777**	**1,822,663**	**1,951,173**	**2,000,126**	**100.00**	**2.51**
AMERICAS	**1,563,934**	**1,644,754**	**1,599,430**	**1,711,075**	**1,766,436**	**88.32**	**3.24**
CARIBBEAN	7,936	7,733	5,906	6,023	6,570	0.33	9.08
Antigua and Barbuda	9	5	17	41	14	0.00	-65.85
Aruba			1				
Bahamas	79	88	74	89	64	0.00	-28.09
Barbados	28	37	56	60	61	0.00	1.67
Bermuda	17	23	9	20	18	0.00	-10.00
British Virgin Islands	2	1	1	1	2	0.00	100.00
Cuba	2,398	1,847	1,717	1,940	2,397	0.12	23.56
Dominica	78	53	29	45	49	0.00	8.89
Dominican Republic	4,612	4,688	3,038	2,720	2,864	0.14	5.29
Grenada	26	10	28	9	15	0.00	66.67
Guadeloupe	153	277	220	192	231	0.01	20.31
Haiti	96	113	156	235	209	0.01	-11.06
Jamaica	138	168	182	276	240	0.01	-13.04
Martinique					1	0.00	
Montserrat				3	14	0.00	366.67
Netherlands Antilles			3	2			
Puerto Rico	5	6	18	4	10	0.00	150.00
Saint Kitts and Nevis	15	6	17	24	30	0.00	25.00
Saint Lucia	9	14	21	13	28	0.00	115.38
Saint Vincent and the Grenadines	7	20	33	20	21	0.00	5.00
Trinidad and Tobago	236	341	260	323	295	0.01	-8.67
Turks and Caicos Islands	26	22	16	4	3	0.00	-25.00
United States Virgin Islands	2	14	10	2	4	0.00	100.00
CENTRAL AMERICA	892,696	933,817	930,258	1,010,753	1,035,885	51.79	2.49
Belize	37,191	43,816	35,960	35,481	40,303	2.02	13.59
Costa Rica	46,504	48,088	42,039	44,984	46,417	2.32	3.19
El Salvador	507,802	485,888	542,316	604,871	638,058	31.90	5.49
Honduras	211,456	258,765	223,010	235,680	220,497	11.02	-6.44
Nicaragua	77,688	83,819	74,362	77,238	77,691	3.88	0.59
Panama	12,055	13,441	12,571	12,499	12,919	0.65	3.36
NORTH AMERICA	604,813	645,521	604,596	631,947	652,275	32.61	3.22
Canada	47,675	46,774	42,719	53,696	52,955	2.65	-1.38
Mexico	105,456	127,691	132,661	144,076	152,506	7.62	5.85
United States of America	451,682	471,056	429,216	434,175	446,814	22.34	2.91
SOUTH AMERICA	58,489	57,683	58,670	62,352	71,706	3.59	15.00
Argentina	10,973	11,519	12,178	12,165	11,481	0.57	-5.62
Bolivia	1,139	890	932	890	1,055	0.05	18.54
Brazil	7,444	7,640	7,313	7,382	8,922	0.45	20.86
Chile	6,605	6,262	6,390	6,514	6,565	0.33	0.78
Colombia	16,930	15,710	15,520	16,478	23,293	1.16	41.36
Ecuador	2,413	2,581	2,470	3,175	3,334	0.17	5.01
French Guiana	10	25	4	17	5	0.00	-70.59
Guyana	49	47	50	88	97	0.00	10.23
Paraguay	574	576	538	713	691	0.03	-3.09
Peru	4,095	3,524	3,819	3,898	4,948	0.25	26.94
Suriname	11	29	47	25	17	0.00	-32.00
Uruguay	1,979	2,121	1,984	1,941	1,815	0.09	-6.49
Venezuela	6,267	6,759	7,425	9,066	9,483	0.47	4.60
EAST ASIA AND THE PACIFIC	**28,558**	**33,954**	**33,052**	**39,082**	**40,741**	**2.04**	**4.24**
NORTH-EAST ASIA	**17,898**	**20,098**	**20,602**	**22,234**	**20,717**	**1.04**	**-6.82**
China	594	809	1,385	1,853	2,687	0.13	45.01
Japan	5,110	7,081	8,238	8,853	7,220	0.36	-18.45
Korea, Dem. People's Republic of	16	16	122	63	62	0.00	-1.59
Korea, Republic of	9,361	8,810	8,506	8,257	8,182	0.41	-0.91
Taiwan, Province of China	2,817	3,382	2,351	3,208	2,566	0.13	-20.01

297

Yearbook of Tourism Statistics, Data 2009 – 2013, 2015 Edition

GUATEMALA

2. Arrivals of non-resident visitors at national borders, by country of residence

	2009	2010	2011	2012	2013	Market share 2013	% Change 2013-2012
SOUTH-EAST ASIA	837	1,080	1,427	1,253	1,394	0.07	11.25
Brunei Darussalam	4	2		2			
Cambodia	15	9	9	3	3	0.00	
Indonesia	34	60	89	84	112	0.01	33.33
Lao People's Democratic Republic	9	26	246	79	70	0.00	-11.39
Malaysia	140	359	275	202	200	0.01	-0.99
Myanmar	13	11	7	9	24	0.00	166.67
Philippines	447	350	457	556	575	0.03	3.42
Singapore	117	195	179	196	220	0.01	12.24
Thailand	47	61	136	106	174	0.01	64.15
Timor-Leste	3		2				
Viet Nam	8	7	27	16	16	0.00	
AUSTRALASIA	9,567	12,591	10,866	15,401	18,359	0.92	19.21
Australia	7,931	10,520	9,048	13,221	15,827	0.79	19.71
New Zealand	1,636	2,071	1,818	2,180	2,532	0.13	16.15
MELANESIA	15	39	31	48	101	0.01	110.42
Fiji	9	27	21	44	88	0.00	100.00
New Caledonia	2	3	1		6	0.00	
Papua New Guinea	1	5	7	4	1	0.00	-75.00
Solomon Islands					3	0.00	
Vanuatu	3	4	2		3	0.00	
MICRONESIA	149	51	43	45	83	0.00	84.44
Cocos (Keeling) Islands	8	16	7	5	7	0.00	40.00
Guam	122	25	12	12	24	0.00	100.00
Kiribati	1	2	2	9	18	0.00	100.00
Marshall Islands	1		2	4	2	0.00	-50.00
Micronesia, Federated States of	17	8	20	13	31	0.00	138.46
Palau				2	1	0.00	-50.00
POLYNESIA	58	35	25	61	21	0.00	-65.57
French Polynesia	4	6	14	3	10	0.00	233.33
Samoa		3	5	1	2	0.00	100.00
Tonga		1		1			
Tuvalu	1		2				
Wallis and Futuna Islands	53	25	4	56	9	0.00	-83.93
OTHER EAST ASIA AND THE PACIFIC	34	60	58	40	66	0.00	65.00
Other countries of Asia	34	60	58	40	66	0.00	65.00
EUROPE	180,387	189,586	184,356	196,590	187,832	9.39	-4.45
CENTRAL/EASTERN EUROPE	12,066	10,718	10,834	11,046	13,611	0.68	23.22
Armenia	14	9	19	17	18	0.00	5.88
Azerbaijan	1	2	5	9	6	0.00	-33.33
Belarus	30	38	18	10	1	0.00	-90.00
Bulgaria	234	261	235	268	555	0.03	107.09
Czech Republic	4,475	3,160	1,551	1,930	2,148	0.11	11.30
Estonia	275	255	245	275	235	0.01	-14.55
Georgia	17	15	184	16	22	0.00	37.50
Hungary	531	777	482	579	792	0.04	36.79
Kazakhstan	6	17	15	38	17	0.00	-55.26
Kyrgyzstan	4	3	6	2	9	0.00	350.00
Lithuania	258	339	263	582	383	0.02	-34.19
Poland	3,498	2,591	3,071	3,166	3,054	0.15	-3.54
Republic of Moldova	17	15	11	16	24	0.00	50.00
Romania	180	665	515	366	1,056	0.05	188.52
Russian Federation	1,312	1,687	2,653	2,574	3,767	0.19	46.35
Slovakia	879	564	1,000	487	717	0.04	47.23
Tajikistan		3	3	13	9	0.00	-30.77
Turkmenistan	2	2	2	8	1	0.00	-87.50
Ukraine	314	309	548	685	797	0.04	16.35
Uzbekistan	19	6	8	5			

Yearbook of Tourism Statistics, Data 2009 – 2013, 2015 Edition

GUATEMALA

2. Arrivals of non-resident visitors at national borders, by country of residence

	2009	2010	2011	2012	2013	Market share 2013	% Change 2013-2012
NORTHERN EUROPE	**42,167**	**42,900**	**39,615**	**46,532**	**44,101**	**2.20**	**-5.22**
Denmark	4,621	4,373	4,076	4,521	3,825	0.19	-15.39
Finland	1,353	1,378	1,327	1,182	1,313	0.07	11.08
Iceland	97	173	144	135	102	0.01	-24.44
Ireland	2,777	2,904	2,835	2,989	2,883	0.14	-3.55
Norway	3,073	3,342	2,922	2,490	2,835	0.14	13.86
Svalbard and Jan Mayen Islands	3			2	1	0.00	-50.00
Sweden	5,020	4,169	3,770	3,927	3,908	0.20	-0.48
United Kingdom	25,223	26,561	24,541	31,286	29,234	1.46	-6.56
SOUTHERN EUROPE	**41,038**	**44,916**	**45,706**	**46,269**	**45,084**	**2.25**	**-2.56**
Albania	51	31	39	47	45	0.00	-4.26
Andorra	15	31	60	41	69	0.00	68.29
Bosnia and Herzegovina	5	12	16	1	22	0.00	2,100.00
Croatia	113	148	151	204	264	0.01	29.41
Gibraltar	1	5	12	1	2	0.00	100.00
Greece	615	682	576	713	683	0.03	-4.21
Holy See	8	12	6	9	10	0.00	11.11
Italy	12,630	14,582	16,819	17,577	14,946	0.75	-14.97
Malta	141	58	96	83	62	0.00	-25.30
Montenegro	9	3	13	2	1	0.00	-50.00
Portugal	971	1,040	942	1,197	1,081	0.05	-9.69
San Marino	12	10	8	5	15	0.00	200.00
Serbia	6	5	3	11	1	0.00	-90.91
Slovenia	540	448	518	567	646	0.03	13.93
Spain	25,863	27,788	26,426	25,774	26,868	1.34	4.24
TFYR of Macedonia	35	34	10	32	32	0.00	
Yugoslavia, SFR (former)	23	27	11	5	337	0.02	6,640.00
WESTERN EUROPE	**77,235**	**80,445**	**76,160**	**80,968**	**74,207**	**3.71**	**-8.35**
Austria	3,109	3,244	3,090	3,525	4,622	0.23	31.12
Belgium	5,866	6,868	6,127	5,456	5,291	0.26	-3.02
France	28,022	26,503	24,874	27,870	24,009	1.20	-13.85
Germany	21,334	20,979	20,516	22,835	22,437	1.12	-1.74
Liechtenstein	18	65	23	18	14	0.00	-22.22
Luxembourg	93	67	99	72	77	0.00	6.94
Monaco	5	2	6	5	13	0.00	160.00
Netherlands	12,818	16,661	15,093	14,840	11,211	0.56	-24.45
Switzerland	5,970	6,056	6,332	6,347	6,533	0.33	2.93
EAST MEDITERRANEAN EUROPE	**7,721**	**10,466**	**11,895**	**11,509**	**10,641**	**0.53**	**-7.54**
Cyprus	37	31	52	89	75	0.00	-15.73
Israel	7,330	9,762	11,282	10,719	9,838	0.49	-8.22
Turkey	354	673	561	701	728	0.04	3.85
OTHER EUROPE	**160**	**141**	**146**	**266**	**188**	**0.01**	**-29.32**
Other countries of Europe	160	141	146	266	188	0.01	-29.32
MIDDLE EAST	**467**	**431**	**537**	**578**	**785**	**0.04**	**35.81**
Bahrain	2	4	5	7	32	0.00	357.14
Iraq	9	4	8	21	22	0.00	4.76
Jordan	88	75	63	107	81	0.00	-24.30
Kuwait	7	3	6	10	3	0.00	-70.00
Lebanon	60	46	48	61	120	0.01	96.72
Libya	9	1	1				
Oman	3	1	14	19	2	0.00	-89.47
Qatar	155	179	263	256	270	0.01	5.47
Saudi Arabia	13	15	19	10	22	0.00	120.00
United Arab Emirates	80	66	91	64	210	0.01	228.13
Yemen	1	14			1	0.00	
Other countries of Middle East	40	23	19	23	22	0.00	-4.35

Yearbook of Tourism Statistics, Data 2009 – 2013, 2015 Edition

GUATEMALA

2. Arrivals of non-resident visitors at national borders, by country of residence

	2009	2010	2011	2012	2013	Market share 2013	% Change 2013-2012
SOUTH ASIA	**1,253**	**5,174**	**3,549**	**1,931**	**2,023**	**0.10**	**4.76**
Afghanistan	18	38	26	57	13	0.00	-77.19
Bangladesh	20	28	16	20	18	0.00	-10.00
India	1,088	4,985	3,409	1,692	1,869	0.09	10.46
Iran, Islamic Republic of	26	15	19	43	19	0.00	-55.81
Maldives		4	1	1			
Nepal	13	31	15	20	23	0.00	15.00
Pakistan	38	41	46	76	65	0.00	-14.47
Sri Lanka	50	32	17	22	16	0.00	-27.27
NOT SPECIFIED	**2,269**	**1,878**	**1,739**	**1,917**	**2,309**	**0.12**	**20.45**
Other countries of the World	2,269	1,878	1,739	1,917	2,309	0.12	20.45

Yearbook of Tourism Statistics, Data 2009 – 2013, 2015 Edition

GUINEA

1. Arrivals of non-resident tourists at national borders, by nationality

		2009	2010	2011	2012	2013	Market share 2013	% Change 2013-2012
TOTAL	(*)			131,070	96,064	56,146	100.00	-41.55
AFRICA				41,540	37,312	19,422	34.59	-47.95
EAST AFRICA				888	696	639	1.14	-8.19
Burundi				128	100	57	0.10	-43.00
Comoros				12	30	18	0.03	-40.00
Djibouti				24	48	12	0.02	-75.00
Ethiopia				190	184	47	0.08	-74.46
Kenya				78	36	160	0.28	344.44
Madagascar				98	52	95	0.17	82.69
Malawi				16		2	0.00	
Mauritius				12	6	29	0.05	383.33
Mozambique				54	42	17	0.03	-59.52
Reunion				6				
Rwanda				120	30	73	0.13	143.33
Somalia				18	14			
Uganda				24	6	29	0.05	383.33
United Republic of Tanzania				56	36			
Zambia				28	68	10	0.02	-85.29
Zimbabwe				24	44	90	0.16	104.55
CENTRAL AFRICA				2,486	1,631	1,410	2.51	-13.55
Angola				208	219	168	0.30	-23.29
Cameroon				1,066	760	618	1.10	-18.68
Central African Republic				64	30	24	0.04	-20.00
Chad				108	78	140	0.25	79.49
Congo				692	378	345	0.61	-8.73
Democratic Republic of the Congo				16	16			
Equatorial Guinea				36	6	6	0.01	
Gabon				296	144	109	0.19	-24.31
NORTH AFRICA				2,286	1,309	1,743	3.10	33.16
Algeria				508	360	127	0.23	-64.72
Morocco				1,200	557	1,146	2.04	105.75
Sudan				40	6	55	0.10	816.67
Tunisia				538	386	415	0.74	7.51
SOUTHERN AFRICA				1,628	1,058	615	1.10	-41.87
Namibia				6	6	4	0.01	-33.33
South Africa				1,622	1,052	611	1.09	-41.92
WEST AFRICA				34,252	32,618	15,015	26.74	-53.97
Benin				1,124	1,028	737	1.31	-28.31
Burkina Faso				1,578	1,295	741	1.32	-42.78
Cabo Verde				30	36	14	0.02	-61.11
Côte d'Ivoire				6,376	3,648	3,268	5.82	-10.42
Gambia				354	248	226	0.40	-8.87
Ghana				1,086	692	480	0.85	-30.64
Guinea-Bissau				424	1,158	57	0.10	-95.08
Liberia				1,750	548	273	0.49	-50.18
Mali				5,194	3,838	1,931	3.44	-49.69
Mauritania				974	980	325	0.58	-66.84
Niger				188	119	293	0.52	146.22
Nigeria				1,718	6,943	887	1.58	-87.22
Senegal				9,686	8,644	4,012	7.15	-53.59
Sierra Leone				2,710	2,379	1,214	2.16	-48.97
Togo				1,060	1,062	557	0.99	-47.55
AMERICAS				16,348	7,935	5,715	10.18	-27.98
CARIBBEAN				126	54	51	0.09	-5.56
Cuba				60	42	44	0.08	4.76
Guadeloupe				6	6			
Haiti				18	6	3	0.01	-50.00
Trinidad and Tobago				42		4	0.01	
NORTH AMERICA				11,064	5,763	5,173	9.21	-10.24

301

GUINEA

1. Arrivals of non-resident tourists at national borders, by nationality

	2009	2010	2011	2012	2013	Market share 2013	% Change 2013-2012
Canada			3,136	1,984	1,229	2.19	-38.05
Mexico			68	28	7	0.01	-75.00
United States of America			7,860	3,751	3,937	7.01	4.96
SOUTH AMERICA			**5,158**	**2,118**	**491**	**0.87**	**-76.82**
Argentina			54	22	5	0.01	-77.27
Brazil			4,668	1,846	359	0.64	-80.55
Chile			24	18	7	0.01	-61.11
Colombia			126	42	29	0.05	-30.95
Peru			78	64	2	0.00	-96.88
Uruguay			6	6			
Venezuela			18	6			
Other countries of South America			184	114	89	0.16	-21.93
EAST ASIA AND THE PACIFIC			**10,006**	**5,204**	**5,888**	**10.49**	**13.14**
NORTH-EAST ASIA			**7,092**	**3,665**	**4,989**	**8.89**	**36.13**
China			5,906	2,739	4,447	7.92	62.36
Japan			372	242	228	0.41	-5.79
Korea, Dem. People's Republic of			754	666	276	0.49	-58.56
Korea, Republic of			18	12	30	0.05	150.00
Taiwan, Province of China			42	6	8	0.01	33.33
SOUTH-EAST ASIA			**720**	**420**	**339**	**0.60**	**-19.29**
Cambodia			58	18			
Indonesia			46	40	36	0.06	-10.00
Lao People's Democratic Republic			34		9	0.02	
Malaysia			100	118	49	0.09	-58.47
Philippines			236	186	121	0.22	-34.95
Singapore			6		6	0.01	
Thailand			134	16	38	0.07	137.50
Viet Nam			106	42	80	0.14	90.48
AUSTRALASIA			**2,110**	**1,060**	**553**	**0.98**	**-47.83**
Australia			2,016	1,000	484	0.86	-51.60
New Zealand			94	60	69	0.12	15.00
MELANESIA			**84**	**59**	**7**	**0.01**	**-88.14**
Fiji			6	6	5	0.01	-16.67
New Caledonia			78	53	2	0.00	-96.23
EUROPE			**49,436**	**33,949**	**20,069**	**35.74**	**-40.88**
CENTRAL/EASTERN EUROPE			**3,162**	**1,914**	**1,531**	**2.73**	**-20.01**
Armenia			18	12			
Azerbaijan			16	16	1	0.00	-93.75
Belarus			202	130	30	0.05	-76.92
Bulgaria			66	36	17	0.03	-52.78
Czech Republic			48	18	19	0.03	5.56
Georgia			18	6			
Hungary			30	30	16	0.03	-46.67
Kazakhstan			18	12	7	0.01	-41.67
Lithuania			12	6	27	0.05	350.00
Poland			124	60	89	0.16	48.33
Republic of Moldova			6	6	4	0.01	-33.33
Romania			128	76	120	0.21	57.89
Russian Federation			1,676	986	886	1.58	-10.14
Slovakia			6	6	20	0.04	233.33
Tajikistan			6	6	1	0.00	-83.33
Turkmenistan			36	20			
Ukraine			746	488	294	0.52	-39.75
Uzbekistan			6				
NORTHERN EUROPE			**3,242**	**1,910**	**1,365**	**2.43**	**-28.53**
Denmark			132	98	39	0.07	-60.20
Finland			100	52	34	0.06	-34.62
Iceland			28	22	31	0.06	40.91
Ireland			244	152	106	0.19	-30.26

302

GUINEA

1. Arrivals of non-resident tourists at national borders, by nationality

	2009	2010	2011	2012	2013	Market share 2013	% Change 2013-2012
Norway			126	44	63	0.11	43.18
Sweden			260	166	136	0.24	-18.07
United Kingdom			2,352	1,376	956	1.70	-30.52
SOUTHERN EUROPE			**5,474**	**4,528**	**2,363**	**4.21**	**-47.81**
Albania			24	24	7	0.01	-70.83
Andorra			22	6			
Bosnia and Herzegovina			18				
Croatia			30	18	24	0.04	33.33
Greece			38	12	39	0.07	225.00
Italy			1,790	920	726	1.29	-21.09
Malta			18	6	4	0.01	-33.33
Portugal			1,836	866	668	1.19	-22.86
Serbia			46	6	4	0.01	-33.33
Spain			1,652	2,670	891	1.59	-66.63
WESTERN EUROPE			**36,230**	**24,935**	**14,047**	**25.02**	**-43.67**
Austria			30	18	32	0.06	77.78
Belgium			2,752	1,721	1,511	2.69	-12.20
France			28,400	19,714	10,141	18.06	-48.56
Germany			2,340	1,116	1,012	1.80	-9.32
Luxembourg			24	18	13	0.02	-27.78
Netherlands			1,956	1,888	901	1.60	-52.28
Switzerland			728	460	437	0.78	-5.00
EAST MEDITERRANEAN EUROPE			**1,328**	**662**	**763**	**1.36**	**15.26**
Israel			646	310	163	0.29	-47.42
Turkey			682	352	600	1.07	70.45
MIDDLE EAST			**2,148**	**1,749**	**1,143**	**2.04**	**-34.65**
Egypt			176	145	204	0.36	40.69
Iraq			18	18	7	0.01	-61.11
Jordan			54	38	10	0.02	-73.68
Lebanon			1,564	1,412	681	1.21	-51.77
Libya			12	6	18	0.03	200.00
Palestine			24		5	0.01	
Saudi Arabia			120	90	86	0.15	-4.44
Syrian Arab Republic			154	40	20	0.04	-50.00
Other countries of Middle East			26		112	0.20	
SOUTH ASIA			**2,736**	**3,034**	**1,550**	**2.76**	**-48.91**
Afghanistan			42	36	6	0.01	-83.33
Bangladesh			6	12	14	0.02	16.67
India			2,454	2,914	1,444	2.57	-50.45
Iran, Islamic Republic of			58	16	27	0.05	68.75
Nepal			28	22	4	0.01	-81.82
Pakistan			136	28	36	0.06	28.57
Sri Lanka			12	6	19	0.03	216.67
NOT SPECIFIED			**8,856**	**6,881**	**2,359**	**4.20**	**-65.72**
Nationals Residing Abroad			8,856	6,881	2,359	4.20	-65.72

303

GUINEA

1. Arrivals of non-resident tourists at national borders, by country of residence

		2009	2010	2011	2012	2013	Market share 2013	% Change 2013-2012
TOTAL	(*)			**131,070**	**96,064**	**56,146**	**100.00**	**-41.55**
AFRICA				**44,195**	**40,014**	**20,189**	**35.96**	**-49.55**
EAST AFRICA				**918**	**674**	**617**	**1.10**	**-8.46**
Burundi				146	94	46	0.08	-51.06
Comoros				12	30	32	0.06	6.67
Djibouti				24	48	10	0.02	-79.17
Ethiopia				202	190	50	0.09	-73.68
Kenya				108	54	160	0.28	196.30
Madagascar				82	36	93	0.17	158.33
Malawi				16		2	0.00	
Mauritius				12	6	16	0.03	166.67
Mozambique				60	42	23	0.04	-45.24
Reunion				6				
Rwanda				96	18	52	0.09	188.89
Somalia				18	14			
Uganda				54	30	28	0.05	-6.67
United Republic of Tanzania				42	36	6	0.01	-83.33
Zambia				28	68	10	0.02	-85.29
Zimbabwe				12	8	89	0.16	1,012.50
CENTRAL AFRICA				**2,828**	**1,889**	**2,043**	**3.64**	**8.15**
Angola				336	451	200	0.36	-55.65
Cameroon				920	616	590	1.05	-4.22
Central African Republic				52	24	18	0.03	-25.00
Chad				108	84	138	0.25	64.29
Congo				602	336	297	0.53	-11.61
Democratic Republic of the Congo				38	16			
Equatorial Guinea				78	32	669	1.19	1,990.63
Gabon				542	330	124	0.22	-62.42
Other countries of Central Africa				152		7	0.01	
NORTH AFRICA				**2,436**	**1,410**	**1,765**	**3.14**	**25.18**
Algeria				462	290	112	0.20	-61.38
Morocco				1,372	626	1,201	2.14	91.85
Sudan				40	12	53	0.09	341.67
Tunisia				562	482	399	0.71	-17.22
SOUTHERN AFRICA				**1,724**	**1,172**	**616**	**1.10**	**-47.44**
Namibia				6	6	2	0.00	-66.67
South Africa				1,718	1,166	614	1.09	-47.34
WEST AFRICA				**36,289**	**34,869**	**15,148**	**26.98**	**-56.56**
Benin				1,106	928	680	1.21	-26.72
Burkina Faso				1,563	1,353	722	1.29	-46.64
Cabo Verde				30	36	14	0.02	-61.11
Côte d'Ivoire				7,426	3,552	3,483	6.20	-1.94
Gambia				438	296	217	0.39	-26.69
Ghana				1,370	994	557	0.99	-43.96
Guinea-Bissau				327	210	59	0.11	-71.90
Liberia				1,489	482	228	0.41	-52.70
Mali				5,330	3,562	1,867	3.33	-47.59
Mauritania				878	679	273	0.49	-59.79
Niger				244	729	284	0.51	-61.04
Nigeria				1,585	9,039	818	1.46	-90.95
Senegal				11,289	10,015	4,350	7.75	-56.57
Sierra Leone				1,942	1,668	984	1.75	-41.01
Togo				1,272	1,326	612	1.09	-53.85
AMERICAS				**17,943**	**8,816**	**6,119**	**10.90**	**-30.59**
CARIBBEAN				**170**	**92**	**61**	**0.11**	**-33.70**
Cuba				60	42	44	0.08	4.76
Haiti				24	18	1	0.00	-94.44
Puerto Rico				28	16			
Saba				16	16	12	0.02	-25.00

Yearbook of Tourism Statistics, Data 2009 – 2013, 2015 Edition

GUINEA

1. Arrivals of non-resident tourists at national borders, by country of residence

	2009	2010	2011	2012	2013	Market share 2013	% Change 2013-2012
Trinidad and Tobago			42		4	0.01	
NORTH AMERICA			**12,627**	**6,622**	**5,629**	**10.03**	**-15.00**
Canada			3,542	2,072	1,262	2.25	-39.09
Mexico			56	22	6	0.01	-72.73
United States of America			9,029	4,528	4,361	7.77	-3.69
SOUTH AMERICA			**5,146**	**2,102**	**429**	**0.76**	**-79.59**
Argentina			54	22	3	0.01	-86.36
Brazil			4,608	1,790	336	0.60	-81.23
Chile			24	12	10	0.02	-16.67
Colombia			132	36	27	0.05	-25.00
Peru			72	64	1	0.00	-98.44
Venezuela			34	22			
Other countries of South America			222	156	52	0.09	-66.67
EAST ASIA AND THE PACIFIC			**9,608**	**5,046**	**5,715**	**10.18**	**13.26**
NORTH-EAST ASIA			**6,918**	**3,585**	**4,893**	**8.71**	**36.49**
China			5,790	2,667	4,396	7.83	64.83
Japan			350	216	208	0.37	-3.70
Korea, Dem. People's Republic of			742	684	253	0.45	-63.01
Korea, Republic of			12	12	29	0.05	141.67
Taiwan, Province of China			24	6	7	0.01	16.67
SOUTH-EAST ASIA			**642**	**386**	**334**	**0.59**	**-13.47**
Cambodia			40	6	2	0.00	-66.67
Indonesia			46	40	42	0.07	5.00
Lao People's Democratic Republic			22		8	0.01	
Malaysia			80	98	45	0.08	-54.08
Philippines			208	164	117	0.21	-28.66
Singapore			12	24	7	0.01	-70.83
Thailand			134	18	27	0.05	50.00
Viet Nam			100	36	86	0.15	138.89
AUSTRALASIA			**1,920**	**967**	**478**	**0.85**	**-50.57**
Australia			1,866	924	413	0.74	-55.30
New Zealand			54	43	65	0.12	51.16
MELANESIA			**128**	**108**	**10**	**0.02**	**-90.74**
Fiji			68	68	8	0.01	-88.24
New Caledonia			60	40	2	0.00	-95.00
EUROPE			**54,500**	**37,403**	**21,475**	**38.25**	**-42.58**
CENTRAL/EASTERN EUROPE			**3,204**	**1,972**	**1,578**	**2.81**	**-19.98**
Armenia			18	12			
Azerbaijan			16	16	1	0.00	-93.75
Belarus				112	28	0.05	-75.00
Bulgaria			66	36	17	0.03	-52.78
Czech Republic			54	24	16	0.03	-33.33
Czech Republic/Slovakia			6		16	0.03	
Georgia			24	18			
Hungary			30	30	16	0.03	-46.67
Kazakhstan			12	12	7	0.01	-41.67
Lithuania			12	6	27	0.05	350.00
Poland			90	32	87	0.15	171.88
Republic of Moldova			18	6	4	0.01	-33.33
Romania			122	70	109	0.19	55.71
Russian Federation			1,704	962	875	1.56	-9.04
Slovakia			6	6	35	0.06	483.33
Tajikistan			6	6	1	0.00	-83.33
Turkmenistan			20	4			
Ukraine			994	620	339	0.60	-45.32
Uzbekistan			6				
NORTHERN EUROPE			**3,152**	**1,775**	**1,350**	**2.40**	**-23.94**
Denmark			120	86	31	0.06	-63.95
Finland			94	52	32	0.06	-38.46

305

Yearbook of Tourism Statistics, Data 2009 – 2013, 2015 Edition

GUINEA

1. Arrivals of non-resident tourists at national borders, by country of residence

	2009	2010	2011	2012	2013	Market share 2013	% Change 2013-2012
Iceland			28	22	29	0.05	31.82
Ireland			216	130	102	0.18	-21.54
Isle of Man			6				
Norway			132	48	68	0.12	41.67
Sweden			254	118	142	0.25	20.34
United Kingdom			2,302	1,319	946	1.68	-28.28
SOUTHERN EUROPE			**6,161**	**4,906**	**2,387**	**4.25**	**-51.35**
Albania			24	24	8	0.01	-66.67
Andorra			12	12			
Bosnia and Herzegovina			24				
Croatia			24	18	23	0.04	27.78
Greece			24	12	33	0.06	175.00
Italy			1,893	994	740	1.32	-25.55
Malta			18	6	10	0.02	66.67
Portugal			1,874	900	658	1.17	-26.89
Serbia			30	6	4	0.01	-33.33
Spain			2,238	2,934	911	1.62	-68.95
WESTERN EUROPE			**40,693**	**28,118**	**15,431**	**27.48**	**-45.12**
Austria			34	18	28	0.05	55.56
Belgium			3,394	1,897	1,712	3.05	-9.75
France			31,666	21,207	11,092	19.76	-47.70
Germany			2,529	1,576	1,122	2.00	-28.81
Luxembourg			42	24	16	0.03	-33.33
Netherlands			1,908	2,196	934	1.66	-57.47
Switzerland			1,120	1,200	527	0.94	-56.08
EAST MEDITERRANEAN EUROPE			**1,290**	**632**	**729**	**1.30**	**15.35**
Israel			618	280	160	0.28	-42.86
Turkey			672	352	569	1.01	61.65
MIDDLE EAST			**2,236**	**1,815**	**1,169**	**2.08**	**-35.59**
Egypt			230	151	198	0.35	31.13
Iraq			12	12	6	0.01	-50.00
Jordan			48	32	8	0.01	-75.00
Kuwait			6	12	4	0.01	-66.67
Lebanon			1,536	1,412	662	1.18	-53.12
Libya			18	6	18	0.03	200.00
Palestine			24		5	0.01	
Qatar			6	2	12	0.02	500.00
Saudi Arabia			174	126	152	0.27	20.63
Syrian Arab Republic			154	40	18	0.03	-55.00
United Arab Emirates			28	22	86	0.15	290.91
SOUTH ASIA			**2,588**	**2,970**	**1,479**	**2.63**	**-50.20**
Afghanistan			30	24	4	0.01	-83.33
India			2,348	2,874	1,396	2.49	-51.43
Iran, Islamic Republic of			58	16	23	0.04	43.75
Nepal			28	22	12	0.02	-45.45
Pakistan			112	28	25	0.04	-10.71
Sri Lanka			12	6	19	0.03	216.67

306

GUINEA

3. Arrivals of non-resident tourists in hotels and similar establishments, by country of residence

	2009	2010	2011	2012	2013	Market share 2013	% Change 2013-2012
TOTAL (*)			62,724	34,841	16,053	100.00	-53.92
AFRICA			24,086	17,188	6,343	39.51	-63.10
EAST AFRICA			450	257	216	1.35	-15.95
Burundi			44	32	11	0.07	-65.63
Comoros			6	14			
Djibouti			12	16	4	0.02	-75.00
Ethiopia			166	33	18	0.11	-45.45
Kenya			66	6	41	0.26	583.33
Madagascar			58	46	30	0.19	-34.78
Mauritius			6		15	0.09	
Mozambique			12	30	4	0.02	-86.67
Rwanda			18	18	6	0.04	-66.67
Somalia			6	10			
Uganda			30	6	9	0.06	50.00
United Republic of Tanzania			14	6	4	0.02	-33.33
Zambia			6	32	8	0.05	-75.00
Zimbabwe			6	8	66	0.41	725.00
CENTRAL AFRICA			1,204	713	556	3.46	-22.02
Angola			144	120	28	0.17	-76.67
Cameroon			414	321	181	1.13	-43.61
Central African Republic			40	18			
Chad			30	48	50	0.31	4.17
Congo			324	161	92	0.57	-42.86
Democratic Republic of the Congo			16	16			
Equatorial Guinea			56	6	179	1.12	2,883.33
Gabon			180	23	26	0.16	13.04
NORTH AFRICA			1,946	369	481	3.00	30.35
Algeria			306	130	30	0.19	-76.92
Morocco			1,150	131	309	1.92	135.88
Sudan			12		13	0.08	
Tunisia			478	108	129	0.80	19.44
SOUTHERN AFRICA			996	452	213	1.33	-52.88
Namibia			6		2	0.01	
South Africa			990	452	211	1.31	-53.32
WEST AFRICA			19,490	15,397	4,877	30.38	-68.32
Benin			644	402	254	1.58	-36.82
Burkina Faso			1,063	696	342	2.13	-50.86
Cabo Verde			6	22	4	0.02	-81.82
Côte d'Ivoire			2,822	1,509	1,034	6.44	-31.48
Gambia			330	98	54	0.34	-44.90
Ghana			1,008	185	179	1.12	-3.24
Guinea-Bissau			164	409	10	0.06	-97.56
Liberia			1,134	77	61	0.38	-20.78
Mali			4,096	871	540	3.36	-38.00
Mauritania			516	495	83	0.52	-83.23
Niger			180	82	98	0.61	19.51
Nigeria			848	2,473	188	1.17	-92.40
Senegal			5,505	5,033	1,626	10.13	-67.69
Sierra Leone			540	720	175	1.09	-75.69
Togo			634	590	229	1.43	-61.19
Other countries of West Africa				1,735			
AMERICAS			6,991	3,164	1,319	8.22	-58.31
CARIBBEAN			98		17	0.11	
Cuba			12		17	0.11	
Haiti			6				
Puerto Rico			28				
Saba			16				
Trinidad and Tobago			36				
NORTH AMERICA			4,331	2,502	1,147	7.15	-54.16

307

GUINEA

3. Arrivals of non-resident tourists in hotels and similar establishments, by country of residence

	2009	2010	2011	2012	2013	Market share 2013	% Change 2013-2012
Canada			1,530	1,025	342	2.13	-66.63
Mexico			24	12	4	0.02	-66.67
United States of America			2,777	1,465	801	4.99	-45.32
SOUTH AMERICA			**2,518**	**662**	**153**	**0.95**	**-76.89**
Argentina			54	6	3	0.02	-50.00
Brazil			2,356	600	125	0.78	-79.17
Chile			6		1	0.01	
Colombia			30	6	12	0.07	100.00
Peru			28	14	1	0.01	-92.86
Uruguay				6			
Venezuela			28	6			
Other countries of South America			16	24	11	0.07	-54.17
OTHER AMERICAS			**44**		**2**	**0.01**	
Other countries of the Americas			44		2	0.01	
EAST ASIA AND THE PACIFIC			**4,724**	**1,851**	**1,772**	**11.04**	**-4.27**
NORTH-EAST ASIA			**3,068**	**1,242**	**1,530**	**9.53**	**23.19**
China			2,404	910	1,347	8.39	48.02
Japan			194	96	93	0.58	-3.13
Korea, Dem. People's Republic of			452	234	72	0.45	-69.23
Korea, Republic of			12	2	18	0.11	800.00
Taiwan, Province of China			6				
SOUTH-EAST ASIA			**414**	**114**	**69**	**0.43**	**-39.47**
Cambodia			34	12			
Indonesia			22		9	0.06	
Malaysia			44	63	9	0.06	-85.71
Philippines			122	39	29	0.18	-25.64
Singapore			6		1	0.01	
Thailand			128		3	0.02	
Viet Nam			58		18	0.11	
AUSTRALASIA			**1,184**	**453**	**171**	**1.07**	**-62.25**
Australia			1,152	433	146	0.91	-66.28
New Zealand			32	20	25	0.16	25.00
MELANESIA			**58**	**42**	**2**	**0.01**	**-95.24**
Fiji			20	6	2	0.01	-66.67
New Caledonia			38	36			
EUROPE			**24,309**	**11,296**	**6,009**	**37.43**	**-46.80**
CENTRAL/EASTERN EUROPE			**1,648**	**746**	**415**	**2.59**	**-44.37**
Azerbaijan			16	16			
Belarus			78	57	8	0.05	-85.96
Bulgaria			60		5	0.03	
Czech Republic			12	6	10	0.06	66.67
Hungary			18	13	4	0.02	-69.23
Kazakhstan			34				
Lithuania			12	6	13	0.08	116.67
Poland			32	26	16	0.10	-38.46
Republic of Moldova			6				
Romania			92	58	13	0.08	-77.59
Russian Federation			658	445	241	1.50	-45.84
Slovakia			6		4	0.02	
Tajikistan			6				
Turkmenistan				18			
Ukraine			618	101	101	0.63	
NORTHERN EUROPE			**1,594**	**808**	**392**	**2.44**	**-51.49**
Denmark			90	18	6	0.04	-66.67
Finland			42	10	12	0.07	20.00
Iceland			22		4	0.02	
Ireland			96	42	21	0.13	-50.00
Norway			54	40	32	0.20	-20.00
Sweden			66	57	40	0.25	-29.82

Yearbook of Tourism Statistics, Data 2009 – 2013, 2015 Edition

GUINEA

3. Arrivals of non-resident tourists in hotels and similar establishments, by country of residence

	2009	2010	2011	2012	2013	Market share 2013	% Change 2013-2012
United Kingdom			1,224	641	277	1.73	-56.79
SOUTHERN EUROPE			**3,275**	**1,289**	**791**	**4.93**	**-38.63**
Andorra			12	6			
Bosnia and Herzegovina			12				
Croatia			6		7	0.04	
Greece			18	6	12	0.07	100.00
Italy			1,113	291	304	1.89	4.47
Malta			6				
Portugal			990	243	150	0.93	-38.27
Serbia			6	6			
Spain			1,112	737	318	1.98	-56.85
WESTERN EUROPE			**17,018**	**8,266**	**4,272**	**26.61**	**-48.32**
Austria			28	12	7	0.04	-41.67
Belgium			1,064	625	324	2.02	-48.16
France			14,097	6,345	3,372	21.01	-46.86
Germany			827	428	243	1.51	-43.22
Luxembourg			12	6	7	0.04	16.67
Netherlands			544	615	180	1.12	-70.73
Switzerland			446	235	139	0.87	-40.85
EAST MEDITERRANEAN EUROPE			**774**	**187**	**139**	**0.87**	**-25.67**
Israel			374	72	50	0.31	-30.56
Turkey			400	115	89	0.55	-22.61
MIDDLE EAST			**1,366**	**303**	**257**	**1.60**	**-15.18**
Egypt			178	33	41	0.26	24.24
Iraq			12		1	0.01	
Jordan			34		2	0.01	
Kuwait			18		1	0.01	
Lebanon			856	252	125	0.78	-50.40
Libya			18		7	0.04	
Palestine			12				
Qatar			6		6	0.04	
Saudi Arabia			120	12	35	0.22	191.67
Syrian Arab Republic			84	6	1	0.01	-83.33
United Arab Emirates			28		38	0.24	
SOUTH ASIA			**1,248**	**1,039**	**353**	**2.20**	**-66.03**
Afghanistan			24	12			
Bangladesh				12	5	0.03	-58.33
India			1,160	961	331	2.06	-65.56
Iran, Islamic Republic of			6	4	4	0.02	
Nepal			22	22	1	0.01	-95.45
Pakistan			36	22	4	0.02	-81.82
Sri Lanka				6	8	0.05	33.33

Yearbook of Tourism Statistics, Data 2009 – 2013, 2015 Edition

GUYANA

1. Arrivals of non-resident tourists at national borders, by country of residence

		2009	2010	2011	2012	2013	Market share 2013	% Change 2013-2012
TOTAL	(*)	**141,281**	**151,926**	**156,871**	**176,642**			
AMERICAS		**130,979**	**141,200**	**107,247**	**124,602**			
CARIBBEAN		**28,026**	**29,487**					
All countries of the Caribbean		28,026	29,487					
NORTH AMERICA		**100,767**	**108,347**	**107,247**	**124,602**			
Canada		23,812	25,381	23,965	25,977			
United States of America		76,955	82,966	83,282	98,625			
OTHER AMERICAS		**2,186**	**3,366**					
Other countries of the Americas		2,186	3,366					
EUROPE		**8,277**	**8,357**	**8,284**	**8,877**			
OTHER EUROPE		**8,277**	**8,357**	**8,284**	**8,877**			
All countries of Europe		8,277	8,357	8,284	8,877			
NOT SPECIFIED		**2,025**	**2,369**	**41,340**	**43,163**			
Other countries of the World		2,025	2,369	41,340	43,163			

Yearbook of Tourism Statistics, Data 2009 – 2013, 2015 Edition

HAITI

1. Arrivals of non-resident tourists at national borders, by country of residence

		2009	2010	2011	2012	2013	Market share 2013	% Change 2013-2012
TOTAL	(*)	**387,218**	**254,732**	**348,755**				
AMERICAS		**335,135**	**220,791**	**309,024**				
CARIBBEAN		**24,989**	**9,954**	**11,552**				
Dominican Republic		9,910	3,168	4,487				
Jamaica		6,050	689	819				
Other countries of the Caribbean		9,029	6,097	6,246				
NORTH AMERICA		**300,288**	**204,485**	**288,014**				
Canada		31,017	20,119	19,568				
Mexico		1,047	1,123	1,024				
United States of America		268,224	183,243	267,422				
OTHER AMERICAS		**9,858**	**6,352**	**9,458**				
Other countries of the Americas		9,858	6,352	9,458				
EUROPE		**24,573**	**26,755**	**31,437**				
WESTERN EUROPE		**12,508**	**14,261**	**18,432**				
France		12,508	14,261	18,432				
OTHER EUROPE		**12,065**	**12,494**	**13,005**				
Other countries of Europe		12,065	12,494	13,005				
NOT SPECIFIED		**27,510**	**7,186**	**8,294**				
Other countries of the World		27,510	7,186	8,294				

Yearbook of Tourism Statistics, Data 2009 – 2013, 2015 Edition

HONDURAS

1. Arrivals of non-resident tourists at national borders, by nationality

	2009	2010	2011	2012	2013	Market share 2013	% Change 2013-2012
TOTAL (*)	835,531	862,548	871,468	894,677	863,012	100.00	-3.54
AFRICA	303	409	431	730	669	0.08	-8.36
EAST AFRICA	36	46	49	80	73	0.01	-8.75
Ethiopia	8	10	12	20	19	0.00	-5.00
Kenya	20	25	26	42	38	0.00	-9.52
Zimbabwe	8	11	11	18	16	0.00	-11.11
CENTRAL AFRICA	12	15	16	25	23	0.00	-8.00
Cameroon	7	10	10	15	14	0.00	-6.67
Congo	2	2	2	4	3	0.00	-25.00
Gabon	3	3	4	6	6	0.00	
NORTH AFRICA	13	16	17	30	26	0.00	-13.33
Algeria	1	1	2	2	3	0.00	50.00
Morocco	10	13	13	24	19	0.00	-20.83
Tunisia	2	2	2	4	4	0.00	
SOUTHERN AFRICA	195	266	279	482	443	0.05	-8.09
South Africa	195	266	279	482	443	0.05	-8.09
WEST AFRICA	30	42	46	73	61	0.01	-16.44
Côte d'Ivoire	4	6	6	10			
Ghana	3	5	5	8	8	0.00	
Nigeria	23	31	35	55	53	0.01	-3.64
OTHER AFRICA	17	24	24	40	43	0.00	7.50
Other countries of Africa	17	24	24	40	43	0.00	7.50
AMERICAS	744,218	753,154	758,751	734,399	713,928	82.73	-2.79
CARIBBEAN	5,226	7,060	6,479	9,935	10,428	1.21	4.96
Antigua and Barbuda	8	10	9	15	16	0.00	6.67
Bahamas	46	64	59	90	95	0.01	5.56
Barbados	19	26	23	34	34	0.00	
Bermuda	1	2	1	2	2	0.00	
Cayman Islands	1,544	2,058	1,912	2,867	2,989	0.35	4.26
Cuba	1,381	1,874	1,731	2,653	2,799	0.32	5.50
Dominica	17	24	19	33	33	0.00	
Dominican Republic	1,382	1,846	1,694	2,622	2,744	0.32	4.65
Haiti	220	321	283	441	477	0.06	8.16
Jamaica	251	333	308	477	499	0.06	4.61
Puerto Rico	114	155	143	219	225	0.03	2.74
Saint Vincent and the Grenadines	12	14	12	19	19	0.00	
Trinidad and Tobago	72	97	86	134	141	0.02	5.22
Other countries of the Caribbean	159	236	199	329	355	0.04	7.90
CENTRAL AMERICA	394,717	434,800	409,642	389,570	362,977	42.06	-6.83
Belize	1,986	2,179	2,057	1,969	1,805	0.21	-8.33
Costa Rica	21,831	24,073	22,825	21,629	20,199	2.34	-6.61
El Salvador	145,157	159,755	150,343	142,961	133,256	15.44	-6.79
Guatemala	111,220	122,641	115,768	110,230	103,115	11.95	-6.45
Nicaragua	106,598	117,342	110,299	104,904	97,233	11.27	-7.31
Panama	7,925	8,810	8,350	7,877	7,369	0.85	-6.45
NORTH AMERICA	325,248	285,593	316,620	292,022	296,042	34.30	1.38
Canada	19,062	16,838	18,530	17,086	17,339	2.01	1.48
Mexico	23,513	20,613	22,968	21,045	21,423	2.48	1.80
Saint Pierre and Miquelon	6	5	5	4	4	0.00	
United States of America	282,667	248,137	275,117	253,887	257,276	29.81	1.33
SOUTH AMERICA	19,027	25,701	26,010	42,872	44,481	5.15	3.75
Argentina	3,690	4,990	5,046	8,404	8,703	1.01	3.56
Bolivia	697	936	960	1,567	1,627	0.19	3.83
Brazil	1,957	2,658	2,684	4,418	4,589	0.53	3.87
Chile	2,381	3,209	3,257	5,346	5,554	0.64	3.89
Colombia	4,545	6,143	6,210	10,239	10,629	1.23	3.81
Ecuador	1,341	1,803	1,817	2,981	3,087	0.36	3.56
French Guiana	15	21	21	34	36	0.00	5.88
Guyana	46	58	57	101	104	0.01	2.97

312

HONDURAS

1. Arrivals of non-resident tourists at national borders, by nationality

	2009	2010	2011	2012	2013	Market share 2013	% Change 2013-2012
Paraguay	229	306	307	506	532	0.06	5.14
Peru	1,625	2,190	2,220	3,653	3,795	0.44	3.89
Suriname	10	13	12	22	23	0.00	4.55
Uruguay	605	823	829	1,358	1,411	0.16	3.90
Venezuela	1,886	2,551	2,590	4,243	4,391	0.51	3.49
EAST ASIA AND THE PACIFIC	**10,475**	**14,143**	**16,346**	**29,860**	**26,543**	**3.08**	**-11.11**
NORTH-EAST ASIA	**7,642**	**10,337**	**11,933**	**21,828**	**19,382**	**2.25**	**-11.21**
China	1,831	2,539	2,865	5,280	4,695	0.54	-11.08
Hong Kong, China	12	19	20	35	33	0.00	-5.71
Japan	2,873	3,889	4,466	8,158	7,217	0.84	-11.53
Korea, Dem. People's Republic of	1,670	2,280	2,660	4,762	4,289	0.50	-9.93
Korea, Republic of	1,180	1,523	1,792	3,390	2,945	0.34	-13.13
Taiwan, Province of China	76	87	130	203	203	0.02	
SOUTH-EAST ASIA	**560**	**767**	**881**	**1,588**	**1,437**	**0.17**	**-9.51**
Indonesia	68	90	101	178	158	0.02	-11.24
Malaysia	77	104	122	219	201	0.02	-8.22
Philippines	398	549	633	1,146	1,035	0.12	-9.69
Thailand	17	24	25	45	43	0.00	-4.44
AUSTRALASIA	**2,054**	**2,740**	**3,191**	**5,815**	**5,160**	**0.60**	**-11.26**
Australia	1,650	2,206	2,569	4,683	4,148	0.48	-11.42
New Zealand	404	534	622	1,132	1,012	0.12	-10.60
OTHER EAST ASIA AND THE PACIFIC	**219**	**299**	**341**	**629**	**564**	**0.07**	**-10.33**
Other countries of Asia	219	299	341	629	564	0.07	-10.33
EUROPE	**79,375**	**93,268**	**94,099**	**126,379**	**119,208**	**13.81**	**-5.67**
CENTRAL/EASTERN EUROPE	**1,890**	**2,172**	**2,235**	**2,952**	**2,815**	**0.33**	**-4.64**
Bulgaria	491	544	582	747	717	0.08	-4.02
Czech Republic/Slovakia	316	371	373	501	475	0.06	-5.19
Hungary	78	90	94	121	117	0.01	-3.31
Poland	400	486	488	651	613	0.07	-5.84
Romania	100	119	121	159	153	0.02	-3.77
Russian Federation	382	421	433	584	563	0.07	-3.60
Ukraine	123	141	144	189	177	0.02	-6.35
NORTHERN EUROPE	**17,289**	**20,073**	**20,255**	**27,395**	**25,748**	**2.98**	**-6.01**
Denmark	1,798	2,120	2,146	2,860	2,700	0.31	-5.59
Finland	651	757	763	1,013	961	0.11	-5.13
Iceland	107	124	125	168	157	0.02	-6.55
Ireland	875	1,004	1,027	1,392	1,312	0.15	-5.75
Norway	1,297	1,489	1,494	2,064	1,928	0.22	-6.59
Sweden	2,580	2,969	2,958	4,009	3,767	0.44	-6.04
United Kingdom	9,981	11,610	11,742	15,889	14,923	1.73	-6.08
SOUTHERN EUROPE	**30,919**	**36,738**	**37,149**	**49,546**	**46,894**	**5.43**	**-5.35**
Andorra	11	13	13	16	16	0.00	
Croatia	43	52	48	69	66	0.01	-4.35
Greece	239	286	274	383	364	0.04	-4.96
Italy	17,392	20,773	20,977	27,739	26,358	3.05	-4.98
Malta	12	14	13	18	18	0.00	
Portugal	309	371	365	500	473	0.05	-5.40
Spain	12,913	15,229	15,459	20,821	19,599	2.27	-5.87
WESTERN EUROPE	**27,707**	**32,446**	**32,577**	**43,970**	**41,363**	**4.79**	**-5.93**
Austria	829	971	981	1,310	1,231	0.14	-6.03
Belgium	1,966	2,315	2,351	3,193	2,994	0.35	-6.23
France	5,878	6,853	6,872	9,282	8,695	1.01	-6.32
Germany	10,459	12,183	12,219	16,583	15,626	1.81	-5.77
Luxembourg	24	26	26	37	34	0.00	-8.11
Netherlands	5,359	6,381	6,393	8,538	8,059	0.93	-5.61
Switzerland	3,192	3,717	3,735	5,027	4,724	0.55	-6.03
EAST MEDITERRANEAN EUROPE	**1,532**	**1,797**	**1,840**	**2,458**	**2,330**	**0.27**	**-5.21**
Cyprus	8	8	8	11	10	0.00	-9.09
Israel	1,457	1,713	1,756	2,344	2,223	0.26	-5.16

313

Yearbook of Tourism Statistics, Data 2009 – 2013, 2015 Edition

HONDURAS

1. Arrivals of non-resident tourists at national borders, by nationality

	2009	2010	2011	2012	2013	Market share 2013	% Change 2013-2012
Turkey	67	76	76	103	97	0.01	-5.83
OTHER EUROPE	**38**	**42**	**43**	**58**	**58**	**0.01**	
Other countries of Europe	38	42	43	58	58	0.01	
MIDDLE EAST	**156**	**210**	**245**	**450**	**313**	**0.04**	**-30.44**
Egypt	40	57	65	119	70	0.01	-41.18
Jordan	27	36	41	77	69	0.01	-10.39
Kuwait	8	9	14	22	20	0.00	-9.09
Lebanon	16	21	23	47	30	0.00	-36.17
Libya	2	2	3	4	2	0.00	-50.00
Palestine	58	77	90	166	111	0.01	-33.13
Syrian Arab Republic	5	8	9	15	11	0.00	-26.67
SOUTH ASIA	**376**	**513**	**598**	**1,071**	**715**	**0.08**	**-33.24**
Bangladesh	8	12	12	24	21	0.00	-12.50
India	297	408	479	852	544	0.06	-36.15
Iran, Islamic Republic of	17	22	25	45	46	0.01	2.22
Pakistan	35	46	53	97	67	0.01	-30.93
Sri Lanka	19	25	29	53	37	0.00	-30.19
NOT SPECIFIED	**628**	**851**	**998**	**1,788**	**1,636**	**0.19**	**-8.50**
Other countries of the World	628	851	998	1,788	1,636	0.19	-8.50

Yearbook of Tourism Statistics, Data 2009 – 2013, 2015 Edition

HONG KONG, CHINA

1. Arrivals of non-resident tourists at national borders, by country of residence

	2009	2010	2011	2012	2013	Market share 2013	% Change 2013-2012
TOTAL	16,926,100	20,085,155	22,316,073	23,770,195	25,661,072	100.00	7.95
AFRICA	101,700	105,322	98,132	89,548	89,343	0.35	-0.23
SOUTHERN AFRICA	32,100	36,993	38,550	34,485	34,446	0.13	-0.11
South Africa	32,100	36,993	38,550	34,485	34,446	0.13	-0.11
OTHER AFRICA	69,600	68,329	59,582	55,063	54,897	0.21	-0.30
Other countries of Africa	69,600	68,329	59,582	55,063	54,897	0.21	-0.30
AMERICAS	1,107,600	1,245,553	1,279,072	1,247,581	1,163,788	4.54	-6.72
CENTRAL AMERICA	12,500	13,749	13,620	13,049	12,789	0.05	-1.99
Honduras	700	777	707	819	755	0.00	-7.81
Other countries of Central America	11,800	12,972	12,913	12,230	12,034	0.05	-1.60
NORTH AMERICA	1,031,600	1,150,848	1,174,102	1,142,545	1,058,181	4.12	-7.38
Canada	260,700	290,827	291,454	278,028	246,679	0.96	-11.28
Mexico	15,100	21,269	21,642	22,887	25,143	0.10	9.86
United States of America	755,800	838,752	861,006	841,630	786,359	3.06	-6.57
SOUTH AMERICA	63,500	80,956	91,350	91,987	92,818	0.36	0.90
Argentina	7,200	10,169	10,300	10,278	10,772	0.04	4.81
Brazil	19,500	27,840	34,579	33,174	33,990	0.13	2.46
Venezuela	10,100	10,711	12,174	12,754	11,360	0.04	-10.93
Other countries of South America	26,700	32,236	34,297	35,781	36,696	0.14	2.56
EAST ASIA AND THE PACIFIC	14,169,300	16,966,228	19,178,636	20,671,911	22,613,497	88.12	9.39
NORTH-EAST ASIA	11,708,400	14,088,673	16,118,154	17,655,990	19,537,142	76.14	10.65
China	9,663,600	11,678,055	13,599,768	15,110,372	17,089,509	66.60	13.10
Japan	779,600	823,575	787,220	774,426	607,877	2.37	-21.51
Korea, Republic of	401,600	587,866	670,835	725,783	745,367	2.90	2.70
Macao, China	249,800	274,616	281,678	291,219	308,711	1.20	6.01
Taiwan, Province of China	613,800	724,561	778,653	754,190	785,678	3.06	4.18
SOUTH-EAST ASIA	1,890,100	2,254,040	2,438,931	2,397,188	2,477,975	9.66	3.37
Indonesia	263,900	340,147	379,915	370,161	379,744	1.48	2.59
Malaysia	326,300	424,491	452,172	434,212	466,578	1.82	7.45
Philippines	455,800	493,092	542,967	585,760	584,727	2.28	-0.18
Singapore	456,700	527,560	585,727	530,561	521,620	2.03	-1.69
Thailand	303,200	356,060	380,647	388,681	426,797	1.66	9.81
Viet Nam	64,900	91,461	73,072	63,596	72,736	0.28	14.37
Other countries of South-East Asia	19,300	21,229	24,431	24,217	25,773	0.10	6.43
AUSTRALASIA	535,400	585,199	575,332	567,838	545,996	2.13	-3.85
Australia	462,600	505,907	500,225	495,441	476,324	1.86	-3.86
New Zealand	72,800	79,292	75,107	72,397	69,672	0.27	-3.76
OTHER EAST ASIA AND THE PACIFIC	35,400	38,316	46,219	50,895	52,384	0.20	2.93
Other countries of Asia	31,400	32,222	39,945	44,906	46,182	0.18	2.84
Other countries of Oceania	4,000	6,094	6,274	5,989	6,202	0.02	3.56
EUROPE	1,271,600	1,379,350	1,395,740	1,440,964	1,451,840	5.66	0.75
CENTRAL/EASTERN EUROPE	32,100	60,880	88,572	125,919	146,221	0.57	16.12
Russian Federation	32,100	60,880	88,572	125,919	146,221	0.57	16.12
NORTHERN EUROPE	515,500	525,472	515,207	534,913	517,696	2.02	-3.22
Denmark	21,300	22,325	22,157	20,770	20,297	0.08	-2.28
Finland	25,900	23,981	20,672	19,861	18,899	0.07	-4.84
Norway	14,800	15,712	15,290	15,404	14,886	0.06	-3.36
Sweden	38,100	41,888	43,932	42,486	41,089	0.16	-3.29
United Kingdom	415,400	421,566	413,156	436,392	422,525	1.65	-3.18
SOUTHERN EUROPE	119,300	130,783	131,718	128,324	127,847	0.50	-0.37
Italy	69,100	76,918	75,509	74,431	73,770	0.29	-0.89
Portugal	8,700	8,380	11,354	12,530	13,550	0.05	8.14
Spain	41,500	45,485	44,855	41,363	40,527	0.16	-2.02
WESTERN EUROPE	465,500	507,015	496,148	483,982	477,050	1.86	-1.43
Austria	18,400	20,310	19,156	19,057	18,886	0.07	-0.90
Belgium	23,500	24,977	24,145	23,554	24,687	0.10	4.81
France	156,300	173,604	168,653	163,210	163,596	0.64	0.24
Germany	156,500	170,170	163,975	161,970	158,702	0.62	-2.02
Netherlands	73,800	77,895	78,543	73,616	67,729	0.26	-8.00

315

HONG KONG, CHINA

1. Arrivals of non-resident tourists at national borders, by country of residence

	2009	2010	2011	2012	2013	Market share 2013	% Change 2013-2012
Switzerland	37,000	40,059	41,676	42,575	43,450	0.17	2.06
EAST MEDITERRANEAN EUROPE	**54,100**	**61,932**	**59,864**	**57,285**	**58,892**	**0.23**	**2.81**
Israel	38,900	43,292	39,931	38,187	38,892	0.15	1.85
Turkey	15,200	18,640	19,933	19,098	20,000	0.08	4.72
OTHER EUROPE	**85,100**	**93,268**	**104,231**	**110,541**	**124,134**	**0.48**	**12.30**
Other countries of Europe	85,100	93,268	104,231	110,541	124,134	0.48	12.30
MIDDLE EAST	**44,500**	**52,669**	**52,395**	**51,152**	**57,997**	**0.23**	**13.38**
Bahrain	1,200	1,696	1,609	1,487	1,577	0.01	6.05
Egypt	4,700	5,488	5,278	5,275	6,123	0.02	16.08
Jordan	3,700	4,205	3,973	3,433	3,641	0.01	6.06
Kuwait	3,200	4,369	5,337	4,839	5,034	0.02	4.03
Saudi Arabia	11,700	17,224	15,025	14,731	15,863	0.06	7.68
United Arab Emirates	11,900	11,290	12,428	12,616	15,986	0.06	26.71
Other countries of Middle East	8,100	8,397	8,745	8,771	9,773	0.04	11.42
SOUTH ASIA	**231,400**	**336,033**	**312,098**	**269,039**	**284,607**	**1.11**	**5.79**
India	231,400	336,033	312,098	269,039	284,607	1.11	5.79

Yearbook of Tourism Statistics, Data 2009 – 2013, 2015 Edition

HONG KONG, CHINA

2. Arrivals of non-resident visitors at national borders, by country of residence

	2009	2010	2011	2012	2013	Market share 2013	% Change 2013-2012
TOTAL	29,590,654	36,030,331	41,921,310	48,615,113	54,298,804	100.00	11.69
AFRICA	182,384	204,105	192,854	173,355	167,879	0.31	-3.16
EAST AFRICA	52,958	58,583	54,292	48,267	49,043	0.09	1.61
Burundi	20	27	12	15	10	0.00	-33.33
Comoros	29	52	71	56	81	0.00	44.64
Djibouti	61	42	88	43	60	0.00	39.53
Eritrea	20	30	19	20	28	0.00	40.00
Ethiopia	905	902	637	1,007	710	0.00	-29.49
Kenya	4,941	4,839	4,955	4,180	5,661	0.01	35.43
Madagascar	4,645	4,277	4,005	3,322	3,129	0.01	-5.81
Malawi	1,014	1,200	1,205	1,128	914	0.00	-18.97
Mauritius	18,421	23,217	21,914	18,382	16,994	0.03	-7.55
Mozambique	1,558	2,100	2,344	1,962	1,903	0.00	-3.01
Rwanda	352	432	298	383	362	0.00	-5.48
Seychelles	446	572	565	522	1,812	0.00	247.13
Somalia	9	6	4	1	9	0.00	800.00
Uganda	4,936	4,338	3,991	3,004	2,932	0.01	-2.40
United Republic of Tanzania	11,260	10,745	8,334	8,842	8,735	0.02	-1.21
Zambia	2,849	3,553	3,577	3,396	3,523	0.01	3.74
Zimbabwe	1,492	2,251	2,273	2,004	2,180	0.00	8.78
CENTRAL AFRICA	4,093	3,638	3,142	3,168	2,414	0.00	-23.80
Angola	522	538	748	660	591	0.00	-10.45
Cameroon	1,228	706	597	426	360	0.00	-15.49
Central African Republic	86	96	54	57	68	0.00	19.30
Chad	315	218	135	136	128	0.00	-5.88
Congo	372	270	209	235	173	0.00	-26.38
Democratic Republic of the Congo	1,165	1,393	1,014	1,198	643	0.00	-46.33
Equatorial Guinea	74	78	114	128	154	0.00	20.31
Gabon	330	331	253	312	281	0.00	-9.94
Sao Tome and Principe	1	8	18	16	16	0.00	
NORTH AFRICA	18,861	20,947	17,841	17,491	17,127	0.03	-2.08
Algeria	10,833	10,943	9,700	8,770	7,846	0.01	-10.54
Morocco	4,854	5,737	4,972	4,828	5,664	0.01	17.32
South Sudan				3	10	0.00	233.33
Sudan	147	102	90	81	132	0.00	62.96
Tunisia	3,027	4,165	3,079	3,809	3,475	0.01	-8.77
SOUTHERN AFRICA	65,484	81,785	84,364	74,045	71,126	0.13	-3.94
Botswana	2,252	2,838	2,594	1,774	1,134	0.00	-36.08
Lesotho	143	274	302	275	235	0.00	-14.55
Namibia	546	637	995	1,102	1,223	0.00	10.98
South Africa	62,246	77,658	79,989	70,660	68,355	0.13	-3.26
Swaziland	297	378	484	234	179	0.00	-23.50
WEST AFRICA	40,988	39,152	33,209	30,384	28,169	0.05	-7.29
Benin	2,244	2,135	2,217	1,777	1,697	0.00	-4.50
Burkina Faso	2,356	2,562	1,667	2,832	2,573	0.00	-9.15
Cabo Verde	296	294	238	243	214	0.00	-11.93
Côte d'Ivoire	450	390	262	365	403	0.00	10.41
Gambia	2,465	2,575	2,412	2,354	1,862	0.00	-20.90
Ghana	873	681	748	532	386	0.00	-27.44
Guinea	6,143	6,056	4,896	4,315	3,450	0.01	-20.05
Guinea-Bissau	1,489	876	486	327	67	0.00	-79.51
Liberia	252	286	279	150	38	0.00	-74.67
Mali	8,613	8,559	7,759	6,455	6,677	0.01	3.44
Mauritania	417	464	368	393	391	0.00	-0.51
Niger	3,446	3,150	2,708	2,577	2,998	0.01	16.34
Nigeria	9,870	9,189	7,584	6,509	5,690	0.01	-12.58
Senegal	1,154	962	724	831	923	0.00	11.07
Sierra Leone	195	283	256	166	204	0.00	22.89
Togo	725	690	605	558	596	0.00	6.81

317

HONG KONG, CHINA

2. Arrivals of non-resident visitors at national borders, by country of residence

	2009	2010	2011	2012	2013	Market share 2013	% Change 2013-2012
OTHER AFRICA				6			
Other countries of Africa				6			
AMERICAS	1,567,807	1,749,558	1,821,096	1,777,842	1,665,562	3.07	-6.32
CARIBBEAN	7,941	8,436	8,872	8,492	8,274	0.02	-2.57
Antigua and Barbuda	105	156	127	151	111	0.00	-26.49
Bahamas	392	481	513	393	365	0.00	-7.12
Barbados	191	215	152	191	260	0.00	36.13
Cuba	252	349	422	507	448	0.00	-11.64
Dominica	416	359	325	325	290	0.00	-10.77
Dominican Republic	1,874	2,088	2,138	1,872	1,775	0.00	-5.18
Grenada	31	44	51	52	55	0.00	5.77
Haiti	98	115	126	133	158	0.00	18.80
Jamaica	2,932	2,869	3,268	2,959	2,801	0.01	-5.34
Saint Kitts and Nevis	181	264	361	528	717	0.00	35.80
Saint Lucia	68	90	51	69	53	0.00	-23.19
Saint Vincent and the Grenadines	53	40	25	38	22	0.00	-42.11
Trinidad and Tobago	1,348	1,366	1,313	1,274	1,219	0.00	-4.32
CENTRAL AMERICA	11,258	12,560	12,706	12,034	11,561	0.02	-3.93
Belize	2,631	2,529	2,638	2,287	2,527	0.00	10.49
Costa Rica	2,365	3,018	3,237	2,841	2,619	0.00	-7.81
El Salvador	431	477	522	535	498	0.00	-6.92
Guatemala	1,279	1,393	1,419	1,623	1,561	0.00	-3.82
Honduras	944	1,113	1,147	1,271	1,183	0.00	-6.92
Nicaragua	60	90	101	99	125	0.00	26.26
Panama	3,548	3,940	3,642	3,378	3,048	0.01	-9.77
NORTH AMERICA	1,452,058	1,604,013	1,652,971	1,608,263	1,496,941	2.76	-6.92
Canada	361,922	404,252	410,591	392,519	353,954	0.65	-9.83
Mexico	20,063	28,342	30,044	30,987	33,146	0.06	6.97
United States of America (*)	1,070,073	1,171,419	1,212,336	1,184,757	1,109,841	2.04	-6.32
SOUTH AMERICA	96,547	124,549	146,547	149,053	148,786	0.27	-0.18
Argentina	9,570	13,281	13,892	13,642	14,453	0.03	5.94
Bolivia	1,750	2,063	2,670	2,794	2,401	0.00	-14.07
Brazil	33,730	47,821	60,672	58,799	58,845	0.11	0.08
Chile	8,452	10,215	11,812	12,657	13,047	0.02	3.08
Colombia	15,079	19,760	20,826	22,419	22,953	0.04	2.38
Ecuador	2,742	3,237	3,992	4,020	4,474	0.01	11.29
French Guiana	8	2	7	1			
Guyana	432	460	463	399	379	0.00	-5.01
Paraguay	838	865	905	784	800	0.00	2.04
Peru	5,708	6,308	6,717	7,315	7,146	0.01	-2.31
Suriname	2,873	2,782	3,050	3,188	3,032	0.01	-4.89
Uruguay	1,685	2,273	2,402	2,249	2,630	0.00	16.94
Venezuela	13,680	15,482	19,139	20,786	18,626	0.03	-10.39
OTHER AMERICAS	3						
Other countries of the Americas	3						
EAST ASIA AND THE PACIFIC	25,659,422	31,548,245	37,378,369	44,166,015	49,914,821	91.93	13.02
NORTH-EAST ASIA	22,474,913	27,852,166	33,418,532	40,245,889	45,977,243	84.67	14.24
China	17,956,731	22,684,388	28,100,129	34,911,395	40,745,277	75.04	16.71
Japan	1,204,490	1,316,618	1,283,687	1,254,602	1,057,033	1.95	-15.75
Korea, Dem. People's Republic of	174	69	46	103	109	0.00	5.83
Korea, Republic of	618,694	891,024	1,020,996	1,078,458	1,083,543	2.00	0.47
Macao, China	671,276	780,293	843,221	883,479	958,215	1.76	8.46
Mongolia	13,904	15,024	21,720	29,107	32,968	0.06	13.26
Taiwan, Province of China	2,009,644	2,164,750	2,148,733	2,088,745	2,100,098	3.87	0.54
SOUTH-EAST ASIA	2,476,546	2,927,555	3,201,966	3,179,331	3,220,159	5.93	1.28
Brunei Darussalam	11,675	11,031	10,904	10,789	9,765	0.02	-9.49
Cambodia	10,588	12,273	12,120	11,914	12,312	0.02	3.34
Indonesia	353,631	453,235	520,795	511,893	517,487	0.95	1.09
Lao People's Democratic Republic	1,229	1,309	2,441	2,456	2,085	0.00	-15.11

318

HONG KONG, CHINA

2. Arrivals of non-resident visitors at national borders, by country of residence

		2009	2010	2011	2012	2013	Market share 2013	% Change 2013-2012
Malaysia		441,698	578,877	632,858	624,859	649,124	1.20	3.88
Myanmar		5,459	5,821	8,387	8,558	10,176	0.02	18.91
Philippines		563,750	603,030	659,829	709,753	705,319	1.30	-0.62
Singapore		623,730	709,777	793,887	728,224	700,065	1.29	-3.87
Thailand		387,728	449,812	480,497	501,759	534,676	0.98	6.56
Timor-Leste		243	173	135	129	196	0.00	51.94
Viet Nam		76,815	102,217	80,113	68,997	78,954	0.15	14.43
AUSTRALASIA		**701,668**	**758,837**	**747,687**	**730,832**	**707,408**	**1.30**	**-3.21**
Australia		600,085	650,681	644,596	632,462	609,714	1.12	-3.60
New Zealand	(*)	101,583	108,156	103,091	98,370	97,694	0.18	-0.69
MELANESIA		**4,439**	**7,697**	**7,738**	**7,584**	**7,804**	**0.01**	**2.90**
Fiji		2,498	5,955	5,631	5,359	5,647	0.01	5.37
Papua New Guinea		1,567	1,269	1,595	1,641	1,656	0.00	0.91
Solomon Islands		129	121	200	251	188	0.00	-25.10
Vanuatu		245	352	312	333	313	0.00	-6.01
MICRONESIA		**1,070**	**1,116**	**1,396**	**1,331**	**1,174**	**0.00**	**-11.80**
Kiribati		96	246	593	611	548	0.00	-10.31
Marshall Islands		273	276	387	464	384	0.00	-17.24
Micronesia, Federated States of		77	100	76	32	61	0.00	90.63
Nauru		624	494	340	224	181	0.00	-19.20
POLYNESIA		**739**	**834**	**1,008**	**993**	**993**	**0.00**	
Samoa		141	199	246	268	323	0.00	20.52
Tonga		473	532	651	590	585	0.00	-0.85
Tuvalu		125	103	111	135	85	0.00	-37.04
OTHER EAST ASIA AND THE PACIFIC		**47**	**40**	**42**	**55**	**40**	**0.00**	**-27.27**
Other countries of Oceania		47	40	42	55	40	0.00	-27.27
EUROPE		**1,709,478**	**1,876,192**	**1,912,917**	**1,973,211**	**1,998,798**	**3.68**	**1.30**
CENTRAL/EASTERN EUROPE		**113,476**	**171,974**	**232,052**	**294,979**	**354,003**	**0.65**	**20.01**
Armenia		131	213	380	290	388	0.00	33.79
Azerbaijan		349	543	558	851	833	0.00	-2.12
Belarus		722	1,115	1,354	1,518	1,696	0.00	11.73
Bulgaria		3,760	4,465	4,673	5,304	5,619	0.01	5.94
Czech Republic		10,185	10,176	11,445	10,683	11,049	0.02	3.43
Estonia		3,619	3,993	3,766	4,325	4,341	0.01	0.37
Georgia		271	262	444	351	309	0.00	-11.97
Hungary		7,748	10,170	9,459	8,968	9,177	0.02	2.33
Kazakhstan		2,018	2,658	3,207	8,580	17,292	0.03	101.54
Kyrgyzstan		209	317	428	478	590	0.00	23.43
Latvia		2,247	2,190	2,280	2,783	2,752	0.01	-1.11
Lithuania		2,526	2,673	3,161	3,702	3,736	0.01	0.92
Poland		21,477	24,641	26,889	23,896	27,709	0.05	15.96
Republic of Moldova		176	219	322	220	263	0.00	19.55
Romania		7,102	9,363	10,162	10,175	11,221	0.02	10.28
Russian Federation		42,980	86,800	131,537	186,461	223,664	0.41	19.95
Slovakia		3,462	4,085	4,351	4,907	4,954	0.01	0.96
Tajikistan		57	105	137	90	85	0.00	-5.56
Turkmenistan		16	16	124	42	20	0.00	-52.38
Ukraine		3,859	7,321	16,617	20,718	27,666	0.05	33.54
Uzbekistan		533	649	758	614	631	0.00	2.77
Other countries Central/East Europe		29			23	8	0.00	-65.22
NORTHERN EUROPE		**672,389**	**682,010**	**673,278**	**694,849**	**668,752**	**1.23**	**-3.76**
Denmark		27,688	29,156	28,781	26,941	26,187	0.05	-2.80
Finland		34,359	33,559	31,356	30,079	28,241	0.05	-6.11
Iceland		1,295	1,415	1,431	1,426	1,417	0.00	-0.63
Ireland		26,876	26,657	28,169	27,108	26,517	0.05	-2.18
Norway		19,377	20,940	19,870	20,326	19,173	0.04	-5.67
Sweden		48,810	54,590	57,114	55,731	53,787	0.10	-3.49
United Kingdom		513,984	515,693	506,557	533,238	513,430	0.95	-3.71
SOUTHERN EUROPE		**191,060**	**212,677**	**217,394**	**215,778**	**215,517**	**0.40**	**-0.12**

319

HONG KONG, CHINA

2. Arrivals of non-resident visitors at national borders, by country of residence

		2009	2010	2011	2012	2013	Market share 2013	% Change 2013-2012
Albania		309	238	230	377	491	0.00	30.24
Andorra		136	104	108	93	134	0.00	44.09
Bosnia and Herzegovina		441	498	446	442	469	0.00	6.11
Croatia		2,610	2,824	2,962	3,262	3,434	0.01	5.27
Greece		8,397	8,784	8,346	8,189	8,537	0.02	4.25
Holy See		11	5	5	5	6	0.00	20.00
Italy		103,315	118,915	117,199	115,610	112,927	0.21	-2.32
Malta		707	949	798	861	769	0.00	-10.69
Montenegro					497	515	0.00	3.62
Portugal		15,122	13,623	19,094	21,708	24,074	0.04	10.90
San Marino		94	152	111	92	91	0.00	-1.09
Serbia					2,963	3,418	0.01	15.36
Serbia and Montenegro		980	1,320	2,174				
Slovenia		2,253	2,327	2,544	2,751	2,251	0.00	-18.18
Spain		56,108	62,350	62,787	58,301	57,751	0.11	-0.94
TFYR of Macedonia		577	588	590	627	650	0.00	3.67
WESTERN EUROPE		**631,970**	**689,383**	**676,699**	**660,833**	**654,051**	**1.20**	**-1.03**
Austria		24,116	26,944	25,638	25,819	25,903	0.05	0.33
Belgium		31,560	33,398	32,783	31,937	33,144	0.06	3.78
France	(*)	217,568	239,964	233,880	226,118	227,760	0.42	0.73
Germany		210,828	230,436	223,544	222,820	220,604	0.41	-0.99
Liechtenstein		230	282	311	335	311	0.00	-7.16
Luxembourg		1,744	1,941	1,674	1,432	1,728	0.00	20.67
Monaco		376	204	135	163	166	0.00	1.84
Netherlands		99,450	106,544	107,564	100,068	91,820	0.17	-8.24
Switzerland		46,098	49,670	51,170	52,141	52,615	0.10	0.91
EAST MEDITERRANEAN EUROPE		**100,583**	**120,148**	**113,494**	**106,772**	**106,475**	**0.20**	**-0.28**
Cyprus		1,626	1,777	1,920	1,276	1,403	0.00	9.95
Israel		65,266	72,914	69,525	66,807	66,630	0.12	-0.26
Turkey		33,691	45,457	42,049	38,689	38,442	0.07	-0.64
MIDDLE EAST		**74,536**	**90,813**	**84,564**	**78,023**	**83,789**	**0.15**	**7.39**
Bahrain		1,664	2,466	2,094	1,860	2,051	0.00	10.27
Egypt		9,505	11,777	10,764	10,839	12,187	0.02	12.44
Iraq		117	175	183	192	207	0.00	7.81
Jordan		11,588	14,806	17,647	14,362	13,171	0.02	-8.29
Kuwait		4,155	5,916	6,878	5,912	6,033	0.01	2.05
Lebanon		1,257	1,349	1,332	1,303	1,203	0.00	-7.67
Libya		64	81	11	25	54	0.00	116.00
Oman		986	1,387	1,364	1,227	1,291	0.00	5.22
Qatar		2,087	1,876	2,109	2,264	3,722	0.01	64.40
Saudi Arabia		19,035	28,401	21,192	19,107	19,872	0.04	4.00
Syrian Arab Republic		596	741	651	618	536	0.00	-13.27
United Arab Emirates		16,195	13,624	14,549	14,410	17,818	0.03	23.65
Yemen		7,218	8,111	5,735	5,857	5,601	0.01	-4.37
Other countries of Middle East		69	103	55	47	43	0.00	-8.51
SOUTH ASIA		**396,914**	**561,323**	**531,401**	**446,667**	**467,955**	**0.86**	**4.77**
Afghanistan		57	80	135	147	118	0.00	-19.73
Bangladesh		6,040	4,968	4,848	4,917	5,512	0.01	12.10
Bhutan		696	767	980	945	1,057	0.00	11.85
India		366,646	530,910	498,063	414,158	434,648	0.80	4.95
Iran, Islamic Republic of		2,035	2,650	3,218	2,858	2,492	0.00	-12.81
Maldives		348	439	766	547	723	0.00	32.18
Nepal		5,060	5,454	6,476	6,906	7,723	0.01	11.83
Pakistan		9,992	9,713	9,958	9,592	9,031	0.02	-5.85
Sri Lanka		6,040	6,342	6,957	6,597	6,651	0.01	0.82
NOT SPECIFIED		**113**	**95**	**109**				
Other countries of the World		113	95	109				

Yearbook of Tourism Statistics, Data 2009 – 2013, 2015 Edition

HUNGARY

1. Arrivals of non-resident tourists at national borders, by nationality

	2009	2010	2011	2012	2013	Market share 2013	% Change 2013-2012
TOTAL	9,058,000	9,511,000	10,250,000	10,353,000	10,676,000	100.00	3.12
AFRICA	22,000	23,000	26,000	26,000	27,000	0.25	3.85
OTHER AFRICA	22,000	23,000	26,000	26,000	27,000	0.25	3.85
All countries of Africa	22,000	23,000	26,000	26,000	27,000	0.25	3.85
AMERICAS	548,000	536,000	606,000	567,000	602,000	5.64	6.17
NORTH AMERICA	393,000	390,000	442,000	402,000	428,000	4.01	6.47
United States of America	393,000	390,000	442,000	402,000	428,000	4.01	6.47
OTHER AMERICAS	155,000	146,000	164,000	165,000	174,000	1.63	5.45
Other countries of the Americas	155,000	146,000	164,000	165,000	174,000	1.63	5.45
EAST ASIA AND THE PACIFIC	389,000	381,000	411,000	404,000	571,000	5.35	41.34
AUSTRALASIA	63,000	65,000	68,000	69,000	78,000	0.73	13.04
Australia	63,000	65,000	68,000	69,000	78,000	0.73	13.04
OTHER EAST ASIA AND THE PACIFIC	326,000	316,000	343,000	335,000	493,000	4.62	47.16
All countries of Asia	326,000	316,000	343,000	335,000	493,000	4.62	47.16
EUROPE	8,099,000	8,571,000	9,207,000	9,356,000	9,476,000	88.76	1.28
CENTRAL/EASTERN EUROPE	2,421,000	2,657,000	2,806,000	3,145,000	3,574,000	33.48	13.64
Bulgaria	51,000	134,000	116,000	125,000	127,000	1.19	1.60
Czech Republic	250,000	271,000	315,000	334,000	530,000	4.96	58.68
Poland	612,000	556,000	422,000	694,000	728,000	6.82	4.90
Romania	721,000	912,000	1,153,000	1,092,000	945,000	8.85	-13.46
Russian Federation	70,000						
Slovakia	510,000	586,000	600,000	679,000	943,000	8.83	38.88
Ukraine	207,000	198,000	200,000	221,000	301,000	2.82	36.20
NORTHERN EUROPE	310,000	319,000	338,000	304,000	374,000	3.50	23.03
United Kingdom	310,000	319,000	338,000	304,000	374,000	3.50	23.03
SOUTHERN EUROPE	645,000	689,000	821,000	822,000	745,000	6.98	-9.37
Croatia	53,000	32,000	54,000	48,000	28,000	0.26	-41.67
Italy	373,000	330,000	428,000	387,000	437,000	4.09	12.92
Serbia and Montenegro	211,000	313,000	333,000	381,000	270,000	2.53	-29.13
Slovenia	8,000	14,000	6,000	6,000	10,000	0.09	66.67
WESTERN EUROPE	3,714,000	3,850,000	4,016,000	4,037,000	3,630,000	34.00	-10.08
Austria	922,000	935,000	965,000	1,005,000	834,000	7.81	-17.01
France	232,000	250,000	283,000	257,000	236,000	2.21	-8.17
Germany	2,182,000	2,266,000	2,287,000	2,399,000	2,068,000	19.37	-13.80
Netherlands	203,000	224,000	262,000	196,000	300,000	2.81	53.06
Switzerland	175,000	175,000	219,000	180,000	192,000	1.80	6.67
OTHER EUROPE	1,009,000	1,056,000	1,226,000	1,048,000	1,153,000	10.80	10.02
Other countries of Europe	1,009,000	1,056,000	1,226,000	1,048,000	1,153,000	10.80	10.02

Yearbook of Tourism Statistics, Data 2009 – 2013, 2015 Edition

HUNGARY

2. Arrivals of non-resident visitors at national borders, by nationality

	2009	2010	2011	2012	2013	Market share 2013	% Change 2013-2012
TOTAL	40,624,000	39,905,000	41,304,000	43,565,000	43,665,000	100.00	0.23
AFRICA	22,000	23,000	26,000	26,000	28,000	0.06	7.69
OTHER AFRICA	22,000	23,000	26,000	26,000	28,000	0.06	7.69
All countries of Africa	22,000	23,000	26,000	26,000	28,000	0.06	7.69
AMERICAS	557,000	547,000	615,000	577,000	623,000	1.43	7.97
NORTH AMERICA	397,000	391,000	443,000	412,000	448,000	1.03	8.74
United States of America	397,000	391,000	443,000	412,000	448,000	1.03	8.74
OTHER AMERICAS	160,000	156,000	172,000	165,000	175,000	0.40	6.06
Other countries of the Americas	160,000	156,000	172,000	165,000	175,000	0.40	6.06
EAST ASIA AND THE PACIFIC	439,000	448,000	515,000	459,000	599,000	1.37	30.50
AUSTRALASIA	63,000	65,000	68,000	69,000	78,000	0.18	13.04
Australia	63,000	65,000	68,000	69,000	78,000	0.18	13.04
OTHER EAST ASIA AND THE PACIFIC	376,000	383,000	447,000	390,000	521,000	1.19	33.59
All countries of Asia	376,000	383,000	447,000	390,000	521,000	1.19	33.59
EUROPE	39,606,000	38,887,000	40,148,000	42,503,000	42,415,000	97.14	-0.21
CENTRAL/EASTERN EUROPE	22,546,000	21,571,000	21,858,000	23,822,000	23,385,000	53.56	-1.83
Bulgaria	1,234,000	1,191,000	1,380,000	1,443,000	1,178,000	2.70	-18.36
Czech Republic	1,077,000	1,003,000	916,000	1,041,000	1,188,000	2.72	14.12
Poland	1,566,000	1,540,000	1,331,000	1,603,000	1,827,000	4.18	13.97
Romania	7,783,000	7,614,000	7,575,000	7,901,000	7,274,000	16.66	-7.94
Russian Federation	106,000						
Slovakia	9,095,000	8,404,000	8,825,000	9,971,000	10,016,000	22.94	0.45
Ukraine	1,685,000	1,819,000	1,831,000	1,863,000	1,902,000	4.36	2.09
NORTHERN EUROPE	359,000	356,000	395,000	357,000	422,000	0.97	18.21
United Kingdom	359,000	356,000	395,000	357,000	422,000	0.97	18.21
SOUTHERN EUROPE	4,217,000	4,153,000	4,952,000	4,301,000	5,166,000	11.83	20.11
Croatia	971,000	868,000	934,000	756,000	824,000	1.89	8.99
Italy	625,000	581,000	663,000	577,000	646,000	1.48	11.96
Serbia and Montenegro	2,203,000	2,329,000	2,964,000	2,658,000	3,343,000	7.66	25.77
Slovenia	418,000	375,000	391,000	310,000	353,000	0.81	13.87
WESTERN EUROPE	10,490,000	10,724,000	10,665,000	11,255,000	10,953,000	25.08	-2.68
Austria	6,437,000	6,696,000	6,649,000	7,233,000	7,118,000	16.30	-1.59
France	364,000	351,000	391,000	346,000	342,000	0.78	-1.16
Germany	3,130,000	3,135,000	3,026,000	3,188,000	2,859,000	6.55	-10.32
Netherlands	306,000	320,000	326,000	274,000	383,000	0.88	39.78
Switzerland	253,000	222,000	273,000	214,000	251,000	0.57	17.29
OTHER EUROPE	1,994,000	2,083,000	2,278,000	2,768,000	2,489,000	5.70	-10.08
Other countries of Europe	1,994,000	2,083,000	2,278,000	2,768,000	2,489,000	5.70	-10.08

Yearbook of Tourism Statistics, Data 2009 – 2013, 2015 Edition

HUNGARY

3. Arrivals of non-resident tourists in hotels and similar establishments, by nationality

	2009	2010	2011	2012	2013	Market share 2013	% Change 2013-2012
TOTAL	2,914,328	3,183,753	3,518,363	3,825,319	4,006,962	100.00	4.75
AFRICA	9,571	9,947	11,400	14,011	16,449	0.41	17.40
OTHER AFRICA	9,571	9,947	11,400	14,011	16,449	0.41	17.40
All countries of Africa	9,571	9,947	11,400	14,011	16,449	0.41	17.40
AMERICAS	182,413	214,547	242,138	246,436	283,322	7.07	14.97
NORTH AMERICA	155,707	184,479	199,950	196,353	226,501	5.65	15.35
Canada	17,665	21,039	24,128	23,878	28,586	0.71	19.72
United States of America	138,042	163,440	175,822	172,475	197,915	4.94	14.75
OTHER AMERICAS	26,706	30,068	42,188	50,083	56,821	1.42	13.45
Other countries of the Americas	26,706	30,068	42,188	50,083	56,821	1.42	13.45
EAST ASIA AND THE PACIFIC	89,195	98,067	96,087	103,996	109,673	2.74	5.46
NORTH-EAST ASIA	70,422	76,317	69,154	76,180	76,586	1.91	0.53
Japan	70,422	76,317	69,154	76,180	76,586	1.91	0.53
OTHER EAST ASIA AND THE PACIFIC	18,773	21,750	26,933	27,816	33,087	0.83	18.95
All countries of Oceania	18,773	21,750	26,933	27,816	33,087	0.83	18.95
EUROPE	2,511,491	2,656,958	2,931,505	3,195,555	3,360,271	83.86	5.15
CENTRAL/EASTERN EUROPE	647,068	725,302	839,953	931,518	1,005,600	25.10	7.95
Bulgaria	22,690	24,805	28,742	33,238	33,627	0.84	1.17
Czech Republic	115,168	127,431	154,907	161,940	175,083	4.37	8.12
Poland	103,917	115,761	133,278	145,919	160,480	4.01	9.98
Romania	191,318	195,544	201,579	202,283	199,860	4.99	-1.20
Russian Federation	81,794	102,043	120,917	156,083	194,390	4.85	24.54
Slovakia	61,563	67,047	86,011	97,083	107,503	2.68	10.73
Ukraine	70,618	92,671	114,519	134,972	134,657	3.36	-0.23
NORTHERN EUROPE	341,800	353,109	382,369	431,987	476,567	11.89	10.32
Denmark	28,550	30,214	30,465	32,139	36,175	0.90	12.56
Finland	40,683	36,612	37,703	41,423	49,783	1.24	20.18
Norway	32,237	29,730	34,856	43,929	49,303	1.23	12.23
Sweden	55,833	56,182	65,785	81,495	85,781	2.14	5.26
United Kingdom	184,497	200,371	213,560	233,001	255,525	6.38	9.67
SOUTHERN EUROPE	384,787	412,039	471,352	509,075	501,991	12.53	-1.39
Croatia	26,210	29,419	31,846	33,959	35,022	0.87	3.13
Greece	35,427	35,040	40,796	33,931	34,888	0.87	2.82
Italy	165,085	175,412	187,503	218,026	221,127	5.52	1.42
Serbia	28,484	43,824	54,456	59,743	62,556	1.56	4.71
Slovenia	18,629	21,286	25,083	24,025	23,688	0.59	-1.40
Spain	110,952	107,058	131,668	139,391	124,710	3.11	-10.53
WESTERN EUROPE	954,389	1,044,024	1,073,518	1,126,580	1,106,098	27.60	-1.82
Austria	234,358	248,742	269,049	270,337	260,618	6.50	-3.60
Belgium	39,585	44,673	51,203	63,012	64,302	1.60	2.05
France	125,694	127,364	138,902	134,176	136,435	3.40	1.68
Germany	446,624	466,939	479,212	505,284	489,359	12.21	-3.15
Netherlands	59,651	89,565	80,569	99,002	94,463	2.36	-4.58
Switzerland	48,477	66,741	54,583	54,769	60,921	1.52	11.23
EAST MEDITERRANEAN EUROPE	63,489	85,204	90,116	100,054	118,809	2.97	18.74
Israel	42,027	50,956	50,970	50,638	64,176	1.60	26.73
Turkey	21,462	34,248	39,146	49,416	54,633	1.36	10.56
OTHER EUROPE	119,958	37,280	74,197	96,341	151,206	3.77	56.95
Other countries of Europe	119,958	37,280	74,197	96,341	151,206	3.77	56.95
NOT SPECIFIED	121,658	204,234	237,233	265,321	237,247	5.92	-10.58
Other countries of the World	121,658	204,234	237,233	265,321	237,247	5.92	-10.58

Yearbook of Tourism Statistics, Data 2009 – 2013, 2015 Edition

HUNGARY

4. Arrivals of non-resident tourists in all types of accommodation establishments, by nationality

		2009	2010	2011	2012	2013	Market share 2013	% Change 2013-2012
TOTAL	(*)	3,227,942	3,462,021	3,821,751	4,163,641	4,387,692	100.00	5.38
AFRICA		9,925	10,096	11,775	14,512	17,415	0.40	20.00
OTHER AFRICA		9,925	10,096	11,775	14,512	17,415	0.40	20.00
All countries of Africa		9,925	10,096	11,775	14,512	17,415	0.40	20.00
AMERICAS		187,101	218,240	242,920	254,759	304,912	6.95	19.69
NORTH AMERICA		158,738	187,007	202,767	200,746	237,233	5.41	18.18
Canada		18,403	21,796	24,786	25,001	31,365	0.71	25.45
United States of America		140,335	165,211	177,981	175,745	205,868	4.69	17.14
OTHER AMERICAS		28,363	31,233	40,153	54,013	67,679	1.54	25.30
Other countries of the Americas		28,363	31,233	40,153	54,013	67,679	1.54	25.30
EAST ASIA AND THE PACIFIC		91,807	100,527	98,532	107,739	116,994	2.67	8.59
NORTH-EAST ASIA		71,124	76,862	69,724	77,093	77,516	1.77	0.55
Japan		71,124	76,862	69,724	77,093	77,516	1.77	0.55
OTHER EAST ASIA AND THE PACIFIC		20,683	23,665	28,808	30,646	39,478	0.90	28.82
All countries of Oceania		20,683	23,665	28,808	30,646	39,478	0.90	28.82
EUROPE		2,815,773	2,927,419	3,225,209	3,516,155	3,700,396	84.34	5.24
CENTRAL/EASTERN EUROPE		753,458	821,967	948,785	1,050,912	1,126,815	25.68	7.22
Bulgaria		23,500	25,407	29,351	34,196	35,299	0.80	3.23
Czech Republic		135,715	148,623	178,585	187,513	197,692	4.51	5.43
Poland		151,674	155,983	178,607	194,035	214,216	4.88	10.40
Romania		204,436	207,974	216,164	217,631	213,876	4.87	-1.73
Russian Federation		82,982	103,766	123,394	159,014	196,889	4.49	23.82
Slovakia		82,773	85,558	105,495	119,872	130,390	2.97	8.77
Ukraine		72,378	94,656	117,189	138,651	138,453	3.16	-0.14
NORTHERN EUROPE		366,885	374,116	405,568	454,118	502,472	11.45	10.65
Denmark		39,001	38,473	40,233	40,121	43,340	0.99	8.02
Finland		42,827	38,747	40,320	43,569	52,089	1.19	19.56
Norway		33,018	30,560	35,523	44,916	50,181	1.14	11.72
Sweden		58,359	58,212	68,067	83,993	88,419	2.02	5.27
United Kingdom		193,680	208,124	221,425	241,519	268,443	6.12	11.15
SOUTHERN EUROPE		401,260	427,578	490,656	532,569	526,757	12.01	-1.09
Croatia		27,714	30,615	33,190	36,028	36,829	0.84	2.22
Greece		35,849	35,422	41,901	34,478	35,486	0.81	2.92
Italy		173,161	183,259	197,495	229,022	232,596	5.30	1.56
Serbia		29,721	45,639	56,506	62,266	65,889	1.50	5.82
Slovenia		21,134	23,378	27,571	27,171	26,906	0.61	-0.98
Spain		113,681	109,265	133,993	143,604	129,051	2.94	-10.13
WESTERN EUROPE		1,103,623	1,136,390	1,208,229	1,275,531	1,263,325	28.79	-0.96
Austria		259,108	272,579	294,931	297,053	286,292	6.52	-3.62
Belgium		46,522	51,199	57,920	71,257	76,789	1.75	7.76
France		138,554	139,851	150,733	144,723	148,996	3.40	2.95
Germany		520,280	528,753	542,333	570,147	552,043	12.58	-3.18
Netherlands		86,927	89,565	103,947	133,537	133,385	3.04	-0.11
Switzerland		52,232	54,443	58,365	58,814	65,820	1.50	11.91
EAST MEDITERRANEAN EUROPE		64,415	86,057	91,679	101,527	121,338	2.77	19.51
Israel		42,405	51,220	51,644	50,972	64,876	1.48	27.28
Turkey		22,010	34,837	40,035	50,555	56,462	1.29	11.68
OTHER EUROPE		126,132	81,311	80,292	101,498	159,689	3.64	57.33
Other countries of Europe		126,132	81,311	80,292	101,498	159,689	3.64	57.33
NOT SPECIFIED		123,336	205,739	243,315	270,476	247,975	5.65	-8.32
Other countries of the World		123,336	205,739	243,315	270,476	247,975	5.65	-8.32

324

HUNGARY

5. Overnight stays of non-resident tourists in hotels and similar establishments, by nationality

	2009	2010	2011	2012	2013	Market share 2013	% Change 2013-2012
TOTAL	7,773,329	8,316,706	9,049,109	9,938,268	10,367,322	100.00	4.32
AFRICA	28,315	28,972	32,381	38,352	46,908	0.45	22.31
OTHER AFRICA	28,315	28,972	32,381	38,352	46,908	0.45	22.31
All countries of Africa	28,315	28,972	32,381	38,352	46,908	0.45	22.31
AMERICAS	485,368	550,633	606,830	636,912	706,885	6.82	10.99
NORTH AMERICA	412,744	472,962	481,637	506,926	564,118	5.44	11.28
Canada	50,865	61,184	38,887	65,583	77,040	0.74	17.47
United States of America	361,879	411,778	442,750	441,343	487,078	4.70	10.36
OTHER AMERICAS	72,624	77,671	125,193	129,986	142,767	1.38	9.83
Other countries of the Americas	72,624	77,671	125,193	129,986	142,767	1.38	9.83
EAST ASIA AND THE PACIFIC	185,957	202,183	197,889	220,355	244,209	2.36	10.83
NORTH-EAST ASIA	139,650	145,782	133,383	151,366	159,859	1.54	5.61
Japan	139,650	145,782	133,383	151,366	159,859	1.54	5.61
OTHER EAST ASIA AND THE PACIFIC	46,307	56,401	64,506	68,989	84,350	0.81	22.27
All countries of Oceania	46,307	56,401	64,506	68,989	84,350	0.81	22.27
EUROPE	6,835,685	7,069,678	7,675,611	8,469,994	8,931,097	86.15	5.44
CENTRAL/EASTERN EUROPE	1,464,910	1,677,433	1,988,959	2,260,108	2,530,403	24.41	11.96
Bulgaria	36,692	40,363	46,792	56,899	53,968	0.52	-5.15
Czech Republic	318,781	365,528	436,830	455,921	491,359	4.74	7.77
Poland	240,593	262,951	303,445	330,566	370,686	3.58	12.14
Romania	329,784	336,707	371,405	373,292	369,224	3.56	-1.09
Russian Federation	273,503	366,850	451,762	600,829	757,871	7.31	26.14
Slovakia	129,017	143,945	190,760	213,295	235,327	2.27	10.33
Ukraine	136,540	161,089	187,965	229,306	251,968	2.43	9.88
NORTHERN EUROPE	957,323	952,168	1,016,500	1,189,080	1,302,786	12.57	9.56
Denmark	92,387	95,861	93,296	103,323	111,966	1.08	8.37
Finland	121,467	110,951	112,380	128,643	149,903	1.45	16.53
Norway	105,990	98,273	111,958	139,836	153,647	1.48	9.88
Sweden	162,166	162,052	185,170	235,276	247,769	2.39	5.31
United Kingdom	475,313	485,031	513,696	582,002	639,501	6.17	9.88
SOUTHERN EUROPE	966,244	1,019,444	1,139,061	1,280,332	1,230,316	11.87	-3.91
Croatia	58,010	52,425	58,672	67,575	67,113	0.65	-0.68
Greece	92,239	89,828	103,515	91,646	93,354	0.90	1.86
Italy	439,644	473,325	497,632	594,475	593,362	5.72	-0.19
Serbia	57,158	85,099	104,301	116,684	122,197	1.18	4.72
Slovenia	34,888	44,575	49,089	54,652	46,066	0.44	-15.71
Spain	284,305	274,192	325,852	355,300	308,224	2.97	-13.25
WESTERN EUROPE	2,966,372	3,057,326	3,154,810	3,309,743	3,199,158	30.86	-3.34
Austria	612,313	642,781	687,892	682,035	650,808	6.28	-4.58
Belgium	109,171	121,516	130,676	173,812	181,111	1.75	4.20
France	316,279	325,358	347,309	347,765	353,008	3.41	1.51
Germany	1,618,558	1,631,723	1,624,048	1,690,581	1,600,419	15.44	-5.33
Netherlands	158,134	173,896	202,135	256,165	241,404	2.33	-5.76
Switzerland	151,917	162,052	162,750	159,385	172,408	1.66	8.17
EAST MEDITERRANEAN EUROPE	185,442	326,027	253,624	279,846	336,771	3.25	20.34
Israel	135,885	164,938	165,843	176,147	223,476	2.16	26.87
Turkey	49,557	161,089	87,781	103,699	113,295	1.09	9.25
OTHER EUROPE	295,394	37,280	122,657	150,885	331,663	3.20	119.81
Other countries of Europe	295,394	37,280	122,657	150,885	331,663	3.20	119.81
NOT SPECIFIED	238,004	465,240	536,398	572,655	438,223	4.23	-23.48
Other countries of the World	238,004	465,240	536,398	572,655	438,223	4.23	-23.48

325

HUNGARY

6. Overnight stays of non-resident tourists in all types of accommodation establishments, by nationality

	2009	2010	2011	2012	2013	Market share 2013	% Change 2013-2012
TOTAL (*)	9,220,148	9,613,728	10,410,774	11,392,183	11,982,883	100.00	5.19
AFRICA	29,759	29,377	33,368	40,085	50,684	0.42	26.44
OTHER AFRICA	29,759	29,377	33,368	40,085	50,684	0.42	26.44
All countries of Africa	29,759	29,377	33,368	40,085	50,684	0.42	26.44
AMERICAS	496,724	562,147	619,267	658,983	763,245	6.37	15.82
NORTH AMERICA	420,976	481,793	520,328	519,585	592,020	4.94	13.94
Canada	52,405	63,528	70,394	69,012	84,406	0.70	22.31
United States of America	368,571	418,265	449,934	450,573	507,614	4.24	12.66
OTHER AMERICAS	75,748	80,354	98,939	139,398	171,225	1.43	22.83
Other countries of the Americas	75,748	80,354	98,939	139,398	171,225	1.43	22.83
EAST ASIA AND THE PACIFIC	192,130	208,421	203,628	229,573	264,473	2.21	15.20
NORTH-EAST ASIA	141,170	147,423	134,717	153,447	162,860	1.36	6.13
Japan	141,170	147,423	134,717	153,447	162,860	1.36	6.13
OTHER EAST ASIA AND THE PACIFIC	50,960	60,998	68,911	76,126	101,613	0.85	33.48
All countries of Oceania	50,960	60,998	68,911	76,126	101,613	0.85	33.48
EUROPE	8,259,704	8,514,590	9,010,668	9,878,386	10,429,312	87.04	5.58
CENTRAL/EASTERN EUROPE	1,790,603	1,969,392	2,321,340	2,623,178	2,753,616	22.98	4.97
Bulgaria	38,316	42,150	48,308	59,165	59,105	0.49	-0.10
Czech Republic	385,272	436,071	514,308	538,591	565,490	4.72	4.99
Poland	393,422	393,513	448,060	485,062	538,910	4.50	11.10
Romania	369,782	370,014	415,493	419,030	411,065	3.43	-1.90
Russian Federation	278,833	374,026	461,953	614,077	627,337	5.24	2.16
Slovakia	182,950	186,946	236,311	266,985	289,311	2.41	8.36
Ukraine	142,028	166,672	196,907	240,268	262,398	2.19	9.21
NORTHERN EUROPE	1,076,805	1,056,682	1,131,776	1,290,491	1,415,497	11.81	9.69
Denmark	169,644	158,707	162,864	159,645	166,783	1.39	4.47
Finland	127,176	117,858	121,890	135,265	156,864	1.31	15.97
Norway	108,534	101,356	114,464	143,481	156,887	1.31	9.34
Sweden	169,936	169,013	193,588	243,988	256,537	2.14	5.14
United Kingdom	501,515	509,748	538,970	608,112	678,426	5.66	11.56
SOUTHERN EUROPE	1,010,473	1,064,731	1,201,761	1,340,741	1,297,740	10.83	-3.21
Croatia	62,147	55,614	62,242	73,346	71,433	0.60	-2.61
Greece	93,787	91,650	114,119	93,202	94,977	0.79	1.90
Italy	463,921	497,806	528,785	624,459	627,337	5.24	0.46
Serbia	59,828	90,006	109,055	122,810	130,457	1.09	6.23
Slovenia	40,408	49,267	55,451	61,453	53,587	0.45	-12.80
Spain	290,382	280,388	332,109	365,471	319,949	2.67	-12.46
WESTERN EUROPE	3,881,897	3,863,997	3,957,699	4,177,086	4,120,590	34.39	-1.35
Austria	734,195	755,553	809,500	804,268	804,786	6.72	0.06
Belgium	144,167	154,686	164,605	210,014	235,059	1.96	11.93
France	355,875	364,106	387,038	380,943	390,985	3.26	2.64
Germany	2,155,746	2,102,987	2,082,681	2,146,491	2,030,649	16.95	-5.40
Netherlands	324,521	318,099	336,532	459,543	469,182	3.92	2.10
Switzerland	167,393	168,566	177,343	175,827	189,929	1.59	8.02
EAST MEDITERRANEAN EUROPE	187,581	243,826	258,765	283,906	345,828	2.89	21.81
Israel	136,872	166,009	168,081	176,939	225,549	1.88	27.47
Turkey	50,709	77,817	90,684	106,967	120,279	1.00	12.44
OTHER EUROPE	312,345	315,962	139,327	162,984	496,041	4.14	204.35
Other countries of Europe	312,345	315,962	139,327	162,984	496,041	4.14	204.35
NOT SPECIFIED	241,831	299,193	543,843	585,156	475,169	3.97	-18.80
Other countries of the World	241,831	299,193	543,843	585,156	475,169	3.97	-18.80

326

ICELAND

1. Arrivals of non-resident tourists at national borders, by nationality

		2009	2010	2011	2012	2013	Market share 2013	% Change 2013-2012
TOTAL	(*)	**493,941**	**488,623**	**565,611**	**646,921**	**781,016**	**100.00**	**20.73**
AMERICAS		**54,998**	**64,652**	**95,547**	**113,786**	**143,682**	**18.40**	**26.27**
NORTH AMERICA		**54,998**	**64,652**	**95,547**	**113,786**	**143,682**	**18.40**	**26.27**
Canada		11,074	13,461	17,946	18,760	23,970	3.07	27.77
United States of America		43,924	51,191	77,601	95,026	119,712	15.33	25.98
EAST ASIA AND THE PACIFIC		**12,416**	**10,774**	**15,686**	**24,379**	**29,960**	**3.84**	**22.89**
NORTH-EAST ASIA		**12,416**	**10,774**	**15,686**	**24,379**	**29,960**	**3.84**	**22.89**
China		5,368	5,194	8,784	14,036	17,597	2.25	25.37
Japan		7,048	5,580	6,902	10,343	12,363	1.58	19.53
EUROPE		**328,176**	**318,157**	**354,949**	**425,995**	**499,531**	**63.96**	**17.26**
CENTRAL/EASTERN EUROPE					**19,660**	**22,823**	**2.92**	**16.09**
Poland					14,936	15,835	2.03	6.02
Russian Federation					4,724	6,988	0.89	47.93
NORTHERN EUROPE		**185,460**	**178,132**	**198,470**	**236,324**	**282,224**	**36.14**	**19.42**
Denmark		43,782	42,593	43,765	40,906	43,119	5.52	5.41
Finland		11,610	11,054	12,057	13,684	13,799	1.77	0.84
Norway		36,703	35,868	41,944	51,534	52,707	6.75	2.28
Sweden		31,585	28,109	32,959	35,601	35,491	4.54	-0.31
United Kingdom		61,780	60,508	67,745	94,599	137,108	17.56	44.94
SOUTHERN EUROPE		**27,105**	**22,378**	**26,824**	**29,119**	**33,230**	**4.25**	**14.12**
Italy		13,224	10,068	12,792	13,841	16,213	2.08	17.14
Spain		13,881	12,310	14,032	15,278	17,017	2.18	11.38
WESTERN EUROPE		**115,611**	**117,647**	**129,655**	**140,892**	**161,254**	**20.65**	**14.45**
France		29,786	30,204	36,747	41,570	48,313	6.19	16.22
Germany		56,467	59,453	61,372	65,179	75,814	9.71	16.32
Netherlands		20,217	18,111	20,757	21,305	22,820	2.92	7.11
Switzerland		9,141	9,879	10,779	12,838	14,307	1.83	11.44
NOT SPECIFIED		**98,351**	**95,040**	**99,429**	**82,761**	**107,843**	**13.81**	**30.31**
Other countries of the World		98,351	95,040	99,429	82,761	107,843	13.81	30.31

327

ICELAND

3. Arrivals of non-resident tourists in hotels and similar establishments, by nationality

	2009	2010	2011	2012	2013	Market share 2013	% Change 2013-2012
TOTAL	872,467	836,838	962,947	1,112,885	1,302,880	100.00	17.07
AFRICA	1,851	1,896	1,823	3,525	1,812	0.14	-48.60
OTHER AFRICA	1,851	1,896	1,823	3,525	1,812	0.14	-48.60
All countries of Africa	1,851	1,896	1,823	3,525	1,812	0.14	-48.60
AMERICAS	77,018	80,807	124,044	151,410	210,344	16.14	38.92
NORTH AMERICA	75,172	78,853	121,232	148,240	207,231	15.91	39.79
Canada	14,015	14,189	20,138	20,935	28,461	2.18	35.95
United States of America	61,157	64,664	101,094	127,305	178,770	13.72	40.43
OTHER AMERICAS	1,846	1,954	2,812	3,170	3,113	0.24	-1.80
Other countries of the Americas	1,846	1,954	2,812	3,170	3,113	0.24	-1.80
EAST ASIA AND THE PACIFIC	30,792	27,011	39,075	65,310	96,111	7.38	47.16
NORTH-EAST ASIA	16,099	11,824	16,492	29,686	46,935	3.60	58.10
China	4,910	3,453	5,721	10,365	20,745	1.59	100.14
Japan	11,189	8,371	10,771	19,321	26,190	2.01	35.55
AUSTRALASIA	4,386	4,782	5,905	8,357	9,930	0.76	18.82
Australia	4,386	4,782	5,905	8,357	9,930	0.76	18.82
OTHER EAST ASIA AND THE PACIFIC	10,307	10,405	16,678	27,267	39,246	3.01	43.93
Other countries of Asia	10,307	10,405	16,678	27,267	39,246	3.01	43.93
EUROPE	709,609	682,592	750,175	856,364	994,613	76.34	16.14
NORTHERN EUROPE	243,830	222,030	248,258	291,935	354,304	27.19	21.36
Denmark	48,176	48,568	45,282	48,296	51,387	3.94	6.40
Finland	12,339	9,736	11,588	13,652	14,231	1.09	4.24
Ireland	4,303	3,068	3,608	3,772	4,748	0.36	25.87
Norway	34,318	35,867	41,551	49,359	52,569	4.03	6.50
Sweden	34,639	28,420	35,821	36,324	38,003	2.92	4.62
United Kingdom	110,055	96,371	110,408	140,532	193,366	14.84	37.60
SOUTHERN EUROPE	91,494	64,087	86,607	87,018	102,611	7.88	17.92
Italy	49,968	34,286	45,915	43,556	52,433	4.02	20.38
Spain	41,526	29,801	40,692	43,462	50,178	3.85	15.45
WESTERN EUROPE	334,947	358,877	365,189	424,680	502,490	38.57	18.32
Austria	18,570	17,896	12,477	14,091	18,068	1.39	28.22
Belgium	13,458	16,403	16,029	15,711	21,427	1.64	36.38
France	72,479	74,581	87,925	106,852	123,284	9.46	15.38
Germany	155,330	180,795	172,969	199,709	236,127	18.12	18.24
Netherlands	48,311	40,861	46,586	49,289	54,375	4.17	10.32
Switzerland	26,799	28,341	29,203	39,028	49,209	3.78	26.09
OTHER EUROPE	39,338	37,598	50,121	52,731	35,208	2.70	-33.23
Other countries of Europe	39,338	37,598	50,121	52,731	35,208	2.70	-33.23
NOT SPECIFIED	53,197	44,532	47,830	36,276			
Other countries of the World	53,197	44,532	47,830	36,276			

Yearbook of Tourism Statistics, Data 2009 – 2013, 2015 Edition

ICELAND

4. Arrivals of non-resident tourists in all types of accommodation establishments, by nationality

	2009	2010	2011	2012	2013	Market share 2013	% Change 2013-2012
TOTAL	1,280,785	1,224,275	1,419,436	1,629,245	1,918,096	100.00	17.73
AFRICA	1,963	2,087	2,328	4,159	2,154	0.11	-48.21
SOUTHERN AFRICA					957	0.05	
South Africa					957	0.05	
OTHER AFRICA	1,963	2,087	2,328	4,159	1,197	0.06	-71.22
Other countries of Africa					1,197	0.06	
All countries of Africa	1,963	2,087	2,328	4,159			
AMERICAS	97,632	104,360	164,168	202,143	282,953	14.75	39.98
NORTH AMERICA	95,283	101,932	160,617	197,532	278,485	14.52	40.98
Canada	21,937	22,675	32,811	34,573	46,104	2.40	33.35
Greenland					1,404	0.07	
United States of America	73,346	79,257	127,806	162,959	230,977	12.04	41.74
SOUTH AMERICA					1,693	0.09	
Brazil					1,693	0.09	
OTHER AMERICAS	2,349	2,428	3,551	4,611	2,775	0.14	-39.82
Other countries of the Americas	2,349	2,428	3,551	4,611	2,775	0.14	-39.82
EAST ASIA AND THE PACIFIC	38,194	34,334	49,079	77,872	95,068	4.96	22.08
NORTH-EAST ASIA	18,917	14,783	20,525	35,204	59,341	3.09	68.56
China	6,458	4,940	7,836	13,643	27,677	1.44	102.87
Japan	12,459	9,843	12,689	21,561	29,794	1.55	38.18
Korea, Republic of					1,870	0.10	
AUSTRALASIA					14,684	0.77	
Australia					13,471	0.70	
New Zealand					1,213	0.06	
OTHER EAST ASIA AND THE PACIFIC	19,277	19,551	28,554	42,668	21,043	1.10	-50.68
Other countries of Asia	12,683	12,718	19,971	31,113	20,907	1.09	-32.80
Other countries of Oceania					136	0.01	
All countries of Oceania	6,594	6,833	8,583	11,555			
EUROPE	1,067,316	1,026,282	1,129,501	1,278,966	1,535,814	80.07	20.08
CENTRAL/EASTERN EUROPE					47,328	2.47	
Bulgaria					950	0.05	
Czech Republic					11,007	0.57	
Estonia					1,270	0.07	
Hungary					3,034	0.16	
Latvia					653	0.03	
Lithuania					1,660	0.09	
Poland					9,218	0.48	
Romania					890	0.05	
Russian Federation					16,299	0.85	
Slovakia					1,620	0.08	
Ukraine					727	0.04	
NORTHERN EUROPE	301,735	281,354	316,003	374,673	466,282	24.31	24.45
Denmark	64,994	65,154	61,556	64,112	64,582	3.37	0.73
Faeroe Islands					4,298	0.22	
Finland	15,216	13,519	15,193	18,119	19,900	1.04	9.83
Ireland	6,017	5,060	5,159	6,957	8,671	0.45	24.64
Norway	40,575	42,073	50,309	59,757	66,512	3.47	11.30
Sweden	42,935	36,498	44,141	47,453	51,588	2.69	8.71
United Kingdom	131,998	119,050	139,645	178,275	250,731	13.07	40.64
SOUTHERN EUROPE	134,539	99,621	131,292	138,588	170,801	8.90	23.24
Croatia					385	0.02	
Greece					1,558	0.08	
Italy	69,356	50,330	65,767	66,064	79,540	4.15	20.40
Malta					151	0.01	
Portugal					2,160	0.11	
Slovenia					2,685	0.14	
Spain	65,183	49,291	65,525	72,524	84,322	4.40	16.27
WESTERN EUROPE	567,256	577,666	600,248	678,159	827,625	43.15	22.04

329

ICELAND

4. Arrivals of non-resident tourists in all types of accommodation establishments, by nationality

	2009	2010	2011	2012	2013	Market share 2013	% Change 2013-2012
Austria	29,300	29,097	22,253	25,492	31,938	1.67	25.29
Belgium	26,408	31,187	30,242	30,978	40,867	2.13	31.92
France	134,954	131,011	157,747	183,688	226,242	11.80	23.17
Germany	253,962	270,296	264,121	294,640	357,149	18.62	21.22
Luxembourg					916	0.05	
Netherlands	77,221	68,536	77,143	81,598	92,748	4.84	13.66
Switzerland	45,411	47,539	48,742	61,763	77,765	4.05	25.91
EAST MEDITERRANEAN EUROPE					**22,955**	**1.20**	
Cyprus					88	0.00	
Israel					22,223	1.16	
Turkey					644	0.03	
OTHER EUROPE	**63,786**	**67,641**	**81,958**	**87,546**	**823**	**0.04**	**-99.06**
Other countries of Europe	63,786	67,641	81,958	87,546	823	0.04	-99.06
SOUTH ASIA					**2,107**	**0.11**	
India					2,107	0.11	
NOT SPECIFIED	**75,680**	**57,212**	**74,360**	**66,105**			
Other countries of the World	75,680	57,212	74,360	66,105			

Yearbook of Tourism Statistics, Data 2009 – 2013, 2015 Edition

ICELAND

5. Overnight stays of non-resident tourists in hotels and similar establishments, by nationality

	2009	2010	2011	2012	2013	Market share 2013	% Change 2013-2012
TOTAL	1,581,226	1,518,639	1,722,785	2,028,013	2,346,540	100.00	15.71
AFRICA	4,040	3,438	3,719	6,444	3,515	0.15	-45.45
OTHER AFRICA	4,040	3,438	3,719	6,444	3,515	0.15	-45.45
All countries of Africa	4,040	3,438	3,719	6,444	3,515	0.15	-45.45
AMERICAS	155,021	162,161	255,571	316,071	411,112	17.52	30.07
NORTH AMERICA	151,096	158,645	250,689	310,037	404,778	17.25	30.56
Canada	24,933	25,586	39,609	37,810	50,669	2.16	34.01
United States of America	126,163	133,059	211,080	272,227	354,109	15.09	30.08
OTHER AMERICAS	3,925	3,516	4,882	6,034	6,334	0.27	4.97
Other countries of the Americas	3,925	3,516	4,882	6,034	6,334	0.27	4.97
EAST ASIA AND THE PACIFIC	55,808	46,832	65,197	103,834	153,420	6.54	47.76
NORTH-EAST ASIA	29,991	22,938	30,266	52,481	80,343	3.42	53.09
China	9,129	6,859	10,517	18,323	33,088	1.41	80.58
Japan	20,862	16,079	19,749	34,158	47,255	2.01	38.34
AUSTRALASIA	8,861	7,587	9,525	12,956	17,098	0.73	31.97
Australia	8,861	7,587	9,525	12,956	17,098	0.73	31.97
OTHER EAST ASIA AND THE PACIFIC	16,956	16,307	25,406	38,397	55,979	2.39	45.79
Other countries of Asia	16,956	16,307	25,406	38,397	55,979	2.39	45.79
EUROPE	1,265,037	1,206,950	1,317,486	1,545,993	1,778,493	75.79	15.04
NORTHERN EUROPE	547,293	494,792	547,030	663,301	778,804	33.19	17.41
Denmark	95,197	95,926	90,790	98,302	90,124	3.84	-8.32
Finland	29,984	24,274	27,806	33,993	33,488	1.43	-1.49
Ireland	8,564	6,226	7,176	7,667	11,578	0.49	51.01
Norway	82,226	83,146	96,699	114,522	118,751	5.06	3.69
Sweden	86,403	71,866	86,894	93,371	90,941	3.88	-2.60
United Kingdom	244,919	213,354	237,665	315,446	433,922	18.49	37.56
SOUTHERN EUROPE	121,148	87,693	118,683	117,148	139,655	5.95	19.21
Italy	64,983	45,432	61,570	56,107	69,017	2.94	23.01
Spain	56,165	42,261	57,113	61,041	70,638	3.01	15.72
WESTERN EUROPE	521,739	551,001	560,506	661,821	776,301	33.08	17.30
Austria	26,416	25,481	18,658	20,330	26,888	1.15	32.26
Belgium	19,868	24,708	23,738	24,464	33,179	1.41	35.62
France	100,880	104,495	122,881	151,772	173,468	7.39	14.30
Germany	256,390	285,729	276,296	326,403	383,792	16.36	17.58
Netherlands	78,891	69,496	76,513	82,274	87,791	3.74	6.71
Switzerland	39,294	41,092	42,420	56,578	71,183	3.03	25.81
OTHER EUROPE	74,857	73,464	91,267	103,723	83,733	3.57	-19.27
Other countries of Europe	74,857	73,464	91,267	103,723	83,733	3.57	-19.27
NOT SPECIFIED	101,320	99,258	80,812	55,671			
Other countries of the World	101,320	99,258	80,812	55,671			

Yearbook of Tourism Statistics, Data 2009 – 2013, 2015 Edition

ICELAND

6. Overnight stays of non-resident tourists in all types of accommodation establishments, by nationality

	2009	2010	2011	2012	2013	Market share 2013	% Change 2013-2012
TOTAL	2,134,245	2,144,318	2,444,245	2,879,098	3,366,252	100.00	16.92
AFRICA	4,159	3,714	4,734	7,526	4,331	0.13	-42.45
SOUTHERN AFRICA					1,921	0.06	
South Africa					1,921	0.06	
OTHER AFRICA	4,159	3,714	4,734	7,526	2,410	0.07	-67.98
Other countries of Africa					2,410	0.07	
All countries of Africa	4,159	3,714	4,734	7,526			
AMERICAS	184,803	205,654	329,923	414,201	557,722	16.57	34.65
NORTH AMERICA	180,045	201,158	323,594	405,729	548,483	16.29	35.18
Canada	35,608	40,681	60,922	61,765	81,729	2.43	32.32
Greenland					3,074	0.09	
United States of America	144,437	160,477	262,672	343,964	463,680	13.77	34.80
SOUTH AMERICA					3,553	0.11	
Brazil					3,553	0.11	
OTHER AMERICAS	4,758	4,496	6,329	8,472	5,686	0.17	-32.88
Other countries of the Americas	4,758	4,496	6,329	8,472	5,686	0.17	-32.88
EAST ASIA AND THE PACIFIC	66,561	60,974	83,344	129,325	163,691	4.86	26.57
NORTH-EAST ASIA	34,216	28,781	37,314	62,007	101,894	3.03	64.33
China	11,118	9,453	13,725	23,617	44,841	1.33	89.87
Japan	23,098	19,328	23,589	38,390	54,042	1.61	40.77
Korea, Republic of					3,011	0.09	
AUSTRALASIA					26,920	0.80	
Australia					24,444	0.73	
New Zealand					2,476	0.07	
OTHER EAST ASIA AND THE PACIFIC	32,345	32,193	46,030	67,318	34,877	1.04	-48.19
Other countries of Asia	20,220	20,047	30,254	45,321	34,609	1.03	-23.64
Other countries of Oceania					268	0.01	
All countries of Oceania	12,125	12,146	15,776	21,997			
EUROPE	1,747,898	1,754,128	1,908,585	2,218,283	2,636,376	78.32	18.85
CENTRAL/EASTERN EUROPE					87,660	2.60	
Bulgaria					5,843	0.17	
Czech Republic					16,066	0.48	
Estonia					2,452	0.07	
Hungary					5,872	0.17	
Latvia					1,295	0.04	
Lithuania					2,892	0.09	
Poland					16,589	0.49	
Romania					1,655	0.05	
Russian Federation					30,948	0.92	
Slovakia					2,783	0.08	
Ukraine					1,265	0.04	
NORTHERN EUROPE	637,363	619,523	685,291	826,775	1,014,551	30.14	22.71
Denmark	122,266	129,359	122,978	128,558	124,745	3.71	-2.97
Faeroe Islands					10,655	0.32	
Finland	34,029	33,238	37,677	42,277	44,130	1.31	4.38
Ireland	11,081	10,460	10,078	12,625	17,929	0.53	42.01
Norway	92,493	96,642	114,924	136,589	149,148	4.43	9.19
Sweden	98,890	88,720	103,055	115,176	117,789	3.50	2.27
United Kingdom	278,604	261,104	296,579	391,550	550,155	16.34	40.51
SOUTHERN EUROPE	172,655	134,618	175,958	184,418	231,635	6.88	25.60
Croatia					1,023	0.03	
Greece					2,296	0.07	
Italy	88,020	66,523	86,562	85,228	104,196	3.10	22.26
Malta					310	0.01	
Portugal					3,779	0.11	
Slovenia					4,315	0.13	
Spain	84,635	68,095	89,396	99,190	115,716	3.44	16.66
WESTERN EUROPE	831,728	882,440	909,221	1,052,079	1,272,023	37.79	20.91

332

ICELAND

6. Overnight stays of non-resident tourists in all types of accommodation establishments, by nationality

	2009	2010	2011	2012	2013	Market share 2013	% Change 2013-2012
Austria	40,215	41,476	32,476	35,979	47,124	1.40	30.98
Belgium	35,518	44,855	43,093	46,417	61,111	1.82	31.66
France	175,153	180,137	213,706	255,886	313,213	9.30	22.40
Germany	399,311	430,900	422,704	486,731	579,814	17.22	19.12
Luxembourg					1,536	0.05	
Netherlands	119,007	117,328	128,032	138,860	156,580	4.65	12.76
Switzerland	62,524	67,744	69,210	88,206	112,645	3.35	27.71
EAST MEDITERRANEAN EUROPE					29,120	0.87	
Cyprus					227	0.01	
Israel					27,649	0.82	
Turkey					1,244	0.04	
OTHER EUROPE	**106,152**	**117,547**	**138,115**	**155,011**	**1,387**	**0.04**	**-99.11**
Other countries of Europe	106,152	117,547	138,115	155,011	1,387	0.04	-99.11
SOUTH ASIA					**4,132**	**0.12**	
India					4,132	0.12	
NOT SPECIFIED	**130,824**	**119,848**	**117,659**	**109,763**			
Other countries of the World	130,824	119,848	117,659	109,763			

Yearbook of Tourism Statistics, Data 2009 – 2013, 2015 Edition

INDIA

1. Arrivals of non-resident tourists at national borders, by nationality

		2009	2010	2011	2012	2013	Market share 2013	% Change 2013-2012
TOTAL	(*)	5,167,699	5,775,692	6,309,222	6,577,745	6,967,601	100.00	5.93
AFRICA		158,605	197,090	224,292	251,187	262,148	3.76	4.36
EAST AFRICA		75,618	91,544	99,385	125,772	131,933	1.89	4.90
Burundi		559	703	857	704	577	0.01	-18.04
Comoros		39	133	231	419	1,225	0.02	192.36
Djibouti			561	602	835	907	0.01	8.62
Eritrea		523	638	616	639	653	0.01	2.19
Ethiopia		3,936	3,797	6,411	11,795	14,899	0.21	26.32
Kenya		22,704	29,223	30,045	34,037	40,484	0.58	18.94
Madagascar		883	2,377	1,509	1,497	1,570	0.02	4.88
Malawi		799	1,250	1,132	10,406	1,393	0.02	-86.61
Mauritius		18,866	21,672	22,091	25,013	27,418	0.39	9.62
Mozambique		1,790	2,442	3,118	3,766	4,469	0.06	18.67
Reunion		59	102	29	21	61	0.00	190.48
Rwanda		849	1,344	1,580	1,907	1,780	0.03	-6.66
Seychelles		1,339	1,672	2,330	2,220	2,029	0.03	-8.60
Somalia		525	555	753	701	970	0.01	38.37
Uganda		2,425	3,011	3,615	3,841	3,857	0.06	0.42
United Republic of Tanzania		17,020	17,645	19,470	21,862	23,345	0.34	6.78
Zambia		2,249	2,621	2,944	3,428	3,853	0.06	12.40
Zimbabwe		1,053	1,798	2,052	2,681	2,443	0.04	-8.88
CENTRAL AFRICA		3,389	4,810	7,914	8,811	4,371	0.06	-50.39
Angola		1,248	1,620	1,891	2,263	2,300	0.03	1.63
Cameroon		671	877	912	1,014	999	0.01	-1.48
Central African Republic		9	15	37	62	34	0.00	-45.16
Chad		154	212	1,198	194	268	0.00	38.14
Congo		1,100	1,930	3,623	5,093	551	0.01	-89.18
Equatorial Guinea		8	11	10	7	16	0.00	128.57
Gabon		188	134	226	170	188	0.00	10.59
Sao Tome and Principe		11	11	17	8	15	0.00	87.50
NORTH AFRICA		8,768	11,766	14,529	17,174	20,664	0.30	20.32
Algeria		1,217	1,203	1,635	1,750	2,270	0.03	29.71
Morocco		1,429	1,724	2,328	3,203	5,943	0.09	85.54
Sudan		4,987	7,418	8,414	9,626	8,778	0.13	-8.81
Tunisia		1,135	1,421	2,152	2,595	3,673	0.05	41.54
SOUTHERN AFRICA		47,179	58,271	60,815	53,830	60,534	0.87	12.45
Botswana		491	1,050	837	919	795	0.01	-13.49
Lesotho		290	523	421	365	392	0.01	7.40
Namibia		558	613	593	757	664	0.01	-12.29
South Africa		44,308	55,688	58,430	50,161	58,023	0.83	15.67
Swaziland		1,532	397	534	1,628	660	0.01	-59.46
WEST AFRICA		23,550	30,699	41,649	45,565	44,077	0.63	-3.27
Benin			209	304	189	268	0.00	41.80
Burkina Faso		259	282	262	300	275	0.00	-8.33
Cabo Verde		22	42	21	30	39	0.00	30.00
Côte d'Ivoire		639	680	637	873	1,168	0.02	33.79
Gambia		161	281	380	297	303	0.00	2.02
Ghana		1,381	1,773	2,129	2,390	2,601	0.04	8.83
Guinea		280	310	341	317	491	0.01	54.89
Guinea-Bissau		12	18	34	68	103	0.00	51.47
Liberia		144	177	164	245	371	0.01	51.43
Mali		273	495	815	845	723	0.01	-14.44
Mauritania		190	131	559	869	202	0.00	-76.75
Niger		316	475	600	497	1,152	0.02	131.79
Nigeria		18,338	23,893	33,537	36,762	34,522	0.50	-6.09
Saint Helena			53	51	41	50	0.00	21.95
Senegal		1,077	1,212	1,234	1,202	1,134	0.02	-5.66
Sierra Leone		301	371	289	357	438	0.01	22.69
Togo		157	297	292	283	237	0.00	-16.25

334

INDIA

1. Arrivals of non-resident tourists at national borders, by nationality

	2009	2010	2011	2012	2013	Market share 2013	% Change 2013-2012
OTHER AFRICA	101			35	569	0.01	1,525.71
Other countries of Africa	101			35	569	0.01	1,525.71
AMERICAS	1,097,813	1,236,695	1,300,911	1,360,373	1,410,677	20.25	3.70
CARIBBEAN	3,563	5,135	4,644	4,489	5,745	0.08	27.98
Anguilla		14	8	1	3	0.00	200.00
Antigua and Barbuda	25	65	35	54	39	0.00	-27.78
Bahamas	142	179	212	281	216	0.00	-23.13
Barbados	326	451	428	488	437	0.01	-10.45
Bermuda		29	31	6	3	0.00	-50.00
British Virgin Islands		15	1		808	0.01	
Cayman Islands		12	6	1			
Cuba	259	338	279	231	356	0.01	54.11
Dominica		48	17	26	127	0.00	388.46
Dominican Republic	255	353	459	337	306	0.00	-9.20
Grenada	100	92	107	93	116	0.00	24.73
Guadeloupe	7	5	2		2	0.00	
Haiti	119	89	89	72	74	0.00	2.78
Jamaica	561	892	768	795	952	0.01	19.75
Martinique	8	12	12	31	7	0.00	-77.42
Montserrat		21	32	81	1	0.00	-98.77
Netherlands Antilles	56	75	55	64	46	0.00	-28.13
Puerto Rico		3	7	4	4	0.00	
Saint Kitts and Nevis		91	82	76	145	0.00	90.79
Saint Lucia	50	88	91	118	120	0.00	1.69
Saint Vincent and the Grenadines		47	24	18	30	0.00	66.67
Trinidad and Tobago	1,655	2,193	1,888	1,708	1,864	0.03	9.13
Turks and Caicos Islands		19	10	4	2	0.00	-50.00
United States Virgin Islands		4	1		87	0.00	
CENTRAL AMERICA	2,670	2,616	3,351	3,152	3,766	0.05	19.48
Belize	223	356	351	362	439	0.01	21.27
Costa Rica	561	568	1,042	763	817	0.01	7.08
El Salvador	213	204	215	255	320	0.00	25.49
Guatemala	495	411	429	527	553	0.01	4.93
Honduras	256	195	283	256	295	0.00	15.23
Nicaragua	109	92	85	81	124	0.00	53.09
Panama	813	790	946	908	1,218	0.02	34.14
NORTH AMERICA	1,059,394	1,184,122	1,250,581	1,307,222	1,353,605	19.43	3.55
Canada	224,069	242,372	259,017	256,021	255,222	3.66	-0.31
Mexico	8,185	10,458	10,876	11,254	13,074	0.19	16.17
United States of America	827,140	931,292	980,688	1,039,947	1,085,309	15.58	4.36
SOUTH AMERICA	32,186	44,822	42,335	45,021	47,061	0.68	4.53
Argentina	6,011	7,626	9,391	9,831	10,325	0.15	5.02
Bolivia	280	290	313	334	376	0.01	12.57
Brazil	13,964	15,219	17,268	18,440	18,551	0.27	0.60
Chile	2,961	11,340	3,975	4,640	4,715	0.07	1.62
Colombia	2,945	3,663	4,085	4,381	5,036	0.07	14.95
Ecuador	606	794	1,208	911	993	0.01	9.00
Guyana	387	601	438	359	434	0.01	20.89
Paraguay	116	228	221	266	223	0.00	-16.17
Peru	1,214	1,326	1,592	1,932	1,945	0.03	0.67
Suriname	514	493	558	539	551	0.01	2.23
Uruguay	1,068	1,387	1,199	1,249	1,563	0.02	25.14
Venezuela	2,120	1,855	2,087	2,139	2,349	0.03	9.82
OTHER AMERICAS				489	500	0.01	2.25
Other countries of the Americas				489	500	0.01	2.25
EAST ASIA AND THE PACIFIC	865,439	1,062,536	1,229,632	1,321,643	1,441,034	20.68	9.03
NORTH-EAST ASIA	322,797	411,947	475,951	535,622	547,305	7.85	2.18
China	100,209	119,530	142,218	168,952	174,712	2.51	3.41
Hong Kong, China	1,396	1,507	1,712	1,743	166	0.00	-90.48

Yearbook of Tourism Statistics, Data 2009 – 2013, 2015 Edition

INDIA

1. Arrivals of non-resident tourists at national borders, by nationality

	2009	2010	2011	2012	2013	Market share 2013	% Change 2013-2012
Japan	124,756	168,019	193,525	220,015	220,283	3.16	0.12
Korea, Dem. People's Republic of	4	25	20	181	332	0.00	83.43
Korea, Republic of	70,485	95,587	108,680	109,469	112,619	1.62	2.88
Macao, China	251	669	573	205	269	0.00	31.22
Mongolia	2,232	2,695	3,307	3,418	3,433	0.05	0.44
Taiwan, Province of China	23,464	23,915	25,916	31,639	35,491	0.51	12.17
SOUTH-EAST ASIA	**360,191**	**439,043**	**520,787**	**540,914**	**630,054**	**9.04**	**16.48**
Brunei Darussalam	303	456	556	665	706	0.01	6.17
Cambodia	1,133	1,715	2,076	2,028	2,238	0.03	10.36
Indonesia	20,068	26,171	32,530	29,559	33,747	0.48	14.17
Lao People's Democratic Republic	294	809		973	1,101	0.02	13.16
Malaysia	135,343	179,077	208,196	195,853	242,649	3.48	23.89
Myanmar	12,849	14,719	25,043	30,588	34,916	0.50	14.15
Philippines	21,987	24,534	31,151	33,323	42,224	0.61	26.71
Singapore	95,328	107,487	119,022	131,452	143,025	2.05	8.80
Thailand	67,309	76,617	92,404	105,141	117,136	1.68	11.41
Viet Nam	5,577	7,458	9,809	11,332	12,312	0.18	8.65
AUSTRALASIA	**179,950**	**206,671**	**229,431**	**241,022**	**259,768**	**3.73**	**7.78**
Australia	149,074	169,647	192,592	202,105	218,967	3.14	8.34
New Zealand	30,876	37,024	36,839	38,917	40,801	0.59	4.84
MELANESIA	**2,248**	**2,971**	**2,997**	**3,105**	**3,141**	**0.05**	**1.16**
Fiji	2,031	2,508	2,705	2,793	2,865	0.04	2.58
New Caledonia		4	2	5	8	0.00	60.00
Norfolk Island		7	5	3	2	0.00	-33.33
Papua New Guinea	177	356	242	265	245	0.00	-7.55
Solomon Islands	40						
Vanuatu		96	43	39	21	0.00	-46.15
MICRONESIA	**207**	**463**	**369**	**311**	**349**	**0.01**	**12.22**
Christmas Island, Australia		2	1				
Guam			2	1	3	0.00	200.00
Kiribati	30	143	83	74	90	0.00	21.62
Nauru	177	318	283	236	256	0.00	8.47
POLYNESIA	**46**	**1,441**	**97**	**669**	**417**	**0.01**	**-37.67**
American Samoa		1,077	41	278	244	0.00	-12.23
Cook Islands		2					
French Polynesia		25	33	15	10	0.00	-33.33
Niue			4		1	0.00	
Samoa	31			43			
Tonga		297		283	92	0.00	-67.49
Tuvalu	15	40	19	50	70	0.00	40.00
EUROPE	**1,869,115**	**2,034,709**	**2,173,422**	**2,236,970**	**2,335,353**	**33.52**	**4.40**
CENTRAL/EASTERN EUROPE	**179,088**	**223,327**	**269,414**	**311,380**	**401,430**	**5.76**	**28.92**
Armenia	452	641	686	595	693	0.01	16.47
Azerbaijan	859	800	1,058	1,263	1,308	0.02	3.56
Belarus	2,536	3,493	4,567	6,239	8,239	0.12	32.06
Bulgaria	2,370	2,900	2,890	3,621	3,501	0.05	-3.31
Czech Republic	8,328	9,918	11,256	11,129	10,121	0.15	-9.06
Estonia	3,496	2,594	2,754	3,005	3,469	0.05	15.44
Georgia	687	655	4,179	1,029	1,107	0.02	7.58
Hungary	4,980	6,022	6,900	6,507	6,614	0.09	1.64
Kazakhstan	6,848	8,786	9,810	11,653	14,680	0.21	25.98
Kyrgyzstan	1,208	1,181	1,340	1,348	2,103	0.03	56.01
Latvia	2,498	3,052	2,968	3,029	2,853	0.04	-5.81
Lithuania	2,365	2,598	3,619	3,408	3,492	0.05	2.46
Poland	19,656	25,424	28,499	25,030	23,785	0.34	-4.97
Republic of Moldova	1,502	424	470	541	625	0.01	15.53
Romania	4,808	5,380	5,988	6,338	7,024	0.10	10.82
Russian Federation	94,945	122,048	144,312	177,526	259,120	3.72	45.96
Slovakia	3,092	3,571	4,061	3,850	4,087	0.06	6.16

336

Yearbook of Tourism Statistics, Data 2009 – 2013, 2015 Edition

INDIA

1. Arrivals of non-resident tourists at national borders, by nationality

	2009	2010	2011	2012	2013	Market share 2013	% Change 2013-2012
Tajikistan	749	963	1,359	1,564	1,685	0.02	7.74
Turkmenistan	1,631	1,509	1,946	2,364	3,029	0.04	28.13
Ukraine	12,436	16,462	23,467	29,033	31,826	0.46	9.62
Uzbekistan	3,642	4,906	7,285	9,808	12,069	0.17	23.05
Other countries Central/East Europe				2,500			
NORTHERN EUROPE	**915,655**	**908,900**	**954,614**	**946,520**	**963,039**	**13.82**	**1.75**
Denmark	30,857	35,541	34,683	33,084	30,842	0.44	-6.78
Faeroe Islands		7	6	5	5	0.00	
Finland	24,874	24,089	23,730	22,416	21,212	0.30	-5.37
Iceland	1,821	2,183	2,589	1,673	1,382	0.02	-17.39
Ireland	19,223	20,329	22,089	24,546	27,174	0.39	10.71
Norway	22,092	22,229	24,578	23,569	21,462	0.31	-8.94
Sweden	43,327	45,028	48,690	51,058	48,826	0.70	-4.37
United Kingdom	769,251	759,494	798,249	788,170	809,444	11.62	2.70
Other countries of Northern Europe	4,210			1,999	2,692	0.04	34.67
SOUTHERN EUROPE	**168,155**	**203,898**	**211,408**	**205,663**	**198,699**	**2.85**	**-3.39**
Albania	279	330	394	234	323	0.00	38.03
Andorra	173	157	181	134	195	0.00	45.52
Bosnia and Herzegovina		305	329	293	477	0.01	62.80
Croatia	2,990	3,080	3,375	3,158	3,150	0.05	-0.25
Gibraltar		5	10	1	2	0.00	100.00
Greece	6,664	7,441	7,253	7,493	7,983	0.11	6.54
Italy	77,873	94,100	100,889	98,743	93,951	1.35	-4.85
Malta	499	540	516	614	728	0.01	18.57
Portugal	17,184	21,038	24,061	24,670	29,612	0.42	20.03
San Marino		46	57	130	88	0.00	-32.31
Slovenia	2,049	3,022	2,938	2,794	85	0.00	-96.96
Spain	59,047	72,591	71,405	67,044	62,079	0.89	-7.41
Yugoslavia, SFR (former)	1,397	1,243		355	26	0.00	-92.68
WESTERN EUROPE	**554,595**	**638,637**	**671,642**	**701,386**	**694,796**	**9.97**	**-0.94**
Austria	27,930	32,620	36,483	38,585	36,465	0.52	-5.49
Belgium	34,759	37,709	40,478	42,604	38,091	0.55	-10.59
France	196,462	225,232	231,423	240,674	248,379	3.56	3.20
Germany	191,616	227,720	240,235	254,783	252,003	3.62	-1.09
Liechtenstein		182	174	136	117	0.00	-13.97
Luxembourg	958	1,200	1,256	1,334	1,266	0.02	-5.10
Monaco		84	108	82	107	0.00	30.49
Netherlands	64,580	70,756	75,153	74,800	69,547	1.00	-7.02
Switzerland	38,290	43,134	46,332	48,388	48,821	0.70	0.89
EAST MEDITERRANEAN EUROPE	**51,622**	**59,947**	**66,344**	**71,520**	**74,832**	**1.07**	**4.63**
Cyprus	759	1,008	896	885	1,073	0.02	21.24
Israel	40,581	43,456	48,089	47,649	48,737	0.70	2.28
Turkey	10,282	15,483	17,359	22,986	25,022	0.36	8.86
OTHER EUROPE				**501**	**2,557**	**0.04**	**410.38**
Other countries of Europe				501	2,557	0.04	410.38
MIDDLE EAST	**159,090**	**183,387**	**221,220**	**231,062**	**284,558**	**4.08**	**23.15**
Bahrain	7,901	7,766	9,587	10,045	10,531	0.15	4.84
Egypt	5,869	8,017	8,791	10,571	15,062	0.22	42.48
Iraq	16,400	28,221	30,808	38,826	41,218	0.59	6.16
Jordan	4,301	4,640	5,061	7,356	7,788	0.11	5.87
Kuwait	5,208	4,764	5,370	5,256	8,461	0.12	60.98
Lebanon	3,320	3,730	4,296	4,842	5,788	0.08	19.54
Libya	693	1,280	465	1,620	1,462	0.02	-9.75
Oman	32,971	35,485	40,577	49,759	62,252	0.89	25.11
Palestine	966	1,151	1,241	1,224	1,378	0.02	12.58
Qatar	2,765	2,735	3,266	4,132	4,966	0.07	20.18
Saudi Arabia	15,552	21,599	26,268	32,127	42,892	0.62	33.51
Syrian Arab Republic	3,215	3,586	4,152	3,971	5,013	0.07	26.24
United Arab Emirates	47,234	45,482	66,383	41,664	51,513	0.74	23.64

337

INDIA

1. Arrivals of non-resident tourists at national borders, by nationality

	2009	2010	2011	2012	2013	Market share 2013	% Change 2013-2012
Yemen	12,695	14,931	14,955	18,654	25,019	0.36	34.12
Other countries of Middle East				1,015	1,215	0.02	19.70
SOUTH ASIA	**1,001,401**	**1,047,444**	**1,139,659**	**1,171,499**	**1,215,035**	**17.44**	**3.72**
Afghanistan	50,446	73,389	89,605	95,231	111,370	1.60	16.95
Bangladesh	468,899	431,962	463,543	487,397	524,923	7.53	7.70
Bhutan	10,328	12,048	15,489	15,266	15,016	0.22	-1.64
Iran, Islamic Republic of	34,652	49,265	43,399	40,973	30,527	0.44	-25.49
Maldives	55,159	58,152	53,999	50,428	45,270	0.65	-10.23
Nepal	88,785	104,374	119,131	125,375	113,790	1.63	-9.24
Pakistan	53,137	51,739	48,640	59,846	111,794	1.60	86.80
Sri Lanka	239,995	266,515	305,853	296,983	262,345	3.77	-11.66
NOT SPECIFIED	**16,236**	**13,831**	**20,086**	**5,011**	**18,796**	**0.27**	**275.09**
Other countries of the World	16,236	13,831	20,086	5,011	18,796	0.27	275.09

Yearbook of Tourism Statistics, Data 2009 – 2013, 2015 Edition

INDONESIA

1. Arrivals of non-resident tourists at national borders, by nationality

	2009	2010	2011	2012	2013	Market share 2013	% Change 2013-2012
TOTAL	6,323,730	7,002,944	7,649,731	8,044,462	8,802,129	100.00	9.42
AFRICA	26,637	28,592	31,651	37,306	42,607	0.48	14.21
SOUTHERN AFRICA	12,999	14,287	16,282	17,433	16,928	0.19	-2.90
South Africa	12,999	14,287	16,282	17,433	16,928	0.19	-2.90
OTHER AFRICA	13,638	14,305	15,369	19,873	25,679	0.29	29.22
Other countries of Africa	13,638	14,305	15,369	19,873	25,679	0.29	29.22
AMERICAS	237,670	255,465	293,306	312,526	343,573	3.90	9.93
CENTRAL AMERICA	4,587	881	1,044	1,800	1,533	0.02	-14.83
All countries of Central America	4,587	881	1,044	1,800	1,533	0.02	-14.83
NORTH AMERICA	209,046	226,026	260,334	275,844	301,760	3.43	9.40
Canada	43,948	48,349	57,129	58,245	65,385	0.74	12.26
United States of America	165,098	177,677	203,205	217,599	236,375	2.69	8.63
SOUTH AMERICA	24,037	21,364	26,193	28,155	32,752	0.37	16.33
All countries of South America	24,037	21,364	26,193	28,155	32,752	0.37	16.33
OTHER AMERICAS		7,194	5,735	6,727	7,528	0.09	11.91
Other countries of the Americas		7,194	5,735	6,727	7,528	0.09	11.91
EAST ASIA AND THE PACIFIC	4,741,596	5,350,445	5,848,604	6,159,068	6,689,446	76.00	8.61
NORTH-EAST ASIA	1,461,827	1,511,249	1,652,613	1,818,053	2,049,097	23.28	12.71
China	444,598	511,188	594,997	726,088	858,140	9.75	18.19
Hong Kong, China	63,801	73,658	84,985	81,782	95,258	1.08	16.48
Japan	488,320	416,151	423,113	463,486	497,399	5.65	7.32
Korea, Republic of	260,314	296,060	320,596	328,989	351,154	3.99	6.74
Taiwan, Province of China	204,794	214,192	228,922	217,708	247,146	2.81	13.52
SOUTH-EAST ASIA	2,637,066	2,958,976	3,131,818	3,246,001	3,490,162	39.65	7.52
Brunei Darussalam	13,668	35,874	38,679	16,423	16,932	0.19	3.10
Cambodia	1,975	5,265	4,628	5,058	31,001	0.35	512.91
Lao People's Democratic Republic	969	1,932	1,914	2,000	6,251	0.07	212.55
Malaysia	1,041,053	1,171,737	1,173,351	1,269,089	1,380,686	15.69	8.79
Myanmar	18,128	15,582	22,304	29,718	2,361	0.03	-92.06
Philippines	196,429	171,181	210,029	236,866	247,573	2.81	4.52
Singapore	1,138,071	1,206,360	1,324,839	1,324,706	1,432,060	16.27	8.10
Thailand	93,381	111,645	115,036	114,867	125,059	1.42	8.87
Viet Nam	20,785	24,929	31,106	33,598	43,249	0.49	28.72
Other countries of South-East Asia	112,607	214,471	209,932	213,676	204,990	2.33	-4.07
AUSTRALASIA	609,245	814,920	985,834	1,012,323	1,051,763	11.95	3.90
Australia	571,541	769,585	933,376	952,717	983,911	11.18	3.27
New Zealand	37,704	45,335	52,458	59,606	67,852	0.77	13.83
OTHER EAST ASIA AND THE PACIFIC	33,458	65,300	78,339	82,691	98,424	1.12	19.03
Other countries of Asia	30,344	60,410	71,742	77,529	93,490	1.06	20.59
Other countries of Oceania	3,114	4,890	6,597	5,162	4,934	0.06	-4.42
EUROPE	1,028,405	1,048,543	1,110,871	1,174,079	1,285,097	14.60	9.46
CENTRAL/EASTERN EUROPE	144,951	145,817	164,358	175,827	188,456	2.14	7.18
USSR (former)	77,018	83,836	96,438	99,448	99,872	1.13	0.43
Other countries Central/East Europe	67,933	61,981	67,920	76,379	88,584	1.01	15.98
NORTHERN EUROPE	257,342	262,295	278,615	299,144	322,213	3.66	7.71
Denmark	20,062	17,565	19,950	21,168	22,890	0.26	8.13
Finland	15,591	11,566	13,137	15,035	15,074	0.17	0.26
Norway	16,261	16,226	17,803	17,118	18,174	0.21	6.17
Sweden	22,166	24,603	26,504	26,097	29,281	0.33	12.20
United Kingdom	183,262	192,335	201,221	219,726	236,794	2.69	7.77
SOUTHERN EUROPE	77,559	81,414	86,574	97,048	114,282	1.30	17.76
Italy	38,028	39,211	42,256	46,651	56,705	0.64	21.55
Portugal	11,331	11,629	13,661	15,406	18,194	0.21	18.10
Spain	28,200	30,574	30,657	34,991	39,383	0.45	12.55
WESTERN EUROPE	536,310	540,997	564,771	580,353	636,754	7.23	9.72
Austria	17,399	16,889	17,374	19,120	21,645	0.25	13.21
Belgium	25,781	24,493	24,579	28,243	34,414	0.39	21.85
France	165,656	160,913	171,736	184,273	201,917	2.29	9.57
Germany	133,032	144,411	149,110	158,212	173,470	1.97	9.64

339

INDONESIA

1. Arrivals of non-resident tourists at national borders, by nationality

	2009	2010	2011	2012	2013	Market share 2013	% Change 2013-2012
Netherlands	154,932	158,957	163,268	152,749	161,402	1.83	5.66
Switzerland	39,510	35,334	38,704	37,756	43,906	0.50	16.29
OTHER EUROPE	**12,243**	**18,020**	**16,553**	**21,707**	**23,392**	**0.27**	**7.76**
Other countries of Europe	12,243	18,020	16,553	21,707	23,392	0.27	7.76
MIDDLE EAST	**113,935**	**143,002**	**163,497**	**144,386**	**187,439**	**2.13**	**29.82**
Bahrain	746	832	879	981	1,176	0.01	19.88
Egypt	3,316	3,650	4,469	6,115	8,091	0.09	32.31
Kuwait	5,875	2,729	4,164	4,738	7,919	0.09	67.14
Qatar	6,579	5,076	4,501	1,265	1,332	0.02	5.30
Saudi Arabia	73,000	94,440	110,908	92,667	121,890	1.38	31.54
United Arab Emirates	3,871	4,970	4,720	6,154	9,891	0.11	60.72
Yemen	3,522	5,597	6,729	5,025	6,851	0.08	36.34
Other countries of Middle East	17,026	25,708	27,127	27,441	30,289	0.34	10.38
SOUTH ASIA	**175,487**	**176,897**	**201,802**	**217,097**	**253,967**	**2.89**	**16.98**
Bangladesh	6,347	5,557	6,394	5,998	8,132	0.09	35.58
India	156,545	159,373	181,791	196,983	231,266	2.63	17.40
Pakistan	5,880	5,772	6,598	5,330	6,281	0.07	17.84
Sri Lanka	6,715	6,195	7,019	8,786	8,288	0.09	-5.67

Yearbook of Tourism Statistics, Data 2009 – 2013, 2015 Edition

INDONESIA

1. Arrivals of non-resident tourists at national borders, by country of residence

	2009	2010	2011	2012	2013	Market share 2013	% Change 2013-2012
TOTAL	6,323,730	7,002,944	7,649,731	8,044,462	8,802,129	100.00	9.42
AFRICA	28,375	27,200	31,640	41,583	51,298	0.58	23.36
SOUTHERN AFRICA	15,831	12,691	15,579	17,228	21,757	0.25	26.29
South Africa	15,831	12,691	15,579	17,228	21,757	0.25	26.29
OTHER AFRICA	12,544	14,509	16,061	24,355	29,541	0.34	21.29
Other countries of Africa	12,544	14,509	16,061	24,355	29,541	0.34	21.29
AMERICAS	229,824	258,584	297,061	312,209	333,150	3.78	6.71
CENTRAL AMERICA	5,923	1,491	2,315	2,951	2,781	0.03	-5.76
All countries of Central America	5,923	1,491	2,315	2,951	2,781	0.03	-5.76
NORTH AMERICA	205,631	223,520	258,562	269,352	290,932	3.31	8.01
Canada	35,400	43,159	54,287	56,501	56,798	0.65	0.53
United States of America	170,231	180,361	204,275	212,851	234,134	2.66	10.00
SOUTH AMERICA	18,270	23,288	26,566	27,165	30,168	0.34	11.05
All countries of South America	18,270	23,288	26,566	27,165	30,168	0.34	11.05
OTHER AMERICAS		10,285	9,618	12,741	9,269	0.11	-27.25
Other countries of the Americas		10,285	9,618	12,741	9,269	0.11	-27.25
EAST ASIA AND THE PACIFIC	4,834,790	5,375,990	5,923,760	6,236,626	6,756,802	76.76	8.34
NORTH-EAST ASIA	1,398,507	1,455,116	1,601,386	1,756,179	2,000,703	22.73	13.92
China	395,013	469,365	574,179	686,779	807,429	9.17	17.57
Hong Kong, China	67,967	78,339	86,646	90,560	112,785	1.28	24.54
Japan	475,766	418,971	412,623	450,687	491,574	5.58	9.07
Korea, Republic of	256,522	274,999	306,061	311,618	343,627	3.90	10.27
Taiwan, Province of China	203,239	213,442	221,877	216,535	245,288	2.79	13.28
SOUTH-EAST ASIA	2,772,684	3,052,285	3,284,664	3,375,291	3,581,420	40.69	6.11
Brunei Darussalam	15,709	39,063	48,193	27,734	23,309	0.26	-15.96
Malaysia	1,179,366	1,277,476	1,302,237	1,335,531	1,430,989	16.26	7.15
Philippines	162,463	189,486	223,779	229,806	246,497	2.80	7.26
Singapore	1,272,862	1,373,126	1,505,588	1,565,478	1,634,149	18.57	4.39
Thailand	109,547	123,825	141,771	149,760	141,349	1.61	-5.62
Viet Nam	14,456	28,196	36,917	40,084	39,770	0.45	-0.78
Other countries of South-East Asia	18,281	21,113	26,179	26,898	65,357	0.74	142.98
AUSTRALASIA	616,030	803,905	967,792	1,017,452	1,064,468	12.09	4.62
Australia	584,437	771,792	931,109	961,595	997,984	11.34	3.78
New Zealand	31,593	32,113	36,683	55,857	66,484	0.76	19.03
OTHER EAST ASIA AND THE PACIFIC	47,569	64,684	69,918	87,704	110,211	1.25	25.66
Other countries of Asia	41,115	58,783	62,761	80,490	102,917	1.17	27.86
Other countries of Oceania	6,454	5,901	7,157	7,214	7,294	0.08	1.11
EUROPE	978,369	1,038,420	1,045,865	1,108,521	1,243,005	14.12	12.13
CENTRAL/EASTERN EUROPE	129,969	139,426	152,801	165,786	174,581	1.98	5.31
Russian Federation	72,829	79,398	87,426	95,731	96,543	1.10	0.85
Other countries Central/East Europe	57,140	60,028	65,375	70,055	78,038	0.89	11.40
NORTHERN EUROPE	244,143	264,815	268,722	289,594	311,247	3.54	7.48
Denmark	19,010	16,755	17,817	22,814	20,096	0.23	-11.91
Finland	18,688	13,740	14,117	14,828	15,949	0.18	7.56
Norway	16,141	17,482	16,578	17,562	18,903	0.21	7.64
Sweden	21,033	24,579	27,525	22,303	27,620	0.31	23.84
United Kingdom	169,271	192,259	192,685	212,087	228,679	2.60	7.82
SOUTHERN EUROPE	81,623	81,716	82,811	94,562	128,267	1.46	35.64
Italy	40,448	38,908	46,145	48,382	63,043	0.72	30.30
Portugal	29,119	13,165	11,070	16,785	24,853	0.28	48.07
Spain	12,056	29,643	25,596	29,395	40,371	0.46	37.34
WESTERN EUROPE	508,052	533,918	525,671	541,484	608,697	6.92	12.41
Austria	16,771	16,472	15,041	17,226	20,497	0.23	18.99
Belgium	23,836	22,328	22,551	24,129	28,329	0.32	17.41
France	159,924	163,110	148,381	170,046	190,853	2.17	12.24
Germany	128,649	145,244	145,160	148,146	168,110	1.91	13.48
Netherlands	143,485	151,836	159,063	146,591	158,181	1.80	7.91
Switzerland	35,387	34,928	35,475	35,346	42,727	0.49	20.88

341

INDONESIA

1. Arrivals of non-resident tourists at national borders, by country of residence

	2009	2010	2011	2012	2013	Market share 2013	% Change 2013-2012
OTHER EUROPE	**14,582**	**18,545**	**15,860**	**17,095**	**20,213**	**0.23**	**18.24**
Other countries of Europe	14,582	18,545	15,860	17,095	20,213	0.23	18.24
MIDDLE EAST	**122,069**	**144,661**	**175,885**	**148,788**	**188,676**	**2.14**	**26.81**
Bahrain	740	1,889	1,675	1,910	1,766	0.02	-7.54
Egypt	3,031	3,235	2,942	5,160	6,194	0.07	20.04
Kuwait	7,606	5,819	5,014	5,959	8,122	0.09	36.30
Saudi Arabia	92,032	105,549	128,784	95,213	123,702	1.41	29.92
Other countries of Middle East	18,660	28,169	37,470	40,546	48,892	0.56	20.58
SOUTH ASIA	**130,303**	**158,089**	**175,520**	**196,735**	**229,198**	**2.60**	**16.50**
Bangladesh	6,324	8,724	8,991	12,050	10,567	0.12	-12.31
India	110,658	137,027	154,237	168,187	201,009	2.28	19.52
Pakistan	7,580	6,314	6,085	6,028	6,213	0.07	3.07
Sri Lanka	5,741	6,024	6,207	10,470	11,409	0.13	8.97

Yearbook of Tourism Statistics, Data 2009 – 2013, 2015 Edition

INDONESIA

3. Arrivals of non-resident tourists in hotels and similar establishments, by country of residence

	2009	2010	2011	2012	2013	Market share 2013	% Change 2013-2012
TOTAL	5,359,218	5,588,783	6,045,250	6,350,697	6,924,167	100.00	9.03
AFRICA	21,174	23,120	24,603	33,288	37,903	0.55	13.86
OTHER AFRICA	21,174	23,120	24,603	33,288	37,903	0.55	13.86
All countries of Africa	21,174	23,120	24,603	33,288	37,903	0.55	13.86
AMERICAS	185,259	210,438	170,264	238,521	253,170	3.66	6.14
CENTRAL AMERICA	5,201	1,260	1,987	2,258	2,175	0.03	-3.68
All countries of Central America	5,201	1,260	1,987	2,258	2,175	0.03	-3.68
NORTH AMERICA	163,674	181,180	139,925	203,774	219,343	3.17	7.64
Canada	27,711	33,200	41,964	43,424	43,592	0.63	0.39
United States of America	135,963	147,980	97,961	160,350	175,751	2.54	9.60
SOUTH AMERICA	16,384	20,416	21,223	23,047	24,735	0.36	7.32
All countries of South America	16,384	20,416	21,223	23,047	24,735	0.36	7.32
OTHER AMERICAS		7,582	7,129	9,442	6,917	0.10	-26.74
Other countries of the Americas		7,582	7,129	9,442	6,917	0.10	-26.74
EAST ASIA AND THE PACIFIC	4,161,852	4,259,161	4,705,662	4,899,415	5,309,223	76.68	8.36
NORTH-EAST ASIA	1,239,025	1,120,241	1,248,584	1,407,692	1,586,828	22.92	12.73
China	339,804	365,297	447,912	565,707	653,200	9.43	15.47
Hong Kong, China	59,967	61,860	64,945	74,318	94,547	1.37	27.22
Japan	444,071	280,671	282,152	316,617	342,497	4.95	8.17
Korea, Republic of	217,456	231,063	266,138	262,952	288,790	4.17	9.83
Taiwan, Province of China	177,727	181,350	187,437	188,098	207,794	3.00	10.47
SOUTH-EAST ASIA	2,463,107	2,428,002	2,612,808	2,609,396	2,775,291	40.08	6.36
Brunei Darussalam	10,904	26,856	37,230	20,761	18,119	0.26	-12.73
Malaysia	1,058,092	1,075,004	1,090,476	1,094,949	1,172,606	16.93	7.09
Philippines	125,899	117,348	144,464	144,836	155,023	2.24	7.03
Singapore	1,159,110	1,077,207	1,179,577	1,179,670	1,234,510	17.83	4.65
Thailand	87,299	102,440	120,196	124,632	121,796	1.76	-2.28
Other countries of South-East Asia	21,803	29,147	40,865	44,548	73,237	1.06	64.40
AUSTRALASIA	431,052	666,043	791,269	814,709	864,504	12.49	6.11
Australia	405,082	639,636	766,025	773,598	815,143	11.77	5.37
New Zealand	25,970	26,407	25,244	41,111	49,361	0.71	20.07
OTHER EAST ASIA AND THE PACIFIC	28,668	44,875	53,001	67,618	82,600	1.19	22.16
Other countries of Asia	23,949	40,685	47,894	62,687	77,450	1.12	23.55
Other countries of Oceania	4,719	4,190	5,107	4,931	5,150	0.07	4.44
EUROPE	805,587	880,989	867,694	917,623	1,012,408	14.62	10.33
CENTRAL/EASTERN EUROPE	111,354	123,035	131,738	136,386	147,200	2.13	7.93
USSR (former)	63,973	71,879	77,827	78,362	84,205	1.22	7.46
Other countries Central/East Europe	47,381	51,156	53,911	58,024	62,995	0.91	8.57
NORTHERN EUROPE	196,578	221,313	219,603	239,932	242,752	3.51	1.18
Denmark	16,158	14,769	16,277	19,673	16,796	0.24	-14.62
Finland	16,093	11,971	12,166	12,551	13,582	0.20	8.21
Norway	13,683	15,777	14,876	14,440	14,903	0.22	3.21
Sweden	18,348	21,540	22,976	19,489	24,242	0.35	24.39
United Kingdom	132,296	157,256	153,308	173,779	173,229	2.50	-0.32
SOUTHERN EUROPE	65,710	66,474	67,842	77,372	106,859	1.54	38.11
Italy	29,551	31,208	37,494	38,857	52,562	0.76	35.27
Portugal			9,255	13,789	20,894	0.30	51.53
Spain			21,093	24,726	33,403	0.48	35.09
Spain,Portugal	36,159	35,266					
WESTERN EUROPE	419,673	454,452	435,532	450,877	499,468	7.21	10.78
Austria	12,646	13,850	12,245	14,699	17,164	0.25	16.77
Belgium	19,523	19,476	18,293	19,969	24,525	0.35	22.82
France	135,691	141,744	123,323	143,067	156,368	2.26	9.30
Germany	105,490	122,015	119,879	124,138	137,790	1.99	11.00
Netherlands	116,644	126,671	132,048	119,160	127,518	1.84	7.01
Switzerland	29,679	30,696	29,744	29,844	36,103	0.52	20.97
OTHER EUROPE	12,272	15,715	12,979	13,056	16,129	0.23	23.54
Other countries of Europe	12,272	15,715	12,979	13,056	16,129	0.23	23.54
MIDDLE EAST	96,208	115,263	156,974	131,488	161,826	2.34	23.07

 Yearbook of Tourism Statistics, Data 2009 – 2013, 2015 Edition

INDONESIA

3. Arrivals of non-resident tourists in hotels and similar establishments, by country of residence

	2009	2010	2011	2012	2013	Market share 2013	% Change 2013-2012
Bahrain	525	1,379	1,490	1,548	1,133	0.02	-26.81
Egypt	2,302	2,263	1,941	3,701	4,658	0.07	25.86
Kuwait			3,303	4,461	6,327	0.09	41.83
Saudi Arabia	77,738	85,665	119,521	89,466	111,326	1.61	24.43
Other countries of Middle East	15,643	25,956	30,719	32,312	38,382	0.55	18.79
SOUTH ASIA	**89,138**	**99,812**	**120,053**	**130,362**	**149,637**	**2.16**	**14.79**
Bangladesh	4,550	5,551	7,203	9,471	7,629	0.11	-19.45
India	75,499	85,142	104,373	109,464	130,186	1.88	18.93
Pakistan	5,459	4,928	4,308	4,245	3,828	0.06	-9.82
Sri Lanka	3,630	4,191	4,169	7,182	7,994	0.12	11.31

Yearbook of Tourism Statistics, Data 2009 – 2013, 2015 Edition

IRAN, ISLAMIC REPUBLIC OF

2. Arrivals of non-resident visitors at national borders, by nationality

	2009	2010	2011	2012	2013	Market share 2013	% Change 2013-2012
TOTAL	2,116,245	2,938,054	3,353,713	3,833,577	4,768,836	100.00	24.40
AFRICA	4,080	5,568	6,831	11,938	17,000	0.36	42.40
EAST AFRICA	785	946	1,979	2,991	4,482	0.09	49.85
Ethiopia	182	349	479	1,117	1,390	0.03	24.44
Kenya	349	309	352	426	625	0.01	46.71
Somalia	41	74	204	156	448	0.01	187.18
Uganda	196	91	79	249	233	0.00	-6.43
United Republic of Tanzania			795	867	1,668	0.03	92.39
Zimbabwe	17	123	70	176	118	0.00	-32.95
NORTH AFRICA	1,326	1,437	1,482	4,281	5,323	0.11	24.34
Algeria	247	422	280	662	735	0.02	11.03
Morocco	241	198	173	1,249	2,259	0.05	80.86
Sudan	584	530	608	1,358	1,248	0.03	-8.10
Tunisia	254	287	421	1,012	1,081	0.02	6.82
WEST AFRICA	814	868	349	2,065	2,641	0.06	27.89
Gambia	33	17	6	27	15	0.00	-44.44
Ghana	86	114	86	367	545	0.01	48.50
Guinea	67	76	67	40	34	0.00	-15.00
Mali	51	53	70	124	92	0.00	-25.81
Mauritania	19	52	21	89	84	0.00	-5.62
Nigeria	365	383	38	1,298	1,729	0.04	33.20
Senegal	193	173	61	120	142	0.00	18.33
OTHER AFRICA	1,155	2,317	3,021	2,601	4,554	0.10	75.09
Other countries of Africa	1,155	2,317	3,021	2,601	4,554	0.10	75.09
AMERICAS	6,151	7,146	6,463	5,913	6,866	0.14	16.12
CARIBBEAN	141	53	94	133	112	0.00	-15.79
Bahamas	1	1		3	1	0.00	-66.67
Cuba	121	26	74	83	73	0.00	-12.05
Dominican Republic	19	26	20	47	38	0.00	-19.15
CENTRAL AMERICA	13	17	20	32	46	0.00	43.75
Guatemala	3	1	15	10	17	0.00	70.00
Panama	10	16	5	22	29	0.00	31.82
NORTH AMERICA	3,766	4,336	4,287	2,529	3,415	0.07	35.03
Canada	1,826	2,540	2,506	2,150	1,392	0.03	-35.26
Mexico	196	187	202	176	280	0.01	59.09
United States of America	1,744	1,609	1,579	203	1,743	0.04	758.62
SOUTH AMERICA	1,323	1,686	1,538	1,979	1,994	0.04	0.76
Argentina	188	193	214	344	305	0.01	-11.34
Brazil	588	835	735	727	809	0.02	11.28
Chile	89	67	84	98	79	0.00	-19.39
Colombia	111	116	109	162	167	0.00	3.09
Ecuador	56	92	97	186	143	0.00	-23.12
Peru	42	43	41	56	54	0.00	-3.57
Uruguay	40	35	40	27	30	0.00	11.11
Venezuela	209	305	218	379	407	0.01	7.39
OTHER AMERICAS	908	1,054	524	1,240	1,299	0.03	4.76
Other countries of the Americas	908	1,054	524	1,240	1,299	0.03	4.76
EAST ASIA AND THE PACIFIC	27,831	33,624	52,596	92,218	124,699	2.61	35.22
NORTH-EAST ASIA	18,960	22,088	37,497	40,817	51,440	1.08	26.03
China	4,378	7,648	22,728	26,160	34,795	0.73	33.01
Japan	5,647	5,592	4,937	5,143	5,809	0.12	12.95
Korea, Dem. People's Republic of	96	77	108	328	470	0.01	43.29
Korea, Republic of	7,270	7,017	8,075	8,117	8,867	0.19	9.24
Mongolia	21	42	52	67	82	0.00	22.39
Taiwan, Province of China	1,548	1,712	1,597	1,002	1,417	0.03	41.42
SOUTH-EAST ASIA	6,018	8,122	10,533	46,609	67,217	1.41	44.21
Indonesia	1,510	1,916	2,725	3,738	3,660	0.08	-2.09
Malaysia	187	1,748	3,157	3,779	3,628	0.08	-4.00
Philippines	2,046	2,399	2,286	36,420	56,550	1.19	55.27

345

IRAN, ISLAMIC REPUBLIC OF

2. Arrivals of non-resident visitors at national borders, by nationality

	2009	2010	2011	2012	2013	Market share 2013	% Change 2013-2012
Singapore	26	178	883	612	698	0.01	14.05
Thailand	2,094	1,689	1,348	1,647	2,243	0.05	36.19
Viet Nam	155	192	134	413	438	0.01	6.05
AUSTRALASIA	**2,853**	**3,414**	**4,399**	**4,222**	**5,238**	**0.11**	**24.06**
Australia	2,853	3,414	3,849	4,218	5,144	0.11	21.95
New Zealand			550	4	94	0.00	2,250.00
OTHER EAST ASIA AND THE PACIFIC			**167**	**570**	**804**	**0.02**	**41.05**
Other countries East Asia/Pacific			167	570	804	0.02	41.05
EUROPE	**856,435**	**1,172,489**	**1,473,742**	**1,327,724**	**1,779,638**	**37.32**	**34.04**
CENTRAL/EASTERN EUROPE	**482,542**	**813,294**	**907,696**	**871,163**	**1,303,687**	**27.34**	**49.65**
Armenia	1,154	1,023	6,777	7,089	7,280	0.15	2.69
Azerbaijan	383,588	690,333	732,201	677,457	1,077,713	22.60	59.08
Bulgaria	489	1,431	1,158	1,020	1,019	0.02	-0.10
Czech Republic	554	821	845	724	931	0.02	28.59
Georgia	323	194	3,203	3,359	7,103	0.15	111.46
Hungary	483	525	606	818	681	0.01	-16.75
Kazakhstan	613	1,222	1,794	1,904	2,261	0.05	18.75
Kyrgyzstan	188	402	560	821	1,010	0.02	23.02
Lithuania	81	133	212	171	280	0.01	63.74
Poland	821	1,052	1,066	7,718	1,864	0.04	-75.85
Romania	1,368	1,340	1,194	1,088	1,111	0.02	2.11
Russian Federation	6,155	11,281	13,413	14,146	19,159	0.40	35.44
Tajikistan	2,327	3,222	3,754	4,953	5,849	0.12	18.09
Turkmenistan	80,533	95,000	135,683	141,533	169,618	3.56	19.84
Ukraine	2,853	3,819	2,614	5,393	5,210	0.11	-3.39
Uzbekistan	1,012	1,496	2,616	2,969	2,598	0.05	-12.50
NORTHERN EUROPE	**16,026**	**17,195**	**16,482**	**16,897**	**18,958**	**0.40**	**12.20**
Denmark	2,142	2,158	2,016	2,184	2,538	0.05	16.21
Finland	673	578	680	679	776	0.02	14.29
Iceland	100	30	71	49	40	0.00	-18.37
Ireland	638	701	730	689	738	0.02	7.11
Norway	1,806	1,655	1,840	1,836	2,610	0.05	42.16
Sweden	3,941	4,257	4,594	7,618	6,807	0.14	-10.65
United Kingdom	6,726	7,816	6,551	3,842	5,449	0.11	41.83
SOUTHERN EUROPE	**16,073**	**14,117**	**15,149**	**15,012**	**20,732**	**0.43**	**38.10**
Albania	88	72	87	101	98	0.00	-2.97
Bosnia and Herzegovina	124	189	223	233	369	0.01	58.37
Greece	945	758	702	1,163	1,572	0.03	35.17
Italy	10,982	9,167	10,010	9,576	13,019	0.27	35.95
Montenegro		18	35	24	29	0.00	20.83
Portugal	502	505	504	623	713	0.01	14.45
Serbia	183	341	427	431	482	0.01	11.83
Slovenia	713	544	489	588	842	0.02	43.20
Spain	2,536	2,523	2,672	2,273	3,608	0.08	58.73
WESTERN EUROPE	**38,882**	**37,790**	**35,327**	**31,117**	**42,818**	**0.90**	**37.60**
Austria	4,200	3,480	3,292	2,692	3,319	0.07	23.29
Belgium	489	1,431	1,444	1,284	1,613	0.03	25.62
France	8,037	6,057	5,993	5,863	7,271	0.15	24.02
Germany	18,072	18,488	16,851	17,981	21,242	0.45	18.14
Luxembourg	41	44	41	42	48	0.00	14.29
Netherlands	5,739	6,240	5,466	1,268	6,953	0.15	448.34
Switzerland	2,304	2,050	2,240	1,987	2,372	0.05	19.38
EAST MEDITERRANEAN EUROPE	**300,015**	**288,165**	**419,973**	**392,757**	**391,400**	**8.21**	**-0.35**
Cyprus	187	134	120	142	117	0.00	-17.61
Turkey	299,828	288,031	419,853	392,615	391,283	8.21	-0.34
OTHER EUROPE	**2,897**	**1,928**	**79,115**	**778**	**2,043**	**0.04**	**162.60**
Other countries of Europe	2,897	1,928	79,115	778	2,043	0.04	162.60
MIDDLE EAST	**518,819**	**740,004**	**782,096**	**1,332,984**	**1,976,623**	**41.45**	**48.29**
Bahrain	14,689	36,837	13,362	44,249	60,569	1.27	36.88

346

IRAN, ISLAMIC REPUBLIC OF

2. Arrivals of non-resident visitors at national borders, by nationality

	2009	2010	2011	2012	2013	Market share 2013	% Change 2013-2012
Egypt	857	975	1,415	3,199	3,687	0.08	15.25
Iraq	440,989	548,008	589,074	1,055,447	1,603,920	33.63	51.97
Jordan	850	860	786	1,091	1,252	0.03	14.76
Kuwait	16,302	49,572	54,641	68,454	81,646	1.71	19.27
Lebanon	11,947	17,416	20,484	18,586	36,353	0.76	95.59
Libya	103	128	261	478	148	0.00	-69.04
Oman	7,707	10,816	9,798	12,120	16,671	0.35	37.55
Palestine	167	96	197	419	432	0.01	3.10
Qatar	1,300	2,568	2,417	2,921	2,522	0.05	-13.66
Saudi Arabia	14,601	60,107	74,275	111,049	155,196	3.25	39.75
Syrian Arab Republic	4,117	2,891	8,442	8,886	7,457	0.16	-16.08
United Arab Emirates	5,022	9,607	6,719	5,506	6,152	0.13	11.73
Yemen	168	123	225	579	618	0.01	6.74
SOUTH ASIA	**314,314**	**413,180**	**426,896**	**537,825**	**621,224**	**13.03**	**15.51**
Afghanistan	175,155	214,649	202,369	308,183	392,559	8.23	27.38
Bangladesh	655	653	819	1,891	2,651	0.06	40.19
India	22,277	23,903	34,770	54,263	70,705	1.48	30.30
Maldives	46	44	49	28	43	0.00	53.57
Nepal	187	208	235	829	1,156	0.02	39.45
Pakistan	115,459	173,068	187,920	170,754	151,470	3.18	-11.29
Sri Lanka	535	655	734	1,877	2,640	0.06	40.65
NOT SPECIFIED	**388,615**	**566,043**	**605,089**	**524,975**	**242,786**	**5.09**	**-53.75**
Other countries of the World	388,615	566,043	605,089	378,137	76,344	1.60	-79.81
Nationals Residing Abroad				146,838	166,442	3.49	13.35

Yearbook of Tourism Statistics, Data 2009 – 2013, 2015 Edition

IRAQ

2. Arrivals of non-resident visitors at national borders, by nationality

	2009	2010	2011	2012	2013	Market share 2013	% Change 2013-2012
TOTAL	1,261,921	1,517,766	1,510,174	1,111,492	891,836	100.00	-19.76
AFRICA	24	44	34	856	182	0.02	-78.74
EAST AFRICA	5	44	34	856	182	0.02	-78.74
Madagascar	3			37	49	0.01	32.43
Mauritius		44	8	10	20	0.00	100.00
United Republic of Tanzania	2		26	809	113	0.01	-86.03
WEST AFRICA	19						
Nigeria	19						
AMERICAS	42	30	26	1,070	767	0.09	-28.32
NORTH AMERICA	42	30	26	1,070	767	0.09	-28.32
Canada		6	11	491	300	0.03	-38.90
United States of America	42	24	15	579	467	0.05	-19.34
EAST ASIA AND THE PACIFIC		35	122	71	208	0.02	192.96
NORTH-EAST ASIA		1	2				
Japan		1	2				
SOUTH-EAST ASIA		34	120	71	208	0.02	192.96
Indonesia		34	120	71	208	0.02	192.96
EUROPE	8,564	3,483	6,878	19,290	17,255	1.93	-10.55
CENTRAL/EASTERN EUROPE	7,775	2,246	5,776	12,923	15,490	1.74	19.86
Azerbaijan	7,717	2,246	5,776	12,923	15,490	1.74	19.86
Russian Federation	58						
NORTHERN EUROPE		28	44	1,407	646	0.07	-54.09
Ireland		1		17			
United Kingdom		27	44	1,390	646	0.07	-53.53
WESTERN EUROPE	27		12	134	150	0.02	11.94
France	27		12	134	150	0.02	11.94
EAST MEDITERRANEAN EUROPE	762	1,209	1,046	4,826	969	0.11	-79.92
Turkey	762	1,209	1,046	4,826	969	0.11	-79.92
MIDDLE EAST	10,752	15,076	10,187	395	146	0.02	-63.04
Bahrain	6,258	7,021	3,052				
Jordan		130	9				
Kuwait	94	820	171				
Lebanon	1,916	4,466	5,476	5			
Saudi Arabia	2,423	2,490	1,162				
Syrian Arab Republic		104	287	251	40	0.00	-84.06
United Arab Emirates	35	45	27	5	20	0.00	300.00
Yemen	26		3	134	86	0.01	-35.82
SOUTH ASIA	1,194,149	1,443,151	1,480,125	1,064,726	859,859	96.41	-19.24
Afghanistan	382	1,673	7,674	8,845	8,857	0.99	0.14
Bangladesh	346	11		305			
India	13,876	13,860	17,949	27,530	25,726	2.88	-6.55
Iran, Islamic Republic of	1,161,541	1,413,792	1,430,908	989,787	787,195	88.27	-20.47
Pakistan	18,004	13,815	23,594	38,259	38,081	4.27	-0.47
NOT SPECIFIED	48,390	55,947	12,802	25,084	13,419	1.50	-46.50
Other countries of the World	48,390	55,947	12,802	25,084	13,419	1.50	-46.50

Yearbook of Tourism Statistics, Data 2009 – 2013, 2015 Edition

IRELAND

1. Arrivals of non-resident tourists at national borders, by country of residence

		2009	2010	2011	2012	2013	Market share 2013	% Change 2013-2012
TOTAL		7,189,000	7,134,000	7,630,000	7,549,000	8,261,000	100.00	9.43
AFRICA		43,000			40,000	38,000	0.46	-5.00
OTHER AFRICA		43,000			40,000	38,000	0.46	-5.00
All countries of Africa		43,000			40,000	38,000	0.46	-5.00
AMERICAS		921,000	864,000	917,000	988,000	1,092,000	13.22	10.53
NORTH AMERICA		891,000	864,000	917,000	940,000	1,039,000	12.58	10.53
Canada		82,000	86,000	99,000	107,000	115,000	1.39	7.48
United States of America		809,000	778,000	818,000	833,000	924,000	11.19	10.92
OTHER AMERICAS		30,000			48,000	53,000	0.64	10.42
Other countries of the Americas		30,000			48,000	53,000	0.64	10.42
EAST ASIA AND THE PACIFIC		233,000	135,000	141,000	289,000	341,000	4.13	17.99
NORTH-EAST ASIA		11,000						
Japan		11,000						
AUSTRALASIA		132,000	135,000	141,000	158,000	192,000	2.32	21.52
Australia		113,000						
New Zealand		19,000						
Australia, New Zealand			135,000	141,000	158,000	192,000	2.32	21.52
OTHER EAST ASIA AND THE PACIFIC		90,000			131,000	149,000	1.80	13.74
Other countries East Asia/Pacific		90,000			131,000	149,000	1.80	13.74
EUROPE		5,992,000	5,959,000	6,361,000	6,232,000	6,790,000	82.19	8.95
CENTRAL/EASTERN EUROPE		258,000			159,000	152,000	1.84	-4.40
Czech Republic		35,000						
Poland		223,000			159,000	152,000	1.84	-4.40
NORTHERN EUROPE		3,769,000	3,948,000	4,129,000	4,098,000	4,567,000	55.28	11.44
Denmark		45,000			42,000	51,000	0.62	21.43
Sweden		59,000			70,000	72,000	0.87	2.86
United Kingdom	(*)	3,665,000	3,948,000	4,129,000	3,986,000	4,444,000	53.79	11.49
SOUTHERN EUROPE		532,000	428,000	450,000	479,000	475,000	5.75	-0.84
Italy		276,000	214,000	213,000	240,000	226,000	2.74	-5.83
Spain		256,000	214,000	237,000	239,000	249,000	3.01	4.18
WESTERN EUROPE		1,128,000	725,000	820,000	1,164,000	1,242,000	15.03	6.70
Austria		45,000			46,000	51,000	0.62	10.87
Belgium		93,000			82,000	95,000	1.15	15.85
France		390,000	344,000	400,000	384,000	409,000	4.95	6.51
Germany		408,000	381,000	420,000	437,000	466,000	5.64	6.64
Netherlands		134,000			137,000	148,000	1.79	8.03
Switzerland		58,000			78,000	73,000	0.88	-6.41
OTHER EUROPE		305,000	858,000	962,000	332,000	354,000	4.29	6.63
Other countries of Europe		305,000	858,000	962,000	332,000	354,000	4.29	6.63
NOT SPECIFIED			176,000	211,000				
Other countries of the World			176,000	211,000				

Yearbook of Tourism Statistics, Data 2009 – 2013, 2015 Edition

IRELAND

6. Overnight stays of non-resident tourists in all types of accommodation establishments, by country of residence

		2009	2010	2011	2012	2013	Market share 2013	% Change 2013-2012
TOTAL	(*)	**52,917,000**	**53,045,000**	**55,248,000**	**52,075,000**	**55,934,000**	**100.00**	**7.41**
AMERICAS		**8,252,000**	**8,780,000**	**8,904,000**	**8,775,000**	**9,563,000**	**17.10**	**8.98**
NORTH AMERICA		**8,252,000**	**8,780,000**	**8,904,000**	**8,775,000**	**9,563,000**	**17.10**	**8.98**
Canada		1,019,000	1,064,000	1,055,000				
United States of America		7,233,000	7,716,000	7,849,000				
All countries of North America					8,775,000	9,563,000	17.10	8.98
EAST ASIA AND THE PACIFIC		**1,565,000**			**1,835,000**	**2,284,000**	**4.08**	**24.47**
AUSTRALASIA		**1,565,000**			**1,835,000**	**2,284,000**	**4.08**	**24.47**
Australia		1,565,000			1,835,000	2,284,000	4.08	24.47
EUROPE		**39,935,000**	**39,662,000**	**41,374,000**	**38,409,000**	**40,573,000**	**72.54**	**5.63**
NORTHERN EUROPE		**15,438,000**	**18,624,000**	**18,217,000**	**17,102,000**	**18,689,000**	**33.41**	**9.28**
United Kingdom	(*)	15,438,000	18,624,000	18,217,000	17,102,000	18,689,000	33.41	9.28
SOUTHERN EUROPE		**5,667,000**	**4,648,000**	**5,740,000**	**2,353,000**	**2,091,000**	**3.74**	**-11.13**
Italy		2,624,000	2,049,000	2,608,000	2,353,000	2,091,000	3.74	-11.13
Spain		3,043,000	2,599,000	3,132,000				
WESTERN EUROPE		**11,412,000**	**7,247,000**	**8,353,000**	**7,553,000**	**8,357,000**	**14.94**	**10.64**
Belgium		754,000						
France		5,049,000	3,531,000	4,491,000	3,615,000	3,879,000	6.93	7.30
Germany		4,044,000	3,716,000	3,862,000	3,938,000	4,478,000	8.01	13.71
Netherlands		954,000						
Switzerland		611,000						
OTHER EUROPE		**7,418,000**	**9,143,000**	**9,064,000**	**11,401,000**	**11,436,000**	**20.45**	**0.31**
Other countries of Europe		7,418,000	9,143,000	9,064,000	11,401,000	11,436,000	20.45	0.31
NOT SPECIFIED		**3,165,000**	**4,603,000**	**4,970,000**	**3,056,000**	**3,514,000**	**6.28**	**14.99**
Other countries of the World		3,165,000	4,603,000	4,970,000	3,056,000	3,514,000	6.28	14.99

Yearbook of Tourism Statistics, Data 2009 – 2013, 2015 Edition

ISRAEL

1. Arrivals of non-resident tourists at national borders, by country of residence

	2009	2010	2011	2012	2013	Market share 2013	% Change 2013-2012
TOTAL (*)	2,321,267	2,803,125	2,820,218	2,885,828	2,961,701	100.00	2.63
AFRICA	75,615	72,080	85,389	71,106	68,597	2.32	-3.53
EAST AFRICA	5,627	8,773	9,276	8,924	9,732	0.33	9.05
Burundi	57	108	53	76	93	0.00	22.37
Comoros			5	1	2	0.00	100.00
Eritrea	59	291	319	369	358	0.01	-2.98
Ethiopia	1,852	3,191	3,445	2,780	2,909	0.10	4.64
Kenya	1,318	2,428	2,744	2,297	2,489	0.08	8.36
Madagascar	79	53	65	79	75	0.00	-5.06
Malawi	83	110	107	106	108	0.00	1.89
Mauritius	291	286	248	376	483	0.02	28.46
Mozambique	50	55	52	170	80	0.00	-52.94
Rwanda	158	158	155	187	314	0.01	67.91
Seychelles	13	18	22	29	47	0.00	62.07
Somalia			2	1	4	0.00	300.00
Uganda	596	658	671	882	935	0.03	6.01
United Republic of Tanzania	584	744	705	683	653	0.02	-4.39
Zambia	130	181	165	174	205	0.01	17.82
Zimbabwe	357	492	518	714	977	0.03	36.83
CENTRAL AFRICA	1,439	1,425	1,696	2,223	2,579	0.09	16.01
Angola	433	598	689	734	1,015	0.03	38.28
Cameroon	400	492	475	491	413	0.01	-15.89
Central African Republic	34	57	113	99	56	0.00	-43.43
Chad	19	8	27	32	37	0.00	15.63
Congo	358	152	178	170	198	0.01	16.47
Democratic Republic of the Congo	64			446	594	0.02	33.18
Equatorial Guinea		36	92	32	67	0.00	109.38
Gabon	131	82	122	219	199	0.01	-9.13
NORTH AFRICA	3,395	3,462	3,568	3,235	3,411	0.12	5.44
Algeria	15	4	12	18	4	0.00	-77.78
Morocco	2,305	2,473	2,409	2,289	2,492	0.08	8.87
Sudan	1	3	24	14	8	0.00	-42.86
Tunisia	1,074	982	1,123	914	907	0.03	-0.77
SOUTHERN AFRICA	18,210	23,694	22,320	24,341	23,758	0.80	-2.40
Lesotho	21	16	18	32	34	0.00	6.25
Namibia	93	2,473	90	233	181	0.01	-22.32
South Africa	18,055	21,130	22,094	23,975	23,501	0.79	-1.98
Swaziland	41	75	118	101	42	0.00	-58.42
WEST AFRICA	46,772	34,296	48,072	32,265	28,856	0.97	-10.57
Benin	88	114	169	183	155	0.01	-15.30
Burkina Faso	141	118	152	206	197	0.01	-4.37
Cabo Verde	59	18	14	35	11	0.00	-68.57
Côte d'Ivoire	938	1,054	798	611	1,230	0.04	101.31
Gambia	13	55	17	59	13	0.00	-77.97
Ghana	488	708	1,146	1,186	1,633	0.06	37.69
Guinea	64	185	34	52	137	0.00	163.46
Guinea-Bissau	8	5	1	8	34	0.00	325.00
Liberia	45	67	63	40	42	0.00	5.00
Mali	32	67	26	41	53	0.00	29.27
Mauritania	5		2	1	1	0.00	
Niger	353	29	33	44	37	0.00	-15.91
Nigeria	43,866	31,616	44,972	29,437	24,557	0.83	-16.58
Senegal	486	110	510	126	547	0.02	334.13
Sierra Leone	40	58	57	44	54	0.00	22.73
Togo	146	92	78	192	155	0.01	-19.27
OTHER AFRICA	172	430	457	118	261	0.01	121.19
Other countries of Africa	172	430	457	118	261	0.01	121.19
AMERICAS	686,651	809,400	776,156	790,983	803,480	27.13	1.58
CARIBBEAN	1,895	2,419	2,366	2,095	2,520	0.09	20.29

351

ISRAEL

1. Arrivals of non-resident tourists at national borders, by country of residence

	2009	2010	2011	2012	2013	Market share 2013	% Change 2013-2012
Antigua and Barbuda	9	22	12	23	18	0.00	-21.74
Bahamas	275	59	95	60	92	0.00	53.33
Barbados	65	42	129	108	110	0.00	1.85
Bermuda	4	3	17	6	8	0.00	33.33
Cayman Islands	17	30	3	34	7	0.00	-79.41
Cuba	146	145	161	159	225	0.01	41.51
Dominica	26	43	34	17	23	0.00	35.29
Dominican Republic	646	1,020	847	659	993	0.03	50.68
Grenada	16	24	24	11	23	0.00	109.09
Haiti	131	118	207	154	128	0.00	-16.88
Jamaica	173	237	193	291	206	0.01	-29.21
Montserrat		1					
Puerto Rico	1	1					
Saint Kitts and Nevis	15	16	16	19	33	0.00	73.68
Saint Lucia	6	71	13	17	16	0.00	-5.88
Saint Vincent and the Grenadines	5	10	14	10	21	0.00	110.00
Trinidad and Tobago	359	575	595	526	613	0.02	16.54
Turks and Caicos Islands	1	2	5	1	4	0.00	300.00
United States Virgin Islands			1				
CENTRAL AMERICA	**5,293**	**7,793**	**6,665**	**8,047**	**7,691**	**0.26**	**-4.42**
Belize	18	30	34	38	39	0.00	2.63
Costa Rica	1,525	2,260	1,995	2,503	2,126	0.07	-15.06
El Salvador	672	1,123	743	879	858	0.03	-2.39
Guatemala	915	1,323	1,125	1,369	1,301	0.04	-4.97
Honduras	394	672	672	699	793	0.03	13.45
Nicaragua	142	172	220	292	301	0.01	3.08
Panama	1,627	2,213	1,876	2,267	2,273	0.08	0.26
NORTH AMERICA	**612,419**	**697,981**	**664,145**	**670,101**	**683,874**	**23.09**	**2.06**
Canada	59,492	70,172	64,388	64,964	65,308	2.21	0.53
Mexico	14,952	22,694	18,711	21,532	21,371	0.72	-0.75
United States of America	537,975	605,115	581,046	583,605	597,195	20.16	2.33
SOUTH AMERICA	**67,044**	**101,207**	**102,980**	**110,740**	**109,395**	**3.69**	**-1.21**
Argentina	16,003	22,286	21,628	23,249	24,461	0.83	5.21
Bolivia	512	607	686	804	784	0.03	-2.49
Brazil	27,891	48,778	53,054	56,637	53,987	1.82	-4.68
Chile	4,244	5,832	5,687	5,470	5,955	0.20	8.87
Colombia	7,896	10,933	9,506	10,984	10,555	0.36	-3.91
Ecuador	2,701	3,495	3,352	3,084	2,756	0.09	-10.64
Guyana	28	41	67	32	32	0.00	
Paraguay	332	524	481	459	697	0.02	51.85
Peru	2,336	3,276	2,811	3,622	3,868	0.13	6.79
Suriname	31	48	42	49	86	0.00	75.51
Uruguay	2,275	2,615	2,556	2,465	2,644	0.09	7.26
Venezuela	2,794	2,768	3,108	3,885	3,569	0.12	-8.13
Other countries of South America	1	4	2		1	0.00	
EAST ASIA AND THE PACIFIC	**94,765**	**142,345**	**147,149**	**171,826**	**182,065**	**6.15**	**5.96**
NORTH-EAST ASIA	**39,503**	**64,219**	**66,233**	**73,429**	**76,859**	**2.60**	**4.67**
China	7,570	12,890	16,806	19,276	24,942	0.84	29.39
Hong Kong, China	2,186	4,052	3,258	4,223	4,796	0.16	13.57
Japan	9,768	13,165	13,444	16,011	13,516	0.46	-15.58
Korea, Dem. People's Republic of		16		24			
Korea, Republic of	17,299	29,953	28,005	28,606	28,067	0.95	-1.88
Macao, China	59	53	49	140	100	0.00	-28.57
Mongolia	107	197	193	178	179	0.01	0.56
Taiwan, Province of China	2,514	3,893	4,478	4,971	5,259	0.18	5.79
SOUTH-EAST ASIA	**28,553**	**43,071**	**48,071**	**63,874**	**67,929**	**2.29**	**6.35**
Brunei Darussalam	1	2	12	2	4	0.00	100.00
Cambodia	24	48	69	113	211	0.01	86.73
Indonesia	9,587	17,742	21,946	27,752	29,463	0.99	6.17

352

Yearbook of Tourism Statistics, Data 2009 – 2013, 2015 Edition

ISRAEL

1. Arrivals of non-resident tourists at national borders, by country of residence

	2009	2010	2011	2012	2013	Market share 2013	% Change 2013-2012
Lao People's Democratic Republic	67	150	240	319	394	0.01	23.51
Malaysia	634	1,583	2,943	6,502	9,168	0.31	41.00
Myanmar		372	343	595	647	0.02	8.74
Philippines	7,321	10,241	9,376	12,187	11,255	0.38	-7.65
Singapore	6,468	8,659	8,270	10,246	10,620	0.36	3.65
Thailand	3,397	2,958	3,227	4,273	3,819	0.13	-10.62
Timor-Leste		1	42	47	32	0.00	-31.91
Viet Nam	1,054	1,315	1,603	1,838	2,316	0.08	26.01
AUSTRALASIA	**26,215**	**34,622**	**32,273**	**33,677**	**36,179**	**1.22**	**7.43**
Australia	23,543	30,738	28,889	30,082	32,486	1.10	7.99
New Zealand	2,672	3,884	3,384	3,595	3,693	0.12	2.73
MELANESIA	**210**	**398**	**530**	**787**	**991**	**0.03**	**25.92**
Fiji	116	194	358	439	540	0.02	23.01
Papua New Guinea	76	178	146	311	428	0.01	37.62
Solomon Islands	6	10	9	16	15	0.00	-6.25
Vanuatu	12	16	17	21	8	0.00	-61.90
MICRONESIA	**4**	**11**	**16**	**7**	**27**	**0.00**	**285.71**
Kiribati		2	3	3	11	0.00	266.67
Micronesia, Federated States of	3	8	3	4	7	0.00	75.00
Palau	1	1	10		9	0.00	
POLYNESIA	**6**	**18**	**26**	**22**	**38**	**0.00**	**72.73**
American Samoa	6	1	1	5	2	0.00	-60.00
Samoa		7	5	17	15	0.00	-11.76
Tonga		10	20		21	0.00	
OTHER EAST ASIA AND THE PACIFIC	**274**	**6**		**30**	**42**	**0.00**	**40.00**
Other countries of Asia	259			6	17	0.00	183.33
Other countries of Oceania	15	6		24	25	0.00	4.17
EUROPE	**1,406,930**	**1,704,345**	**1,730,182**	**1,761,124**	**1,826,015**	**61.65**	**3.68**
CENTRAL/EASTERN EUROPE	**435,618**	**576,584**	**652,760**	**686,727**	**715,909**	**24.17**	**4.25**
Armenia	811	1,503	1,404	1,867	1,871	0.06	0.21
Azerbaijan	2,695	2,912	2,851	3,139	3,007	0.10	-4.21
Belarus	9,655	11,420	11,800	14,229	15,112	0.51	6.21
Bulgaria	6,148	7,165	7,489	7,135	6,741	0.23	-5.52
Czech Republic	10,943	13,709	13,028	13,807	14,976	0.51	8.47
Estonia	3,057	5,252	3,555	3,254	2,467	0.08	-24.19
Georgia	4,555	4,477	4,312	4,349	4,080	0.14	-6.19
Hungary	9,433	11,787	11,418	9,316	14,570	0.49	56.40
Kazakhstan	4,534	6,501	9,603	10,914	9,362	0.32	-14.22
Kyrgyzstan	411	496	634	698	702	0.02	0.57
Latvia	4,168	4,749	5,370	5,573	5,368	0.18	-3.68
Lithuania	4,153	5,124	5,093	5,580	6,467	0.22	15.90
Poland	53,840	69,435	60,410	58,860	67,280	2.27	14.31
Republic of Moldova	3,121	4,434	3,630	3,968	3,580	0.12	-9.78
Romania	28,881	38,475	37,790	39,631	34,597	1.17	-12.70
Russian Federation	231,366	318,472	353,419	380,737	404,989	13.67	6.37
Slovakia	8,143	11,595	10,194	10,119	8,437	0.28	-16.62
Tajikistan	181	251	319	367	630	0.02	71.66
Turkmenistan	165	122	125	232	245	0.01	5.60
Ukraine	46,455	55,296	106,807	109,156	108,019	3.65	-1.04
USSR (former)	13	7	4	3	2	0.00	-33.33
Uzbekistan	2,890	3,402	3,505	3,793	3,407	0.12	-10.18
NORTHERN EUROPE	**230,856**	**247,409**	**251,117**	**246,755**	**260,471**	**8.79**	**5.56**
Denmark	12,740	15,182	18,934	18,604	19,190	0.65	3.15
Finland	17,776	19,503	18,255	17,476	18,716	0.63	7.10
Iceland	234	355	320	315	299	0.01	-5.08
Ireland	7,490	9,145	8,864	7,564	8,074	0.27	6.74
Norway	12,050	14,209	15,993	15,485	16,380	0.55	5.78
Sweden	17,029	20,246	20,739	22,211	24,495	0.83	10.28
United Kingdom	163,537	168,769	168,012	165,100	173,317	5.85	4.98

353

ISRAEL

1. Arrivals of non-resident tourists at national borders, by country of residence

	2009	2010	2011	2012	2013	Market share 2013	% Change 2013-2012
SOUTHERN EUROPE	204,631	264,267	206,805	220,733	217,294	7.34	-1.56
Albania	659	473	545	497	746	0.03	50.10
Andorra	50	66	54	57	74	0.00	29.82
Bosnia and Herzegovina	345	418	643	396	406	0.01	2.53
Croatia	5,291	6,097	5,124	5,317	4,648	0.16	-12.58
Greece	18,408	24,200	18,979	20,419	17,991	0.61	-11.89
Holy See	289	270	250	263	306	0.01	16.35
Italy	116,489	150,176	113,307	126,245	127,739	4.31	1.18
Malta	1,514	2,209	1,215	1,960	1,343	0.05	-31.48
Montenegro		394	322	469	330	0.01	-29.64
Portugal	6,886	13,557	8,458	8,352	8,789	0.30	5.23
San Marino	98	104	64	99	90	0.00	-9.09
Serbia	1,397	2,964	4,063	3,725	4,000	0.14	7.38
Serbia and Montenegro	98	60	113				
Slovenia	2,189	2,560	1,965	2,228	2,180	0.07	-2.15
Spain	48,994	59,737	51,033	50,106	47,885	1.62	-4.43
TFYR of Macedonia	580	621	563	598	767	0.03	28.26
Yugoslavia, SFR (former)	1,344	361	107	2			
WESTERN EUROPE	512,922	591,976	595,797	581,388	602,927	20.36	3.70
Austria	23,574	28,805	27,738	27,936	26,912	0.91	-3.67
Belgium	23,732	31,192	31,769	31,310	32,509	1.10	3.83
France	253,969	274,114	269,454	263,629	292,305	9.87	10.88
Germany	139,806	171,487	170,987	158,463	159,797	5.40	0.84
Liechtenstein	56	76	80	105	124	0.00	18.10
Luxembourg	639	728	776	777	761	0.03	-2.06
Monaco	24	87	44	49	57	0.00	16.33
Netherlands	44,511	53,377	58,668	61,981	52,037	1.76	-16.04
Switzerland	26,611	32,110	36,281	37,138	38,425	1.30	3.47
EAST MEDITERRANEAN EUROPE	22,862	24,109	23,703	25,415	29,289	0.99	15.24
Cyprus	9,428	10,432	10,206	9,165	6,812	0.23	-25.67
Turkey	13,434	13,677	13,497	16,250	22,477	0.76	38.32
OTHER EUROPE	41			106	125	0.00	17.92
Other countries of Europe	41			106	125	0.00	17.92
MIDDLE EAST	18,069	20,928	23,230	27,693	22,517	0.76	-18.69
Bahrain		3	1		4	0.00	
Egypt	2,263	2,586	2,449	3,797	4,062	0.14	6.98
Iraq	123	158	157	167	139	0.00	-16.77
Jordan	15,039	17,824	20,263	23,369	17,936	0.61	-23.25
Kuwait	31	5	8	4	5	0.00	25.00
Lebanon	398	224	239	252	239	0.01	-5.16
Libya	8	3	3	1	2	0.00	100.00
Oman	1	1	4	3	4	0.00	33.33
Qatar	10	9	8	2	5	0.00	150.00
Saudi Arabia		4			1	0.00	
Syrian Arab Republic	125	84	67	61	73	0.00	19.67
United Arab Emirates		15	8		3	0.00	
Yemen	71	12	23	37	44	0.00	18.92
SOUTH ASIA	25,746	43,080	41,425	46,795	43,397	1.47	-7.26
Afghanistan	1	6	2	2			
Bangladesh	10	16	9	16	41	0.00	156.25
Bhutan		4	25	30	60	0.00	100.00
India	23,058	40,109	38,481	42,992	39,025	1.32	-9.23
Iran, Islamic Republic of	400	474	409	304	310	0.01	1.97
Maldives	9	30	64	103	92	0.00	-10.68
Nepal	894	493	471	433	612	0.02	41.34
Pakistan	11	5	9	6	11	0.00	83.33
Sri Lanka	1,363	1,943	1,955	2,909	3,246	0.11	11.58
NOT SPECIFIED	13,491	10,947	16,687	16,301	15,630	0.53	-4.12
Other countries of the World	13,491	10,947	16,687	16,301	15,630	0.53	-4.12

354

ISRAEL

2. Arrivals of non-resident visitors at national borders, by country of residence

		2009	2010	2011	2012	2013	Market share 2013	% Change 2013-2012
TOTAL	(*)	**2,739,737**	**3,443,988**	**3,362,073**	**3,520,347**	**3,539,666**	**100.00**	**0.55**
AFRICA		**78,496**	**72,692**	**88,429**	**74,859**	**70,914**	**2.00**	**-5.27**
EAST AFRICA		**7,795**	**10,777**	**11,258**	**11,469**	**11,242**	**0.32**	**-1.98**
Burundi		57	109	53	76	93	0.00	22.37
Comoros				5	1	2	0.00	100.00
Eritrea		59	291	324	369	359	0.01	-2.71
Ethiopia		3,965	5,118	5,341	5,201	4,217	0.12	-18.92
Kenya		1,358	2,434	2,771	2,308	2,517	0.07	9.06
Madagascar		79	54	67	83	78	0.00	-6.02
Malawi		86	111	107	107	109	0.00	1.87
Mauritius		293	293	279	461	639	0.02	38.61
Mozambique		50	57	55	170	82	0.00	-51.76
Rwanda		158	160	155	187	316	0.01	68.98
Seychelles		13	63	22	32	47	0.00	46.88
Somalia				2	1	4	0.00	300.00
Uganda		598	659	680	883	939	0.03	6.34
United Republic of Tanzania		587	745	705	684	653	0.02	-4.53
Zambia		130	181	167	176	205	0.01	16.48
Zimbabwe		362	502	525	730	982	0.03	34.52
CENTRAL AFRICA		**1,453**	**1,455**	**1,703**	**2,331**	**2,628**	**0.07**	**12.74**
Angola		435	608	765	796	1,017	0.03	27.76
Cameroon		404	494	498	501	416	0.01	-16.97
Central African Republic		37	65	115	103	72	0.00	-30.10
Chad		19	9	27	40	39	0.00	-2.50
Congo		361	157	182	174	200	0.01	14.94
Democratic Republic of the Congo		64			456	613	0.02	34.43
Equatorial Guinea			36	92	34	67	0.00	97.06
Gabon		133	86	24	227	204	0.01	-10.13
NORTH AFRICA		**3,408**	**3,514**	**3,624**	**3,295**	**3,476**	**0.10**	**5.49**
Algeria		15	5	14	18	4	0.00	-77.78
Morocco		2,313	2,516	2,449	2,332	2,551	0.07	9.39
Sudan		1	3	24	20	8	0.00	-60.00
Tunisia		1,079	990	1,137	925	913	0.03	-1.30
SOUTHERN AFRICA		**18,706**	**22,053**	**23,134**	**25,091**	**24,405**	**0.69**	**-2.73**
Lesotho		22	19	20	32	34	0.00	6.25
Namibia		93	105	90	241	156	0.00	-35.27
South Africa		18,550	21,826	22,886	24,713	24,170	0.68	-2.20
Swaziland		41	103	138	105	45	0.00	-57.14
WEST AFRICA		**46,908**	**34,451**	**48,248**	**32,546**	**28,932**	**0.82**	**-11.10**
Benin		88	118	193	226	155	0.00	-31.42
Burkina Faso		142	118	154	208	197	0.01	-5.29
Cabo Verde		59	19	14	36	11	0.00	-69.44
Côte d'Ivoire		969	1,087	802	640	1,255	0.04	96.09
Gambia		13	55	17	59	15	0.00	-74.58
Ghana		516	716	1,155	1,227	1,661	0.05	35.37
Guinea		68	185	36	52	138	0.00	165.38
Liberia		45	68	63	40	42	0.00	5.00
Mali		32	67	26	41	53	0.00	29.27
Mauritania		5		6	1	1	0.00	
Niger		353	29	38	44	37	0.00	-15.91
Nigeria		43,942	31,723	45,093	29,602	24,608	0.70	-16.87
Senegal		486	111	515	132	549	0.02	315.91
Sierra Leone		40	58	57	46	55	0.00	19.57
Togo		150	97	79	192	155	0.00	-19.27
OTHER AFRICA		**226**	**442**	**462**	**127**	**231**	**0.01**	**81.89**
Other countries of Africa		226	442	462	127	231	0.01	81.89
AMERICAS		**734,596**	**879,191**	**855,218**	**844,992**	**843,208**	**23.82**	**-0.21**
CARIBBEAN		**1,989**	**2,622**	**4,625**	**2,414**	**2,693**	**0.08**	**11.56**
Antigua and Barbuda		11	25	15	27	18	0.00	-33.33
Bahamas		276	78	156	67	122	0.00	82.09
Barbados		66	55	138	141	120	0.00	-14.89

355

ISRAEL

2. Arrivals of non-resident visitors at national borders, by country of residence

	2009	2010	2011	2012	2013	Market share 2013	% Change 2013-2012
Bermuda	4	4	19	10	8	0.00	-20.00
Cayman Islands	17	30	3	34	7	0.00	-79.41
Cuba	148	148	172	164	230	0.01	40.24
Dominica	26	45	76	18	26	0.00	44.44
Dominican Republic	655	1,099	1,000	743	1,058	0.03	42.40
Grenada	16	25	26	11	24	0.00	118.18
Haiti	131	128	209	214	134	0.00	-37.38
Jamaica	179	259	2,110	311	212	0.01	-31.83
Puerto Rico	1	3	2		1	0.00	
Saint Kitts and Nevis	15	19	16	19	34	0.00	78.95
Saint Lucia	6	71	17	18	20	0.00	11.11
Saint Vincent and the Grenadines	6	10	17	10	21	0.00	110.00
Trinidad and Tobago	431	621	643	626	654	0.02	4.47
Turks and Caicos Islands	1	2	5	1	4	0.00	300.00
United States Virgin Islands			1				
CENTRAL AMERICA	**5,511**	**8,737**	**7,126**	**8,764**	**8,109**	**0.23**	**-7.47**
Belize	18	30	35	38	39	0.00	2.63
Costa Rica	1,632	2,747	2,401	2,902	2,424	0.07	-16.47
El Salvador	688	1,176	768	926	885	0.03	-4.43
Guatemala	982	1,562	1,221	1,431	1,334	0.04	-6.78
Honduras	400	725	722	727	807	0.02	11.00
Nicaragua	143	200		302	306	0.01	1.32
Panama	1,648	2,297	1,979	2,438	2,314	0.07	-5.09
NORTH AMERICA	**656,313**	**758,790**	**731,744**	**714,214**	**716,410**	**20.24**	**0.31**
Canada	67,183	79,716	76,637	72,105	70,714	2.00	-1.93
Mexico	16,327	27,015	21,236	24,176	22,929	0.65	-5.16
United States of America	572,803	652,059	633,871	617,933	622,767	17.59	0.78
SOUTH AMERICA	**70,113**	**109,037**	**111,719**	**119,595**	**115,995**	**3.28**	**-3.01**
Argentina	16,409	23,364	23,129	24,728	25,713	0.73	3.98
Bolivia	533	749	711	847	818	0.02	-3.42
Brazil	28,945	51,983	56,889	59,403	56,434	1.59	-5.00
Chile	4,700	6,377	6,381	6,032	6,594	0.19	9.32
Colombia	8,291	12,197	11,033	13,232	11,705	0.33	-11.54
Ecuador	2,907	4,206	3,820	3,822	3,296	0.09	-13.76
Guyana	28	42	71	33	36	0.00	9.09
Paraguay	337	544	515	491	704	0.02	43.38
Peru	2,401	3,508	2,950	3,876	4,088	0.12	5.47
Suriname	31	50	45	54	87	0.00	61.11
Uruguay	2,419	2,857	2,774	2,718	2,876	0.08	5.81
Venezuela	3,112	3,160	3,401	4,359	3,644	0.10	-16.40
OTHER AMERICAS	**670**	**5**	**4**	**5**	**1**	**0.00**	**-80.00**
Other countries of the Americas	670	5	4	5	1	0.00	-80.00
EAST ASIA AND THE PACIFIC	**102,996**	**159,938**	**161,588**	**184,839**	**194,634**	**5.50**	**5.30**
NORTH-EAST ASIA	**44,021**	**75,592**	**73,032**	**79,344**	**81,572**	**2.30**	**2.81**
China	7,714	13,258	17,418	19,633	25,410	0.72	29.42
Hong Kong, China	2,335	4,499	3,723	4,830	5,160	0.15	6.83
Japan	10,031	13,866	14,112	16,481	14,167	0.40	-14.04
Korea, Dem. People's Republic of		16	16	29			
Korea, Republic of	21,113	39,644	32,718	32,724	30,935	0.87	-5.47
Macao, China	59	53	52	156	110	0.00	-29.49
Mongolia	109	207	204	185	195	0.01	5.41
Taiwan, Province of China	2,660	4,049	4,789	5,306	5,595	0.16	5.45
SOUTH-EAST ASIA	**29,428**	**43,953**	**49,478**	**66,126**	**68,974**	**1.95**	**4.31**
Brunei Darussalam	1	2	12	2	4	0.00	100.00
Cambodia	24	48	70	114	211	0.01	85.09
Indonesia	9,595	17,823	22,019	27,869	29,568	0.84	6.10
Lao People's Democratic Republic	67	150	240	319	394	0.01	23.51
Malaysia	640	1,611	3,276	6,881	9,275	0.26	34.79
Myanmar		373	345	599	648	0.02	8.18
Philippines	8,077	10,659	9,999	13,560	11,877	0.34	-12.41
Singapore	6,520	8,901	8,487	10,476	10,765	0.30	2.76

Yearbook of Tourism Statistics, Data 2009 – 2013, 2015 Edition

ISRAEL

2. Arrivals of non-resident visitors at national borders, by country of residence

	2009	2010	2011	2012	2013	Market share 2013	% Change 2013-2012
Thailand	3,450	3,051	3,378	4,398	3,870	0.11	-12.01
Timor-Leste		7	42	47	32	0.00	-31.91
Viet Nam	1,054	1,328	1,610	1,861	2,330	0.07	25.20
AUSTRALASIA	**28,627**	**39,950**	**38,481**	**38,492**	**42,876**	**1.21**	**11.39**
Australia	25,465	35,188	34,203	34,071	38,292	1.08	12.39
New Zealand	3,162	4,762	4,278	4,421	4,584	0.13	3.69
MELANESIA	**223**	**404**	**554**	**818**	**1,002**	**0.03**	**22.49**
Fiji	129	200	380	441	551	0.02	24.94
Papua New Guinea	76	178	148	340	428	0.01	25.88
Solomon Islands	6	10	9	16	15	0.00	-6.25
Vanuatu	12	16	17	21	8	0.00	-61.90
MICRONESIA	**4**	**12**	**16**	**7**	**27**	**0.00**	**285.71**
Kiribati		2	3	3	11	0.00	266.67
Micronesia, Federated States of	3	9	3	4	7	0.00	75.00
Palau	1	1	10		9	0.00	
POLYNESIA	**6**	**21**	**27**	**46**	**42**	**0.00**	**-8.70**
American Samoa	6	1	1	5	6	0.00	20.00
Cook Islands		1					
French Polynesia		2					
Samoa		7	6	17	15	0.00	-11.76
Tonga		10	20	24	21	0.00	-12.50
OTHER EAST ASIA AND THE PACIFIC	**687**	**6**		**6**	**141**	**0.00**	**2,250.00**
Other countries of Asia	669			6	116	0.00	1,833.33
Other countries of Oceania	18	6			25	0.00	
EUROPE	**1,764,666**	**2,253,137**	**2,175,690**	**2,323,587**	**2,348,386**	**66.34**	**1.07**
CENTRAL/EASTERN EUROPE	**723,680**	**952,844**	**884,454**	**997,758**	**989,707**	**27.96**	**-0.81**
Armenia	1,170	2,283	1,878	2,587	2,425	0.07	-6.26
Azerbaijan	2,991	3,142	2,994	3,335	3,253	0.09	-2.46
Belarus	14,442	17,760	15,187	20,342	21,540	0.61	5.89
Bulgaria	7,016	8,135	8,304	8,080	7,759	0.22	-3.97
Czech Republic	23,540	25,184	19,037	17,324	16,915	0.48	-2.36
Estonia	4,023	7,695	4,015	3,755	2,905	0.08	-22.64
Georgia	4,675	4,546	4,345	4,443	4,165	0.12	-6.26
Hungary	11,825	15,339	13,745	11,852	16,337	0.46	37.84
Kazakhstan	10,736	12,224	14,607	19,394	17,904	0.51	-7.68
Kyrgyzstan	659	709	750	954	1,030	0.03	7.97
Latvia	5,094	5,722	5,910	6,411	6,185	0.17	-3.53
Lithuania	7,229	9,134	6,969	7,579	8,147	0.23	7.49
Poland	96,880	128,961	95,958	101,912	89,164	2.52	-12.51
Republic of Moldova	3,823	4,619	3,867	4,136	3,757	0.11	-9.16
Romania	30,494	41,306	40,255	42,898	36,659	1.04	-14.54
Russian Federation	408,304	554,364	491,418	587,743	603,125	17.04	2.62
Slovakia	12,909	16,815	13,495	11,523	9,035	0.26	-21.59
Tajikistan	260	283	402	514	727	0.02	41.44
Turkmenistan	236	191	171	321	320	0.01	-0.31
Ukraine	73,924	90,711	137,266	138,313	134,470	3.80	-2.78
USSR (former)	13	7	4	3	2	0.00	-33.33
Uzbekistan	3,437	3,714	3,877	4,339	3,883	0.11	-10.51
NORTHERN EUROPE	**251,791**	**283,555**	**311,362**	**296,384**	**311,775**	**8.81**	**5.19**
Denmark	13,150	15,949	20,688	20,978	21,497	0.61	2.47
Finland	17,952	19,783	18,640	18,320	19,463	0.55	6.24
Iceland	238	384	389	361	362	0.01	0.28
Ireland	8,580	10,427	10,713	8,972	9,200	0.26	2.54
Norway	12,764	15,288	17,981	17,676	18,327	0.52	3.68
Sweden	17,793	21,374	21,857	23,665	25,789	0.73	8.98
United Kingdom	181,314	200,350	221,094	206,412	217,137	6.13	5.20
SOUTHERN EUROPE	**223,946**	**325,218**	**255,735**	**277,204**	**272,237**	**7.69**	**-1.79**
Albania	715	591	625	551	821	0.02	49.00
Andorra	52	87	60	62	75	0.00	20.97
Bosnia and Herzegovina	360	511	690	485	446	0.01	-8.04
Croatia	5,398	6,833	6,791	6,587	4,993	0.14	-24.20

357

ISRAEL

2. Arrivals of non-resident visitors at national borders, by country of residence

	2009	2010	2011	2012	2013	Market share 2013	% Change 2013-2012
Greece	20,642	28,957	19,791	22,050	19,334	0.55	-12.32
Holy See	292	274	256	271	310	0.01	14.39
Italy	125,704	185,383	151,245	170,033	173,150	4.89	1.83
Malta	1,517	2,342	1,437	2,354	1,542	0.04	-34.49
Montenegro		485	401	557	385	0.01	-30.88
Portugal	7,208	15,341	9,569	9,522	9,618	0.27	1.01
San Marino	102	140	82	123	101	0.00	-17.89
Serbia	877	4,720	5,062	4,773	4,908	0.14	2.83
Serbia and Montenegro	1,556	72	113				
Slovenia	2,348	3,332	2,682	3,142	3,146	0.09	0.13
Spain	54,144	74,967	56,210	56,040	52,609	1.49	-6.12
TFYR of Macedonia	694	699	596	652	799	0.02	22.55
Yugoslavia, SFR (former)	2,337	484	125	2			
WESTERN EUROPE	**539,160**	**663,771**	**698,564**	**723,552**	**740,521**	**20.92**	**2.35**
Austria	24,924	32,388	35,164	34,764	33,525	0.95	-3.56
Belgium	26,127	35,255	37,040	36,337	36,203	1.02	-0.37
France	263,885	302,695	300,567	300,573	315,457	8.91	4.95
Germany	148,322	199,942	220,688	239,758	254,021	7.18	5.95
Liechtenstein	59	86	97	124	137	0.00	10.48
Luxembourg	663	837	989	1,025	1,135	0.03	10.73
Monaco	26	104	60	66	78	0.00	18.18
Netherlands	47,587	57,962	63,047	67,850	57,096	1.61	-15.85
Switzerland	27,567	34,502	40,912	43,055	42,869	1.21	-0.43
EAST MEDITERRANEAN EUROPE	**25,735**	**27,749**	**25,575**	**28,583**	**34,020**	**0.96**	**19.02**
Cyprus	11,521	12,699	11,552	11,422	9,635	0.27	-15.65
Turkey	14,214	15,050	14,023	17,161	24,385	0.69	42.10
OTHER EUROPE	**354**			**106**	**126**	**0.00**	**18.87**
Other countries of Europe	354			106	126	0.00	18.87
MIDDLE EAST	**19,085**	**21,645**	**23,891**	**28,292**	**23,040**	**0.65**	**-18.56**
Bahrain		3	1		4	0.00	
Egypt	2,431	2,810	2,663	3,928	4,151	0.12	5.68
Iraq	123	158	157	168	142	0.00	-15.48
Jordan	15,885	18,310	20,708	23,834	18,367	0.52	-22.94
Kuwait	31	7	9	4	5	0.00	25.00
Lebanon	400	228	239	253	239	0.01	-5.53
Libya	8	3	3	1	2	0.00	100.00
Oman	1	1	4	3	4	0.00	33.33
Qatar	10	10	8	2	5	0.00	150.00
Saudi Arabia		4			1	0.00	
Syrian Arab Republic	125	84	67	62	73	0.00	17.74
United Arab Emirates		15	9		3	0.00	
Yemen	71	12	23	37	44	0.00	18.92
SOUTH ASIA	**26,078**	**43,381**	**41,780**	**47,196**	**43,611**	**1.23**	**-7.60**
Afghanistan	1	6	2	2			
Bangladesh	10	17	14	16	41	0.00	156.25
Bhutan		4	25	30	60	0.00	100.00
India	23,374	40,394	38,870	43,360	39,232	1.11	-9.52
Iran, Islamic Republic of	401	476	411	304	311	0.01	2.30
Maldives	9	30		103	92	0.00	-10.68
Nepal	899	493	477	437	614	0.02	40.50
Pakistan	11	5	15	6	11	0.00	83.33
Sri Lanka	1,373	1,956	1,966	2,938	3,250	0.09	10.62
NOT SPECIFIED	**13,820**	**14,004**	**15,477**	**16,582**	**15,873**	**0.45**	**-4.28**
Other countries of the World	13,820	14,004	15,477	16,582	15,873	0.45	-4.28

Yearbook of Tourism Statistics, Data 2009 – 2013, 2015 Edition

ISRAEL

3. Arrivals of non-resident tourists in hotels and similar establishments, by country of residence

		2009	2010	2011	2012	2013	Market share 2013	% Change 2013-2012
TOTAL	(*)	2,620,800	3,237,000	3,231,900	3,170,500	3,135,400	100.00	-1.11
AMERICAS		883,500	1,133,000	1,103,900	1,099,100	1,102,200	35.15	0.28
NORTH AMERICA		814,700	1,010,900	973,100	954,700	945,900	30.17	-0.92
All countries of North America		814,700	1,010,900	973,100	954,700	945,900	30.17	-0.92
SOUTH AMERICA		68,800	122,100	130,800	144,400	156,300	4.99	8.24
All countries of South America	(*)	68,800	122,100	130,800	144,400	156,300	4.99	8.24
EUROPE		1,255,300	1,547,700	1,522,600	1,425,800	1,385,800	44.20	-2.81
OTHER EUROPE		1,255,300	1,547,700	1,522,600	1,425,800	1,385,800	44.20	-2.81
All countries of Europe		1,255,300	1,547,700	1,522,600	1,425,800	1,385,800	44.20	-2.81
NOT SPECIFIED		482,000	556,300	605,400	645,600	647,400	20.65	0.28
Other countries of the World		482,000	556,300	605,400	645,600	647,400	20.65	0.28

Yearbook of Tourism Statistics, Data 2009 – 2013, 2015 Edition

ISRAEL

5. Overnight stays of non-resident tourists in hotels and similar establishments, by country of residence

		2009	2010	2011	2012	2013	Market share 2013	% Change 2013-2012
TOTAL	(*)	8,108,800	9,933,100	9,949,200	9,750,400	9,745,500	100.00	-0.05
AMERICAS		2,628,200	3,313,900	3,212,000	3,179,100	3,193,400	32.77	0.45
NORTH AMERICA		2,421,800	2,958,300	2,828,700	2,785,700	2,744,200	28.16	-1.49
All countries of North America		2,421,800	2,958,300	2,828,700	2,785,700	2,744,200	28.16	-1.49
SOUTH AMERICA		206,400	355,600	383,300	393,400	449,200	4.61	14.18
All countries of South America	(*)	206,400	355,600	383,300	393,400	449,200	4.61	14.18
EUROPE		4,173,300	5,149,700	5,119,000	4,848,700	4,819,400	49.45	-0.60
OTHER EUROPE		4,173,300	5,149,700	5,119,000	4,848,700	4,819,400	49.45	-0.60
All countries of Europe		4,173,300	5,149,700	5,119,000	4,848,700	4,819,400	49.45	-0.60
NOT SPECIFIED		1,307,300	1,469,500	1,618,200	1,722,600	1,732,700	17.78	0.59
Other countries of the World		1,307,300	1,469,500	1,618,200	1,722,600	1,732,700	17.78	0.59

Yearbook of Tourism Statistics, Data 2009 – 2013, 2015 Edition

ITALY

1. Arrivals of non-resident tourists at national borders, by nationality

	2009	2010	2011	2012	2013	Market share 2013	% Change 2013-2012
TOTAL (*)	43,238,919	43,626,118	46,118,848	46,359,908	47,703,911	100.00	2.90
AFRICA	248,441	318,179	280,199	225,208	185,020	0.39	-17.84
EAST AFRICA	34,856	28,227	32,911	29,643	13,325	0.03	-55.05
All countries of East Africa	34,856	28,227	32,911	29,643	13,325	0.03	-55.05
CENTRAL AFRICA	10,830	10,973	13,033	10,561	8,839	0.02	-16.31
All countries of Central Africa	10,830	10,973	13,033	10,561	8,839	0.02	-16.31
NORTH AFRICA	105,245	189,253	124,915	84,161	60,997	0.13	-27.52
Algeria	12,664	7,560	11,303	10,548	17,671	0.04	67.53
Morocco	62,194	145,241	72,468	40,884	15,913	0.03	-61.08
Tunisia	27,363	34,166	34,921	30,398	24,851	0.05	-18.25
Other countries of North Africa	3,024	2,286	6,223	2,331	2,562	0.01	9.91
SOUTHERN AFRICA	64,956	55,431	67,232	54,903	61,706	0.13	12.39
South Africa	64,124	55,431	66,054	53,574	57,543	0.12	7.41
Other countries of Southern Africa	832		1,178	1,329	4,163	0.01	213.24
WEST AFRICA	32,554	34,295	42,108	45,940	40,153	0.08	-12.60
All countries of West Africa	32,554	34,295	42,108	45,940	40,153	0.08	-12.60
AMERICAS	3,390,307	3,501,730	4,067,153	3,910,295	4,476,932	9.38	14.49
CARIBBEAN	20,044	15,363	28,884	24,454	15,290	0.03	-37.47
All countries of the Caribbean	20,044	15,363	28,884	24,454	15,290	0.03	-37.47
CENTRAL AMERICA	19,114	20,173	28,114	31,114	34,612	0.07	11.24
Costa Rica	7,969	8,613	14,904	14,851	17,184	0.04	15.71
Panama	2,336	2,149	2,663	3,238	4,809	0.01	48.52
Other countries of Central America	8,809	9,411	10,547	13,025	12,619	0.03	-3.12
NORTH AMERICA	2,862,090	2,963,977	3,400,653	3,204,846	3,585,912	7.52	11.89
Canada	512,890	561,294	574,527	513,885	573,655	1.20	11.63
Mexico	87,465	74,338	111,543	100,218	128,249	0.27	27.97
United States of America	2,261,735	2,327,342	2,714,583	2,590,359	2,884,008	6.05	11.34
Other countries of North America		1,003		384			
SOUTH AMERICA	489,059	502,217	609,502	649,881	841,118	1.76	29.43
Argentina	138,165	127,537	130,821	159,624	217,174	0.46	36.05
Brazil	188,892	234,199	293,309	310,575	394,696	0.83	27.09
Chile	31,657	47,787	51,437	50,736	61,860	0.13	21.93
Colombia	18,572	15,683	18,433	28,728	45,007	0.09	56.67
Peru	28,052	21,395	23,732	19,159	26,152	0.05	36.50
Venezuela	45,467	36,215	60,891	43,113	61,687	0.13	43.08
Other countries of South America	38,254	19,401	30,879	37,946	34,542	0.07	-8.97
EAST ASIA AND THE PACIFIC	1,299,901	1,324,474	1,512,096	1,528,003	1,795,338	3.76	17.50
NORTH-EAST ASIA	565,451	573,999	640,954	681,887	861,395	1.81	26.33
China	138,210	136,780	209,651	231,022	289,682	0.61	25.39
Hong Kong, China	26,748	26,199	40,524	31,200	31,944	0.07	2.38
Japan	320,591	340,210	314,239	353,547	454,465	0.95	28.54
Korea, Republic of	59,972	59,996	58,490	48,351	68,403	0.14	41.47
Taiwan, Province of China	10,138	8,124	15,946	15,445	15,175	0.03	-1.75
Other countries of North-East Asia	9,792	2,690	2,104	2,322	1,726	0.00	-25.67
SOUTH-EAST ASIA	132,965	119,679	94,826	133,296	126,234	0.26	-5.30
Indonesia	12,474	14,938	9,573	22,823	17,919	0.04	-21.49
Malaysia	16,729	26,154	21,905	23,358	19,742	0.04	-15.48
Philippines	19,154	21,682	14,217	25,627	27,922	0.06	8.96
Singapore	28,743	20,146	28,623	34,124	31,280	0.07	-8.33
Thailand	51,196	33,206	18,444	25,561	22,843	0.05	-10.63
Other countries of South-East Asia	4,669	3,553	2,064	1,803	6,528	0.01	262.06
AUSTRALASIA	597,408	624,205	769,764	709,743	806,100	1.69	13.58
Australia	526,755	548,288	693,265	644,285	707,344	1.48	9.79
New Zealand	70,653	75,917	76,499	65,458	98,756	0.21	50.87
MELANESIA		1,555	2,449	1,316	1,609	0.00	22.26
All countries of Melanesia		1,555	2,449	1,316	1,609	0.00	22.26

361

ITALY

1. Arrivals of non-resident tourists at national borders, by nationality

	2009	2010	2011	2012	2013	Market share 2013	% Change 2013-2012
MICRONESIA		· 1,293	384	882			
All countries of Micronesia		1,293	384	882			
POLYNESIA	4,077	3,743	3,719	879			
American Samoa	1,668	3,743	2,945				
Samoa	776						
Other countries of Polynesia	1,633		774	879			
EUROPE	37,853,912	37,921,219	39,743,414	40,062,889	40,643,734	85.20	1.45
CENTRAL/EASTERN EUROPE	4,366,233	4,894,033	5,246,233	5,867,085	6,109,951	12.81	4.14
Czech Republic	772,544	816,161	953,555	857,473	903,578	1.89	5.38
Hungary	620,833	525,595	504,221	498,110	496,236	1.04	-0.38
Poland	1,033,409	1,124,044	1,182,758	1,327,821	1,318,877	2.76	-0.67
Romania	672,205	672,377	644,841	681,349	689,334	1.45	1.17
Russian Federation	431,470	595,275	745,453	950,061	1,005,099	2.11	5.79
Slovakia	360,843	411,974	388,003	494,401	490,420	1.03	-0.81
Other countries Central/East Europe	474,929	748,607	827,402	1,057,870	1,206,407	2.53	14.04
NORTHERN EUROPE	5,062,988	4,920,559	5,045,420	5,262,553	5,284,682	11.08	0.42
Denmark	451,417	470,812	443,135	534,175	475,535	1.00	-10.98
Finland	216,965	217,226	259,229	251,079	238,967	0.50	-4.82
Ireland	336,040	348,638	279,313	306,675	326,401	0.68	6.43
Norway	261,533	264,516	235,290	312,886	309,576	0.65	-1.06
Sweden	429,538	444,826	625,500	474,650	478,825	1.00	0.88
United Kingdom	3,361,357	3,163,036	3,195,408	3,377,115	3,443,285	7.22	1.96
Other countries of Northern Europe	6,138	11,505	7,545	5,973	12,093	0.03	102.46
SOUTHERN EUROPE	4,023,658	4,621,045	4,595,039	4,167,115	4,365,236	9.15	4.75
Albania	86,930	88,965	139,383	113,873	116,859	0.24	2.62
Bosnia and Herzegovina	107,867	265,236	257,321	381,674	632,767	1.33	65.79
Croatia	261,155	390,919	359,940	273,025	204,273	0.43	-25.18
Greece	438,965	473,474	369,346	307,458	379,412	0.80	23.40
Malta	40,835	58,598	72,553	59,666	75,383	0.16	26.34
Portugal	223,691	284,028	273,900	166,428	213,069	0.45	28.02
Serbia	121,695	267,995	248,613	354,271	587,786	1.23	65.91
Slovenia	245,459	255,651	170,561	191,132	119,230	0.25	-37.62
Spain	2,463,309	2,484,724	2,610,373	2,268,144	1,892,114	3.97	-16.58
Other countries of Southern Europe	33,752	51,455	93,049	51,444	144,343	0.30	180.58
WESTERN EUROPE	24,135,839	23,217,166	24,602,584	24,478,179	24,508,556	51.38	0.12
Austria	3,403,807	3,361,695	3,205,214	3,083,283	3,332,861	6.99	8.09
Belgium	1,112,551	1,104,115	1,397,291	1,253,301	1,318,368	2.76	5.19
France	4,935,031	4,843,586	4,982,877	4,977,292	5,251,927	11.01	5.52
Germany	9,546,257	8,960,697	9,874,509	10,169,734	9,544,536	20.01	-6.15
Luxembourg	108,020	89,597	101,609	101,379	146,733	0.31	44.74
Netherlands	1,922,473	1,592,483	1,758,978	1,710,635	1,810,122	3.79	5.82
Switzerland	2,952,608	3,183,639	3,235,773	3,135,368	3,026,303	6.34	-3.48
Other countries of Western Europe	155,092	81,354	46,333	47,187	77,706	0.16	64.68
EAST MEDITERRANEAN EUROPE	239,402	242,408	231,327	252,056	350,286	0.73	38.97
Israel	72,915	105,578	79,291	71,834	122,739	0.26	70.86
Turkey	166,487	136,830	152,036	180,222	227,547	0.48	26.26
OTHER EUROPE	25,792	26,008	22,811	35,901	25,023	0.05	-30.30
Other countries of Europe	25,792	26,008	22,811	35,901	25,023	0.05	-30.30
MIDDLE EAST	222,200	289,353	246,530	275,989	304,127	0.64	10.20
Egypt	46,559	47,639	42,623	37,676	41,990	0.09	11.45
Jordan	15,429	16,158	27,599	21,114	43,770	0.09	107.30
Lebanon	17,277	16,875	9,708	19,245	15,238	0.03	-20.82
Libya	12,695	14,841	8,687	11,920	22,078	0.05	85.22
Saudi Arabia	15,687	47,494	40,126	50,654	56,418	0.12	11.38
United Arab Emirates	80,049	95,716	62,256	73,776	65,190	0.14	-11.64
Other countries of Middle East	34,504	50,630	55,531	61,604	59,443	0.12	-3.51

362

ITALY

1. Arrivals of non-resident tourists at national borders, by nationality

	2009	2010	2011	2012	2013	Market share 2013	% Change 2013-2012
SOUTH ASIA	**224,158**	**270,007**	**269,061**	**357,196**	**297,814**	**0.62**	**-16.62**
India	139,094	182,552	188,408	251,361	199,253	0.42	-20.73
Iran, Islamic Republic of	31,173	16,912	33,441	31,843	19,608	0.04	-38.42
Pakistan	29,359	33,383	17,669	28,973	24,848	0.05	-14.24
Other countries of South Asia	24,532	37,160	29,543	45,019	54,105	0.11	20.18
NOT SPECIFIED		**1,156**	**395**	**328**	**946**	**0.00**	**188.41**
Other countries of the World		1,156	395	328	946	0.00	188.41

363

ITALY

2. Arrivals of non-resident visitors at national borders, by nationality

	2009	2010	2011	2012	2013	Market share 2013	% Change 2013-2012
TOTAL (*)	71,692,233	73,225,219	75,866,005	76,292,846	76,762,341	100.00	0.62
AFRICA	287,673	377,484	360,837	275,380	253,294	0.33	-8.02
EAST AFRICA	35,510	31,368	37,040	32,521	16,699	0.02	-48.65
All countries of East Africa	35,510	31,368	37,040	32,521	16,699	0.02	-48.65
CENTRAL AFRICA	11,826	11,347	14,197	11,523	11,149	0.01	-3.25
Sao Tome and Principe		74		341			
Other countries of Central Africa		11,273		11,182			
All countries of Central Africa	11,826		14,197		11,149	0.01	
NORTH AFRICA	131,023	231,918	182,336	109,294	117,071	0.15	7.12
Algeria	19,538	17,896	25,264	18,091	46,780	0.06	158.58
Morocco	66,324	150,887	86,979	42,734	20,926	0.03	-51.03
Tunisia	41,266	60,849	63,231	44,214	42,294	0.06	-4.34
Other countries of North Africa	3,895	2,286	6,862	4,255	7,071	0.01	66.18
SOUTHERN AFRICA	71,258	60,088	69,011	57,567	62,261	0.08	8.15
South Africa	70,426	60,088	67,833	56,238	58,098	0.08	3.31
Other countries of Southern Africa	832		1,178	1,329	4,163	0.01	213.24
WEST AFRICA	38,056	42,763	58,253	64,475	46,114	0.06	-28.48
All countries of West Africa	38,056	42,763	58,253	64,475	46,114	0.06	-28.48
AMERICAS	3,760,644	3,968,611	4,828,460	4,757,349	5,404,282	7.04	13.60
CARIBBEAN	20,674	16,603	36,015	27,358	15,486	0.02	-43.39
All countries of the Caribbean	20,674	16,603	36,015	27,358	15,486	0.02	-43.39
CENTRAL AMERICA	21,139	23,661	34,393	37,392	45,048	0.06	20.47
Costa Rica	8,053	9,827	14,904	14,851	17,198	0.02	15.80
Panama	3,055	2,619	3,170	3,238	9,686	0.01	199.14
Other countries of Central America	10,031	11,215	16,319	19,303	18,164	0.02	-5.90
NORTH AMERICA	3,143,205	3,311,017	3,957,155	3,789,802	4,224,902	5.50	11.48
Canada	547,752	604,640	636,858	612,174	646,276	0.84	5.57
Mexico	89,316	77,019	118,782	105,897	130,621	0.17	23.35
United States of America	2,506,137	2,621,863	3,201,515	3,071,347	3,448,005	4.49	12.26
Other countries of North America		7,495		384			
SOUTH AMERICA	575,626	617,330	800,897	902,797	1,118,846	1.46	23.93
Argentina	162,298	155,949	162,180	205,764	259,317	0.34	26.03
Brazil	221,802	274,543	398,721	424,831	515,639	0.67	21.38
Chile	32,032	52,491	53,247	56,281	73,875	0.10	31.26
Colombia	20,317	16,472	20,690	29,125	47,581	0.06	63.37
Peru	28,905	23,924	26,154	23,280	26,152	0.03	12.34
Venezuela	59,717	56,189	97,105	83,285	145,750	0.19	75.00
Other countries of South America	50,555	37,762	42,800	80,231	50,532	0.07	-37.02
EAST ASIA AND THE PACIFIC	1,396,924	1,416,478	1,646,410	1,656,647	1,938,994	2.53	17.04
NORTH-EAST ASIA	610,831	608,046	680,841	722,802	881,249	1.15	21.92
China	145,995	145,991	223,815	251,699	297,513	0.39	18.20
Hong Kong, China	27,466	29,269	50,484	36,787	34,984	0.05	-4.90
Japan	349,710	359,855	326,895	365,304	459,700	0.60	25.84
Korea, Republic of	60,222	60,955	58,836	50,873	70,257	0.09	38.10
Taiwan, Province of China	12,727	8,817	17,598	15,583	16,008	0.02	2.73
Other countries of North-East Asia	14,711	3,159	3,213	2,556	2,787	0.00	9.04
SOUTH-EAST ASIA	143,730	132,132	111,828	149,125	143,857	0.19	-3.53
Indonesia	15,012	17,037	11,008	23,290	19,084	0.02	-18.06
Malaysia	17,734	27,654	22,075	23,915	23,163	0.03	-3.14
Philippines	21,933	25,757	19,567	34,958	33,227	0.04	-4.95
Singapore	31,075	21,699	34,512	35,471	32,652	0.04	-7.95
Thailand	52,307	34,993	22,370	29,112	24,406	0.03	-16.17
Other countries of South-East Asia	5,669	4,992	2,296	2,379	11,325	0.01	376.04
AUSTRALASIA	631,827	665,008	846,988	781,643	912,037	1.19	16.68
Australia	555,249	584,401	765,527	710,073	811,900	1.06	14.34
New Zealand	76,578	80,607	81,461	71,570	100,137	0.13	39.91

Yearbook of Tourism Statistics, Data 2009 – 2013, 2015 Edition

ITALY

2. Arrivals of non-resident visitors at national borders, by nationality

	2009	2010	2011	2012	2013	Market share 2013	% Change 2013-2012
MELANESIA	**160**	**1,555**	**2,449**	**1,316**	**1,851**	**0.00**	**40.65**
All countries of Melanesia	160	1,555	2,449	1,316	1,851	0.00	40.65
MICRONESIA		**1,293**	**384**	**882**			
All countries of Micronesia		1,293	384	882			
POLYNESIA	**10,376**	**8,444**	**3,920**	**879**			
American Samoa	7,077	5,011	3,146				
Samoa	776						
Other countries of Polynesia	2,523	3,433	774				
All countries of Polynesia				879			
EUROPE	**65,745,321**	**66,821,317**	**68,359,168**	**68,800,401**	**68,417,636**	**89.13**	**-0.56**
CENTRAL/EASTERN EUROPE	**5,143,307**	**5,749,328**	**6,211,261**	**7,153,591**	**7,444,314**	**9.70**	**4.06**
Czech Republic	897,923	915,028	1,101,088	1,051,130	1,060,395	1.38	0.88
Hungary	734,637	655,307	658,379	604,932	698,634	0.91	15.49
Poland	1,164,908	1,257,219	1,287,725	1,524,685	1,485,405	1.94	-2.58
Romania	859,744	863,342	982,513	1,059,922	1,124,890	1.47	6.13
Russian Federation	457,208	645,416	792,560	1,045,379	1,085,032	1.41	3.79
Slovakia	410,843	475,148	431,024	606,097	574,613	0.75	-5.19
Other countries Central/East Europe	618,044	937,868	957,972	1,261,446	1,415,345	1.84	12.20
NORTHERN EUROPE	**5,438,643**	**5,239,507**	**5,436,515**	**5,694,281**	**5,660,690**	**7.37**	**-0.59**
Denmark	493,788	516,566	464,582	591,348	544,090	0.71	-7.99
Finland	235,631	237,220	279,397	281,792	264,201	0.34	-6.24
Ireland	349,829	361,657	287,609	318,109	341,118	0.44	7.23
Norway	281,075	282,464	248,948	328,391	326,363	0.43	-0.62
Sweden	455,663	481,502	668,911	518,951	533,414	0.69	2.79
United Kingdom	3,615,588	3,348,204	3,479,523	3,646,810	3,639,411	4.74	-0.20
Other countries of Northern Europe	7,069	11,894	7,545	8,880	12,093	0.02	36.18
SOUTHERN EUROPE	**9,746,658**	**10,250,804**	**10,322,189**	**9,743,174**	**9,751,993**	**12.70**	**0.09**
Albania	97,835	99,047	150,063	147,474	134,645	0.18	-8.70
Bosnia and Herzegovina	152,527	293,249	260,725	410,179	634,652	0.83	54.73
Croatia	1,133,295	1,239,545	1,146,611	1,274,320	1,099,408	1.43	-13.73
Greece	552,039	598,570	467,671	399,267	452,698	0.59	13.38
Malta	87,304	91,671	100,367	77,356	91,718	0.12	18.57
Portugal	274,309	380,725	340,350	247,763	312,484	0.41	26.12
Serbia	159,160	303,033	284,991	404,160	639,733	0.83	58.29
Slovenia	4,225,605	4,116,591	4,394,410	4,070,720	3,937,703	5.13	-3.27
Spain	3,005,610	3,045,843	3,061,249	2,631,346	2,277,657	2.97	-13.44
Other countries of Southern Europe	58,974	82,530	115,752	80,589	171,295	0.22	112.55
WESTERN EUROPE	**45,105,222**	**45,248,161**	**46,052,599**	**45,828,924**	**45,123,507**	**58.78**	**-1.54**
Austria	7,317,666	7,660,061	6,502,564	6,929,749	6,606,530	8.61	-4.66
Belgium	1,288,870	1,248,305	1,672,460	1,441,271	1,479,533	1.93	2.65
France	10,168,307	9,975,720	10,165,234	10,245,551	10,361,116	13.50	1.13
Germany	11,422,068	10,856,813	11,681,707	11,679,304	10,971,379	14.29	-6.06
Luxembourg	129,698	114,445	119,621	114,109	154,348	0.20	35.26
Netherlands	2,148,031	1,806,616	2,079,358	1,923,531	1,959,972	2.55	1.89
Switzerland	12,234,105	13,297,391	13,565,237	13,145,021	12,985,489	16.92	-1.21
Other countries of Western Europe	396,477	288,810	266,418	350,388	605,140	0.79	72.71
EAST MEDITERRANEAN EUROPE	**283,176**	**303,813**	**310,597**	**341,851**	**408,066**	**0.53**	**19.37**
Israel	90,331	142,026	134,292	145,055	167,548	0.22	15.51
Turkey	192,845	161,787	176,305	196,796	240,518	0.31	22.22
OTHER EUROPE	**28,315**	**29,704**	**26,007**	**38,580**	**29,066**	**0.04**	**-24.66**
Other countries of Europe	28,315	29,704	26,007	38,580	29,066	0.04	-24.66
MIDDLE EAST	**260,945**	**349,821**	**362,070**	**380,597**	**415,518**	**0.54**	**9.18**
Egypt	54,427	54,849	70,402	55,029	67,829	0.09	23.26
Jordan	16,431	18,212	29,050	23,595	16,913	0.02	-28.32
Lebanon	20,146	26,459	36,590	45,976	65,433	0.09	42.32
Libya	18,294	26,463	22,568	33,377	30,458	0.04	-8.75
Saudi Arabia	18,841	53,503	43,982	58,149	79,746	0.10	37.14
United Arab Emirates	86,828	112,934	80,829	87,354	80,286	0.10	-8.09

ITALY

2. Arrivals of non-resident visitors at national borders, by nationality

	2009	2010	2011	2012	2013	Market share 2013	% Change 2013-2012
Other countries of Middle East	45,978	57,401	78,649	77,117	74,853	0.10	-2.94
SOUTH ASIA	**240,726**	**290,352**	**308,665**	**422,144**	**331,671**	**0.43**	**-21.43**
India	144,105	189,629	208,132	280,902	210,262	0.27	-25.15
Iran, Islamic Republic of	35,824	24,932	38,683	45,311	27,822	0.04	-38.60
Pakistan	31,719	35,924	23,852	47,849	35,104	0.05	-26.64
Other countries of South Asia	29,078	39,867	37,998	48,082	58,483	0.08	21.63
NOT SPECIFIED		**1,156**	**395**	**328**	**946**	**0.00**	**188.41**
Other countries of the World		1,156	395	328	946	0.00	188.41

Yearbook of Tourism Statistics, Data 2009 – 2013, 2015 Edition

ITALY

3. Arrivals of non-resident tourists in hotels and similar establishments, by nationality

	2009	2010	2011	2012	2013	Market share 2013	% Change 2013-2012
TOTAL (*)	32,632,696	35,020,415	37,983,634	38,867,517	39,989,184	100.00	2.89
AFRICA	250,004	261,939	287,903	301,284	184,501	0.46	-38.76
SOUTHERN AFRICA	52,763	61,542	70,950	73,916	75,318	0.19	1.90
South Africa	52,763	61,542	70,950	73,916	75,318	0.19	1.90
OTHER AFRICA	197,241	200,397	216,953	227,368	109,183	0.27	-51.98
Other countries of Africa	197,241	200,397	216,953	227,368	109,183	0.27	-51.98
AMERICAS	4,949,563	5,503,571	6,002,579	6,034,731	6,166,811	15.42	2.19
NORTH AMERICA	4,134,823	4,503,592	4,740,665	4,699,061	4,787,414	11.97	1.88
Canada	501,488	574,369	601,077	593,357	605,987	1.52	2.13
Mexico	135,467	165,582	187,990	192,534	196,605	0.49	2.11
United States of America	3,497,868	3,763,641	3,951,598	3,913,170	3,984,822	9.96	1.83
SOUTH AMERICA	814,740	999,979	1,261,914	1,335,670	1,379,397	3.45	3.27
Argentina	168,435	205,447	262,304	301,808	339,271	0.85	12.41
Brazil	399,018	533,471	695,086	696,110	670,847	1.68	-3.63
Venezuela	52,114	49,766	59,860	66,269	66,410	0.17	0.21
Other countries of South America	195,173	211,295	244,664	271,483	302,869	0.76	11.56
EAST ASIA AND THE PACIFIC	3,006,496	3,612,759	4,218,725	4,602,744	4,915,535	12.29	6.80
NORTH-EAST ASIA	2,141,170	2,525,936	2,966,141	3,254,060	3,520,669	8.80	8.19
China	696,778	929,308	1,291,762	1,516,406	1,760,320	4.40	16.09
Japan	1,238,474	1,304,394	1,345,981	1,380,879	1,361,430	3.40	-1.41
Korea, Republic of	205,918	292,234	328,398	356,775	398,919	1.00	11.81
AUSTRALASIA	573,459	674,490	736,905	752,878	790,921	1.98	5.05
Australia	501,313	595,227	656,600	665,648	702,333	1.76	5.51
New Zealand	72,146	79,263	80,305	87,230	88,588	0.22	1.56
OTHER EAST ASIA AND THE PACIFIC	291,867	412,333	515,679	595,806	603,945	1.51	1.37
Other countries of Asia	291,867	412,333	515,679	595,806	603,945	1.51	1.37
EUROPE	23,545,983	24,711,162	26,419,114	26,839,941	27,519,958	68.82	2.53
CENTRAL/EASTERN EUROPE	2,181,461	2,524,728	2,978,424	3,132,588	3,403,096	8.51	8.64
Czech Republic	312,073	342,037	357,376	373,893	385,291	0.96	3.05
Estonia	26,268	25,906	36,008	36,805	40,547	0.10	10.17
Hungary	230,371	242,192	256,357	247,323	259,329	0.65	4.85
Latvia	25,918	27,219	35,794	40,874	47,671	0.12	16.63
Lithuania	52,508	54,384	69,716	73,278	88,485	0.22	20.75
Poland	621,581	682,019	761,582	691,355	730,935	1.83	5.72
Russian Federation	838,921	1,069,232	1,372,237	1,578,700	1,753,193	4.38	11.05
Slovakia	73,821	81,739	89,354	90,360	97,645	0.24	8.06
NORTHERN EUROPE	3,902,653	3,941,823	4,032,572	4,184,628	4,238,152	10.60	1.28
Denmark	335,233	344,390	335,989	359,677	359,724	0.90	0.01
Finland	213,831	214,958	228,490	219,454	217,899	0.54	-0.71
Iceland	20,599	19,747	19,094	20,586	19,474	0.05	-5.40
Ireland	335,319	304,677	293,654	299,447	297,695	0.74	-0.59
Norway	271,662	294,226	308,167	331,455	338,409	0.85	2.10
Sweden	428,173	480,807	512,006	499,838	506,766	1.27	1.39
United Kingdom	2,297,836	2,283,018	2,335,172	2,454,171	2,498,185	6.25	1.79
SOUTHERN EUROPE	2,419,587	2,520,293	2,585,925	2,324,785	2,250,779	5.63	-3.18
Croatia	151,649	142,111	143,113	147,138	149,421	0.37	1.55
Greece	328,778	319,467	315,987	266,215	273,558	0.68	2.76
Malta	46,700	51,279	56,031	59,894	70,165	0.18	17.15
Portugal	197,166	214,588	217,714	208,992	203,489	0.51	-2.63
Slovenia	147,442	150,015	161,765	149,011	155,819	0.39	4.57
Spain	1,547,852	1,642,833	1,691,315	1,493,535	1,398,327	3.50	-6.37
WESTERN EUROPE	13,540,694	13,996,316	14,845,638	15,126,929	15,483,278	38.72	2.36
Austria	1,463,284	1,524,404	1,593,639	1,600,731	1,616,711	4.04	1.00
Belgium	783,832	800,229	852,979	860,163	875,174	2.19	1.75
France	2,732,413	2,838,922	3,025,404	3,007,555	3,120,628	7.80	3.76
Germany	6,289,216	6,456,004	6,809,122	6,990,758	7,094,037	17.74	1.48
Luxembourg	54,839	54,209	56,938	58,763	64,691	0.16	10.09
Netherlands	892,568	918,543	956,303	944,519	931,599	2.33	-1.37
Switzerland	1,324,542	1,404,005	1,551,253	1,664,440	1,780,438	4.45	6.97

Yearbook of Tourism Statistics, Data 2009 – 2013, 2015 Edition

ITALY

3. Arrivals of non-resident tourists in hotels and similar establishments, by nationality

	2009	2010	2011	2012	2013	Market share 2013	% Change 2013-2012
EAST MEDITERRANEAN EUROPE	390,511	468,123	511,461	553,266	626,868	1.57	13.30
Cyprus	16,285	19,031	18,516	22,040	20,554	0.05	-6.74
Israel	222,325	252,876	264,895	274,036	301,286	0.75	9.94
Turkey	151,901	196,216	228,050	257,190	305,028	0.76	18.60
OTHER EUROPE	1,111,077	1,259,879	1,465,094	1,517,745	1,517,785	3.80	0.00
Other countries of Europe	1,111,077	1,259,879	1,465,094	1,517,745	1,517,785	3.80	0.00
MIDDLE EAST	212,806	246,834	289,156	319,604	348,709	0.87	9.11
Egypt	37,951	39,664	38,335	41,662	44,745	0.11	7.40
Other countries of Middle East	174,855	207,170	250,821	277,942	303,964	0.76	9.36
SOUTH ASIA	147,569	184,676	236,277	258,854	259,173	0.65	0.12
India	147,569	184,676	236,277	258,854	259,173	0.65	0.12
NOT SPECIFIED	520,275	499,474	529,880	510,359	594,497	1.49	16.49
Other countries of the World	520,275	499,474	529,880	510,359	594,497	1.49	16.49

Yearbook of Tourism Statistics, Data 2009 – 2013, 2015 Edition

ITALY

4. Arrivals of non-resident tourists in all types of accommodation establishments, by nationality

	2009	2010	2011	2012	2013	Market share 2013	% Change 2013-2012
TOTAL	41,124,722	43,794,338	47,460,809	48,738,575	50,263,236	100.00	3.13
AFRICA	277,994	289,502	323,857	342,175	215,283	0.43	-37.08
SOUTHERN AFRICA	63,038	71,950	84,255	89,643	91,646	0.18	2.23
South Africa	63,038	71,950	84,255	89,643	91,646	0.18	2.23
OTHER AFRICA	214,956	217,552	239,602	252,532	123,637	0.25	-51.04
Other countries of Africa	214,956	217,552	239,602	252,532	123,637	0.25	-51.04
AMERICAS	5,571,671	6,195,100	6,785,181	6,851,313	7,041,606	14.01	2.78
NORTH AMERICA	4,670,934	5,090,819	5,387,397	5,364,985	5,489,403	10.92	2.32
Canada	588,776	670,055	708,380	706,427	724,606	1.44	2.57
Mexico	153,481	185,244	212,345	216,009	221,861	0.44	2.71
United States of America	3,928,677	4,235,520	4,466,672	4,442,549	4,542,936	9.04	2.26
SOUTH AMERICA	900,737	1,104,281	1,397,784	1,486,328	1,552,203	3.09	4.43
Argentina	190,837	231,503	297,233	341,330	385,379	0.77	12.91
Brazil	436,377	580,610	757,691	765,174	747,065	1.49	-2.37
Venezuela	57,583	55,240	66,316	72,990	74,552	0.15	2.14
Other countries of South America	215,940	236,928	276,544	306,834	345,207	0.69	12.51
EAST ASIA AND THE PACIFIC	3,278,798	3,921,679	4,574,445	4,998,069	5,368,972	10.68	7.42
NORTH-EAST ASIA	2,250,841	2,643,095	3,111,195	3,422,883	3,721,204	7.40	8.72
China	727,570	965,857	1,342,518	1,583,479	1,850,206	3.68	16.84
Japan	1,298,068	1,363,444	1,410,677	1,449,115	1,432,051	2.85	-1.18
Korea, Republic of	225,203	313,794	358,000	390,289	438,947	0.87	12.47
AUSTRALASIA	713,880	836,382	910,092	933,340	986,591	1.96	5.71
Australia	613,799	729,960	803,884	820,562	870,857	1.73	6.13
New Zealand	100,081	106,422	106,208	112,778	115,734	0.23	2.62
OTHER EAST ASIA AND THE PACIFIC	314,077	442,202	553,158	641,846	661,177	1.32	3.01
Other countries of Asia	314,077	442,202	553,158	641,846	661,177	1.32	3.01
EUROPE	31,044,562	32,383,435	34,630,439	35,377,771	36,347,208	72.31	2.74
CENTRAL/EASTERN EUROPE	2,833,442	3,234,612	3,766,341	3,947,068	4,299,709	8.55	8.93
Czech Republic	540,417	584,478	612,930	639,847	651,197	1.30	1.77
Estonia	31,158	31,398	41,453	43,278	49,520	0.10	14.42
Hungary	335,402	350,577	367,577	348,665	363,648	0.72	4.30
Latvia	30,731	32,855	43,591	49,650	59,216	0.12	19.27
Lithuania	60,105	63,081	81,269	86,885	108,067	0.22	24.38
Poland	811,024	888,472	989,436	919,013	981,351	1.95	6.78
Russian Federation	894,659	1,140,432	1,474,137	1,707,998	1,926,911	3.83	12.82
Slovakia	129,946	143,319	155,948	151,732	159,799	0.32	5.32
NORTHERN EUROPE	4,780,832	4,842,851	4,948,929	5,154,472	5,244,767	10.43	1.75
Denmark	582,009	601,085	579,740	626,425	619,236	1.23	-1.15
Finland	249,324	251,453	269,455	258,618	257,866	0.51	-0.29
Iceland	24,337	23,868	22,552	23,627	22,672	0.05	-4.04
Ireland	402,495	365,193	351,383	361,263	366,346	0.73	1.41
Norway	324,784	350,400	369,221	395,285	407,664	0.81	3.13
Sweden	513,491	574,731	609,826	599,239	615,721	1.22	2.75
United Kingdom	2,684,392	2,676,121	2,746,752	2,890,015	2,955,262	5.88	2.26
SOUTHERN EUROPE	2,769,729	2,879,943	2,967,086	2,679,426	2,610,854	5.19	-2.56
Croatia	175,431	163,619	166,120	169,870	172,882	0.34	1.77
Greece	355,853	344,641	342,634	290,038	299,289	0.60	3.19
Malta	52,995	58,543	64,817	69,618	82,394	0.16	18.35
Portugal	220,538	239,012	242,831	232,512	228,853	0.46	-1.57
Slovenia	203,988	206,354	220,852	205,581	212,597	0.42	3.41
Spain	1,760,924	1,867,774	1,929,832	1,711,807	1,614,839	3.21	-5.66
WESTERN EUROPE	18,980,303	19,502,832	20,753,343	21,289,604	21,773,755	43.32	2.27
Austria	1,948,791	2,011,317	2,115,524	2,110,605	2,113,848	4.21	0.15
Belgium	994,999	1,013,042	1,079,541	1,103,629	1,136,286	2.26	2.96
France	3,332,807	3,449,866	3,689,634	3,700,775	3,879,255	7.72	4.82
Germany	9,085,679	9,302,743	9,873,213	10,192,697	10,329,271	20.55	1.34
Luxembourg	64,037	64,329	67,008	70,917	75,519	0.15	6.49
Netherlands	1,836,907	1,851,034	1,933,447	1,959,306	1,925,017	3.83	-1.75
Switzerland	1,717,083	1,810,501	1,994,976	2,151,675	2,314,559	4.60	7.57

369

ITALY

4. Arrivals of non-resident tourists in all types of accommodation establishments, by nationality

	2009	2010	2011	2012	2013	Market share 2013	% Change 2013-2012
EAST MEDITERRANEAN EUROPE	**434,714**	**520,028**	**568,428**	**616,250**	**705,354**	**1.40**	**14.46**
Cyprus	17,388	20,569	19,958	24,174	23,343	0.05	-3.44
Israel	252,455	289,049	302,765	315,476	351,559	0.70	11.44
Turkey	164,871	210,410	245,705	276,600	330,452	0.66	19.47
OTHER EUROPE	**1,245,542**	**1,403,169**	**1,626,312**	**1,690,951**	**1,712,769**	**3.41**	**1.29**
Other countries of Europe	1,245,542	1,403,169	1,626,312	1,690,951	1,712,769	3.41	1.29
MIDDLE EAST	**226,341**	**261,281**	**306,390**	**339,554**	**372,813**	**0.74**	**9.79**
Egypt	41,295	43,160	41,998	45,124	48,960	0.10	8.50
Other countries of Middle East	185,046	218,121	264,392	294,430	323,853	0.64	9.99
SOUTH ASIA	**157,708**	**197,152**	**251,631**	**276,229**	**279,232**	**0.56**	**1.09**
India	157,708	197,152	251,631	276,229	279,232	0.56	1.09
NOT SPECIFIED	**567,648**	**546,189**	**588,866**	**553,464**	**638,122**	**1.27**	**15.30**
Other countries of the World	567,648	546,189	588,866	553,464	638,122	1.27	15.30

Yearbook of Tourism Statistics, Data 2009 – 2013, 2015 Edition

ITALY

5. Overnight stays of non-resident tourists in hotels and similar establishments, by nationality

	2009	2010	2011	2012	2013	Market share 2013	% Change 2013-2012
TOTAL (*)	106,828,579	111,551,526	120,014,027	122,700,343	126,330,288	100.00	2.96
AFRICA	781,987	782,638	1,127,921	1,196,970	632,159	0.50	-47.19
SOUTHERN AFRICA	155,501	170,553	206,296	212,829	215,482	0.17	1.25
South Africa	155,501	170,553	206,296	212,829	215,482	0.17	1.25
OTHER AFRICA	626,486	612,085	921,625	984,141	416,677	0.33	-57.66
Other countries of Africa	626,486	612,085	921,625	984,141	416,677	0.33	-57.66
AMERICAS	12,259,124	13,412,419	14,774,746	14,693,766	15,119,084	11.97	2.89
NORTH AMERICA	10,195,123	10,979,562	11,795,941	11,571,920	11,850,708	9.38	2.41
Canada	1,301,640	1,459,085	1,656,449	1,552,994	1,594,486	1.26	2.67
Mexico	329,798	380,543	425,837	428,562	440,945	0.35	2.89
United States of America	8,563,685	9,139,934	9,713,655	9,590,364	9,815,277	7.77	2.35
SOUTH AMERICA	2,064,001	2,432,857	2,978,805	3,121,846	3,268,376	2.59	4.69
Argentina	433,805	516,089	641,449	702,862	787,033	0.62	11.98
Brazil	976,487	1,247,397	1,582,610	1,598,437	1,571,282	1.24	-1.70
Venezuela	153,638	141,684	165,396	177,622	191,224	0.15	7.66
Other countries of South America	500,071	527,687	589,350	642,925	718,837	0.57	11.81
EAST ASIA AND THE PACIFIC	6,033,692	6,925,435	7,924,700	8,619,225	9,029,703	7.15	4.76
NORTH-EAST ASIA	3,868,385	4,323,597	4,939,757	5,419,732	5,756,384	4.56	6.21
China	1,120,082	1,404,270	1,895,228	2,265,575	2,536,935	2.01	11.98
Japan	2,341,372	2,414,679	2,471,480	2,559,377	2,567,519	2.03	0.32
Korea, Republic of	406,931	504,648	573,049	594,780	651,930	0.52	9.61
AUSTRALASIA	1,434,028	1,662,709	1,838,566	1,920,914	1,994,117	1.58	3.81
Australia	1,243,145	1,451,206	1,624,804	1,687,234	1,758,300	1.39	4.21
New Zealand	190,883	211,503	213,762	233,680	235,817	0.19	0.91
OTHER EAST ASIA AND THE PACIFIC	731,279	939,129	1,146,377	1,278,579	1,279,202	1.01	0.05
Other countries of Asia	731,279	939,129	1,146,377	1,278,579	1,279,202	1.01	0.05
EUROPE	85,394,447	87,994,204	93,501,667	95,504,674	98,533,355	78.00	3.17
CENTRAL/EASTERN EUROPE	7,928,309	9,119,265	10,368,002	11,034,914	12,011,884	9.51	8.85
Czech Republic	1,375,188	1,478,895	1,542,005	1,577,270	1,593,566	1.26	1.03
Estonia	80,156	87,842	115,715	127,023	124,636	0.10	-1.88
Hungary	748,646	765,236	804,953	763,811	794,124	0.63	3.97
Latvia	86,140	85,843	102,640	128,949	141,985	0.11	10.11
Lithuania	142,040	148,652	185,029	198,109	250,823	0.20	26.61
Poland	2,216,059	2,412,767	2,487,718	2,356,455	2,455,369	1.94	4.20
Russian Federation	2,965,533	3,801,556	4,752,783	5,501,906	6,252,558	4.95	13.64
Slovakia	314,547	338,474	377,159	381,391	398,823	0.32	4.57
NORTHERN EUROPE	14,317,327	14,231,652	14,809,878	15,217,421	15,630,475	12.37	2.71
Denmark	1,269,074	1,287,186	1,268,999	1,342,876	1,377,381	1.09	2.57
Finland	740,426	733,575	779,682	743,494	752,774	0.60	1.25
Iceland	80,874	71,863	70,991	77,106	81,627	0.06	5.86
Ireland	1,300,099	1,165,921	1,119,810	1,143,677	1,144,569	0.91	0.08
Norway	949,952	992,868	1,039,100	1,111,229	1,178,537	0.93	6.06
Sweden	1,537,476	1,703,565	1,825,339	1,790,342	1,852,668	1.47	3.48
United Kingdom	8,439,426	8,276,674	8,705,957	9,008,697	9,242,919	7.32	2.60
SOUTHERN EUROPE	6,556,123	6,710,662	6,885,335	6,268,166	6,120,874	4.85	-2.35
Croatia	453,271	412,143	393,114	413,243	419,708	0.33	1.56
Greece	891,998	853,639	829,791	736,400	746,876	0.59	1.42
Malta	148,209	171,231	175,554	195,912	225,388	0.18	15.05
Portugal	560,775	568,408	581,631	566,741	554,871	0.44	-2.09
Slovenia	421,663	427,894	456,855	418,719	428,486	0.34	2.33
Spain	4,080,207	4,277,347	4,448,390	3,937,151	3,745,545	2.96	-4.87
WESTERN EUROPE	52,011,396	52,891,926	55,747,098	57,041,534	58,474,272	46.29	2.51
Austria	5,085,735	5,273,070	5,584,362	5,535,023	5,580,473	4.42	0.82
Belgium	3,094,207	3,088,377	3,229,371	3,278,599	3,366,983	2.67	2.70
France	7,780,100	7,956,900	8,621,882	8,588,324	9,028,387	7.15	5.12
Germany	27,768,674	28,091,376	29,306,486	30,232,994	30,750,733	24.34	1.71
Luxembourg	253,555	249,711	264,721	269,209	281,035	0.22	4.39
Netherlands	3,160,459	3,193,313	3,267,142	3,249,696	3,228,291	2.56	-0.66
Switzerland	4,868,666	5,039,179	5,473,134	5,887,689	6,238,370	4.94	5.96

Yearbook of Tourism Statistics, Data 2009 – 2013, 2015 Edition

ITALY

5. Overnight stays of non-resident tourists in hotels and similar establishments, by nationality

	2009	2010	2011	2012	2013	Market share 2013	% Change 2013-2012
EAST MEDITERRANEAN EUROPE	1,075,768	1,270,977	1,408,162	1,506,884	1,713,836	1.36	13.73
Cyprus	52,742	61,417	58,012	62,828	62,377	0.05	-0.72
Israel	605,880	716,764	779,624	823,066	909,597	0.72	10.51
Turkey	417,146	492,796	570,526	620,990	741,862	0.59	19.46
OTHER EUROPE	3,505,524	3,769,722	4,283,192	4,435,755	4,582,014	3.63	3.30
Other countries of Europe	3,505,524	3,769,722	4,283,192	4,435,755	4,582,014	3.63	3.30
MIDDLE EAST	708,535	773,622	886,737	958,997	1,013,418	0.80	5.67
Egypt	135,776	140,341	146,560	170,050	148,615	0.12	-12.61
Other countries of Middle East	572,759	633,281	740,177	788,947	864,803	0.68	9.61
SOUTH ASIA	337,851	387,672	479,236	512,474	519,179	0.41	1.31
India	337,851	387,672	479,236	512,474	519,179	0.41	1.31
NOT SPECIFIED	1,312,943	1,275,536	1,319,020	1,214,237	1,483,390	1.17	22.17
Other countries of the World	1,312,943	1,275,536	1,319,020	1,214,237	1,483,390	1.17	22.17

Yearbook of Tourism Statistics, Data 2009 – 2013, 2015 Edition

ITALY

6. Overnight stays of non-resident tourists in all types of accommodation establishments, by nationality

	2009	2010	2011	2012	2013	Market share 2013	% Change 2013-2012
TOTAL	159,493,866	165,202,498	176,474,062	180,594,988	184,793,382	100.00	2.32
AFRICA	1,028,095	1,027,597	1,501,871	1,623,414	880,265	0.48	-45.78
SOUTHERN AFRICA	191,669	210,938	255,991	271,223	274,164	0.15	1.08
South Africa	191,669	210,938	255,991	271,223	274,164	0.15	1.08
OTHER AFRICA	836,426	816,659	1,245,880	1,352,191	606,101	0.33	-55.18
Other countries of Africa	836,426	816,659	1,245,880	1,352,191	606,101	0.33	-55.18
AMERICAS	14,513,549	15,883,627	17,500,991	17,569,754	18,125,304	9.81	3.16
NORTH AMERICA	12,080,237	13,046,664	14,038,324	13,902,922	14,258,723	7.72	2.56
Canada	1,612,960	1,798,679	2,024,178	1,948,324	2,009,093	1.09	3.12
Mexico	387,160	440,692	498,265	505,152	523,572	0.28	3.65
United States of America	10,080,117	10,807,293	11,515,881	11,449,446	11,726,058	6.35	2.42
SOUTH AMERICA	2,433,312	2,836,963	3,462,667	3,666,832	3,866,581	2.09	5.45
Argentina	519,315	609,771	757,589	834,321	929,334	0.50	11.39
Brazil	1,137,182	1,427,733	1,809,011	1,848,507	1,830,635	0.99	-0.97
Venezuela	178,425	163,986	191,695	205,270	223,406	0.12	8.84
Other countries of South America	598,390	635,473	704,372	778,734	883,206	0.48	13.42
EAST ASIA AND THE PACIFIC	6,970,551	7,961,682	9,088,145	9,855,149	10,465,753	5.66	6.20
NORTH-EAST ASIA	4,287,190	4,733,489	5,416,203	5,939,640	6,345,316	3.43	6.83
China	1,254,039	1,564,035	2,089,115	2,496,287	2,829,861	1.53	13.36
Japan	2,534,836	2,593,846	2,665,424	2,765,414	2,765,168	1.50	-0.01
Korea, Republic of	498,315	575,608	661,664	677,939	750,287	0.41	10.67
AUSTRALASIA	1,846,456	2,147,422	2,367,349	2,462,893	2,613,408	1.41	6.11
Australia	1,572,543	1,861,752	2,081,771	2,157,363	2,292,708	1.24	6.27
New Zealand	273,913	285,670	285,578	305,530	320,700	0.17	4.97
OTHER EAST ASIA AND THE PACIFIC	836,905	1,080,771	1,304,593	1,452,616	1,507,029	0.82	3.75
Other countries of Asia	836,905	1,080,771	1,304,593	1,452,616	1,507,029	0.82	3.75
EUROPE	134,234,320	137,485,494	145,229,651	148,463,381	151,819,761	82.16	2.26
CENTRAL/EASTERN EUROPE	11,995,567	13,662,293	15,195,030	15,889,109	17,197,966	9.31	8.24
Czech Republic	2,841,017	3,077,661	3,168,776	3,248,662	3,246,993	1.76	-0.05
Estonia	100,553	108,633	134,152	150,105	154,869	0.08	3.17
Hungary	1,366,001	1,453,372	1,482,498	1,348,087	1,395,769	0.76	3.54
Latvia	109,296	111,807	135,326	163,930	185,253	0.10	13.01
Lithuania	174,487	186,380	231,275	249,281	319,103	0.17	28.01
Poland	3,400,700	3,736,189	3,883,908	3,742,801	3,963,625	2.14	5.90
Russian Federation	3,294,957	4,208,604	5,318,880	6,179,785	7,111,178	3.85	15.07
Slovakia	708,556	779,647	840,215	806,458	821,176	0.44	1.83
NORTHERN EUROPE	19,652,109	19,686,308	20,103,858	20,755,513	21,293,968	11.52	2.59
Denmark	3,208,729	3,311,712	3,139,703	3,375,537	3,401,183	1.84	0.76
Finland	901,719	903,041	958,010	913,647	921,514	0.50	0.86
Iceland	96,917	89,837	84,211	92,809	96,907	0.05	4.42
Ireland	1,706,869	1,533,856	1,448,777	1,507,394	1,584,550	0.86	5.12
Norway	1,255,530	1,316,970	1,366,480	1,455,664	1,534,189	0.83	5.39
Sweden	2,013,300	2,193,686	2,311,576	2,278,494	2,373,896	1.28	4.19
United Kingdom	10,469,045	10,337,206	10,795,101	11,131,968	11,381,729	6.16	2.24
SOUTHERN EUROPE	7,989,916	8,146,446	8,350,266	7,640,643	7,428,117	4.02	-2.78
Croatia	640,887	559,823	526,812	542,024	540,261	0.29	-0.33
Greece	1,022,691	971,217	952,829	845,787	856,229	0.46	1.23
Malta	177,540	202,203	207,217	230,219	266,882	0.14	15.93
Portugal	651,567	671,622	680,305	660,028	643,759	0.35	-2.46
Slovenia	664,166	678,568	718,615	663,959	655,396	0.35	-1.29
Spain	4,833,065	5,063,013	5,264,488	4,698,626	4,465,590	2.42	-4.96
WESTERN EUROPE	88,733,229	89,590,427	94,427,763	96,742,865	98,059,201	53.06	1.36
Austria	8,078,701	8,226,147	8,670,900	8,505,045	8,367,288	4.53	-1.62
Belgium	4,434,026	4,425,339	4,614,934	4,749,059	4,879,723	2.64	2.75
France	10,447,586	10,623,637	11,432,007	11,369,866	11,900,230	6.44	4.66
Germany	47,278,488	47,801,927	50,199,797	51,752,263	52,224,949	28.26	0.91
Luxembourg	309,707	308,829	320,997	328,186	338,480	0.18	3.14
Netherlands	10,875,329	10,674,451	11,043,799	11,303,681	11,144,216	6.03	-1.41
Switzerland	7,309,392	7,530,097	8,145,329	8,734,765	9,204,315	4.98	5.38

373

ITALY

6. Overnight stays of non-resident tourists in all types of accommodation establishments, by nationality

	2009	2010	2011	2012	2013	Market share 2013	% Change 2013-2012
EAST MEDITERRANEAN EUROPE	**1,267,778**	**1,491,744**	**1,648,181**	**1,761,347**	**2,013,905**	**1.09**	**14.34**
Cyprus	57,348	67,900	63,995	71,342	72,902	0.04	2.19
Israel	734,500	871,404	936,832	987,903	1,095,855	0.59	10.93
Turkey	475,930	552,440	647,354	702,102	845,148	0.46	20.37
OTHER EUROPE	**4,595,721**	**4,908,276**	**5,504,553**	**5,673,904**	**5,826,604**	**3.15**	**2.69**
Other countries of Europe	4,595,721	4,908,276	5,504,553	5,673,904	5,826,604	3.15	2.69
MIDDLE EAST	**818,238**	**874,432**	**1,001,851**	**1,090,134**	**1,160,748**	**0.63**	**6.48**
Egypt	170,842	170,056	181,312	202,086	180,033	0.10	-10.91
Other countries of Middle East	647,396	704,376	820,539	888,048	980,715	0.53	10.43
SOUTH ASIA	**394,709**	**461,311**	**554,886**	**591,731**	**607,973**	**0.33**	**2.74**
India	394,709	461,311	554,886	591,731	607,973	0.33	2.74
NOT SPECIFIED	**1,534,404**	**1,508,355**	**1,596,667**	**1,401,425**	**1,733,578**	**0.94**	**23.70**
Other countries of the World	1,534,404	1,508,355	1,596,667	1,401,425	1,733,578	0.94	23.70

Yearbook of Tourism Statistics, Data 2009 – 2013, 2015 Edition

JAMAICA

1. Arrivals of non-resident tourists at national borders, by country of residence

		2009	2010	2011	2012	2013	Market share 2013	% Change 2013-2012
TOTAL	(*)	**1,831,097**	**1,921,678**	**1,951,752**	**1,986,085**	**2,008,409**	**100.00**	**1.12**
AFRICA		**1,237**	**1,169**	**1,200**	**1,651**	**1,370**	**0.07**	**-17.02**
OTHER AFRICA		**1,237**	**1,169**	**1,200**	**1,651**	**1,370**	**0.07**	**-17.02**
All countries of Africa		1,237	1,169	1,200	1,651	1,370	0.07	-17.02
AMERICAS		**1,542,976**	**1,639,875**	**1,687,308**	**1,750,890**	**1,759,380**	**87.60**	**0.48**
CARIBBEAN		**62,823**	**56,031**	**63,360**	**62,196**	**55,877**	**2.78**	**-10.16**
Antigua and Barbuda		2,554	2,235	2,290	2,457	1,845	0.09	-24.91
Aruba		400	398	409	496	438	0.02	-11.69
Bahamas		5,031	4,884	5,999	5,481	5,216	0.26	-4.83
Barbados		5,027	4,469	5,422	5,315	4,439	0.22	-16.48
Bermuda		3,369	3,112	2,710	2,683	2,568	0.13	-4.29
British Virgin Islands		1,025	1,054	1,031	1,205	941	0.05	-21.91
Cayman Islands		23,384	18,409	18,035	16,536	16,234	0.81	-1.83
Cuba		1,067	562	646	748	1,285	0.06	71.79
Curaçao		1,279	778	893	886	969	0.05	9.37
Dominica		543	387	418	434	328	0.02	-24.42
Dominican Republic		1,111	1,038	1,293	1,298	1,559	0.08	20.11
Grenada		640	450	527	518	448	0.02	-13.51
Guadeloupe		121	185	322	448	145	0.01	-67.63
Haiti		288	447	392	511	498	0.02	-2.54
Montserrat		154	149	143	181	129	0.01	-28.73
Puerto Rico		1,346	1,447	1,486	1,559	1,481	0.07	-5.00
Saint Kitts and Nevis		1,103	950	913	981	907	0.05	-7.54
Saint Lucia		1,308	990	1,055	1,157	916	0.05	-20.83
Saint Vincent and the Grenadines		595	445	676	612	478	0.02	-21.90
Sint Maarten		789	941	1,079	1,352	1,057	0.05	-21.82
Trinidad and Tobago		9,622	10,330	15,513	14,947	11,437	0.57	-23.48
Turks and Caicos Islands		1,445	1,545	1,522	1,804	1,895	0.09	5.04
Other countries of the Caribbean		622	826	586	587	664	0.03	13.12
CENTRAL AMERICA		**3,441**	**3,251**	**3,655**	**4,635**	**7,106**	**0.35**	**53.31**
Belize		592	481	612	670	600	0.03	-10.45
Costa Rica		799	758	846	1,328	3,018	0.15	127.26
El Salvador		177	142	174	180	214	0.01	18.89
Guatemala		348	527	501	628	684	0.03	8.92
Honduras		156	131	203	159	354	0.02	122.64
Nicaragua		85	76	102	60	101	0.01	68.33
Panama		1,284	1,136	1,217	1,610	2,135	0.11	32.61
NORTH AMERICA		**1,465,338**	**1,570,118**	**1,606,627**	**1,663,208**	**1,673,360**	**83.32**	**0.61**
Canada		290,307	325,191	378,938	403,200	399,331	19.88	-0.96
Mexico		2,187	1,984	2,124	2,339	2,767	0.14	18.30
United States of America		1,172,844	1,242,943	1,225,565	1,257,669	1,271,262	63.30	1.08
SOUTH AMERICA		**11,374**	**10,475**	**13,666**	**20,851**	**23,037**	**1.15**	**10.48**
Argentina		1,695	1,779	2,168	3,739	4,625	0.23	23.70
Bolivia		34	51	56	28	85	0.00	203.57
Brazil		1,550	1,683	1,597	2,071	2,771	0.14	33.80
Chile		893	741	1,023	3,654	5,005	0.25	36.97
Colombia		1,001	1,110	1,489	4,062	3,625	0.18	-10.76
Ecuador		1,844	1,481	2,979	2,464	1,864	0.09	-24.35
Guyana		2,079	1,827	2,376	2,288	1,860	0.09	-18.71
Paraguay		30	22	58	40	83	0.00	107.50
Peru		465	393	485	791	1,045	0.05	32.11
Suriname		431	441	480	500	512	0.03	2.40
Uruguay		190	139	168	381	505	0.03	32.55
Venezuela		1,145	786	759	750	1,019	0.05	35.87
Other countries of South America		17	22	28	83	38	0.00	-54.22
EAST ASIA AND THE PACIFIC		**7,138**	**6,760**	**7,429**	**8,220**	**8,651**	**0.43**	**5.24**
NORTH-EAST ASIA		**4,013**	**3,703**	**4,281**	**4,681**	**5,025**	**0.25**	**7.35**
China		1,142	1,302	1,703	2,102	2,420	0.12	15.13
Japan		2,511	1,950	2,027	2,092	2,177	0.11	4.06

Yearbook of Tourism Statistics, Data 2009 – 2013, 2015 Edition

JAMAICA

1. Arrivals of non-resident tourists at national borders, by country of residence

	2009	2010	2011	2012	2013	Market share 2013	% Change 2013-2012
Korea, Republic of	291	375	477	350	369	0.02	5.43
Taiwan, Province of China	69	76	74	137	59	0.00	-56.93
SOUTH-EAST ASIA	**450**	**587**	**424**	**481**	**444**	**0.02**	**-7.69**
Philippines	322	479	323	364	309	0.02	-15.11
Singapore	128	108	101	117	135	0.01	15.38
AUSTRALASIA	**2,218**	**2,121**	**2,269**	**2,597**	**2,742**	**0.14**	**5.58**
Australia	1,903	1,869	2,040	2,254	2,462	0.12	9.23
New Zealand	315	252	229	343	280	0.01	-18.37
OTHER EAST ASIA AND THE PACIFIC	**457**	**349**	**455**	**461**	**440**	**0.02**	**-4.56**
Other countries of Asia	457	349	455	461	440	0.02	-4.56
EUROPE	**277,931**	**272,139**	**253,749**	**223,268**	**236,641**	**11.78**	**5.99**
CENTRAL/EASTERN EUROPE	**4,336**	**4,533**	**4,893**	**4,350**	**15,499**	**0.77**	**256.30**
Czech Republic/Slovakia	578	473	772	615	1,214	0.06	97.40
Hungary	276	389	286	317	316	0.02	-0.32
Poland	1,294	1,299	1,443	1,199	1,183	0.06	-1.33
Russian Federation	1,744	1,945	1,976	1,701	12,286	0.61	622.28
Ukraine	444	427	416	518	500	0.02	-3.47
NORTHERN EUROPE	**191,225**	**190,825**	**179,726**	**151,433**	**158,713**	**7.90**	**4.81**
Denmark	794	772	648	615	632	0.03	2.76
Finland	526	427	451	427	477	0.02	11.71
Ireland	2,838	2,737	2,459	2,071	1,913	0.10	-7.63
Norway	958	915	1,054	1,030	1,159	0.06	12.52
Sweden	1,597	1,619	1,607	2,059	3,217	0.16	56.24
United Kingdom	184,512	184,355	173,507	145,231	151,315	7.53	4.19
SOUTHERN EUROPE	**36,703**	**34,107**	**23,492**	**18,136**	**12,134**	**0.60**	**-33.09**
Greece	291	249	273	208	201	0.01	-3.37
Italy	14,588	13,700	11,700	9,672	7,808	0.39	-19.27
Portugal	9,056	10,076	4,686	3,906	1,556	0.08	-60.16
Spain	12,768	10,082	6,833	4,350	2,569	0.13	-40.94
WESTERN EUROPE	**42,848**	**40,233**	**43,079**	**46,763**	**47,492**	**2.36**	**1.56**
Austria	2,623	2,641	2,545	2,377	2,174	0.11	-8.54
Belgium	6,610	5,228	5,276	4,882	4,703	0.23	-3.67
France	3,779	3,762	4,748	9,253	12,087	0.60	30.63
Germany	20,220	18,857	19,939	20,236	19,658	0.98	-2.86
Luxembourg	248	207	212	202	236	0.01	16.83
Netherlands	7,023	6,677	7,200	6,714	5,515	0.27	-17.86
Switzerland	2,345	2,861	3,159	3,099	3,119	0.16	0.65
EAST MEDITERRANEAN EUROPE	**1,132**	**824**	**704**	**840**	**830**	**0.04**	**-1.19**
Israel	879	683	597	639	636	0.03	-0.47
Turkey	253	141	107	201	194	0.01	-3.48
OTHER EUROPE	**1,687**	**1,617**	**1,855**	**1,746**	**1,973**	**0.10**	**13.00**
Other countries of Europe	1,687	1,617	1,855	1,746	1,973	0.10	13.00
MIDDLE EAST	**532**	**542**	**649**	**608**	**680**	**0.03**	**11.84**
Saudi Arabia	19	16	36	31	45	0.00	45.16
Other countries of Middle East	513	526	613	577	635	0.03	10.05
SOUTH ASIA	**1,248**	**1,152**	**1,362**	**1,397**	**1,596**	**0.08**	**14.24**
India	1,232	1,127	1,330	1,375	1,567	0.08	13.96
Pakistan	16	25	32	22	29	0.00	31.82
NOT SPECIFIED	**35**	**41**	**55**	**51**	**91**	**0.00**	**78.43**
Other countries of the World	35	41	55	51	91	0.00	78.43

376

JAMAICA

6. Overnight stays of non-resident tourists in all types of accommodation establishments, by country of residence

		2009	2010	2011	2012	2013	Market share 2013	% Change 2013-2012
TOTAL	(*)	15,535,167	15,903,420	15,932,132	16,051,021	16,080,663	100.00	0.18
AMERICAS		11,655,659	12,155,998	12,430,885	12,941,576	12,804,094	79.62	-1.06
CARIBBEAN		426,111	395,983	410,946	420,302	380,279	2.36	-9.52
All countries of the Caribbean		426,111	395,983	410,946	420,302	380,279	2.36	-9.52
NORTH AMERICA		11,110,489	11,641,691	11,885,744	12,331,159	12,194,225	75.83	-1.11
Canada, United States		11,110,489	11,641,691	11,885,744	12,331,159	12,194,225	75.83	-1.11
OTHER AMERICAS		119,059	118,324	134,195	190,115	229,590	1.43	20.76
Other countries of the Americas	(*)	119,059	118,324	134,195	190,115	229,590	1.43	20.76
EUROPE		3,740,515	3,608,147	3,344,357	2,952,823	3,060,133	19.03	3.63
OTHER EUROPE		3,740,515	3,608,147	3,344,357	2,952,823	3,060,133	19.03	3.63
All countries of Europe	(*)	3,740,515	3,608,147	3,344,357	2,952,823	3,060,133	19.03	3.63
NOT SPECIFIED		138,993	139,275	156,890	156,622	216,436	1.35	38.19
Other countries of the World		138,993	139,275	156,890	156,622	216,436	1.35	38.19

Yearbook of Tourism Statistics, Data 2009 – 2013, 2015 Edition

JAPAN

2. Arrivals of non-resident visitors at national borders, by nationality

	2009	2010	2011	2012	2013	Market share 2013	% Change 2013-2012
TOTAL (*)	6,789,658	8,611,175	6,218,752	8,358,105	10,363,904	100.00	24.00
AFRICA	17,219	19,076	16,777	21,074	22,955	0.22	8.93
SOUTHERN AFRICA	4,290	4,635	3,942	5,708	5,828	0.06	2.10
South Africa	4,290	4,635	3,942	5,708	5,828	0.06	2.10
WEST AFRICA	2,090	2,333	1,834	2,541	2,408	0.02	-5.23
Ghana	792	957	799	1,095	1,049	0.01	-4.20
Nigeria	1,298	1,376	1,035	1,446	1,359	0.01	-6.02
OTHER AFRICA	10,839	12,108	11,001	12,825	14,719	0.14	14.77
Other countries of Africa	10,839	12,108	11,001	12,825	14,719	0.14	14.77
AMERICAS	908,098	945,377	716,808	927,552	1,031,911	9.96	11.25
CENTRAL AMERICA		357	291	346	381	0.00	10.12
El Salvador		357	291	346	381	0.00	10.12
NORTH AMERICA	869,129	899,785	680,266	870,566	975,384	9.41	12.04
Canada	152,756	153,303	101,299	135,355	152,766	1.47	12.86
Mexico	16,454	19,248	13,080	18,502	23,338	0.23	26.14
United States of America	699,919	727,234	565,887	716,709	799,280	7.71	11.52
SOUTH AMERICA	32,398	38,137	31,038	49,870	48,413	0.47	-2.92
Argentina	4,379	4,896	3,768	5,239	6,357	0.06	21.34
Bolivia	459	518	384	477	587	0.01	23.06
Brazil	16,899	21,393	18,470	32,111	27,105	0.26	-15.59
Chile	2,667	3,053	2,579	3,538	4,031	0.04	13.93
Colombia	2,973	3,052	2,238	3,308	4,176	0.04	26.24
Ecuador	683	845	480	754	869	0.01	15.25
Peru	2,164	2,452	1,857	2,306	2,369	0.02	2.73
Venezuela	2,174	1,928	1,262	2,137	2,919	0.03	36.59
OTHER AMERICAS	6,571	7,098	5,213	6,770	7,733	0.07	14.22
Other countries of the Americas	6,571	7,098	5,213	6,770	7,733	0.07	14.22
EAST ASIA AND THE PACIFIC	4,940,971	6,653,648	4,796,321	6,488,700	8,239,562	79.50	26.98
NORTH-EAST ASIA	4,092,862	5,660,930	4,083,956	5,447,709	6,775,139	65.37	24.37
China	1,006,085	1,412,875	1,043,246	1,425,100	1,314,437	12.68	-7.77
Hong Kong, China	449,568	508,691	364,865	481,665	745,881	7.20	54.85
Korea, Republic of	1,586,772	2,439,816	1,658,073	2,042,775	2,456,165	23.70	20.24
Macao, China	17,199	21,330	13,292	19,040	32,797	0.32	72.25
Mongolia	8,946	9,940	10,506	13,376	15,038	0.15	12.43
Taiwan, Province of China	1,024,292	1,268,278	993,974	1,465,753	2,210,821	21.33	50.83
SOUTH-EAST ASIA	592,793	722,112	515,154	789,317	1,168,664	11.28	48.06
Brunei Darussalam	1,138	1,388	971	1,378	1,986	0.02	44.12
Cambodia	3,008	3,189	3,069	3,662	4,842	0.05	32.22
Indonesia	63,617	80,632	61,911	101,460	136,797	1.32	34.83
Lao People's Democratic Republic	2,145	2,209	2,111	2,676	3,243	0.03	21.19
Malaysia	89,509	114,519	81,516	130,183	176,521	1.70	35.59
Myanmar	4,905	5,095	5,106	6,924	9,533	0.09	37.68
Philippines	71,485	77,377	63,099	85,037	108,351	1.05	27.42
Singapore	145,224	180,960	111,354	142,201	189,280	1.83	33.11
Thailand	177,541	214,881	144,969	260,640	453,642	4.38	74.05
Viet Nam	34,221	41,862	41,048	55,156	84,469	0.82	53.15
AUSTRALASIA	243,226	257,812	186,574	238,257	281,523	2.72	18.16
Australia	211,659	225,751	162,578	206,404	244,569	2.36	18.49
New Zealand	31,567	32,061	23,996	31,853	36,954	0.36	16.01
OTHER EAST ASIA AND THE PACIFIC	12,090	12,794	10,637	13,417	14,236	0.14	6.10
Other countries of Asia	9,103	9,734	8,061	10,161	10,873	0.10	7.01
Other countries of Oceania	2,987	3,060	2,576	3,256	3,363	0.03	3.29
EUROPE	820,128	877,284	582,787	796,761	931,074	8.98	16.86
CENTRAL/EASTERN EUROPE	76,200	84,204	58,191	84,353	103,223	1.00	22.37
Bulgaria	2,434	2,238	1,783	2,345	2,659	0.03	13.39
Czech Republic	4,943	5,319	4,525	5,485	6,869	0.07	25.23
Hungary	4,455	4,371	3,182	4,531	5,170	0.05	14.10
Poland	8,638	10,253	7,451	10,668	15,525	0.15	45.53
Romania	3,550	4,664	3,227	4,797	5,293	0.05	10.34

378

JAPAN

2. Arrivals of non-resident visitors at national borders, by nationality

	2009	2010	2011	2012	2013	Market share 2013	% Change 2013-2012
Russian Federation	46,952	51,457	33,793	50,176	60,502	0.58	20.58
Slovakia	1,786	2,192	1,356	2,161	2,397	0.02	10.92
Ukraine	3,442	3,710	2,874	4,190	4,808	0.05	14.75
NORTHERN EUROPE	**259,062**	**266,428**	**200,414**	**256,112**	**285,702**	**2.76**	**11.55**
Denmark	13,116	14,606	10,821	13,594	15,065	0.15	10.82
Finland	17,797	16,960	10,943	15,529	16,523	0.16	6.40
Iceland		589	546	732	767	0.01	4.78
Ireland	10,450	10,738	8,294	10,358	11,258	0.11	8.69
Norway	9,855	10,302	7,905	11,447	14,085	0.14	23.05
Sweden	26,384	29,188	21,806	30,458	36,206	0.35	18.87
United Kingdom	181,460	184,045	140,099	173,994	191,798	1.85	10.23
SOUTHERN EUROPE	**116,229**	**123,728**	**65,312**	**101,075**	**130,354**	**1.26**	**28.97**
Croatia	1,325	1,402	918	1,335	1,593	0.02	19.33
Greece	4,350	4,363	2,459	3,074	4,031	0.04	31.13
Italy	59,607	62,394	34,035	51,801	67,228	0.65	29.78
Montenegro		70	41	65	63	0.00	-3.08
Portugal	8,463	10,313	6,227	8,408	11,604	0.11	38.01
Serbia		973	754	1,185	1,374	0.01	15.95
Serbia and Montenegro		137	64				
Spain	42,484	44,076	20,814	35,207	44,461	0.43	26.28
WESTERN EUROPE	**333,803**	**365,507**	**235,749**	**320,558**	**369,238**	**3.56**	**15.19**
Austria	13,684	14,440	8,539	11,633	13,015	0.13	11.88
Belgium	13,899	15,981	10,708	14,608	16,558	0.16	13.35
France	141,251	151,011	95,438	130,142	154,892	1.49	19.02
Germany	110,692	124,360	80,772	108,898	121,776	1.18	11.83
Luxembourg		873	432	682	814	0.01	19.35
Netherlands	31,186	32,837	23,450	30,266	33,861	0.33	11.88
Switzerland	23,091	26,005	16,410	24,329	28,322	0.27	16.41
EAST MEDITERRANEAN EUROPE	**20,043**	**24,118**	**13,508**	**20,921**	**26,942**	**0.26**	**28.78**
Israel	12,205	14,189	6,931	10,413	14,478	0.14	39.04
Turkey	7,838	9,929	6,577	10,508	12,464	0.12	18.61
OTHER EUROPE	**14,791**	**13,299**	**9,613**	**13,742**	**15,615**	**0.15**	**13.63**
Other countries of Europe	14,791	13,299	9,613	13,742	15,615	0.15	13.63
MIDDLE EAST	**7,332**	**10,448**	**7,106**	**10,706**	**12,809**	**0.12**	**19.64**
Egypt	3,402	3,589	2,584	3,651	3,742	0.04	2.49
Lebanon		935	611	820	948	0.01	15.61
Saudi Arabia	2,750	3,749	2,866	4,208	5,227	0.05	24.22
United Arab Emirates	1,180	2,175	1,045	2,027	2,892	0.03	42.67
SOUTH ASIA	**95,270**	**104,679**	**98,460**	**112,814**	**125,104**	**1.21**	**10.89**
Bangladesh	6,360	6,213	6,118	6,310	6,900	0.07	9.35
India	58,918	66,819	59,354	68,914	75,095	0.72	8.97
Iran, Islamic Republic of	4,898	4,831	3,787	4,187	3,148	0.03	-24.81
Nepal	9,221	9,484	11,041	13,082	18,065	0.17	38.09
Pakistan	7,335	7,762	8,120	9,196	9,011	0.09	-2.01
Sri Lanka	8,538	9,570	10,040	11,125	12,885	0.12	15.82
NOT SPECIFIED	**640**	**663**	**493**	**498**	**489**	**0.00**	**-1.81**
Other countries of the World	640	663	493	498	489	0.00	-1.81

 Yearbook of Tourism Statistics, Data 2009 – 2013, 2015 Edition

JORDAN

1. Arrivals of non-resident tourists at national borders, by nationality

	2009	2010	2011	2012	2013	Market share 2013	% Change 2013-2012
TOTAL	3,788,890	4,207,408	3,959,654	4,162,367	3,945,363	100.00	-5.21
AFRICA	46,387	49,762	49,947	55,002	55,472	1.41	0.85
EAST AFRICA	3,587	4,666	4,342	6,913	8,693	0.22	25.75
Djibouti	49	26	25	42	38	0.00	-9.52
Eritrea	358	407	367	346	625	0.02	80.64
Ethiopia	2,113	3,106	2,264	4,581	6,570	0.17	43.42
Kenya	486	599	1,191	1,253	706	0.02	-43.66
Mauritius	234	296	299	431	570	0.01	32.25
Somalia	347	232	196	260	184	0.00	-29.23
CENTRAL AFRICA	92	164	363	620	811	0.02	30.81
Chad	92	164	363	620	811	0.02	30.81
NORTH AFRICA	32,490	34,354	32,072	32,931	32,613	0.83	-0.97
Algeria	6,166	6,270	7,400	9,330	9,626	0.24	3.17
Morocco	4,782	4,293	3,337	4,024	4,158	0.11	3.33
Sudan	17,589	19,511	17,843	15,589	14,914	0.38	-4.33
Tunisia	3,953	4,280	3,492	3,988	3,915	0.10	-1.83
SOUTHERN AFRICA	8,072	8,193	9,792	10,595	9,687	0.25	-8.57
South Africa	8,072	8,193	9,792	10,595	9,687	0.25	-8.57
WEST AFRICA	739	449	581	695	1,063	0.03	52.95
Mauritania	229	10	16	15	10	0.00	-33.33
Nigeria	448	364	478	584	987	0.03	69.01
Senegal	62	75	87	96	66	0.00	-31.25
OTHER AFRICA	1,407	1,936	2,797	3,248	2,605	0.07	-19.80
Other countries of Africa	1,407	1,936	2,797	3,248	2,605	0.07	-19.80
AMERICAS	189,776	215,121	189,283	198,631	188,073	4.77	-5.32
NORTH AMERICA	177,563	194,439	168,862	174,639	163,781	4.15	-6.22
Canada	18,682	34,960	27,785	28,512	26,144	0.66	-8.31
Mexico	2,944	5,373	3,565	4,703	4,641	0.12	-1.32
United States of America	155,937	154,106	137,512	141,424	132,996	3.37	-5.96
SOUTH AMERICA	8,691	16,222	15,582	18,681	19,510	0.49	4.44
Argentina	2,111	3,172	2,446	3,507	3,367	0.09	-3.99
Brazil	4,495	8,215	8,317	9,133	10,870	0.28	19.02
Chile	75	1,952	1,794	1,862	1,785	0.05	-4.14
Colombia	1,244	1,510	1,835	2,810	2,299	0.06	-18.19
Venezuela	766	1,373	1,190	1,369	1,189	0.03	-13.15
OTHER AMERICAS	3,522	4,460	4,839	5,311	4,782	0.12	-9.96
Other countries of the Americas	3,522	4,460	4,839	5,311	4,782	0.12	-9.96
EAST ASIA AND THE PACIFIC	138,404	148,981	154,149	174,733	177,130	4.49	1.37
NORTH-EAST ASIA	35,239	49,738	46,348	50,881	55,224	1.40	8.54
China	12,594	13,882	12,118	12,389	15,501	0.39	25.12
Hong Kong, China	200	436	1,931	2,151	2,712	0.07	26.08
Japan	12,506	18,779	12,480	14,823	14,866	0.38	0.29
Korea, Dem. People's Republic of	25	14	52	10	10	0.00	
Korea, Republic of	8,297	14,307	17,678	18,101	18,577	0.47	2.63
Taiwan, Province of China	1,617	2,320	2,089	3,407	3,558	0.09	4.43
SOUTH-EAST ASIA	76,496	64,716	78,892	95,221	94,075	2.38	-1.20
Brunei Darussalam		247	312	399	244	0.01	-38.85
Indonesia	39,165	32,282	39,551	41,149	39,645	1.00	-3.66
Malaysia	6,922	11,890	15,585	22,855	25,085	0.64	9.76
Philippines	25,249	11,893	13,058	15,745	15,645	0.40	-0.64
Singapore	2,373	4,544	5,410	7,647	8,183	0.21	7.01
Thailand	2,651	3,860	4,976	7,393	5,248	0.13	-29.01
Viet Nam	136			33	25	0.00	-24.24
AUSTRALASIA	25,952	33,716	28,120	27,114	25,945	0.66	-4.31
Australia	21,620	28,420	23,926	23,178	22,391	0.57	-3.40
New Zealand	4,332	5,296	4,194	3,936	3,554	0.09	-9.71
MELANESIA	347	418	268	261	139	0.00	-46.74
Fiji	347	418	268	261	139	0.00	-46.74
OTHER EAST ASIA AND THE PACIFIC	370	393	521	1,256	1,747	0.04	39.09

Yearbook of Tourism Statistics, Data 2009 – 2013, 2015 Edition

JORDAN

1. Arrivals of non-resident tourists at national borders, by nationality

	2009	2010	2011	2012	2013	Market share 2013	% Change 2013-2012
Other countries of Asia	370	393	521	1,256	1,747	0.04	39.09
EUROPE	**602,394**	**744,992**	**626,886**	**590,204**	**536,744**	**13.60**	**-9.06**
CENTRAL/EASTERN EUROPE	**48,230**	**69,403**	**64,738**	**66,191**	**58,792**	**1.49**	**-11.18**
Belarus		1,096	1,091	1,216	1,286	0.03	5.76
Bulgaria	2,151	2,051	1,855	1,815	1,650	0.04	-9.09
Czech Republic	2,802	2,738	2,592	2,356	2,050	0.05	-12.99
Hungary	1,978	5,857	4,360	4,121	5,378	0.14	30.50
Poland	9,073	9,944	10,513	11,904	9,323	0.24	-21.68
Romania	3,428	4,437	4,536	4,195	3,971	0.10	-5.34
Russian Federation	20,777	29,292	25,173	25,724	22,181	0.56	-13.77
Slovakia	1,749	1,087	1,672	1,126	937	0.02	-16.79
Ukraine	5,302	7,608	7,780	8,647	7,229	0.18	-16.40
Other countries Central/East Europe	970	5,293	5,166	5,087	4,787	0.12	-5.90
NORTHERN EUROPE	**101,601**	**109,933**	**113,995**	**110,311**	**107,674**	**2.73**	**-2.39**
Denmark	6,057	8,730	11,840	8,944	8,396	0.21	-6.13
Finland	6,498	4,808	3,189	3,147	3,145	0.08	-0.06
Iceland	186	210	261	294	232	0.01	-21.09
Ireland	3,715	4,816	3,950	4,262	3,896	0.10	-8.59
Norway	7,072	7,815	12,182	8,838	8,802	0.22	-0.41
Sweden	14,902	16,373	15,066	14,981	16,027	0.41	6.98
United Kingdom	63,171	67,181	67,507	69,845	67,176	1.70	-3.82
SOUTHERN EUROPE	**84,909**	**115,546**	**68,713**	**76,725**	**76,140**	**1.93**	**-0.76**
Bosnia and Herzegovina	708	801	612	639	566	0.01	-11.42
Croatia	864	1,420	1,155	973	919	0.02	-5.55
Greece	4,768	5,222	3,351	3,368	3,440	0.09	2.14
Holy See	136						
Italy	43,529	57,747	36,484	39,631	39,381	1.00	-0.63
Malta	229	306	264	384	314	0.01	-18.23
Portugal	3,528	5,203	2,573	2,697	2,883	0.07	6.90
Serbia				1,370	1,485	0.04	8.39
Serbia and Montenegro	573	86					
Slovenia	1,318	1,688	983	1,195	1,078	0.03	-9.79
Spain	29,256	42,657	22,944	25,764	25,141	0.64	-2.42
TFYR of Macedonia		304	201	416	666	0.02	60.10
Other countries of Southern Europe		112	146	288	267	0.01	-7.29
WESTERN EUROPE	**141,501**	**196,284**	**156,370**	**139,488**	**130,109**	**3.30**	**-6.72**
Austria	6,522	9,581	8,874	6,457	6,468	0.16	0.17
Belgium	12,296	16,983	15,942	14,375	11,655	0.30	-18.92
France	53,637	74,893	51,956	41,812	36,891	0.94	-11.77
Germany	41,622	61,080	52,245	47,274	49,595	1.26	4.91
Luxembourg	341	490	326	360	269	0.01	-25.28
Netherlands	18,545	23,604	19,561	22,586	18,767	0.48	-16.91
Switzerland	8,538	9,653	7,466	6,624	6,464	0.16	-2.42
EAST MEDITERRANEAN EUROPE	**220,704**	**234,853**	**205,682**	**182,133**	**163,448**	**4.14**	**-10.26**
Cyprus	1,563	1,768	1,567	1,785	1,256	0.03	-29.64
Israel	185,489	197,276	172,465	162,789	147,232	3.73	-9.56
Turkey	33,652	35,809	31,650	17,559	14,960	0.38	-14.80
OTHER EUROPE	**5,449**	**18,973**	**17,388**	**15,356**	**581**	**0.01**	**-96.22**
Other countries of Europe	5,449	18,973	17,388	15,356	581	0.01	-96.22
MIDDLE EAST	**1,867,473**	**2,054,551**	**1,892,950**	**2,007,452**	**1,827,755**	**46.33**	**-8.95**
Bahrain	44,983	28,475	19,473	20,072	17,293	0.44	-13.85
Egypt	39,885	55,978	53,673	61,251	61,262	1.55	0.02
Iraq	212,670	235,121	286,031	367,476	321,028	8.14	-12.64
Kuwait	89,682	57,767	46,450	49,647	57,034	1.45	14.88
Lebanon	96,064	104,168	69,020	53,638	49,218	1.25	-8.24
Libya	34,261	45,898	22,168	97,906	78,911	2.00	-19.40
Oman	16,192	15,633	12,154	13,729	13,730	0.35	0.01
Palestine	285,610	324,116	348,257	367,574	382,759	9.70	4.13
Qatar	13,310	9,146	7,234	8,721	14,484	0.37	66.08

Yearbook of Tourism Statistics, Data 2009 – 2013, 2015 Edition

JORDAN

1. Arrivals of non-resident tourists at national borders, by nationality

	2009	2010	2011	2012	2013	Market share 2013	% Change 2013-2012
Saudi Arabia	644,360	541,401	516,608	582,037	547,087	13.87	-6.00
Syrian Arab Republic	310,471	571,824	455,595	316,303	204,248	5.18	-35.43
United Arab Emirates	27,565	22,682	15,894	16,513	19,531	0.50	18.28
Yemen	52,420	42,342	40,393	52,585	61,170	1.55	16.33
SOUTH ASIA	**71,778**	**65,243**	**77,078**	**77,759**	**75,012**	**1.90**	**-3.53**
Afghanistan	1,786	1,133	1,056	566	782	0.02	38.16
Bangladesh	7,239	2,948	3,224	2,778	3,898	0.10	40.32
India	29,760	40,342	51,550	54,202	49,646	1.26	-8.41
Iran, Islamic Republic of	1,216	866	960	855	696	0.02	-18.60
Nepal	4,021	1,159	917	662	528	0.01	-20.24
Pakistan	12,396	8,643	8,945	7,426	7,653	0.19	3.06
Sri Lanka	15,360	10,152	10,426	11,270	11,809	0.30	4.78
NOT SPECIFIED	**872,678**	**928,758**	**969,361**	**1,058,586**	**1,085,177**	**27.51**	**2.51**
Other countries of the World	11,260						
Nationals Residing Abroad	861,418	928,758	969,361	1,058,586	1,085,177	27.51	2.51

Yearbook of Tourism Statistics, Data 2009 – 2013, 2015 Edition

JORDAN

2. Arrivals of non-resident visitors at national borders, by nationality

	2009	2010	2011	2012	2013	Market share 2013	% Change 2013-2012
TOTAL	7,084,552	8,078,380	6,812,436	6,314,250	5,388,918	100.00	-14.65
AFRICA	63,584	68,722	58,144	59,239	58,747	1.09	-0.83
EAST AFRICA	4,867	5,179	4,879	7,460	9,122	0.17	22.28
Djibouti	53	49	44	79	72	0.00	-8.86
Eritrea	453	407	367	347	625	0.01	80.12
Ethiopia	2,675	3,106	2,264	4,581	6,570	0.12	43.42
Kenya	662	629	1,313	1,400	779	0.01	-44.36
Mauritius	296	336	332	484	779	0.01	60.95
Somalia	728	652	559	569	297	0.01	-47.80
CENTRAL AFRICA	116	164	363	620	811	0.02	30.81
Chad	116	164	363	620	811	0.02	30.81
NORTH AFRICA	47,418	52,083	38,983	35,769	34,898	0.65	-2.44
Algeria	12,258	18,453	11,494	10,250	10,027	0.19	-2.18
Morocco	5,331	4,417	3,423	4,101	4,231	0.08	3.17
Sudan	24,047	22,769	20,109	16,898	16,460	0.31	-2.59
Tunisia	5,782	6,444	3,957	4,520	4,180	0.08	-7.52
SOUTHERN AFRICA	8,496	8,860	10,493	11,339	10,312	0.19	-9.06
South Africa	8,496	8,860	10,493	11,339	10,312	0.19	-9.06
WEST AFRICA	892	455	588	702	1,070	0.02	52.42
Mauritania	246	10	16	15	10	0.00	-33.33
Nigeria	567	370	485	590	993	0.02	68.31
Senegal	79	75	87	97	67	0.00	-30.93
OTHER AFRICA	1,795	1,981	2,838	3,349	2,534	0.05	-24.34
Other countries of Africa	1,795	1,981	2,838	3,349	2,534	0.05	-24.34
AMERICAS	230,436	250,246	216,890	226,374	215,071	3.99	-4.99
NORTH AMERICA	212,871	224,556	192,123	197,389	185,852	3.45	-5.84
Canada	33,939	39,048	30,970	31,940	29,225	0.54	-8.50
Mexico	3,978	6,843	4,506	6,060	5,839	0.11	-3.65
United States of America	174,954	178,665	156,647	159,389	150,788	2.80	-5.40
SOUTH AMERICA	13,191	20,279	19,253	22,671	23,617	0.44	4.17
Argentina	3,289	4,698	3,579	4,728	4,767	0.09	0.82
Brazil	5,686	9,939	10,110	11,064	12,808	0.24	15.76
Chile	1,607	2,338	2,167	2,129	2,093	0.04	-1.69
Colombia	1,314	1,817	2,109	3,251	2,652	0.05	-18.43
Venezuela	1,295	1,487	1,288	1,499	1,297	0.02	-13.48
OTHER AMERICAS	4,374	5,411	5,514	6,314	5,602	0.10	-11.28
Other countries of the Americas	4,374	5,411	5,514	6,314	5,602	0.10	-11.28
EAST ASIA AND THE PACIFIC	157,281	173,664	169,649	186,976	188,473	3.50	0.80
NORTH-EAST ASIA	39,219	50,541	47,169	51,895	56,233	1.04	8.36
China	13,979	13,976	12,208	12,491	15,689	0.29	25.60
Hong Kong, China	268	439	1,975	2,186	2,748	0.05	25.71
Japan	13,052	19,052	12,829	15,321	15,279	0.28	-0.27
Korea, Dem. People's Republic of	27	14	52	10	10	0.00	
Korea, Republic of	10,043	14,559	17,859	18,225	18,683	0.35	2.51
Taiwan, Province of China	1,850	2,501	2,246	3,662	3,824	0.07	4.42
SOUTH-EAST ASIA	86,178	84,780	90,155	102,889	100,920	1.87	-1.91
Indonesia	44,202	40,729	42,792	43,604	41,371	0.77	-5.12
Malaysia	7,822	12,600	15,977	23,209	25,263	0.47	8.85
Philippines	28,448	22,315	20,572	20,697	20,407	0.38	-1.40
Singapore	2,636	5,078	5,546	7,746	8,281	0.15	6.91
Thailand	2,920	3,860	4,976	7,393	5,248	0.10	-29.01
Viet Nam	150	198	292	240	350	0.01	45.83
AUSTRALASIA	30,866	37,095	31,065	29,972	28,882	0.54	-3.64
Australia	25,714	31,025	26,175	25,300	24,661	0.46	-2.53
New Zealand	5,152	6,070	4,890	4,672	4,221	0.08	-9.65
MELANESIA	413	536	353	371	215	0.00	-42.05
Fiji	413	536	353	371	215	0.00	-42.05
OTHER EAST ASIA AND THE PACIFIC	605	712	907	1,849	2,223	0.04	20.23
Other countries of Asia	605	712	907	1,849	2,223	0.04	20.23

383

Yearbook of Tourism Statistics, Data 2009 – 2013, 2015 Edition

JORDAN

2. Arrivals of non-resident visitors at national borders, by nationality

	2009	2010	2011	2012	2013	Market share 2013	% Change 2013-2012
EUROPE	930,747	1,117,010	897,386	767,148	671,598	12.46	-12.46
CENTRAL/EASTERN EUROPE	128,805	156,416	112,894	112,991	92,921	1.72	-17.76
Belarus	1,420	1,545	1,345	1,660	2,019	0.04	21.63
Bulgaria	2,690	2,906	2,398	2,169	2,061	0.04	-4.98
Czech Republic	8,668	8,303	4,786	3,292	2,729	0.05	-17.10
Hungary	3,377	7,518	5,016	4,614	5,904	0.11	27.96
Poland	19,946	24,563	15,266	15,492	12,488	0.23	-19.39
Romania	4,972	5,444	5,357	6,055	4,847	0.09	-19.95
Russian Federation	70,132	79,142	56,624	60,252	46,439	0.86	-22.93
Slovakia	3,122	3,678	2,629	1,653	1,257	0.02	-23.96
Ukraine	11,051	12,509	10,685	11,236	9,058	0.17	-19.38
Other countries Central/East Europe	3,427	10,808	8,788	6,568	6,119	0.11	-6.84
NORTHERN EUROPE	135,048	152,623	141,555	135,840	130,452	2.42	-3.97
Denmark	7,441	9,490	13,044	10,088	9,470	0.18	-6.13
Finland	7,116	7,727	6,197	7,888	8,437	0.16	6.96
Iceland	186	210	261	294	232	0.00	-21.09
Ireland	4,317	5,386	4,210	4,550	4,245	0.08	-6.70
Norway	8,275	9,327	14,293	10,381	10,391	0.19	0.10
Sweden	16,274	17,505	15,877	15,800	16,875	0.31	6.80
United Kingdom	91,439	102,978	87,673	86,839	80,802	1.50	-6.95
SOUTHERN EUROPE	97,477	129,596	75,403	85,178	84,930	1.58	-0.29
Bosnia and Herzegovina	2,328	2,213	1,227	916	687	0.01	-25.00
Croatia	1,115	1,599	1,247	1,160	1,035	0.02	-10.78
Greece	5,138	5,458	3,505	3,493	3,565	0.07	2.06
Holy See	160						
Italy	49,403	65,756	40,861	45,180	45,906	0.85	1.61
Malta	269	306	264	384	314	0.01	-18.23
Portugal	3,856	5,565	2,717	2,867	3,002	0.06	4.71
Serbia				1,697	1,792	0.03	5.60
Serbia and Montenegro	627	96					
Slovenia	1,522	1,749	1,006	1,233	1,114	0.02	-9.65
Spain	30,325	44,190	23,875	27,101	26,246	0.49	-3.15
TFYR of Macedonia	2,734	2,556	552	835	953	0.02	14.13
Other countries of Southern Europe		108	149	312	316	0.01	1.28
WESTERN EUROPE	176,800	240,861	179,792	165,592	156,684	2.91	-5.38
Austria	7,340	9,881	9,103	6,773	6,859	0.13	1.27
Belgium	17,862	21,375	18,578	16,053	13,014	0.24	-18.93
France	65,884	102,890	63,076	50,601	42,193	0.78	-16.62
Germany	56,110	69,460	59,074	59,549	66,528	1.23	11.72
Luxembourg	341	552	364	406	305	0.01	-24.88
Netherlands	19,876	25,842	21,114	24,527	20,249	0.38	-17.44
Switzerland	9,387	10,861	8,483	7,683	7,536	0.14	-1.91
EAST MEDITERRANEAN EUROPE	381,926	416,741	369,643	251,852	205,981	3.82	-18.21
Cyprus	1,580	1,987	1,761	2,005	1,412	0.03	-29.58
Israel	226,759	243,975	211,889	203,740	184,618	3.43	-9.39
Turkey	153,587	170,779	155,993	46,107	19,951	0.37	-56.73
OTHER EUROPE	10,691	20,773	18,099	15,695	630	0.01	-95.99
Other countries of Europe	10,691	20,773	18,099	15,695	630	0.01	-95.99
MIDDLE EAST	5,133,608	5,418,565	4,366,252	3,897,092	3,048,572	56.57	-21.77
Bahrain	86,092	100,221	43,645	35,941	28,359	0.53	-21.10
Egypt	548,068	383,168	326,511	353,827	262,950	4.88	-25.68
Iraq	283,464	241,482	292,129	373,107	325,291	6.04	-12.82
Kuwait	140,638	142,110	69,420	66,690	78,415	1.46	17.58
Lebanon	177,860	189,612	108,638	65,859	58,772	1.09	-10.76
Libya	38,985	48,685	23,264	101,938	79,680	1.48	-21.83
Oman	18,497	21,440	13,730	14,333	14,297	0.27	-0.25
Palestine	386,573	408,383	441,574	470,241	474,347	8.80	0.87
Qatar	17,787	15,725	9,127	9,688	15,544	0.29	60.45
Saudi Arabia	1,193,168	1,332,680	1,074,190	1,144,118	1,079,361	20.03	-5.66

384

Yearbook of Tourism Statistics, Data 2009 – 2013, 2015 Edition

JORDAN

2. Arrivals of non-resident visitors at national borders, by nationality

	2009	2010	2011	2012	2013	Market share 2013	% Change 2013-2012
Syrian Arab Republic	2,165,646	2,451,995	1,903,749	1,190,201	548,663	10.18	-53.90
United Arab Emirates	35,182	36,932	18,045	17,530	20,736	0.38	18.29
Yemen	41,648	46,132	42,230	53,619	62,157	1.15	15.92
SOUTH ASIA	**82,169**	**101,060**	**114,361**	**97,247**	**99,270**	**1.84**	**2.08**
Afghanistan	2,135	2,826	2,518	1,069	1,417	0.03	32.55
Bangladesh	8,105	5,387	5,428	3,784	4,898	0.09	29.44
India	34,061	51,461	64,971	60,913	57,784	1.07	-5.14
Iran, Islamic Republic of	1,364	1,037	1,132	897	707	0.01	-21.18
Nepal	4,428	5,445	4,807	2,732	2,100	0.04	-23.13
Pakistan	15,014	21,489	23,339	14,774	18,539	0.34	25.48
Sri Lanka	17,062	13,415	12,166	13,078	13,825	0.26	5.71
NOT SPECIFIED	**486,727**	**949,113**	**989,754**	**1,080,174**	**1,107,187**	**20.55**	**2.50**
Other countries of the World	15,303						
Nationals Residing Abroad	471,424	949,113	989,754	1,080,174	1,107,187	20.55	2.50

Yearbook of Tourism Statistics, Data 2009 – 2013, 2015 Edition

KAZAKHSTAN

2. Arrivals of non-resident visitors at national borders, by country of residence

	2009	2010	2011	2012	2013	Market share 2013	% Change 2013-2012
TOTAL	3,774,352	4,097,387	5,685,132	6,163,204	6,841,085	100.00	11.00
AFRICA	2,530	3,315	2,195	11,470	2,240	0.03	-80.47
EAST AFRICA	106	1,677	141	8,572	250	0.00	-97.08
Ethiopia	11	17	21	22	14	0.00	-36.36
Kenya	52	56	51	130	100	0.00	-23.08
Madagascar	1	8	3	10	7	0.00	-30.00
Uganda	6	1,567	30	8,361	55	0.00	-99.34
United Republic of Tanzania	16	1	7	12	22	0.00	83.33
Zambia	5	2	8	17	34	0.00	100.00
Zimbabwe	15	26	21	20	18	0.00	-10.00
CENTRAL AFRICA	859	15	43	46	51	0.00	10.87
Angola	7	5	2	11	13	0.00	18.18
Chad	831	2	5	6	3	0.00	-50.00
Congo	21	8	36	29	35	0.00	20.69
NORTH AFRICA	346	418	506	699	360	0.01	-48.50
Algeria	150	138	130	165	143	0.00	-13.33
Morocco	86	140	183	404	114	0.00	-71.78
Sudan	41	45	50	44	33	0.00	-25.00
Tunisia	69	95	143	86	70	0.00	-18.60
SOUTHERN AFRICA	969	958	1,114	1,497	1,174	0.02	-21.58
South Africa	969	958	1,114	1,497	1,174	0.02	-21.58
WEST AFRICA	250	247	391	656	405	0.01	-38.26
Burkina Faso	3	5	8	13	16	0.00	23.08
Côte d'Ivoire	6	15	11	13	8	0.00	-38.46
Ghana	41	40	43	42	27	0.00	-35.71
Guinea-Bissau	1	1			2	0.00	
Liberia	2	4	2	11	5	0.00	-54.55
Mali	2	3	19	17	6	0.00	-64.71
Mauritania	6	6	16	9	7	0.00	-22.22
Niger	11	2	7	27	5	0.00	-81.48
Nigeria	152	156	249	493	313	0.00	-36.51
Senegal	26	15	36	31	16	0.00	-48.39
AMERICAS	27,563	27,715	29,308	34,241	29,910	0.44	-12.65
CARIBBEAN	264	329	498	349	452	0.01	29.51
Anguilla	1	2			1	0.00	
Barbados	1	3	5	11	7	0.00	-36.36
Cuba	201	233	293	288	377	0.01	30.90
Dominica		6	6		12	0.00	
Jamaica	6	3		8	21	0.00	162.50
Saint Lucia	5	48	171	14	2	0.00	-85.71
Trinidad and Tobago	50	34	23	28	32	0.00	14.29
CENTRAL AMERICA	83	132	54	120	114	0.00	-5.00
Costa Rica	14	17	12	51	38	0.00	-25.49
El Salvador	31	68	22	40	43	0.00	7.50
Guatemala	4	12	3	2	14	0.00	600.00
Honduras	21	15	8	9	13	0.00	44.44
Panama	13	20	9	18	6	0.00	-66.67
NORTH AMERICA	25,731	25,794	27,054	31,909	27,623	0.40	-13.43
Canada	4,944	5,155	5,393	6,024	4,798	0.07	-20.35
Mexico	130	178	198	279	317	0.00	13.62
United States of America	20,657	20,461	21,463	25,606	22,508	0.33	-12.10
SOUTH AMERICA	1,485	1,460	1,702	1,863	1,721	0.03	-7.62
Argentina	308	258	255	274	244	0.00	-10.95
Brazil	546	425	608	727	508	0.01	-30.12
Chile	59	178	158	167	118	0.00	-29.34
Colombia	266	255	239	212	140	0.00	-33.96
Ecuador	59	49	47	51	32	0.00	-37.25
Peru	33	61	62	71	119	0.00	67.61
Uruguay	6	32	5	13	48	0.00	269.23

Yearbook of Tourism Statistics, Data 2009 – 2013, 2015 Edition

KAZAKHSTAN

2. Arrivals of non-resident visitors at national borders, by country of residence

	2009	2010	2011	2012	2013	Market share 2013	% Change 2013-2012
Venezuela	208	202	328	348	512	0.01	47.13
EAST ASIA AND THE PACIFIC	**170,560**	**148,951**	**177,944**	**200,012**	**249,069**	**3.64**	**24.53**
NORTH-EAST ASIA	**159,471**	**137,670**	**166,583**	**187,142**	**239,111**	**3.50**	**27.77**
China	134,251	108,630	128,312	154,226	205,066	3.00	32.96
Hong Kong, China	13	49	71	426	1,009	0.01	136.85
Japan	4,271	4,428	4,720	6,049	5,202	0.08	-14.00
Korea, Dem. People's Republic of	106	182	125	49	77	0.00	57.14
Korea, Republic of	12,627	13,740	16,589	16,963	16,620	0.24	-2.02
Macao, China			1		1	0.00	
Mongolia	7,944	10,419	11,305	9,077	10,750	0.16	18.43
Taiwan, Province of China	259	222	5,460	352	386	0.01	9.66
SOUTH-EAST ASIA	**7,226**	**7,535**	**7,748**	**8,488**	**6,207**	**0.09**	**-26.87**
Cambodia	20	21	4	19	8	0.00	-57.89
Indonesia	622	504	692	723	747	0.01	3.32
Lao People's Democratic Republic	31	17	10	25	81	0.00	224.00
Malaysia	1,223	1,488	2,194	2,179	2,300	0.03	5.55
Myanmar	5	19	42	39	48	0.00	23.08
Philippines	3,366	3,708	3,215	3,035	1,398	0.02	-53.94
Singapore	483	437	491	736	685	0.01	-6.93
Thailand	1,122	1,153	908	984	685	0.01	-30.39
Viet Nam	354	188	192	748	255	0.00	-65.91
AUSTRALASIA	**3,856**	**3,737**	**3,596**	**4,347**	**3,735**	**0.05**	**-14.08**
Australia	3,224	3,158	2,980	3,628	3,166	0.05	-12.73
New Zealand	632	579	616	719	569	0.01	-20.86
MELANESIA	**6**	**4**	**17**	**27**	**15**	**0.00**	**-44.44**
Papua New Guinea	6	4	17	27	15	0.00	-44.44
POLYNESIA	**1**	**5**		**8**	**1**	**0.00**	**-87.50**
Samoa	1	5		8	1	0.00	-87.50
EUROPE	**3,539,975**	**3,875,397**	**5,436,269**	**5,874,175**	**6,522,838**	**95.35**	**11.04**
CENTRAL/EASTERN EUROPE	**3,337,708**	**3,668,845**	**5,227,740**	**5,585,175**	**6,262,043**	**91.54**	**12.12**
Armenia	12,659	18,121	26,093	37,337	54,244	0.79	45.28
Azerbaijan	39,750	54,386	63,849	83,811	112,617	1.65	34.37
Belarus	11,218	12,411	13,302	20,399	55,090	0.81	170.06
Bulgaria	1,368	1,539	1,591	2,194	3,622	0.05	65.09
Czech Republic	2,097	2,141	2,531	3,645	4,111	0.06	12.78
Estonia	639	600	715	1,074	869	0.01	-19.09
Georgia	7,081	7,661	10,536	11,686	12,462	0.18	6.64
Hungary	2,832	2,846	3,455	4,452	3,559	0.05	-20.06
Kyrgyzstan	864,912	930,493	1,539,885	1,454,124	1,382,706	20.21	-4.91
Latvia	1,238	1,638	1,614	2,785	3,479	0.05	24.92
Lithuania	2,553	2,541	3,194	4,824	8,465	0.12	75.48
Poland	4,172	4,400	5,157	7,405	8,208	0.12	10.84
Republic of Moldova	7,379	8,483	9,425	12,028	16,695	0.24	38.80
Romania	2,071	2,110	2,820	3,139	2,400	0.04	-23.54
Russian Federation	934,972	1,041,978	1,346,594	1,371,306	1,780,574	26.03	29.85
Slovakia	826	1,058	1,084	1,524	1,478	0.02	-3.02
Tajikistan	193,518	162,387	187,956	176,212	186,214	2.72	5.68
Turkmenistan	24,119	22,537	26,369	40,185	47,711	0.70	18.73
Ukraine	65,210	50,074	49,272	58,428	82,971	1.21	42.01
Uzbekistan	1,159,094	1,341,441	1,932,298	2,288,617	2,494,568	36.46	9.00
NORTHERN EUROPE	**32,691**	**33,425**	**33,727**	**36,176**	**29,365**	**0.43**	**-18.83**
Denmark	918	976	969	1,206	959	0.01	-20.48
Finland	1,225	1,292	1,152	1,825	1,545	0.02	-15.34
Iceland	71	68	35	109	134	0.00	22.94
Ireland	1,053	1,213	1,469	2,125	1,670	0.02	-21.41
Norway	1,739	2,458	2,218	1,482	915	0.01	-38.26
Sweden	1,155	1,507	1,554	1,947	1,753	0.03	-9.96
United Kingdom	26,530	25,911	26,330	27,482	22,389	0.33	-18.53
SOUTHERN EUROPE	**19,702**	**21,323**	**21,162**	**28,310**	**31,761**	**0.46**	**12.19**

387

KAZAKHSTAN

2. Arrivals of non-resident visitors at national borders, by country of residence

	2009	2010	2011	2012	2013	Market share 2013	% Change 2013-2012
Albania	87	106	125	441	371	0.01	-15.87
Bosnia and Herzegovina	122	165	207	321	339	0.00	5.61
Croatia	977	999	1,102	1,506	1,276	0.02	-15.27
Greece	1,205	1,518	1,211	1,523	1,835	0.03	20.49
Italy	13,920	14,223	15,161	18,445	14,961	0.22	-18.89
Malta	25	46	48	87	84	0.00	-3.45
Portugal	428	465	517	676	690	0.01	2.07
Serbia	449	953	23	1,424	7,954	0.12	458.57
Slovenia	444	477	511	694	853	0.01	22.91
Spain	2,045	2,371	2,257	3,193	3,398	0.05	6.42
WESTERN EUROPE	**92,572**	**95,202**	**88,217**	**132,467**	**102,405**	**1.50**	**-22.69**
Austria	2,234	2,566	2,395	8,447	3,870	0.06	-54.18
Belgium	2,100	2,325	1,886	2,275	2,184	0.03	-4.00
France	7,788	8,606	9,141	12,394	10,245	0.15	-17.34
Germany	73,891	74,311	67,725	100,911	75,491	1.10	-25.19
Liechtenstein	11	13	27	3	73	0.00	2,333.33
Luxembourg	73	94	82	103	93	0.00	-9.71
Monaco	10	8	1	21	18	0.00	-14.29
Netherlands	4,857	5,372	5,035	5,983	8,198	0.12	37.02
Switzerland	1,608	1,907	1,925	2,330	2,233	0.03	-4.16
EAST MEDITERRANEAN EUROPE	**57,302**	**56,602**	**65,423**	**92,047**	**97,264**	**1.42**	**5.67**
Cyprus	74	114	81	148	116	0.00	-21.62
Israel	4,572	4,212	4,614	6,042	5,078	0.07	-15.95
Turkey	52,656	52,276	60,728	85,857	92,070	1.35	7.24
MIDDLE EAST	**4,808**	**5,164**	**5,103**	**5,391**	**4,220**	**0.06**	**-21.72**
Bahrain	30	26	60	67	97	0.00	44.78
Egypt	1,114	1,112	1,024	1,038	768	0.01	-26.01
Iraq	110	153	191	275	221	0.00	-19.64
Jordan	528	731	672	785	509	0.01	-35.16
Kuwait	130	104	102	53	161	0.00	203.77
Lebanon	693	779	799	724	519	0.01	-28.31
Libya	72	59	44	36	77	0.00	113.89
Oman	82	130	122	155	130	0.00	-16.13
Palestine	164	152	192	185	94	0.00	-49.19
Qatar	121	99	173	284	201	0.00	-29.23
Saudi Arabia	478	381	329	378	294	0.00	-22.22
Syrian Arab Republic	517	594	541	569	235	0.00	-58.70
United Arab Emirates	769	844	854	842	914	0.01	8.55
SOUTH ASIA	**22,232**	**20,671**	**22,894**	**24,624**	**21,720**	**0.32**	**-11.79**
Afghanistan	4,366	2,362	2,236	2,525	2,262	0.03	-10.42
Bangladesh	511	360	284	217	221	0.00	1.84
Bhutan	6	7	10	8	16	0.00	100.00
India	11,734	11,904	13,778	14,716	9,929	0.15	-32.53
Iran, Islamic Republic of	3,071	3,714	3,876	4,265	7,283	0.11	70.76
Nepal	110	95	124	116	102	0.00	-12.07
Pakistan	2,324	2,069	2,437	2,236	1,738	0.03	-22.27
Sri Lanka	110	160	149	541	169	0.00	-68.76
NOT SPECIFIED	**6,684**	**16,174**	**11,419**	**13,291**	**11,088**	**0.16**	**-16.58**
Other countries of the World	6,684	16,174	11,419	13,291	11,088	0.16	-16.58

KENYA

2. Arrivals of non-resident visitors at national borders, by country of residence

	2009	2010	2011	2012	2013	Market share 2013	% Change 2013-2012
TOTAL	1,490,448	1,609,110	1,822,885	1,710,829	1,519,551	100.00	-11.18
AFRICA	157,592	278,812	354,517	309,619	286,202	18.83	-7.56
OTHER AFRICA	157,592	278,812	354,517	309,619	286,202	18.83	-7.56
All countries of Africa	157,592	278,812	354,517	309,619	286,202	18.83	-7.56
AMERICAS	110,783	130,928	186,036	189,800	165,856	10.91	-12.62
OTHER AMERICAS	110,783	130,928	186,036	189,800	165,856	10.91	-12.62
All countries of the Americas	110,783	130,928	186,036	189,800	165,856	10.91	-12.62
EAST ASIA AND THE PACIFIC	122,023	162,119	217,497	206,358	124,590	8.20	-39.62
OTHER EAST ASIA AND THE PACIFIC	122,023	162,119	217,497	206,358	124,590	8.20	-39.62
All countries of Asia	122,023	162,119	217,497	206,358	124,590	8.20	-39.62
EUROPE	1,040,037	932,343	930,527	865,359	825,729	54.34	-4.58
OTHER EUROPE	1,040,037	932,343	930,527	865,359	825,729	54.34	-4.58
All countries of Europe	1,040,037	932,343	930,527	865,359	825,729	54.34	-4.58
NOT SPECIFIED	60,013	104,908	134,308	139,693	117,174	7.71	-16.12
Other countries of the World	60,013	104,908	134,308	139,693	117,174	7.71	-16.12

Yearbook of Tourism Statistics, Data 2009 – 2013, 2015 Edition

KENYA

5. Overnight stays of non-resident tourists in hotels and similar establishments, by country of residence

	2009	2010	2011	2012	2013	Market share 2013	% Change 2013-2012
TOTAL	4,062,400	4,260,100	4,353,400	4,027,000	3,840,100	100.00	-4.64
AFRICA	485,700	451,700	479,400	475,600	499,900	13.02	5.11
EAST AFRICA	174,100	129,400	144,700	151,000	174,700	4.55	15.70
Uganda	103,000	67,900	76,200	81,800	110,200	2.87	34.72
United Republic of Tanzania	71,100	61,500	68,500	69,200	64,500	1.68	-6.79
NORTH AFRICA	25,400	28,300	30,900	23,900	29,000	0.76	21.34
All countries of North Africa	25,400	28,300	30,900	23,900	29,000	0.76	21.34
SOUTHERN AFRICA	87,800	88,100	88,400	88,200	91,100	2.37	3.29
All countries of Southern Africa	87,800	88,100	88,400	88,200	91,100	2.37	3.29
WEST AFRICA	45,400	55,100	63,100	55,900	63,300	1.65	13.24
All countries of West Africa	45,400	55,100	63,100	55,900	63,300	1.65	13.24
OTHER AFRICA	153,000	150,800	152,300	156,600	141,800	3.69	-9.45
Other countries of Africa	153,000	150,800	152,300	156,600	141,800	3.69	-9.45
AMERICAS	325,700	347,100	386,900	387,500	393,200	10.24	1.47
NORTH AMERICA	292,300	314,000	348,500	347,400	356,400	9.28	2.59
Canada	58,500	59,800	64,700	55,900	61,800	1.61	10.55
United States of America	233,800	254,200	283,800	291,500	294,600	7.67	1.06
OTHER AMERICAS	33,400	33,100	38,400	40,100	36,800	0.96	-8.23
Other countries of the Americas	33,400	33,100	38,400	40,100	36,800	0.96	-8.23
EAST ASIA AND THE PACIFIC	166,900	194,600	248,600	281,000	270,700	7.05	-3.67
NORTH-EAST ASIA	71,000	91,500	132,600	155,900	154,000	4.01	-1.22
China	33,200	50,700	89,600	114,000	105,900	2.76	-7.11
Japan	37,800	40,800	43,000	41,900	48,100	1.25	14.80
AUSTRALASIA	54,900	60,200	63,000	56,900	62,300	1.62	9.49
Australia, New Zealand	54,900	60,200	63,000	56,900	62,300	1.62	9.49
OTHER EAST ASIA AND THE PACIFIC	41,000	42,900	53,000	68,200	54,400	1.42	-20.23
Other countries of Asia	41,000	42,900	53,000	68,200	54,400	1.42	-20.23
EUROPE	2,798,100	2,933,400	2,870,700	2,547,200	2,320,700	60.43	-8.89
NORTHERN EUROPE	1,007,000	1,048,800	879,100	676,100	641,800	16.71	-5.07
United Kingdom	909,700	964,700	765,900	521,600	498,300	12.98	-4.47
Scandinavia	97,300	84,100	113,200	154,500	143,500	3.74	-7.12
SOUTHERN EUROPE	383,200	651,000	495,300	415,500	234,800	6.11	-43.49
Italy	383,200	651,000	495,300	415,500	234,800	6.11	-43.49
WESTERN EUROPE	1,044,900	869,000	1,012,300	1,007,100	961,900	25.05	-4.49
France	231,800	222,700	239,500	160,000	113,900	2.97	-28.81
Germany	685,600	563,200	677,000	748,900	751,100	19.56	0.29
Switzerland	127,500	83,100	95,800	98,200	96,900	2.52	-1.32
OTHER EUROPE	363,000	364,600	484,000	448,500	482,200	12.56	7.51
Other countries of Europe	363,000	364,600	484,000	448,500	482,200	12.56	7.51
MIDDLE EAST	37,500	36,600	43,600	50,200	50,600	1.32	0.80
All countries of Middle East	37,500	36,600	43,600	50,200	50,600	1.32	0.80
SOUTH ASIA	83,300	91,100	110,100	110,300	101,100	2.63	-8.34
India	83,300	91,100	110,100	110,300	101,100	2.63	-8.34
NOT SPECIFIED	165,200	205,600	214,100	175,200	203,900	5.31	16.38
Other countries of the World	165,200	205,600	214,100	175,200	203,900	5.31	16.38

Yearbook of Tourism Statistics, Data 2009 – 2013, 2015 Edition

KIRIBATI

1. Arrivals of non-resident tourists at national borders, by nationality

		2009	2010	2011	2012	2013	Market share 2013	% Change 2013-2012
TOTAL	(*)	**3,944**	**4,701**	**5,264**	**4,907**	**5,868**	**100.00**	**19.58**
AMERICAS		**699**	**827**	**1,063**	**682**	**1,387**	**23.64**	**103.37**
NORTH AMERICA		**699**	**827**	**1,063**	**682**	**1,387**	**23.64**	**103.37**
Canada		47	51	67		52	0.89	
United States of America		652	776	996	682	1,335	22.75	95.75
EAST ASIA AND THE PACIFIC		**2,695**	**3,240**	**2,887**	**2,514**	**3,501**	**59.66**	**39.26**
NORTH-EAST ASIA		**288**	**429**	**298**	**200**	**285**	**4.86**	**42.50**
Japan		234	244	236	200	216	3.68	8.00
Taiwan, Province of China		54	185	62		69	1.18	
AUSTRALASIA		**1,286**	**1,383**	**1,432**	**1,343**	**1,658**	**28.25**	**23.45**
Australia		934	913	809	857	1,060	18.06	23.69
New Zealand		352	470	623	486	598	10.19	23.05
OTHER EAST ASIA AND THE PACIFIC		**1,121**	**1,428**	**1,157**	**971**	**1,558**	**26.55**	**60.45**
Other countries of Asia		379	387			463	7.89	
Other countries of Oceania		742	1,041	1,157	971	1,095	18.66	12.77
EUROPE		**382**	**368**	**412**	**328**	**629**	**10.72**	**91.77**
NORTHERN EUROPE		**135**	**153**	**226**	**109**	**142**	**2.42**	**30.28**
United Kingdom		135	153	226	109	142	2.42	30.28
SOUTHERN EUROPE		**11**	**14**			**5**	**0.09**	
Italy		11	14			5	0.09	
WESTERN EUROPE		**185**	**144**	**112**	**219**	**132**	**2.25**	**-39.73**
France		120	72	43		50	0.85	
Germany		50	55	69	219	62	1.06	-71.69
Switzerland		15	17			20	0.34	
OTHER EUROPE		**51**	**57**	**74**		**350**	**5.96**	
Other countries of Europe		51	57	74		350	5.96	
NOT SPECIFIED		**168**	**266**	**902**	**1,383**	**351**	**5.98**	**-74.62**
Other countries of the World		168	266	902	1,383	351	5.98	-74.62

Yearbook of Tourism Statistics, Data 2009 – 2013, 2015 Edition

KOREA, REPUBLIC OF

2. Arrivals of non-resident visitors at national borders, by nationality

	2009	2010	2011	2012	2013	Market share 2013	% Change 2013-2012
TOTAL (*)	7,817,533	8,797,658	9,794,796	11,140,028	12,175,550	100.00	9.30
AFRICA	22,487	26,892	30,334	32,237	33,564	0.28	4.12
EAST AFRICA	4,874	5,949	7,438	7,836	8,217	0.07	4.86
Burundi	14	27	70	49	67	0.00	36.73
Comoros	6		13	38	23	0.00	-39.47
Djibouti	12	13	14	10	10	0.00	
Eritrea	11	18	29	39	25	0.00	-35.90
Ethiopia	439	599	915	967	1,424	0.01	47.26
Kenya	816	1,017	1,312	1,528	1,638	0.01	7.20
Madagascar	107	88	109	161	230	0.00	42.86
Malawi	28	94	101	102	132	0.00	29.41
Mauritius	495	567	502	558	1,004	0.01	79.93
Mozambique	83	90	174	198	310	0.00	56.57
Reunion			3	3	3	0.00	
Rwanda	109	121	229	258	246	0.00	-4.65
Seychelles	43	83	71	84	79	0.00	-5.95
Somalia	11	9	16	23	17	0.00	-26.09
Uganda	246	295	402	475	600	0.00	26.32
United Republic of Tanzania	2,175	2,534	3,060	2,807	1,955	0.02	-30.35
Zambia	93	124	160	251	171	0.00	-31.87
Zimbabwe	186	270	258	285	283	0.00	-0.70
CENTRAL AFRICA	1,028	1,440	1,674	2,233	1,881	0.02	-15.76
Angola	314	438	476	850	734	0.01	-13.65
Cameroon	318	386	444	564	546	0.00	-3.19
Central African Republic	6	25	35	41	9	0.00	-78.05
Chad	4	21	36	28	19	0.00	-32.14
Congo	90	63	103	103	75	0.00	-27.18
Democratic Republic of the Congo	157	328	327	298	348	0.00	16.78
Equatorial Guinea	6	34	40	48	13	0.00	-72.92
Gabon	127	140	204	294	132	0.00	-55.10
Sao Tome and Principe	6	5	9	7	5	0.00	-28.57
NORTH AFRICA	3,198	3,536	4,168	4,675	5,029	0.04	7.57
Algeria	667	804	1,000	1,209	1,017	0.01	-15.88
Morocco	943	887	1,280	1,242	1,670	0.01	34.46
South Sudan			4	82	66	0.00	-19.51
Sudan	965	1,085	978	1,053	984	0.01	-6.55
Tunisia	623	760	905	1,088	1,292	0.01	18.75
Western Sahara			1	1			
SOUTHERN AFRICA	7,768	9,869	10,172	10,674	11,028	0.09	3.32
Botswana	23	27	57	96	114	0.00	18.75
Lesotho	13	20	31	30	30	0.00	
Namibia	163	154	183	172	143	0.00	-16.86
South Africa	7,530	9,633	9,833	10,298	10,560	0.09	2.54
Swaziland	39	35	68	78	181	0.00	132.05
WEST AFRICA	5,619	6,098	6,882	6,817	7,409	0.06	8.68
Benin	73	52	77	78	59	0.00	-24.36
Burkina Faso	26	46	80	92	61	0.00	-33.70
Cabo Verde	20	29	23	34	16	0.00	-52.94
Côte d'Ivoire	180	206	142	181	191	0.00	5.52
Gambia	34	27	41	71	41	0.00	-42.25
Ghana	1,673	2,062	2,214	2,024	2,320	0.02	14.62
Guinea	87	45	110	109	103	0.00	-5.50
Guinea-Bissau	3	6	14	16	13	0.00	-18.75
Liberia	89	105	158	138	163	0.00	18.12
Mali	75	53	96	82	129	0.00	57.32
Mauritania	8	14	43	84	22	0.00	-73.81
Niger	28	38	63	43	41	0.00	-4.65
Nigeria	3,024	3,032	3,390	3,453	3,781	0.03	9.50
Saint Helena	5	9	14	6			

392

KOREA, REPUBLIC OF

2. Arrivals of non-resident visitors at national borders, by nationality

	2009	2010	2011	2012	2013	Market share 2013	% Change 2013-2012
Senegal	228	274	330	314	343	0.00	9.24
Sierra Leone	29	45	35	33	50	0.00	51.52
Togo	37	55	52	59	76	0.00	28.81
OTHER AFRICA					2		
Other countries of Africa					2		
AMERICAS	751,697	813,860	827,383	876,149	915,622	7.52	4.51
CARIBBEAN	1,292	1,731	2,058	2,612	6,495	0.05	148.66
Antigua and Barbuda	16	28	22	33	20	0.00	-39.39
Bahamas	33	75	83	72	114	0.00	58.33
Barbados	36	58	79	56	98	0.00	75.00
Bermuda		4	2	1			
British Virgin Islands	50	109	112	50	4	0.00	-92.00
Cuba	132	85	221	80	190	0.00	137.50
Dominica	38	37	40	54	273	0.00	405.56
Dominican Republic	344	343	451	517	624	0.01	20.70
Grenada	8	12	28	31	37	0.00	19.35
Haiti	42	66	86	133	299	0.00	124.81
Jamaica	312	442	500	811	2,725	0.02	236.00
Montserrat	4	4					
Netherlands Antilles		16	10	42	2	0.00	-95.24
Puerto Rico	4	4	7	22	8	0.00	-63.64
Saint Kitts and Nevis	19	24	54	88	110	0.00	25.00
Saint Lucia	30	11	22	39	164	0.00	320.51
Saint Vincent and the Grenadines	44	91	34	205	1,046	0.01	410.24
Trinidad and Tobago	180	322	271	378	781	0.01	106.61
Turks and Caicos Islands			36				
CENTRAL AMERICA	2,994	3,873	3,734	4,342	5,679	0.05	30.79
Belize	70	53	39	61	73	0.00	19.67
Costa Rica	548	669	757	968	948	0.01	-2.07
El Salvador	639	694	685	574	542	0.00	-5.57
Guatemala	581	680	742	753	828	0.01	9.96
Honduras	620	918	762	903	2,038	0.02	125.69
Nicaragua	133	316	191	314	406	0.00	29.30
Panama	403	543	558	769	844	0.01	9.75
NORTH AMERICA	726,048	782,037	792,085	836,323	866,908	7.12	3.66
Canada	109,249	121,214	122,223	128,431	133,640	1.10	4.06
Mexico	5,472	7,934	8,359	10,026	10,953	0.09	9.25
United States of America	611,327	652,889	661,503	697,866	722,315	5.93	3.50
SOUTH AMERICA	21,356	26,206	29,503	32,865	36,539	0.30	11.18
Argentina	2,350	3,196	2,984	3,316	3,296	0.03	-0.60
Bolivia	451	534	572	648	897	0.01	38.43
Brazil	10,145	12,747	14,639	15,761	15,739	0.13	-0.14
Chile	1,735	2,109	2,828	3,245	3,299	0.03	1.66
Colombia	2,376	2,303	2,674	3,233	4,088	0.03	26.45
Ecuador	546	815	868	944	1,110	0.01	17.58
Guyana	77	58	50	214	173	0.00	-19.16
Paraguay	377	451	445	510	440	0.00	-13.73
Peru	1,690	2,127	2,424	2,687	4,615	0.04	71.75
Suriname	38	40	54	93	65	0.00	-30.11
Uruguay	150	206	280	357	418	0.00	17.09
Venezuela	1,421	1,620	1,685	1,857	2,399	0.02	29.19
OTHER AMERICAS	7	13	3	7	1	0.00	-85.71
Other countries of the Americas	7	13	3	7	1	0.00	-85.71
EAST ASIA AND THE PACIFIC	6,029,612	6,769,195	7,678,884	8,913,347	9,825,755	80.70	10.24
NORTH-EAST ASIA	5,037,628	5,583,188	6,277,955	7,346,617	8,109,401	66.60	10.38
China	1,342,317	1,875,157	2,220,196	2,836,892	4,326,869	35.54	52.52
Hong Kong, China	215,769	228,582	280,849	360,027	400,435	3.29	11.22
Japan	3,053,311	3,023,009	3,289,051	3,518,792	2,747,750	22.57	-21.91
Macao, China	7,157	8,130	11,647	21,557	25,945	0.21	20.36

Yearbook of Tourism Statistics, Data 2009 – 2013, 2015 Edition

KOREA, REPUBLIC OF

2. Arrivals of non-resident visitors at national borders, by nationality

	2009	2010	2011	2012	2013	Market share 2013	% Change 2013-2012
Mongolia	38,446	41,958	48,004	61,116	63,740	0.52	4.29
Taiwan, Province of China	380,628	406,352	428,208	548,233	544,662	4.47	-0.65
SOUTH-EAST ASIA	**860,971**	**1,039,112**	**1,244,309**	**1,399,359**	**1,555,117**	**12.77**	**11.13**
Brunei Darussalam	925	1,268	1,434	2,070	2,188	0.02	5.70
Cambodia	6,041	7,194	12,438	18,567	21,172	0.17	14.03
Indonesia	80,988	95,239	124,474	149,247	189,189	1.55	26.76
Lao People's Democratic Republic	1,104	1,999	2,477	3,294	5,526	0.05	67.76
Malaysia	80,105	113,675	156,281	178,082	207,727	1.71	16.65
Myanmar	56,044	57,916	70,168	67,917	63,470	0.52	-6.55
Philippines	271,962	297,452	337,268	331,346	400,686	3.29	20.93
Singapore	96,622	112,855	124,565	154,073	174,567	1.43	13.30
Thailand	190,972	260,718	309,143	387,441	372,878	3.06	-3.76
Timor-Leste	230	583	530	815	644	0.01	-20.98
Viet Nam	75,978	90,213	105,531	106,507	117,070	0.96	9.92
AUSTRALASIA	**123,106**	**139,382**	**149,102**	**158,358**	**152,665**	**1.25**	**-3.60**
Australia	99,153	112,409	122,494	128,812	123,560	1.01	-4.08
New Zealand	23,953	26,973	26,608	29,546	29,105	0.24	-1.49
MELANESIA	**4,517**	**4,827**	**4,299**	**4,739**	**4,766**	**0.04**	**0.57**
Fiji	4,127	4,486	3,856	4,224	4,326	0.04	2.41
New Caledonia			3				
Papua New Guinea	251	214	261	256	238	0.00	-7.03
Solomon Islands	109	94	130	174	144	0.00	-17.24
Vanuatu	30	33	49	85	58	0.00	-31.76
MICRONESIA	**2,119**	**1,423**	**1,834**	**2,481**	**2,104**	**0.02**	**-15.20**
Kiribati	1,909	1,254	1,605	2,019	1,769	0.01	-12.38
Marshall Islands	45	67	55	148	78	0.00	-47.30
Micronesia, Federated States of	77	66	86	72	95	0.00	31.94
Nauru	11	9	25	53	29	0.00	-45.28
Palau	77	27	63	189	133	0.00	-29.63
POLYNESIA	**700**	**457**	**419**	**719**	**508**	**0.00**	**-29.35**
American Samoa	8	9	4	3	1	0.00	-66.67
French Polynesia	4	6	69	2			
Samoa	137	172	92	174	126	0.00	-27.59
Tonga	111	139	112	193	106	0.00	-45.08
Tuvalu	440	131	142	347	275	0.00	-20.75
OTHER EAST ASIA AND THE PACIFIC	**571**	**806**	**966**	**1,074**	**1,194**	**0.01**	**11.17**
Other countries of Asia	567	806	966	1,067	1,190	0.01	11.53
Other countries of Oceania	4			7	4	0.00	-42.86
EUROPE	**645,624**	**708,948**	**752,961**	**807,244**	**863,541**	**7.09**	**6.97**
CENTRAL/EASTERN EUROPE	**224,765**	**256,329**	**279,822**	**305,854**	**322,033**	**2.64**	**5.29**
Armenia	207	195	283	323	311	0.00	-3.72
Azerbaijan	506	679	706	761	800	0.01	5.12
Belarus	813	772	859	968	1,477	0.01	52.58
Bulgaria	6,220	7,525	8,103	7,186	7,880	0.06	9.66
Czech Republic	6,307	6,589	7,103	8,353	11,903	0.10	42.50
Estonia	771	759	905	944	893	0.01	-5.40
Georgia	677	687	842	803	588	0.00	-26.77
Hungary	2,144	2,365	2,384	2,703	3,182	0.03	17.72
Kazakhstan	5,699	7,417	8,421	11,039	13,158	0.11	19.20
Kyrgyzstan	2,652	2,424	2,109	2,783	3,424	0.03	23.03
Latvia	1,958	2,559	2,111	2,259	1,988	0.02	-12.00
Lithuania	1,142	1,366	1,572	1,827	1,622	0.01	-11.22
Poland	10,598	11,555	13,451	13,656	13,300	0.11	-2.61
Republic of Moldova	178	191	218	221	352	0.00	59.28
Romania	6,601	8,699	9,780	10,650	12,259	0.10	15.11
Russian Federation	137,054	150,730	154,835	166,721	175,360	1.44	5.18
Slovakia	1,682	1,841	2,558	2,833	2,701	0.02	-4.66
Tajikistan	410	696	1,171	1,433	1,548	0.01	8.03
Turkmenistan	196	196	199	363	374	0.00	3.03

394

KOREA, REPUBLIC OF

2. Arrivals of non-resident visitors at national borders, by nationality

	2009	2010	2011	2012	2013	Market share 2013	% Change 2013-2012
Ukraine	22,597	25,373	31,162	27,782	24,299	0.20	-12.54
Uzbekistan	16,353	23,711	31,050	42,246	44,614	0.37	5.61
NORTHERN EUROPE	**137,223**	**147,564**	**158,582**	**166,003**	**185,069**	**1.52**	**11.49**
Denmark	7,813	7,978	8,435	8,952	9,595	0.08	7.18
Faeroe Islands			1				
Finland	9,131	9,339	10,320	9,973	10,728	0.09	7.57
Iceland	214	308	384	418	427	0.00	2.15
Ireland	5,991	6,257	7,199	7,035	7,416	0.06	5.42
Norway	10,968	12,821	13,371	13,958	18,318	0.15	31.24
Sweden	11,941	13,351	14,228	15,495	17,711	0.15	14.30
United Kingdom	91,165	97,510	104,644	110,172	120,874	0.99	9.71
SOUTHERN EUROPE	**56,433**	**61,626**	**65,085**	**72,490**	**85,823**	**0.70**	**18.39**
Albania	101	122	143	164	190	0.00	15.85
Andorra	23	26	17	36	18	0.00	-50.00
Bosnia and Herzegovina	42	75	52	69	77	0.00	11.59
Croatia	6,001	5,755	6,117	5,780	6,799	0.06	17.63
Greece	7,885	7,975	8,802	8,600	8,585	0.07	-0.17
Holy See	8	12	5	8	6	0.00	-25.00
Italy	22,894	25,686	26,442	28,941	38,715	0.32	33.77
Malta	148	212	240	206	237	0.00	15.05
Montenegro	347	1,287	1,522	1,434	1,213	0.01	-15.41
Portugal	5,003	5,574	6,397	8,702	8,648	0.07	-0.62
San Marino	30	5	27	5	7	0.00	40.00
Serbia	503	1,047	1,304	1,498	2,303	0.02	53.74
Serbia and Montenegro	1,684	81	51	18	3	0.00	-83.33
Slovenia	974	973	924	1,080	1,290	0.01	19.44
Spain	10,691	12,590	12,884	15,833	17,513	0.14	10.61
TFYR of Macedonia	99	206	158	116	219	0.00	88.79
WESTERN EUROPE	**204,308**	**214,440**	**220,186**	**230,570**	**238,106**	**1.96**	**3.27**
Austria	8,017	8,956	9,227	9,750	9,811	0.08	0.63
Belgium	6,828	7,803	7,793	8,894	9,267	0.08	4.19
France	61,426	66,192	69,459	71,140	75,947	0.62	6.76
Germany	97,691	98,119	99,468	102,262	100,803	0.83	-1.43
Liechtenstein	34	26	49	41	60	0.00	46.34
Luxembourg	451	465	480	437	555	0.00	27.00
Monaco	11	12	17	60	22	0.00	-63.33
Netherlands	20,358	22,669	23,279	25,886	28,916	0.24	11.71
Switzerland	9,492	10,198	10,414	12,100	12,725	0.10	5.17
EAST MEDITERRANEAN EUROPE	**22,552**	**28,751**	**28,986**	**32,065**	**32,238**	**0.26**	**0.54**
Cyprus	359	438	472	531	618	0.01	16.38
Israel	9,784	11,993	11,216	12,244	11,922	0.10	-2.63
Turkey	12,409	16,320	17,298	19,290	19,698	0.16	2.12
OTHER EUROPE	**343**	**238**	**300**	**262**	**272**	**0.00**	**3.82**
Other countries of Europe	343	238	300	262	272	0.00	3.82
MIDDLE EAST	**19,759**	**24,574**	**29,340**	**34,693**	**39,669**	**0.33**	**14.34**
Bahrain	296	261	328	367	383	0.00	4.36
Egypt	3,852	5,138	5,845	5,753	6,585	0.05	14.46
Iraq	1,975	2,210	2,090	2,695	2,788	0.02	3.45
Jordan	3,007	3,137	3,520	3,521	2,971	0.02	-15.62
Kuwait	463	870	1,047	1,116	1,587	0.01	42.20
Lebanon	824	1,198	1,335	1,172	1,116	0.01	-4.78
Libya	2,162	1,726	800	3,246	3,265	0.03	0.59
Oman	366	721	873	1,001	836	0.01	-16.48
Palestine	207	257	253	266	314	0.00	18.05
Qatar	318	311	506	676	777	0.01	14.94
Saudi Arabia	3,040	3,875	6,904	7,970	10,219	0.08	28.22
Syrian Arab Republic	1,829	1,853	2,263	2,024	1,549	0.01	-23.47
United Arab Emirates	887	2,433	2,958	3,866	6,098	0.05	57.73
Yemen	533	584	618	1,020	1,181	0.01	15.78

Yearbook of Tourism Statistics, Data 2009 – 2013, 2015 Edition

KOREA, REPUBLIC OF

2. Arrivals of non-resident visitors at national borders, by nationality

	2009	2010	2011	2012	2013	Market share 2013	% Change 2013-2012
SOUTH ASIA	**113,740**	**134,503**	**148,431**	**146,655**	**187,704**	**1.54**	**27.99**
Afghanistan	611	780	1,028	972	1,039	0.01	6.89
Bangladesh	6,718	8,899	9,302	9,243	10,083	0.08	9.09
Bhutan	180	250	278	311	290	0.00	-6.75
India	72,779	86,547	92,047	91,700	123,235	1.01	34.39
Iran, Islamic Republic of	7,854	8,387	9,532	6,568	5,342	0.04	-18.67
Maldives	263	279	354	324	209	0.00	-35.49
Nepal	6,994	7,574	10,095	13,698	22,316	0.18	62.91
Pakistan	8,935	9,270	10,121	9,691	9,371	0.08	-3.30
Sri Lanka	9,406	12,517	15,674	14,148	15,819	0.13	11.81
NOT SPECIFIED	**234,614**	**319,686**	**327,463**	**329,703**	**309,695**	**2.54**	**-6.07**
Other countries of the World	194	192	203	145	200	0.00	37.93
Nationals Residing Abroad	234,420	319,494	327,260	329,558	309,495	2.54	-6.09

Yearbook of Tourism Statistics, Data 2009 – 2013, 2015 Edition

KUWAIT

2. Arrivals of non-resident visitors at national borders, by nationality

	2009	2010	2011	2012	2013	Market share 2013	% Change 2013-2012
TOTAL	**5,087,781**	**5,207,785**	**5,574,302**	**5,728,697**	**6,216,936**	**100.00**	**8.52**
AFRICA	**73,260**	**95,080**	**113,314**	**113,437**	**131,878**	**2.12**	**16.26**
EAST AFRICA	**28,071**	**50,575**	**69,836**	**65,704**	**78,101**	**1.26**	**18.87**
Burundi	14	11	22	15	62	0.00	313.33
Comoros	166	425	303	411	460	0.01	11.92
Djibouti	95	92	82	116	174	0.00	50.00
Eritrea	1,207	1,044	969	976	1,075	0.02	10.14
Ethiopia	21,109	43,611	63,866	57,541	65,180	1.05	13.28
Kenya	1,293	1,622	1,416	1,396	1,481	0.02	6.09
Madagascar	600	705	458	1,978	3,510	0.06	77.45
Malawi	40	50	92	102	153	0.00	50.00
Mauritius	124	143	86	103	108	0.00	4.85
Mozambique	31	17	32	37	30	0.00	-18.92
Rwanda	1	3	15	18	54	0.00	200.00
Seychelles	35	24	34	32	44	0.00	37.50
Somalia	2,674	2,170	1,935	1,948	1,963	0.03	0.77
Uganda	203	131	117	574	2,936	0.05	411.50
United Republic of Tanzania	169	211	212	235	437	0.01	85.96
Zambia	39	75	10	23	57	0.00	147.83
Zimbabwe	271	241	187	199	377	0.01	89.45
CENTRAL AFRICA	**1,465**	**1,219**	**949**	**745**	**1,242**	**0.02**	**66.71**
Angola	21	12	20	34	46	0.00	35.29
Cameroon	82	108	50	60	126	0.00	110.00
Central African Republic	101	32	34	37	31	0.00	-16.22
Chad	1,216	1,032	794	571	835	0.01	46.23
Congo	2		7	5	45	0.00	800.00
Democratic Republic of the Congo	35	30	36	26	72	0.00	176.92
Gabon	8	5	8	12	87	0.00	625.00
NORTH AFRICA	**29,498**	**31,462**	**31,973**	**36,551**	**40,004**	**0.64**	**9.45**
Algeria	3,201	3,694	3,566	4,116	4,259	0.07	3.47
Morocco	11,086	11,808	11,451	13,006	13,978	0.22	7.47
Sudan	8,302	8,043	9,049	10,420	13,053	0.21	25.27
Tunisia	6,909	7,917	7,907	9,009	8,714	0.14	-3.27
SOUTHERN AFRICA	**5,568**	**5,337**	**4,550**	**4,494**	**5,358**	**0.09**	**19.23**
Botswana	5	6	29	37	42	0.00	13.51
Lesotho	1	62	13	23	73	0.00	217.39
Namibia	4	15	13	9	30	0.00	233.33
South Africa	5,350	5,023	4,424	4,312	5,098	0.08	18.23
Swaziland	208	231	71	113	115	0.00	1.77
WEST AFRICA	**8,657**	**6,485**	**5,960**	**5,937**	**7,141**	**0.11**	**20.28**
Benin	172	203	226	260	281	0.00	8.08
Burkina Faso	60	70	101	97	162	0.00	67.01
Cabo Verde	4	2		6	3	0.00	-50.00
Côte d'Ivoire	84	58	89	71	102	0.00	43.66
Gambia	37	54	66	72	123	0.00	70.83
Ghana	5,045	3,084	2,662	2,331	2,307	0.04	-1.03
Guinea	108	97	70	78	129	0.00	65.38
Guinea-Bissau		21	6	13	20	0.00	53.85
Liberia	263	288	224	221	229	0.00	3.62
Mali	101	120	143	238	676	0.01	184.03
Mauritania	294	266	293	387	516	0.01	33.33
Niger	147	173	189	189	223	0.00	17.99
Nigeria	1,615	1,281	1,173	1,170	1,377	0.02	17.69
Saint Helena	1		1	3	4	0.00	33.33
Senegal	410	336	385	443	452	0.01	2.03
Sierra Leone	121	133	158	247	293	0.00	18.62
Togo	195	299	174	111	244	0.00	119.82
OTHER AFRICA	**1**	**2**	**46**	**6**	**32**	**0.00**	**433.33**
Other countries of Africa	1	2	46	6	32	0.00	433.33

Yearbook of Tourism Statistics, Data 2009 – 2013, 2015 Edition

KUWAIT

2. Arrivals of non-resident visitors at national borders, by nationality

	2009	2010	2011	2012	2013	Market share 2013	% Change 2013-2012
AMERICAS	229,288	226,943	222,973	184,619	174,906	2.81	-5.26
CARIBBEAN	516	478	578	671	722	0.01	7.60
Aruba	1	6	4		1	0.00	
Bahamas	4	17	15	11	12	0.00	9.09
Barbados	21	12	11	10	4	0.00	-60.00
Bermuda	1	4	8	31	1	0.00	-96.77
Cuba	44	18	33	65	36	0.00	-44.62
Curaçao			1				
Dominican Republic	177	165	196	248	287	0.00	15.73
Grenada	24	30	13	17	40	0.00	135.29
Haiti	41	31	72	84	77	0.00	-8.33
Jamaica	59	61	88	93	91	0.00	-2.15
Saint Kitts and Nevis		4	2	7	34	0.00	385.71
Saint Lucia	4	7	7	5	6	0.00	20.00
Saint Vincent and the Grenadines			3	1	1	0.00	
Trinidad and Tobago	140	123	125	99	132	0.00	33.33
CENTRAL AMERICA	423	399	290	290	322	0.01	11.03
Belize	162	175	153	127	113	0.00	-11.02
Costa Rica	27	21	24	19	22	0.00	15.79
El Salvador	127	159	50	39	20	0.00	-48.72
Guatemala	26	10	20	36	71	0.00	97.22
Honduras	40	4	21	10	13	0.00	30.00
Nicaragua	8	4	2	4	17	0.00	325.00
Panama	33	26	20	55	66	0.00	20.00
NORTH AMERICA	224,756	222,270	218,016	179,569	169,930	2.73	-5.37
Canada	40,440	41,156	39,130	39,060	39,968	0.64	2.32
Mexico	374	276	369	385	514	0.01	33.51
United States of America	183,942	180,838	178,517	140,124	129,448	2.08	-7.62
SOUTH AMERICA	3,588	3,789	4,081	4,081	3,918	0.06	-3.99
Argentina	514	441	609	532	485	0.01	-8.83
Bolivia	66	99	86	80	88	0.00	10.00
Brazil	1,143	1,374	1,252	1,209	1,286	0.02	6.37
Chile	103	99	72	91	75	0.00	-17.58
Colombia	542	420	410	469	451	0.01	-3.84
Ecuador	130	166	138	197	105	0.00	-46.70
French Guiana	6	20		2			
Guyana	8	20	17	23	24	0.00	4.35
Paraguay	14	6	9	7	30	0.00	328.57
Peru	77	42	52	149	111	0.00	-25.50
Suriname	19	9	12	26	32	0.00	23.08
Uruguay	33	29	51	48	59	0.00	22.92
Venezuela	933	1,064	1,373	1,248	1,172	0.02	-6.09
OTHER AMERICAS	5	7	8	8	14	0.00	75.00
Other countries of the Americas	5	7	8	8	14	0.00	75.00
EAST ASIA AND THE PACIFIC	249,653	229,734	226,602	230,571	231,957	3.73	0.60
NORTH-EAST ASIA	20,855	25,571	31,941	32,188	35,250	0.57	9.51
China	8,207	10,925	14,208	13,283	15,428	0.25	16.15
Hong Kong, China	212	244	211	218	269	0.00	23.39
Japan	4,606	4,959	4,798	5,291	5,072	0.08	-4.14
Korea, Dem. People's Republic of	728		442	354	273	0.00	-22.88
Korea, Republic of	6,838	9,111	11,677	12,731	13,833	0.22	8.66
Macao, China	3	4	10	4	4	0.00	
Mongolia	106	170	399	197	187	0.00	-5.08
Taiwan, Province of China	155	158	196	110	184	0.00	67.27
SOUTH-EAST ASIA	207,446	184,929	179,100	184,353	183,499	2.95	-0.46
Brunei Darussalam	31	37	14	21	7	0.00	-66.67
Cambodia	100	64	70	113	81	0.00	-28.32
Indonesia	63,419	35,664	25,793	17,693	13,800	0.22	-22.00
Lao People's Democratic Republic	72	20	14	34	25	0.00	-26.47

398

KUWAIT

2. Arrivals of non-resident visitors at national borders, by nationality

	2009	2010	2011	2012	2013	Market share 2013	% Change 2013-2012
Malaysia	3,495	4,105	4,320	4,294	4,733	0.08	10.22
Myanmar	332	188	376	297	288	0.00	-3.03
Philippines	130,417	135,182	139,988	154,389	156,952	2.52	1.66
Singapore	1,275	1,457	1,323	1,174	1,126	0.02	-4.09
Thailand	7,561	7,631	6,670	5,544	6,132	0.10	10.61
Timor-Leste	7	8	6	7	4	0.00	-42.86
Viet Nam	737	573	526	787	351	0.01	-55.40
AUSTRALASIA	**20,293**	**18,557**	**15,293**	**13,821**	**13,025**	**0.21**	**-5.76**
Australia	16,990	15,306	12,543	11,180	10,495	0.17	-6.13
New Zealand	3,303	3,251	2,750	2,641	2,530	0.04	-4.20
MELANESIA	**941**	**565**	**147**	**92**	**94**	**0.00**	**2.17**
Fiji	941	565	147	92	94	0.00	2.17
MICRONESIA	**33**	**45**	**22**	**16**	**9**	**0.00**	**-43.75**
Marshall Islands	4	7	5	3	1	0.00	-66.67
Palau	29	38	17	13	8	0.00	-38.46
POLYNESIA	**19**	**16**	**15**	**13**	**17**	**0.00**	**30.77**
Cook Islands	12	8	9	7	5	0.00	-28.57
Samoa	3	1		1			
Tonga	4	7	6	5	12	0.00	140.00
OTHER EAST ASIA AND THE PACIFIC	**66**	**51**	**84**	**88**	**63**	**0.00**	**-28.41**
Other countries of Asia	66	51	84	88	63	0.00	-28.41
EUROPE	**184,248**	**191,455**	**188,306**	**185,227**	**200,837**	**3.23**	**8.43**
CENTRAL/EASTERN EUROPE	**21,729**	**25,211**	**20,218**	**19,788**	**21,690**	**0.35**	**9.61**
Armenia	464	526	586	643	807	0.01	25.51
Azerbaijan	289	290	340	410	519	0.01	26.59
Belarus	602	454	376	287	388	0.01	35.19
Bulgaria	3,301	3,490	3,223	3,365	3,325	0.05	-1.19
Czech Republic	686	1,353	779	617	667	0.01	8.10
Czech Republic/Slovakia				1	2	0.00	100.00
Estonia	29	38	33	51	65	0.00	27.45
Georgia	2,731	1,832	1,135	551	534	0.01	-3.09
Hungary	1,197	1,380	1,345	1,497	1,583	0.03	5.74
Kazakhstan	197	238	277	218	320	0.01	46.79
Kyrgyzstan	512	634	696	649	826	0.01	27.27
Latvia	63	85	98	152	142	0.00	-6.58
Lithuania	108	107	120	209	188	0.00	-10.05
Poland	1,593	1,955	1,806	1,781	1,960	0.03	10.05
Republic of Moldova	60	54	52	86	41	0.00	-52.33
Romania	3,688	5,609	3,499	3,480	3,947	0.06	13.42
Russian Federation	3,969	2,579	3,190	3,119	3,263	0.05	4.62
Slovakia	576	2,772	915	693	772	0.01	11.40
Tajikistan	69	118	129	208	376	0.01	80.77
Turkmenistan	36	48	12	33	22	0.00	-33.33
Ukraine	981	1,050	1,051	1,141	1,424	0.02	24.80
Uzbekistan	578	599	556	597	519	0.01	-13.07
NORTHERN EUROPE	**83,734**	**83,947**	**87,000**	**86,222**	**87,864**	**1.41**	**1.90**
Denmark	3,367	3,206	3,063	3,279	3,304	0.05	0.76
Finland	1,094	1,025	1,097	930	930	0.01	
Iceland	139	81	110	105	105	0.00	
Ireland	2,936	3,000	3,174	3,424	3,441	0.06	0.50
Norway	2,566	2,659	2,433	1,962	1,545	0.02	-21.25
Sweden	6,512	6,614	6,826	6,820	5,539	0.09	-18.78
United Kingdom	67,120	67,362	70,297	69,702	73,000	1.17	4.73
SOUTHERN EUROPE	**24,125**	**25,325**	**24,199**	**24,349**	**29,736**	**0.48**	**22.12**
Albania	98	199	205	224	171	0.00	-23.66
Andorra	2	2	7	8	3	0.00	-62.50
Bosnia and Herzegovina	1,509	1,124	1,327	904	816	0.01	-9.73
Croatia	615	806	774	658	899	0.01	36.63
Greece	1,887	2,416	2,759	2,510	2,909	0.05	15.90

Yearbook of Tourism Statistics, Data 2009 – 2013, 2015 Edition

KUWAIT

2. Arrivals of non-resident visitors at national borders, by nationality

	2009	2010	2011	2012	2013	Market share 2013	% Change 2013-2012
Holy See	11						
Italy	11,222	10,925	10,021	11,002	13,598	0.22	23.60
Malta	116	222	169	223	230	0.00	3.14
Montenegro		11	33	48	38	0.00	-20.83
Portugal	867	1,141	989	1,449	2,019	0.03	39.34
San Marino	10	3	7	8	12	0.00	50.00
Serbia	235	628	923	942	1,150	0.02	22.08
Serbia and Montenegro	1,430						
Slovenia	153	286	231	296	386	0.01	30.41
Spain	5,118	6,771	6,382	5,691	7,046	0.11	23.81
TFYR of Macedonia	852	791	372	386	459	0.01	18.91
WESTERN EUROPE	**42,666**	**44,451**	**44,669**	**43,486**	**48,923**	**0.79**	**12.50**
Austria	1,984	1,997	1,914	1,690	1,826	0.03	8.05
Belgium	2,374	2,755	2,407	2,035	2,100	0.03	3.19
France	14,907	15,084	15,209	15,844	15,818	0.25	-0.16
Germany	14,159	15,283	14,962	14,455	18,082	0.29	25.09
Liechtenstein	18	13	23	70	13	0.00	-81.43
Luxembourg	111	97	87	104	95	0.00	-8.65
Monaco	3	6		3	3	0.00	
Netherlands	7,070	7,101	7,869	7,243	8,919	0.14	23.14
Switzerland	2,040	2,115	2,198	2,042	2,067	0.03	1.22
EAST MEDITERRANEAN EUROPE	**11,893**	**11,764**	**11,653**	**10,868**	**12,214**	**0.20**	**12.38**
Cyprus	323	286	380	614	573	0.01	-6.68
Turkey	11,570	11,478	11,273	10,254	11,641	0.19	13.53
OTHER EUROPE	**101**	**757**	**567**	**514**	**410**	**0.01**	**-20.23**
Other countries of Europe	101	757	567	514	410	0.01	-20.23
MIDDLE EAST	**2,996,469**	**3,103,394**	**3,434,185**	**3,609,287**	**3,950,556**	**63.55**	**9.46**
Bahrain	125,962	122,192	121,482	163,783	230,269	3.70	40.59
Egypt	540,708	569,452	594,099	646,093	710,415	11.43	9.96
Iraq	89,908	69,080	70,058	76,757	77,213	1.24	0.59
Jordan	90,023	94,480	97,267	103,020	112,618	1.81	9.32
Lebanon	119,998	117,686	104,739	108,277	111,408	1.79	2.89
Libya	535	677	455	773	914	0.01	18.24
Oman	16,711	18,035	17,865	19,782	20,922	0.34	5.76
Palestine	7,480	7,622	6,640	6,775	6,831	0.11	0.83
Qatar	32,170	30,873	33,023	35,861	39,048	0.63	8.89
Saudi Arabia	1,613,460	1,708,661	2,063,815	2,160,291	2,365,262	38.05	9.49
Syrian Arab Republic	306,561	307,949	269,013	227,429	199,456	3.21	-12.30
United Arab Emirates	41,763	45,957	45,659	49,458	64,749	1.04	30.92
Yemen	11,190	10,730	10,070	10,988	11,451	0.18	4.21
SOUTH ASIA	**1,316,151**	**1,327,607**	**1,351,987**	**1,355,377**	**1,474,763**	**23.72**	**8.81**
Afghanistan	20,045	12,607	12,457	12,467	13,120	0.21	5.24
Bangladesh	104,757	102,390	107,817	105,983	108,788	1.75	2.65
Bhutan	36	72	123	77	125	0.00	62.34
India	733,117	751,059	789,694	826,526	917,539	14.76	11.01
Iran, Islamic Republic of	89,219	81,136	72,067	72,432	76,384	1.23	5.46
Maldives	16	14	41	49	90	0.00	83.67
Nepal	54,209	52,971	53,812	47,546	50,909	0.82	7.07
Pakistan	219,502	228,028	215,194	200,037	215,742	3.47	7.85
Sri Lanka	95,250	99,330	100,782	90,260	92,066	1.48	2.00
NOT SPECIFIED	**38,712**	**33,572**	**36,935**	**50,179**	**52,039**	**0.84**	**3.71**
Other countries of the World	38,712	33,572	36,935	50,179	52,039	0.84	3.71

Yearbook of Tourism Statistics, Data 2009 – 2013, 2015 Edition

KYRGYZSTAN

2. Arrivals of non-resident visitors at national borders, by country of residence

	2009	2010	2011	2012	2013	Market share 2013	% Change 2013-2012
TOTAL	1,394,175	854,900	2,277,554	2,405,954	3,075,963	100.00	27.85
AMERICAS	12,986	8,753	17,739	18,947	22,143	0.72	16.87
NORTH AMERICA	12,986	8,753	17,739	18,947	22,143	0.72	16.87
Canada	1,976	1,706	1,917	2,240	1,980	0.06	-11.61
United States of America	11,010	7,047	15,822	16,707	20,163	0.66	20.69
EAST ASIA AND THE PACIFIC	32,366	23,898	33,247	34,263	38,705	1.26	12.96
NORTH-EAST ASIA	29,950	22,432	31,498	32,096	36,455	1.19	13.58
China	22,919	18,384	25,315	24,115	30,056	0.98	24.64
Japan	2,119	988	2,487	2,324	2,675	0.09	15.10
Korea, Republic of	4,912	3,060	3,696	5,657	3,724	0.12	-34.17
SOUTH-EAST ASIA	267	86	127	249	210	0.01	-15.66
Malaysia	267	86	127	249	210	0.01	-15.66
AUSTRALASIA	2,149	1,380	1,622	1,918	2,040	0.07	6.36
Australia	1,810	1,196	1,389	1,680	1,737	0.06	3.39
New Zealand	339	184	233	238	303	0.01	27.31
EUROPE	1,332,286	804,293	2,208,239	2,333,206	2,983,093	96.98	27.85
CENTRAL/EASTERN EUROPE	1,291,048	775,438	2,168,520	2,284,717	2,926,901	95.15	28.11
Armenia	425	307	1,001	889	1,327	0.04	49.27
Azerbaijan	1,244	1,315	4,005	3,618	3,470	0.11	-4.09
Belarus	1,038	548	1,703	1,337	1,911	0.06	42.93
Czech Republic	339	141	81	130	342	0.01	163.08
Georgia	910	624	910	1,008	1,293	0.04	28.27
Hungary	447	222	369	456	497	0.02	8.99
Kazakhstan	687,326	541,710	864,963	1,675,644	2,156,041	70.09	28.67
Lithuania	296	175	422	588	618	0.02	5.10
Poland	813	453	702	991	1,003	0.03	1.21
Republic of Moldova	880	472	1,224	821	1,423	0.05	73.33
Russian Federation	158,820	134,436	1,020,575	364,591	448,881	14.59	23.12
Tajikistan	239,342	68,311	50,946	72,087	114,121	3.71	58.31
Turkmenistan	5,430	5,002	310	431	513	0.02	19.03
Ukraine	4,287	1,582	9,102	3,538	4,933	0.16	39.43
Uzbekistan	189,451	20,140	212,207	158,588	190,528	6.19	20.14
NORTHERN EUROPE	5,760	6,970	4,543	6,387	6,412	0.21	0.39
Denmark	89	77	137	274	387	0.01	41.24
Finland	303	180	174	280	189	0.01	-32.50
Ireland	631	349	276	300	304	0.01	1.33
Norway	545	383	518	962	877	0.03	-8.84
Sweden	316	221	240	363	385	0.01	6.06
United Kingdom	3,876	5,760	3,198	4,208	4,270	0.14	1.47
SOUTHERN EUROPE	2,824	1,374	2,124	2,053	2,479	0.08	20.75
Italy	1,321	914	1,477	1,131	1,754	0.06	55.08
Spain	1,503	460	647	922	725	0.02	-21.37
WESTERN EUROPE	18,290	11,788	16,572	20,554	20,756	0.67	0.98
Austria	1,072	558	525	868	1,063	0.03	22.47
Belgium	968	430	596	741	1,139	0.04	53.71
France	3,209	1,818	3,743	3,935	5,247	0.17	33.34
Germany	9,850	7,278	8,607	11,734	9,215	0.30	-21.47
Netherlands	1,220	709	852	1,222	1,366	0.04	11.78
Switzerland	1,971	995	2,249	2,054	2,726	0.09	32.72
EAST MEDITERRANEAN EUROPE	14,364	8,723	16,480	19,495	26,545	0.86	36.16
Israel	988	591	745	1,106	1,134	0.04	2.53
Turkey	13,376	8,132	15,735	18,389	25,411	0.83	38.19
MIDDLE EAST	205	93	126	271	1,271	0.04	369.00
Saudi Arabia	205	93	126	271	1,271	0.04	369.00
SOUTH ASIA	7,134	4,996	7,351	7,321	6,620	0.22	-9.58
Afghanistan	474	420	551	610	626	0.02	2.62
India	1,744	1,788	2,029	2,801	3,075	0.10	9.78
Iran, Islamic Republic of	2,987	1,497	2,696	1,935	1,265	0.04	-34.63
Pakistan	1,929	1,291	2,075	1,975	1,654	0.05	-16.25
NOT SPECIFIED	9,198	12,867	10,852	11,946	24,131	0.78	102.00
Other countries of the World	9,198	12,867	10,852	11,946	24,131	0.78	102.00

401

LAO PEOPLE´S DEMOCRATIC REPUBLIC

2. Arrivals of non-resident visitors at national borders, by nationality

	2009	2010	2011	2012	2013	Market share 2013	% Change 2013-2012
TOTAL	1,969,990	2,513,028	2,723,564	3,330,072	3,779,490	100.00	13.50
AMERICAS	53,348	67,291	69,990	75,851	85,899	2.27	13.25
NORTH AMERICA	50,294	63,419	64,514	70,124	78,740	2.08	12.29
Canada	10,955	13,637	14,422	16,744	17,132	0.45	2.32
United States of America	39,339	49,782	50,092	53,380	61,608	1.63	15.41
OTHER AMERICAS	3,054	3,872	5,476	5,727	7,159	0.19	25.00
Other countries of the Americas	3,054	3,872	5,476	5,727	7,159	0.19	25.00
EAST ASIA AND THE PACIFIC	1,818,291	2,256,705	2,461,424	3,057,840	3,468,560	91.77	13.43
NORTH-EAST ASIA	176,702	226,588	228,410	299,708	380,247	10.06	26.87
China	128,226	161,854	150,791	199,857	245,033	6.48	22.60
Japan	28,081	34,076	37,883	42,026	48,644	1.29	15.75
Korea, Republic of	17,876	27,312	34,707	53,829	81,799	2.16	51.96
Taiwan, Province of China	2,519	3,346	5,029	3,996	4,771	0.13	19.39
SOUTH-EAST ASIA	1,611,009	1,990,932	2,191,224	2,712,478	3,041,233	80.47	12.12
Brunei Darussalam	267	197	354	533	582	0.02	9.19
Cambodia	7,530	6,908	7,561	15,140	12,180	0.32	-19.55
Indonesia	3,158	2,245	3,338	4,256	4,888	0.13	14.85
Malaysia	13,816	15,427	17,702	22,785	26,035	0.69	14.26
Myanmar	1,794	1,652	1,765	1,730	1,947	0.05	12.54
Philippines	8,331	10,341	11,847	14,281	16,318	0.43	14.26
Singapore	5,286	6,087	7,130	10,545	9,685	0.26	-8.16
Thailand	1,274,064	1,517,064	1,579,941	1,937,612	2,059,434	54.49	6.29
Viet Nam	296,763	431,011	561,586	705,596	910,164	24.08	28.99
AUSTRALASIA	27,688	34,931	36,759	39,296	40,901	1.08	4.08
Australia	24,209	30,538	31,874	33,878	35,450	0.94	4.64
New Zealand	3,479	4,393	4,885	5,418	5,451	0.14	0.61
OTHER EAST ASIA AND THE PACIFIC	2,892	4,254	5,031	6,358	6,179	0.16	-2.82
Other countries East Asia/Pacific	2,892	4,254	5,031	6,358	6,179	0.16	-2.82
EUROPE	94,039	181,840	185,771	189,043	215,930	5.71	14.22
CENTRAL/EASTERN EUROPE	2,861	4,835	7,019	8,642	11,649	0.31	34.80
Russian Federation	2,861	4,835	7,019	8,642	11,649	0.31	34.80
NORTHERN EUROPE	4	54,207	52,237	53,693	57,787	1.53	7.62
Denmark	2,977	5,359	4,769	5,054	4,586	0.12	-9.26
Finland	1,985	2,470	2,742	2,962	2,735	0.07	-7.66
Norway	2,221	2,845	3,178	3,307	3,531	0.09	6.77
Sweden	4,150	6,261	5,926	6,676	5,194	0.14	-22.20
United Kingdom	27,044	37,272	35,622	35,694	41,741	1.10	16.94
SOUTHERN EUROPE	8,980	11,848	12,080	10,863	14,382	0.38	32.39
Greece	537	578	451	366	433	0.01	18.31
Italy	5,481	7,075	6,977	6,289	8,822	0.23	40.28
Spain	2,962	4,195	4,652	4,208	5,127	0.14	21.84
WESTERN EUROPE	70,134	93,658	93,595	98,843	112,531	2.98	13.85
Austria	2,450	2,565	3,801	2,860	3,339	0.09	16.75
Belgium	3,868	5,012	5,241	6,284	6,046	0.16	-3.79
France	31,775	44,844	44,399	46,903	52,411	1.39	11.74
Germany	17,710	22,583	21,280	23,417	29,250	0.77	24.91
Netherlands	8,504	10,032	9,164	9,283	10,899	0.29	17.41
Switzerland	5,827	8,622	9,710	10,096	10,586	0.28	4.85
EAST MEDITERRANEAN EUROPE	2,236	3,700	4,232	3,241	3,364	0.09	3.80
Israel	2,236	3,700	4,232	3,241	3,364	0.09	3.80
OTHER EUROPE	9,824	13,592	16,608	13,761	16,217	0.43	17.85
Other countries of Europe	9,824	13,592	16,608	13,761	16,217	0.43	17.85
SOUTH ASIA	2,280	3,321	3,227	3,275	4,551	0.12	38.96
India	2,280	3,321	3,227	3,275	4,551	0.12	38.96
NOT SPECIFIED	2,032	3,871	3,152	4,063	4,550	0.12	11.99
Other countries of the World	2,032	3,871	3,152	4,063	4,550	0.12	11.99

402

LATVIA

2. Arrivals of non-resident visitors at national borders, by country of residence

	2009	2010	2011	2012	2013	Market share 2013	% Change 2013-2012
TOTAL (*)	**4,726,585**	**5,042,260**	**5,538,393**				
AFRICA	**5,059**	**7,422**	**4,345**				
EAST AFRICA	**317**	**144**	**656**				
United Republic of Tanzania	317	144	656				
CENTRAL AFRICA			**143**				
Congo			143				
NORTH AFRICA	**3,671**	**5,190**	**1,135**				
Algeria	660	583	188				
Morocco	1,877	3,509	947				
Tunisia	1,134	1,098					
SOUTHERN AFRICA	**460**	**146**	**1,081**				
South Africa	460	146	1,081				
WEST AFRICA	**611**	**1,942**	**1,330**				
Gambia			286				
Ghana		343					
Liberia		175					
Niger	611		279				
Nigeria		1,424	765				
AMERICAS	**60,256**	**62,408**	**76,550**				
CARIBBEAN	**472**	**808**	**383**				
Cuba	292	808	383				
Jamaica	180						
NORTH AMERICA	**55,904**	**54,772**	**70,354**				
Canada	9,099	10,417	9,074				
Mexico	1,273	2,553	1,704				
United States of America	45,532	41,802	59,576				
SOUTH AMERICA	**3,880**	**6,828**	**5,813**				
Argentina	460	1,291	764				
Brazil	1,438	3,148	1,970				
Chile	493	1,729	1,756				
Peru		197	143				
Suriname		144					
Uruguay	1,163	319	711				
Venezuela	326		469				
EAST ASIA AND THE PACIFIC	**35,405**	**47,040**	**49,521**				
NORTH-EAST ASIA	**17,030**	**27,595**	**26,769**				
China	5,042	13,131	13,500				
Hong Kong, China	652		596				
Japan	7,937	10,483	10,072				
Korea, Republic of	1,973	2,402	1,323				
Mongolia	1,426	1,291	1,278				
Taiwan, Province of China		288					
SOUTH-EAST ASIA	**9,513**	**8,786**	**9,142**				
Indonesia	4,166	3,170	2,120				
Malaysia	1,134	2,336	711				
Philippines	1,736	2,233	2,093				
Singapore	360						
Thailand	2,117	726	3,081				
Viet Nam		321	1,137				
AUSTRALASIA	**8,862**	**10,659**	**13,610**				
Australia	5,040	5,738	9,340				
New Zealand	3,822	4,921	4,270				
EUROPE	**4,611,254**	**4,901,853**	**5,386,291**				
CENTRAL/EASTERN EUROPE	**3,450,735**	**3,537,615**	**3,879,175**				
Armenia	2,029	9,441	8,045				
Azerbaijan	4,305	4,376	3,115				
Belarus	113,276	101,469	125,854				
Bulgaria	5,708	10,733	11,860				
Czech Republic	28,881	31,279	42,145				

403

LATVIA

2. Arrivals of non-resident visitors at national borders, by country of residence

	2009	2010	2011	2012	2013	Market share 2013	% Change 2013-2012
Estonia	946,292	957,038	1,040,672				
Georgia	17,266	23,885	16,882				
Hungary	10,517	15,821	14,339				
Kazakhstan	19,380	19,036	23,005				
Kyrgyzstan	1,991	1,127	3,854				
Lithuania	1,731,017	1,707,920	1,788,940				
Poland	201,811	210,457	234,118				
Republic of Moldova	9,467	10,239	8,548				
Romania	3,827	8,713	7,070				
Russian Federation	297,328	348,070	449,797				
Slovakia	8,267	11,759	12,381				
Tajikistan	1,798	4,063	3,879				
Turkmenistan	116	736	188				
Ukraine	37,462	46,528	62,322				
Uzbekistan	9,997	14,925	22,161				
NORTHERN EUROPE	**704,111**	**857,075**	**908,149**				
Denmark	51,798	65,418	63,997				
Finland	172,919	202,644	188,915				
Iceland	4,986	6,130	16,418				
Ireland	21,539	22,282	25,593				
Norway	87,446	121,438	150,077				
Sweden	271,840	352,486	351,185				
United Kingdom	93,583	86,677	111,964				
SOUTHERN EUROPE	**85,709**	**113,331**	**138,023**				
Albania	180	146					
Andorra			379				
Bosnia and Herzegovina	163	144					
Croatia	3,544	4,007	8,692				
Greece	4,065	6,666	6,581				
Italy	41,392	53,482	71,540				
Malta	3,814	4,285	3,964				
Montenegro		197					
Portugal	9,164	12,927	13,956				
Serbia		2,355	523				
Slovenia	2,728	4,709	4,818				
Spain	18,145	22,108	26,100				
TFYR of Macedonia	2,514	2,305	1,470				
WESTERN EUROPE	**348,770**	**360,688**	**431,176**				
Austria	9,918	16,045	21,419				
Belgium	23,802	41,150	48,766				
France	35,513	35,490	49,204				
Germany	226,461	218,449	249,112				
Liechtenstein	681	806	1,422				
Luxembourg	2,699	5,837	7,129				
Monaco	940	351	848				
Netherlands	31,053	28,833	32,048				
Switzerland	17,703	13,727	21,228				
EAST MEDITERRANEAN EUROPE	**21,929**	**33,144**	**29,768**				
Cyprus	2,711	5,511	3,015				
Israel	9,601	15,699	18,464				
Turkey	9,617	11,934	8,289				
MIDDLE EAST	**1,924**	**7,514**	**1,858**				
Bahrain		175	191				
Egypt	635	1,027	140				
Iraq		146	383				
Jordan	158	197	188				
Kuwait		1,303	765				
Lebanon	455	2,949					
Qatar		1,055					

Yearbook of Tourism Statistics, Data 2009 – 2013, 2015 Edition

LATVIA

2. Arrivals of non-resident visitors at national borders, by country of residence

	2009	2010	2011	2012	2013	Market share 2013	% Change 2013-2012
Saudi Arabia	180	144					
Syrian Arab Republic		518					
United Arab Emirates	496		191				
SOUTH ASIA	**7,790**	**11,283**	**11,063**				
Afghanistan		526					
Bangladesh	180	197					
India	3,737	7,147	7,790				
Iran, Islamic Republic of	2,305	1,467	188				
Nepal			564				
Pakistan	1,568	1,946	2,333				
Sri Lanka			188				
NOT SPECIFIED	**4,897**	**4,740**	**8,765**				
Other countries of the World	4,897	4,740	8,765				

Yearbook of Tourism Statistics, Data 2009 – 2013, 2015 Edition

LATVIA

4. Arrivals of non-resident tourists in all types of accommodation establishments, by country of residence

	2009	2010	2011	2012	2013	Market share 2013	% Change 2013-2012
TOTAL	753,875	877,774	1,063,294	1,096,274	1,249,814	100.00	14.01
AFRICA	347	428	786	866	1,206	0.10	39.26
EAST AFRICA	15	19	59	44	102	0.01	131.82
Kenya	7	12	44	18	27	0.00	50.00
Uganda	3		10	9	18	0.00	100.00
United Republic of Tanzania	4	5	2	8	45	0.00	462.50
Zimbabwe	1	2	3	9	12	0.00	33.33
CENTRAL AFRICA	28	32	54	62	70	0.01	12.90
Angola	2	2	11	36	17	0.00	-52.78
Cameroon	15	11	21	13	20	0.00	53.85
Central African Republic	6	15	21	5	5	0.00	
Congo		3	1	3	22	0.00	633.33
Democratic Republic of the Congo	5	1		5	6	0.00	20.00
NORTH AFRICA	56	97	167	133	251	0.02	88.72
Algeria	16	18	15	52	67	0.01	28.85
Morocco	26	64	54	50	144	0.01	188.00
Tunisia	14	15	98	31	40	0.00	29.03
SOUTHERN AFRICA	165	182	353	466	494	0.04	6.01
Namibia		11	6	12	18	0.00	50.00
South Africa	126	132	151	241	286	0.02	18.67
Swaziland	39	39	196	213	190	0.02	-10.80
WEST AFRICA	83	98	153	161	289	0.02	79.50
Gambia			1	3			
Ghana	7	1	14	16	13	0.00	-18.75
Liberia		2	2	9	17	0.00	88.89
Mauritania	2	2	9		30	0.00	
Niger	3	15	18	14	135	0.01	864.29
Nigeria	30	29	46	51	32	0.00	-37.25
Senegal	1	11	2	12	6	0.00	-50.00
Sierra Leone	40	38	61	56	56	0.00	
AMERICAS	19,027	22,589	24,820	28,926	34,356	2.75	18.77
CARIBBEAN	26	29	25	43	143	0.01	232.56
Antigua and Barbuda	1	1	5	3	20	0.00	566.67
Barbados	9				13	0.00	
Cuba	7	13	19	25	92	0.01	268.00
Dominican Republic	7			3	6	0.00	100.00
Jamaica	2	15	1	12	12	0.00	
CENTRAL AMERICA	53	70	94	58	79	0.01	36.21
Belize	2	1		14	4	0.00	-71.43
Costa Rica	43	33	57	26	45	0.00	73.08
Guatemala		21	17	6	17	0.00	183.33
Panama	8	15	20	12	13	0.00	8.33
NORTH AMERICA	17,737	21,001	22,212	25,993	30,809	2.47	18.53
Canada	2,418	2,703	3,587	3,298	3,772	0.30	14.37
Greenland	4	11	3	57	6	0.00	-89.47
Mexico	486	424	507	452	509	0.04	12.61
United States of America	14,829	17,863	18,115	22,186	26,522	2.12	19.54
SOUTH AMERICA	1,211	1,489	2,489	2,832	3,325	0.27	17.41
Argentina	165	320	362	439	583	0.05	32.80
Bolivia	10	11	1	7	15	0.00	114.29
Brazil	801	848	1,647	1,577	2,017	0.16	27.90
Chile	86	85	173	518	233	0.02	-55.02
Colombia	73	68	87	81	223	0.02	175.31
Ecuador	6	8	13	25	57	0.00	128.00
Peru	15	40	54	39	34	0.00	-12.82
Suriname			22	9	16	0.00	77.78
Uruguay	8	66	38	102	37	0.00	-63.73
Venezuela	47	43	92	35	110	0.01	214.29
EAST ASIA AND THE PACIFIC	14,389	15,482	18,426	24,482	31,399	2.51	28.25

406

Yearbook of Tourism Statistics, Data 2009 – 2013, 2015 Edition

LATVIA

4. Arrivals of non-resident tourists in all types of accommodation establishments, by country of residence

	2009	2010	2011	2012	2013	Market share 2013	% Change 2013-2012
NORTH-EAST ASIA	**9,684**	**9,991**	**11,802**	**16,501**	**22,527**	**1.80**	**36.52**
China	1,593	1,963	2,893	3,666	6,319	0.51	72.37
Hong Kong, China	97	144	435	653	1,335	0.11	104.44
Japan	6,690	5,428	5,843	7,322	8,988	0.72	22.75
Korea, Dem. People's Republic of	447	397	383				
Korea, Republic of	332	1,562	1,475	2,385	2,129	0.17	-10.73
Mongolia	30	19	20	17	29	0.00	70.59
Taiwan, Province of China	495	478	753	2,458	3,727	0.30	51.63
SOUTH-EAST ASIA	**979**	**1,395**	**1,421**	**2,516**	**2,956**	**0.24**	**17.49**
Indonesia	159	123	104	132	263	0.02	99.24
Lao People's Democratic Republic	2	116	19	10	17	0.00	70.00
Malaysia	137	51	117	253	380	0.03	50.20
Philippines	108	125	277	336	384	0.03	14.29
Singapore	103	171	328	453	420	0.03	-7.28
Thailand	448	777	487	1,280	1,397	0.11	9.14
Viet Nam	22	32	89	52	95	0.01	82.69
AUSTRALASIA	**3,726**	**4,096**	**5,203**	**5,465**	**5,916**	**0.47**	**8.25**
Australia	3,395	3,636	4,616	4,679	5,454	0.44	16.56
New Zealand	331	460	587	786	462	0.04	-41.22
EUROPE	**713,375**	**827,934**	**1,007,215**	**1,027,617**	**1,174,264**	**93.96**	**14.27**
CENTRAL/EASTERN EUROPE	**265,867**	**338,473**	**447,263**	**508,235**	**643,905**	**51.52**	**26.69**
Armenia	171	290	669	833	565	0.05	-32.17
Azerbaijan	487	738	1,434	1,388	2,301	0.18	65.78
Belarus	14,901	15,247	16,682	21,545	29,408	2.35	36.50
Bulgaria	1,318	1,467	1,785	1,835	2,142	0.17	16.73
Czech Republic	5,948	5,226	5,600	6,434	6,852	0.55	6.50
Estonia	58,762	62,906	81,979	87,026	105,558	8.45	21.29
Georgia	1,169	1,172	1,491	1,481	1,864	0.15	25.86
Hungary	2,122	2,873	4,375	2,823	3,304	0.26	17.04
Kazakhstan	484	1,157	1,665	2,716	3,315	0.27	22.05
Kyrgyzstan	51	151	184	135	184	0.01	36.30
Lithuania	71,811	84,509	100,561	93,270	109,118	8.73	16.99
Poland	24,038	27,447	35,309	32,103	39,785	3.18	23.93
Republic of Moldova	338	425	560	536	619	0.05	15.49
Romania	1,982	2,699	2,771	3,006	3,341	0.27	11.14
Russian Federation	72,227	119,007	174,343	232,552	310,266	24.82	33.42
Slovakia	1,332	1,602	2,587	3,125	3,525	0.28	12.80
Tajikistan	94	132	100	125	144	0.01	15.20
Turkmenistan	40	22	52	224	144	0.01	-35.71
Ukraine	7,667	9,479	12,746	13,015	16,155	1.29	24.13
Uzbekistan	925	1,924	2,370	4,063	5,315	0.43	30.81
NORTHERN EUROPE	**231,602**	**262,686**	**290,767**	**253,113**	**247,278**	**19.79**	**-2.31**
Denmark	12,686	12,859	15,075	16,871	15,590	1.25	-7.59
Finland	72,024	79,655	90,991	74,172	63,515	5.08	-14.37
Iceland	485	840	1,108	910	1,746	0.14	91.87
Ireland	6,012	4,380	4,190	4,099	4,474	0.36	9.15
Norway	49,190	64,273	72,309	67,643	66,160	5.29	-2.19
Sweden	55,609	61,155	63,135	51,458	55,799	4.46	8.44
United Kingdom	35,596	39,524	43,959	37,960	39,994	3.20	5.36
SOUTHERN EUROPE	**47,724**	**52,053**	**68,429**	**61,474**	**66,474**	**5.32**	**8.13**
Albania	76	118	286	246	156	0.01	-36.59
Andorra	32	31	69	46	163	0.01	254.35
Bosnia and Herzegovina	99	87	134	251	569	0.05	126.69
Croatia	626	815	529	881	785	0.06	-10.90
Gibraltar		2	13	13	10	0.00	-23.08
Greece	2,836	3,216	3,431	2,884	3,956	0.32	37.17
Italy	27,303	27,510	37,963	33,205	31,826	2.55	-4.15
Malta	184	160	251	399	569	0.05	42.61
Montenegro	14	10	37	52	19	0.00	-63.46

407

LATVIA

4. Arrivals of non-resident tourists in all types of accommodation establishments, by country of residence

	2009	2010	2011	2012	2013	Market share 2013	% Change 2013-2012
Portugal	2,638	2,958	3,212	2,393	2,875	0.23	20.14
San Marino	13	3	32	17	6	0.00	-64.71
Serbia	221	236	515	308	530	0.04	72.08
Slovenia	1,048	1,144	1,222	1,400	1,634	0.13	16.71
Spain	12,551	15,706	20,680	19,239	23,199	1.86	20.58
TFYR of Macedonia	83	57	55	140	177	0.01	26.43
WESTERN EUROPE	**159,010**	**162,488**	**184,053**	**188,712**	**199,745**	**15.98**	**5.85**
Austria	8,543	6,554	8,515	8,197	11,251	0.90	37.26
Belgium	8,811	11,005	13,092	11,140	10,238	0.82	-8.10
France	18,296	19,032	19,635	20,912	22,568	1.81	7.92
Germany	93,739	98,305	113,064	120,447	122,737	9.82	1.90
Liechtenstein	18	14	107	59	223	0.02	277.97
Luxembourg	925	826	857	948	977	0.08	3.06
Monaco	77	118	127	49	96	0.01	95.92
Netherlands	18,893	18,113	18,358	17,682	20,628	1.65	16.66
Switzerland	9,708	8,521	10,298	9,278	11,027	0.88	18.85
EAST MEDITERRANEAN EUROPE	**9,172**	**12,234**	**16,703**	**16,083**	**16,862**	**1.35**	**4.84**
Cyprus	780	408	632	575	751	0.06	30.61
Israel	3,586	4,328	6,216	6,045	7,126	0.57	17.88
Turkey	4,806	7,498	9,855	9,463	8,985	0.72	-5.05
MIDDLE EAST	**478**	**648**	**972**	**1,210**	**1,324**	**0.11**	**9.42**
Bahrain	12	16	10	11	35	0.00	218.18
Egypt	196	208	282	407	326	0.03	-19.90
Iraq	67	91	62	89	88	0.01	-1.12
Jordan	11	22	17	36	54	0.00	50.00
Kuwait	41	30	85	88	83	0.01	-5.68
Lebanon	22	87	80	89	93	0.01	4.49
Libya	8	57	55	46	47	0.00	2.17
Qatar		4	8	20	22	0.00	10.00
Saudi Arabia	24	27	130	153	116	0.01	-24.18
Syrian Arab Republic	20	29	49	39	82	0.01	110.26
United Arab Emirates	77	75	192	231	370	0.03	60.17
Yemen		2	2	1	8	0.00	700.00
SOUTH ASIA	**1,081**	**1,418**	**2,029**	**2,055**	**2,260**	**0.18**	**9.98**
Afghanistan	19	87	109	99	111	0.01	12.12
Bangladesh	28	22	11	44	35	0.00	-20.45
India	867	913	1,411	1,422	1,548	0.12	8.86
Iran, Islamic Republic of	94	159	210	187	319	0.03	70.59
Nepal	1	19	57	55	48	0.00	-12.73
Pakistan	51	174	190	209	144	0.01	-31.10
Sri Lanka	21	44	41	39	55	0.00	41.03
NOT SPECIFIED	**5,178**	**9,275**	**9,046**	**11,118**	**5,005**	**0.40**	**-54.98**
Other countries of the World	5,178	9,275	9,046	11,118	5,005	0.40	-54.98

Yearbook of Tourism Statistics, Data 2009 – 2013, 2015 Edition

LATVIA

6. Overnight stays of non-resident tourists in all types of accommodation establishments, by country of residence

	2009	2010	2011	2012	2013	Market share 2013	% Change 2013-2012
TOTAL	1,699,562	1,912,336	2,257,021	2,429,093	2,639,434	100.00	8.66
AFRICA	555	1,019	1,762	1,846	2,595	0.10	40.57
EAST AFRICA	35	105	278	107	228	0.01	113.08
Kenya	13	53	262	76	81	0.00	6.58
Uganda	14		11	12	33	0.00	175.00
United Republic of Tanzania	4	34	2	8	50	0.00	525.00
Zimbabwe	4	18	3	11	64	0.00	481.82
CENTRAL AFRICA	43	126	135	97	145	0.01	49.48
Angola	2	4	14	44	21	0.00	-52.27
Cameroon	19	56	46	31	69	0.00	122.58
Central African Republic	15	60	74	11	12	0.00	9.09
Congo	7	5	1	3	35	0.00	1,066.67
Democratic Republic of the Congo		1		8	8	0.00	
NORTH AFRICA	104	187	348	474	498	0.02	5.06
Algeria	20	51	43	312	146	0.01	-53.21
Morocco	42	91	100	113	260	0.01	130.09
Tunisia	42	45	205	49	92	0.00	87.76
SOUTHERN AFRICA	235	378	758	824	1,138	0.04	38.11
Namibia		27	8	16	27	0.00	68.75
South Africa	235	293	352	499	796	0.03	59.52
Swaziland		58	398	309	315	0.01	1.94
WEST AFRICA	138	223	243	344	586	0.02	70.35
Gambia			1	3			
Ghana	12	5	24	37	15	0.00	-59.46
Liberia		8	2	20	37	0.00	85.00
Mauritania	12	28	15		62	0.00	
Niger	8	15	31	67	309	0.01	361.19
Nigeria	58	60	86	115	46	0.00	-60.00
Senegal	1	21	4	22	12	0.00	-45.45
Sierra Leone	47	86	80	80	105	0.00	31.25
AMERICAS	47,030	58,740	60,081	64,557	85,644	3.24	32.66
CARIBBEAN	68	64	47	65	212	0.01	226.15
Antigua and Barbuda	1	1	5	3	49	0.00	1,533.33
Barbados	28				26	0.00	
Cuba	20	32	40	34	98	0.00	188.24
Dominican Republic	12			3	12	0.00	300.00
Jamaica	7	31	2	25	27	0.00	8.00
CENTRAL AMERICA	79	90	180	107	184	0.01	71.96
Belize	5	2		20	6	0.00	-70.00
Costa Rica	61	41	74	53	114	0.00	115.09
Guatemala		24	43	20	27	0.00	35.00
Panama	13	23	63	14	37	0.00	164.29
NORTH AMERICA	44,268	55,451	54,514	59,040	77,089	2.92	30.57
Canada	5,212	6,306	8,575	7,517	9,494	0.36	26.30
Greenland	12	28	9	61	18	0.00	-70.49
Mexico	764	886	1,065	921	940	0.04	2.06
United States of America	38,280	48,231	44,865	50,541	66,637	2.52	31.85
SOUTH AMERICA	2,615	3,135	5,340	5,345	8,159	0.31	52.65
Argentina	405	683	912	866	1,154	0.04	33.26
Bolivia	60	23	4	7	29	0.00	314.29
Brazil	1,650	1,841	3,495	3,137	5,456	0.21	73.92
Chile	163	156	402	756	483	0.02	-36.11
Colombia	139	151	163	154	418	0.02	171.43
Ecuador	11	10	19	64	97	0.00	51.56
Peru	38	83	84	85	81	0.00	-4.71
Suriname			25	25	43	0.00	72.00
Uruguay	43	123	69	161	84	0.00	-47.83
Venezuela	106	65	167	90	314	0.01	248.89
EAST ASIA AND THE PACIFIC	27,824	29,406	36,012	47,884	58,639	2.22	22.46

409

LATVIA

6. Overnight stays of non-resident tourists in all types of accommodation establishments, by country of residence

	2009	2010	2011	2012	2013	Market share 2013	% Change 2013-2012
NORTH-EAST ASIA	17,912	17,792	21,506	30,590	39,124	1.48	27.90
China	3,231	3,804	5,521	7,533	12,034	0.46	59.75
Hong Kong, China	174	306	764	1,281	2,056	0.08	60.50
Japan	11,967	9,680	9,924	12,765	15,776	0.60	23.59
Korea, Dem. People's Republic of	607	691	995				
Korea, Republic of	1,026	2,555	2,903	4,686	4,221	0.16	-9.92
Mongolia	119	35	27	55	65	0.00	18.18
Taiwan, Province of China	788	721	1,372	4,270	4,972	0.19	16.44
SOUTH-EAST ASIA	2,221	2,602	2,748	5,039	5,732	0.22	13.75
Indonesia	380	231	189	350	403	0.02	15.14
Lao People's Democratic Republic	3	124	19	10	18	0.00	80.00
Malaysia	267	114	189	496	670	0.03	35.08
Philippines	360	257	561	733	778	0.03	6.14
Singapore	290	448	856	1,033	859	0.03	-16.84
Thailand	863	1,345	762	2,310	2,254	0.09	-2.42
Viet Nam	58	83	172	107	750	0.03	600.93
AUSTRALASIA	7,691	9,012	11,758	12,255	13,783	0.52	12.47
Australia	7,004	8,063	10,581	10,525	12,736	0.48	21.01
New Zealand	687	949	1,177	1,730	1,047	0.04	-39.48
EUROPE	1,609,225	1,785,749	2,132,688	2,282,680	2,468,729	93.53	8.15
CENTRAL/EASTERN EUROPE	649,913	740,745	973,489	1,162,662	1,375,581	52.12	18.31
Armenia	480	724	1,225	1,403	1,130	0.04	-19.46
Azerbaijan	1,242	1,956	3,790	5,849	8,569	0.32	46.50
Belarus	131,484	82,616	83,329	91,620	100,672	3.81	9.88
Bulgaria	2,542	3,757	3,492	5,678	6,583	0.25	15.94
Czech Republic	10,749	10,946	11,265	15,099	15,596	0.59	3.29
Estonia	90,246	95,985	127,749	136,610	161,585	6.12	18.28
Georgia	2,808	2,403	5,385	8,273	9,162	0.35	10.75
Hungary	4,443	5,051	7,877	5,572	6,797	0.26	21.98
Kazakhstan	1,314	2,692	4,139	9,238	12,363	0.47	33.83
Kyrgyzstan	247	607	1,273	531	545	0.02	2.64
Lithuania	120,457	128,760	180,541	162,918	190,592	7.22	16.99
Poland	42,185	45,193	57,819	58,108	66,462	2.52	14.38
Republic of Moldova	1,061	1,437	1,069	1,032	1,425	0.05	38.08
Romania	4,417	6,220	6,445	7,431	7,086	0.27	-4.64
Russian Federation	196,582	320,130	433,560	587,953	702,067	26.60	19.41
Slovakia	2,893	3,685	5,554	9,804	7,713	0.29	-21.33
Tajikistan	535	729	589	563	260	0.01	-53.82
Turkmenistan	75	44	174	363	502	0.02	38.29
Ukraine	33,855	22,303	29,562	38,613	51,805	1.96	34.16
Uzbekistan	2,298	5,507	8,652	16,004	24,667	0.93	54.13
NORTHERN EUROPE	493,328	556,115	603,010	551,047	518,730	19.65	-5.86
Denmark	25,518	26,245	31,180	37,565	33,162	1.26	-11.72
Finland	153,309	160,956	181,742	154,407	122,783	4.65	-20.48
Iceland	992	2,341	2,720	2,055	3,575	0.14	73.97
Ireland	13,878	10,192	9,291	9,119	9,767	0.37	7.11
Norway	118,591	159,181	172,330	162,957	157,717	5.98	-3.22
Sweden	102,788	105,615	111,434	102,058	104,465	3.96	2.36
United Kingdom	78,252	91,585	94,313	82,886	87,261	3.31	5.28
SOUTHERN EUROPE	106,701	110,926	141,046	131,532	129,890	4.92	-1.25
Albania	196	203	357	322	280	0.01	-13.04
Andorra	106	64	146	89	286	0.01	221.35
Bosnia and Herzegovina	169	146	324	532	1,194	0.05	124.44
Croatia	1,310	2,193	1,202	2,411	2,126	0.08	-11.82
Gibraltar		5	41	33	18	0.00	-45.45
Greece	6,696	7,019	8,080	6,436	8,422	0.32	30.86
Italy	60,433	59,453	78,070	71,760	64,774	2.45	-9.74
Malta	358	312	461	899	1,400	0.05	55.73
Montenegro	15	12	141	111	103	0.00	-7.21

410

LATVIA

6. Overnight stays of non-resident tourists in all types of accommodation establishments, by country of residence

	2009	2010	2011	2012	2013	Market share 2013	% Change 2013-2012
Portugal	5,945	6,747	7,180	6,059	6,611	0.25	9.11
San Marino	25	10	156	22	15	0.00	-31.82
Serbia	522	569	1,141	730	1,017	0.04	39.32
Slovenia	2,166	2,590	2,397	3,147	3,249	0.12	3.24
Spain	28,518	31,442	41,256	38,725	40,045	1.52	3.41
TFYR of Macedonia	242	161	94	256	350	0.01	36.72
WESTERN EUROPE	**334,139**	**346,917**	**377,006**	**399,804**	**402,071**	**15.23**	**0.57**
Austria	17,078	13,441	16,638	17,162	22,063	0.84	28.56
Belgium	19,468	25,151	28,577	23,519	21,425	0.81	-8.90
France	39,470	38,734	40,432	43,736	48,614	1.84	11.15
Germany	197,465	209,921	225,812	252,943	239,359	9.07	-5.37
Liechtenstein	36	23	178	110	303	0.01	175.45
Luxembourg	2,052	1,794	1,867	2,110	1,928	0.07	-8.63
Monaco	121	152	208	124	211	0.01	70.16
Netherlands	38,297	39,743	42,179	40,303	44,269	1.68	9.84
Switzerland	20,152	17,958	21,115	19,797	23,899	0.91	20.72
EAST MEDITERRANEAN EUROPE	**25,144**	**31,046**	**38,137**	**37,635**	**42,457**	**1.61**	**12.81**
Cyprus	1,722	1,191	1,927	1,694	2,142	0.08	26.45
Israel	10,417	13,519	15,036	14,815	19,380	0.73	30.81
Turkey	13,005	16,336	21,174	21,126	20,935	0.79	-0.90
MIDDLE EAST	**1,389**	**1,817**	**2,096**	**2,987**	**3,681**	**0.14**	**23.23**
Bahrain	24	51	18	12	86	0.00	616.67
Egypt	499	692	776	1,117	1,233	0.05	10.38
Iraq	386	156	118	292	192	0.01	-34.25
Jordan	64	90	46	69	129	0.00	86.96
Kuwait	73	37	123	182	189	0.01	3.85
Lebanon	73	228	177	187	288	0.01	54.01
Libya	13	160	99	128	96	0.00	-25.00
Qatar		4	12	44	50	0.00	13.64
Saudi Arabia	73	80	278	392	384	0.01	-2.04
Syrian Arab Republic	38	122	104	111	182	0.01	63.96
United Arab Emirates	146	195	341	446	836	0.03	87.44
Yemen		2	4	7	16	0.00	128.57
SOUTH ASIA	**2,360**	**5,410**	**4,457**	**6,161**	**9,169**	**0.35**	**48.82**
Afghanistan	34	191	229	177	153	0.01	-13.56
Bangladesh	46	49	28	67	62	0.00	-7.46
India	1,941	4,521	3,302	3,951	6,644	0.25	68.16
Iran, Islamic Republic of	203	282	344	672	1,170	0.04	74.11
Nepal	1	48	97	392	281	0.01	-28.32
Pakistan	75	262	408	821	386	0.01	-52.98
Sri Lanka	60	57	49	81	473	0.02	483.95
NOT SPECIFIED	**11,179**	**30,195**	**19,925**	**22,978**	**10,977**	**0.42**	**-52.23**
Other countries of the World	11,179	30,195	19,925	22,978	10,977	0.42	-52.23

Yearbook of Tourism Statistics, Data 2009 – 2013, 2015 Edition

LEBANON

1. Arrivals of non-resident tourists at national borders, by nationality

	2009	2010	2011	2012	2013	Market share 2013	% Change 2013-2012
TOTAL (*)	1,844,106	2,167,989	1,655,051	1,365,845	1,274,362	100.00	-6.70
AFRICA	66,140	66,225	82,643	82,368	85,450	6.71	3.74
EAST AFRICA	24,536	21,616	43,095	43,484	46,968	3.69	8.01
Burundi	26	2	18	20	44	0.00	120.00
Comoros	60	95	186	171	81	0.01	-52.63
Djibouti	64	54	42	68	27	0.00	-60.29
Eritrea	709	616	468	305	253	0.02	-17.05
Ethiopia	18,031	18,676	39,158	39,321	41,223	3.23	4.84
Kenya	431	635	1,687	1,763	2,872	0.23	62.90
Madagascar	4,085	375	280	389	728	0.06	87.15
Malawi	87	93	93	113	122	0.01	7.96
Mauritius	133	87	128	104	80	0.01	-23.08
Mozambique	39	61	97	110	139	0.01	26.36
Rwanda	87	31	35	53	58	0.00	9.43
Seychelles	62	48	35	37	27	0.00	-27.03
Somalia	223	402	308	424	512	0.04	20.75
Uganda	89	106	106	100	206	0.02	106.00
United Republic of Tanzania	245	179	289	315	383	0.03	21.59
Zambia	73	76	91	96	111	0.01	15.63
Zimbabwe	92	80	74	95	102	0.01	7.37
CENTRAL AFRICA	1,997	1,583	1,848	2,012	2,116	0.17	5.17
Angola	78	75	96	89	122	0.01	37.08
Cameroon	450	402	560	882	873	0.07	-1.02
Central African Republic	102	81	66	55	66	0.01	20.00
Chad	107	59	58	41	52	0.00	26.83
Congo	500	319	415	441	460	0.04	4.31
Equatorial Guinea	21	22	16	8	27	0.00	237.50
Gabon	737	625	633	488	516	0.04	5.74
Sao Tome and Principe	2		4	8			
NORTH AFRICA	22,904	25,572	20,327	20,087	19,672	1.54	-2.07
Algeria	4,648	5,377	4,223	4,005	4,009	0.31	0.10
Morocco	7,503	7,830	6,318	6,219	6,767	0.53	8.81
Sudan	4,377	4,723	3,813	3,720	3,349	0.26	-9.97
Tunisia	6,376	7,642	5,973	6,143	5,547	0.44	-9.70
SOUTHERN AFRICA	2,382	2,451	2,026	2,162	1,985	0.16	-8.19
Botswana	5	2	1	2	3	0.00	50.00
Lesotho	7	4	3	2	3	0.00	50.00
Namibia	44	22	22	19	17	0.00	-10.53
South Africa	2,326	2,418	2,000	2,139	1,958	0.15	-8.46
Swaziland		5			4	0.00	
WEST AFRICA	14,321	15,003	15,347	14,623	14,709	1.15	0.59
Benin	406	412	515	422	435	0.03	3.08
Burkina Faso	494	491	613	566	577	0.05	1.94
Cabo Verde	13	7	7	4	10	0.00	150.00
Côte d'Ivoire	2,618	2,851	2,055	1,847	1,733	0.14	-6.17
Gambia	231	293	317	358	421	0.03	17.60
Ghana	3,187	3,435	4,115	3,940	4,002	0.31	1.57
Guinea	529	574	627	516	427	0.03	-17.25
Guinea-Bissau	89	62	67	43	81	0.01	88.37
Liberia	258	225	213	224	246	0.02	9.82
Mali	184	247	255	291	193	0.02	-33.68
Mauritania	233	182	179	221	194	0.02	-12.22
Niger	183	140	122	107	113	0.01	5.61
Nigeria	2,475	2,828	2,703	2,628	2,623	0.21	-0.19
Senegal	1,997	1,796	1,809	1,502	1,386	0.11	-7.72
Sierra Leone	1,073	1,071	1,163	1,181	1,157	0.09	-2.03
Togo	351	389	587	773	1,111	0.09	43.73

Yearbook of Tourism Statistics, Data 2009 – 2013, 2015 Edition

LEBANON

1. Arrivals of non-resident tourists at national borders, by nationality

	2009	2010	2011	2012	2013	Market share 2013	% Change 2013-2012
AMERICAS	232,694	248,725	222,671	221,174	209,580	16.45	-5.24
CARIBBEAN	815	895	842	858	953	0.07	11.07
Antigua and Barbuda	61	60	41	27	67	0.01	148.15
Bahamas	3	3	6	5	3	0.00	-40.00
Barbados	10	10	4	12	6	0.00	-50.00
Cuba	209	167	133	138	140	0.01	1.45
Dominican Republic	236	335	414	354	421	0.03	18.93
Grenada	27	18	14	17	17	0.00	
Haiti	63	55	31	36	28	0.00	-22.22
Jamaica	69	57	37	57	24	0.00	-57.89
Puerto Rico		1		1	1	0.00	
Saint Kitts and Nevis	9	22	58	82	151	0.01	84.15
Saint Lucia	4	7	1	4	2	0.00	-50.00
Saint Vincent and the Grenadines	34	37	29	41	15	0.00	-63.41
Trinidad and Tobago	90	123	74	84	78	0.01	-7.14
CENTRAL AMERICA	1,286	1,400	1,095	1,064	1,005	0.08	-5.55
Belize	218	261	219	217	237	0.02	9.22
Costa Rica	119	247	93	93	76	0.01	-18.28
El Salvador	132	109	62	64	36	0.00	-43.75
Guatemala	129	150	72	60	133	0.01	121.67
Honduras	31	59	42	36	58	0.00	61.11
Nicaragua	32	21	25	16	19	0.00	18.75
Panama	625	553	582	578	446	0.03	-22.84
NORTH AMERICA	201,377	214,607	192,243	188,365	177,013	13.89	-6.03
Canada	87,144	88,002	79,978	75,751	71,841	5.64	-5.16
Mexico	2,332	3,303	2,100	2,075	1,689	0.13	-18.60
United States of America	111,901	123,302	110,165	110,539	103,483	8.12	-6.38
SOUTH AMERICA	29,216	31,823	28,491	30,887	30,609	2.40	-0.90
Argentina	1,542	2,114	1,397	1,432	1,258	0.10	-12.15
Bolivia	82	105	94	103	80	0.01	-22.33
Brazil	13,332	15,371	13,431	13,383	13,603	1.07	1.64
Chile	642	822	740	604	515	0.04	-14.74
Colombia	1,440	1,370	1,202	1,203	974	0.08	-19.04
Ecuador	290	399	355	296	226	0.02	-23.65
Paraguay	574	584	556	577	534	0.04	-7.45
Peru	178	287	233	238	208	0.02	-12.61
Suriname	71	93	38	48	41	0.00	-14.58
Uruguay	143	143	135	136	136	0.01	
Venezuela	10,922	10,535	10,310	12,867	13,034	1.02	1.30
EAST ASIA AND THE PACIFIC	128,919	133,451	112,163	101,518	98,001	7.69	-3.46
NORTH-EAST ASIA	10,088	14,782	11,164	8,019	8,523	0.67	6.29
China	3,895	5,938	4,862	3,564	3,793	0.30	6.43
Hong Kong, China	136	215	126	88	85	0.01	-3.41
Japan	2,562	3,906	2,186	1,541	1,398	0.11	-9.28
Korea, Dem. People's Republic of	35	84	63	72	307	0.02	326.39
Korea, Republic of	3,168	4,200	3,606	2,571	2,827	0.22	9.96
Mongolia	18	25	31	42	20	0.00	-52.38
Taiwan, Province of China	274	414	290	141	93	0.01	-34.04
SOUTH-EAST ASIA	54,772	58,236	44,615	41,623	44,323	3.48	6.49
Brunei Darussalam	40	24	83	56	67	0.01	19.64
Cambodia	11	229	240	251	197	0.02	-21.51
Indonesia	10,567	10,525	8,446	9,218	10,816	0.85	17.34
Lao People's Democratic Republic	3	1	14		1	0.00	
Malaysia	3,587	4,901	4,580	3,598	3,252	0.26	-9.62
Myanmar	48	47	65	37	52	0.00	40.54
Philippines	39,384	41,174	30,172	27,620	29,172	2.29	5.62
Singapore	626	828	517	432	296	0.02	-31.48
Thailand	288	308	355	307	370	0.03	20.52
Viet Nam	218	199	143	104	100	0.01	-3.85

413

LEBANON

1. Arrivals of non-resident tourists at national borders, by nationality

	2009	2010	2011	2012	2013	Market share 2013	% Change 2013-2012
AUSTRALASIA	63,899	60,302	56,249	51,734	44,780	3.51	-13.44
Australia	62,140	58,150	54,522	50,261	43,560	3.42	-13.33
New Zealand	1,759	2,152	1,727	1,473	1,220	0.10	-17.18
MELANESIA	160	130	134	142	375	0.03	164.08
Fiji	158	129	133	140	375	0.03	167.86
Papua New Guinea	1	1	1				
Vanuatu	1			2			
POLYNESIA			1	1			
Tonga			1	1			
EUROPE	454,742	550,866	487,150	445,758	435,494	34.17	-2.30
CENTRAL/EASTERN EUROPE	39,616	47,248	43,164	39,565	42,988	3.37	8.65
Armenia	1,810	2,123	1,889	1,617	1,972	0.15	21.95
Azerbaijan	222	255	261	306	268	0.02	-12.42
Belarus	1,972	2,379	2,279	2,383	2,217	0.17	-6.97
Bulgaria	1,842	2,591	2,167	2,020	2,177	0.17	7.77
Czech Republic	2,140	2,780	1,838	1,820	1,646	0.13	-9.56
Estonia	186	380	416	132	110	0.01	-16.67
Georgia	223	344	393	422	411	0.03	-2.61
Hungary	1,657	1,886	1,411	1,168	1,103	0.09	-5.57
Kazakhstan	497	555	567	598	626	0.05	4.68
Kyrgyzstan	143	161	225	157	150	0.01	-4.46
Latvia	400	614	597	353	367	0.03	3.97
Lithuania	453	725	709	512	536	0.04	4.69
Poland	4,397	4,906	3,837	3,118	3,010	0.24	-3.46
Republic of Moldova	1,275	1,439	1,461	1,366	1,377	0.11	0.81
Romania	3,933	4,639	4,190	4,272	4,844	0.38	13.39
Russian Federation	9,838	12,175	11,121	9,954	11,942	0.94	19.97
Slovakia	1,024	1,143	1,014	738	705	0.06	-4.47
Tajikistan	66	92	80	91	139	0.01	52.75
Turkmenistan	54	57	72	88	60	0.00	-31.82
Ukraine	7,024	7,484	8,140	8,450	8,812	0.69	4.28
Uzbekistan	460	520	497		516	0.04	
NORTHERN EUROPE	104,587	121,219	108,408	100,284	96,774	7.59	-3.50
Denmark	18,078	19,332	16,830	13,937	12,590	0.99	-9.66
Finland	1,661	2,391	1,810	2,392	3,095	0.24	29.39
Iceland	153	211	143	81	80	0.01	-1.23
Ireland	3,222	4,050	4,953	5,232	4,444	0.35	-15.06
Norway	4,552	5,484	4,697	4,088	4,050	0.32	-0.93
Sweden	26,894	29,512	26,752	24,340	24,011	1.88	-1.35
United Kingdom	50,027	60,239	53,223	50,214	48,504	3.81	-3.41
SOUTHERN EUROPE	58,699	66,961	52,268	49,020	48,246	3.79	-1.58
Albania	95	98	87	99	111	0.01	12.12
Andorra	9	14	3	4	8	0.00	100.00
Bosnia and Herzegovina	306	361	251	286	253	0.02	-11.54
Croatia	679	779	641	729	708	0.06	-2.88
Greece	8,041	9,328	7,695	7,532	7,987	0.63	6.04
Holy See	68	79	109	155	93	0.01	-40.00
Italy	32,619	36,625	28,808	25,539	24,980	1.96	-2.19
Malta	252	300	258	216	232	0.02	7.41
Portugal	1,707	2,091	1,701	1,475	1,801	0.14	22.10
San Marino	13	17	10	3	9	0.00	200.00
Serbia	678	1,212	1,091	1,055	1,392	0.11	31.94
Serbia and Montenegro	390	70		13	13	0.00	
Slovenia	314	385	292	290	340	0.03	17.24
Spain	13,343	15,417	11,301	11,472	10,156	0.80	-11.47
TFYR of Macedonia	185	185	21	152	163	0.01	7.24
WESTERN EUROPE	230,620	263,433	239,734	220,810	216,224	16.97	-2.08
Austria	4,252	5,823	5,002	4,665	4,574	0.36	-1.95
Belgium	13,661	15,379	13,497	12,873	12,979	1.02	0.82

414

LEBANON

1. Arrivals of non-resident tourists at national borders, by nationality

	2009	2010	2011	2012	2013	Market share 2013	% Change 2013-2012
France	120,408	139,534	128,999	120,134	117,688	9.24	-2.04
Germany	69,847	76,854	68,401	62,160	61,123	4.80	-1.67
Liechtenstein	17	13	20	20	12	0.00	-40.00
Luxembourg	378	406	357	232	232	0.02	
Monaco	55	60	85	26	27	0.00	3.85
Netherlands	10,268	11,824	10,281	9,298	8,677	0.68	-6.68
Switzerland	11,734	13,540	12,935	11,402	10,912	0.86	-4.30
Other countries of Western Europe			157				
EAST MEDITERRANEAN EUROPE	**21,220**	**52,005**	**43,576**	**36,079**	**31,262**	**2.45**	**-13.35**
Cyprus	8,241	9,325	7,932	7,229	7,439	0.58	2.90
Turkey	12,979	42,680	35,644	28,850	23,823	1.87	-17.42
MIDDLE EAST	**761,852**	**867,898**	**560,273**	**436,964**	**381,422**	**29.93**	**-12.71**
Bahrain	25,218	25,096	9,493	7,365	5,481	0.43	-25.58
Egypt	57,379	67,773	62,825	64,017	63,578	4.99	-0.69
Iraq	101,561	129,847	129,294	126,982	141,986	11.14	11.82
Jordan	223,793	274,615	129,640	89,100	78,018	6.12	-12.44
Kuwait	102,537	95,824	61,756	40,121	29,598	2.32	-26.23
Libya	3,913	4,570	2,484	5,094	5,837	0.46	14.59
Oman	5,717	6,639	4,494	3,128	2,189	0.17	-30.02
Qatar	19,358	18,436	11,171	5,124	1,800	0.14	-64.87
Saudi Arabia	173,294	191,066	111,701	72,658	40,958	3.21	-43.63
United Arab Emirates	42,974	46,923	32,058	17,742	6,709	0.53	-62.19
Yemen	6,108	7,109	5,357	5,633	5,268	0.41	-6.48
SOUTH ASIA	**197,941**	**299,087**	**188,242**	**76,157**	**63,356**	**4.97**	**-16.81**
Afghanistan	450	420	383	432	502	0.04	16.20
Bangladesh	16,047	19,980	23,730	20,557	20,946	1.64	1.89
Bhutan	19	7	4	13	29	0.00	123.08
India	13,946	16,117	15,378	13,513	12,889	1.01	-4.62
Iran, Islamic Republic of	145,706	241,514	131,870	28,134	16,130	1.27	-42.67
Maldives	5	7	5	36	10	0.00	-72.22
Nepal	8,435	6,975	4,560	3,803	3,813	0.30	0.26
Pakistan	3,336	3,729	3,448	2,992	2,878	0.23	-3.81
Sri Lanka	9,997	10,338	8,864	6,677	6,159	0.48	-7.76
NOT SPECIFIED	**1,818**	**1,737**	**1,909**	**1,906**	**1,059**	**0.08**	**-44.44**
Other countries of the World	1,818	1,737	1,909	1,906	1,059	0.08	-44.44

Yearbook of Tourism Statistics, Data 2009 – 2013, 2015 Edition

LESOTHO

2. Arrivals of non-resident visitors at national borders, by country of residence

	2009	2010	2011	2012	2013	Market share 2013	% Change 2013-2012
TOTAL	343,743	425,870	398,149	422,597	432,966	100.00	2.45
AFRICA	314,218	400,823	379,507	403,763	408,371	94.32	1.14
EAST AFRICA	6,905	6,135	4,550	5,911	6,325	1.46	7.00
Kenya	301	386	261	246	273	0.06	10.98
Malawi	430	333	295	309	372	0.09	20.39
Mauritius	136	112	97	125	126	0.03	0.80
Mozambique	210	302	359	610	426	0.10	-30.16
Uganda	269	268	205	204	275	0.06	34.80
United Republic of Tanzania	240	208	144	204	213	0.05	4.41
Zambia	806	707	570	662	855	0.20	29.15
Zimbabwe	4,513	3,819	2,619	3,551	3,785	0.87	6.59
SOUTHERN AFRICA	306,121	393,645	374,161	397,159	401,228	92.67	1.02
Botswana	2,060	1,922	1,419	1,752	2,200	0.51	25.57
South Africa	302,655	390,849	371,867	394,336	397,696	91.85	0.85
Swaziland	1,406	874	875	1,071	1,332	0.31	24.37
WEST AFRICA	206	233	154	132	197	0.05	49.24
Ghana	84	61	59	42	144	0.03	242.86
Nigeria	122	172	95	90	53	0.01	-41.11
OTHER AFRICA	986	810	642	561	621	0.14	10.70
Other countries of Africa	986	810	642	561	621	0.14	10.70
AMERICAS	4,122	3,907	3,180	3,059	3,410	0.79	11.47
NORTH AMERICA	4,017	3,739	3,080	2,940	3,305	0.76	12.41
Canada	805	662	502	718	626	0.14	-12.81
United States of America	3,212	3,077	2,578	2,222	2,679	0.62	20.57
OTHER AMERICAS	105	168	100	119	105	0.02	-11.76
Other countries of the Americas	105	168	100	119	105	0.02	-11.76
EAST ASIA AND THE PACIFIC	5,150	3,938	2,407	2,783	4,032	0.93	44.88
NORTH-EAST ASIA	2,378	1,728	860	1,159	1,558	0.36	34.43
China	2,233	1,596	724	998	1,360	0.31	36.27
Taiwan, Province of China	145	132	136	161	198	0.05	22.98
AUSTRALASIA	770	871	621	609	985	0.23	61.74
Australia	770	871	621	609	985	0.23	61.74
OTHER EAST ASIA AND THE PACIFIC	2,002	1,339	926	1,015	1,489	0.34	46.70
Other countries of Asia	2,002	1,339	926	1,015	1,489	0.34	46.70
EUROPE	19,726	16,719	12,751	12,672	16,841	3.89	32.90
NORTHERN EUROPE	5,552	4,723	3,201	2,398	3,217	0.74	34.15
Denmark	248	232	117	152	222	0.05	46.05
Ireland	397	349	189	230	293	0.07	27.39
Sweden	288	316	310	205	322	0.07	57.07
United Kingdom	4,619	3,826	2,585	1,811	2,380	0.55	31.42
SOUTHERN EUROPE	422	213	291	310	342	0.08	10.32
Italy	422	213	291	310	342	0.08	10.32
WESTERN EUROPE	10,862	9,653	7,485	7,906	10,717	2.48	35.56
France	1,592	1,342	668	566	1,120	0.26	97.88
Germany	5,015	4,425	3,927	3,746	4,727	1.09	26.19
Netherlands	4,255	3,886	2,890	3,594	4,870	1.12	35.50
OTHER EUROPE	2,890	2,130	1,774	2,058	2,565	0.59	24.64
Other countries of Europe	2,890	2,130	1,774	2,058	2,565	0.59	24.64
MIDDLE EAST	177	70	13	13	48	0.01	269.23
All countries of Middle East	177	70	13	13	48	0.01	269.23
SOUTH ASIA	256	285	261	212	259	0.06	22.17
India	256	285	261	212	259	0.06	22.17
NOT SPECIFIED	94	128	30	95	5	0.00	-94.74
Other countries of the World	94	128	30	95	5	0.00	-94.74

Yearbook of Tourism Statistics, Data 2009 – 2013, 2015 Edition

LIECHTENSTEIN

3. Arrivals of non-resident tourists in hotels and similar establishments, by country of residence

	2009	2010	2011	2012	2013	Market share 2013	% Change 2013-2012
TOTAL	**52,285**	**49,804**	**53,326**	**53,598**	**52,379**	**100.00**	**-2.27**
AFRICA	**171**	**132**	**138**	**382**	**183**	**0.35**	**-52.09**
SOUTHERN AFRICA	**75**	**57**	**73**	**72**	**97**	**0.19**	**34.72**
South Africa	75	57	73	72	97	0.19	34.72
OTHER AFRICA	**96**	**75**	**65**	**310**	**86**	**0.16**	**-72.26**
Other countries of Africa	96	75	65	310	86	0.16	-72.26
AMERICAS	**2,260**	**2,397**	**2,714**	**3,293**	**3,214**	**6.14**	**-2.40**
NORTH AMERICA	**1,941**	**2,088**	**2,323**	**2,507**	**2,566**	**4.90**	**2.35**
Canada	222	255	343	291	305	0.58	4.81
Mexico	28	23	47	60	110	0.21	83.33
United States of America	1,691	1,810	1,933	2,156	2,151	4.11	-0.23
SOUTH AMERICA	**154**	**176**	**230**	**394**	**392**	**0.75**	**-0.51**
Brazil	154	176	230	394	392	0.75	-0.51
OTHER AMERICAS	**165**	**133**	**161**	**392**	**256**	**0.49**	**-34.69**
Other countries of the Americas	165	133	161	392	256	0.49	-34.69
EAST ASIA AND THE PACIFIC	**1,330**	**1,656**	**1,858**	**2,220**	**2,629**	**5.02**	**18.42**
NORTH-EAST ASIA	**637**	**752**	**994**	**1,147**	**1,297**	**2.48**	**13.08**
China	147	272	399	498	730	1.39	46.59
Hong Kong, China	31	43	45	70	90	0.17	28.57
Japan	361	316	400	445	347	0.66	-22.02
Korea, Republic of	49	71	87	83	90	0.17	8.43
Taiwan, Province of China	49	50	63	51	40	0.08	-21.57
AUSTRALASIA	**219**	**289**	**280**	**354**	**383**	**0.73**	**8.19**
Australia	219	289	280	354	383	0.73	8.19
OTHER EAST ASIA AND THE PACIFIC	**474**	**615**	**584**	**719**	**949**	**1.81**	**31.99**
Other countries of Asia	474	615	554	659	873	1.67	32.47
Other countries of Oceania			30	60	76	0.15	26.67
EUROPE	**48,210**	**45,393**	**48,252**	**46,154**	**46,123**	**88.06**	**-0.07**
CENTRAL/EASTERN EUROPE	**2,531**	**2,453**	**3,016**	**3,131**	**3,941**	**7.52**	**25.87**
Bulgaria	93	93	95	69	108	0.21	56.52
Czech Republic	511	550	650	625	669	1.28	7.04
Estonia	63	15	32	46	85	0.16	84.78
Hungary	624	521	548	442	442	0.84	
Latvia	44	51	37	84	65	0.12	-22.62
Lithuania	38	49	85	42	34	0.06	-19.05
Poland	282	323	352	329	434	0.83	31.91
Romania	122	119	163	199	176	0.34	-11.56
Russian Federation	593	572	911	962	1,353	2.58	40.64
Slovakia	161	160	143	218	299	0.57	37.16
Ukraine				115	276	0.53	140.00
NORTHERN EUROPE	**3,808**	**3,404**	**4,143**	**3,813**	**3,699**	**7.06**	**-2.99**
Denmark	428	504	508	571	524	1.00	-8.23
Finland	278	173	287	349	288	0.55	-17.48
Iceland	45	39	67	50	33	0.06	-34.00
Ireland	117	128	133	149	128	0.24	-14.09
Norway	282	357	424	398	440	0.84	10.55
Sweden	444	362	457	443	526	1.00	18.74
United Kingdom	2,214	1,841	2,267	1,853	1,760	3.36	-5.02
SOUTHERN EUROPE	**2,879**	**2,912**	**2,970**	**3,099**	**2,893**	**5.52**	**-6.65**
Croatia	83	60	56	55	82	0.16	49.09
Greece	235	231	192	150	163	0.31	8.67
Italy	1,775	1,844	1,973	2,151	1,909	3.64	-11.25
Malta	20	17	38	58	29	0.06	-50.00
Portugal	180	153	164	146	130	0.25	-10.96
Slovenia	125	86	78	126	82	0.16	-34.92
Spain	461	521	469	413	498	0.95	20.58
WESTERN EUROPE	**38,656**	**36,177**	**37,451**	**35,746**	**35,203**	**67.21**	**-1.52**
Austria	2,525	2,355	2,447	2,294	2,464	4.70	7.41
Belgium	1,063	811	1,071	1,029	1,029	1.96	

417

LIECHTENSTEIN

3. Arrivals of non-resident tourists in hotels and similar establishments, by country of residence

	2009	2010	2011	2012	2013	Market share 2013	% Change 2013-2012
France	1,121	1,163	1,270	1,138	1,362	2.60	19.68
Germany	16,697	15,518	14,341	13,284	13,506	25.79	1.67
Luxembourg	630	605	564	412	358	0.68	-13.11
Netherlands	1,086	1,112	1,167	1,156	1,199	2.29	3.72
Switzerland	15,534	14,613	16,591	16,433	15,285	29.18	-6.99
EAST MEDITERRANEAN EUROPE	**68**	**131**	**129**	**152**	**149**	**0.28**	**-1.97**
Cyprus	3	16	15	19	21	0.04	10.53
Turkey	65	115	114	133	128	0.24	-3.76
OTHER EUROPE	**268**	**316**	**543**	**213**	**238**	**0.45**	**11.74**
Other countries of Europe	268	316	543	213	238	0.45	11.74
SOUTH ASIA	**84**	**70**	**96**	**65**	**52**	**0.10**	**-20.00**
India	84	70	96	65	52	0.10	-20.00
NOT SPECIFIED	**230**	**156**	**268**	**1,484**	**178**	**0.34**	**-88.01**
Other countries of the World	230	156	268	1,484	178	0.34	-88.01

Yearbook of Tourism Statistics, Data 2009 – 2013, 2015 Edition

LIECHTENSTEIN

4. Arrivals of non-resident tourists in all types of accommodation establishments, by country of residence

	2009	2010	2011	2012	2013	Market share 2013	% Change 2013-2012
TOTAL				62,382	59,640	100.00	-4.40
AFRICA				391	197	0.33	-49.62
SOUTHERN AFRICA				73	105	0.18	43.84
South Africa				73	105	0.18	43.84
OTHER AFRICA				318	92	0.15	-71.07
Other countries of Africa				318	92	0.15	-71.07
AMERICAS				3,545	3,364	5.64	-5.11
NORTH AMERICA				2,729	2,676	4.49	-1.94
Canada				361	335	0.56	-7.20
Mexico				61	111	0.19	81.97
United States of America				2,307	2,230	3.74	-3.34
SOUTH AMERICA				401	417	0.70	3.99
Brazil				401	417	0.70	3.99
OTHER AMERICAS				415	271	0.45	-34.70
Other countries of the Americas				415	271	0.45	-34.70
EAST ASIA AND THE PACIFIC				2,452	2,837	4.76	15.70
NORTH-EAST ASIA				1,263	1,377	2.31	9.03
China				542	770	1.29	42.07
Hong Kong, China				75	95	0.16	26.67
Japan				481	358	0.60	-25.57
Korea, Republic of				102	100	0.17	-1.96
Taiwan, Province of China				63	54	0.09	-14.29
AUSTRALASIA				407	418	0.70	2.70
Australia				407	418	0.70	2.70
OTHER EAST ASIA AND THE PACIFIC				782	1,042	1.75	33.25
Other countries of Asia				700	953	1.60	36.14
Other countries of Oceania				82	89	0.15	8.54
EUROPE				54,440	53,012	88.89	-2.62
CENTRAL/EASTERN EUROPE				3,416	4,268	7.16	24.94
Bulgaria				73	111	0.19	52.05
Czech Republic				714	791	1.33	10.78
Estonia				55	85	0.14	54.55
Hungary				469	480	0.80	2.35
Latvia				85	79	0.13	-7.06
Lithuania				42	45	0.08	7.14
Poland				410	487	0.82	18.78
Romania				211	191	0.32	-9.48
Russian Federation				997	1,385	2.32	38.92
Slovakia				234	332	0.56	41.88
Ukraine				126	282	0.47	123.81
NORTHERN EUROPE				4,345	4,094	6.86	-5.78
Denmark				651	607	1.02	-6.76
Finland				373	326	0.55	-12.60
Iceland				53	39	0.07	-26.42
Ireland				184	146	0.24	-20.65
Norway				456	481	0.81	5.48
Sweden				483	564	0.95	16.77
United Kingdom				2,145	1,931	3.24	-9.98
SOUTHERN EUROPE				3,348	3,239	5.43	-3.26
Croatia				63	92	0.15	46.03
Greece				153	167	0.28	9.15
Italy				2,307	2,120	3.55	-8.11
Malta				58	29	0.05	-50.00
Portugal				154	144	0.24	-6.49
Slovenia				137	107	0.18	-21.90
Spain				476	580	0.97	21.85
WESTERN EUROPE				42,954	40,994	68.74	-4.56
Austria				2,585	2,663	4.47	3.02
Belgium				1,154	1,102	1.85	-4.51

Yearbook of Tourism Statistics, Data 2009 – 2013, 2015 Edition

LIECHTENSTEIN

4. Arrivals of non-resident tourists in all types of accommodation establishments, by country of residence

	2009	2010	2011	2012	2013	Market share 2013	% Change 2013-2012
France				1,301	1,435	2.41	10.30
Germany				16,728	16,287	27.31	-2.64
Luxembourg				419	385	0.65	-8.11
Netherlands				1,529	1,471	2.47	-3.79
Switzerland				19,238	17,651	29.60	-8.25
EAST MEDITERRANEAN EUROPE				**158**	**156**	**0.26**	**-1.27**
Cyprus				19	23	0.04	21.05
Turkey				139	133	0.22	-4.32
OTHER EUROPE				**219**	**261**	**0.44**	**19.18**
Other countries of Europe				219	261	0.44	19.18
SOUTH ASIA				**70**	**52**	**0.09**	**-25.71**
India				70	52	0.09	-25.71
NOT SPECIFIED				**1,484**	**178**	**0.30**	**-88.01**
Other countries of the World				1,484	178	0.30	-88.01

Yearbook of Tourism Statistics, Data 2009 – 2013, 2015 Edition

LIECHTENSTEIN

5. Overnight stays of non-resident tourists in hotels and similar establishments, by country of residence

	2009	2010	2011	2012	2013	Market share 2013	% Change 2013-2012
TOTAL	**117,806**	**111,458**	**112,459**	**111,345**	**111,533**	**100.00**	**0.17**
AFRICA	**556**	**326**	**357**	**605**	**292**	**0.26**	**-51.74**
SOUTHERN AFRICA	**135**	**115**	**185**	**178**	**139**	**0.12**	**-21.91**
South Africa	135	115	185	178	139	0.12	-21.91
OTHER AFRICA	**421**	**211**	**172**	**427**	**153**	**0.14**	**-64.17**
Other countries of Africa	421	211	172	427	153	0.14	-64.17
AMERICAS	**4,452**	**4,679**	**5,463**	**6,781**	**6,141**	**5.51**	**-9.44**
NORTH AMERICA	**3,934**	**4,117**	**4,729**	**5,086**	**5,063**	**4.54**	**-0.45**
Canada	519	524	503	450	639	0.57	42.00
Mexico	102	62	109	206	249	0.22	20.87
United States of America	3,313	3,531	4,117	4,430	4,175	3.74	-5.76
SOUTH AMERICA	**213**	**226**	**360**	**645**	**558**	**0.50**	**-13.49**
Brazil	213	226	360	645	558	0.50	-13.49
OTHER AMERICAS	**305**	**336**	**374**	**1,050**	**520**	**0.47**	**-50.48**
Other countries of the Americas	305	336	374	1,050	520	0.47	-50.48
EAST ASIA AND THE PACIFIC	**3,155**	**3,682**	**3,837**	**4,793**	**5,201**	**4.66**	**8.51**
NORTH-EAST ASIA	**1,575**	**1,829**	**2,161**	**2,721**	**2,677**	**2.40**	**-1.62**
China	383	593	864	1,205	1,381	1.24	14.61
Hong Kong, China	54	58	96	101	153	0.14	51.49
Japan	836	719	764	1,038	794	0.71	-23.51
Korea, Republic of	169	261	231	266	196	0.18	-26.32
Taiwan, Province of China	133	198	206	111	153	0.14	37.84
AUSTRALASIA	**333**	**432**	**420**	**593**	**587**	**0.53**	**-1.01**
Australia	333	432	420	593	587	0.53	-1.01
OTHER EAST ASIA AND THE PACIFIC	**1,247**	**1,421**	**1,256**	**1,479**	**1,937**	**1.74**	**30.97**
Other countries of Asia	1,247	1,421	1,195	1,379	1,784	1.60	29.37
Other countries of Oceania			61	100	153	0.14	53.00
EUROPE	**109,141**	**102,267**	**101,780**	**95,938**	**98,636**	**88.44**	**2.81**
CENTRAL/EASTERN EUROPE	**4,295**	**4,219**	**5,029**	**5,707**	**6,770**	**6.07**	**18.63**
Bulgaria	194	174	151	115	189	0.17	64.35
Czech Republic	801	757	940	914	1,106	0.99	21.01
Estonia	131	21	62	52	99	0.09	90.38
Hungary	877	970	851	950	751	0.67	-20.95
Latvia	112	284	49	129	117	0.10	-9.30
Lithuania	55	78	98	77	68	0.06	-11.69
Poland	502	557	675	579	880	0.79	51.99
Romania	220	220	280	483	408	0.37	-15.53
Russian Federation	1,025	846	1,587	1,763	2,152	1.93	22.06
Slovakia	378	312	336	439	589	0.53	34.17
Ukraine				206	411	0.37	99.51
NORTHERN EUROPE	**8,263**	**6,678**	**7,302**	**6,190**	**6,080**	**5.45**	**-1.78**
Denmark	822	856	967	990	826	0.74	-16.57
Finland	493	294	395	509	492	0.44	-3.34
Iceland	151	70	217	112	67	0.06	-40.18
Ireland	243	342	280	217	252	0.23	16.13
Norway	381	490	629	498	586	0.53	17.67
Sweden	1,046	673	771	661	767	0.69	16.04
United Kingdom	5,127	3,953	4,043	3,203	3,090	2.77	-3.53
SOUTHERN EUROPE	**5,076**	**6,147**	**5,439**	**4,879**	**4,716**	**4.23**	**-3.34**
Croatia	129	135	100	96	161	0.14	67.71
Greece	532	854	434	303	348	0.31	14.85
Italy	3,146	3,216	3,644	3,242	3,050	2.73	-5.92
Malta	29	46	124	148	52	0.05	-64.86
Portugal	288	438	239	219	212	0.19	-3.20
Slovenia	149	139	141	196	130	0.12	-33.67
Spain	803	1,319	757	675	763	0.68	13.04
WESTERN EUROPE	**90,965**	**84,219**	**81,884**	**78,440**	**80,349**	**72.04**	**2.43**
Austria	4,705	4,217	4,273	3,923	4,358	3.91	11.09
Belgium	4,174	3,176	3,890	3,783	3,442	3.09	-9.01

421

LIECHTENSTEIN

5. Overnight stays of non-resident tourists in hotels and similar establishments, by country of residence

	2009	2010	2011	2012	2013	Market share 2013	% Change 2013-2012
France	2,002	2,119	2,238	1,937	2,635	2.36	36.04
Germany	39,996	37,337	32,454	28,464	31,644	28.37	11.17
Luxembourg	2,591	2,833	2,178	1,463	1,217	1.09	-16.81
Netherlands	2,404	2,090	2,130	2,221	2,320	2.08	4.46
Switzerland	35,093	32,447	34,721	36,649	34,733	31.14	-5.23
EAST MEDITERRANEAN EUROPE	**144**	**449**	**290**	**300**	**297**	**0.27**	**-1.00**
Cyprus	6	26	31	38	49	0.04	28.95
Turkey	138	423	259	262	248	0.22	-5.34
OTHER EUROPE	**398**	**555**	**1,836**	**422**	**424**	**0.38**	**0.47**
Other countries of Europe	398	555	1,836	422	424	0.38	0.47
SOUTH ASIA	**148**	**166**	**205**	**239**	**147**	**0.13**	**-38.49**
India	148	166	205	239	147	0.13	-38.49
NOT SPECIFIED	**354**	**338**	**817**	**2,989**	**1,116**	**1.00**	**-62.66**
Other countries of the World	354	338	817	2,989	1,116	1.00	-62.66

Yearbook of Tourism Statistics, Data 2009 – 2013, 2015 Edition

LIECHTENSTEIN

6. Overnight stays of non-resident tourists in all types of accommodation establishments, by country of residence

	2009	2010	2011	2012	2013	Market share 2013	% Change 2013-2012
TOTAL				136,276	132,491	100.00	-2.78
AFRICA				619	333	0.25	-46.20
SOUTHERN AFRICA				181	156	0.12	-13.81
South Africa				181	156	0.12	-13.81
OTHER AFRICA				438	177	0.13	-59.59
Other countries of Africa				438	177	0.13	-59.59
AMERICAS				7,705	6,740	5.09	-12.52
NORTH AMERICA				5,942	5,526	4.17	-7.00
Canada				808	927	0.70	14.73
Mexico				209	261	0.20	24.88
United States of America				4,925	4,338	3.27	-11.92
SOUTH AMERICA				658	642	0.48	-2.43
Brazil				658	642	0.48	-2.43
OTHER AMERICAS				1,105	572	0.43	-48.24
Other countries of the Americas				1,105	572	0.43	-48.24
EAST ASIA AND THE PACIFIC				5,447	5,833	4.40	7.09
NORTH-EAST ASIA				3,048	2,895	2.19	-5.02
China				1,345	1,470	1.11	9.29
Hong Kong, China				113	178	0.13	57.52
Japan				1,119	826	0.62	-26.18
Korea, Republic of				340	217	0.16	-36.18
Taiwan, Province of China				131	204	0.15	55.73
AUSTRALASIA				722	678	0.51	-6.09
Australia				722	678	0.51	-6.09
OTHER EAST ASIA AND THE PACIFIC				1,677	2,260	1.71	34.76
Other countries of Asia				1,503	2,062	1.56	37.19
Other countries of Oceania				174	198	0.15	13.79
EUROPE				119,267	118,322	89.31	-0.79
CENTRAL/EASTERN EUROPE				6,521	7,809	5.89	19.75
Bulgaria				123	205	0.15	66.67
Czech Republic				1,149	1,517	1.14	32.03
Estonia				61	99	0.07	62.30
Hungary				1,012	917	0.69	-9.39
Latvia				130	190	0.14	46.15
Lithuania				77	85	0.06	10.39
Poland				910	1,073	0.81	17.91
Romania				504	431	0.33	-14.48
Russian Federation				1,855	2,205	1.66	18.87
Slovakia				478	654	0.49	36.82
Ukraine				222	433	0.33	95.05
NORTHERN EUROPE				7,274	7,174	5.41	-1.37
Denmark				1,162	1,089	0.82	-6.28
Finland				556	609	0.46	9.53
Iceland				140	73	0.06	-47.86
Ireland				270	281	0.21	4.07
Norway				626	705	0.53	12.62
Sweden				763	874	0.66	14.55
United Kingdom				3,757	3,543	2.67	-5.70
SOUTHERN EUROPE				5,327	5,661	4.27	6.27
Croatia				125	193	0.15	54.40
Greece				315	356	0.27	13.02
Italy				3,465	3,619	2.73	4.44
Malta				148	52	0.04	-64.86
Portugal				239	252	0.19	5.44
Slovenia				216	208	0.16	-3.70
Spain				819	981	0.74	19.78
WESTERN EUROPE				99,363	96,856	73.10	-2.52
Austria				4,442	4,700	3.55	5.81
Belgium				4,240	3,673	2.77	-13.37

423

LIECHTENSTEIN

6. Overnight stays of non-resident tourists in all types of accommodation establishments, by country of residence

	2009	2010	2011	2012	2013	Market share 2013	% Change 2013-2012
France				2,395	2,792	2.11	16.58
Germany				39,238	39,901	30.12	1.69
Luxembourg				1,490	1,258	0.95	-15.57
Netherlands				3,153	3,193	2.41	1.27
Switzerland				44,405	41,339	31.20	-6.90
EAST MEDITERRANEAN EUROPE				**345**	**327**	**0.25**	**-5.22**
Cyprus				38	73	0.06	92.11
Turkey				307	254	0.19	-17.26
OTHER EUROPE				**437**	**495**	**0.37**	**13.27**
Other countries of Europe				437	495	0.37	13.27
SOUTH ASIA				**249**	**147**	**0.11**	**-40.96**
India				249	147	0.11	-40.96
NOT SPECIFIED				**2,989**	**1,116**	**0.84**	**-62.66**
Other countries of the World				2,989	1,116	0.84	-62.66

Yearbook of Tourism Statistics, Data 2009 – 2013, 2015 Edition

LITHUANIA

3. Arrivals of non-resident tourists in hotels and similar establishments, by country of residence

	2009	2010	2011	2012	2013	Market share 2013	% Change 2013-2012
TOTAL	684,471	760,885	909,274	1,008,138	1,098,496	100.00	8.96
AFRICA	1,151	1,493	3,009	1,697	1,772	0.16	4.42
OTHER AFRICA	1,151	1,493	3,009	1,697	1,772	0.16	4.42
All countries of Africa	1,151	1,493	3,009	1,697	1,772	0.16	4.42
AMERICAS	18,760	24,209	30,879	33,984	33,933	3.09	-0.15
NORTH AMERICA	17,066	21,713	27,445	26,725	28,654	2.61	7.22
Canada	1,698	2,858	3,705	2,714	1,985	0.18	-26.86
United States of America	15,368	18,855	23,740	24,011	26,669	2.43	11.07
OTHER AMERICAS	1,694	2,496	3,434	7,259	5,279	0.48	-27.28
Other countries of the Americas	1,694	2,496	3,434	7,259	5,279	0.48	-27.28
EAST ASIA AND THE PACIFIC	17,873	20,555	29,574	37,716	38,384	3.49	1.77
NORTH-EAST ASIA	9,779	10,779	13,613	14,926	14,631	1.33	-1.98
China	2,298	3,236	5,278	5,877	5,138	0.47	-12.57
Japan	7,481	7,543	8,335	9,049	9,493	0.86	4.91
OTHER EAST ASIA AND THE PACIFIC	8,094	9,776	15,961	22,790	23,753	2.16	4.23
Other countries of Asia	4,603	6,523	12,087	18,552	19,597	1.78	5.63
All countries of Oceania	3,491	3,253	3,874	4,238	4,156	0.38	-1.93
EUROPE	646,687	714,628	845,812	934,741	1,024,407	93.26	9.59
CENTRAL/EASTERN EUROPE	336,708	391,181	464,477	540,191	620,001	56.44	14.77
Belarus	39,861	56,786	77,431	98,302	138,172	12.58	40.56
Bulgaria	1,409	1,131	1,694	1,525	1,808	0.16	18.56
Czech Republic	9,270	6,564	6,779	7,555	7,068	0.64	-6.45
Estonia	27,348	29,986	35,188	36,919	38,144	3.47	3.32
Hungary	2,073	2,941	3,462	3,569	3,970	0.36	11.24
Latvia	55,832	60,460	59,764	67,121	72,200	6.57	7.57
Poland	115,661	125,988	130,426	117,280	117,133	10.66	-0.13
Romania	2,377	2,074	3,892	2,923	3,466	0.32	18.58
Russian Federation	70,707	93,907	128,874	183,651	208,004	18.94	13.26
Slovakia	1,635	1,732	2,557	2,050	2,507	0.23	22.29
Ukraine	7,055	8,413	12,270	17,680	25,969	2.36	46.88
Other countries Central/East Europe	3,480	1,199	2,140	1,616	1,560	0.14	-3.47
NORTHERN EUROPE	105,808	122,044	131,045	144,588	147,870	13.46	2.27
Denmark	12,007	15,026	16,581	19,751	19,220	1.75	-2.69
Finland	29,055	33,093	34,502	35,845	30,440	2.77	-15.08
Iceland	1,718	823	907	1,668	1,569	0.14	-5.94
Ireland	4,481	3,513	4,075	5,111	4,070	0.37	-20.37
Norway	15,342	16,141	19,177	25,824	27,856	2.54	7.87
Sweden	18,463	19,265	24,472	21,120	23,308	2.12	10.36
United Kingdom	24,742	34,183	31,331	35,269	41,407	3.77	17.40
SOUTHERN EUROPE	37,093	39,664	56,579	51,394	51,258	4.67	-0.26
Greece	2,942	2,646	3,254	2,402	3,201	0.29	33.26
Italy	19,926	21,180	29,151	27,697	26,750	2.44	-3.42
Portugal	2,065	2,030	2,660	2,121	2,739	0.25	29.14
Spain	12,160	13,808	21,514	19,174	18,568	1.69	-3.16
WESTERN EUROPE	144,525	137,348	163,603	181,886	186,984	17.02	2.80
Austria	6,478	5,902	6,484	7,882	7,781	0.71	-1.28
Belgium	6,889	7,066	7,088	8,201	10,774	0.98	31.37
France	20,287	21,367	23,223	23,470	21,803	1.98	-7.10
Germany	97,486	90,207	109,439	126,297	128,620	11.71	1.84
Luxembourg	816	523	694	686	988	0.09	44.02
Netherlands	8,255	8,573	11,773	10,642	11,891	1.08	11.74
Switzerland	4,314	3,710	4,902	4,708	5,127	0.47	8.90
EAST MEDITERRANEAN EUROPE	7,346	8,028	12,140	12,326	12,627	1.15	2.44
Israel	4,521	5,045	6,679	7,652	6,534	0.59	-14.61
Turkey	2,825	2,983	5,461	4,674	6,093	0.55	30.36
OTHER EUROPE	15,207	16,363	17,968	4,356	5,667	0.52	30.10
Other countries of Europe	15,207	16,363	17,968	4,356	5,667	0.52	30.10

425

Yearbook of Tourism Statistics, Data 2009 – 2013, 2015 Edition

LITHUANIA

4. Arrivals of non-resident tourists in all types of accommodation establishments, by country of residence

	2009	2010	2011	2012	2013	Market share 2013	% Change 2013-2012
TOTAL	752,389	840,368	1,003,843	1,125,338	1,234,919	100.00	9.74
AFRICA	1,177	1,523	3,034	1,762	1,836	0.15	4.20
OTHER AFRICA	1,177	1,523	3,034	1,762	1,836	0.15	4.20
All countries of Africa	1,177	1,523	3,034	1,762	1,836	0.15	4.20
AMERICAS	20,489	25,247	32,302	36,132	36,052	2.92	-0.22
NORTH AMERICA	18,756	22,665	28,727	27,955	29,948	2.43	7.13
Canada	1,795	2,999	3,877	2,876	2,143	0.17	-25.49
United States of America	16,961	19,666	24,850	25,079	27,805	2.25	10.87
SOUTH AMERICA	1,020	1,282	1,543	1,889	1,506	0.12	-20.28
Brazil	1,020	1,282	1,543	1,889	1,506	0.12	-20.28
OTHER AMERICAS	713	1,300	2,032	6,288	4,598	0.37	-26.88
Other countries of the Americas	713	1,300	2,032	6,288	4,598	0.37	-26.88
EAST ASIA AND THE PACIFIC	18,470	21,283	30,829	39,502	41,530	3.36	5.13
NORTH-EAST ASIA	11,015	12,283	16,547	18,083	18,647	1.51	3.12
China	2,515	3,309	5,522	6,124	5,591	0.45	-8.70
Japan	7,599	7,654	8,528	9,465	10,079	0.82	6.49
Korea, Republic of	901	1,320	2,497	2,494	2,977	0.24	19.37
AUSTRALASIA	3,686	3,702	4,130	4,532	4,131	0.33	-8.85
Australia	3,686	3,702	4,130	4,532	4,131	0.33	-8.85
OTHER EAST ASIA AND THE PACIFIC	3,769	5,298	10,152	16,887	18,752	1.52	11.04
Other countries of Asia	3,769	5,298	10,152	16,887	18,752	1.52	11.04
EUROPE	712,253	792,315	937,678	1,047,942	1,155,501	93.57	10.26
CENTRAL/EASTERN EUROPE	376,163	438,864	517,221	613,300	707,654	57.30	15.38
Belarus	52,193	71,436	92,248	117,037	162,158	13.13	38.55
Bulgaria	1,522	1,189	1,764	1,657	1,911	0.15	15.33
Czech Republic	10,066	8,618	7,852	8,522	8,368	0.68	-1.81
Estonia	30,340	32,527	37,409	39,712	42,086	3.41	5.98
Hungary	2,159	3,587	3,670	3,740	4,158	0.34	11.18
Latvia	62,815	66,519	66,145	76,431	83,223	6.74	8.89
Poland	125,662	135,856	139,632	127,033	127,330	10.31	0.23
Romania	2,554	2,275	4,192	3,211	3,810	0.31	18.65
Russian Federation	78,690	105,869	148,267	214,337	243,599	19.73	13.65
Slovakia	1,753	1,888	2,768	2,254	2,680	0.22	18.90
Ukraine	8,409	9,100	13,274	19,366	28,331	2.29	46.29
NORTHERN EUROPE	109,537	127,264	136,906	150,961	155,705	12.61	3.14
Denmark	12,338	15,416	16,925	20,149	19,795	1.60	-1.76
Finland	30,211	35,137	36,483	37,545	33,249	2.69	-11.44
Iceland	1,742	845	929	1,687	1,602	0.13	-5.04
Ireland	4,577	3,875	4,317	5,673	4,680	0.38	-17.50
Norway	15,657	16,846	20,092	26,461	29,169	2.36	10.23
Sweden	19,101	19,747	25,303	21,694	23,043	1.87	6.22
United Kingdom	25,911	35,398	32,857	37,752	44,167	3.58	16.99
SOUTHERN EUROPE	39,869	43,487	63,057	58,258	57,678	4.67	-1.00
Greece	2,964	2,680	3,326	2,474	3,266	0.26	32.01
Italy	20,689	22,547	31,490	30,137	28,912	2.34	-4.06
Malta	205	217	293	471	561	0.05	19.11
Portugal	2,175	2,238	2,809	2,308	2,871	0.23	24.39
Slovenia	1,124	1,254	2,404	1,713	1,668	0.14	-2.63
Spain	12,712	14,551	22,735	21,155	20,400	1.65	-3.57
WESTERN EUROPE	161,068	157,463	189,695	207,914	213,982	17.33	2.92
Austria	6,833	6,249	6,948	8,257	8,370	0.68	1.37
Belgium	7,104	7,585	7,852	8,800	11,489	0.93	30.56
France	21,641	23,248	25,684	26,423	24,645	2.00	-6.73
Germany	110,163	105,832	128,930	144,975	148,599	12.03	2.50
Luxembourg	816	544	724	953	1,008	0.08	5.77
Netherlands	9,876	9,997	14,137	13,322	14,050	1.14	5.46
Switzerland	4,635	4,008	5,420	5,184	5,821	0.47	12.29

Yearbook of Tourism Statistics, Data 2009 – 2013, 2015 Edition

LITHUANIA

4. Arrivals of non-resident tourists in all types of accommodation establishments, by country of residence

	2009	2010	2011	2012	2013	Market share 2013	% Change 2013-2012
EAST MEDITERRANEAN EUROPE	**8,142**	**9,015**	**13,180**	**13,452**	**14,356**	**1.16**	**6.72**
Cyprus	401	500	374	403	762	0.06	89.08
Israel	4,830	5,413	7,151	8,159	7,072	0.57	-13.32
Turkey	2,911	3,102	5,655	4,890	6,522	0.53	33.37
OTHER EUROPE	**17,474**	**16,222**	**17,619**	**4,057**	**6,126**	**0.50**	**51.00**
Other countries of Europe	17,474	16,222	17,619	4,057	6,126	0.50	51.00

Yearbook of Tourism Statistics, Data 2009 – 2013, 2015 Edition

LITHUANIA

5. Overnight stays of non-resident tourists in hotels and similar establishments, by country of residence

	2009	2010	2011	2012	2013	Market share 2013	% Change 2013-2012
TOTAL	1,322,983	1,509,883	1,818,031	2,001,745	2,169,087	100.00	8.36
AFRICA	2,715	3,157	6,812	4,350	4,024	0.19	-7.49
OTHER AFRICA	2,715	3,157	6,812	4,350	4,024	0.19	-7.49
All countries of Africa	2,715	3,157	6,812	4,350	4,024	0.19	-7.49
AMERICAS	40,088	59,025	61,071	73,610	78,525	3.62	6.68
NORTH AMERICA	36,248	54,101	54,552	56,683	65,691	3.03	15.89
Canada	3,745	5,732	6,829	5,946	4,790	0.22	-19.44
United States of America	32,503	48,369	47,723	50,737	60,901	2.81	20.03
OTHER AMERICAS	3,840	4,924	6,519	16,927	12,834	0.59	-24.18
Other countries of the Americas	3,840	4,924	6,519	16,927	12,834	0.59	-24.18
EAST ASIA AND THE PACIFIC	35,196	37,487	56,241	75,291	81,188	3.74	7.83
NORTH-EAST ASIA	16,887	17,161	20,261	24,383	24,751	1.14	1.51
China	4,418	5,238	8,497	10,363	9,567	0.44	-7.68
Japan	12,469	11,923	11,764	14,020	15,184	0.70	8.30
OTHER EAST ASIA AND THE PACIFIC	18,309	20,326	35,980	50,908	56,437	2.60	10.86
Other countries of Asia	10,847	13,905	28,007	41,863	47,152	2.17	12.63
All countries of Oceania	7,462	6,421	7,973	9,045	9,285	0.43	2.65
EUROPE	1,244,984	1,410,214	1,693,907	1,848,494	2,005,350	92.45	8.49
CENTRAL/EASTERN EUROPE	624,685	753,271	881,220	1,053,051	1,175,659	54.20	11.64
Belarus	73,816	108,583	129,163	163,837	223,628	10.31	36.49
Bulgaria	2,854	2,420	3,528	3,160	3,841	0.18	21.55
Czech Republic	24,506	11,032	13,326	23,299	14,272	0.66	-38.74
Estonia	44,169	46,544	54,845	56,726	60,450	2.79	6.56
Hungary	5,159	6,435	7,348	6,887	8,387	0.39	21.78
Latvia	84,599	92,477	93,217	104,194	110,996	5.12	6.53
Poland	204,378	246,085	249,892	249,640	223,783	10.32	-10.36
Romania	5,462	4,652	8,091	5,416	7,564	0.35	39.66
Russian Federation	146,956	203,133	285,646	397,950	454,352	20.95	14.17
Slovakia	3,085	3,451	5,063	3,820	5,391	0.25	41.13
Ukraine	21,360	16,152	25,799	34,606	49,685	2.29	43.57
Other countries Central/East Europe	8,341	12,307	5,302	3,516	13,310	0.61	278.56
NORTHERN EUROPE	207,753	231,042	263,691	282,594	299,325	13.80	5.92
Denmark	26,270	27,659	34,651	33,219	39,039	1.80	17.52
Finland	53,112	63,220	68,419	68,497	57,564	2.65	-15.96
Iceland	2,801	1,662	1,945	3,526	3,479	0.16	-1.33
Ireland	9,414	6,973	8,300	10,589	9,028	0.42	-14.74
Norway	34,846	34,285	44,958	57,954	63,490	2.93	9.55
Sweden	32,824	33,684	44,739	39,081	42,083	1.94	7.68
United Kingdom	48,486	63,559	60,679	69,728	84,642	3.90	21.39
SOUTHERN EUROPE	78,652	94,657	135,791	112,408	111,503	5.14	-0.81
Greece	6,330	6,983	7,987	6,594	7,485	0.35	13.51
Italy	41,795	46,442	62,312	58,525	56,095	2.59	-4.15
Portugal	5,670	6,366	8,207	4,963	7,270	0.34	46.48
Spain	24,857	34,866	57,285	42,326	40,653	1.87	-3.95
WESTERN EUROPE	282,261	283,045	339,932	355,547	366,638	16.90	3.12
Austria	12,625	10,587	12,548	13,762	9,028	0.42	-34.40
Belgium	15,180	14,489	15,229	16,721	24,646	1.14	47.40
France	39,308	55,419	58,285	44,354	53,772	2.48	21.23
Germany	189,777	178,337	218,073	244,118	241,047	11.11	-1.26
Luxembourg	1,355	914	1,171	1,156	1,776	0.08	53.63
Netherlands	15,792	16,313	25,667	26,725	26,797	1.24	0.27
Switzerland	8,224	6,986	8,959	8,711	9,572	0.44	9.88
EAST MEDITERRANEAN EUROPE	21,266	24,039	34,704	36,231	39,849	1.84	9.99
Israel	12,060	14,643	19,530	23,186	22,757	1.05	-1.85
Turkey	9,206	9,396	15,174	13,045	17,092	0.79	31.02
OTHER EUROPE	30,367	24,160	38,569	8,663	12,376	0.57	42.86
Other countries of Europe	30,367	24,160	38,569	8,663	12,376	0.57	42.86

Yearbook of Tourism Statistics, Data 2009 – 2013, 2015 Edition

LITHUANIA

6. Overnight stays of non-resident tourists in all types of accommodation establishments, by country of residence

	2009	2010	2011	2012	2013	Market share 2013	% Change 2013-2012
TOTAL	1,758,447	1,999,251	2,377,346	2,622,298	2,838,638	100.00	8.25
AFRICA	2,827	3,224	6,866	4,548	4,384	0.15	-3.61
OTHER AFRICA	2,827	3,224	6,866	4,548	4,384	0.15	-3.61
All countries of Africa	2,827	3,224	6,866	4,548	4,384	0.15	-3.61
AMERICAS	46,043	61,964	65,530	80,172	85,875	3.03	7.11
NORTH AMERICA	42,022	56,913	58,767	61,331	71,032	2.50	15.82
Canada	4,103	6,027	7,507	6,533	5,243	0.18	-19.75
United States of America	37,919	50,886	51,260	54,798	65,789	2.32	20.06
SOUTH AMERICA	2,508	2,486	3,068	3,815	3,351	0.12	-12.16
Brazil	2,508	2,486	3,068	3,815	3,351	0.12	-12.16
OTHER AMERICAS	1,513	2,565	3,695	15,026	11,492	0.40	-23.52
Other countries of the Americas	1,513	2,565	3,695	15,026	11,492	0.40	-23.52
EAST ASIA AND THE PACIFIC	41,574	39,360	59,084	82,555	103,606	3.65	25.50
NORTH-EAST ASIA	24,785	20,276	25,505	29,684	31,019	1.09	4.50
China	9,896	5,350	8,920	10,807	10,400	0.37	-3.77
Japan	12,686	12,140	12,101	14,902	16,319	0.57	9.51
Korea, Republic of	2,203	2,786	4,484	3,975	4,300	0.15	8.18
AUSTRALASIA	7,837	7,416	8,507	9,577	10,317	0.36	7.73
Australia	7,837	7,416	8,507	9,577	10,317	0.36	7.73
OTHER EAST ASIA AND THE PACIFIC	8,952	11,668	25,072	43,294	62,270	2.19	43.83
Other countries of Asia	8,952	11,668	25,072	43,294	62,270	2.19	43.83
EUROPE	1,668,003	1,894,703	2,245,866	2,455,023	2,644,773	93.17	7.73
CENTRAL/EASTERN EUROPE	912,678	1,076,511	1,244,497	1,475,705	1,623,678	57.20	10.03
Belarus	250,314	293,417	312,565	353,382	424,704	14.96	20.18
Bulgaria	3,021	2,535	3,769	3,727	4,218	0.15	13.17
Czech Republic	25,897	13,466	14,892	25,140	16,685	0.59	-33.63
Estonia	49,918	51,342	60,523	63,621	69,486	2.45	9.22
Hungary	5,527	12,226	7,682	7,255	8,690	0.31	19.78
Latvia	100,225	109,891	112,104	127,773	137,595	4.85	7.69
Poland	239,067	281,286	277,979	277,327	249,189	8.78	-10.15
Romania	7,995	5,119	8,885	6,087	8,155	0.29	33.97
Russian Federation	195,401	282,318	412,645	568,669	643,869	22.68	13.22
Slovakia	3,342	3,769	5,446	4,588	5,733	0.20	24.96
Ukraine	31,971	21,142	28,007	38,136	55,354	1.95	45.15
NORTHERN EUROPE	217,638	242,990	278,985	297,733	318,986	11.24	7.14
Denmark	27,026	28,433	35,615	34,531	40,835	1.44	18.26
Finland	55,508	67,439	73,608	72,116	63,509	2.24	-11.93
Iceland	2,878	1,699	1,980	3,594	3,602	0.13	0.22
Ireland	9,640	7,900	8,848	12,096	10,250	0.36	-15.26
Norway	36,123	36,180	47,301	59,667	66,375	2.34	11.24
Sweden	34,507	34,916	46,967	40,871	43,861	1.55	7.32
United Kingdom	51,956	66,423	64,666	74,858	90,554	3.19	20.97
SOUTHERN EUROPE	84,565	102,852	151,723	127,869	124,536	4.39	-2.61
Greece	6,377	7,109	8,224	6,721	7,620	0.27	13.38
Italy	43,550	49,094	67,187	63,756	60,457	2.13	-5.17
Malta	508	609	990	936	1,310	0.05	39.96
Portugal	6,002	6,780	8,544	5,339	7,513	0.26	40.72
Slovenia	2,129	2,541	5,802	3,703	3,243	0.11	-12.42
Spain	25,999	36,719	60,976	47,414	44,393	1.56	-6.37
WESTERN EUROPE	389,675	407,441	491,336	502,212	514,796	18.14	2.51
Austria	13,225	11,104	13,435	14,336	16,213	0.57	13.09
Belgium	15,675	15,546	16,494	17,815	26,102	0.92	46.52
France	42,650	59,466	62,955	50,824	59,509	2.10	17.09
Germany	288,365	293,747	356,978	374,229	368,203	12.97	-1.61
Luxembourg	1,355	958	1,224	1,795	1,828	0.06	1.84
Netherlands	19,214	19,133	30,454	33,649	31,318	1.10	-6.93
Switzerland	9,191	7,487	9,796	9,564	11,623	0.41	21.53

Yearbook of Tourism Statistics, Data 2009 – 2013, 2015 Edition

LITHUANIA

6. Overnight stays of non-resident tourists in all types of accommodation establishments, by country of residence

	2009	2010	2011	2012	2013	Market share 2013	% Change 2013-2012
EAST MEDITERRANEAN EUROPE	**26,648**	**30,720**	**41,852**	**43,535**	**50,406**	**1.78**	**15.78**
Cyprus	868	1,041	800	1,009	1,762	0.06	74.63
Israel	16,133	19,988	25,394	29,028	30,400	1.07	4.73
Turkey	9,647	9,691	15,658	13,498	18,244	0.64	35.16
OTHER EUROPE	**36,799**	**34,189**	**37,473**	**7,969**	**12,371**	**0.44**	**55.24**
Other countries of Europe	36,799	34,189	37,473	7,969	12,371	0.44	55.24

Yearbook of Tourism Statistics, Data 2009 – 2013, 2015 Edition

LUXEMBOURG

3. Arrivals of non-resident tourists in hotels and similar establishments, by country of residence

	2009	2010	2011	2012	2013	Market share 2013	% Change 2013-2012
TOTAL (*)	651,273	651,532	684,580	770,279	762,783	100.00	-0.97
AFRICA	3,021	2,775	9,768	13,908	4,416	0.58	-68.25
SOUTHERN AFRICA	476	832	905	1,067	691	0.09	-35.24
South Africa	476	832	905	1,067	691	0.09	-35.24
OTHER AFRICA	2,545	1,943	8,863	12,841	3,725	0.49	-70.99
Other countries of Africa	2,545	1,943	8,863	12,841	3,725	0.49	-70.99
AMERICAS	25,816	27,426	35,405	35,730	36,083	4.73	0.99
NORTH AMERICA	21,146	21,485	20,493	22,885	28,665	3.76	25.26
Canada	3,564	3,485	3,261	4,198	4,051	0.53	-3.50
United States of America	17,582	18,000	17,232	18,687	24,614	3.23	31.72
SOUTH AMERICA	2,167	2,473	2,264	3,472	3,050	0.40	-12.15
Brazil	2,167	2,473	2,264	3,472	3,050	0.40	-12.15
OTHER AMERICAS	2,503	3,468	12,648	9,373	4,368	0.57	-53.40
Other countries of the Americas	2,503	3,468	12,648	9,373	4,368	0.57	-53.40
EAST ASIA AND THE PACIFIC	28,792	32,969	52,156	71,246	56,591	7.42	-20.57
NORTH-EAST ASIA	17,628	20,400	32,149	48,872	38,855	5.09	-20.50
China	13,608	15,529	25,697	40,974	31,896	4.18	-22.16
Japan	3,308	3,431	5,275	6,879	5,903	0.77	-14.19
Korea, Republic of	712	1,440	1,177	1,019	1,056	0.14	3.63
AUSTRALASIA	1,838	2,102	2,127	2,557	2,509	0.33	-1.88
Australia	1,838	2,102	2,127	2,557	2,509	0.33	-1.88
OTHER EAST ASIA AND THE PACIFIC	9,326	10,467	17,880	19,817	15,227	2.00	-23.16
Other countries of Asia	9,326	10,467	17,880	19,817	15,227	2.00	-23.16
EUROPE	591,200	586,879	587,251	649,395	665,693	87.27	2.51
CENTRAL/EASTERN EUROPE	20,936	23,506	24,398	28,435	32,673	4.28	14.90
Bulgaria	1,229	1,008	1,176	1,177	1,327	0.17	12.74
Czech Republic	2,397	2,719	1,931	2,809	2,881	0.38	2.56
Estonia	481	518	520	555	822	0.11	48.11
Hungary	1,754	1,628	1,635	2,218	2,550	0.33	14.97
Latvia	463	531	483	554	727	0.10	31.23
Lithuania	796	679	724	1,048	1,188	0.16	13.36
Poland	4,002	5,267	4,936	5,091	5,512	0.72	8.27
Romania	2,222	2,637	2,625	2,865	3,518	0.46	22.79
Russian Federation	6,470	7,125	8,913	9,918	11,189	1.47	12.82
Slovakia	678	859	803	981	1,091	0.14	11.21
Ukraine	444	535	652	1,219	1,868	0.24	53.24
NORTHERN EUROPE	65,478	64,742	56,410	65,154	80,173	10.51	23.05
Denmark	7,550	6,681	3,964	4,134	5,232	0.69	26.56
Finland	2,423	2,442	2,132	2,404	3,048	0.40	26.79
Iceland	463	712	769	676	720	0.09	6.51
Ireland	2,423	2,505	2,344	2,641	4,410	0.58	66.98
Norway	2,243	2,219	2,040	2,072	2,914	0.38	40.64
Sweden	5,441	5,847	4,672	4,475	5,644	0.74	26.12
United Kingdom	44,935	44,336	40,489	48,752	58,205	7.63	19.39
SOUTHERN EUROPE	42,553	42,723	41,086	43,563	48,336	6.34	10.96
Greece	2,207	2,263	1,930	2,039	2,365	0.31	15.99
Italy	18,672	17,738	17,603	17,865	21,118	2.77	18.21
Malta	569	470	455	476	597	0.08	25.42
Portugal	7,106	7,702	8,134	8,619	7,902	1.04	-8.32
Slovenia	908	1,042	740	852	852	0.11	
Spain	13,091	13,508	12,224	13,712	15,502	2.03	13.05
WESTERN EUROPE	451,308	445,137	448,836	492,861	486,311	63.75	-1.33
Austria	4,995	5,484	5,539	5,463	5,608	0.74	2.65
Belgium	146,911	147,935	152,191	169,733	165,718	21.73	-2.37
France	104,923	112,343	115,994	122,164	117,019	15.34	-4.21
Germany	95,866	92,209	97,017	106,266	112,066	14.69	5.46
Netherlands	79,588	70,048	61,891	70,887	66,714	8.75	-5.89
Switzerland	19,025	17,118	16,204	18,348	19,186	2.52	4.57

Yearbook of Tourism Statistics, Data 2009 – 2013, 2015 Edition

LUXEMBOURG

3. Arrivals of non-resident tourists in hotels and similar establishments, by country of residence

	2009	2010	2011	2012	2013	Market share 2013	% Change 2013-2012
EAST MEDITERRANEAN EUROPE	**2,991**	**3,485**	**3,894**	**6,553**	**13,333**	**1.75**	**103.46**
Cyprus	444	422	335	404	506	0.07	25.25
Turkey	2,547	3,063	3,559	6,149	12,827	1.68	108.60
OTHER EUROPE	**7,934**	**7,286**	**12,627**	**12,829**	**4,867**	**0.64**	**-62.06**
Other countries of Europe	7,934	7,286	12,627	12,829	4,867	0.64	-62.06
NOT SPECIFIED	**2,444**	**1,483**					
Other countries of the World	2,444	1,483					

Yearbook of Tourism Statistics, Data 2009 – 2013, 2015 Edition

LUXEMBOURG

4. Arrivals of non-resident tourists in all types of accommodation establishments, by country of residence

	2009	2010	2011	2012	2013	Market share 2013	% Change 2013-2012
TOTAL	846,685	805,472	870,484	950,423	944,528	100.00	-0.62
AFRICA	3,296	2,886	10,091	14,358	4,726	0.50	-67.08
SOUTHERN AFRICA	519	870	986	1,278	832	0.09	-34.90
South Africa	519	870	986	1,278	832	0.09	-34.90
OTHER AFRICA	2,777	2,016	9,105	13,080	3,894	0.41	-70.23
Other countries of Africa	2,777	2,016	9,105	13,080	3,894	0.41	-70.23
AMERICAS	28,720	28,975	37,969	38,751	39,205	4.15	1.17
NORTH AMERICA	23,289	22,565	22,156	24,979	30,847	3.27	23.49
Canada	4,211	3,736	3,752	4,650	4,561	0.48	-1.91
United States of America	19,078	18,829	18,404	20,329	26,286	2.78	29.30
SOUTH AMERICA	2,514	2,622	2,546	3,880	3,482	0.37	-10.26
Brazil	2,514	2,622	2,546	3,880	3,482	0.37	-10.26
OTHER AMERICAS	2,917	3,788	13,267	9,892	4,876	0.52	-50.71
Other countries of the Americas	2,917	3,788	13,267	9,892	4,876	0.52	-50.71
EAST ASIA AND THE PACIFIC	32,039	34,879	55,643	74,997	60,342	6.39	-19.54
NORTH-EAST ASIA	19,221	21,262	34,147	50,911	41,006	4.34	-19.46
China	14,271	15,933	26,544	42,286	33,335	3.53	-21.17
Japan	3,706	3,575	5,628	7,133	6,205	0.66	-13.01
Korea, Republic of	1,244	1,754	1,975	1,492	1,466	0.16	-1.74
AUSTRALASIA	2,616	2,594	2,762	3,235	3,075	0.33	-4.95
Australia	2,616	2,594	2,762	3,235	3,075	0.33	-4.95
OTHER EAST ASIA AND THE PACIFIC	10,202	11,023	18,734	20,851	16,261	1.72	-22.01
Other countries of Asia	10,202	11,023	18,734	20,851	16,261	1.72	-22.01
EUROPE	779,128	737,093	766,781	822,317	840,255	88.96	2.18
CENTRAL/EASTERN EUROPE	23,708	25,079	27,642	31,533	35,832	3.79	13.63
Bulgaria	1,369	1,080	1,305	1,282	1,389	0.15	8.35
Czech Republic	2,986	3,090	2,450	3,437	3,262	0.35	-5.09
Estonia	507	531	595	615	1,261	0.13	105.04
Hungary	2,096	1,836	1,865	2,467	2,790	0.30	13.09
Latvia	473	570	1,000	594	765	0.08	28.79
Lithuania	828	731	771	1,237	1,265	0.13	2.26
Poland	5,033	5,810	5,942	6,084	6,511	0.69	7.02
Romania	2,336	2,750	2,831	3,143	3,870	0.41	23.13
Russian Federation	6,852	7,248	9,274	10,266	11,616	1.23	13.15
Slovakia	778	895	935	1,181	1,215	0.13	2.88
Ukraine	450	538	674	1,227	1,888	0.20	53.87
NORTHERN EUROPE	77,291	75,161	67,525	75,005	89,904	9.52	19.86
Denmark	9,452	7,866	5,550	5,646	6,605	0.70	16.99
Finland	3,131	2,817	2,755	2,880	3,841	0.41	33.37
Iceland	504	737	833	705	764	0.08	8.37
Ireland	2,858	2,993	2,760	3,185	4,709	0.50	47.85
Norway	2,818	2,535	2,309	2,510	3,303	0.35	31.59
Sweden	6,092	6,291	5,313	4,996	6,233	0.66	24.76
United Kingdom	52,436	51,922	48,005	55,083	64,449	6.82	17.00
SOUTHERN EUROPE	47,003	45,351	45,075	48,493	53,360	5.65	10.04
Greece	2,310	2,369	2,015	2,234	2,580	0.27	15.49
Italy	20,345	18,691	19,036	19,683	23,275	2.46	18.25
Malta	571	472	459	478	600	0.06	25.52
Portugal	7,650	8,023	8,766	9,665	8,670	0.92	-10.29
Slovenia	1,215	1,304	964	1,077	1,137	0.12	5.57
Spain	14,912	14,492	13,835	15,356	17,098	1.81	11.34
WESTERN EUROPE	619,886	580,404	607,628	647,410	642,408	68.01	-0.77
Austria	5,567	5,967	6,083	6,232	6,125	0.65	-1.72
Belgium	172,251	167,501	177,543	192,585	189,827	20.10	-1.43
France	114,001	118,447	124,862	131,112	125,726	13.31	-4.11
Germany	118,334	108,927	119,439	129,169	137,193	14.53	6.21
Netherlands	189,081	161,150	161,631	168,407	162,650	17.22	-3.42
Switzerland	20,652	18,412	18,070	19,905	20,887	2.21	4.93

433

Yearbook of Tourism Statistics, Data 2009 – 2013, 2015 Edition

LUXEMBOURG

4. Arrivals of non-resident tourists in all types of accommodation establishments, by country of residence

	2009	2010	2011	2012	2013	Market share 2013	% Change 2013-2012
EAST MEDITERRANEAN EUROPE	**3,043**	**3,508**	**3,969**	**6,708**	**13,448**	**1.42**	**100.48**
Cyprus	449	424	338	425	518	0.05	21.88
Turkey	2,594	3,084	3,631	6,283	12,930	1.37	105.79
OTHER EUROPE	**8,197**	**7,590**	**14,942**	**13,168**	**5,303**	**0.56**	**-59.73**
Other countries of Europe	8,197	7,590	14,942	13,168	5,303	0.56	-59.73
NOT SPECIFIED	**3,502**	**1,639**					
Other countries of the World	3,502	1,639					

Yearbook of Tourism Statistics, Data 2009 – 2013, 2015 Edition

LUXEMBOURG

5. Overnight stays of non-resident tourists in hotels and similar establishments, by country of residence

	2009	2010	2011	2012	2013	Market share 2013	% Change 2013-2012
TOTAL (*)	1,191,576	1,163,204	1,288,696	1,423,870	1,414,696	100.00	-0.64
AFRICA	8,016	7,856	22,001	29,145	11,267	0.80	-61.34
SOUTHERN AFRICA	1,337	2,656	3,071	3,239	2,207	0.16	-31.86
South Africa	1,337	2,656	3,071	3,239	2,207	0.16	-31.86
OTHER AFRICA	6,679	5,200	18,930	25,906	9,060	0.64	-65.03
Other countries of Africa	6,679	5,200	18,930	25,906	9,060	0.64	-65.03
AMERICAS	58,393	64,060	75,391	80,833	79,555	5.62	-1.58
NORTH AMERICA	48,641	50,618	46,982	54,059	63,189	4.47	16.89
Canada	8,780	7,928	8,039	10,745	9,973	0.70	-7.18
United States of America	39,861	42,690	38,943	43,314	53,216	3.76	22.86
SOUTH AMERICA	4,750	5,527	5,095	6,669	6,102	0.43	-8.50
Brazil	4,750	5,527	5,095	6,669	6,102	0.43	-8.50
OTHER AMERICAS	5,002	7,915	23,314	20,105	10,264	0.73	-48.95
Other countries of the Americas	5,002	7,915	23,314	20,105	10,264	0.73	-48.95
EAST ASIA AND THE PACIFIC	56,218	61,246	93,855	115,337	98,990	7.00	-14.17
NORTH-EAST ASIA	27,369	28,401	42,155	59,665	49,516	3.50	-17.01
China	19,863	19,392	32,377	48,117	38,175	2.70	-20.66
Japan	6,280	5,770	7,854	9,720	9,387	0.66	-3.43
Korea, Republic of	1,226	3,239	1,924	1,828	1,954	0.14	6.89
AUSTRALASIA	3,687	3,991	4,211	4,991	5,298	0.37	6.15
Australia	3,687	3,991	4,211	4,991	5,298	0.37	6.15
OTHER EAST ASIA AND THE PACIFIC	25,162	28,854	47,489	50,681	44,176	3.12	-12.84
Other countries of Asia	25,162	28,854	47,489	50,681	44,176	3.12	-12.84
EUROPE	1,064,704	1,026,366	1,097,449	1,198,555	1,224,884	86.58	2.20
CENTRAL/EASTERN EUROPE	49,797	54,477	53,058	63,340	75,757	5.36	19.60
Bulgaria	3,296	2,943	2,758	3,022	4,138	0.29	36.93
Czech Republic	7,541	6,567	4,627	6,994	6,751	0.48	-3.47
Estonia	1,105	1,103	1,162	1,119	2,172	0.15	94.10
Hungary	5,207	4,936	4,346	5,572	7,481	0.53	34.26
Latvia	1,206	1,141	970	1,267	1,925	0.14	51.93
Lithuania	1,481	1,511	1,469	2,477	2,664	0.19	7.55
Poland	10,196	12,786	13,063	14,611	16,197	1.14	10.85
Romania	5,655	6,795	7,043	7,218	9,956	0.70	37.93
Russian Federation	11,545	12,820	14,428	16,742	18,580	1.31	10.98
Slovakia	1,783	2,857	1,897	2,341	2,585	0.18	10.42
Ukraine	782	1,018	1,295	1,977	3,308	0.23	67.32
NORTHERN EUROPE	125,773	119,926	117,024	131,853	151,586	10.72	14.97
Denmark	13,205	11,695	7,228	6,958	9,929	0.70	42.70
Finland	5,081	4,908	5,150	5,096	6,421	0.45	26.00
Iceland	1,205	1,707	2,161	2,105	2,249	0.16	6.84
Ireland	5,883	6,450	7,116	6,833	9,856	0.70	44.24
Norway	3,970	3,923	4,456	4,254	5,587	0.39	31.34
Sweden	9,782	10,599	8,573	7,969	10,728	0.76	34.62
United Kingdom	86,647	80,644	82,340	98,638	106,816	7.55	8.29
SOUTHERN EUROPE	83,460	82,209	85,893	93,598	101,860	7.20	8.83
Greece	5,546	4,902	4,825	5,065	5,619	0.40	10.94
Italy	36,223	34,743	36,473	38,447	46,121	3.26	19.96
Malta	2,078	1,906	1,953	2,120	2,713	0.19	27.97
Portugal	13,610	14,380	16,727	17,433	16,089	1.14	-7.71
Slovenia	2,531	2,688	1,754	2,482	1,868	0.13	-24.74
Spain	23,472	23,590	24,161	28,051	29,450	2.08	4.99
WESTERN EUROPE	780,844	746,740	808,545	874,424	862,806	60.99	-1.33
Austria	11,642	11,656	12,064	12,124	10,990	0.78	-9.35
Belgium	249,866	241,942	277,712	293,433	284,690	20.12	-2.98
France	169,769	180,836	196,638	204,432	200,540	14.18	-1.90
Germany	172,075	161,798	178,605	200,925	211,938	14.98	5.48
Netherlands	143,938	120,316	113,156	129,181	120,280	8.50	-6.89
Switzerland	33,554	30,192	30,370	34,329	34,368	2.43	0.11

Yearbook of Tourism Statistics, Data 2009 – 2013, 2015 Edition

LUXEMBOURG

5. Overnight stays of non-resident tourists in hotels and similar establishments, by country of residence

	2009	2010	2011	2012	2013	Market share 2013	% Change 2013-2012
EAST MEDITERRANEAN EUROPE	**5,820**	**6,381**	**7,716**	**10,477**	**18,839**	**1.33**	**79.81**
Cyprus	1,230	1,013	1,372	1,865	1,913	0.14	2.57
Turkey	4,590	5,368	6,344	8,612	16,926	1.20	96.54
OTHER EUROPE	**19,010**	**16,633**	**25,213**	**24,863**	**14,036**	**0.99**	**-43.55**
Other countries of Europe	19,010	16,633	25,213	24,863	14,036	0.99	-43.55
NOT SPECIFIED	**4,245**	**3,676**					
Other countries of the World	4,245	3,676					

Yearbook of Tourism Statistics, Data 2009 – 2013, 2015 Edition

LUXEMBOURG

6. Overnight stays of non-resident tourists in all types of accommodation establishments, by country of residence

	2009	2010	2011	2012	2013	Market share 2013	% Change 2013-2012
TOTAL	2,073,813	1,717,130	2,064,093	2,296,608	2,316,471	100.00	0.86
AFRICA	8,572	8,071	22,800	30,503	12,086	0.52	-60.38
SOUTHERN AFRICA	1,423	2,694	3,326	3,635	2,469	0.11	-32.08
South Africa	1,423	2,694	3,326	3,635	2,469	0.11	-32.08
OTHER AFRICA	7,149	5,377	19,474	26,868	9,617	0.42	-64.21
Other countries of Africa	7,149	5,377	19,474	26,868	9,617	0.42	-64.21
AMERICAS	63,780	67,259	79,840	86,513	85,995	3.71	-0.60
NORTH AMERICA	52,651	53,059	50,008	57,903	67,235	2.90	16.12
Canada	9,891	8,353	8,860	11,592	11,005	0.48	-5.06
United States of America	42,760	44,706	41,148	46,311	56,230	2.43	21.42
SOUTH AMERICA	5,512	5,801	5,504	7,439	6,896	0.30	-7.30
Brazil	5,512	5,801	5,504	7,439	6,896	0.30	-7.30
OTHER AMERICAS	5,617	8,399	24,328	21,171	11,864	0.51	-43.96
Other countries of the Americas	5,617	8,399	24,328	21,171	11,864	0.51	-43.96
EAST ASIA AND THE PACIFIC	61,095	63,983	99,411	122,276	105,906	4.57	-13.39
NORTH-EAST ASIA	29,513	29,617	44,874	63,360	53,392	2.30	-15.73
China	20,679	19,874	33,516	50,497	40,763	1.76	-19.28
Japan	6,912	6,092	8,407	10,176	9,929	0.43	-2.43
Korea, Republic of	1,922	3,651	2,951	2,687	2,700	0.12	0.48
AUSTRALASIA	4,925	4,669	5,397	6,161	6,281	0.27	1.95
Australia	4,925	4,669	5,397	6,161	6,281	0.27	1.95
OTHER EAST ASIA AND THE PACIFIC	26,657	29,697	49,140	52,755	46,233	2.00	-12.36
Other countries of Asia	26,657	29,697	49,140	52,755	46,233	2.00	-12.36
EUROPE	1,933,744	1,573,840	1,862,042	2,057,316	2,112,484	91.19	2.68
CENTRAL/EASTERN EUROPE	57,424	58,302	61,280	79,394	84,862	3.66	6.89
Bulgaria	3,672	3,047	3,023	3,249	4,350	0.19	33.89
Czech Republic	8,570	7,281	5,727	8,328	7,415	0.32	-10.96
Estonia	1,140	1,114	1,305	1,230	3,061	0.13	148.86
Hungary	5,960	5,415	5,215	6,154	8,086	0.35	31.39
Latvia	1,216	1,319	1,768	1,347	1,986	0.09	47.44
Lithuania	1,592	1,705	1,794	2,880	2,931	0.13	1.77
Poland	13,403	14,089	16,213	26,263	19,565	0.84	-25.50
Romania	6,453	7,214	7,568	7,894	11,639	0.50	47.44
Russian Federation	12,260	13,067	14,962	17,395	19,382	0.84	11.42
Slovakia	2,362	3,025	2,345	2,669	2,999	0.13	12.36
Ukraine	796	1,026	1,360	1,985	3,448	0.15	73.70
NORTHERN EUROPE	157,494	143,376	145,982	157,376	175,622	7.58	11.59
Denmark	18,830	14,415	11,684	11,415	14,103	0.61	23.55
Finland	6,138	5,457	6,290	5,872	7,927	0.34	35.00
Iceland	1,347	1,811	2,344	2,156	2,361	0.10	9.51
Ireland	7,197	7,727	8,142	7,929	10,470	0.45	32.05
Norway	5,322	4,335	4,954	5,386	6,240	0.27	15.86
Sweden	11,139	11,267	9,918	8,955	11,802	0.51	31.79
United Kingdom	107,521	98,364	102,650	115,663	122,719	5.30	6.10
SOUTHERN EUROPE	92,853	87,590	95,746	105,925	113,462	4.90	7.12
Greece	5,756	5,111	5,048	5,439	6,059	0.26	11.40
Italy	39,770	36,700	40,117	42,051	50,165	2.17	19.30
Malta	2,082	1,913	1,959	2,122	2,719	0.12	28.13
Portugal	15,692	15,528	19,077	21,956	19,349	0.84	-11.87
Slovenia	3,108	3,191	2,098	2,883	2,357	0.10	-18.24
Spain	26,445	25,147	27,447	31,474	32,813	1.42	4.25
WESTERN EUROPE	1,600,560	1,261,046	1,520,436	1,678,111	1,703,941	73.56	1.54
Austria	12,777	12,722	13,057	13,881	12,621	0.54	-9.08
Belgium	378,659	331,401	395,668	451,833	451,206	19.48	-0.14
France	197,235	202,414	221,887	227,987	226,744	9.79	-0.55
Germany	239,284	208,162	241,641	273,328	295,698	12.77	8.18
Netherlands	736,007	474,036	614,304	673,515	679,257	29.32	0.85
Switzerland	36,598	32,311	33,879	37,567	38,415	1.66	2.26

Yearbook of Tourism Statistics, Data 2009 – 2013, 2015 Edition

LUXEMBOURG

6. Overnight stays of non-resident tourists in all types of accommodation establishments, by country of residence

	2009	2010	2011	2012	2013	Market share 2013	% Change 2013-2012
EAST MEDITERRANEAN EUROPE	**5,928**	**6,418**	**7,845**	**10,772**	**19,153**	**0.83**	**77.80**
Cyprus	1,254	1,019	1,377	1,907	1,934	0.08	1.42
Turkey	4,674	5,399	6,468	8,865	17,219	0.74	94.24
OTHER EUROPE	**19,485**	**17,108**	**30,753**	**25,738**	**15,444**	**0.67**	**-40.00**
Other countries of Europe	19,485	17,108	30,753	25,738	15,444	0.67	-40.00
NOT SPECIFIED	**6,622**	**3,977**					
Other countries of the World	6,622	3,977					

Yearbook of Tourism Statistics, Data 2009 – 2013, 2015 Edition

MACAO, CHINA

2. Arrivals of non-resident visitors at national borders, by nationality

		2009	2010	2011	2012	2013	Market share 2013	% Change 2013-2012
TOTAL	(*)	21,752,751	24,965,411	28,002,279	28,082,292	29,324,822	100.00	4.42
AFRICA		16,702	21,736	25,161	27,945	31,317	0.11	12.07
EAST AFRICA		2,015	2,932	3,950	4,509	4,936	0.02	9.47
Burundi		33	31	39	74	187	0.00	152.70
Ethiopia		61	99	101	180	259	0.00	43.89
Kenya		181	263	423	579	1,027	0.00	77.37
Madagascar		219	339	342	343	392	0.00	14.29
Malawi		4	12	32	22	6	0.00	-72.73
Mauritius		549	705	672	570	570	0.00	
Mozambique		364	435	321	442	441	0.00	-0.23
Rwanda		31	36	97	114	124	0.00	8.77
Seychelles		126	163	164	169	242	0.00	43.20
Somalia		19	17	31	34	68	0.00	100.00
Uganda		84	369	1,156	1,262	799	0.00	-36.69
United Republic of Tanzania		247	320	439	504	642	0.00	27.38
Zambia		36	53	54	69	72	0.00	4.35
Zimbabwe		61	90	79	147	107	0.00	-27.21
CENTRAL AFRICA		2,517	3,138	4,236	5,076	5,347	0.02	5.34
Angola		1,029	1,329	1,673	1,756	1,957	0.01	11.45
Cameroon		611	411	330	374	447	0.00	19.52
Congo		189	223	355	490	636	0.00	29.80
Democratic Republic of the Congo		636	1,099	1,808	2,378	2,150	0.01	-9.59
Equatorial Guinea		6	11	22	23	22	0.00	-4.35
Gabon		30	35	19	31	88	0.00	183.87
Sao Tome and Principe		16	30	29	24	47	0.00	95.83
NORTH AFRICA		1,177	1,300	1,310	1,639	1,863	0.01	13.67
Algeria		235	235	203	396	303	0.00	-23.48
Morocco		421	482	527	530	740	0.00	39.62
Sudan		136	151	281	377	397	0.00	5.31
Tunisia		385	432	299	336	423	0.00	25.89
SOUTHERN AFRICA		4,287	4,675	5,301	4,743	5,215	0.02	9.95
Botswana		17	12	39	21	179	0.00	752.38
Lesotho		7	3	5	10	17	0.00	70.00
Namibia		28	32	60	41	35	0.00	-14.63
South Africa		4,231	4,624	5,186	4,663	4,976	0.02	6.71
Swaziland		4	4	11	8	8	0.00	
WEST AFRICA		6,366	7,544	7,891	8,103	10,139	0.03	25.13
Benin		47	92	183	184	641	0.00	248.37
Burkina Faso		48	72	80	47	90	0.00	91.49
Cabo Verde		167	221	198	250	299	0.00	19.60
Côte d'Ivoire		159	156	146	218	287	0.00	31.65
Gambia		136	125	159	171	146	0.00	-14.62
Ghana		309	453	396	399	412	0.00	3.26
Guinea		385	607	915	1,100	1,197	0.00	8.82
Guinea-Bissau		265	170	191	160	223	0.00	39.38
Liberia		58	64	205	136	105	0.00	-22.79
Mali		1,969	3,310	3,969	3,427	3,636	0.01	6.10
Mauritania		40	38	68	49	75	0.00	53.06
Niger		212	226	392	603	1,262	0.00	109.29
Nigeria		2,061	1,371	201	224	236	0.00	5.36
Senegal		200	276	374	511	754	0.00	47.55
Sierra Leone		72	49	91	203	199	0.00	-1.97
Togo		238	314	323	421	577	0.00	37.05
OTHER AFRICA		340	2,147	2,473	3,875	3,817	0.01	-1.50
Other countries of Africa		340	2,147	2,473	3,875	3,817	0.01	-1.50
AMERICAS		278,788	297,154	310,564	306,528	289,944	0.99	-5.41
CARIBBEAN		760	1,003	1,015	1,114	1,497	0.01	34.38
Antigua and Barbuda		6	17	8	5	8	0.00	60.00
Bahamas		24	15	34	43	29	0.00	-32.56

Yearbook of Tourism Statistics, Data 2009 – 2013, 2015 Edition

MACAO, CHINA

2. Arrivals of non-resident visitors at national borders, by nationality

	2009	2010	2011	2012	2013	Market share 2013	% Change 2013-2012
Barbados	20	20	11	22	29	0.00	31.82
British Virgin Islands					1	0.00	
Cuba	58	80	51	60	266	0.00	343.33
Dominica	40	56	33	63	47	0.00	-25.40
Dominican Republic	249	321	349	373	376	0.00	0.80
Grenada	6	7	19	10	90	0.00	800.00
Haiti	12	15	16	15	73	0.00	386.67
Jamaica	165	189	209	194	163	0.00	-15.98
Puerto Rico	7	3	1	4	2	0.00	-50.00
Saint Kitts and Nevis	49	82	118	160	228	0.00	42.50
Saint Lucia	3	5	9	4	2	0.00	-50.00
Saint Vincent and the Grenadines	7	9	1	2	2	0.00	
Trinidad and Tobago	114	184	156	159	181	0.00	13.84
CENTRAL AMERICA	**2,409**	**2,676**	**2,755**	**2,719**	**3,268**	**0.01**	**20.19**
Belize	427	497	543	542	750	0.00	38.38
Costa Rica	786	842	869	737	966	0.00	31.07
El Salvador	56	64	82	49	104	0.00	112.24
Guatemala	218	197	181	247	296	0.00	19.84
Honduras	150	150	174	226	297	0.00	31.42
Nicaragua	15	28	22	39	30	0.00	-23.08
Panama	757	898	884	879	825	0.00	-6.14
NORTH AMERICA	**258,057**	**272,567**	**281,199**	**277,284**	**259,307**	**0.88**	**-6.48**
Canada	74,791	79,152	79,816	83,442	74,159	0.25	-11.13
Mexico	3,679	5,145	5,368	5,182	5,749	0.02	10.94
United States of America	179,587	188,270	196,015	188,660	179,399	0.61	-4.91
SOUTH AMERICA	**17,562**	**20,908**	**25,594**	**25,411**	**25,872**	**0.09**	**1.81**
Argentina	1,335	1,675	1,544	1,718	2,189	0.01	27.42
Bolivia	205	186	204	177	272	0.00	53.67
Brazil	7,525	8,347	10,501	10,288	9,782	0.03	-4.92
Chile	939	1,142	1,329	1,371	1,493	0.01	8.90
Colombia	1,939	2,309	3,567	3,854	3,850	0.01	-0.10
Ecuador	445	605	682	819	746	0.00	-8.91
Guyana	103	95	98	87	103	0.00	18.39
Paraguay	65	81	86	56	76	0.00	35.71
Peru	1,383	1,340	1,379	1,471	1,599	0.01	8.70
Suriname	152	177	199	186	167	0.00	-10.22
Uruguay	153	217	167	152	208	0.00	36.84
Venezuela	3,318	4,734	5,838	5,232	5,387	0.02	2.96
OTHER AMERICAS			1				
Other countries of the Americas			1				
EAST ASIA AND THE PACIFIC	**21,077,816**	**24,193,292**	**27,206,644**	**27,293,574**	**28,528,455**	**97.28**	**4.52**
NORTH-EAST ASIA	**19,598,355**	**22,740,428**	**25,762,927**	**25,903,793**	**27,169,635**	**92.65**	**4.89**
China	10,988,796	13,228,418	16,161,927	16,900,964	18,631,640	63.54	10.24
Hong Kong, China	6,727,020	7,465,961	7,582,998	7,081,137	6,764,211	23.07	-4.48
Japan	379,346	413,529	396,050	396,010	290,462	0.99	-26.65
Korea, Dem. People's Republic of	1,038	1,161	1,167	1,318	1,793	0.01	36.04
Korea, Republic of	204,832	331,786	398,832	444,786	473,965	1.62	6.56
Mongolia	4,255	5,183	6,450	7,157	7,023	0.02	-1.87
Taiwan, Province of China	1,293,068	1,294,390	1,215,503	1,072,421	1,000,541	3.41	-6.70
SOUTH-EAST ASIA	**1,344,190**	**1,324,534**	**1,314,196**	**1,257,800**	**1,230,787**	**4.20**	**-2.15**
Brunei Darussalam	1,940	1,829	1,816	1,772	1,559	0.01	-12.02
Cambodia	3,854	4,359	4,467	4,367	4,416	0.02	1.12
Indonesia	191,494	208,468	220,454	209,110	208,378	0.71	-0.35
Lao People's Democratic Republic	977	843	1,196	1,292	1,245	0.00	-3.64
Malaysia	332,551	338,042	324,503	301,788	290,941	0.99	-3.59
Myanmar	4,081	4,920	4,500	4,573	4,931	0.02	7.83
Philippines	247,573	247,803	268,713	283,862	273,924	0.93	-3.50
Singapore	256,556	257,213	280,588	205,688	189,617	0.65	-7.81
Thailand	242,592	212,441	196,362	231,293	238,497	0.81	3.11

Yearbook of Tourism Statistics, Data 2009 – 2013, 2015 Edition

MACAO, CHINA

2. Arrivals of non-resident visitors at national borders, by nationality

	2009	2010	2011	2012	2013	Market share 2013	% Change 2013-2012
Timor-Leste	144	151	174	151	162	0.00	7.28
Viet Nam	62,428	48,465	11,423	13,904	17,117	0.06	23.11
AUSTRALASIA	**134,337**	**126,360**	**126,717**	**127,678**	**123,937**	**0.42**	**-2.93**
Australia	120,449	111,777	111,823	113,287	109,541	0.37	-3.31
New Zealand	13,888	14,583	14,894	14,391	14,396	0.05	0.03
MELANESIA	**576**	**839**	**809**	**908**	**937**	**0.00**	**3.19**
Fiji	306	465	366	379	494	0.00	30.34
Papua New Guinea	91	80	101	125	133	0.00	6.40
Solomon Islands	126	186	251	272	265	0.00	-2.57
Vanuatu	53	108	91	132	45	0.00	-65.91
MICRONESIA	**202**	**153**	**208**	**334**	**247**	**0.00**	**-26.05**
Kiribati	3	4	7	24	25	0.00	4.17
Marshall Islands	46	46	112	240	190	0.00	-20.83
Micronesia, Federated States of	1	28	7	4	1	0.00	-75.00
Nauru	152	75	74	62	30	0.00	-51.61
Palau			8	4	1	0.00	-75.00
POLYNESIA	**156**	**186**	**232**	**238**	**203**	**0.00**	**-14.71**
Samoa	9	19	9	24	4	0.00	-83.33
Tonga	137	163	219	211	194	0.00	-8.06
Tuvalu	10	4	4	3	5	0.00	66.67
OTHER EAST ASIA AND THE PACIFIC		**792**	**1,555**	**2,823**	**2,709**	**0.01**	**-4.04**
Other countries of Asia		792	1,555	2,823	2,709	0.01	-4.04
EUROPE	**253,927**	**264,408**	**270,531**	**280,551**	**290,405**	**0.99**	**3.51**
CENTRAL/EASTERN EUROPE	**21,224**	**27,315**	**32,394**	**43,997**	**48,749**	**0.17**	**10.80**
Belarus	282	363	507	628	829	0.00	32.01
Bulgaria	779	800	888	1,136	1,136	0.00	
Czech Republic/Slovakia	1,895	1,552	1,946	1,738	1,762	0.01	1.38
Estonia	604	540	407	645	549	0.00	-14.88
Hungary	1,544	2,141	1,686	1,732	1,711	0.01	-1.21
Latvia	337	332	338	412	697	0.00	69.17
Lithuania	373	406	444	516	465	0.00	-9.88
Poland	3,872	4,515	4,847	4,255	4,744	0.02	11.49
Republic of Moldova	58	100	79	147	163	0.00	10.88
Romania	1,978	2,465	2,167	2,313	2,285	0.01	-1.21
Russian Federation	7,809	11,698	16,511	26,855	30,533	0.10	13.70
Slovakia	838	937	758	1,210	983	0.00	-18.76
Ukraine	855	1,466	1,816	2,410	2,892	0.01	20.00
NORTHERN EUROPE	**84,226**	**80,141**	**81,305**	**79,245**	**80,976**	**0.28**	**2.18**
Denmark	3,556	3,434	3,599	3,260	3,340	0.01	2.45
Faeroe Islands					2	0.00	
Finland	4,474	3,807	3,316	3,411	3,439	0.01	0.82
Iceland	166	167	109	156	156	0.00	
Ireland	3,550	3,256	3,359	3,524	3,747	0.01	6.33
Norway	2,285	2,449	2,442	2,491	2,435	0.01	-2.25
Sweden	6,698	6,569	6,825	6,915	6,525	0.02	-5.64
United Kingdom	63,497	60,459	61,655	59,488	61,332	0.21	3.10
SOUTHERN EUROPE	**34,892**	**37,910**	**37,540**	**38,696**	**41,263**	**0.14**	**6.63**
Albania	87	122	90	80	100	0.00	25.00
Andorra	19	37	34	22	38	0.00	72.73
Bosnia and Herzegovina	25	50	52	44	61	0.00	38.64
Croatia	373	404	354	527	570	0.00	8.16
Greece	1,048	1,028	908	1,094	1,079	0.00	-1.37
Holy See	9	4	1	2			
Italy	12,223	13,459	13,119	13,003	13,479	0.05	3.66
Malta	78	64	98	127	89	0.00	-29.92
Montenegro	6	24	22	35	40	0.00	14.29
Portugal	12,437	13,577	13,339	14,496	16,033	0.05	10.60
San Marino	10	16	7	16	3	0.00	-81.25

441

Yearbook of Tourism Statistics, Data 2009 – 2013, 2015 Edition

MACAO, CHINA

2. Arrivals of non-resident visitors at national borders, by nationality

	2009	2010	2011	2012	2013	Market share 2013	% Change 2013-2012
Serbia	251	272	422	495	585	0.00	18.18
Slovenia	329	329	303	453	307	0.00	-32.23
Spain	7,919	8,449	8,690	8,198	8,788	0.03	7.20
TFYR of Macedonia	71	75	101	104	91	0.00	-12.50
Yugoslavia, SFR (former)	7						
WESTERN EUROPE	**95,369**	**99,079**	**100,433**	**100,777**	**101,916**	**0.35**	**1.13**
Austria	4,233	4,482	4,095	4,378	4,237	0.01	-3.22
Belgium	4,497	4,793	4,681	4,261	4,779	0.02	12.16
France	39,158	41,420	42,662	42,480	43,467	0.15	2.32
Germany	28,176	28,820	28,800	29,310	29,696	0.10	1.32
Liechtenstein	40	41	57	39	53	0.00	35.90
Luxembourg	203	277	254	239	276	0.00	15.48
Monaco	19	24	17	32	46	0.00	43.75
Netherlands	12,897	12,667	12,776	12,519	11,709	0.04	-6.47
Switzerland	6,146	6,555	7,091	7,519	7,653	0.03	1.78
EAST MEDITERRANEAN EUROPE	**16,638**	**19,963**	**18,859**	**17,836**	**17,499**	**0.06**	**-1.89**
Cyprus	219	228	238	204	281	0.00	37.75
Israel	14,021	16,721	14,694	13,551	12,808	0.04	-5.48
Turkey	2,398	3,014	3,927	4,081	4,410	0.02	8.06
OTHER EUROPE	**1,578**				**2**	**0.00**	
Other countries of Europe	1,578				2	0.00	
MIDDLE EAST	**7,549**	**9,844**	**12,158**	**14,144**	**14,939**	**0.05**	**5.62**
Bahrain	123	205	164	200	202	0.00	1.00
Egypt	927	1,251	1,563	1,875	1,991	0.01	6.19
Iraq	136	209	217	301	236	0.00	-21.59
Jordan	453	656	835	884	873	0.00	-1.24
Kuwait	654	1,041	1,464	1,623	1,905	0.01	17.38
Lebanon	1,501	1,890	2,393	2,634	2,493	0.01	-5.35
Libya	410	320	325	666	993	0.00	49.10
Oman	104	131	148	81	126	0.00	55.56
Palestine	185	268	186	209	163	0.00	-22.01
Qatar	149	255	266	284	471	0.00	65.85
Saudi Arabia	1,405	1,869	2,324	2,772	3,250	0.01	17.24
Syrian Arab Republic	699	766	1,049	1,135	254	0.00	-77.62
United Arab Emirates	560	652	797	914	1,362	0.00	49.02
Yemen	243	331	427	566	620	0.00	9.54
SOUTH ASIA	**117,933**	**178,977**	**177,221**	**159,550**	**169,762**	**0.58**	**6.40**
Afghanistan	277	162	157	237	260	0.00	9.70
Bangladesh	1,673	1,023	272	294	1,190	0.00	304.76
Bhutan	126	116	205	198	196	0.00	-1.01
India	107,575	169,116	169,682	150,838	159,907	0.55	6.01
Iran, Islamic Republic of	1,333	3,673	3,208	3,761	3,696	0.01	-1.73
Maldives	130	157	135	111	173	0.00	55.86
Nepal	2,885	2,109	2,019	2,439	2,405	0.01	-1.39
Pakistan	3,129	2,042	975	1,052	1,218	0.00	15.78
Sri Lanka	805	579	568	620	717	0.00	15.65
NOT SPECIFIED	**36**						
Other countries of the World	36						

442

MACAO, CHINA

2. Arrivals of non-resident visitors at national borders, by country of residence

		2009	2010	2011	2012	2013	Market share 2013	% Change 2013-2012
TOTAL	(*)	**21,752,751**	**24,965,411**	**28,002,279**	**28,082,292**	**29,324,822**	**100.00**	**4.42**
AFRICA		**16,803**	**22,845**	**24,864**	**26,990**	**29,429**	**0.10**	**9.04**
EAST AFRICA		**2,019**	**2,939**	**3,949**	**4,512**	**4,801**	**0.02**	**6.41**
Burundi		33	34	39	76	103	0.00	35.53
Ethiopia		61	99	101	177	257	0.00	45.20
Kenya		182	261	424	578	1,024	0.00	77.16
Madagascar		219	341	342	344	392	0.00	13.95
Malawi		4	12	31	22	6	0.00	-72.73
Mauritius		548	706	673	569	569	0.00	
Mozambique		364	435	322	442	440	0.00	-0.45
Reunion				1	1			
Rwanda		31	36	98	114	124	0.00	8.77
Seychelles		126	163	164	169	240	0.00	42.01
Somalia		22	19	28	36	68	0.00	88.89
Uganda		84	372	1,155	1,264	785	0.00	-37.90
United Republic of Tanzania		247	320	440	505	644	0.00	27.52
Zambia		36	53	55	69	42	0.00	-39.13
Zimbabwe		62	88	76	146	107	0.00	-26.71
CENTRAL AFRICA		**2,521**	**3,140**	**4,245**	**5,077**	**5,052**	**0.02**	**-0.49**
Angola		1,031	1,330	1,674	1,755	1,945	0.01	10.83
Cameroon		611	405	332	372	387	0.00	4.03
Congo		189	224	354	489	508	0.00	3.89
Democratic Republic of the Congo		637	1,099	1,808	2,376	2,120	0.01	-10.77
Equatorial Guinea		6	10	23	23	18	0.00	-21.74
Gabon		31	42	25	38	27	0.00	-28.95
Sao Tome and Principe		16	30	29	24	47	0.00	95.83
NORTH AFRICA		**1,555**	**2,882**	**1,510**	**1,927**	**1,857**	**0.01**	**-3.63**
Algeria		235	235	202	397	301	0.00	-24.18
Morocco		423	482	526	531	741	0.00	39.55
Sudan		135	150	282	375	395	0.00	5.33
Tunisia		762	2,015	500	624	420	0.00	-32.69
SOUTHERN AFRICA		**4,285**	**4,675**	**5,302**	**4,749**	**5,053**	**0.02**	**6.40**
Botswana		18	11	40	22	23	0.00	4.55
Lesotho		7	4	5	10	12	0.00	20.00
Namibia		28	32	60	41	30	0.00	-26.83
South Africa		4,228	4,624	5,185	4,667	4,981	0.02	6.73
Swaziland		4	4	12	9	7	0.00	-22.22
WEST AFRICA		**6,375**	**7,541**	**7,880**	**8,092**	**9,590**	**0.03**	**18.51**
Benin		49	91	183	187	279	0.00	49.20
Burkina Faso		48	72	80	47	86	0.00	82.98
Cabo Verde		167	213	190	242	226	0.00	-6.61
Côte d'Ivoire		159	157	149	216	286	0.00	32.41
Gambia		135	125	159	171	145	0.00	-15.20
Ghana		308	454	393	399	349	0.00	-12.53
Guinea		384	608	916	1,099	1,189	0.00	8.19
Guinea-Bissau		267	170	189	159	206	0.00	29.56
Liberia		59	64	205	137	107	0.00	-21.90
Mali		1,971	3,309	3,968	3,429	3,637	0.01	6.07
Mauritania		38	37	67	47	74	0.00	57.45
Niger		211	227	393	603	1,249	0.00	107.13
Nigeria		2,061	1,368	195	220	237	0.00	7.73
Saint Helena		8	8	4	2	1	0.00	-50.00
Senegal		200	276	374	511	750	0.00	46.77
Sierra Leone		72	49	92	203	198	0.00	-2.46
Togo		238	313	323	420	571	0.00	35.95
OTHER AFRICA		**48**	**1,668**	**1,978**	**2,633**	**3,076**	**0.01**	**16.82**
Other countries of Africa		48	1,668	1,978	2,633	3,076	0.01	16.82

Yearbook of Tourism Statistics, Data 2009 – 2013, 2015 Edition

MACAO, CHINA

2. Arrivals of non-resident visitors at national borders, by country of residence

	2009	2010	2011	2012	2013	Market share 2013	% Change 2013-2012
AMERICAS	278,661	297,137	310,608	306,521	288,691	0.98	-5.82
CARIBBEAN	837	1,091	1,050	1,152	1,239	0.00	7.55
Antigua and Barbuda	7	17	8	5	8	0.00	60.00
Aruba				1			
Bahamas	23	18	36	49	35	0.00	-28.57
Barbados	21	20	10	21	28	0.00	33.33
Bermuda	11	2	3	12	4	0.00	-66.67
Cayman Islands	11	15	9	11	2	0.00	-81.82
Cuba	59	79	52	60	135	0.00	125.00
Curaçao	1		2				
Dominica	68	87	50	72	48	0.00	-33.33
Dominican Republic	252	326	349	373	373	0.00	
Grenada	6	7	18	10	10	0.00	
Guadeloupe		2			1	0.00	
Haiti	10	14	16	15	17	0.00	13.33
Jamaica	168	194	209	194	163	0.00	-15.98
Martinique	4	1			1	0.00	
Netherlands Antilles	2	1					
Puerto Rico	3	2	2		2	0.00	
Saint Kitts and Nevis	62	101	118	164	226	0.00	37.80
Saint Lucia	4	4	9	4	3	0.00	-25.00
Saint Vincent and the Grenadines	6	9	2	2	2	0.00	
Sint Maarten	5	4	1				
Trinidad and Tobago	114	186	156	159	178	0.00	11.95
Turks and Caicos Islands		1			3	0.00	
United States Virgin Islands		1					
CENTRAL AMERICA	2,418	2,695	2,755	2,717	2,851	0.01	4.93
Belize	431	509	542	542	746	0.00	37.64
Costa Rica	788	846	869	738	731	0.00	-0.95
El Salvador	57	64	84	48	48	0.00	
Guatemala	219	196	181	247	241	0.00	-2.43
Honduras	151	152	173	226	232	0.00	2.65
Nicaragua	15	28	22	39	30	0.00	-23.08
Panama	757	900	884	877	823	0.00	-6.16
NORTH AMERICA	257,923	272,547	281,249	277,372	259,418	0.88	-6.47
Canada	74,744	79,148	79,818	83,459	74,213	0.25	-11.08
Greenland	3						
Mexico	3,676	5,145	5,364	5,183	5,678	0.02	9.55
Saint Pierre and Miquelon			2				
United States of America	179,500	188,254	196,065	188,730	179,527	0.61	-4.88
SOUTH AMERICA	17,483	20,804	25,554	25,280	25,183	0.09	-0.38
Argentina	1,217	1,546	1,506	1,590	1,659	0.01	4.34
Bolivia	205	187	203	175	268	0.00	53.14
Brazil	7,521	8,346	10,505	10,283	9,785	0.03	-4.84
Chile	946	1,147	1,327	1,371	1,488	0.01	8.53
Colombia	1,936	2,302	3,564	3,854	3,848	0.01	-0.16
Ecuador	448	605	682	819	672	0.00	-17.95
Falkland Islands, Malvinas	2			1			
French Guiana		1		1	2	0.00	100.00
Guyana	104	96	98	87	97	0.00	11.49
Paraguay	67	82	85	55	75	0.00	36.36
Peru	1,389	1,341	1,376	1,473	1,543	0.01	4.75
Suriname	155	177	199	185	165	0.00	-10.81
Uruguay	164	225	174	158	219	0.00	38.61
Venezuela	3,329	4,749	5,835	5,228	5,362	0.02	2.56
EAST ASIA AND THE PACIFIC	21,078,253	24,192,340	27,206,922	27,294,670	28,532,561	97.30	4.54
NORTH-EAST ASIA	19,599,207	22,739,551	25,763,275	25,904,934	27,173,120	92.66	4.90

Yearbook of Tourism Statistics, Data 2009 – 2013, 2015 Edition

MACAO, CHINA

2. Arrivals of non-resident visitors at national borders, by country of residence

	2009	2010	2011	2012	2013	Market share 2013	% Change 2013-2012
China	10,989,533	13,229,058	16,162,747	16,902,499	18,632,207	63.54	10.23
Hong Kong, China	6,727,822	7,466,139	7,582,923	7,081,153	6,766,044	23.07	-4.45
Japan	379,241	413,507	396,023	395,989	290,622	0.99	-26.61
Korea, Dem. People's Republic of	1,038	1,160	1,167	1,318	1,781	0.01	35.13
Korea, Republic of	204,767	331,768	398,807	444,773	474,269	1.62	6.63
Mongolia	4,255	5,185	6,446	7,150	7,008	0.02	-1.99
Taiwan, Province of China	1,292,551	1,292,734	1,215,162	1,072,052	1,001,189	3.41	-6.61
SOUTH-EAST ASIA	**1,343,831**	**1,324,445**	**1,314,107**	**1,257,757**	**1,231,428**	**4.20**	**-2.09**
Brunei Darussalam	1,943	1,842	1,819	1,786	1,566	0.01	-12.32
Cambodia	3,849	4,348	4,431	4,357	4,332	0.01	-0.57
Indonesia	191,425	208,440	220,423	209,084	208,481	0.71	-0.29
Lao People's Democratic Republic	976	840	1,189	1,286	1,244	0.00	-3.27
Malaysia	332,529	338,058	324,509	301,802	291,136	0.99	-3.53
Myanmar	4,083	4,922	4,481	4,552	4,913	0.02	7.93
Philippines	247,459	247,770	268,710	283,881	274,103	0.93	-3.44
Singapore	256,520	257,196	280,602	205,692	189,751	0.65	-7.75
Thailand	242,514	212,442	196,375	231,295	238,635	0.81	3.17
Timor-Leste	145	150	174	154	162	0.00	5.19
Viet Nam	62,388	48,437	11,394	13,868	17,105	0.06	23.34
AUSTRALASIA	**134,275**	**126,353**	**126,724**	**127,694**	**123,967**	**0.42**	**-2.92**
Australia	120,395	111,771	111,827	113,295	109,566	0.37	-3.29
New Zealand	13,880	14,582	14,897	14,399	14,401	0.05	0.01
MELANESIA	**580**	**849**	**813**	**908**	**930**	**0.00**	**2.42**
Fiji	306	472	367	379	493	0.00	30.08
New Caledonia	2		1				
Papua New Guinea	92	80	101	126	128	0.00	1.59
Solomon Islands	127	189	253	272	265	0.00	-2.57
Vanuatu	53	108	91	131	44	0.00	-66.41
MICRONESIA	**203**	**156**	**210**	**323**	**217**	**0.00**	**-32.82**
Kiribati	3	3	9	21	15	0.00	-28.57
Marshall Islands	44	47	111	232	174	0.00	-25.00
Micronesia, Federated States of	1	28	7	4	1	0.00	-75.00
Nauru	154	78	74	62	26	0.00	-58.06
Northern Mariana Islands	1		1				
Palau			8	4	1	0.00	-75.00
POLYNESIA	**157**	**199**	**236**	**240**	**199**	**0.00**	**-17.08**
Samoa	9	19	9	24	4	0.00	-83.33
Tonga	138	175	223	213	192	0.00	-9.86
Tuvalu	10	4	4	3	3	0.00	
Wallis and Futuna Islands		1					
OTHER EAST ASIA AND THE PACIFIC		**787**	**1,557**	**2,814**	**2,700**	**0.01**	**-4.05**
Other countries of Asia		787	1,557	2,814	2,700	0.01	-4.05
EUROPE	**253,816**	**264,431**	**270,603**	**280,524**	**290,344**	**0.99**	**3.50**
CENTRAL/EASTERN EUROPE	**21,239**	**27,356**	**32,414**	**43,997**	**48,753**	**0.17**	**10.81**
Belarus	282	361	508	628	827	0.00	31.69
Bulgaria	778	803	889	1,136	1,136	0.00	
Czech Republic	1,895	1,552	1,945	1,740	1,764	0.01	1.38
Estonia	608	547	407	646	549	0.00	-15.02
Hungary	1,544	2,139	1,686	1,734	1,712	0.01	-1.27
Latvia	348	353	339	412	698	0.00	69.42
Lithuania	373	406	444	516	466	0.00	-9.69
Poland	3,878	4,522	4,854	4,258	4,750	0.02	11.55
Republic of Moldova	57	101	80	147	163	0.00	10.88
Romania	1,978	2,467	2,172	2,313	2,288	0.01	-1.08
Russian Federation	7,806	11,702	16,512	26,844	30,528	0.10	13.72
Slovakia	837	938	758	1,210	982	0.00	-18.84
Ukraine	855	1,465	1,820	2,413	2,890	0.01	19.77
NORTHERN EUROPE	**84,114**	**80,133**	**81,311**	**79,230**	**81,031**	**0.28**	**2.27**

445

MACAO, CHINA

2. Arrivals of non-resident visitors at national borders, by country of residence

	2009	2010	2011	2012	2013	Market share 2013	% Change 2013-2012
Denmark	3,560	3,436	3,605	3,264	3,345	0.01	2.48
Faeroe Islands					2	0.00	
Finland	4,475	3,808	3,317	3,412	3,441	0.01	0.85
Iceland	160	167	104	149	188	0.00	26.17
Ireland	3,551	3,257	3,360	3,527	3,749	0.01	6.29
Norway	2,286	2,452	2,450	2,492	2,445	0.01	-1.89
Sweden	6,698	6,574	6,838	6,918	6,531	0.02	-5.59
United Kingdom	63,384	60,439	61,637	59,468	61,330	0.21	3.13
SOUTHERN EUROPE	**34,890**	**37,912**	**37,547**	**38,685**	**41,158**	**0.14**	**6.39**
Albania	99	122	91	78	99	0.00	26.92
Andorra	12	30	29	18	26	0.00	44.44
Bosnia and Herzegovina	26	50	52	45	61	0.00	35.56
Croatia	373	404	353	529	571	0.00	7.94
Gibraltar	1	1			2	0.00	
Greece	1,049	1,028	910	1,095	1,037	0.00	-5.30
Holy See	10	4	1	2			
Italy	12,229	13,461	13,121	13,004	13,487	0.05	3.71
Malta	80	65	99	127	89	0.00	-29.92
Montenegro	6	23	21	32	39	0.00	21.88
Portugal	12,429	13,583	13,339	14,497	16,034	0.05	10.60
San Marino	11	16	13	18	3	0.00	-83.33
Serbia	252	272	423	493	585	0.00	18.66
Slovenia	329	329	303	455	308	0.00	-32.31
Spain	7,914	8,448	8,691	8,190	8,723	0.03	6.51
TFYR of Macedonia	70	76	101	102	92	0.00	-9.80
Yugoslavia, SFR (former)					2	0.00	
WESTERN EUROPE	**95,361**	**99,062**	**100,476**	**100,780**	**101,893**	**0.35**	**1.10**
Austria	4,234	4,474	4,096	4,375	4,238	0.01	-3.13
Belgium	4,497	4,792	4,680	4,261	4,782	0.02	12.23
France	39,165	41,417	42,710	42,486	43,440	0.15	2.25
Germany	28,172	28,820	28,811	29,320	29,717	0.10	1.35
Liechtenstein	38	41	56	39	54	0.00	38.46
Luxembourg	206	280	250	239	261	0.00	9.21
Monaco	19	24	17	33	46	0.00	39.39
Netherlands	12,888	12,664	12,769	12,506	11,697	0.04	-6.47
Switzerland	6,142	6,550	7,087	7,521	7,658	0.03	1.82
EAST MEDITERRANEAN EUROPE	**16,635**	**19,968**	**18,855**	**17,832**	**17,509**	**0.06**	**-1.81**
Cyprus	220	228	238	203	281	0.00	38.42
Israel	14,022	16,725	14,694	13,551	12,816	0.04	-5.42
Turkey	2,393	3,015	3,923	4,078	4,412	0.02	8.19
OTHER EUROPE	**1,577**						
Other countries of Europe	1,577						
MIDDLE EAST	**7,520**	**9,829**	**12,153**	**14,131**	**14,901**	**0.05**	**5.45**
Bahrain	122	206	164	198	202	0.00	2.02
Egypt	926	1,256	1,563	1,878	1,992	0.01	6.07
Iraq	129	209	216	299	223	0.00	-25.42
Jordan	455	653	836	886	872	0.00	-1.58
Kuwait	654	1,045	1,465	1,623	1,904	0.01	17.31
Lebanon	1,504	1,888	2,396	2,641	2,490	0.01	-5.72
Libya	411	320	325	666	991	0.00	48.80
Oman	98	121	145	76	119	0.00	56.58
Palestine	186	268	187	209	164	0.00	-21.53
Qatar	147	255	266	284	471	0.00	65.85
Saudi Arabia	1,384	1,859	2,314	2,755	3,243	0.01	17.71
Syrian Arab Republic	700	766	1,051	1,136	250	0.00	-77.99
United Arab Emirates	561	653	798	914	1,365	0.00	49.34
Yemen	243	330	427	566	615	0.00	8.66
SOUTH ASIA	**117,677**	**178,829**	**177,129**	**159,456**	**168,896**	**0.58**	**5.92**

Yearbook of Tourism Statistics, Data 2009 – 2013, 2015 Edition

MACAO, CHINA

2. Arrivals of non-resident visitors at national borders, by country of residence

	2009	2010	2011	2012	2013	Market share 2013	% Change 2013-2012
Afghanistan	273	161	150	238	209	0.00	-12.18
Bangladesh	1,566	905	209	210	294	0.00	40.00
Bhutan	125	116	204	200	190	0.00	-5.00
India	107,513	169,096	169,660	150,825	160,019	0.55	6.10
Iran, Islamic Republic of	1,334	3,673	3,208	3,754	3,672	0.01	-2.18
Maldives	132	157	135	112	173	0.00	54.46
Nepal	2,827	2,102	2,019	2,444	2,405	0.01	-1.60
Pakistan	3,103	2,042	976	1,052	1,218	0.00	15.78
Sri Lanka	804	577	568	621	716	0.00	15.30
NOT SPECIFIED	**21**						
Other countries of the World	21						

Yearbook of Tourism Statistics, Data 2009 – 2013, 2015 Edition

MACAO, CHINA

3. Arrivals of non-resident tourists in hotels and similar establishments, by country of residence

	2009	2010	2011	2012	2013	Market share 2013	% Change 2013-2012
TOTAL	6,398,389	7,288,172	8,051,777	8,885,266	10,016,020	100.00	12.73
AMERICAS	82,845	88,656	97,085	107,911	113,388	1.13	5.08
NORTH AMERICA	82,845	88,035	84,947	98,425	101,202	1.01	2.82
Canada	27,450	29,782	26,726	31,510	29,219	0.29	-7.27
United States of America	55,395	58,253	58,221	66,915	71,983	0.72	7.57
OTHER AMERICAS		621	12,138	9,486	12,186	0.12	28.46
Other countries of the Americas		621	12,138	9,486	12,186	0.12	28.46
EAST ASIA AND THE PACIFIC	6,031,777	6,872,856	7,651,544	8,455,145	9,454,063	94.39	11.81
NORTH-EAST ASIA	5,431,239	6,278,219	7,055,066	7,867,123	8,843,414	88.29	12.41
China	3,282,433	4,012,193	4,703,663	5,372,718	6,319,488	63.09	17.62
Hong Kong, China	1,600,074	1,620,471	1,632,010	1,701,857	1,743,107	17.40	2.42
Japan	210,856	228,266	233,069	243,533	181,664	1.81	-25.40
Korea, Republic of	79,636	127,455	152,314	186,240	213,328	2.13	14.54
Taiwan, Province of China	258,240	289,834	334,010	362,775	385,827	3.85	6.35
SOUTH-EAST ASIA	506,663	495,914	499,169	479,988	494,554	4.94	3.03
Indonesia	77,325	82,884	84,971	81,535	92,353	0.92	13.27
Malaysia	114,284	120,180	120,932	117,632	123,959	1.24	5.38
Philippines	65,964	69,675	72,284	70,161	65,074	0.65	-7.25
Singapore	126,732	115,951	117,212	99,617	99,725	1.00	0.11
Thailand	122,358	107,224	103,770	111,043	113,443	1.13	2.16
AUSTRALASIA	46,829	48,207	49,672	57,517	59,926	0.60	4.19
Australia	41,512	42,472	43,167	50,268	51,987	0.52	3.42
New Zealand	5,317	5,735	6,505	7,249	7,939	0.08	9.52
OTHER EAST ASIA AND THE PACIFIC	47,046	50,516	47,637	50,517	56,169	0.56	11.19
Other countries of Asia	47,046	50,199	37,170	43,476	52,758	0.53	21.35
Other countries of Oceania		317	10,467	7,041	3,411	0.03	-51.56
EUROPE	79,823	81,524	93,773	100,596	107,246	1.07	6.61
NORTHERN EUROPE	19,782	18,633	20,170	21,504	23,510	0.23	9.33
United Kingdom	19,782	18,633	20,170	21,504	23,510	0.23	9.33
SOUTHERN EUROPE	11,563	13,213	15,254	20,214	18,144	0.18	-10.24
Italy	4,842	5,681	6,625	6,829	6,647	0.07	-2.67
Portugal	6,721	7,532	8,629	13,385	11,497	0.11	-14.11
WESTERN EUROPE	22,312	22,033	24,022	23,882	26,048	0.26	9.07
France	13,572	12,070	13,897	14,399	15,987	0.16	11.03
Germany	8,740	9,963	10,125	9,483	10,061	0.10	6.10
OTHER EUROPE	26,166	27,645	34,327	34,996	39,544	0.39	13.00
Other countries of Europe	26,166	27,645	34,327	34,996	39,544	0.39	13.00
SOUTH ASIA	78,458	120,737	123,902	106,028	137,457	1.37	29.64
India	78,458	120,737	123,902	106,028	137,457	1.37	29.64
NOT SPECIFIED	125,486	124,399	85,473	115,586	203,866	2.04	76.38
Other countries of the World	125,486	124,399	85,473	115,586	203,866	2.04	76.38

Yearbook of Tourism Statistics, Data 2009 – 2013, 2015 Edition

MACAO, CHINA

5. Overnight stays of non-resident tourists in hotels and similar establishments, by country of residence

	2009	2010	2011	2012	2013	Market share 2013	% Change 2013-2012
TOTAL	9,133,979	10,663,207	11,684,464	11,613,908	13,079,951	100.00	12.62
AMERICAS	213,020	248,369	352,432	283,727	270,326	2.07	-4.72
NORTH AMERICA	213,020	240,415	241,506	261,459	239,956	1.83	-8.22
Canada	47,649	57,705	54,858	62,353	60,146	0.46	-3.54
United States of America	165,371	182,710	186,648	199,106	179,810	1.37	-9.69
OTHER AMERICAS		7,954	110,926	22,268	30,370	0.23	36.38
Other countries of the Americas		7,954	110,926	22,268	30,370	0.23	36.38
EAST ASIA AND THE PACIFIC	8,100,050	9,452,054	10,532,958	10,383,847	11,657,755	89.13	12.27
NORTH-EAST ASIA	7,037,836	8,344,807	9,365,089	9,251,701	10,485,305	80.16	13.33
China	4,062,398	5,083,252	5,989,362	5,944,896	6,927,007	52.96	16.52
Hong Kong, China	2,023,718	2,132,874	2,145,908	1,992,862	2,242,051	17.14	12.50
Japan	378,152	398,449	415,574	427,857	327,879	2.51	-23.37
Korea, Republic of	134,561	224,940	230,636	274,254	351,022	2.68	27.99
Taiwan, Province of China	439,007	505,292	583,609	611,832	637,346	4.87	4.17
SOUTH-EAST ASIA	851,843	874,810	866,073	847,906	865,897	6.62	2.12
Indonesia	148,912	165,835	167,433	161,147	149,813	1.15	-7.03
Malaysia	183,356	194,114	181,783	184,560	209,393	1.60	13.46
Philippines	120,162	132,299	131,776	130,208	112,400	0.86	-13.68
Singapore	204,341	199,476	207,728	188,801	192,665	1.47	2.05
Thailand	195,072	183,086	177,353	183,190	201,626	1.54	10.06
AUSTRALASIA	113,761	133,095	130,536	145,137	134,866	1.03	-7.08
Australia	99,876	115,017	110,536	119,315	110,648	0.85	-7.26
New Zealand	13,885	18,078	20,000	25,822	24,218	0.19	-6.21
OTHER EAST ASIA AND THE PACIFIC	96,610	99,342	171,260	139,103	171,687	1.31	23.42
Other countries of Asia	96,610	94,730	74,000	124,910	162,785	1.24	30.32
Other countries of Oceania		4,612	97,260	14,193	8,902	0.07	-37.28
EUROPE	205,509	254,450	244,901	263,355	275,668	2.11	4.68
NORTHERN EUROPE	49,530	67,347	60,256	56,589	63,756	0.49	12.67
United Kingdom	49,530	67,347	60,256	56,589	63,756	0.49	12.67
SOUTHERN EUROPE	28,959	36,835	32,257	51,622	56,663	0.43	9.77
Italy	12,654	17,130	15,321	23,174	27,119	0.21	17.02
Portugal	16,305	19,705	16,936	28,448	29,544	0.23	3.85
WESTERN EUROPE	47,680	57,986	58,020	64,302	62,304	0.48	-3.11
France	29,061	33,194	34,682	37,057	37,956	0.29	2.43
Germany	18,619	24,792	23,338	27,245	24,348	0.19	-10.63
OTHER EUROPE	79,340	92,282	94,368	90,842	92,945	0.71	2.32
Other countries of Europe	79,340	92,282	94,368	90,842	92,945	0.71	2.32
SOUTH ASIA	142,338	208,342	223,133	257,577	306,637	2.34	19.05
India	142,338	208,342	223,133	257,577	306,637	2.34	19.05
NOT SPECIFIED	473,062	499,992	331,040	425,402	569,565	4.35	33.89
Other countries of the World	473,062	499,992	331,040	425,402	569,565	4.35	33.89

Yearbook of Tourism Statistics, Data 2009 – 2013, 2015 Edition

MADAGASCAR

1. Arrivals of non-resident tourists at national borders, by nationality

	2009	2010	2011	2012	2013	Market share 2013	% Change 2013-2012
TOTAL	162,687	196,052	225,055	255,942	196,375	100.00	-23.27
AFRICA	36,732	40,083	39,176	45,179	34,874	17.76	-22.81
EAST AFRICA	28,304	29,927	27,847	34,196	27,936	14.23	-18.31
Comoros	348	517	4,468	5,969	4,069	2.07	-31.83
Kenya	103		363	571	397	0.20	-30.47
Mauritius	6,507	7,845	7,261	8,418	5,498	2.80	-34.69
Reunion	21,149	21,565	15,360	18,760	17,752	9.04	-5.37
Seychelles	197		395	478	220	0.11	-53.97
SOUTHERN AFRICA	6,507	7,842	7,121	5,967	3,743	1.91	-37.27
South Africa	6,507	7,842	7,121	5,967	3,743	1.91	-37.27
OTHER AFRICA	1,921	2,314	4,208	5,016	3,195	1.63	-36.30
Other countries of Africa	1,921	2,314	4,208	5,016	3,195	1.63	-36.30
AMERICAS	4,881	5,882	9,870	10,071	6,328	3.22	-37.17
NORTH AMERICA	4,881	5,882	9,193	9,291	5,762	2.93	-37.98
Canada, United States	4,881	5,882	9,193	9,291	5,762	2.93	-37.98
OTHER AMERICAS			677	780	566	0.29	-27.44
Other countries of the Americas			677	780	566	0.29	-27.44
EAST ASIA AND THE PACIFIC	5,694	6,861	22,955	23,414	11,877	6.05	-49.27
NORTH-EAST ASIA	1,627	1,960	2,925	2,434	369	0.19	-84.84
Japan	1,627	1,960	2,925	2,434	369	0.19	-84.84
OTHER EAST ASIA AND THE PACIFIC	4,067	4,901	20,030	20,980	11,508	5.86	-45.15
Other countries of Asia	4,067	4,901	20,030	20,980	11,508	5.86	-45.15
EUROPE	110,869	143,226	153,054	177,278	142,102	72.36	-19.84
NORTHERN EUROPE	3,253	3,920	10,730	11,146	4,008	2.04	-64.04
United Kingdom	3,253	3,920	9,213	9,029	4,008	2.04	-55.61
Scandinavia			1,517	2,117			
SOUTHERN EUROPE	4,881	17,645	9,182	11,302	31,180	15.88	175.88
Italy	4,881	17,645	7,162	8,932	29,841	15.20	234.09
Portugal				499	202	0.10	-59.52
Spain			2,020	1,871	1,137	0.58	-39.23
WESTERN EUROPE	101,516	121,153	130,081	151,914	103,752	52.83	-31.70
France	95,985	111,750	114,471	137,578	93,180	47.45	-32.27
Germany	3,253	5,882	6,504	6,028	3,992	2.03	-33.78
Switzerland	2,278	3,521	3,902	3,650	3,193	1.63	-12.52
Benelux			5,204	4,658	3,387	1.72	-27.29
OTHER EUROPE	1,219	508	3,061	2,916	3,162	1.61	8.44
Other countries of Europe	1,219	508	3,061	2,916	3,162	1.61	8.44
NOT SPECIFIED	4,511				1,194	0.61	
Other countries of the World	4,511				1,194	0.61	

Yearbook of Tourism Statistics, Data 2009 – 2013, 2015 Edition

MADAGASCAR

5. Overnight stays of non-resident tourists in hotels and similar establishments, by nationality

	2009	2010	2011	2012	2013	Market share 2013	% Change 2013-2012
TOTAL (*)	**2,413,073**	**3,298,025**	**3,763,549**				
AFRICA	**326,804**	**624,549**	**615,279**				
EAST AFRICA	**183,528**	**420,529**	**401,949**				
Comoros	5,916	8,789	76,519				
Kenya	927		4,051				
Mauritius	45,549	109,830	100,825				
Reunion	126,336	301,910	214,252				
Seychelles	4,800		6,302				
SOUTHERN AFRICA	**110,619**	**164,682**	**141,785**				
South Africa	110,619	164,682	141,785				
OTHER AFRICA	**32,657**	**39,338**	**71,545**				
Other countries of Africa	32,657	39,338	71,545				
AMERICAS	**82,977**	**99,994**	**167,576**				
NORTH AMERICA	**82,977**	**99,994**	**156,098**				
Canada, United States	82,977	99,994	156,098				
OTHER AMERICAS			**11,478**				
Other countries of the Americas			11,478				
EAST ASIA AND THE PACIFIC	**96,798**	**116,637**	**390,245**				
NORTH-EAST ASIA	**27,659**	**33,320**	**49,737**				
Japan	27,659	33,320	49,737				
OTHER EAST ASIA AND THE PACIFIC	**69,139**	**83,317**	**340,508**				
Other countries of Asia	69,139	83,317	340,508				
EUROPE	**1,888,450**	**2,456,845**	**2,590,449**				
NORTHERN EUROPE	**55,301**	**66,640**	**191,296**				
United Kingdom	55,301	66,640	153,037				
Scandinavia			38,259				
SOUTHERN EUROPE	**102,501**	**317,610**	**163,254**				
Italy	102,501	317,610	128,821				
Spain			34,433				
WESTERN EUROPE	**1,725,772**	**2,065,483**	**2,193,049**				
France	1,631,745	1,899,750	1,947,401				
Germany	55,301	105,876	117,074				
Switzerland	38,726	59,857	66,189				
Benelux			62,385				
OTHER EUROPE	**4,876**	**7,112**	**42,850**				
Other countries of Europe	4,876	7,112	42,850				
NOT SPECIFIED	**18,044**						
Other countries of the World	18,044						

Yearbook of Tourism Statistics, Data 2009 – 2013, 2015 Edition

MALAWI

1. Arrivals of non-resident tourists at national borders, by country of residence

	2009	2010	2011	2012	2013	Market share 2013	% Change 2013-2012
TOTAL (*)	755,031	746,129	767,000	769,722			
AFRICA	574,172	562,379	588,306	631,107			
EAST AFRICA	462,612	439,600	449,237	482,076			
Mozambique	188,694	159,580	196,629	249,341			
Zambia	102,956	80,428	95,766	42,638			
Zimbabwe	77,281	128,387	131,756	89,802			
Other countries of East Africa	93,681	71,205	25,086	100,295			
SOUTHERN AFRICA	100,958	102,342	115,051	142,540			
All countries of Southern Africa	100,958	102,342	115,051	142,540			
OTHER AFRICA	10,602	20,437	24,018	6,491			
Other countries of Africa	10,602	20,437	24,018	6,491			
AMERICAS	46,120	45,893	44,735	28,390			
NORTH AMERICA	43,766	44,572	43,778	27,061			
Canada, United States	43,766	44,572	43,778	27,061			
OTHER AMERICAS	2,354	1,321	957	1,329			
Other countries of the Americas	2,354	1,321	957	1,329			
EAST ASIA AND THE PACIFIC	12,142	20,456	10,247	6,710			
OTHER EAST ASIA AND THE PACIFIC	12,142	20,456	10,247	6,710			
All countries of Asia	12,142	20,456	10,247	6,710			
EUROPE	105,054	104,779	102,389	91,786			
NORTHERN EUROPE	54,476	53,897	51,936	52,128			
United Kingdom/Ireland	54,476	53,897	51,936	52,128			
OTHER EUROPE	50,578	50,882	50,453	39,658			
Other countries of Europe	50,578	50,882	50,453	39,658			
MIDDLE EAST	1,691	2,310	3,400	2,351			
All countries of Middle East	1,691	2,310	3,400	2,351			
SOUTH ASIA	14,299	8,338	15,894	4,160			
All countries of South Asia	14,299	8,338	15,894	4,160			
NOT SPECIFIED	1,553	1,974	2,029	5,218			
Other countries of the World	1,553	1,974	2,029	5,218			

Yearbook of Tourism Statistics, Data 2009 – 2013, 2015 Edition

MALAWI

6. Overnight stays of non-resident tourists in all types of accommodation establishments, by country of residence

	2009	2010	2011	2012	2013	Market share 2013	% Change 2013-2012
TOTAL	5,167,246	6,056,990	5,820,695				
AFRICA	3,252,681	3,818,821	3,566,241				
EAST AFRICA	2,347,201	2,689,880	2,508,426				
Mozambique	622,690	622,362	668,539				
Zambia	391,233	450,396	497,983				
Zimbabwe	587,336	893,709	1,040,872				
Other countries of East Africa	745,942	723,413	301,032				
SOUTHERN AFRICA	798,276	1,012,063	908,903				
All countries of Southern Africa	798,276	1,012,063	908,903				
OTHER AFRICA	107,204	116,878	148,912				
Other countries of Africa	107,204	116,878	148,912				
AMERICAS	496,825	559,693	549,546				
NORTH AMERICA	477,993	545,796	542,847				
Canada, United States	477,993	545,796	542,847				
OTHER AMERICAS	18,832	13,897	6,699				
Other countries of the Americas	18,832	13,897	6,699				
EAST ASIA AND THE PACIFIC	194,272	157,350	336,767				
OTHER EAST ASIA AND THE PACIFIC	194,272	157,350	336,767				
All countries of Asia	194,272	157,350	336,767				
EUROPE	1,198,620	1,489,710	1,352,721				
NORTHERN EUROPE	629,257	805,066	727,104				
United Kingdom/Ireland	629,257	805,066	727,104				
OTHER EUROPE	569,363	684,644	625,617				
Other countries of Europe	569,363	684,644	625,617				
NOT SPECIFIED	24,848	31,416	15,420				
Other countries of the World	24,848	31,416	15,420				

Yearbook of Tourism Statistics, Data 2009 – 2013, 2015 Edition

MALAYSIA

1. Arrivals of non-resident tourists at national borders, by country of residence

	2009	2010	2011	2012	2013	Market share 2013	% Change 2013-2012
TOTAL (*)	23,646,191	24,577,196	24,714,324	25,032,722	25,715,460	100.00	2.73
AFRICA	84,549	41,615	111,182	98,765	100,873	0.39	2.13
EAST AFRICA	24,322		26,754	25,275	29,376	0.11	16.23
British Indian Ocean Territory	19		2	1	2	0.00	100.00
Burundi	28		42	22	28	0.00	27.27
Comoros	48		229	268	364	0.00	35.82
Djibouti	187		213	564	178	0.00	-68.44
Ethiopia	411		371	184	652	0.00	254.35
Kenya	3,296		3,523	3,702	3,755	0.01	1.43
Madagascar	212		297	309	421	0.00	36.25
Malawi	177		326	289	281	0.00	-2.77
Mauritius	11,523		10,850	12,342	14,038	0.05	13.74
Mozambique	180		264	226	280	0.00	23.89
Reunion	1		3				
Rwanda	53		129	130	123	0.00	-5.38
Seychelles	899		926	614	534	0.00	-13.03
Somalia	1,514		2,381		2,262	0.01	
Uganda	1,253		1,998	1,740	1,754	0.01	0.80
United Republic of Tanzania	2,545		2,254	2,782	2,736	0.01	-1.65
Zambia	431		887	807	827	0.00	2.48
Zimbabwe	1,545		2,059	1,295	1,141	0.00	-11.89
CENTRAL AFRICA	791		1,126	1,165	1,366	0.01	17.25
Angola	75		217	144	135	0.00	-6.25
Cameroon	409		469	549	573	0.00	4.37
Central African Republic	3		5	1	3	0.00	200.00
Chad	140		223	186	219	0.00	17.74
Congo	76		75	144	142	0.00	-1.39
Democratic Republic of the Congo			1				
Equatorial Guinea	28		56	55	132	0.00	140.00
Gabon	27		77	85	162	0.00	90.59
Sao Tome and Principe	33		3	1			
NORTH AFRICA	18,586	15,220	25,422	24,562	23,894	0.09	-2.72
Algeria	2,424		2,718	3,401	4,723	0.02	38.87
Morocco	2,864	2,043	2,881	3,533	4,161	0.02	17.78
Sudan	10,993	10,914	13,703	14,343	10,831	0.04	-24.49
Tunisia	2,305	2,263	2,892	3,285	4,179	0.02	27.21
Western Sahara			3,228				
SOUTHERN AFRICA	25,275	26,395	34,584	25,285	23,677	0.09	-6.36
Botswana	1,288		1,424	1,080	596	0.00	-44.81
Lesotho	118		134	113	120	0.00	6.19
Namibia	197		326	334	352	0.00	5.39
South Africa	23,556	26,395	31,441	23,635	22,473	0.09	-4.92
Swaziland	116		185	123	136	0.00	10.57
Other countries of Southern Africa			1,074				
WEST AFRICA	15,575		23,296	22,478	22,560	0.09	0.36
Benin	60		179	83	165	0.00	98.80
Burkina Faso	61		71	67	60	0.00	-10.45
Cabo Verde	20		17	14	25	0.00	78.57
Côte d'Ivoire	109		179	160	293	0.00	83.13
Gambia	180		198	168	141	0.00	-16.07
Ghana	831		1,197	1,157	1,240	0.00	7.17
Guinea	706		888	881	747	0.00	-15.21
Guinea-Bissau	30		135	28	37	0.00	32.14
Liberia	162		108	138	154	0.00	11.59
Mali	213		138	107	101	0.00	-5.61
Mauritania	163		152		163	0.00	
Niger	22		59	19	38	0.00	100.00
Nigeria	12,421		18,916	18,792	18,359	0.07	-2.30
Saint Helena	15		11				

454

MALAYSIA

1. Arrivals of non-resident tourists at national borders, by country of residence

	2009	2010	2011	2012	2013	Market share 2013	% Change 2013-2012
Senegal	386		676	479	461	0.00	-3.76
Sierra Leone	135		279	321	464	0.00	44.55
Togo	61		93	64	112	0.00	75.00
AMERICAS	**345,768**	**342,521**	**339,645**	**362,250**	**377,283**	**1.47**	**4.15**
CARIBBEAN	**1,306**		**2,159**	**2,629**	**2,262**	**0.01**	**-13.96**
Anguilla			5	1	4	0.00	300.00
Antigua and Barbuda	9		14	4	9	0.00	125.00
Aruba	3		56	14	13	0.00	-7.14
Bahamas	70		49	39	54	0.00	38.46
Barbados	73		450	84	85	0.00	1.19
Bermuda	1						
British Virgin Islands			2		2	0.00	
Cayman Islands			1				
Cuba	161		174	217	332	0.00	53.00
Curaçao					69	0.00	
Dominica	15		38		69	0.00	
Dominican Republic	107		134	129	195	0.00	51.16
Grenada	7		9	7	15	0.00	114.29
Guadeloupe	1		1				
Haiti	17		27	30	59	0.00	96.67
Jamaica	168		236	1,160	224	0.00	-80.69
Martinique				1			
Montserrat			3	1			
Netherlands Antilles	60		73		4	0.00	
Puerto Rico	17		2				
Saint Kitts and Nevis	19		138	143	170	0.00	18.88
Saint Lucia	13		10	14	14	0.00	
Saint Vincent and the Grenadines	10		9		9	0.00	
Trinidad and Tobago	545		723	771	934	0.00	21.14
Turks and Caicos Islands	10		5	14	1	0.00	-92.86
CENTRAL AMERICA	**1,370**		**6,825**	**1,814**	**1,829**	**0.01**	**0.83**
Belize	156		134	78	116	0.00	48.72
Costa Rica	536		641	728	662	0.00	-9.07
El Salvador	96		203	180	204	0.00	13.33
Guatemala	210		362	349	297	0.00	-14.90
Honduras	142		179	169	139	0.00	-17.75
Nicaragua	47		5,251	40	71	0.00	77.50
Panama	183		55	270	340	0.00	25.93
NORTH AMERICA	**321,468**	**328,680**	**302,773**	**333,049**	**343,078**	**1.33**	**3.01**
Canada	88,080	91,701	86,015	86,931	88,904	0.35	2.27
Greenland	1		1				
Mexico	4,816	4,014	2	5,984	7,238	0.03	20.96
United States of America	228,571	232,965	216,755	240,134	246,936	0.96	2.83
SOUTH AMERICA	**21,624**	**13,841**	**27,888**	**24,758**	**30,114**	**0.12**	**21.63**
Argentina	6,098	6,014	8,929	5,430	5,776	0.02	6.37
Bolivia	201		198	199	288	0.00	44.72
Brazil	7,529	6,072	9,254	9,540	12,897	0.05	35.19
Chile	2,286		3,403	3,379	3,965	0.02	17.34
Colombia	1,401		1,721	1,861	1,952	0.01	4.89
Ecuador	5		536	610	777	0.00	27.38
French Guiana	2		1				
Guyana	46		54	44	67	0.00	52.27
Paraguay	99	121	125	98	147	0.00	50.00
Peru	1,105		1,075	1,261	1,453	0.01	15.23
Suriname	152		110	140	148	0.00	5.71
Uruguay	364		470	430	516	0.00	20.00
Venezuela	2,336	1,634	2,012	1,766	2,128	0.01	20.50

Yearbook of Tourism Statistics, Data 2009 – 2013, 2015 Edition

MALAYSIA

1. Arrivals of non-resident tourists at national borders, by country of residence

	2009	2010	2011	2012	2013	Market share 2013	% Change 2013-2012
EAST ASIA AND THE PACIFIC	20,830,330	21,605,363	21,667,502	21,945,509	22,567,904	87.76	2.84
NORTH-EAST ASIA	1,844,375	2,021,337	2,138,812	2,559,216	2,868,924	11.16	12.10
China	1,015,550	1,130,261	1,245,475	1,557,960	1,790,079	6.96	14.90
Hong Kong, China	4,199		4,716	794	1,284	0.00	61.71
Japan	395,746	415,881	386,974	470,008	513,076	2.00	9.16
Korea, Dem. People's Republic of	693		1,013	772	932	0.00	20.73
Korea, Republic of	227,312	264,052	263,428	283,977	274,622	1.07	-3.29
Macao, China	7		345	31	60	0.00	93.55
Mongolia	2,999		3,078	3,155	2,605	0.01	-17.43
Taiwan, Province of China	197,869	211,143	233,783	242,519	286,266	1.11	18.04
SOUTH-EAST ASIA	18,386,363	18,937,179	18,885,302	18,809,736	19,105,915	74.30	1.57
Brunei Darussalam	1,061,357	1,124,406	1,239,404	1,258,070	1,238,871	4.82	-1.53
Cambodia	43,146	48,618	49,472	50,179	64,534	0.25	28.61
Indonesia	2,405,360	2,506,509	2,134,381	2,382,606	2,548,021	9.91	6.94
Lao People's Democratic Republic	36,663	38,111	29,520	38,364	35,676	0.14	-7.01
Myanmar	60,338	72,792	81,946	83,473	90,740	0.35	8.71
Philippines	447,470	486,790	362,101	508,744	557,147	2.17	9.51
Singapore	12,733,082	13,042,004	13,372,647	13,014,268	13,178,774	51.25	1.26
Thailand	1,449,262	1,458,678	1,442,048	1,263,024	1,156,452	4.50	-8.44
Viet Nam	149,685	159,271	173,783	211,008	235,700	0.92	11.70
AUSTRALASIA	596,386	646,847	639,798	573,674	589,517	2.29	2.76
Australia	533,382	580,695	558,411	507,948	526,342	2.05	3.62
New Zealand	63,004	66,152	81,387	65,726	63,175	0.25	-3.88
MELANESIA	2,797		3,043	2,743	3,271	0.01	19.25
Fiji	1,130		1,391	1,237	1,519	0.01	22.80
New Caledonia	2		1				
Papua New Guinea	1,466		1,325	1,303	1,477	0.01	13.35
Solomon Islands	157		244	194	209	0.00	7.73
Vanuatu	42		82	9	66	0.00	633.33
MICRONESIA	138		90	64	108	0.00	68.75
Kiribati	45		29	30	19	0.00	-36.67
Marshall Islands	12		7	2	17	0.00	750.00
Micronesia, Federated States of	20		12	9	21	0.00	133.33
Nauru	47		25	12	28	0.00	133.33
Palau	11		17	11	23	0.00	109.09
Other countries of Micronesia	3						
POLYNESIA	271		254	76	169	0.00	122.37
American Samoa	1		20	1	45	0.00	4,400.00
French Polynesia	1		1		1	0.00	
Samoa	59		87		42	0.00	
Tonga	160		120	74	61	0.00	-17.57
Tuvalu	50		26	1	20	0.00	1,900.00
OTHER EAST ASIA AND THE PACIFIC			203				
Other countries of Oceania			203				
EUROPE	1,165,807	1,133,235	1,136,443	1,161,319	1,226,655	4.77	5.63
CENTRAL/EASTERN EUROPE	80,115	68,670	112,303	124,730	145,062	0.56	16.30
Armenia	152		235	273	347	0.00	27.11
Azerbaijan	544		913	1,024	1,228	0.00	19.92
Belarus	854		1,295	1,311	1,840	0.01	40.35
Bulgaria	1,614		2,585	2,694	3,386	0.01	25.69
Czech Republic	6,774	6,753	6,818	7,219	7,602	0.03	5.31
Hungary	4,242		4,385	4,584	5,661	0.02	23.49
Kazakhstan	5,493	10,527	17,462	20,188	19,840	0.08	-1.72
Kyrgyzstan	844		1,677	1,795	2,136	0.01	19.00
Lithuania	1,100		1,720	1,788	2,051	0.01	14.71
Poland	12,544	12,358	13,055	13,432	16,397	0.06	22.07
Romania	2,844		3,398	3,709	6,009	0.02	62.01
Russian Federation	29,202	32,075	38,918	44,765	53,203	0.21	18.85
Slovakia	2,472		3,112	3,451	3,723	0.01	7.88

456

Yearbook of Tourism Statistics, Data 2009 – 2013, 2015 Edition

MALAYSIA

1. Arrivals of non-resident tourists at national borders, by country of residence

	2009	2010	2011	2012	2013	Market share 2013	% Change 2013-2012
Tajikistan	491		499	489	517	0.00	5.73
Turkmenistan	626		750	799	940	0.00	17.65
Ukraine	3,125		6,229	6,312	8,591	0.03	36.11
Uzbekistan	7,194	6,957	9,252	10,897	11,591	0.05	6.37
NORTHERN EUROPE	**579,898**	**571,079**	**533,492**	**526,748**	**548,729**	**2.13**	**4.17**
Denmark	25,916	24,869	22,269	24,408	25,312	0.10	3.70
Faeroe Islands	2						
Finland	20,912	21,355	19,969	19,342	18,952	0.07	-2.02
Iceland	633		690	737	749	0.00	1.63
Ireland	25,347	23,146	22,593	21,639	24,459	0.10	13.03
Norway	22,487	22,773	19,891	19,996	22,325	0.09	11.65
Svalbard and Jan Mayen Islands			2	1			
Sweden	49,509	48,971	44,138	38,418	43,460	0.17	13.12
United Kingdom	435,091	429,965	403,940	402,207	413,472	1.61	2.80
Other countries of Northern Europe	1						
SOUTHERN EUROPE	**86,932**	**72,770**	**82,101**	**84,588**	**89,536**	**0.35**	**5.85**
Albania	292		298	316	290	0.00	-8.23
Andorra	36		18	16	36	0.00	125.00
Bosnia and Herzegovina	482		540	528	539	0.00	2.08
Croatia	1,334		1,728	1,948	2,147	0.01	10.22
Greece	3,105		2,624	3,199	3,676	0.01	14.91
Holy See	8		12	5	9	0.00	80.00
Italy	46,352	47,068	43,864	44,330	45,253	0.18	2.08
Malta	410		654	640	764	0.00	19.38
Portugal	11,685	6,264	9,842	9,198	10,109	0.04	9.90
San Marino	43		43	10	21	0.00	110.00
Serbia and Montenegro	259		363	691	526	0.00	-23.88
Spain	22,771	19,438	22,104	23,594	26,162	0.10	10.88
Yugoslavia, SFR (former)	155		11	113	4	0.00	-96.46
WESTERN EUROPE	**410,032**	**411,567**	**399,340**	**414,798**	**427,995**	**1.66**	**3.18**
Austria	14,491	10,891	13,082	13,679	14,722	0.06	7.62
Belgium	16,721	15,275	16,436	17,151	18,502	0.07	7.88
France	110,054	111,175	127,980	136,172	145,108	0.56	6.56
Germany	128,288	130,896	124,670	131,277	136,749	0.53	4.17
Liechtenstein	54		85	84	110	0.00	30.95
Luxembourg	732	549	666	629	615	0.00	-2.23
Monaco	30		29	42	43	0.00	2.38
Netherlands	111,139	114,887	90,590	88,404	83,955	0.33	-5.03
Switzerland	28,523	27,894	25,802	27,360	28,191	0.11	3.04
EAST MEDITERRANEAN EUROPE	**8,830**	**9,149**	**9,207**	**10,455**	**15,333**	**0.06**	**46.66**
Cyprus	558		617	528	2,497	0.01	372.92
Israel	7		13	18	61	0.00	238.89
Turkey	8,265	9,149	8,577	9,909	12,775	0.05	28.92
MIDDLE EAST	**196,854**	**166,636**	**236,987**	**265,603**	**274,393**	**1.07**	**3.31**
Bahrain	6,114		7,128	5,624	5,737	0.02	2.01
Egypt	11,006	11,709	15,359	16,804	21,053	0.08	25.29
Iraq	8,680		13,568	21,939	27,869	0.11	27.03
Jordan	7,713		9,012	8,529	9,468	0.04	11.01
Kuwait	20,170	17,632	22,833	22,759	22,195	0.09	-2.48
Lebanon	5,187		4,887	4,503	5,016	0.02	11.39
Libya	3,187		2,881	6,214	7,707	0.03	24.03
Oman	15,280	16,377	22,062	24,977	26,601	0.10	6.50
Qatar	4,257	3,965	5,727	7,742	7,264	0.03	-6.17
Saudi Arabia	77,082	86,771	87,693	102,365	94,986	0.37	-7.21
Syrian Arab Republic	5,909	4,537	7,241	9,413	9,850	0.04	4.64
United Arab Emirates	22,108	25,645	24,212	18,233	19,830	0.08	8.76
Yemen	10,161		14,384	16,501	16,817	0.07	1.92

457

MALAYSIA

1. Arrivals of non-resident tourists at national borders, by country of residence

	2009	2010	2011	2012	2013	Market share 2013	% Change 2013-2012
SOUTH ASIA	**929,954**	**997,156**	**1,124,647**	**1,185,201**	**1,156,003**	**4.50**	**-2.46**
Afghanistan	1,026		757	1,710	1,815	0.01	6.14
Bangladesh	87,443	63,886	65,603	86,465	134,663	0.52	55.74
Bhutan	417		503	535	357	0.00	-33.27
India	589,838	690,849	693,056	691,271	650,989	2.53	-5.83
Iran, Islamic Republic of	101,664	116,252	139,617	127,404	78,316	0.30	-38.53
Maldives	11,001		11,702	11,833	12,267	0.05	3.67
Nepal	18,898	2,983	81,791	123,173	132,148	0.51	7.29
Pakistan	69,581	65,101	73,046	79,989	81,397	0.32	1.76
Sri Lanka	50,086	58,085	58,572	62,821	64,051	0.25	1.96
NOT SPECIFIED	**92,929**	**290,670**	**97,918**	**14,075**	**12,349**	**0.05**	**-12.26**
Other countries of the World	92,929	290,670	97,918	14,075	12,349	0.05	-12.26

Yearbook of Tourism Statistics, Data 2009 – 2013, 2015 Edition

MALDIVES

1. Arrivals of non-resident tourists at national borders, by nationality

		2009	2010	2011	2012	2013	Market share 2013	% Change 2013-2012
TOTAL	(*)	**655,852**	**791,917**	**931,333**	**958,027**	**1,125,202**	**100.00**	**17.45**
AFRICA		**5,034**	**5,628**	**6,452**	**7,095**	**8,271**	**0.74**	**16.58**
EAST AFRICA		**596**	**643**	**776**	**815**	**930**	**0.08**	**14.11**
Comoros		1	5	12	16	28	0.00	75.00
Djibouti		2	5		3	4	0.00	33.33
Eritrea		22	11	19	20	31	0.00	55.00
Ethiopia		34	57	35	69	67	0.01	-2.90
Kenya		143	168	155	224	198	0.02	-11.61
Madagascar		5	5	7	15	17	0.00	13.33
Malawi		6	10	10	7	10	0.00	42.86
Mauritius		218	185	229	211	242	0.02	14.69
Mozambique		15	24	62	32	41	0.00	28.13
Seychelles		47	50	81	38	22	0.00	-42.11
Somalia		3		7	7	10	0.00	42.86
Uganda		10	14	30	14	20	0.00	42.86
United Republic of Tanzania		43	50	45	63	95	0.01	50.79
Zambia		17	21	21	39	44	0.00	12.82
Zimbabwe		30	38	63	57	69	0.01	21.05
Other countries of East Africa						32	0.00	
CENTRAL AFRICA		**43**	**61**	**61**	**85**	**148**	**0.01**	**74.12**
Angola		21	35	29	46	80	0.01	73.91
Cameroon		15	19	16	27	37	0.00	37.04
Chad				3	1			
Congo		7	7	13	11	31	0.00	181.82
NORTH AFRICA		**1,205**	**1,341**	**1,579**	**1,805**	**2,058**	**0.18**	**14.02**
Algeria		252	264	326	364	407	0.04	11.81
Morocco		476	464	552	621	637	0.06	2.58
Sudan		112	139	137	171	222	0.02	29.82
Tunisia		365	474	564	649	792	0.07	22.03
SOUTHERN AFRICA		**3,014**	**3,195**	**3,740**	**4,020**	**4,571**	**0.41**	**13.71**
Botswana				12				
Lesotho		1	1		1			
Namibia		34	32	40	33	53	0.00	60.61
South Africa		2,975	3,157	3,684	3,967	4,503	0.40	13.51
Swaziland		4	5	4	19	15	0.00	-21.05
WEST AFRICA		**159**	**356**	**149**	**301**	**293**	**0.03**	**-2.66**
Burkina Faso					2	2	0.00	
Cabo Verde		5	6	6	8			
Côte d'Ivoire		13	17	34				
Gambia		2	4	5	11	2	0.00	-81.82
Ghana		18	25	21	31	25	0.00	-19.35
Guinea		5	12	8	5	9	0.00	80.00
Liberia		3	4	9	1	10	0.00	900.00
Mali		4	2	5	2	11	0.00	450.00
Mauritania		3	81	8	1	2	0.00	100.00
Nigeria		91	186	13	202	197	0.02	-2.48
Senegal		11	12	33	29	18	0.00	-37.93
Sierra Leone		4	4	7	8	6	0.00	-25.00
Togo			3		1	11	0.00	1,000.00
OTHER AFRICA		**17**	**32**	**147**	**69**	**271**	**0.02**	**292.75**
Other countries of Africa		17	32	147	69	271	0.02	292.75
AMERICAS		**15,159**	**18,601**	**23,654**	**26,774**	**32,970**	**2.93**	**23.14**
CARIBBEAN		**69**	**102**	**110**	**186**	**220**	**0.02**	**18.28**
Antigua and Barbuda			3	2	48	1	0.00	-97.92
Bahamas		4		7	2	6	0.00	200.00
Barbados		2	7	7	5	4	0.00	-20.00
Cuba		33	21	24	28	16	0.00	-42.86
Dominica		8	26	24	25	27	0.00	8.00
Grenada		2		1	3			

459

Yearbook of Tourism Statistics, Data 2009 – 2013, 2015 Edition

MALDIVES

1. Arrivals of non-resident tourists at national borders, by nationality

	2009	2010	2011	2012	2013	Market share 2013	% Change 2013-2012
Haiti		1	3	6	1	0.00	-83.33
Jamaica	4	10	10	11	99	0.01	800.00
Saint Lucia		6	6	1	1	0.00	
Trinidad and Tobago	16	28	26	57	65	0.01	14.04
CENTRAL AMERICA	**80**	**88**	**98**	**131**	**145**	**0.01**	**10.69**
Belize	5	10	4	5	5	0.00	
Costa Rica	16	12	26	42	49	0.00	16.67
El Salvador	7	14	11	16	5	0.00	-68.75
Guatemala	9	11	17	4	11	0.00	175.00
Honduras	1	6	5	9	8	0.00	-11.11
Nicaragua	3	5	2	3	4	0.00	33.33
Panama	39	30	33	52	63	0.01	21.15
NORTH AMERICA	**12,986**	**15,850**	**19,925**	**21,959**	**27,118**	**2.41**	**23.49**
Canada	3,043	3,815	4,690	5,070	6,098	0.54	20.28
Mexico	505	553	745	840	986	0.09	17.38
United States of America	9,438	11,482	14,490	16,049	20,034	1.78	24.83
SOUTH AMERICA	**2,018**	**2,554**	**3,474**	**4,454**	**5,362**	**0.48**	**20.39**
Argentina	274	288	457	621	745	0.07	19.97
Bolivia	9	19	20	18	27	0.00	50.00
Brazil	1,304	1,761	2,342	3,061	3,675	0.33	20.06
Chile	57	72	105	101	175	0.02	73.27
Colombia	110	151	178	210	251	0.02	19.52
Ecuador	25	34	36	35			
Paraguay	17	18	30	42	37	0.00	-11.90
Peru	55	48	89	92	123	0.01	33.70
Suriname	1		1				
Uruguay	31	18	37	55	42	0.00	-23.64
Venezuela	135	145	179	219	287	0.03	31.05
OTHER AMERICAS	**6**	**7**	**47**	**44**	**125**	**0.01**	**184.09**
Other countries of the Americas	6	7	47	44	125	0.01	184.09
EAST ASIA AND THE PACIFIC	**137,946**	**214,026**	**303,018**	**339,183**	**467,718**	**41.57**	**37.90**
NORTH-EAST ASIA	**115,434**	**186,414**	**265,096**	**294,397**	**408,113**	**36.27**	**38.63**
China	60,666	118,961	198,655	229,551	331,719	29.48	44.51
Japan	36,641	38,791	35,782	36,438	39,463	3.51	8.30
Korea, Republic of	16,135	24,808	25,285	23,933	30,306	2.69	26.63
Mongolia	17	23	29		69	0.01	
Taiwan, Province of China	1,975	3,831	5,305	4,430	6,522	0.58	47.22
Other countries of North-East Asia			40	45	34	0.00	-24.44
SOUTH-EAST ASIA	**14,095**	**16,807**	**23,726**	**27,960**	**40,844**	**3.63**	**46.08**
Brunei Darussalam	16	34	46		83	0.01	
Cambodia	15	14	54		111	0.01	
Indonesia	677	818	1,283	1,772	2,511	0.22	41.70
Lao People's Democratic Republic	24	30	58		111	0.01	
Malaysia	3,139	3,894	6,055	6,766	10,875	0.97	60.73
Myanmar	60	76	139		430	0.04	
Philippines	979	1,066	1,652	2,265	3,040	0.27	34.22
Singapore	5,214	5,332	7,990	9,625	11,143	0.99	15.77
Thailand	3,813	5,397	6,214	6,896	11,705	1.04	69.74
Viet Nam	158	146	234		831	0.07	
Other countries of South-East Asia			1	636	4	0.00	-99.37
AUSTRALASIA	**8,383**	**10,725**	**14,168**	**16,787**	**18,706**	**1.66**	**11.43**
Australia	7,392	9,622	12,778	15,208	16,915	1.50	11.22
New Zealand	991	1,103	1,390	1,579	1,791	0.16	13.43
MELANESIA	**11**	**18**	**19**	**19**	**26**	**0.00**	**36.84**
Fiji	11	17	19	19	24	0.00	26.32
Vanuatu		1			2	0.00	
MICRONESIA	**5**	**3**		**2**	**3**	**0.00**	**50.00**
Kiribati	5	2		2	1	0.00	-50.00
Marshall Islands		1			2	0.00	

Yearbook of Tourism Statistics, Data 2009 – 2013, 2015 Edition

MALDIVES

1. Arrivals of non-resident tourists at national borders, by nationality

	2009	2010	2011	2012	2013	Market share 2013	% Change 2013-2012
POLYNESIA		2	1		2	0.00	
Tonga		2	1		2	0.00	
OTHER EAST ASIA AND THE PACIFIC	18	57	8	18	24	0.00	33.33
Other countries of Asia	13	49					
Other countries of Oceania	5	8	8	18	24	0.00	33.33
EUROPE	462,192	505,421	537,769	517,809	527,274	46.86	1.83
CENTRAL/EASTERN EUROPE	62,374	75,378	95,247	100,097	119,568	10.63	19.45
Armenia	79	134	162	185	354	0.03	91.35
Azerbaijan	244	275	288	486	775	0.07	59.47
Belarus	812	898	1,161	1,509	2,030	0.18	34.53
Bulgaria	902	1,051	1,368	1,479	1,882	0.17	27.25
Czech Republic	3,851	5,137	6,471	5,588	6,421	0.57	14.91
Estonia	262	205	230	362	498	0.04	37.57
Georgia	60	77	74	114	154	0.01	35.09
Hungary	1,848	2,434	2,596	2,408	2,796	0.25	16.11
Kazakhstan	1,756	1,572	1,731	2,875	3,131	0.28	8.90
Kyrgyzstan	66	59	83	135	135	0.01	
Latvia	383	406	485	621	822	0.07	32.37
Lithuania	446	623	638	777	971	0.09	24.97
Poland	3,357	3,795	4,158	3,918	6,668	0.59	70.19
Republic of Moldova	219	266	321	360	439	0.04	21.94
Romania	1,247	1,290	1,656	1,879	2,423	0.22	28.95
Russian Federation	40,014	49,111	63,936	66,378	76,479	6.80	15.22
Slovakia	1,970	2,348	2,822	2,636	2,758	0.25	4.63
Tajikistan	21	22	43	32	59	0.01	84.38
Turkmenistan	39	42	28	28	65	0.01	132.14
Ukraine	4,643	5,445	6,729	8,044	10,362	0.92	28.82
Uzbekistan	155	188	233	277	346	0.03	24.91
Other countries Central/East Europe			34	6			
NORTHERN EUROPE	116,491	126,222	119,388	107,350	103,104	9.16	-3.96
Denmark	1,722	2,422	3,173	3,493	4,055	0.36	16.09
Finland	1,088	1,281	1,535	1,402	1,549	0.14	10.49
Iceland	26	56	57	64	62	0.01	-3.13
Ireland	2,420	2,514	2,444	2,483	2,590	0.23	4.31
Norway	2,120	2,153	2,775	2,902	3,281	0.29	13.06
Sweden	3,165	3,638	4,896	5,230	5,694	0.51	8.87
United Kingdom	105,950	114,158	104,508	91,776	85,869	7.63	-6.44
Other countries of Northern Europe					4	0.00	
SOUTHERN EUROPE	109,297	111,109	104,072	81,287	79,364	7.05	-2.37
Albania	127	119	144	142	188	0.02	32.39
Andorra	10	31	24	21	40	0.00	90.48
Bosnia and Herzegovina	101	109	170	239	194	0.02	-18.83
Croatia	548	551	626	801	709	0.06	-11.49
Greece	5,406	4,630	3,009	2,058	1,841	0.16	-10.54
Italy	89,292	89,621	83,088	62,687	57,854	5.14	-7.71
Malta	130	221	214	252	240	0.02	-4.76
Montenegro	12	24	30	39	95	0.01	143.59
Portugal	4,822	4,555	4,434	3,660	4,617	0.41	26.15
Serbia	127	575	723	852	884	0.08	3.76
Slovenia	1,324	1,647	1,609	1,295	1,243	0.11	-4.02
Spain	7,279	8,912	9,710	8,824	11,040	0.98	25.11
TFYR of Macedonia	119	114	194	203	278	0.02	36.95
Other countries of Southern Europe			97	214	141	0.01	-34.11
WESTERN EUROPE	169,027	185,433	211,755	220,817	212,651	18.90	-3.70
Austria	13,274	14,944	16,655	18,164	18,140	1.61	-0.13
Belgium	3,437	4,386	5,738	5,141	5,130	0.46	-0.21
France	50,373	54,789	59,694	56,775	54,328	4.83	-4.31
Germany	69,085	77,108	90,517	98,351	93,598	8.32	-4.83
Liechtenstein	148	148	177	140	171	0.02	22.14

MALDIVES

1. Arrivals of non-resident tourists at national borders, by nationality

	2009	2010	2011	2012	2013	Market share 2013	% Change 2013-2012
Luxembourg	519	575	725	659	670	0.06	1.67
Monaco	53	35	52	53	59	0.01	11.32
Netherlands	5,355	5,682	5,693	6,077	6,453	0.57	6.19
Switzerland	26,783	27,766	32,504	35,457	34,102	3.03	-3.82
EAST MEDITERRANEAN EUROPE	**4,517**	**7,166**	**7,307**	**8,256**	**12,583**	**1.12**	**52.41**
Cyprus	379	416	332	271	213	0.02	-21.40
Israel	1,380	2,113	2,433	2,569	3,253	0.29	26.63
Turkey	2,758	4,637	4,542	5,416	9,117	0.81	68.33
OTHER EUROPE	**486**	**113**		**2**	**4**	**0.00**	**100.00**
Other countries of Europe	486	113		2	4	0.00	100.00
MIDDLE EAST	**9,525**	**11,629**	**14,570**	**21,843**	**32,050**	**2.85**	**46.73**
Bahrain	438	629	612	679	780	0.07	14.87
Egypt	559	689	864	1,168	1,671	0.15	43.07
Iraq	53	72	113	132	348	0.03	163.64
Jordan	538	577	607	744	1,179	0.10	58.47
Kuwait	1,181	1,409	1,797	2,987	4,622	0.41	54.74
Lebanon	984	1,145	1,346	1,666	1,817	0.16	9.06
Libya	82	131	32	130	230	0.02	76.92
Oman	321	272	418	727	915	0.08	25.86
Palestine	84	77	121	164	319	0.03	94.51
Qatar	418	595	872	1,521	2,827	0.25	85.86
Saudi Arabia	3,036	4,040	5,005	7,263	10,477	0.93	44.25
Syrian Arab Republic	191	234	398	447	656	0.06	46.76
United Arab Emirates	1,580	1,699	2,292	4,047	5,936	0.53	46.68
Yemen	60	60	93	168	273	0.02	62.50
SOUTH ASIA	**25,996**	**36,612**	**45,870**	**45,323**	**56,796**	**5.05**	**25.31**
Afghanistan	30	155	134	57	91	0.01	59.65
Bangladesh	388	525	1,496	1,221	1,906	0.17	56.10
Bhutan	45	47	93	54	53	0.00	-1.85
India	15,850	25,756	30,978	31,721	38,014	3.38	19.84
Iran, Islamic Republic of	637	779	1,321	1,295	1,350	0.12	4.25
Nepal	167	222	336	258	289	0.03	12.02
Pakistan	1,046	1,256	1,842	1,857	2,693	0.24	45.02
Sri Lanka	7,833	7,872	9,670	8,860	12,400	1.10	39.95
NOT SPECIFIED					**123**	**0.01**	
Other countries of the World					123	0.01	

Yearbook of Tourism Statistics, Data 2009 – 2013, 2015 Edition

MALI

1. Arrivals of non-resident tourists at national borders, by nationality

		2009	2010	2011	2012	2013	Market share 2013	% Change 2013-2012
TOTAL	(*)	**160,012**	**169,305**	**159,782**	**101,335**			
AFRICA		**44,589**	**47,175**	**52,467**	**60,166**			
WEST AFRICA		**27,408**	**29,872**	**33,983**				
All countries of West Africa		27,408	29,872	33,983				
OTHER AFRICA		**17,181**	**17,303**	**18,484**	**60,166**			
Other countries of Africa		17,181	17,303	18,484				
All countries of Africa					60,166			
AMERICAS		**26,992**	**23,692**	**20,826**	**5,956**			
NORTH AMERICA		**26,992**	**23,692**	**20,826**				
Canada		10,091	6,147	5,644				
United States of America		16,901	17,545	15,182				
OTHER AMERICAS					**5,956**			
All countries of the Americas					5,956			
EAST ASIA AND THE PACIFIC		**1,307**	**2,668**	**3,148**	**5,517**			
NORTH-EAST ASIA		**1,307**	**2,668**	**3,148**				
Japan		1,307	2,668	3,148				
OTHER EAST ASIA AND THE PACIFIC					**5,517**			
All countries East Asia/Pacific					5,517			
EUROPE		**72,872**	**82,837**	**68,752**	**29,164**			
CENTRAL/EASTERN EUROPE		**3,547**	**5,596**	**5,580**				
Russian Federation		737	1,541	1,355				
Other countries Central/East Europe		2,810	4,055	4,225				
NORTHERN EUROPE		**5,964**	**6,297**	**5,911**				
United Kingdom		4,173	4,422	3,595				
Scandinavia		1,791	1,875	2,316				
SOUTHERN EUROPE		**9,695**	**12,392**	**10,766**				
Italy		5,307	6,878	5,955				
Spain		4,388	5,514	4,811				
WESTERN EUROPE		**53,666**	**58,552**	**46,495**				
Austria		660	1,906	1,648				
France		38,261	42,883	30,207				
Germany		5,380	4,937	5,428				
Switzerland		2,723	2,520	2,815				
Benelux		6,642	6,306	6,397				
OTHER EUROPE					**29,164**			
All countries of Europe					29,164			
MIDDLE EAST		**2,946**	**2,948**	**3,910**	**529**			
All countries of Middle East		2,946	2,948	3,910	529			
NOT SPECIFIED		**11,306**	**9,985**	**10,679**	**3**			
Other countries of the World		11,306	9,985	10,679	3			

Yearbook of Tourism Statistics, Data 2009 – 2013, 2015 Edition

MALI

1. Arrivals of non-resident tourists at national borders, by country of residence

	2009	2010	2011	2012	2013	Market share 2013	% Change 2013-2012
TOTAL (*)					120,901	100.00	
AFRICA					52,657	43.55	
EAST AFRICA					2,522	2.09	
Burundi					211	0.17	
Comoros					17	0.01	
Djibouti					20	0.02	
Ethiopia					612	0.51	
Kenya					559	0.46	
Madagascar					79	0.07	
Malawi					90	0.07	
Mauritius					8	0.01	
Mozambique					109	0.09	
Rwanda					264	0.22	
Somalia					2	0.00	
Uganda					115	0.10	
United Republic of Tanzania					206	0.17	
Zambia					112	0.09	
Zimbabwe					118	0.10	
CENTRAL AFRICA					5,954	4.92	
Angola					197	0.16	
Cameroon					974	0.81	
Central African Republic					110	0.09	
Chad					352	0.29	
Congo					2,363	1.95	
Democratic Republic of the Congo					431	0.36	
Equatorial Guinea					19	0.02	
Gabon					1,497	1.24	
Sao Tome and Principe					11	0.01	
NORTH AFRICA					6,927	5.73	
Algeria					1,529	1.26	
Morocco					3,544	2.93	
Sudan					105	0.09	
Tunisia					1,749	1.45	
SOUTHERN AFRICA					1,753	1.45	
Botswana					14	0.01	
Lesotho					5	0.00	
Namibia					16	0.01	
South Africa					1,693	1.40	
Swaziland					25	0.02	
WEST AFRICA					35,501	29.36	
Benin					1,464	1.21	
Burkina Faso					3,359	2.78	
Cabo Verde					21	0.02	
Côte d'Ivoire					8,020	6.63	
Gambia					223	0.18	
Ghana					2,041	1.69	
Guinea					2,841	2.35	
Guinea-Bissau					911	0.75	
Liberia					119	0.10	
Mauritania					1,714	1.42	
Niger					1,377	1.14	
Nigeria					1,556	1.29	
Senegal					10,202	8.44	
Sierra Leone					131	0.11	
Togo					1,522	1.26	
AMERICAS					6,296	5.21	
CARIBBEAN					84	0.07	
Cuba					23	0.02	
Dominican Republic					1	0.00	

Yearbook of Tourism Statistics, Data 2009 – 2013, 2015 Edition

MALI

1. Arrivals of non-resident tourists at national borders, by country of residence

	2009	2010	2011	2012	2013	Market share 2013	% Change 2013-2012
Haiti					54	0.04	
Jamaica					6	0.00	
CENTRAL AMERICA					**63**	**0.05**	
Costa Rica					4	0.00	
Guatemala					1	0.00	
Honduras					2	0.00	
Nicaragua					2	0.00	
Panama					54	0.04	
NORTH AMERICA					**5,971**	**4.94**	
Canada					1,515	1.25	
Mexico					23	0.02	
United States of America					4,433	3.67	
SOUTH AMERICA					**178**	**0.15**	
Argentina					14	0.01	
Brazil					85	0.07	
Chile					10	0.01	
Colombia					36	0.03	
Ecuador					2	0.00	
Guyana					2	0.00	
Peru					3	0.00	
Uruguay					9	0.01	
Venezuela					17	0.01	
EAST ASIA AND THE PACIFIC					**4,191**	**3.47**	
NORTH-EAST ASIA					**2,881**	**2.38**	
China					2,612	2.16	
Japan					105	0.09	
Korea, Republic of					161	0.13	
Taiwan, Province of China					3	0.00	
SOUTH-EAST ASIA					**329**	**0.27**	
Cambodia					12	0.01	
Indonesia					46	0.04	
Malaysia					22	0.02	
Philippines					172	0.14	
Singapore					4	0.00	
Thailand					40	0.03	
Viet Nam					33	0.03	
AUSTRALASIA					**961**	**0.79**	
Australia					908	0.75	
New Zealand					53	0.04	
MELANESIA					**20**	**0.02**	
New Caledonia					20	0.02	
EUROPE					**54,815**	**45.34**	
CENTRAL/EASTERN EUROPE					**1,072**	**0.89**	
Bulgaria					67	0.06	
Czech Republic					13	0.01	
Estonia					7	0.01	
Hungary					27	0.02	
Latvia					6	0.00	
Lithuania					3	0.00	
Poland					43	0.04	
Romania					71	0.06	
Russian Federation					427	0.35	
Slovakia					24	0.02	
Ukraine					381	0.32	
Uzbekistan					1	0.00	
Other countries Central/East Europe					2	0.00	
NORTHERN EUROPE					**1,389**	**1.15**	
Denmark					212	0.18	
Finland					47	0.04	

465

Yearbook of Tourism Statistics, Data 2009 – 2013, 2015 Edition

MALI

1. Arrivals of non-resident tourists at national borders, by country of residence

	2009	2010	2011	2012	2013	Market share 2013	% Change 2013-2012
Iceland					39	0.03	
Ireland					42	0.03	
Norway					117	0.10	
Sweden					211	0.17	
United Kingdom					721	0.60	
SOUTHERN EUROPE					**5,076**	**4.20**	
Croatia					19	0.02	
Greece					40	0.03	
Italy					1,453	1.20	
Malta					7	0.01	
Portugal					508	0.42	
Serbia					17	0.01	
Slovenia					1	0.00	
Spain					3,031	2.51	
WESTERN EUROPE					**46,483**	**38.45**	
Austria					50	0.04	
Belgium					1,135	0.94	
France					42,711	35.33	
Germany					1,246	1.03	
Luxembourg					43	0.04	
Netherlands					676	0.56	
Switzerland					622	0.51	
EAST MEDITERRANEAN EUROPE					**795**	**0.66**	
Cyprus					7	0.01	
Israel					43	0.04	
Turkey					745	0.62	
MIDDLE EAST					**1,316**	**1.09**	
Egypt					196	0.16	
Jordan					7	0.01	
Kuwait					16	0.01	
Lebanon					389	0.32	
Libya					249	0.21	
Oman					1	0.00	
Palestine					8	0.01	
Qatar					26	0.02	
Saudi Arabia					240	0.20	
Syrian Arab Republic					58	0.05	
United Arab Emirates					114	0.09	
Yemen					12	0.01	
SOUTH ASIA					**1,577**	**1.30**	
Afghanistan					16	0.01	
Bangladesh					37	0.03	
India					1,344	1.11	
Iran, Islamic Republic of					52	0.04	
Nepal					5	0.00	
Pakistan					106	0.09	
Sri Lanka					17	0.01	
NOT SPECIFIED					**49**	**0.04**	
Other countries of the World					49	0.04	

Yearbook of Tourism Statistics, Data 2009 – 2013, 2015 Edition

MALI

3. Arrivals of non-resident tourists in hotels and similar establishments, by country of residence

	2009	2010	2011	2012	2013	Market share 2013	% Change 2013-2012
TOTAL				31,620	57,223	100.00	80.97
AFRICA				13,302	15,635	27.32	17.54
WEST AFRICA				9,243	10,122	17.69	9.51
All countries of West Africa				9,243	10,122	17.69	9.51
OTHER AFRICA				4,059	5,513	9.63	35.82
Other countries of Africa				4,059	5,513	9.63	35.82
AMERICAS				5,581	10,211	17.84	82.96
NORTH AMERICA				5,581	10,211	17.84	82.96
Canada				894	584	1.02	-34.68
United States of America				4,687	9,627	16.82	105.40
EAST ASIA AND THE PACIFIC				457	411	0.72	-10.07
NORTH-EAST ASIA				457	411	0.72	-10.07
Japan				457	411	0.72	-10.07
EUROPE				9,159	14,137	24.71	54.35
CENTRAL/EASTERN EUROPE				526	2,974	5.20	465.40
Russian Federation				105	298	0.52	183.81
Other countries Central/East Europe				421	2,676	4.68	535.63
NORTHERN EUROPE				896	3,867	6.76	331.58
United Kingdom				485	3,576	6.25	637.32
Scandinavia				411	291	0.51	-29.20
SOUTHERN EUROPE				1,705	1,033	1.81	-39.41
Italy				819	571	1.00	-30.28
Spain				886	462	0.81	-47.86
WESTERN EUROPE				6,032	6,263	10.94	3.83
Austria				184	341	0.60	85.33
France				4,006	3,115	5.44	-22.24
Germany				709	655	1.14	-7.62
Switzerland				348	465	0.81	33.62
Benelux				785	1,687	2.95	114.90
MIDDLE EAST				184	538	0.94	192.39
All countries of Middle East				184	538	0.94	192.39
NOT SPECIFIED				2,937	16,291	28.47	454.68
Other countries of the World				2,937	16,291	28.47	454.68

Yearbook of Tourism Statistics, Data 2009 – 2013, 2015 Edition

MALI

5. Overnight stays of non-resident tourists in hotels and similar establishments, by country of residence

	2009	2010	2011	2012	2013	Market share 2013	% Change 2013-2012
TOTAL	352,801	290,936	283,729	61,187	102,640	100.00	67.75
AFRICA	107,972	97,038	93,136	26,928	30,662	29.87	13.87
WEST AFRICA	66,435	64,929	59,451	17,593	17,152	16.71	-2.51
All countries of West Africa	66,435	64,929	59,451	17,593	17,152	16.71	-2.51
OTHER AFRICA	41,537	32,109	33,685	9,335	13,510	13.16	44.72
Other countries of Africa	41,537	32,109	33,685	9,335	13,510	13.16	44.72
AMERICAS	57,747	41,200	30,877	9,608	12,827	12.50	33.50
NORTH AMERICA	57,747	41,200	30,877	9,608	12,827	12.50	33.50
Canada	20,859	10,326	9,534	1,683	1,490	1.45	-11.47
United States of America	36,888	30,874	21,343	7,925	11,337	11.05	43.05
EAST ASIA AND THE PACIFIC	1,307	4,448	5,358	1,071	1,153	1.12	7.66
NORTH-EAST ASIA	1,307	4,448	5,358	1,071	1,153	1.12	7.66
Japan	1,307	4,448	5,358	1,071	1,153	1.12	7.66
EUROPE	157,888	123,796	94,768	17,253	34,870	33.97	102.11
CENTRAL/EASTERN EUROPE	8,007	7,380	9,299	903	5,727	5.58	534.22
Russian Federation	1,947	2,005	3,760	218	970	0.95	344.95
Other countries Central/East Europe	6,060	5,375	5,539	685	4,757	4.63	594.45
NORTHERN EUROPE	13,956	9,167	8,078	1,421	6,780	6.61	377.13
United Kingdom	9,986	6,712	5,028	710	5,889	5.74	729.44
Scandinavia	3,970	2,455	3,050	711	891	0.87	25.32
SOUTHERN EUROPE	20,471	17,563	15,348	2,947	2,658	2.59	-9.81
Italy	11,081	9,720	7,970	1,330	1,439	1.40	8.20
Spain	9,390	7,843	7,378	1,617	1,219	1.19	-24.61
WESTERN EUROPE	115,454	89,686	62,043	11,982	19,705	19.20	64.46
Austria	1,355	2,898	2,077	503	907	0.88	80.32
France	81,028	65,721	37,776	7,333	13,552	13.20	84.81
Germany	12,824	8,094	8,234	2,178	1,674	1.63	-23.14
Switzerland	6,155	3,716	3,972	503	1,128	1.10	124.25
Benelux	14,092	9,257	9,984	1,465	2,444	2.38	66.83
MIDDLE EAST	6,101	4,409	4,969	435	1,180	1.15	171.26
All countries of Middle East	6,101	4,409	4,969	435	1,180	1.15	171.26
NOT SPECIFIED	21,786	20,045	54,621	5,892	21,948	21.38	272.51
Other countries of the World	21,786	20,045	54,621	5,892	21,948	21.38	272.51

Yearbook of Tourism Statistics, Data 2009 – 2013, 2015 Edition

MALTA

1. Arrivals of non-resident tourists at national borders, by nationality

	2009	2010	2011	2012	2013	Market share 2013	% Change 2013-2012
TOTAL (*)	1,182,489	1,338,841	1,415,018	1,443,414	1,582,153	100.00	9.61
AMERICAS	13,943	16,418	16,499	18,027	19,502	1.23	8.18
NORTH AMERICA	13,943	16,418	16,499	18,027	19,502	1.23	8.18
United States of America	13,943	16,418	16,499	18,027	19,502	1.23	8.18
EUROPE	1,088,750	1,221,398	1,303,990	1,327,982	1,431,600	90.48	7.80
CENTRAL/EASTERN EUROPE	56,944	64,231	71,666	94,878	118,033	7.46	24.41
Bulgaria	4,960	3,189	3,304	4,701	6,896	0.44	46.69
Czech Republic	6,796	5,923	7,738	8,810	7,698	0.49	-12.62
Estonia	749	1,510	1,480	1,850	1,944	0.12	5.08
Hungary	7,848	7,747	7,867	7,344	12,992	0.82	76.91
Latvia	908	1,170	1,307	1,768	2,907	0.18	64.42
Lithuania	2,168	1,673	2,160	6,987	10,020	0.63	43.41
Poland	7,139	12,070	13,557	20,085	23,889	1.51	18.94
Romania	5,557	4,280	6,094	6,598	7,014	0.44	6.30
Russian Federation	17,239	22,727	24,191	31,562	40,048	2.53	26.89
Slovakia	3,580	3,942	3,968	5,173	4,625	0.29	-10.59
NORTHERN EUROPE	489,582	533,165	559,452	566,370	589,952	37.29	4.16
Denmark	21,268	28,830	33,203	34,065	33,839	2.14	-0.66
Finland	9,697	11,922	7,457	7,590	6,878	0.43	-9.38
Ireland	24,328	25,185	26,886	27,731	30,224	1.91	8.99
Norway	6,470	15,006	13,146	14,152	18,752	1.19	32.50
Sweden	29,347	37,123	39,977	41,557	45,600	2.88	9.73
United Kingdom	398,472	415,099	438,783	441,275	454,659	28.74	3.03
SOUTHERN EUROPE	223,151	300,681	278,992	274,940	301,422	19.05	9.63
Croatia			2,347	950	2,272	0.14	139.16
Greece	7,641	5,880	4,341	3,113	4,580	0.29	47.12
Italy	161,736	219,663	201,774	202,200	233,777	14.78	15.62
Portugal	4,347	4,320	3,858	4,511	3,591	0.23	-20.39
Slovenia	4,129	2,976	3,584	3,943	3,924	0.25	-0.48
Spain	45,298	67,842	63,088	60,223	53,278	3.37	-11.53
WESTERN EUROPE	300,777	313,876	355,488	360,540	391,157	24.72	8.49
Austria	21,217	19,908	19,647	19,827	25,739	1.63	29.82
Belgium	23,746	24,296	31,742	27,279	28,948	1.83	6.12
France	71,931	86,516	103,629	107,893	116,533	7.37	8.01
Germany	127,374	126,193	134,306	137,500	147,110	9.30	6.99
Luxembourg	2,052	2,016	2,221	3,091	2,639	0.17	-14.62
Netherlands	33,418	33,425	38,897	39,191	41,486	2.62	5.86
Switzerland	21,039	21,522	25,046	25,759	28,702	1.81	11.43
EAST MEDITERRANEAN EUROPE	18,296	9,445	38,392	31,254	31,036	1.96	-0.70
Cyprus	18,296	9,445	7,384	4,842	4,321	0.27	-10.76
Israel			31,008	26,412	26,715	1.69	1.15
MIDDLE EAST	14,282	15,864	6,273	17,217	34,621	2.19	101.09
Libya	14,282	15,864	6,273	17,217	34,621	2.19	101.09
NOT SPECIFIED	65,514	85,161	88,256	80,188	96,430	6.09	20.25
Other countries of the World	65,514	85,161	88,256	80,188	96,430	6.09	20.25

469

MALTA

4. Arrivals of non-resident tourists in all types of accommodation establishments, by country of residence

	2009	2010	2011	2012	2013	Market share 2013	% Change 2013-2012
TOTAL (*)	1,182,490	1,338,841	1,415,018	1,443,414	1,582,153	100.00	9.61
AMERICAS	13,943	16,418	16,499	18,027	19,502	1.23	8.18
NORTH AMERICA	13,943	16,418	16,499	18,027	19,502	1.23	8.18
United States of America	13,943	16,418	16,499	18,027	19,502	1.23	8.18
EUROPE	1,012,578	1,155,257	1,235,127	1,245,129	1,334,559	84.35	7.18
CENTRAL/EASTERN EUROPE	17,240	22,727	24,191	31,526	40,048	2.53	27.03
Russian Federation	17,240	22,727	24,191	31,526	40,048	2.53	27.03
NORTHERN EUROPE	489,579	533,165	559,452	566,369	589,951	37.29	4.16
Ireland	24,328	25,185	26,886	27,731	30,224	1.91	8.99
United Kingdom	398,472	415,099	438,783	441,275	454,659	28.74	3.03
Scandinavia	66,779	92,881	93,783	97,363	105,068	6.64	7.91
SOUTHERN EUROPE	207,035	287,505	267,209	263,373	289,327	18.29	9.85
Croatia			2,347	950	2,272	0.14	139.16
Italy	161,737	219,663	201,774	202,200	233,777	14.78	15.62
Spain	45,298	67,842	63,088	60,223	53,278	3.37	-11.53
WESTERN EUROPE	298,724	311,860	353,267	357,449	388,518	24.56	8.69
Austria	21,218	19,908	19,647	19,827	25,739	1.63	29.82
Belgium	23,746	24,296	31,742	27,279	28,948	1.83	6.12
France	71,930	86,516	103,629	107,893	116,533	7.37	8.01
Germany	127,373	126,193	134,306	137,500	147,110	9.30	6.99
Netherlands	33,419	33,425	38,897	39,191	41,486	2.62	5.86
Switzerland	21,038	21,522	25,046	25,759	28,702	1.81	11.43
EAST MEDITERRANEAN EUROPE			31,008	26,412	26,715	1.69	1.15
Israel			31,008	26,412	26,715	1.69	1.15
MIDDLE EAST	14,281	15,864	6,273	17,217	34,621	2.19	101.09
Libya	14,281	15,864	6,273	17,217	34,621	2.19	101.09
NOT SPECIFIED	141,688	151,302	157,119	163,041	193,471	12.23	18.66
Other countries of the World	141,688	151,302	157,119	163,041	193,471	12.23	18.66

Yearbook of Tourism Statistics, Data 2009 – 2013, 2015 Edition

MALTA

6. Overnight stays of non-resident tourists in all types of accommodation establishments, by country of residence

		2009	2010	2011	2012	2013	Market share 2013	% Change 2013-2012
TOTAL	(*)	9,949,378	11,147,939	11,241,472	11,859,521	12,890,268	100.00	8.69
AMERICAS		114,541	139,709	119,969	137,719	158,890	1.23	15.37
NORTH AMERICA		114,541	139,709	119,969	137,719	158,890	1.23	15.37
United States of America		114,541	139,709	119,969	137,719	158,890	1.23	15.37
EUROPE		8,993,721	9,920,734	10,209,195	10,646,241	11,469,913	88.98	7.74
CENTRAL/EASTERN EUROPE		591,026	659,779	692,470	965,864	1,153,191	8.95	19.39
Bulgaria		35,645	29,122	28,180	33,028	66,317	0.51	100.79
Czech Republic		76,763	56,429	76,737	98,596	71,008	0.55	-27.98
Estonia		10,158	16,269	10,437	10,271	15,871	0.12	54.52
Hungary		68,005	62,922	60,787	55,742	102,804	0.80	84.43
Latvia		4,729	7,117	7,073	11,796	26,268	0.20	122.69
Lithuania		14,645	14,947	15,792	52,299	76,673	0.59	46.61
Poland		71,659	101,998	105,688	155,095	195,786	1.52	26.24
Romania		40,121	32,082	37,409	48,365	59,575	0.46	23.18
Russian Federation		232,977	299,778	303,191	445,322	490,753	3.81	10.20
Slovakia		36,324	39,115	47,176	55,350	48,136	0.37	-13.03
NORTHERN EUROPE		4,325,798	4,730,479	4,794,073	4,867,776	5,103,494	39.59	4.84
Denmark		170,647	230,067	266,978	288,811	275,434	2.14	-4.63
Finland		81,805	98,306	63,455	59,865	57,237	0.44	-4.39
Ireland		185,294	197,767	207,794	217,901	241,849	1.88	10.99
Norway		49,544	126,460	107,090	118,517	148,302	1.15	25.13
Sweden		206,049	262,985	280,661	291,042	337,033	2.61	15.80
United Kingdom		3,632,459	3,814,894	3,868,095	3,891,640	4,043,639	31.37	3.91
SOUTHERN EUROPE		1,508,633	1,911,801	1,741,014	1,743,807	1,884,626	14.62	8.08
Croatia				14,201	9,315	16,171	0.13	73.60
Greece		41,136	26,711	16,557	11,607	27,845	0.22	139.90
Italy		993,826	1,275,909	1,153,785	1,200,524	1,375,812	10.67	14.60
Portugal		27,624	23,353	22,813	33,037	22,416	0.17	-32.15
Slovenia		29,385	19,961	24,058	24,587	33,222	0.26	35.12
Spain		416,662	565,867	509,600	464,737	409,160	3.17	-11.96
WESTERN EUROPE		2,489,995	2,573,613	2,804,904	2,931,679	3,191,287	24.76	8.86
Austria		165,497	150,029	145,874	147,309	200,768	1.56	36.29
Belgium		190,777	181,393	219,733	196,293	224,399	1.74	14.32
France		586,106	669,289	762,385	813,240	890,573	6.91	9.51
Germany		1,072,509	1,093,633	1,127,521	1,200,873	1,255,420	9.74	4.54
Luxembourg		19,350	14,146	17,475	21,409	21,589	0.17	0.84
Netherlands		272,852	277,998	311,012	321,426	339,891	2.64	5.74
Switzerland		182,904	187,125	220,904	231,129	258,647	2.01	11.91
EAST MEDITERRANEAN EUROPE		78,269	45,062	176,734	137,115	137,315	1.07	0.15
Cyprus		78,269	45,062	31,750	18,102	19,178	0.15	5.94
Israel				144,984	119,013	118,137	0.92	-0.74
MIDDLE EAST		103,103	131,773	42,928	114,715	204,958	1.59	78.67
Libya		103,103	131,773	42,928	114,715	204,958	1.59	78.67
NOT SPECIFIED		738,013	955,723	869,380	960,846	1,056,507	8.20	9.96
Other countries of the World		738,013	955,723	869,380	960,846	1,056,507	8.20	9.96

Yearbook of Tourism Statistics, Data 2009 – 2013, 2015 Edition

MARSHALL ISLANDS

1. Arrivals of non-resident tourists at national borders, by nationality

	2009	2010	2011	2012	2013	Market share 2013	% Change 2013-2012
TOTAL (*)	5,372	4,563	4,555				
AMERICAS	1,614	1,712	1,619				
NORTH AMERICA	1,519	1,700	1,594				
Canada	44	46	45				
United States of America	1,475	1,654	1,549				
OTHER AMERICAS	95	12	25				
Other countries of the Americas	95	12	25				
EAST ASIA AND THE PACIFIC	3,501	2,622	2,681				
NORTH-EAST ASIA	1,909	1,164	1,030				
China	129	105	126				
Japan	1,431	585	464				
Korea, Republic of	49	52	57				
Taiwan, Province of China	300	422	383				
SOUTH-EAST ASIA	240	274	232				
Philippines	240	274	232				
AUSTRALASIA	307	321	357				
Australia	216	202	245				
New Zealand	91	119	112				
MELANESIA	95	116	120				
Fiji	95	116	120				
MICRONESIA	505	508	752				
Guam	16	14	56				
Kiribati	97	69	54				
Micronesia, Federated States of	327	338	539				
Nauru	6	24	8				
Palau	59	63	95				
POLYNESIA	16	14	11				
Tuvalu	16	14	11				
OTHER EAST ASIA AND THE PACIFIC	429	225	179				
Other countries of Asia	369	74	63				
Other countries of Oceania	60	151	116				
EUROPE	207	211	209				
NORTHERN EUROPE	20	53	63				
United Kingdom	20	53	63				
WESTERN EUROPE	31	39	18				
Germany	31	39	18				
OTHER EUROPE	156	119	128				
Other countries of Europe	156	119	128				
NOT SPECIFIED	50	18	46				
Other countries of the World	50	18	46				

Yearbook of Tourism Statistics, Data 2009 – 2013, 2015 Edition

MARSHALL ISLANDS

1. Arrivals of non-resident tourists at national borders, by country of residence

		2009	2010	2011	2012	2013	Market share 2013	% Change 2013-2012
TOTAL	(*)	**5,372**	**4,563**	**4,559**	**4,578**			
AMERICAS		**1,354**	**1,332**	**1,322**	**1,140**			
NORTH AMERICA		**1,297**	**1,323**	**1,297**	**1,126**			
Canada		41	26	26	24			
United States of America		1,256	1,297	1,271	1,102			
OTHER AMERICAS		**57**	**9**	**25**	**14**			
Other countries of the Americas		57	9	25	14			
EAST ASIA AND THE PACIFIC		**3,263**	**2,934**	**2,877**	**3,145**			
NORTH-EAST ASIA		**1,731**	**1,080**	**946**	**960**			
China		89	79	83	87			
Japan		1,349	557	435	448			
Korea, Republic of		38	40	50	62			
Taiwan, Province of China		255	404	378	363			
SOUTH-EAST ASIA		**196**	**216**	**194**	**187**			
Philippines		196	216	194	187			
AUSTRALASIA		**271**	**274**	**313**	**309**			
Australia		177	164	204	192			
New Zealand		94	110	109	117			
MELANESIA		**119**	**138**	**152**	**194**			
Fiji		119	138	152	194			
MICRONESIA		**654**	**861**	**982**	**1,243**			
Guam		193	325	293	232			
Kiribati		76	59	48	90			
Micronesia, Federated States of		319	383	536	363			
Nauru		5	24	10	511			
Palau		61	70	95	47			
POLYNESIA		**8**	**14**	**10**	**17**			
Tuvalu		8	14	10	17			
OTHER EAST ASIA AND THE PACIFIC		**284**	**351**	**280**	**235**			
Other countries of Asia		207	85	70	52			
Other countries of Oceania		77	266	210	183			
EUROPE		**153**	**144**	**137**	**115**			
NORTHERN EUROPE		**14**	**26**	**37**	**31**			
United Kingdom		14	26	37	31			
WESTERN EUROPE		**24**	**28**	**10**	**15**			
Germany		24	28	10	15			
OTHER EUROPE		**115**	**90**	**90**	**69**			
Other countries of Europe		115	90	90	69			
NOT SPECIFIED		**602**	**153**	**223**	**178**			
Other countries of the World		602	153	223	178			

Yearbook of Tourism Statistics, Data 2009 – 2013, 2015 Edition

MARSHALL ISLANDS

6. Overnight stays of non-resident tourists in all types of accommodation establishments, by country of residence

	2009	2010	2011	2012	2013	Market share 2013	% Change 2013-2012
TOTAL	**27,648**	**33,705**	**34,521**				
AMERICAS	**11,408**	**12,390**	**13,183**				
NORTH AMERICA	**10,950**	**12,301**	**11,010**				
Canada	485	452	276				
United States of America	10,465	11,849	10,734				
OTHER AMERICAS	**458**	**89**	**2,173**				
Other countries of the Americas	458	89	2,173				
EAST ASIA AND THE PACIFIC	**12,847**	**19,563**	**19,660**				
NORTH-EAST ASIA	**5,150**	**7,079**	**5,842**				
China	351	326	473				
Japan	3,616	3,882	2,860				
Korea, Republic of	118	183	423				
Taiwan, Province of China	1,065	2,688	2,086				
SOUTH-EAST ASIA	**1,190**	**1,054**	**1,199**				
Philippines	1,190	1,054	1,199				
AUSTRALASIA	**1,787**	**2,115**	**2,755**				
Australia	1,167	1,497	1,839				
New Zealand	620	618	916				
MELANESIA	**790**	**983**	**1,715**				
Fiji	790	983	1,715				
MICRONESIA	**2,708**	**4,686**	**5,864**				
Guam	770	1,614	1,181				
Kiribati	458	762	833				
Micronesia, Federated States of	1,110	1,738	2,972				
Nauru	43	158	67				
Palau	327	414	811				
POLYNESIA		**52**	**56**				
Tuvalu		52	56				
OTHER EAST ASIA AND THE PACIFIC	**1,222**	**3,594**	**2,229**				
Other countries of Asia	885	560	386				
Other countries of Oceania	337	3,034	1,843				
EUROPE	**1,850**	**836**	**939**				
NORTHERN EUROPE	**998**	**227**	**296**				
United Kingdom	998	227	296				
WESTERN EUROPE	**116**	**169**	**37**				
Germany	116	169	37				
OTHER EUROPE	**736**	**440**	**606**				
Other countries of Europe	736	440	606				
NOT SPECIFIED	**1,543**	**916**	**739**				
Other countries of the World	1,543	916	739				

Yearbook of Tourism Statistics, Data 2009 – 2013, 2015 Edition

MARTINIQUE

1. Arrivals of non-resident tourists at national borders, by country of residence

		2009	2010	2011	2012	2013	Market share 2013	% Change 2013-2012
TOTAL	(*)	**441,648**	**478,060**	**496,538**	**487,769**	**489,705**	**100.00**	**0.40**
AMERICAS		**63,145**	**85,239**	**86,363**	**77,648**	**68,157**	**13.92**	**-12.22**
CARIBBEAN		**46,624**	**56,961**	**57,761**	**52,464**	**45,354**	**9.26**	**-13.55**
Barbados		1,164	2,871	2,842	1,226	1,054	0.22	-14.03
Dominica		1,166	3,648	2,841	1,598	1,380	0.28	-13.64
Guadeloupe		38,094	39,863	42,844	45,556	39,386	8.04	-13.54
Saint Lucia		5,601	8,201	3,997	1,856	1,607	0.33	-13.42
Other countries of the Caribbean		599	2,378	5,237	2,228	1,927	0.39	-13.51
NORTH AMERICA		**7,582**	**15,998**	**15,389**	**11,558**	**10,993**	**2.24**	**-4.89**
Canada		1,292	9,535	9,570	9,154	8,010	1.64	-12.50
United States of America		6,290	6,463	5,819	2,404	2,983	0.61	24.08
SOUTH AMERICA		**8,939**	**12,280**	**13,213**	**13,626**	**11,810**	**2.41**	**-13.33**
French Guiana		7,141	9,878	10,368	13,626	11,810	2.41	-13.33
Venezuela		1,798	2,402	2,845				
EUROPE		**367,030**	**389,306**	**404,670**	**407,783**	**419,053**	**85.57**	**2.76**
NORTHERN EUROPE		**1,606**	**2,595**	**2,775**	**2,708**	**4,265**	**0.87**	**57.50**
United Kingdom/Ireland		938	1,610	1,427	1,549	3,061	0.63	97.61
Scandinavia		668	985	1,348	1,159	1,204	0.25	3.88
SOUTHERN EUROPE		**2,029**	**2,349**	**2,497**	**3,057**	**2,066**	**0.42**	**-32.42**
Italy		2,029	2,349	2,497	3,057	2,066	0.42	-32.42
WESTERN EUROPE		**362,994**	**383,570**	**397,285**	**397,883**	**405,905**	**82.89**	**2.02**
France		354,846	372,426	385,358	384,526	391,708	79.99	1.87
Germany		1,011	2,480	2,567	3,946	4,174	0.85	5.78
Switzerland		2,314	2,706	2,138	3,182	3,485	0.71	9.52
Benelux		4,823	5,958	7,222	6,229	6,538	1.34	4.96
OTHER EUROPE		**401**	**792**	**2,113**	**4,135**	**6,817**	**1.39**	**64.86**
Other countries of Europe		401	792	2,113	4,135	6,817	1.39	64.86
NOT SPECIFIED		**11,473**	**3,515**	**5,505**	**2,338**	**2,495**	**0.51**	**6.72**
Other countries of the World		11,473	3,515	5,505	2,338	2,495	0.51	6.72

475

MARTINIQUE

3. Arrivals of non-resident tourists in hotels and similar establishments, by nationality

	2009	2010	2011	2012	2013	Market share 2013	% Change 2013-2012
TOTAL	174,400	177,826	192,816	176,625	158,663	100.00	-10.17
AMERICAS	17,003	27,085	17,954	20,870	18,010	11.35	-13.70
CARIBBEAN	12,393	17,774	12,230	15,158	13,828	8.72	-8.77
All countries of the Caribbean	12,393	17,774	12,230	15,158	13,828	8.72	-8.77
NORTH AMERICA	4,610	9,311	5,724	5,712	4,182	2.64	-26.79
Canada	463	4,771	3,326	4,504	2,272	1.43	-49.56
United States of America	4,147	4,540	2,398	1,208	1,910	1.20	58.11
EUROPE	153,504	149,458	172,978	155,083	138,190	87.10	-10.89
WESTERN EUROPE	147,766	141,923	163,720	143,705	122,003	76.89	-15.10
France	147,766	141,923	163,720	143,705	122,003	76.89	-15.10
OTHER EUROPE	5,738	7,535	9,258	11,378	16,187	10.20	42.27
Other countries of Europe	5,738	7,535	9,258	11,378	16,187	10.20	42.27
NOT SPECIFIED	3,893	1,283	1,884	672	2,463	1.55	266.52
Other countries of the World	3,893	1,283	1,884	672	2,463	1.55	266.52

Yearbook of Tourism Statistics, Data 2009 – 2013, 2015 Edition

MARTINIQUE

4. Arrivals of non-resident tourists in all types of accommodation establishments, by nationality

	2009	2010	2011	2012	2013	Market share 2013	% Change 2013-2012
TOTAL	441,648	478,059	496,538	487,768	489,706	100.00	0.40
AMERICAS	63,146	85,238	86,363	77,648	68,158	13.92	-12.22
CARIBBEAN	55,564	69,240	70,974	66,090	57,165	11.67	-13.50
All countries of the Caribbean	55,564	69,240	70,974	66,090	57,165	11.67	-13.50
NORTH AMERICA	7,582	15,998	15,389	11,558	10,993	2.24	-4.89
Canada	1,292	9,535	9,570	9,154	8,010	1.64	-12.50
United States of America	6,290	6,463	5,819	2,404	2,983	0.61	24.08
EUROPE	367,029	389,306	404,669	407,782	419,053	85.57	2.76
WESTERN EUROPE	354,846	372,426	385,358	384,526	391,708	79.99	1.87
France	354,846	372,426	385,358	384,526	391,708	79.99	1.87
OTHER EUROPE	12,183	16,880	19,311	23,256	27,345	5.58	17.58
Other countries of Europe	12,183	16,880	19,311	23,256	27,345	5.58	17.58
NOT SPECIFIED	11,473	3,515	5,506	2,338	2,495	0.51	6.72
Other countries of the World	11,473	3,515	5,506	2,338	2,495	0.51	6.72

477

MARTINIQUE

5. Overnight stays of non-resident tourists in hotels and similar establishments, by country of residence

	2009	2010	2011	2012	2013	Market share 2013	% Change 2013-2012
TOTAL	1,388,809	1,401,434	1,652,360	1,379,000	1,362,000	100.00	-1.23
AMERICAS	136,376	150,450	209,708	101,492	89,971	6.61	-11.35
CARIBBEAN	120,020	86,951	168,141	83,839	45,981	3.38	-45.16
All countries of the Caribbean	120,020	86,951	168,141	83,839	45,981	3.38	-45.16
NORTH AMERICA	16,356	63,499	41,567	17,653	43,990	3.23	149.19
Canada	3,720	39,177	23,881	13,577	33,248	2.44	144.88
United States of America	12,636	24,322	17,686	4,076	10,742	0.79	163.54
EUROPE	1,222,866	1,243,668	1,421,020	1,271,315	1,250,052	91.78	-1.67
WESTERN EUROPE	1,189,611	1,198,467	1,367,728	1,179,920	1,111,123	81.58	-5.83
France	1,189,611	1,198,467	1,367,728	1,179,920	1,111,123	81.58	-5.83
OTHER EUROPE	33,255	45,201	53,292	91,395	138,929	10.20	52.01
Other countries of Europe	33,255	45,201	53,292	91,395	138,929	10.20	52.01
NOT SPECIFIED	29,567	7,316	21,632	6,193	21,977	1.61	254.87
Other countries of the World	29,567	7,316	21,632	6,193	21,977	1.61	254.87

Yearbook of Tourism Statistics, Data 2009 – 2013, 2015 Edition

MARTINIQUE

6. Overnight stays of non-resident tourists in all types of accommodation establishments, by nationality

	2009	2010	2011	2012	2013	Market share 2013	% Change 2013-2012
TOTAL	5,793,364	6,368,874	6,196,064	6,900,859	7,300,698	100.00	5.79
AMERICAS	576,397	773,454	786,369	733,498	598,909	8.20	-18.35
CARIBBEAN	508,269	579,527	630,498	667,264	491,733	6.74	-26.31
All countries of the Caribbean	508,269	579,527	630,498	667,264	491,733	6.74	-26.31
NORTH AMERICA	68,128	193,927	155,871	66,234	107,176	1.47	61.81
Canada	15,495	134,233	89,551	51,167	81,472	1.12	59.23
United States of America	52,633	59,694	66,320	15,067	25,704	0.35	70.60
EUROPE	5,093,806	5,561,063	5,328,580	6,126,217	6,614,415	90.60	7.97
WESTERN EUROPE	4,955,283	5,387,193	5,128,744	5,781,703	6,253,551	85.66	8.16
France	4,955,283	5,387,193	5,128,744	5,781,703	6,253,551	85.66	8.16
OTHER EUROPE	138,523	173,870	199,836	344,514	360,864	4.94	4.75
Other countries of Europe	138,523	173,870	199,836	344,514	360,864	4.94	4.75
NOT SPECIFIED	123,161	34,357	81,115	41,144	87,374	1.20	112.36
Other countries of the World	123,161	34,357	81,115	41,144	87,374	1.20	112.36

Yearbook of Tourism Statistics, Data 2009 – 2013, 2015 Edition

MAURITIUS

1. Arrivals of non-resident tourists at national borders, by country of residence

	2009	2010	2011	2012	2013	Market share 2013	% Change 2013-2012
TOTAL	**871,356**	**934,827**	**964,642**	**965,441**	**993,106**	**100.00**	**2.87**
AFRICA	**203,846**	**225,754**	**230,673**	**264,786**	**277,190**	**27.91**	**4.68**
EAST AFRICA	**125,773**	**140,190**	**139,415**	**167,787**	**173,400**	**17.46**	**3.35**
Burundi	63	76	80	69	80	0.01	15.94
Comoros	606	746	969	1,076	1,147	0.12	6.60
Djibouti	20	26	25	52	38	0.00	-26.92
Eritrea	7	11	17	14	15	0.00	7.14
Ethiopia	128	88	155	160	334	0.03	108.75
Kenya	1,386	1,548	1,914	2,705	2,865	0.29	5.91
Madagascar	8,333	9,833	11,449	13,563	13,943	1.40	2.80
Malawi	150	185	197	279	233	0.02	-16.49
Mozambique	377	396	414	637	699	0.07	9.73
Reunion	104,946	114,914	113,000	139,169	143,114	14.41	2.83
Rwanda	62	86	75	98	151	0.02	54.08
Seychelles	7,532	10,160	8,485	6,779	7,187	0.72	6.02
Somalia	3	1	7	12	7	0.00	-41.67
Uganda	174	164	264	429	537	0.05	25.17
United Republic of Tanzania	325	321	481	551	625	0.06	13.43
Zambia	335	431	388	626	899	0.09	43.61
Zimbabwe	1,326	1,204	1,495	1,568	1,526	0.15	-2.68
CENTRAL AFRICA	**466**	**519**	**621**	**818**	**1,369**	**0.14**	**67.36**
Angola	123	155	208	330	505	0.05	53.03
Cameroon	147	160	183	163	159	0.02	-2.45
Central African Republic	5	10	12	9	7	0.00	-22.22
Chad	4	8	13	9	12	0.00	33.33
Congo	144	147	155	203	411	0.04	102.46
Democratic Republic of the Congo	3	2			1	0.00	
Equatorial Guinea		4	8	7	3	0.00	-57.14
Gabon	38	30	39	92	266	0.03	189.13
Sao Tome and Principe	2	3	3	5	5	0.00	
NORTH AFRICA	**1,024**	**913**	**1,091**	**1,029**	**1,152**	**0.12**	**11.95**
Algeria	242	223	289	139	216	0.02	55.40
Morocco	389	328	348	372	445	0.04	19.62
Sudan	55	64	64	101	90	0.01	-10.89
Tunisia	338	298	390	417	401	0.04	-3.84
SOUTHERN AFRICA	**75,446**	**82,944**	**87,856**	**91,076**	**96,539**	**9.72**	**6.00**
Botswana	450	487	435	550	666	0.07	21.09
Lesotho	86	107	125	168	145	0.01	-13.69
Namibia	615	761	856	1,047	1,237	0.12	18.15
South Africa	74,176	81,458	86,232	89,058	94,208	9.49	5.78
Swaziland	119	131	208	253	283	0.03	11.86
WEST AFRICA	**1,065**	**1,186**	**1,683**	**1,808**	**2,279**	**0.23**	**26.05**
Benin	42	44	72	66	68	0.01	3.03
Burkina Faso	36	42	46	53	50	0.01	-5.66
Cabo Verde	31	53	33	33	28	0.00	-15.15
Côte d'Ivoire	152	157	211	200	208	0.02	4.00
Gambia	16	26	37	64	57	0.01	-10.94
Ghana	254	263	299	382	435	0.04	13.87
Guinea	18	16	68	30	45	0.00	50.00
Guinea-Bissau	5	2	2	14	4	0.00	-71.43
Liberia	5	16	13	15	22	0.00	46.67
Mali	34	29	57	28	33	0.00	17.86
Mauritania	32	16	11	70	74	0.01	5.71
Niger	13	8	19	55	98	0.01	78.18
Nigeria	272	318	481	574	908	0.09	58.19
Senegal	129	152	222	141	179	0.02	26.95
Sierra Leone	8	18	42	27	28	0.00	3.70
Togo	18	26	70	56	42	0.00	-25.00
OTHER AFRICA	**72**	**2**	**7**	**2,268**	**2,451**	**0.25**	**8.07**

Yearbook of Tourism Statistics, Data 2009 – 2013, 2015 Edition

MAURITIUS

1. Arrivals of non-resident tourists at national borders, by country of residence

	2009	2010	2011	2012	2013	Market share 2013	% Change 2013-2012
Other countries of Africa	72	2	7	2,268	2,451	0.25	8.07
AMERICAS	**13,071**	**13,724**	**14,424**	**16,079**	**15,279**	**1.54**	**-4.98**
CARIBBEAN	**100**	**119**	**159**	**248**	**206**	**0.02**	**-16.94**
Anguilla	1			1			
Antigua and Barbuda		2		8	4	0.00	-50.00
Bahamas	1	7	6	18	27	0.00	50.00
Barbados	7	6	4	12	9	0.00	-25.00
Bermuda	3			4	17	0.00	325.00
Cuba	17	22	27	11	9	0.00	-18.18
Dominica	5	3	2	9	4	0.00	-55.56
Dominican Republic	3	11	17	4	13	0.00	225.00
Grenada	4	5	2	1	5	0.00	400.00
Guadeloupe				19	38	0.00	100.00
Haiti	9	13	15	16	15	0.00	-6.25
Jamaica	19	23	31	27	17	0.00	-37.04
Martinique	1			65	20	0.00	-69.23
Trinidad and Tobago	30	27	55	53	28	0.00	-47.17
CENTRAL AMERICA	**39**	**50**	**38**	**46**	**70**	**0.01**	**52.17**
Belize	8	1	4	4	7	0.00	75.00
Costa Rica	8	9	15	9	15	0.00	66.67
El Salvador	4	5	4	7	8	0.00	14.29
Guatemala	6	12	6	7	14	0.00	100.00
Honduras	9	19	9	19	20	0.00	5.26
Nicaragua	4	4			6	0.00	
NORTH AMERICA	**10,600**	**11,054**	**10,870**	**11,227**	**10,341**	**1.04**	**-7.89**
Canada	3,532	3,619	3,887	4,736	4,435	0.45	-6.36
Mexico	117	119	113	117	129	0.01	10.26
United States of America	6,951	7,316	6,870	6,374	5,777	0.58	-9.37
SOUTH AMERICA	**2,208**	**2,469**	**3,330**	**4,331**	**4,285**	**0.43**	**-1.06**
Argentina	498	627	657	742	890	0.09	19.95
Bolivia	10	12	7	7	15	0.00	114.29
Brazil	1,331	1,459	2,235	3,217	2,886	0.29	-10.29
Chile	124	137	153	137	253	0.03	84.67
Colombia	64	57	79	52	67	0.01	28.85
Ecuador	15	28	27	16	15	0.00	-6.25
Guyana	7	5	13	22	18	0.00	-18.18
Paraguay	17	14	21	12	18	0.00	50.00
Peru	73	68	67	48	32	0.00	-33.33
Suriname	17	8	21	4	16	0.00	300.00
Uruguay	25	15	18	40	45	0.00	12.50
Venezuela	27	39	32	34	30	0.00	-11.76
OTHER AMERICAS	**124**	**32**	**27**	**227**	**377**	**0.04**	**66.08**
Other countries of the Americas	124	32	27	227	377	0.04	66.08
EAST ASIA AND THE PACIFIC	**26,534**	**30,911**	**45,590**	**54,737**	**79,088**	**7.96**	**44.49**
NORTH-EAST ASIA	**10,109**	**11,486**	**20,197**	**27,852**	**49,544**	**4.99**	**77.88**
China	6,925	7,609	15,133	20,885	41,913	4.22	100.68
Hong Kong, China	382	415	593	1,269	1,449	0.15	14.18
Japan	1,351	1,485	1,545	1,641	1,768	0.18	7.74
Korea, Republic of	704	1,067	1,935	2,651	2,778	0.28	4.79
Macao, China	1		1	11	34	0.00	209.09
Mongolia	16	13	3	9	6	0.00	-33.33
Taiwan, Province of China	730	897	987	1,386	1,596	0.16	15.15
SOUTH-EAST ASIA	**5,227**	**7,138**	**8,605**	**8,464**	**9,964**	**1.00**	**17.72**
Brunei Darussalam	18	5	10	34	29	0.00	-14.71
Cambodia	11	66	69	33	34	0.00	3.03
Indonesia	853	1,275	1,615	1,626	1,852	0.19	13.90
Lao People's Democratic Republic	1	2	2	13	5	0.00	-61.54
Malaysia	1,164	1,438	1,989	1,967	3,174	0.32	61.36
Myanmar	21	14	71	50	63	0.01	26.00

481

MAURITIUS

1. Arrivals of non-resident tourists at national borders, by country of residence

	2009	2010	2011	2012	2013	Market share 2013	% Change 2013-2012
Philippines	1,022	1,773	1,850	1,801	1,821	0.18	1.11
Singapore	1,657	1,909	2,461	2,078	2,112	0.21	1.64
Thailand	187	230	190	286	331	0.03	15.73
Viet Nam	293	426	348	576	543	0.05	-5.73
AUSTRALASIA	**11,113**	**12,219**	**16,725**	**17,737**	**19,061**	**1.92**	**7.46**
Australia	10,363	11,493	15,726	17,009	18,393	1.85	8.14
New Zealand	750	726	999	728	668	0.07	-8.24
MELANESIA	**21**	**22**	**30**	**108**	**103**	**0.01**	**-4.63**
Fiji	13	17	19	33	24	0.00	-27.27
New Caledonia				50	50	0.01	
Papua New Guinea	2	2	4	10	6	0.00	-40.00
Solomon Islands			4	7	5	0.00	-28.57
Vanuatu	6	3	3	8	18	0.00	125.00
MICRONESIA	**1**			**4**	**5**	**0.00**	**25.00**
Kiribati				3	4	0.00	33.33
Nauru	1			1	1	0.00	
POLYNESIA	**2**			**521**	**332**	**0.03**	**-36.28**
American Samoa	1			508	324	0.03	-36.22
Cook Islands	1			1	1	0.00	
French Polynesia				12	7	0.00	-41.67
OTHER EAST ASIA AND THE PACIFIC	**61**	**46**	**33**	**51**	**79**	**0.01**	**54.90**
Other countries of Asia	54	40	27	23	24	0.00	4.35
Other countries of Oceania	7	6	6	28	55	0.01	96.43
EUROPE	**579,897**	**605,790**	**610,181**	**561,210**	**547,598**	**55.14**	**-2.43**
CENTRAL/EASTERN EUROPE	**19,445**	**19,944**	**26,692**	**35,415**	**31,569**	**3.18**	**-10.86**
Armenia	24	32	48	60	78	0.01	30.00
Azerbaijan	47	73	78	86	165	0.02	91.86
Belarus	169	149	223	441	428	0.04	-2.95
Bulgaria	511	498	639	613	597	0.06	-2.61
Czech Republic	3,487	3,477	4,081	5,247	5,543	0.56	5.64
Estonia	989	549	288	303	256	0.03	-15.51
Georgia	18	34	8	31	29	0.00	-6.45
Hungary	1,382	1,376	1,231	1,013	820	0.08	-19.05
Kazakhstan	276	282	204	210	207	0.02	-1.43
Latvia	268	219	250	297	329	0.03	10.77
Lithuania	309	343	372	369	361	0.04	-2.17
Poland	2,880	2,560	2,995	2,862	2,998	0.30	4.75
Republic of Moldova	68	59	79	70	49	0.00	-30.00
Romania	814	960	1,055	962	1,221	0.12	26.92
Russian Federation	5,626	6,615	12,224	19,429	14,905	1.50	-23.28
Slovakia	1,172	1,366	1,263	1,488	1,580	0.16	6.18
Tajikistan	1	4	3	2	7	0.00	250.00
Turkmenistan	5	3	1	14	10	0.00	-28.57
Ukraine	1,178	1,206	1,485	1,754	1,876	0.19	6.96
USSR (former)	19		2	19	13	0.00	-31.58
Uzbekistan	37	50	24	77	45	0.00	-41.56
Other countries Central/East Europe	165	89	139	68	52	0.01	-23.53
NORTHERN EUROPE	**120,206**	**114,926**	**104,004**	**102,320**	**112,686**	**11.35**	**10.13**
Denmark	2,770	2,678	2,549	2,453	3,282	0.33	33.80
Faeroe Islands	1			16	6	0.00	-62.50
Finland	3,600	4,026	3,133	2,330	1,866	0.19	-19.91
Iceland	55	44	38	48	45	0.00	-6.25
Ireland	4,249	3,460	2,717	2,009	1,807	0.18	-10.05
Norway	2,475	2,674	3,060	3,521	3,086	0.31	-12.35
Sweden	5,060	4,496	4,325	4,295	4,577	0.46	6.57
United Kingdom	101,996	97,548	88,182	87,648	98,017	9.87	11.83
SOUTHERN EUROPE	**72,015**	**70,548**	**68,109**	**53,916**	**43,488**	**4.38**	**-19.34**
Albania	71	49	73	43	26	0.00	-39.53
Andorra	30	17	20	35	59	0.01	68.57

482

MAURITIUS

1. Arrivals of non-resident tourists at national borders, by country of residence

	2009	2010	2011	2012	2013	Market share 2013	% Change 2013-2012
Bosnia and Herzegovina	37	44	36	44	21	0.00	-52.27
Croatia	244	272	368	341	291	0.03	-14.66
Gibraltar				2	6	0.00	200.00
Greece	1,766	1,447	1,342	998	835	0.08	-16.33
Italy	56,736	56,540	52,747	40,009	31,205	3.14	-22.01
Malta	206	247	365	221	211	0.02	-4.52
Portugal	2,098	2,680	2,426	1,799	1,620	0.16	-9.95
San Marino	52	115	59	41	31	0.00	-24.39
Serbia and Montenegro	91	20	10	4	2	0.00	-50.00
Slovenia	1,106	991	841	885	688	0.07	-22.26
Spain	9,549	8,096	9,801	9,473	8,441	0.85	-10.89
TFYR of Macedonia	29	30	21	21	52	0.01	147.62
WESTERN EUROPE	**366,947**	**398,851**	**409,702**	**368,139**	**358,437**	**36.09**	**-2.64**
Austria	8,106	9,255	8,822	8,151	7,937	0.80	-2.63
Belgium	10,254	10,214	12,029	10,967	11,566	1.16	5.46
France	275,599	302,185	302,004	262,100	244,752	24.65	-6.62
Germany	51,279	52,886	56,331	55,186	60,530	6.10	9.68
Liechtenstein	61	80	98	80	79	0.01	-1.25
Luxembourg	591	615	710	943	1,008	0.10	6.89
Monaco	181	174	167	276	310	0.03	12.32
Netherlands	5,527	4,865	5,179	4,434	4,499	0.45	1.47
Switzerland	15,349	18,577	24,362	26,002	27,756	2.79	6.75
EAST MEDITERRANEAN EUROPE	**1,263**	**1,496**	**1,674**	**1,420**	**1,418**	**0.14**	**-0.14**
Cyprus	278	314	291	241	160	0.02	-33.61
Israel	391	425	574	541	552	0.06	2.03
Turkey	594	757	809	638	706	0.07	10.66
OTHER EUROPE	**21**	**25**					
Other countries of Europe	21	25					
MIDDLE EAST	**5,702**	**6,012**	**6,448**	**8,902**	**12,659**	**1.27**	**42.20**
Bahrain	72	69	52	139	181	0.02	30.22
Egypt	395	402	468	401	514	0.05	28.18
Iraq	11	26	29	17	17	0.00	
Jordan	178	156	153	109	184	0.02	68.81
Kuwait	112	101	199	234	279	0.03	19.23
Lebanon	326	323	360	313	441	0.04	40.89
Libya	69	53	20	25	62	0.01	148.00
Oman	52	57	78	173	235	0.02	35.84
Palestine	9	22	7	6	10	0.00	66.67
Qatar	59	49	58	243	362	0.04	48.97
Saudi Arabia	1,161	1,197	1,188	1,782	2,136	0.22	19.87
Syrian Arab Republic	101	64	41	39	56	0.01	43.59
United Arab Emirates	3,141	3,470	3,780	5,403	8,161	0.82	51.05
Yemen	16	23	15	18	21	0.00	16.67
SOUTH ASIA	**41,014**	**51,348**	**55,743**	**58,606**	**59,722**	**6.01**	**1.90**
Bangladesh	496	207	226	1,264	525	0.05	-58.47
Bhutan	1	3	1	3	6	0.00	100.00
India	39,252	49,779	53,955	55,197	57,255	5.77	3.73
Iran, Islamic Republic of	133	149	308	235	221	0.02	-5.96
Maldives	18	28	48	64	48	0.00	-25.00
Nepal	80	124	264	211	180	0.02	-14.69
Pakistan	621	771	698	946	994	0.10	5.07
Sri Lanka	413	287	243	686	493	0.05	-28.13
NOT SPECIFIED	**1,292**	**1,288**	**1,583**	**1,121**	**1,570**	**0.16**	**40.05**
Other countries of the World	1,292	1,288	1,583	1,121	1,570	0.16	40.05

Yearbook of Tourism Statistics, Data 2009 – 2013, 2015 Edition

MAURITIUS

6. Overnight stays of non-resident tourists in all types of accommodation establishments, by country of residence

	2009	2010	2011	2012	2013	Market share 2013	% Change 2013-2012
TOTAL	8,639,304	9,651,244	10,000,136	10,461,126	10,834,907	100.00	3.57
AFRICA	1,826,343	1,773,320	1,994,346	2,302,416	2,267,088	20.92	-1.53
EAST AFRICA	1,167,314	1,010,854	1,200,888	1,426,649	1,338,644	12.35	-6.17
Comoros	8,503	13,472	18,014	21,786	24,683	0.23	13.30
Kenya	11,767	12,684	17,600	20,768	21,901	0.20	5.46
Madagascar	96,282	108,972	125,848	143,169	205,807	1.90	43.75
Reunion	969,927	769,924	943,649	1,159,028	1,001,960	9.25	-13.55
Seychelles	67,976	94,302	80,522	63,574	67,712	0.62	6.51
Zimbabwe	12,859	11,500	15,255	18,324	16,581	0.15	-9.51
SOUTHERN AFRICA	602,983	697,026	720,138	753,993	780,188	7.20	3.47
South Africa	602,983	697,026	720,138	753,993	780,188	7.20	3.47
OTHER AFRICA	56,046	65,440	73,320	121,774	148,256	1.37	21.75
Other countries of Africa	56,046	65,440	73,320	121,774	148,256	1.37	21.75
AMERICAS	131,044	144,272	162,574	201,437	201,130	1.86	-0.15
NORTH AMERICA	112,498	122,432	135,525	162,275	161,216	1.49	-0.65
Canada	58,423	59,091	67,860	102,280	99,775	0.92	-2.45
United States of America	54,075	63,341	67,665	59,995	61,441	0.57	2.41
OTHER AMERICAS	18,546	21,840	27,049	39,162	39,914	0.37	1.92
Other countries of the Americas	18,546	21,840	27,049	39,162	39,914	0.37	1.92
EAST ASIA AND THE PACIFIC	373,044	462,784	577,234	779,127	934,215	8.62	19.91
NORTH-EAST ASIA	84,888	108,456	180,207	262,860	400,053	3.69	52.19
China	69,196	93,492	162,914	241,543	378,981	3.50	56.90
Hong Kong, China	4,211	4,934	6,533	10,921	10,543	0.10	-3.46
Japan	11,481	10,030	10,760	10,396	10,529	0.10	1.28
SOUTH-EAST ASIA	21,884	24,624	26,500	32,560	40,345	0.37	23.91
Malaysia	10,554	11,799	11,695	15,275	19,550	0.18	27.99
Singapore	11,330	12,825	14,805	17,285	20,795	0.19	20.31
AUSTRALASIA	138,665	151,744	200,337	225,318	227,459	2.10	0.95
Australia	138,665	151,744	200,337	225,318	227,459	2.10	0.95
OTHER EAST ASIA AND THE PACIFIC	127,607	177,960	170,190	258,389	266,358	2.46	3.08
Other countries of Asia	117,511	166,432	158,991	248,232	250,374	2.31	0.86
Other countries of Oceania	10,096	11,528	11,199	10,157	15,984	0.15	57.37
EUROPE	5,917,949	6,805,697	6,720,887	6,617,993	6,838,694	63.12	3.33
NORTHERN EUROPE	1,344,549	1,265,664	1,151,836	1,260,377	1,420,594	13.11	12.71
Sweden	62,581	55,107	50,680	48,995	57,240	0.53	16.83
United Kingdom	1,281,968	1,210,557	1,101,156	1,211,382	1,363,354	12.58	12.55
SOUTHERN EUROPE	597,089	593,727	578,087	462,777	393,588	3.63	-14.95
Italy	512,033	526,028	501,289	391,495	323,399	2.98	-17.39
Spain	85,056	67,699	76,798	71,282	70,189	0.65	-1.53
WESTERN EUROPE	3,566,833	4,502,055	4,488,216	4,291,654	4,462,111	41.18	3.97
Austria	92,209	112,541	104,758	95,919	96,826	0.89	0.95
Belgium	138,764	138,874	150,952	154,761	159,050	1.47	2.77
France	2,498,920	3,296,234	3,190,400	2,985,267	3,081,030	28.44	3.21
Germany	579,531	657,888	686,431	677,082	729,164	6.73	7.69
Netherlands	59,667	52,667	56,328	50,552	48,207	0.44	-4.64
Switzerland	197,742	243,851	299,347	328,073	347,834	3.21	6.02
OTHER EUROPE	409,478	444,251	502,748	603,185	562,401	5.19	-6.76
Other countries of Europe	409,478	444,251	502,748	603,185	562,401	5.19	-6.76
SOUTH ASIA	376,783	414,939	488,810	552,374	582,864	5.38	5.52
India	376,783	414,939	488,810	552,374	582,864	5.38	5.52
NOT SPECIFIED	14,141	50,232	56,285	7,779	10,916	0.10	40.33
Other countries of the World	14,141	50,232	56,285	7,779	10,916	0.10	40.33

Yearbook of Tourism Statistics, Data 2009 – 2013, 2015 Edition

MEXICO

1. Arrivals of non-resident tourists at national borders, by nationality

		2009	2010	2011	2012	2013	Market share 2013	% Change 2013-2012
TOTAL		22,346,260	23,289,749	23,403,263	23,402,545	24,150,514	100.00	3.20
AFRICA		9,884	15,005	14,701	15,578	17,721	0.07	13.76
OTHER AFRICA		9,884	15,005	14,701	15,578	17,721	0.07	13.76
All countries of Africa		9,884	15,005	14,701	15,578	17,721	0.07	13.76
AMERICAS		20,178,443	20,867,904	21,152,561	21,540,885	22,088,031	91.46	2.54
CARIBBEAN		40,965	39,249	40,873	44,881	48,887	0.20	8.93
Cuba		40,965	39,249	40,873	44,881	48,887	0.20	8.93
CENTRAL AMERICA		94,843	103,426	88,837	118,452	129,401	0.54	9.24
Costa Rica		42,107	53,152	44,415	59,361	62,507	0.26	5.30
Guatemala		52,736	50,274	44,422	59,091	66,894	0.28	13.21
NORTH AMERICA		19,484,056	19,987,581	20,117,762	20,229,713	20,539,175	85.05	1.53
Canada		1,222,410	1,460,418	1,563,146	1,571,543	1,599,425	6.62	1.77
United States of America	(*)	18,261,646	18,527,163	18,554,616	18,658,170	18,939,750	78.42	1.51
SOUTH AMERICA		401,457	542,831	688,018	881,324	1,047,595	4.34	18.87
Argentina		127,107	170,467	200,687	251,221	257,820	1.07	2.63
Brazil		68,211	117,658	196,266	248,899	267,507	1.11	7.48
Chile		54,179	67,661	76,379	88,148	94,647	0.39	7.37
Colombia		68,493	102,177	125,882	163,725	262,653	1.09	60.42
Venezuela		83,467	84,868	88,804	129,331	164,968	0.68	27.55
OTHER AMERICAS		157,122	194,817	217,071	266,515	322,973	1.34	21.18
Other countries of the Americas		157,122	194,817	217,071	266,515	322,973	1.34	21.18
EAST ASIA AND THE PACIFIC		78,407	101,129	112,642	133,302	156,475	0.65	17.38
NORTH-EAST ASIA		78,407	101,129	112,642	133,302	156,475	0.65	17.38
Japan		52,229	66,164	72,339	85,687	97,226	0.40	13.47
Korea, Republic of		26,178	34,965	40,303	47,615	59,249	0.25	24.43
EUROPE		1,188,286	1,417,935	1,509,736	1,619,164	1,724,875	7.14	6.53
NORTHERN EUROPE		257,367	295,831	330,071	363,142	414,039	1.71	14.02
United Kingdom		257,367	295,831	330,071	363,142	414,039	1.71	14.02
SOUTHERN EUROPE		350,528	469,085	473,679	474,221	469,659	1.94	-0.96
Italy		108,547	133,292	150,690	156,532	154,325	0.64	-1.41
Portugal		26,312	48,630	43,459	38,877	33,079	0.14	-14.91
Spain		215,669	287,163	279,530	278,812	282,255	1.17	1.23
WESTERN EUROPE		418,570	462,343	479,626	500,107	506,369	2.10	1.25
Belgium		30,173	31,188	30,344	29,924	29,783	0.12	-0.47
France		164,236	170,250	186,778	202,855	199,866	0.83	-1.47
Germany		140,754	163,266	165,133	172,841	187,141	0.77	8.27
Netherlands		58,317	68,964	67,821	63,159	57,700	0.24	-8.64
Switzerland		25,090	28,675	29,550	31,328	31,879	0.13	1.76
OTHER EUROPE		161,821	190,676	226,360	281,694	334,808	1.39	18.86
Other countries of Europe		161,821	190,676	226,360	281,694	334,808	1.39	18.86
NOT SPECIFIED		891,241	887,776	613,623	93,616	163,412	0.68	74.56
Other countries of the World		891,241	887,776	613,623	93,616	163,412	0.68	74.56

485

MEXICO

1. Arrivals of non-resident tourists at national borders, by country of residence

		2009	2010	2011	2012	2013	Market share 2013	% Change 2013-2012
TOTAL	(*)	22,346,261	23,289,749	23,403,274	23,402,545	24,150,514	100.00	3.20
AMERICAS		18,874,985	19,128,045	19,314,307	19,397,096	19,788,668	81.94	2.02
NORTH AMERICA		18,874,985	19,128,045	19,314,307	19,397,096	19,788,668	81.94	2.02
Canada		613,339	600,882	759,691	738,926	848,918	3.52	14.89
United States of America		18,261,646	18,527,163	18,554,616	18,658,170	18,939,750	78.42	1.51
NOT SPECIFIED		3,471,276	4,161,704	4,088,967	4,005,449	4,361,846	18.06	8.90
Other countries of the World		3,471,276	4,161,704	4,088,967	4,005,449	4,361,846	18.06	8.90

Yearbook of Tourism Statistics, Data 2009 – 2013, 2015 Edition

MICRONESIA, FEDERATED STATES OF

1. Arrivals of non-resident tourists at national borders, by country of residence

	2009	2010	2011	2012	2013	Market share 2013	% Change 2013-2012
TOTAL (*)	47,538	44,738	35,378	38,263	42,109	100.00	10.05
AMERICAS	8,585	9,194	7,951	7,569	8,358	19.85	10.42
NORTH AMERICA	8,585	9,194	7,951	7,569	8,358	19.85	10.42
Canada	404	399	283	252	391	0.93	55.16
United States of America	8,181	8,795	7,668	7,317	7,967	18.92	8.88
EAST ASIA AND THE PACIFIC	35,808	32,576	24,776	27,866	30,382	72.15	9.03
NORTH-EAST ASIA	16,940	13,781	8,832	9,591	9,101	21.61	-5.11
China	12,712	9,387	4,692	4,652	4,531	10.76	-2.60
Japan	4,228	4,394	4,140	4,939	4,570	10.85	-7.47
SOUTH-EAST ASIA	5,970	5,436	4,659	5,356	6,486	15.40	21.10
Philippines	5,970	5,436	4,659	5,356	6,486	15.40	21.10
AUSTRALASIA	2,772	1,626	1,607	1,595	1,739	4.13	9.03
Australia	2,403	1,350	1,321	1,355	1,429	3.39	5.46
New Zealand	369	276	286	240	310	0.74	29.17
OTHER EAST ASIA AND THE PACIFIC	10,126	11,733	9,678	11,324	13,056	31.01	15.29
Other countries of Asia	8,069	9,223	7,225	8,953	10,472	24.87	16.97
Other countries of Oceania	2,057	2,510	2,453	2,371	2,584	6.14	8.98
EUROPE	2,851	2,725	2,429	2,489	2,981	7.08	19.77
OTHER EUROPE	2,851	2,725	2,429	2,489	2,981	7.08	19.77
All countries of Europe	2,851	2,725	2,429	2,489	2,981	7.08	19.77
NOT SPECIFIED	294	243	222	339	388	0.92	14.45
Other countries of the World	294	243	222	339	388	0.92	14.45

Yearbook of Tourism Statistics, Data 2009 – 2013, 2015 Edition

MONACO

3. Arrivals of non-resident tourists in hotels and similar establishments, by nationality

	2009	2010	2011	2012	2013	Market share 2013	% Change 2013-2012
TOTAL	**264,540**	**279,166**	**294,901**	**292,027**	**327,942**	**100.00**	**12.30**
AFRICA	**2,342**	**2,881**	**2,836**	**3,765**	**3,738**	**1.14**	**-0.72**
OTHER AFRICA	**2,342**	**2,881**	**2,836**	**3,765**	**3,738**	**1.14**	**-0.72**
All countries of Africa	2,342	2,881	2,836	3,765	3,738	1.14	-0.72
AMERICAS	**27,456**	**30,863**	**33,143**	**38,241**	**46,374**	**14.14**	**21.27**
NORTH AMERICA	**22,919**	**25,373**	**27,887**	**32,661**	**42,058**	**12.82**	**28.77**
Canada	3,330	3,938	4,652	4,944	4,774	1.46	-3.44
Mexico	602	738	904	1,001	741	0.23	-25.97
United States of America	18,987	20,697	22,331	26,716	36,543	11.14	36.78
SOUTH AMERICA	**3,221**	**3,814**	**3,558**	**3,963**	**3,055**	**0.93**	**-22.91**
Argentina	686	659	611	883	586	0.18	-33.64
Brazil	2,535	3,155	2,947	3,080	2,469	0.75	-19.84
OTHER AMERICAS	**1,316**	**1,676**	**1,698**	**1,617**	**1,261**	**0.38**	**-22.02**
Other countries of the Americas	1,316	1,676	1,698	1,617	1,261	0.38	-22.02
EAST ASIA AND THE PACIFIC	**10,222**	**11,783**	**14,650**	**15,893**	**16,931**	**5.16**	**6.53**
NORTH-EAST ASIA	**6,920**	**7,414**	**9,308**	**9,346**	**9,135**	**2.79**	**-2.26**
China	1,796	2,888	4,311	3,770	3,661	1.12	-2.89
Japan	5,124	4,526	4,997	5,576	5,474	1.67	-1.83
AUSTRALASIA	**3,302**	**4,369**	**5,342**	**6,547**	**7,796**	**2.38**	**19.08**
Australia	3,302	4,369	5,342	6,547	7,796	2.38	19.08
EUROPE	**216,280**	**223,207**	**232,827**	**221,937**	**226,172**	**68.97**	**1.91**
CENTRAL/EASTERN EUROPE	**13,795**	**14,899**	**17,229**	**14,360**	**18,770**	**5.72**	**30.71**
Russian Federation	13,795	14,899	17,229	14,360	18,770	5.72	30.71
NORTHERN EUROPE	**36,575**	**37,524**	**38,124**	**37,330**	**35,969**	**10.97**	**-3.65**
Denmark	1,602	1,710	1,562	1,360	1,188	0.36	-12.65
Norway	1,549	1,639	2,319	1,702	1,719	0.52	1.00
Sweden	2,357	2,526	2,892	2,445	2,801	0.85	14.56
United Kingdom	31,067	31,649	31,351	31,823	30,261	9.23	-4.91
SOUTHERN EUROPE	**60,052**	**61,870**	**60,116**	**49,385**	**49,536**	**15.11**	**0.31**
Italy	52,951	55,129	53,081	43,614	44,130	13.46	1.18
Portugal	1,111	1,069	1,232	1,055	1,053	0.32	-0.19
Spain	5,990	5,672	5,803	4,716	4,353	1.33	-7.70
WESTERN EUROPE	**87,640**	**91,800**	**99,470**	**97,949**	**102,017**	**31.11**	**4.15**
Austria	2,125	2,485	2,539	2,354	2,484	0.76	5.52
Belgium	4,632	4,509	4,821	5,154	5,508	1.68	6.87
France	56,685	61,234	65,659	64,561	63,934	19.50	-0.97
Germany	11,587	11,070	13,002	12,015	14,234	4.34	18.47
Netherlands	4,741	4,342	4,608	4,292	4,066	1.24	-5.27
Switzerland	7,870	8,160	8,841	9,573	11,791	3.60	23.17
EAST MEDITERRANEAN EUROPE	**1,468**	**1,269**	**1,397**	**1,480**	**2,076**	**0.63**	**40.27**
Israel	1,468	1,269	1,397	1,480	2,076	0.63	40.27
OTHER EUROPE	**16,750**	**15,845**	**16,491**	**21,433**	**17,804**	**5.43**	**-16.93**
Other countries of Europe	16,750	15,845	16,491	21,433	17,804	5.43	-16.93
MIDDLE EAST	**4,333**	**5,039**	**5,386**	**5,446**	**8,501**	**2.59**	**56.10**
All countries of Middle East	4,333	5,039	5,386	5,446	8,501	2.59	56.10
NOT SPECIFIED	**3,907**	**5,393**	**6,059**	**6,745**	**26,226**	**8.00**	**288.82**
Other countries of the World	3,907	5,393	6,059	6,745	26,226	8.00	288.82

488

MONACO

5. Overnight stays of non-resident tourists in hotels and similar establishments, by nationality

	2009	2010	2011	2012	2013	Market share 2013	% Change 2013-2012
TOTAL	778,451	817,011	852,578	802,434	892,795	100.00	11.26
AFRICA	7,351	8,773	8,775	10,536	13,037	1.46	23.74
OTHER AFRICA	7,351	8,773	8,775	10,536	13,037	1.46	23.74
All countries of Africa	7,351	8,773	8,775	10,536	13,037	1.46	23.74
AMERICAS	92,791	103,292	106,963	113,560	115,207	12.90	1.45
NORTH AMERICA	79,625	86,965	91,537	98,492	102,162	11.44	3.73
Canada	10,798	12,561	14,932	14,711	12,238	1.37	-16.81
Mexico	1,638	2,095	2,472	2,484	2,167	0.24	-12.76
United States of America	67,189	72,309	74,133	81,297	87,757	9.83	7.95
SOUTH AMERICA	9,062	10,863	9,962	10,139	9,457	1.06	-6.73
Argentina	2,567	2,464	2,089	2,308	2,219	0.25	-3.86
Brazil	6,495	8,399	7,873	7,831	7,238	0.81	-7.57
OTHER AMERICAS	4,104	5,464	5,464	4,929	3,588	0.40	-27.21
Other countries of the Americas	4,104	5,464	5,464	4,929	3,588	0.40	-27.21
EAST ASIA AND THE PACIFIC	29,885	32,747	38,571	36,726	38,746	4.34	5.50
NORTH-EAST ASIA	19,513	19,485	23,415	21,574	19,899	2.23	-7.76
China	4,118	6,361	9,484	7,611	7,037	0.79	-7.54
Japan	15,395	13,124	13,931	13,963	12,862	1.44	-7.89
AUSTRALASIA	10,372	13,262	15,156	15,152	18,847	2.11	24.39
Australia	10,372	13,262	15,156	15,152	18,847	2.11	24.39
EUROPE	619,478	636,189	661,030	600,244	618,157	69.24	2.98
CENTRAL/EASTERN EUROPE	65,409	70,750	78,084	61,707	66,328	7.43	7.49
Russian Federation	65,409	70,750	78,084	61,707	66,328	7.43	7.49
NORTHERN EUROPE	111,182	113,894	114,311	102,779	114,604	12.84	11.51
Denmark	4,348	4,846	4,394	3,742	3,390	0.38	-9.41
Norway	4,365	4,528	6,397	4,359	4,840	0.54	11.03
Sweden	8,186	8,395	8,479	6,805	7,742	0.87	13.77
United Kingdom	94,283	96,125	95,041	87,873	98,632	11.05	12.24
SOUTHERN EUROPE	151,080	155,649	153,932	121,199	118,320	13.25	-2.38
Italy	131,312	136,767	134,476	103,804	103,911	11.64	0.10
Portugal	3,486	3,345	3,602	2,610	2,754	0.31	5.52
Spain	16,282	15,537	15,854	14,785	11,655	1.31	-21.17
WESTERN EUROPE	234,101	241,745	259,067	241,444	256,101	28.69	6.07
Austria	8,214	8,926	8,377	7,109	8,400	0.94	18.16
Belgium	17,023	16,352	16,280	15,188	18,329	2.05	20.68
France	132,822	143,867	153,985	144,933	141,608	15.86	-2.29
Germany	38,001	35,831	41,176	36,281	43,324	4.85	19.41
Netherlands	13,919	12,229	13,002	11,026	11,278	1.26	2.29
Switzerland	24,122	24,540	26,247	26,907	33,162	3.71	23.25
EAST MEDITERRANEAN EUROPE	5,451	4,642	5,090	4,707	5,991	0.67	27.28
Israel	5,451	4,642	5,090	4,707	5,991	0.67	27.28
OTHER EUROPE	52,255	49,509	50,546	68,408	56,813	6.36	-16.95
Other countries of Europe	52,255	49,509	50,546	68,408	56,813	6.36	-16.95
MIDDLE EAST	17,550	20,968	21,529	21,593	31,352	3.51	45.20
All countries of Middle East	17,550	20,968	21,529	21,593	31,352	3.51	45.20
NOT SPECIFIED	11,396	15,042	15,710	19,775	76,296	8.55	285.82
Other countries of the World	11,396	15,042	15,710	19,775	76,296	8.55	285.82

Yearbook of Tourism Statistics, Data 2009 – 2013, 2015 Edition

MONGOLIA

1. Arrivals of non-resident tourists at national borders, by nationality

	2009	2010	2011	2012	2013	Market share 2013	% Change 2013-2012
TOTAL	411,497	456,963	460,360	475,892	417,813	100.00	-12.20
AFRICA	434	595					
EAST AFRICA	85	145					
Burundi		58					
Eritrea	1						
Ethiopia	16	16					
Kenya	15	13					
Madagascar	2	2					
Malawi	3						
Mauritius	7	16					
Mozambique	3	11					
Reunion	3	1					
Rwanda	4	1					
Uganda	12	8					
United Republic of Tanzania	4	6					
Zambia	7	3					
Zimbabwe	8	10					
CENTRAL AFRICA	30	21					
Angola	1						
Cameroon	16	12					
Central African Republic	4	1					
Chad		8					
Congo	9						
NORTH AFRICA	42	73					
Algeria	11	17					
Morocco	14	35					
Sudan	12						
Tunisia	5	21					
SOUTHERN AFRICA	216	271					
Lesotho		1					
Namibia	1	4					
South Africa	197	258					
Swaziland	18	8					
WEST AFRICA	61	85					
Benin	1	8					
Burkina Faso	1	4					
Gambia	1	1					
Ghana	27	24					
Guinea-Bissau		1					
Liberia	4	6					
Mali	1	3					
Mauritania		1					
Niger	13	12					
Nigeria	9	21					
Senegal	3	1					
Sierra Leone		2					
Togo	1	1					
AMERICAS	14,161	16,486	18,596	18,415	17,304	4.14	-6.03
CARIBBEAN	43	42					
Barbados		1					
Bermuda	2						
Cuba	25	26					
Dominica	2	2					
Haiti	4	4					
Jamaica	1	3					
Trinidad and Tobago	9	6					
CENTRAL AMERICA	30	39					
Belize		3					
Costa Rica	5	6					

490

MONGOLIA

1. Arrivals of non-resident tourists at national borders, by nationality

	2009	2010	2011	2012	2013	Market share 2013	% Change 2013-2012
El Salvador	4	6					
Guatemala	6	5					
Honduras	9	11					
Nicaragua		1					
Panama	6	7					
NORTH AMERICA	**13,663**	**15,799**	**18,596**	**18,415**	**17,304**	**4.14**	**-6.03**
Canada	2,255	2,864	3,173	2,828	2,603	0.62	-7.96
Mexico	73	127					
United States of America	11,335	12,808	15,423	15,587	14,701	3.52	-5.68
SOUTH AMERICA	**425**	**606**					
Argentina	68	179					
Bolivia	2	11					
Brazil	159	225					
Chile	84	59					
Colombia	32	32					
Ecuador	11	7					
Guyana	1						
Paraguay	4	4					
Peru	41	51					
Uruguay	10	24					
Venezuela	13	14					
EAST ASIA AND THE PACIFIC	**241,097**	**264,401**	**274,086**	**306,257**	**254,578**	**60.93**	**-16.87**
NORTH-EAST ASIA	**233,067**	**253,808**	**263,806**	**295,214**	**246,041**	**58.89**	**-16.66**
China	181,523	194,333	200,010	228,547	178,326	42.68	-21.97
Hong Kong, China	434	791	1,878	1,888	1,729	0.41	-8.42
Japan	11,399	14,140	14,988	17,119	18,178	4.35	6.19
Korea, Dem. People's Republic of	342	1,068	1,072	1,012	625	0.15	-38.24
Korea, Republic of	38,272	42,231	43,994	44,360	45,178	10.81	1.84
Macao, China	11	10					
Taiwan, Province of China	1,086	1,235	1,864	2,288	2,005	0.48	-12.37
SOUTH-EAST ASIA	**3,586**	**4,229**	**2,226**	**2,589**	**1,772**	**0.42**	**-31.56**
Brunei Darussalam	7	3					
Cambodia	85	34					
Indonesia	203	246	428	607			
Lao People's Democratic Republic	92	58					
Malaysia	846	926					
Myanmar	7	8					
Philippines	600	823	1,798	1,982	1,772	0.42	-10.60
Singapore	922	1,170					
Thailand	443	546					
Viet Nam	381	415					
AUSTRALASIA	**4,431**	**6,325**	**8,054**	**8,454**	**6,765**	**1.62**	**-19.98**
Australia	3,721	5,443	7,093	7,480	6,765	1.62	-9.56
New Zealand	710	882	961	974			
MELANESIA	**7**	**29**					
Fiji		15					
Papua New Guinea	1	12					
Solomon Islands	6	1					
Vanuatu		1					
POLYNESIA	**6**	**10**					
American Samoa		2					
Samoa	2	5					
Tonga	4	3					
EUROPE	**153,785**	**173,381**	**147,710**	**132,166**	**121,320**	**29.04**	**-8.21**
CENTRAL/EASTERN EUROPE	**117,535**	**132,127**	**112,892**	**96,602**	**87,379**	**20.91**	**-9.55**
Armenia	120	75					
Azerbaijan	75	76					
Belarus	188	177					
Bulgaria	89	123					

491

MONGOLIA

1. Arrivals of non-resident tourists at national borders, by nationality

	2009	2010	2011	2012	2013	Market share 2013	% Change 2013-2012
Czech Republic	815	841					
Estonia	35	91					
Georgia	50	69					
Hungary	281	330					
Kazakhstan	5,053	5,757	7,973	10,523	11,422	2.73	8.54
Kyrgyzstan	205	238					
Latvia	28	45					
Lithuania	53	79					
Poland	1,048	1,163	1,172	1,292	1,489	0.36	15.25
Republic of Moldova	40	40					
Romania	84	106					
Russian Federation	107,911	121,705	102,738	83,707	74,468	17.82	-11.04
Slovakia	196	184					
Tajikistan	112	30					
Turkmenistan	2	4					
Ukraine	967	818	1,009	1,080			
Uzbekistan	183	176					
NORTHERN EUROPE	**10,254**	**11,179**	**9,312**	**8,928**	**6,391**	**1.53**	**-28.42**
Denmark	660	676	729	717			
Finland	843	945					
Iceland	25	18					
Ireland	508	490					
Norway	737	816					
Sweden	1,634	1,625	1,463	1,407			
United Kingdom	5,847	6,609	7,120	6,804	6,391	1.53	-6.07
SOUTHERN EUROPE	**4,393**	**4,730**	**2,737**	**2,769**	**2,682**	**0.64**	**-3.14**
Albania	4	15					
Andorra	3	2					
Bosnia and Herzegovina	17	27					
Croatia	41	37					
Greece	92	126					
Italy	2,415	2,750	2,737	2,769	2,682	0.64	-3.14
Malta	4	9					
Portugal	278	192					
Serbia and Montenegro	57	60					
Slovenia	154	154					
Spain	1,315	1,340					
TFYR of Macedonia	13	18					
WESTERN EUROPE	**20,457**	**23,420**	**21,918**	**22,191**	**22,148**	**5.30**	**-0.19**
Austria	1,105	1,118					
Belgium	807	964					
France	6,702	7,527	7,570	7,553	7,407	1.77	-1.93
Germany	6,858	8,095	8,545	8,909	9,499	2.27	6.62
Liechtenstein	10						
Luxembourg	37	78					
Netherlands	2,775	3,244	3,239	2,999	2,594	0.62	-13.50
Switzerland	2,163	2,394	2,564	2,730	2,648	0.63	-3.00
EAST MEDITERRANEAN EUROPE	**1,146**	**1,925**	**851**	**1,676**	**2,720**	**0.65**	**62.29**
Cyprus	6	11					
Israel	619	757					
Turkey	521	1,157	851	1,676	2,720	0.65	62.29
MIDDLE EAST	**645**	**616**					
Bahrain	3	9					
Egypt	37	34					
Iraq	10	18					
Jordan	18	81					
Kuwait	107	233					
Lebanon	7	3					
Libya	20	26					

492

Yearbook of Tourism Statistics, Data 2009 – 2013, 2015 Edition

MONGOLIA

1. Arrivals of non-resident tourists at national borders, by nationality

	2009	2010	2011	2012	2013	Market share 2013	% Change 2013-2012
Oman	28	8					
Palestine	2						
Qatar	223	39					
Saudi Arabia	49	34					
Syrian Arab Republic	104	102					
United Arab Emirates	19	11					
Yemen	18	18					
SOUTH ASIA	**1,327**	**1,473**	**1,478**	**1,340**	**1,519**	**0.36**	**13.36**
Afghanistan	31	17					
Bangladesh	91	82					
Bhutan	9	31					
India	941	940	1,478	1,340	1,519	0.36	13.36
Iran, Islamic Republic of	63	219					
Maldives	7	5					
Pakistan	115	110					
Sri Lanka	70	69					
NOT SPECIFIED	**48**	**11**	**18,490**	**17,714**	**23,092**	**5.53**	**30.36**
Other countries of the World	48	11	18,490	17,714	23,092	5.53	30.36

Yearbook of Tourism Statistics, Data 2009 – 2013, 2015 Edition

MONGOLIA

2. Arrivals of non-resident visitors at national borders, by nationality

	2009	2010	2011	2012	2013	Market share 2013	% Change 2013-2012
TOTAL	467,989	557,452	627,007	623,839	515,205	100.00	-17.41
AFRICA	418	597					
EAST AFRICA	87	148					
Burundi		58					
Eritrea	1						
Ethiopia	16	16					
Kenya	15	13					
Madagascar	2	2					
Malawi	3	3					
Mauritius	9	16					
Mozambique	3	11					
Reunion	3	1					
Rwanda	4	1					
Uganda	12	8					
United Republic of Tanzania	4	6					
Zambia	7	3					
Zimbabwe	8	10					
CENTRAL AFRICA	33	25					
Angola	1						
Cameroon	17	12					
Central African Republic	4	1					
Congo	11	8					
Equatorial Guinea		4					
NORTH AFRICA	43	73					
Algeria	11	17					
Morocco	15	35					
Sudan	12						
Tunisia	5	21					
SOUTHERN AFRICA	187	271					
Lesotho		1					
Namibia	1	4					
South Africa	168	258					
Swaziland	18	8					
WEST AFRICA	68	80					
Benin	1	8					
Burkina Faso	1						
Gambia	2	1					
Ghana	31	24					
Guinea	1	1					
Liberia	4	6					
Mali	1						
Mauritania		1					
Niger	14	13					
Nigeria	9	22					
Senegal	3	1					
Sierra Leone		2					
Togo	1	1					
AMERICAS	14,202	16,686	20,156	21,077	19,376	3.76	-8.07
CARIBBEAN	44	43					
Barbados		1					
Bermuda	2						
Cuba	26	27					
Dominica		2					
Dominican Republic	2						
Haiti	4	4					
Jamaica	1	3					
Trinidad and Tobago	9	6					
CENTRAL AMERICA	30	38					
Belize		3					

494

Yearbook of Tourism Statistics, Data 2009 – 2013, 2015 Edition

MONGOLIA

2. Arrivals of non-resident visitors at national borders, by nationality

	2009	2010	2011	2012	2013	Market share 2013	% Change 2013-2012
Costa Rica	5	6					
El Salvador	4	6					
Guatemala	6	5					
Honduras	9	11					
Panama	6	7					
NORTH AMERICA	**13,854**	**15,996**	**20,156**	**21,077**	**19,376**	**3.76**	**-8.07**
Canada	2,273	2,887	3,711	3,714	3,342	0.65	-10.02
Mexico	73	127					
United States of America	11,508	12,982	16,445	17,363	16,034	3.11	-7.65
SOUTH AMERICA	**274**	**609**					
Argentina	68	179					
Bolivia	2	11					
Brazil		227					
Chile	84	59					
Colombia	31	32					
Ecuador	11	7					
Falkland Islands, Malvinas	9	1					
Paraguay	4	4					
Peru	42	51					
Uruguay	10	24					
Venezuela	13	14					
EAST ASIA AND THE PACIFIC	**292,096**	**360,681**	**418,673**	**443,954**	**342,615**	**66.50**	**-22.83**
NORTH-EAST ASIA	**283,964**	**350,016**	**409,033**	**430,410**	**332,263**	**64.49**	**-22.80**
China	232,038	290,061	346,984	361,506	261,468	50.75	-27.67
Hong Kong, China	435	793	1,903	1,924	1,776	0.34	-7.69
Japan	11,496	14,279	15,336	17,642	18,751	3.64	6.29
Korea, Dem. People's Republic of	343	1,080		1,516	1,720	0.33	13.46
Korea, Republic of	38,551	42,551	44,810	45,489	46,498	9.03	2.22
Macao, China	11	10					
Taiwan, Province of China	1,090	1,242		2,333	2,050	0.40	-12.13
SOUTH-EAST ASIA	**3,629**	**4,273**	**600**	**2,984**	**1,824**	**0.35**	**-38.87**
Brunei Darussalam	7	2					
Cambodia	85	34					
Indonesia	204	198	600	919			
Lao People's Democratic Republic	93	66					
Malaysia	853	927					
Myanmar	7	8					
Philippines	607	828					
Singapore	931	1,173		2,065	1,824	0.35	-11.67
Thailand	447	603					
Viet Nam	395	434					
AUSTRALASIA	**4,457**	**6,353**	**9,040**	**10,560**	**8,528**	**1.66**	**-19.24**
Australia	3,741	5,471	7,981	9,348	8,528	1.66	-8.77
New Zealand	716	882	1,059	1,212			
MELANESIA	**40**	**29**					
Fiji	23	15					
Papua New Guinea	11	12					
Solomon Islands	6	1					
Vanuatu		1					
POLYNESIA	**6**	**10**					
American Samoa		2					
Samoa	2	5					
Tonga	4	3					
EUROPE	**154,374**	**177,256**	**143,555**	**136,698**	**125,009**	**24.26**	**-8.55**
CENTRAL/EASTERN EUROPE	**119,072**	**136,065**	**114,145**	**99,798**	**89,829**	**17.44**	**-9.99**
Armenia	120	75					
Azerbaijan	77	78					
Belarus	191	182					
Bulgaria	90	124					

495

MONGOLIA

2. Arrivals of non-resident visitors at national borders, by nationality

	2009	2010	2011	2012	2013	Market share 2013	% Change 2013-2012
Czech Republic	826	860					
Estonia	36	91					
Georgia	50	75					
Hungary	289	337					
Kazakhstan	5,094	5,792	8,140	10,697	11,574	2.25	8.20
Kyrgyzstan	209	242					
Latvia	28	45					
Lithuania	10	79					
Poland	1,058	1,170		1,313	1,507	0.29	14.78
Republic of Moldova	42	40					
Romania	85	110					
Russian Federation	109,391	125,543	104,916	86,584	76,748	14.90	-11.36
Slovakia	199	186					
Tajikistan	112	30					
Turkmenistan	2	4					
Ukraine	978	824	1,089	1,204			
Uzbekistan	185	178					
NORTHERN EUROPE	**10,365**	**10,818**	**9,669**	**9,560**	**6,939**	**1.35**	**-27.42**
Denmark	662	676	734	733			
Finland	862	949					
Iceland	25	18					
Ireland	510	492					
Norway	744	823					
Sweden	1,667	1,632	1,499	1,458			
United Kingdom	5,895	6,228	7,436	7,369	6,939	1.35	-5.84
SOUTHERN EUROPE	**3,097**	**4,833**		**2,811**	**2,733**	**0.53**	**-2.77**
Albania	4	15					
Andorra	3	2					
Bosnia and Herzegovina	18	28					
Croatia	50	69					
Greece	95	126					
Italy	2,417	2,819		2,811	2,733	0.53	-2.77
Malta	4	9					
Portugal	278	192					
Serbia and Montenegro	60	60					
Slovenia	154	154					
Spain		1,340					
TFYR of Macedonia	14	19					
WESTERN EUROPE	**20,693**	**23,576**	**19,741**	**22,649**	**22,578**	**4.38**	**-0.31**
Austria	1,113	1,122					
Belgium	826	966					
France	6,737	7,543	7,708	7,716	7,586	1.47	-1.68
Germany	6,995	8,220	8,750	9,150	9,703	1.88	6.04
Liechtenstein	10						
Luxembourg	37	78					
Netherlands	2,791	3,248	3,283	3,038	2,613	0.51	-13.99
Switzerland	2,184	2,399		2,745	2,676	0.52	-2.51
EAST MEDITERRANEAN EUROPE	**1,147**	**1,964**		**1,880**	**2,930**	**0.57**	**55.85**
Cyprus	6	11					
Israel	604	759					
Turkey	537	1,194		1,880	2,930	0.57	55.85
MIDDLE EAST	**612**	**619**					
Bahrain	3	9					
Egypt	37	34					
Iraq	10	18					
Jordan	20	81					
Kuwait	107	233					
Lebanon	20	26					
Libya		3					

496

Yearbook of Tourism Statistics, Data 2009 – 2013, 2015 Edition

MONGOLIA

2. Arrivals of non-resident visitors at national borders, by nationality

	2009	2010	2011	2012	2013	Market share 2013	% Change 2013-2012
Oman		8					
Palestine	2	2					
Qatar	223	39					
Saudi Arabia	49	34					
Syrian Arab Republic	104	102					
United Arab Emirates	19	11					
Yemen	18	19					
SOUTH ASIA	**1,447**	**1,597**	**1,611**	**1,546**	**1,758**	**0.34**	**13.71**
Afghanistan	38	26					
Bangladesh	91	84					
Bhutan	11	31					
India	952	949	1,611	1,546	1,758	0.34	13.71
Iran, Islamic Republic of	63	219					
Maldives	7	5					
Nepal	98	98					
Pakistan	117	116					
Sri Lanka	70	69					
NOT SPECIFIED	**4,840**	**16**	**43,012**	**20,564**	**26,447**	**5.13**	**28.61**
Other countries of the World	4,840	16	43,012	20,564	26,447	5.13	28.61

Yearbook of Tourism Statistics, Data 2009 – 2013, 2015 Edition

MONTENEGRO

3. Arrivals of non-resident tourists in hotels and similar establishments, by nationality

		2009	2010	2011	2012	2013	Market share 2013	% Change 2013-2012
TOTAL		467,650	485,780	523,631	557,401	603,973	100.00	8.36
AMERICAS		7,694	8,655	8,158	9,494	11,035	1.83	16.23
NORTH AMERICA		7,694	8,655	8,158	9,494	11,035	1.83	16.23
Canada		1,310	1,500	1,709	2,107	2,282	0.38	8.31
United States of America		6,384	7,155	6,449	7,387	8,753	1.45	18.49
EAST ASIA AND THE PACIFIC		2,222	3,946	3,980	4,582	5,406	0.90	17.98
NORTH-EAST ASIA		510	790	1,200	1,464	2,082	0.34	42.21
Japan		510	790	1,200	1,464	2,082	0.34	42.21
AUSTRALASIA		1,712	3,156	2,780	3,118	3,324	0.55	6.61
Australia		1,411	1,626	2,392	2,584	2,676	0.44	3.56
New Zealand		301	1,530	388	534	648	0.11	21.35
EUROPE		452,663	466,751	502,089	529,154	570,852	94.52	7.88
CENTRAL/EASTERN EUROPE		108,438	136,046	156,128	180,058	209,734	34.73	16.48
Belarus		766	889	1,121	2,153	3,285	0.54	52.58
Bulgaria		4,787	4,337	4,489	5,241	5,485	0.91	4.66
Czech Republic		11,309	11,735	14,321	16,390	16,753	2.77	2.21
Estonia		217	928	204	526	446	0.07	-15.21
Hungary		7,417	8,548	8,336	8,506	9,092	1.51	6.89
Latvia		171	551	217	448	1,016	0.17	126.79
Lithuania		927	1,027	1,080	1,266	1,004	0.17	-20.70
Poland		11,003	13,568	18,737	23,230	27,570	4.56	18.68
Romania		5,632	7,722	9,321	10,495	9,010	1.49	-14.15
Russian Federation		56,226	73,981	83,055	90,656	114,284	18.92	26.06
Slovakia		4,212	5,049	5,644	5,793	4,735	0.78	-18.26
Ukraine		5,771	7,711	9,603	15,354	17,054	2.82	11.07
NORTHERN EUROPE		26,800	27,746	27,815	27,325	32,931	5.45	20.52
Denmark		943	1,150	1,076	1,312	1,603	0.27	22.18
Finland		1,632	1,469	1,591	1,399	1,671	0.28	19.44
Iceland		179	397	188	256	380	0.06	48.44
Ireland		1,404	1,474	1,333	1,528	1,885	0.31	23.36
Norway		3,390	3,462	3,638	3,133	4,761	0.79	51.96
Sweden		7,128	7,077	6,927	6,003	6,502	1.08	8.31
United Kingdom		12,124	12,717	13,062	13,694	16,129	2.67	17.78
SOUTHERN EUROPE		245,089	229,371	226,106	224,952	217,779	36.06	-3.19
Albania		16,377	17,205	17,536	17,427	19,044	3.15	9.28
Bosnia and Herzegovina		24,060	22,885	22,504	21,495	23,039	3.81	7.18
Croatia		12,103	12,808	12,058	12,851	13,517	2.24	5.18
Greece		2,937	3,346	3,975	3,340	4,413	0.73	32.13
Italy		18,136	19,695	25,064	23,180	21,093	3.49	-9.00
Portugal		460	571	883	763	2,540	0.42	232.90
Serbia	(*)	143,198	128,160	121,344	123,197	111,713	18.50	-9.32
Slovenia		16,683	15,578	14,048	14,456	12,855	2.13	-11.07
Spain		1,497	2,336	2,060	2,039	2,784	0.46	36.54
TFYR of Macedonia		9,638	6,787	6,634	6,204	6,781	1.12	9.30
WESTERN EUROPE		51,040	55,249	60,481	68,675	77,296	12.80	12.55
Austria		6,835	7,125	8,264	9,225	11,548	1.91	25.18
Belgium		5,359	5,584	5,571	5,165	6,781	1.12	31.29
France		19,060	21,091	23,546	27,266	30,454	5.04	11.69
Germany		14,177	13,853	16,507	19,263	19,921	3.30	3.42
Luxembourg		708	240	279	523	467	0.08	-10.71
Netherlands		2,356	2,281	2,521	2,671	3,073	0.51	15.05
Switzerland		2,545	5,075	3,793	4,562	5,052	0.84	10.74
EAST MEDITERRANEAN EUROPE		13,819	15,979	18,752	23,506	26,528	4.39	12.86
Israel		11,003	9,875	11,013	11,419	9,118	1.51	-20.15
Turkey		2,816	6,104	7,739	12,087	17,410	2.88	44.04
OTHER EUROPE		7,477	2,360	12,807	4,638	6,584	1.09	41.96
Other countries of Europe		7,477	2,360	12,807	4,638	6,584	1.09	41.96
NOT SPECIFIED		5,071	6,428	9,404	14,171	16,680	2.76	17.71
Other countries of the World		5,071	6,428	9,404	14,171	16,680	2.76	17.71

498

Yearbook of Tourism Statistics, Data 2009 – 2013, 2015 Edition

MONTENEGRO

4. Arrivals of non-resident tourists in all types of accommodation establishments, by nationality

	2009	2010	2011	2012	2013	Market share 2013	% Change 2013-2012
TOTAL	1,043,933	1,087,794	1,201,099	1,264,163	1,324,403	100.00	4.77
AMERICAS	8,255	10,622	12,661	13,136	13,434	1.01	2.27
NORTH AMERICA	8,255	10,622	12,661	13,136	13,434	1.01	2.27
Canada	1,557	1,853	2,087	2,912	3,020	0.23	3.71
United States of America	6,698	8,769	10,574	10,224	10,414	0.79	1.86
EAST ASIA AND THE PACIFIC	2,426	3,241	4,918	6,392	6,870	0.52	7.48
NORTH-EAST ASIA	515	863	1,431	1,748	2,231	0.17	27.63
Japan	515	863	1,431	1,748	2,231	0.17	27.63
AUSTRALASIA	1,911	2,378	3,487	4,644	4,639	0.35	-0.11
Australia	1,597	1,909	2,962	4,032	3,921	0.30	-2.75
New Zealand	314	469	525	612	718	0.05	17.32
EUROPE	1,028,084	1,066,715	1,171,855	1,226,970	1,281,691	96.77	4.46
CENTRAL/EASTERN EUROPE	260,417	293,303	415,839	442,111	517,718	39.09	17.10
Belarus	1,480	6,400	7,706	20,504	20,734	1.57	1.12
Bulgaria	6,163	5,604	5,237	7,181	7,117	0.54	-0.89
Czech Republic	25,928	24,085	24,702	26,847	27,286	2.06	1.64
Estonia	276	1,162	414	1,246	1,046	0.08	-16.05
Hungary	32,631	28,838	17,264	15,857	17,677	1.33	11.48
Latvia	1,662	741	500	1,031	1,377	0.10	33.56
Lithuania	2,583	4,261	5,046	5,390	4,911	0.37	-8.89
Poland	15,039	25,381	39,544	39,131	44,764	3.38	14.40
Romania	7,895	14,471	22,923	23,108	18,867	1.42	-18.35
Russian Federation	145,557	150,194	244,924	243,647	300,177	22.67	23.20
Slovakia	8,908	7,699	10,729	9,427	8,113	0.61	-13.94
Ukraine	12,295	24,467	36,850	48,742	65,649	4.96	34.69
NORTHERN EUROPE	31,626	42,617	49,570	43,142	50,390	3.80	16.80
Denmark	1,191	1,549	1,531	2,580	2,820	0.21	9.30
Finland	1,710	1,579	2,211	1,916	2,107	0.16	9.97
Iceland	192	425	634	423	580	0.04	37.12
Ireland	1,493	3,424	4,204	3,479	3,363	0.25	-3.33
Norway	5,156	6,754	8,657	6,267	8,069	0.61	28.75
Sweden	7,776	8,390	8,429	9,108	9,566	0.72	5.03
United Kingdom	14,108	20,496	23,904	19,369	23,885	1.80	23.32
SOUTHERN EUROPE	590,011	567,447	533,952	570,445	525,076	39.65	-7.95
Albania	39,252	37,601	27,388	27,428	25,971	1.96	-5.31
Bosnia and Herzegovina	101,874	103,025	97,497	95,271	91,453	6.91	-4.01
Croatia	15,677	17,497	20,195	24,015	23,358	1.76	-2.74
Greece	2,970	3,487	4,373	3,886	4,881	0.37	25.60
Italy	42,549	39,987	34,403	36,113	31,066	2.35	-13.98
Portugal	8,466	808	5,504	959	2,715	0.20	183.11
Serbia (*)	338,893	314,836	299,617	337,245	303,135	22.89	-10.11
Slovenia	18,891	22,472	20,027	18,463	16,651	1.26	-9.81
Spain	1,528	3,317	2,343	2,501	3,349	0.25	33.91
TFYR of Macedonia	19,911	24,417	22,605	24,564	22,497	1.70	-8.41
WESTERN EUROPE	79,661	100,388	96,925	103,458	112,145	8.47	8.40
Austria	12,204	12,454	12,994	15,865	16,889	1.28	6.45
Belgium	7,473	8,146	7,201	5,983	8,169	0.62	36.54
France	33,080	42,099	28,336	33,122	36,602	2.76	10.51
Germany	18,329	25,381	33,427	32,648	34,722	2.62	6.35
Luxembourg	1,386	2,469	862	728	1,335	0.10	83.38
Netherlands	4,225	3,468	6,647	5,669	5,501	0.42	-2.96
Switzerland	2,964	6,371	7,458	9,443	8,927	0.67	-5.46
EAST MEDITERRANEAN EUROPE	14,054	16,841	30,671	25,590	28,505	2.15	11.39
Israel	11,142	10,595	11,799	12,393	10,077	0.76	-18.69
Turkey	2,912	6,246	18,872	13,197	18,428	1.39	39.64
OTHER EUROPE	52,315	46,119	44,898	42,224	47,857	3.61	13.34
Other countries of Europe	52,315	46,119	44,898	42,224	47,857	3.61	13.34
NOT SPECIFIED	5,168	7,216	11,665	17,665	22,408	1.69	26.85
Other countries of the World	5,168	7,216	11,665	17,665	22,408	1.69	26.85

Yearbook of Tourism Statistics, Data 2009 – 2013, 2015 Edition

MONTENEGRO

5. Overnight stays of non-resident tourists in hotels and similar establishments, by nationality

		2009	2010	2011	2012	2013	Market share 2013	% Change 2013-2012
TOTAL		2,388,133	2,478,239	2,647,592	2,702,819	2,920,695	100.00	8.06
AMERICAS		23,107	26,188	22,764	25,796	27,337	0.94	5.97
NORTH AMERICA		23,107	26,188	22,764	25,796	27,337	0.94	5.97
Canada		3,904	4,474	5,410	5,810	5,838	0.20	0.48
United States of America		19,203	21,714	17,354	19,986	21,499	0.74	7.57
EAST ASIA AND THE PACIFIC		5,650	6,789	8,448	10,371	10,629	0.36	2.49
NORTH-EAST ASIA		1,274	1,570	1,863	2,586	2,818	0.10	8.97
Japan		1,274	1,570	1,863	2,586	2,818	0.10	8.97
AUSTRALASIA		4,376	5,219	6,585	7,785	7,811	0.27	0.33
Australia		3,688	4,402	5,718	6,645	6,624	0.23	-0.32
New Zealand		688	817	867	1,140	1,187	0.04	4.12
EUROPE		2,344,820	2,426,615	2,591,984	2,638,548	2,843,694	97.36	7.77
CENTRAL/EASTERN EUROPE		691,409	873,732	1,031,655	1,153,493	1,366,010	46.77	18.42
Belarus		5,772	5,850	7,975	16,032	23,397	0.80	45.94
Bulgaria		13,126	10,393	14,252	13,792	14,712	0.50	6.67
Czech Republic		74,237	73,549	93,548	108,887	113,776	3.90	4.49
Estonia		786	6,330	595	1,325	1,415	0.05	6.79
Hungary		31,177	36,354	38,862	34,549	37,786	1.29	9.37
Latvia		447	1,994	674	1,586	2,183	0.07	37.64
Lithuania		2,852	2,894	3,146	3,710	2,299	0.08	-38.03
Poland		42,923	46,968	81,995	94,093	120,399	4.12	27.96
Romania		23,243	39,380	46,193	43,191	35,970	1.23	-16.72
Russian Federation		428,511	571,981	644,972	691,089	866,102	29.65	25.32
Slovakia		27,401	28,877	36,013	41,589	30,473	1.04	-26.73
Ukraine		40,934	49,162	63,430	103,650	117,498	4.02	13.36
NORTHERN EUROPE		135,368	134,194	130,969	122,557	144,408	4.94	17.83
Denmark		3,011	4,279	3,093	4,210	4,853	0.17	15.27
Finland		7,023	5,410	6,818	5,091	4,812	0.16	-5.48
Iceland		371	1,599	576	672	848	0.03	26.19
Ireland		5,237	5,073	5,483	4,947	6,462	0.22	30.62
Norway		14,585	15,277	17,258	13,109	21,065	0.72	60.69
Sweden		39,607	38,576	36,036	28,598	32,166	1.10	12.48
United Kingdom		65,534	63,980	61,705	65,930	74,202	2.54	12.55
SOUTHERN EUROPE		1,221,678	1,097,605	1,057,412	997,660	921,791	31.56	-7.60
Albania		37,464	43,006	42,293	44,324	40,963	1.40	-7.58
Bosnia and Herzegovina		122,548	106,738	100,511	96,225	101,151	3.46	5.12
Croatia		29,637	31,594	27,673	28,831	31,378	1.07	8.83
Greece		5,258	5,981	6,485	6,914	8,002	0.27	15.74
Italy		59,227	62,686	78,588	69,962	59,216	2.03	-15.36
Portugal		1,329	1,877	3,821	2,466	11,151	0.38	352.19
Serbia	(*)	854,589	760,121	722,192	668,541	603,777	20.67	-9.69
Slovenia		68,335	58,540	50,581	57,588	38,880	1.33	-32.49
Spain		4,393	5,906	4,887	4,835	5,724	0.20	18.39
TFYR of Macedonia		38,898	21,156	20,381	17,974	21,549	0.74	19.89
WESTERN EUROPE		241,266	226,532	290,992	314,012	349,257	11.96	11.22
Austria		19,655	22,242	27,062	31,152	41,778	1.43	34.11
Belgium		32,337	32,645	33,272	27,627	31,683	1.08	14.68
France		91,804	100,579	121,896	133,768	150,680	5.16	12.64
Germany		76,936	42,145	87,427	95,736	96,377	3.30	0.67
Luxembourg		3,732	749	1,037	1,577	1,577	0.05	
Netherlands		7,871	6,028	7,010	8,367	7,667	0.26	-8.37
Switzerland		8,931	22,144	13,288	15,785	19,495	0.67	23.50
EAST MEDITERRANEAN EUROPE		25,003	26,419	31,428	36,671	41,775	1.43	13.92
Israel		19,311	16,509	18,862	19,733	15,317	0.52	-22.38
Turkey		5,692	9,910	12,566	16,938	26,458	0.91	56.20
OTHER EUROPE		30,096	68,133	49,528	14,155	20,453	0.70	44.49
Other countries of Europe		30,096	68,133	49,528	14,155	20,453	0.70	44.49
NOT SPECIFIED		14,556	18,647	24,396	28,104	39,035	1.34	38.89
Other countries of the World		14,556	18,647	24,396	28,104	39,035	1.34	38.89

500

MONTENEGRO

6. Overnight stays of non-resident tourists in all types of accommodation establishments, by nationality

	2009	2010	2011	2012	2013	Market share 2013	% Change 2013-2012
TOTAL	6,694,514	6,977,860	7,818,803	8,143,007	8,414,215	100.00	3.33
AMERICAS	28,765	41,051	54,025	52,414	45,515	0.54	-13.16
NORTH AMERICA	28,765	41,051	54,025	52,414	45,515	0.54	-13.16
Canada	6,120	7,231	8,739	11,079	11,251	0.13	1.55
United States of America	22,645	33,820	45,286	41,335	34,264	0.41	-17.11
EAST ASIA AND THE PACIFIC	7,259	10,266	16,248	23,841	21,968	0.26	-7.86
NORTH-EAST ASIA	1,288	2,050	3,025	3,829	3,546	0.04	-7.39
Japan	1,288	2,050	3,025	3,829	3,546	0.04	-7.39
AUSTRALASIA	5,971	8,216	13,223	20,012	18,422	0.22	-7.95
Australia	5,113	6,675	11,141	18,395	16,761	0.20	-8.88
New Zealand	858	1,541	2,082	1,617	1,661	0.02	2.72
EUROPE	6,642,906	6,901,660	7,706,203	8,016,866	8,268,953	98.27	3.14
CENTRAL/EASTERN EUROPE	1,818,803	2,059,195	2,870,291	3,182,304	3,684,014	43.78	15.77
Belarus	14,187	45,636	52,935	134,914	135,989	1.62	0.80
Bulgaria	23,307	18,967	18,849	25,002	24,090	0.29	-3.65
Czech Republic	171,643	165,050	171,107	174,634	177,406	2.11	1.59
Estonia	1,350	8,857	2,641	5,956	5,366	0.06	-9.91
Hungary	205,259	183,031	98,577	79,743	91,746	1.09	15.05
Latvia	11,371	2,966	2,683	4,684	5,025	0.06	7.28
Lithuania	18,088	27,592	32,329	34,139	32,097	0.38	-5.98
Poland	123,557	84,053	214,927	196,888	227,413	2.70	15.50
Romania	38,061	84,838	142,281	118,313	98,391	1.17	-16.84
Russian Federation	1,060,458	1,217,978	1,791,616	1,988,533	2,367,000	28.13	19.03
Slovakia	61,841	52,353	71,168	65,716	51,709	0.61	-21.31
Ukraine	89,681	167,874	271,178	353,782	467,782	5.56	32.22
NORTHERN EUROPE	190,487	255,749	302,763	241,045	275,759	3.28	14.40
Denmark	5,371	7,606	6,717	11,635	12,606	0.15	8.35
Finland	7,777	6,370	10,771	8,382	7,021	0.08	-16.24
Iceland	454	1,795	3,303	1,514	1,883	0.02	24.37
Ireland	6,150	18,458	26,199	18,397	17,202	0.20	-6.50
Norway	43,620	55,550	66,008	47,487	59,172	0.70	24.61
Sweden	47,696	50,542	50,219	51,401	55,541	0.66	8.05
United Kingdom	79,419	115,428	139,546	102,229	122,334	1.45	19.67
SOUTHERN EUROPE	3,846,545	3,575,364	3,582,990	3,714,245	3,357,203	39.90	-9.61
Albania	191,826	189,074	162,323	159,811	104,310	1.24	-34.73
Bosnia and Herzegovina	778,439	731,633	750,341	679,317	631,588	7.51	-7.03
Croatia	59,767	66,161	89,876	107,786	102,040	1.21	-5.33
Greece	5,498	6,794	9,106	10,753	11,062	0.13	2.87
Italy	225,976	199,617	143,938	151,366	124,663	1.48	-17.64
Portugal	42,710	3,381	31,572	3,712	12,456	0.15	235.56
Serbia (*)	2,298,717	2,097,051	2,109,159	2,353,370	2,115,867	25.15	-10.09
Slovenia	84,578	106,016	136,108	82,380	63,495	0.75	-22.92
Spain	4,504	11,676	6,483	7,281	12,195	0.14	67.49
TFYR of Macedonia	154,530	163,961	144,084	158,469	179,527	2.13	13.29
WESTERN EUROPE	458,024	601,875	507,588	532,595	565,416	6.72	6.16
Austria	57,588	58,785	59,475	71,006	75,394	0.90	6.18
Belgium	46,834	48,063	43,677	31,745	39,252	0.47	23.65
France	193,983	233,959	152,395	167,215	186,653	2.22	11.62
Germany	109,893	151,843	182,724	184,984	190,827	2.27	3.16
Luxembourg	10,192	13,947	4,180	2,716	5,688	0.07	109.43
Netherlands	27,647	66,161	31,472	33,371	27,880	0.33	-16.45
Switzerland	11,887	29,117	33,665	41,558	39,722	0.47	-4.42
EAST MEDITERRANEAN EUROPE	26,407	30,739	53,884	48,230	53,089	0.63	10.07
Israel	20,163	19,729	22,815	24,209	19,784	0.24	-18.28
Turkey	6,244	11,010	31,069	24,021	33,305	0.40	38.65
OTHER EUROPE	302,640	378,738	388,687	298,447	333,472	3.96	11.74
Other countries of Europe	302,640	378,738	388,687	298,447	333,472	3.96	11.74
NOT SPECIFIED	15,584	24,883	42,327	49,886	77,779	0.92	55.91
Other countries of the World	15,584	24,883	42,327	49,886	77,779	0.92	55.91

MONTSERRAT

1. Arrivals of non-resident tourists at national borders, by country of residence

	2009	2010	2011	2012	2013	Market share 2013	% Change 2013-2012
TOTAL	6,324	5,981	5,395	7,310	7,202	100.00	-1.48
AMERICAS	4,252	4,353	3,749	4,845	4,882	67.79	0.76
CARIBBEAN	2,267	2,259	1,881	2,390	2,591	35.98	8.41
All countries of the Caribbean	2,267	2,259	1,881	2,390	2,591	35.98	8.41
NORTH AMERICA	1,973	2,069	1,846	2,455	2,291	31.81	-6.68
Canada	367	404	320	505	516	7.16	2.18
United States of America	1,606	1,665	1,526	1,950	1,775	24.65	-8.97
OTHER AMERICAS	12	25	22				
Other countries of the Americas	12	25	22				
EAST ASIA AND THE PACIFIC	3	1	14				
NORTH-EAST ASIA	3	1	14				
Japan	3	1	14				
EUROPE	2,044	1,573	1,535	2,342	2,220	30.82	-5.21
NORTHERN EUROPE	1,870	1,385	1,333	2,148	1,821	25.28	-15.22
Sweden	6	5	4				
United Kingdom	1,864	1,380	1,329	2,148	1,821	25.28	-15.22
SOUTHERN EUROPE	31	21	27				
Italy	18	11	19				
Spain	13	10	8				
WESTERN EUROPE	94	114	117				
Belgium	12	13	6				
France	47	51	60				
Germany	18	30	31				
Netherlands	5	1	7				
Switzerland	12	19	13				
OTHER EUROPE	49	53	58	194	399	5.54	105.67
Other countries of Europe	49	53	58	194	399	5.54	105.67
NOT SPECIFIED	25	54	97	123	100	1.39	-18.70
Other countries of the World	25	54	97	123	100	1.39	-18.70

Yearbook of Tourism Statistics, Data 2009 – 2013, 2015 Edition

MONTSERRAT

2. Arrivals of non-resident visitors at national borders, by country of residence

	2009	2010	2011	2012	2013	Market share 2013	% Change 2013-2012
TOTAL	**7,335**	**7,707**	**7,392**				
AMERICAS	**5,081**	**5,540**	**5,078**				
CARIBBEAN	**2,950**	**3,119**	**2,778**				
All countries of the Caribbean	2,950	3,119	2,778				
NORTH AMERICA	**2,112**	**2,384**	**2,270**				
Canada	378	471	396				
United States of America	1,734	1,913	1,874				
OTHER AMERICAS	**19**	**37**	**30**				
Other countries of the Americas	19	37	30				
EUROPE	**2,221**	**2,102**	**2,102**				
NORTHERN EUROPE	**1,991**	**1,848**	**1,851**				
United Kingdom	1,991	1,848	1,851				
OTHER EUROPE	**230**	**254**	**251**				
Other countries of Europe	230	254	251				
NOT SPECIFIED	**33**	**65**	**212**				
Other countries of the World	33	65	212				

503

MOROCCO

1. Arrivals of non-resident tourists at national borders, by nationality

	2009	2010	2011	2012	2013	Market share 2013	% Change 2013-2012
TOTAL	8,341,237	9,288,338	9,342,133	9,375,156	10,046,264	100.00	7.16
AFRICA	222,990	255,888	290,596	316,715	330,579	3.29	4.38
EAST AFRICA	4,076	4,744	6,795	6,779	6,625	0.07	-2.27
Burundi	137	193	189	314	217	0.00	-30.89
Comoros	324	470	411	401	557	0.01	38.90
Djibouti	381	435	361	452	401	0.00	-11.28
Eritrea	90	83	116	121	125	0.00	3.31
Ethiopia	479	502	549	532	767	0.01	44.17
Kenya	883	874	870	1,067	1,107	0.01	3.75
Madagascar	348	359	406	396	485	0.00	22.47
Malawi	122	75	27	77	331	0.00	329.87
Mauritius	540	667	2,527	1,253	1,088	0.01	-13.17
Mozambique	47	53	101	155	121	0.00	-21.94
Reunion	30	266	10	314	45	0.00	-85.67
Rwanda	99	110	250	722	165	0.00	-77.15
Seychelles	34	57	60	73	112	0.00	53.42
Somalia	100	77	235	149	150	0.00	0.67
Uganda	138	153	173	191	397	0.00	107.85
United Republic of Tanzania	131	118	178	200	227	0.00	13.50
Zambia	58	88	192	178	120	0.00	-32.58
Zimbabwe	135	164	140	184	210	0.00	14.13
CENTRAL AFRICA	19,668	22,052	26,073	26,406	24,673	0.25	-6.56
Angola	1,426	2,926	4,231	2,378	1,015	0.01	-57.32
Cameroon	3,703	3,869	3,443	3,175	3,307	0.03	4.16
Central African Republic	375	855	937	776	826	0.01	6.44
Chad	268	413	430	513	481	0.00	-6.24
Congo	6,905	7,906	10,228	12,210	11,718	0.12	-4.03
Democratic Republic of the Congo	990	592	1,043	446	1,352	0.01	203.14
Equatorial Guinea	1,993	1,937	1,885	2,939	1,497	0.01	-49.06
Gabon	3,927	3,496	3,792	3,820	4,385	0.04	14.79
Sao Tome and Principe	81	58	84	149	92	0.00	-38.26
NORTH AFRICA	95,241	106,537	124,339	137,198	149,076	1.48	8.66
Algeria	59,512	68,183	80,741	93,195	103,215	1.03	10.75
Sudan	1,916	2,019	2,487	2,353	2,350	0.02	-0.13
Tunisia	33,813	36,335	41,111	41,650	43,511	0.43	4.47
SOUTHERN AFRICA	3,765	4,739	4,117	5,362	4,302	0.04	-19.77
Botswana	76	56	95	111	126	0.00	13.51
Lesotho		1	27	37	32	0.00	-13.51
Namibia	90	53	69	88	60	0.00	-31.82
South Africa	3,585	4,547	3,887	5,089	4,036	0.04	-20.69
Swaziland	14	82	39	37	48	0.00	29.73
WEST AFRICA	100,240	117,816	129,272	140,970	145,903	1.45	3.50
Benin	1,237	1,369	1,234	1,265	1,549	0.02	22.45
Burkina Faso	2,434	2,742	2,589	2,870	3,388	0.03	18.05
Cabo Verde	456	139	279	255	625	0.01	145.10
Côte d'Ivoire	9,795	12,315	14,666	14,024	15,530	0.15	10.74
Gambia	649	708	959	821	781	0.01	-4.87
Ghana	894	781	871	1,061	1,110	0.01	4.62
Guinea	7,756	14,297	10,005	12,042	11,506	0.11	-4.45
Guinea-Bissau	4,176	1,085	3,667	517	2,849	0.03	451.06
Liberia	370	398	347	664	549	0.01	-17.32
Mali	10,483	12,441	15,225	16,436	18,193	0.18	10.69
Mauritania	25,267	30,576	34,528	39,035	39,399	0.39	0.93
Niger	4,854	4,933	5,713	6,465	6,032	0.06	-6.70
Nigeria	1,685	1,592	2,025	1,596	1,991	0.02	24.75
Senegal	28,878	32,969	36,067	42,785	41,203	0.41	-3.70
Sierra Leone	364	439	323	295	326	0.00	10.51
Togo	942	1,032	774	839	872	0.01	3.93

504

Yearbook of Tourism Statistics, Data 2009 – 2013, 2015 Edition

MOROCCO

1. Arrivals of non-resident tourists at national borders, by nationality

	2009	2010	2011	2012	2013	Market share 2013	% Change 2013-2012
AMERICAS	214,666	250,995	239,576	257,892	294,609	2.93	14.24
CARIBBEAN	1,760	1,560	2,170	3,648	2,214	0.02	-39.31
Anguilla	2						
Bahamas	47	45	86	89	115	0.00	29.21
Barbados	101	163	793	1,854	508	0.01	-72.60
Bermuda	142	10	13	17	8	0.00	-52.94
Cuba	410	252	176	187	190	0.00	1.60
Dominica	199	260	207	277	214	0.00	-22.74
Dominican Republic	7	27	11	62	35	0.00	-43.55
Grenada	35	28	29	20	38	0.00	90.00
Guadeloupe	32	41	38	12	7	0.00	-41.67
Haiti	51	296	283	191	271	0.00	41.88
Jamaica	401	129	124	574	325	0.00	-43.38
Martinique	11			2			
Puerto Rico	97	231	193	177	261	0.00	47.46
Trinidad and Tobago	225	78	217	186	242	0.00	30.11
CENTRAL AMERICA	1,376	3,620	1,301	1,515	1,399	0.01	-7.66
Belize	194	38	9	307	115	0.00	-62.54
Costa Rica	271	315	307	346	442	0.00	27.75
El Salvador	231	189	187	170	168	0.00	-1.18
Guatemala	330	278	421	200	239	0.00	19.50
Honduras	147	2,558	162	280	152	0.00	-45.71
Nicaragua	76	72	66	83	45	0.00	-45.78
Panama	127	170	149	129	238	0.00	84.50
NORTH AMERICA	181,410	210,958	200,421	215,686	240,792	2.40	11.64
Canada	54,789	67,925	63,237	69,206	70,923	0.71	2.48
Greenland					3	0.00	
Mexico	5,477	7,647	6,756	6,432	9,833	0.10	52.88
United States of America	121,144	135,376	130,427	140,045	160,033	1.59	14.27
Hawaii, USA		10	1	3			
SOUTH AMERICA	30,120	34,857	35,684	37,043	50,204	0.50	35.53
Argentina	8,077	9,615	8,447	10,062	10,006	0.10	-0.56
Bolivia	252	263	287	317	311	0.00	-1.89
Brazil	10,978	13,049	14,552	15,142	25,639	0.26	69.32
Chile	2,788	3,516	3,611	3,543	4,145	0.04	16.99
Colombia	2,032	2,473	2,386	2,138	2,505	0.02	17.17
Ecuador	622	555	630	515	627	0.01	21.75
Guyana	16	15	3	5	18	0.00	260.00
Paraguay	155	197	163	191	201	0.00	5.24
Peru	1,724	2,164	1,960	1,672	3,497	0.03	109.15
Suriname	48	59	250	50	20	0.00	-60.00
Uruguay	1,383	1,082	1,323	1,095	1,282	0.01	17.08
Venezuela	2,045	1,869	2,072	2,313	1,953	0.02	-15.56
EAST ASIA AND THE PACIFIC	77,674	99,648	96,612	113,302	124,567	1.24	9.94
NORTH-EAST ASIA	35,801	48,273	46,199	61,187	63,958	0.64	4.53
China	4,129	5,769	5,882	6,899	7,871	0.08	14.09
Hong Kong, China	1,154	1,340	1,066	1,968	2,619	0.03	33.08
Japan	19,149	24,366	22,861	30,306	32,184	0.32	6.20
Korea, Dem. People's Republic of	620	1	912		1,177	0.01	
Korea, Republic of	10,001	15,795	14,484	21,092	18,750	0.19	-11.10
Mongolia	39	38	45	66	39	0.00	-40.91
Taiwan, Province of China	709	964	949	856	1,318	0.01	53.97
SOUTH-EAST ASIA	16,613	21,081	21,424	23,530	29,240	0.29	24.27
Brunei Darussalam	64	50	76	100	214	0.00	114.00
Cambodia	25	76	202	92	179	0.00	94.57
Indonesia	2,572	3,606	3,974	4,618	5,055	0.05	9.46
Lao People's Democratic Republic	161	208	164	71	173	0.00	143.66
Malaysia	2,101	2,801	2,302	2,877	4,518	0.04	57.04
Myanmar	109	107	82	106	150	0.00	41.51

505

MOROCCO

1. Arrivals of non-resident tourists at national borders, by nationality

	2009	2010	2011	2012	2013	Market share 2013	% Change 2013-2012
Philippines	7,989	10,170	10,697	11,486	13,938	0.14	21.35
Singapore	1,412	1,832	1,662	2,096	2,701	0.03	28.86
Thailand	1,838	1,986	1,951	1,708	1,783	0.02	4.39
Viet Nam	342	245	314	376	529	0.01	40.69
AUSTRALASIA	**25,201**	**29,879**	**28,541**	**27,935**	**31,120**	**0.31**	**11.40**
Australia	20,531	24,690	23,502	22,812	26,117	0.26	14.49
New Zealand	4,670	5,189	5,039	5,123	5,003	0.05	-2.34
MELANESIA	**59**	**394**	**430**	**486**	**183**	**0.00**	**-62.35**
Fiji	33	28	27	413	19	0.00	-95.40
Vanuatu	26	366	403	73	164	0.00	124.66
MICRONESIA		**8**	**18**	**56**	**66**	**0.00**	**17.86**
Guam			1				
Kiribati		8	17	56	66	0.00	17.86
POLYNESIA		**13**		**108**			
American Samoa		13		108			
EUROPE	**3,624,438**	**4,144,878**	**4,138,271**	**4,106,768**	**4,308,029**	**42.88**	**4.90**
CENTRAL/EASTERN EUROPE	**92,623**	**118,083**	**124,862**	**122,399**	**162,447**	**1.62**	**32.72**
Armenia	244	96	279	541	226	0.00	-58.23
Azerbaijan	384	334	237	209	224	0.00	7.18
Belarus	264	360	446	477	778	0.01	63.10
Bulgaria	4,013	4,419	3,990	4,283	4,587	0.05	7.10
Czech Republic	5,685	5,647	10,435	11,729	20,511	0.20	74.87
Estonia	1,096	1,970	2,629	2,423	3,441	0.03	42.01
Georgia	222	388	184	201	216	0.00	7.46
Hungary	5,175	5,171	4,657	3,950	4,471	0.04	13.19
Kazakhstan	218	225	225	300	345	0.00	15.00
Kyrgyzstan	61	45	34	61	74	0.00	21.31
Latvia	400	355	537	1,035	1,909	0.02	84.44
Lithuania	2,093	2,753	3,644	2,871	3,963	0.04	38.04
Poland	34,686	42,040	49,933	41,768	47,994	0.48	14.91
Republic of Moldova	137	201	135	167	501	0.00	200.00
Romania	10,974	11,834	13,172	12,386	14,335	0.14	15.74
Russian Federation	19,114	32,460	22,620	29,644	47,138	0.47	59.01
Slovakia	3,387	5,026	7,013	5,834	5,226	0.05	-10.42
Turkmenistan	8				11	0.00	
Ukraine	4,368	4,509	4,562	4,353	6,345	0.06	45.76
Uzbekistan	94	250	130	167	152	0.00	-8.98
NORTHERN EUROPE	**327,190**	**423,568**	**452,352**	**439,730**	**505,220**	**5.03**	**14.89**
Denmark	10,512	14,863	22,153	18,253	22,444	0.22	22.96
Finland	8,874	6,045	5,263	5,658	8,043	0.08	42.15
Iceland	1,402	844	981	970	1,299	0.01	33.92
Ireland	17,974	20,341	15,446	14,242	16,591	0.17	16.49
Norway	10,934	15,255	21,847	17,469	19,107	0.19	9.38
Svalbard and Jan Mayen Islands	14	1	15	6	6	0.00	
Sweden	24,535	28,159	34,506	25,785	34,405	0.34	33.43
United Kingdom	252,945	338,060	352,141	357,347	403,325	4.01	12.87
SOUTHERN EUROPE	**890,051**	**1,039,551**	**991,667**	**997,001**	**994,912**	**9.90**	**-0.21**
Albania	584	213	283	504	797	0.01	58.13
Andorra	872	563	676	2,008	786	0.01	-60.86
Bosnia and Herzegovina	329	358	267	406	376	0.00	-7.39
Croatia	1,598	2,141	1,922	1,422	2,195	0.02	54.36
Gibraltar	1			2	11	0.00	450.00
Greece	7,875	7,844	5,340	5,266	5,856	0.06	11.20
Italy	177,915	233,224	211,405	196,186	234,912	2.34	19.74
Malta	812	792	768	897	1,212	0.01	35.12
Portugal	53,079	63,077	72,995	54,194	60,143	0.60	10.98
San Marino	40	59	43	38	63	0.00	65.79
Serbia	824	1,111	997	1,323	1,573	0.02	18.90
Slovenia	2,897	3,274	3,429	3,614	3,796	0.04	5.04

506

MOROCCO

1. Arrivals of non-resident tourists at national borders, by nationality

	2009	2010	2011	2012	2013	Market share 2013	% Change 2013-2012
Spain	642,817	726,540	693,255	730,882	682,834	6.80	-6.57
TFYR of Macedonia	116	240	210	194	328	0.00	69.07
Yugoslavia, SFR (former)	292	115	77	65	30	0.00	-53.85
WESTERN EUROPE	**2,283,962**	**2,523,278**	**2,537,790**	**2,510,551**	**2,599,321**	**25.87**	**3.54**
Austria	13,581	17,731	13,956	14,758	17,439	0.17	18.17
Belgium	188,108	221,371	258,620	255,290	272,593	2.71	6.78
France	1,699,201	1,827,453	1,775,961	1,769,710	1,782,056	17.74	0.70
Germany	174,384	205,417	219,576	199,349	237,852	2.37	19.31
Liechtenstein	210	103	112	258	389	0.00	50.78
Luxembourg	3,509	4,141	3,991	4,188	4,874	0.05	16.38
Monaco	294	344	317	297	283	0.00	-4.71
Netherlands	139,611	175,078	197,642	204,767	210,859	2.10	2.98
Switzerland	65,064	71,640	67,615	61,934	72,976	0.73	17.83
EAST MEDITERRANEAN EUROPE	**30,612**	**40,398**	**31,600**	**37,087**	**46,129**	**0.46**	**24.38**
Cyprus	438	481	450	504	690	0.01	36.90
Israel	13,466	19,190	8,985	10,819	18,199	0.18	68.21
Turkey	16,708	20,727	22,165	25,764	27,240	0.27	5.73
MIDDLE EAST	**134,659**	**142,091**	**152,326**	**198,387**	**248,636**	**2.47**	**25.33**
Bahrain	2,956	3,028	2,870	3,188	3,228	0.03	1.25
Egypt	16,614	16,543	13,689	18,417	22,450	0.22	21.90
Iraq	1,486	1,688	2,085	2,571	2,666	0.03	3.70
Jordan	4,907	4,945	4,877	5,338	6,133	0.06	14.89
Kuwait	9,131	9,111	12,649	15,669	18,649	0.19	19.02
Lebanon	6,835	7,332	6,337	6,665	6,721	0.07	0.84
Libya	17,174	20,456	18,037	45,400	84,102	0.84	85.25
Oman	4,076	4,305	3,777	5,718	5,460	0.05	-4.51
Palestine	1,321	1,337	1,304	1,549	1,583	0.02	2.19
Qatar	2,732	2,976	3,183	4,190	4,384	0.04	4.63
Saudi Arabia	48,780	51,219	62,887	70,666	75,265	0.75	6.51
Syrian Arab Republic	4,505	4,782	4,342	4,587	2,833	0.03	-38.24
United Arab Emirates	12,496	12,659	14,552	12,576	13,183	0.13	4.83
Yemen	1,646	1,710	1,737	1,853	1,979	0.02	6.80
SOUTH ASIA	**11,753**	**12,242**	**12,486**	**14,425**	**14,145**	**0.14**	**-1.94**
Afghanistan	123	143	330	697	200	0.00	-71.31
Bangladesh	547	546	942	744	475	0.00	-36.16
Bhutan				8			
India	6,995	7,936	7,640	9,343	9,784	0.10	4.72
Iran, Islamic Republic of	959	519	519	515	425	0.00	-17.48
Maldives	64	58	50	78	157	0.00	101.28
Nepal	212	272	289	353	288	0.00	-18.41
Pakistan	2,343	2,157	2,172	2,080	2,262	0.02	8.75
Sri Lanka	510	611	544	607	554	0.01	-8.73
NOT SPECIFIED	**4,055,057**	**4,382,596**	**4,412,266**	**4,367,667**	**4,725,699**	**47.04**	**8.20**
Other countries of the World	6,778	4,693	4,016	4,240	2,768	0.03	-34.72
Nationals Residing Abroad	4,048,279	4,377,903	4,408,250	4,363,427	4,722,931	47.01	8.24

Yearbook of Tourism Statistics, Data 2009 – 2013, 2015 Edition

MOROCCO

3. Arrivals of non-resident tourists in hotels and similar establishments, by nationality

	2009	2010	2011	2012	2013	Market share 2013	% Change 2013-2012
TOTAL (*)	3,669,087	4,077,535	3,455,696	3,569,611	4,010,339	100.00	12.35
AFRICA	101,948	117,966	133,845	140,390	150,734	3.76	7.37
NORTH AFRICA	52,294	62,050	71,389	84,231	93,878	2.34	11.45
Algeria	35,543	42,718	50,217	61,055	68,574	1.71	12.32
Tunisia	16,751	19,332	21,172	23,176	25,304	0.63	9.18
WEST AFRICA	5,139	6,445	7,308	7,766	8,951	0.22	15.26
Mauritania	5,139	6,445	7,308	7,766	8,951	0.22	15.26
OTHER AFRICA	44,515	49,471	55,148	48,393	47,905	1.19	-1.01
Other countries of Africa	44,515	49,471	55,148	48,393	47,905	1.19	-1.01
AMERICAS	129,806	152,223	127,013	143,707	169,269	4.22	17.79
NORTH AMERICA	129,806	152,223	127,013	143,707	169,269	4.22	17.79
Canada	28,094	32,546	28,629	31,584	33,034	0.82	4.59
United States of America	101,712	119,677	98,384	112,123	136,235	3.40	21.50
EAST ASIA AND THE PACIFIC	44,999	60,862	54,835	77,385	86,488	2.16	11.76
NORTH-EAST ASIA	44,999	60,862	54,835	77,385	86,488	2.16	11.76
Japan	44,999	60,862	54,835	77,385	86,488	2.16	11.76
EUROPE	2,913,714	3,164,721	2,634,037	2,615,669	2,804,944	69.94	7.24
CENTRAL/EASTERN EUROPE	71,921	90,785	90,224	93,733	111,817	2.79	19.29
Commonwealth Independent States	71,921	90,785	90,224	93,733	111,817	2.79	19.29
NORTHERN EUROPE	255,464	333,058	327,033	307,881	348,879	8.70	13.32
Denmark	5,235	7,225	10,321	7,810	11,767	0.29	50.67
Finland	5,920	2,368	2,487	2,363	4,601	0.11	94.71
Norway	4,570	6,892	10,833	7,437	7,311	0.18	-1.69
Sweden	15,173	17,089	18,237	11,336	15,869	0.40	39.99
United Kingdom	224,566	299,484	285,155	278,935	309,331	7.71	10.90
SOUTHERN EUROPE	655,169	692,452	489,534	492,301	533,540	13.30	8.38
Italy	208,211	241,119	156,827	157,405	171,533	4.28	8.98
Portugal	41,877	50,817	44,636	40,401	41,550	1.04	2.84
Spain	405,081	400,516	288,071	294,495	320,457	7.99	8.82
WESTERN EUROPE	1,931,160	2,048,426	1,727,246	1,721,754	1,810,708	45.15	5.17
Austria	12,688	15,824	11,588	10,944	13,859	0.35	26.64
Belgium	111,039	111,056	117,688	110,785	119,085	2.97	7.49
France	1,422,823	1,474,509	1,206,521	1,205,641	1,238,120	30.87	2.69
Germany	227,808	270,965	251,097	243,699	279,870	6.98	14.84
Netherlands	112,334	127,023	102,250	113,327	118,244	2.95	4.34
Switzerland	44,468	49,049	38,102	37,358	41,530	1.04	11.17
MIDDLE EAST	128,002	131,274	133,680	187,636	241,751	6.03	28.84
Egypt	12,114	12,217	11,531	11,952	14,392	0.36	20.41
Libya	10,209	12,517	11,283	29,912	61,248	1.53	104.76
Saudi Arabia	44,932	46,315	52,454	70,328	79,426	1.98	12.94
Syrian Arab Republic	2,023	2,302	2,111	2,366	2,240	0.06	-5.33
United Arab Emirates	12,153	11,527	10,259	13,646	15,555	0.39	13.99
Other countries of Middle East	46,571	46,396	46,042	59,432	68,890	1.72	15.91
NOT SPECIFIED	350,618	450,489	372,286	404,824	557,153	13.89	37.63
Other countries of the World	332,366	434,523	353,721	389,768	540,177	13.47	38.59
Nationals Residing Abroad	18,252	15,966	18,565	15,056	16,976	0.42	12.75

508

MOROCCO

5. Overnight stays of non-resident tourists in hotels and similar establishments, by nationality

	2009	2010	2011	2012	2013	Market share 2013	% Change 2013-2012
TOTAL (*)	12,520,803	13,954,610	12,418,682	12,547,875	13,931,125	100.00	11.02
AFRICA	291,101	330,275	366,492	409,379	438,169	3.15	7.03
NORTH AFRICA	155,336	184,025	211,251	251,341	281,051	2.02	11.82
Algeria	106,274	129,270	150,366	182,919	205,877	1.48	12.55
Tunisia	49,062	54,755	60,885	68,422	75,174	0.54	9.87
WEST AFRICA	10,940	17,320	17,595	17,772	20,692	0.15	16.43
Mauritania	10,940	17,320	17,595	17,772	20,692	0.15	16.43
OTHER AFRICA	124,825	128,930	137,646	140,266	136,426	0.98	-2.74
Other countries of Africa	124,825	128,930	137,646	140,266	136,426	0.98	-2.74
AMERICAS	319,839	363,015	311,801	346,109	396,862	2.85	14.66
NORTH AMERICA	319,839	363,015	311,801	346,109	396,862	2.85	14.66
Canada	73,286	76,900	72,380	76,451	82,145	0.59	7.45
United States of America	246,553	286,115	239,421	269,658	314,717	2.26	16.71
EAST ASIA AND THE PACIFIC	78,306	102,374	89,612	116,451	129,545	0.93	11.24
NORTH-EAST ASIA	78,306	102,374	89,612	116,451	129,545	0.93	11.24
Japan	78,306	102,374	89,612	116,451	129,545	0.93	11.24
EUROPE	10,485,295	11,548,134	10,147,295	9,929,159	10,653,591	76.47	7.30
CENTRAL/EASTERN EUROPE	321,288	438,862	367,048	393,251	510,955	3.67	29.93
Commonwealth Independent States	321,288	438,862	367,048	393,251	510,955	3.67	29.93
NORTHERN EUROPE	1,077,219	1,487,413	1,523,310	1,465,977	1,667,741	11.97	13.76
Denmark	14,677	22,978	41,141	27,014	37,863	0.27	40.16
Finland	35,196	7,021	8,067	7,626	20,239	0.15	165.39
Norway	15,077	25,524	42,984	26,438	26,145	0.19	-1.11
Sweden	82,299	86,339	91,511	44,350	65,175	0.47	46.96
United Kingdom	929,970	1,345,551	1,339,607	1,360,549	1,518,319	10.90	11.60
SOUTHERN EUROPE	1,592,660	1,734,905	1,318,904	1,175,300	1,267,230	9.10	7.82
Italy	571,376	657,142	460,409	368,571	401,112	2.88	8.83
Portugal	99,294	132,303	152,048	122,346	151,832	1.09	24.10
Spain	921,990	945,460	706,447	684,383	714,286	5.13	4.37
WESTERN EUROPE	7,494,128	7,886,954	6,938,033	6,894,631	7,207,665	51.74	4.54
Austria	32,857	39,869	29,947	28,915	33,740	0.24	16.69
Belgium	582,277	589,418	641,405	590,649	659,138	4.73	11.60
France	5,550,236	5,814,996	4,906,723	4,931,278	5,052,091	36.26	2.45
Germany	895,617	946,323	944,226	909,016	991,489	7.12	9.07
Netherlands	292,937	340,763	290,086	306,427	333,399	2.39	8.80
Switzerland	140,204	155,585	125,646	128,346	137,808	0.99	7.37
MIDDLE EAST	472,371	436,613	469,267	651,987	790,419	5.67	21.23
Egypt	33,508	35,422	38,504	39,397	47,959	0.34	21.73
Libya	23,995	30,617	28,560	79,585	169,217	1.21	112.62
Saudi Arabia	220,651	183,672	209,654	270,825	287,878	2.07	6.30
Syrian Arab Republic	7,677	7,995	12,888	6,811	5,360	0.04	-21.30
United Arab Emirates	27,607	27,864	26,388	30,531	34,187	0.25	11.97
Other countries of Middle East	158,933	151,043	153,273	224,838	245,818	1.76	9.33
NOT SPECIFIED	873,891	1,174,199	1,034,215	1,094,790	1,522,539	10.93	39.07
Other countries of the World	843,189	1,145,382	996,625	1,061,635	1,490,179	10.70	40.37
Nationals Residing Abroad	30,702	28,817	37,590	33,155	32,360	0.23	-2.40

Yearbook of Tourism Statistics, Data 2009 – 2013, 2015 Edition

MOZAMBIQUE

2. Arrivals of non-resident visitors at national borders, by country of residence

	2009	2010	2011	2012	2013	Market share 2013	% Change 2013-2012
TOTAL (*)	1,711,147	1,836,143	2,012,640	2,205,853	1,969,716	100.00	-10.71
AFRICA	1,442,962	1,465,793	1,584,095	1,580,523	1,411,327	71.65	-10.71
EAST AFRICA	408,964	377,152	386,764	468,476	419,328	21.29	-10.49
Malawi	114,849	228,092	215,374	264,723	236,385	12.00	-10.70
Zambia	10,031		20,126	5,732	6,120	0.31	6.77
Zimbabwe	284,084	149,060	151,264	198,021	176,823	8.98	-10.70
SOUTHERN AFRICA	991,290	985,599	1,091,825	1,035,964	939,024	47.67	-9.36
South Africa	803,720	946,583	950,941	971,868	872,017	44.27	-10.27
Swaziland	187,570	39,016	140,884	64,096	67,007	3.40	4.54
OTHER AFRICA	42,708	103,042	105,506	76,083	52,975	2.69	-30.37
Other countries of Africa	42,708	103,042	105,506	76,083	52,975	2.69	-30.37
AMERICAS	46,363	102,041	106,670	135,488	120,984	6.14	-10.71
NORTH AMERICA	25,788	21,292	36,228	76,603	68,403	3.47	-10.70
United States of America	25,788	21,292	36,228	76,603	68,403	3.47	-10.70
OTHER AMERICAS	20,575	80,749	70,442	58,885	52,581	2.67	-10.71
Other countries of the Americas	20,575	80,749	70,442	58,885	52,581	2.67	-10.71
EAST ASIA AND THE PACIFIC	22,240	28,211	33,293	28,661	25,593	1.30	-10.70
OTHER EAST ASIA AND THE PACIFIC	22,240	28,211	33,293	28,661	25,593	1.30	-10.70
All countries of Asia	22,240	28,211	33,293	28,661	25,593	1.30	-10.70
EUROPE	192,502	219,089	272,868	444,506	396,922	20.15	-10.70
NORTHERN EUROPE	33,184	50,420	70,442	57,322	51,186	2.60	-10.70
United Kingdom	33,184	50,420	70,442	57,322	51,186	2.60	-10.70
SOUTHERN EUROPE	37,353	25,810	67,214	86,504	77,244	3.92	-10.70
Portugal	37,353	25,810	67,214	86,504	77,244	3.92	-10.70
OTHER EUROPE	121,965	142,859	135,212	300,680	268,492	13.63	-10.71
Other countries of Europe	121,965	142,859	135,212	300,680	268,492	13.63	-10.71
NOT SPECIFIED	7,080	21,009	15,714	16,675	14,890	0.76	-10.70
Other countries of the World	7,080	21,009	15,714	16,675	14,890	0.76	-10.70

510

MYANMAR

1. Arrivals of non-resident tourists at national borders, by nationality

	2009	2010	2011	2012	2013	Market share 2013	% Change 2013-2012
TOTAL	762,547	791,505	816,369	1,058,995	2,044,307	100.00	93.04
AFRICA	764	816	993	1,598	2,688	0.13	68.21
OTHER AFRICA	764	816	993	1,598	2,688	0.13	68.21
All countries of Africa	764	816	993	1,598	2,688	0.13	68.21
AMERICAS	18,662	20,580	27,745	47,609	67,253	3.29	41.26
NORTH AMERICA	17,440	18,911	25,365	44,074	62,628	3.06	42.10
Canada	2,387	2,407	3,685	6,485	8,975	0.44	38.40
United States of America	15,053	16,504	21,680	37,589	53,653	2.62	42.74
OTHER AMERICAS	1,222	1,669	2,380	3,535	4,625	0.23	30.83
Other countries of the Americas	1,222	1,669	2,380	3,535	4,625	0.23	30.83
EAST ASIA AND THE PACIFIC	676,361	688,267	679,603	848,063	1,747,299	85.47	106.03
NORTH-EAST ASIA	144,261	167,155	185,722	238,185	350,038	17.12	46.96
China	101,932	113,672	120,953	128,804	187,770	9.19	45.78
Hong Kong, China	2,747	3,081	3,820	4,826	7,874	0.39	63.16
Japan	13,809	16,186	21,321	47,690	68,761	3.36	44.18
Korea, Republic of	12,508	18,930	22,524	34,805	54,934	2.69	57.83
Taiwan, Province of China	12,276	14,170	15,542	22,060	30,699	1.50	39.16
Other countries of North-East Asia	989	1,116	1,562				
SOUTH-EAST ASIA	524,011	512,278	482,128	583,397	1,273,859	62.31	118.35
Indonesia	2,072	2,398	2,968	5,637	10,274	0.50	82.26
Malaysia	9,668	16,186	23,287	30,499	39,758	1.94	30.36
Philippines	1,888	2,169	2,878	4,753	7,578	0.37	59.44
Singapore	10,712	12,114	15,391	26,296	39,140	1.91	48.84
Thailand	496,932	472,978	427,954	501,957	1,155,454	56.52	130.19
Viet Nam	1,864	5,609	7,703	11,472	17,453	0.85	52.14
Other countries of South-East Asia	875	824	1,947	2,783	4,202	0.21	50.99
AUSTRALASIA	7,993	8,686	11,603	20,603	28,036	1.37	36.08
Australia	7,163	7,693	10,415	18,261	24,718	1.21	35.36
New Zealand	830	993	1,188	2,342	3,318	0.16	41.67
OTHER EAST ASIA AND THE PACIFIC	96	148	150	5,878	95,366	4.66	1,522.42
Other countries of Asia	84	139	131	5,831	95,323	4.66	1,534.76
Other countries of Oceania	12	9	19	47	43	0.00	-8.51
EUROPE	53,150	65,935	88,517	139,373	168,346	8.23	20.79
CENTRAL/EASTERN EUROPE	4,623	6,117	7,622	9,077	10,183	0.50	12.18
Russian Federation	2,070	2,757	3,496	3,749	4,117	0.20	9.82
Other countries Central/East Europe	2,553	3,360	4,126	5,328	6,066	0.30	13.85
NORTHERN EUROPE	7,770	9,504	13,765	24,296	40,891	2.00	68.30
Denmark	882	1,247	1,527		3,628	0.18	
Sweden	717	917	1,182		4,060	0.20	
United Kingdom	6,171	7,340	11,056	24,296	33,203	1.62	36.66
SOUTHERN EUROPE	10,456	12,981	16,369	17,518	17,316	0.85	-1.15
Italy	5,975	7,169	9,710	10,830	11,728	0.57	8.29
Spain	4,481	5,812	6,659	6,688	5,588	0.27	-16.45
WESTERN EUROPE	28,477	35,084	47,800	69,277	91,404	4.47	31.94
Austria	1,447	1,896	1,964	3,489	3,959	0.19	13.47
Belgium	1,848	2,411	3,376	4,627	5,946	0.29	28.51
France	10,458	13,143	19,414	30,064	35,462	1.73	17.96
Germany	9,608	11,082	14,006	23,063	27,712	1.36	20.16
Netherlands	1,887	2,384	3,495		8,778	0.43	
Switzerland	3,229	4,168	5,545	8,034	9,547	0.47	18.83
OTHER EUROPE	1,824	2,249	2,961	19,205	8,552	0.42	-55.47
Other countries of Europe	1,824	2,249	2,961	19,205	8,552	0.42	-55.47
MIDDLE EAST	1,564	2,208	2,607	3,747	3,396	0.17	-9.37
All countries of Middle East	1,564	2,208	2,607	3,747	3,396	0.17	-9.37
SOUTH ASIA	12,046	13,699	16,904	18,605	55,325	2.71	197.37
Bangladesh	1,212	1,441	1,988	1,737	1,981	0.10	14.05
India	8,609	9,849	12,318	16,868	52,284	2.56	209.96
Pakistan	733	794			1,060	0.05	
Other countries of South Asia	1,492	1,615	2,598				

511

MYANMAR

5. Overnight stays of non-resident tourists in hotels and similar establishments, by nationality

	2009	2010	2011	2012	2013	Market share 2013	% Change 2013-2012
TOTAL	2,067,863	2,485,504	3,129,408	4,013,667	6,301,127	100.00	56.99
AFRICA	6,494	6,536	7,944	11,186	18,816	0.30	68.21
OTHER AFRICA	6,494	6,536	7,944	11,186	18,816	0.30	68.21
All countries of Africa	6,494	6,536	7,944	11,186	18,816	0.30	68.21
AMERICAS	158,628	164,632	221,960	333,263	470,771	7.47	41.26
NORTH AMERICA	148,241	151,288	202,920	308,518	438,396	6.96	42.10
Canada	20,290	19,256	29,480	45,395	62,825	1.00	38.40
United States of America	127,951	132,032	173,440	263,123	375,571	5.96	42.74
OTHER AMERICAS	10,387	13,344	19,040	24,745	32,375	0.51	30.83
Other countries of the Americas	10,387	13,344	19,040	24,745	32,375	0.51	30.83
EAST ASIA AND THE PACIFIC	1,335,282	1,659,600	2,035,280	2,537,143	4,440,765	70.48	75.03
NORTH-EAST ASIA	668,696	796,992	1,014,296	1,121,302	1,769,726	28.09	57.83
China	308,899	369,128	496,144	495,635	633,850	10.06	27.89
Hong Kong, China	23,350	24,648	30,560	33,782	55,118	0.87	63.16
Japan	117,377	129,488	170,568	333,830	481,327	7.64	44.18
Korea, Republic of	106,318	151,440	180,192	243,635	384,538	6.10	57.83
Taiwan, Province of China	104,346	113,360	124,336		214,893	3.41	
Other countries of North-East Asia	8,406	8,928	12,496	14,420			
SOUTH-EAST ASIA	597,830	791,936	926,960	1,057,959	1,777,811	28.21	68.04
Indonesia	17,613	19,184	23,744		71,918	1.14	
Malaysia	82,178	129,488	186,296	213,493	278,306	4.42	30.36
Philippines	16,048	17,352	23,024		53,046	0.84	
Singapore	91,053	96,912	123,128	184,072	273,980	4.35	48.84
Thailand	367,660	477,536	493,568	660,394	978,390	15.53	48.15
Viet Nam	15,844	44,872	61,624		122,171	1.94	
Other countries of South-East Asia	7,434	6,592	15,576				
AUSTRALASIA	67,940	69,488	92,824	144,221	196,252	3.11	36.08
Australia	60,885	61,544	83,320	127,827	173,026	2.75	35.36
New Zealand	7,055	7,944	9,504	16,394	23,226	0.37	41.67
OTHER EAST ASIA AND THE PACIFIC	816	1,184	1,200	213,661	696,976	11.06	226.21
Other countries of Asia	714	1,112	1,048	213,332	696,675	11.06	226.57
Other countries of Oceania	102	72	152	329	301	0.00	-8.51
EUROPE	451,774	527,480	708,136	975,611	1,178,422	18.70	20.79
CENTRAL/EASTERN EUROPE	39,295	48,936	60,976	63,539	71,281	1.13	12.18
Russian Federation	17,595	22,056	27,968	26,243	28,819	0.46	9.82
Other countries Central/East Europe	21,700	26,880	33,008	37,296	42,462	0.67	13.85
NORTHERN EUROPE	66,045	76,032	110,120	170,072	286,237	4.54	68.30
Denmark	7,497	9,976	12,216		25,396	0.40	
Sweden	6,095	7,336	9,456		28,420	0.45	
United Kingdom	52,453	58,720	88,448	170,072	232,421	3.69	36.66
SOUTHERN EUROPE	88,876	103,848	130,952	122,626	121,212	1.92	-1.15
Italy	50,788	57,352	77,680	75,810	82,096	1.30	8.29
Spain	38,088	46,496	53,272	46,816	39,116	0.62	-16.45
WESTERN EUROPE	242,054	280,672	382,400	484,939	639,828	10.15	31.94
Austria	12,300	15,168	15,712	24,423	27,713	0.44	13.47
Belgium	15,708	19,288	27,008	32,389	41,622	0.66	28.51
France	88,893	105,144	155,312	210,448	248,234	3.94	17.96
Germany	81,668	88,656	112,048	161,441	193,984	3.08	20.16
Netherlands	16,039	19,072	27,960		61,446	0.98	
Switzerland	27,446	33,344	44,360	56,238	66,829	1.06	18.83
OTHER EUROPE	15,504	17,992	23,688	134,435	59,864	0.95	-55.47
Other countries of Europe	15,504	17,992	23,688	134,435	59,864	0.95	-55.47
MIDDLE EAST	13,294	17,664	20,856	26,229	23,772	0.38	-9.37
All countries of Middle East	13,294	17,664	20,856	26,229	23,772	0.38	-9.37
SOUTH ASIA	102,391	109,592	135,232	130,235	168,581	2.68	29.44
Bangladesh	10,302	11,528	15,904	12,159	13,867	0.22	14.05
India	73,177	78,792	98,544	118,076	147,294	2.34	24.75
Pakistan	6,230	6,352			7,420	0.12	
Other countries of South Asia	12,682	12,920	20,784				

512

NAMIBIA

1. Arrivals of non-resident tourists at national borders, by nationality

	2009	2010	2011	2012	2013	Market share 2013	% Change 2013-2012
TOTAL	980,178	984,098	1,027,230	1,078,935	1,176,041	100.00	9.00
AFRICA	723,762	714,287	784,580	826,688	912,861	77.62	10.42
EAST AFRICA	86,175	91,896	104,065	134,535	155,358	13.21	15.48
Zambia	54,333	54,229	61,120	80,515	98,792	8.40	22.70
Zimbabwe	31,842	37,667	42,945	54,020	56,566	4.81	4.71
CENTRAL AFRICA	309,127	296,825	361,480	379,842	426,025	36.23	12.16
Angola	309,127	296,825	361,480	379,842	426,025	36.23	12.16
SOUTHERN AFRICA	312,697	309,158	301,588	294,666	309,011	26.28	4.87
Botswana	26,918	31,503	28,658	25,273	31,829	2.71	25.94
South Africa	285,779	277,655	272,930	269,393	277,182	23.57	2.89
OTHER AFRICA	15,763	16,408	17,447	17,645	22,467	1.91	27.33
Other countries of Africa	15,763	16,408	17,447	17,645	22,467	1.91	27.33
AMERICAS	26,657	26,175	24,828	26,635	29,097	2.47	9.24
NORTH AMERICA	24,940	22,793	22,790	24,243	26,116	2.22	7.73
Canada	4,860	4,967	4,844	5,539	6,959	0.59	25.64
United States of America	20,080	17,826	17,946	18,704	19,157	1.63	2.42
SOUTH AMERICA	1,717	3,382	2,038	2,392	2,981	0.25	24.62
Brazil	1,717	3,382	2,038	2,392	2,981	0.25	24.62
EAST ASIA AND THE PACIFIC	11,484	11,294	11,668	13,803	16,891	1.44	22.37
NORTH-EAST ASIA	5,119	4,228	4,035	5,830	9,910	0.84	69.98
China	5,119	4,228	4,035	5,830	9,910	0.84	69.98
AUSTRALASIA	6,365	7,066	7,633	7,973	6,981	0.59	-12.44
Australia	6,365	7,066	7,633	7,973	6,981	0.59	-12.44
EUROPE	206,496	219,070	194,430	198,219	199,655	16.98	0.72
CENTRAL/EASTERN EUROPE	1,806	1,762	1,898	2,293	2,168	0.18	-5.45
Russian Federation	1,806	1,762	1,898	2,293	2,168	0.18	-5.45
NORTHERN EUROPE	36,720	36,308	31,699	31,522	31,603	2.69	0.26
United Kingdom	28,039	25,717	21,584	21,035	23,185	1.97	10.22
Scandinavia	8,681	10,591	10,115	10,487	8,418	0.72	-19.73
SOUTHERN EUROPE	26,176	27,962	25,650	26,810	28,585	2.43	6.62
Italy	12,095	10,767	11,207	9,335	8,780	0.75	-5.95
Portugal	8,653	9,124	8,774	12,679	14,048	1.19	10.80
Spain	5,428	8,071	5,669	4,796	5,757	0.49	20.04
WESTERN EUROPE	135,460	147,015	129,415	130,304	130,790	11.12	0.37
Austria	7,201	7,197	6,016	6,288	5,875	0.50	-6.57
Belgium	5,647	7,024	6,170	5,739	7,329	0.62	27.71
France	15,044	17,039	13,729	15,937	15,911	1.35	-0.16
Germany	81,974	87,072	79,721	80,127	79,551	6.76	-0.72
Netherlands	14,503	16,078	12,346	11,890	10,276	0.87	-13.57
Switzerland	11,091	12,605	11,433	10,323	11,848	1.01	14.77
OTHER EUROPE	6,334	6,023	5,768	7,290	6,509	0.55	-10.71
Other countries of Europe	6,334	6,023	5,768	7,290	6,509	0.55	-10.71
NOT SPECIFIED	11,779	13,272	11,724	13,590	17,537	1.49	29.04
Other countries of the World	11,779	13,272	11,724	13,590	17,537	1.49	29.04

513

NAMIBIA

2. Arrivals of non-resident visitors at national borders, by nationality

	2009	2010	2011	2012	2013	Market share 2013	% Change 2013-2012
TOTAL		1,114,423	1,163,395	1,245,240	1,327,142	100.00	6.58
AFRICA		833,316	909,399	976,217	1,049,827	79.10	7.54
EAST AFRICA		160,981	168,949	226,330	221,683	16.70	-2.05
Zambia		122,383	123,973	170,721	162,086	12.21	-5.06
Zimbabwe		38,598	44,976	55,609	59,597	4.49	7.17
CENTRAL AFRICA		319,987	393,968	411,000	465,675	35.09	13.30
Angola		319,987	393,968	411,000	465,675	35.09	13.30
SOUTHERN AFRICA		335,507	328,157	320,075	338,560	25.51	5.78
Botswana		36,032	33,008	28,217	35,325	2.66	25.19
South Africa		299,475	295,149	291,858	303,235	22.85	3.90
OTHER AFRICA		16,841	18,325	18,812	23,909	1.80	27.09
Other countries of Africa		16,841	18,325	18,812	23,909	1.80	27.09
AMERICAS		28,470	26,427	28,625	31,643	2.38	10.54
NORTH AMERICA		24,811	24,225	26,192	28,642	2.16	9.35
Canada		5,233	5,052	5,938	7,532	0.57	26.84
United States of America		19,578	19,173	20,254	21,110	1.59	4.23
SOUTH AMERICA		3,659	2,202	2,433	3,001	0.23	23.35
Brazil		3,659	2,202	2,433	3,001	0.23	23.35
EAST ASIA AND THE PACIFIC		11,581	11,998	14,595	17,799	1.34	21.95
NORTH-EAST ASIA		4,300	4,085	6,109	10,358	0.78	69.55
China		4,300	4,085	6,109	10,358	0.78	69.55
AUSTRALASIA		7,281	7,913	8,486	7,441	0.56	-12.31
Australia		7,281	7,913	8,486	7,441	0.56	-12.31
EUROPE		227,519	202,694	209,905	208,428	15.71	-0.70
CENTRAL/EASTERN EUROPE		1,762	2,496	2,821	2,290	0.17	-18.82
Russian Federation		1,762	2,496	2,821	2,290	0.17	-18.82
NORTHERN EUROPE		38,417	34,077	34,828	33,586	2.53	-3.57
United Kingdom		27,460	23,368	23,150	24,678	1.86	6.60
Scandinavia		10,957	10,709	11,678	8,908	0.67	-23.72
SOUTHERN EUROPE		30,707	27,558	29,118	30,532	2.30	4.86
Italy		10,866	11,566	9,591	9,033	0.68	-5.82
Portugal		11,576	10,039	14,134	15,412	1.16	9.04
Spain		8,265	5,953	5,393	6,087	0.46	12.87
WESTERN EUROPE		150,422	132,291	134,716	134,871	10.16	0.12
Austria		7,360	6,065	6,480	5,991	0.45	-7.55
Belgium		7,176	6,255	5,809	7,774	0.59	33.83
France		17,187	14,115	16,784	16,516	1.24	-1.60
Germany		88,950	81,423	82,695	81,813	6.16	-1.07
Netherlands		16,954	12,741	12,351	10,580	0.80	-14.34
Switzerland		12,795	11,692	10,597	12,197	0.92	15.10
OTHER EUROPE		6,211	6,272	8,422	7,149	0.54	-15.12
Other countries of Europe		6,211	6,272	8,422	7,149	0.54	-15.12
NOT SPECIFIED		13,537	12,877	15,898	19,445	1.47	22.31
Other countries of the World		13,537	12,877	15,898	19,445	1.47	22.31

Yearbook of Tourism Statistics, Data 2009 – 2013, 2015 Edition

NEPAL

1. Arrivals of non-resident tourists at national borders, by nationality

	2009	2010	2011	2012	2013	Market share 2013	% Change 2013-2012
TOTAL	**509,956**	**602,867**	**736,215**	**803,092**	**797,616**	**100.00**	**-0.68**
AFRICA	**435**	**461**	**2,239**	**1,324**			
EAST AFRICA	**141**	**219**	**349**				
Kenya	141	219	223				
Mauritius			126				
NORTH AFRICA	**252**	**173**	**231**				
Algeria	196	53	131				
Morocco	42	92	76				
Tunisia	14	28	24				
SOUTHERN AFRICA			**1,243**	**1,324**			
South Africa			1,243	1,324			
WEST AFRICA	**42**	**69**	**416**				
Benin			321				
Nigeria	42	69	95				
AMERICAS	**45,528**	**51,508**	**62,505**	**67,203**	**59,487**	**7.46**	**-11.48**
CARIBBEAN	**294**	**9**	**53**				
Bahamas	294	9	53				
CENTRAL AMERICA	**297**	**30**	**33**				
Costa Rica	297	30	33				
NORTH AMERICA	**41,695**	**47,437**	**55,735**	**63,956**	**59,487**	**7.46**	**-6.99**
Canada	8,965	9,322	11,404	13,507	12,132	1.52	-10.18
Mexico	687	1,690	1,456	1,464			
United States of America	32,043	36,425	42,875	48,985	47,355	5.94	-3.33
SOUTH AMERICA	**3,242**	**4,032**	**6,684**	**3,247**			
Argentina	923	1,102	2,226	1,617			
Bolivia	201	55	29				
Brazil	1,167	1,794	1,859	1,630			
Chile	270	606	493				
Colombia	459	392	402				
Peru			129				
Suriname			115				
Uruguay			1,226				
Venezuela	222	83	205				
EAST ASIA AND THE PACIFIC	**133,009**	**152,420**	**195,914**	**230,911**	**260,073**	**32.61**	**12.63**
NORTH-EAST ASIA	**70,912**	**90,129**	**120,214**	**135,335**	**169,249**	**21.22**	**25.06**
China	32,272	46,360	61,917	71,861	113,179	14.19	57.50
Japan	22,445	23,332	26,283	28,642	26,694	3.35	-6.80
Korea, Dem. People's Republic of			196				
Korea, Republic of	16,145	20,320	24,488	26,004	19,714	2.47	-24.19
Mongolia	50	117	362				
Taiwan, Province of China			6,968	8,828	9,662	1.21	9.45
SOUTH-EAST ASIA	**44,163**	**43,460**	**52,642**	**69,789**	**65,982**	**8.27**	**-5.46**
Brunei Darussalam	401	37	18				
Cambodia	319	227	141	862			
Indonesia	729	1,075	1,027	1,500			
Malaysia	5,527	6,752	7,381	11,780	18,842	2.36	59.95
Myanmar	2,600	1,633	328	9,470			
Philippines	1,247	2,362	2,399	1,757			
Singapore	5,344	8,937	6,985	5,626	6,171	0.77	9.69
Thailand	27,397	21,528	33,541	36,618	40,969	5.14	11.88
Timor-Leste			112				
Viet Nam	599	909	710	2,176			
AUSTRALASIA	**17,900**	**18,767**	**22,923**	**25,787**	**24,842**	**3.11**	**-3.66**
Australia	15,461	16,243	19,824	22,030	22,034	2.76	0.02
New Zealand	2,439	2,524	3,099	3,757	2,808	0.35	-25.26
MELANESIA	**34**	**64**	**135**				
Fiji	34	64	26				
Vanuatu			109				

515

NEPAL

1. Arrivals of non-resident tourists at national borders, by nationality

		2009	2010	2011	2012	2013	Market share 2013	% Change 2013-2012
EUROPE		**151,792**	**181,836**	**207,447**	**216,964**	**153,973**	**19.30**	**-29.03**
CENTRAL/EASTERN EUROPE		**8,553**	**18,875**	**15,426**	**24,672**	**12,774**	**1.60**	**-48.22**
Armenia				113				
Azerbaijan				147				
Belarus				249				
Bulgaria		326	327	302	1,229			
Czech Republic		1,307	2,831	2,121	3,592	1,123	0.14	-68.74
Estonia		90	225	87				
Hungary		514	1,895	726				
Kazakhstan		148	170	211				
Latvia				224				
Lithuania				282				
Poland		1,784	3,842	3,152	5,689	3,438	0.43	-39.57
Romania				501	1,336			
Russian Federation		3,262	6,846	5,554	9,673	8,213	1.03	-15.09
Slovakia		426	436	564	1,267			
Ukraine		696	2,303	1,193	1,886			
NORTHERN EUROPE		**47,728**	**51,706**	**57,166**	**60,626**	**47,393**	**5.94**	**-21.83**
Denmark		4,464	4,359	6,138	7,118	5,320	0.67	-25.26
Finland		1,408	3,284	2,276	2,464			
Iceland		179	76	171				
Ireland		1,643	3,249	2,168	2,018			
Norway		2,329	2,647	3,240	3,280	2,551	0.32	-22.23
Sweden		2,323	3,000	4,082	4,452	3,854	0.48	-13.43
United Kingdom		35,382	35,091	39,091	41,294	35,668	4.47	-13.62
SOUTHERN EUROPE		**23,209**	**29,262**	**33,614**	**31,039**	**20,386**	**2.56**	**-34.32**
Andorra				305				
Croatia		585	130	198				
Greece	(*)	979	2,763	1,068	691			
Italy		7,982	10,226	12,621	14,614	9,974	1.25	-31.75
Portugal		657	2,431	1,281	1,185			
Serbia				167				
Slovenia				201				
Spain		13,006	13,712	16,037	14,549	10,412	1.31	-28.43
TFYR of Macedonia				1,736				
WESTERN EUROPE		**65,905**	**74,588**	**92,602**	**91,788**	**67,983**	**8.52**	**-25.93**
Austria		3,245	3,389	3,998	3,797	3,131	0.39	-17.54
Belgium		4,832	5,275	6,368	6,286	5,328	0.67	-15.24
France		22,154	24,550	26,720	28,805	21,842	2.74	-24.17
Germany		19,246	22,583	27,472	30,409	22,263	2.79	-26.79
Luxembourg				188				
Netherlands		11,147	13,471	16,836	15,445	10,516	1.32	-31.91
Switzerland		5,281	5,320	11,020	7,046	4,903	0.61	-30.41
EAST MEDITERRANEAN EUROPE		**6,397**	**7,405**	**8,639**	**8,839**	**5,437**	**0.68**	**-38.49**
Israel		5,879	4,594	6,519	7,151	5,437	0.68	-23.97
Turkey		518	2,811	2,120	1,688			
MIDDLE EAST		**922**	**1,580**	**4,130**	**1,209**			
Bahrain		262	224	325				
Egypt		182	237	287				
Jordan				200				
Kuwait				139				
Lebanon				793				
Oman				389				
Qatar				259				
Saudi Arabia		279	536	743	1,209			
Syrian Arab Republic				165				
United Arab Emirates		199	583	830				

Yearbook of Tourism Statistics, Data 2009 – 2013, 2015 Edition

NEPAL

1. Arrivals of non-resident tourists at national borders, by nationality

	2009	2010	2011	2012	2013	Market share 2013	% Change 2013-2012
SOUTH ASIA	**152,785**	**193,510**	**235,983**	**261,813**	**240,496**	**30.15**	**-8.14**
Afghanistan	512	442	508	503			
Bangladesh	15,385	16,470	17,563	16,764	22,410	2.81	33.68
Bhutan	1,849	4,742	3,301	4,183			
India	93,884	120,898	149,504	165,815	180,974	22.69	9.14
Iran, Islamic Republic of	570	809	522				
Maldives	257	245	318				
Pakistan	3,966	4,373	4,383	5,072	4,376	0.55	-13.72
Sri Lanka	36,362	45,531	59,884	69,476	32,736	4.10	-52.88
NOT SPECIFIED	**25,485**	**21,552**	**27,997**	**23,668**	**83,587**	**10.48**	**253.16**
Other countries of the World	25,485	21,552	27,997	23,668	83,587	10.48	253.16

Yearbook of Tourism Statistics, Data 2009 – 2013, 2015 Edition

NEPAL

1. Arrivals of non-resident tourists at national borders, by country of residence

	2009	2010	2011	2012	2013	Market share 2013	% Change 2013-2012
TOTAL	509,956	602,867	736,215	803,092	797,616	100.00	-0.68
AFRICA	481	437	3,017	1,321			
EAST AFRICA	183	191	494				
Kenya	183	191	494				
CENTRAL AFRICA			966				
Angola			966				
NORTH AFRICA	280	185					
Algeria	246	112					
Morocco	34	73					
SOUTHERN AFRICA			1,244	1,321			
South Africa			1,244	1,321			
WEST AFRICA	18	61	313				
Benin			313				
Nigeria	18	61					
AMERICAS	42,567	49,637	62,430	65,212	59,487	7.46	-8.78
CARIBBEAN	311	28					
Bahamas	311	28					
CENTRAL AMERICA	300	27					
Costa Rica	300	27					
NORTH AMERICA	38,772	45,763	54,321	62,180	59,487	7.46	-4.33
Canada	7,827	9,024	10,705	12,885	12,132	1.52	-5.84
Mexico	657	1,779	1,645	1,383			
United States of America	30,288	34,960	41,971	47,912	47,355	5.94	-1.16
SOUTH AMERICA	3,184	3,819	8,109	3,032			
Argentina	913	1,060	2,898	1,552			
Bolivia	192	32					
Brazil	1,150	1,682	2,363	1,480			
Chile	271	580	638				
Colombia	433	367	490				
Uruguay			1,720				
Venezuela	225	98					
EAST ASIA AND THE PACIFIC	135,232	148,074	201,134	227,273	258,502	32.41	13.74
NORTH-EAST ASIA	70,360	85,621	121,506	133,349	169,243	21.22	26.92
China	33,487	44,694	64,115	71,380	113,173	14.19	58.55
Japan	21,066	21,594	25,856	27,993	26,694	3.35	-4.64
Korea, Republic of	15,757	19,247	24,202	25,129	19,714	2.47	-21.55
Mongolia	50	86	307				
Taiwan, Province of China			7,026	8,847	9,662	1.21	9.21
SOUTH-EAST ASIA	47,791	44,706	56,903	68,185	65,982	8.27	-3.23
Brunei Darussalam	439	73					
Cambodia	411	251	270	871			
Indonesia	754	891	1,167	1,357			
Malaysia	5,157	6,376	7,126	11,932	18,842	2.36	57.91
Myanmar	2,601	1,538	1,678	8,043			
Philippines	1,351	2,361	2,384	1,734			
Singapore	6,976	10,345	8,648	7,018	6,171	0.77	-12.07
Thailand	29,388	22,318	34,587	35,315	40,969	5.14	16.01
Viet Nam	714	553	1,043	1,915			
AUSTRALASIA	17,042	17,687	22,725	25,739	23,277	2.92	-9.57
Australia	14,897	15,636	19,949	22,272	20,469	2.57	-8.10
New Zealand	2,145	2,051	2,776	3,467	2,808	0.35	-19.01
MELANESIA	39	60					
Fiji	39	60					
EUROPE	143,814	169,694	212,729	211,322	153,973	19.30	-27.14
CENTRAL/EASTERN EUROPE	8,290	17,687	22,935	23,560	12,774	1.60	-45.78
Belarus			268				
Bulgaria	308	457	1,204	1,200			
Czech Republic	1,284	2,540	4,170	3,505	1,123	0.14	-67.96
Estonia	93	202					

518

NEPAL

1. Arrivals of non-resident tourists at national borders, by country of residence

		2009	2010	2011	2012	2013	Market share 2013	% Change 2013-2012
Hungary		496	1,775	736				
Kazakhstan		152	159	259				
Latvia				273				
Lithuania				271				
Poland		1,654	3,502	4,196	5,107	3,438	0.43	-32.68
Romania				939	1,195			
Russian Federation		3,204	6,472	7,881	9,486	8,213	1.03	-13.42
Slovakia		412	366	1,028	1,195			
Ukraine		687	2,214	1,710	1,872			
NORTHERN EUROPE		**44,076**	**46,803**	**55,321**	**58,933**	**47,393**	**5.94**	**-19.58**
Denmark		4,198	4,295	5,955	6,852	5,320	0.67	-22.36
Finland		1,297	2,890	2,380	2,320			
Iceland		180	102	399				
Ireland		1,524	2,806	2,333	1,740			
Norway		2,190	2,492	3,268	3,270	2,551	0.32	-21.99
Sweden		2,096	2,758	4,005	4,387	3,854	0.48	-12.15
United Kingdom		32,591	31,460	36,981	40,364	35,668	4.47	-11.63
SOUTHERN EUROPE		**22,668**	**27,685**	**33,823**	**30,351**	**20,386**	**2.56**	**-32.83**
Andorra				296				
Croatia		623	120	229				
Greece	(*)	938	2,593	1,114	643			
Italy		7,632	9,594	12,257	14,191	9,974	1.25	-29.72
Portugal		600	2,168	1,346	1,027			
Slovenia				224				
Spain		12,875	13,210	15,593	14,490	10,412	1.31	-28.14
TFYR of Macedonia				2,764				
WESTERN EUROPE		**62,414**	**70,505**	**91,842**	**89,723**	**67,983**	**8.52**	**-24.23**
Austria		3,139	3,146	3,885	3,706	3,131	0.39	-15.52
Belgium		4,653	5,036	6,347	6,429	5,328	0.67	-17.13
France		20,907	23,032	26,131	27,684	21,842	2.74	-21.10
Germany		17,927	21,146	26,866	29,682	22,263	2.79	-24.99
Liechtenstein				261				
Luxembourg				237				
Netherlands		10,377	12,659	16,343	14,727	10,516	1.32	-28.59
Switzerland		5,411	5,486	11,772	7,495	4,903	0.61	-34.58
EAST MEDITERRANEAN EUROPE		**6,366**	**7,014**	**8,808**	**8,755**	**5,437**	**0.68**	**-37.90**
Israel		5,863	4,314	6,593	7,087	5,437	0.68	-23.28
Turkey		503	2,700	2,215	1,668			
MIDDLE EAST		**4,891**	**7,524**	**12,857**	**1,652**			
Bahrain		518	481	578				
Egypt		140	137					
Kuwait				294				
Lebanon				892				
Oman				733				
Qatar				1,692				
Saudi Arabia		494	755	1,231	1,652			
United Arab Emirates		3,739	6,151	7,437				
SOUTH ASIA		**150,951**	**177,704**	**234,599**	**253,980**	**240,496**	**30.15**	**-5.31**
Afghanistan		594	483	561	570			
Bangladesh		15,746	14,681	18,133	16,970	22,410	2.81	32.06
Bhutan		1,866	4,413	4,291	3,990			
India		91,994	108,077	147,037	165,139	180,974	22.69	9.59
Iran, Islamic Republic of		536	689	467				
Maldives		259	227	310				
Pakistan		3,637	3,742	4,015	4,891	4,376	0.55	-10.53
Sri Lanka		36,319	45,392	59,785	62,420	32,736	4.10	-47.56
NOT SPECIFIED		**32,020**	**49,797**	**9,449**	**42,332**	**85,158**	**10.68**	**101.17**
Other countries of the World		32,020	49,797	9,449	42,332	85,158	10.68	101.17

Yearbook of Tourism Statistics, Data 2009 – 2013, 2015 Edition

NETHERLANDS

3. Arrivals of non-resident tourists in hotels and similar establishments, by country of residence

	2009	2010	2011	2012	2013	Market share 2013	% Change 2013-2012
TOTAL (*)	7,754,300	8,726,800	9,026,500	9,356,700	10,019,000	100.00	7.08
AFRICA	81,700	100,300	112,100	110,100	119,000	1.19	8.08
OTHER AFRICA	81,700	100,300	112,100	110,100	119,000	1.19	8.08
All countries of Africa	81,700	100,300	112,100	110,100	119,000	1.19	8.08
AMERICAS	1,010,100	1,215,400	1,311,300	1,313,800	1,327,000	13.24	1.00
NORTH AMERICA	864,800	1,021,400	1,077,500	1,062,900	1,058,000	10.56	-0.46
Canada	103,300	127,200	131,500	131,400	139,000	1.39	5.78
United States of America	761,500	894,200	946,000	931,500	919,000	9.17	-1.34
OTHER AMERICAS	145,300	194,000	233,800	250,900	269,000	2.68	7.21
Other countries of the Americas	145,300	194,000	233,800	250,900	269,000	2.68	7.21
EAST ASIA AND THE PACIFIC	554,800	627,000	684,800	775,500	848,000	8.46	9.35
NORTH-EAST ASIA	258,400	281,000	316,100	363,600	407,000	4.06	11.94
China	122,500	124,300	155,700	172,800	192,000	1.92	11.11
Japan	99,300	119,000	110,500	136,300	150,000	1.50	10.05
Korea, Republic of	22,900	23,200	25,300	27,800	39,000	0.39	40.29
Taiwan, Province of China	13,700	14,500	24,600	26,700	26,000	0.26	-2.62
SOUTH-EAST ASIA	13,800	21,200	23,600	32,100	38,000	0.38	18.38
Indonesia	13,800	21,200	23,600	32,100	38,000	0.38	18.38
AUSTRALASIA	96,700	129,700	142,700	150,400	149,000	1.49	-0.93
Australia	84,700	115,600	127,100	134,200	132,000	1.32	-1.64
New Zealand	12,000	14,100	15,600	16,200	17,000	0.17	4.94
OTHER EAST ASIA AND THE PACIFIC	185,900	195,100	202,400	229,400	254,000	2.54	10.72
Other countries of Asia	176,100	181,100	190,600	220,200	242,000	2.42	9.90
Other countries of Oceania	9,800	14,000	11,800	9,200	12,000	0.12	30.43
EUROPE	6,058,300	6,720,500	6,850,500	7,080,300	7,646,000	76.32	7.99
CENTRAL/EASTERN EUROPE	223,100	264,700	304,300	329,800	381,000	3.80	15.52
Czech Republic	28,200	32,600	36,100	37,800	39,000	0.39	3.17
Hungary	22,800	26,600	30,300	30,500	34,000	0.34	11.48
Poland	68,200	80,600	88,300	94,000	104,000	1.04	10.64
Russian Federation	95,100	114,800	139,000	153,800	190,000	1.90	23.54
Slovakia	8,800	10,100	10,600	13,700	14,000	0.14	2.19
NORTHERN EUROPE	1,781,000	1,983,000	1,937,700	2,055,800	2,142,000	21.38	4.19
Denmark	117,500	135,500	122,600	121,600	130,000	1.30	6.91
Finland	42,900	49,200	62,800	62,200	63,000	0.63	1.29
Iceland	5,400	7,100	8,000	8,300	9,000	0.09	8.43
Ireland	105,400	109,300	87,300	93,300	92,000	0.92	-1.39
Norway	85,900	96,100	104,000	114,800	119,000	1.19	3.66
Sweden	93,700	108,400	119,600	132,200	134,000	1.34	1.36
United Kingdom	1,330,200	1,477,400	1,433,400	1,523,400	1,595,000	15.92	4.70
SOUTHERN EUROPE	776,400	934,500	919,300	892,000	925,000	9.23	3.70
Greece	45,900	44,800	41,500	36,200	36,000	0.36	-0.55
Italy	343,800	411,600	407,600	405,200	437,000	4.36	7.85
Portugal	50,900	53,200	60,000	54,700	67,000	0.67	22.49
Spain	335,800	424,900	410,200	395,900	385,000	3.84	-2.75
WESTERN EUROPE	2,807,500	3,132,100	3,254,400	3,360,300	3,695,000	36.88	9.96
Austria	63,600	69,000	78,100	75,300	84,000	0.84	11.55
Belgium	712,500	796,500	808,100	884,600	972,000	9.70	9.88
France	497,900	577,900	584,100	558,700	603,000	6.02	7.93
Germany	1,357,000	1,485,100	1,562,100	1,600,300	1,782,000	17.79	11.35
Luxembourg	31,400	40,000	38,300	43,900	44,000	0.44	0.23
Switzerland	145,100	163,600	183,700	197,500	210,000	2.10	6.33
EAST MEDITERRANEAN EUROPE	104,200	121,800	144,700	157,600	182,000	1.82	15.48
Israel	60,600	69,600	86,200	85,700	99,000	0.99	15.52
Turkey	43,600	52,200	58,500	71,900	83,000	0.83	15.44
OTHER EUROPE	366,100	284,400	290,100	284,800	321,000	3.20	12.71
Other countries of Europe	366,100	284,400	290,100	284,800	321,000	3.20	12.71
SOUTH ASIA	49,400	63,600	67,800	77,000	79,000	0.79	2.60
India	49,400	63,600	67,800	77,000	79,000	0.79	2.60

Yearbook of Tourism Statistics, Data 2009 – 2013, 2015 Edition

NETHERLANDS

4. Arrivals of non-resident tourists in all types of accommodation establishments, by country of residence

	2009	2010	2011	2012	2013	Market share 2013	% Change 2013-2012
TOTAL (*)	9,920,600	10,883,200	11,299,500	11,679,600	12,785,000	100.00	9.46
AFRICA	83,600	103,300	114,400	112,000	121,000	0.95	8.04
OTHER AFRICA	83,600	103,300	114,400	112,000	121,000	0.95	8.04
All countries of Africa	83,600	103,300	114,400	112,000	121,000	0.95	8.04
AMERICAS	1,017,700	1,223,000	1,319,800	1,322,800	1,337,000	10.46	1.07
OTHER AMERICAS	1,017,700	1,223,000	1,319,800	1,322,800	1,337,000	10.46	1.07
All countries of the Americas	1,017,700	1,223,000	1,319,800	1,322,800	1,337,000	10.46	1.07
EAST ASIA AND THE PACIFIC	673,400	770,100	849,700	949,300	1,040,000	8.13	9.55
OTHER EAST ASIA AND THE PACIFIC	673,400	770,100	849,700	949,300	1,040,000	8.13	9.55
All countries of Asia	563,900	622,800	690,800	786,000	875,000	6.84	11.32
All countries of Oceania	109,500	147,300	158,900	163,300	165,000	1.29	1.04
EUROPE	8,145,900	8,786,800	9,015,600	9,295,500	10,287,000	80.46	10.67
NORTHERN EUROPE	1,644,500	1,819,100	1,770,100	1,887,200	1,966,000	15.38	4.18
Denmark	135,200	150,200	136,900	135,500	144,000	1.13	6.27
Sweden	100,600	113,400	124,900	138,100	142,000	1.11	2.82
United Kingdom	1,408,700	1,555,500	1,508,300	1,613,600	1,680,000	13.14	4.12
SOUTHERN EUROPE	719,600	882,700	863,000	840,600	856,000	6.70	1.83
Italy	368,400	443,000	437,700	434,500	461,000	3.61	6.10
Spain	351,200	439,700	425,300	406,100	395,000	3.09	-2.73
WESTERN EUROPE	4,654,200	4,954,300	5,191,200	5,330,600	6,081,000	47.56	14.08
Belgium	1,171,800	1,256,800	1,345,000	1,461,800	1,673,000	13.09	14.45
France	574,300	668,500	666,400	641,700	680,000	5.32	5.97
Germany	2,744,000	2,847,700	2,978,000	3,009,600	3,495,000	27.34	16.13
Switzerland	164,100	181,300	201,800	217,500	233,000	1.82	7.13
OTHER EUROPE	1,127,600	1,130,700	1,191,300	1,237,100	1,384,000	10.83	11.87
Other countries of Europe	1,127,600	1,130,700	1,191,300	1,237,100	1,384,000	10.83	11.87

Yearbook of Tourism Statistics, Data 2009 – 2013, 2015 Edition

NETHERLANDS

5. Overnight stays of non-resident tourists in hotels and similar establishments, by country of residence

	2009	2010	2011	2012	2013	Market share 2013	% Change 2013-2012
TOTAL (*)	14,428,600	16,175,000	16,684,900	17,065,600	18,349,000	100.00	7.52
AFRICA	160,500	194,400	211,600	210,500	218,000	1.19	3.56
OTHER AFRICA	160,500	194,400	211,600	210,500	218,000	1.19	3.56
All countries of Africa	160,500	194,400	211,600	210,500	218,000	1.19	3.56
AMERICAS	1,825,900	2,185,800	2,282,400	2,299,100	2,373,000	12.93	3.21
NORTH AMERICA	1,539,500	1,812,800	1,835,700	1,814,000	1,843,000	10.04	1.60
Canada	192,800	240,500	244,900	246,900	266,000	1.45	7.74
United States of America	1,346,700	1,572,300	1,590,800	1,567,100	1,577,000	8.59	0.63
OTHER AMERICAS	286,400	373,000	446,700	485,100	530,000	2.89	9.26
Other countries of the Americas	286,400	373,000	446,700	485,100	530,000	2.89	9.26
EAST ASIA AND THE PACIFIC	977,200	1,102,100	1,240,600	1,376,000	1,467,000	7.99	6.61
NORTH-EAST ASIA	426,200	465,400	541,600	590,600	647,000	3.53	9.55
China	200,500	202,700	253,200	266,500	297,000	1.62	11.44
Japan	162,300	196,800	196,700	228,800	247,000	1.35	7.95
Korea, Republic of	38,000	38,900	45,700	48,200	60,000	0.33	24.48
Taiwan, Province of China	25,400	27,000	46,000	47,100	43,000	0.23	-8.70
SOUTH-EAST ASIA	28,300	39,000	44,200	61,300	69,000	0.38	12.56
Indonesia	28,300	39,000	44,200	61,300	69,000	0.38	12.56
AUSTRALASIA	188,200	248,600	281,900	295,500	294,000	1.60	-0.51
Australia	164,800	222,800	251,700	264,000	261,000	1.42	-1.14
New Zealand	23,400	25,800	30,200	31,500	33,000	0.18	4.76
OTHER EAST ASIA AND THE PACIFIC	334,500	349,100	372,900	428,600	457,000	2.49	6.63
Other countries of Asia	318,600	325,500	349,900	411,600	436,000	2.38	5.93
Other countries of Oceania	15,900	23,600	23,000	17,000	21,000	0.11	23.53
EUROPE	11,368,600	12,563,900	12,813,400	13,037,900	14,150,000	77.12	8.53
CENTRAL/EASTERN EUROPE	427,000	497,100	590,600	632,200	728,000	3.97	15.15
Czech Republic	52,400	61,600	66,400	72,900	76,000	0.41	4.25
Hungary	41,700	49,400	59,000	54,900	63,000	0.34	14.75
Poland	130,400	146,600	169,500	174,700	185,000	1.01	5.90
Russian Federation	185,200	220,700	275,300	303,900	379,000	2.07	24.71
Slovakia	17,300	18,800	20,400	25,800	25,000	0.14	-3.10
NORTHERN EUROPE	3,226,600	3,570,700	3,495,900	3,697,400	3,853,000	21.00	4.21
Denmark	215,000	256,700	237,600	223,200	238,000	1.30	6.63
Finland	79,300	90,800	118,500	117,200	115,000	0.63	-1.88
Iceland	9,900	12,300	15,000	15,300	17,000	0.09	11.11
Ireland	197,000	189,000	156,700	164,900	166,000	0.90	0.67
Norway	162,200	176,900	188,600	211,500	223,000	1.22	5.44
Sweden	163,300	189,600	208,500	233,300	242,000	1.32	3.73
United Kingdom	2,399,900	2,655,400	2,571,000	2,732,000	2,852,000	15.54	4.39
SOUTHERN EUROPE	1,544,300	1,846,800	1,827,900	1,738,700	1,817,000	9.90	4.50
Greece	91,700	87,300	81,600	71,400	70,000	0.38	-1.96
Italy	678,500	822,300	822,100	808,900	886,000	4.83	9.53
Portugal	95,600	103,300	113,500	105,200	130,000	0.71	23.57
Spain	678,500	833,900	810,700	753,200	731,000	3.98	-2.95
WESTERN EUROPE	5,259,600	5,862,400	6,066,800	6,131,900	6,793,000	37.02	10.78
Austria	129,000	130,800	157,600	144,700	164,000	0.89	13.34
Belgium	1,176,500	1,301,100	1,312,700	1,437,900	1,592,000	8.68	10.72
France	875,400	1,020,300	1,022,500	974,100	1,072,000	5.84	10.05
Germany	2,752,100	3,029,200	3,149,600	3,125,200	3,490,000	19.02	11.67
Luxembourg	60,200	81,000	79,200	81,000	85,000	0.46	4.94
Switzerland	266,400	300,000	345,200	369,000	390,000	2.13	5.69
EAST MEDITERRANEAN EUROPE	200,000	244,000	281,000	311,500	372,000	2.03	19.42
Israel	121,200	149,900	172,000	178,200	216,000	1.18	21.21
Turkey	78,800	94,100	109,000	133,300	156,000	0.85	17.03
OTHER EUROPE	711,100	542,900	551,200	526,200	587,000	3.20	11.55
Other countries of Europe	711,100	542,900	551,200	526,200	587,000	3.20	11.55
SOUTH ASIA	96,400	128,800	136,900	142,100	141,000	0.77	-0.77
India	96,400	128,800	136,900	142,100	141,000	0.77	-0.77

Yearbook of Tourism Statistics, Data 2009 – 2013, 2015 Edition

NETHERLANDS

6. Overnight stays of non-resident tourists in all types of accommodation establishments, by country of residence

	2009	2010	2011	2012	2013	Market share 2013	% Change 2013-2012
TOTAL (*)	25,013,600	26,799,600	27,738,900	27,898,500	31,771,000	100.00	13.88
AFRICA	171,200	209,100	224,200	219,400	229,000	0.72	4.38
OTHER AFRICA	171,200	209,100	224,200	219,400	229,000	0.72	4.38
All countries of Africa	171,200	209,100	224,200	219,400	229,000	0.72	4.38
AMERICAS	1,861,200	2,222,400	2,319,900	2,339,800	2,424,000	7.63	3.60
OTHER AMERICAS	1,861,200	2,222,400	2,319,900	2,339,800	2,424,000	7.63	3.60
All countries of the Americas	1,861,200	2,222,400	2,319,900	2,339,800	2,424,000	7.63	3.60
EAST ASIA AND THE PACIFIC	1,237,300	1,434,100	1,602,600	1,746,100	1,903,000	5.99	8.99
OTHER EAST ASIA AND THE PACIFIC	1,237,300	1,434,100	1,602,600	1,746,100	1,903,000	5.99	8.99
All countries of Asia	1,022,800	1,148,800	1,281,800	1,420,300	1,574,000	4.95	10.82
All countries of Oceania	214,500	285,300	320,800	325,800	329,000	1.04	0.98
EUROPE	21,743,900	22,934,000	23,592,200	23,593,200	27,215,000	85.66	15.35
NORTHERN EUROPE	3,242,200	3,542,800	3,433,900	3,653,000	3,828,000	12.05	4.79
Denmark	289,400	315,000	298,500	279,500	298,000	0.94	6.62
Sweden	181,500	204,700	226,700	251,100	272,000	0.86	8.32
United Kingdom	2,771,300	3,023,100	2,908,700	3,122,400	3,258,000	10.25	4.34
SOUTHERN EUROPE	1,467,500	1,787,400	1,770,200	1,672,200	1,724,000	5.43	3.10
Italy	741,200	901,600	905,400	885,700	955,000	3.01	7.82
Spain	726,300	885,800	864,800	786,500	769,000	2.42	-2.23
WESTERN EUROPE	14,689,900	15,315,100	15,946,200	15,778,600	18,822,000	59.24	19.29
Belgium	3,039,200	3,196,000	3,460,700	3,710,100	4,393,000	13.83	18.41
France	1,137,200	1,345,800	1,301,400	1,269,000	1,357,000	4.27	6.93
Germany	10,172,700	10,403,700	10,759,300	10,354,700	12,579,000	39.59	21.48
Switzerland	340,800	369,600	424,800	444,800	493,000	1.55	10.84
OTHER EUROPE	2,344,300	2,288,700	2,441,900	2,489,400	2,841,000	8.94	14.12
Other countries of Europe	2,344,300	2,288,700	2,441,900	2,489,400	2,841,000	8.94	14.12

Yearbook of Tourism Statistics, Data 2009 – 2013, 2015 Edition

NEW CALEDONIA

1. Arrivals of non-resident tourists at national borders, by country of residence

	2009	2010	2011	2012	2013	Market share 2013	% Change 2013-2012
TOTAL (*)	99,379	98,562	111,875	112,204	107,753	100.00	-3.97
AFRICA	1,980	2,238	1,904	1,468	729	0.68	-50.34
EAST AFRICA	1,653	1,946	1,566	1,109	348	0.32	-68.62
Reunion	1,653	1,946	1,566	1,109	348	0.32	-68.62
OTHER AFRICA	327	292	338	359	381	0.35	6.13
Other countries of Africa	327	292	338	359	381	0.35	6.13
AMERICAS	2,518	2,891	2,889	2,956	3,106	2.88	5.07
CARIBBEAN	229	289	275	210	196	0.18	-6.67
All countries of the Caribbean (*)	229	289	275	210	196	0.18	-6.67
NORTH AMERICA	2,045	2,255	2,289	2,466	2,527	2.35	2.47
Canada	1,150	1,182	1,192	1,383	1,511	1.40	9.26
United States of America	895	1,073	1,097	1,083	1,016	0.94	-6.19
SOUTH AMERICA	22	27	18	26	39	0.04	50.00
Argentina	22	27	18	26	39	0.04	50.00
OTHER AMERICAS	222	320	307	254	344	0.32	35.43
Other countries of the Americas	222	320	307	254	344	0.32	35.43
EAST ASIA AND THE PACIFIC	63,213	64,573	68,172	64,548	59,898	55.59	-7.20
NORTH-EAST ASIA	21,415	21,165	21,546	20,976	19,027	17.66	-9.29
China	166	499	649	774	401	0.37	-48.19
Hong Kong, China	111	89	98	120	164	0.15	36.67
Japan	18,926	18,534	18,455	17,430	15,674	14.55	-10.07
Korea, Republic of	2,212	2,043	2,344	2,652	2,788	2.59	5.13
AUSTRALASIA	25,218	23,957	23,507	23,971	22,056	20.47	-7.99
Australia	18,567	17,551	17,040	17,729	15,722	14.59	-11.32
New Zealand	6,651	6,406	6,467	6,242	6,334	5.88	1.47
MELANESIA	2,869	3,652	4,061	3,891	3,950	3.67	1.52
Vanuatu	2,869	3,652	4,061	3,891	3,950	3.67	1.52
POLYNESIA	10,550	11,999	12,998	11,354	10,709	9.94	-5.68
French Polynesia	4,096	4,940	4,935	4,258	3,946	3.66	-7.33
Wallis and Futuna Islands	6,454	7,059	8,063	7,096	6,763	6.28	-4.69
OTHER EAST ASIA AND THE PACIFIC	3,161	3,800	6,060	4,356	4,156	3.86	-4.59
Other countries of Asia	2,274	2,122	2,744	3,021	2,723	2.53	-9.86
Other countries of Oceania	887	1,678	3,316	1,335	1,433	1.33	7.34
EUROPE	31,652	28,859	38,886	43,231	44,020	40.85	1.83
NORTHERN EUROPE	495	474	598	567	576	0.53	1.59
United Kingdom	495	474	598	567	576	0.53	1.59
SOUTHERN EUROPE	650	736	571	717	718	0.67	0.14
Italy	650	736	571	717	718	0.67	0.14
WESTERN EUROPE	28,606	26,021	35,852	39,999	40,563	37.64	1.41
France	27,335	24,960	34,647	38,746	39,183	36.36	1.13
Germany	765	584	691	704	755	0.70	7.24
Switzerland	506	477	514	549	625	0.58	13.84
OTHER EUROPE	1,901	1,628	1,865	1,948	2,163	2.01	11.04
Other countries of Europe	1,901	1,628	1,865	1,948	2,163	2.01	11.04
NOT SPECIFIED	16	1	24	1			
Other countries of the World	16	1	24	1			

Yearbook of Tourism Statistics, Data 2009 – 2013, 2015 Edition

NEW CALEDONIA

3. Arrivals of non-resident tourists in hotels and similar establishments, by country of residence

		2009	2010	2011	2012	2013	Market share 2013	% Change 2013-2012
TOTAL	(*)	114,842	133,385	142,437	121,497	117,393	100.00	-3.38
EAST ASIA AND THE PACIFIC		63,428	73,683	65,362	56,444	58,985	50.25	4.50
NORTH-EAST ASIA		28,776	31,173	27,573	23,582	23,642	20.14	0.25
Japan		28,776	31,173	27,573	23,582	23,642	20.14	0.25
AUSTRALASIA		34,652	42,510	37,789	32,862	35,343	30.11	7.55
Australia		24,115	25,789	26,406	22,923	25,069	21.35	9.36
New Zealand		10,537	16,721	11,383	9,939	10,274	8.75	3.37
EUROPE		33,673	38,286	50,674	43,962	41,126	35.03	-6.45
WESTERN EUROPE		33,673	38,286	50,674	43,962	41,126	35.03	-6.45
France		33,673	38,286	50,674	43,962	41,126	35.03	-6.45
NOT SPECIFIED		17,741	21,416	26,401	21,091	17,282	14.72	-18.06
Other countries of the World		17,741	21,416	26,401	21,091	17,282	14.72	-18.06

Yearbook of Tourism Statistics, Data 2009 – 2013, 2015 Edition

NEW CALEDONIA

5. Overnight stays of non-resident tourists in hotels and similar establishments, by country of residence

		2009	2010	2011	2012	2013	Market share 2013	% Change 2013-2012
TOTAL	(*)	**304,274**	**279,406**	**316,228**	**288,020**	**285,560**	**100.00**	**-0.85**
EAST ASIA AND THE PACIFIC		**139,827**	**131,591**	**137,817**	**131,680**	**138,988**	**48.67**	**5.55**
NORTH-EAST ASIA		**62,322**	**57,168**	**59,367**	**55,867**	**57,000**	**19.96**	**2.03**
Japan		62,322	57,168	59,367	55,867	57,000	19.96	2.03
AUSTRALASIA		**77,505**	**74,423**	**78,450**	**75,813**	**81,988**	**28.71**	**8.15**
Australia		52,926	48,810	53,296	50,538	55,444	19.42	9.71
New Zealand		24,579	25,613	25,154	25,275	26,544	9.30	5.02
EUROPE		**113,793**	**97,060**	**122,168**	**110,632**	**104,858**	**36.72**	**-5.22**
WESTERN EUROPE		**113,793**	**97,060**	**122,168**	**110,632**	**104,858**	**36.72**	**-5.22**
France		113,793	97,060	122,168	110,632	104,858	36.72	-5.22
NOT SPECIFIED		**50,654**	**50,755**	**56,243**	**45,708**	**41,714**	**14.61**	**-8.74**
Other countries of the World		50,654	50,755	56,243	45,708	41,714	14.61	-8.74

Yearbook of Tourism Statistics, Data 2009 – 2013, 2015 Edition

NEW ZEALAND

2. Arrivals of non-resident visitors at national borders, by country of residence

		2009	2010	2011	2012	2013	Market share 2013	% Change 2013-2012
TOTAL	(*)	2,447,532	2,510,759	2,594,196	2,554,784	2,710,416	100.00	6.09
AFRICA		22,155	20,425	30,199	18,720	18,304	0.68	-2.22
EAST AFRICA		1,776	2,015	2,322	1,856	1,968	0.07	6.03
Burundi					16			
Comoros				41				
Eritrea		18						
Ethiopia		68	46	128	80	64	0.00	-20.00
Kenya		385	325	374	384	400	0.01	4.17
Madagascar		70		16	48			
Malawi		21	130	56	80	144	0.01	80.00
Mauritius		204	199	309	192	288	0.01	50.00
Mozambique			29	62	112	64	0.00	-42.86
Reunion		151	341	354	224	160	0.01	-28.57
Rwanda		27			32	48	0.00	50.00
Seychelles		23	100	48	80	32	0.00	-60.00
Somalia						32	0.00	
Uganda		116	98	149	64	64	0.00	
United Republic of Tanzania		182	237	239	96	144	0.01	50.00
Zambia		72	159	213	128	128	0.00	
Zimbabwe		439	322	333	320	400	0.01	25.00
Other countries of East Africa			29					
CENTRAL AFRICA		155	144	194	224	208	0.01	-7.14
Angola		64	74	66	48	64	0.00	33.33
Cameroon			24		48			
Chad		41		25		16	0.00	
Congo		23		16	48	48	0.00	
Democratic Republic of the Congo				25	16	16	0.00	
Equatorial Guinea		27		46		32	0.00	
Gabon			46	16	64	32	0.00	-50.00
NORTH AFRICA		220	162	360	144	192	0.01	33.33
Algeria		23	22	96	32			
Morocco		72		48	48	32	0.00	-33.33
South Sudan						32	0.00	
Sudan		80	120	125	64	96	0.00	50.00
Tunisia		45	20	91		32	0.00	
SOUTHERN AFRICA		19,535	17,719	26,700	15,984	15,440	0.57	-3.40
Botswana		93	174	105	96	128	0.00	33.33
Lesotho		23						
Namibia		155	144	261	176	96	0.00	-45.45
South Africa		19,214	17,401	26,286	15,712	15,184	0.56	-3.36
Swaziland		50		48		32	0.00	
WEST AFRICA		469	385	623	512	496	0.02	-3.13
Burkina Faso				46	32			
Cabo Verde						32	0.00	
Côte d'Ivoire				16				
Gambia			24	16				
Ghana		165	168	196	192	128	0.00	-33.33
Guinea						32	0.00	
Liberia		28				32	0.00	
Mali				40		48	0.00	
Mauritania			29	57				
Niger		27						
Nigeria		249	164	208	176	192	0.01	9.09
Saint Helena					32	16	0.00	-50.00
Senegal					64	16	0.00	-75.00
Sierra Leone				20	16			
Togo				24				

527

Yearbook of Tourism Statistics, Data 2009 – 2013, 2015 Edition

NEW ZEALAND

2. Arrivals of non-resident visitors at national borders, by country of residence

	2009	2010	2011	2012	2013	Market share 2013	% Change 2013-2012
AMERICAS	275,849	268,358	268,501	253,136	279,216	10.30	10.30
CARIBBEAN	1,509	1,272	1,513	1,280	1,376	0.05	7.50
Anguilla				16			
Antigua and Barbuda	93		32	16	16	0.00	
Aruba			30				
Bahamas	119	29	78	64	112	0.00	75.00
Barbados	123	55	86	32	64	0.00	100.00
Bermuda	343	282	293	224	176	0.01	-21.43
British Virgin Islands	44	47	46	64	48	0.00	-25.00
Cayman Islands	227	202	255	272	224	0.01	-17.65
Cuba	18	53	16	16	48	0.00	200.00
Curaçao				32	16	0.00	-50.00
Dominica	47	25		16			
Dominican Republic	45		40	112	64	0.00	-42.86
Grenada		29		16	16	0.00	
Guadeloupe	21		16	16	16	0.00	
Haiti		20					
Jamaica	89	176	149	80	128	0.00	60.00
Martinique	23				32	0.00	
Netherlands Antilles	18	24	66				
Puerto Rico	89	178	138	64	112	0.00	75.00
Saint Kitts and Nevis			16	16			
Saint Lucia			32	16	16	0.00	
Saint Vincent and the Grenadines			16	16			
Sint Maarten					48	0.00	
Trinidad and Tobago	112	128	163	112	176	0.01	57.14
Turks and Caicos Islands	98		16	64	64	0.00	
United States Virgin Islands		24	25	16			
CENTRAL AMERICA	397	588	404	528	528	0.02	
Belize		25			16	0.00	
Costa Rica	114	217	165	192	224	0.01	16.67
El Salvador	23	51	16		16	0.00	
Guatemala	95	79	52	128	96	0.00	-25.00
Honduras		67			16	0.00	
Nicaragua	28		16	32	32	0.00	
Panama	137	149	155	176	128	0.00	-27.27
NORTH AMERICA	249,531	241,574	236,947	227,344	253,184	9.34	11.37
Canada	48,656	48,942	49,154	46,448	48,192	1.78	3.75
Greenland	23		36	64	16	0.00	-75.00
Mexico	3,060	2,923	3,043	3,152	3,552	0.13	12.69
United States of America	197,792	189,709	184,714	177,680	201,424	7.43	13.36
SOUTH AMERICA	24,412	24,924	29,637	23,984	24,128	0.89	0.60
Argentina	6,237	5,654	9,695	6,048	4,640	0.17	-23.28
Bolivia	73	105	32	80	32	0.00	-60.00
Brazil	11,355	11,796	11,587	10,272	10,624	0.39	3.43
Chile	4,369	4,938	5,382	4,848	5,728	0.21	18.15
Colombia	776	765	1,026	848	1,184	0.04	39.62
Ecuador	162	99	181	128	176	0.01	37.50
Falkland Islands, Malvinas	21	20	68	16	64	0.00	300.00
French Guiana	28	22					
Paraguay	75	95	120	64	32	0.00	-50.00
Peru	325	419	366	432	416	0.02	-3.70
Suriname	23	55		16	16	0.00	
Uruguay	716	776	902	976	928	0.03	-4.92
Venezuela	252	180	278	256	288	0.01	12.50
EAST ASIA AND THE PACIFIC	1,561,724	1,649,581	1,695,043	1,741,744	1,857,184	68.52	6.63
NORTH-EAST ASIA	274,383	323,835	311,337	367,728	405,184	14.95	10.19
China	102,259	122,712	145,524	197,024	228,928	8.45	16.19
Hong Kong, China	23,572	24,287	25,397	26,272	28,080	1.04	6.88

528

NEW ZEALAND

2. Arrivals of non-resident visitors at national borders, by country of residence

	2009	2010	2011	2012	2013	Market share 2013	% Change 2013-2012
Japan	78,426	87,735	68,963	72,080	74,560	2.75	3.44
Korea, Dem. People's Republic of	23	29					
Korea, Republic of	52,921	67,309	52,787	52,896	50,992	1.88	-3.60
Macao, China	458	450	504	624	640	0.02	2.56
Mongolia	140	121	187	192	208	0.01	8.33
Taiwan, Province of China	16,584	21,192	17,975	18,640	21,776	0.80	16.82
SOUTH-EAST ASIA	**90,894**	**96,989**	**116,580**	**110,096**	**121,808**	**4.49**	**10.64**
Brunei Darussalam	1,340	1,369	1,192	1,072	1,008	0.04	-5.97
Cambodia	646	586	609	640	784	0.03	22.50
Indonesia	9,506	9,787	11,450	12,256	13,712	0.51	11.88
Lao People's Democratic Republic	248	226	222	240	272	0.01	13.33
Malaysia	19,702	21,843	35,011	29,424	28,976	1.07	-1.52
Myanmar	114	144	178	192	288	0.01	50.00
Philippines	7,572	8,240	8,563	9,568	10,432	0.38	9.03
Singapore	29,582	30,300	38,680	36,400	42,256	1.56	16.09
Thailand	19,728	21,434	17,523	16,944	20,704	0.76	22.19
Timor-Leste	89	292	238	144	240	0.01	66.67
Viet Nam	2,367	2,768	2,914	3,216	3,136	0.12	-2.49
AUSTRALASIA	**1,082,680**	**1,119,879**	**1,156,426**	**1,155,792**	**1,218,016**	**44.94**	**5.38**
Australia	1,082,680	1,119,879	1,156,426	1,155,792	1,218,016	44.94	5.38
MELANESIA	**46,642**	**45,885**	**47,946**	**48,624**	**51,072**	**1.88**	**5.03**
Fiji	23,608	20,853	21,619	22,432	24,112	0.89	7.49
New Caledonia	15,217	16,148	16,597	16,752	17,280	0.64	3.15
Norfolk Island	798	931	961	848	688	0.03	-18.87
Papua New Guinea	1,764	2,293	2,784	2,368	2,656	0.10	12.16
Solomon Islands	1,027	1,130	1,341	1,360	1,232	0.05	-9.41
Vanuatu	4,228	4,530	4,644	4,864	5,104	0.19	4.93
MICRONESIA	**1,040**	**874**	**1,024**	**880**	**1,168**	**0.04**	**32.73**
Guam	210	154	162	160	208	0.01	30.00
Kiribati	549	577	670	512	528	0.02	3.13
Marshall Islands	121	47	48	64	80	0.00	25.00
Micronesia, Federated States of	94		16	64	80	0.00	25.00
Nauru	66	47	48	32	128	0.00	300.00
Northern Mariana Islands			32		48	0.00	
Palau		49	48	48	96	0.00	100.00
POLYNESIA	**66,085**	**62,094**	**61,698**	**58,624**	**59,888**	**2.21**	**2.16**
American Samoa	1,174	1,228	1,109	1,008	1,008	0.04	
Cook Islands	11,042	10,577	11,309	9,856	9,632	0.36	-2.27
French Polynesia	19,632	19,090	16,785	15,552	15,376	0.57	-1.13
Niue	2,151	1,889	1,959	2,032	2,048	0.08	0.79
Pitcairn	44		16	16	16	0.00	
Samoa	17,678	16,250	16,787	16,192	16,544	0.61	2.17
Tokelau	232	291	227	224	256	0.01	14.29
Tonga	13,469	12,167	12,914	13,200	14,432	0.53	9.33
Tuvalu	381	316	390	320	384	0.01	20.00
Wallis and Futuna Islands	282	286	202	224	192	0.01	-14.29
OTHER EAST ASIA AND THE PACIFIC		**25**	**32**		**48**	**0.00**	
Other countries of Oceania		25	32		48	0.00	
EUROPE	**491,498**	**465,308**	**475,955**	**411,376**	**424,352**	**15.66**	**3.15**
CENTRAL/EASTERN EUROPE	**16,987**	**16,451**	**17,719**	**17,808**	**19,184**	**0.71**	**7.73**
Armenia	73	42		16	32	0.00	100.00
Azerbaijan	119	29	48	96	64	0.00	-33.33
Belarus	75	123	98	80	96	0.00	20.00
Bulgaria	450	303	394	528	448	0.02	-15.15
Czech Republic	3,811	3,605	3,877	3,712	3,744	0.14	0.86
Estonia	421	330	306	288	352	0.01	22.22
Georgia		26	155		16	0.00	
Hungary	1,157	1,191	1,145	1,072	1,216	0.04	13.43
Kazakhstan	203	144	157	208	176	0.01	-15.38

529

NEW ZEALAND

2. Arrivals of non-resident visitors at national borders, by country of residence

	2009	2010	2011	2012	2013	Market share 2013	% Change 2013-2012
Kyrgyzstan		53		16	32	0.00	100.00
Latvia	417	306	189	208	304	0.01	46.15
Lithuania	258	204	143	336	336	0.01	
Poland	2,433	2,546	2,759	2,752	3,200	0.12	16.28
Republic of Moldova	69	47	16	48	16	0.00	-66.67
Romania	862	863	921	800	880	0.03	10.00
Russian Federation	3,952	4,135	5,112	5,024	5,488	0.20	9.24
Slovakia	778	789	644	800	832	0.03	4.00
Tajikistan	27		16	48	16	0.00	-66.67
Turkmenistan	24						
Ukraine	1,817	1,715	1,677	1,712	1,904	0.07	11.21
Uzbekistan	41		62	64	32	0.00	-50.00
NORTHERN EUROPE	**304,697**	**277,185**	**275,942**	**228,800**	**231,392**	**8.54**	**1.13**
Denmark	10,172	9,854	9,194	8,256	8,864	0.33	7.36
Faeroe Islands	52	121	102	32	80	0.00	150.00
Finland	3,951	3,942	3,817	3,632	4,112	0.15	13.22
Iceland	301	225	414	656	496	0.02	-24.39
Ireland	17,055	13,290	16,302	11,120	10,208	0.38	-8.20
Norway	3,861	4,325	4,359	3,968	4,352	0.16	9.68
Sweden	10,867	11,114	11,438	11,488	11,648	0.43	1.39
United Kingdom	258,438	234,314	230,316	189,648	191,632	7.07	1.05
SOUTHERN EUROPE	**22,536**	**22,749**	**22,396**	**20,704**	**20,240**	**0.75**	**-2.24**
Albania			16	16			
Andorra	18	25	48	32	64	0.00	100.00
Bosnia and Herzegovina			16		16	0.00	
Croatia	211	311	247	240	320	0.01	33.33
Gibraltar	41		66	96	48	0.00	-50.00
Greece	941	723	787	656	592	0.02	-9.76
Italy	8,460	8,617	8,952	8,576	8,704	0.32	1.49
Malta	311	352	344	320	288	0.01	-10.00
Montenegro	24		36	32	32	0.00	
Portugal	1,077	1,072	1,036	848	928	0.03	9.43
San Marino	27		16				
Serbia	162	134	140	112	176	0.01	57.14
Slovenia	670	748	698	640	672	0.02	5.00
Spain	10,539	10,747	9,946	9,024	8,304	0.31	-7.98
TFYR of Macedonia	55	20	48	96	48	0.00	-50.00
Other countries of Southern Europe				16	48	0.00	200.00
WESTERN EUROPE	**139,345**	**140,657**	**153,003**	**138,352**	**147,456**	**5.44**	**6.58**
Austria	6,819	6,930	6,909	7,184	7,328	0.27	2.00
Belgium	4,962	5,051	5,198	4,736	5,040	0.19	6.42
France	23,227	24,579	36,607	24,944	26,976	1.00	8.15
Germany	64,564	64,648	63,719	63,776	69,808	2.58	9.46
Liechtenstein	27	54	121	80	80	0.00	
Luxembourg	353	476	504	368	528	0.02	43.48
Monaco	96	173	161	144	128	0.00	-11.11
Netherlands	24,300	23,378	23,608	21,424	21,248	0.78	-0.82
Switzerland	14,997	15,368	16,176	15,696	16,320	0.60	3.98
EAST MEDITERRANEAN EUROPE	**7,933**	**8,266**	**6,895**	**5,712**	**6,080**	**0.22**	**6.44**
Cyprus	371	277	284	352	448	0.02	27.27
Israel	6,768	6,993	5,592	4,528	4,832	0.18	6.71
Turkey	794	996	1,019	832	800	0.03	-3.85
MIDDLE EAST	**15,234**	**16,097**	**16,246**	**13,264**	**13,920**	**0.51**	**4.95**
Bahrain	756	668	712	496	480	0.02	-3.23
Egypt	344	382	446	336	288	0.01	-14.29
Iraq	220	213	339	176	160	0.01	-9.09
Jordan	152	111	93	96	192	0.01	100.00
Kuwait	504	444	576	464	464	0.02	
Lebanon	109	146	89	80	80	0.00	

Yearbook of Tourism Statistics, Data 2009 – 2013, 2015 Edition

NEW ZEALAND

2. Arrivals of non-resident visitors at national borders, by country of residence

	2009	2010	2011	2012	2013	Market share 2013	% Change 2013-2012
Libya	73	53	16		64	0.00	
Oman	718	778	623	656	608	0.02	-7.32
Palestine		29	16		48	0.00	
Qatar	867	1,130	1,138	1,136	1,360	0.05	19.72
Saudi Arabia	4,292	4,418	4,189	3,088	2,912	0.11	-5.70
Syrian Arab Republic	88	26	16	32	32	0.00	
United Arab Emirates	7,088	7,699	7,977	6,672	7,232	0.27	8.39
Yemen	23		16	32			
SOUTH ASIA	**28,461**	**32,948**	**31,927**	**33,104**	**34,640**	**1.28**	**4.64**
Afghanistan	166	252	277	272	256	0.01	-5.88
Bangladesh	380	493	377	384	416	0.02	8.33
Bhutan	23		46	32			
India	25,336	29,486	28,262	29,856	30,976	1.14	3.75
Iran, Islamic Republic of	341	420	505	352	336	0.01	-4.55
Maldives	198	125	140	112	96	0.00	-14.29
Nepal	220	289	227	240	256	0.01	6.67
Pakistan	674	627	606	528	656	0.02	24.24
Sri Lanka	1,123	1,256	1,487	1,328	1,648	0.06	24.10
NOT SPECIFIED	**52,611**	**58,042**	**76,325**	**83,440**	**82,800**	**3.05**	**-0.77**
Other countries of the World	30,077	37,064	46,587	50,896	55,584	2.05	9.21
Nationals Residing Abroad	22,534	20,978	29,738	32,544	27,216	1.00	-16.37

Yearbook of Tourism Statistics, Data 2009 – 2013, 2015 Edition

NICARAGUA

1. Arrivals of non-resident tourists at national borders, by nationality

	2009	2010	2011	2012	2013	Market share 2013	% Change 2013-2012
TOTAL	931,904	1,011,251	1,060,031	1,179,581	1,229,410	100.00	4.22
AFRICA	563	605	487	622	864	0.07	38.91
EAST AFRICA	89	88	87	91	122	0.01	34.07
Burundi			1				
Djibouti	9	1	1	3	3	0.00	
Ethiopia	10	22	6	9	14	0.00	55.56
Kenya	12	10	18	12	26	0.00	116.67
Madagascar	1	2	1	1	7	0.00	600.00
Malawi	2	1	5		3	0.00	
Mauritius	8	10		3	3	0.00	
Mozambique	5	6	8	6	9	0.00	50.00
Rwanda	2	1	6		3	0.00	
Seychelles	6	7					
Somalia	3	4	8	8	11	0.00	37.50
Uganda	11	8	13	13	17	0.00	30.77
United Republic of Tanzania	11	12	14	18	18	0.00	
Zambia	2		3	5	3	0.00	-40.00
Zimbabwe	7	4	3	13	5	0.00	-61.54
CENTRAL AFRICA	29	22	18	18	23	0.00	27.78
Angola	7	5	5	6	8	0.00	33.33
Cameroon	10	7	3	4	5	0.00	25.00
Central African Republic	4	7	5	2	4	0.00	100.00
Congo			3	4	3	0.00	-25.00
Equatorial Guinea	6				2	0.00	
Gabon	2	3	2	2	1	0.00	-50.00
NORTH AFRICA	38	45	42	54	68	0.01	25.93
Algeria	16	13	11	14	18	0.00	28.57
Morocco	19	23	25	31	45	0.00	45.16
Sudan	1	1					
Tunisia	2	8	6	9	5	0.00	-44.44
SOUTHERN AFRICA	255	282	237	276	358	0.03	29.71
Botswana	2	3	8	4	3	0.00	-25.00
Lesotho		6		1			
Namibia	5		1	4	15	0.00	275.00
South Africa	244	271	223	259	337	0.03	30.12
Swaziland	4	2	5	8	3	0.00	-62.50
WEST AFRICA	74	55	49	86	110	0.01	27.91
Burkina Faso			2	15	5	0.00	-66.67
Cabo Verde	9	8		1			
Côte d'Ivoire	23						
Gambia		2	1	3	2	0.00	-33.33
Ghana	9	14	22	17	41	0.00	141.18
Guinea	8	1	1	2	7	0.00	250.00
Guinea-Bissau		1		3	1	0.00	-66.67
Mali	2	3	1	1	1	0.00	
Mauritania		1					
Niger	1			3	8	0.00	166.67
Nigeria	11	18	18	32	33	0.00	3.13
Senegal	9	4	4	7	7	0.00	
Sierra Leone	1	3		2	2	0.00	
Togo	1				3	0.00	
OTHER AFRICA	78	113	54	97	183	0.01	88.66
Other countries of Africa	78	113	54	97	183	0.01	88.66
AMERICAS	769,799	846,897	893,498	999,987	1,031,698	83.92	3.17
CARIBBEAN	5,032	4,530	4,770	5,707	6,485	0.53	13.63
Antigua and Barbuda	3	4	2	16	9	0.00	-43.75
Aruba	2	1			2	0.00	
Bahamas	29	37	59	66	52	0.00	-21.21
Barbados	33	27	34	30	39	0.00	30.00

Yearbook of Tourism Statistics, Data 2009 – 2013, 2015 Edition

NICARAGUA

1. Arrivals of non-resident tourists at national borders, by nationality

	2009	2010	2011	2012	2013	Market share 2013	% Change 2013-2012
Bermuda	6	8	11	14	16	0.00	14.29
Bonaire	2	2	1				
Cayman Islands	154	121	88	109	107	0.01	-1.83
Cuba	2,487	2,383	2,238	2,251	2,572	0.21	14.26
Dominica	24	11	33	10	21	0.00	110.00
Dominican Republic	1,882	1,618	1,794	2,658	3,021	0.25	13.66
Grenada	20	3	16	15	15	0.00	
Guadeloupe	2	4	1		2	0.00	
Haiti	81	51	114	91	128	0.01	40.66
Jamaica	131	132	122	141	199	0.02	41.13
Martinique			1	1			
Montserrat	1						
Netherlands Antilles		4	1				
Puerto Rico	15	4	5	9	6	0.00	-33.33
Saint Lucia	8	9	12	15	8	0.00	-46.67
Saint Vincent and the Grenadines	57	23	41	119	59	0.00	-50.42
Trinidad and Tobago	87	78	180	142	208	0.02	46.48
United States Virgin Islands	8	10	17	20	21	0.00	5.00
CENTRAL AMERICA	**494,107**	**573,489**	**611,947**	**682,672**	**707,976**	**57.59**	**3.71**
Belize	593	578	537	625	607	0.05	-2.88
Costa Rica	111,861	125,811	136,466	160,108	163,758	13.32	2.28
El Salvador	121,069	135,455	138,120	152,741	150,963	12.28	-1.16
Guatemala	67,317	76,695	83,408	92,877	94,957	7.72	2.24
Honduras	176,120	214,776	230,965	251,804	273,015	22.21	8.42
Panama	17,147	20,174	22,451	24,517	24,676	2.01	0.65
NORTH AMERICA	**250,232**	**247,857**	**253,431**	**287,523**	**291,818**	**23.74**	**1.49**
Canada	24,161	23,597	25,676	30,710	33,832	2.75	10.17
Mexico	13,423	13,781	13,769	15,967	14,947	1.22	-6.39
United States of America	212,648	210,479	213,986	240,846	243,039	19.77	0.91
SOUTH AMERICA	**20,428**	**21,021**	**23,350**	**24,085**	**25,419**	**2.07**	**5.54**
Argentina	3,638	3,779	3,771	4,339	4,523	0.37	4.24
Bolivia	740	752	883	761	821	0.07	7.88
Brazil	2,667	3,226	3,659	3,665	3,898	0.32	6.36
Chile	1,685	1,585	1,920	1,823	1,872	0.15	2.69
Colombia	4,001	4,204	4,869	4,779	5,051	0.41	5.69
Ecuador	1,263	1,282	1,509	1,694	1,632	0.13	-3.66
Guyana	53	32	22	48	29	0.00	-39.58
Paraguay	142	152	209	210	196	0.02	-6.67
Peru	2,386	2,347	2,233	2,309	2,103	0.17	-8.92
Suriname	30	11	13	61	40	0.00	-34.43
Uruguay	615	596	730	660	737	0.06	11.67
Venezuela	3,208	3,055	3,532	3,736	4,517	0.37	20.90
EAST ASIA AND THE PACIFIC	**11,982**	**10,620**	**10,252**	**10,785**	**12,302**	**1.00**	**14.07**
NORTH-EAST ASIA	**5,357**	**5,093**	**5,255**	**5,533**	**5,805**	**0.47**	**4.92**
China	641	404	303	354	481	0.04	35.88
Hong Kong, China	17	31	18	15	42	0.00	180.00
Japan	1,542	1,669	1,747	1,984	1,756	0.14	-11.49
Korea, Republic of	1,992	2,095	2,316	2,209	2,257	0.18	2.17
Mongolia			1	1			
Taiwan, Province of China	1,165	894	870	970	1,269	0.10	30.82
SOUTH-EAST ASIA	**3,194**	**1,864**	**1,087**	**885**	**1,148**	**0.09**	**29.72**
Indonesia	782	86	124	61	63	0.01	3.28
Lao People's Democratic Republic		2			1	0.00	
Malaysia	50	50	50	49	59	0.00	20.41
Myanmar	140	81	47	20	37	0.00	85.00
Philippines	2,056	1,533	741	558	802	0.07	43.73
Singapore	43	41	52	55	72	0.01	30.91
Thailand	90	46	59	120	76	0.01	-36.67
Viet Nam	33	25	14	22	38	0.00	72.73

Yearbook of Tourism Statistics, Data 2009 – 2013, 2015 Edition

NICARAGUA

1. Arrivals of non-resident tourists at national borders, by nationality

	2009	2010	2011	2012	2013	Market share 2013	% Change 2013-2012
AUSTRALASIA	**3,412**	**3,645**	**3,901**	**4,353**	**5,337**	**0.43**	**22.61**
Australia	2,787	3,017	3,255	3,665	4,402	0.36	20.11
New Zealand	625	628	646	688	935	0.08	35.90
MELANESIA	**3**	**7**	**3**	**5**	**3**	**0.00**	**-40.00**
Fiji	1	4	2	4	1	0.00	-75.00
Papua New Guinea	2	3	1	1	2	0.00	100.00
MICRONESIA	**11**	**11**	**6**	**8**	**8**	**0.00**	
Micronesia, Federated States of	11	11	6	8	8	0.00	
POLYNESIA	**5**			**1**	**1**	**0.00**	
French Polynesia	5				1	0.00	
Tonga				1			
EUROPE	**71,540**	**73,644**	**75,948**	**79,435**	**82,916**	**6.74**	**4.38**
CENTRAL/EASTERN EUROPE	**2,788**	**3,112**	**2,934**	**3,319**	**4,607**	**0.37**	**38.81**
Armenia		3	3	4	5	0.00	25.00
Azerbaijan	2	2	2	3	2	0.00	-33.33
Belarus			2	44	39	0.00	-11.36
Bulgaria	97	106	88	95	93	0.01	-2.11
Czech Republic	453	587	470	566	690	0.06	21.91
Czech Republic/Slovakia	87	120	131	162	184	0.01	13.58
Estonia	51	57	64	29	62	0.01	113.79
Georgia	55	65	35	38	9	0.00	-76.32
Hungary	245	205	157	187	208	0.02	11.23
Kazakhstan	6	8	8	13	21	0.00	61.54
Kyrgyzstan		5	1		3	0.00	
Latvia	50	18	4	40	42	0.00	5.00
Lithuania	39	35	92	85	77	0.01	-9.41
Poland	489	550	595	595	835	0.07	40.34
Republic of Moldova	7	4	4	6	7	0.00	16.67
Romania	221	172	208	189	519	0.04	174.60
Russian Federation	770	1,003	893	1,044	1,499	0.12	43.58
Tajikistan	3		2		4	0.00	
Turkmenistan	4	4		1			
Ukraine	206	163	171	216	308	0.03	42.59
Uzbekistan	3	5	4	2			
NORTHERN EUROPE	**19,119**	**17,729**	**18,071**	**17,975**	**19,060**	**1.55**	**6.04**
Denmark	2,230	2,117	2,101	2,099	1,951	0.16	-7.05
Finland	784	766	617	718	758	0.06	5.57
Iceland	115	81	101	93	75	0.01	-19.35
Ireland	1,047	1,101	992	1,051	1,252	0.10	19.12
Norway	1,610	1,822	1,757	1,704	1,742	0.14	2.23
Sweden	2,572	2,318	2,396	2,658	2,678	0.22	0.75
United Kingdom	10,761	9,524	10,107	9,652	10,604	0.86	9.86
SOUTHERN EUROPE	**16,559**	**17,823**	**17,680**	**18,808**	**19,476**	**1.58**	**3.55**
Albania	8	5	3	8	8	0.00	
Andorra	9	13	13	8	6	0.00	-25.00
Bosnia and Herzegovina	2	2	7	9	5	0.00	-44.44
Croatia	64	65	50	86	60	0.00	-30.23
Greece	215	196	195	175	191	0.02	9.14
Holy See	2	1	3	2	2	0.00	
Italy	5,118	5,613	5,541	5,781	5,959	0.48	3.08
Malta	9	8	10	20	19	0.00	-5.00
Portugal	349	361	349	426	474	0.04	11.27
San Marino				2	1	0.00	-50.00
Serbia	1	22	26	33	43	0.00	30.30
Serbia and Montenegro	35						
Slovenia	125	164	164	198	191	0.02	-3.54
Spain	10,616	11,338	11,305	12,052	12,506	1.02	3.77
TFYR of Macedonia	6	7	9	8	5	0.00	-37.50
Yugoslavia, SFR (former)		28	5		6	0.00	

534

NICARAGUA

1. Arrivals of non-resident tourists at national borders, by nationality

	2009	2010	2011	2012	2013	Market share 2013	% Change 2013-2012
WESTERN EUROPE	**31,236**	**33,161**	**35,141**	**36,874**	**37,215**	**3.03**	**0.92**
Austria	1,388	1,399	1,576	1,653	1,916	0.16	15.91
Belgium	2,542	3,538	3,266	2,822	2,528	0.21	-10.42
France	6,496	7,065	7,131	7,648	7,824	0.64	2.30
Germany	10,834	11,048	12,118	13,255	13,936	1.13	5.14
Liechtenstein	5	14	6	5	12	0.00	140.00
Luxembourg	74	75	67	95	86	0.01	-9.47
Monaco	2			3	10	0.00	233.33
Netherlands	6,418	6,468	7,178	7,370	6,764	0.55	-8.22
Switzerland	3,477	3,554	3,799	4,023	4,139	0.34	2.88
EAST MEDITERRANEAN EUROPE	**1,838**	**1,819**	**2,122**	**2,459**	**2,558**	**0.21**	**4.03**
Cyprus	15	22	14	11	14	0.00	27.27
Israel	1,618	1,595	1,895	2,187	2,273	0.18	3.93
Turkey	205	202	213	261	271	0.02	3.83
MIDDLE EAST	**164**	**133**	**143**	**193**	**216**	**0.02**	**11.92**
Bahrain	1	4			3	0.00	
Egypt	11	14	27	26	22	0.00	-15.38
Iraq	1			3	2	0.00	-33.33
Jordan	15	24	27	35	41	0.00	17.14
Kuwait	4	2	6	4	12	0.00	200.00
Lebanon	22	18	10	14	16	0.00	14.29
Libya	61	49	35	38	45	0.00	18.42
Palestine	13	8	19	43	42	0.00	-2.33
Qatar		1	8				
Saudi Arabia	4	6	3	20	19	0.00	-5.00
Syrian Arab Republic	4	1	1	4	6	0.00	50.00
United Arab Emirates	28	4	7	6	6	0.00	
Yemen		2			2	0.00	
SOUTH ASIA	**733**	**2,089**	**1,573**	**818**	**3,714**	**0.30**	**354.03**
Afghanistan	2		3		88	0.01	
Bangladesh	35	17	14	13	14	0.00	7.69
India	513	1,935	1,410	562	3,446	0.28	513.17
Iran, Islamic Republic of	105	105	95	195	102	0.01	-47.69
Maldives			1	1			
Nepal	11	7	7	7	22	0.00	214.29
Pakistan	34	13	10	20	24	0.00	20.00
Sri Lanka	33	12	33	20	18	0.00	-10.00
NOT SPECIFIED	**77,123**	**77,263**	**78,130**	**87,741**	**97,700**	**7.95**	**11.35**
Other countries of the World	2	53	50	36	68	0.01	88.89
Nationals Residing Abroad	77,121	77,210	78,080	87,705	97,632	7.94	11.32

Yearbook of Tourism Statistics, Data 2009 – 2013, 2015 Edition

NIGER

1. Arrivals of non-resident tourists at national borders, by nationality

	2009	2010	2011	2012	2013	Market share 2013	% Change 2013-2012
TOTAL	**65,883**	**74,278**	**82,370**	**94,149**	**123,289**	**100.00**	**30.95**
AFRICA	**42,312**	**47,702**	**52,881**	**56,798**	**69,514**	**56.38**	**22.39**
OTHER AFRICA	**42,312**	**47,702**	**52,881**	**56,798**	**69,514**	**56.38**	**22.39**
All countries of Africa	42,312	47,702	52,881	56,798	69,514	56.38	22.39
AMERICAS	**4,078**	**4,598**	**5,107**	**7,156**	**11,092**	**9.00**	**55.00**
NORTH AMERICA	**3,947**	**4,450**	**4,942**	**6,888**	**10,816**	**8.77**	**57.03**
Canada	1,373	1,548	1,719	2,266	4,518	3.66	99.38
United States of America	2,574	2,902	3,223	4,622	6,298	5.11	36.26
OTHER AMERICAS	**131**	**148**	**165**	**268**	**276**	**0.22**	**2.99**
Other countries of the Americas	131	148	165	268	276	0.22	2.99
EAST ASIA AND THE PACIFIC	**3,158**	**3,560**	**3,954**	**6,231**	**9,840**	**7.98**	**57.92**
NORTH-EAST ASIA	**2,259**	**2,547**	**2,829**	**4,007**	**6,187**	**5.02**	**54.40**
Japan	2,259	2,547	2,829	4,007	6,187	5.02	54.40
OTHER EAST ASIA AND THE PACIFIC	**899**	**1,013**	**1,125**	**2,224**	**3,653**	**2.96**	**64.25**
Other countries of Asia	899	1,013	1,125	2,224	3,653	2.96	64.25
EUROPE	**16,335**	**18,418**	**20,428**	**23,964**	**32,843**	**26.64**	**37.05**
SOUTHERN EUROPE	**961**	**1,085**	**1,109**	**1,353**	**2,871**	**2.33**	**112.20**
Italy	961	1,085	1,109	1,353	2,871	2.33	112.20
WESTERN EUROPE	**15,255**	**17,331**	**19,237**	**21,759**	**28,492**	**23.11**	**30.94**
France	13,209	14,892	16,519	18,097	23,517	19.07	29.95
Germany	953	1,207	1,345	1,720	2,465	2.00	43.31
Benelux	1,093	1,232	1,373	1,942	2,510	2.04	29.25
OTHER EUROPE	**119**	**2**	**82**	**852**	**1,480**	**1.20**	**73.71**
Other countries of Europe	119	2	82	852	1,480	1.20	73.71

536

NIGERIA

2. Arrivals of non-resident visitors at national borders, by nationality

	2009	2010	2011	2012	2013	Market share 2013	% Change 2013-2012
TOTAL (*)	6,053,318	6,113,384	3,765,400	4,673,136	4,037,808	100.00	-13.60
AFRICA	4,175,489	4,185,492	872,285	1,091,802	1,280,787	31.72	17.31
EAST AFRICA	192,077	192,803	35,887	114,790	63,762	1.58	-44.45
Burundi				2,922			
Djibouti				1,152			
Eritrea				780			
Ethiopia	80,941	81,053	6,307	15,434	8,383	0.21	-45.68
Kenya	41,872	41,981	22,720	39,362	8,704	0.22	-77.89
Madagascar				4,140			
Malawi				1,776	2,049	0.05	15.37
Mozambique	21,669	21,757		1,674			
Rwanda	288	379	1,520	4,080	3,288	0.08	-19.41
Somalia	576	677		5,460			
Uganda	3,860	3,886	2,720	9,410	5,383	0.13	-42.79
United Republic of Tanzania	17,575	17,666	1,900	13,074	15,183	0.38	16.13
Zambia	2,439	2,483	720	6,622	2,340	0.06	-64.66
Zimbabwe	22,857	22,921		8,904	18,432	0.46	107.01
CENTRAL AFRICA	510,574	511,231	270,151	283,496	272,860	6.76	-3.75
Angola	13,385	13,496		24,324			
Cameroon	233,274	233,370	205,920	174,544	158,647	3.93	-9.11
Central African Republic	15,984	16,035	2,731	8,472			
Chad	185,527	185,633	48,400	12,790	34,231	0.85	167.64
Congo	16,803	16,852	3,560	34,158	42,295	1.05	23.82
Democratic Republic of the Congo	16,801	16,908	4,720	8,530			
Equatorial Guinea	1,123	1,195	2,900	796			
Gabon	27,065	27,114	1,920	18,730	37,687	0.93	101.21
Sao Tome and Principe	612	628		1,152			
NORTH AFRICA	397,936	398,485	17,030	37,316	11,148	0.28	-70.13
Algeria	79,547	79,658		8,178	3,078	0.08	-62.36
Morocco	125,272	125,421		6,468	8,070	0.20	24.77
South Sudan				5,082			
Sudan	137,128	137,288	15,480	11,230			
Tunisia	55,989	56,118	1,550	6,358			
SOUTHERN AFRICA	84,346	90,682	42,440	95,474	66,487	1.65	-30.36
Botswana	14,129	14,220		10,278			
Lesotho	13,706	13,812		2,964			
Namibia	36,479	36,556		7,140	6,912	0.17	-3.19
South Africa	20,032	26,094	42,440	74,384	59,575	1.48	-19.91
Swaziland				708			
WEST AFRICA	2,990,556	2,992,291	506,777	560,726	866,530	21.46	54.54
Benin	855,605	855,712	65,760	58,110	83,767	2.07	44.15
Burkina Faso	69,380	69,459	10,000	11,934	33,000	0.82	176.52
Cabo Verde	598	624	4,280	3,914			
Côte d'Ivoire	110,650	110,839	17,720	17,348	41,143	1.02	137.16
Gambia	39,475	39,587		15,558	33,158	0.82	113.13
Ghana	45,157	45,406	177,640	169,720	95,287	2.36	-43.86
Guinea	42,764	42,836	38,800	22,272	43,447	1.08	95.07
Guinea-Bissau				20,616			
Liberia	234,160	234,254	26,000	14,428	38,839	0.96	169.19
Mali	80,745	80,793	29,200	29,918	64,183	1.59	114.53
Mauritania	2,093	2,284	5,017	7,740			
Niger	1,273,378	1,273,550	64,400	93,370	297,607	7.37	218.74
Senegal	126,201	126,464	30,920	35,754	49,207	1.22	37.63
Sierra Leone	36,185	36,257	12,960	14,536	32,079	0.79	120.69
Togo	74,165	74,226	24,080	45,508	54,813	1.36	20.45
AMERICAS	256,055	257,581	176,880	478,144	240,661	5.96	-49.67
CARIBBEAN	31,469	31,841	37,760	28,182	4,231	0.10	-84.99
Antigua and Barbuda				588			
Bahamas				2,496			
Barbados	3,987	4,064		1,386			
Cuba	4,527	4,609	9,960	2,854			

537

NIGERIA

2. Arrivals of non-resident visitors at national borders, by nationality

	2009	2010	2011	2012	2013	Market share 2013	% Change 2013-2012
Dominican Republic	1,274	1,342	800	624			
Grenada				3,054			
Haiti	557	574					
Jamaica	10,063	10,139	16,720	6,482	4,231	0.10	-34.73
Trinidad and Tobago	11,061	11,113	10,280	10,698			
CENTRAL AMERICA	**1,231**	**1,292**		**2,748**			
Costa Rica	697	726					
Honduras				240			
Nicaragua	534	566					
Panama				2,508			
NORTH AMERICA	**153,248**	**153,707**	**109,800**	**393,886**	**236,430**	**5.86**	**-39.98**
Canada	22,573	22,678	13,320	51,084	36,535	0.90	-28.48
Mexico	51,339	51,454		5,892			
United States of America	79,336	79,575	96,480	336,910	199,895	4.95	-40.67
SOUTH AMERICA	**70,107**	**70,741**	**29,320**	**53,328**			
Argentina	13,895	14,105		10,110			
Bolivia	1,325	1,396		642			
Brazil	26,458	26,547	10,080	19,920			
Chile	12,731	12,777	19,240	11,358			
Colombia	10,565	10,603		6,078			
Guyana	669	718		630			
Paraguay	1,801	1,852		1,740			
Peru	1,668	1,697		1,032			
Uruguay				246			
Venezuela	995	1,046		1,572			
EAST ASIA AND THE PACIFIC	**351,092**	**352,351**	**339,879**	**415,138**	**180,934**	**4.48**	**-56.42**
NORTH-EAST ASIA	**191,873**	**192,579**	**270,940**	**290,608**	**154,545**	**3.83**	**-46.82**
China	75,904	76,143	241,280	227,694	113,779	2.82	-50.03
Hong Kong, China	36,532	36,710		5,028			
Japan	27,130	27,340	26,300	41,988	24,231	0.60	-42.29
Korea, Republic of	2,974	2,859	3,360	13,750	16,535	0.41	20.25
Taiwan, Province of China	49,333	49,527		2,124			
Other countries of North-East Asia				24			
SOUTH-EAST ASIA	**151,250**	**151,690**	**45,659**	**58,830**	**26,389**	**0.65**	**-55.14**
Brunei Darussalam				822			
Indonesia	37,177	37,199	6,440	7,924	2,383	0.06	-69.93
Malaysia	38,220	38,291	17,499	15,072	10,079	0.25	-33.13
Myanmar	181	230					
Philippines	31,460	31,569	11,120	18,568	13,927	0.34	-24.99
Singapore	25,500	25,611	10,600	12,718			
Thailand	18,712	18,790		3,726			
AUSTRALASIA	**7,969**	**8,082**	**23,280**	**65,460**			
Australia	5,332	5,404	10,880	32,996			
New Zealand	2,637	2,678	12,400	32,464			
MELANESIA				**240**			
Fiji				240			
EUROPE	**1,000,609**	**1,002,737**	**448,853**	**699,122**	**319,246**	**7.91**	**-54.34**
CENTRAL/EASTERN EUROPE	**194,019**	**194,379**	**56,973**	**81,552**	**23,506**	**0.58**	**-71.18**
Azerbaijan				1,584			
Belarus				168			
Bulgaria	30,713	30,752	7,920	12,952			
Czech Republic				8,014	14,737	0.36	83.89
Czech Republic/Slovakia	24,853	24,905	7,293				
Estonia				3,186			
Georgia				4,338			
Hungary	37,057	37,096		3,312	1,182	0.03	-64.31
Poland	27,822	27,893	18,120	15,164	6,535	0.16	-56.90
Romania	47,457	47,546	5,080	11,498			
Russian Federation	26,117	26,187	12,560	14,846			
Slovakia				1,008			
Ukraine			6,000	5,482	1,052	0.03	-80.81

538

NIGERIA

2. Arrivals of non-resident visitors at national borders, by nationality

	2009	2010	2011	2012	2013	Market share 2013	% Change 2013-2012
NORTHERN EUROPE	**234,341**	**234,791**	**233,301**	**234,072**	**147,223**	**3.65**	**-37.10**
Denmark	35,481	35,550	21,141	14,702			
Finland	39,697	39,775	14,240	15,238			
Iceland				7,710			
Ireland	22,332	22,371	2,240	5,970	1,152	0.03	-80.70
Norway	27,558	27,589	5,920	10,922			
Sweden	25,215	25,277	480	8,466	5,760	0.14	-31.96
United Kingdom	84,058	84,229	189,280	171,064	140,311	3.47	-17.98
SOUTHERN EUROPE	**212,533**	**213,016**	**48,558**	**109,006**	**25,322**	**0.63**	**-76.77**
Bosnia and Herzegovina				354			
Croatia			530	3,628			
Greece	4,420	4,468	5,559	12,848			
Italy	142,712	142,813	26,480	45,754	11,201	0.28	-75.52
Malta				1,590			
Montenegro				4,686			
Portugal	17,321	17,392	9,120	12,958			
Serbia				4,142			
Spain	45,332	45,514	6,869	23,022	14,121	0.35	-38.66
Yugoslavia, SFR (former)	2,748	2,829		24			
WESTERN EUROPE	**305,584**	**306,161**	**94,541**	**225,452**	**92,277**	**2.29**	**-59.07**
Austria	9,171	9,250	880	16,596			
Belgium	14,881	14,982	6,320	17,588			
France	134,609	134,718	19,200	58,934	32,295	0.80	-45.20
Germany	131,309	131,418	47,360	90,950	43,447	1.08	-52.23
Luxembourg	2,414	2,485					
Netherlands	11,673	11,781	16,880	34,164	16,535	0.41	-51.60
Switzerland	1,527	1,527	3,901	7,220			
EAST MEDITERRANEAN EUROPE	**54,132**	**54,390**	**15,480**	**49,040**	**30,918**	**0.77**	**-36.95**
Cyprus	6,183	6,254					
Israel	32,890	33,029	13,680	18,482	7,687	0.19	-58.41
Turkey	15,059	15,107	1,800	30,558	23,231	0.58	-23.98
MIDDLE EAST	**109,559**	**110,692**	**38,423**	**113,260**	**62,350**	**1.54**	**-44.95**
Bahrain				558			
Egypt	35,674	35,779	9,223	21,880	12,295	0.30	-43.81
Iraq	8,265	8,301		1,938			
Jordan	4,201	4,253		660	2,304	0.06	249.09
Kuwait	1,599	1,648		6,144			
Lebanon	41,601	41,683	24,840	60,544	37,687	0.93	-37.75
Libya	10,474	10,518	1,840	1,440			
Oman				980			
Palestine				4,746			
Saudi Arabia	4,163	4,224	1,120	5,148	2,000	0.05	-61.15
Syrian Arab Republic	1,983	2,661		3,426	3,456	0.09	0.88
United Arab Emirates			1,400	5,562	4,608	0.11	-17.15
Yemen	1,599	1,625		234			
SOUTH ASIA	**142,858**	**143,412**	**212,920**	**220,544**	**97,763**	**2.42**	**-55.67**
Afghanistan	871	883					
Bangladesh	957	1,006		14,262			
India	57,028	57,229	202,200	181,144	89,159	2.21	-50.78
Iran, Islamic Republic of	20,871	20,913		1,680			
Nepal	114	158					
Pakistan	60,617	60,699	10,720	20,944	8,604	0.21	-58.92
Sri Lanka	2,400	2,524		2,514			
NOT SPECIFIED	**17,656**	**61,119**	**1,676,160**	**1,655,126**	**1,856,067**	**45.97**	**12.14**
Other countries of the World	17,656	61,119		2,248			
Nationals Residing Abroad			1,676,160	1,652,878	1,856,067	45.97	12.29

Yearbook of Tourism Statistics, Data 2009 – 2013, 2015 Edition

NIUE

1. Arrivals of non-resident tourists at national borders, by country of residence

	2009	2010	2011	2012	2013	Market share 2013	% Change 2013-2012
TOTAL (*)	4,662	6,214	6,094	5,047	7,047	100.00	39.63
AMERICAS	203	298	1,176	139	183	2.60	31.65
NORTH AMERICA	189	290	1,165	139	183	2.60	31.65
Canada	32	60	239	40	67	0.95	67.50
United States of America	157	230	926	99	116	1.65	17.17
OTHER AMERICAS	14	8	11				
Other countries of the Americas	14	8	11				
EAST ASIA AND THE PACIFIC	3,550	4,156	4,432	4,550	6,386	90.62	40.35
NORTH-EAST ASIA	20	35	30	12	38	0.54	216.67
China	6	22	6	1	8	0.11	700.00
Japan	14	13	24	11	30	0.43	172.73
AUSTRALASIA	3,151	3,474	4,166	4,387	6,137	87.09	39.89
Australia	461	539	611	551	648	9.20	17.60
New Zealand	2,690	2,935	3,555	3,836	5,489	77.89	43.09
OTHER EAST ASIA AND THE PACIFIC	379	647	236	151	211	2.99	39.74
Other countries of Asia	146	445	20	17			
Other countries of Oceania	233	202	216	134	211	2.99	57.46
EUROPE	889	1,602	402	331	405	5.75	22.36
NORTHERN EUROPE	71	138	108	75	105	1.49	40.00
Denmark	24	35					
United Kingdom	47	103	108	75	105	1.49	40.00
SOUTHERN EUROPE	17	13					
Italy	17	13					
WESTERN EUROPE	682	1,255	99	94	118	1.67	25.53
Austria	38	60					
France	101	45	48	46	66	0.94	43.48
Germany	475	1,043	51	48	52	0.74	8.33
Netherlands	17	27					
Switzerland	51	80					
OTHER EUROPE	119	196	195	162	182	2.58	12.35
Other countries of Europe	119	196	195	162	182	2.58	12.35
NOT SPECIFIED	20	158	84	27	73	1.04	170.37
Other countries of the World	20	158	84	27	73	1.04	170.37

Yearbook of Tourism Statistics, Data 2009 – 2013, 2015 Edition

NORTHERN MARIANA ISLANDS

2. Arrivals of non-resident visitors at national borders, by nationality

	2009	2010	2011	2012	2013	Market share 2013	% Change 2013-2012
TOTAL	353,956	379,091	340,957				
AMERICAS	29,555	27,319	24,155				
NORTH AMERICA	29,555	27,319	24,155				
Canada	296	193	175				
United States of America	29,259	27,126	23,980				
EAST ASIA AND THE PACIFIC	316,064	345,874	310,394				
NORTH-EAST ASIA	310,475	343,043	306,862				
China	29,528	41,623	54,186				
Hong Kong, China	286	369	2,005				
Japan	191,111	185,032	142,946				
Korea, Republic of	89,132	115,811	107,503				
Taiwan, Province of China	418	208	222				
SOUTH-EAST ASIA	1,660	772	565				
Philippines	1,591	703	544				
Thailand	69	69	21				
AUSTRALASIA	2,584	977	2,037				
Australia	2,584	977	2,037				
MICRONESIA	1,345	1,082	930				
Micronesia, Federated States of	911	813	665				
Palau	434	269	265				
EUROPE	7,309	4,961	5,646				
CENTRAL/EASTERN EUROPE	6,222	4,391	5,276				
Russian Federation	6,222	4,391	5,276				
OTHER EUROPE	1,087	570	370				
Other countries of Europe	1,087	570	370				
NOT SPECIFIED	1,028	937	762				
Other countries of the World	1,028	937	762				

Yearbook of Tourism Statistics, Data 2009 – 2013, 2015 Edition

NORWAY

1. Arrivals of non-resident tourists at national borders, by nationality

	2009	2010	2011	2012	2013	Market share 2013	% Change 2013-2012
TOTAL (*)	**4,346,000**	**4,767,000**	**4,963,000**				
AMERICAS	**132,000**	**160,000**	**164,000**				
NORTH AMERICA	**132,000**	**160,000**	**164,000**				
United States of America	132,000	160,000	164,000				
EAST ASIA AND THE PACIFIC	**25,000**	**28,000**	**27,000**				
NORTH-EAST ASIA	**25,000**	**28,000**	**27,000**				
Japan	25,000	28,000	27,000				
EUROPE	**3,943,000**	**4,313,000**	**4,471,000**				
CENTRAL/EASTERN EUROPE	**257,000**	**288,000**	**303,000**				
Poland	188,000	206,000	195,000				
Russian Federation	69,000	82,000	108,000				
NORTHERN EUROPE	**2,319,000**	**2,438,000**	**2,490,000**				
Denmark	539,000	545,000	538,000				
Finland	239,000	250,000	294,000				
Sweden	1,239,000	1,336,000	1,339,000				
United Kingdom	302,000	307,000	319,000				
SOUTHERN EUROPE	**130,000**	**143,000**	**156,000**				
Italy	62,000	69,000	85,000				
Spain	68,000	74,000	71,000				
WESTERN EUROPE	**1,039,000**	**1,188,000**	**1,200,000**				
Austria	28,000	31,000	36,000				
Belgium	37,000	51,000	47,000				
France	128,000	133,000	134,000				
Germany	617,000	730,000	719,000				
Netherlands	188,000	194,000	203,000				
Switzerland	41,000	49,000	61,000				
OTHER EUROPE	**198,000**	**256,000**	**322,000**				
Other countries of Europe	198,000	256,000	322,000				
NOT SPECIFIED	**246,000**	**266,000**	**301,000**				
Other countries of the World	246,000	266,000	301,000				

Yearbook of Tourism Statistics, Data 2009 – 2013, 2015 Edition

NORWAY

5. Overnight stays of non-resident tourists in hotels and similar establishments, by nationality

	2009	2010	2011	2012	2013	Market share 2013	% Change 2013-2012
TOTAL (*)	4,426,610	4,798,028	4,898,885	5,050,573	5,067,588	100.00	0.34
AFRICA	28,469	28,419	40,329	38,472	37,375	0.74	-2.85
SOUTHERN AFRICA	5,031	5,353	6,345	6,649	10,492	0.21	57.80
South Africa	5,031	5,353	6,345	6,649	10,492	0.21	57.80
OTHER AFRICA	23,438	23,066	33,984	31,823	26,883	0.53	-15.52
Other countries of Africa	23,438	23,066	33,984	31,823	26,883	0.53	-15.52
AMERICAS	302,991	366,634	375,674	378,381	390,397	7.70	3.18
NORTH AMERICA	274,233	328,883	327,916	318,391	327,814	6.47	2.96
Canada	18,180	20,205	21,913	24,743	33,257	0.66	34.41
Mexico	5,367	6,532	7,249	6,765	11,816	0.23	74.66
United States of America	250,686	302,146	298,754	286,883	282,741	5.58	-1.44
SOUTH AMERICA	28,758	37,751	47,758	59,990	62,583	1.23	4.32
Brazil	15,079	21,025	28,757	36,966	36,181	0.71	-2.12
Other countries of South America	13,679	16,726	19,001	23,024	26,402	0.52	14.67
EAST ASIA AND THE PACIFIC	330,286	401,483	462,263	522,880	602,267	11.88	15.18
NORTH-EAST ASIA	159,991	199,541	225,682	260,871	292,086	5.76	11.97
China	41,562	63,617	86,179	86,007	141,923	2.80	65.01
Japan	95,316	100,836	97,875	116,397	99,786	1.97	-14.27
Korea, Republic of	23,113	35,088	41,628	58,467	50,377	0.99	-13.84
AUSTRALASIA	28,252	36,583	41,247	45,460	53,458	1.05	17.59
Australia	28,252	36,583	41,247	45,460	53,458	1.05	17.59
OTHER EAST ASIA AND THE PACIFIC	142,043	165,359	195,334	216,549	256,723	5.07	18.55
Other countries of Asia	132,018	154,496	182,245	198,878	234,271	4.62	17.80
Other countries of Oceania	10,025	10,863	13,089	17,671	22,452	0.44	27.06
EUROPE	3,764,864	4,001,492	4,020,619	4,110,840	4,037,549	79.67	-1.78
CENTRAL/EASTERN EUROPE	301,251	359,614	368,179	384,790	397,796	7.85	3.38
Czech Republic	20,231	22,819	30,770	21,299	22,319	0.44	4.79
Estonia	11,150	8,710	8,073	12,021	12,097	0.24	0.63
Hungary	9,051	10,338	9,645	13,801	11,837	0.23	-14.23
Latvia	9,421	12,242	13,958	13,446	15,079	0.30	12.14
Lithuania	11,439	18,004	17,536	23,758	22,678	0.45	-4.55
Poland	111,350	132,445	122,886	125,272	125,792	2.48	0.42
Russian Federation	111,524	135,869	143,854	152,246	161,822	3.19	6.29
Slovakia	5,796	8,244	7,806	8,445	9,104	0.18	7.80
Ukraine	11,289	10,943	13,651	14,502	17,068	0.34	17.69
NORTHERN EUROPE	1,620,761	1,670,595	1,673,142	1,858,270	1,819,511	35.90	-2.09
Denmark	512,279	519,076	491,279	516,216	452,441	8.93	-12.35
Finland	66,825	75,487	76,315	78,871	110,277	2.18	39.82
Iceland	11,722	15,746	16,981	22,048	26,183	0.52	18.75
Ireland	16,587	19,045	23,816	24,101	21,064	0.42	-12.60
Sweden	568,062	601,797	610,446	707,737	701,432	13.84	-0.89
United Kingdom	445,286	439,444	454,305	509,297	508,114	10.03	-0.23
SOUTHERN EUROPE	375,647	403,304	393,948	314,386	296,178	5.84	-5.79
Greece	15,564	14,048	11,979	9,987	12,017	0.24	20.33
Italy	157,245	168,845	152,965	124,238	125,558	2.48	1.06
Malta	836	1,193	1,415	1,714	1,500	0.03	-12.49
Portugal	17,567	17,124	16,730	15,040	11,899	0.23	-20.88
Slovenia	2,904	4,758	4,298	4,526	4,234	0.08	-6.45
Spain	181,531	197,336	206,561	158,881	140,970	2.78	-11.27
WESTERN EUROPE	1,301,354	1,378,192	1,357,629	1,296,919	1,171,331	23.11	-9.68
Austria	30,850	37,485	37,609	42,118	39,688	0.78	-5.77
Belgium	38,672	49,761	47,412	54,754	50,929	1.00	-6.99
France	209,560	219,043	211,972	206,800	203,635	4.02	-1.53
Germany	664,459	708,652	699,776	651,739	565,648	11.16	-13.21
Liechtenstein	1,122	1,595	1,445	2,216	2,094	0.04	-5.51
Luxembourg	3,140	2,665	3,156	5,466	3,182	0.06	-41.79
Netherlands	291,484	285,860	278,474	254,000	219,143	4.32	-13.72
Switzerland	62,067	73,131	77,785	79,826	87,012	1.72	9.00

543

NORWAY

5. Overnight stays of non-resident tourists in hotels and similar establishments, by nationality

	2009	2010	2011	2012	2013	Market share 2013	% Change 2013-2012
EAST MEDITERRANEAN EUROPE	**9,171**	**12,135**	**10,801**	**12,109**	**13,365**	**0.26**	**10.37**
Cyprus	1,372	1,729	1,334	1,743	2,043	0.04	17.21
Turkey	7,799	10,406	9,467	10,366	11,322	0.22	9.22
OTHER EUROPE	**156,680**	**177,652**	**216,920**	**244,366**	**339,368**	**6.70**	**38.88**
Other countries of Europe	156,680	177,652	216,920	244,366	339,368	6.70	38.88

Yearbook of Tourism Statistics, Data 2009 – 2013, 2015 Edition

NORWAY

6. Overnight stays of non-resident tourists in all types of accommodation establishments, by nationality

	2009	2010	2011	2012	2013	Market share 2013	% Change 2013-2012
TOTAL	7,525,174	7,903,186	7,844,241	7,940,468	7,687,797	100.00	-3.18
AFRICA	42,319	34,507	44,678	41,114	42,127	0.55	2.46
SOUTHERN AFRICA	6,012	5,831	6,979	7,283	13,635	0.18	87.22
South Africa	6,012	5,831	6,979	7,283	13,635	0.18	87.22
OTHER AFRICA	36,307	28,676	37,699	33,831	28,492	0.37	-15.78
Other countries of Africa	36,307	28,676	37,699	33,831	28,492	0.37	-15.78
AMERICAS	324,554	388,266	400,579	403,177	421,146	5.48	4.46
NORTH AMERICA	292,442	346,739	349,229	339,205	353,655	4.60	4.26
Canada	21,873	24,328	25,876	28,857	38,072	0.50	31.93
Mexico	6,230	6,975	7,977	7,069	12,413	0.16	75.60
United States of America	264,339	315,436	315,376	303,279	303,170	3.94	-0.04
SOUTH AMERICA	32,112	41,527	51,350	63,972	67,491	0.88	5.50
Brazil	16,827	22,882	30,862	39,491	38,999	0.51	-1.25
Other countries of South America	15,285	18,645	20,488	24,481	28,492	0.37	16.38
EAST ASIA AND THE PACIFIC	365,700	431,898	495,132	560,092	665,841	8.66	18.88
NORTH-EAST ASIA	175,722	210,155	238,111	275,257	322,792	4.20	17.27
China	51,795	68,133	91,715	93,532	161,876	2.11	73.07
Japan	98,607	104,014	101,124	119,558	103,874	1.35	-13.12
Korea, Republic of	25,320	38,008	45,272	62,167	57,042	0.74	-8.24
AUSTRALASIA	34,724	43,917	48,411	53,863	61,294	0.80	13.80
Australia	34,724	43,917	48,411	53,863	61,294	0.80	13.80
OTHER EAST ASIA AND THE PACIFIC	155,254	177,826	208,610	230,972	281,755	3.66	21.99
Other countries of Asia	143,214	165,176	194,103	211,918	257,639	3.35	21.57
Other countries of Oceania	12,040	12,650	14,507	19,054	24,116	0.31	26.57
EUROPE	6,792,601	7,048,515	6,903,852	6,936,085	6,558,683	85.31	-5.44
CENTRAL/EASTERN EUROPE	571,836	668,528	701,684	755,442	736,536	9.58	-2.50
Czech Republic	79,855	91,349	95,136	81,629	72,749	0.95	-10.88
Estonia	30,536	25,314	26,867	26,990	32,751	0.43	21.34
Hungary	13,048	14,941	15,276	19,607	16,791	0.22	-14.36
Latvia	28,430	34,933	37,113	36,966	33,929	0.44	-8.22
Lithuania	45,764	59,391	71,296	96,856	83,575	1.09	-13.71
Poland	203,962	235,939	233,399	255,374	242,112	3.15	-5.19
Russian Federation	141,166	172,811	186,401	198,201	211,743	2.75	6.83
Slovakia	15,685	20,566	19,456	22,038	21,999	0.29	-0.18
Ukraine	13,390	13,284	16,740	17,781	20,887	0.27	17.47
NORTHERN EUROPE	2,563,567	2,587,196	2,493,677	2,656,497	2,638,448	34.32	-0.68
Denmark	949,997	914,053	841,484	865,597	835,116	10.86	-3.52
Finland	146,013	148,685	147,471	139,806	163,033	2.12	16.61
Iceland	16,519	20,834	25,025	29,487	34,262	0.45	16.19
Ireland	20,807	24,358	27,303	28,694	25,315	0.33	-11.78
Sweden	905,649	958,838	932,923	1,022,597	999,308	13.00	-2.28
United Kingdom	524,582	520,428	519,471	570,316	581,414	7.56	1.95
SOUTHERN EUROPE	481,830	515,286	497,120	400,182	382,982	4.98	-4.30
Greece	17,006	15,604	13,367	11,236	13,260	0.17	18.01
Italy	211,861	222,540	200,287	166,257	164,224	2.14	-1.22
Malta	1,075	1,289	1,506	1,889	1,793	0.02	-5.08
Portugal	21,252	21,368	20,994	18,936	18,516	0.24	-2.22
Slovenia	8,446	8,847	7,359	7,795	10,333	0.13	32.56
Spain	222,190	245,638	253,607	194,069	174,856	2.27	-9.90
WESTERN EUROPE	2,980,764	3,061,582	2,954,387	2,820,996	2,412,233	31.38	-14.49
Austria	66,930	76,045	75,953	76,320	67,579	0.88	-11.45
Belgium	72,873	88,866	84,820	95,455	81,669	1.06	-14.44
France	298,526	318,280	309,784	301,197	285,482	3.71	-5.22
Germany	1,590,305	1,637,206	1,594,621	1,511,995	1,309,466	17.03	-13.39
Liechtenstein	1,614	2,084	1,942	2,811	2,609	0.03	-7.19
Luxembourg	7,602	6,427	4,573	7,775	5,907	0.08	-24.03
Netherlands	825,603	799,515	742,328	677,831	519,983	6.76	-23.29
Switzerland	117,311	133,159	140,366	147,612	139,538	1.82	-5.47

Yearbook of Tourism Statistics, Data 2009 – 2013, 2015 Edition

NORWAY

6. Overnight stays of non-resident tourists in all types of accommodation establishments, by nationality

	2009	2010	2011	2012	2013	Market share 2013	% Change 2013-2012
EAST MEDITERRANEAN EUROPE	**10,262**	**13,559**	**11,755**	**13,476**	**14,818**	**0.19**	**9.96**
Cyprus	1,473	1,789	1,378	2,085	2,232	0.03	7.05
Turkey	8,789	11,770	10,377	11,391	12,586	0.16	10.49
OTHER EUROPE	**184,342**	**202,364**	**245,229**	**289,492**	**373,666**	**4.86**	**29.08**
Other countries of Europe	184,342	202,364	245,229	289,492	373,666	4.86	29.08

Yearbook of Tourism Statistics, Data 2009 – 2013, 2015 Edition

OMAN

2. Arrivals of non-resident visitors at national borders, by nationality

	2009	2010	2011	2012	2013	Market share 2013	% Change 2013-2012
TOTAL	1,584,000	1,500,000	1,393,000	1,967,000	2,122,000	100.00	7.88
EUROPE	270,000	270,000	250,000	321,000	371,000	17.48	15.58
OTHER EUROPE	270,000	270,000	250,000	321,000	371,000	17.48	15.58
All countries of Europe	270,000	270,000	250,000	321,000	371,000	17.48	15.58
MIDDLE EAST	967,000	841,000	802,000	884,000	1,015,000	47.83	14.82
All countries of Middle East	967,000	841,000	802,000	884,000	1,015,000	47.83	14.82
SOUTH ASIA	249,000	291,000	258,000	359,000	435,000	20.50	21.17
All countries of South Asia	249,000	291,000	258,000	359,000	435,000	20.50	21.17
NOT SPECIFIED	98,000	98,000	83,000	403,000	301,000	14.18	-25.31
Other countries of the World	98,000	98,000	83,000	403,000	301,000	14.18	-25.31

Yearbook of Tourism Statistics, Data 2009 – 2013, 2015 Edition

PAKISTAN

1. Arrivals of non-resident tourists at national borders, by nationality

	2009	2010	2011	2012	2013	Market share 2013	% Change 2013-2012
TOTAL	854,905	906,818	1,161,254	966,277			
AFRICA	14,659	15,290	24,691	19,853			
EAST AFRICA	5,428	5,127	8,471	6,648			
Burundi	3	2	16	15			
Comoros	8	11	180	155			
Djibouti	85	40	220	146			
Eritrea	15	10	26	9			
Ethiopia	544	309	304	266			
Kenya	1,489	1,447	2,429	1,605			
Madagascar	69	88	174	94			
Malawi	234	263	572	477			
Mauritius	554	513	1,039	871			
Mozambique	567	650	1,141	1,044			
Reunion			6	5			
Rwanda	308	18	32	18			
Seychelles	9	4	18	19			
Somalia	347	335	523	489			
Uganda	67	63	179	133			
United Republic of Tanzania	772	913	991	813			
Zambia	216	288	323	207			
Zimbabwe	141	173	298	282			
CENTRAL AFRICA	109	95	216	253			
Angola	26	24	46	29			
Cameroon	38	41	73	36			
Chad	31	2	74	155			
Congo	14	26	14	23			
Gabon		2	9	10			
NORTH AFRICA	2,109	1,929	3,256	2,593			
Algeria	203	142	360	10			
Morocco	495	329	518	692			
Sudan	1,242	1,250	2,015	1,518			
Tunisia	169	208	363	373			
SOUTHERN AFRICA	6,136	7,282	11,007	8,535			
Botswana	36	46	58	49			
Lesotho	80	84	91	81			
Namibia	123	9	28	35			
South Africa	5,846	7,093	10,748	8,291			
Swaziland	51	50	82	79			
WEST AFRICA	877	857	1,741	1,824			
Benin	5	5	5	3			
Burkina Faso	4	3	3	4			
Gambia	11	5	25	17			
Ghana	118	108	144	117			
Guinea	14	14	17	25			
Guinea-Bissau	1	1	4	2			
Liberia	50	12	22	21			
Mali	14	19	88	26			
Mauritania	19	43	20	42			
Niger	41	14	36	38			
Nigeria	499	560	1,197	1,430			
Senegal	63	36	120	58			
Sierra Leone	25	33	43	32			
Togo	13	4	17	9			
AMERICAS	162,451	168,421	250,740	201,865			
CARIBBEAN	287	233	286	242			
Anguilla	2	7	6	5			
Antigua and Barbuda	9	8	17	13			
Cuba	16	22	60	21			
Dominica	23	47	14	6			

548

Yearbook of Tourism Statistics, Data 2009 – 2013, 2015 Edition

PAKISTAN

1. Arrivals of non-resident tourists at national borders, by nationality

	2009	2010	2011	2012	2013	Market share 2013	% Change 2013-2012
Grenada	27	32	37	26			
Haiti	2	2	6	1			
Jamaica	4	8	25	24			
Netherlands Antilles	56	11	8	10			
Puerto Rico	54	2	2				
Trinidad and Tobago	94	94	111	136			
CENTRAL AMERICA	**348**	**341**	**379**	**238**			
Belize	27	25	13	39			
Costa Rica	11	28	16	18			
El Salvador	15	8	6	8			
Guatemala	20	18	9	12			
Honduras	61	38	154	27			
Nicaragua	23	11	9	15			
Panama	191	213	172	119			
NORTH AMERICA	**160,614**	**166,765**	**248,287**	**199,937**			
Canada	42,954	46,228	79,941	65,168			
Mexico	195	168	188	173			
United States of America	117,465	120,369	168,158	134,596			
SOUTH AMERICA	**1,202**	**1,082**	**1,788**	**1,448**			
Argentina	177	236	344	250			
Bolivia	42	30	44	45			
Brazil	271	322	500	467			
Chile	206	139	292	155			
Colombia	117	134	220	142			
Ecuador	125	29	86	116			
Guyana	13	14	21	14			
Paraguay	9	5	22	12			
Peru	163	78	128	145			
Suriname	3	2	9	10			
Uruguay	25	22	13	9			
Venezuela	51	71	109	83			
EAST ASIA AND THE PACIFIC	**88,984**	**89,748**	**140,015**	**115,293**			
NORTH-EAST ASIA	**42,813**	**41,745**	**63,472**	**55,712**			
China	29,996	27,887	42,708	39,017			
Hong Kong, China	7	9	16	14			
Japan	6,705	7,077	9,918	8,242			
Korea, Dem. People's Republic of	218	389	248	108			
Korea, Republic of	4,926	5,390	9,359	7,450			
Macao, China	1	2	96	143			
Mongolia	33	50	35	58			
Taiwan, Province of China	927	941	1,092	680			
SOUTH-EAST ASIA	**31,443**	**32,645**	**54,312**	**40,554**			
Brunei Darussalam	67	60	104	79			
Cambodia	81	79	181	110			
Indonesia	3,099	3,314	5,775	4,117			
Lao People's Democratic Republic	22	28	23	49			
Malaysia	5,027	5,420	7,915	5,766			
Myanmar	2,213	2,546	4,532	3,449			
Philippines	15,603	15,871	27,207	19,940			
Singapore	2,585	2,461	3,549	3,191			
Thailand	2,170	2,269	4,177	3,414			
Timor-Leste	1		2				
Viet Nam	575	597	847	439			
AUSTRALASIA	**14,597**	**15,283**	**22,084**	**18,878**			
Australia	13,223	13,931	20,026	17,257			
New Zealand	1,374	1,352	2,058	1,621			
MELANESIA	**131**	**75**	**147**	**149**			
Fiji	128	68	139	144			
Papua New Guinea	3	7	8	5			

Yearbook of Tourism Statistics, Data 2009 – 2013, 2015 Edition

PAKISTAN

1. Arrivals of non-resident tourists at national borders, by nationality

	2009	2010	2011	2012	2013	Market share 2013	% Change 2013-2012
EUROPE	378,643	395,644	485,182	429,920			
CENTRAL/EASTERN EUROPE	12,145	11,850	18,032	13,736			
Armenia	12	16	17	10			
Azerbaijan	354	272	448	322			
Belarus	140	134	133	111			
Bulgaria	660	653	897	581			
Czech Republic	1,639	603	640	545			
Czech Republic/Slovakia		222	278	202			
Estonia	70	80	118	71			
Georgia	152	160	246	177			
Hungary	323	327	429	382			
Kazakhstan	396	435	713	560			
Kyrgyzstan	129	215	3	340			
Latvia	182	188	389	363			
Lithuania	174	141	306	251			
Poland	974	980	1,953	1,518			
Republic of Moldova	11	24	41	41			
Romania	624	736	1,692	1,474			
Russian Federation	2,488	2,623	3,991	3,014			
Slovakia	198						
Tajikistan	133	165	318	250			
Turkmenistan	85	166	183	136			
Ukraine	3,048	3,347	4,600	2,960			
Uzbekistan	353	363	637	428			
NORTHERN EUROPE	301,404	316,433	373,972	339,050			
Denmark	5,747	6,980	9,063	7,610			
Finland	525	671	829	719			
Iceland	1,075	27	44	49			
Ireland	2,882	2,938	4,560	4,153			
Norway	12,441	13,744	18,521	16,501			
Sweden	3,383	3,835	4,951	3,958			
United Kingdom	275,351	288,238	336,004	306,060			
SOUTHERN EUROPE	9,287	9,442	14,574	12,479			
Albania	32	26	51	84			
Andorra	2	2	2	4			
Bosnia and Herzegovina	87	79	3	1			
Croatia	311	287	673	428			
Greece	808	701	1,389	966			
Italy	4,385	4,543	6,556	5,524			
Malta	38	55	40	53			
Montenegro				6			
Portugal	687	765	1,469	1,370			
Serbia				143			
Serbia and Montenegro	89		32	3			
Slovenia	90	96	148	106			
Spain	2,736	2,862	4,185	3,771			
TFYR of Macedonia	22	26	26	20			
WESTERN EUROPE	50,840	52,402	69,652	57,058			
Austria	2,301	2,240	3,088	2,235			
Belgium	4,109	4,376	6,266	5,145			
France	10,685	10,887	14,820	12,665			
Germany	21,493	22,555	30,105	24,381			
Liechtenstein	9	14	12	19			
Luxembourg	83	57	51	62			
Monaco	13	9	6	1			
Netherlands	9,976	10,083	12,288	10,040			
Switzerland	2,171	2,181	3,016	2,510			
EAST MEDITERRANEAN EUROPE	4,967	5,517	8,952	7,597			
Cyprus	120	84	130	94			

Yearbook of Tourism Statistics, Data 2009 – 2013, 2015 Edition

PAKISTAN

1. Arrivals of non-resident tourists at national borders, by nationality

	2009	2010	2011	2012	2013	Market share 2013	% Change 2013-2012
Turkey	4,847	5,433	8,822	7,503			
MIDDLE EAST	**27,951**	**28,188**	**40,058**	**34,805**			
Bahrain	3,774	3,403	4,901	5,491			
Egypt	2,305	2,306	3,959	3,997			
Iraq	487	588	723	563			
Jordan	1,493	1,436	2,347	1,756			
Kuwait	477	564	763	743			
Lebanon	736	590	905	735			
Libya	279	277	184	337			
Oman	7,311	6,944	12,107	9,798			
Palestine	259	332	449	213			
Qatar	436	429	661	644			
Saudi Arabia	4,482	5,433	5,955	5,058			
Syrian Arab Republic	1,160	1,191	2,083	1,095			
United Arab Emirates	3,997	3,889	4,167	3,522			
Yemen	755	806	854	853			
SOUTH ASIA	**178,242**	**204,136**	**212,351**	**158,164**			
Afghanistan	96,617	110,922	79,291	33,734			
Bangladesh	6,941	6,333	8,750	5,484			
Bhutan	38	44	78	85			
India	42,694	43,751	84,074	77,232			
Iran, Islamic Republic of	26,557	37,722	30,793	34,084			
Maldives	187	141	301	212			
Nepal	1,569	1,345	2,012	2,283			
Sri Lanka	3,639	3,878	7,052	5,050			
NOT SPECIFIED	**3,975**	**5,391**	**8,217**	**6,377**			
Other countries of the World	3,975	5,391	8,217	6,377			

Yearbook of Tourism Statistics, Data 2009 – 2013, 2015 Edition

PALAU

1. Arrivals of non-resident tourists at national borders, by country of residence

	2009	2010	2011	2012	2013	Market share 2013	% Change 2013-2012
TOTAL (*)	71,887	85,593	109,057	118,754	105,066	100.00	-11.53
AMERICAS	5,193	5,809	5,890	6,529	6,618	6.30	1.36
NORTH AMERICA	5,193	5,809	5,890	6,529	6,618	6.30	1.36
United States of America	5,193	5,809	5,890	6,529	6,618	6.30	1.36
EAST ASIA AND THE PACIFIC	62,970	75,701	98,658	107,128	91,801	87.37	-14.31
NORTH-EAST ASIA	56,843	67,841	93,513	102,695	87,716	83.49	-14.59
China	534	725	1,699	4,471	8,804	8.38	96.91
Hong Kong, China	334	493	701	756	856	0.81	13.23
Japan	26,688	29,318	37,800	39,353	35,642	33.92	-9.43
Korea, Republic of	13,009	15,144	15,681	19,465	16,871	16.06	-13.33
Taiwan, Province of China	16,278	22,161	37,632	38,650	25,543	24.31	-33.91
SOUTH-EAST ASIA	998	1,139	1,123	932	804	0.77	-13.73
Philippines	998	913	913	746	804	0.77	7.77
Singapore		226	210	186			
AUSTRALASIA	700	1,241	1,134	1,366	1,277	1.22	-6.52
Australia, New Zealand	700	1,241	1,134	1,366	1,277	1.22	-6.52
MICRONESIA	4,429	5,480	2,888	2,135	2,004	1.91	-6.14
Guam	3,374	3,336	1,932	1,230	1,219	1.16	-0.89
Micronesia, Federated States of	1,055	1,487	637	710	785	0.75	10.56
Northern Mariana Islands		657	319	195			
EUROPE	2,923	3,402	3,535	4,353	5,018	4.78	15.28
CENTRAL/EASTERN EUROPE	295	562	577	664	811	0.77	22.14
Russian Federation	295	562	577	664	811	0.77	22.14
NORTHERN EUROPE	373	311	260	284	330	0.31	16.20
United Kingdom	373	311	260	284	330	0.31	16.20
SOUTHERN EUROPE	327	384	273	397	255	0.24	-35.77
Italy	327	384	273	397	255	0.24	-35.77
WESTERN EUROPE	854	1,123	1,317	1,498	1,933	1.84	29.04
France		245	279	269	254	0.24	-5.58
Germany	629	662	749	946	1,290	1.23	36.36
Switzerland	225	216	289	283	389	0.37	37.46
OTHER EUROPE	1,074	1,022	1,108	1,510	1,689	1.61	11.85
Other countries of Europe	1,074	1,022	1,108	1,510	1,689	1.61	11.85
NOT SPECIFIED	801	681	974	744	1,629	1.55	118.95
Other countries of the World	801	681	974	744	1,629	1.55	118.95

Yearbook of Tourism Statistics, Data 2009 – 2013, 2015 Edition

PALESTINE

3. Arrivals of non-resident tourists in hotels and similar establishments, by nationality

	2009	2010	2011	2012	2013	Market share 2013	% Change 2013-2012
TOTAL (*)	395,622	521,927	448,500	490,110	545,464	100.00	11.29
AFRICA	11,736	14,126	27,837	24,331	32,853	6.02	35.03
OTHER AFRICA	11,736	14,126	27,837	24,331	32,853	6.02	35.03
All countries of Africa	11,736	14,126	27,837	24,331	32,853	6.02	35.03
AMERICAS	62,958	87,721	56,701	53,766	68,036	12.47	26.54
NORTH AMERICA	49,890	72,354	42,813	40,626	53,838	9.87	32.52
Canada, United States	49,890	72,354	42,813	40,626	53,838	9.87	32.52
OTHER AMERICAS	13,068	15,367	13,888	13,140	14,198	2.60	8.05
Other countries of the Americas	13,068	15,367	13,888	13,140	14,198	2.60	8.05
EAST ASIA AND THE PACIFIC	41,157	67,218	58,394	51,911	64,141	11.76	23.56
AUSTRALASIA	1,580	4,553	4,944	3,761	3,494	0.64	-7.10
Australia, New Zealand	1,580	4,553	4,944	3,761	3,494	0.64	-7.10
OTHER EAST ASIA AND THE PACIFIC	39,577	62,665	53,450	48,150	60,647	11.12	25.95
All countries of Asia	39,577	62,665	53,450	48,150	60,647	11.12	25.95
EUROPE	275,694	350,543	300,768	353,349	372,841	68.35	5.52
EAST MEDITERRANEAN EUROPE	44,195	44,003	44,065	66,518	76,441	14.01	14.92
Israel	44,195	44,003	44,065	66,518	76,441	14.01	14.92
OTHER EUROPE	231,499	306,540	256,703	286,831	296,400	54.34	3.34
Other countries of Europe	231,499	306,540	256,703	286,831	296,400	54.34	3.34
MIDDLE EAST	4,077	2,319	4,800	6,753	7,593	1.39	12.44
All countries of Middle East	4,077	2,319	4,800	6,753	7,593	1.39	12.44

Yearbook of Tourism Statistics, Data 2009 – 2013, 2015 Edition

PALESTINE

5. Overnight stays of non-resident tourists in hotels and similar establishments, by nationality

	2009	2010	2011	2012	2013	Market share 2013	% Change 2013-2012
TOTAL (*)	926,312	1,165,519	1,112,523	1,162,530	1,326,193	100.00	14.08
AFRICA	19,442	27,088	50,363	43,988	100,256	7.56	127.92
OTHER AFRICA	19,442	27,088	50,363	43,988	100,256	7.56	127.92
All countries of Africa	19,442	27,088	50,363	43,988	100,256	7.56	127.92
AMERICAS	149,612	190,830	149,938	140,999	161,095	12.15	14.25
NORTH AMERICA	120,508	157,176	110,217	106,283	125,626	9.47	18.20
Canada, United States	120,508	157,176	110,217	106,283	125,626	9.47	18.20
OTHER AMERICAS	29,104	33,654	39,721	34,716	35,469	2.67	2.17
Other countries of the Americas	29,104	33,654	39,721	34,716	35,469	2.67	2.17
EAST ASIA AND THE PACIFIC	89,195	150,976	140,001	129,663	150,720	11.36	16.24
AUSTRALASIA	3,633	8,705	10,273	9,076	7,238	0.55	-20.25
Australia, New Zealand	3,633	8,705	10,273	9,076	7,238	0.55	-20.25
OTHER EAST ASIA AND THE PACIFIC	85,562	142,271	129,728	120,587	143,482	10.82	18.99
All countries of Asia	85,562	142,271	129,728	120,587	143,482	10.82	18.99
EUROPE	660,388	787,729	752,319	819,420	885,306	66.76	8.04
EAST MEDITERRANEAN EUROPE	80,312	77,191	73,538	112,443	140,183	10.57	24.67
Israel	80,312	77,191	73,538	112,443	140,183	10.57	24.67
OTHER EUROPE	580,076	710,538	678,781	706,977	745,123	56.19	5.40
Other countries of Europe	580,076	710,538	678,781	706,977	745,123	56.19	5.40
MIDDLE EAST	7,675	8,896	19,902	28,460	28,816	2.17	1.25
All countries of Middle East	7,675	8,896	19,902	28,460	28,816	2.17	1.25

Yearbook of Tourism Statistics, Data 2009 – 2013, 2015 Edition

PANAMA

2. Arrivals of non-resident visitors at national borders, by country of residence

		2009	2010	2011	2012	2013	Market share 2013	% Change 2013-2012
TOTAL	(*)	**1,054,663**	**1,162,713**	**1,310,292**	**1,478,282**	**1,527,228**	**100.00**	**3.31**
AFRICA		851	1,000	1,921	1,919	2,990	0.20	55.81
EAST AFRICA				337	240	422	0.03	75.83
Burundi				9	6	9	0.00	50.00
Comoros				10	3	13	0.00	333.33
Djibouti				1	2	1	0.00	-50.00
Eritrea				10	3	7	0.00	133.33
Ethiopia				40	20	45	0.00	125.00
Kenya				57	71	139	0.01	95.77
Madagascar				11	8	16	0.00	100.00
Malawi				7	4	7	0.00	75.00
Mauritius				19	28	47	0.00	67.86
Mozambique				22	14	15	0.00	7.14
Reunion				5		3	0.00	
Rwanda				6	3	18	0.00	500.00
Seychelles				10	9			
Somalia				2	1	9	0.00	800.00
Uganda				43	24	29	0.00	20.83
United Republic of Tanzania				29	25	19	0.00	-24.00
Zambia				27	8	14	0.00	75.00
Zimbabwe				29	11	31	0.00	181.82
CENTRAL AFRICA				329	389	592	0.04	52.19
Angola				226	304	518	0.03	70.39
Cameroon				24	31	20	0.00	-35.48
Central African Republic				1	1	6	0.00	500.00
Chad				4	4			
Congo				13	15	8	0.00	-46.67
Democratic Republic of the Congo				28	23	10	0.00	-56.52
Gabon				22	8	22	0.00	175.00
Sao Tome and Principe				11	3	8	0.00	166.67
NORTH AFRICA				133	214	709	0.05	231.31
Algeria				42	34	63	0.00	85.29
Morocco				53	52	87	0.01	67.31
Sudan				11	4	7	0.00	75.00
Tunisia				22	23	50	0.00	117.39
Western Sahara				5	101	502	0.03	397.03
SOUTHERN AFRICA		279	319	726	719	791	0.05	10.01
Botswana				3	9	18	0.00	100.00
Lesotho				10	4	7	0.00	75.00
Namibia				32	20	25	0.00	25.00
South Africa		279	319	668	680	733	0.05	7.79
Swaziland				13	6	8	0.00	33.33
WEST AFRICA				396	357	441	0.03	23.53
Benin				7	8	15	0.00	87.50
Burkina Faso				18	6	11	0.00	83.33
Cabo Verde				24	18	13	0.00	-27.78
Côte d'Ivoire				12	9	20	0.00	122.22
Gambia				13	6	2	0.00	-66.67
Ghana				82	87	119	0.01	36.78
Guinea				22	46	42	0.00	-8.70
Guinea-Bissau				13	13	14	0.00	7.69
Liberia				11	10	8	0.00	-20.00
Mali				12	10	16	0.00	60.00
Mauritania				4	5	21	0.00	320.00
Niger				15	16	16	0.00	
Nigeria				114	80	105	0.01	31.25
Senegal				26	23	28	0.00	21.74
Sierra Leone				4	15	6	0.00	-60.00
Togo				19	5	5	0.00	

Yearbook of Tourism Statistics, Data 2009 – 2013, 2015 Edition

PANAMA

2. Arrivals of non-resident visitors at national borders, by country of residence

	2009	2010	2011	2012	2013	Market share 2013	% Change 2013-2012
OTHER AFRICA	572	681			35	0.00	
Other countries of Africa	572	681			35	0.00	
AMERICAS	916,458	1,006,007	1,134,147	1,284,902	1,311,442	85.87	2.07
CARIBBEAN	28,787	30,546	32,677	36,837	41,780	2.74	13.42
Anguilla			2	13	8	0.00	-38.46
Antigua and Barbuda			103	136	187	0.01	37.50
Aruba			53	78	179	0.01	129.49
Bahamas	393	373	626	1,178	1,302	0.09	10.53
Barbados	421	451	485	629	549	0.04	-12.72
Bermuda	194	142	186	283	207	0.01	-26.86
British Virgin Islands			3		14	0.00	
Cayman Islands			115	627	445	0.03	-29.03
Cuba	5,032	5,025	5,461	5,960	8,245	0.54	38.34
Curaçao	40	106	86	73	196	0.01	168.49
Dominica			152	141	137	0.01	-2.84
Dominican Republic	9,649	11,704	13,412	15,935	16,281	1.07	2.17
Grenada			148	142	148	0.01	4.23
Haiti	5,759	4,462	4,081	2,658	2,549	0.17	-4.10
Jamaica	3,345	2,763	2,857	3,294	3,847	0.25	16.79
Martinique			2	6	2	0.00	-66.67
Montserrat			1	3			
Puerto Rico	664	1,069	750	798	1,447	0.09	81.33
Saint Kitts and Nevis			110	151	160	0.01	5.96
Saint Lucia			132	165	212	0.01	28.48
Saint Vincent and the Grenadines			143	140	185	0.01	32.14
Trinidad and Tobago			3,718	4,376	5,433	0.36	24.15
Turks and Caicos Islands			42	36	29	0.00	-19.44
United States Virgin Islands			3	10	3	0.00	-70.00
Other countries of the Caribbean	3,290	4,451	6	5	15	0.00	200.00
CENTRAL AMERICA	100,477	114,080	111,545	123,702	137,937	9.03	11.51
Belize	736	1,070	967	1,051	941	0.06	-10.47
Costa Rica	37,759	39,524	40,524	42,978	48,945	3.20	13.88
El Salvador	15,569	16,547	16,696	20,820	21,510	1.41	3.31
Guatemala	26,064	32,780	27,107	27,913	30,641	2.01	9.77
Honduras	10,383	12,270	13,921	16,400	17,441	1.14	6.35
Nicaragua	9,966	11,889	12,330	14,540	18,459	1.21	26.95
NORTH AMERICA	316,945	348,999	383,896	424,441	372,760	24.41	-12.18
Canada	37,849	48,029	52,731	62,792	52,341	3.43	-16.64
Mexico	44,904	48,132	51,422	57,803	60,296	3.95	4.31
United States of America	234,190	252,837	279,742	303,843	260,122	17.03	-14.39
Other countries of North America	2	1	1	3	1	0.00	-66.67
SOUTH AMERICA	470,249	512,382	606,029	699,922	758,965	49.70	8.44
Argentina	41,989	47,216	62,357	66,623	72,730	4.76	9.17
Bolivia	4,942	6,744	9,544	12,327	12,115	0.79	-1.72
Brazil	24,338	31,520	47,890	59,687	67,518	4.42	13.12
Chile	13,035	16,232	19,020	21,095	25,189	1.65	19.41
Colombia	177,224	219,250	218,962	244,890	264,715	17.33	8.10
Ecuador	22,172	30,861	43,975	59,782	70,571	4.62	18.05
French Guiana			19	17	24	0.00	41.18
Guyana			1,001	1,192	1,066	0.07	-10.57
Paraguay	821	1,078	1,319	3,955	3,838	0.25	-2.96
Peru	11,853	15,431	22,382	30,824	33,273	2.18	7.95
Suriname			213	281	255	0.02	-9.25
Uruguay	10,556	11,400	11,163	11,898	11,286	0.74	-5.14
Venezuela	162,581	131,608	168,184	187,351	196,385	12.86	4.82
Other countries of South America	738	1,042					

Yearbook of Tourism Statistics, Data 2009 – 2013, 2015 Edition

PANAMA

2. Arrivals of non-resident visitors at national borders, by country of residence

	2009	2010	2011	2012	2013	Market share 2013	% Change 2013-2012
EAST ASIA AND THE PACIFIC	22,550	27,020	26,993	30,503	28,823	1.89	-5.51
NORTH-EAST ASIA	4,715	5,485	16,574	18,940	16,763	1.10	-11.49
China			6,661	7,714	6,905	0.45	-10.49
Hong Kong, China			35	28	71	0.00	153.57
Japan	3,133	3,988	4,525	5,043	4,515	0.30	-10.47
Korea, Dem. People's Republic of			298	10	4	0.00	-60.00
Korea, Republic of			3,486	4,511	3,780	0.25	-16.20
Macao, China			18	9	3	0.00	-66.67
Mongolia			74	98	10	0.00	-89.80
Taiwan, Province of China	1,582	1,497	1,477	1,527	1,475	0.10	-3.41
SOUTH-EAST ASIA			6,502	6,694	7,456	0.49	11.38
Brunei Darussalam			7	2	9	0.00	350.00
Cambodia			32	12	12	0.00	
Indonesia			519	390	619	0.04	58.72
Lao People's Democratic Republic			6	8	7	0.00	-12.50
Malaysia			183	214	251	0.02	17.29
Myanmar			260	209	326	0.02	55.98
Philippines			4,608	5,141	5,379	0.35	4.63
Singapore			425	407	430	0.03	5.65
Thailand			214	191	234	0.02	22.51
Timor-Leste			8		9	0.00	
Viet Nam			240	120	180	0.01	50.00
AUSTRALASIA	2,925	3,243	3,791	4,709	4,480	0.29	-4.86
Australia	2,352	2,439	3,139	3,990	3,740	0.24	-6.27
New Zealand	573	804	652	719	740	0.05	2.92
MELANESIA			16	10	15	0.00	50.00
Fiji			12	4	7	0.00	75.00
Papua New Guinea			4	6	8	0.00	33.33
MICRONESIA			11	10	59	0.00	490.00
Guam				1	21	0.00	2,000.00
Kiribati			3	5	33	0.00	560.00
Micronesia, Federated States of			8	4	5	0.00	25.00
POLYNESIA			33	32	22	0.00	-31.25
Cook Islands			13	7	3	0.00	-57.14
Samoa			15	13	16	0.00	23.08
Tuvalu			5	12	3	0.00	-75.00
OTHER EAST ASIA AND THE PACIFIC	14,910	18,292	66	108	28	0.00	-74.07
Other countries of Asia	14,823	18,214	6	20	28	0.00	40.00
Other countries of Oceania	87	78	60	88			
EUROPE	114,729	128,595	141,728	155,213	178,575	11.69	15.05
CENTRAL/EASTERN EUROPE			10,353	10,857	11,928	0.78	9.86
Armenia			5	12	30	0.00	150.00
Azerbaijan			8	5	20	0.00	300.00
Belarus			85	93	110	0.01	18.28
Bulgaria			423	494	523	0.03	5.87
Czech Republic			530	632	737	0.05	16.61
Czech Republic/Slovakia				174			
Estonia			221	132	183	0.01	38.64
Georgia			108	91	107	0.01	17.58
Hungary			352	407	506	0.03	24.32
Kazakhstan			44	53	43	0.00	-18.87
Kyrgyzstan			6	5	10	0.00	100.00
Latvia			356	359	325	0.02	-9.47
Lithuania			238	205	249	0.02	21.46
Poland			1,583	1,714	2,024	0.13	18.09
Republic of Moldova			28	59	37	0.00	-37.29
Romania			733	1,006	1,110	0.07	10.34
Russian Federation			3,284	3,156	3,337	0.22	5.74
Slovakia			207	251	290	0.02	15.54

557

PANAMA

2. Arrivals of non-resident visitors at national borders, by country of residence

	2009	2010	2011	2012	2013	Market share 2013	% Change 2013-2012
Tajikistan			2	1	2	0.00	100.00
Turkmenistan			6	6	2	0.00	-66.67
Ukraine			2,125	1,994	2,272	0.15	13.94
Uzbekistan			9	8	11	0.00	37.50
NORTHERN EUROPE	**10,818**	**11,181**	**22,468**	**21,301**	**21,205**	**1.39**	**-0.45**
Denmark			1,917	1,892	1,985	0.13	4.92
Finland			3,236	1,061	1,018	0.07	-4.05
Iceland			141	154	124	0.01	-19.48
Ireland			1,203	1,253	1,228	0.08	-2.00
Norway			1,568	1,670	1,674	0.11	0.24
Sweden			2,843	2,858	2,886	0.19	0.98
United Kingdom	10,818	11,181	11,560	12,413	12,290	0.80	-0.99
SOUTHERN EUROPE	**39,633**	**47,660**	**53,423**	**62,129**	**77,683**	**5.09**	**25.04**
Albania			80	102	62	0.00	-39.22
Andorra			175	200	191	0.01	-4.50
Bosnia and Herzegovina			9	17	38	0.00	123.53
Croatia			408	478	473	0.03	-1.05
Greece	1,034	1,001	1,062	982	1,201	0.08	22.30
Holy See			2	9	7	0.00	-22.22
Italy	13,399	15,814	16,295	17,039	17,503	1.15	2.72
Malta			30	28	38	0.00	35.71
Portugal			2,668	3,106	3,105	0.20	-0.03
San Marino			4	8	9	0.00	12.50
Serbia and Montenegro				15	160	0.01	966.67
Slovenia			117	198	234	0.02	18.18
Spain	25,200	30,845	32,560	39,928	54,633	3.58	36.83
TFYR of Macedonia			13	19	29	0.00	52.63
WESTERN EUROPE	**33,567**	**36,345**	**46,497**	**51,416**	**58,814**	**3.85**	**14.39**
Austria			1,906	1,973	1,939	0.13	-1.72
Belgium			3,172	3,292	2,803	0.18	-14.85
France	11,166	11,665	12,361	13,731	14,977	0.98	9.07
Germany	9,087	9,742	12,847	14,396	15,855	1.04	10.13
Liechtenstein			42	51	49	0.00	-3.92
Luxembourg			75	94	105	0.01	11.70
Monaco			8	4	8	0.00	100.00
Netherlands	9,610	10,732	11,110	12,181	17,323	1.13	42.21
Switzerland	3,704	4,206	4,976	5,694	5,755	0.38	1.07
EAST MEDITERRANEAN EUROPE	**6,800**	**7,826**	**8,858**	**9,478**	**8,815**	**0.58**	**-7.00**
Cyprus			53	65	62	0.00	-4.62
Israel	6,800	7,826	8,312	8,625	7,425	0.49	-13.91
Turkey			493	788	1,328	0.09	68.53
OTHER EUROPE	**23,911**	**25,583**	**129**	**32**	**130**	**0.01**	**306.25**
Other countries of Europe	23,911	25,583	129	32	130	0.01	306.25
MIDDLE EAST	**75**	**91**	**787**	**955**	**770**	**0.05**	**-19.37**
Bahrain			4	7	13	0.00	85.71
Egypt	75	91	91	104	121	0.01	16.35
Iraq			16	17	16	0.00	-5.88
Jordan			106	83	43	0.00	-48.19
Kuwait			45	19	56	0.00	194.74
Lebanon			246	458	194	0.01	-57.64
Libya			9	34	30	0.00	-11.76
Oman			9	10	24	0.00	140.00
Palestine			97	77	54	0.00	-29.87
Qatar			17	22	59	0.00	168.18
Saudi Arabia			64	58	63	0.00	8.62
Syrian Arab Republic			60	36	36	0.00	
United Arab Emirates			16	21	48	0.00	128.57
Yemen			7	9	13	0.00	44.44

Yearbook of Tourism Statistics, Data 2009 – 2013, 2015 Edition

PANAMA

2. Arrivals of non-resident visitors at national borders, by country of residence

	2009	2010	2011	2012	2013	Market share 2013	% Change 2013-2012
SOUTH ASIA			**4,716**	**4,790**	**4,628**	**0.30**	**-3.38**
Afghanistan			19	2	8	0.00	300.00
Bangladesh			68	65	108	0.01	66.15
India			4,297	4,393	4,176	0.27	-4.94
Iran, Islamic Republic of			62	53	56	0.00	5.66
Maldives			14	3	11	0.00	266.67
Nepal			18	12	15	0.00	25.00
Pakistan			152	147	154	0.01	4.76
Sri Lanka			86	115	100	0.01	-13.04

Yearbook of Tourism Statistics, Data 2009 – 2013, 2015 Edition

PAPUA NEW GUINEA

2. Arrivals of non-resident visitors at national borders, by country of residence

	2009	2010	2011	2012	2013	Market share 2013	% Change 2013-2012
TOTAL	125,891	146,350	165,059	175,203	182,188	100.00	3.99
AFRICA	877	1,056	1,671	1,481	1,149	0.63	-22.42
OTHER AFRICA	877	1,056	1,671	1,481	1,149	0.63	-22.42
All countries of Africa	877	1,056	1,671	1,481	1,149	0.63	-22.42
AMERICAS	9,029	10,869	11,715	11,985	13,214	7.25	10.25
NORTH AMERICA	8,567	10,362	11,024	11,235	12,449	6.83	10.81
Canada	1,937	1,927	2,067	1,899	1,886	1.04	-0.68
United States of America	6,630	8,435	8,957	9,336	10,563	5.80	13.14
SOUTH AMERICA	21	14	8	11	47	0.03	327.27
Chile	21	14	8	11	47	0.03	327.27
OTHER AMERICAS	441	493	683	739	718	0.39	-2.84
Other countries of the Americas	441	493	683	739	718	0.39	-2.84
EAST ASIA AND THE PACIFIC	102,717	119,610	131,593	142,789	149,428	82.02	4.65
NORTH-EAST ASIA	10,064	12,220	12,098	13,104	12,842	7.05	-2.00
China	6,492	7,435	7,063	7,736	7,866	4.32	1.68
Japan	2,767	3,804	3,500	3,492	3,167	1.74	-9.31
Korea, Republic of	805	981	1,535	1,876	1,809	0.99	-3.57
SOUTH-EAST ASIA	15,092	19,072	24,869	30,561	34,902	19.16	14.20
Indonesia	1,831	2,249	2,377	3,253	7,313	4.01	124.81
Malaysia	5,017	5,915	6,563	6,009	4,793	2.63	-20.24
Philippines	7,333	9,551	14,292	19,314	21,048	11.55	8.98
Singapore	911	1,357	1,637	1,985	1,748	0.96	-11.94
AUSTRALASIA	72,527	82,398	86,451	89,523	91,904	50.44	2.66
Australia	66,842	75,355	77,396	80,276	83,616	45.90	4.16
New Zealand	5,685	7,043	9,055	9,247	8,288	4.55	-10.37
OTHER EAST ASIA AND THE PACIFIC	5,034	5,920	8,175	9,601	9,780	5.37	1.86
Other countries of Asia	1,270	2,064	3,418	4,732	4,416	2.42	-6.68
Other countries of Oceania	3,764	3,856	4,757	4,869	5,364	2.94	10.17
EUROPE	9,022	12,065	15,130	13,468	13,238	7.27	-1.71
CENTRAL/EASTERN EUROPE	411	559	575	452	380	0.21	-15.93
Russian Federation	411	559	575	452	380	0.21	-15.93
NORTHERN EUROPE	4,067	5,445	6,315	5,431	5,636	3.09	3.77
United Kingdom	3,669	5,102	5,753	4,893	4,962	2.72	1.41
Scandinavia	398	343	562	538	674	0.37	25.28
SOUTHERN EUROPE	293	270	453	550	339	0.19	-38.36
Italy	293	270	453	550	339	0.19	-38.36
WESTERN EUROPE	2,318	3,141	4,495	4,162	4,361	2.39	4.78
France	584	830	1,271	1,059	1,278	0.70	20.68
Germany	1,219	1,680	2,480	2,407	2,487	1.37	3.32
Netherlands	515	631	744	696	596	0.33	-14.37
EAST MEDITERRANEAN EUROPE	144	55	132	134	194	0.11	44.78
Israel	144	55	132	134	194	0.11	44.78
OTHER EUROPE	1,789	2,595	3,160	2,739	2,328	1.28	-15.01
Other countries of Europe	1,789	2,595	3,160	2,739	2,328	1.28	-15.01
SOUTH ASIA	2,382	2,750	4,950	5,480	5,159	2.83	-5.86
India	2,382	2,750	4,950	5,480	5,159	2.83	-5.86
NOT SPECIFIED	1,864						
Other countries of the World	1,864						

Yearbook of Tourism Statistics, Data 2009 – 2013, 2015 Edition

PARAGUAY

1. Arrivals of non-resident tourists at national borders, by nationality

	2009	2010	2011	2012	2013	Market share 2013	% Change 2013-2012
TOTAL (*)	439,246	465,363	523,740	579,305	609,901	100.00	5.28
AFRICA	401	386	354	593	746	0.12	25.80
EAST AFRICA	103	91	34	63	47	0.01	-25.40
Burundi	2	1		2	1	0.00	-50.00
Ethiopia	10	9	3	4	3	0.00	-25.00
Kenya	15	18	13	14	8	0.00	-42.86
Madagascar	6	3	5	5	1	0.00	-80.00
Malawi	5	4		2	1	0.00	-50.00
Mauritius			1		2	0.00	
Mozambique	6	7	4	13	5	0.00	-61.54
Rwanda			2	2	1	0.00	-50.00
Somalia	1						
Uganda	4	1	3	5	11	0.00	120.00
United Republic of Tanzania	14	14	1	10	10	0.00	
Zambia	8	6	1	6	2	0.00	-66.67
Zimbabwe	32	28	1		2	0.00	
CENTRAL AFRICA	39	62	58	142	348	0.06	145.07
Angola	28	40	40	115	335	0.05	191.30
Cameroon	3	13	5	5	5	0.00	
Central African Republic			3	4	1	0.00	-75.00
Congo	5	6	4	9	2	0.00	-77.78
Equatorial Guinea	3	3	6	9	5	0.00	-44.44
NORTH AFRICA	12	8	6	41	36	0.01	-12.20
Algeria	6	4	1	2	2	0.00	
Morocco	4	1	4	33	27	0.00	-18.18
Sudan				1			
Tunisia	2	3	1	5	7	0.00	40.00
SOUTHERN AFRICA	185	192	220	286	255	0.04	-10.84
Botswana	3	2					
Lesotho	1			1			
Namibia	3	9	3	4	1	0.00	-75.00
South Africa	176	181	216	281	254	0.04	-9.61
Swaziland	2		1				
WEST AFRICA	62	33	33	54	55	0.01	1.85
Benin	3			2			
Burkina Faso	8	4	2	3			
Cabo Verde	8	2	8	5	3	0.00	-40.00
Côte d'Ivoire	3	4	1	3	5	0.00	66.67
Gambia	3	1					
Ghana	9	9	1	7	8	0.00	14.29
Guinea	3	1			3	0.00	
Guinea-Bissau			4	2	1	0.00	-50.00
Liberia	2			1			
Mauritania	2			2			
Nigeria	17	9	15	22	21	0.00	-4.55
Senegal	3	3	2	7	14	0.00	100.00
Sierra Leone	1						
OTHER AFRICA			3	7	5	0.00	-28.57
Other countries of Africa			3	7	5	0.00	-28.57
AMERICAS	394,649	432,963	480,529	519,208	552,806	90.64	6.47
CARIBBEAN	612	316	683	916	1,143	0.19	24.78
Anguilla		1	3	2	43	0.01	2,050.00
Antigua and Barbuda	2	1	1	1	3	0.00	200.00
Bahamas	4		5	5	11	0.00	120.00
Barbados	6	2	9	3	3	0.00	
Cuba	337	190	381	553	755	0.12	36.53
Dominican Republic	113	96	219	274	251	0.04	-8.39
Haiti	33	13	29	34	38	0.01	11.76
Jamaica	15	9	14	18	26	0.00	44.44

Yearbook of Tourism Statistics, Data 2009 – 2013, 2015 Edition

PARAGUAY

1. Arrivals of non-resident tourists at national borders, by nationality

	2009	2010	2011	2012	2013	Market share 2013	% Change 2013-2012
Martinique				1			
Puerto Rico	1	1	3	2	1	0.00	-50.00
Saint Lucia	2		1	1	2	0.00	100.00
Saint Vincent and the Grenadines	89		1	3			
Trinidad and Tobago	10	3	12	13	5	0.00	-61.54
Other countries of the Caribbean			5	6	5	0.00	-16.67
CENTRAL AMERICA	**1,546**	**868**	**1,901**	**3,022**	**2,923**	**0.48**	**-3.28**
Belize	9	1	103	10	19	0.00	90.00
Costa Rica	346	253	526	816	660	0.11	-19.12
El Salvador	250	166	239	361	375	0.06	3.88
Guatemala	361	202	298	593	575	0.09	-3.04
Honduras	120	45	134	231	273	0.04	18.18
Nicaragua	144	64	163	254	239	0.04	-5.91
Panama	316	137	438	757	782	0.13	3.30
NORTH AMERICA	**18,858**	**13,290**	**15,454**	**23,522**	**24,886**	**4.08**	**5.80**
Canada	2,669	1,647	1,606	2,292	2,223	0.36	-3.01
Mexico	2,177	1,501	2,563	3,950	3,986	0.65	0.91
United States of America	14,012	10,142	11,285	17,280	18,677	3.06	8.08
SOUTH AMERICA	**373,633**	**418,489**	**462,491**	**491,748**	**523,854**	**85.89**	**6.53**
Argentina	196,149	218,418	222,901	254,328	271,897	44.58	6.91
Bolivia	13,203	11,646	23,256	18,202	18,674	3.06	2.59
Brazil	131,429	159,280	176,440	171,925	191,451	31.39	11.36
Chile	11,115	9,829	11,706	11,780	11,042	1.81	-6.26
Colombia	3,017	2,482	4,177	7,129	7,279	1.19	2.10
Ecuador	1,266	779	1,815	2,369	2,184	0.36	-7.81
Guyana	3	4	15	21	7	0.00	-66.67
Peru	5,044	4,141	6,219	7,909	6,394	1.05	-19.16
Suriname	2		23	26	6	0.00	-76.92
Uruguay	11,130	11,216	14,154	15,448	12,801	2.10	-17.13
Venezuela	1,275	694	1,784	2,611	2,119	0.35	-18.84
Other countries of South America			1				
EAST ASIA AND THE PACIFIC	**8,478**	**7,177**	**8,037**	**11,971**	**12,039**	**1.97**	**0.57**
NORTH-EAST ASIA	**7,743**	**6,574**	**7,408**	**10,888**	**11,234**	**1.84**	**3.18**
China	218	193	363	741	813	0.13	9.72
Hong Kong, China	1	2	1				
Japan	3,319	3,134	2,666	3,947	4,435	0.73	12.36
Korea, Republic of	3,672	2,917	3,923	5,571	5,252	0.86	-5.73
Mongolia	2	1		2			
Taiwan, Province of China	531	327	455	627	734	0.12	17.07
SOUTH-EAST ASIA	**189**	**152**	**138**	**241**	**265**	**0.04**	**9.96**
Cambodia	2			2	2	0.00	
Indonesia	96	56	29	24	39	0.01	62.50
Lao People's Democratic Republic		3	11	2	1	0.00	-50.00
Malaysia	26	40	16	23	30	0.00	30.43
Myanmar	1			2			
Philippines	43	32	62	105	133	0.02	26.67
Singapore	2	5	7	12	10	0.00	-16.67
Thailand	8	11	4	22	18	0.00	-18.18
Viet Nam	11	5	9	49	32	0.01	-34.69
AUSTRALASIA	**543**	**447**	**472**	**825**	**526**	**0.09**	**-36.24**
Australia	391	319	341	694	435	0.07	-37.32
New Zealand	152	128	131	131	91	0.01	-30.53
MELANESIA	**3**	**3**	**1**	**3**	**1**	**0.00**	**-66.67**
Fiji	3	2					
Papua New Guinea		1		3	1	0.00	-66.67
Solomon Islands			1				
MICRONESIA		**1**					
Guam		1					

Yearbook of Tourism Statistics, Data 2009 – 2013, 2015 Edition

PARAGUAY

1. Arrivals of non-resident tourists at national borders, by nationality

	2009	2010	2011	2012	2013	Market share 2013	% Change 2013-2012
OTHER EAST ASIA AND THE PACIFIC			18	14	13	0.00	-7.14
Other countries of Asia			16	3	2	0.00	-33.33
Other countries of Oceania			2	11	11	0.00	
EUROPE	34,716	24,280	34,014	46,279	43,068	7.06	-6.94
CENTRAL/EASTERN EUROPE	1,040	745	1,035	1,552	1,394	0.23	-10.18
Armenia	3	3	7	12	5	0.00	-58.33
Azerbaijan	5		4	3	1	0.00	-66.67
Belarus	14	3					
Bulgaria	22	20	51	69	80	0.01	15.94
Czech Republic	142	83	160	280	162	0.03	-42.14
Estonia	51	48	24	53	24	0.00	-54.72
Georgia	1			5	4	0.00	-20.00
Hungary	102	18	81	122	93	0.02	-23.77
Kazakhstan	2			6	5	0.00	-16.67
Latvia	25	11	26	31	44	0.01	41.94
Lithuania	24	11	19	19	32	0.01	68.42
Poland	353	195	292	448	389	0.06	-13.17
Republic of Moldova	1		7	19	13	0.00	-31.58
Romania	1	2	2	4	14	0.00	250.00
Russian Federation	202	196	265	263	362	0.06	37.64
Slovakia	51	22	35	74	75	0.01	1.35
Ukraine	41	133	57	133	90	0.01	-32.33
Uzbekistan			5	11	1	0.00	-90.91
NORTHERN EUROPE	3,666	2,456	3,668	5,086	4,180	0.69	-17.81
Denmark	323	213	431	646	412	0.07	-36.22
Finland	132	103	137	205	160	0.03	-21.95
Iceland	15	15	20	28	24	0.00	-14.29
Ireland	307	229	230	261	240	0.04	-8.05
Norway	321	218	342	463	371	0.06	-19.87
Sweden	518	296	531	1,017	623	0.10	-38.74
United Kingdom	2,050	1,382	1,977	2,466	2,350	0.39	-4.70
SOUTHERN EUROPE	11,416	7,772	12,138	16,974	17,203	2.82	1.35
Albania	1	3	6	8	2	0.00	-75.00
Andorra	1	1	11	11	4	0.00	-63.64
Bosnia and Herzegovina	4			4	2	0.00	-50.00
Croatia	55	10	24	38	37	0.01	-2.63
Greece	116	176	101	150	83	0.01	-44.67
Holy See	29	4	7	8	7	0.00	-12.50
Italy	3,270	2,376	3,008	4,185	4,148	0.68	-0.88
Malta	3	3	7	12	9	0.00	-25.00
Portugal	336	238	557	720	763	0.13	5.97
San Marino				1			
Serbia and Montenegro	8	3			38	0.01	
Slovenia	32	29	50	34	39	0.01	14.71
Spain	7,557	4,929	8,364	11,801	12,070	1.98	2.28
TFYR of Macedonia	4		3	2	1	0.00	-50.00
WESTERN EUROPE	18,053	12,969	16,551	21,339	19,062	3.13	-10.67
Austria	706	610	702	930	821	0.13	-11.72
Belgium	701	436	521	949	804	0.13	-15.28
France	3,414	2,568	3,632	4,512	4,272	0.70	-5.32
Germany	10,289	7,173	9,057	11,486	10,105	1.66	-12.02
Liechtenstein	5	5	5	6	3	0.00	-50.00
Luxembourg	23	19	51	38	37	0.01	-2.63
Monaco	3			30	1	0.00	-96.67
Netherlands	1,065	701	859	1,223	1,132	0.19	-7.44
Switzerland	1,847	1,457	1,724	2,165	1,887	0.31	-12.84
EAST MEDITERRANEAN EUROPE	541	332	618	1,322	1,216	0.20	-8.02
Cyprus	22	2	8	22	17	0.00	-22.73
Israel	462	298	508	1,030	998	0.16	-3.11

Yearbook of Tourism Statistics, Data 2009 – 2013, 2015 Edition

PARAGUAY

1. Arrivals of non-resident tourists at national borders, by nationality

	2009	2010	2011	2012	2013	Market share 2013	% Change 2013-2012
Turkey	57	32	102	270	201	0.03	-25.56
OTHER EUROPE		6	4	6	13	0.00	116.67
Other countries of Europe		6	4	6	13	0.00	116.67
MIDDLE EAST	654	348	468	718	684	0.11	-4.74
Egypt	22	8	22	32	24	0.00	-25.00
Iraq	8	4	10	6	7	0.00	16.67
Jordan	6	10	8	29	5	0.00	-82.76
Kuwait	1		1	2	2	0.00	
Lebanon	583	316	399	593	561	0.09	-5.40
Libya			1	2	2	0.00	
Palestine	4	3	7	14	4	0.00	-71.43
Qatar	4	1		3	19	0.00	533.33
Saudi Arabia	11	1	2	1	11	0.00	1,000.00
Syrian Arab Republic	10	4	7	13	26	0.00	100.00
United Arab Emirates	5	1	11	23	23	0.00	
SOUTH ASIA	348	209	338	536	558	0.09	4.10
Afghanistan	3	2			6	0.00	
Bangladesh	24	16	28	92	104	0.02	13.04
India	258	177	281	398	390	0.06	-2.01
Iran, Islamic Republic of	26	8	9	8	7	0.00	-12.50
Maldives	1						
Nepal	5	1	1	8	27	0.00	237.50
Pakistan	28	5	18	25	21	0.00	-16.00
Sri Lanka	3		1	5	3	0.00	-40.00

Yearbook of Tourism Statistics, Data 2009 – 2013, 2015 Edition

PERU

1. Arrivals of non-resident tourists at national borders, by country of residence

		2009	2010	2011	2012	2013	Market share 2013	% Change 2013-2012
TOTAL	(*)	**2,139,961**	**2,299,187**	**2,597,803**	**2,845,623**	**3,163,639**	**100.00**	**11.18**
AFRICA		**3,478**	**3,714**	**4,247**	**4,406**	**4,257**	**0.13**	**-3.38**
NORTH AFRICA		**136**	**130**	**229**	**225**	**241**	**0.01**	**7.11**
Morocco		136	130	229	225	241	0.01	7.11
SOUTHERN AFRICA		**2,444**	**2,689**	**2,994**	**2,943**	**2,672**	**0.08**	**-9.21**
South Africa		2,444	2,689	2,994	2,943	2,672	0.08	-9.21
OTHER AFRICA		**898**	**895**	**1,024**	**1,238**	**1,344**	**0.04**	**8.56**
Other countries of Africa		898	895	1,024	1,238	1,344	0.04	8.56
AMERICAS		**1,581,215**	**1,746,961**	**1,996,759**	**2,190,815**	**2,473,451**	**78.18**	**12.90**
CARIBBEAN		**10,936**	**9,793**	**8,613**	**7,952**	**8,145**	**0.26**	**2.43**
Aruba		254	253	286	307	355	0.01	15.64
Cuba		5,139	4,855	4,172	3,755	3,562	0.11	-5.14
Dominican Republic		4,676	3,719	3,234	2,800	2,962	0.09	5.79
Puerto Rico		501	506	557	591	664	0.02	12.35
Trinidad and Tobago		366	460	364	499	602	0.02	20.64
CENTRAL AMERICA		**25,285**	**27,537**	**31,860**	**34,840**	**37,479**	**1.18**	**7.57**
Costa Rica		7,842	8,765	9,302	9,319	9,489	0.30	1.82
El Salvador		2,938	2,663	4,948	5,746	5,404	0.17	-5.95
Guatemala		2,971	2,797	3,451	3,486	3,829	0.12	9.84
Honduras		1,375	1,477	1,930	1,988	2,349	0.07	18.16
Nicaragua		1,203	1,117	1,269	1,393	1,287	0.04	-7.61
Panama		8,956	10,718	10,960	12,908	15,121	0.48	17.14
NORTH AMERICA		**509,543**	**508,284**	**515,394**	**559,809**	**610,418**	**19.29**	**9.04**
Canada		54,595	52,955	57,454	61,362	62,820	1.99	2.38
Mexico		28,623	38,097	46,005	51,229	60,270	1.91	17.65
United States of America		426,325	417,232	411,935	447,218	487,328	15.40	8.97
SOUTH AMERICA		**1,034,279**	**1,198,782**	**1,433,730**	**1,586,366**	**1,816,415**	**57.42**	**14.50**
Argentina		121,172	127,062	147,403	158,950	155,145	4.90	-2.39
Bolivia		93,408	86,181	88,042	101,546	111,983	3.54	10.28
Brazil		82,764	87,674	117,537	126,085	143,538	4.54	13.84
Chile		464,153	595,944	741,717	806,929	886,485	28.02	9.86
Colombia		87,225	98,642	112,816	133,975	134,725	4.26	0.56
Ecuador		136,054	152,445	160,841	176,071	208,358	6.59	18.34
Paraguay		3,914	3,914	4,631	4,756	5,104	0.16	7.32
Uruguay		8,648	8,219	10,303	11,846	12,509	0.40	5.60
Venezuela		36,789	38,469	50,185	65,930	158,215	5.00	139.97
Other countries of South America		152	232	255	278	353	0.01	26.98
OTHER AMERICAS		**1,172**	**2,565**	**7,162**	**1,848**	**994**	**0.03**	**-46.21**
Other countries of the Americas		1,172	2,565	7,162	1,848	994	0.03	-46.21
EAST ASIA AND THE PACIFIC		**104,232**	**96,851**	**117,314**	**138,821**	**153,562**	**4.85**	**10.62**
NORTH-EAST ASIA		**59,525**	**53,129**	**71,190**	**86,042**	**99,201**	**3.14**	**15.29**
China		9,257	9,484	11,896	12,180	12,864	0.41	5.62
Hong Kong, China		369	615	952	1,027	1,455	0.05	41.67
Japan		40,018	30,604	43,794	56,526	67,639	2.14	19.66
Korea, Republic of		7,824	10,157	12,059	13,318	14,000	0.44	5.12
Taiwan, Province of China		2,057	2,269	2,489	2,991	3,243	0.10	8.43
SOUTH-EAST ASIA		**5,846**	**6,360**	**8,159**	**8,537**	**9,826**	**0.31**	**15.10**
Indonesia		1,114	1,432	1,533	1,584	1,891	0.06	19.38
Malaysia		748	916	1,246	1,155	1,556	0.05	34.72
Philippines		2,492	2,268	2,628	2,701	2,597	0.08	-3.85
Singapore		661	868	1,348	1,252	1,523	0.05	21.65
Thailand		603	647	799	1,023	1,316	0.04	28.64
Viet Nam		228	229	605	822	943	0.03	14.72
AUSTRALASIA		**36,210**	**35,022**	**35,570**	**41,361**	**41,779**	**1.32**	**1.01**
Australia		30,947	29,659	30,436	35,745	36,373	1.15	1.76
New Zealand		5,263	5,363	5,134	5,616	5,406	0.17	-3.74

565

PERU

1. Arrivals of non-resident tourists at national borders, by country of residence

	2009	2010	2011	2012	2013	Market share 2013	% Change 2013-2012
OTHER EAST ASIA AND THE PACIFIC	2,651	2,340	2,395	2,881	2,756	0.09	-4.34
Other countries of Asia	2,580	2,275	2,341	2,786	2,659	0.08	-4.56
Other countries of Oceania	71	65	54	95	97	0.00	2.11
EUROPE	446,431	447,061	474,961	506,136	526,770	16.65	4.08
CENTRAL/EASTERN EUROPE	29,153	27,934	32,033	34,712	39,821	1.26	14.72
Belarus	6,340	7,316	8,216	8,867	9,735	0.31	9.79
Bulgaria	753	686	917	1,064	965	0.03	-9.30
Czech Republic	3,569	3,052	3,211	3,568	4,336	0.14	21.52
Hungary	1,439	1,230	1,334	1,369	1,877	0.06	37.11
Lithuania	441	487	523	600	844	0.03	40.67
Poland	7,510	6,140	6,268	6,076	7,960	0.25	31.01
Romania	1,252	1,237	1,511	1,794	1,975	0.06	10.09
Russian Federation	5,373	5,487	7,429	8,469	8,966	0.28	5.87
Slovakia	991	910	898	1,139	1,280	0.04	12.38
Ukraine	1,485	1,389	1,726	1,766	1,883	0.06	6.63
NORTHERN EUROPE	89,125	83,751	85,130	87,140	88,240	2.79	1.26
Denmark	5,903	5,760	6,023	5,884	5,761	0.18	-2.09
Finland	2,334	2,451	2,445	2,628	2,865	0.09	9.02
Ireland	7,587	6,346	5,525	5,655	5,904	0.19	4.40
Norway	5,701	5,675	5,827	5,923	5,913	0.19	-0.17
Sweden	8,971	9,337	9,895	10,664	11,014	0.35	3.28
United Kingdom	58,629	54,182	55,415	56,386	56,783	1.79	0.70
SOUTHERN EUROPE	138,149	145,197	157,673	165,400	178,491	5.64	7.91
Croatia	944	681	864	884	848	0.03	-4.07
Greece	1,659	1,632	1,476	1,233	1,288	0.04	4.46
Italy	40,426	41,831	45,192	46,845	47,624	1.51	1.66
Portugal	3,344	3,506	4,027	4,600	5,249	0.17	14.11
Slovenia	1,062	881	883	797	915	0.03	14.81
Spain	90,714	96,666	105,231	111,041	122,567	3.87	10.38
WESTERN EUROPE	173,585	174,407	183,740	201,669	203,868	6.44	1.09
Austria	6,087	6,454	6,791	7,498	7,813	0.25	4.20
Belgium	5,864	4,755	4,534	5,128	4,670	0.15	-8.93
France	66,071	66,985	72,900	81,851	81,904	2.59	0.06
Germany	51,864	53,201	56,197	62,051	62,570	1.98	0.84
Netherlands	25,530	24,795	24,486	24,831	25,299	0.80	1.88
Switzerland	18,169	18,217	18,832	20,310	21,612	0.68	6.41
EAST MEDITERRANEAN EUROPE	14,477	13,928	14,356	14,662	13,780	0.44	-6.02
Israel	13,657	12,978	12,809	13,082	11,809	0.37	-9.73
Turkey	820	950	1,547	1,580	1,971	0.06	24.75
OTHER EUROPE	1,942	1,844	2,029	2,553	2,570	0.08	0.67
Other countries of Europe	1,942	1,844	2,029	2,553	2,570	0.08	0.67
MIDDLE EAST	131	141	222	225	209	0.01	-7.11
Egypt	131	141	222	225	209	0.01	-7.11
SOUTH ASIA	3,406	3,526	3,471	4,165	4,454	0.14	6.94
India	3,406	3,526	3,471	4,165	4,454	0.14	6.94
NOT SPECIFIED	1,068	933	829	1,055	936	0.03	-11.28
Other countries of the World	1,068	933	829	1,055	936	0.03	-11.28

Yearbook of Tourism Statistics, Data 2009 – 2013, 2015 Edition

PERU

3. Arrivals of non-resident tourists in hotels and similar establishments, by nationality

	2009	2010	2011	2012	2013	Market share 2013	% Change 2013-2012
TOTAL	**4,059,014**	**4,462,298**	**4,766,963**	**7,269,167**	**8,179,292**	**100.00**	**12.52**
AMERICAS	**2,021,589**	**2,300,796**	**2,017,479**	**3,884,946**	**4,616,580**	**56.44**	**18.83**
NORTH AMERICA	**1,109,434**	**1,227,329**	**475,384**	**1,826,870**	**2,041,133**	**24.95**	**11.73**
Canada	165,713	179,678	223,217	272,979	276,544	3.38	1.31
Mexico	69,120	97,777	137,520	191,485	228,900	2.80	19.54
United States of America	874,601	949,874	114,647	1,362,406	1,535,689	18.78	12.72
SOUTH AMERICA	**912,155**	**1,073,467**	**1,542,095**	**2,058,076**	**2,575,447**	**31.49**	**25.14**
Argentina	204,232	234,462	347,494	417,004	441,404	5.40	5.85
Bolivia	41,763	48,319	56,450	72,627	87,444	1.07	20.40
Brazil	199,894	213,883	339,093	412,988	488,078	5.97	18.18
Chile	191,920	248,683	358,837	517,213	637,253	7.79	23.21
Colombia	131,621	168,969	233,127	338,628	407,430	4.98	20.32
Ecuador	95,301	106,889	128,030	157,149	199,685	2.44	27.07
Venezuela	47,424	52,262	79,064	142,467	314,153	3.84	120.51
EAST ASIA AND THE PACIFIC	**158,367**	**114,899**	**213,352**	**285,360**	**284,676**	**3.48**	**-0.24**
NORTH-EAST ASIA	**158,367**	**114,899**	**213,352**	**285,360**	**284,676**	**3.48**	**-0.24**
Japan	158,367	114,899	213,352	285,360	284,676	3.48	-0.24
EUROPE	**841,389**	**887,560**	**1,081,458**	**1,315,664**	**1,299,693**	**15.89**	**-1.21**
SOUTHERN EUROPE	**336,865**	**363,845**	**449,851**	**515,704**	**565,381**	**6.91**	**9.63**
Italy	107,860	116,684	148,266	167,350	165,690	2.03	-0.99
Spain	229,005	247,161	301,585	348,354	399,691	4.89	14.74
WESTERN EUROPE	**504,524**	**523,715**	**631,607**	**799,960**	**734,312**	**8.98**	**-8.21**
France	326,158	327,450	380,874	480,853	417,726	5.11	-13.13
Germany	178,366	196,265	250,733	319,107	316,586	3.87	-0.79
NOT SPECIFIED	**1,037,669**	**1,159,043**	**1,454,674**	**1,783,197**	**1,978,343**	**24.19**	**10.94**
Other countries of the World	1,037,669	1,159,043	1,454,674	1,783,197	1,978,343	24.19	10.94

Yearbook of Tourism Statistics, Data 2009 – 2013, 2015 Edition

PERU

5. Overnight stays of non-resident tourists in hotels and similar establishments, by nationality

	2009	2010	2011	2012	2013	Market share 2013	% Change 2013-2012
TOTAL	**7,606,573**	**8,363,391**	**10,321,554**	**13,542,209**	**15,392,968**	**100.00**	**13.67**
AMERICAS	**4,057,047**	**4,554,278**	**5,627,872**	**7,698,361**	**9,169,212**	**59.57**	**19.11**
NORTH AMERICA	**2,124,065**	**2,287,320**	**2,620,153**	**3,311,925**	**3,717,242**	**24.15**	**12.24**
Canada	320,233	334,181	400,066	487,676	489,294	3.18	0.33
Mexico	156,493	227,763	279,418	417,129	534,096	3.47	28.04
United States of America	1,647,339	1,725,376	1,940,669	2,407,120	2,693,852	17.50	11.91
SOUTH AMERICA	**1,932,982**	**2,266,958**	**3,007,719**	**4,386,436**	**5,451,970**	**35.42**	**24.29**
Argentina	422,642	475,615	647,130	845,376	876,549	5.69	3.69
Bolivia	77,613	90,743	102,858	136,401	163,098	1.06	19.57
Brazil	423,388	457,088	663,047	868,090	1,006,138	6.54	15.90
Chile	391,320	507,885	715,078	1,130,507	1,320,795	8.58	16.83
Colombia	307,110	384,878	447,295	733,558	832,127	5.41	13.44
Ecuador	193,559	219,380	249,836	326,237	415,487	2.70	27.36
Venezuela	117,350	131,369	182,475	346,267	837,776	5.44	141.95
EAST ASIA AND THE PACIFIC	**231,348**	**176,330**	**350,998**	**426,493**	**422,939**	**2.75**	**-0.83**
NORTH-EAST ASIA	**231,348**	**176,330**	**350,998**	**426,493**	**422,939**	**2.75**	**-0.83**
Japan	231,348	176,330	350,998	426,493	422,939	2.75	-0.83
EUROPE	**1,451,432**	**1,522,074**	**1,816,534**	**2,300,629**	**2,354,222**	**15.29**	**2.33**
SOUTHERN EUROPE	**601,067**	**655,986**	**802,753**	**997,616**	**1,120,088**	**7.28**	**12.28**
Italy	200,986	204,828	270,370	301,443	301,749	1.96	0.10
Spain	400,081	451,158	532,383	696,173	818,339	5.32	17.55
WESTERN EUROPE	**850,365**	**866,088**	**1,013,781**	**1,303,013**	**1,234,134**	**8.02**	**-5.29**
France	510,473	504,193	576,014	743,204	671,424	4.36	-9.66
Germany	339,892	361,895	437,767	559,809	562,710	3.66	0.52
NOT SPECIFIED	**1,866,746**	**2,110,709**	**2,526,150**	**3,116,726**	**3,446,595**	**22.39**	**10.58**
Other countries of the World	1,866,746	2,110,709	2,526,150	3,116,726	3,446,595	22.39	10.58

Yearbook of Tourism Statistics, Data 2009 – 2013, 2015 Edition

PHILIPPINES

1. Arrivals of non-resident tourists at national borders, by country of residence

	2009	2010	2011	2012	2013	Market share 2013	% Change 2013-2012
TOTAL	3,017,099	3,520,472	3,917,454	4,272,811	4,681,307	100.00	9.56
AFRICA	3,082	3,584	4,193	5,163	5,515	0.12	6.82
SOUTHERN AFRICA	2,311	2,774	3,221	3,691	3,979	0.08	7.80
South Africa	2,311	2,774	3,221	3,691	3,979	0.08	7.80
WEST AFRICA	771	810	972	1,472	1,536	0.03	4.35
Nigeria	771	810	972	1,472	1,536	0.03	4.35
AMERICAS	686,293	711,356	747,656	783,295	814,589	17.40	4.00
NORTH AMERICA	682,696	707,706	743,448	778,162	808,531	17.27	3.90
Canada	99,012	106,345	117,423	123,699	131,381	2.81	6.21
Mexico	1,147	1,195	1,498	1,837	2,586	0.06	40.77
United States of America	582,537	600,166	624,527	652,626	674,564	14.41	3.36
SOUTH AMERICA	3,597	3,650	4,208	5,133	6,058	0.13	18.02
Argentina	687	684	786	1,112	1,259	0.03	13.22
Brazil	1,595	1,652	2,078	2,559	3,043	0.07	18.91
Colombia	573	581	689	754	989	0.02	31.17
Peru	422	403	391	433	478	0.01	10.39
Venezuela	320	330	264	275	289	0.01	5.09
EAST ASIA AND THE PACIFIC	1,643,595	2,064,400	2,404,758	2,666,888	2,997,380	64.03	12.39
NORTH-EAST ASIA	1,202,995	1,563,013	1,844,942	2,038,987	2,298,597	49.10	12.73
China	155,019	187,446	243,137	250,883	426,352	9.11	69.94
Hong Kong, China	122,786	133,746	112,106	118,666	126,008	2.69	6.19
Japan	324,980	358,744	375,496	412,474	433,705	9.26	5.15
Korea, Republic of	497,936	740,622	925,204	1,031,155	1,165,789	24.90	13.06
Macao, China			7,261	9,298	7,644	0.16	-17.79
Taiwan, Province of China	102,274	142,455	181,738	216,511	139,099	2.97	-35.75
SOUTH-EAST ASIA	255,586	298,176	331,672	375,190	422,061	9.02	12.49
Brunei Darussalam	3,592	4,072	5,247	5,992	8,297	0.18	38.47
Cambodia	1,942	2,244	2,469	2,661	3,228	0.07	21.31
Indonesia	29,188	31,997	34,542	36,627	45,582	0.97	24.45
Lao People's Democratic Republic	831	1,079	971	1,088	1,062	0.02	-2.39
Malaysia	68,679	79,694	91,752	114,513	109,437	2.34	-4.43
Myanmar	5,445	3,983	3,246	4,290	4,948	0.11	15.34
Singapore	98,305	121,083	137,802	148,215	175,034	3.74	18.09
Thailand	34,212	36,713	37,862	40,987	47,874	1.02	16.80
Viet Nam	13,392	17,311	17,781	20,817	26,599	0.57	27.78
AUSTRALASIA	142,852	158,792	183,518	205,250	228,806	4.89	11.48
Australia	132,330	147,469	170,736	191,150	213,023	4.55	11.44
New Zealand	10,522	11,323	12,782	14,100	15,783	0.34	11.94
MELANESIA	2,835	3,475	3,594	4,726	5,668	0.12	19.93
Papua New Guinea	2,835	3,475	3,594	4,726	5,668	0.12	19.93
MICRONESIA	39,327	40,944	41,032	42,735	42,248	0.90	-1.14
Guam	39,323	40,928	41,013	42,695	42,204	0.90	-1.15
Nauru	4	16	19	40	44	0.00	10.00
EUROPE	329,840	360,991	402,073	442,686	479,472	10.24	8.31
CENTRAL/EASTERN EUROPE	16,522	21,821	27,171	37,916	46,907	1.00	23.71
Poland	2,372	2,917	3,263	4,187	5,653	0.12	35.01
Russian Federation	10,674	14,642	20,185	28,270	35,404	0.76	25.24
Other countries Central/East Europe	3,476	4,262	3,723	5,459	5,850	0.12	7.16
NORTHERN EUROPE	138,950	150,178	164,205	181,978	196,441	4.20	7.95
Denmark	10,971	11,609	13,004	13,556	13,618	0.29	0.46
Finland	3,331	4,024	4,780	5,399	5,906	0.13	9.39
Ireland	5,475	5,368	6,023	8,362	10,576	0.23	26.48
Norway	14,781	16,742	17,959	19,572	20,625	0.44	5.38
Sweden	13,383	15,510	17,973	21,807	22,957	0.49	5.27
United Kingdom	91,009	96,925	104,466	113,282	122,759	2.62	8.37
SOUTHERN EUROPE	29,281	32,388	45,781	43,268	43,079	0.92	-0.44
Andorra			12,250	7,333	4,840	0.10	-34.00
Greece	1,666	2,104	1,855	1,834	1,879	0.04	2.45
Italy	15,047	16,350	15,798	16,740	17,668	0.38	5.54

569

PHILIPPINES

1. Arrivals of non-resident tourists at national borders, by country of residence

	2009	2010	2011	2012	2013	Market share 2013	% Change 2013-2012
Portugal	865	1,175	1,230	1,466	1,566	0.03	6.82
Spain	11,703	12,759	14,648	15,895	17,126	0.37	7.74
WESTERN EUROPE	**138,946**	**149,193**	**157,265**	**170,498**	**181,639**	**3.88**	**6.53**
Austria	10,974	11,537	11,603	11,718	12,106	0.26	3.31
Belgium	9,729	10,512	10,959	11,649	11,454	0.24	-1.67
France	24,572	27,302	29,591	33,709	39,042	0.83	15.82
Germany	55,912	58,725	61,193	67,023	70,949	1.52	5.86
Luxembourg	462	666	555	647	586	0.01	-9.43
Netherlands	18,586	19,227	21,029	22,195	22,595	0.48	1.80
Switzerland	18,711	21,224	22,335	23,557	24,907	0.53	5.73
EAST MEDITERRANEAN EUROPE	**6,141**	**7,411**	**7,651**	**9,026**	**11,406**	**0.24**	**26.37**
Israel	4,061	4,525	4,990	5,895	7,675	0.16	30.20
Turkey	2,080	2,886	2,661	3,131	3,731	0.08	19.16
MIDDLE EAST	**46,811**	**48,716**	**55,829**	**57,275**	**68,916**	**1.47**	**20.32**
Bahrain	3,014	3,334	3,304	3,528	3,424	0.07	-2.95
Egypt	1,036	1,135	1,389	1,619	1,763	0.04	8.89
Jordan	635	691	755	756	833	0.02	10.19
Kuwait	9,605	5,230	5,430	4,877	5,048	0.11	3.51
Qatar	2,932	3,378	3,602	3,771	3,724	0.08	-1.25
Saudi Arabia	19,101	22,214	27,945	30,040	38,969	0.83	29.72
United Arab Emirates	10,488	12,734	13,404	12,684	15,155	0.32	19.48
SOUTH ASIA	**46,960**	**50,914**	**61,259**	**63,860**	**69,333**	**1.48**	**8.57**
Bangladesh	2,107	2,569	2,862	3,188	3,244	0.07	1.76
India	32,817	34,581	42,844	46,395	52,206	1.12	12.53
Iran, Islamic Republic of	4,256	5,516	6,258	5,017	3,652	0.08	-27.21
Nepal	1,411	1,794	1,874	2,107	2,403	0.05	14.05
Pakistan	2,705	2,722	3,344	3,541	3,765	0.08	6.33
Sri Lanka	3,664	3,732	4,077	3,612	4,063	0.09	12.49
NOT SPECIFIED	**260,518**	**280,511**	**241,686**	**253,644**	**246,102**	**5.26**	**-2.97**
Other countries of the World	62,597	52,066	34,534	37,701	42,490	0.91	12.70
Nationals Residing Abroad (*)	197,921	228,445	207,152	215,943	203,612	4.35	-5.71

Yearbook of Tourism Statistics, Data 2009 – 2013, 2015 Edition

PHILIPPINES

4. Arrivals of non-resident tourists in all types of accommodation establishments, by country of residence

		2009	2010	2011	2012	2013	Market share 2013	% Change 2013-2012
TOTAL	(*)	**2,960,282**	**3,461,007**	**3,884,055**	**4,237,935**	**4,637,026**	**100.00**	**9.42**
AFRICA		**2,950**	**3,466**	**4,152**	**5,118**	**5,426**	**0.12**	**6.02**
SOUTHERN AFRICA		**2,180**	**2,657**	**3,181**	**3,646**	**3,891**	**0.08**	**6.72**
South Africa		2,180	2,657	3,181	3,646	3,891	0.08	6.72
WEST AFRICA		**770**	**809**	**971**	**1,472**	**1,535**	**0.03**	**4.28**
Nigeria		770	809	971	1,472	1,535	0.03	4.28
AMERICAS		**684,028**	**709,423**	**745,291**	**782,046**	**811,835**	**17.51**	**3.81**
NORTH AMERICA		**680,833**	**706,129**	**741,124**	**776,948**	**805,850**	**17.38**	**3.72**
Canada		98,563	106,062	117,055	123,412	130,841	2.82	6.02
Mexico		1,095	1,124	1,475	1,814	2,571	0.06	41.73
United States of America		581,175	598,943	622,594	651,722	672,438	14.50	3.18
SOUTH AMERICA		**3,195**	**3,294**	**4,167**	**5,098**	**5,985**	**0.13**	**17.40**
Argentina		665	644	781	1,107	1,245	0.03	12.47
Brazil		1,492	1,565	2,060	2,547	3,015	0.07	18.37
Colombia		437	505	681	750	979	0.02	30.53
Peru		282	254	383	424	461	0.01	8.73
Venezuela		319	326	262	270	285	0.01	5.56
EAST ASIA AND THE PACIFIC		**1,612,169**	**2,034,014**	**2,377,612**	**2,637,300**	**2,963,308**	**63.91**	**12.36**
NORTH-EAST ASIA		**1,189,983**	**1,551,201**	**1,828,624**	**2,020,515**	**2,278,755**	**49.14**	**12.78**
China		146,566	180,346	238,126	245,153	417,408	9.00	70.26
Hong Kong, China		122,715	133,721	112,076	118,579	125,571	2.71	5.90
Japan		323,638	357,660	374,128	410,976	433,309	9.34	5.43
Korea, Republic of		496,031	738,258	923,691	1,029,617	1,164,152	25.11	13.07
Taiwan, Province of China		101,033	141,216	180,603	216,190	138,315	2.98	-36.02
SOUTH-EAST ASIA		**240,037**	**282,845**	**321,147**	**365,207**	**409,483**	**8.83**	**12.12**
Brunei Darussalam		3,576	4,052	5,210	5,985	8,294	0.18	38.58
Cambodia		1,940	2,242	2,440	2,660	3,228	0.07	21.35
Indonesia		24,030	27,207	31,640	34,231	42,307	0.91	23.59
Lao People's Democratic Republic		831	1,078	942	1,088	1,062	0.02	-2.39
Malaysia		67,616	78,116	90,133	112,923	107,816	2.33	-4.52
Myanmar		1,763	1,693	1,652	1,995	2,578	0.06	29.22
Singapore		98,113	120,961	137,741	147,963	173,462	3.74	17.23
Thailand		32,594	35,359	36,970	40,337	47,503	1.02	17.77
Viet Nam		9,574	12,137	14,419	18,025	23,233	0.50	28.89
AUSTRALASIA		**140,000**	**155,560**	**183,221**	**204,119**	**227,165**	**4.90**	**11.29**
Australia		129,608	144,432	170,480	190,080	211,462	4.56	11.25
New Zealand		10,392	11,128	12,741	14,039	15,703	0.34	11.85
MELANESIA		**2,822**	**3,464**	**3,588**	**4,724**	**5,658**	**0.12**	**19.77**
Papua New Guinea		2,822	3,464	3,588	4,724	5,658	0.12	19.77
MICRONESIA		**39,327**	**40,944**	**41,032**	**42,735**	**42,247**	**0.91**	**-1.14**
Guam		39,323	40,928	41,013	42,695	42,204	0.91	-1.15
Nauru		4	16	19	40	43	0.00	7.50
EUROPE		**314,335**	**341,812**	**384,006**	**427,235**	**465,674**	**10.04**	**9.00**
CENTRAL/EASTERN EUROPE		**12,593**	**17,427**	**25,178**	**35,237**	**43,446**	**0.94**	**23.30**
Poland		1,958	2,403	3,035	3,847	4,988	0.11	29.66
Russian Federation		8,843	12,643	19,388	27,526	34,327	0.74	24.71
Commonwealth Independent States		1,792	2,381	2,755	3,864	4,131	0.09	6.91
NORTHERN EUROPE		**134,152**	**144,198**	**162,000**	**179,309**	**194,822**	**4.20**	**8.65**
Denmark		10,915	11,541	12,952	13,536	13,585	0.29	0.36
Finland		3,310	4,013	4,780	5,396	5,892	0.13	9.19
Ireland		5,398	5,260	5,997	8,330	10,555	0.23	26.71
Norway		14,758	16,692	17,930	19,527	20,584	0.44	5.41
Sweden		13,345	15,404	17,949	21,725	22,861	0.49	5.23
United Kingdom		86,426	91,288	102,392	110,795	121,345	2.62	9.52
SOUTHERN EUROPE		**26,726**	**29,662**	**33,283**	**35,665**	**37,998**	**0.82**	**6.54**
Greece		1,583	1,977	1,751	1,760	1,769	0.04	0.51
Italy		13,165	14,118	15,711	16,660	17,600	0.38	5.64
Portugal		814	1,123	1,217	1,387	1,545	0.03	11.39
Spain		11,164	12,444	14,604	15,858	17,084	0.37	7.73

571

PHILIPPINES

4. Arrivals of non-resident tourists in all types of accommodation establishments, by country of residence

	2009	2010	2011	2012	2013	Market share 2013	% Change 2013-2012
WESTERN EUROPE	**135,031**	**143,440**	**156,012**	**168,159**	**178,115**	**3.84**	**5.92**
Austria	10,728	11,056	11,550	11,622	11,929	0.26	2.64
Belgium	9,547	10,392	10,917	11,595	11,406	0.25	-1.63
France	23,584	26,360	29,540	33,268	38,970	0.84	17.14
Germany	54,007	55,904	60,355	65,551	68,168	1.47	3.99
Luxembourg	449	655	550	644	573	0.01	-11.02
Netherlands	18,322	18,858	20,861	22,060	22,427	0.48	1.66
Switzerland	18,394	20,215	22,239	23,419	24,642	0.53	5.22
EAST MEDITERRANEAN EUROPE	**5,833**	**7,085**	**7,533**	**8,865**	**11,293**	**0.24**	**27.39**
Israel	4,057	4,521	4,990	5,895	7,671	0.17	30.13
Turkey	1,776	2,564	2,543	2,970	3,622	0.08	21.95
MIDDLE EAST	**46,775**	**48,641**	**55,782**	**57,237**	**68,897**	**1.49**	**20.37**
Bahrain	3,014	3,334	3,304	3,528	3,424	0.07	-2.95
Egypt	1,001	1,063	1,342	1,581	1,746	0.04	10.44
Jordan	635	691	755	756	832	0.02	10.05
Kuwait	9,605	5,230	5,430	4,877	5,047	0.11	3.49
Qatar	2,932	3,378	3,602	3,771	3,724	0.08	-1.25
Saudi Arabia	19,100	22,214	27,945	30,040	38,969	0.84	29.72
United Arab Emirates	10,488	12,731	13,404	12,684	15,155	0.33	19.48
SOUTH ASIA	**41,634**	**45,410**	**57,366**	**60,039**	**65,091**	**1.40**	**8.41**
Bangladesh	1,923	2,333	2,680	2,978	3,140	0.07	5.44
India	29,293	30,691	40,195	43,578	49,006	1.06	12.46
Iran, Islamic Republic of	4,232	5,513	6,237	5,016	3,652	0.08	-27.19
Nepal	1,389	1,762	1,853	2,092	2,249	0.05	7.50
Pakistan	2,674	2,647	3,272	3,517	3,659	0.08	4.04
Sri Lanka	2,123	2,464	3,129	2,858	3,385	0.07	18.44
NOT SPECIFIED	**258,391**	**278,241**	**259,846**	**268,960**	**256,795**	**5.54**	**-4.52**
Other countries of the World	60,470	49,796	52,694	53,017	53,183	1.15	0.31
Nationals Residing Abroad (*)	197,921	228,445	207,152	215,943	203,612	4.39	-5.71

Yearbook of Tourism Statistics, Data 2009 – 2013, 2015 Edition

POLAND

2. Arrivals of non-resident visitors at national borders, by nationality

	2009	2010	2011	2012	2013	Market share 2013	% Change 2013-2012
TOTAL (*)	53,839,000	58,340,000	60,745,000	67,390,000	72,310,000	100.00	7.30
AFRICA	20,000	20,000	15,000	15,000	15,000	0.02	
OTHER AFRICA	20,000	20,000	15,000	15,000	15,000	0.02	
All countries of Africa	20,000	20,000	15,000	15,000	15,000	0.02	
AMERICAS	338,000	395,000	400,000	425,000	425,000	0.59	
NORTH AMERICA	298,000	340,000	365,000	390,000	390,000	0.54	
Canada	68,000	75,000	80,000	90,000	80,000	0.11	-11.11
Mexico			15,000				
United States of America	230,000	265,000	270,000	300,000	310,000	0.43	3.33
SOUTH AMERICA	10,000	15,000	25,000	25,000	25,000	0.03	
Argentina			10,000	10,000	10,000	0.01	
Brazil	10,000	15,000	15,000	15,000	15,000	0.02	
OTHER AMERICAS	30,000	40,000	10,000	10,000	10,000	0.01	
Other countries of the Americas	30,000	40,000	10,000	10,000	10,000	0.01	
EAST ASIA AND THE PACIFIC	207,000	280,000	300,000	320,000	355,000	0.49	10.94
NORTH-EAST ASIA	100,000	135,000	135,000	135,000	170,000	0.24	25.93
China	25,000	35,000	40,000	40,000	45,000	0.06	12.50
Hong Kong, China	5,000	5,000	5,000	5,000	5,000	0.01	
Japan	35,000	60,000	45,000	40,000	45,000	0.06	12.50
Korea, Republic of	35,000	35,000	35,000	40,000	65,000	0.09	62.50
Taiwan, Province of China			10,000	10,000	10,000	0.01	
SOUTH-EAST ASIA			30,000	30,000	30,000	0.04	
Indonesia			5,000	5,000	5,000	0.01	
Malaysia			5,000	5,000	5,000	0.01	
Philippines			5,000	5,000	5,000	0.01	
Singapore			10,000	10,000	10,000	0.01	
Thailand			5,000	5,000	5,000	0.01	
AUSTRALASIA	37,000	55,000	65,000	85,000	85,000	0.12	
Australia	37,000	55,000	55,000	75,000	75,000	0.10	
New Zealand			10,000	10,000	10,000	0.01	
OTHER EAST ASIA AND THE PACIFIC	70,000	90,000	70,000	70,000	70,000	0.10	
Other countries East Asia/Pacific	70,000	90,000	70,000	70,000	70,000	0.10	
EUROPE	53,220,000	57,540,000	59,950,000	66,545,000	71,430,000	98.78	7.34
CENTRAL/EASTERN EUROPE	24,170,000	28,475,000	31,030,000	36,410,000	38,905,000	53.80	6.85
Armenia			20,000	20,000	20,000	0.03	
Belarus	2,360,000	3,090,000	3,450,000	3,920,000	3,950,000	5.46	0.77
Bulgaria	85,000	80,000	85,000	100,000	90,000	0.12	-10.00
Czech Republic	8,180,000	9,240,000	10,840,000	12,380,000	13,380,000	18.50	8.08
Estonia	130,000	115,000	120,000	110,000	120,000	0.17	9.09
Georgia			5,000	5,000	5,000	0.01	
Hungary	225,000	220,000	230,000	235,000	245,000	0.34	4.26
Kazakhstan			40,000	40,000	40,000	0.06	
Latvia	390,000	350,000	360,000	385,000	365,000	0.50	-5.19
Lithuania	2,640,000	2,690,000	2,420,000	3,010,000	2,890,000	4.00	-3.99
Republic of Moldova			40,000	40,000	40,000	0.06	
Romania	90,000	120,000	120,000	125,000	135,000	0.19	8.00
Russian Federation	1,210,000	1,530,000	1,850,000	2,670,000	3,570,000	4.94	33.71
Slovakia	5,040,000	6,010,000	5,620,000	6,630,000	6,725,000	9.30	1.43
Ukraine	3,820,000	5,030,000	5,830,000	6,740,000	7,330,000	10.14	8.75
NORTHERN EUROPE	1,085,000	1,150,000	1,100,000	1,205,000	1,350,000	1.87	12.03
Denmark	120,000	125,000	110,000	110,000	140,000	0.19	27.27
Finland	75,000	90,000	95,000	85,000	95,000	0.13	11.76
Iceland			5,000	5,000	5,000	0.01	
Ireland	80,000	80,000	85,000	120,000	95,000	0.13	-20.83
Norway	120,000	120,000	120,000	140,000	190,000	0.26	35.71
Sweden	190,000	195,000	185,000	205,000	205,000	0.28	
United Kingdom	500,000	540,000	500,000	540,000	620,000	0.86	14.81
SOUTHERN EUROPE	550,000	580,000	630,000	660,000	685,000	0.95	3.79
Croatia	30,000	20,000	20,000	20,000	20,000	0.03	

Yearbook of Tourism Statistics, Data 2009 – 2013, 2015 Edition

POLAND

2. Arrivals of non-resident visitors at national borders, by nationality

	2009	2010	2011	2012	2013	Market share 2013	% Change 2013-2012
Greece	45,000	35,000	40,000	50,000	30,000	0.04	-40.00
Italy	255,000	285,000	315,000	320,000	335,000	0.46	4.69
Portugal	70,000	75,000	70,000	80,000	45,000	0.06	-43.75
Serbia			10,000	10,000	10,000	0.01	
Slovenia	20,000	20,000	20,000	20,000	20,000	0.03	
Spain	130,000	145,000	155,000	160,000	225,000	0.31	40.63
WESTERN EUROPE	**27,145,000**	**27,030,000**	**26,975,000**	**27,960,000**	**30,165,000**	**41.72**	**7.89**
Austria	325,000	345,000	355,000	360,000	355,000	0.49	-1.39
Belgium	110,000	125,000	130,000	140,000	130,000	0.18	-7.14
France	240,000	260,000	280,000	280,000	310,000	0.43	10.71
Germany	26,070,000	25,860,000	25,740,000	26,720,000	28,900,000	39.97	8.16
Luxembourg	5,000	10,000	20,000	10,000	5,000	0.01	-50.00
Netherlands	335,000	370,000	390,000	390,000	400,000	0.55	2.56
Switzerland	60,000	60,000	60,000	60,000	65,000	0.09	8.33
EAST MEDITERRANEAN EUROPE	**120,000**	**145,000**	**175,000**	**200,000**	**215,000**	**0.30**	**7.50**
Cyprus	5,000	5,000		5,000	5,000	0.01	
Israel	60,000	70,000	90,000	90,000	90,000	0.12	
Turkey	55,000	70,000	85,000	105,000	120,000	0.17	14.29
OTHER EUROPE	**150,000**	**160,000**	**40,000**	**110,000**	**110,000**	**0.15**	
Other countries of Europe	150,000	160,000	40,000	110,000	110,000	0.15	
MIDDLE EAST	**15,000**	**15,000**	**15,000**	**15,000**	**15,000**	**0.02**	
All countries of Middle East	15,000	15,000	15,000	15,000	15,000	0.02	
SOUTH ASIA	**20,000**	**30,000**	**20,000**	**20,000**	**20,000**	**0.03**	
India	10,000	15,000	15,000	15,000	15,000	0.02	
Other countries of South Asia	10,000	15,000	5,000	5,000	5,000	0.01	
NOT SPECIFIED	**19,000**	**60,000**	**45,000**	**50,000**	**50,000**	**0.07**	
Other countries of the World	19,000	60,000	45,000	50,000	50,000	0.07	

Yearbook of Tourism Statistics, Data 2009 – 2013, 2015 Edition

POLAND

3. Arrivals of non-resident tourists in hotels and similar establishments, by country of residence

		2009	2010	2011	2012	2013	Market share 2013	% Change 2013-2012
TOTAL	(*)	**3,394,053**	**3,667,358**	**3,907,422**	**4,369,548**	**4,686,963**	**100.00**	**7.26**
AFRICA		**8,089**	**8,370**	**7,530**	**9,272**	**12,832**	**0.27**	**38.40**
EAST AFRICA		**615**	**1,065**	**618**	**1,198**	**1,488**	**0.03**	**24.21**
Burundi		39	33	42	43	35	0.00	-18.60
Comoros		4	2		3	5	0.00	66.67
Djibouti		23	4	8	1	3	0.00	200.00
Eritrea					2			
Ethiopia		112	205	54	331	163	0.00	-50.76
Kenya		153	173	167	266	343	0.01	28.95
Madagascar		5	36	17	15	21	0.00	40.00
Malawi		10	12	4	58	23	0.00	-60.34
Mauritius		23	57	33	47	81	0.00	72.34
Mozambique		5	13	21	41	3	0.00	-92.68
Reunion		1			3			
Rwanda		14	138	25	126	225	0.00	78.57
Seychelles		18	17	20	58	33	0.00	-43.10
Somalia		23	45	52	36	23	0.00	-36.11
Uganda		60	98	68	87	149	0.00	71.26
United Republic of Tanzania		34	171	37	28	173	0.00	517.86
Zambia		29	32	14	25	71	0.00	184.00
Zimbabwe		62	29	56	28	137	0.00	389.29
CENTRAL AFRICA		**656**	**822**	**655**	**802**	**1,855**	**0.04**	**131.30**
Angola		292	581	402	389	1,176	0.03	202.31
Cameroon		95	86	80	113	109	0.00	-3.54
Central African Republic		36	37	80	70	290	0.01	314.29
Chad		25	3	4	62	108	0.00	74.19
Congo		147	88	71	52	157	0.00	201.92
Democratic Republic of the Congo		43	23	15	112	7	0.00	-93.75
Equatorial Guinea			4	3	2	8	0.00	300.00
Gabon		18			2			
NORTH AFRICA		**2,402**	**3,005**	**2,841**	**3,200**	**4,361**	**0.09**	**36.28**
Algeria		962	1,556	1,632	1,655	2,566	0.05	55.05
Morocco		533	826	500	683	853	0.02	24.89
Sudan		71	56	116	171	71	0.00	-58.48
Tunisia		481	498	574	658	854	0.02	29.79
Western Sahara		355	69	19	33	17	0.00	-48.48
SOUTHERN AFRICA		**2,207**	**1,755**	**2,090**	**2,286**	**3,003**	**0.06**	**31.36**
Botswana		125	60	5	24	33	0.00	37.50
Lesotho		1	5	5	4	5	0.00	25.00
Namibia		124	26	48	48	63	0.00	31.25
South Africa		1,765	1,664	2,032	2,210	2,901	0.06	31.27
Swaziland		192				1	0.00	
WEST AFRICA		**2,209**	**1,723**	**1,326**	**1,786**	**2,125**	**0.05**	**18.98**
Benin		37	26	15	20	59	0.00	195.00
Burkina Faso		4	15	23	1	17	0.00	1,600.00
Cabo Verde		8	7	14	1			
Côte d'Ivoire		14	138	36	159	43	0.00	-72.96
Gambia		17	33	4	10	29	0.00	190.00
Ghana		31	78	65	59	105	0.00	77.97
Guinea		27	5	10	29	59	0.00	103.45
Guinea-Bissau		2		14	16			
Liberia		7	20	12	33	7	0.00	-78.79
Mali		19	28	27	36	26	0.00	-27.78
Mauritania		46	15	23	15	77	0.00	413.33
Niger		364	382	164	211	359	0.01	70.14
Nigeria		945	609	571	877	906	0.02	3.31
Saint Helena		22	24	7	6	10	0.00	66.67
Senegal		409	145	91	92	139	0.00	51.09
Sierra Leone		243	195	232	211	258	0.01	22.27
Togo		14	3	18	10	31	0.00	210.00
AMERICAS		**171,859**	**203,579**	**208,953**	**237,516**	**266,804**	**5.69**	**12.33**

575

Yearbook of Tourism Statistics, Data 2009 – 2013, 2015 Edition

POLAND

3. Arrivals of non-resident tourists in hotels and similar establishments, by country of residence

	2009	2010	2011	2012	2013	Market share 2013	% Change 2013-2012
CARIBBEAN	**735**	**673**	**1,662**	**1,399**	**1,103**	**0.02**	**-21.16**
Anguilla	12						
Antigua and Barbuda	9			14			
Aruba	16	11	3	36	21	0.00	-41.67
Bahamas	28	100	599	106	41	0.00	-61.32
Barbados	120	59	26	24	22	0.00	-8.33
Bermuda	23	13	28	252	24	0.00	-90.48
British Virgin Islands	1						
Cayman Islands	20	20	13	218	16	0.00	-92.66
Cuba	224	232	255	110	279	0.01	153.64
Dominica	8	18	31	15	148	0.00	886.67
Dominican Republic	28	54	122	199	44	0.00	-77.89
Grenada	2			3	6	0.00	100.00
Guadeloupe	11		1	59	13	0.00	-77.97
Haiti	12	16	40	23	10	0.00	-56.52
Jamaica	124	48	73	65	90	0.00	38.46
Martinique	2		3	2			
Netherlands Antilles	1			7			
Puerto Rico	80	86	451	224	317	0.01	41.52
Saint Kitts and Nevis	3						
Trinidad and Tobago	10	16	17	42	72	0.00	71.43
Turks and Caicos Islands	1						
CENTRAL AMERICA	**580**	**665**	**680**	**863**	**986**	**0.02**	**14.25**
Belize	90	36	65	155	97	0.00	-37.42
Costa Rica	192	150	195	270	272	0.01	0.74
El Salvador	57	54	106	57	137	0.00	140.35
Guatemala	49	64	56	96	100	0.00	4.17
Honduras	88	167	173	162	222	0.00	37.04
Nicaragua	33	135	31	55	23	0.00	-58.18
Panama	71	59	54	68	135	0.00	98.53
NORTH AMERICA	**158,082**	**186,488**	**190,195**	**214,478**	**239,749**	**5.12**	**11.78**
Canada	21,468	25,478	26,549	29,459	28,338	0.60	-3.81
Greenland	5	1			1	0.00	
Mexico	3,355	3,598	5,051	5,049	6,010	0.13	19.03
United States of America	133,254	157,411	158,595	179,970	205,400	4.38	14.13
SOUTH AMERICA	**12,462**	**15,753**	**16,416**	**20,776**	**24,966**	**0.53**	**20.17**
Argentina	2,063	2,046	2,967	2,913	4,257	0.09	46.14
Bolivia	605	1,041	1,036	1,055	1,133	0.02	7.39
Brazil	6,955	9,488	9,310	12,941	14,802	0.32	14.38
Chile	748	887	1,007	916	1,112	0.02	21.40
Colombia	437	571	719	1,085	1,025	0.02	-5.53
Ecuador	253	176	125	207	299	0.01	44.44
Falkland Islands, Malvinas	84	1	7	9	475	0.01	5,177.78
French Guiana	2	1	4	6	2	0.00	-66.67
Guyana	1	3	85	68	16	0.00	-76.47
Paraguay	14	61	74	50	64	0.00	28.00
Peru	450	280	270	435	350	0.01	-19.54
Suriname	65	33					
Uruguay	278	464	463	536	393	0.01	-26.68
Venezuela	507	701	349	555	1,038	0.02	87.03
EAST ASIA AND THE PACIFIC	**111,645**	**141,195**	**145,032**	**151,606**	**180,153**	**3.84**	**18.83**
NORTH-EAST ASIA	**86,574**	**109,545**	**103,918**	**106,092**	**130,401**	**2.78**	**22.91**
China	18,990	25,421	32,000	33,855	36,816	0.79	8.75
Hong Kong, China	3,403	3,912	4,566	3,824	5,374	0.11	40.53
Japan	32,860	48,772	37,353	38,685	47,200	1.01	22.01
Korea, Dem. People's Republic of	11,709	15,859	14,364	12,485	4,396	0.09	-64.79
Korea, Republic of	17,786	13,734	13,291	14,265	32,976	0.70	131.17
Macao, China	55	62	48	37	179	0.00	383.78
Mongolia	389	490	376	380	433	0.01	13.95
Taiwan, Province of China	1,382	1,295	1,920	2,561	3,027	0.06	18.20
SOUTH-EAST ASIA	**8,568**	**10,647**	**17,916**	**20,289**	**22,533**	**0.48**	**11.06**

POLAND

3. Arrivals of non-resident tourists in hotels and similar establishments, by country of residence

	2009	2010	2011	2012	2013	Market share 2013	% Change 2013-2012
Brunei Darussalam	5	54	12	14	28	0.00	100.00
Cambodia	7	38	11	11	3	0.00	-72.73
Indonesia	1,013	885	2,522	3,092	3,760	0.08	21.60
Lao People's Democratic Republic	17	16	43	161	41	0.00	-74.53
Malaysia	952	1,170	2,041	3,024	3,028	0.06	0.13
Myanmar	10	2	3	58	97	0.00	67.24
Philippines	991	824	2,317	1,212	1,838	0.04	51.65
Singapore	2,052	4,004	5,738	7,452	8,164	0.17	9.55
Thailand	1,651	1,987	3,545	3,176	3,596	0.08	13.22
Timor-Leste		1	3	4	72	0.00	1,700.00
Viet Nam	1,870	1,666	1,681	2,085	1,906	0.04	-8.59
AUSTRALASIA	**16,363**	**20,883**	**23,091**	**25,031**	**27,107**	**0.58**	**8.29**
Australia	14,713	18,647	20,988	22,484	24,686	0.53	9.79
New Zealand	1,650	2,236	2,103	2,547	2,421	0.05	-4.95
MELANESIA	**94**	**35**	**65**	**153**	**76**	**0.00**	**-50.33**
Fiji	46	8	14	66	36	0.00	-45.45
New Caledonia	13	8	35	74	37	0.00	-50.00
Norfolk Island	27						
Papua New Guinea	8	19	16	13	3	0.00	-76.92
MICRONESIA	**3**	**2**	**14**	**5**	**9**	**0.00**	**80.00**
Guam	3	2	8	2	5	0.00	150.00
Micronesia, Federated States of			6	3	4	0.00	33.33
POLYNESIA	**43**	**83**	**28**	**36**	**27**	**0.00**	**-25.00**
American Samoa	28			5			
French Polynesia	9	36	24	31	27	0.00	-12.90
Samoa	5						
Tonga	1	47	4				
EUROPE	**3,063,367**	**3,260,437**	**3,494,942**	**3,891,459**	**4,131,452**	**88.15**	**6.17**
CENTRAL/EASTERN EUROPE	**639,280**	**727,434**	**870,726**	**1,104,337**	**1,225,672**	**26.15**	**10.99**
Armenia	2,376	3,119	3,521	3,671	3,960	0.08	7.87
Azerbaijan	915	720	793	899	1,394	0.03	55.06
Belarus	63,213	72,545	93,956	141,443	182,874	3.90	29.29
Bulgaria	8,450	9,297	9,488	10,416	10,832	0.23	3.99
Czech Republic	66,975	68,726	77,388	84,857	82,068	1.75	-3.29
Estonia	31,558	30,510	34,057	34,970	37,331	0.80	6.75
Georgia	1,780	1,979	1,663	1,790	2,529	0.05	41.28
Hungary	40,192	41,239	44,522	51,620	50,364	1.07	-2.43
Kazakhstan	2,369	2,494	3,650	3,251	3,860	0.08	18.73
Kyrgyzstan	95	184	288	354	341	0.01	-3.67
Latvia	34,689	40,106	46,530	53,849	59,017	1.26	9.60
Lithuania	88,702	87,690	91,868	94,756	97,543	2.08	2.94
Republic of Moldova	2,077	2,099	2,349	2,550	2,494	0.05	-2.20
Romania	17,785	23,302	24,693	27,234	32,162	0.69	18.10
Russian Federation	149,529	198,801	255,376	361,642	376,891	8.04	4.22
Slovakia	33,244	36,316	42,123	43,613	47,283	1.01	8.41
Tajikistan	47	164	60	132	139	0.00	5.30
Turkmenistan	31	26	56	117	60	0.00	-48.72
Ukraine	94,935	107,365	137,399	185,942	233,473	4.98	25.56
Uzbekistan	318	752	946	1,231	1,057	0.02	-14.13
NORTHERN EUROPE	**671,581**	**692,474**	**698,763**	**769,810**	**795,507**	**16.97**	**3.34**
Denmark	81,265	74,855	78,987	83,707	79,503	1.70	-5.02
Faeroe Islands	4						
Finland	42,831	52,596	59,813	57,081	52,762	1.13	-7.57
Iceland	1,662	2,531	1,750	2,534	2,323	0.05	-8.33
Ireland	37,327	38,081	37,775	49,747	37,797	0.81	-24.02
Norway	86,554	96,225	98,166	125,957	147,466	3.15	17.08
Svalbard and Jan Mayen Islands	11	2					
Sweden	97,659	93,584	97,968	108,503	119,828	2.56	10.44
United Kingdom	324,268	334,600	324,304	342,281	355,828	7.59	3.96
SOUTHERN EUROPE	**323,206**	**349,942**	**400,845**	**408,597**	**402,009**	**8.58**	**-1.61**
Albania	1,384	1,313	1,631	1,551	2,381	0.05	53.51

577

POLAND

3. Arrivals of non-resident tourists in hotels and similar establishments, by country of residence

	2009	2010	2011	2012	2013	Market share 2013	% Change 2013-2012
Andorra	122	372	276	282	267	0.01	-5.32
Bosnia and Herzegovina	1,167	774	1,131	1,273	1,077	0.02	-15.40
Croatia	6,067	6,570	7,757	11,971	8,824	0.19	-26.29
Gibraltar	26	38	46	135	102	0.00	-24.44
Greece	15,014	12,218	14,071	15,978	11,950	0.25	-25.21
Holy See	161	138	108		145	0.00	
Italy	168,068	181,952	195,474	201,393	203,213	4.34	0.90
Malta	515	714	1,285	1,260	1,258	0.03	-0.16
Montenegro	126	153	372	360	458	0.01	27.22
Portugal	16,659	18,212	19,771	22,500	18,146	0.39	-19.35
San Marino	116	26	179	27	395	0.01	1,362.96
Serbia	1,793	4,014	3,537	3,992	5,357	0.11	34.19
Slovenia	8,176	7,869	9,005	9,306	9,646	0.21	3.65
Spain	103,125	114,920	145,465	137,689	138,003	2.94	0.23
TFYR of Macedonia	687	659	737	880	787	0.02	-10.57
WESTERN EUROPE	**1,286,299**	**1,335,250**	**1,360,478**	**1,435,839**	**1,536,531**	**32.78**	**7.01**
Austria	50,882	54,543	57,533	58,663	59,779	1.28	1.90
Belgium	50,908	57,511	60,923	57,447	58,942	1.26	2.60
France	156,874	166,367	177,404	175,231	180,558	3.85	3.04
Germany	903,444	928,727	928,048	1,002,624	1,087,300	23.20	8.45
Liechtenstein	1,122	246	337	262	388	0.01	48.09
Luxembourg	2,732	3,271	3,363	3,289	3,410	0.07	3.68
Monaco	398	278	207	207	253	0.01	22.22
Netherlands	89,011	92,260	98,327	99,291	105,018	2.24	5.77
Switzerland	30,928	32,047	34,336	38,825	40,883	0.87	5.30
EAST MEDITERRANEAN EUROPE	**143,001**	**155,337**	**164,130**	**172,876**	**171,733**	**3.66**	**-0.66**
Cyprus	2,413	2,194	1,976	2,359	2,296	0.05	-2.67
Israel	126,974	138,007	143,915	150,034	146,712	3.13	-2.21
Turkey	13,614	15,136	18,239	20,483	22,725	0.48	10.95
MIDDLE EAST	**6,591**	**6,658**	**8,620**	**13,860**	**15,306**	**0.33**	**10.43**
Bahrain	157	213	159	177	196	0.00	10.73
Egypt	1,277	1,422	1,546	2,288	2,456	0.05	7.34
Iraq	554	421	657	846	885	0.02	4.61
Jordan	274	201	408	389	490	0.01	25.96
Kuwait	519	484	676	573	1,056	0.02	84.29
Lebanon	836	461	610	688	1,154	0.02	67.73
Libya	207	281	308	479	992	0.02	107.10
Oman	40	96	26	160	162	0.00	1.25
Qatar	297	285	237	2,691	628	0.01	-76.66
Saudi Arabia	1,022	1,476	2,216	3,202	3,627	0.08	13.27
Syrian Arab Republic	290	299	467	395	304	0.01	-23.04
United Arab Emirates	1,080	989	1,271	1,740	3,315	0.07	90.52
Yemen	38	30	39	232	41	0.00	-82.33
SOUTH ASIA	**12,962**	**14,644**	**16,266**	**19,228**	**20,466**	**0.44**	**6.44**
Afghanistan	1,224	1,219	1,440	1,646	2,047	0.04	24.36
Bangladesh	765	784	918	1,306	1,698	0.04	30.02
Bhutan	262	394	107	20	66	0.00	230.00
India	8,231	9,226	10,826	12,963	13,590	0.29	4.84
Iran, Islamic Republic of	1,567	2,147	1,892	2,270	1,902	0.04	-16.21
Maldives	8	46	15	31	4	0.00	-87.10
Nepal	169	110	85	63	191	0.00	203.17
Pakistan	644	583	806	787	800	0.02	1.65
Sri Lanka	92	135	177	142	168	0.00	18.31
NOT SPECIFIED	**19,540**	**32,475**	**26,079**	**46,607**	**59,950**	**1.28**	**28.63**
Other countries of the World	19,540	32,475	26,079	46,607	59,950	1.28	28.63

578

POLAND

4. Arrivals of non-resident tourists in all types of accommodation establishments, by country of residence

	2009	2010	2011	2012	2013	Market share 2013	% Change 2013-2012
TOTAL	3,861,942	4,134,970	4,409,550	4,940,248	5,204,935	100.00	5.36
AFRICA	8,783	9,318	9,209	11,862	14,205	0.27	19.75
EAST AFRICA	689	1,231	788	1,346	1,655	0.03	22.96
Burundi	45	33	42	46	36	0.00	-21.74
Comoros	4	2		3	5	0.00	66.67
Djibouti	23	4	9	1	3	0.00	200.00
Eritrea				2			
Ethiopia	135	228	78	342	188	0.00	-45.03
Kenya	161	218	203	313	385	0.01	23.00
Madagascar	6	38	19	16	32	0.00	100.00
Malawi	10	15	7	60	33	0.00	-45.00
Mauritius	24	61	36	51	85	0.00	66.67
Mozambique	5	13	24	41	3	0.00	-92.68
Reunion	1			3			
Rwanda	14	147	28	130	238	0.00	83.08
Seychelles	18	17	20	73	34	0.00	-53.42
Somalia	24	84	52	38	24	0.00	-36.84
Uganda	75	110	102	107	176	0.00	64.49
United Republic of Tanzania	42	178	45	48	178	0.00	270.83
Zambia	32	47	61	29	77	0.00	165.52
Zimbabwe	70	36	62	43	158	0.00	267.44
CENTRAL AFRICA	740	930	711	860	2,033	0.04	136.40
Angola	295	619	419	413	1,281	0.02	210.17
Cameroon	114	115	102	131	140	0.00	6.87
Central African Republic	38	46	81	70	290	0.01	314.29
Chad	31	8	4	62	113	0.00	82.26
Congo	167	114	87	66	192	0.00	190.91
Democratic Republic of the Congo	51	24	15	114	9	0.00	-92.11
Equatorial Guinea		4	3	2	8	0.00	300.00
Gabon	44			2			
NORTH AFRICA	2,537	3,294	3,162	3,654	4,841	0.09	32.48
Algeria	1,022	1,644	1,778	1,893	2,828	0.05	49.39
Morocco	560	950	581	774	960	0.02	24.03
Sudan	76	64	137	177	79	0.00	-55.37
Tunisia	524	567	647	777	957	0.02	23.17
Western Sahara	355	69	19	33	17	0.00	-48.48
SOUTHERN AFRICA	2,314	1,892	2,457	2,431	3,225	0.06	32.66
Botswana	125	60	5	37	34	0.00	-8.11
Lesotho	2	11	5	4	5	0.00	25.00
Namibia	130	26	281	52	68	0.00	30.77
South Africa	1,865	1,795	2,166	2,338	3,117	0.06	33.32
Swaziland	192				1	0.00	
WEST AFRICA	2,503	1,971	2,091	3,571	2,451	0.05	-31.36
Benin	38	26	16	20	63	0.00	215.00
Burkina Faso	25	15	26	1	23	0.00	2,200.00
Cabo Verde	8	7	14	1			
Côte d'Ivoire	34	142	36	164	46	0.00	-71.95
Gambia	23	35	7	10	29	0.00	190.00
Ghana	36	91	89	80	139	0.00	73.75
Guinea	43	17	11	38	76	0.00	100.00
Guinea-Bissau	2		14	16			
Liberia	7	20	13	34	9	0.00	-73.53
Mali	20	30	27	1,167	31	0.00	-97.34
Mauritania	48	15	24	18	82	0.00	355.56
Niger	377	455	213	563	376	0.01	-33.21
Nigeria	1,059	720	1,224	1,097	1,112	0.02	1.37
Saint Helena	51	24	7	14	13	0.00	-7.14
Senegal	471	175	119	122	162	0.00	32.79
Sierra Leone	243	195	233	215	258	0.00	20.00
Togo	18	4	18	11	32	0.00	190.91
AMERICAS	184,464	217,610	225,130	256,431	284,437	5.46	10.92

579

Yearbook of Tourism Statistics, Data 2009 – 2013, 2015 Edition

POLAND

4. Arrivals of non-resident tourists in all types of accommodation establishments, by country of residence

	2009	2010	2011	2012	2013	Market share 2013	% Change 2013-2012
CARIBBEAN	**773**	**751**	**1,719**	**1,466**	**1,219**	**0.02**	**-16.85**
Anguilla	12						
Antigua and Barbuda	9			14			
Aruba	17	11	3	39	29	0.00	-25.64
Bahamas	33	108	600	108	41	0.00	-62.04
Barbados	132	65	26	25	73	0.00	192.00
Bermuda	25	13	28	252	24	0.00	-90.48
British Virgin Islands	1						
Cayman Islands	20	20	13	218	16	0.00	-92.66
Cuba	231	279	277	129	296	0.01	129.46
Dominica	8	18	31	19	149	0.00	684.21
Dominican Republic	30	56	126	205	56	0.00	-72.68
Grenada	2			3	6	0.00	100.00
Guadeloupe	12	3	1	60	13	0.00	-78.33
Haiti	13	17	48	26	13	0.00	-50.00
Jamaica	126	48	75	86	95	0.00	10.47
Martinique	2		3	2			
Netherlands Antilles	1			7			
Puerto Rico	85	93	457	230	333	0.01	44.78
Saint Kitts and Nevis	3						
Trinidad and Tobago	10	20	31	43	75	0.00	74.42
Turks and Caicos Islands	1						
CENTRAL AMERICA	**1,516**	**1,437**	**1,294**	**1,569**	**1,805**	**0.03**	**15.04**
Belize	90	41	68	155	99	0.00	-36.13
Costa Rica	198	249	220	299	290	0.01	-3.01
El Salvador	59	56	111	61	147	0.00	140.98
Guatemala	55	74	65	118	116	0.00	-1.69
Honduras	930	777	722	785	973	0.02	23.95
Nicaragua	113	143	45	64	31	0.00	-51.56
Panama	71	97	63	87	149	0.00	71.26
NORTH AMERICA	**168,322**	**197,815**	**203,052**	**229,348**	**253,084**	**4.86**	**10.35**
Canada	24,197	28,135	29,289	32,797	31,464	0.60	-4.06
Greenland	5	2			1	0.00	
Mexico	3,697	4,082	5,765	5,979	6,883	0.13	15.12
United States of America	140,423	165,596	167,998	190,572	214,736	4.13	12.68
SOUTH AMERICA	**13,853**	**17,607**	**19,065**	**24,048**	**28,329**	**0.54**	**17.80**
Argentina	2,265	2,339	3,230	3,406	4,684	0.09	37.52
Bolivia	620	1,046	1,047	1,075	1,190	0.02	10.70
Brazil	7,689	10,467	10,890	14,826	16,687	0.32	12.55
Chile	882	1,019	1,229	1,170	1,474	0.03	25.98
Colombia	498	643	941	1,226	1,229	0.02	0.24
Ecuador	306	254	180	321	347	0.01	8.10
Falkland Islands, Malvinas	84	1	7	13	475	0.01	3,553.85
French Guiana	2	1	4	6	2	0.00	-66.67
Guyana	1	3	89	70	16	0.00	-77.14
Paraguay	17	89	77	68	68	0.00	
Peru	509	386	370	534	486	0.01	-8.99
Suriname	69	33					
Uruguay	326	517	547	673	535	0.01	-20.51
Venezuela	585	809	454	660	1,136	0.02	72.12
EAST ASIA AND THE PACIFIC	**120,014**	**151,559**	**156,583**	**166,143**	**193,544**	**3.72**	**16.49**
NORTH-EAST ASIA	**90,107**	**113,881**	**108,818**	**112,234**	**135,860**	**2.61**	**21.05**
China	20,033	26,578	33,182	35,547	38,490	0.74	8.28
Hong Kong, China	3,566	4,231	4,958	4,246	5,776	0.11	36.03
Japan	34,386	50,499	39,202	41,080	49,245	0.95	19.88
Korea, Dem. People's Republic of	12,022	16,413	15,006	13,205	4,430	0.09	-66.45
Korea, Republic of	17,901	13,943	13,702	14,716	33,841	0.65	129.96
Macao, China	65	63	52	51	184	0.00	260.78
Mongolia	559	644	591	597	579	0.01	-3.02
Taiwan, Province of China	1,575	1,510	2,125	2,792	3,315	0.06	18.73
SOUTH-EAST ASIA	**9,230**	**11,838**	**18,986**	**21,461**	**23,641**	**0.45**	**10.16**

580

POLAND

4. Arrivals of non-resident tourists in all types of accommodation establishments, by country of residence

	2009	2010	2011	2012	2013	Market share 2013	% Change 2013-2012
Brunei Darussalam	5	54	16	19	28	0.00	47.37
Cambodia	7	41	13	13	3	0.00	-76.92
Indonesia	1,169	980	2,578	3,200	3,881	0.07	21.28
Lao People's Democratic Republic	18	17	47	161	44	0.00	-72.67
Malaysia	1,138	1,403	2,242	3,241	3,239	0.06	-0.06
Myanmar	10	2	6	61	99	0.00	62.30
Philippines	1,015	1,025	2,489	1,309	1,928	0.04	47.29
Singapore	2,146	4,243	6,025	7,793	8,548	0.16	9.69
Thailand	1,712	2,116	3,730	3,320	3,675	0.07	10.69
Timor-Leste		1	3	4	72	0.00	1,700.00
Viet Nam	2,010	1,956	1,837	2,340	2,124	0.04	-9.23
AUSTRALASIA	**20,527**	**25,700**	**28,662**	**32,252**	**33,927**	**0.65**	**5.19**
Australia	18,216	22,902	25,959	29,002	30,759	0.59	6.06
New Zealand	2,311	2,798	2,703	3,250	3,168	0.06	-2.52
MELANESIA	**96**	**53**	**71**	**155**	**80**	**0.00**	**-48.39**
Fiji	48	8	19	67	39	0.00	-41.79
New Caledonia	13	26	36	74	37	0.00	-50.00
Norfolk Island	27						
Papua New Guinea	8	19	16	14	4	0.00	-71.43
MICRONESIA	**5**	**2**	**14**	**5**	**9**	**0.00**	**80.00**
Guam	3	2	8	2	5	0.00	150.00
Micronesia, Federated States of			6	3	4	0.00	33.33
Nauru	2						
POLYNESIA	**49**	**85**	**32**	**36**	**27**	**0.00**	**-25.00**
American Samoa	28			5			
French Polynesia	15	38	28	31	27	0.00	-12.90
Samoa	5						
Tonga	1	47	4				
EUROPE	**3,507,918**	**3,696,478**	**3,966,041**	**4,423,222**	**4,614,444**	**88.66**	**4.32**
CENTRAL/EASTERN EUROPE	**743,407**	**830,132**	**993,938**	**1,247,106**	**1,365,104**	**26.23**	**9.46**
Armenia	2,485	3,203	3,651	3,765	4,071	0.08	8.13
Azerbaijan	998	830	903	1,021	1,605	0.03	57.20
Belarus	71,485	81,928	107,304	163,655	205,606	3.95	25.63
Bulgaria	9,539	10,203	10,584	11,955	12,248	0.24	2.45
Czech Republic	78,708	79,603	89,567	97,638	93,205	1.79	-4.54
Estonia	34,592	32,486	36,152	37,505	39,636	0.76	5.68
Georgia	2,364	2,174	2,032	2,271	3,226	0.06	42.05
Hungary	48,063	48,153	52,708	59,266	59,568	1.14	0.51
Kazakhstan	2,638	2,815	4,013	3,946	4,626	0.09	17.23
Kyrgyzstan	125	237	378	527	455	0.01	-13.66
Latvia	38,112	43,265	50,691	58,587	62,461	1.20	6.61
Lithuania	101,950	100,255	103,789	105,732	108,356	2.08	2.48
Republic of Moldova	2,625	3,210	2,931	3,152	3,248	0.06	3.05
Romania	20,552	25,836	27,371	30,270	35,261	0.68	16.49
Russian Federation	161,353	214,544	280,975	394,371	405,020	7.78	2.70
Slovakia	41,627	45,401	50,928	52,445	54,471	1.05	3.86
Tajikistan	49	196	109	192	158	0.00	-17.71
Turkmenistan	37	27	59	119	65	0.00	-45.38
Ukraine	125,707	134,930	168,738	219,305	270,666	5.20	23.42
Uzbekistan	398	836	1,055	1,384	1,152	0.02	-16.76
NORTHERN EUROPE	**717,561**	**744,176**	**747,170**	**852,062**	**846,814**	**16.27**	**-0.62**
Denmark	87,299	79,932	84,630	88,926	84,378	1.62	-5.11
Faeroe Islands	8						
Finland	47,492	58,511	64,834	61,373	57,041	1.10	-7.06
Iceland	1,785	2,722	1,905	2,661	2,505	0.05	-5.86
Ireland	40,525	42,122	41,243	81,133	41,632	0.80	-48.69
Norway	91,042	102,124	104,421	132,661	153,409	2.95	15.64
Svalbard and Jan Mayen Islands	11	2					
Sweden	108,850	102,784	106,586	117,968	129,780	2.49	10.01
United Kingdom	340,549	355,979	343,551	367,340	378,069	7.26	2.92
SOUTHERN EUROPE	**350,611**	**381,226**	**435,968**	**451,844**	**437,069**	**8.40**	**-3.27**

581

POLAND

4. Arrivals of non-resident tourists in all types of accommodation establishments, by country of residence

	2009	2010	2011	2012	2013	Market share 2013	% Change 2013-2012
Albania	1,477	1,418	1,702	1,679	2,606	0.05	55.21
Andorra	130	373	290	290	276	0.01	-4.83
Bosnia and Herzegovina	1,239	852	1,276	1,464	1,157	0.02	-20.97
Croatia	7,090	7,564	8,852	14,087	9,704	0.19	-31.11
Gibraltar	26	38	46	135	102	0.00	-24.44
Greece	15,601	12,805	14,702	16,780	12,765	0.25	-23.93
Holy See	204	141	155		152	0.00	
Italy	180,442	194,892	208,737	217,980	217,753	4.18	-0.10
Malta	584	775	1,373	1,450	1,355	0.03	-6.55
Montenegro	170	188	383	453	507	0.01	11.92
Portugal	18,285	20,299	22,181	25,433	20,182	0.39	-20.65
San Marino	118	32	197	28	396	0.01	1,314.29
Serbia	2,374	4,855	4,726	5,477	6,959	0.13	27.06
Slovenia	9,251	8,866	10,014	10,372	10,878	0.21	4.88
Spain	112,831	126,883	160,397	155,203	151,328	2.91	-2.50
TFYR of Macedonia	789	1,245	937	1,013	949	0.02	-6.32
WESTERN EUROPE	**1,550,661**	**1,582,580**	**1,621,143**	**1,694,605**	**1,788,651**	**34.36**	**5.55**
Austria	54,810	59,050	62,469	64,365	65,026	1.25	1.03
Belgium	56,663	63,964	66,987	63,853	65,438	1.26	2.48
France	174,044	187,267	198,572	195,938	200,949	3.86	2.56
Germany	1,126,573	1,128,378	1,141,632	1,212,837	1,289,255	24.77	6.30
Liechtenstein	1,149	267	351	275	394	0.01	43.27
Luxembourg	2,838	3,593	3,565	3,568	3,631	0.07	1.77
Monaco	415	300	219	239	260	0.00	8.79
Netherlands	101,006	105,631	110,934	112,160	119,817	2.30	6.83
Switzerland	33,163	34,130	36,414	41,370	43,881	0.84	6.07
EAST MEDITERRANEAN EUROPE	**145,678**	**158,364**	**167,822**	**177,605**	**176,806**	**3.40**	**-0.45**
Cyprus	2,532	2,255	2,048	2,453	2,515	0.05	2.53
Israel	128,419	139,567	145,572	152,064	148,546	2.85	-2.31
Turkey	14,727	16,542	20,202	23,088	25,745	0.49	11.51
MIDDLE EAST	**7,061**	**7,198**	**9,264**	**14,637**	**16,197**	**0.31**	**10.66**
Bahrain	165	229	159	185	204	0.00	10.27
Egypt	1,398	1,565	1,756	2,572	2,767	0.05	7.58
Iraq	614	520	767	890	970	0.02	8.99
Jordan	313	228	433	403	502	0.01	24.57
Kuwait	543	498	680	584	1,073	0.02	83.73
Lebanon	866	500	632	755	1,228	0.02	62.65
Libya	229	303	347	541	1,110	0.02	105.18
Oman	42	99	27	171	168	0.00	-1.75
Qatar	325	288	265	2,709	631	0.01	-76.71
Saudi Arabia	1,085	1,535	2,304	3,352	3,727	0.07	11.19
Syrian Arab Republic	338	328	489	439	373	0.01	-15.03
United Arab Emirates	1,105	1,074	1,361	1,798	3,397	0.07	88.93
Yemen	38	31	44	238	47	0.00	-80.25
SOUTH ASIA	**14,134**	**18,472**	**17,072**	**20,524**	**21,435**	**0.41**	**4.44**
Afghanistan	1,248	3,757	1,458	1,676	2,108	0.04	25.78
Bangladesh	791	859	928	1,337	1,718	0.03	28.50
Bhutan	263	398	109	20	81	0.00	305.00
India	8,943	9,952	11,324	13,551	14,198	0.27	4.77
Iran, Islamic Republic of	1,648	2,255	2,048	2,489	2,013	0.04	-19.12
Maldives	9	46	16	41	6	0.00	-85.37
Nepal	419	325	121	135	248	0.00	83.70
Pakistan	695	727	878	1,125	886	0.02	-21.24
Sri Lanka	118	153	190	150	177	0.00	18.00
NOT SPECIFIED	**19,568**	**34,335**	**26,251**	**47,429**	**60,673**	**1.17**	**27.92**
Other countries of the World	19,568	34,335	26,251	47,429	60,673	1.17	27.92

Yearbook of Tourism Statistics, Data 2009 – 2013, 2015 Edition

POLAND

5. Overnight stays of non-resident tourists in hotels and similar establishments, by country of residence

	2009	2010	2011	2012	2013	Market share 2013	% Change 2013-2012
TOTAL (*)	7,478,048	8,029,202	8,397,392	9,424,550	10,129,465	100.00	7.48
AFRICA	20,722	20,737	20,073	21,635	30,603	0.30	41.45
EAST AFRICA	1,466	2,180	1,583	2,065	3,902	0.04	88.96
Burundi	74	46	74	51	61	0.00	19.61
Comoros	4	4		7	42	0.00	500.00
Djibouti	52	4	16	2	11	0.00	450.00
Eritrea				4			
Ethiopia	156	365	151	467	494	0.00	5.78
Kenya	517	409	382	445	1,249	0.01	180.67
Madagascar	7	100	66	23	27	0.00	17.39
Malawi	27	29	21	73	146	0.00	100.00
Mauritius	32	136	83	150	167	0.00	11.33
Mozambique	9	48	58	55	9	0.00	-83.64
Reunion	2			14			
Rwanda	30	224	196	171	338	0.00	97.66
Seychelles	33	47	31	139	102	0.00	-26.62
Somalia	49	107	93	58	64	0.00	10.34
Uganda	188	298	192	174	324	0.00	86.21
United Republic of Tanzania	39	212	74	100	310	0.00	210.00
Zambia	68	59	43	55	233	0.00	323.64
Zimbabwe	179	92	103	77	325	0.00	322.08
CENTRAL AFRICA	1,421	1,604	1,908	1,647	3,883	0.04	135.76
Angola	595	1,212	954	720	2,467	0.02	242.64
Cameroon	163	124	159	287	340	0.00	18.47
Central African Republic	175	65	553	251	407	0.00	62.15
Chad	93	4	16	130	248	0.00	90.77
Congo	263	165	182	122	378	0.00	209.84
Democratic Republic of the Congo	105	28	37	126	22	0.00	-82.54
Equatorial Guinea		6	7	7	21	0.00	200.00
Gabon	27			4			
NORTH AFRICA	5,582	8,007	7,787	8,336	9,733	0.10	16.76
Algeria	2,144	4,051	4,081	4,290	5,168	0.05	20.47
Morocco	1,273	2,597	1,644	1,780	2,058	0.02	15.62
Sudan	167	144	234	312	214	0.00	-31.41
Tunisia	1,396	1,085	1,783	1,871	2,231	0.02	19.24
Western Sahara	602	130	45	83	62	0.00	-25.30
SOUTHERN AFRICA	5,288	4,490	5,498	6,077	8,292	0.08	36.45
Botswana	132	79	25	37	103	0.00	178.38
Lesotho	7	13	19	11	81	0.00	636.36
Namibia	233	60	130	74	167	0.00	125.68
South Africa	4,628	4,338	5,324	5,955	7,940	0.08	33.33
Swaziland	288				1	0.00	
WEST AFRICA	6,965	4,456	3,297	3,510	4,793	0.05	36.55
Benin	116	94	51	41	201	0.00	390.24
Burkina Faso	4	25	76	2	86	0.00	4,200.00
Cabo Verde	16	14	42	3			
Côte d'Ivoire	38	168	68	216	106	0.00	-50.93
Gambia	34	83	5	35	153	0.00	337.14
Ghana	62	183	335	134	313	0.00	133.58
Guinea	118	17	24	44	152	0.00	245.45
Guinea-Bissau	3		14	16			
Liberia	11	56	38	34	18	0.00	-47.06
Mali	35	57	92	60	119	0.00	98.33
Mauritania	86	28	28	16	134	0.00	737.50
Niger	651	1,017	365	511	746	0.01	45.99
Nigeria	3,737	1,664	1,443	1,822	1,741	0.02	-4.45
Saint Helena	61	31	8	14	12	0.00	-14.29
Senegal	1,376	651	338	177	353	0.00	99.44
Sierra Leone	587	365	350	373	459	0.00	23.06
Togo	30	3	20	12	200	0.00	1,566.67
AMERICAS	388,543	450,356	463,590	529,995	593,518	5.86	11.99

583

POLAND

5. Overnight stays of non-resident tourists in hotels and similar establishments, by country of residence

	2009	2010	2011	2012	2013	Market share 2013	% Change 2013-2012
CARIBBEAN	1,732	1,558	4,019	3,248	2,776	0.03	-14.53
Anguilla	14						
Antigua and Barbuda	18			52			
Aruba	26	15	16	124	42	0.00	-66.13
Bahamas	59	195	1,539	327	69	0.00	-78.90
Barbados	173	110	73	74	49	0.00	-33.78
Bermuda	35	14	116	546	110	0.00	-79.85
British Virgin Islands	1						
Cayman Islands	50	56	27	325	35	0.00	-89.23
Cuba	639	541	669	252	869	0.01	244.84
Dominica	21	59	79	56	278	0.00	396.43
Dominican Republic	235	189	336	540	110	0.00	-79.63
Grenada	2			3	6	0.00	100.00
Guadeloupe	17		5	128	18	0.00	-85.94
Haiti	19	56	159	61	64	0.00	4.92
Jamaica	248	136	156	151	260	0.00	72.19
Martinique	2		34	5			
Netherlands Antilles	1			7			
Puerto Rico	145	143	738	423	729	0.01	72.34
Saint Kitts and Nevis	6						
Trinidad and Tobago	19	44	72	174	137	0.00	-21.26
Turks and Caicos Islands	2						
CENTRAL AMERICA	1,300	1,266	1,432	1,498	2,007	0.02	33.98
Belize	131	77	105	172	272	0.00	58.14
Costa Rica	350	273	417	525	530	0.01	0.95
El Salvador	112	88	184	104	230	0.00	121.15
Guatemala	150	119	176	165	172	0.00	4.24
Honduras	334	317	309	314	467	0.00	48.73
Nicaragua	74	257	96	118	61	0.00	-48.31
Panama	149	135	145	100	275	0.00	175.00
NORTH AMERICA	357,942	413,234	415,694	474,561	532,066	5.25	12.12
Canada	46,492	55,395	56,280	64,034	63,745	0.63	-0.45
Greenland	19	2			1	0.00	
Mexico	7,397	8,960	12,902	11,670	14,009	0.14	20.04
United States of America	304,034	348,877	346,512	398,857	454,311	4.49	13.90
SOUTH AMERICA	27,569	34,298	42,445	50,688	56,669	0.56	11.80
Argentina	4,465	4,458	7,237	6,664	9,089	0.09	36.39
Bolivia	1,699	2,309	2,513	2,255	2,612	0.03	15.83
Brazil	15,431	21,052	25,389	32,285	33,929	0.33	5.09
Chile	1,469	1,807	2,274	2,102	2,683	0.03	27.64
Colombia	1,359	1,407	1,868	3,023	2,993	0.03	-0.99
Ecuador	528	400	266	407	666	0.01	63.64
Falkland Islands, Malvinas	86	2	8	39	647	0.01	1,558.97
French Guiana	7	1	39	16	2	0.00	-87.50
Guyana	3	3	143	260	75	0.00	-71.15
Paraguay	30	168	225	89	128	0.00	43.82
Peru	783	607	610	1,303	839	0.01	-35.61
Suriname	93	66					
Uruguay	461	802	1,148	920	780	0.01	-15.22
Venezuela	1,155	1,216	725	1,325	2,226	0.02	68.00
EAST ASIA AND THE PACIFIC	221,960	292,648	280,049	279,046	333,469	3.29	19.50
NORTH-EAST ASIA	164,718	224,414	197,875	188,460	235,700	2.33	25.07
China	35,840	54,866	62,809	61,416	67,694	0.67	10.22
Hong Kong, China	6,777	7,856	8,510	6,887	9,118	0.09	32.39
Japan	70,599	101,297	72,520	71,331	92,350	0.91	29.47
Korea, Dem. People's Republic of	22,619	30,110	23,309	19,579	7,375	0.07	-62.33
Korea, Republic of	25,273	26,802	25,621	24,216	52,384	0.52	116.32
Macao, China	195	102	91	90	310	0.00	244.44
Mongolia	735	850	731	681	866	0.01	27.17
Taiwan, Province of China	2,680	2,531	4,284	4,260	5,603	0.06	31.53
SOUTH-EAST ASIA	20,774	22,646	32,559	36,881	39,054	0.39	5.89

584

Yearbook of Tourism Statistics, Data 2009 – 2013, 2015 Edition

POLAND

5. Overnight stays of non-resident tourists in hotels and similar establishments, by country of residence

	2009	2010	2011	2012	2013	Market share 2013	% Change 2013-2012
Brunei Darussalam	13	80	18	43	109	0.00	153.49
Cambodia	26	70	67	26	6	0.00	-76.92
Indonesia	1,971	2,038	4,304	5,434	6,136	0.06	12.92
Lao People's Democratic Republic	37	33	51	371	67	0.00	-81.94
Malaysia	4,976	5,137	4,677	6,958	6,151	0.06	-11.60
Myanmar	17	5	7	369	125	0.00	-66.12
Philippines	2,512	1,724	4,362	3,184	4,250	0.04	33.48
Singapore	4,244	6,770	9,276	11,419	12,190	0.12	6.75
Thailand	3,420	3,694	6,585	5,694	6,398	0.06	12.36
Timor-Leste		1	6	4	142	0.00	3,450.00
Viet Nam	3,558	3,094	3,206	3,379	3,480	0.03	2.99
AUSTRALASIA	**36,154**	**45,265**	**49,371**	**53,312**	**58,235**	**0.57**	**9.23**
Australia	31,439	40,306	44,741	48,087	52,970	0.52	10.15
New Zealand	4,715	4,959	4,630	5,225	5,265	0.05	0.77
MELANESIA	**215**	**109**	**183**	**328**	**425**	**0.00**	**29.57**
Fiji	93	20	53	149	208	0.00	39.60
New Caledonia	26	13	61	146	209	0.00	43.15
Norfolk Island	84						
Papua New Guinea	12	76	69	33	8	0.00	-75.76
MICRONESIA	**13**	**2**	**22**	**7**	**18**	**0.00**	**157.14**
Guam	13	2	16	4	5	0.00	25.00
Micronesia, Federated States of			6	3	13	0.00	333.33
POLYNESIA	**86**	**212**	**39**	**58**	**37**	**0.00**	**-36.21**
American Samoa	46			7			
French Polynesia	27	150	25	51	37	0.00	-27.45
Samoa	11						
Tonga	2	62	14				
EUROPE	**6,757,450**	**7,147,489**	**7,514,760**	**8,427,889**	**8,980,415**	**88.66**	**6.56**
CENTRAL/EASTERN EUROPE	**1,133,044**	**1,245,609**	**1,422,092**	**1,730,382**	**1,933,340**	**19.09**	**11.73**
Armenia	6,664	7,830	9,317	8,689	10,481	0.10	20.62
Azerbaijan	2,364	2,039	2,513	2,101	3,759	0.04	78.91
Belarus	84,504	100,399	126,589	179,082	232,565	2.30	29.87
Bulgaria	19,447	17,852	21,385	26,910	23,458	0.23	-12.83
Czech Republic	145,521	150,899	153,983	154,324	145,645	1.44	-5.62
Estonia	38,970	36,553	42,981	43,990	45,802	0.45	4.12
Georgia	15,936	15,851	4,661	4,359	5,503	0.05	26.24
Hungary	80,692	84,227	90,651	105,085	104,873	1.04	-0.20
Kazakhstan	4,897	5,254	7,445	7,319	7,966	0.08	8.84
Kyrgyzstan	232	582	899	978	762	0.01	-22.09
Latvia	42,741	48,878	57,067	65,900	74,854	0.74	13.59
Lithuania	118,738	116,183	119,978	127,015	133,516	1.32	5.12
Republic of Moldova	10,731	5,771	5,537	5,348	6,316	0.06	18.10
Romania	43,429	50,647	56,908	58,105	66,927	0.66	15.18
Russian Federation	277,456	313,057	383,731	545,314	567,373	5.60	4.05
Slovakia	64,611	88,294	94,274	87,996	101,671	1.00	15.54
Tajikistan	216	440	109	352	399	0.00	13.35
Turkmenistan	67	63	212	267	104	0.00	-61.05
Ukraine	175,161	199,268	241,771	303,120	398,075	3.93	31.33
Uzbekistan	667	1,522	2,081	4,128	3,291	0.03	-20.28
NORTHERN EUROPE	**1,513,900**	**1,537,774**	**1,559,441**	**1,746,135**	**1,817,737**	**17.95**	**4.10**
Denmark	195,061	172,905	178,090	185,650	178,456	1.76	-3.88
Faeroe Islands	4						
Finland	89,536	106,234	121,936	118,466	112,900	1.11	-4.70
Iceland	3,475	5,545	3,949	5,520	5,547	0.05	0.49
Ireland	91,898	94,366	94,655	118,593	86,815	0.86	-26.80
Norway	211,537	240,910	245,009	323,810	382,415	3.78	18.10
Svalbard and Jan Mayen Islands	23	15					
Sweden	206,559	195,175	203,457	228,752	259,625	2.56	13.50
United Kingdom	715,807	722,624	712,345	765,344	791,979	7.82	3.48
SOUTHERN EUROPE	**703,608**	**739,941**	**837,877**	**872,896**	**854,519**	**8.44**	**-2.11**
Albania	3,213	3,178	3,982	3,967	5,036	0.05	26.95

585

Yearbook of Tourism Statistics, Data 2009 – 2013, 2015 Edition

POLAND

5. Overnight stays of non-resident tourists in hotels and similar establishments, by country of residence

	2009	2010	2011	2012	2013	Market share 2013	% Change 2013-2012
Andorra	193	930	548	610	666	0.01	9.18
Bosnia and Herzegovina	2,502	4,599	3,211	3,461	2,752	0.03	-20.49
Croatia	13,765	16,812	17,822	24,057	19,467	0.19	-19.08
Gibraltar	37	144	103	186	187	0.00	0.54
Greece	36,397	26,242	28,691	33,920	26,854	0.27	-20.83
Holy See	374	246	174		336	0.00	
Italy	374,970	397,485	420,638	441,178	439,816	4.34	-0.31
Malta	1,398	2,439	4,021	4,742	3,841	0.04	-19.00
Montenegro	347	336	1,063	900	1,154	0.01	28.22
Portugal	35,512	36,687	44,338	50,841	40,965	0.40	-19.43
San Marino	257	58	305	46	590	0.01	1,182.61
Serbia	4,962	8,466	9,486	9,616	11,849	0.12	23.22
Slovenia	17,139	15,482	16,692	18,421	19,109	0.19	3.73
Spain	210,777	225,405	285,020	279,252	280,400	2.77	0.41
TFYR of Macedonia	1,765	1,432	1,783	1,699	1,497	0.01	-11.89
WESTERN EUROPE	**3,127,648**	**3,327,263**	**3,370,504**	**3,740,328**	**4,035,091**	**39.84**	**7.88**
Austria	100,498	100,215	107,819	109,842	110,946	1.10	1.01
Belgium	99,348	113,774	118,769	114,189	117,299	1.16	2.72
France	312,494	324,221	350,702	342,627	350,434	3.46	2.28
Germany	2,377,950	2,540,966	2,533,533	2,896,873	3,156,785	31.16	8.97
Liechtenstein	1,497	486	605	417	687	0.01	64.75
Luxembourg	4,937	6,836	6,533	6,481	6,652	0.07	2.64
Monaco	601	386	337	329	354	0.00	7.60
Netherlands	170,440	179,677	187,680	195,957	212,510	2.10	8.45
Switzerland	59,883	60,702	64,526	73,613	79,424	0.78	7.89
EAST MEDITERRANEAN EUROPE	**279,250**	**296,902**	**324,846**	**338,148**	**339,728**	**3.35**	**0.47**
Cyprus	6,334	5,928	4,180	5,410	5,117	0.05	-5.42
Israel	242,475	258,838	281,377	287,972	288,183	2.84	0.07
Turkey	30,441	32,136	39,289	44,766	46,428	0.46	3.71
MIDDLE EAST	**17,626**	**20,015**	**25,821**	**37,648**	**34,711**	**0.34**	**-7.80**
Bahrain	763	883	865	794	370	0.00	-53.40
Egypt	3,743	4,493	4,955	6,052	6,651	0.07	9.90
Iraq	941	750	2,043	1,633	1,664	0.02	1.90
Jordan	530	457	977	867	1,237	0.01	42.68
Kuwait	1,195	1,332	1,898	1,565	2,173	0.02	38.85
Lebanon	1,505	1,036	1,233	1,508	2,263	0.02	50.07
Libya	397	862	586	1,363	3,133	0.03	129.86
Oman	163	635	269	474	389	0.00	-17.93
Qatar	1,522	2,765	1,384	9,693	1,732	0.02	-82.13
Saudi Arabia	2,568	3,508	7,264	8,272	8,536	0.08	3.19
Syrian Arab Republic	522	520	959	822	659	0.01	-19.83
United Arab Emirates	3,700	2,730	3,245	4,308	5,809	0.06	34.84
Yemen	77	44	143	297	95	0.00	-68.01
SOUTH ASIA	**33,415**	**39,877**	**46,033**	**49,213**	**55,807**	**0.55**	**13.40**
Afghanistan	2,928	4,590	6,255	7,509	8,050	0.08	7.20
Bangladesh	1,959	1,628	2,899	2,768	3,667	0.04	32.48
Bhutan	278	399	212	37	128	0.00	245.95
India	22,201	26,395	29,273	31,599	36,213	0.36	14.60
Iran, Islamic Republic of	4,014	4,990	4,948	5,215	4,383	0.04	-15.95
Maldives	11	126	34	67	4	0.00	-94.03
Nepal	466	204	187	121	1,427	0.01	1,079.34
Pakistan	1,368	1,212	1,711	1,540	1,586	0.02	2.99
Sri Lanka	190	333	514	357	349	0.00	-2.24
NOT SPECIFIED	**38,332**	**58,080**	**47,066**	**79,124**	**100,942**	**1.00**	**27.57**
Other countries of the World	38,332	58,080	47,066	79,124	100,942	1.00	27.57

Yearbook of Tourism Statistics, Data 2009 – 2013, 2015 Edition

POLAND

6. Overnight stays of non-resident tourists in all types of accommodation establishments, by country of residence

	2009	2010	2011	2012	2013	Market share 2013	% Change 2013-2012
TOTAL	9,609,447	10,064,628	10,620,264	11,754,585	12,361,678	100.00	5.16
AFRICA	23,095	25,862	26,068	41,919	37,557	0.30	-10.41
EAST AFRICA	1,803	2,958	2,152	2,685	4,711	0.04	75.46
Burundi	83	46	74	69	71	0.00	2.90
Comoros	4	4		7	42	0.00	500.00
Djibouti	52	4	17	2	11	0.00	450.00
Eritrea				4			
Ethiopia	229	527	244	548	656	0.01	19.71
Kenya	538	629	528	593	1,381	0.01	132.88
Madagascar	15	106	78	24	67	0.00	179.17
Malawi	27	34	24	75	167	0.00	122.67
Mauritius	33	152	89	162	174	0.00	7.41
Mozambique	9	48	61	55	9	0.00	-83.64
Reunion	2			14			
Rwanda	30	235	200	198	561	0.00	183.33
Seychelles	33	47	31	154	104	0.00	-32.47
Somalia	51	222	93	60	66	0.00	10.00
Uganda	238	343	262	268	463	0.00	72.76
United Republic of Tanzania	65	261	137	221	319	0.00	44.34
Zambia	79	108	144	67	258	0.00	285.07
Zimbabwe	315	192	170	164	362	0.00	120.73
CENTRAL AFRICA	1,744	1,957	2,367	2,266	6,261	0.05	176.30
Angola	654	1,365	1,074	1,024	4,196	0.03	309.77
Cameroon	254	212	467	516	410	0.00	-20.54
Central African Republic	187	95	555	251	407	0.00	62.15
Chad	101	9	16	130	267	0.00	105.38
Congo	350	232	211	204	936	0.01	358.82
Democratic Republic of the Congo	118	38	37	130	24	0.00	-81.54
Equatorial Guinea		6	7	7	21	0.00	200.00
Gabon	80			4			
NORTH AFRICA	6,064	10,117	9,495	10,642	11,183	0.09	5.08
Algeria	2,435	4,270	4,726	5,835	5,693	0.05	-2.43
Morocco	1,331	4,174	2,530	2,018	2,358	0.02	16.85
Sudan	176	154	277	409	261	0.00	-36.19
Tunisia	1,520	1,389	1,917	2,297	2,809	0.02	22.29
Western Sahara	602	130	45	83	62	0.00	-25.30
SOUTHERN AFRICA	5,747	4,871	6,472	6,583	8,942	0.07	35.83
Botswana	132	79	25	179	104	0.00	-41.90
Lesotho	23	19	19	11	81	0.00	636.36
Namibia	240	60	803	79	180	0.00	127.85
South Africa	5,064	4,713	5,625	6,314	8,576	0.07	35.83
Swaziland	288				1	0.00	
WEST AFRICA	7,737	5,959	5,582	19,743	6,460	0.05	-67.28
Benin	117	94	52	41	228	0.00	456.10
Burkina Faso	75	25	82	2	125	0.00	6,150.00
Cabo Verde	16	14	42	3			
Côte d'Ivoire	130	176	68	227	112	0.00	-50.66
Gambia	70	85	10	35	153	0.00	337.14
Ghana	91	215	436	315	438	0.00	39.05
Guinea	140	36	25	57	189	0.00	231.58
Guinea-Bissau	3		14	16			
Liberia	11	56	40	35	20	0.00	-42.86
Mali	38	59	92	11,865	139	0.00	-98.83
Mauritania	88	28	33	21	190	0.00	804.76
Niger	674	2,057	477	2,815	847	0.01	-69.91
Nigeria	4,129	1,939	3,183	2,914	2,662	0.02	-8.65
Saint Helena	90	31	8	46	33	0.00	-28.26
Senegal	1,444	774	649	953	661	0.01	-30.64
Sierra Leone	587	365	351	379	459	0.00	21.11
Togo	34	5	20	19	204	0.00	973.68
AMERICAS	427,512	493,842	510,862	584,420	644,044	5.21	10.20

587

POLAND

6. Overnight stays of non-resident tourists in all types of accommodation establishments, by country of residence

	2009	2010	2011	2012	2013	Market share 2013	% Change 2013-2012
CARIBBEAN	1,883	1,761	4,232	3,610	3,149	0.03	-12.77
Anguilla	14						
Antigua and Barbuda	18			52			
Aruba	27	15	16	133	58	0.00	-56.39
Bahamas	69	212	1,540	329	69	0.00	-79.03
Barbados	239	123	73	76	184	0.00	142.11
Bermuda	41	14	116	546	110	0.00	-79.85
British Virgin Islands	1						
Cayman Islands	50	56	27	325	35	0.00	-89.23
Cuba	685	672	723	470	1,004	0.01	113.62
Dominica	21	59	79	62	279	0.00	350.00
Dominican Republic	245	191	343	551	138	0.00	-74.95
Grenada	2			3	6	0.00	100.00
Guadeloupe	19	4	5	129	18	0.00	-86.05
Haiti	20	57	167	69	73	0.00	5.80
Jamaica	252	136	177	222	266	0.00	19.82
Martinique	2		34	5			
Netherlands Antilles	1			7			
Puerto Rico	150	171	843	443	758	0.01	71.11
Saint Kitts and Nevis	6						
Trinidad and Tobago	19	51	89	188	151	0.00	-19.68
Turks and Caicos Islands	2						
CENTRAL AMERICA	3,628	3,300	2,758	2,786	3,122	0.03	12.06
Belize	131	82	114	172	274	0.00	59.30
Costa Rica	374	639	481	629	587	0.00	-6.68
El Salvador	114	102	192	116	270	0.00	132.76
Guatemala	156	137	192	226	221	0.00	-2.21
Honduras	2,438	1,510	1,489	1,276	1,389	0.01	8.86
Nicaragua	266	271	132	187	74	0.00	-60.43
Panama	149	559	158	180	307	0.00	70.56
NORTH AMERICA	390,051	448,751	454,374	518,771	572,751	4.63	10.41
Canada	54,822	64,142	64,778	74,125	73,159	0.59	-1.30
Greenland	19	3			1	0.00	
Mexico	8,251	10,631	15,572	15,161	17,482	0.14	15.31
United States of America	326,959	373,975	374,024	429,485	482,109	3.90	12.25
SOUTH AMERICA	31,950	40,030	49,498	59,253	65,022	0.53	9.74
Argentina	5,121	5,381	7,838	7,829	9,953	0.08	27.13
Bolivia	1,729	2,318	2,535	2,401	2,704	0.02	12.62
Brazil	17,624	23,497	29,395	37,098	38,629	0.31	4.13
Chile	1,759	2,195	2,742	2,683	3,596	0.03	34.03
Colombia	1,522	1,662	2,584	3,393	3,660	0.03	7.87
Ecuador	839	841	383	890	797	0.01	-10.45
Falkland Islands, Malvinas	86	2	8	43	647	0.01	1,404.65
French Guiana	7	1	39	16	2	0.00	-87.50
Guyana	3	3	151	263	75	0.00	-71.48
Paraguay	37	280	234	116	141	0.00	21.55
Peru	918	851	812	1,620	1,384	0.01	-14.57
Suriname	97	66					
Uruguay	571	959	1,282	1,244	1,000	0.01	-19.61
Venezuela	1,637	1,974	1,495	1,657	2,434	0.02	46.89
EAST ASIA AND THE PACIFIC	243,534	317,019	311,619	316,140	371,741	3.01	17.59
NORTH-EAST ASIA	174,133	234,855	212,601	205,016	253,281	2.05	23.54
China	39,383	58,167	66,542	66,094	73,852	0.60	11.74
Hong Kong, China	7,054	8,553	9,866	8,137	10,111	0.08	24.26
Japan	74,193	105,300	76,584	76,459	98,201	0.79	28.44
Korea, Dem. People's Republic of	23,418	31,279	25,940	20,892	7,425	0.06	-64.46
Korea, Republic of	25,589	27,208	26,483	25,312	54,492	0.44	115.28
Macao, China	220	117	96	125	317	0.00	153.60
Mongolia	1,034	1,166	2,309	3,252	2,613	0.02	-19.65
Taiwan, Province of China	3,242	3,065	4,781	4,745	6,270	0.05	32.14
SOUTH-EAST ASIA	23,467	25,495	36,413	41,565	44,062	0.36	6.01

Yearbook of Tourism Statistics, Data 2009 – 2013, 2015 Edition

POLAND

6. Overnight stays of non-resident tourists in all types of accommodation establishments, by country of residence

	2009	2010	2011	2012	2013	Market share 2013	% Change 2013-2012
Brunei Darussalam	13	80	25	55	109	0.00	98.18
Cambodia	26	75	73	32	6	0.00	-81.25
Indonesia	3,305	2,279	4,514	5,727	6,469	0.05	12.96
Lao People's Democratic Republic	47	34	57	371	70	0.00	-81.13
Malaysia	5,315	5,601	5,163	7,382	6,621	0.05	-10.31
Myanmar	17	5	16	458	130	0.00	-71.62
Philippines	2,613	2,241	5,331	3,569	4,789	0.04	34.18
Singapore	4,429	7,457	9,858	12,100	13,035	0.11	7.73
Thailand	3,571	4,004	7,135	5,977	6,538	0.05	9.39
Timor-Leste		1	6	4	142	0.00	3,450.00
Viet Nam	4,131	3,718	4,235	5,890	6,153	0.05	4.47
AUSTRALASIA	**45,594**	**56,287**	**62,351**	**69,158**	**73,910**	**0.60**	**6.87**
Australia	39,392	50,090	56,364	62,359	66,921	0.54	7.32
New Zealand	6,202	6,197	5,987	6,799	6,989	0.06	2.79
MELANESIA	**217**	**166**	**189**	**336**	**433**	**0.00**	**28.87**
Fiji	95	20	58	150	215	0.00	43.33
New Caledonia	26	70	62	146	209	0.00	43.15
Norfolk Island	84						
Papua New Guinea	12	76	69	40	9	0.00	-77.50
MICRONESIA	**26**	**2**	**22**	**7**	**18**	**0.00**	**157.14**
Guam	13	2	16	4	5	0.00	25.00
Micronesia, Federated States of			6	3	13	0.00	333.33
Nauru	13						
POLYNESIA	**97**	**214**	**43**	**58**	**37**	**0.00**	**-36.21**
American Samoa	46			7			
French Polynesia	38	152	29	51	37	0.00	-27.45
Samoa	11						
Tonga	2	62	14				
EUROPE	**8,802,443**	**9,083,870**	**9,644,744**	**10,633,849**	**11,104,507**	**89.83**	**4.43**
CENTRAL/EASTERN EUROPE	**1,428,204**	**1,525,689**	**1,734,920**	**2,115,244**	**2,336,037**	**18.90**	**10.44**
Armenia	6,982	8,089	9,618	9,124	10,915	0.09	19.63
Azerbaijan	2,932	2,514	2,902	2,694	4,818	0.04	78.84
Belarus	110,874	128,721	166,008	238,604	283,592	2.29	18.85
Bulgaria	24,208	20,935	26,336	38,530	33,909	0.27	-11.99
Czech Republic	185,282	182,037	182,488	189,133	177,932	1.44	-5.92
Estonia	45,398	39,420	46,080	47,396	49,667	0.40	4.79
Georgia	19,092	16,480	6,384	6,266	7,753	0.06	23.73
Hungary	98,695	102,314	109,595	123,885	127,793	1.03	3.15
Kazakhstan	6,461	6,955	8,796	10,688	10,842	0.09	1.44
Kyrgyzstan	330	696	1,185	1,603	973	0.01	-39.30
Latvia	48,525	54,450	64,043	73,418	80,439	0.65	9.56
Lithuania	146,607	139,407	141,070	149,516	156,601	1.27	4.74
Republic of Moldova	12,394	8,453	6,669	7,772	8,314	0.07	6.97
Romania	55,041	69,533	74,049	75,598	77,561	0.63	2.60
Russian Federation	314,452	356,019	439,405	622,810	649,653	5.26	4.31
Slovakia	87,764	110,548	116,362	122,817	127,045	1.03	3.44
Tajikistan	222	1,032	1,023	587	609	0.00	3.75
Turkmenistan	95	64	221	271	115	0.00	-57.56
Ukraine	261,125	275,695	330,374	389,880	524,027	4.24	34.41
Uzbekistan	1,725	2,327	2,312	4,652	3,479	0.03	-25.21
NORTHERN EUROPE	**1,646,811**	**1,678,802**	**1,690,748**	**1,926,102**	**1,962,193**	**15.87**	**1.87**
Denmark	215,086	189,395	195,853	202,961	194,219	1.57	-4.31
Faeroe Islands	50						
Finland	98,262	117,164	132,129	128,060	122,077	0.99	-4.67
Iceland	4,085	5,935	4,246	5,911	6,648	0.05	12.47
Ireland	100,562	106,780	103,997	163,073	98,312	0.80	-39.71
Norway	224,005	256,073	261,127	342,015	400,101	3.24	16.98
Svalbard and Jan Mayen Islands	23	15					
Sweden	242,071	226,951	233,081	261,647	292,044	2.36	11.62
United Kingdom	762,667	776,489	760,315	822,435	848,792	6.87	3.20
SOUTHERN EUROPE	**777,522**	**826,288**	**923,809**	**981,454**	**943,017**	**7.63**	**-3.92**

589

POLAND

6. Overnight stays of non-resident tourists in all types of accommodation establishments, by country of residence

	2009	2010	2011	2012	2013	Market share 2013	% Change 2013-2012
Albania	3,620	3,433	4,200	4,546	6,835	0.06	50.35
Andorra	209	938	569	632	687	0.01	8.70
Bosnia and Herzegovina	2,852	4,942	3,769	4,095	3,044	0.02	-25.67
Croatia	16,447	19,381	20,682	29,322	22,191	0.18	-24.32
Gibraltar	37	144	103	186	187	0.00	0.54
Greece	38,505	28,300	30,780	36,866	29,900	0.24	-18.90
Holy See	497	252	234		353	0.00	
Italy	408,730	430,151	454,508	484,326	476,444	3.85	-1.63
Malta	1,578	2,756	4,229	5,238	4,143	0.03	-20.90
Montenegro	558	456	1,091	1,202	1,305	0.01	8.57
Portugal	39,842	41,738	50,117	57,890	45,927	0.37	-20.67
San Marino	271	84	419	48	606	0.00	1,162.50
Serbia	7,610	11,012	12,420	13,457	15,860	0.13	17.86
Slovenia	20,070	17,862	18,644	21,950	22,073	0.18	0.56
Spain	234,380	252,341	318,698	319,562	311,489	2.52	-2.53
TFYR of Macedonia	2,316	12,498	3,346	2,134	1,973	0.02	-7.54
WESTERN EUROPE	**4,656,940**	**4,742,259**	**4,953,847**	**5,253,697**	**5,497,885**	**44.48**	**4.65**
Austria	111,382	112,274	119,380	122,456	124,406	1.01	1.59
Belgium	114,459	131,160	133,359	130,282	134,199	1.09	3.01
France	359,408	380,666	403,854	397,709	403,687	3.27	1.50
Germany	3,797,376	3,828,542	4,002,950	4,287,737	4,485,153	36.28	4.60
Liechtenstein	1,528	513	633	452	699	0.01	54.65
Luxembourg	5,348	7,763	7,066	7,270	7,256	0.06	-0.19
Monaco	710	500	378	493	376	0.00	-23.73
Netherlands	201,404	214,978	216,947	227,623	254,496	2.06	11.81
Switzerland	65,325	65,863	69,280	79,675	87,613	0.71	9.96
EAST MEDITERRANEAN EUROPE	**292,966**	**310,832**	**341,420**	**357,352**	**365,375**	**2.96**	**2.25**
Cyprus	6,839	6,165	4,617	5,754	5,660	0.05	-1.63
Israel	252,245	267,809	288,906	294,459	294,619	2.38	0.05
Turkey	33,882	36,858	47,897	57,139	65,096	0.53	13.93
MIDDLE EAST	**20,722**	**23,400**	**29,779**	**42,596**	**40,659**	**0.33**	**-4.55**
Bahrain	782	899	865	825	381	0.00	-53.82
Egypt	4,807	5,022	6,191	7,848	9,272	0.08	18.14
Iraq	1,178	1,359	2,533	1,810	1,996	0.02	10.28
Jordan	739	579	1,184	943	1,258	0.01	33.40
Kuwait	1,349	1,399	1,919	1,602	2,225	0.02	38.89
Lebanon	1,641	1,156	1,275	1,694	2,593	0.02	53.07
Libya	582	1,004	786	1,602	3,975	0.03	148.13
Oman	169	640	270	532	396	0.00	-25.56
Qatar	1,710	2,795	1,719	9,953	1,762	0.01	-82.30
Saudi Arabia	2,798	3,712	7,519	9,277	8,804	0.07	-5.10
Syrian Arab Republic	720	869	1,192	1,355	1,269	0.01	-6.35
United Arab Emirates	4,170	3,897	4,174	4,852	6,625	0.05	36.54
Yemen	77	69	152	303	103	0.00	-66.01
SOUTH ASIA	**53,656**	**58,210**	**49,475**	**54,589**	**59,172**	**0.48**	**8.40**
Afghanistan	2,966	8,622	6,285	7,597	8,206	0.07	8.02
Bangladesh	2,495	1,827	2,916	2,830	3,747	0.03	32.40
Bhutan	280	403	214	37	154	0.00	316.22
India	34,300	34,791	31,282	34,304	38,067	0.31	10.97
Iran, Islamic Republic of	4,397	5,342	5,604	6,055	4,976	0.04	-17.82
Maldives	13	126	35	79	6	0.00	-92.41
Nepal	7,272	4,466	384	626	1,789	0.01	185.78
Pakistan	1,590	2,240	2,220	2,671	1,865	0.02	-30.18
Sri Lanka	343	393	535	390	362	0.00	-7.18
NOT SPECIFIED	**38,485**	**62,425**	**47,717**	**81,072**	**103,998**	**0.84**	**28.28**
Other countries of the World	38,485	62,425	47,717	81,072	103,998	0.84	28.28

Yearbook of Tourism Statistics, Data 2009 – 2013, 2015 Edition

PORTUGAL

3. Arrivals of non-resident tourists in hotels and similar establishments, by country of residence

	2009	2010	2011	2012	2013	Market share 2013	% Change 2013-2012
TOTAL	5,911,079	6,256,808	6,792,220	7,043,478	7,630,090	100.00	8.33
AFRICA	72,785	73,519	82,981	95,137	119,321	1.56	25.42
SOUTHERN AFRICA	6,941	8,497	10,208	9,276	9,521	0.12	2.64
South Africa	6,941	8,497	10,208	9,276	9,521	0.12	2.64
OTHER AFRICA	65,844	65,022	72,773	85,861	109,800	1.44	27.88
Other countries of Africa	65,844	65,022	72,773	85,861	109,800	1.44	27.88
AMERICAS	607,432	743,093	860,255	933,643	1,017,301	13.33	8.96
NORTH AMERICA	285,548	322,548	351,429	384,735	429,515	5.63	11.64
Canada	59,676	69,459	86,492	95,000	105,927	1.39	11.50
United States of America	225,872	253,089	264,937	289,735	323,588	4.24	11.68
SOUTH AMERICA	260,801	355,226	433,344	472,061	498,964	6.54	5.70
Brazil	260,801	355,226	433,344	472,061	498,964	6.54	5.70
OTHER AMERICAS	61,083	65,319	75,482	76,847	88,822	1.16	15.58
Other countries of the Americas	61,083	65,319	75,482	76,847	88,822	1.16	15.58
EAST ASIA AND THE PACIFIC	181,740	221,740	253,807	293,323	404,495	5.30	37.90
NORTH-EAST ASIA	88,383	114,810	125,097	150,282	191,599	2.51	27.49
China	21,647	29,089	37,258	51,602	73,036	0.96	41.54
Japan	56,727	60,942	57,857	63,788	78,364	1.03	22.85
Korea, Republic of	10,009	24,779	29,982	34,892	40,199	0.53	15.21
AUSTRALASIA	25,334	29,481	34,051	35,987	42,236	0.55	17.36
Australia	25,334	29,481	34,051	35,987	42,236	0.55	17.36
OTHER EAST ASIA AND THE PACIFIC	68,023	77,449	94,659	107,054	170,660	2.24	59.41
Other countries of Asia	62,224	71,211	88,336	98,387	133,056	1.74	35.24
Other countries of Oceania	5,799	6,238	6,323	8,667	37,604	0.49	333.88
EUROPE	5,049,122	5,218,456	5,595,177	5,721,375	6,088,973	79.80	6.42
CENTRAL/EASTERN EUROPE	171,187	203,747	258,004	288,133	325,105	4.26	12.83
Bulgaria	6,584	7,043	6,842	8,213	8,819	0.12	7.38
Hungary	16,646	16,422	18,165	19,027	19,056	0.25	0.15
Poland	72,596	82,609	102,417	99,158	112,309	1.47	13.26
Romania	19,942	21,101	22,591	27,020	30,387	0.40	12.46
USSR (former)	55,419	76,572	107,989	134,715	154,534	2.03	14.71
NORTHERN EUROPE	1,386,825	1,431,672	1,535,947	1,610,067	1,743,234	22.85	8.27
Denmark	76,368	86,693	74,899	78,833	84,522	1.11	7.22
Finland	74,647	75,031	70,353	57,282	61,168	0.80	6.78
Iceland	2,213	4,135	2,546	4,090	2,371	0.03	-42.03
Ireland	146,703	148,647	154,546	174,430	189,642	2.49	8.72
Norway	55,776	58,085	64,889	68,913	79,485	1.04	15.34
Sweden	79,878	86,906	84,460	95,346	105,554	1.38	10.71
United Kingdom	951,240	972,175	1,084,254	1,131,173	1,220,492	16.00	7.90
SOUTHERN EUROPE	1,615,501	1,666,233	1,696,479	1,510,420	1,521,419	19.94	0.73
Greece	17,570	14,417	18,221	17,852	12,796	0.17	-28.32
Italy	309,075	344,508	363,427	334,539	307,639	4.03	-8.04
Spain	1,288,856	1,307,308	1,314,831	1,158,029	1,200,984	15.74	3.71
WESTERN EUROPE	1,723,294	1,798,845	1,950,529	2,149,338	2,360,088	30.93	9.81
Austria	68,680	63,340	67,583	83,285	71,996	0.94	-13.55
Belgium	136,618	135,527	146,513	158,116	160,654	2.11	1.61
France	527,501	542,195	619,753	695,242	784,278	10.28	12.81
Germany	636,281	643,359	650,096	714,182	802,543	10.52	12.37
Luxembourg	11,103	10,597	12,887	14,450	17,553	0.23	21.47
Netherlands	287,335	304,404	338,848	355,166	380,809	4.99	7.22
Switzerland	55,776	99,423	114,849	128,897	142,255	1.86	10.36
EAST MEDITERRANEAN EUROPE	6,618	8,740	11,083	14,390	18,996	0.25	32.01
Turkey	6,618	8,740	11,083	14,390	18,996	0.25	32.01
OTHER EUROPE	145,697	109,219	143,135	149,027	120,131	1.57	-19.39
Other countries of Europe	145,697	109,219	143,135	149,027	120,131	1.57	-19.39

Yearbook of Tourism Statistics, Data 2009 – 2013, 2015 Edition

PORTUGAL

4. Arrivals of non-resident tourists in all types of accommodation establishments, by country of residence

	2009	2010	2011	2012	2013	Market share 2013	% Change 2013-2012
TOTAL	6,439,022	6,756,354	7,263,644	7,503,252	8,096,941	100.00	7.91
AFRICA	73,882	75,446	84,319	96,330	121,335	1.50	25.96
SOUTHERN AFRICA	7,163	8,944	10,464	9,522	9,774	0.12	2.65
South Africa	7,163	8,944	10,464	9,522	9,774	0.12	2.65
OTHER AFRICA	66,719	66,502	73,855	86,808	111,561	1.38	28.51
Other countries of Africa	66,719	66,502	73,855	86,808	111,561	1.38	28.51
AMERICAS	622,683	759,506	874,361	946,990	1,029,242	12.71	8.69
NORTH AMERICA	290,834	328,002	356,165	389,313	434,279	5.36	11.55
Canada	62,058	71,851	88,732	97,289	108,410	1.34	11.43
United States of America	228,776	256,151	267,433	292,024	325,869	4.02	11.59
SOUTH AMERICA	268,913	363,871	440,787	479,115	504,473	6.23	5.29
Brazil	268,913	363,871	440,787	479,115	504,473	6.23	5.29
OTHER AMERICAS	62,936	67,633	77,409	78,562	90,490	1.12	15.18
Other countries of the Americas	62,936	67,633	77,409	78,562	90,490	1.12	15.18
EAST ASIA AND THE PACIFIC	190,419	229,173	261,440	301,056	412,305	5.09	36.95
NORTH-EAST ASIA	89,799	116,108	126,292	151,600	192,762	2.38	27.15
China	21,929	29,424	37,587	51,932	73,639	0.91	41.80
Japan	57,641	61,690	58,492	64,578	78,797	0.97	22.02
Korea, Republic of	10,229	24,994	30,213	35,090	40,326	0.50	14.92
AUSTRALASIA	30,308	33,143	38,225	39,382	45,740	0.56	16.14
Australia	30,308	33,143	38,225	39,382	45,740	0.56	16.14
OTHER EAST ASIA AND THE PACIFIC	70,312	79,922	96,923	110,074	173,803	2.15	57.90
Other countries of Asia	62,887	72,417	89,359	100,100	134,717	1.66	34.58
Other countries of Oceania	7,425	7,505	7,564	9,974	39,086	0.48	291.88
EUROPE	5,552,038	5,692,229	6,043,524	6,158,876	6,534,059	80.70	6.09
CENTRAL/EASTERN EUROPE	181,256	212,829	266,584	296,495	333,779	4.12	12.57
Bulgaria	6,941	7,358	7,178	8,473	9,116	0.11	7.59
Hungary	17,694	17,271	18,933	19,655	19,997	0.25	1.74
Poland	79,323	89,095	108,350	104,807	117,773	1.45	12.37
Romania	20,622	21,885	23,395	27,976	31,242	0.39	11.67
USSR (former)	56,676	77,220	108,728	135,584	155,651	1.92	14.80
NORTHERN EUROPE	1,436,703	1,478,999	1,576,701	1,652,120	1,791,078	22.12	8.41
Denmark	79,924	89,879	78,116	81,984	87,853	1.09	7.16
Finland	76,455	76,757	72,518	58,842	62,875	0.78	6.85
Iceland	2,231	4,192	2,566	4,115	2,375	0.03	-42.28
Ireland	149,809	151,786	156,990	176,895	192,669	2.38	8.92
Norway	57,199	59,380	66,291	70,229	80,643	1.00	14.83
Sweden	81,962	88,864	86,822	97,579	108,484	1.34	11.18
United Kingdom	989,123	1,008,141	1,113,398	1,162,476	1,256,179	15.51	8.06
SOUTHERN EUROPE	1,767,778	1,818,614	1,836,104	1,623,828	1,635,910	20.20	0.74
Greece	18,319	14,722	18,657	18,027	13,573	0.17	-24.71
Italy	330,105	364,908	382,711	350,167	321,835	3.97	-8.09
Spain	1,419,354	1,438,984	1,434,736	1,255,634	1,300,502	16.06	3.57
WESTERN EUROPE	2,006,249	2,057,084	2,203,102	2,415,414	2,626,760	32.44	8.75
Austria	72,873	67,169	71,523	87,454	76,509	0.94	-12.52
Belgium	154,990	152,851	162,325	175,004	176,137	2.18	0.65
France	663,022	666,958	747,153	826,798	911,957	11.26	10.30
Germany	702,542	695,247	701,458	770,115	863,799	10.67	12.16
Luxembourg	11,745	11,078	13,487	15,109	18,149	0.22	20.12
Netherlands	337,349	356,749	384,694	402,891	428,233	5.29	6.29
Switzerland	63,728	107,032	122,462	138,043	151,976	1.88	10.09
EAST MEDITERRANEAN EUROPE	6,737	8,873	11,347	14,583	19,313	0.24	32.44
Turkey	6,737	8,873	11,347	14,583	19,313	0.24	32.44
OTHER EUROPE	153,315	115,830	149,686	156,436	127,219	1.57	-18.68
Other countries of Europe	153,315	115,830	149,686	156,436	127,219	1.57	-18.68

Yearbook of Tourism Statistics, Data 2009 – 2013, 2015 Edition

PORTUGAL

5. Overnight stays of non-resident tourists in hotels and similar establishments, by country of residence

	2009	2010	2011	2012	2013	Market share 2013	% Change 2013-2012
TOTAL	23,214,377	23,608,207	26,003,760	27,256,580	29,359,790	100.00	7.72
AFRICA	266,501	268,870	292,404	338,084	419,500	1.43	24.08
SOUTHERN AFRICA	23,388	26,925	33,413	25,908	26,681	0.09	2.98
South Africa	23,388	26,925	33,413	25,908	26,681	0.09	2.98
OTHER AFRICA	243,113	241,945	258,991	312,176	392,819	1.34	25.83
Other countries of Africa	243,113	241,945	258,991	312,176	392,819	1.34	25.83
AMERICAS	1,482,342	1,785,586	2,064,495	2,273,438	2,513,373	8.56	10.55
NORTH AMERICA	738,068	800,925	864,745	948,880	1,085,680	3.70	14.42
Canada	207,890	224,106	252,847	286,008	316,555	1.08	10.68
United States of America	530,178	576,819	611,898	662,872	769,125	2.62	16.03
SOUTH AMERICA	595,511	828,510	1,015,458	1,139,398	1,209,521	4.12	6.15
Brazil	595,511	828,510	1,015,458	1,139,398	1,209,521	4.12	6.15
OTHER AMERICAS	148,763	156,151	184,292	185,160	218,172	0.74	17.83
Other countries of the Americas	148,763	156,151	184,292	185,160	218,172	0.74	17.83
EAST ASIA AND THE PACIFIC	433,282	484,508	556,593	637,694	844,288	2.88	32.40
NORTH-EAST ASIA	172,618	214,763	231,637	276,771	348,905	1.19	26.06
China	47,124	59,812	74,861	101,363	142,976	0.49	41.05
Japan	108,278	117,721	113,267	127,254	149,557	0.51	17.53
Korea, Republic of	17,216	37,230	43,509	48,154	56,372	0.19	17.07
AUSTRALASIA	67,630	74,038	87,805	89,244	106,442	0.36	19.27
Australia	67,630	74,038	87,805	89,244	106,442	0.36	19.27
OTHER EAST ASIA AND THE PACIFIC	193,034	195,707	237,151	271,679	388,941	1.32	43.16
Other countries of Asia	172,936	180,177	220,043	239,642	294,842	1.00	23.03
Other countries of Oceania	20,098	15,530	17,108	32,037	94,099	0.32	193.72
EUROPE	21,032,252	21,069,243	23,090,268	24,007,364	25,582,629	87.13	6.56
CENTRAL/EASTERN EUROPE	652,778	754,449	994,900	1,098,295	1,267,411	4.32	15.40
Bulgaria	18,382	19,896	21,726	27,648	29,978	0.10	8.43
Hungary	55,551	57,445	62,971	69,333	69,982	0.24	0.94
Poland	301,687	338,544	429,573	392,070	458,778	1.56	17.01
Romania	69,866	66,225	84,854	98,843	116,009	0.40	17.37
USSR (former)	207,292	272,339	395,776	510,401	592,664	2.02	16.12
NORTHERN EUROPE	7,989,061	7,857,143	8,574,675	8,916,653	9,722,457	33.11	9.04
Denmark	388,854	434,122	362,288	397,075	420,736	1.43	5.96
Finland	401,017	393,782	380,438	310,769	326,107	1.11	4.94
Iceland	16,250	28,494	9,334	26,173	9,041	0.03	-65.46
Ireland	872,146	826,785	865,949	991,997	1,088,906	3.71	9.77
Norway	263,453	273,625	290,201	329,975	395,308	1.35	19.80
Sweden	377,660	405,382	407,902	439,122	502,640	1.71	14.46
United Kingdom	5,669,681	5,494,953	6,258,563	6,421,542	6,979,719	23.77	8.69
SOUTHERN EUROPE	4,065,206	4,190,547	4,419,837	3,993,159	3,936,573	13.41	-1.42
Greece	58,225	43,452	56,515	49,496	37,930	0.13	-23.37
Italy	803,211	869,313	918,210	867,038	799,607	2.72	-7.78
Spain	3,203,770	3,277,782	3,445,112	3,076,625	3,099,036	10.56	0.73
WESTERN EUROPE	7,896,037	7,895,256	8,611,941	9,455,535	10,191,869	34.71	7.79
Austria	307,855	266,003	289,739	307,531	280,543	0.96	-8.78
Belgium	552,940	510,108	567,767	605,980	621,127	2.12	2.50
France	1,595,447	1,619,416	1,931,067	2,224,668	2,569,043	8.75	15.48
Germany	3,341,911	3,279,012	3,392,161	3,684,847	4,078,995	13.89	10.70
Luxembourg	45,284	42,866	48,786	54,617	67,173	0.23	22.99
Netherlands	1,789,147	1,843,369	1,992,895	2,137,313	2,085,943	7.10	-2.40
Switzerland	263,453	334,482	389,526	440,579	489,045	1.67	11.00
EAST MEDITERRANEAN EUROPE	18,114	22,902	29,759	35,903	46,985	0.16	30.87
Turkey	18,114	22,902	29,759	35,903	46,985	0.16	30.87
OTHER EUROPE	411,056	348,946	459,156	507,819	417,334	1.42	-17.82
Other countries of Europe	411,056	348,946	459,156	507,819	417,334	1.42	-17.82

Yearbook of Tourism Statistics, Data 2009 – 2013, 2015 Edition

PORTUGAL

6. Overnight stays of non-resident tourists in all types of accommodation establishments, by country of residence

	2009	2010	2011	2012	2013	Market share 2013	% Change 2013-2012
TOTAL	25,024,678	25,386,084	27,860,103	29,033,970	31,093,919	100.00	7.09
AFRICA	269,905	277,411	296,810	342,420	425,356	1.37	24.22
SOUTHERN AFRICA	23,973	27,914	34,176	26,371	27,225	0.09	3.24
South Africa	23,973	27,914	34,176	26,371	27,225	0.09	3.24
OTHER AFRICA	245,932	249,497	262,634	316,049	398,131	1.28	25.97
Other countries of Africa	245,932	249,497	262,634	316,049	398,131	1.28	25.97
AMERICAS	1,518,453	1,829,088	2,106,853	2,314,958	2,544,713	8.18	9.92
NORTH AMERICA	749,296	813,649	876,451	960,788	1,096,598	3.53	14.14
Canada	212,555	229,296	258,611	291,668	322,531	1.04	10.58
United States of America	536,741	584,353	617,840	669,120	774,067	2.49	15.68
SOUTH AMERICA	616,386	854,456	1,041,180	1,164,721	1,226,067	3.94	5.27
Brazil	616,386	854,456	1,041,180	1,164,721	1,226,067	3.94	5.27
OTHER AMERICAS	152,771	160,983	189,222	189,449	222,048	0.71	17.21
Other countries of the Americas	152,771	160,983	189,222	189,449	222,048	0.71	17.21
EAST ASIA AND THE PACIFIC	453,336	502,231	597,457	661,926	863,221	2.78	30.41
NORTH-EAST ASIA	175,146	217,356	233,912	279,314	351,759	1.13	25.94
China	47,693	60,429	75,579	102,173	144,828	0.47	41.75
Japan	109,890	119,251	114,441	128,635	150,362	0.48	16.89
Korea, Republic of	17,563	37,676	43,892	48,506	56,569	0.18	16.62
AUSTRALASIA	78,953	83,014	111,130	99,660	113,917	0.37	14.31
Australia	78,953	83,014	111,130	99,660	113,917	0.37	14.31
OTHER EAST ASIA AND THE PACIFIC	199,237	201,861	252,415	282,952	397,545	1.28	40.50
Other countries of Asia	174,717	183,800	225,945	245,691	299,302	0.96	21.82
Other countries of Oceania	24,520	18,061	26,470	37,261	98,243	0.32	163.66
EUROPE	22,782,984	22,777,354	24,858,983	25,714,666	27,260,629	87.67	6.01
CENTRAL/EASTERN EUROPE	677,274	779,780	1,025,421	1,123,240	1,293,077	4.16	15.12
Bulgaria	19,181	20,720	22,734	28,737	31,385	0.10	9.21
Hungary	57,811	59,376	66,734	71,085	72,762	0.23	2.36
Poland	317,452	354,935	450,480	408,135	473,878	1.52	16.11
Romania	72,354	70,499	87,232	102,565	119,515	0.38	16.53
USSR (former)	210,476	274,250	398,241	512,718	595,537	1.92	16.15
NORTHERN EUROPE	8,299,604	8,145,104	8,863,685	9,207,166	10,047,251	32.31	9.12
Denmark	403,189	448,050	376,360	411,428	434,027	1.40	5.49
Finland	409,470	401,517	392,306	319,010	335,611	1.08	5.20
Iceland	16,275	28,633	9,404	26,244	9,050	0.03	-65.52
Ireland	889,769	844,271	880,667	1,005,917	1,107,995	3.56	10.15
Norway	277,630	288,228	303,621	340,562	404,187	1.30	18.68
Sweden	391,407	419,147	424,754	455,496	521,046	1.68	14.39
United Kingdom	5,911,864	5,715,258	6,476,573	6,648,509	7,235,335	23.27	8.83
SOUTHERN EUROPE	4,475,777	4,616,274	4,853,777	4,340,144	4,260,372	13.70	-1.84
Greece	63,374	44,081	57,720	50,042	39,981	0.13	-20.11
Italy	852,761	913,932	970,194	906,315	834,335	2.68	-7.94
Spain	3,559,642	3,658,261	3,825,863	3,383,787	3,386,056	10.89	0.07
WESTERN EUROPE	8,885,462	8,846,151	9,604,981	10,479,786	11,177,251	35.95	6.66
Austria	319,275	276,170	301,794	319,237	292,472	0.94	-8.38
Belgium	618,754	574,808	632,650	673,453	679,226	2.18	0.86
France	1,980,920	1,989,283	2,325,934	2,648,302	2,976,322	9.57	12.39
Germany	3,567,813	3,479,508	3,615,029	3,896,194	4,292,934	13.81	10.18
Luxembourg	47,388	44,751	52,382	57,716	69,356	0.22	20.17
Netherlands	2,066,269	2,125,748	2,261,326	2,415,700	2,348,618	7.55	-2.78
Switzerland	285,043	355,883	415,866	469,184	518,323	1.67	10.47
EAST MEDITERRANEAN EUROPE	18,360	23,207	30,301	36,432	48,649	0.16	33.53
Turkey	18,360	23,207	30,301	36,432	48,649	0.16	33.53
OTHER EUROPE	426,507	366,838	480,818	527,898	434,029	1.40	-17.78
Other countries of Europe	426,507	366,838	480,818	527,898	434,029	1.40	-17.78

Yearbook of Tourism Statistics, Data 2009 – 2013, 2015 Edition

PUERTO RICO

1. Arrivals of non-resident tourists at national borders, by country of residence

		2009	2010	2011	2012	2013	Market share 2013	% Change 2013-2012
TOTAL	(*)	**3,183,252**	**3,185,606**	**3,047,915**	**3,069,087**	**3,199,700**	**100.00**	**4.26**
AMERICAS		**2,704,074**	**2,639,721**	**2,593,837**	**2,587,942**	**2,738,600**	**85.59**	**5.82**
CARIBBEAN		**13,007**	**8,823**	**7,231**	**6,924**	**8,200**	**0.26**	**18.43**
United States Virgin Islands		13,007	8,823	7,231	6,924	8,200	0.26	18.43
NORTH AMERICA		**2,691,067**	**2,630,898**	**2,586,606**	**2,581,018**	**2,730,400**	**85.33**	**5.79**
United States of America		2,691,067	2,630,898	2,586,606	2,581,018	2,730,400	85.33	5.79
NOT SPECIFIED		**479,178**	**545,885**	**454,078**	**481,145**	**461,100**	**14.41**	**-4.17**
Other countries of the World		479,178	545,885	454,078	481,145	461,100	14.41	-4.17

595

PUERTO RICO

3. Arrivals of non-resident tourists in hotels and similar establishments, by country of residence

	2009	2010	2011	2012	2013	Market share 2013	% Change 2013-2012
TOTAL (*)	1,280,937	1,349,449	1,414,587	1,504,659	1,584,897	100.00	5.33
AFRICA	1,456	1,327	1,361	1,490	1,700	0.11	14.09
OTHER AFRICA	1,456	1,327	1,361	1,490	1,700	0.11	14.09
All countries of Africa	1,456	1,327	1,361	1,490	1,700	0.11	14.09
AMERICAS	1,218,956	1,289,492	1,355,328	1,442,372	1,527,382	96.37	5.89
CARIBBEAN	30,714	30,275	30,903	32,673	33,147	2.09	1.45
Cuba	25	30	49	50	40	0.00	-20.00
Dominican Republic	5,948	6,056	6,123	6,497	6,797	0.43	4.62
United States Virgin Islands			1,804	2,222	2,506	0.16	12.78
Other countries of the Caribbean (*)	24,741	24,189	22,927	23,904	23,804	1.50	-0.42
CENTRAL AMERICA	3,243	3,272	3,615	4,285	4,729	0.30	10.36
Belize	19	38	50	52	68	0.00	30.77
Costa Rica	690	785	795	1,260	1,249	0.08	-0.87
El Salvador	98	113	175	161	229	0.01	42.24
Guatemala	422	443	550	532	586	0.04	10.15
Honduras	91	142	159	166	221	0.01	33.13
Nicaragua	49	45	75	72	160	0.01	122.22
Panama	788	766	888	976	1,201	0.08	23.05
Other countries of Central America	1,086	940	923	1,066	1,015	0.06	-4.78
NORTH AMERICA	1,173,826	1,244,696	1,308,692	1,390,897	1,474,112	93.01	5.98
Canada	15,012	19,632	23,290	23,379	21,590	1.36	-7.65
Mexico	8,388	8,195	8,057	9,435	9,354	0.59	-0.86
United States of America	1,150,426	1,216,869	1,277,345	1,358,083	1,443,168	91.06	6.27
SOUTH AMERICA	11,173	11,249	12,118	14,517	15,394	0.97	6.04
Argentina	1,961	2,230	2,035	2,563	2,681	0.17	4.60
Bolivia	450	463	453	467	499	0.03	6.85
Brazil	1,882	1,916	2,300	2,650	2,367	0.15	-10.68
Chile	650	637	649	803	791	0.05	-1.49
Colombia	2,023	2,123	2,501	2,942	3,254	0.21	10.61
Ecuador	186	159	175	251	299	0.02	19.12
French Guiana	5	3	18	11	17	0.00	54.55
Guyana	15	17	27	24	45	0.00	87.50
Paraguay	27	64	41	83	58	0.00	-30.12
Peru	335	380	418	549	564	0.04	2.73
Suriname	20	30	19	42	72	0.00	71.43
Uruguay	142	193	169	416	213	0.01	-48.80
Venezuela	2,465	2,403	2,909	3,329	4,172	0.26	25.32
Other countries of South America	1,012	631	404	387	362	0.02	-6.46
EAST ASIA AND THE PACIFIC	2,997	3,342	3,926	4,808	4,785	0.30	-0.48
NORTH-EAST ASIA	1,194	1,240	1,584	1,862	1,892	0.12	1.61
China	448	514	636	687	814	0.05	18.49
Hong Kong, China	86	81	91	136	139	0.01	2.21
Japan	642	625	805	976	898	0.06	-7.99
Taiwan, Province of China	18	20	52	63	41	0.00	-34.92
SOUTH-EAST ASIA	199	162	209	217	330	0.02	52.07
Philippines	113	153	186	173	270	0.02	56.07
Thailand	86	9	23	44	60	0.00	36.36
AUSTRALASIA	861	891	1,261	1,410	1,279	0.08	-9.29
Australia	781	813	1,175	1,309	1,154	0.07	-11.84
New Zealand	80	78	86	101	125	0.01	23.76
OTHER EAST ASIA AND THE PACIFIC	743	1,049	872	1,319	1,284	0.08	-2.65
Other countries of Asia	743	1,049	872	1,319	1,284	0.08	-2.65
EUROPE	29,951	24,315	26,231	32,332	32,852	2.07	1.61
CENTRAL/EASTERN EUROPE	1,431	1,101	1,334	1,644	2,040	0.13	24.09
Bulgaria	16	28	64	11	13	0.00	18.18
Czech Republic	82	78	113	177	157	0.01	-11.30
Hungary	46	48	110	94	97	0.01	3.19
Poland	161	82	142	190	158	0.01	-16.84
Romania	40	33	44	81	63	0.00	-22.22

596

PUERTO RICO

3. Arrivals of non-resident tourists in hotels and similar establishments, by country of residence

	2009	2010	2011	2012	2013	Market share 2013	% Change 2013-2012
Russian Federation	879	746	771	909	1,386	0.09	52.48
Slovakia		27	10	53	37	0.00	-30.19
Baltic countries	207	59	80	129	129	0.01	
NORTHERN EUROPE	**5,087**	**6,015**	**6,216**	**6,684**	**8,089**	**0.51**	**21.02**
Denmark	656	612	670	669	757	0.05	13.15
Finland	241	369	354	394	551	0.03	39.85
Iceland	11	33	34	29	55	0.00	89.66
Ireland	313	346	487	479	770	0.05	60.75
Norway	301	358	348	460	626	0.04	36.09
Sweden	677	762	852	891	1,185	0.07	33.00
United Kingdom	2,888	3,535	3,471	3,762	4,145	0.26	10.18
SOUTHERN EUROPE	**9,081**	**6,972**	**6,873**	**7,581**	**6,889**	**0.43**	**-9.13**
Albania	38	53	62	67	63	0.00	-5.97
Gibraltar	33	3	4	24	34	0.00	41.67
Greece	437	442	407	470	466	0.03	-0.85
Italy	1,413	1,306	1,404	1,874	1,940	0.12	3.52
Malta	16	14	7	13	2	0.00	-84.62
Portugal	296	146	210	241	181	0.01	-24.90
San Marino	12	6	3	8	7	0.00	-12.50
Spain	6,754	4,739	4,666	4,740	4,121	0.26	-13.06
Yugoslavia, SFR (former)	82	263	110	144	75	0.00	-47.92
WESTERN EUROPE	**6,253**	**6,738**	**7,999**	**11,216**	**10,248**	**0.65**	**-8.63**
Austria	215	265	351	353	379	0.02	7.37
Belgium	479	636	566	625	558	0.04	-10.72
France	1,499	1,521	1,933	2,463	2,550	0.16	3.53
Germany	2,676	2,932	3,586	5,459	4,870	0.31	-10.79
Luxembourg	25	29	45	52	48	0.00	-7.69
Netherlands	784	808	823	1,376	1,113	0.07	-19.11
Switzerland	575	547	695	888	730	0.05	-17.79
EAST MEDITERRANEAN EUROPE	**414**	**431**	**561**	**629**	**613**	**0.04**	**-2.54**
Israel	310	355	480	424	497	0.03	17.22
Turkey	104	76	81	205	116	0.01	-43.41
OTHER EUROPE	**7,685**	**3,058**	**3,248**	**4,578**	**4,973**	**0.31**	**8.63**
Other countries of Europe	7,685	3,058	3,248	4,578	4,973	0.31	8.63
MIDDLE EAST	**111**	**135**	**38**	**66**	**85**	**0.01**	**28.79**
Egypt	9	85	3	20	19	0.00	-5.00
Iraq				1			
Saudi Arabia	102	50	35	45	66	0.00	46.67
SOUTH ASIA	**210**	**167**	**338**	**346**	**434**	**0.03**	**25.43**
India	210	167	338	346	434	0.03	25.43
NOT SPECIFIED	**27,256**	**30,671**	**27,365**	**23,245**	**17,659**	**1.11**	**-24.03**
Other countries of the World (*)	27,256	30,671	27,365	23,245	17,659	1.11	-24.03

Yearbook of Tourism Statistics, Data 2009 – 2013, 2015 Edition

QATAR

1. Arrivals of non-resident tourists at national borders, by country of residence

	2009	2010	2011	2012	2013	Market share 2013	% Change 2013-2012
TOTAL	2,361,650	1,699,568	2,057,157	2,346,359	2,611,451	100.00	11.30
AFRICA	61,142	70,037	84,436	92,856	95,033	3.64	2.34
OTHER AFRICA	61,142	70,037	84,436	92,856	95,033	3.64	2.34
All countries of Africa	61,142	70,037	84,436	92,856	95,033	3.64	2.34
AMERICAS	967,485	92,121	101,829	117,100	130,438	4.99	11.39
OTHER AMERICAS	967,485	92,121	101,829	117,100	130,438	4.99	11.39
All countries of the Americas	967,485	92,121	101,829	117,100	130,438	4.99	11.39
EAST ASIA AND THE PACIFIC	99,035	115,297	130,203	153,125	165,000	6.32	7.76
OTHER EAST ASIA AND THE PACIFIC	99,035	115,297	130,203	153,125	165,000	6.32	7.76
All countries East Asia/Pacific	99,035	115,297	130,203	153,125	165,000	6.32	7.76
EUROPE	231,386	265,099	301,843	365,840	409,140	15.67	11.84
OTHER EUROPE	231,386	265,099	301,843	365,840	409,140	15.67	11.84
All countries of Europe	231,386	265,099	301,843	365,840	409,140	15.67	11.84
MIDDLE EAST	723,300	823,510	1,057,492	1,178,915	1,323,291	50.67	12.25
Bahrain	83,824	87,188	89,677	102,735	113,533	4.35	10.51
Kuwait	41,282	43,957	59,486	58,382	77,320	2.96	32.44
Oman	76,438	83,053	86,650	100,965	102,600	3.93	1.62
Saudi Arabia	273,118	338,632	498,645	574,112	673,350	25.78	17.29
United Arab Emirates	81,602	90,720	111,247	116,671	123,460	4.73	5.82
Other countries of Middle East	167,036	179,960	211,787	226,050	233,028	8.92	3.09
SOUTH ASIA	279,302	333,504	381,354	438,523	488,549	18.71	11.41
All countries of South Asia	279,302	333,504	381,354	438,523	488,549	18.71	11.41

Yearbook of Tourism Statistics, Data 2009 – 2013, 2015 Edition

REPUBLIC OF MOLDOVA

2. Arrivals of non-resident visitors at national borders, by nationality

		2009	2010	2011	2012	2013	Market share 2013	% Change 2013-2012
TOTAL	(*)	9,189	8,956	10,788	12,797	13,150	100.00	2.76
AFRICA		2	2	14		1	0.01	
CENTRAL AFRICA				1				
Congo				1				
NORTH AFRICA			1	2				
Algeria			1	2				
SOUTHERN AFRICA			1	5		1	0.01	
South Africa			1	3		1	0.01	
Swaziland				2				
WEST AFRICA		2		6				
Benin		2						
Ghana				5				
Mauritania				1				
AMERICAS		232	524	651	593	621	4.72	4.72
CARIBBEAN				23				
British Virgin Islands				23				
NORTH AMERICA		227	490	611	577	614	4.67	6.41
Canada		33	38	53	40	35	0.27	-12.50
Mexico			1		3			
United States of America		194	451	558	534	579	4.40	8.43
SOUTH AMERICA		5	34	17	16	7	0.05	-56.25
Argentina		2	1	2				
Bolivia		1			1			
Brazil			29	11	15	7	0.05	-53.33
Colombia		1						
Ecuador		1						
Peru			3	4				
Venezuela			1					
EAST ASIA AND THE PACIFIC		107	162	545	375	444	3.38	18.40
NORTH-EAST ASIA		106	133	487	305	369	2.81	20.98
China		8	27	166	75	65	0.49	-13.33
Japan		76	93	258	193	265	2.02	37.31
Korea, Republic of			12	23	37	25	0.19	-32.43
Mongolia			1			14	0.11	
Taiwan, Province of China		22		40				
SOUTH-EAST ASIA		1	3	34	25			
Philippines			1	1				
Singapore		1		2				
Thailand			2	2	8			
Viet Nam				29	17			
AUSTRALASIA			26	24	45	75	0.57	66.67
Australia			25	16	40	71	0.54	77.50
New Zealand			1	8	5	4	0.03	-20.00
EUROPE		8,837	8,229	9,559	11,753	12,020	91.41	2.27
CENTRAL/EASTERN EUROPE		4,744	4,685	5,459	6,567	6,743	51.28	2.68
Armenia		49	23	39	21	28	0.21	33.33
Azerbaijan		76	29	13	41	109	0.83	165.85
Belarus		176	105	44	57	64	0.49	12.28
Bulgaria		380	324	289	401	246	1.87	-38.65
Czech Republic		40	24	57	93	108	0.82	16.13
Estonia		42	70	76	58	136	1.03	134.48
Georgia		53	7	85	19	52	0.40	173.68
Hungary		31	18	84	79	40	0.30	-49.37
Kazakhstan		56	23	16	29	18	0.14	-37.93
Kyrgyzstan		15	5	11	19	14	0.11	-26.32
Latvia		14	80	40	35	28	0.21	-20.00
Lithuania		34	12	69	88	105	0.80	19.32
Poland		291	204	371	505	823	6.26	62.97
Romania		765	1,698	1,600	1,782	2,307	17.54	29.46

Yearbook of Tourism Statistics, Data 2009 – 2013, 2015 Edition

REPUBLIC OF MOLDOVA

2. Arrivals of non-resident visitors at national borders, by nationality

	2009	2010	2011	2012	2013	Market share 2013	% Change 2013-2012
Russian Federation	1,713	1,327	1,404	2,204	1,604	12.20	-27.22
Slovakia	11	6	52	130	16	0.12	-87.69
Tajikistan	4		3	9	2	0.02	-77.78
Turkmenistan	2		12	2			
Ukraine	979	730	1,189	987	1,042	7.92	5.57
Uzbekistan	13		5	8	1	0.01	-87.50
NORTHERN EUROPE	**1,032**	**625**	**965**	**1,031**	**1,000**	**7.60**	**-3.01**
Denmark	100	15	54	26	20	0.15	-23.08
Finland	84	66	128	49	92	0.70	87.76
Ireland	10	7	12	19	22	0.17	15.79
Norway	35	33	87	66	87	0.66	31.82
Sweden	59	99	334	207	276	2.10	33.33
United Kingdom	744	405	350	664	503	3.83	-24.25
SOUTHERN EUROPE	**612**	**764**	**789**	**920**	**1,394**	**10.60**	**51.52**
Albania	3		3	4	54	0.41	1,250.00
Bosnia and Herzegovina	2	2	52	4	7	0.05	75.00
Croatia	85	37	12	12	63	0.48	425.00
Greece	118	91	86	78	100	0.76	28.21
Italy	258	474	445	622	593	4.51	-4.66
Montenegro			3	2	251	1.91	12,450.00
Portugal	44	5	14	8	43	0.33	437.50
San Marino			50				
Serbia		19	16	55	67	0.51	21.82
Serbia and Montenegro	26						
Slovenia	8	53	31	55	115	0.87	109.09
Spain	60	79	69	72	98	0.75	36.11
TFYR of Macedonia	8	4	8	8	3	0.02	-62.50
WESTERN EUROPE	**1,265**	**1,392**	**1,689**	**2,209**	**2,167**	**16.48**	**-1.90**
Austria	147	103	95	269	308	2.34	14.50
Belgium	17	103	46	129	82	0.62	-36.43
France	196	283	248	155	364	2.77	134.84
Germany	460	482	1,001	1,275	798	6.07	-37.41
Luxembourg		2	2	1	39	0.30	3,800.00
Netherlands	154	311	219	288	336	2.56	16.67
Switzerland	291	108	78	92	240	1.83	160.87
EAST MEDITERRANEAN EUROPE	**1,184**	**763**	**657**	**1,026**	**716**	**5.44**	**-30.21**
Cyprus	26	12	42	44	12	0.09	-72.73
Israel	156	225	138	163	147	1.12	-9.82
Turkey	1,002	526	477	819	557	4.24	-31.99
MIDDLE EAST	**5**	**24**	**10**	**45**	**26**	**0.20**	**-42.22**
Egypt		19		6	1	0.01	-83.33
Iraq	1	1		2	5	0.04	150.00
Jordan		1		1	6	0.05	500.00
Kuwait			1	2			
Lebanon	1	1		17	10	0.08	-41.18
Syrian Arab Republic	3		3	16			
United Arab Emirates		2	6	1	4	0.03	300.00
SOUTH ASIA	**6**	**15**	**9**	**18**	**13**	**0.10**	**-27.78**
Afghanistan		12					
Bangladesh			1				
India	5	2	6	12	13	0.10	8.33
Iran, Islamic Republic of	1	1	1	5			
Pakistan			1	1			
NOT SPECIFIED				**13**	**25**	**0.19**	**92.31**
Other countries of the World				13	25	0.19	92.31

Yearbook of Tourism Statistics, Data 2009 – 2013, 2015 Edition

REPUBLIC OF MOLDOVA

4. Arrivals of non-resident tourists in all types of accommodation establishments, by nationality

	2009	2010	2011	2012	2013	Market share 2013	% Change 2013-2012
TOTAL (*)	59,563	63,593	75,000	88,956	95,640	100.00	7.51
AFRICA	127	127	300	340	524	0.55	54.12
OTHER AFRICA	127	127	300	340	524	0.55	54.12
All countries of Africa	127	127	300	340	524	0.55	54.12
AMERICAS	3,703	3,666	5,245	7,146	6,353	6.64	-11.10
NORTH AMERICA	3,636	3,524	4,960	6,855	5,683	5.94	-17.10
Canada	274	388	495	444	424	0.44	-4.50
United States of America	3,328	3,132	4,419	6,338	4,666	4.88	-26.38
Other countries of North America	34	4	46	73	593	0.62	712.33
SOUTH AMERICA	60	108	201	235	370	0.39	57.45
All countries of South America	60	108	201	235	370	0.39	57.45
OTHER AMERICAS	7	34	84	56	300	0.31	435.71
Other countries of the Americas	7	34	84	56	300	0.31	435.71
EAST ASIA AND THE PACIFIC	806	1,006	1,968	2,068	2,180	2.28	5.42
NORTH-EAST ASIA	453	525	985	1,122	1,062	1.11	-5.35
China	144	188	518	555	315	0.33	-43.24
Japan	309	337	467	567	747	0.78	31.75
OTHER EAST ASIA AND THE PACIFIC	353	481	983	946	1,118	1.17	18.18
Other countries of Asia	220	426	837	727	861	0.90	18.43
All countries of Oceania	133	55	146	219	257	0.27	17.35
EUROPE	54,927	58,794	67,487	79,402	86,583	90.53	9.04
CENTRAL/EASTERN EUROPE	31,669	36,332	40,749	45,698	53,471	55.91	17.01
Armenia	252	167	324	313	322	0.34	2.88
Azerbaijan	451	332	471	611	810	0.85	32.57
Belarus	1,379	932	923	1,194	1,446	1.51	21.11
Bulgaria	1,458	1,384	1,163	1,373	1,657	1.73	20.68
Czech Republic	684	438	1,145	771	826	0.86	7.13
Estonia	241	504	456	373	547	0.57	46.65
Georgia	259	433	616	717	793	0.83	10.60
Hungary	450	480	755	552	656	0.69	18.84
Kazakhstan	362	247	247	453	324	0.34	-28.48
Kyrgyzstan	124	510	112	147	84	0.09	-42.86
Latvia	178	273	332	249	503	0.53	102.01
Lithuania	440	400	506	600	665	0.70	10.83
Poland	1,639	1,390	1,872	2,295	2,677	2.80	16.64
Romania	8,796	15,403	16,097	17,549	21,030	21.99	19.84
Russian Federation	7,314	6,484	7,840	9,244	11,003	11.50	19.03
Slovakia	240	198	292	263	341	0.36	29.66
Tajikistan	117	60	186	377	164	0.17	-56.50
Turkmenistan	39	268	30	82	109	0.11	32.93
Ukraine	7,115	6,083	7,194	8,216	9,287	9.71	13.04
Uzbekistan	131	346	188	319	227	0.24	-28.84
NORTHERN EUROPE	4,112	4,062	5,215	5,956	5,444	5.69	-8.60
Denmark	367	302	311	383	395	0.41	3.13
Finland	360	764	510	386	504	0.53	30.57
Ireland	385	172	466	328	267	0.28	-18.60
Norway	377	342	598	461	597	0.62	29.50
Sweden	781	889	1,432	1,144	1,056	1.10	-7.69
United Kingdom	1,842	1,593	1,898	3,254	2,625	2.74	-19.33
SOUTHERN EUROPE	6,157	6,118	7,272	8,197	8,170	8.54	-0.33
Albania	37	139	104	144	118	0.12	-18.06
Bosnia and Herzegovina	36	106	162	93	140	0.15	50.54
Croatia	233	221	247	191	183	0.19	-4.19
Greece	923	598	648	762	652	0.68	-14.44
Italy	3,777	3,942	4,447	5,001	5,084	5.32	1.66
Montenegro			49	60	235	0.25	291.67
Portugal	138	148	347	147	263	0.27	78.91
Serbia		148	201	237	198	0.21	-16.46
Serbia and Montenegro	157						

601

Yearbook of Tourism Statistics, Data 2009 – 2013, 2015 Edition

REPUBLIC OF MOLDOVA

4. Arrivals of non-resident tourists in all types of accommodation establishments, by nationality

	2009	2010	2011	2012	2013	Market share 2013	% Change 2013-2012
Slovenia	283	345	388	632	369	0.39	-41.61
Spain	573	471	679	930	928	0.97	-0.22
WESTERN EUROPE	**8,390**	**7,966**	**9,011**	**11,003**	**12,369**	**12.93**	**12.41**
Austria	927	820	1,003	1,124	1,554	1.62	38.26
Belgium	388	405	577	678	708	0.74	4.42
France	1,805	1,479	2,130	2,103	2,256	2.36	7.28
Germany	2,959	3,468	3,863	5,520	5,934	6.20	7.50
Luxembourg	77	22	31	34	86	0.09	152.94
Netherlands	979	1,283	1,036	977	1,224	1.28	25.28
Switzerland	1,255	489	371	567	607	0.63	7.05
EAST MEDITERRANEAN EUROPE	**3,969**	**3,837**	**4,306**	**7,701**	**6,603**	**6.90**	**-14.26**
Cyprus			204	249	201	0.21	-19.28
Israel	878	1,299	1,321	1,654	1,802	1.88	8.95
Turkey	3,091	2,538	2,781	5,798	4,600	4.81	-20.66
OTHER EUROPE	**630**	**479**	**934**	**847**	**526**	**0.55**	**-37.90**
Other countries of Europe	630	479	934	847	526	0.55	-37.90

Yearbook of Tourism Statistics, Data 2009 – 2013, 2015 Edition

REPUBLIC OF MOLDOVA

6. Overnight stays of non-resident tourists in all types of accommodation establishments, by nationality

	2009	2010	2011	2012	2013	Market share 2013	% Change 2013-2012
TOTAL (*)	147,762	162,755	173,893	190,766	216,115	100.00	13.29
AFRICA	293	401	687	598	863	0.40	44.31
OTHER AFRICA	293	401	687	598	863	0.40	44.31
All countries of Africa	293	401	687	598	863	0.40	44.31
AMERICAS	11,410	12,780	12,646	13,854	12,942	5.99	-6.58
NORTH AMERICA	11,185	12,097	10,963	13,382	12,069	5.58	-9.81
Canada	1,079	1,500	1,208	1,016	896	0.41	-11.81
United States of America	10,032	10,593	9,565	12,195	10,479	4.85	-14.07
Other countries of North America	74	4	190	171	694	0.32	305.85
SOUTH AMERICA	207	560	918	395	530	0.25	34.18
All countries of South America	207	560	918	395	530	0.25	34.18
OTHER AMERICAS	18	123	765	77	343	0.16	345.45
Other countries of the Americas	18	123	765	77	343	0.16	345.45
EAST ASIA AND THE PACIFIC	2,268	2,817	5,481	4,378	4,687	2.17	7.06
NORTH-EAST ASIA	1,374	1,429	2,978	2,648	2,415	1.12	-8.80
China	514	569	1,771	1,245	916	0.42	-26.43
Japan	860	860	1,207	1,403	1,499	0.69	6.84
OTHER EAST ASIA AND THE PACIFIC	894	1,388	2,503	1,730	2,272	1.05	31.33
Other countries of Asia	639	1,188	2,181	1,353	1,782	0.82	31.71
All countries of Oceania	255	200	322	377	490	0.23	29.97
EUROPE	133,791	146,757	155,079	171,936	197,623	91.44	14.94
CENTRAL/EASTERN EUROPE	75,438	86,134	93,390	100,362	120,979	55.98	20.54
Armenia	897	641	948	695	884	0.41	27.19
Azerbaijan	1,260	1,074	1,237	1,347	2,029	0.94	50.63
Belarus	6,151	3,092	3,188	3,759	4,077	1.89	8.46
Bulgaria	2,867	2,512	2,815	3,512	3,120	1.44	-11.16
Czech Republic	1,297	918	2,288	2,464	1,896	0.88	-23.05
Estonia	604	1,099	1,140	924	1,532	0.71	65.80
Georgia	821	1,169	1,449	1,442	1,684	0.78	16.78
Hungary	1,028	1,146	1,497	1,113	1,314	0.61	18.06
Kazakhstan	962	724	653	963	875	0.40	-9.14
Kyrgyzstan	431	1,377	346	441	362	0.17	-17.91
Latvia	455	799	741	554	1,383	0.64	149.64
Lithuania	1,089	1,006	1,103	1,227	1,404	0.65	14.43
Poland	3,964	3,084	4,211	4,235	5,507	2.55	30.04
Romania	19,144	37,728	36,487	37,969	45,516	21.06	19.88
Russian Federation	20,114	17,043	20,117	21,615	28,862	13.35	33.53
Slovakia	491	511	573	570	753	0.35	32.11
Tajikistan	328	199	458	1,159	412	0.19	-64.45
Turkmenistan	324	538	121	183	182	0.08	-0.55
Ukraine	12,834	10,811	13,596	15,551	18,672	8.64	20.07
Uzbekistan	377	663	422	639	515	0.24	-19.41
NORTHERN EUROPE	10,776	11,016	12,803	12,569	12,154	5.62	-3.30
Denmark	1,191	712	803	917	1,047	0.48	14.18
Finland	941	2,102	1,251	719	1,112	0.51	54.66
Ireland	945	528	1,345	713	612	0.28	-14.17
Norway	1,103	1,045	1,437	1,105	1,318	0.61	19.28
Sweden	1,941	2,195	3,177	2,742	2,511	1.16	-8.42
United Kingdom	4,655	4,434	4,790	6,373	5,554	2.57	-12.85
SOUTHERN EUROPE	14,161	15,658	17,816	19,743	18,577	8.60	-5.91
Albania	92	309	254	365	273	0.13	-25.21
Bosnia and Herzegovina	126	289	340	232	476	0.22	105.17
Croatia	538	628	611	444	367	0.17	-17.34
Greece	2,053	1,556	1,300	1,568	1,558	0.72	-0.64
Italy	9,044	10,287	11,274	12,809	11,638	5.39	-9.14
Montenegro			110	174	378	0.17	117.24
Portugal	284	335	1,004	427	556	0.26	30.21
Serbia		374	456	674	560	0.26	-16.91
Serbia and Montenegro	356						

603

Yearbook of Tourism Statistics, Data 2009 – 2013, 2015 Edition

REPUBLIC OF MOLDOVA

6. Overnight stays of non-resident tourists in all types of accommodation establishments, by nationality

	2009	2010	2011	2012	2013	Market share 2013	% Change 2013-2012
Slovenia	495	750	859	1,310	811	0.38	-38.09
Spain	1,173	1,130	1,608	1,740	1,960	0.91	12.64
WESTERN EUROPE	**19,535**	**19,495**	**20,502**	**22,437**	**27,012**	**12.50**	**20.39**
Austria	1,827	1,819	2,086	2,184	3,808	1.76	74.36
Belgium	949	880	1,140	1,319	1,388	0.64	5.23
France	4,296	3,653	4,675	4,404	4,774	2.21	8.40
Germany	7,305	8,790	9,112	10,728	12,616	5.84	17.60
Luxembourg	154	46	43	70	181	0.08	158.57
Netherlands	2,381	3,100	2,490	2,553	2,891	1.34	13.24
Switzerland	2,623	1,207	956	1,179	1,354	0.63	14.84
EAST MEDITERRANEAN EUROPE	**12,341**	**13,151**	**9,212**	**15,583**	**18,076**	**8.36**	**16.00**
Cyprus			554	507	395	0.18	-22.09
Israel	2,470	4,472	3,631	4,686	6,135	2.84	30.92
Turkey	9,871	8,679	5,027	10,390	11,546	5.34	11.13
OTHER EUROPE	**1,540**	**1,303**	**1,356**	**1,242**	**825**	**0.38**	**-33.57**
Other countries of Europe	1,540	1,303	1,356	1,242	825	0.38	-33.57

Yearbook of Tourism Statistics, Data 2009 – 2013, 2015 Edition

REUNION

1. Arrivals of non-resident tourists at national borders, by country of residence

		2009	2010	2011	2012	2013	Market share 2013	% Change 2013-2012
TOTAL	(*)	**421,900**	**420,200**	**471,300**	**446,500**	**416,000**	**100.00**	**-6.83**
AFRICA		**41,600**	**34,000**	**42,500**	**46,100**	**45,600**	**10.96**	**-1.08**
EAST AFRICA		**20,300**	**18,400**	**18,200**				
Mauritius		20,300	18,400	18,200				
OTHER AFRICA		**21,300**	**15,600**	**24,300**	**46,100**	**45,600**	**10.96**	**-1.08**
Other countries of Africa		21,300	15,600	24,300				
All countries of Africa	(*)				46,100	45,600	10.96	-1.08
EUROPE		**364,300**	**367,900**	**406,100**	**379,400**	**358,900**	**86.27**	**-5.40**
WESTERN EUROPE		**344,300**	**346,200**	**381,600**	**355,900**	**337,200**	**81.06**	**-5.25**
France		344,300	346,200	381,600	355,900	337,200	81.06	-5.25
OTHER EUROPE		**20,000**	**21,700**	**24,500**	**23,500**	**21,700**	**5.22**	**-7.66**
Other countries of Europe		20,000	21,700	24,500	23,500	21,700	5.22	-7.66
NOT SPECIFIED		**16,000**	**18,300**	**22,700**	**21,000**	**11,500**	**2.76**	**-45.24**
Other countries of the World		16,000	18,300	22,700	21,000	11,500	2.76	-45.24

Yearbook of Tourism Statistics, Data 2009 – 2013, 2015 Edition

ROMANIA

2. Arrivals of non-resident visitors at national borders, by country of residence

	2009	2010	2011	2012	2013	Market share 2013	% Change 2013-2012
TOTAL	7,575,298	7,498,307	7,611,124	7,936,694	8,018,576	100.00	1.03
AFRICA	12,803	14,464	15,568	16,325	17,380	0.22	6.46
EAST AFRICA	968	1,293	1,469	1,510	1,502	0.02	-0.53
Burundi	6	8	10	17	11	0.00	-35.29
Comoros	3	7	1	6	8	0.00	33.33
Djibouti	1		1		2	0.00	
Eritrea	6	6	11	7	8	0.00	14.29
Ethiopia	36	44	69	65	97	0.00	49.23
Kenya	100	118	153	155	183	0.00	18.06
Madagascar	84	102	76	73	68	0.00	-6.85
Mauritius	532	695	712	706	692	0.01	-1.98
Mozambique	21	21	14	24	50	0.00	108.33
Rwanda	13	14	14	12	16	0.00	33.33
Somalia	3	8	9	15	10	0.00	-33.33
Uganda	23	31	30	50	30	0.00	-40.00
United Republic of Tanzania	75	176	273	230	216	0.00	-6.09
Zambia	18	17	25	39	35	0.00	-10.26
Zimbabwe	47	46	71	111	76	0.00	-31.53
CENTRAL AFRICA	645	653	789	710	706	0.01	-0.56
Angola	126	97	149	150	164	0.00	9.33
Cameroon	269	316	359	313	282	0.00	-9.90
Central African Republic	26	13	14	16	18	0.00	12.50
Chad	5	8	8	10	7	0.00	-30.00
Congo	183	119	130	91	86	0.00	-5.49
Democratic Republic of the Congo	15	43	79	80	95	0.00	18.75
Equatorial Guinea	1	11	7	14	18	0.00	28.57
Gabon	18	45	42	34	35	0.00	2.94
Sao Tome and Principe	2	1	1	2	1	0.00	-50.00
NORTH AFRICA	8,029	9,165	9,492	9,878	10,937	0.14	10.72
Algeria	761	748	896	957	1,216	0.02	27.06
Morocco	2,197	2,472	2,887	3,302	3,798	0.05	15.02
Sudan	334	356	296	231	222	0.00	-3.90
Tunisia	4,737	5,589	5,413	5,388	5,701	0.07	5.81
SOUTHERN AFRICA	1,249	1,465	1,834	2,104	1,901	0.02	-9.65
Botswana	8	10	10	17	7	0.00	-58.82
Lesotho	1	2	1	4	3	0.00	-25.00
Namibia	15	59	51	42	37	0.00	-11.90
South Africa	1,225	1,394	1,772	2,041	1,854	0.02	-9.16
WEST AFRICA	1,912	1,860	1,963	2,091	2,309	0.03	10.43
Benin	47	34	53	45	80	0.00	77.78
Burkina Faso	38	21	31	47	47	0.00	
Cabo Verde	63	84	69	66	56	0.00	-15.15
Côte d'Ivoire	150	160	192	173	161	0.00	-6.94
Gambia	11	15	6	10	11	0.00	10.00
Ghana	149	143	177	132	194	0.00	46.97
Guinea	144	69	66	71	62	0.00	-12.68
Guinea-Bissau	3	5	9	17	7	0.00	-58.82
Liberia	15	11	17	12	4	0.00	-66.67
Mali	20	21	19	30	39	0.00	30.00
Mauritania	49	35	23	12	22	0.00	83.33
Niger	24	39	28	12	13	0.00	8.33
Nigeria	911	948	1,023	1,144	1,309	0.02	14.42
Senegal	249	218	198	237	241	0.00	1.69
Sierra Leone	15	37	30	32	15	0.00	-53.13
Togo	24	20	22	51	48	0.00	-5.88
OTHER AFRICA		28	21	32	25	0.00	-21.88
Other countries of Africa		28	21	32	25	0.00	-21.88
AMERICAS	168,744	170,757	182,169	207,627	208,942	2.61	0.63
CARIBBEAN	545	542	505	674	753	0.01	11.72

606

ROMANIA

2. Arrivals of non-resident visitors at national borders, by country of residence

	2009	2010	2011	2012	2013	Market share 2013	% Change 2013-2012
Cuba	390	311	245	354	432	0.01	22.03
Dominican Republic	102	160	186	233	193	0.00	-17.17
Haiti	16	21	13	22	26	0.00	18.18
Jamaica	37	50	61	65	102	0.00	56.92
CENTRAL AMERICA	**695**	**834**	**918**	**982**	**1,222**	**0.02**	**24.44**
Belize	1	4	11	9	5	0.00	-44.44
Costa Rica	237	301	272	248	320	0.00	29.03
El Salvador	55	69	70	68	106	0.00	55.88
Guatemala	142	172	151	159	185	0.00	16.35
Honduras	132	168	268	338	423	0.01	25.15
Nicaragua	49	45	75	53	60	0.00	13.21
Panama	79	75	71	107	123	0.00	14.95
NORTH AMERICA	**158,019**	**158,688**	**168,589**	**192,557**	**192,178**	**2.40**	**-0.20**
Canada	36,592	38,740	41,595	44,964	45,501	0.57	1.19
Mexico	2,293	2,999	3,659	3,853	4,404	0.05	14.30
United States of America	119,134	116,949	123,335	143,740	142,273	1.77	-1.02
SOUTH AMERICA	**9,485**	**10,427**	**11,949**	**13,236**	**14,637**	**0.18**	**10.58**
Argentina	1,961	1,841	2,193	2,317	2,437	0.03	5.18
Bolivia	194	181	204	158	201	0.00	27.22
Brazil	3,741	4,331	5,216	5,856	6,435	0.08	9.89
Chile	681	768	885	1,095	1,499	0.02	36.89
Colombia	680	787	744	956	1,196	0.01	25.10
Ecuador	532	538	543	584	532	0.01	-8.90
Guyana	6	5	9	9	10	0.00	11.11
Paraguay	89	112	120	132	180	0.00	36.36
Peru	630	792	900	981	958	0.01	-2.34
Suriname	5	13	17	39	27	0.00	-30.77
Uruguay	205	270	251	332	329	0.00	-0.90
Venezuela	761	789	867	777	833	0.01	7.21
OTHER AMERICAS		**266**	**208**	**178**	**152**	**0.00**	**-14.61**
Other countries of the Americas		266	208	178	152	0.00	-14.61
EAST ASIA AND THE PACIFIC	**70,145**	**79,098**	**92,027**	**97,728**	**103,441**	**1.29**	**5.85**
NORTH-EAST ASIA	**41,899**	**44,748**	**51,524**	**55,417**	**57,561**	**0.72**	**3.87**
China	19,681	17,796	18,570	19,991	21,502	0.27	7.56
Hong Kong, China	788	824	1,225	2,230	2,775	0.03	24.44
Japan	10,345	12,333	13,544	14,252	13,359	0.17	-6.27
Korea, Dem. People's Republic of	96	114	114	120	77	0.00	-35.83
Korea, Republic of	10,109	12,628	16,077	16,370	17,150	0.21	4.76
Mongolia	233	150	181	180	148	0.00	-17.78
Taiwan, Province of China	647	903	1,813	2,274	2,550	0.03	12.14
SOUTH-EAST ASIA	**14,662**	**20,829**	**25,072**	**26,324**	**28,561**	**0.36**	**8.50**
Cambodia	25	27	38	48	16	0.00	-66.67
Indonesia	1,279	2,001	2,405	3,104	3,342	0.04	7.67
Lao People's Democratic Republic	6	5		10	7	0.00	-30.00
Malaysia	1,293	2,078	1,764	1,728	2,109	0.03	22.05
Myanmar	850	664	1,324	842	651	0.01	-22.68
Philippines	7,824	13,372	16,668	17,328	18,996	0.24	9.63
Singapore	548	593	735	1,014	1,106	0.01	9.07
Thailand	1,159	1,027	984	805	1,054	0.01	30.93
Viet Nam	1,678	1,062	1,154	1,445	1,280	0.02	-11.42
AUSTRALASIA	**13,502**	**13,323**	**15,263**	**15,847**	**17,128**	**0.21**	**8.08**
Australia	11,218	11,117	12,976	13,272	14,252	0.18	7.38
New Zealand	2,284	2,206	2,287	2,575	2,876	0.04	11.69
MELANESIA	**41**	**23**	**16**				
Fiji	41	23	16				
OTHER EAST ASIA AND THE PACIFIC	**41**	**175**	**152**	**140**	**191**	**0.00**	**36.43**
Other countries East Asia/Pacific	41	175	152	140	191	0.00	36.43
EUROPE	**7,278,936**	**7,179,264**	**7,266,677**	**7,556,131**	**7,624,865**	**95.09**	**0.91**
CENTRAL/EASTERN EUROPE	**5,065,085**	**5,008,381**	**4,955,252**	**5,157,216**	**5,234,100**	**65.27**	**1.49**

607

ROMANIA

2. Arrivals of non-resident visitors at national borders, by country of residence

	2009	2010	2011	2012	2013	Market share 2013	% Change 2013-2012
Armenia	1,511	1,836	2,067	2,450	2,709	0.03	10.57
Azerbaijan	2,499	3,191	4,024	5,821	6,450	0.08	10.81
Belarus	42,933	56,757	56,871	95,496	143,113	1.78	49.86
Bulgaria	877,287	786,452	797,382	943,501	1,135,567	14.16	20.36
Czech Republic	100,656	79,709	80,145	96,437	89,891	1.12	-6.79
Estonia	3,913	4,471	3,981	3,978	5,021	0.06	26.22
Georgia	7,573	9,900	16,617	21,684	22,088	0.28	1.86
Hungary	1,836,334	1,734,844	1,545,502	1,547,014	1,442,567	17.99	-6.75
Kazakhstan	1,266	1,948	2,226	2,723	3,026	0.04	11.13
Kyrgyzstan	114	183	288	226	188	0.00	-16.81
Latvia	3,760	3,669	4,425	4,239	5,639	0.07	33.03
Lithuania	10,155	9,153	8,771	10,810	10,251	0.13	-5.17
Poland	222,783	237,922	249,731	300,794	299,724	3.74	-0.36
Republic of Moldova	1,042,871	1,216,140	1,330,322	1,120,272	995,118	12.41	-11.17
Russian Federation	73,203	91,907	119,502	158,983	176,066	2.20	10.75
Slovakia	113,990	97,676	84,310	100,061	99,807	1.24	-0.25
Tajikistan	48	84	94	61	58	0.00	-4.92
Turkmenistan	129	207	348	314	296	0.00	-5.73
Ukraine	723,813	672,065	648,394	739,545	793,612	9.90	7.31
Uzbekistan	242	219	252	233	296	0.00	27.04
Other countries Central/East Europe	5	48		2,574	2,613	0.03	1.52
NORTHERN EUROPE	**165,980**	**154,462**	**184,131**	**183,365**	**168,011**	**2.10**	**-8.37**
Denmark	13,168	10,827	13,652	14,225	11,756	0.15	-17.36
Finland	8,975	8,266	10,549	7,337	6,753	0.08	-7.96
Iceland	1,075	2,122	1,767	2,015	1,695	0.02	-15.88
Ireland	11,071	10,046	13,054	12,533	11,422	0.14	-8.86
Norway	8,714	7,608	10,446	9,372	9,676	0.12	3.24
Sweden	19,363	23,964	25,559	25,301	22,365	0.28	-11.60
United Kingdom	103,614	91,629	109,104	112,582	104,344	1.30	-7.32
SOUTHERN EUROPE	**804,001**	**827,506**	**879,960**	**898,597**	**933,267**	**11.64**	**3.86**
Albania	4,919	4,720	6,757	7,142	8,100	0.10	13.41
Bosnia and Herzegovina	3,971	3,603	5,952	7,188	8,848	0.11	23.09
Croatia	25,192	20,326	19,362	19,335	20,113	0.25	4.02
Greece	89,747	70,593	83,083	76,786	76,039	0.95	-0.97
Holy See	8	9	7	7	11	0.00	57.14
Italy	374,702	330,909	352,310	340,138	332,355	4.14	-2.29
Malta	1,083	1,465	1,603	3,142	1,809	0.02	-42.43
Montenegro				2,537	2,899	0.04	14.27
Portugal	20,209	47,460	47,234	41,496	52,695	0.66	26.99
San Marino	156	217	231	236	219	0.00	-7.20
Serbia				286,291	318,617	3.97	11.29
Serbia and Montenegro	170,025	243,775	250,531				
Slovenia	34,563	23,224	16,774	19,081	23,339	0.29	22.32
Spain	66,952	63,306	77,101	74,048	64,328	0.80	-13.13
TFYR of Macedonia	12,474	17,899	19,015	21,170	23,895	0.30	12.87
WESTERN EUROPE	**901,923**	**834,887**	**882,888**	**961,144**	**932,914**	**11.63**	**-2.94**
Austria	180,579	177,544	192,814	217,629	199,641	2.49	-8.27
Belgium	36,772	42,407	49,856	47,081	48,020	0.60	1.99
France	150,052	131,050	153,118	149,769	135,668	1.69	-9.42
Germany	442,805	394,387	381,336	439,219	448,344	5.59	2.08
Liechtenstein	151	214	479	388	319	0.00	-17.78
Luxembourg	980	854	1,329	1,234	832	0.01	-32.58
Monaco	17	27	25	25	36	0.00	44.00
Netherlands	66,947	66,157	78,315	76,134	71,290	0.89	-6.36
Switzerland	23,620	22,247	25,616	29,665	28,764	0.36	-3.04
EAST MEDITERRANEAN EUROPE	**341,947**	**354,028**	**364,446**	**355,809**	**356,573**	**4.45**	**0.21**
Cyprus	8,492	7,955	10,408	8,742	7,168	0.09	-18.01
Israel	75,918	81,179	83,376	79,984	94,706	1.18	18.41
Turkey	257,537	264,894	270,662	267,083	254,699	3.18	-4.64

Yearbook of Tourism Statistics, Data 2009 – 2013, 2015 Edition

ROMANIA

2. Arrivals of non-resident visitors at national borders, by country of residence

	2009	2010	2011	2012	2013	Market share 2013	% Change 2013-2012
MIDDLE EAST	**26,520**	**33,482**	**33,500**	**36,608**	**41,648**	**0.52**	**13.77**
Bahrain	67	90	101	98	111	0.00	13.27
Egypt	4,405	6,191	6,397	7,036	6,600	0.08	-6.20
Iraq	2,300	2,470	2,634	3,005	3,685	0.05	22.63
Jordan	2,385	2,532	2,520	2,228	2,474	0.03	11.04
Kuwait	427	421	532	636	901	0.01	41.67
Lebanon	5,051	5,267	4,884	5,045	5,065	0.06	0.40
Libya	220	326	184	555	771	0.01	38.92
Oman	103	121	204	91	233	0.00	156.04
Palestine	554	587	573	528	563	0.01	6.63
Qatar	89	77	133	141	152	0.00	7.80
Saudi Arabia	583	563	853	831	1,137	0.01	36.82
Syrian Arab Republic	9,846	14,193	13,839	15,732	19,050	0.24	21.09
United Arab Emirates	395	480	473	492	676	0.01	37.40
Yemen	95	164	173	190	230	0.00	21.05
SOUTH ASIA	**17,083**	**20,825**	**20,710**	**21,832**	**21,720**	**0.27**	**-0.51**
Afghanistan	185	218	203	243	194	0.00	-20.16
Bangladesh	456	274	202	227	209	0.00	-7.93
India	6,662	8,861	9,040	9,964	9,785	0.12	-1.80
Iran, Islamic Republic of	7,416	8,873	8,626	8,602	8,742	0.11	1.63
Maldives	53	129	36	21	23	0.00	9.52
Nepal	65	223	186	138	146	0.00	5.80
Pakistan	1,689	1,770	1,848	2,020	2,034	0.03	0.69
Sri Lanka	557	477	569	617	587	0.01	-4.86
NOT SPECIFIED	**1,067**	**417**	**473**	**443**	**580**	**0.01**	**30.93**
Other countries of the World	1,067	417	473	443	580	0.01	30.93

Yearbook of Tourism Statistics, Data 2009 – 2013, 2015 Edition

ROMANIA

3. Arrivals of non-resident tourists in hotels and similar establishments, by country of residence

	2009	2010	2011	2012	2013	Market share 2013	% Change 2013-2012
TOTAL	1,255,703	1,326,770	1,495,892	1,542,663	1,595,612	100.00	3.43
AFRICA	7,435	8,854	10,279	13,810	13,438	0.84	-2.69
SOUTHERN AFRICA	2,040	1,699	2,167	1,769	2,166	0.14	22.44
South Africa	2,040	1,699	2,167	1,769	2,166	0.14	22.44
OTHER AFRICA	5,395	7,155	8,112	12,041	11,272	0.71	-6.39
Other countries of Africa (*)	5,395	7,155	8,112	12,041	11,272	0.71	-6.39
AMERICAS	93,504	105,103	107,815	112,960	113,694	7.13	0.65
NORTH AMERICA	88,063	98,057	100,257	103,919	104,527	6.55	0.59
Canada	10,732	12,176	11,995	13,313	13,341	0.84	0.21
Mexico	1,411	1,535	2,429	3,289	2,420	0.15	-26.42
United States of America	75,920	84,346	85,833	87,317	88,766	5.56	1.66
SOUTH AMERICA	1,815	2,634	2,985	4,027	3,571	0.22	-11.32
Brazil	1,815	2,634	2,985	4,027	3,571	0.22	-11.32
OTHER AMERICAS	3,626	4,412	4,573	5,014	5,596	0.35	11.61
Other countries of the Americas	3,626	4,412	4,573	5,014	5,596	0.35	11.61
EAST ASIA AND THE PACIFIC	46,837	53,655	66,058	70,877	77,886	4.88	9.89
NORTH-EAST ASIA	22,165	26,284	30,690	34,550	37,725	2.36	9.19
China	6,929	5,939	9,054	11,138	13,037	0.82	17.05
Japan	11,752	13,296	16,432	17,311	16,638	1.04	-3.89
Korea, Republic of	3,484	7,049	5,204	6,101	8,050	0.50	31.95
AUSTRALASIA	5,313	6,082	6,942	6,611	7,127	0.45	7.81
Australia	5,313	6,082	6,942	6,611	7,127	0.45	7.81
OTHER EAST ASIA AND THE PACIFIC	19,359	21,289	28,426	29,716	33,034	2.07	11.17
Other countries of Asia	17,389	19,075	24,855	26,556	30,757	1.93	15.82
Other countries of Oceania	1,970	2,214	3,571	3,160	2,277	0.14	-27.94
EUROPE	1,086,564	1,135,729	1,290,559	1,323,019	1,364,739	85.53	3.15
CENTRAL/EASTERN EUROPE	202,403	198,687	255,980	261,292	286,953	17.98	9.82
Bulgaria	23,764	24,544	31,287	35,657	41,643	2.61	16.79
Czech Republic	18,530	17,085	19,726	20,701	20,116	1.26	-2.83
Estonia	850	1,334	1,297	1,834	2,435	0.15	32.77
Hungary	75,569	76,720	86,300	69,868	74,730	4.68	6.96
Latvia	1,550	1,590	1,652	1,687	2,322	0.15	37.64
Lithuania	1,351	1,907	2,086	3,416	3,621	0.23	6.00
Poland	29,689	35,657	45,719	47,311	58,710	3.68	24.09
Republic of Moldova	19,893	7,455	25,757	28,635	29,819	1.87	4.13
Russian Federation	13,101	14,714	19,265	26,320	27,062	1.70	2.82
Slovakia	7,510	7,735	9,533	10,313	10,766	0.67	4.39
Ukraine	10,596	9,946	13,358	15,550	15,729	0.99	1.15
NORTHERN EUROPE	115,105	114,568	130,062	144,497	138,115	8.66	-4.42
Denmark	11,104	11,092	13,870	18,650	10,072	0.63	-45.99
Finland	7,366	6,366	6,047	5,294	4,666	0.29	-11.86
Ireland	6,957	7,695	7,922	8,004	6,805	0.43	-14.98
Norway	8,004	7,456	8,628	10,770	13,767	0.86	27.83
Sweden	10,893	10,534	12,813	14,164	14,442	0.91	1.96
United Kingdom	70,781	71,425	80,782	87,615	88,363	5.54	0.85
SOUTHERN EUROPE	252,712	263,205	301,490	306,116	305,270	19.13	-0.28
Greece	36,706	35,825	36,779	33,887	38,239	2.40	12.84
Italy	141,131	144,603	171,778	172,835	171,759	10.76	-0.62
Malta	665	654	741	813	853	0.05	4.92
Montenegro	543	422	550	691	643	0.04	-6.95
Portugal	7,446	8,694	10,393	11,868	9,780	0.61	-17.59
Serbia	7,868	6,714	9,103	11,887	13,152	0.82	10.64
Slovenia	5,362	5,640	5,272	6,504	7,375	0.46	13.39
Spain	52,991	60,653	66,874	67,631	63,469	3.98	-6.15
WESTERN EUROPE	404,019	411,763	449,449	465,616	465,724	29.19	0.02
Austria	57,791	61,104	61,757	59,295	54,882	3.44	-7.44
Belgium	22,815	23,126	23,986	26,631	28,349	1.78	6.45
France	99,246	98,121	108,078	111,160	111,290	6.97	0.12

610

ROMANIA

3. Arrivals of non-resident tourists in hotels and similar establishments, by country of residence

	2009	2010	2011	2012	2013	Market share 2013	% Change 2013-2012
Germany	170,994	175,751	196,915	205,227	205,759	12.90	0.26
Luxembourg	1,143	1,047	1,415	1,301	1,426	0.09	9.61
Netherlands	36,594	36,337	40,474	43,636	44,277	2.77	1.47
Switzerland	15,436	16,277	16,824	18,366	19,741	1.24	7.49
EAST MEDITERRANEAN EUROPE	**80,780**	**101,914**	**119,567**	**118,401**	**135,602**	**8.50**	**14.53**
Cyprus	5,230	5,454	5,553	4,392	5,069	0.32	15.41
Israel	53,606	71,630	86,647	81,282	93,971	5.89	15.61
Turkey	21,944	24,830	27,367	32,727	36,562	2.29	11.72
OTHER EUROPE	**31,545**	**45,592**	**34,011**	**27,097**	**33,075**	**2.07**	**22.06**
Other countries of Europe	31,545	45,592	34,011	27,097	33,075	2.07	22.06
NOT SPECIFIED	**21,363**	**23,429**	**21,181**	**21,997**	**25,855**	**1.62**	**17.54**
Other countries of the World	21,363	23,429	21,181	21,997	25,855	1.62	17.54

Yearbook of Tourism Statistics, Data 2009 – 2013, 2015 Edition

ROMANIA

4. Arrivals of non-resident tourists in all types of accommodation establishments, by country of residence

	2009	2010	2011	2012	2013	Market share 2013	% Change 2013-2012
TOTAL	1,275,590	1,346,343	1,516,699	1,653,361	1,715,559	100.00	3.76
AFRICA	7,437	8,875	10,292	14,078	13,751	0.80	-2.32
SOUTHERN AFRICA	2,040	1,699	2,170	1,814	2,225	0.13	22.66
South Africa	2,040	1,699	2,170	1,814	2,225	0.13	22.66
OTHER AFRICA	5,397	7,176	8,122	12,264	11,526	0.67	-6.02
Other countries of Africa (*)	5,397	7,176	8,122	12,264	11,526	0.67	-6.02
AMERICAS	93,625	105,210	107,889	116,410	117,562	6.85	0.99
NORTH AMERICA	88,162	98,119	100,329	107,016	108,116	6.30	1.03
Canada	10,780	12,198	12,027	13,813	13,967	0.81	1.11
Mexico	1,411	1,536	2,429	3,289	2,524	0.15	-23.26
United States of America	75,971	84,385	85,873	89,914	91,625	5.34	1.90
SOUTH AMERICA	1,818	2,647	2,986	4,158	3,707	0.22	-10.85
Brazil	1,818	2,647	2,986	4,158	3,707	0.22	-10.85
OTHER AMERICAS	3,645	4,444	4,574	5,236	5,739	0.33	9.61
Other countries of the Americas	3,645	4,444	4,574	5,236	5,739	0.33	9.61
EAST ASIA AND THE PACIFIC	43,531	53,722	66,162	75,235	79,559	4.64	5.75
NORTH-EAST ASIA	18,714	26,307	30,732	35,177	38,414	2.24	9.20
China	6,946	5,952	9,071	11,390	13,329	0.78	17.02
Japan	11,768	13,298	16,437	17,605	16,974	0.99	-3.58
Korea, Republic of		7,057	5,224	6,182	8,111	0.47	31.20
AUSTRALASIA	5,405	6,100	6,982	6,970	7,430	0.43	6.60
Australia	5,405	6,100	6,982	6,970	7,430	0.43	6.60
OTHER EAST ASIA AND THE PACIFIC	19,412	21,315	28,448	33,088	33,715	1.97	1.89
Other countries of Asia	17,419	19,079	24,866	29,843	31,355	1.83	5.07
Other countries of Oceania	1,993	2,236	3,582	3,245	2,360	0.14	-27.27
EUROPE	1,106,150	1,155,107	1,311,175	1,425,522	1,478,645	86.19	3.73
CENTRAL/EASTERN EUROPE	206,716	215,813	259,482	293,665	330,147	19.24	12.42
Bulgaria	23,820	24,615	31,363	37,287	43,751	2.55	17.34
Czech Republic	18,804	17,237	20,107	22,083	22,246	1.30	0.74
Estonia	852	1,341	1,314	2,173	2,589	0.15	19.14
Hungary	76,906	77,568	87,245	89,599	99,261	5.79	10.78
Latvia	1,551	1,601	1,698	2,004	2,477	0.14	23.60
Lithuania	1,490	1,932	2,202	3,636	3,796	0.22	4.40
Poland	31,579	37,338	47,055	52,154	64,152	3.74	23.00
Republic of Moldova	20,094	21,479	25,952	28,988	33,668	1.96	16.14
Russian Federation	13,402	14,900	19,507	27,893	29,302	1.71	5.05
Slovakia	7,561	7,784	9,566	11,001	11,678	0.68	6.15
Ukraine	10,657	10,018	13,473	16,847	17,227	1.00	2.26
NORTHERN EUROPE	115,898	115,143	130,456	151,714	145,146	8.46	-4.33
Denmark	11,162	11,148	13,904	20,285	11,004	0.64	-45.75
Finland	7,409	6,383	6,060	5,567	4,934	0.29	-11.37
Ireland	6,989	7,707	7,955	8,339	7,161	0.42	-14.13
Norway	8,037	7,496	8,645	11,160	14,242	0.83	27.62
Sweden	10,944	10,589	12,856	14,669	15,049	0.88	2.59
United Kingdom	71,357	71,820	81,036	91,694	92,756	5.41	1.16
SOUTHERN EUROPE	252,673	263,631	301,814	319,739	321,057	18.71	0.41
Greece	36,735	35,855	36,851	34,877	39,360	2.29	12.85
Italy	141,568	145,421	172,500	181,812	181,894	10.60	0.05
Malta				834	870	0.05	4.32
Montenegro	543	422	550	691	659	0.04	-4.63
Portugal	7,456	8,702	10,399	12,299	10,145	0.59	-17.51
Serbia	7,881	6,721	9,118	11,903	13,959	0.81	17.27
Slovenia	5,423	5,761	5,361	6,771	7,795	0.45	15.12
Spain	53,067	60,749	67,035	70,552	66,375	3.87	-5.92
WESTERN EUROPE	417,626	425,718	464,776	505,862	506,238	29.51	0.07
Austria	58,401	61,435	62,158	63,143	58,765	3.43	-6.93
Belgium	23,197	23,787	24,608	26,911	30,299	1.77	12.59
France	100,330	99,417	109,586	117,929	118,649	6.92	0.61

612

ROMANIA

4. Arrivals of non-resident tourists in all types of accommodation establishments, by country of residence

	2009	2010	2011	2012	2013	Market share 2013	% Change 2013-2012
Germany	181,084	184,986	207,144	229,823	228,592	13.32	-0.54
Luxembourg	1,145	1,051	1,419	1,343	1,491	0.09	11.02
Netherlands	37,713	38,091	42,500	47,058	47,378	2.76	0.68
Switzerland	15,756	16,951	17,361	19,655	21,064	1.23	7.17
EAST MEDITERRANEAN EUROPE	**75,657**	**96,637**	**114,089**	**119,944**	**140,113**	**8.17**	**16.82**
Cyprus				4,499	5,123	0.30	13.87
Israel	53,649	71,672	86,679	81,324	96,615	5.63	18.80
Turkey	22,008	24,965	27,410	34,121	38,375	2.24	12.47
OTHER EUROPE	**37,580**	**38,165**	**40,558**	**34,598**	**35,944**	**2.10**	**3.89**
Other countries of Europe	37,580	38,165	40,558	34,598	35,944	2.10	3.89
NOT SPECIFIED	**24,847**	**23,429**	**21,181**	**22,116**	**26,042**	**1.52**	**17.75**
Other countries of the World	24,847	23,429	21,181	22,116	26,042	1.52	17.75

Yearbook of Tourism Statistics, Data 2009 – 2013, 2015 Edition

ROMANIA

5. Overnight stays of non-resident tourists in hotels and similar establishments, by country of residence

	2009	2010	2011	2012	2013	Market share 2013	% Change 2013-2012
TOTAL	2,581,861	2,684,868	2,981,991	3,001,482	3,167,791	100.00	5.54
AFRICA	18,184	23,426	23,548	42,163	31,779	1.00	-24.63
SOUTHERN AFRICA	4,002	3,178	3,829	4,190	4,184	0.13	-0.14
South Africa	4,002	3,178	3,829	4,190	4,184	0.13	-0.14
OTHER AFRICA	14,182	20,248	19,719	37,973	27,595	0.87	-27.33
Other countries of Africa (*)	14,182	20,248	19,719	37,973	27,595	0.87	-27.33
AMERICAS	170,573	198,570	212,355	209,596	212,093	6.70	1.19
NORTH AMERICA	159,421	183,035	194,951	190,313	192,794	6.09	1.30
Canada	21,066	25,197	23,651	25,520	24,926	0.79	-2.33
Mexico	3,315	3,351	12,705	7,492	5,573	0.18	-25.61
United States of America	135,040	154,487	158,595	157,301	162,295	5.12	3.17
SOUTH AMERICA	3,874	6,067	7,098	8,608	7,866	0.25	-8.62
Brazil	3,874	6,067	7,098	8,608	7,866	0.25	-8.62
OTHER AMERICAS	7,278	9,468	10,306	10,675	11,433	0.36	7.10
Other countries of the Americas	7,278	9,468	10,306	10,675	11,433	0.36	7.10
EAST ASIA AND THE PACIFIC	105,115	119,100	132,534	136,306	154,762	4.89	13.54
NORTH-EAST ASIA	50,614	54,157	62,670	67,069	71,243	2.25	6.22
China	21,192	18,053	21,376	21,344	27,098	0.86	26.96
Japan	20,512	22,430	28,121	33,393	28,522	0.90	-14.59
Korea, Republic of	8,910	13,674	13,173	12,332	15,623	0.49	26.69
AUSTRALASIA	9,923	11,522	12,131	12,090	13,082	0.41	8.21
Australia	9,923	11,522	12,131	12,090	13,082	0.41	8.21
OTHER EAST ASIA AND THE PACIFIC	44,578	53,421	57,733	57,147	70,437	2.22	23.26
Other countries of Asia	40,813	49,218	51,455	51,280	65,824	2.08	28.36
Other countries of Oceania	3,765	4,203	6,278	5,867	4,613	0.15	-21.37
EUROPE	2,251,663	2,304,829	2,579,355	2,577,697	2,723,445	85.97	5.65
CENTRAL/EASTERN EUROPE	446,927	436,309	520,780	533,570	611,609	19.31	14.63
Bulgaria	59,893	45,659	55,885	64,774	75,333	2.38	16.30
Czech Republic	33,645	30,753	34,630	36,198	38,901	1.23	7.47
Estonia	1,946	2,928	3,028	3,374	4,119	0.13	22.08
Hungary	162,445	160,426	177,408	139,181	147,823	4.67	6.21
Latvia	3,249	3,102	4,015	3,662	4,715	0.15	28.75
Lithuania	2,901	3,917	5,090	5,960	7,501	0.24	25.86
Poland	53,712	66,623	90,223	97,457	146,872	4.64	50.70
Republic of Moldova	54,155	53,905	64,764	79,480	82,258	2.60	3.50
Russian Federation	32,195	33,111	42,220	54,284	56,194	1.77	3.52
Slovakia	19,954	15,351	18,866	20,942	20,037	0.63	-4.32
Ukraine	22,832	20,534	24,651	28,258	27,856	0.88	-1.42
NORTHERN EUROPE	228,647	226,529	244,293	264,952	260,105	8.21	-1.83
Denmark	24,824	25,096	30,441	34,373	20,930	0.66	-39.11
Finland	16,039	13,286	11,880	10,721	9,169	0.29	-14.48
Ireland	14,976	15,276	16,665	16,887	13,979	0.44	-17.22
Norway	16,898	14,729	16,700	19,829	27,171	0.86	37.03
Sweden	20,102	20,232	24,080	26,485	27,506	0.87	3.86
United Kingdom	135,808	137,910	144,527	156,657	161,350	5.09	3.00
SOUTHERN EUROPE	507,959	523,380	613,432	595,229	607,540	19.18	2.07
Greece	70,431	72,042	96,144	70,022	82,170	2.59	17.35
Italy	295,924	296,427	339,963	336,515	350,887	11.08	4.27
Malta	1,380	1,515	1,548	1,740	1,824	0.06	4.83
Montenegro	804	945	976	1,648	1,269	0.04	-23.00
Portugal	16,543	19,887	23,061	23,332	20,571	0.65	-11.83
Serbia	16,730	12,938	18,721	23,048	24,843	0.78	7.79
Slovenia	10,267	10,471	9,220	13,600	13,320	0.42	-2.06
Spain	95,880	109,155	123,799	125,324	112,656	3.56	-10.11
WESTERN EUROPE	799,412	815,312	871,327	867,814	867,483	27.38	-0.04
Austria	97,786	106,226	106,751	103,132	97,005	3.06	-5.94
Belgium	43,758	44,536	44,800	44,844	51,289	1.62	14.37
France	190,815	188,372	209,504	205,082	197,731	6.24	-3.58

Yearbook of Tourism Statistics, Data 2009 – 2013, 2015 Edition

ROMANIA

5. Overnight stays of non-resident tourists in hotels and similar establishments, by country of residence

	2009	2010	2011	2012	2013	Market share 2013	% Change 2013-2012
Germany	362,888	373,442	398,247	400,850	399,305	12.61	-0.39
Luxembourg	2,184	2,187	3,216	2,717	2,603	0.08	-4.20
Netherlands	74,330	71,810	79,283	79,924	86,089	2.72	7.71
Switzerland	27,651	28,739	29,526	31,265	33,461	1.06	7.02
EAST MEDITERRANEAN EUROPE	**190,199**	**224,505**	**253,783**	**257,997**	**297,068**	**9.38**	**15.14**
Cyprus	9,400	10,326	10,003	8,543	9,357	0.30	9.53
Israel	135,782	164,384	188,320	186,727	214,394	6.77	14.82
Turkey	45,017	49,795	55,460	62,727	73,317	2.31	16.88
OTHER EUROPE	**78,519**	**78,794**	**75,740**	**58,135**	**79,640**	**2.51**	**36.99**
Other countries of Europe	78,519	78,794	75,740	58,135	79,640	2.51	36.99
NOT SPECIFIED	**36,326**	**38,943**	**34,199**	**35,720**	**45,712**	**1.44**	**27.97**
Other countries of the World	36,326	38,943	34,199	35,720	45,712	1.44	27.97

Yearbook of Tourism Statistics, Data 2009 – 2013, 2015 Edition

ROMANIA

6. Overnight stays of non-resident tourists in all types of accommodation establishments, by country of residence

	2009	2010	2011	2012	2013	Market share 2013	% Change 2013-2012
TOTAL	2,667,666	2,766,581	3,066,882	3,291,504	3,471,152	100.00	5.46
AFRICA	18,189	23,488	23,593	42,679	32,521	0.94	-23.80
SOUTHERN AFRICA	4,002	3,178	3,832	4,260	4,351	0.13	2.14
South Africa	4,002	3,178	3,832	4,260	4,351	0.13	2.14
OTHER AFRICA	14,187	20,310	19,761	38,419	28,170	0.81	-26.68
Other countries of Africa (*)	14,187	20,310	19,761	38,419	28,170	0.81	-26.68
AMERICAS	171,091	198,914	212,822	218,254	220,770	6.36	1.15
NORTH AMERICA	159,896	183,222	195,397	198,130	200,671	5.78	1.28
Canada	21,247	25,253	23,935	26,744	26,244	0.76	-1.87
Mexico	3,315	3,356	12,705	7,492	5,793	0.17	-22.68
United States of America	135,334	154,613	158,757	163,894	168,634	4.86	2.89
SOUTH AMERICA	3,877	6,191	7,112	8,859	8,195	0.24	-7.50
Brazil	3,877	6,191	7,112	8,859	8,195	0.24	-7.50
OTHER AMERICAS	7,318	9,501	10,313	11,265	11,904	0.34	5.67
Other countries of the Americas	7,318	9,501	10,313	11,265	11,904	0.34	5.67
EAST ASIA AND THE PACIFIC	96,778	119,225	132,896	145,509	158,918	4.58	9.22
NORTH-EAST ASIA	41,826	54,202	62,753	68,550	72,965	2.10	6.44
China	21,246	18,088	21,399	22,039	28,037	0.81	27.22
Japan	20,580	22,432	28,161	34,033	29,170	0.84	-14.29
Korea, Republic of		13,682	13,193	12,478	15,758	0.45	26.29
AUSTRALASIA	10,233	11,552	12,275	12,937	13,786	0.40	6.56
Australia	10,233	11,552	12,275	12,937	13,786	0.40	6.56
OTHER EAST ASIA AND THE PACIFIC	44,719	53,471	57,868	64,022	72,167	2.08	12.72
Other countries of Asia	40,869	49,242	51,568	57,993	67,394	1.94	16.21
Other countries of Oceania	3,850	4,229	6,300	6,029	4,773	0.14	-20.83
EUROPE	2,336,372	2,386,011	2,663,372	2,849,023	3,012,926	86.80	5.75
CENTRAL/EASTERN EUROPE	457,693	444,325	528,763	605,455	709,418	20.44	17.17
Bulgaria	60,040	45,759	56,050	67,846	79,227	2.28	16.77
Czech Republic	34,118	31,073	35,199	39,605	45,008	1.30	13.64
Estonia	1,950	2,955	3,049	3,792	4,482	0.13	18.20
Hungary	165,613	162,723	179,414	182,858	203,063	5.85	11.05
Latvia	3,252	3,143	4,079	4,181	5,108	0.15	22.17
Lithuania	3,047	3,957	5,214	6,341	7,831	0.23	23.50
Poland	56,975	69,657	92,456	106,646	156,258	4.50	46.52
Republic of Moldova	54,667	54,336	65,273	80,767	91,487	2.64	13.27
Russian Federation	34,968	34,594	44,182	59,499	63,089	1.82	6.03
Slovakia	20,060	15,409	18,926	22,763	23,024	0.66	1.15
Ukraine	23,003	20,719	24,921	31,157	30,841	0.89	-1.01
NORTHERN EUROPE	230,426	227,879	245,200	285,534	276,461	7.96	-3.18
Denmark	25,002	25,222	30,512	41,260	22,478	0.65	-45.52
Finland	16,142	13,328	11,905	11,318	9,651	0.28	-14.73
Ireland	15,043	15,305	16,788	18,044	15,218	0.44	-15.66
Norway	17,060	14,972	16,790	21,855	29,359	0.85	34.34
Sweden	20,206	20,389	24,148	27,548	28,863	0.83	4.77
United Kingdom	136,973	138,663	145,057	165,509	170,892	4.92	3.25
SOUTHERN EUROPE	507,754	523,743	613,633	627,659	647,861	18.66	3.22
Greece	70,512	72,084	96,269	72,438	86,459	2.49	19.36
Italy	296,735	297,839	341,121	358,352	376,222	10.84	4.99
Malta				1,769	1,850	0.05	4.58
Montenegro	804	945	976	1,648	1,349	0.04	-18.14
Portugal	16,553	19,899	23,077	24,203	21,643	0.62	-10.58
Serbia	16,775	12,966	18,756	23,077	26,702	0.77	15.71
Slovenia	10,365	10,718	9,362	14,053	14,104	0.41	0.36
Spain	96,010	109,292	124,072	132,119	119,532	3.44	-9.53
WESTERN EUROPE	869,499	883,149	943,652	996,962	986,452	28.42	-1.05
Austria	100,275	107,867	107,869	113,203	106,576	3.07	-5.85
Belgium	44,527	45,745	45,925	48,089	55,044	1.59	14.46
France	192,790	190,658	211,765	218,216	212,548	6.12	-2.60

Yearbook of Tourism Statistics, Data 2009 – 2013, 2015 Edition

ROMANIA

6. Overnight stays of non-resident tourists in all types of accommodation establishments, by country of residence

	2009	2010	2011	2012	2013	Market share 2013	% Change 2013-2012
Germany	424,532	429,369	460,013	494,004	480,591	13.85	-2.72
Luxembourg	2,212	2,215	3,228	2,776	2,756	0.08	-0.72
Netherlands	76,684	76,523	83,998	86,357	92,338	2.66	6.93
Switzerland	28,479	30,772	30,854	34,317	36,599	1.05	6.65
EAST MEDITERRANEAN EUROPE	**180,973**	**214,719**	**243,940**	**260,933**	**306,008**	**8.82**	**17.27**
Cyprus				8,728	9,468	0.27	8.48
Israel	135,837	164,601	188,409	186,799	219,614	6.33	17.57
Turkey	45,136	50,118	55,531	65,406	76,926	2.22	17.61
OTHER EUROPE	**90,027**	**92,196**	**88,184**	**72,480**	**86,726**	**2.50**	**19.66**
Other countries of Europe	90,027	92,196	88,184	72,480	86,726	2.50	19.66
NOT SPECIFIED	**45,236**	**38,943**	**34,199**	**36,039**	**46,017**	**1.33**	**27.69**
Other countries of the World	45,236	38,943	34,199	36,039	46,017	1.33	27.69

Yearbook of Tourism Statistics, Data 2009 – 2013, 2015 Edition

RUSSIAN FEDERATION

2. Arrivals of non-resident visitors at national borders, by nationality

	2009	2010	2011	2012	2013	Market share 2013	% Change 2013-2012
TOTAL	21,338,650	22,281,217	24,932,061	28,176,502	30,792,091	100.00	9.28
AFRICA	34,649	36,833	40,116	40,149	55,884	0.18	39.19
EAST AFRICA	4,871	5,041	5,320	5,461	9,343	0.03	71.09
British Indian Ocean Territory	28	182	69	9	15	0.00	66.67
Burundi	120	108	133	146	147	0.00	0.68
Comoros	51	63	23	43	60	0.00	39.53
Djibouti	24	72	135	119	109	0.00	-8.40
Eritrea	58	69	59	107	99	0.00	-7.48
Ethiopia	368	420	427	585	844	0.00	44.27
Kenya	958	1,062	1,194	1,304	1,473	0.00	12.96
Madagascar	243	198	177	193	233	0.00	20.73
Malawi	59	53	52	46	290	0.00	530.43
Mauritius	79	590	676	653	827	0.00	26.65
Mozambique	1,105	158	267	201	252	0.00	25.37
Rwanda	34	41	68	61	97	0.00	59.02
Seychelles	515	200	323	228	309	0.00	35.53
Somalia	75	116	155	62	92	0.00	48.39
Uganda	195	403	238	315	2,332	0.01	640.32
United Republic of Tanzania	378	502	504	497	1,097	0.00	120.72
Zambia	295	444	404	473	625	0.00	32.14
Zimbabwe	286	360	416	419	442	0.00	5.49
CENTRAL AFRICA	3,531	2,981	3,996	4,094	4,531	0.01	10.67
Angola	1,033	1,091	1,513	1,673	1,857	0.01	11.00
Cameroon	806	785	751	744	1,015	0.00	36.42
Central African Republic	144	24	9	31	67	0.00	116.13
Chad	123	121	105	158	155	0.00	-1.90
Congo	551	328	510	638	526	0.00	-17.55
Democratic Republic of the Congo	672	416	777	505	483	0.00	-4.36
Equatorial Guinea	117	132	217	225	261	0.00	16.00
Gabon	75	71	106	83	147	0.00	77.11
Sao Tome and Principe	10	13	8	37	20	0.00	-45.95
NORTH AFRICA	9,786	10,090	11,731	13,377	21,031	0.07	57.22
Algeria	3,140	2,564	3,350	3,636	3,723	0.01	2.39
Morocco	3,679	4,146	4,796	5,208	7,882	0.03	51.34
Sudan	1,157	1,220	1,276	1,383	1,453	0.00	5.06
Tunisia	1,809	2,159	2,307	3,149	7,973	0.03	153.19
Western Sahara	1	1	2	1			
SOUTHERN AFRICA	7,830	8,695	9,094	9,811	11,897	0.04	21.26
Botswana	66	123	119	181	302	0.00	66.85
Lesotho	16	58	11	8	16	0.00	100.00
Namibia	232	416	423	511	656	0.00	28.38
South Africa	7,447	8,022	8,468	9,039	10,817	0.04	19.67
Swaziland	69	76	73	72	106	0.00	47.22
WEST AFRICA	8,631	10,026	9,975	7,406	9,082	0.03	22.63
Benin	150	215	198	211	246	0.00	16.59
Burkina Faso	32	56	57	62	119	0.00	91.94
Cabo Verde	137	323	338	728	764	0.00	4.95
Côte d'Ivoire	446	425	482	963	656	0.00	-31.88
Gambia	21	38	45	66	112	0.00	69.70
Ghana	822	890	1,040	1,081	1,326	0.00	22.66
Guinea	209	283	459	370	392	0.00	5.95
Guinea-Bissau	121	749	117	128	136	0.00	6.25
Liberia	3,768	3,746	4,169	89	176	0.00	97.75
Mali	169	270	242	275	335	0.00	21.82
Mauritania	79	131	76	91	87	0.00	-4.40
Niger	51	24	51	28	64	0.00	128.57
Nigeria	2,244	2,552	2,370	2,864	3,922	0.01	36.94
Senegal	148	198	205	294	555	0.00	88.78
Sierra Leone	136	65	74	80	119	0.00	48.75

618

RUSSIAN FEDERATION

2. Arrivals of non-resident visitors at national borders, by nationality

	2009	2010	2011	2012	2013	Market share 2013	% Change 2013-2012
Togo	98	61	52	76	73	0.00	-3.95
AMERICAS	**469,112**	**420,512**	**439,039**	**443,873**	**493,673**	**1.60**	**11.22**
CARIBBEAN	**52,965**	**33,947**	**16,313**	**7,472**	**13,139**	**0.04**	**75.84**
Anguilla	7	1,183	72	73	12	0.00	-83.56
Antigua and Barbuda	4,860	5,673	4,074	130	52	0.00	-60.00
Bahamas	29,122	18,871	4,693	92	276	0.00	200.00
Barbados	670	492	437	86	97	0.00	12.79
Bermuda	9,254	457	75	74	61	0.00	-17.57
British Virgin Islands	11		69	9	41	0.00	355.56
Cayman Islands	919	267	331	3	1	0.00	-66.67
Cuba	4,172	4,053	4,099	5,239	9,625	0.03	83.72
Dominica	330	213	208	24	27	0.00	12.50
Dominican Republic	667	690	523	611	1,023	0.00	67.43
Grenada	114	45	39	21	43	0.00	104.76
Haiti	68	66	99	79	181	0.00	129.11
Jamaica	630	447	386	399	817	0.00	104.76
Martinique	15						
Netherlands Antilles	256		130	8			
Puerto Rico	15	15	7	2	3	0.00	50.00
Saint Kitts and Nevis	238	120	97	104	90	0.00	-13.46
Saint Lucia	139	62	67	56	106	0.00	89.29
Saint Vincent and the Grenadines	1,227	999	524	67	177	0.00	164.18
Trinidad and Tobago	251	294	383	395	507	0.00	28.35
CENTRAL AMERICA	**21,065**	**12,854**	**10,379**	**4,260**	**4,887**	**0.02**	**14.72**
Belize	1,199	1,208	706	50	63	0.00	26.00
Costa Rica	454	710	778	938	1,101	0.00	17.38
El Salvador	245	198	143	270	320	0.00	18.52
Guatemala	1,202	1,002	903	811	925	0.00	14.06
Honduras	5,397	3,022	1,290	718	1,055	0.00	46.94
Nicaragua	455	396	559	686	679	0.00	-1.02
Panama	12,113	6,318	6,000	787	744	0.00	-5.46
NORTH AMERICA	**354,963**	**324,394**	**344,244**	**357,714**	**388,716**	**1.26**	**8.67**
Canada	59,537	48,559	52,238	54,730	61,234	0.20	11.88
Greenland	1	8	8	2	1	0.00	-50.00
Mexico	10,058	13,767	16,759	16,431	21,527	0.07	31.01
United States of America	285,367	262,060	275,239	286,551	305,954	0.99	6.77
SOUTH AMERICA	**40,119**	**49,317**	**68,103**	**74,427**	**86,931**	**0.28**	**16.80**
Argentina	9,598	9,044	12,316	13,976	15,944	0.05	14.08
Bolivia	354	365	349	520	452	0.00	-13.08
Brazil	15,540	21,950	29,840	33,647	37,386	0.12	11.11
Chile	3,207	3,438	5,093	5,710	6,495	0.02	13.75
Colombia	3,794	4,620	7,105	8,514	10,760	0.03	26.38
Ecuador	1,233	1,495	1,479	1,726	3,168	0.01	83.55
Falkland Islands, Malvinas	57	355	1	2			
French Guiana			2,930	6			
Guyana	60	66	87	119	137	0.00	15.13
Paraguay	198	185	253	259	294	0.00	13.51
Peru	1,601	3,351	3,168	3,720	4,629	0.02	24.44
Suriname	8	25	6	13	28	0.00	115.38
Uruguay	813	896	1,090	1,479	1,818	0.01	22.92
Venezuela	3,656	3,527	4,386	4,736	5,820	0.02	22.89
EAST ASIA AND THE PACIFIC	**1,294,719**	**1,358,186**	**1,547,594**	**1,903,926**	**1,938,415**	**6.30**	**1.81**
NORTH-EAST ASIA	**1,068,706**	**1,121,871**	**1,279,709**	**1,585,441**	**1,568,982**	**5.10**	**-1.04**
China	718,581	747,640	845,588	978,988	1,071,515	3.48	9.45
Hong Kong, China	8,169	14,852	19,872	20,491	20,099	0.07	-1.91
Japan	74,159	78,188	76,204	86,806	102,408	0.33	17.97
Korea, Dem. People's Republic of	18,686	21,167	18,901	22,071	23,604	0.08	6.95
Korea, Republic of	84,166	90,622	91,335	94,922	107,942	0.35	13.72
Macao, China	104	95	226	358	974	0.00	172.07

Yearbook of Tourism Statistics, Data 2009 – 2013, 2015 Edition

RUSSIAN FEDERATION

2. Arrivals of non-resident visitors at national borders, by nationality

	2009	2010	2011	2012	2013	Market share 2013	% Change 2013-2012
Mongolia	156,997	157,367	212,117	365,236	226,673	0.74	-37.94
Taiwan, Province of China	7,844	11,940	15,466	16,569	15,767	0.05	-4.84
SOUTH-EAST ASIA	**185,855**	**196,816**	**225,345**	**267,773**	**314,237**	**1.02**	**17.35**
Brunei Darussalam	211	58	81	263	195	0.00	-25.86
Cambodia	416	443	281	299	294	0.00	-1.67
Indonesia	24,841	14,448	18,313	18,572	21,088	0.07	13.55
Lao People's Democratic Republic	114	252	259	221	497	0.00	124.89
Malaysia	11,844	16,508	14,988	15,126	16,127	0.05	6.62
Myanmar	3,467	5,424	7,054	7,432	8,157	0.03	9.76
Philippines	79,365	81,385	99,405	130,541	149,213	0.48	14.30
Singapore	10,226	12,283	14,412	12,983	13,674	0.04	5.32
Thailand	14,562	15,192	17,023	19,375	23,919	0.08	23.45
Viet Nam	40,809	50,823	53,529	62,961	81,073	0.26	28.77
AUSTRALASIA	**36,948**	**36,199**	**40,800**	**50,130**	**54,385**	**0.18**	**8.49**
Australia	31,931	30,584	34,868	43,105	46,861	0.15	8.71
New Zealand	5,017	5,615	5,932	7,025	7,524	0.02	7.10
MELANESIA	**492**	**604**	**178**	**128**	**240**	**0.00**	**87.50**
Fiji	39	43	46	53	210	0.00	296.23
New Caledonia	3	1		4			
Papua New Guinea	4	44	3	51	17	0.00	-66.67
Solomon Islands	3	434	5	4	4	0.00	
Vanuatu	443	82	124	16	9	0.00	-43.75
MICRONESIA	**2,468**	**2,575**	**1,460**	**380**	**395**	**0.00**	**3.95**
Guam	1	29	3		5	0.00	
Kiribati	118	347	278	133	227	0.00	70.68
Marshall Islands	2,342	2,189	1,170	221	120	0.00	-45.70
Micronesia, Federated States of		1	2	3	13	0.00	333.33
Nauru	6	3	4	11	22	0.00	100.00
Northern Mariana Islands		4		2			
Palau	1	2	3	10	8	0.00	-20.00
POLYNESIA	**250**	**121**	**102**	**74**	**176**	**0.00**	**137.84**
American Samoa	1	11	5	3	2	0.00	-33.33
French Polynesia				1			
Pitcairn		13		1			
Samoa	27		6	22	86	0.00	290.91
Tokelau	1						
Tonga	9	12	3	9	22	0.00	144.44
Tuvalu	212	85	88	38	66	0.00	73.68
EUROPE	**18,790,566**	**19,568,815**	**21,895,885**	**24,740,959**	**27,229,286**	**88.43**	**10.06**
CENTRAL/EASTERN EUROPE	**15,578,448**	**16,370,280**	**18,333,305**	**20,910,996**	**23,185,490**	**75.30**	**10.88**
Armenia	379,525	459,040	550,349	700,332	882,864	2.87	26.06
Azerbaijan	892,435	979,778	1,045,525	1,116,238	1,196,759	3.89	7.21
Belarus	286,495	259,191	267,233	372,942	418,207	1.36	12.14
Bulgaria	37,704	38,446	42,031	45,312	47,154	0.15	4.07
Czech Republic	38,356	40,565	46,776	62,980	76,530	0.25	21.51
Estonia	920,497	474,949	519,402	494,282	430,164	1.40	-12.97
Georgia	19,846	24,568	30,415	35,511	48,440	0.16	36.41
Hungary	19,791	20,736	23,241	23,047	27,155	0.09	17.82
Kazakhstan	2,590,688	2,747,358	3,049,406	3,630,342	3,848,899	12.50	6.02
Kyrgyzstan	406,504	552,909	592,960	623,970	763,418	2.48	22.35
Latvia	516,838	569,330	571,374	461,162	391,304	1.27	-15.15
Lithuania	600,785	760,728	622,740	553,896	539,308	1.75	-2.63
Poland	434,529	394,872	704,610	1,190,003	1,644,657	5.34	38.21
Republic of Moldova	884,999	988,084	1,070,637	1,194,291	1,374,690	4.46	15.11
Romania	14,072	17,884	21,993	24,792	30,886	0.10	24.58
Slovakia	15,863	18,512	20,445	24,161	27,554	0.09	14.04
Tajikistan	674,572	830,160	955,455	1,134,150	1,348,828	4.38	18.93
Turkmenistan	27,704	35,017	39,579	43,720	40,238	0.13	-7.96
Ukraine	5,604,433	5,574,067	6,072,775	6,502,543	7,080,991	23.00	8.90

Yearbook of Tourism Statistics, Data 2009 – 2013, 2015 Edition

RUSSIAN FEDERATION

2. Arrivals of non-resident visitors at national borders, by nationality

	2009	2010	2011	2012	2013	Market share 2013	% Change 2013-2012
Uzbekistan	1,212,812	1,584,086	2,086,359	2,677,322	2,967,444	9.64	10.84
NORTHERN EUROPE	**1,452,439**	**1,371,633**	**1,594,248**	**1,766,457**	**1,809,125**	**5.88**	**2.42**
Denmark	30,316	33,121	35,814	34,908	36,262	0.12	3.88
Faeroe Islands	25	24	31	4	12	0.00	200.00
Finland	1,057,575	1,012,621	1,211,519	1,375,614	1,388,016	4.51	0.90
Iceland	1,627	1,437	1,798	1,976	2,695	0.01	36.39
Ireland	14,078	11,990	14,214	13,270	14,691	0.05	10.71
Norway	49,488	45,340	48,614	50,115	54,433	0.18	8.62
Svalbard and Jan Mayen Islands	97						
Sweden	59,438	54,253	60,840	58,900	53,340	0.17	-9.44
United Kingdom	239,795	212,847	221,418	231,670	259,676	0.84	12.09
SOUTHERN EUROPE	**470,045**	**479,838**	**502,013**	**485,404**	**562,503**	**1.83**	**15.88**
Albania	1,681	1,086	1,193	1,111	1,623	0.01	46.08
Andorra	107	127	209	196	181	0.00	-7.65
Bosnia and Herzegovina	5,669	5,970	6,292	8,311	10,791	0.04	29.84
Croatia	11,954	14,638	15,295	15,990	18,276	0.06	14.30
Gibraltar	4,467	3,711	4,657	1			
Greece	39,130	33,296	33,569	36,474	48,280	0.16	32.37
Holy See			13	23	17	0.00	-26.09
Italy	190,862	198,002	207,476	212,411	225,933	0.73	6.37
Malta	21,970	27,204	10,251	2,079	2,158	0.01	3.80
Montenegro	4,302	4,691	4,752	5,403	6,137	0.02	13.59
Portugal	16,281	18,434	15,814	15,398	14,952	0.05	-2.90
San Marino	179	201	133	140	130	0.00	-7.14
Serbia	44,342	47,939	57,177	70,371	107,601	0.35	52.91
Slovenia	10,569	11,160	12,285	12,622	13,296	0.04	5.34
Spain	115,975	110,601	129,730	101,536	109,089	0.35	7.44
TFYR of Macedonia	2,557	2,778	3,167	3,338	4,039	0.01	21.00
WESTERN EUROPE	**1,008,243**	**1,034,731**	**1,087,880**	**1,142,411**	**1,144,034**	**3.72**	**0.14**
Austria	69,715	67,606	70,388	71,367	46,861	0.15	-34.34
Belgium	32,575	33,571	36,430	37,025	40,316	0.13	8.89
France	185,082	194,218	213,473	225,343	225,860	0.73	0.23
Germany	592,313	611,367	629,391	671,676	686,557	2.23	2.22
Liechtenstein	244	205	281	258	294	0.00	13.95
Luxembourg	1,993	1,912	2,263	2,503	2,597	0.01	3.76
Monaco	148	168	127	175	249	0.00	42.29
Netherlands	78,752	80,720	87,549	81,212	86,402	0.28	6.39
Switzerland	47,421	44,964	47,978	52,852	54,898	0.18	3.87
EAST MEDITERRANEAN EUROPE	**281,391**	**312,333**	**378,439**	**435,691**	**528,134**	**1.72**	**21.22**
Cyprus	14,961	15,338	14,950	6,288	6,160	0.02	-2.04
Israel	89,098	100,291	114,380	123,974	136,827	0.44	10.37
Turkey	177,332	196,704	249,109	305,429	385,147	1.25	26.10
MIDDLE EAST	**38,009**	**41,496**	**41,881**	**50,774**	**58,570**	**0.19**	**15.35**
Bahrain	222	494	282	508	538	0.00	5.91
Egypt	9,983	10,273	11,561	13,344	18,692	0.06	40.08
Iraq	1,549	2,760	2,639	3,823	4,693	0.02	22.76
Jordan	2,649	3,024	3,215	3,383	4,775	0.02	41.15
Kuwait	649	386	348	556	610	0.00	9.71
Lebanon	4,035	4,510	4,619	5,871	6,502	0.02	10.75
Libya	979	1,316	442	615	762	0.00	23.90
Oman	580	623	593	699	844	0.00	20.74
Palestine	749	1,200	1,173	1,307	1,197	0.00	-8.42
Qatar	203	369	242	279	289	0.00	3.58
Saudi Arabia	1,151	1,390	1,288	1,143	1,590	0.01	39.11
Syrian Arab Republic	13,188	12,882	13,260	16,826	14,990	0.05	-10.91
United Arab Emirates	1,070	1,083	1,137	1,404	1,675	0.01	19.30
Yemen	1,002	1,186	1,082	1,016	1,413	0.00	39.07

Yearbook of Tourism Statistics, Data 2009 – 2013, 2015 Edition

RUSSIAN FEDERATION

2. Arrivals of non-resident visitors at national borders, by nationality

	2009	2010	2011	2012	2013	Market share 2013	% Change 2013-2012
SOUTH ASIA	**93,311**	**89,407**	**98,557**	**122,798**	**137,489**	**0.45**	**11.96**
Afghanistan	7,258	7,336	7,457	8,424	8,651	0.03	2.69
Bangladesh	1,464	1,580	1,498	1,905	2,185	0.01	14.70
Bhutan	26	57	45	86	69	0.00	-19.77
India	59,815	53,364	60,191	80,127	95,542	0.31	19.24
Iran, Islamic Republic of	18,607	20,576	21,575	23,085	20,657	0.07	-10.52
Maldives	105	122	100	94	151	0.00	60.64
Nepal	1,171	1,237	1,563	1,866	1,944	0.01	4.18
Pakistan	3,347	3,262	4,121	4,597	5,074	0.02	10.38
Sri Lanka	1,518	1,873	2,007	2,614	3,216	0.01	23.03
NOT SPECIFIED	**618,284**	**765,968**	**868,989**	**874,023**	**878,774**	**2.85**	**0.54**
Other countries of the World	618,284	765,968	868,989	874,023	878,774	2.85	0.54

Yearbook of Tourism Statistics, Data 2009 – 2013, 2015 Edition

RWANDA

2. Arrivals of non-resident visitors at national borders, by nationality

	2009	2010	2011	2012	2013	Market share 2013	% Change 2013-2012
TOTAL	662,556	666,001	908,009	1,075,789	1,137,436	100.00	5.73
AFRICA	559,668	546,904	773,841	940,921	993,416	87.34	5.58
EAST AFRICA	241,826	287,330	370,515	445,427	483,701	42.53	8.59
Burundi	69,304	72,316	75,824	77,600	100,452	8.83	29.45
Comoros	42	33	57	50	47	0.00	-6.00
Djibouti	66	255	197	103	83	0.01	-19.42
Eritrea	421	658	677	626	582	0.05	-7.03
Ethiopia	697	948	1,040	1,120	1,050	0.09	-6.25
Kenya	30,721	37,193	44,020	60,433	56,194	4.94	-7.01
Madagascar	241	303	436	427	647	0.06	51.52
Malawi	278	566	422	388	556	0.05	43.30
Mauritius	101	105	172	263	336	0.03	27.76
Mozambique	161	221	177	254	170	0.01	-33.07
Seychelles	16	37	41	54	35	0.00	-35.19
Somalia	263	134	169	126	135	0.01	7.14
Uganda	106,622	133,089	191,927	207,090	235,267	20.68	13.61
United Republic of Tanzania	31,784	40,286	53,560	94,912	86,143	7.57	-9.24
Zambia	412	336	637	866	903	0.08	4.27
Zimbabwe	697	850	1,159	1,115	1,101	0.10	-1.26
CENTRAL AFRICA	305,221	245,838	386,066	477,617	490,767	43.15	2.75
Angola	146	268	173	154	163	0.01	5.84
Cameroon	1,127	1,232	1,323	1,206	1,173	0.10	-2.74
Central African Republic	131	147	167	178	181	0.02	1.69
Chad	174	318	446	281	276	0.02	-1.78
Congo	121	134	236	133	442	0.04	232.33
Democratic Republic of the Congo	302,786	242,976	383,099	474,634	488,339	42.93	2.89
Equatorial Guinea	659	722	542	827	5	0.00	-99.40
Gabon	77	41	80	204	188	0.02	-7.84
NORTH AFRICA	880	947	1,163	1,218	981	0.09	-19.46
Algeria	197	97	109	133	219	0.02	64.66
Morocco	87	173	189	92	82	0.01	-10.87
Sudan	404	509	507	492	392	0.03	-20.33
Tunisia	192	168	358	501	288	0.03	-42.51
SOUTHERN AFRICA	6,216	6,097	8,570	8,291	8,449	0.74	1.91
Botswana	89	98	235	146	157	0.01	7.53
Lesotho	108	46	55	54	183	0.02	238.89
Namibia	59	39	62	204	205	0.02	0.49
South Africa	5,903	5,839	8,085	7,703	7,614	0.67	-1.16
Swaziland	57	75	133	184	290	0.03	57.61
WEST AFRICA	5,522	6,690	7,479	7,946	8,570	0.75	7.85
Benin	542	761	745	615	752	0.07	22.28
Burkina Faso	573	488	729	543	456	0.04	-16.02
Côte d'Ivoire	612	712	787	754	995	0.09	31.96
Gambia	147	103	149	146	103	0.01	-29.45
Ghana	692	995	1,098	1,078	1,670	0.15	54.92
Liberia	183	243	249	200	155	0.01	-22.50
Mali	366	452	539	669	569	0.05	-14.95
Mauritania	140	192	183	122	156	0.01	27.87
Niger	85	249	247	266	336	0.03	26.32
Nigeria	1,027	1,149	1,356	2,130	2,212	0.19	3.85
Senegal	630	785	820	840	625	0.05	-25.60
Sierra Leone	327	372	351	317	202	0.02	-36.28
Togo	198	189	226	266	339	0.03	27.44
OTHER AFRICA	3	2	48	422	948	0.08	124.64
Other countries of Africa	3	2	48	422	948	0.08	124.64
AMERICAS	28,116	33,189	37,919	35,032	40,776	3.58	16.40
CARIBBEAN	151	150	180	271	311	0.03	14.76
Barbados	14	26	22	11	24	0.00	118.18
Haiti	115	96	138	247	238	0.02	-3.64

623

Yearbook of Tourism Statistics, Data 2009 – 2013, 2015 Edition

RWANDA

2. Arrivals of non-resident visitors at national borders, by nationality

	2009	2010	2011	2012	2013	Market share 2013	% Change 2013-2012
Jamaica	22	28	20	13	49	0.00	276.92
CENTRAL AMERICA	**101**	**42**	**65**	**214**	**137**	**0.01**	**-35.98**
Costa Rica	9	6	6	110	50	0.00	-54.55
Guatemala	77	22	40	56	42	0.00	-25.00
Nicaragua	15	5	5	47	45	0.00	-4.26
Panama		9	14	1			
NORTH AMERICA	**25,437**	**30,700**	**35,366**	**31,212**	**36,401**	**3.20**	**16.63**
Canada	5,689	6,991	6,964	6,952	6,988	0.61	0.52
Mexico	170	298	321	219	231	0.02	5.48
United States of America	19,578	23,411	28,081	24,041	29,182	2.57	21.38
SOUTH AMERICA	**2,427**	**2,297**	**2,308**	**3,335**	**3,927**	**0.35**	**17.75**
Argentina	83	79	127	139	163	0.01	17.27
Brazil	193	220	308	299	277	0.02	-7.36
Chile	25	67	36	62	65	0.01	4.84
Colombia	61	68	73	128	146	0.01	14.06
Guyana	10	8	4	5	14	0.00	180.00
Peru	47	115	81	166	160	0.01	-3.61
Uruguay	1,590	1,231	1,139	2,194	2,286	0.20	4.19
Venezuela	19	33	35	35	30	0.00	-14.29
Other countries of South America	399	476	505	307	786	0.07	156.03
EAST ASIA AND THE PACIFIC	**8,059**	**10,521**	**12,868**	**12,481**	**15,791**	**1.39**	**26.52**
NORTH-EAST ASIA	**4,467**	**5,909**	**6,906**	**6,758**	**9,140**	**0.80**	**35.25**
China	2,965	4,062	4,533	4,077	5,831	0.51	43.02
Japan	1,110	1,042	1,195	1,597	1,520	0.13	-4.82
Korea, Republic of	372	775	940	955	1,646	0.14	72.36
Taiwan, Province of China	20	30	238	129	143	0.01	10.85
SOUTH-EAST ASIA	**1,013**	**1,604**	**1,181**	**1,409**	**1,589**	**0.14**	**12.78**
Indonesia	77	64	120	315	328	0.03	4.13
Malaysia	103	196	178	199	137	0.01	-31.16
Philippines	588	908	399	582	433	0.04	-25.60
Thailand	217	407	455	277	627	0.06	126.35
Viet Nam	28	29	29	36	64	0.01	77.78
AUSTRALASIA	**2,541**	**2,997**	**4,446**	**3,526**	**4,181**	**0.37**	**18.58**
Australia	2,068	2,453	3,863	3,029	3,339	0.29	10.23
New Zealand	473	544	583	497	842	0.07	69.42
MELANESIA	**38**	**11**	**9**	**21**	**22**	**0.00**	**4.76**
Fiji	38	11	9	21	22	0.00	4.76
OTHER EAST ASIA AND THE PACIFIC			**326**	**767**	**859**	**0.08**	**11.99**
Other countries of Asia			324	755	844	0.07	11.79
Other countries of Oceania			2	12	15	0.00	25.00
EUROPE	**46,968**	**54,253**	**66,961**	**66,472**	**65,158**	**5.73**	**-1.98**
CENTRAL/EASTERN EUROPE	**2,339**	**2,853**	**2,553**	**3,309**	**2,682**	**0.24**	**-18.95**
Armenia	14	29	29	2	14	0.00	600.00
Belarus	41	28	23	32	34	0.00	6.25
Bulgaria	72	176	95	153	76	0.01	-50.33
Czech Republic	119	302	243	615	311	0.03	-49.43
Estonia	18	10	32	37	44	0.00	18.92
Hungary	43	62	82	103	108	0.01	4.85
Kazakhstan	63	68	75	22	17	0.00	-22.73
Poland	466	574	651	602	546	0.05	-9.30
Republic of Moldova	2		14	39	22	0.00	-43.59
Romania	170	369	262	186	274	0.02	47.31
Russian Federation	534	960	700	932	914	0.08	-1.93
Ukraine	797	275	347	586	322	0.03	-45.05
NORTHERN EUROPE	**14,650**	**16,154**	**20,485**	**20,865**	**20,002**	**1.76**	**-4.14**
Denmark	627	745	947	1,140	990	0.09	-13.16
Finland	350	435	482	532	561	0.05	5.45
Norway	839	923	985	1,195	1,086	0.10	-9.12
Sweden	2,092	1,903	2,393	2,903	2,661	0.23	-8.34

624

Yearbook of Tourism Statistics, Data 2009 – 2013, 2015 Edition

RWANDA

2. Arrivals of non-resident visitors at national borders, by nationality

	2009	2010	2011	2012	2013	Market share 2013	% Change 2013-2012
United Kingdom	10,295	10,824	13,915	13,355	12,792	1.12	-4.22
Other countries of Northern Europe	447	1,324	1,763	1,740	1,912	0.17	9.89
SOUTHERN EUROPE	**5,201**	**5,714**	**6,729**	**7,313**	**7,997**	**0.70**	**9.35**
Bosnia and Herzegovina	116	54	137	54	31	0.00	-42.59
Croatia	89	104	119	140	119	0.01	-15.00
Holy See		2	4	1	3	0.00	200.00
Italy	3,409	3,456	4,338	4,511	5,530	0.49	22.59
Portugal	125	298	261	318	232	0.02	-27.04
Serbia	67	181	177	65	167	0.01	156.92
Slovenia	42	79	108	121	96	0.01	-20.66
Spain	1,353	1,540	1,585	2,103	1,819	0.16	-13.50
WESTERN EUROPE	**23,607**	**28,138**	**35,665**	**33,848**	**33,509**	**2.95**	**-1.00**
Austria	395	707	949	672	505	0.04	-24.85
Belgium	8,166	10,100	11,870	9,192	9,241	0.81	0.53
France	5,058	5,990	7,090	7,931	7,712	0.68	-2.76
Germany	5,652	6,157	7,741	9,180	8,465	0.74	-7.79
Luxembourg	80	136	1,676	120	119	0.01	-0.83
Netherlands	2,979	3,376	4,403	4,388	5,099	0.45	16.20
Switzerland	1,277	1,672	1,936	2,365	2,368	0.21	0.13
EAST MEDITERRANEAN EUROPE	**1,171**	**1,394**	**1,529**	**1,137**	**968**	**0.09**	**-14.86**
Israel	467	455	563	520	305	0.03	-41.35
Turkey	704	939	966	617	663	0.06	7.46
MIDDLE EAST	**2,104**	**2,784**	**2,308**	**1,989**	**2,446**	**0.22**	**22.98**
Egypt	462	772	642	369	395	0.03	7.05
Jordan	66	96	84	86	66	0.01	-23.26
Kuwait	7	9	4	7	43	0.00	514.29
Lebanon	829	925	831	600	838	0.07	39.67
Libya	164	398	185	47	157	0.01	234.04
Oman	495	521	434	640	721	0.06	12.66
Saudi Arabia	42	32	36	79	89	0.01	12.66
Syrian Arab Republic	13	20	32	51	32	0.00	-37.25
United Arab Emirates	26	11	18	6	17	0.00	183.33
Other countries of Middle East			42	104	88	0.01	-15.38
SOUTH ASIA	**16,931**	**17,794**	**13,774**	**16,914**	**17,629**	**1.55**	**4.23**
Bangladesh	346	388	343	497	858	0.08	72.64
India	13,085	16,178	12,347	14,947	14,839	1.30	-0.72
Iran, Islamic Republic of	65	39	66	167	199	0.02	19.16
Nepal	140	127	100	176	184	0.02	4.55
Pakistan	2,961	552	470	731	912	0.08	24.76
Sri Lanka	334	510	403	292	329	0.03	12.67
Other countries of South Asia			45	104	308	0.03	196.15
NOT SPECIFIED	**710**	**556**	**338**	**1,980**	**2,220**	**0.20**	**12.12**
Other countries of the World	710	556	338	1,980	2,220	0.20	12.12

Yearbook of Tourism Statistics, Data 2009 – 2013, 2015 Edition

SAINT KITTS AND NEVIS

1. Arrivals of non-resident tourists at national borders, by country of residence

		2009	2010	2011	2012	2013	Market share 2013	% Change 2013-2012
TOTAL	(*)	**93,081**	**98,329**	**101,701**	**104,240**	**106,904**	**100.00**	**2.56**
AMERICAS		**83,233**	**85,940**	**89,099**	**91,378**	**93,319**	**87.29**	**2.12**
CARIBBEAN		**22,410**	**21,176**	**18,893**	**17,317**	**17,732**	**16.59**	**2.40**
All countries of the Caribbean		22,410	21,176	18,893	17,317	17,732	16.59	2.40
NORTH AMERICA		**60,823**	**64,764**	**70,206**	**74,061**	**75,587**	**70.71**	**2.06**
Canada		6,413	6,054	5,961	7,073	7,202	6.74	1.82
United States of America		54,410	58,710	64,245	66,988	68,385	63.97	2.09
EUROPE		**6,496**	**8,455**	**8,047**	**7,975**	**8,451**	**7.91**	**5.97**
NORTHERN EUROPE		**6,496**	**8,455**	**8,047**	**7,975**	**8,451**	**7.91**	**5.97**
United Kingdom		6,496	8,455	8,047	7,975	8,451	7.91	5.97
NOT SPECIFIED		**3,352**	**3,934**	**4,555**	**4,887**	**5,134**	**4.80**	**5.05**
Other countries of the World		3,352	3,934	4,555	4,887	5,134	4.80	5.05

Yearbook of Tourism Statistics, Data 2009 – 2013, 2015 Edition

SAINT LUCIA

1. Arrivals of non-resident tourists at national borders, by country of residence

	2009	2010	2011	2012	2013	Market share 2013	% Change 2013-2012
TOTAL (*)	**278,491**	**305,937**	**312,404**	**306,801**	**318,626**	**100.00**	**3.85**
AMERICAS	**189,805**	**216,734**	**216,461**	**212,189**	**228,617**	**71.75**	**7.74**
CARIBBEAN	**60,183**	**53,998**	**56,929**	**56,067**	**60,521**	**18.99**	**7.94**
Anguilla			120	176	146	0.05	-17.05
Antigua and Barbuda	2,141	2,126	1,941	2,041	1,858	0.58	-8.97
Aruba			58	45	33	0.01	-26.67
Bahamas			179	222	258	0.08	16.22
Barbados	9,269	7,201	7,016	6,851	6,575	2.06	-4.03
Bermuda			190	172	171	0.05	-0.58
Bonaire			18	16	5	0.00	-68.75
British Virgin Islands			270	429	370	0.12	-13.75
Cuba			187	149	371	0.12	148.99
Curaçao			123	181	74	0.02	-59.12
Dominica	2,996	3,070	3,168	2,208	1,949	0.61	-11.73
Dominican Republic	133	115	109	136	110	0.03	-19.12
Grenada	1,763	1,489	1,584	1,518	1,434	0.45	-5.53
Guadeloupe			2,525	2,020	1,853	0.58	-8.27
Haiti	127	116	110	255	231	0.07	-9.41
Jamaica	2,123	1,756	1,804	1,593	1,551	0.49	-2.64
Martinique			23,326	19,114	18,924	5.94	-0.99
Montserrat			74	66	95	0.03	43.94
Netherlands Antilles		654	87		1	0.00	
Puerto Rico	931	829	1,505	559	259	0.08	-53.67
Saint Kitts and Nevis	915	840	677	602	764	0.24	26.91
Saint Vincent and the Grenadines	2,657	2,509	2,438	2,253	2,280	0.72	1.20
Sint Maarten			261	80	46	0.01	-42.50
Trinidad and Tobago	9,139	8,788	8,259	12,608	18,050	5.66	43.16
Turks and Caicos Islands			30	86	140	0.04	62.79
United States Virgin Islands	828	675	675	541	599	0.19	10.72
Other countries of the Caribbean	27,161	23,830	195	2,146	2,374	0.75	10.62
CENTRAL AMERICA			**113**	**96**	**145**	**0.05**	**51.04**
Belize			113	96	145	0.05	51.04
NORTH AMERICA	**127,248**	**161,239**	**157,749**	**152,774**	**164,316**	**51.57**	**7.55**
Canada	28,563	32,154	35,393	37,709	35,985	11.29	-4.57
United States of America	98,685	129,085	122,356	115,065	128,331	40.28	11.53
SOUTH AMERICA	**1,849**	**1,089**	**1,670**	**1,585**	**1,795**	**0.56**	**13.25**
Guyana	1,849	1,089	1,546	1,466	1,679	0.53	14.53
Suriname			124	119	116	0.04	-2.52
OTHER AMERICAS	**525**	**408**		**1,667**	**1,840**	**0.58**	**10.38**
Other countries of the Americas	525	408		1,667	1,840	0.58	10.38
EAST ASIA AND THE PACIFIC	**207**	**183**	**224**	**170**	**185**	**0.06**	**8.82**
NORTH-EAST ASIA	**207**	**183**	**224**	**170**	**185**	**0.06**	**8.82**
Japan	207	183	224	170	185	0.06	8.82
EUROPE	**84,238**	**85,695**	**91,759**	**93,400**	**88,492**	**27.77**	**-5.25**
NORTHERN EUROPE	**72,374**	**68,136**	**73,758**	**76,449**	**71,705**	**22.50**	**-6.21**
Sweden	521	719	699	772	837	0.26	8.42
United Kingdom	71,853	67,417	73,059	75,677	70,868	22.24	-6.35
SOUTHERN EUROPE	**1,229**	**1,465**	**1,605**	**1,195**	**1,077**	**0.34**	**-9.87**
Italy	925	1,134	1,239	829	746	0.23	-10.01
Spain	304	331	366	366	331	0.10	-9.56
WESTERN EUROPE	**8,707**	**11,843**	**12,294**	**10,758**	**10,782**	**3.38**	**0.22**
Austria	308	579	399	399	332	0.10	-16.79
Belgium	241	264	255	257	227	0.07	-11.67
France	5,356	5,822	7,428	5,467	5,464	1.71	-0.05
Germany	2,416	4,142	3,041	3,165	3,316	1.04	4.77
Netherlands		400	320	644	555	0.17	-13.82
Switzerland	386	636	851	826	888	0.28	7.51
OTHER EUROPE	**1,928**	**4,251**	**4,102**	**4,998**	**4,928**	**1.55**	**-1.40**
Other countries of Europe	1,928	4,251	4,102	4,998	4,928	1.55	-1.40
NOT SPECIFIED	**4,241**	**3,325**	**3,960**	**1,042**	**1,332**	**0.42**	**27.83**
Other countries of the World	4,241	3,325	3,960	1,042	1,332	0.42	27.83

Yearbook of Tourism Statistics, Data 2009 – 2013, 2015 Edition

SAINT VINCENT AND THE GRENADINES

1. Arrivals of non-resident tourists at national borders, by country of residence

	2009	2010	2011	2012	2013	Market share 2013	% Change 2013-2012
TOTAL (*)	75,446	72,478	73,866	74,364	71,725	100.00	-3.55
AMERICAS	55,424	53,933	52,391	52,724	50,078	69.82	-5.02
CARIBBEAN	26,835	23,968	23,272	22,768	21,745	30.32	-4.49
Antigua and Barbuda	1,093	921	847	914	895	1.25	-2.08
Barbados	8,335	7,375	6,562	6,665	6,033	8.41	-9.48
Grenada	1,521	1,075	1,007	946	977	1.36	3.28
Netherlands Antilles	419	294	375	388	329	0.46	-15.21
Saint Lucia	2,122	1,917	1,937	1,862	1,769	2.47	-4.99
Trinidad and Tobago	7,346	6,709	7,110	7,290	6,946	9.68	-4.72
Other countries of the Caribbean	5,999	5,677	5,434	4,703	4,796	6.69	1.98
NORTH AMERICA	26,979	28,759	27,883	28,878	27,252	38.00	-5.63
Canada	6,820	7,208	6,719	7,424	7,146	9.96	-3.74
United States of America	20,159	21,551	21,164	21,454	20,106	28.03	-6.28
OTHER AMERICAS	1,610	1,206	1,236	1,078	1,081	1.51	0.28
Other countries of the Americas	1,610	1,206	1,236	1,078	1,081	1.51	0.28
EUROPE	19,097	17,665	20,549	20,410	20,401	28.44	-0.04
NORTHERN EUROPE	14,054	12,957	15,650	15,878	16,021	22.34	0.90
Ireland	209	190	199	194	193	0.27	-0.52
Norway	144	148	165	163	148	0.21	-9.20
Sweden	354	483	391	498	497	0.69	-0.20
United Kingdom	13,347	12,136	14,895	15,023	15,183	21.17	1.07
SOUTHERN EUROPE	1,591	1,265	1,208	1,108	910	1.27	-17.87
Italy	1,429	1,105	1,037	965	756	1.05	-21.66
Spain	162	160	171	143	154	0.21	7.69
WESTERN EUROPE	2,427	2,468	2,516	2,431	2,445	3.41	0.58
Belgium	151	141	171	104	126	0.18	21.15
France	1,113	994	1,051	1,069	945	1.32	-11.60
Germany	731	824	744	742	791	1.10	6.60
Netherlands	67	193	166	98	143	0.20	45.92
Switzerland	365	316	384	418	440	0.61	5.26
OTHER EUROPE	1,025	975	1,175	993	1,025	1.43	3.22
Other countries of Europe	1,025	975	1,175	993	1,025	1.43	3.22
NOT SPECIFIED	925	880	926	1,230	1,246	1.74	1.30
Other countries of the World	925	880	926	1,230	1,246	1.74	1.30

Yearbook of Tourism Statistics, Data 2009 – 2013, 2015 Edition

SAINT VINCENT AND THE GRENADINES

2. Arrivals of non-resident visitors at national borders, by country of residence

		2009	2010	2011	2012	2013	Market share 2013	% Change 2013-2012
TOTAL	(*)	**80,631**	**77,564**	**77,807**	**77,415**	**74,388**	**100.00**	**-3.91**
AMERICAS		**57,967**	**56,592**	**54,516**	**54,199**	**51,666**	**69.45**	**-4.67**
CARIBBEAN		**28,507**	**25,654**	**24,628**	**23,656**	**22,772**	**30.61**	**-3.74**
Antigua and Barbuda		1,132	971	889	940	920	1.24	-2.13
Barbados		8,926	8,014	7,507	7,015	6,445	8.66	-8.13
Grenada		1,709	1,204	1,097	969	1,036	1.39	6.91
Netherlands Antilles		422	374	386	394	337	0.45	-14.47
Saint Lucia		2,347	2,139	2,133	1,971	1,882	2.53	-4.52
Trinidad and Tobago		7,754	7,092	7,415	7,446	7,153	9.62	-3.93
Other countries of the Caribbean		6,217	5,860	5,201	4,921	4,999	6.72	1.59
NORTH AMERICA		**27,812**	**29,682**	**28,601**	**29,419**	**27,762**	**37.32**	**-5.63**
Canada		7,120	7,565	6,957	7,602	7,336	9.86	-3.50
United States of America		20,692	22,117	21,644	21,817	20,426	27.46	-6.38
OTHER AMERICAS		**1,648**	**1,256**	**1,287**	**1,124**	**1,132**	**1.52**	**0.71**
Other countries of the Americas		1,648	1,256	1,287	1,124	1,132	1.52	0.71
EUROPE		**21,697**	**20,041**	**22,323**	**21,933**	**21,334**	**28.68**	**-2.73**
NORTHERN EUROPE		**16,036**	**14,715**	**16,890**	**17,011**	**16,671**	**22.41**	**-2.00**
Ireland		266	225	227	226	202	0.27	-10.62
Norway		146	165	170	164	154	0.21	-6.10
Sweden		381	498	408	511	509	0.68	-0.39
United Kingdom		15,243	13,827	16,085	16,110	15,806	21.25	-1.89
SOUTHERN EUROPE		**1,699**	**1,230**	**1,261**	**1,162**	**964**	**1.30**	**-17.04**
Italy		1,530	1,067	1,079	1,017	809	1.09	-20.45
Spain		169	163	182	145	155	0.21	6.90
WESTERN EUROPE		**2,791**	**2,832**	**2,910**	**2,589**	**2,577**	**3.46**	**-0.46**
Belgium		146	146	178	110	129	0.17	17.27
France		1,213	1,086	1,228	1,110	1,038	1.40	-6.49
Germany		969	1,058	885	816	840	1.13	2.94
Netherlands		67	196	180	109	145	0.19	33.03
Switzerland		396	346	439	444	425	0.57	-4.28
OTHER EUROPE		**1,171**	**1,264**	**1,262**	**1,171**	**1,122**	**1.51**	**-4.18**
Other countries of Europe		1,171	1,264	1,262	1,171	1,122	1.51	-4.18
NOT SPECIFIED		**967**	**931**	**968**	**1,283**	**1,388**	**1.87**	**8.18**
Other countries of the World		967	931	968	1,283	1,388	1.87	8.18

Yearbook of Tourism Statistics, Data 2009 – 2013, 2015 Edition

SAMOA

2. Arrivals of non-resident visitors at national borders, by country of residence

	2009	2010	2011	2012	2013	Market share 2013	% Change 2013-2012
TOTAL	129,305	129,500	127,603	134,694	124,673	100.00	-7.44
AMERICAS	9,794	9,238	7,875	7,948	7,540	6.05	-5.13
NORTH AMERICA	9,794	9,238	7,875	7,948	7,540	6.05	-5.13
Canada	530	580	450	351	396	0.32	12.82
United States of America	9,264	8,658	7,425	7,597	7,144	5.73	-5.96
EAST ASIA AND THE PACIFIC	113,425	115,163	114,798	122,573	111,607	89.52	-8.95
NORTH-EAST ASIA	1,794	1,866	2,044	2,359	2,015	1.62	-14.58
China	1,193	1,356	1,512	1,671	1,520	1.22	-9.04
Japan	601	510	532	688	452	0.36	-34.30
Korea, Republic of					43	0.03	
AUSTRALASIA	79,094	81,252	80,121	87,968	81,506	65.38	-7.35
Australia	24,507	23,415	25,197	28,161	28,261	22.67	0.36
New Zealand	54,587	57,837	54,924	59,807	53,245	42.71	-10.97
MELANESIA	2,538	2,636	2,646	2,876	2,708	2.17	-5.84
Fiji	2,538	2,636	2,646	2,876	2,708	2.17	-5.84
POLYNESIA	24,491	23,847	24,787	23,392	20,311	16.29	-13.17
American Samoa	24,298	23,737	24,582	23,180	20,194	16.20	-12.88
Cook Islands	193	110	205	212	117	0.09	-44.81
OTHER EAST ASIA AND THE PACIFIC	5,508	5,562	5,200	5,978	5,067	4.06	-15.24
Other countries of Asia	1,627	1,927	1,500	2,301	1,481	1.19	-35.64
Other countries of Oceania	3,881	3,635	3,700	3,677	3,586	2.88	-2.47
EUROPE	5,547	4,658	4,055	3,487	3,464	2.78	-0.66
NORTHERN EUROPE	2,392	2,171	1,601	1,351	1,168	0.94	-13.55
United Kingdom	1,719	1,306	1,163	1,031	862	0.69	-16.39
Scandinavia	673	865	438	320	306	0.25	-4.38
WESTERN EUROPE	1,633	1,228	1,291	1,149	1,052	0.84	-8.44
Germany	1,450	1,089	1,151	1,003	955	0.77	-4.79
Benelux	183	139	140	146	97	0.08	-33.56
OTHER EUROPE	1,522	1,259	1,163	987	1,244	1.00	26.04
Other countries of Europe	1,522	1,259	1,163	987	1,244	1.00	26.04
NOT SPECIFIED	539	441	875	686	2,062	1.65	200.58
Other countries of the World	539	441	875	686	2,062	1.65	200.58

Yearbook of Tourism Statistics, Data 2009 – 2013, 2015 Edition

SAN MARINO

2. Arrivals of non-resident visitors at national borders, by nationality

	2009	2010	2011	2012	2013	Market share 2013	% Change 2013-2012
TOTAL	2,055,705	1,976,481	2,038,359	1,869,393	1,905,021	100.00	1.91
AFRICA	130	275	206	357	450	0.02	26.05
EAST AFRICA	97	96					
Mozambique		96					
Somalia	97						
CENTRAL AFRICA				100	102	0.01	2.00
Congo				100	102	0.01	2.00
NORTH AFRICA		44		138	189	0.01	36.96
Algeria		29					
Morocco		15		51	121	0.01	137.25
Tunisia				87	68	0.00	-21.84
SOUTHERN AFRICA	33	135	206	52	159	0.01	205.77
South Africa	33	135	206	52	159	0.01	205.77
WEST AFRICA				67			
Senegal				67			
AMERICAS	12,063	12,142	19,225	17,721	17,328	0.91	-2.22
CARIBBEAN			71	120			
Cuba			54	50			
Puerto Rico			17	70			
CENTRAL AMERICA			52	100	28	0.00	-72.00
Costa Rica			52				
Panama				100	28	0.00	-72.00
NORTH AMERICA	10,084	8,188	13,878	10,914	10,505	0.55	-3.75
Canada	3,371	3,115	3,462	3,056	2,935	0.15	-3.96
Mexico	228	70	140	521	345	0.02	-33.78
United States of America	6,485	5,003	10,276	7,337	7,225	0.38	-1.53
SOUTH AMERICA	1,979	3,954	5,224	6,587	6,795	0.36	3.16
Argentina	665	1,514	1,639	1,724	1,782	0.09	3.36
Bolivia				113	151	0.01	33.63
Brazil	1,033	1,904	3,394	4,043	3,466	0.18	-14.27
Chile		221			87	0.00	
Colombia		105		265	75	0.00	-71.70
Ecuador	72	33	56		273	0.01	
Paraguay				71	62	0.00	-12.68
Peru				153	242	0.01	58.17
Uruguay		40		42	63	0.00	50.00
Venezuela	209	60	103	176	594	0.03	237.50
Other countries of South America		77	32				
EAST ASIA AND THE PACIFIC	18,790	18,386	19,930	21,715	22,199	1.17	2.23
NORTH-EAST ASIA	16,045	14,952	16,731	17,807	18,897	0.99	6.12
China	9,041	10,189	12,206	14,363	13,828	0.73	-3.72
Hong Kong, China				136	354	0.02	160.29
Japan	4,998	4,281	3,590	2,933	4,096	0.22	39.65
Korea, Dem. People's Republic of	41						
Korea, Republic of	1,965	454	786	358	452	0.02	26.26
Mongolia					24	0.00	
Taiwan, Province of China		28	149	17	143	0.01	741.18
SOUTH-EAST ASIA	960	1,327	1,602	1,616	1,590	0.08	-1.61
Indonesia	67	208	209	152	104	0.01	-31.58
Malaysia	246	282	308	696	829	0.04	19.11
Myanmar					22	0.00	
Philippines	610	757	699	563	481	0.03	-14.56
Singapore					64	0.00	
Thailand	37	80	363	205	79	0.00	-61.46
Viet Nam			23		11	0.00	
AUSTRALASIA	1,785	2,107	1,597	2,292	1,712	0.09	-25.31
Australia	1,657	2,004	1,483	2,207	1,550	0.08	-29.77
New Zealand	128	103	114	85	162	0.01	90.59

Yearbook of Tourism Statistics, Data 2009 – 2013, 2015 Edition

SAN MARINO

2. Arrivals of non-resident visitors at national borders, by nationality

	2009	2010	2011	2012	2013	Market share 2013	% Change 2013-2012
EUROPE	**2,023,438**	**1,944,198**	**1,997,416**	**1,828,558**	**1,864,530**	**97.87**	**1.97**
CENTRAL/EASTERN EUROPE	**170,000**	**224,078**	**269,567**	**268,902**	**299,503**	**15.72**	**11.38**
Armenia	63	79		19	99	0.01	421.05
Belarus	1,371	1,378	973	1,869	2,859	0.15	52.97
Bulgaria	3,810	2,560	2,991	4,157	5,037	0.26	21.17
Czech Republic	12,363	12,011	10,838	11,621	10,365	0.54	-10.81
Estonia	2,387	2,428	3,471	3,819	3,115	0.16	-18.43
Georgia	196	119	27	94	45	0.00	-52.13
Hungary	6,604	6,784	6,542	4,516	3,961	0.21	-12.29
Kazakhstan	50	100	23	245	195	0.01	-20.41
Latvia	1,141	1,116	1,643	1,340	1,051	0.06	-21.57
Lithuania	5,179	5,000	6,266	3,971	3,838	0.20	-3.35
Poland	54,556	57,208	52,725	45,926	44,101	2.31	-3.97
Republic of Moldova	424	200	91	241	307	0.02	27.39
Romania	4,490	4,599	5,004	3,626	4,419	0.23	21.87
Russian Federation	71,212	123,517	170,781	176,613	210,635	11.06	19.26
Slovakia	1,971	1,994	2,827	3,992	3,168	0.17	-20.64
Ukraine	3,733	4,915	5,365	6,288	5,836	0.31	-7.19
Uzbekistan	50	70					
Other countries Central/East Europe	400			565	472	0.02	-16.46
NORTHERN EUROPE	**17,971**	**13,389**	**14,720**	**15,767**	**15,403**	**0.81**	**-2.31**
Denmark	1,901	2,035	1,450	1,824	1,325	0.07	-27.36
Finland	3,993	3,852	3,780	3,824	4,818	0.25	25.99
Iceland		46	276	338	170	0.01	-49.70
Ireland	230	305	260	360	139	0.01	-61.39
Norway	2,837	2,019	1,702	2,686	1,411	0.07	-47.47
Sweden	2,742	2,384	3,329	3,207	2,807	0.15	-12.47
United Kingdom	5,868	2,748	3,923	3,528	4,733	0.25	34.16
Other countries of Northern Europe	400						
SOUTHERN EUROPE	**1,513,729**	**1,415,331**	**1,416,209**	**1,263,728**	**1,239,703**	**65.08**	**-1.90**
Albania	773	379	258	222	53	0.00	-76.13
Andorra		132		45	225	0.01	400.00
Bosnia and Herzegovina	427	1,517	1,819	2,010	1,595	0.08	-20.65
Croatia	4,447	4,074	4,060	3,368	3,648	0.19	8.31
Greece	8,493	6,100	5,848	1,426	1,293	0.07	-9.33
Italy	1,483,490	1,381,570	1,385,681	1,238,576	1,217,761	63.92	-1.68
Malta	16	88	311	455	600	0.03	31.87
Portugal	629	565	463	481	530	0.03	10.19
Serbia and Montenegro	7,467	12,951	9,640	10,043	8,154	0.43	-18.81
Slovenia	6,271	5,616	4,693	4,224	2,829	0.15	-33.03
Spain	1,066	2,027	3,344	1,652	2,902	0.15	75.67
TFYR of Macedonia	83	238	92	58	82	0.00	41.38
Other countries of Southern Europe	567	74		1,168	31	0.00	-97.35
WESTERN EUROPE	**320,268**	**289,484**	**295,388**	**278,389**	**307,138**	**16.12**	**10.33**
Austria	23,838	21,544	23,672	20,714	18,972	1.00	-8.41
Belgium	21,684	18,342	18,291	15,766	17,271	0.91	9.55
France	69,199	62,358	61,498	56,650	59,255	3.11	4.60
Germany	127,913	110,676	111,885	113,820	136,132	7.15	19.60
Luxembourg	1,533	1,989	2,298	2,865	2,390	0.13	-16.58
Monaco			16				
Netherlands	33,553	32,035	33,068	26,496	25,321	1.33	-4.43
Switzerland	42,548	42,540	44,660	42,078	47,797	2.51	13.59
EAST MEDITERRANEAN EUROPE	**1,470**	**1,916**	**1,532**	**1,772**	**2,783**	**0.15**	**57.05**
Cyprus	185	81			162	0.01	
Israel	979	977	927	832	824	0.04	-0.96
Turkey	306	858	605	940	1,797	0.09	91.17

632

SAN MARINO

2. Arrivals of non-resident visitors at national borders, by nationality

	2009	2010	2011	2012	2013	Market share 2013	% Change 2013-2012
MIDDLE EAST	393	457	469	281	158	0.01	-43.77
Egypt		20	166	93			
Iraq		12		50			
Jordan			19	121	27	0.00	-77.69
Lebanon		59	201		69	0.00	
Saudi Arabia	38		27	17	62	0.00	264.71
Syrian Arab Republic	355	366	56				
SOUTH ASIA	130	364	428	556	356	0.02	-35.97
Bangladesh	130	199			55	0.00	
India		105	216	338	204	0.01	-39.64
Iran, Islamic Republic of		60		183	18	0.00	-90.16
Sri Lanka			212	35	79	0.00	125.71
NOT SPECIFIED	761	659	685	205			
Other countries of the World	761	659	685	205			

Yearbook of Tourism Statistics, Data 2009 – 2013, 2015 Edition

SAO TOME AND PRINCIPE

1. Arrivals of non-resident tourists at national borders, by nationality

	2009	2010	2011	2012	2013	Market share 2013	% Change 2013-2012
TOTAL		7,963	12,221				
AFRICA		2,123	2,992				
EAST AFRICA		24					
Mozambique		24					
CENTRAL AFRICA		1,484					
Angola		1,105					
Cameroon		71					
Chad		2					
Congo		24					
Equatorial Guinea		138					
Gabon		144					
NORTH AFRICA		2					
Morocco		2					
SOUTHERN AFRICA		80					
South Africa		80					
WEST AFRICA		486					
Benin		9					
Cabo Verde		251					
Côte d'Ivoire		4					
Ghana		6					
Guinea-Bissau		6					
Mali		5					
Nigeria		198					
Senegal		7					
OTHER AFRICA		47	2,992				
Other countries of Africa		47					
All countries of Africa			2,992				
AMERICAS		489	980				
CARIBBEAN		1					
Cuba		1					
NORTH AMERICA		327					
Canada		47					
United States of America		280					
SOUTH AMERICA		139					
Brazil		139					
OTHER AMERICAS		22	980				
Other countries of the Americas		22					
All countries of the Americas			980				
EAST ASIA AND THE PACIFIC		85	491				
NORTH-EAST ASIA		79					
China		13					
Japan		23					
Taiwan, Province of China		43					
SOUTH-EAST ASIA		6					
Philippines		6					
OTHER EAST ASIA AND THE PACIFIC			491				
All countries East Asia/Pacific			491				
EUROPE		5,090	6,704				
NORTHERN EUROPE		262					
Denmark		6					
Norway		11					
Sweden		16					
United Kingdom		229					
SOUTHERN EUROPE		3,807					
Italy		80					
Portugal		3,578					
Spain		149					
WESTERN EUROPE		942					
Austria		23					

634

SAO TOME AND PRINCIPE

1. Arrivals of non-resident tourists at national borders, by nationality

	2009	2010	2011	2012	2013	Market share 2013	% Change 2013-2012
Belgium		52					
France		514					
Germany		193					
Netherlands		115					
Switzerland		45					
OTHER EUROPE		**79**	**6,704**				
Other countries of Europe		79					
All countries of Europe			6,704				
MIDDLE EAST		**27**	**87**				
Lebanon		27					
All countries of Middle East			87				
SOUTH ASIA		**5**	**967**				
India		5					
All countries of South Asia			967				
NOT SPECIFIED		**144**					
Other countries of the World		144					

Yearbook of Tourism Statistics, Data 2009 – 2013, 2015 Edition

SAUDI ARABIA

1. Arrivals of non-resident tourists at national borders, by nationality

	2009	2010	2011	2012	2013	Market share 2013	% Change 2013-2012
TOTAL	10,896,712	10,850,188	17,497,887	14,276,196	13,380,351	100.00	-6.28
AFRICA	260,717	368,610	790,301	1,138,839	551,537	4.12	-51.57
EAST AFRICA	12,142	22,313	74,904	118,494	57,226	0.43	-51.71
Burundi	16		85	12	21	0.00	75.00
Comoros	229	1,051	2,761	4,558	1,075	0.01	-76.42
Djibouti	348	429	1,220	422	256	0.00	-39.34
Eritrea	1,282	2,804	14,156	6,851	2,042	0.02	-70.19
Ethiopia	4,086	9,628	38,080	93,479	50,387	0.38	-46.10
Kenya	1,858	1,825	6,723	4,776	1,165	0.01	-75.61
Madagascar	53		171	164			
Malawi	787		2,015	183	16	0.00	-91.26
Mauritius		1,677	1,414	1,837	449	0.00	-75.56
Mozambique	207		1,232	997	38	0.00	-96.19
Rwanda			59	26	11	0.00	-57.69
Somalia	1,623	1,268	3,880	2,320	1,001	0.01	-56.85
Uganda	229	758	630	405	303	0.00	-25.19
United Republic of Tanzania			1,525	1,468	344	0.00	-76.57
Zambia	72		261	319	49	0.00	-84.64
Zimbabwe	739		492	438	69	0.00	-84.25
Other countries of East Africa	613	2,873	200	239			
CENTRAL AFRICA	5,104	3,888	7,196	171,174	1,922	0.01	-98.88
Angola	13		599	12	1	0.00	-91.67
Cameroon	2,504	1,029	1,357	1,311	767	0.01	-41.50
Central African Republic	36		73	49	39	0.00	-20.41
Chad	2,465	2,686	4,832	3,861	1,017	0.01	-73.66
Congo	37		221	165,799	74	0.00	-99.96
Equatorial Guinea	8		5	1			
Gabon	41		97	133	24	0.00	-81.95
Other countries of Central Africa		173	12	8			
NORTH AFRICA	205,734	256,445	581,493	537,483	457,923	3.42	-14.80
Algeria	64,015	96,097	124,163	226,139	4,522	0.03	-98.00
Morocco	41,108	60,995	108,339	97,546	9,248	0.07	-90.52
Sudan	88,269	65,352	298,344	159,581	437,287	3.27	174.02
Tunisia	12,342	34,001	50,647	54,217	6,866	0.05	-87.34
SOUTHERN AFRICA	14,144	25,203	41,244	54,861	24,957	0.19	-54.51
Botswana	52		67	97	24	0.00	-75.26
Lesotho	29		126	60	8	0.00	-86.67
Namibia	16		80	110	38	0.00	-65.45
South Africa	14,024	24,996	40,910	54,477	24,798	0.19	-54.48
Swaziland	23		59	78	89	0.00	14.10
Other countries of Southern Africa		207	2	39			
WEST AFRICA	23,593	60,761	85,464	256,827	9,509	0.07	-96.30
Benin	234		693	475	99	0.00	-79.16
Burkina Faso	390		1,361	878	163	0.00	-81.44
Côte d'Ivoire	149		512	341	146	0.00	-57.18
Gambia	91		398	226	74	0.00	-67.26
Ghana	954	1,568	3,244	1,593	2,435	0.02	52.86
Guinea	219		892	654	447	0.00	-31.65
Guinea-Bissau	6		86	50	46	0.00	-8.00
Liberia	102		103	64	57	0.00	-10.94
Mali	465						
Mauritania	1,128	2,354	4,261	3,474	1,001	0.01	-71.19
Niger	609	1,965	2,905	2,839	725	0.01	-74.46
Nigeria	17,759	51,090	66,599	241,868	3,135	0.02	-98.70
Senegal	399	1,175	2,232	862	491	0.00	-43.04
Sierra Leone	123		241	462	57	0.00	-87.66
Togo	120		255	129	69	0.00	-46.51
Other countries of West Africa	845	2,609	1,682	2,912	564	0.00	-80.63

Yearbook of Tourism Statistics, Data 2009 – 2013, 2015 Edition

SAUDI ARABIA

1. Arrivals of non-resident tourists at national borders, by nationality

	2009	2010	2011	2012	2013	Market share 2013	% Change 2013-2012
AMERICAS	56,841	53,432	182,105	162,863	74,898	0.56	-54.01
CARIBBEAN	309	1,369	1,479	1,178	566	0.00	-51.95
Bahamas			26	12	4	0.00	-66.67
Barbados	12		49	39	12	0.00	-69.23
British Virgin Islands	7						
Cuba	4	1,092	29	16	17	0.00	6.25
Dominica			54	62	74	0.00	19.35
Dominican Republic	6						
Haiti	3		15	5	3	0.00	-40.00
Jamaica	17	277	82	47	15	0.00	-68.09
Puerto Rico				366			
Saint Lucia			5	2			
Trinidad and Tobago	260		1,219	629	441	0.00	-29.89
CENTRAL AMERICA	320		814	846	110	0.00	-87.00
Belize	15		75	34	13	0.00	-61.76
Costa Rica	33		178	27	44	0.00	62.96
El Salvador	33		160	525			
Guatemala	12		41	29	31	0.00	6.90
Honduras	22		102	145	10	0.00	-93.10
Nicaragua	151		24	14	4	0.00	-71.43
Panama	54		234	72	8	0.00	-88.89
NORTH AMERICA	53,476	50,043	169,002	97,569	71,215	0.53	-27.01
Canada	11,468	11,716	67,877	17,321	7,660	0.06	-55.78
Mexico	231	550	1,432	245	296	0.00	20.82
United States of America	41,777	37,777	99,693	80,003	63,259	0.47	-20.93
SOUTH AMERICA	2,736	2,020	10,810	63,175	3,007	0.02	-95.24
Argentina	1,468	351	1,294	469	453	0.00	-3.41
Bolivia	17		162	42	45	0.00	7.14
Brazil	735	935	2,154	1,237	1,195	0.01	-3.40
Chile	37		229	93	99	0.00	6.45
Colombia	176		2,020	352	464	0.00	31.82
Ecuador	14		203	95	74	0.00	-22.11
Paraguay	7		21	7	6	0.00	-14.29
Peru	39		257	65	82	0.00	26.15
Suriname	1		12	60,166	9	0.00	-99.99
Uruguay	11		97	56	49	0.00	-12.50
Venezuela	231	734	4,361	593	531	0.00	-10.46
OTHER AMERICAS				95			
Other countries of the Americas				95			
EAST ASIA AND THE PACIFIC	362,500	485,534	844,723	1,016,597	407,220	3.04	-59.94
NORTH-EAST ASIA	39,022	40,655	66,644	64,020	52,815	0.39	-17.50
China	18,298	20,416	24,409	19,436	10,937	0.08	-43.73
Hong Kong, China	237		30	11,011	5,723	0.04	-48.02
Japan	6,539	9,210	16,410	11,803	13,477	0.10	14.18
Korea, Republic of	13,842	10,932	25,738	21,742	22,663	0.17	4.24
Mongolia	105		51	24	14	0.00	-41.67
Other countries of North-East Asia	1	97	6	4	1	0.00	-75.00
SOUTH-EAST ASIA	320,255	436,692	734,899	934,987	335,096	2.50	-64.16
Brunei Darussalam	5,134	4,927	2,281	3,613	734	0.01	-79.68
Cambodia	48	26	146	86	55	0.00	-36.05
Indonesia	205,374	235,636	404,903	676,764	257,899	1.93	-61.89
Malaysia	62,749	152,396	110,148	165,086	16,097	0.12	-90.25
Myanmar	479	3,149	1,244	1,180	383	0.00	-67.54
Philippines	35,213	28,053	197,463	63,114	42,324	0.32	-32.94
Singapore	4,875	5,935	9,375	20,095	15,319	0.11	-23.77
Thailand	5,217	3,425	8,108	4,880	1,883	0.01	-61.41
Viet Nam	1,166	3,145	1,231	169	402	0.00	137.87
AUSTRALASIA	3,192	8,187	42,988	17,518	19,280	0.14	10.06
Australia	2,794	6,036	37,450	14,568	14,097	0.11	-3.23

637

SAUDI ARABIA

1. Arrivals of non-resident tourists at national borders, by nationality

	2009	2010	2011	2012	2013	Market share 2013	% Change 2013-2012
New Zealand	398	2,151	5,538	2,950	5,183	0.04	75.69
MELANESIA	**20**		**32**	**15**	**6**	**0.00**	**-60.00**
Fiji	20		32	15	6	0.00	-60.00
MICRONESIA			**131**	**30**	**23**	**0.00**	**-23.33**
Kiribati			1	20	23	0.00	15.00
Marshall Islands			130	10			
POLYNESIA	**11**		**12**	**20**			
American Samoa	11		1	19			
French Polynesia			5	1			
Tonga			6				
OTHER EAST ASIA AND THE PACIFIC			**17**	**7**			
Other countries of Oceania			17	7			
EUROPE	**444,667**	**367,238**	**722,534**	**982,253**	**321,951**	**2.41**	**-67.22**
CENTRAL/EASTERN EUROPE	**13,633**	**24,465**	**47,048**	**30,596**	**13,335**	**0.10**	**-56.42**
Armenia	42		45	36	118	0.00	227.78
Azerbaijan	552	974	1,762	1,719	360	0.00	-79.06
Belarus	116		434	232	357	0.00	53.88
Bulgaria	170		756	603	907	0.01	50.41
Czech Republic	2,233		2,447	725	1,114	0.01	53.66
Estonia	39		116	60	115	0.00	91.67
Georgia	33		197	169	217	0.00	28.40
Hungary	271		987	740	965	0.01	30.41
Kazakhstan	176	4,207	2,146	2,750	293	0.00	-89.35
Kyrgyzstan				482	114	0.00	-76.35
Latvia	80		221	233	136	0.00	-41.63
Lithuania	58		138	156	112	0.00	-28.21
Poland	476	909	2,319	2,157	2,320	0.02	7.56
Republic of Moldova	22		60	39	44	0.00	12.82
Romania	626	1,040	3,504	1,748	1,954	0.01	11.78
Russian Federation	3,540	3,418	5,894	4,985	2,099	0.02	-57.89
Slovakia	156		767	387	485	0.00	25.32
Tajikistan	877		1,045	1,651	457	0.00	-72.32
Turkmenistan	174		720	886	62	0.00	-93.00
Ukraine	738	1,212	2,560	2,996	671	0.01	-77.60
Uzbekistan	2,792	9,084	5,547	7,018	424	0.00	-93.96
Other countries Central/East Europe	462	3,621	15,383	824	11	0.00	-98.67
NORTHERN EUROPE	**182,008**	**113,147**	**283,717**	**156,026**	**109,810**	**0.82**	**-29.62**
Denmark	1,906	4,823	8,446	3,905	2,883	0.02	-26.17
Finland	669	1,100	2,774	1,868	1,656	0.01	-11.35
Iceland	69	76	258	256	166	0.00	-35.16
Ireland	4,853	4,155	11,757	7,401	6,493	0.05	-12.27
Norway	1,918	1,742	3,564	2,895	1,338	0.01	-53.78
Sweden	2,126	3,107	5,724	4,441	2,826	0.02	-36.37
United Kingdom	170,467	98,144	251,194	135,260	94,448	0.71	-30.17
SOUTHERN EUROPE	**26,836**	**19,506**	**45,105**	**33,656**	**42,613**	**0.32**	**26.61**
Albania	129	195	332	251	103	0.00	-58.96
Andorra	1		2	4	13	0.00	225.00
Bosnia and Herzegovina	281	552	885	799	454	0.00	-43.18
Croatia	910	398	1,143	1,292	1,058	0.01	-18.11
Greece	1,831	1,677	7,266	3,435	3,579	0.03	4.19
Italy	11,504	9,599	23,743	16,026	19,415	0.15	21.15
Malta	61	183	497	190	255	0.00	34.21
Portugal	856	1,049	2,281	2,161	2,566	0.02	18.74
San Marino	3						
Serbia	12						
Slovenia	97	137	221	296	292	0.00	-1.35
Spain	10,999	5,460	8,392	8,788	14,878	0.11	69.30
Other countries of Southern Europe	152	256	343	414			

Yearbook of Tourism Statistics, Data 2009 – 2013, 2015 Edition

SAUDI ARABIA

1. Arrivals of non-resident tourists at national borders, by nationality

	2009	2010	2011	2012	2013	Market share 2013	% Change 2013-2012
WESTERN EUROPE	66,012	80,667	148,438	107,085	103,144	0.77	-3.68
Austria	9,954	3,726	5,377	3,601	4,702	0.04	30.57
Belgium	2,797	5,383	8,240	6,777	4,718	0.04	-30.38
France	20,720	28,802	68,663	37,496	48,982	0.37	30.63
Germany	22,940	28,818	39,202	30,587	28,911	0.22	-5.48
Liechtenstein			4	6			
Luxembourg	64		148	109	78	0.00	-28.44
Netherlands	5,213	10,412	19,057	15,721	9,714	0.07	-38.21
Switzerland	4,324	3,421	7,747	12,788	6,039	0.05	-52.78
Other countries of Western Europe		105					
EAST MEDITERRANEAN EUROPE	156,178	129,453	198,226	654,890	53,049	0.40	-91.90
Cyprus	2,167	526	1,147	758	817	0.01	7.78
Turkey	154,011	128,927	197,079	654,132	52,232	0.39	-92.02
MIDDLE EAST	8,677,688	8,244,721	11,098,731	8,063,169	8,728,345	65.23	8.25
Bahrain	624,793	820,132	1,220,651	1,012,397	826,618	6.18	-18.35
Egypt	538,287	763,901	1,157,812	1,142,021	1,709,015	12.77	49.65
Iraq	64,138	171,913	44,862	165,896	291	0.00	-99.82
Jordan	517,167	451,099	1,666,814	1,352,257	1,885,686	14.09	39.45
Kuwait	2,475,318	2,507,813	2,578,541	1,855,774	1,751,617	13.09	-5.61
Lebanon	58,337	116,129	164,157	111,810	179,675	1.34	60.70
Libya	27,835	42,976	1,651	86,674	306	0.00	-99.65
Oman	165,875	176,687	373,421	357,811	293,218	2.19	-18.05
Palestine	14,487	26,084	82,814	11,982	115,222	0.86	861.63
Qatar	1,470,382	843,762	1,058,300	810,336	689,188	5.15	-14.95
Syrian Arab Republic	730,306	254,140	765,908	86,129	28,597	0.21	-66.80
United Arab Emirates	1,889,187	1,957,613	1,531,429	861,735	654,638	4.89	-24.03
Yemen	101,576	112,472	452,371	205,657	594,274	4.44	188.96
Other countries of Middle East				2,690			
SOUTH ASIA	1,094,282	1,330,271	3,858,203	2,902,963	3,293,803	24.62	13.46
Afghanistan	5,140	8,793	24,403	17,238	7,342	0.05	-57.41
Bangladesh	23,698	188,584	407,697	93,593	110,720	0.83	18.30
Bhutan			1,590	4	3	0.00	-25.00
India	247,075	389,116	1,501,308	998,779	1,695,846	12.67	69.79
Iran, Islamic Republic of	413,656	220,051	559,690	506,192	1,079	0.01	-99.79
Maldives	2,456	3,466	1,729	1,942	202	0.00	-89.60
Nepal	32,694	25,841	57,586	40,342	48,770	0.36	20.89
Pakistan	336,255	465,571	1,219,287	1,172,470	1,400,546	10.47	19.45
Sri Lanka	33,308	28,779	84,913	72,403	29,295	0.22	-59.54
Other countries of South Asia		70					
NOT SPECIFIED	17	382	1,290	9,512	2,597	0.02	-72.70
Other countries of the World	17	382	1,290	9,512	2,597	0.02	-72.70

Yearbook of Tourism Statistics, Data 2009 – 2013, 2015 Edition

SERBIA

3. Arrivals of non-resident tourists in hotels and similar establishments, by nationality

	2009	2010	2011	2012	2013	Market share 2013	% Change 2013-2012
TOTAL	569,535	612,989	680,365	707,173	767,058	100.00	8.47
AMERICAS	15,064	17,459	18,005	19,790	21,062	2.75	6.43
NORTH AMERICA	15,064	17,459	18,005	19,790	21,062	2.75	6.43
Canada	3,429	4,081	4,177	4,581	5,110	0.67	11.55
United States of America	11,635	13,378	13,828	15,209	15,952	2.08	4.89
EAST ASIA AND THE PACIFIC	6,897	8,798	10,647	12,713	18,033	2.35	41.85
NORTH-EAST ASIA	2,379	2,842	3,846	5,026	9,694	1.26	92.88
China					5,159	0.67	
Japan	2,379	2,842	3,846	5,026	4,535	0.59	-9.77
AUSTRALASIA	4,518	5,956	6,801	7,687	8,339	1.09	8.48
Australia	4,001	5,329	6,096	6,993	7,540	0.98	7.82
New Zealand	517	627	705	694	799	0.10	15.13
EUROPE	532,804	566,315	630,597	649,788	696,246	90.77	7.15
CENTRAL/EASTERN EUROPE	111,019	114,325	128,645	142,357	167,430	21.83	17.61
Bulgaria	22,472	22,912	25,626	31,767	38,031	4.96	19.72
Czech Republic	8,346	9,147	8,613	9,070	10,958	1.43	20.82
Hungary	14,666	15,050	17,144	18,281	20,966	2.73	14.69
Poland	20,624	18,997	19,810	19,504	24,709	3.22	26.69
Romania	21,073	22,478	28,292	29,337	30,667	4.00	4.53
Russian Federation	15,712	19,827	22,957	28,478	35,389	4.61	24.27
Slovakia	8,126	5,914	6,203	5,920	6,710	0.87	13.34
NORTHERN EUROPE	30,722	34,321	40,246	44,420	45,117	5.88	1.57
Denmark	2,996	3,378	3,634	5,007	4,692	0.61	-6.29
Finland	1,533	1,831	2,523	1,963	2,189	0.29	11.51
Iceland	321	339	342	518	398	0.05	-23.17
Ireland	1,452	1,583	1,849	1,855	1,755	0.23	-5.39
Norway	3,948	4,881	5,126	6,268	6,178	0.81	-1.44
Sweden	6,089	6,637	9,341	11,136	12,065	1.57	8.34
United Kingdom	14,383	15,672	17,431	17,673	17,840	2.33	0.94
SOUTHERN EUROPE	269,557	286,275	310,181	304,853	283,209	36.92	-7.10
Bosnia and Herzegovina	56,705	55,805	56,639	53,980	43,837	5.71	-18.79
Croatia	38,667	43,870	48,073	43,682	46,816	6.10	7.17
Greece	21,927	23,026	25,128	25,690	33,507	4.37	30.43
Italy	28,847	30,651	36,255	47,551	38,919	5.07	-18.15
Montenegro	40,108	38,026	39,096	36,467	31,760	4.14	-12.91
Portugal	1,239	1,414	1,666	1,678	1,644	0.21	-2.03
Slovenia	50,156	61,938	68,735	60,027	59,210	7.72	-1.36
Spain	5,048	5,667	6,275	5,679	5,399	0.70	-4.93
TFYR of Macedonia	26,860	25,878	28,314	30,099	22,117	2.88	-26.52
WESTERN EUROPE	93,665	103,716	113,684	116,138	115,928	15.11	-0.18
Austria	20,585	22,978	23,948	23,476	21,435	2.79	-8.69
Belgium	4,288	4,929	6,530	6,248	5,856	0.76	-6.27
France	15,073	16,734	16,559	17,896	17,729	2.31	-0.93
Germany	37,348	40,739	45,774	46,420	47,945	6.25	3.29
Luxembourg	249	393	386	467	393	0.05	-15.85
Netherlands	9,668	10,601	11,173	11,220	11,207	1.46	-0.12
Switzerland	6,454	7,342	9,314	10,411	11,363	1.48	9.14
EAST MEDITERRANEAN EUROPE	16,044	16,562	21,762	21,498	31,230	4.07	45.27
Israel	2,599	3,009	3,286	3,781	3,799	0.50	0.48
Turkey	13,445	13,553	18,476	17,717	27,431	3.58	54.83
OTHER EUROPE	11,797	11,116	16,079	20,522	53,332	6.95	159.88
Other countries of Europe	11,797	11,116	16,079	20,522	53,332	6.95	159.88
NOT SPECIFIED	14,770	20,417	21,116	24,882	31,717	4.13	27.47
Other countries of the World	14,770	20,417	21,116	24,882	31,717	4.13	27.47

Yearbook of Tourism Statistics, Data 2009 – 2013, 2015 Edition

SERBIA

4. Arrivals of non-resident tourists in all types of accommodation establishments, by nationality

	2009	2010	2011	2012	2013	Market share 2013	% Change 2013-2012
TOTAL	**645,022**	**682,681**	**764,167**	**809,967**	**921,768**	**100.00**	**13.80**
AMERICAS	**16,266**	**18,554**	**19,180**	**21,641**	**24,277**	**2.63**	**12.18**
NORTH AMERICA	**16,266**	**18,554**	**19,180**	**21,641**	**24,277**	**2.63**	**12.18**
Canada	3,969	4,408	4,542	5,140	6,073	0.66	18.15
United States of America	12,297	14,146	14,638	16,501	18,204	1.97	10.32
EAST ASIA AND THE PACIFIC	**8,160**	**9,903**	**12,193**	**14,997**	**22,898**	**2.48**	**52.68**
NORTH-EAST ASIA	**2,929**	**3,011**	**3,988**	**5,251**	**10,913**	**1.18**	**107.83**
China					5,783	0.63	
Japan	2,929	3,011	3,988	5,251	5,130	0.56	-2.30
AUSTRALASIA	**5,231**	**6,892**	**8,205**	**9,746**	**11,985**	**1.30**	**22.97**
Australia	4,613	6,137	7,283	8,772	10,713	1.16	22.13
New Zealand	618	755	922	974	1,272	0.14	30.60
EUROPE	**602,599**	**632,964**	**710,757**	**745,959**	**836,803**	**90.78**	**12.18**
CENTRAL/EASTERN EUROPE	**120,985**	**123,547**	**139,951**	**159,172**	**197,722**	**21.45**	**24.22**
Bulgaria	24,476	24,582	28,054	35,243	43,430	4.71	23.23
Czech Republic	9,271	9,844	9,278	10,042	12,924	1.40	28.70
Hungary	16,291	16,276	18,660	20,315	24,528	2.66	20.74
Poland	22,304	20,672	21,548	23,323	30,003	3.25	28.64
Romania	22,876	23,907	30,628	32,042	35,495	3.85	10.78
Russian Federation	17,312	21,636	25,236	31,628	43,070	4.67	36.18
Slovakia	8,455	6,630	6,547	6,579	8,272	0.90	25.73
NORTHERN EUROPE	**33,294**	**38,037**	**44,250**	**49,524**	**53,932**	**5.85**	**8.90**
Denmark	3,208	3,633	3,872	5,471	5,714	0.62	4.44
Finland	1,728	1,999	2,692	2,223	2,672	0.29	20.20
Iceland	337	350	361	539	466	0.05	-13.54
Ireland	1,665	1,782	2,070	2,049	2,128	0.23	3.86
Norway	4,203	5,176	5,340	6,765	7,152	0.78	5.72
Sweden	6,531	7,071	9,917	12,186	13,945	1.51	14.43
United Kingdom	15,622	18,026	19,998	20,291	21,855	2.37	7.71
SOUTHERN EUROPE	**318,803**	**331,827**	**364,725**	**361,045**	**381,406**	**41.38**	**5.64**
Bosnia and Herzegovina	63,981	63,560	65,960	62,276	68,117	7.39	9.38
Croatia	40,243	46,367	50,625	47,229	53,394	5.79	13.05
Greece	24,155	24,726	26,400	26,900	37,025	4.02	37.64
Italy	37,321	34,221	38,105	50,580	43,376	4.71	-14.24
Montenegro	61,752	56,888	66,636	64,703	67,658	7.34	4.57
Portugal	1,425	1,647	1,856	1,967	2,005	0.22	1.93
Slovenia	54,766	66,686	74,674	65,723	67,498	7.32	2.70
Spain	5,581	6,151	6,850	6,584	6,758	0.73	2.64
TFYR of Macedonia	29,579	31,581	33,619	35,083	35,575	3.86	1.40
WESTERN EUROPE	**99,672**	**110,777**	**121,992**	**129,206**	**137,393**	**14.91**	**6.34**
Austria	21,464	24,075	25,245	25,216	24,740	2.68	-1.89
Belgium	4,529	5,339	7,131	7,090	6,984	0.76	-1.50
France	16,542	18,339	18,191	20,219	21,747	2.36	7.56
Germany	39,497	42,672	48,159	50,896	55,468	6.02	8.98
Luxembourg	261	415	443	485	416	0.05	-14.23
Netherlands	10,357	12,082	12,963	14,027	14,846	1.61	5.84
Switzerland	7,022	7,855	9,860	11,273	13,192	1.43	17.02
EAST MEDITERRANEAN EUROPE	**16,701**	**16,973**	**22,618**	**24,822**	**36,654**	**3.98**	**47.67**
Israel	2,780	3,131	3,422	3,957	4,217	0.46	6.57
Turkey	13,921	13,842	19,196	20,865	32,437	3.52	55.46
OTHER EUROPE	**13,144**	**11,803**	**17,221**	**22,190**	**29,696**	**3.22**	**33.83**
Other countries of Europe	13,144	11,803	17,221	22,190	29,696	3.22	33.83
NOT SPECIFIED	**17,997**	**21,260**	**22,037**	**27,370**	**37,790**	**4.10**	**38.07**
Other countries of the World	17,997	21,260	22,037	27,370	37,790	4.10	38.07

Yearbook of Tourism Statistics, Data 2009 – 2013, 2015 Edition

SERBIA

5. Overnight stays of non-resident tourists in hotels and similar establishments, by nationality

	2009	2010	2011	2012	2013	Market share 2013	% Change 2013-2012
TOTAL	1,184,154	1,235,654	1,387,148	1,518,577	1,616,648	100.00	6.46
AMERICAS	40,704	45,661	46,997	52,065	57,357	3.55	10.16
NORTH AMERICA	40,704	45,661	46,997	52,065	57,357	3.55	10.16
Canada	9,172	9,917	10,701	10,677	12,505	0.77	17.12
United States of America	31,532	35,744	36,296	41,388	44,852	2.77	8.37
EAST ASIA AND THE PACIFIC	15,231	19,862	23,426	30,700	40,678	2.52	32.50
NORTH-EAST ASIA	5,744	7,397	8,372	13,241	21,112	1.31	59.44
China					10,239	0.63	
Japan	5,744	7,397	8,372	13,241	10,873	0.67	-17.88
AUSTRALASIA	9,487	12,465	15,054	17,459	19,566	1.21	12.07
Australia	8,451	11,106	13,694	15,943	17,901	1.11	12.28
New Zealand	1,036	1,359	1,360	1,516	1,665	0.10	9.83
EUROPE	1,080,313	1,111,912	1,261,918	1,369,692	1,411,991	87.34	3.09
CENTRAL/EASTERN EUROPE	224,885	218,272	258,003	297,214	341,215	21.11	14.80
Bulgaria	42,260	39,597	48,307	69,132	63,886	3.95	-7.59
Czech Republic	16,901	17,994	17,651	18,704	29,389	1.82	57.13
Hungary	25,316	24,745	32,547	34,495	45,060	2.79	30.63
Poland	30,006	28,547	30,972	32,308	37,131	2.30	14.93
Romania	41,141	42,033	53,871	54,673	58,679	3.63	7.33
Russian Federation	46,001	53,578	62,182	75,717	93,704	5.80	23.76
Slovakia	23,260	11,778	12,473	12,185	13,366	0.83	9.69
NORTHERN EUROPE	74,015	82,990	103,776	118,183	114,026	7.05	-3.52
Denmark	7,018	7,591	9,700	14,361	13,027	0.81	-9.29
Finland	3,703	4,294	6,456	4,442	5,077	0.31	14.30
Iceland	984	984	1,121	1,742	1,225	0.08	-29.68
Ireland	3,486	4,945	5,517	4,961	4,578	0.28	-7.72
Norway	9,947	12,146	14,754	20,862	18,374	1.14	-11.93
Sweden	13,688	14,196	21,531	26,670	27,819	1.72	4.31
United Kingdom	35,189	38,834	44,697	45,145	43,926	2.72	-2.70
SOUTHERN EUROPE	538,648	545,550	594,178	634,472	564,889	34.94	-10.97
Bosnia and Herzegovina	120,214	105,503	113,626	110,186	87,964	5.44	-20.17
Croatia	74,597	82,410	85,443	81,838	84,950	5.25	3.80
Greece	43,540	42,996	46,509	48,737	60,175	3.72	23.47
Italy	67,493	73,909	86,436	138,308	95,627	5.92	-30.86
Montenegro	84,625	76,308	81,189	80,002	70,279	4.35	-12.15
Portugal	3,204	3,190	4,774	4,314	4,278	0.26	-0.83
Slovenia	84,333	102,904	110,715	102,682	105,308	6.51	2.56
Spain	12,199	12,982	16,002	14,082	13,803	0.85	-1.98
TFYR of Macedonia	48,443	45,348	49,484	54,323	42,505	2.63	-21.76
WESTERN EUROPE	187,357	206,361	229,549	239,176	232,220	14.36	-2.91
Austria	38,048	41,667	42,618	42,882	38,117	2.36	-11.11
Belgium	9,074	9,767	14,165	13,367	12,196	0.75	-8.76
France	31,762	37,555	36,865	40,827	38,976	2.41	-4.53
Germany	74,311	78,984	90,227	93,342	93,217	5.77	-0.13
Luxembourg	552	768	922	1,046	909	0.06	-13.10
Netherlands	18,567	21,740	24,331	24,923	23,697	1.47	-4.92
Switzerland	15,043	15,880	20,421	22,789	25,108	1.55	10.18
EAST MEDITERRANEAN EUROPE	27,302	29,482	39,681	39,397	55,614	3.44	41.16
Israel	6,092	7,256	8,015	8,613	9,231	0.57	7.18
Turkey	21,210	22,226	31,666	30,784	46,383	2.87	50.67
OTHER EUROPE	28,106	29,257	36,731	41,250	104,027	6.43	152.19
Other countries of Europe	28,106	29,257	36,731	41,250	104,027	6.43	152.19
NOT SPECIFIED	47,906	58,219	54,807	66,120	106,622	6.60	61.26
Other countries of the World	47,906	58,219	54,807	66,120	106,622	6.60	61.26

SERBIA

6. Overnight stays of non-resident tourists in all types of accommodation establishments, by nationality

	2009	2010	2011	2012	2013	Market share 2013	% Change 2013-2012
TOTAL	1,469,102	1,452,156	1,643,054	1,796,217	1,988,393	100.00	10.70
AMERICAS	49,939	49,310	50,817	57,733	64,966	3.27	12.53
NORTH AMERICA	49,939	49,310	50,817	57,733	64,966	3.27	12.53
Canada	14,918	11,072	12,235	12,387	15,023	0.76	21.28
United States of America	35,021	38,238	38,582	45,346	49,943	2.51	10.14
EAST ASIA AND THE PACIFIC	26,500	23,359	27,310	36,330	53,377	2.68	46.92
NORTH-EAST ASIA	12,448	8,805	9,515	14,754	27,193	1.37	84.31
China					14,047	0.71	
Japan	12,448	8,805	9,515	14,754	13,146	0.66	-10.90
AUSTRALASIA	14,052	14,554	17,795	21,576	26,184	1.32	21.36
Australia	12,543	13,002	16,118	19,717	23,792	1.20	20.67
New Zealand	1,509	1,552	1,677	1,859	2,392	0.12	28.67
EUROPE	1,306,508	1,312,069	1,501,808	1,623,215	1,732,896	87.15	6.76
CENTRAL/EASTERN EUROPE	267,327	248,357	300,646	349,377	413,037	20.77	18.22
Bulgaria	46,507	44,448	55,689	76,622	74,232	3.73	-3.12
Czech Republic	21,683	20,026	19,436	21,598	33,562	1.69	55.39
Hungary	30,505	27,793	41,005	42,259	52,822	2.66	25.00
Poland	36,123	32,276	35,180	40,350	46,346	2.33	14.86
Romania	47,572	47,068	59,911	62,916	67,983	3.42	8.05
Russian Federation	59,488	62,583	75,308	91,517	120,899	6.08	32.11
Slovakia	25,449	14,163	14,117	14,115	17,193	0.86	21.81
NORTHERN EUROPE	87,239	92,626	117,722	131,641	133,909	6.73	1.72
Denmark	7,799	8,354	10,239	15,286	15,213	0.77	-0.48
Finland	4,908	4,734	6,900	5,262	6,115	0.31	16.21
Iceland	1,008	1,034	1,235	1,782	1,420	0.07	-20.31
Ireland	5,158	5,382	6,194	5,362	5,292	0.27	-1.31
Norway	10,937	13,165	15,533	22,515	20,499	1.03	-8.95
Sweden	16,133	15,729	23,388	29,443	32,209	1.62	9.39
United Kingdom	41,296	44,228	54,233	51,991	53,161	2.67	2.25
SOUTHERN EUROPE	671,078	679,677	744,260	779,817	783,277	39.39	0.44
Bosnia and Herzegovina	157,106	147,569	165,538	148,784	155,868	7.84	4.76
Croatia	79,955	89,693	93,339	91,645	100,483	5.05	9.64
Greece	48,503	46,284	50,318	52,509	67,262	3.38	28.10
Italy	82,382	80,980	91,039	148,147	105,985	5.33	-28.46
Montenegro	127,404	120,774	129,455	132,083	137,520	6.92	4.12
Portugal	4,891	4,614	5,732	5,509	5,284	0.27	-4.08
Slovenia	96,332	114,471	124,517	115,718	121,997	6.14	5.43
Spain	17,308	15,541	19,103	17,335	17,799	0.90	2.68
TFYR of Macedonia	57,197	59,751	65,219	68,087	71,079	3.57	4.39
WESTERN EUROPE	211,359	226,895	255,112	270,834	275,498	13.86	1.72
Austria	42,388	45,998	48,472	47,900	45,038	2.27	-5.97
Belgium	9,935	10,799	15,551	15,146	14,245	0.72	-5.95
France	38,735	42,194	41,277	45,698	47,166	2.37	3.21
Germany	81,926	84,203	96,875	103,325	107,840	5.42	4.37
Luxembourg	617	821	1,121	1,096	942	0.05	-14.05
Netherlands	20,419	25,510	29,778	32,315	31,107	1.56	-3.74
Switzerland	17,339	17,370	22,038	25,354	29,160	1.47	15.01
EAST MEDITERRANEAN EUROPE	31,717	31,222	42,316	44,909	65,186	3.28	45.15
Israel	7,268	7,691	8,473	9,070	10,169	0.51	12.12
Turkey	24,449	23,531	33,843	35,839	55,017	2.77	53.51
OTHER EUROPE	37,788	33,292	41,752	46,637	61,989	3.12	32.92
Other countries of Europe	37,788	33,292	41,752	46,637	61,989	3.12	32.92
NOT SPECIFIED	86,155	67,418	63,119	78,939	137,154	6.90	73.75
Other countries of the World	86,155	67,418	63,119	78,939	137,154	6.90	73.75

Yearbook of Tourism Statistics, Data 2009 – 2013, 2015 Edition

SEYCHELLES

1. Arrivals of non-resident tourists at national borders, by country of residence

	2009	2010	2011	2012	2013	Market share 2013	% Change 2013-2012
TOTAL	**157,541**	**174,529**	**194,476**	**208,034**	**230,272**	**100.00**	**10.69**
AFRICA	**18,499**	**22,163**	**24,422**	**25,435**	**27,060**	**11.75**	**6.39**
EAST AFRICA	**8,936**	**10,402**	**11,905**	**10,927**	**11,142**	**4.84**	**1.97**
Burundi	25	22	18	31	52	0.02	67.74
Comoros	28	63	264	58	54	0.02	-6.90
Djibouti	91	48	62	52	83	0.04	59.62
Eritrea					6	0.00	
Ethiopia	77	46	79	683	936	0.41	37.04
Kenya	870	1,018	1,163	1,645	1,955	0.85	18.84
Madagascar	316	349	590	289	321	0.14	11.07
Malawi	15	21	36	65	80	0.03	23.08
Mauritius	3,476	3,631	3,867	2,868	3,322	1.44	15.83
Mozambique	62	52	131	141	143	0.06	1.42
Reunion	3,389	4,483	4,789	4,115	2,869	1.25	-30.28
Rwanda	59	45	20	74	121	0.05	63.51
Somalia		6	28	26	22	0.01	-15.38
Uganda	154	136	185	261	414	0.18	58.62
United Republic of Tanzania	136	229	274	227	338	0.15	48.90
Zambia	94	92	146	180	238	0.10	32.22
Zimbabwe	144	161	253	212	188	0.08	-11.32
CENTRAL AFRICA	**164**	**135**	**168**	**305**	**437**	**0.19**	**43.28**
Angola	76	52	94	86	199	0.09	131.40
Cameroon	38	11	12	71	65	0.03	-8.45
Central African Republic					4	0.00	
Chad					8	0.00	
Congo					53	0.02	
Democratic Republic of the Congo	39	59	56	113	89	0.04	-21.24
Equatorial Guinea					11	0.00	
Gabon	11	13	6	35	7	0.00	-80.00
Sao Tome and Principe					1	0.00	
NORTH AFRICA	**291**	**359**	**522**	**564**	**643**	**0.28**	**14.01**
Algeria	32	40	126	47	48	0.02	2.13
Morocco	131	101	166	182	196	0.09	7.69
South Sudan				37	59	0.03	59.46
Sudan	50	55	68	108	130	0.06	20.37
Tunisia	78	163	162	190	210	0.09	10.53
SOUTHERN AFRICA	**8,446**	**10,797**	**10,958**	**12,710**	**13,677**	**5.94**	**7.61**
Botswana	86	162	185	143	172	0.07	20.28
Lesotho	13	20	14	14	22	0.01	57.14
Namibia	116	126	127	170	164	0.07	-3.53
South Africa	8,208	10,425	10,559	12,351	13,294	5.77	7.64
Swaziland	23	64	73	32	25	0.01	-21.88
WEST AFRICA	**468**	**294**	**366**	**661**	**1,023**	**0.44**	**54.77**
Benin					5	0.00	
Burkina Faso					5	0.00	
Cabo Verde					3	0.00	
Côte d'Ivoire	22	21	24	50	27	0.01	-46.00
Gambia					2	0.00	
Ghana	73	43	105	87	132	0.06	51.72
Guinea					10	0.00	
Guinea-Bissau					1	0.00	
Liberia					7	0.00	
Mali					8	0.00	
Mauritania					2	0.00	
Niger					3	0.00	
Nigeria	346	206	206	497	776	0.34	56.14
Saint Helena					3	0.00	
Senegal	27	24	31	27	17	0.01	-37.04
Sierra Leone					5	0.00	
Togo					17	0.01	

Yearbook of Tourism Statistics, Data 2009 – 2013, 2015 Edition

SEYCHELLES

1. Arrivals of non-resident tourists at national borders, by country of residence

	2009	2010	2011	2012	2013	Market share 2013	% Change 2013-2012
OTHER AFRICA	194	176	503	268	138	0.06	-48.51
Other countries of Africa	194	176	503	268	138	0.06	-48.51
AMERICAS	4,541	3,960	4,730	5,590	6,145	2.67	9.93
CARIBBEAN					88	0.04	
Bahamas					1	0.00	
Barbados					3	0.00	
Bermuda					4	0.00	
Cayman Islands					4	0.00	
Cuba					21	0.01	
Dominica					5	0.00	
Dominican Republic					6	0.00	
Guadeloupe					1	0.00	
Jamaica					22	0.01	
Martinique					3	0.00	
Puerto Rico					9	0.00	
Saint Kitts and Nevis					2	0.00	
Trinidad and Tobago					7	0.00	
CENTRAL AMERICA					14	0.01	
Belize					1	0.00	
Costa Rica					2	0.00	
El Salvador					3	0.00	
Guatemala					2	0.00	
Honduras					3	0.00	
Panama					3	0.00	
NORTH AMERICA	4,139	3,488	3,956	4,710	5,031	2.18	6.82
Canada	493	640	666	720	859	0.37	19.31
Greenland					1	0.00	
Mexico	73	59	79	67	87	0.04	29.85
United States of America	3,573	2,789	3,211	3,923	4,084	1.77	4.10
SOUTH AMERICA	254	286	556	613	1,012	0.44	65.09
Argentina	115	126	208	252	296	0.13	17.46
Bolivia					9	0.00	
Brazil	139	160	348	361	550	0.24	52.35
Chile					41	0.02	
Colombia					25	0.01	
Falkland Islands, Malvinas					5	0.00	
Paraguay					2	0.00	
Peru					30	0.01	
Suriname					4	0.00	
Uruguay					26	0.01	
Venezuela					24	0.01	
OTHER AMERICAS	148	186	218	267			
Other countries of the Americas	148	186	218	267			
EAST ASIA AND THE PACIFIC	3,523	4,179	5,664	8,969	13,023	5.66	45.20
NORTH-EAST ASIA	1,512	1,738	3,302	6,515	10,266	4.46	57.57
China	919	1,078	2,124	4,484	7,745	3.36	72.73
Hong Kong, China	73	98	129	198	558	0.24	181.82
Japan	378	299	541	962	823	0.36	-14.45
Korea, Dem. People's Republic of					54	0.02	
Korea, Republic of	84	214	472	748	916	0.40	22.46
Macao, China					5	0.00	
Mongolia					29	0.01	
Taiwan, Province of China	58	49	36	123	136	0.06	10.57
SOUTH-EAST ASIA	1,131	1,324	1,214	1,093	1,024	0.44	-6.31
Brunei Darussalam					12	0.01	
Cambodia					2	0.00	
Indonesia	96	125	174	169	119	0.05	-29.59
Malaysia	159	147	175	163	128	0.06	-21.47
Myanmar					3	0.00	
Philippines	216	226	213	298	266	0.12	-10.74

645

SEYCHELLES

1. Arrivals of non-resident tourists at national borders, by country of residence

	2009	2010	2011	2012	2013	Market share 2013	% Change 2013-2012
Singapore	511	625	526	321	315	0.14	-1.87
Thailand	149	201	126	142	151	0.07	6.34
Viet Nam					28	0.01	
AUSTRALASIA	**796**	**1,049**	**1,091**	**1,219**	**1,688**	**0.73**	**38.47**
Australia	675	928	980	1,083	1,494	0.65	37.95
New Zealand	121	121	111	136	194	0.08	42.65
MELANESIA					**13**	**0.01**	
Fiji					5	0.00	
New Caledonia					6	0.00	
Papua New Guinea					2	0.00	
MICRONESIA					**4**	**0.00**	
Guam					2	0.00	
Kiribati					1	0.00	
Micronesia, Federated States of					1	0.00	
POLYNESIA					**28**	**0.01**	
French Polynesia					9	0.00	
Samoa					19	0.01	
OTHER EAST ASIA AND THE PACIFIC	**84**	**68**	**57**	**142**			
Other countries East Asia/Pacific	35	24	28	121			
Other countries of Oceania	49	44	29	21			
EUROPE	**122,322**	**132,254**	**144,144**	**146,492**	**160,926**	**69.89**	**9.85**
CENTRAL/EASTERN EUROPE	**13,210**	**14,411**	**15,962**	**22,693**	**26,158**	**11.36**	**15.27**
Armenia				35	70	0.03	100.00
Azerbaijan				98	164	0.07	67.35
Belarus	56	100	128	203	243	0.11	19.70
Bulgaria	218	220	352	569	400	0.17	-29.70
Czech Republic	1,392	1,303	1,849	2,058	2,342	1.02	13.80
Estonia	68	66	96	188	255	0.11	35.64
Georgia					39	0.02	
Hungary	695	632	677	894	910	0.40	1.79
Kazakhstan	153	182	212	402	521	0.23	29.60
Kyrgyzstan				9	19	0.01	111.11
Latvia	108	119	127	169	164	0.07	-2.96
Lithuania		107	70	148	294	0.13	98.65
Poland	824	961	1,005	1,289	2,995	1.30	132.35
Republic of Moldova					40	0.02	
Romania	272	333	445	567	674	0.29	18.87
Russian Federation	8,098	8,942	8,840	13,494	14,367	6.24	6.47
Slovakia	223	384	592	654	725	0.31	10.86
Tajikistan				2	8	0.00	300.00
Turkmenistan				8	3	0.00	-62.50
Ukraine	915	890	1,343	1,821	1,884	0.82	3.46
Uzbekistan				16	41	0.02	156.25
Other countries Central/East Europe	188	172	226	69			
NORTHERN EUROPE	**13,846**	**15,936**	**17,096**	**15,606**	**18,404**	**7.99**	**17.93**
Channel Islands					11	0.00	
Denmark	737	727	814	1,185	1,071	0.47	-9.62
Finland	518	694	619	542	701	0.30	29.34
Iceland	3	5	26	9	19	0.01	111.11
Ireland	58	450	362	365	562	0.24	53.97
Isle of Man					9	0.00	
Norway	482	755	856	741	929	0.40	25.37
Sweden	756	983	1,084	1,511	2,505	1.09	65.78
United Kingdom	11,292	12,322	13,335	11,253	12,564	5.46	11.65
Other countries of Northern Europe					33	0.01	
SOUTHERN EUROPE	**30,346**	**29,841**	**30,194**	**27,471**	**26,156**	**11.36**	**-4.79**
Albania	3				9	0.00	
Andorra					16	0.01	
Bosnia and Herzegovina	12	11	7	18	29	0.01	61.11
Croatia	93	65	119	190	170	0.07	-10.53
Gibraltar					5	0.00	

Yearbook of Tourism Statistics, Data 2009 – 2013, 2015 Edition

SEYCHELLES

1. Arrivals of non-resident tourists at national borders, by country of residence

	2009	2010	2011	2012	2013	Market share 2013	% Change 2013-2012
Greece	695	598	561	394	417	0.18	5.84
Italy	26,114	25,602	25,674	23,401	21,767	9.45	-6.98
Malta					81	0.04	
Montenegro					27	0.01	
Portugal	403	552	587	333	441	0.19	32.43
San Marino					40	0.02	
Serbia	107	56	125	173	246	0.11	42.20
Slovenia	311	317	322	351	379	0.16	7.98
Spain	2,599	2,627	2,769	2,580	2,503	1.09	-2.98
TFYR of Macedonia					26	0.01	
Yugoslavia, SFR (former)	9	13	30	31			
WESTERN EUROPE	**63,462**	**70,570**	**79,328**	**78,604**	**88,395**	**38.39**	**12.46**
Austria	2,852	3,446	3,745	4,771	4,667	2.03	-2.18
Belgium	2,185	2,247	2,512	2,372	2,369	1.03	-0.13
France	31,341	35,026	39,370	32,248	35,765	15.53	10.91
Germany	19,736	21,314	23,706	28,163	33,489	14.54	18.91
Liechtenstein					28	0.01	
Luxembourg	301	431	446	424	417	0.18	-1.65
Monaco	153	148	158	194	148	0.06	-23.71
Netherlands	1,297	1,435	1,747	1,850	1,854	0.81	0.22
Switzerland	5,597	6,523	7,644	8,582	9,658	4.19	12.54
EAST MEDITERRANEAN EUROPE	**899**	**1,359**	**1,374**	**1,862**	**1,813**	**0.79**	**-2.63**
Cyprus	177	116	176	126	109	0.05	-13.49
Israel	436	665	661	1,145	1,162	0.50	1.48
Turkey	286	578	537	591	542	0.24	-8.29
OTHER EUROPE	**559**	**137**	**190**	**256**			
Other countries of Europe	559	137	190	256			
MIDDLE EAST	**6,422**	**8,332**	**12,176**	**18,183**	**19,501**	**8.47**	**7.25**
Bahrain	360	280	264	364	413	0.18	13.46
Egypt	92	149	138	234	207	0.09	-11.54
Iraq	5	7	13	22	36	0.02	63.64
Jordan	40	57	51	99	73	0.03	-26.26
Kuwait	141	182	204	357	400	0.17	12.04
Lebanon	155	211	266	355	339	0.15	-4.51
Libya	44	41	20	19	53	0.02	178.95
Oman	68	60	95	108	164	0.07	51.85
Palestine					10	0.00	
Qatar	1,033	1,121	1,390	2,124	2,054	0.89	-3.30
Saudi Arabia	603	785	1,212	1,585	1,796	0.78	13.31
Syrian Arab Republic	26	41	29	15	43	0.02	186.67
United Arab Emirates	3,842	5,387	8,488	12,880	13,895	6.03	7.88
Yemen	10	5	5	18	18	0.01	
Other countries of Middle East	3	6	1	3			
SOUTH ASIA	**2,234**	**3,641**	**3,340**	**3,365**	**3,617**	**1.57**	**7.49**
Afghanistan					26	0.01	
Bangladesh	87	340	43	41	110	0.05	168.29
India	1,616	2,671	2,380	2,546	2,381	1.03	-6.48
Iran, Islamic Republic of	84	122	188	162	161	0.07	-0.62
Maldives	83	68	205	56	99	0.04	76.79
Nepal					37	0.02	
Pakistan	93	117	212	218	277	0.12	27.06
Sri Lanka	232	208	257	253	526	0.23	107.91
Other countries of South Asia	39	115	55	89			

647

SIERRA LEONE

1. Arrivals of non-resident tourists at national borders, by country of residence

		2009	2010	2011	2012	2013	Market share 2013	% Change 2013-2012
TOTAL	(*)	36,775	38,615	52,442	59,730	81,250	100.00	36.03
AFRICA		12,614	10,806	15,885	16,349	21,632	26.62	32.31
EAST AFRICA			663	2,553	1,632	3,342	4.11	104.78
Burundi			12	46	7	9	0.01	28.57
Comoros			24	1				
Djibouti					7	2	0.00	-71.43
Eritrea			9	15		5	0.01	
Ethiopia					41	107	0.13	160.98
Kenya			251	448	504	1,847	2.27	266.47
Madagascar					10	13	0.02	30.00
Malawi			27	167	133	110	0.14	-17.29
Mozambique			2	148	22	62	0.08	181.82
Rwanda			46	145	52	44	0.05	-15.38
Seychelles			21	199	6	2	0.00	-66.67
Somalia			26		3	5	0.01	66.67
Uganda			34	406	169	226	0.28	33.73
United Republic of Tanzania			52	366	168	212	0.26	26.19
Zambia			53	300	257	136	0.17	-47.08
Zimbabwe			106	312	253	562	0.69	122.13
CENTRAL AFRICA			198	636	311	265	0.33	-14.79
Angola			14	46	74	19	0.02	-74.32
Cameroon			139	193	96	115	0.14	19.79
Central African Republic			1	3				
Chad			7	40		6	0.01	
Congo			14	308	104	105	0.13	0.96
Equatorial Guinea			7			12	0.01	
Gabon			4	40	3	8	0.01	166.67
Sao Tome and Principe			12	6	34			
NORTH AFRICA			207	411	104	191	0.24	83.65
Algeria			22	52	21	4	0.00	-80.95
Morocco			92	158	32	70	0.09	118.75
Sudan			49	186	43	31	0.04	-27.91
Tunisia			44	15	8	86	0.11	975.00
SOUTHERN AFRICA			1,018	998	1,857	3,116	3.84	67.80
Botswana			21	47	13	15	0.02	15.38
Lesotho			13	22				
Namibia			37	66	34	30	0.04	-11.76
South Africa			891	852	1,797	3,061	3.77	70.34
Swaziland			56	11	13	10	0.01	-23.08
WEST AFRICA			6,846	11,054	12,445	14,718	18.11	18.26
Benin			17	123	59	143	0.18	142.37
Burkina Faso			90	121	96	65	0.08	-32.29
Cabo Verde			8	17	54	12	0.01	-77.78
Côte d'Ivoire			162	205	508	337	0.41	-33.66
Gambia			509	672	946	591	0.73	-37.53
Ghana			1,594	3,580	3,171	5,695	7.01	79.60
Guinea			297	642	1,304	419	0.52	-67.87
Guinea-Bissau			18	18	82	18	0.02	-78.05
Liberia			270	647	819	418	0.51	-48.96
Mali			129	136	203	99	0.12	-51.23
Mauritania			17	34	34	93	0.11	173.53
Niger			4	16	29	66	0.08	127.59
Nigeria			3,480	4,003	4,348	5,999	7.38	37.97
Senegal			218	689	711	670	0.82	-5.77
Togo			33	151	81	93	0.11	14.81
OTHER AFRICA		12,614	1,874	233				
Other countries of Africa			1,874	233				
All countries of Africa		12,614						
AMERICAS		7,238	7,406	10,707	10,574	19,939	24.54	88.57

648

Yearbook of Tourism Statistics, Data 2009 – 2013, 2015 Edition

SIERRA LEONE

1. Arrivals of non-resident tourists at national borders, by country of residence

	2009	2010	2011	2012	2013	Market share 2013	% Change 2013-2012
CARIBBEAN		278	347	59	167	0.21	183.05
Bahamas					4	0.00	
Barbados					51	0.06	
Cuba					10	0.01	
Haiti		4	3	3	7	0.01	133.33
Jamaica		165	227	40	71	0.09	77.50
Saint Lucia					3	0.00	
Trinidad and Tobago		109	117	16	21	0.03	31.25
CENTRAL AMERICA		13	2	34	11	0.01	-67.65
Costa Rica		12	2	32	7	0.01	-78.13
El Salvador				2	4	0.00	100.00
Guatemala		1					
NORTH AMERICA		5,023	9,911	10,211	19,533	24.04	91.29
Canada		920	3,592	2,240	4,364	5.37	94.82
Mexico		62	249	152	103	0.13	-32.24
United States of America		4,041	6,070	7,819	15,066	18.54	92.68
SOUTH AMERICA		530	214	234	228	0.28	-2.56
Argentina		338	33	99	54	0.07	-45.45
Bolivia					4	0.00	
Brazil		168	127	96	66	0.08	-31.25
Chile		14		25	30	0.04	20.00
Colombia					6	0.01	
Ecuador					10	0.01	
Paraguay		5	2	3			
Peru					11	0.01	
Suriname					2	0.00	
Uruguay		2		1	5	0.01	400.00
Venezuela		3	52	10	40	0.05	300.00
OTHER AMERICAS	7,238	1,562	233	36			
Other countries of the Americas		1,562	233	36			
All countries of the Americas	7,238						
EAST ASIA AND THE PACIFIC	4,068	6,261	9,024	7,817	7,093	8.73	-9.26
NORTH-EAST ASIA		953	4,957	3,177	3,546	4.36	11.61
China		826	4,179	2,257	3,090	3.80	36.91
Japan		89	589	423	243	0.30	-42.55
Korea, Dem. People's Republic of		22	87	192	97	0.12	-49.48
Korea, Republic of		15	101	302	115	0.14	-61.92
Mongolia		1	1	3	1	0.00	-66.67
SOUTH-EAST ASIA		267	403	350	1,084	1.33	209.71
Cambodia		18	10	1			
Indonesia		8	37	57	106	0.13	85.96
Malaysia		16	54	63	51	0.06	-19.05
Philippines		192	257	175	881	1.08	403.43
Singapore		8	12	13	18	0.02	38.46
Thailand		5	12	32	6	0.01	-81.25
Timor-Leste		6					
Viet Nam		14	21	9	22	0.03	144.44
AUSTRALASIA		3,030	3,664	4,272	2,431	2.99	-43.09
Australia		2,653	3,364	4,162	2,313	2.85	-44.43
New Zealand		377	300	110	118	0.15	7.27
MELANESIA				18	31	0.04	72.22
Papua New Guinea				18	31	0.04	72.22
POLYNESIA					1	0.00	
Tonga					1	0.00	
OTHER EAST ASIA AND THE PACIFIC	4,068	2,011					
Other countries of Asia		1,116					
All countries of Asia	4,068						
Other countries of Oceania		895					

649

SIERRA LEONE

1. Arrivals of non-resident tourists at national borders, by country of residence

	2009	2010	2011	2012	2013	Market share 2013	% Change 2013-2012
EUROPE	**10,574**	**10,295**	**13,807**	**15,956**	**25,739**	**31.68**	**61.31**
CENTRAL/EASTERN EUROPE		**499**	**629**	**793**	**1,008**	**1.24**	**27.11**
Azerbaijan		7		13	23	0.03	76.92
Belarus		1	11	21	18	0.02	-14.29
Bulgaria		11	18	34	27	0.03	-20.59
Czech Republic		21	33	28	31	0.04	10.71
Estonia				3	4	0.00	33.33
Georgia				14	1	0.00	-92.86
Hungary		38	59	42	46	0.06	9.52
Kazakhstan		24		11	17	0.02	54.55
Kyrgyzstan		13		10	8	0.01	-20.00
Latvia		165	35	41	44	0.05	7.32
Lithuania		9	23	25	26	0.03	4.00
Poland		12	82	76	88	0.11	15.79
Republic of Moldova				4	6	0.01	50.00
Romania		22	154	197	281	0.35	42.64
Russian Federation		70	149	187	227	0.28	21.39
Slovakia		7	24	30	58	0.07	93.33
Tajikistan		24	2	1			
Ukraine		75	39	56	103	0.13	83.93
NORTHERN EUROPE		**5,478**	**8,202**	**11,173**	**19,169**	**23.59**	**71.57**
Denmark		60	233	288	405	0.50	40.63
Finland		231	94	106	102	0.13	-3.77
Iceland				10	24	0.03	140.00
Ireland		1,204	773	638	830	1.02	30.09
Norway		81	268	461	353	0.43	-23.43
Sweden		51	243	215	364	0.45	69.30
United Kingdom		3,851	6,591	9,455	17,091	21.04	80.76
SOUTHERN EUROPE		**1,459**	**1,168**	**955**	**1,597**	**1.97**	**67.23**
Albania		7		15	1	0.00	-93.33
Andorra				2	3	0.00	50.00
Bosnia and Herzegovina		9		3	5	0.01	66.67
Croatia		14	51	44	72	0.09	63.64
Greece		19	30	33	65	0.08	96.97
Holy See				8			
Italy		480	578	498	843	1.04	69.28
Malta				4	9	0.01	125.00
Montenegro		6		2	1	0.00	-50.00
Portugal		133	53	97	151	0.19	55.67
Serbia		2	6	12	26	0.03	116.67
Slovenia					13	0.02	
Spain		789	450	221	391	0.48	76.92
TFYR of Macedonia				16	17	0.02	6.25
WESTERN EUROPE		**1,983**	**3,630**	**2,699**	**3,715**	**4.57**	**37.64**
Austria		18	54	57	81	0.10	42.11
Belgium		109	334	383	657	0.81	71.54
France		514	1,730	680	991	1.22	45.74
Germany		537	1,033	629	942	1.16	49.76
Luxembourg		5	12	8	2	0.00	-75.00
Monaco				3			
Netherlands		767	387	727	967	1.19	33.01
Switzerland		33	80	212	75	0.09	-64.62
EAST MEDITERRANEAN EUROPE		**267**	**178**	**336**	**250**	**0.31**	**-25.60**
Cyprus		25	9		47	0.06	
Israel		211	128	269	111	0.14	-58.74
Turkey		31	41	67	92	0.11	37.31
OTHER EUROPE	**10,574**	**609**					
Other countries of Europe		609					
All countries of Europe	10,574						

Yearbook of Tourism Statistics, Data 2009 – 2013, 2015 Edition

SIERRA LEONE

1. Arrivals of non-resident tourists at national borders, by country of residence

	2009	2010	2011	2012	2013	Market share 2013	% Change 2013-2012
MIDDLE EAST	1,750	2,667	1,562	5,711	3,727	4.59	-34.74
Egypt		24	66	1,842	150	0.18	-91.86
Iraq		61	28	429	4	0.00	-99.07
Jordan		22	8	8	5	0.01	-37.50
Kuwait		4	16	34	4	0.00	-88.24
Lebanon		1,074	1,343	1,740	3,508	4.32	101.61
Libya		15	28	506	7	0.01	-98.62
Oman				23			
Palestine		88	12	3	6	0.01	100.00
Qatar				41			
Saudi Arabia		138	13	118	18	0.02	-84.75
Syrian Arab Republic		51	29	871	20	0.02	-97.70
United Arab Emirates		17	16	66	4	0.00	-93.94
Yemen		56	3	30	1	0.00	-96.67
Other countries of Middle East		1,117					
All countries of Middle East	1,750						
SOUTH ASIA		1,180	1,457	3,323	2,638	3.25	-20.61
Afghanistan		4	7		5	0.01	
Bangladesh		13	65	112	96	0.12	-14.29
India		1,014	1,148	2,182	2,208	2.72	1.19
Iran, Islamic Republic of		49	48	483	14	0.02	-97.10
Nepal		16	22	32	39	0.05	21.88
Pakistan		61	122	486	231	0.28	-52.47
Sri Lanka		23	45	28	45	0.06	60.71
NOT SPECIFIED	531				482	0.59	
Other countries of the World	531				482	0.59	

Yearbook of Tourism Statistics, Data 2009 – 2013, 2015 Edition

SIERRA LEONE

5. Overnight stays of non-resident tourists in hotels and similar establishments, by country of residence

	2009	2010	2011	2012	2013	Market share 2013	% Change 2013-2012
TOTAL	257,425	270,305	367,094	418,110	568,750	100.00	36.03
AFRICA	81,459	75,142	109,564	130,879	152,523	26.82	16.54
OTHER AFRICA	81,459	75,142	109,564	130,879	152,523	26.82	16.54
All countries of Africa	81,459	75,142	109,564	130,879	152,523	26.82	16.54
AMERICAS	51,436	52,066	73,318	74,004	139,538	24.53	88.55
OTHER AMERICAS	51,436	52,066	73,318	74,004	139,538	24.53	88.55
All countries of the Americas	51,436	52,066	73,318	74,004	139,538	24.53	88.55
EAST ASIA AND THE PACIFIC	28,189	52,256	63,168	74,753	68,194	11.99	-8.77
OTHER EAST ASIA AND THE PACIFIC	28,189	52,256	63,168	74,753	68,194	11.99	-8.77
All countries of Asia	24,605	24,723	37,520	44,723	50,960	8.96	13.95
All countries of Oceania	3,584	27,533	25,648	30,030	17,234	3.03	-42.61
EUROPE	89,705	72,088	96,649	109,669	179,249	31.52	63.45
OTHER EUROPE	89,705	72,088	96,649	109,669	179,249	31.52	63.45
All countries of Europe	89,705	72,088	96,649	109,669	179,249	31.52	63.45
MIDDLE EAST	6,636	18,753	24,395	28,805	29,246	5.14	1.53
All countries of Middle East	6,636	18,753	24,395	28,805	29,246	5.14	1.53

Yearbook of Tourism Statistics, Data 2009 – 2013, 2015 Edition

SINGAPORE

2. Arrivals of non-resident visitors at national borders, by nationality

		2009	2010	2011	2012	2013	Market share 2013	% Change 2013-2012
TOTAL	(*)	**9,682,690**	**11,641,701**	**13,171,303**	**14,496,092**	**15,567,923**	**100.00**	**7.39**
AFRICA		**72,110**	**71,190**	**73,345**	**69,407**	**69,027**	**0.44**	**-0.55**
EAST AFRICA		**9,401**	**10,190**	**9,147**	**9,489**	**9,012**	**0.06**	**-5.03**
Mauritius		9,401	10,190	9,147	9,489	9,012	0.06	-5.03
SOUTHERN AFRICA		**36,740**	**34,330**	**36,714**	**36,972**	**36,372**	**0.23**	**-1.62**
South Africa		36,740	34,330	36,714	36,972	36,372	0.23	-1.62
OTHER AFRICA		**25,969**	**26,670**	**27,484**	**22,946**	**23,643**	**0.15**	**3.04**
Other countries of Africa		25,969	26,670	27,484	22,946	23,643	0.15	3.04
AMERICAS		**538,229**	**610,959**	**666,791**	**713,767**	**744,827**	**4.78**	**4.35**
CARIBBEAN		**4,081**	**4,449**	**4,632**	**3,491**	**3,158**	**0.02**	**-9.54**
All countries of the Caribbean		4,081	4,449	4,632	3,491	3,158	0.02	-9.54
CENTRAL AMERICA		**2,122**	**2,793**	**2,849**	**2,937**	**2,997**	**0.02**	**2.04**
All countries of Central America		2,122	2,793	2,849	2,937	2,997	0.02	2.04
NORTH AMERICA		**508,493**	**575,831**	**622,995**	**662,829**	**689,650**	**4.43**	**4.05**
Canada		101,463	112,059	123,672	129,418	135,434	0.87	4.65
Mexico		6,904	8,641	9,768	11,566	13,286	0.09	14.87
United States of America		400,126	455,131	489,555	521,845	540,930	3.47	3.66
SOUTH AMERICA		**23,533**	**27,886**	**36,315**	**44,510**	**49,022**	**0.31**	**10.14**
Argentina		3,420	4,557	5,430	7,163	7,760	0.05	8.33
Brazil		9,985	12,715	17,828	21,005	22,461	0.14	6.93
Chile		2,698	2,493	3,438	4,271	5,089	0.03	19.15
Colombia		2,712	3,111	4,104	5,509	6,106	0.04	10.84
Uruguay		311	311	555	668	964	0.01	44.31
Venezuela		2,061	2,069	2,304	2,641	3,151	0.02	19.31
Other countries of South America		2,346	2,630	2,656	3,253	3,491	0.02	7.32
EAST ASIA AND THE PACIFIC		**6,487,570**	**8,126,315**	**9,502,765**	**10,590,765**	**11,506,119**	**73.91**	**8.64**
NORTH-EAST ASIA		**2,065,296**	**2,564,646**	**3,270,413**	**3,927,354**	**4,408,086**	**28.32**	**12.24**
China		913,067	1,150,027	1,554,480	2,198,157	2,645,728	16.99	20.36
Hong Kong, China	(*)	177,199	252,993	312,856	138,849			
Japan		521,688	569,676	701,753	816,448	895,051	5.75	9.63
Korea, Dem. People's Republic of		463	136	140	690	1,240	0.01	79.71
Korea, Republic of		284,586	379,294	437,155	469,212	499,136	3.21	6.38
Macao, China	(*)	4,172	10,915	11,706	4,258			
Mongolia		5,466	6,431	8,824	10,225	9,075	0.06	-11.25
Taiwan, Province of China		158,655	195,174	243,499	289,515	357,856	2.30	23.61
SOUTH-EAST ASIA		**3,539,836**	**4,624,705**	**5,202,921**	**5,555,836**	**5,921,369**	**38.04**	**6.58**
Brunei Darussalam		41,951	46,319	46,562	56,918	64,129	0.41	12.67
Cambodia		26,771	32,759	35,782	35,310	40,306	0.26	14.15
Indonesia		1,756,577	2,346,790	2,628,294	2,872,426	3,112,414	19.99	8.35
Lao People's Democratic Republic		3,385	5,024	5,336	7,334	6,845	0.04	-6.67
Malaysia		648,597	832,685	919,061	989,931	1,030,824	6.62	4.13
Myanmar		72,390	81,082	97,476	96,354	101,319	0.65	5.15
Philippines		449,968	570,889	711,063	698,878	733,041	4.71	4.89
Thailand		286,938	398,503	439,378	443,116	459,995	2.95	3.81
Viet Nam		253,259	310,654	319,969	355,569	372,496	2.39	4.76
AUSTRALASIA		**874,752**	**929,568**	**1,021,281**	**1,098,442**	**1,166,764**	**7.49**	**6.22**
Australia		769,549	819,953	888,817	961,774	1,029,156	6.61	7.01
New Zealand		105,203	109,615	132,464	136,668	137,608	0.88	0.69
MELANESIA		**6,244**	**5,923**	**6,783**	**7,831**	**8,848**	**0.06**	**12.99**
Fiji		2,197	1,811	1,892	2,208	2,394	0.02	8.42
New Caledonia		63	53	94	79			
Papua New Guinea		3,984	4,059	4,797	5,544	6,454	0.04	16.41
MICRONESIA		**192**	**157**	**143**	**91**	**27**	**0.00**	**-70.33**
Guam		29	31	26	12			
Nauru		163	126	117	79	27	0.00	-65.82
OTHER EAST ASIA AND THE PACIFIC		**1,250**	**1,316**	**1,224**	**1,211**	**1,025**	**0.01**	**-15.36**
Other countries of Oceania		1,250	1,316	1,224	1,211	1,025	0.01	-15.36

653

SINGAPORE

2. Arrivals of non-resident visitors at national borders, by nationality

	2009	2010	2011	2012	2013	Market share 2013	% Change 2013-2012
EUROPE	1,515,203	1,609,141	1,656,961	1,812,580	1,879,764	12.07	3.71
CENTRAL/EASTERN EUROPE	93,511	101,752	112,706	133,667	153,532	0.99	14.86
Czech Republic	6,480	6,330	6,789	7,705	8,502	0.05	10.34
Hungary	4,351	5,373	5,490	6,296	7,237	0.05	14.95
Poland	13,690	14,773	18,104	23,654	25,951	0.17	9.71
Commonwealth Independent States	68,990	75,276	82,323	96,012	111,842	0.72	16.49
NORTHERN EUROPE	723,371	730,863	726,956	763,152	781,493	5.02	2.40
Denmark	35,651	35,158	32,992	37,760	37,991	0.24	0.61
Finland	18,959	18,659	27,058	36,977	32,382	0.21	-12.43
Ireland	31,987	30,806	29,547	31,264	30,269	0.19	-3.18
Norway	31,936	33,108	33,854	38,142	37,314	0.24	-2.17
Sweden	36,453	40,336	43,042	48,848	51,472	0.33	5.37
United Kingdom	568,385	572,796	560,463	570,161	592,065	3.80	3.84
SOUTHERN EUROPE	106,346	117,726	124,246	143,201	149,297	0.96	4.26
Greece	9,875	8,907	8,162	9,280	8,503	0.05	-8.37
Italy	54,198	59,902	63,808	77,427	80,341	0.52	3.76
Portugal	10,072	12,944	14,670	14,762	16,285	0.10	10.32
Serbia and Montenegro	1,913	1,960	2,182	2,072	2,248	0.01	8.49
Spain	30,288	34,013	35,424	39,660	41,920	0.27	5.70
WESTERN EUROPE	539,217	599,370	633,599	699,216	713,911	4.59	2.10
Austria	19,797	22,693	22,741	26,473	27,854	0.18	5.22
Belgium	20,722	23,787	23,735	25,723	26,733	0.17	3.93
France	147,540	165,255	177,136	198,009	199,980	1.28	1.00
Germany	203,858	231,070	244,815	276,262	278,219	1.79	0.71
Luxembourg	1,138	1,466	1,503	1,610	1,753	0.01	8.88
Netherlands	91,445	92,941	98,021	100,161	101,801	0.65	1.64
Switzerland	54,717	62,158	65,648	70,978	77,571	0.50	9.29
EAST MEDITERRANEAN EUROPE	25,184	30,943	28,680	33,609	36,509	0.23	8.63
Israel	11,283	13,124	12,407	14,062	14,783	0.09	5.13
Turkey	13,901	17,819	16,273	19,547	21,726	0.14	11.15
OTHER EUROPE	27,574	28,487	30,774	39,735	45,022	0.29	13.31
Other countries of Europe	27,574	28,487	30,774	39,735	45,022	0.29	13.31
MIDDLE EAST	35,875	44,730	48,960	51,920	65,277	0.42	25.73
Bahrain	1,708	1,834	1,907	1,884	2,468	0.02	31.00
Egypt	3,813	4,637	4,255	4,272	5,113	0.03	19.69
Jordan	1,057	1,292	1,770	1,489	1,554	0.01	4.37
Kuwait	4,119	6,090	6,182	5,554	8,482	0.05	52.72
Lebanon	1,091	1,310	1,462	1,563	1,570	0.01	0.45
Libya	293	606	207	329	409	0.00	24.32
Saudi Arabia	7,373	8,251	11,740	13,184	14,790	0.10	12.18
United Arab Emirates	10,464	13,194	12,716	13,592	17,761	0.11	30.67
Other countries of Middle East	5,957	7,516	8,721	10,053	13,130	0.08	30.61
SOUTH ASIA	1,033,118	1,178,866	1,221,983	1,255,834	1,299,988	8.35	3.52
Afghanistan	499	370	284	319	424	0.00	32.92
Bangladesh	86,459	92,410	95,896	110,648	119,337	0.77	7.85
India	792,245	907,350	949,698	980,479	1,013,049	6.51	3.32
Iran, Islamic Republic of	25,756	40,385	35,963	21,832	13,532	0.09	-38.02
Nepal	18,441	18,101	16,429	17,490	16,913	0.11	-3.30
Pakistan	25,088	25,236	24,815	26,011	24,984	0.16	-3.95
Sri Lanka	75,610	85,241	90,175	90,513	103,147	0.66	13.96
Other countries of South Asia	9,020	9,773	8,723	8,542	8,602	0.06	0.70
NOT SPECIFIED	585	500	498	1,819	2,921	0.02	60.58
Other countries of the World	585	500	498	1,819	2,921	0.02	60.58

Yearbook of Tourism Statistics, Data 2009 – 2013, 2015 Edition

SINGAPORE

2. Arrivals of non-resident visitors at national borders, by country of residence

		2009	2010	2011	2012	2013	Market share 2013	% Change 2013-2012
TOTAL	(*)	9,682,690	11,641,701	13,171,303	14,496,092	15,567,923	100.00	7.39
AFRICA		72,348	70,436	69,452	64,183	62,580	0.40	-2.50
EAST AFRICA		11,418	11,617	10,527	9,857	8,546	0.05	-13.30
Mauritius		11,418	11,617	10,527	9,857	8,546	0.05	-13.30
SOUTHERN AFRICA		34,451	32,430	33,506	32,739	31,990	0.21	-2.29
South Africa		34,451	32,430	33,506	32,739	31,990	0.21	-2.29
OTHER AFRICA		26,479	26,389	25,419	21,587	22,044	0.14	2.12
Other countries of Africa		26,479	26,389	25,419	21,587	22,044	0.14	2.12
AMERICAS		467,723	524,846	563,742	616,400	641,465	4.12	4.07
CARIBBEAN		2,747	3,082	2,961	3,048	3,141	0.02	3.05
All countries of the Caribbean		2,747	3,082	2,961	3,048	3,141	0.02	3.05
CENTRAL AMERICA		1,441	1,947	1,895	2,060	2,316	0.01	12.43
All countries of Central America		1,441	1,947	1,895	2,060	2,316	0.01	12.43
NORTH AMERICA		445,816	498,803	531,073	574,353	595,949	3.83	3.76
Canada		70,034	75,142	82,932	87,795	92,685	0.60	5.57
Mexico		5,078	6,466	7,565	9,345	11,318	0.07	21.11
United States of America		370,704	417,195	440,576	477,213	491,946	3.16	3.09
SOUTH AMERICA		17,258	20,190	27,141	36,287	39,564	0.25	9.03
Argentina		2,569	3,550	4,234	5,926	6,616	0.04	11.64
Brazil		7,713	9,802	14,209	18,860	19,717	0.13	4.54
Chile		2,287	2,117	2,853	3,400	4,202	0.03	23.59
Colombia		1,570	1,781	2,284	3,544	3,798	0.02	7.17
Uruguay		295	310	635	697	1,023	0.01	46.77
Venezuela		1,259	1,082	1,374	1,731	2,010	0.01	16.12
Other countries of South America		1,565	1,548	1,552	2,129	2,198	0.01	3.24
OTHER AMERICAS		461	824	672	652	495	0.00	-24.08
Other countries of the Americas		461	824	672	652	495	0.00	-24.08
EAST ASIA AND THE PACIFIC		6,785,096	8,474,870	9,887,028	10,987,491	11,920,226	76.57	8.49
NORTH-EAST ASIA		2,163,701	2,664,002	3,379,363	4,018,736	4,492,703	28.86	11.79
China		936,747	1,171,493	1,577,522	2,034,177	2,269,870	14.58	11.59
Hong Kong, China		294,420	387,579	464,375	472,167	539,810	3.47	14.33
Japan		489,987	528,951	656,417	757,116	832,845	5.35	10.00
Korea, Dem. People's Republic of		844	809	899	1,521	1,190	0.01	-21.76
Korea, Republic of		271,987	360,703	414,879	445,184	471,768	3.03	5.97
Macao, China		7,713	16,933	18,159	16,274	17,826	0.11	9.54
Mongolia		5,242	6,348	8,624	10,094	9,086	0.06	-9.99
Taiwan, Province of China		156,761	191,186	238,488	282,203	350,308	2.25	24.13
SOUTH-EAST ASIA		3,684,848	4,821,753	5,414,250	5,779,608	6,166,395	39.61	6.69
Brunei Darussalam		56,531	62,157	62,243	71,755	79,866	0.51	11.30
Cambodia		29,425	34,934	36,520	37,382	44,361	0.28	18.67
Indonesia		1,745,330	2,306,243	2,592,222	2,837,537	3,088,859	19.84	8.86
Lao People's Democratic Republic		3,590	5,196	5,484	7,509	7,302	0.05	-2.76
Malaysia		764,309	1,037,489	1,140,935	1,231,687	1,280,942	8.23	4.00
Myanmar		70,272	78,338	94,184	93,046	99,367	0.64	6.79
Philippines		432,072	544,449	677,723	656,804	687,794	4.42	4.72
Thailand		317,905	430,067	472,708	477,654	497,409	3.20	4.14
Viet Nam		265,414	322,880	332,231	366,234	380,495	2.44	3.89
AUSTRALASIA		924,133	976,348	1,079,034	1,174,074	1,245,626	8.00	6.09
Australia		830,299	880,558	956,039	1,050,373	1,125,179	7.23	7.12
New Zealand		93,834	95,790	122,995	123,701	120,447	0.77	-2.63
MELANESIA		9,489	9,455	10,668	11,239	11,695	0.08	4.06
Fiji		1,826	1,421	1,567	1,528	1,677	0.01	9.75
New Caledonia		1,484	1,514	1,498	1,274	1,022	0.01	-19.78
Papua New Guinea		6,179	6,520	7,603	8,437	8,996	0.06	6.63
MICRONESIA		1,163	1,279	1,651	1,553	1,591	0.01	2.45
Guam		1,062	1,215	1,604	1,487	1,558	0.01	4.77
Nauru		101	64	47	66	33	0.00	-50.00
OTHER EAST ASIA AND THE PACIFIC		1,762	2,033	2,062	2,281	2,216	0.01	-2.85
Other countries of Oceania		1,762	2,033	2,062	2,281	2,216	0.01	-2.85

Yearbook of Tourism Statistics, Data 2009 – 2013, 2015 Edition

SINGAPORE

2. Arrivals of non-resident visitors at national borders, by country of residence

	2009	2010	2011	2012	2013	Market share 2013	% Change 2013-2012
EUROPE	**1,318,260**	**1,386,361**	**1,413,639**	**1,550,934**	**1,605,773**	**10.31**	**3.54**
CENTRAL/EASTERN EUROPE	**88,442**	**95,423**	**104,641**	**123,559**	**142,354**	**0.91**	**15.21**
Czech Republic	6,141	6,098	6,372	7,178	8,073	0.05	12.47
Hungary	4,447	5,673	6,044	6,889	6,366	0.04	-7.59
Poland	11,200	11,594	14,095	18,905	21,854	0.14	15.60
Commonwealth Independent States	66,654	72,058	78,130	90,587	106,061	0.68	17.08
NORTHERN EUROPE	**601,360**	**594,301**	**582,100**	**610,325**	**621,383**	**3.99**	**1.81**
Denmark	30,571	29,635	27,201	31,479	31,920	0.21	1.40
Finland	16,035	15,611	23,905	33,333	29,375	0.19	-11.87
Ireland	22,720	20,437	18,565	18,965	17,446	0.11	-8.01
Norway	30,354	31,765	32,450	36,803	35,927	0.23	-2.38
Sweden	31,924	35,084	37,368	43,248	45,256	0.29	4.64
United Kingdom	469,756	461,769	442,611	446,497	461,459	2.96	3.35
SOUTHERN EUROPE	**95,021**	**101,531**	**105,549**	**121,450**	**124,871**	**0.80**	**2.82**
Greece	9,250	8,006	7,130	8,137	7,200	0.05	-11.52
Italy	46,770	51,086	53,520	65,557	66,650	0.43	1.67
Portugal	6,600	7,115	8,268	8,429	9,791	0.06	16.16
Serbia and Montenegro	1,530	1,559	1,654	1,549	1,723	0.01	11.23
Spain	30,871	33,765	34,977	37,778	39,507	0.25	4.58
WESTERN EUROPE	**482,467**	**535,112**	**565,232**	**626,904**	**640,962**	**4.12**	**2.24**
Austria	17,505	20,093	19,889	23,264	24,731	0.16	6.31
Belgium	19,267	21,848	22,048	23,831	24,047	0.15	0.91
France	119,728	130,461	140,299	158,923	160,013	1.03	0.69
Germany	183,681	209,263	219,952	252,433	251,560	1.62	-0.35
Luxembourg	2,098	2,551	2,931	2,993	3,305	0.02	10.42
Netherlands	76,359	76,520	81,090	81,603	82,926	0.53	1.62
Switzerland	63,829	74,376	79,023	83,857	94,380	0.61	12.55
EAST MEDITERRANEAN EUROPE	**23,684**	**29,237**	**26,868**	**31,629**	**34,424**	**0.22**	**8.84**
Israel	10,884	12,833	12,137	13,600	14,579	0.09	7.20
Turkey	12,800	16,404	14,731	18,029	19,845	0.13	10.07
OTHER EUROPE	**27,286**	**30,757**	**29,249**	**37,067**	**41,779**	**0.27**	**12.71**
Other countries of Europe	27,286	30,757	29,249	37,067	41,779	0.27	12.71
MIDDLE EAST	**85,709**	**101,461**	**113,287**	**117,950**	**134,919**	**0.87**	**14.39**
Bahrain	3,152	3,536	3,605	3,379	3,824	0.02	13.17
Egypt	3,861	4,746	3,829	3,630	3,782	0.02	4.19
Jordan	684	769	1,054	954	1,086	0.01	13.84
Kuwait	5,750	8,368	8,278	7,621	10,613	0.07	39.26
Lebanon	784	866	1,187	1,047	1,155	0.01	10.32
Libya	184	358	109	181	272	0.00	50.28
Saudi Arabia	10,815	12,633	17,041	17,969	19,896	0.13	10.72
United Arab Emirates	49,529	56,476	62,736	65,552	72,553	0.47	10.68
Other countries of Middle East	10,950	13,709	15,448	17,617	21,738	0.14	23.39
SOUTH ASIA	**953,364**	**1,083,673**	**1,124,022**	**1,151,365**	**1,201,527**	**7.72**	**4.36**
Afghanistan	544	434	373	347	396	0.00	14.12
Bangladesh	86,637	92,312	95,531	110,673	119,324	0.77	7.82
India	725,624	828,994	868,991	894,993	933,553	6.00	4.31
Iran, Islamic Republic of	23,917	36,932	32,434	18,553	10,956	0.07	-40.95
Nepal	15,183	14,303	12,757	13,425	12,738	0.08	-5.12
Pakistan	22,280	21,927	20,928	21,206	20,248	0.13	-4.52
Sri Lanka	70,010	78,973	83,991	83,359	95,606	0.61	14.69
Other countries of South Asia	9,169	9,798	9,017	8,809	8,706	0.06	-1.17
NOT SPECIFIED	**190**	**54**	**133**	**7,769**	**1,433**	**0.01**	**-81.55**
Other countries of the World	190	54	133	7,769	1,433	0.01	-81.55

Yearbook of Tourism Statistics, Data 2009 – 2013, 2015 Edition

SINT MAARTEN

1. Arrivals of non-resident tourists at national borders, by nationality

	2009	2010	2011	2012	2013	Market share 2013	% Change 2013-2012
TOTAL (*)	440,185	443,136	424,340	456,720	466,955	100.00	2.24
AMERICAS	309,659	307,871	291,734	318,833	333,275	71.37	4.53
CARIBBEAN	25,266	23,780	23,314	24,236	24,967	5.35	3.02
Antigua and Barbuda	3,416	2,708	2,401	2,128	1,869	0.40	-12.17
Dominican Republic	2,880	2,789	3,199	3,518	3,815	0.82	8.44
Haiti	3,130	2,919	3,179	3,167	2,944	0.63	-7.04
Saint Kitts and Nevis	3,744	3,340	2,758	2,497	2,704	0.58	8.29
Trinidad and Tobago	2,450	2,391	2,603	3,031	4,269	0.91	40.84
Other countries of the Caribbean	9,646	9,633	9,174	9,895	9,366	2.01	-5.35
NORTH AMERICA	272,708	269,877	252,460	278,964	292,488	62.64	4.85
Canada	32,277	33,498	33,256	40,426	46,300	9.92	14.53
United States of America	240,431	236,379	219,204	238,538	246,188	52.72	3.21
SOUTH AMERICA	7,241	9,977	11,072	10,964	10,868	2.33	-0.88
Argentina	904	876	2,052	2,362	2,398	0.51	1.52
Brazil	2,975	6,050	5,766	4,849	4,725	1.01	-2.56
Chile	168	198	418	338	469	0.10	38.76
Venezuela	3,194	2,853	2,836	3,415	3,276	0.70	-4.07
OTHER AMERICAS	4,444	4,237	4,888	4,669	4,952	1.06	6.06
Other countries of the Americas	4,444	4,237	4,888	4,669	4,952	1.06	6.06
EUROPE	98,341	101,118	101,712	105,196	103,643	22.20	-1.48
CENTRAL/EASTERN EUROPE	389	559	594	822	935	0.20	13.75
Russian Federation	389	559	594	822	935	0.20	13.75
SOUTHERN EUROPE	3,835	3,479	3,593	4,054	3,870	0.83	-4.54
Italy	3,835	3,479	3,593	4,054	3,870	0.83	-4.54
WESTERN EUROPE	81,393	84,330	83,146	83,877	82,735	17.72	-1.36
France (*)	66,177	67,833	66,539	67,463	66,716	14.29	-1.11
Netherlands	15,216	16,497	16,607	16,414	16,019	3.43	-2.41
OTHER EUROPE	12,724	12,750	14,379	16,443	16,103	3.45	-2.07
Other countries of Europe	12,724	12,750	14,379	16,443	16,103	3.45	-2.07
NOT SPECIFIED	32,185	34,147	30,894	32,691	30,037	6.43	-8.12
Other countries of the World	32,185	34,147	30,894	32,691	30,037	6.43	-8.12

Yearbook of Tourism Statistics, Data 2009 – 2013, 2015 Edition

SLOVAKIA

4. Arrivals of non-resident tourists in all types of accommodation establishments, by nationality

	2009	2010	2011	2012	2013	Market share 2013	% Change 2013-2012
TOTAL	1,298,075	1,326,639	1,460,361	1,527,500	1,669,948	100.00	9.33
AFRICA	1,946	2,684	2,926	5,183	5,365	0.32	3.51
EAST AFRICA	51	78	73	139	302	0.02	117.27
Kenya	51	78	73	139	302	0.02	117.27
NORTH AFRICA	92	105	99	261	168	0.01	-35.63
Tunisia	92	105	99	261	168	0.01	-35.63
SOUTHERN AFRICA	490	845	624	1,202	1,696	0.10	41.10
South Africa	490	845	624	1,202	1,696	0.10	41.10
OTHER AFRICA	1,313	1,656	2,130	3,581	3,199	0.19	-10.67
Other countries of Africa	1,313	1,656	2,130	3,581	3,199	0.19	-10.67
AMERICAS	30,137	36,198	43,172	46,250	52,149	3.12	12.75
CARIBBEAN	28	45	24	38	20	0.00	-47.37
Dominican Republic	28	45	24	38	20	0.00	-47.37
NORTH AMERICA	25,897	29,513	34,935	38,388	43,740	2.62	13.94
Canada	4,177	4,861	6,762	6,571	6,220	0.37	-5.34
Mexico	905	2,601	1,691	1,689	1,705	0.10	0.95
United States of America	20,815	22,051	26,482	30,128	35,815	2.14	18.88
SOUTH AMERICA	2,084	2,751	3,870	4,446	5,815	0.35	30.79
Argentina	400	592	561	998	1,096	0.07	9.82
Brazil	1,684	2,159	3,309	3,448	4,719	0.28	36.86
OTHER AMERICAS	2,128	3,889	4,343	3,378	2,574	0.15	-23.80
Other countries of the Americas	2,128	3,889	4,343	3,378	2,574	0.15	-23.80
EAST ASIA AND THE PACIFIC	53,748	65,064	72,073	80,037	84,732	5.07	5.87
NORTH-EAST ASIA	35,471	43,279	47,898	53,892	52,505	3.14	-2.57
China	6,540	8,337	11,857	16,317	15,882	0.95	-2.67
Japan	11,351	11,523	8,865	10,117	9,444	0.57	-6.65
Korea, Republic of	17,580	23,419	27,176	27,458	27,179	1.63	-1.02
SOUTH-EAST ASIA	1,164	954	1,160	1,388	2,896	0.17	108.65
Thailand	1,164	954	1,160	1,388	2,896	0.17	108.65
AUSTRALASIA	4,656	5,535	5,190	6,272	6,688	0.40	6.63
Australia	4,014	4,881	4,545	5,413	5,739	0.34	6.02
New Zealand	642	654	645	859	949	0.06	10.48
OTHER EAST ASIA AND THE PACIFIC	12,457	15,296	17,825	18,485	22,643	1.36	22.49
Other countries of Asia	12,457	15,296	17,825	18,485	22,643	1.36	22.49
EUROPE	1,209,816	1,219,740	1,336,504	1,389,146	1,521,290	91.10	9.51
CENTRAL/EASTERN EUROPE	737,179	743,991	834,124	855,721	932,051	55.81	8.92
Belarus	2,967	3,506	4,319	5,841	9,369	0.56	60.40
Bulgaria	5,626	5,416	6,517	8,037	8,578	0.51	6.73
Czech Republic	425,414	433,321	477,159	491,136	492,713	29.50	0.32
Estonia	3,250	3,209	2,952	3,918	4,234	0.25	8.07
Hungary	56,111	51,324	59,000	59,885	68,832	4.12	14.94
Latvia	4,472	4,734	5,460	5,843	6,442	0.39	10.25
Lithuania	12,602	13,182	15,046	15,062	15,872	0.95	5.38
Poland	164,712	161,851	172,001	163,754	167,751	10.05	2.44
Republic of Moldova	512	440	381	485	654	0.04	34.85
Romania	17,513	18,381	20,551	21,485	23,147	1.39	7.74
Russian Federation	23,382	26,968	35,122	40,817	54,471	3.26	33.45
Ukraine	20,618	21,659	35,616	39,458	79,988	4.79	102.72
NORTHERN EUROPE	77,934	79,581	82,524	90,579	97,583	5.84	7.73
Denmark	7,810	7,153	7,774	9,343	9,700	0.58	3.82
Finland	7,941	7,537	11,982	8,362	7,762	0.46	-7.18
Iceland	180	293	239	433	626	0.04	44.57
Ireland	4,898	6,829	6,853	6,814	7,224	0.43	6.02
Norway	4,174	5,054	6,224	7,823	9,741	0.58	24.52
Sweden	10,616	11,754	9,976	11,163	12,275	0.74	9.96
United Kingdom	42,315	40,961	39,476	46,641	50,255	3.01	7.75
SOUTHERN EUROPE	107,455	110,470	117,591	117,423	130,421	7.81	11.07
Albania	228	240	380	410	443	0.03	8.05
Bosnia and Herzegovina	1,281	989	1,390	1,606	3,891	0.23	142.28

658

Yearbook of Tourism Statistics, Data 2009 – 2013, 2015 Edition

SLOVAKIA

4. Arrivals of non-resident tourists in all types of accommodation establishments, by nationality

	2009	2010	2011	2012	2013	Market share 2013	% Change 2013-2012
Croatia	13,360	12,283	13,487	12,518	14,933	0.89	19.29
Greece	3,748	3,815	5,130	4,617	4,586	0.27	-0.67
Italy	50,982	54,439	51,957	50,377	53,969	3.23	7.13
Malta	1,227	994	231	418	563	0.03	34.69
Montenegro	112	300	372	511	583	0.03	14.09
Portugal	2,243	2,732	3,323	3,189	3,672	0.22	15.15
Serbia	3,301	4,891	7,972	9,738	10,880	0.65	11.73
Slovenia	12,614	11,953	12,901	14,145	15,075	0.90	6.57
Spain	17,549	16,926	19,635	17,969	19,355	1.16	7.71
TFYR of Macedonia	810	908	813	1,925	2,471	0.15	28.36
WESTERN EUROPE	**264,350**	**260,562**	**275,390**	**288,024**	**317,025**	**18.98**	**10.07**
Austria	50,065	51,678	58,983	65,621	73,862	4.42	12.56
Belgium	14,671	14,460	15,242	16,292	16,879	1.01	3.60
France	34,045	32,967	35,931	35,347	35,831	2.15	1.37
Germany	133,989	131,674	133,431	135,897	153,814	9.21	13.18
Liechtenstein	121	148	163	234	318	0.02	35.90
Luxembourg	548	489	419	623	663	0.04	6.42
Netherlands	20,759	18,776	18,499	20,759	20,743	1.24	-0.08
Switzerland	10,152	10,370	12,722	13,251	14,915	0.89	12.56
EAST MEDITERRANEAN EUROPE	**12,471**	**14,394**	**16,450**	**20,666**	**24,675**	**1.48**	**19.40**
Cyprus	1,371	1,358	1,686	1,884	1,128	0.07	-40.13
Israel	8,232	9,690	10,281	13,016	15,307	0.92	17.60
Turkey	2,868	3,346	4,483	5,766	8,240	0.49	42.91
OTHER EUROPE	**10,427**	**10,742**	**10,425**	**16,733**	**19,535**	**1.17**	**16.75**
Other countries of Europe	10,427	10,742	10,425	16,733	19,535	1.17	16.75
MIDDLE EAST	**516**	**551**	**579**	**1,182**	**1,142**	**0.07**	**-3.38**
Egypt	516	551	579	1,182	1,142	0.07	-3.38
SOUTH ASIA	**1,290**	**1,495**	**2,537**	**2,892**	**4,128**	**0.25**	**42.74**
India	1,290	1,495	2,537	2,892	4,128	0.25	42.74
NOT SPECIFIED	**622**	**907**	**2,570**	**2,810**	**1,142**	**0.07**	**-59.36**
Other countries of the World	622	907	2,570	2,810	1,142	0.07	-59.36

SLOVAKIA

6. Overnight stays of non-resident tourists in all types of accommodation establishments, by nationality

	2009	2010	2011	2012	2013	Market share 2013	% Change 2013-2012
TOTAL	3,769,136	3,806,609	4,038,635	4,101,201	4,340,009	100.00	5.82
AFRICA	8,178	9,637	8,557	20,333	12,339	0.28	-39.32
EAST AFRICA	167	162	165	395	687	0.02	73.92
Kenya	167	162	165	395	687	0.02	73.92
NORTH AFRICA	204	399	323	925	446	0.01	-51.78
Tunisia	204	399	323	925	446	0.01	-51.78
SOUTHERN AFRICA	1,402	2,752	1,543	3,252	2,988	0.07	-8.12
South Africa	1,402	2,752	1,543	3,252	2,988	0.07	-8.12
OTHER AFRICA	6,405	6,324	6,526	15,761	8,218	0.19	-47.86
Other countries of Africa	6,405	6,324	6,526	15,761	8,218	0.19	-47.86
AMERICAS	72,794	86,304	101,260	102,521	105,385	2.43	2.79
CARIBBEAN	47	140	29	190	78	0.00	-58.95
Dominican Republic	47	140	29	190	78	0.00	-58.95
NORTH AMERICA	62,510	70,966	82,879	86,145	88,952	2.05	3.26
Canada	10,473	12,824	18,237	15,348	13,846	0.32	-9.79
Mexico	2,053	4,139	4,585	4,409	3,915	0.09	-11.20
United States of America	49,984	54,003	60,057	66,388	71,191	1.64	7.23
SOUTH AMERICA	5,395	6,365	9,710	9,440	11,079	0.26	17.36
Argentina	780	1,141	1,140	1,978	2,046	0.05	3.44
Brazil	4,615	5,224	8,570	7,462	9,033	0.21	21.05
OTHER AMERICAS	4,842	8,833	8,642	6,746	5,276	0.12	-21.79
Other countries of the Americas	4,842	8,833	8,642	6,746	5,276	0.12	-21.79
EAST ASIA AND THE PACIFIC	135,461	174,993	194,358	205,150	196,127	4.52	-4.40
NORTH-EAST ASIA	68,548	87,571	103,510	104,367	88,521	2.04	-15.18
China	10,441	16,839	19,519	23,643	24,526	0.57	3.73
Japan	18,995	20,187	16,443	16,404	16,519	0.38	0.70
Korea, Republic of	39,112	50,545	67,548	64,320	47,476	1.09	-26.19
SOUTH-EAST ASIA	5,433	4,200	2,092	2,581	4,396	0.10	70.32
Thailand	5,433	4,200	2,092	2,581	4,396	0.10	70.32
AUSTRALASIA	5,204	13,723	13,716	16,887	15,856	0.37	-6.11
Australia	4,014	12,383	12,517	15,057	14,216	0.33	-5.59
New Zealand	1,190	1,340	1,199	1,830	1,640	0.04	-10.38
OTHER EAST ASIA AND THE PACIFIC	56,276	69,499	75,040	81,315	87,354	2.01	7.43
Other countries of Asia	56,276	69,499	75,040	81,315	87,354	2.01	7.43
EUROPE	3,540,645	3,527,429	3,719,751	3,758,567	4,011,507	92.43	6.73
CENTRAL/EASTERN EUROPE	2,201,102	2,210,346	2,399,523	2,396,826	2,568,215	59.18	7.15
Belarus	10,701	10,369	12,490	17,053	26,407	0.61	54.85
Bulgaria	13,292	10,488	12,871	16,967	16,711	0.39	-1.51
Czech Republic	1,300,870	1,350,234	1,422,506	1,412,870	1,387,482	31.97	-1.80
Estonia	9,243	7,744	8,026	9,623	10,709	0.25	11.29
Hungary	136,921	120,304	143,575	131,570	141,872	3.27	7.83
Latvia	10,649	11,618	11,776	13,099	15,648	0.36	19.46
Lithuania	27,824	26,889	31,117	32,295	35,748	0.82	10.69
Poland	479,774	453,067	471,178	441,447	442,755	10.20	0.30
Republic of Moldova	1,650	1,405	1,049	1,325	1,826	0.04	37.81
Romania	45,619	49,722	57,218	53,860	56,241	1.30	4.42
Russian Federation	88,213	94,325	125,636	151,838	198,522	4.57	30.75
Ukraine	76,346	74,181	102,081	114,879	234,294	5.40	103.95
NORTHERN EUROPE	178,415	188,546	192,381	203,464	212,348	4.89	4.37
Denmark	20,702	19,167	21,984	25,018	26,224	0.60	4.82
Finland	18,751	19,126	32,776	18,042	16,138	0.37	-10.55
Iceland	390	932	532	1,154	1,459	0.03	26.43
Ireland	10,460	15,453	15,614	15,042	15,825	0.36	5.21
Norway	10,295	11,717	14,223	20,424	22,668	0.52	10.99
Sweden	22,633	26,935	22,444	23,717	25,616	0.59	8.01
United Kingdom	95,184	95,216	84,808	100,067	104,418	2.41	4.35
SOUTHERN EUROPE	238,003	238,555	243,681	254,649	270,113	6.22	6.07
Albania	485	656	966	824	976	0.02	18.45
Bosnia and Herzegovina	3,713	2,774	2,773	3,549	7,189	0.17	102.56

Yearbook of Tourism Statistics, Data 2009 – 2013, 2015 Edition

SLOVAKIA

6. Overnight stays of non-resident tourists in all types of accommodation establishments, by nationality

	2009	2010	2011	2012	2013	Market share 2013	% Change 2013-2012
Croatia	29,444	26,330	26,782	25,870	27,799	0.64	7.46
Greece	8,195	8,997	11,311	9,998	9,510	0.22	-4.88
Italy	110,885	118,579	110,966	107,401	111,080	2.56	3.43
Malta	5,767	2,196	625	1,143	1,281	0.03	12.07
Montenegro	408	704	641	2,049	1,397	0.03	-31.82
Portugal	5,643	6,216	7,246	7,648	8,375	0.19	9.51
Serbia	10,923	14,662	18,483	23,774	24,993	0.58	5.13
Slovenia	23,050	23,067	24,194	30,648	34,966	0.81	14.09
Spain	37,781	32,577	37,978	36,995	38,511	0.89	4.10
TFYR of Macedonia	1,709	1,797	1,716	4,750	4,036	0.09	-15.03
WESTERN EUROPE	**837,451**	**786,851**	**774,616**	**766,711**	**806,146**	**18.57**	**5.14**
Austria	122,449	120,900	125,499	135,907	150,125	3.46	10.46
Belgium	35,435	35,022	35,093	36,404	36,539	0.84	0.37
France	75,680	69,368	79,757	74,902	73,441	1.69	-1.95
Germany	527,821	490,780	462,503	443,663	466,577	10.75	5.16
Liechtenstein	519	399	323	383	477	0.01	24.54
Luxembourg	1,312	1,337	902	1,209	1,366	0.03	12.99
Netherlands	53,063	46,894	42,861	47,626	48,483	1.12	1.80
Switzerland	21,172	22,151	27,678	26,617	29,138	0.67	9.47
EAST MEDITERRANEAN EUROPE	**65,988**	**79,283**	**87,033**	**106,567**	**121,497**	**2.80**	**14.01**
Cyprus	6,892	7,618	7,884	6,405	4,240	0.10	-33.80
Israel	52,570	64,270	69,636	86,818	102,280	2.36	17.81
Turkey	6,526	7,395	9,513	13,344	14,977	0.35	12.24
OTHER EUROPE	**19,686**	**23,848**	**22,517**	**30,350**	**33,188**	**0.76**	**9.35**
Other countries of Europe	19,686	23,848	22,517	30,350	33,188	0.76	9.35
MIDDLE EAST	**2,051**	**2,754**	**3,127**	**4,138**	**4,885**	**0.11**	**18.05**
Egypt	2,051	2,754	3,127	4,138	4,885	0.11	18.05
SOUTH ASIA	**3,207**	**4,063**	**6,628**	**6,348**	**7,834**	**0.18**	**23.41**
India	3,207	4,063	6,628	6,348	7,834	0.18	23.41
NOT SPECIFIED	**6,800**	**1,429**	**4,954**	**4,144**	**1,932**	**0.04**	**-53.38**
Other countries of the World	6,800	1,429	4,954	4,144	1,932	0.04	-53.38

Yearbook of Tourism Statistics, Data 2009 – 2013, 2015 Edition

SLOVENIA

3. Arrivals of non-resident tourists in hotels and similar establishments, by nationality

	2009	2010	2011	2012	2013	Market share 2013	% Change 2013-2012
TOTAL	1,411,352	1,422,382	1,528,057	1,592,858	1,639,871	100.00	2.95
AFRICA	2,518	2,779	3,642	3,982	4,544	0.28	14.11
SOUTHERN AFRICA	780	956	1,419	1,868	1,874	0.11	0.32
South Africa	780	956	1,419	1,868	1,874	0.11	0.32
OTHER AFRICA	1,738	1,823	2,223	2,114	2,670	0.16	26.30
Other countries of Africa	1,738	1,823	2,223	2,114	2,670	0.16	26.30
AMERICAS	49,459	52,235	56,002	62,145	70,409	4.29	13.30
NORTH AMERICA	42,694	45,032	46,660	51,635	56,610	3.45	9.63
Canada	7,124	7,435	8,050	8,634	8,857	0.54	2.58
United States of America	33,327	35,487	38,455	42,986	47,717	2.91	11.01
Other countries of North America	2,243	2,110	155	15	36	0.00	140.00
SOUTH AMERICA	2,776	3,057	3,772	5,185	7,992	0.49	54.14
Brazil	2,776	3,057	3,772	5,185	7,992	0.49	54.14
OTHER AMERICAS	3,989	4,146	5,570	5,325	5,807	0.35	9.05
Other countries of the Americas	3,989	4,146	5,570	5,325	5,807	0.35	9.05
EAST ASIA AND THE PACIFIC	84,457	84,888	95,273	119,400	131,022	7.99	9.73
NORTH-EAST ASIA	57,894	53,090	55,091	68,952	74,754	4.56	8.41
China	5,319	7,613	10,078	13,860	17,998	1.10	29.86
Japan	47,641	39,502	34,187	39,764	34,786	2.12	-12.52
Korea, Republic of	4,934	5,975	10,826	15,328	21,970	1.34	43.33
AUSTRALASIA	14,477	15,551	15,423	14,923	16,624	1.01	11.40
Australia	12,325	13,035	13,604	13,095	14,440	0.88	10.27
New Zealand	2,152	2,516	1,819	1,828	2,184	0.13	19.47
OTHER EAST ASIA AND THE PACIFIC	12,086	16,247	24,759	35,525	39,644	2.42	11.59
Other countries of Asia	11,226	15,706	24,040	34,727	38,162	2.33	9.89
Other countries of Oceania	860	541	719	798	1,482	0.09	85.71
EUROPE	1,274,918	1,282,480	1,373,140	1,407,331	1,433,896	87.44	1.89
CENTRAL/EASTERN EUROPE	168,285	178,106	209,763	228,112	229,943	14.02	0.80
Bulgaria	16,135	15,654	18,147	17,087	19,231	1.17	12.55
Czech Republic	25,225	24,702	27,897	28,336	30,051	1.83	6.05
Estonia	1,438	1,568	1,860	1,775	1,564	0.10	-11.89
Hungary	38,814	36,844	42,088	42,320	41,052	2.50	-3.00
Latvia	2,670	3,041	2,444	2,346	2,211	0.13	-5.75
Lithuania	1,979	1,787	2,127	2,104	2,796	0.17	32.89
Poland	21,556	20,924	23,729	26,813	26,724	1.63	-0.33
Romania	15,453	16,204	17,944	18,056	17,494	1.07	-3.11
Russian Federation	25,045	30,414	38,019	47,054	50,213	3.06	6.71
Slovakia	11,363	12,093	13,181	14,114	13,953	0.85	-1.14
Ukraine	8,607	14,875	22,327	28,107	24,654	1.50	-12.29
NORTHERN EUROPE	103,143	91,464	95,261	91,268	93,831	5.72	2.81
Denmark	8,058	9,277	10,139	9,103	8,425	0.51	-7.45
Finland	14,071	11,953	12,559	11,387	11,529	0.70	1.25
Iceland	1,179	659	1,482	1,469	1,366	0.08	-7.01
Ireland	7,481	5,127	5,132	4,190	4,121	0.25	-1.65
Norway	5,759	5,637	5,343	5,561	6,915	0.42	24.35
Sweden	11,959	10,844	11,759	12,771	13,056	0.80	2.23
United Kingdom	54,636	47,967	48,847	46,787	48,419	2.95	3.49
SOUTHERN EUROPE	556,443	578,563	589,086	572,097	578,528	35.28	1.12
Bosnia and Herzegovina	23,432	23,899	25,224	24,855	26,221	1.60	5.50
Croatia	82,404	82,584	87,602	88,298	91,689	5.59	3.84
Greece	6,651	6,050	6,150	6,419	7,214	0.44	12.39
Italy	352,163	348,103	348,128	340,350	339,930	20.73	-0.12
Malta	2,183	2,195	2,664	2,348	3,503	0.21	49.19
Montenegro	3,871	6,543	6,214	6,278	7,080	0.43	12.77
Portugal	6,091	5,763	5,821	4,786	4,260	0.26	-10.99
Serbia	46,489	67,104	70,350	67,054	68,073	4.15	1.52
Spain	23,390	23,114	24,444	20,989	18,636	1.14	-11.21
TFYR of Macedonia	9,769	13,208	12,489	10,720	11,922	0.73	11.21

Yearbook of Tourism Statistics, Data 2009 – 2013, 2015 Edition

SLOVENIA

3. Arrivals of non-resident tourists in hotels and similar establishments, by nationality

	2009	2010	2011	2012	2013	Market share 2013	% Change 2013-2012
WESTERN EUROPE	**405,634**	**391,862**	**432,070**	**460,389**	**464,544**	**28.33**	**0.90**
Austria	169,240	164,237	181,515	198,388	198,847	12.13	0.23
Belgium	22,617	22,394	28,400	29,122	30,033	1.83	3.13
France	39,921	37,258	39,326	38,208	41,150	2.51	7.70
Germany	125,269	123,041	134,573	142,568	141,387	8.62	-0.83
Luxembourg	1,107	968	1,066	1,297	1,022	0.06	-21.20
Netherlands	25,355	23,309	24,294	26,297	26,364	1.61	0.25
Switzerland	22,125	20,655	22,896	24,509	25,741	1.57	5.03
EAST MEDITERRANEAN EUROPE	**31,931**	**32,817**	**35,791**	**42,414**	**48,148**	**2.94**	**13.52**
Cyprus	587	713	570	852	1,084	0.07	27.23
Israel	23,770	21,848	22,298	28,989	33,923	2.07	17.02
Turkey	7,574	10,256	12,923	12,573	13,141	0.80	4.52
OTHER EUROPE	**9,482**	**9,668**	**11,169**	**13,051**	**18,902**	**1.15**	**44.83**
Other countries of Europe	9,482	9,668	11,169	13,051	18,902	1.15	44.83

Yearbook of Tourism Statistics, Data 2009 – 2013, 2015 Edition

SLOVENIA

4. Arrivals of non-resident tourists in all types of accommodation establishments, by nationality

	2009	2010	2011	2012	2013	Market share 2013	% Change 2013-2012
TOTAL	1,823,931	1,869,106	2,036,652	2,155,612	2,258,570	100.00	4.78
AFRICA	2,911	3,396	4,437	4,919	5,682	0.25	15.51
SOUTHERN AFRICA	898	1,132	1,773	2,258	2,298	0.10	1.77
South Africa	898	1,132	1,773	2,258	2,298	0.10	1.77
OTHER AFRICA	2,013	2,264	2,664	2,661	3,384	0.15	27.17
Other countries of Africa	2,013	2,264	2,664	2,661	3,384	0.15	27.17
AMERICAS	55,336	61,941	67,613	75,923	88,344	3.91	16.36
NORTH AMERICA	47,777	53,368	56,627	63,037	71,327	3.16	13.15
Canada	8,410	9,598	10,583	11,251	12,081	0.53	7.38
United States of America	37,050	41,566	45,796	51,754	59,202	2.62	14.39
Other countries of North America	2,317	2,204	248	32	44	0.00	37.50
SOUTH AMERICA	2,998	3,591	4,290	6,075	9,475	0.42	55.97
Brazil	2,998	3,591	4,290	6,075	9,475	0.42	55.97
OTHER AMERICAS	4,561	4,982	6,696	6,811	7,542	0.33	10.73
Other countries of the Americas	4,561	4,982	6,696	6,811	7,542	0.33	10.73
EAST ASIA AND THE PACIFIC	90,168	94,653	106,067	133,006	147,845	6.55	11.16
NORTH-EAST ASIA	58,958	55,314	57,934	73,089	79,594	3.52	8.90
China	5,638	8,234	11,050	15,294	19,801	0.88	29.47
Japan	48,182	40,455	35,321	41,398	36,437	1.61	-11.98
Korea, Republic of	5,138	6,625	11,563	16,397	23,356	1.03	42.44
AUSTRALASIA	18,379	21,318	21,524	21,407	24,939	1.10	16.50
Australia	15,308	17,695	18,461	18,216	21,229	0.94	16.54
New Zealand	3,071	3,623	3,063	3,191	3,710	0.16	16.26
OTHER EAST ASIA AND THE PACIFIC	12,831	18,021	26,609	38,510	43,312	1.92	12.47
Other countries of Asia	11,793	17,071	25,631	37,361	41,433	1.83	10.90
Other countries of Oceania	1,038	950	978	1,149	1,879	0.08	63.53
EUROPE	1,675,516	1,709,116	1,858,535	1,941,764	2,016,699	89.29	3.86
CENTRAL/EASTERN EUROPE	240,190	255,552	299,936	326,586	340,416	15.07	4.23
Bulgaria	19,507	18,833	21,800	20,937	23,618	1.05	12.81
Czech Republic	52,417	53,205	58,817	63,077	65,464	2.90	3.78
Estonia	1,958	2,072	2,525	2,593	2,612	0.12	0.73
Hungary	55,370	55,325	63,096	62,856	63,953	2.83	1.75
Latvia	3,339	3,997	3,274	3,385	3,563	0.16	5.26
Lithuania	3,045	2,821	3,386	3,356	4,792	0.21	42.79
Poland	32,607	33,320	39,626	43,583	46,478	2.06	6.64
Romania	18,660	19,462	21,799	22,298	22,380	0.99	0.37
Russian Federation	26,842	32,690	41,360	52,476	57,576	2.55	9.72
Slovakia	16,329	17,427	19,720	21,258	21,936	0.97	3.19
Ukraine	10,116	16,400	24,533	30,767	28,044	1.24	-8.85
NORTHERN EUROPE	132,595	128,875	134,236	132,008	142,308	6.30	7.80
Denmark	13,723	15,255	16,576	16,120	16,025	0.71	-0.59
Finland	16,549	15,082	15,629	14,412	15,824	0.70	9.80
Iceland	1,436	882	1,785	1,817	1,603	0.07	-11.78
Ireland	9,354	7,715	7,719	6,667	7,403	0.33	11.04
Norway	7,150	7,448	6,876	7,314	8,729	0.39	19.35
Sweden	14,955	14,028	14,986	16,614	18,057	0.80	8.69
United Kingdom	69,428	68,465	70,665	69,064	74,667	3.31	8.11
SOUTHERN EUROPE	663,976	691,750	715,444	705,766	717,469	31.77	1.66
Bosnia and Herzegovina	26,881	27,299	29,356	30,372	31,948	1.41	5.19
Croatia	104,045	103,134	110,377	113,647	118,772	5.26	4.51
Greece	7,434	6,822	6,885	7,580	8,187	0.36	8.01
Italy	417,771	412,137	420,247	414,041	414,192	18.34	0.04
Malta	2,389	2,401	2,926	2,637	3,938	0.17	49.34
Montenegro	4,188	7,277	6,801	7,126	7,985	0.35	12.05
Portugal	7,330	7,422	7,644	6,586	6,629	0.29	0.65
Serbia	51,388	76,156	80,995	78,207	80,622	3.57	3.09
Spain	31,409	33,670	35,687	32,563	30,575	1.35	-6.11
TFYR of Macedonia	11,141	15,432	14,526	13,007	14,621	0.65	12.41

664

SLOVENIA

4. Arrivals of non-resident tourists in all types of accommodation establishments, by nationality

	2009	2010	2011	2012	2013	Market share 2013	% Change 2013-2012
WESTERN EUROPE	**590,074**	**581,231**	**651,247**	**707,735**	**731,504**	**32.39**	**3.36**
Austria	207,366	201,756	222,192	240,113	242,892	10.75	1.16
Belgium	33,845	35,209	45,312	48,817	54,213	2.40	11.05
France	60,527	62,104	67,019	67,619	72,027	3.19	6.52
Germany	195,240	194,386	218,894	238,352	242,951	10.76	1.93
Luxembourg	1,381	1,253	1,495	1,713	1,440	0.06	-15.94
Netherlands	63,803	58,941	65,548	78,049	82,698	3.66	5.96
Switzerland	27,912	27,582	30,787	33,072	35,283	1.56	6.69
EAST MEDITERRANEAN EUROPE	**37,774**	**40,442**	**44,562**	**54,427**	**63,116**	**2.79**	**15.96**
Cyprus	616	778	685	1,069	1,301	0.06	21.70
Israel	29,110	28,713	30,153	39,595	46,862	2.07	18.35
Turkey	8,048	10,951	13,724	13,763	14,953	0.66	8.65
OTHER EUROPE	**10,907**	**11,266**	**13,110**	**15,242**	**21,886**	**0.97**	**43.59**
Other countries of Europe	10,907	11,266	13,110	15,242	21,886	0.97	43.59

Yearbook of Tourism Statistics, Data 2009 – 2013, 2015 Edition

SLOVENIA

5. Overnight stays of non-resident tourists in hotels and similar establishments, by nationality

	2009	2010	2011	2012	2013	Market share 2013	% Change 2013-2012
TOTAL	3,684,005	3,715,473	4,005,927	4,150,042	4,202,067	100.00	1.25
AFRICA	6,896	8,440	13,187	13,143	12,899	0.31	-1.86
SOUTHERN AFRICA	2,157	2,662	3,784	5,124	4,233	0.10	-17.39
South Africa	2,157	2,662	3,784	5,124	4,233	0.10	-17.39
OTHER AFRICA	4,739	5,778	9,403	8,019	8,666	0.21	8.07
Other countries of Africa	4,739	5,778	9,403	8,019	8,666	0.21	8.07
AMERICAS	111,159	119,261	126,276	143,875	153,327	3.65	6.57
NORTH AMERICA	96,441	104,688	106,094	121,353	124,616	2.97	2.69
Canada	16,506	17,617	18,867	19,196	19,120	0.46	-0.40
United States of America	74,623	82,616	86,927	102,127	105,429	2.51	3.23
Other countries of North America	5,312	4,455	300	30	67	0.00	123.33
SOUTH AMERICA	5,939	5,967	7,542	10,763	16,026	0.38	48.90
Brazil	5,939	5,967	7,542	10,763	16,026	0.38	48.90
OTHER AMERICAS	8,779	8,606	12,640	11,759	12,685	0.30	7.87
Other countries of the Americas	8,779	8,606	12,640	11,759	12,685	0.30	7.87
EAST ASIA AND THE PACIFIC	136,049	137,284	162,107	188,119	204,328	4.86	8.62
NORTH-EAST ASIA	80,420	73,738	81,305	95,921	100,987	2.40	5.28
China	10,300	14,152	19,411	20,377	25,881	0.62	27.01
Japan	63,160	51,986	48,299	56,741	49,880	1.19	-12.09
Korea, Republic of	6,960	7,600	13,595	18,803	25,226	0.60	34.16
AUSTRALASIA	28,017	31,344	32,339	30,266	32,242	0.77	6.53
Australia	23,856	26,066	27,807	26,759	28,058	0.67	4.85
New Zealand	4,161	5,278	4,532	3,507	4,184	0.10	19.30
OTHER EAST ASIA AND THE PACIFIC	27,612	32,202	48,463	61,932	71,099	1.69	14.80
Other countries of Asia	25,755	31,073	46,973	60,264	68,216	1.62	13.20
Other countries of Oceania	1,857	1,129	1,490	1,668	2,883	0.07	72.84
EUROPE	3,429,901	3,450,488	3,704,357	3,804,905	3,831,513	91.18	0.70
CENTRAL/EASTERN EUROPE	496,286	539,062	638,430	743,398	732,436	17.43	-1.47
Bulgaria	27,247	26,025	29,260	26,532	29,108	0.69	9.71
Czech Republic	58,710	60,630	69,988	73,604	80,780	1.92	9.75
Estonia	4,092	3,802	4,942	4,690	3,967	0.09	-15.42
Hungary	98,547	93,131	107,350	105,551	102,561	2.44	-2.83
Latvia	5,345	6,042	5,633	5,299	5,374	0.13	1.42
Lithuania	5,019	4,566	5,043	4,970	9,380	0.22	88.73
Poland	50,074	45,255	48,668	60,238	50,001	1.19	-16.99
Romania	34,094	32,495	37,521	36,902	35,212	0.84	-4.58
Russian Federation	156,770	198,832	243,471	327,339	315,252	7.50	-3.69
Slovakia	27,064	30,401	33,652	33,925	35,639	0.85	5.05
Ukraine	29,324	37,883	52,902	64,348	65,162	1.55	1.26
NORTHERN EUROPE	321,163	291,261	294,406	277,083	292,789	6.97	5.67
Denmark	23,222	20,128	23,411	20,694	19,370	0.46	-6.40
Finland	38,173	32,708	32,683	29,691	32,382	0.77	9.06
Iceland	2,148	2,046	3,757	4,511	4,408	0.10	-2.28
Ireland	23,926	15,968	16,274	12,474	11,385	0.27	-8.73
Norway	14,950	14,217	12,896	13,423	17,981	0.43	33.96
Sweden	31,747	27,130	28,353	32,974	34,504	0.82	4.64
United Kingdom	186,997	179,064	177,032	163,316	172,759	4.11	5.78
SOUTHERN EUROPE	1,341,168	1,393,598	1,405,182	1,339,865	1,326,645	31.57	-0.99
Bosnia and Herzegovina	59,005	55,120	56,482	55,459	58,010	1.38	4.60
Croatia	215,855	209,972	216,121	220,376	219,725	5.23	-0.30
Greece	14,491	12,672	13,431	11,814	14,682	0.35	24.28
Italy	839,009	828,083	825,344	777,204	752,881	17.92	-3.13
Malta	10,988	11,251	13,778	11,774	16,794	0.40	42.64
Montenegro	9,530	15,855	14,695	14,705	16,343	0.39	11.14
Portugal	11,893	11,596	10,464	10,264	8,709	0.21	-15.15
Serbia	114,736	177,041	180,134	172,199	172,722	4.11	0.30
Spain	45,173	46,002	49,827	45,061	42,889	1.02	-4.82
TFYR of Macedonia	20,488	26,006	24,906	21,009	23,890	0.57	13.71

Yearbook of Tourism Statistics, Data 2009 – 2013, 2015 Edition

SLOVENIA

5. Overnight stays of non-resident tourists in hotels and similar establishments, by nationality

	2009	2010	2011	2012	2013	Market share 2013	% Change 2013-2012
WESTERN EUROPE	**1,157,061**	**1,114,777**	**1,235,962**	**1,282,037**	**1,279,389**	**30.45**	**-0.21**
Austria	519,130	499,393	545,235	568,879	566,875	13.49	-0.35
Belgium	75,620	79,154	102,023	102,642	107,165	2.55	4.41
France	80,481	73,371	81,216	77,458	85,964	2.05	10.98
Germany	361,572	354,612	392,345	407,787	393,520	9.36	-3.50
Luxembourg	3,291	2,322	2,583	3,061	2,339	0.06	-23.59
Netherlands	63,999	61,056	62,746	69,393	67,767	1.61	-2.34
Switzerland	52,968	44,869	49,814	52,817	55,759	1.33	5.57
EAST MEDITERRANEAN EUROPE	**86,554**	**87,128**	**97,138**	**119,742**	**148,207**	**3.53**	**23.77**
Cyprus	1,990	2,148	1,609	2,047	2,434	0.06	18.91
Israel	67,898	67,081	70,864	93,654	119,292	2.84	27.38
Turkey	16,666	17,899	24,665	24,041	26,481	0.63	10.15
OTHER EUROPE	**27,669**	**24,662**	**33,239**	**42,780**	**52,047**	**1.24**	**21.66**
Other countries of Europe	27,669	24,662	33,239	42,780	52,047	1.24	21.66

Yearbook of Tourism Statistics, Data 2009 – 2013, 2015 Edition

SLOVENIA

6. Overnight stays of non-resident tourists in all types of accommodation establishments, by nationality

	2009	2010	2011	2012	2013	Market share 2013	% Change 2013-2012
TOTAL	4,936,293	4,997,031	5,463,931	5,777,204	5,962,251	100.00	3.20
AFRICA	8,185	11,340	15,500	16,912	16,092	0.27	-4.85
SOUTHERN AFRICA	2,452	3,162	4,768	6,663	5,296	0.09	-20.52
South Africa	2,452	3,162	4,768	6,663	5,296	0.09	-20.52
OTHER AFRICA	5,733	8,178	10,732	10,249	10,796	0.18	5.34
Other countries of Africa	5,733	8,178	10,732	10,249	10,796	0.18	5.34
AMERICAS	127,357	141,414	153,840	176,654	193,667	3.25	9.63
NORTH AMERICA	109,694	124,012	129,885	147,823	157,266	2.64	6.39
Canada	20,102	22,772	24,894	25,175	26,310	0.44	4.51
United States of America	84,076	96,648	104,503	122,580	130,877	2.20	6.77
Other countries of North America	5,516	4,592	488	68	79	0.00	16.18
SOUTH AMERICA	6,580	6,971	8,565	12,728	18,821	0.32	47.87
Brazil	6,580	6,971	8,565	12,728	18,821	0.32	47.87
OTHER AMERICAS	11,083	10,431	15,390	16,103	17,580	0.29	9.17
Other countries of the Americas	11,083	10,431	15,390	16,103	17,580	0.29	9.17
EAST ASIA AND THE PACIFIC	154,321	161,964	186,139	221,794	241,315	4.05	8.80
NORTH-EAST ASIA	83,401	77,954	87,599	104,552	110,161	1.85	5.36
China	11,263	15,477	21,785	23,530	29,321	0.49	24.61
Japan	64,712	53,761	50,840	60,278	53,200	0.89	-11.74
Korea, Republic of	7,426	8,716	14,974	20,744	27,640	0.46	33.24
AUSTRALASIA	36,915	44,098	45,274	44,093	48,658	0.82	10.35
Australia	30,786	36,419	38,064	37,793	41,532	0.70	9.89
New Zealand	6,129	7,679	7,210	6,300	7,126	0.12	13.11
OTHER EAST ASIA AND THE PACIFIC	34,005	39,912	53,266	73,149	82,496	1.38	12.78
Other countries of Asia	31,538	36,743	51,129	70,597	78,684	1.32	11.46
Other countries of Oceania	2,467	3,169	2,137	2,552	3,812	0.06	49.37
EUROPE	4,646,430	4,682,313	5,108,452	5,361,844	5,511,177	92.43	2.79
CENTRAL/EASTERN EUROPE	691,285	742,046	874,432	1,004,619	1,028,666	17.25	2.39
Bulgaria	33,699	32,426	36,436	33,521	37,361	0.63	11.46
Czech Republic	124,415	127,165	141,937	157,175	166,532	2.79	5.95
Estonia	5,246	4,874	6,442	6,451	6,549	0.11	1.52
Hungary	147,338	144,215	165,059	161,233	164,059	2.75	1.75
Latvia	7,630	8,222	7,941	8,095	8,812	0.15	8.86
Lithuania	7,550	6,706	7,964	7,717	15,008	0.25	94.48
Poland	80,495	82,639	93,128	108,312	105,825	1.77	-2.30
Romania	44,590	40,959	48,216	48,736	45,993	0.77	-5.63
Russian Federation	163,903	208,341	257,173	350,319	348,098	5.84	-0.63
Slovakia	39,935	43,376	50,424	49,830	55,039	0.92	10.45
Ukraine	36,484	43,123	59,712	73,230	75,390	1.26	2.95
NORTHERN EUROPE	409,201	396,526	409,066	394,226	427,947	7.18	8.55
Denmark	42,790	40,059	47,605	46,625	48,026	0.81	3.00
Finland	44,915	39,947	41,012	37,625	43,218	0.72	14.87
Iceland	3,139	2,531	4,804	5,314	4,993	0.08	-6.04
Ireland	28,984	22,053	22,536	18,716	18,937	0.32	1.18
Norway	18,504	18,876	16,561	17,735	22,250	0.37	25.46
Sweden	39,039	34,592	35,819	42,096	45,898	0.77	9.03
United Kingdom	231,830	238,468	240,729	226,115	244,625	4.10	8.19
SOUTHERN EUROPE	1,643,436	1,688,496	1,740,156	1,687,064	1,676,870	28.12	-0.60
Bosnia and Herzegovina	77,281	66,611	70,478	72,080	76,621	1.29	6.30
Croatia	288,170	274,380	291,186	297,647	296,966	4.98	-0.23
Greece	16,911	14,435	15,312	14,717	16,857	0.28	14.54
Italy	1,004,783	987,268	1,005,222	957,027	929,327	15.59	-2.89
Malta	11,637	11,921	14,529	12,551	18,236	0.31	45.30
Montenegro	10,410	17,759	16,446	17,497	18,762	0.31	7.23
Portugal	15,055	15,071	14,146	14,262	14,777	0.25	3.61
Serbia	131,177	201,683	209,971	203,807	206,322	3.46	1.23
Spain	62,432	67,276	71,737	69,396	67,346	1.13	-2.95
TFYR of Macedonia	25,580	32,092	31,129	28,080	31,656	0.53	12.74

Yearbook of Tourism Statistics, Data 2009 – 2013, 2015 Edition

SLOVENIA

6. Overnight stays of non-resident tourists in all types of accommodation establishments, by nationality

	2009	2010	2011	2012	2013	Market share 2013	% Change 2013-2012
WESTERN EUROPE	**1,767,215**	**1,718,709**	**1,923,304**	**2,074,958**	**2,126,541**	**35.67**	**2.49**
Austria	642,242	619,259	674,194	695,555	699,850	11.74	0.62
Belgium	111,140	117,980	152,612	168,219	184,816	3.10	9.87
France	130,752	130,968	143,478	145,968	154,148	2.59	5.60
Germany	577,961	578,262	646,696	692,648	690,687	11.58	-0.28
Luxembourg	4,116	2,922	3,619	4,087	3,280	0.06	-19.75
Netherlands	233,539	208,654	234,390	295,679	314,860	5.28	6.49
Switzerland	67,465	60,664	68,315	72,802	78,900	1.32	8.38
EAST MEDITERRANEAN EUROPE	**102,913**	**106,872**	**122,855**	**152,195**	**190,530**	**3.20**	**25.19**
Cyprus	2,042	2,292	1,880	2,486	3,152	0.05	26.79
Israel	82,258	84,657	93,915	122,174	155,816	2.61	27.54
Turkey	18,613	19,923	27,060	27,535	31,562	0.53	14.63
OTHER EUROPE	**32,380**	**29,664**	**38,639**	**48,782**	**60,623**	**1.02**	**24.27**
Other countries of Europe	32,380	29,664	38,639	48,782	60,623	1.02	24.27

Yearbook of Tourism Statistics, Data 2009 – 2013, 2015 Edition

SOLOMON ISLANDS

1. Arrivals of non-resident tourists at national borders, by country of residence

	2009	2010	2011	2012	2013	Market share 2013	% Change 2013-2012
TOTAL	**18,308**	**20,521**	**22,941**	**23,925**	**24,431**	**100.00**	**2.11**
AMERICAS	**1,122**	**975**	**1,232**	**1,445**	**1,309**	**5.36**	**-9.41**
NORTH AMERICA	**1,122**	**975**	**1,232**	**1,445**	**1,309**	**5.36**	**-9.41**
Canada	88	113	192	111	148	0.61	33.33
United States of America	1,034	862	1,040	1,334	1,161	4.75	-12.97
EAST ASIA AND THE PACIFIC	**15,886**	**18,255**	**20,480**	**21,166**	**21,776**	**89.13**	**2.88**
NORTH-EAST ASIA	**938**	**627**	**771**	**694**	**682**	**2.79**	**-1.73**
Hong Kong, China	65	38	130	80	81	0.33	1.25
Japan	873	589	641	614	601	2.46	-2.12
AUSTRALASIA	**10,266**	**12,461**	**13,116**	**12,826**	**13,086**	**53.56**	**2.03**
Australia	8,902	10,751	11,392	11,079	11,181	45.77	0.92
New Zealand	1,364	1,710	1,724	1,747	1,905	7.80	9.04
MELANESIA	**2,323**	**2,757**	**3,774**	**4,123**	**4,623**	**18.92**	**12.13**
Fiji	917	991	1,204	1,555	1,800	7.37	15.76
Papua New Guinea	1,098	1,361	2,057	1,973	2,019	8.26	2.33
Vanuatu	308	405	513	595	804	3.29	35.13
OTHER EAST ASIA AND THE PACIFIC	**2,359**	**2,410**	**2,819**	**3,523**	**3,385**	**13.86**	**-3.92**
Other countries of Asia	1,409	1,825	2,056	2,105	2,625	10.74	24.70
Other countries of Oceania	950	585	763	1,418	760	3.11	-46.40
EUROPE	**1,091**	**1,014**	**941**	**1,061**	**1,122**	**4.59**	**5.75**
NORTHERN EUROPE	**419**	**432**	**380**	**385**	**460**	**1.88**	**19.48**
United Kingdom	419	432	380	385	460	1.88	19.48
SOUTHERN EUROPE	**66**	**39**	**80**	**93**	**83**	**0.34**	**-10.75**
Italy	66	39	80	93	83	0.34	-10.75
WESTERN EUROPE	**232**	**236**	**235**	**262**	**292**	**1.20**	**11.45**
France	81	82	60	88	93	0.38	5.68
Germany	100	101	111	117	136	0.56	16.24
Netherlands	51	53	64	57	63	0.26	10.53
OTHER EUROPE	**374**	**307**	**246**	**321**	**287**	**1.17**	**-10.59**
Other countries of Europe	374	307	246	321	287	1.17	-10.59
NOT SPECIFIED	**209**	**277**	**288**	**253**	**224**	**0.92**	**-11.46**
Other countries of the World	209	277	288	253	224	0.92	-11.46

Yearbook of Tourism Statistics, Data 2009 – 2013, 2015 Edition

SOUTH AFRICA

1. Arrivals of non-resident tourists at national borders, by country of residence

		2009	2010	2011	2012	2013	Market share 2013	% Change 2013-2012
TOTAL	(*)	**7,011,865**	**8,073,552**	**8,339,354**	**9,188,368**	**9,536,568**	**100.00**	**3.79**
AFRICA		**5,083,145**	**5,733,499**	**6,129,606**	**6,648,201**	**6,846,702**	**71.79**	**2.99**
EAST AFRICA		**2,587,771**	**2,950,813**	**3,036,469**	**3,389,016**	**3,539,373**	**37.11**	**4.44**
Burundi		960	891	1,010	1,472	1,772	0.02	20.38
Comoros		155	209	198	276	369	0.00	33.70
Djibouti		78	79	97	92	91	0.00	-1.09
Eritrea		579	602	666	904	720	0.01	-20.35
Ethiopia		10,651	9,397	9,125	7,862	9,049	0.09	15.10
Kenya		25,581	29,089	30,279	32,992	35,582	0.37	7.85
Madagascar		2,623	3,075	2,962	4,813	6,424	0.07	33.47
Malawi		139,605	126,120	135,577	142,063	170,345	1.79	19.91
Mauritius		13,625	16,329	16,545	18,233	19,341	0.20	6.08
Mozambique		983,739	1,051,502	1,076,753	1,104,404	1,116,735	11.71	1.12
Reunion		596	348	3		1	0.00	
Rwanda		2,841	2,931	2,838	3,429	3,647	0.04	6.36
Seychelles		2,166	2,861	3,182	3,292	4,849	0.05	47.30
Somalia		2,863	2,706	829	206	115	0.00	-44.17
Uganda		12,257	13,627	14,450	15,522	17,161	0.18	10.56
United Republic of Tanzania		14,732	19,641	28,645	35,928	38,099	0.40	6.04
Zambia		147,089	157,692	160,302	169,555	179,914	1.89	6.11
Zimbabwe		1,227,631	1,513,714	1,553,008	1,847,973	1,935,159	20.29	4.72
CENTRAL AFRICA		**85,071**	**87,644**	**87,613**	**99,185**	**111,120**	**1.17**	**12.03**
Angola		37,254	38,543	39,217	47,714	57,041	0.60	19.55
Cameroon		4,531	6,461	5,357	6,234	6,203	0.07	-0.50
Central African Republic		120	170	143	191	197	0.00	3.14
Chad		251	252	339	414	486	0.01	17.39
Congo		6,347	4,437	3,337	3,868	4,551	0.05	17.66
Democratic Republic of the Congo		30,982	31,285	32,582	32,956	34,066	0.36	3.37
Equatorial Guinea		343	311	319	406	497	0.01	22.41
Gabon		5,077	6,052	6,199	7,168	7,864	0.08	9.71
Sao Tome and Principe		166	133	120	234	215	0.00	-8.12
NORTH AFRICA		**5,270**	**8,479**	**5,745**	**6,018**	**6,658**	**0.07**	**10.63**
Algeria		1,210	3,529	1,259	1,539	2,082	0.02	35.28
Morocco		933	1,563	1,364	1,611	1,601	0.02	-0.62
Sudan		2,087	2,080	1,891	1,665	1,511	0.02	-9.25
Tunisia		1,027	1,212	1,221	1,182	1,440	0.02	21.83
Western Sahara		13	95	10	21	24	0.00	14.29
SOUTHERN AFRICA		**2,338,784**	**2,606,273**	**2,902,488**	**3,039,950**	**3,056,893**	**32.05**	**0.56**
Botswana		484,258	507,042	477,937	452,159	537,131	5.63	18.79
Lesotho		1,048,550	1,275,838	1,526,597	1,618,222	1,461,267	15.32	-9.70
Namibia		177,863	190,903	197,835	200,841	222,028	2.33	10.55
Swaziland		628,113	632,490	700,119	768,728	836,467	8.77	8.81
WEST AFRICA		**66,220**	**80,226**	**97,291**	**114,027**	**131,758**	**1.38**	**15.55**
Benin		1,293	1,234	1,299	1,553	1,930	0.02	24.28
Burkina Faso		588	628	697	816	1,052	0.01	28.92
Cabo Verde		602	554	534	635	785	0.01	23.62
Côte d'Ivoire		2,182	2,716	1,781	2,415	2,988	0.03	23.73
Gambia		631	748	805	1,142	1,051	0.01	-7.97
Ghana		11,395	18,435	18,538	22,953	27,361	0.29	19.20
Guinea		1,334	1,931	2,127	2,990	2,866	0.03	-4.15
Guinea-Bissau		174	230	198	212	193	0.00	-8.96
Liberia		498	545	586	708	716	0.01	1.13
Mali		792	1,190	1,192	1,268	1,516	0.02	19.56
Mauritania		118	271	269	241	445	0.00	84.65
Niger		244	293	296	369	533	0.01	44.44
Nigeria		42,651	46,853	64,402	73,282	84,552	0.89	15.38
Saint Helena		143	119	80	52	59	0.00	13.46
Senegal		2,333	3,005	2,965	3,600	3,926	0.04	9.06
Sierra Leone		766	955	930	991	995	0.01	0.40

671

SOUTH AFRICA

1. Arrivals of non-resident tourists at national borders, by country of residence

	2009	2010	2011	2012	2013	Market share 2013	% Change 2013-2012
Togo	476	519	592	800	790	0.01	-1.25
OTHER AFRICA	**29**	**64**		**5**	**900**	**0.01**	**17,900.00**
Other countries of Africa	29	64		5	900	0.01	17,900.00
AMERICAS	**333,528**	**458,249**	**433,135**	**513,610**	**545,492**	**5.72**	**6.21**
CARIBBEAN	**2,062**	**3,479**	**3,275**	**4,169**	**4,711**	**0.05**	**13.00**
Antigua and Barbuda	28	96	83	51	66	0.00	29.41
Bahamas	78	142	137	153	165	0.00	7.84
Barbados	126	207	174	168	126	0.00	-25.00
Bermuda	65	73	58	45	63	0.00	40.00
British Virgin Islands	26	4		3	2	0.00	-33.33
Cuba	577	1,247	1,139	1,801	2,008	0.02	11.49
Dominica	55	116	109	173	154	0.00	-10.98
Grenada	20	33	37	31	35	0.00	12.90
Haiti	179	192	98	98	141	0.00	43.88
Jamaica	497	695	663	743	688	0.01	-7.40
Puerto Rico	6	4	3	3	3	0.00	
Saint Lucia	38	41	43	36	41	0.00	13.89
Saint Vincent and the Grenadines	18	43	36	21	33	0.00	57.14
Trinidad and Tobago	347	585	693	839	1,182	0.01	40.88
Turks and Caicos Islands	1	1	2	4	4	0.00	
United States Virgin Islands	1						
CENTRAL AMERICA	**966**	**3,736**	**1,262**	**1,498**	**1,681**	**0.02**	**12.22**
Belize	66	59	57	78	61	0.00	-21.79
Costa Rica	284	921	401	372	510	0.01	37.10
El Salvador	113	391	93	146	124	0.00	-15.07
Guatemala	182	569	181	278	273	0.00	-1.80
Honduras	102	1,330	188	284	270	0.00	-4.93
Nicaragua	57	88	80	80	119	0.00	48.75
Panama	162	378	262	260	324	0.00	24.62
NORTH AMERICA	**278,360**	**353,572**	**348,627**	**396,923**	**420,042**	**4.40**	**5.82**
Canada	45,330	55,263	57,767	66,802	68,587	0.72	2.67
Greenland	32	9					
Mexico	2,674	15,923	3,246	3,477	4,077	0.04	17.26
United States of America	230,324	282,377	287,614	326,644	347,378	3.64	6.35
SOUTH AMERICA	**51,752**	**97,172**	**79,864**	**110,920**	**118,968**	**1.25**	**7.26**
Argentina	9,787	21,701	13,817	17,514	19,423	0.20	10.90
Bolivia	549	722	690	1,371	1,561	0.02	13.86
Brazil	32,256	53,756	54,183	78,376	82,730	0.87	5.56
Chile	2,581	7,260	3,210	3,507	4,036	0.04	15.08
Colombia	1,582	3,146	1,831	2,627	2,833	0.03	7.84
Ecuador	418	1,004	626	750	810	0.01	8.00
Falkland Islands, Malvinas	5	2					
French Guiana	67	38		4			
Guyana	293	273	246	254	211	0.00	-16.93
Paraguay	384	1,170	530	692	760	0.01	9.83
Peru	1,577	2,731	2,185	2,944	3,246	0.03	10.26
Suriname	64	95	91	69	73	0.00	5.80
Uruguay	944	2,683	1,162	1,370	1,575	0.02	14.96
Venezuela	1,245	2,591	1,293	1,442	1,710	0.02	18.59
OTHER AMERICAS	**388**	**290**	**107**	**100**	**90**	**0.00**	**-10.00**
Other countries of the Americas	388	290	107	100	90	0.00	-10.00
EAST ASIA AND THE PACIFIC	**216,051**	**293,141**	**304,704**	**401,353**	**436,852**	**4.58**	**8.84**
NORTH-EAST ASIA	**87,140**	**123,223**	**138,377**	**197,840**	**226,373**	**2.37**	**14.42**
China	34,561	65,920	84,862	132,327	151,053	1.58	14.15
Hong Kong, China	7,522	2,389	21	7	3	0.00	-57.14
Japan	20,513	27,577	26,284	34,415	41,099	0.43	19.42
Korea, Dem. People's Republic of	125	420	254	402	617	0.01	53.48
Korea, Republic of	14,311	17,489	18,290	19,817	21,756	0.23	9.78
Macao, China	122	74	1	6	1	0.00	-83.33

Yearbook of Tourism Statistics, Data 2009 – 2013, 2015 Edition

SOUTH AFRICA

1. Arrivals of non-resident tourists at national borders, by country of residence

	2009	2010	2011	2012	2013	Market share 2013	% Change 2013-2012
Mongolia	89	191	141	180	144	0.00	-20.00
Taiwan, Province of China	9,897	9,163	8,524	10,686	11,700	0.12	9.49
SOUTH-EAST ASIA	**27,405**	**41,759**	**43,542**	**60,563**	**62,131**	**0.65**	**2.59**
Brunei Darussalam	59	58	26	37	51	0.00	37.84
Cambodia	90	173	91	93	133	0.00	43.01
Indonesia	3,361	5,158	4,279	6,113	6,254	0.07	2.31
Lao People's Democratic Republic	19	72	74	107	48	0.00	-55.14
Malaysia	7,025	9,175	10,337	10,044	10,544	0.11	4.98
Myanmar	232	401	339	459	471	0.00	2.61
Philippines	3,359	9,553	9,203	16,238	17,011	0.18	4.76
Singapore	6,663	6,660	7,874	8,896	10,603	0.11	19.19
Thailand	5,300	7,174	7,468	8,693	9,103	0.10	4.72
Timor-Leste	17	17	3	1	42	0.00	4,100.00
Viet Nam	1,280	3,318	3,848	9,882	7,871	0.08	-20.35
AUSTRALASIA	**100,795**	**127,706**	**122,365**	**142,524**	**147,840**	**1.55**	**3.73**
Australia	82,753	107,905	103,506	120,315	124,898	1.31	3.81
New Zealand	18,042	19,801	18,859	22,209	22,942	0.24	3.30
MELANESIA	**229**	**217**	**281**	**270**	**345**	**0.00**	**27.78**
Fiji	157	119	151	182	171	0.00	-6.04
New Caledonia	4		2				
Norfolk Island	4		1				
Papua New Guinea	46	71	91	62	127	0.00	104.84
Solomon Islands	12	12	29	13	12	0.00	-7.69
Vanuatu	6	15	7	13	35	0.00	169.23
MICRONESIA	**132**	**75**	**46**	**40**	**42**	**0.00**	**5.00**
Christmas Island, Australia	18	3					
Cocos (Keeling) Islands	16	27	1	3			
Guam	24	6	2				
Kiribati	4	11	12	14	16	0.00	14.29
Marshall Islands	7	2	9	7	4	0.00	-42.86
Micronesia, Federated States of	12	8	4	3	6	0.00	100.00
Nauru	13	2	14	6	7	0.00	16.67
Northern Mariana Islands	29	15	1	6	7	0.00	16.67
Palau	9	1	3	1	2	0.00	100.00
POLYNESIA	**270**	**134**	**87**	**105**	**85**	**0.00**	**-19.05**
Cook Islands	4			1			
French Polynesia	140	55	4	3	2	0.00	-33.33
Pitcairn	4	2					
Samoa	97	46	48	53	54	0.00	1.89
Tokelau	6	7	2	3			
Tonga	18	20	24	27	17	0.00	-37.04
Tuvalu	1	4	9	18	12	0.00	-33.33
OTHER EAST ASIA AND THE PACIFIC	**80**	**27**	**6**	**11**	**36**	**0.00**	**227.27**
Other countries of Asia	27	10	1	1	32	0.00	3,100.00
Other countries of Oceania	53	17	5	10	4	0.00	-60.00
EUROPE	**1,248,467**	**1,354,579**	**1,306,794**	**1,434,177**	**1,517,015**	**15.91**	**5.78**
CENTRAL/EASTERN EUROPE	**38,908**	**47,576**	**43,370**	**52,766**	**54,848**	**0.58**	**3.95**
Armenia	58	133	100	163	186	0.00	14.11
Azerbaijan	136	280	160	237	304	0.00	28.27
Belarus	449	573	665	665	650	0.01	-2.26
Bulgaria	1,927	2,515	2,233	2,838	2,963	0.03	4.40
Czech Republic	5,889	6,058	6,169	6,922	6,894	0.07	-0.40
Estonia	754	959	676	776	976	0.01	25.77
Georgia	160	251	194	171	233	0.00	36.26
Hungary	2,480	3,115	2,882	3,253	3,321	0.03	2.09
Kazakhstan	517	743	619	590	649	0.01	10.00
Kyrgyzstan	105	37	7		78	0.00	
Latvia	693	646	608	704	674	0.01	-4.26
Lithuania	859	785	773	1,057	1,082	0.01	2.37

673

Yearbook of Tourism Statistics, Data 2009 – 2013, 2015 Edition

SOUTH AFRICA

1. Arrivals of non-resident tourists at national borders, by country of residence

	2009	2010	2011	2012	2013	Market share 2013	% Change 2013-2012
Poland	9,257	9,970	9,962	11,722	12,856	0.13	9.67
Republic of Moldova	114	181	149	205	167	0.00	-18.54
Romania	2,221	2,309	2,188	2,937	2,852	0.03	-2.89
Russian Federation	8,893	11,551	10,487	13,350	13,546	0.14	1.47
Slovakia	1,964	3,730	2,093	2,619	2,831	0.03	8.09
Tajikistan	31	44	53	49	39	0.00	-20.41
Turkmenistan	28	31	18	48	28	0.00	-41.67
Ukraine	2,233	3,469	3,142	4,276	4,307	0.05	0.72
Uzbekistan	140	196	192	184	212	0.00	15.22
NORTHERN EUROPE	**568,656**	**579,063**	**542,563**	**566,984**	**569,416**	**5.97**	**0.43**
Channel Islands	7	6		2			
Denmark	22,540	24,212	22,970	25,149	25,968	0.27	3.26
Faeroe Islands	46	23					
Finland	9,404	10,511	10,090	10,203	10,605	0.11	3.94
Iceland	492	694	598	733	807	0.01	10.10
Ireland	35,166	30,518	29,098	28,862	27,593	0.29	-4.40
Isle of Man	45	50	13		3	0.00	
Norway	18,140	19,330	20,556	23,156	24,343	0.26	5.13
Sweden	36,335	40,662	38,754	40,856	43,498	0.46	6.47
United Kingdom	446,481	453,057	420,484	438,023	436,599	4.58	-0.33
SOUTHERN EUROPE	**114,372**	**140,473**	**131,426**	**149,220**	**164,027**	**1.72**	**9.92**
Albania	175	223	115	110	156	0.00	41.82
Andorra	66	62	32	52	73	0.00	40.38
Bosnia and Herzegovina	173	267	267	254	219	0.00	-13.78
Croatia	1,103	1,266	1,159	1,672	1,655	0.02	-1.02
Gibraltar	14	6		1	2	0.00	100.00
Greece	7,296	8,172	5,822	6,157	6,380	0.07	3.62
Holy See	13	8	10	27			
Italy	50,305	54,645	54,628	61,318	67,259	0.71	9.69
Malta	473	568	550	567	664	0.01	17.11
Portugal	26,895	40,677	40,302	48,213	52,580	0.55	9.06
San Marino	36	25	41	38	24	0.00	-36.84
Serbia and Montenegro	1,138	441	254	235	1,915	0.02	714.89
Slovenia	958	2,211	1,037	1,178	1,063	0.01	-9.76
Spain	25,727	31,902	27,209	29,398	32,037	0.34	8.98
WESTERN EUROPE	**502,348**	**556,227**	**559,664**	**629,451**	**691,362**	**7.25**	**9.84**
Austria	17,210	20,389	21,841	25,179	28,787	0.30	14.33
Belgium	36,720	39,304	40,478	44,125	46,262	0.49	4.84
France	103,985	115,401	105,420	122,244	133,787	1.40	9.44
Germany	196,643	215,800	235,774	266,333	300,739	3.15	12.92
Liechtenstein	237	200	213	271	280	0.00	3.32
Luxembourg	1,309	1,259	1,271	1,488	1,707	0.02	14.72
Monaco	94	61	93	68	104	0.00	52.94
Netherlands	114,431	124,088	113,846	117,936	120,763	1.27	2.40
Switzerland	31,719	39,725	40,728	51,807	58,933	0.62	13.75
EAST MEDITERRANEAN EUROPE	**24,183**	**31,240**	**29,771**	**35,756**	**37,362**	**0.39**	**4.49**
Cyprus	1,585	1,972	1,672	1,659	1,634	0.02	-1.51
Israel	14,950	19,353	17,751	20,640	22,116	0.23	7.15
Turkey	7,648	9,915	10,348	13,457	13,612	0.14	1.15
MIDDLE EAST	**19,262**	**21,151**	**20,168**	**22,869**	**25,837**	**0.27**	**12.98**
Bahrain	174	294	177	194	203	0.00	4.64
Egypt	4,999	5,967	6,251	7,308	7,908	0.08	8.21
Iraq	310	333	285	296	303	0.00	2.36
Jordan	1,509	1,938	1,696	1,818	2,169	0.02	19.31
Kuwait	550	651	632	650	956	0.01	47.08
Lebanon	1,933	3,183	2,720	3,252	3,333	0.03	2.49
Libya	1,181	1,711	977	951	1,441	0.02	51.52
Oman	298	433	349	426	411	0.00	-3.52
Palestine	147	305	245	241	208	0.00	-13.69

674

SOUTH AFRICA

1. Arrivals of non-resident tourists at national borders, by country of residence

	2009	2010	2011	2012	2013	Market share 2013	% Change 2013-2012
Qatar	399	361	231	303	237	0.00	-21.78
Saudi Arabia	5,328	3,570	4,733	5,305	6,303	0.07	18.81
Syrian Arab Republic	420	707	498	573	602	0.01	5.06
United Arab Emirates	1,728	1,332	1,072	1,180	1,296	0.01	9.83
Yemen	286	366	302	372	467	0.00	25.54
SOUTH ASIA	**74,938**	**97,552**	**119,147**	**142,010**	**144,545**	**1.52**	**1.79**
Afghanistan	998	675	206	184	296	0.00	60.87
Bangladesh	2,943	3,829	3,900	5,480	4,896	0.05	-10.66
Bhutan	9	35	27	36	45	0.00	25.00
India	55,203	71,587	90,367	106,774	112,100	1.18	4.99
Iran, Islamic Republic of	4,037	4,566	4,773	3,806	2,720	0.03	-28.53
Maldives	38	86	36	35	46	0.00	31.43
Nepal	309	543	490	456	626	0.01	37.28
Pakistan	9,596	13,359	16,221	20,799	19,474	0.20	-6.37
Sri Lanka	1,805	2,872	3,127	4,440	4,342	0.05	-2.21
NOT SPECIFIED	**36,474**	**115,381**	**25,800**	**26,148**	**20,125**	**0.21**	**-23.03**
Other countries of the World	36,474	115,381	25,800	26,148	20,125	0.21	-23.03

Yearbook of Tourism Statistics, Data 2009 – 2013, 2015 Edition

SOUTH AFRICA

2. Arrivals of non-resident visitors at national borders, by country of residence

		2009	2010	2011	2012	2013	Market share 2013	% Change 2013-2012
TOTAL	(*)	**9,531,615**	**11,303,087**	**12,097,490**	**13,069,034**	**14,317,908**	**100.00**	**9.56**
AFRICA		**7,406,780**	**8,725,042**	**9,654,943**	**10,305,075**	**11,402,212**	**79.64**	**10.65**
EAST AFRICA		**3,259,300**	**3,837,056**	**4,115,170**	**4,725,255**	**5,487,975**	**38.33**	**16.14**
Burundi		1,041	952	1,049	1,535	1,850	0.01	20.52
Comoros		164	237	228	286	418	0.00	46.15
Djibouti		81	86	102	94	91	0.00	-3.19
Eritrea		617	645	718	950	734	0.01	-22.74
Ethiopia		10,971	9,857	9,618	8,459	9,590	0.07	13.37
Kenya		27,734	32,081	33,651	36,354	38,626	0.27	6.25
Madagascar		2,756	3,208	3,099	4,978	6,695	0.05	34.49
Malawi		149,524	137,023	146,432	151,553	180,519	1.26	19.11
Mauritius		15,525	19,743	19,893	20,525	21,825	0.15	6.33
Mozambique		1,324,445	1,328,731	1,389,253	1,502,618	1,754,003	12.25	16.73
Reunion		632	370	3		1	0.00	
Rwanda		3,103	3,076	3,014	3,604	3,826	0.03	6.16
Seychelles		2,367	3,115	3,588	3,571	5,132	0.04	43.71
Somalia		2,876	2,714	836	223	121	0.00	-45.74
Uganda		13,675	15,597	17,024	17,625	19,163	0.13	8.73
United Republic of Tanzania		16,238	21,827	32,059	39,645	42,016	0.29	5.98
Zambia		160,995	172,215	174,782	181,206	191,703	1.34	5.79
Zimbabwe		1,526,556	2,085,579	2,279,821	2,752,029	3,211,662	22.43	16.70
CENTRAL AFRICA		**87,973**	**90,143**	**90,087**	**102,181**	**114,301**	**0.80**	**11.86**
Angola		38,814	39,535	39,952	48,608	58,065	0.41	19.46
Cameroon		4,731	6,737	5,610	6,585	6,479	0.05	-1.61
Central African Republic		125	175	144	200	202	0.00	1.00
Chad		260	262	355	432	501	0.00	15.97
Congo		6,654	4,623	3,393	3,945	4,623	0.03	17.19
Democratic Republic of the Congo		31,569	32,077	33,811	34,348	35,571	0.25	3.56
Equatorial Guinea		430	347	351	441	526	0.00	19.27
Gabon		5,218	6,244	6,346	7,379	8,115	0.06	9.97
Sao Tome and Principe		172	143	125	243	219	0.00	-9.88
NORTH AFRICA		**5,653**	**8,855**	**6,115**	**6,245**	**6,944**	**0.05**	**11.19**
Algeria		1,359	3,586	1,346	1,623	2,143	0.01	32.04
Morocco		963	1,642	1,444	1,686	1,693	0.01	0.42
Sudan		2,198	2,216	2,043	1,709	1,624	0.01	-4.97
Tunisia		1,119	1,316	1,270	1,206	1,456	0.01	20.73
Western Sahara		14	95	12	21	28	0.00	33.33
SOUTHERN AFRICA		**3,983,336**	**4,703,731**	**5,340,433**	**5,351,099**	**5,653,832**	**39.49**	**5.66**
Botswana		822,305	829,518	782,223	717,813	886,947	6.19	23.56
Lesotho		1,890,976	2,610,507	3,160,694	3,122,796	3,056,859	21.35	-2.11
Namibia		212,098	226,541	235,780	234,205	263,290	1.84	12.42
Swaziland		1,057,957	1,037,165	1,161,736	1,276,285	1,446,736	10.10	13.36
WEST AFRICA		**70,372**	**85,174**	**103,137**	**120,289**	**138,219**	**0.97**	**14.91**
Benin		1,363	1,334	1,387	1,628	2,014	0.01	23.71
Burkina Faso		637	643	732	834	1,111	0.01	33.21
Cabo Verde		679	636	603	713	876	0.01	22.86
Côte d'Ivoire		2,303	2,789	1,839	2,498	3,069	0.02	22.86
Gambia		722	801	845	1,187	1,078	0.01	-9.18
Ghana		12,419	19,948	20,134	24,857	29,383	0.21	18.21
Guinea		1,478	2,023	2,239	3,131	3,046	0.02	-2.71
Guinea-Bissau		205	260	216	230	207	0.00	-10.00
Liberia		540	578	639	737	760	0.01	3.12
Mali		832	1,259	1,266	1,298	1,569	0.01	20.88
Mauritania		126	280	278	245	456	0.00	86.12
Niger		273	299	307	380	547	0.00	43.95
Nigeria		44,817	49,418	67,769	76,787	88,096	0.62	14.73
Saint Helena		182	131	81	53	62	0.00	16.98
Senegal		2,408	3,115	3,068	3,713	4,008	0.03	7.95
Sierra Leone		884	1,126	1,115	1,165	1,123	0.01	-3.61

676

SOUTH AFRICA

2. Arrivals of non-resident visitors at national borders, by country of residence

	2009	2010	2011	2012	2013	Market share 2013	% Change 2013-2012
Togo	504	534	619	833	814	0.01	-2.28
OTHER AFRICA	**146**	**83**	**1**	**6**	**941**	**0.01**	**15,583.33**
Other countries of Africa	146	83	1	6	941	0.01	15,583.33
AMERICAS	**376,485**	**505,235**	**488,018**	**566,842**	**602,739**	**4.21**	**6.33**
CARIBBEAN	**2,386**	**3,873**	**3,707**	**4,733**	**5,189**	**0.04**	**9.63**
Antigua and Barbuda	33	112	98	67	83	0.00	23.88
Bahamas	95	143	148	186	176	0.00	-5.38
Barbados	141	221	185	192	136	0.00	-29.17
Bermuda	116	97	62	47	65	0.00	38.30
British Virgin Islands				3	2	0.00	-33.33
Cuba	707	1,362	1,301	2,001	2,160	0.02	7.95
Dominica	56	132	120	218	182	0.00	-16.51
Grenada	21	34	38	31	36	0.00	16.13
Haiti	206	202	120	109	163	0.00	49.54
Jamaica	578	851	785	875	810	0.01	-7.43
Puerto Rico	6	5	6	3	4	0.00	33.33
Saint Lucia	39	41	54	41	43	0.00	4.88
Saint Vincent and the Grenadines	20	46	40	23	38	0.00	65.22
Trinidad and Tobago	366	623	748	932	1,287	0.01	38.09
Turks and Caicos Islands	2	4	2	5	4	0.00	-20.00
CENTRAL AMERICA	**1,113**	**3,945**	**1,535**	**1,676**	**1,813**	**0.01**	**8.17**
Belize	83	65	62	84	67	0.00	-20.24
Costa Rica	335	984	490	489	577	0.00	18.00
El Salvador	123	406	99	151	128	0.00	-15.23
Guatemala	207	597	194	292	293	0.00	0.34
Honduras	132	1,343	202	306	284	0.00	-7.19
Nicaragua	62	97	85	83	126	0.00	51.81
Panama	171	453	403	271	338	0.00	24.72
NORTH AMERICA	**314,769**	**392,007**	**392,937**	**440,472**	**468,674**	**3.27**	**6.40**
Canada	51,233	61,522	64,857	73,620	76,027	0.53	3.27
Greenland	34	11					
Mexico	2,903	16,447	3,556	3,895	4,502	0.03	15.58
United States of America	260,599	314,027	324,524	362,957	388,145	2.71	6.94
SOUTH AMERICA	**57,797**	**105,091**	**89,726**	**119,852**	**126,967**	**0.89**	**5.94**
Argentina	10,656	22,715	14,622	18,204	20,142	0.14	10.65
Bolivia	615	789	774	1,516	1,719	0.01	13.39
Brazil	36,722	59,838	62,083	85,454	88,839	0.62	3.96
Chile	2,911	7,562	3,493	3,733	4,279	0.03	14.63
Colombia	1,656	3,273	1,962	2,729	2,949	0.02	8.06
Ecuador	433	1,047	673	793	890	0.01	12.23
Falkland Islands, Malvinas	5	2					
French Guiana	73	40	1	4			
Guyana	12	5	295	325	255	0.00	-21.54
Paraguay	457	1,250	584	748	804	0.01	7.49
Peru	1,852	3,030	2,452	3,281	3,546	0.02	8.08
Suriname	67	99	91	71	77	0.00	8.45
Uruguay	981	2,738	1,259	1,436	1,654	0.01	15.18
Venezuela	1,357	2,703	1,437	1,558	1,813	0.01	16.37
OTHER AMERICAS	**420**	**319**	**113**	**109**	**96**	**0.00**	**-11.93**
Other countries of the Americas	420	319	113	109	96	0.00	-11.93
EAST ASIA AND THE PACIFIC	**238,400**	**322,335**	**337,159**	**432,223**	**469,989**	**3.28**	**8.74**
NORTH-EAST ASIA	**95,720**	**135,436**	**152,123**	**211,263**	**241,613**	**1.69**	**14.37**
China	36,480	71,921	92,587	140,607	160,324	1.12	14.02
Hong Kong, China	7,821	2,523	25	8	3	0.00	-62.50
Japan	24,424	30,936	29,558	37,097	43,296	0.30	16.71
Korea, Dem. People's Republic of	137	457	292	437	670	0.00	53.32
Korea, Republic of	15,714	18,690	19,639	21,126	23,378	0.16	10.66
Macao, China	132	83	1	6	1	0.00	-83.33
Mongolia	92	200	141	190	153	0.00	-19.47

677

SOUTH AFRICA

2. Arrivals of non-resident visitors at national borders, by country of residence

	2009	2010	2011	2012	2013	Market share 2013	% Change 2013-2012
Taiwan, Province of China	10,920	10,626	9,880	11,792	13,788	0.10	16.93
SOUTH-EAST ASIA	**29,776**	**45,485**	**48,418**	**65,455**	**66,933**	**0.47**	**2.26**
Brunei Darussalam	65	63	26	37	52	0.00	40.54
Cambodia	95	185	105	93	137	0.00	47.31
Indonesia	3,537	5,370	4,506	6,468	6,595	0.05	1.96
Lao People's Democratic Republic	23	88	101	128	53	0.00	-58.59
Malaysia	7,767	9,841	11,192	10,743	11,322	0.08	5.39
Myanmar	271	456	413	510	561	0.00	10.00
Philippines	4,103	11,406	11,925	19,134	19,701	0.14	2.96
Singapore	7,079	7,175	8,504	9,480	11,203	0.08	18.18
Thailand	5,487	7,480	7,733	8,897	9,296	0.06	4.48
Timor-Leste	18	17		1	54	0.00	5,300.00
Viet Nam	1,331	3,404	3,913	9,964	7,959	0.06	-20.12
AUSTRALASIA	**111,609**	**140,935**	**136,187**	**155,053**	**160,907**	**1.12**	**3.78**
Australia	91,951	119,455	115,699	131,209	136,309	0.95	3.89
New Zealand	19,658	21,480	20,488	23,844	24,598	0.17	3.16
MELANESIA	**224**	**219**	**285**	**279**	**365**	**0.00**	**30.82**
Fiji	164	124	154	187	177	0.00	-5.35
New Caledonia	6		2				
Norfolk Island	4	1	1				
Papua New Guinea	32	67	92	62	133	0.00	114.52
Solomon Islands	12	12	29	13	12	0.00	-7.69
Vanuatu	6	15	7	17	43	0.00	152.94
MICRONESIA	**142**	**79**	**46**	**50**	**46**	**0.00**	**-8.00**
Christmas Island, Australia	19	4					
Cocos (Keeling) Islands	17	28	1	3			
Guam	27	6	2				
Kiribati	4	12	12	20	16	0.00	-20.00
Marshall Islands	7	2	9	7	4	0.00	-42.86
Micronesia, Federated States of	13	8	4	3	6	0.00	100.00
Nauru	13	3	14	6	8	0.00	33.33
Northern Mariana Islands	33	15	1	10	10	0.00	
Palau	9	1	3	1	2	0.00	100.00
POLYNESIA	**304**	**148**	**90**	**110**	**87**	**0.00**	**-20.91**
Cook Islands	4	1		1			
French Polynesia	171	64	4	3	2	0.00	-33.33
Pitcairn	4	2					
Samoa	100	50	51	55	55	0.00	
Tokelau	6	7	2	3			
Tonga	18	20	24	30	18	0.00	-40.00
Tuvalu	1	4	9	18	12	0.00	-33.33
OTHER EAST ASIA AND THE PACIFIC	**625**	**33**	**10**	**13**	**38**	**0.00**	**192.31**
Other countries of Asia	551	10	5	1	34	0.00	3,300.00
Other countries of Oceania	74	23	5	12	4	0.00	-66.67
EUROPE	**1,367,291**	**1,473,071**	**1,431,337**	**1,552,241**	**1,629,641**	**11.38**	**4.99**
CENTRAL/EASTERN EUROPE	**42,380**	**51,606**	**47,630**	**57,627**	**59,774**	**0.42**	**3.73**
Armenia	59	146	103	172	189	0.00	9.88
Azerbaijan	140	287	165	241	331	0.00	37.34
Belarus	493	584	707	687	688	0.00	0.15
Bulgaria	2,091	2,684	2,414	3,219	3,417	0.02	6.15
Czech Republic	6,333	6,520	6,662	7,388	7,274	0.05	-1.54
Estonia	779	1,050	732	849	1,025	0.01	20.73
Georgia	168	258	210	198	254	0.00	28.28
Hungary	2,743	3,418	3,072	3,479	3,575	0.02	2.76
Kazakhstan		780	670	636	663	0.00	4.25
Kyrgyzstan	140	73	10	1	79	0.00	7,800.00
Latvia	749	678	648	766	709	0.00	-7.44
Lithuania	1,094	852	829	1,104	1,142	0.01	3.44
Poland	10,106	10,897	11,220	12,883	14,159	0.10	9.90

678

Yearbook of Tourism Statistics, Data 2009 – 2013, 2015 Edition

SOUTH AFRICA

2. Arrivals of non-resident visitors at national borders, by country of residence

	2009	2010	2011	2012	2013	Market share 2013	% Change 2013-2012
Republic of Moldova	124	189	158	209	176	0.00	-15.79
Romania	2,433	2,453	2,318	3,237	3,093	0.02	-4.45
Russian Federation	10,097	12,751	11,756	14,835	14,952	0.10	0.79
Slovakia	2,101	3,971	2,319	2,819	3,045	0.02	8.02
Tajikistan	31	45	55	49	39	0.00	-20.41
Turkmenistan	30	32	19	50	28	0.00	-44.00
Ukraine	2,525	3,733	3,365	4,620	4,720	0.03	2.16
Uzbekistan	144	205	198	185	216	0.00	16.76
NORTHERN EUROPE	**614,635**	**626,504**	**589,965**	**609,428**	**610,638**	**4.26**	**0.20**
Channel Islands	7	8		2			
Denmark	24,535	26,093	25,016	26,897	27,509	0.19	2.28
Faeroe Islands	50	24					
Finland	10,140	11,527	10,960	11,105	11,517	0.08	3.71
Iceland	587	759	684	780	944	0.01	21.03
Ireland	38,280	33,935	31,935	31,358	30,393	0.21	-3.08
Isle of Man	45	53	13	1	3	0.00	200.00
Norway	19,631	20,909	22,425	24,686	25,722	0.18	4.20
Sweden	38,581	43,125	41,155	43,118	45,482	0.32	5.48
United Kingdom	482,779	490,071	457,777	471,481	469,068	3.28	-0.51
SOUTHERN EUROPE	**138,097**	**165,831**	**161,435**	**179,267**	**189,197**	**1.32**	**5.54**
Albania	198	243	128	113	161	0.00	42.48
Andorra	79	76	46	54	75	0.00	38.89
Bosnia and Herzegovina	178	274	268	265	227	0.00	-14.34
Croatia	1,177	1,326	1,213	1,799	1,739	0.01	-3.34
Gibraltar	16	6		1	2	0.00	100.00
Greece	8,576	9,086	6,672	6,805	7,075	0.05	3.97
Italy	59,599	63,255	63,917	69,018	74,951	0.52	8.60
Malta	506	614	593	630	710	0.00	12.70
Portugal	35,428	51,785	54,770	65,583	66,448	0.46	1.32
San Marino	43	27	47	42	26	0.00	-38.10
Slovenia	1,020	2,255	1,113	1,272	2,168	0.02	70.44
Spain	31,277	36,884	32,668	33,685	35,615	0.25	5.73
WESTERN EUROPE	**544,140**	**595,169**	**599,472**	**667,128**	**729,259**	**5.09**	**9.31**
Austria	18,508	21,697	23,294	26,622	30,186	0.21	13.39
Belgium	40,555	43,000	44,432	47,622	49,505	0.35	3.95
France	117,523	127,804	116,873	133,526	144,868	1.01	8.49
Germany	209,644	227,514	248,400	278,539	313,787	2.19	12.65
Liechtenstein	265	220	226	290	292	0.00	0.69
Luxembourg	1,465	1,333	1,343	1,544	1,779	0.01	15.22
Monaco	113	76	113	71	121	0.00	70.42
Netherlands	121,274	130,668	120,523	123,888	126,801	0.89	2.35
Switzerland	34,793	42,857	44,268	55,026	61,920	0.43	12.53
EAST MEDITERRANEAN EUROPE	**26,536**	**33,388**	**32,549**	**38,510**	**40,773**	**0.28**	**5.88**
Cyprus	1,726	2,113	1,821	1,770	1,747	0.01	-1.30
Israel	16,368	20,594	19,489	22,332	24,192	0.17	8.33
Turkey	8,442	10,681	11,239	14,408	14,834	0.10	2.96
OTHER EUROPE	**1,503**	**573**	**286**	**281**			
Other countries of Europe	1,503	573	286	281			
MIDDLE EAST	**20,189**	**22,401**	**21,192**	**23,867**	**26,937**	**0.19**	**12.86**
Bahrain	180	299	178	198	203	0.00	2.53
Egypt	5,227	6,222	6,536	7,674	8,347	0.06	8.77
Iraq	332	340	288	305	309	0.00	1.31
Jordan	1,604	2,103	1,776	2,108	2,509	0.02	19.02
Kuwait	561	680	636	675	973	0.01	44.15
Lebanon	2,148	3,456	2,938	3,396	3,431	0.02	1.03
Libya	1,351	2,078	1,297	1,024	1,555	0.01	51.86
Oman	299	444	354	433	418	0.00	-3.46
Palestine	165	345	282	255	210	0.00	-17.65
Qatar	406	362	237	303	248	0.00	-18.15

SOUTH AFRICA

2. Arrivals of non-resident visitors at national borders, by country of residence

	2009	2010	2011	2012	2013	Market share 2013	% Change 2013-2012
Saudi Arabia	5,415	3,621	4,761	5,327	6,329	0.04	18.81
Syrian Arab Republic	438	722	512	578	618	0.00	6.92
United Arab Emirates	1,771	1,358	1,092	1,214	1,315	0.01	8.32
Yemen	292	371	305	377	472	0.00	25.20
SOUTH ASIA	**82,043**	**109,526**	**134,941**	**159,023**	**162,003**	**1.13**	**1.87**
Afghanistan	1,238	882	220	203	322	0.00	58.62
Bangladesh	3,463	4,821	5,096	6,970	6,590	0.05	-5.45
Bhutan	9	37	27	39	45	0.00	15.38
India	59,878	79,529	101,255	117,904	122,936	0.86	4.27
Iran, Islamic Republic of	4,111	4,637	4,856	3,865	2,785	0.02	-27.94
Maldives	47	88	39	41	56	0.00	36.59
Nepal	345	574	490	464	635	0.00	36.85
Pakistan	10,792	15,428	19,009	24,147	23,389	0.16	-3.14
Sri Lanka	2,160	3,530	3,949	5,390	5,245	0.04	-2.69
NOT SPECIFIED	**40,427**	**145,477**	**29,900**	**29,763**	**24,387**	**0.17**	**-18.06**
Other countries of the World	40,427	145,477	29,900	29,763	24,387	0.17	-18.06

Yearbook of Tourism Statistics, Data 2009 – 2013, 2015 Edition

SPAIN

1. Arrivals of non-resident tourists at national borders, by country of residence

	2009	2010	2011	2012	2013	Market share 2013	% Change 2013-2012
TOTAL	**52,177,640**	**52,676,972**	**56,176,886**	**57,464,496**	**60,661,073**	**100.00**	**5.56**
AFRICA	**267,458**	**302,420**	**508,832**	**491,930**	**484,384**	**0.80**	**-1.53**
OTHER AFRICA	**267,458**	**302,420**	**508,832**	**491,930**	**484,384**	**0.80**	**-1.53**
All countries of Africa	267,458	302,420	508,832	491,930	484,384	0.80	-1.53
AMERICAS	**2,573,760**	**2,617,572**	**2,886,793**	**3,123,095**	**3,073,174**	**5.07**	**-1.60**
NORTH AMERICA	**1,532,615**	**1,509,219**	**1,612,374**	**1,769,402**	**1,706,627**	**2.81**	**-3.55**
Canada	182,604	189,452	216,048	260,898	245,816	0.41	-5.78
Mexico	216,300	185,740	259,028	269,305	265,863	0.44	-1.28
United States of America	1,133,711	1,134,027	1,137,298	1,239,199	1,194,948	1.97	-3.57
SOUTH AMERICA	**536,466**	**586,557**	**823,699**	**972,023**	**965,311**	**1.59**	**-0.69**
Argentina	257,463	276,408	306,759	348,102	363,630	0.60	4.46
Brazil	227,731	241,214	369,909	410,182	394,366	0.65	-3.86
Chile	24,222	17,706	37,671	40,618	57,604	0.09	41.82
Venezuela	27,050	51,229	109,360	173,121	149,711	0.25	-13.52
OTHER AMERICAS	**504,679**	**521,796**	**450,720**	**381,670**	**401,236**	**0.66**	**5.13**
Other countries of the Americas	504,679	521,796	450,720	381,670	401,236	0.66	5.13
EAST ASIA AND THE PACIFIC	**504,634**	**961,998**	**1,176,192**	**1,344,930**	**1,520,167**	**2.51**	**13.03**
NORTH-EAST ASIA	**229,856**	**332,930**	**342,979**	**357,671**	**374,175**	**0.62**	**4.61**
Japan	229,856	332,930	342,979	357,671	374,175	0.62	4.61
OTHER EAST ASIA AND THE PACIFIC	**274,778**	**629,068**	**833,213**	**987,259**	**1,145,992**	**1.89**	**16.08**
Other countries East Asia/Pacific	274,778	629,068	833,213	987,259	1,145,992	1.89	16.08
EUROPE	**48,204,400**	**48,290,225**	**51,420,001**	**52,242,810**	**55,264,613**	**91.10**	**5.78**
CENTRAL/EASTERN EUROPE	**421,993**	**605,276**	**862,841**	**1,202,073**	**1,581,785**	**2.61**	**31.59**
Russian Federation	421,993	605,276	862,841	1,202,073	1,581,785	2.61	31.59
NORTHERN EUROPE	**18,094,666**	**17,191,654**	**18,797,582**	**18,981,669**	**20,472,064**	**33.75**	**7.85**
Denmark	960,009	937,726	909,515	929,258	984,707	1.62	5.97
Finland	517,203	507,161	574,039	581,777	656,897	1.08	12.91
Ireland	1,463,913	1,177,253	1,284,168	1,189,278	1,270,038	2.09	6.79
Norway	886,830	1,016,339	1,120,269	1,250,357	1,517,668	2.50	21.38
Sweden	969,949	1,112,935	1,294,206	1,406,949	1,715,477	2.83	21.93
United Kingdom	13,296,762	12,440,240	13,615,385	13,624,050	14,327,277	23.62	5.16
SOUTHERN EUROPE	**5,331,450**	**5,534,807**	**5,760,483**	**5,452,138**	**4,987,697**	**8.22**	**-8.52**
Greece	81,787	148,881	117,578	89,328	66,133	0.11	-25.97
Italy	3,188,147	3,490,352	3,764,818	3,537,932	3,251,019	5.36	-8.11
Portugal	2,061,516	1,895,574	1,878,087	1,824,878	1,670,545	2.75	-8.46
WESTERN EUROPE	**22,326,428**	**22,655,560**	**23,958,616**	**24,621,651**	**26,052,627**	**42.95**	**5.81**
Austria	506,161	561,190	579,430	564,068	568,311	0.94	0.75
Belgium	1,599,004	1,623,375	1,756,695	1,701,782	1,873,221	3.09	10.07
France	7,955,104	8,125,354	8,375,035	8,913,399	9,525,432	15.70	6.87
Germany	8,935,147	8,814,070	8,975,236	9,318,737	9,854,760	16.25	5.75
Luxembourg	113,782	97,693	133,654	120,066	126,187	0.21	5.10
Netherlands	2,089,048	2,276,393	2,771,903	2,559,989	2,617,460	4.31	2.24
Switzerland	1,128,182	1,157,485	1,366,663	1,443,610	1,487,256	2.45	3.02
OTHER EUROPE	**2,029,863**	**2,302,928**	**2,040,479**	**1,985,279**	**2,170,440**	**3.58**	**9.33**
Other countries of Europe	2,029,863	2,302,928	2,040,479	1,985,279	2,170,440	3.58	9.33
MIDDLE EAST		**68,276**	**110,027**	**170,435**	**216,950**	**0.36**	**27.29**
All countries of Middle East		68,276	110,027	170,435	216,950	0.36	27.29
SOUTH ASIA		**29,615**	**73,842**	**91,296**	**101,785**	**0.17**	**11.49**
All countries of South Asia		29,615	73,842	91,296	101,785	0.17	11.49
NOT SPECIFIED	**627,388**	**406,866**	**1,199**				
Other countries of the World	627,388	406,866	1,199				

681

Yearbook of Tourism Statistics, Data 2009 – 2013, 2015 Edition

SPAIN

3. Arrivals of non-resident tourists in hotels and similar establishments, by country of residence

	2009	2010	2011	2012	2013	Market share 2013	% Change 2013-2012
TOTAL (*)	32,002,230	35,655,543	39,542,091	39,936,727	41,251,542	100.00	3.29
AFRICA	327,060	387,765	421,398	456,897	501,349	1.22	9.73
SOUTHERN AFRICA	38,478	41,754	55,232	64,979	56,705	0.14	-12.73
South Africa	38,478	41,754	55,232	64,979	56,705	0.14	-12.73
OTHER AFRICA	288,582	346,011	366,166	391,918	444,644	1.08	13.45
Other countries of Africa	288,582	346,011	366,166	391,918	444,644	1.08	13.45
AMERICAS	3,198,470	3,835,945	4,345,144	4,195,711	4,150,260	10.06	-1.08
NORTH AMERICA	2,061,419	2,515,894	2,804,083	2,718,880	2,614,834	6.34	-3.83
Canada	259,147	396,790	480,827	470,431	376,993	0.91	-19.86
United States of America	1,532,535	1,813,566	1,994,258	1,958,383	1,942,857	4.71	-0.79
Other countries of North America	269,737	305,538	328,998	290,066	294,984	0.72	1.70
SOUTH AMERICA	297,077	416,112	510,197	445,046	443,889	1.08	-0.26
Brazil	297,077	416,112	510,197	445,046	443,889	1.08	-0.26
OTHER AMERICAS	839,974	903,939	1,030,864	1,031,785	1,091,537	2.65	5.79
Other countries of the Americas	839,974	903,939	1,030,864	1,031,785	1,091,537	2.65	5.79
EAST ASIA AND THE PACIFIC	1,188,417	1,568,090	1,836,473	2,023,202	2,313,317	5.61	14.34
NORTH-EAST ASIA	751,444	989,141	1,081,627	1,163,941	1,354,258	3.28	16.35
China	151,439	206,930	284,511	343,168	441,055	1.07	28.52
Japan	511,770	611,531	607,371	626,086	683,383	1.66	9.15
Korea, Republic of	88,235	170,680	189,745	194,687	229,820	0.56	18.05
AUSTRALASIA	153,006	198,063	244,783	252,789	281,822	0.68	11.49
Australia	153,006	198,063	244,783	252,789	281,822	0.68	11.49
OTHER EAST ASIA AND THE PACIFIC	283,967	380,886	510,063	606,472	677,237	1.64	11.67
Other countries of Asia	251,016	343,701	473,985	572,714	639,779	1.55	11.71
Other countries of Oceania	32,951	37,185	36,078	33,758	37,458	0.09	10.96
EUROPE	26,584,436	29,075,912	32,181,824	32,527,822	33,473,161	81.14	2.91
CENTRAL/EASTERN EUROPE	1,358,788	1,744,666	2,331,130	2,607,080	2,822,450	6.84	8.26
Bulgaria	53,999	63,675	70,231	69,501	62,781	0.15	-9.67
Czech Republic	165,205	163,097	197,668	196,883	169,153	0.41	-14.08
Estonia	29,096	29,435	33,386	34,821	43,191	0.10	24.04
Hungary	83,954	99,470	104,459	107,748	104,206	0.25	-3.29
Latvia	24,899	33,872	35,176	35,594	36,826	0.09	3.46
Lithuania	36,858	40,081	48,818	51,441	57,189	0.14	11.17
Poland	311,680	396,108	512,299	484,494	494,162	1.20	2.00
Romania	149,479	191,711	221,971	203,600	200,647	0.49	-1.45
Russian Federation	430,772	630,965	979,383	1,273,622	1,484,739	3.60	16.58
Slovakia	36,015	44,422	50,017	54,259	52,537	0.13	-3.17
Ukraine	36,831	51,830	77,722	95,117	117,019	0.28	23.03
NORTHERN EUROPE	8,486,289	9,031,576	9,804,697	10,515,445	11,061,086	26.81	5.19
Denmark	366,740	407,404	463,109	466,046	475,730	1.15	2.08
Finland	235,041	248,601	275,427	287,816	327,868	0.79	13.92
Iceland	33,424	32,175	37,859	39,502	39,223	0.10	-0.71
Ireland	550,697	522,505	546,755	564,870	585,472	1.42	3.65
Norway	319,183	388,160	445,760	523,915	614,088	1.49	17.21
Sweden	557,479	645,936	742,767	823,935	919,171	2.23	11.56
United Kingdom	6,423,725	6,786,795	7,293,020	7,809,361	8,099,534	19.63	3.72
SOUTHERN EUROPE	3,553,376	4,031,634	4,259,081	3,657,274	3,356,802	8.14	-8.22
Greece	129,427	175,801	146,534	102,738	99,551	0.24	-3.10
Italy	2,237,467	2,543,005	2,833,011	2,420,081	2,195,871	5.32	-9.26
Malta	26,942	25,416	25,337	26,228	19,597	0.05	-25.28
Portugal	1,125,591	1,250,973	1,214,535	1,070,205	1,009,310	2.45	-5.69
Slovenia	33,949	36,439	39,664	38,022	32,473	0.08	-14.59
WESTERN EUROPE	12,675,716	13,628,825	15,042,738	15,043,814	15,454,875	37.46	2.73
Austria	278,619	337,736	386,465	394,850	375,363	0.91	-4.94
Belgium	950,963	949,796	1,044,485	1,075,231	1,121,392	2.72	4.29
France	3,494,385	3,864,873	4,227,160	4,259,794	4,546,021	11.02	6.72
Germany	6,089,490	6,491,508	7,122,227	7,019,583	7,035,130	17.05	0.22
Luxembourg	63,940	67,048	76,209	67,925	75,865	0.18	11.69
Netherlands	1,272,294	1,323,332	1,485,998	1,494,511	1,497,341	3.63	0.19

682

SPAIN

3. Arrivals of non-resident tourists in hotels and similar establishments, by country of residence

	2009	2010	2011	2012	2013	Market share 2013	% Change 2013-2012
Switzerland	526,025	594,532	700,194	731,920	803,763	1.95	9.82
EAST MEDITERRANEAN EUROPE	**105,216**	**148,736**	**163,239**	**171,639**	**192,408**	**0.47**	**12.10**
Cyprus	15,059	22,236	24,881	22,813	14,893	0.04	-34.72
Turkey	90,157	126,500	138,358	148,826	177,515	0.43	19.28
OTHER EUROPE	**405,051**	**490,475**	**580,939**	**532,570**	**585,540**	**1.42**	**9.95**
Other countries of Europe	405,051	490,475	580,939	532,570	585,540	1.42	9.95
NOT SPECIFIED	**703,847**	**787,831**	**757,252**	**733,095**	**813,455**	**1.97**	**10.96**
Other countries of the World	703,847	787,831	757,252	733,095	813,455	1.97	10.96

Yearbook of Tourism Statistics, Data 2009 – 2013, 2015 Edition

SPAIN

4. Arrivals of non-resident tourists in all types of accommodation establishments, by country of residence

	2009	2010	2011	2012	2013	Market share 2013	% Change 2013-2012
TOTAL (*)	39,204,144	43,182,773	47,652,541	48,100,648	49,798,882	100.00	3.53
AFRICA	347,353	410,199	448,878	491,493	548,957	1.10	11.69
SOUTHERN AFRICA	40,740	44,085	58,672	69,900	62,089	0.12	-11.17
South Africa	40,740	44,085	58,672	69,900	62,089	0.12	-11.17
OTHER AFRICA	306,613	366,114	390,206	421,593	486,868	0.98	15.48
Other countries of Africa	306,613	366,114	390,206	421,593	486,868	0.98	15.48
AMERICAS	3,320,307	3,988,405	4,513,180	4,387,499	4,343,597	8.72	-1.00
NORTH AMERICA	2,140,165	2,605,944	2,908,123	2,840,456	2,736,381	5.49	-3.66
Canada	268,611	409,078	493,819	484,791	391,795	0.79	-19.18
United States of America	1,593,206	1,878,192	2,072,053	2,050,747	2,034,487	4.09	-0.79
Other countries of North America	278,348	318,674	342,251	304,918	310,099	0.62	1.70
SOUTH AMERICA	302,882	424,492	518,838	454,602	454,532	0.91	-0.02
Brazil	302,882	424,492	518,838	454,602	454,532	0.91	-0.02
OTHER AMERICAS	877,260	957,969	1,086,219	1,092,441	1,152,684	2.31	5.51
Other countries of the Americas	877,260	957,969	1,086,219	1,092,441	1,152,684	2.31	5.51
EAST ASIA AND THE PACIFIC	1,261,815	1,662,979	1,942,206	2,161,202	2,432,077	4.88	12.53
NORTH-EAST ASIA	793,987	1,045,961	1,140,985	1,241,938	1,423,192	2.86	14.59
China	159,503	218,795	299,961	365,318	462,845	0.93	26.70
Japan	541,064	647,000	641,263	669,354	719,172	1.44	7.44
Korea, Republic of	93,420	180,166	199,761	207,266	241,175	0.48	16.36
AUSTRALASIA	162,328	210,097	258,774	269,101	295,729	0.59	9.90
Australia	162,328	210,097	258,774	269,101	295,729	0.59	9.90
OTHER EAST ASIA AND THE PACIFIC	305,500	406,921	542,447	650,163	713,156	1.43	9.69
Other countries of Asia	265,680	363,575	499,833	609,682	671,380	1.35	10.12
Other countries of Oceania	39,820	43,346	42,614	40,481	41,776	0.08	3.20
EUROPE	33,534,133	36,291,222	39,953,668	40,284,522	41,623,064	83.58	3.32
CENTRAL/EASTERN EUROPE	1,566,685	1,978,565	2,615,786	2,917,027	3,475,163	6.98	19.13
Bulgaria	64,505	73,704	80,598	79,975	71,190	0.14	-10.98
Czech Republic	199,679	199,577	232,256	227,613	509,560	1.02	123.87
Estonia	34,454	34,017	38,243	40,067	48,985	0.10	22.26
Hungary	101,457	116,380	120,713	123,983	118,182	0.24	-4.68
Latvia	29,976	39,416	40,405	40,956	41,765	0.08	1.98
Lithuania	44,398	46,529	56,253	59,191	64,856	0.13	9.57
Poland	360,792	451,680	577,957	547,845	561,187	1.13	2.44
Romania	180,764	224,675	255,990	234,254	227,504	0.46	-2.88
Russian Federation	466,056	682,985	1,070,095	1,396,309	1,644,910	3.30	17.80
Slovakia	43,699	52,547	58,023	62,436	59,584	0.12	-4.57
Ukraine	40,905	57,055	85,253	104,398	127,440	0.26	22.07
NORTHERN EUROPE	11,786,510	12,380,638	13,497,146	14,181,960	14,608,123	29.33	3.00
Denmark	542,596	582,027	639,841	652,255	665,752	1.34	2.07
Finland	383,557	393,710	436,993	446,778	481,004	0.97	7.66
Iceland	37,265	35,152	41,432	43,358	42,717	0.09	-1.48
Ireland	859,181	805,687	841,266	850,728	907,915	1.82	6.72
Norway	529,197	595,560	692,752	779,100	875,528	1.76	12.38
Sweden	855,881	940,231	1,072,577	1,160,643	954,239	1.92	-17.78
United Kingdom	8,578,833	9,028,271	9,772,285	10,249,098	10,680,968	21.45	4.21
SOUTHERN EUROPE	3,929,014	4,489,711	4,724,264	4,089,018	3,778,277	7.59	-7.60
Greece	138,404	187,438	154,658	109,110	106,476	0.21	-2.41
Italy	2,472,479	2,843,261	3,156,911	2,725,480	2,496,065	5.01	-8.42
Malta	32,232	29,521	29,125	30,181	22,226	0.04	-26.36
Portugal	1,244,957	1,386,989	1,337,852	1,180,495	1,116,682	2.24	-5.41
Slovenia	40,942	42,502	45,718	43,752	36,828	0.07	-15.83
WESTERN EUROPE	15,682,976	16,741,389	18,299,528	18,322,356	18,911,398	37.98	3.21
Austria	317,951	376,581	430,405	434,467	420,080	0.84	-3.31
Belgium	1,116,593	1,122,324	1,226,717	1,265,693	1,319,491	2.65	4.25
France	4,358,571	4,754,050	5,187,844	5,239,738	5,572,154	11.19	6.34
Germany	7,242,350	7,662,337	8,311,039	8,177,033	8,315,494	16.70	1.69
Luxembourg	77,733	78,491	90,899	81,060	89,155	0.18	9.99
Netherlands	1,965,074	2,064,753	2,253,468	2,285,060	2,270,903	4.56	-0.62

684

SPAIN

4. Arrivals of non-resident tourists in all types of accommodation establishments, by country of residence

	2009	2010	2011	2012	2013	Market share 2013	% Change 2013-2012
Switzerland	604,704	682,853	799,156	839,305	924,121	1.86	10.11
EAST MEDITERRANEAN EUROPE	**117,873**	**164,211**	**180,283**	**189,597**	**210,218**	**0.42**	**10.88**
Cyprus	18,136	26,143	28,715	26,250	16,891	0.03	-35.65
Turkey	99,737	138,068	151,568	163,347	193,327	0.39	18.35
OTHER EUROPE	**451,075**	**536,708**	**636,661**	**584,564**	**639,885**	**1.28**	**9.46**
Other countries of Europe	451,075	536,708	636,661	584,564	639,885	1.28	9.46
NOT SPECIFIED	**740,536**	**829,968**	**794,609**	**775,932**	**851,187**	**1.71**	**9.70**
Other countries of the World	740,536	829,968	794,609	775,932	851,187	1.71	9.70

Yearbook of Tourism Statistics, Data 2009 – 2013, 2015 Edition

SPAIN

5. Overnight stays of non-resident tourists in hotels and similar establishments, by country of residence

	2009	2010	2011	2012	2013	Market share 2013	% Change 2013-2012
TOTAL (*)	141,227,941	153,927,193	175,236,929	178,558,302	185,396,231	100.00	3.83
AFRICA	733,420	949,106	930,591	1,009,190	1,151,992	0.62	14.15
SOUTHERN AFRICA	89,509	96,034	125,044	139,306	130,270	0.07	-6.49
South Africa	89,509	96,034	125,044	139,306	130,270	0.07	-6.49
OTHER AFRICA	643,911	853,072	805,547	869,884	1,021,722	0.55	17.45
Other countries of Africa	643,911	853,072	805,547	869,884	1,021,722	0.55	17.45
AMERICAS	7,146,183	8,498,825	9,759,858	9,503,513	9,550,986	5.15	0.50
NORTH AMERICA	4,637,580	5,591,062	6,283,469	6,170,493	6,051,431	3.26	-1.93
Canada	670,029	953,720	1,142,309	1,154,293	942,019	0.51	-18.39
United States of America	3,350,590	3,947,861	4,384,027	4,344,385	4,422,745	2.39	1.80
Other countries of North America	616,961	689,481	757,133	671,815	686,667	0.37	2.21
SOUTH AMERICA	738,504	991,426	1,213,339	1,069,431	1,086,789	0.59	1.62
Brazil	738,504	991,426	1,213,339	1,069,431	1,086,789	0.59	1.62
OTHER AMERICAS	1,770,099	1,916,337	2,263,050	2,263,589	2,412,766	1.30	6.59
Other countries of the Americas	1,770,099	1,916,337	2,263,050	2,263,589	2,412,766	1.30	6.59
EAST ASIA AND THE PACIFIC	2,261,203	2,917,847	3,571,095	3,960,859	4,571,008	2.47	15.40
NORTH-EAST ASIA	1,245,174	1,604,230	1,788,744	1,932,045	2,252,916	1.22	16.61
China	270,323	373,936	499,863	602,425	754,994	0.41	25.33
Japan	845,591	987,041	1,020,401	1,050,969	1,158,516	0.62	10.23
Korea, Republic of	129,260	243,253	268,480	278,651	339,406	0.18	21.80
AUSTRALASIA	337,522	443,068	567,365	600,989	664,170	0.36	10.51
Australia	337,522	443,068	567,365	600,989	664,170	0.36	10.51
OTHER EAST ASIA AND THE PACIFIC	678,507	870,549	1,214,986	1,427,825	1,653,922	0.89	15.84
Other countries of Asia	614,125	796,765	1,136,989	1,355,978	1,571,410	0.85	15.89
Other countries of Oceania	64,382	73,784	77,997	71,847	82,512	0.04	14.84
EUROPE	129,335,156	139,555,580	158,865,426	162,108,857	167,853,068	90.54	3.54
CENTRAL/EASTERN EUROPE	6,127,120	8,149,947	11,568,617	13,237,285	14,738,398	7.95	11.34
Bulgaria	150,467	183,842	229,228	200,735	185,295	0.10	-7.69
Czech Republic	852,714	833,430	1,015,423	967,335	848,511	0.46	-12.28
Estonia	112,131	115,554	127,685	128,215	173,895	0.09	35.63
Hungary	288,085	361,184	384,310	361,400	358,931	0.19	-0.68
Latvia	89,487	104,699	133,056	135,509	139,487	0.08	2.94
Lithuania	145,506	149,572	189,459	193,822	225,119	0.12	16.15
Poland	1,446,449	1,770,454	2,454,487	2,358,614	2,415,076	1.30	2.39
Romania	437,149	606,685	746,507	636,270	630,715	0.34	-0.87
Russian Federation	2,320,571	3,584,505	5,721,742	7,605,640	9,013,764	4.86	18.51
Slovakia	158,274	208,431	235,878	261,702	241,858	0.13	-7.58
Ukraine	126,287	231,591	330,842	388,043	505,747	0.27	30.33
NORTHERN EUROPE	46,823,037	49,576,077	54,944,372	59,394,591	62,606,635	33.77	5.41
Denmark	1,718,683	1,941,915	2,523,244	2,458,862	2,403,696	1.30	-2.24
Finland	1,052,385	1,138,286	1,314,827	1,408,843	1,627,218	0.88	15.50
Iceland	168,506	184,026	222,853	222,089	236,636	0.13	6.55
Ireland	2,473,845	2,235,348	2,444,829	2,599,832	2,771,254	1.49	6.59
Norway	1,738,795	2,018,901	2,338,035	2,939,936	3,290,381	1.77	11.92
Sweden	3,013,007	3,280,840	3,905,603	4,492,215	4,965,404	2.68	10.53
United Kingdom	36,657,816	38,776,761	42,194,981	45,272,814	47,312,046	25.52	4.50
SOUTHERN EUROPE	10,775,541	12,169,405	13,174,074	11,206,385	10,132,882	5.47	-9.58
Greece	345,572	515,089	434,151	291,313	253,936	0.14	-12.83
Italy	7,216,770	8,151,620	9,378,102	8,005,524	7,264,804	3.92	-9.25
Malta	93,297	79,914	76,587	75,728	62,543	0.03	-17.41
Portugal	3,015,623	3,311,143	3,136,338	2,694,631	2,443,335	1.32	-9.33
Slovenia	104,279	111,639	148,896	139,189	108,264	0.06	-22.22
WESTERN EUROPE	64,157,947	67,855,105	76,975,346	76,204,852	77,996,194	42.07	2.35
Austria	1,205,537	1,462,259	1,771,063	1,843,562	1,706,015	0.92	-7.46
Belgium	5,022,613	4,931,948	5,439,535	5,543,961	5,818,996	3.14	4.96
France	9,619,625	10,527,172	12,141,416	12,229,112	13,499,961	7.28	10.39
Germany	39,731,293	41,959,464	47,000,767	45,838,457	45,816,924	24.71	-0.05
Luxembourg	350,637	383,246	446,311	375,713	450,095	0.24	19.80
Netherlands	5,889,819	6,029,492	7,029,259	7,124,152	7,095,819	3.83	-0.40

Yearbook of Tourism Statistics, Data 2009 – 2013, 2015 Edition

SPAIN

5. Overnight stays of non-resident tourists in hotels and similar establishments, by country of residence

	2009	2010	2011	2012	2013	Market share 2013	% Change 2013-2012
Switzerland	2,338,423	2,561,524	3,146,995	3,249,895	3,608,384	1.95	11.03
EAST MEDITERRANEAN EUROPE	**238,353**	**345,569**	**404,789**	**421,251**	**461,484**	**0.25**	**9.55**
Cyprus	39,711	62,822	80,333	66,610	48,293	0.03	-27.50
Turkey	198,642	282,747	324,456	354,641	413,191	0.22	16.51
OTHER EUROPE	**1,213,158**	**1,459,477**	**1,798,228**	**1,644,493**	**1,917,475**	**1.03**	**16.60**
Other countries of Europe	1,213,158	1,459,477	1,798,228	1,644,493	1,917,475	1.03	16.60
NOT SPECIFIED	**1,751,979**	**2,005,835**	**2,109,959**	**1,975,883**	**2,269,177**	**1.22**	**14.84**
Other countries of the World	1,751,979	2,005,835	2,109,959	1,975,883	2,269,177	1.22	14.84

Yearbook of Tourism Statistics, Data 2009 – 2013, 2015 Edition

SPAIN

6. Overnight stays of non-resident tourists in all types of accommodation establishments, by country of residence

	2009	2010	2011	2012	2013	Market share 2013	% Change 2013-2012
TOTAL (*)	200,551,732	213,365,670	239,387,398	243,389,007	252,447,761	100.00	3.72
AFRICA	859,319	1,095,462	1,122,861	1,236,992	1,445,179	0.57	16.83
SOUTHERN AFRICA	104,043	109,534	148,813	170,751	163,425	0.06	-4.29
South Africa	104,043	109,534	148,813	170,751	163,425	0.06	-4.29
OTHER AFRICA	755,276	985,928	974,048	1,066,241	1,281,754	0.51	20.21
Other countries of Africa	755,276	985,928	974,048	1,066,241	1,281,754	0.51	20.21
AMERICAS	7,868,261	9,328,295	10,703,558	10,488,130	10,488,890	4.15	0.01
NORTH AMERICA	5,065,453	6,025,212	6,791,522	6,704,684	6,577,034	2.61	-1.90
Canada	737,643	1,037,280	1,236,127	1,253,006	1,033,318	0.41	-17.53
United States of America	3,667,681	4,237,949	4,733,642	4,711,065	4,793,553	1.90	1.75
Other countries of North America	660,129	749,983	821,753	740,613	750,163	0.30	1.29
SOUTH AMERICA	777,815	1,044,060	1,271,518	1,129,705	1,144,502	0.45	1.31
Brazil	777,815	1,044,060	1,271,518	1,129,705	1,144,502	0.45	1.31
OTHER AMERICAS	2,024,993	2,259,023	2,640,518	2,653,741	2,767,354	1.10	4.28
Other countries of the Americas	2,024,993	2,259,023	2,640,518	2,653,741	2,767,354	1.10	4.28
EAST ASIA AND THE PACIFIC	2,568,167	3,287,927	4,002,207	4,562,148	5,056,795	2.00	10.84
NORTH-EAST ASIA	1,403,007	1,798,522	1,997,308	2,219,576	2,489,114	0.99	12.14
China	303,340	419,353	557,460	690,309	833,027	0.33	20.67
Japan	953,799	1,106,837	1,140,843	1,209,915	1,281,587	0.51	5.92
Korea, Republic of	145,868	272,332	299,005	319,352	374,500	0.15	17.27
AUSTRALASIA	381,097	497,831	632,237	688,679	732,760	0.29	6.40
Australia	381,097	497,831	632,237	688,679	732,760	0.29	6.40
OTHER EAST ASIA AND THE PACIFIC	784,063	991,574	1,372,662	1,653,893	1,834,921	0.73	10.95
Other countries of Asia	693,770	894,655	1,267,649	1,553,878	1,733,846	0.69	11.58
Other countries of Oceania	90,293	96,919	105,013	100,015	101,075	0.04	1.06
EUROPE	187,295,365	197,413,969	221,224,296	224,854,775	232,963,069	92.28	3.61
CENTRAL/EASTERN EUROPE	7,585,061	9,677,280	13,469,486	15,394,925	19,981,977	7.92	29.80
Bulgaria	211,471	237,372	291,118	255,474	233,549	0.09	-8.58
Czech Republic	1,077,379	1,049,358	1,229,957	1,164,490	3,763,191	1.49	223.16
Estonia	158,262	150,113	162,919	163,173	219,241	0.09	34.36
Hungary	405,747	470,963	487,171	459,934	452,522	0.18	-1.61
Latvia	126,069	135,873	170,166	172,445	175,863	0.07	1.98
Lithuania	204,908	193,735	240,894	246,669	283,818	0.11	15.06
Poland	1,774,022	2,089,974	2,869,174	2,779,394	2,835,666	1.12	2.02
Romania	613,919	787,577	946,853	809,676	794,898	0.31	-1.83
Russian Federation	2,632,296	4,014,664	6,381,181	8,546,313	10,322,985	4.09	20.79
Slovakia	222,021	271,056	297,323	333,077	304,934	0.12	-8.45
Ukraine	158,967	276,595	392,730	464,280	595,310	0.24	28.22
NORTHERN EUROPE	76,003,707	78,183,507	85,951,164	90,430,234	92,020,415	36.45	1.76
Denmark	3,255,430	3,406,994	4,020,160	4,071,655	4,043,708	1.60	-0.69
Finland	2,371,404	2,393,517	2,697,213	2,771,719	2,929,949	1.16	5.71
Iceland	215,399	224,600	269,255	265,731	278,556	0.11	4.83
Ireland	5,068,140	4,436,198	4,714,176	4,921,387	5,270,029	2.09	7.08
Norway	3,945,740	4,119,934	4,760,661	5,591,788	5,881,784	2.33	5.19
Sweden	5,691,244	5,892,123	6,763,657	7,413,587	5,170,345	2.05	-30.26
United Kingdom	55,456,350	57,710,141	62,726,042	65,394,367	68,446,044	27.11	4.67
SOUTHERN EUROPE	12,657,316	14,381,746	15,460,472	13,410,809	12,219,108	4.84	-8.89
Greece	402,901	576,043	482,437	323,535	288,256	0.11	-10.90
Italy	8,435,329	9,667,736	11,041,379	9,656,938	8,862,250	3.51	-8.23
Malta	131,634	104,342	97,762	96,380	78,854	0.03	-18.18
Portugal	3,540,535	3,889,037	3,650,401	3,156,812	2,853,251	1.13	-9.62
Slovenia	146,917	144,588	188,493	177,144	136,497	0.05	-22.95
WESTERN EUROPE	89,180,373	92,992,328	103,685,146	103,142,076	105,924,063	41.96	2.70
Austria	1,511,202	1,753,595	2,110,051	2,154,338	2,014,622	0.80	-6.49
Belgium	6,358,928	6,328,795	6,954,129	7,143,548	7,451,420	2.95	4.31
France	14,649,330	15,660,542	17,938,395	18,113,925	19,713,529	7.81	8.83
Germany	51,053,217	52,986,209	58,302,711	56,834,642	57,519,527	22.78	1.21
Luxembourg	449,023	453,613	545,132	482,364	554,273	0.22	14.91
Netherlands	12,250,266	12,646,078	14,008,577	14,433,571	14,255,782	5.65	-1.23

688

SPAIN

6. Overnight stays of non-resident tourists in all types of accommodation establishments, by country of residence

	2009	2010	2011	2012	2013	Market share 2013	% Change 2013-2012
Switzerland	2,908,407	3,163,496	3,826,151	3,979,688	4,414,910	1.75	10.94
EAST MEDITERRANEAN EUROPE	**311,405**	**425,169**	**495,850**	**509,072**	**547,260**	**0.22**	**7.50**
Cyprus	55,704	82,365	102,883	84,767	60,889	0.02	-28.17
Turkey	255,701	342,804	392,967	424,305	486,371	0.19	14.63
OTHER EUROPE	**1,557,503**	**1,753,939**	**2,162,178**	**1,967,659**	**2,270,246**	**0.90**	**15.38**
Other countries of Europe	1,557,503	1,753,939	2,162,178	1,967,659	2,270,246	0.90	15.38
NOT SPECIFIED	**1,960,620**	**2,240,017**	**2,334,476**	**2,246,962**	**2,493,828**	**0.99**	**10.99**
Other countries of the World	1,960,620	2,240,017	2,334,476	2,246,962	2,493,828	0.99	10.99

Yearbook of Tourism Statistics, Data 2009 – 2013, 2015 Edition

SRI LANKA

1. Arrivals of non-resident tourists at national borders, by nationality

	2009	2010	2011	2012	2013	Market share 2013	% Change 2013-2012
TOTAL (*)	**447,890**	**654,476**	**855,975**	**1,005,605**	**1,274,593**	**100.00**	**26.75**
AFRICA	**1,591**	**2,249**	**6,736**	**6,912**	**7,717**	**0.61**	**11.65**
OTHER AFRICA	**1,591**	**2,249**	**6,736**	**6,912**	**7,717**	**0.61**	**11.65**
All countries of Africa	1,591	2,249	6,736	6,912	7,717	0.61	11.65
AMERICAS	**25,710**	**41,146**	**54,825**	**57,695**	**73,112**	**5.74**	**26.72**
NORTH AMERICA	**25,044**	**40,552**	**53,658**	**56,694**	**70,003**	**5.49**	**23.48**
Canada	10,785	21,231	26,090	28,786	30,382	2.38	5.54
United States of America	14,259	19,321	27,568	27,908	39,621	3.11	41.97
OTHER AMERICAS	**666**	**594**	**1,167**	**1,001**	**3,109**	**0.24**	**210.59**
Other countries of the Americas	666	594	1,167	1,001	3,109	0.24	210.59
EAST ASIA AND THE PACIFIC	**75,503**	**110,816**	**141,751**	**175,910**	**255,401**	**20.04**	**45.19**
NORTH-EAST ASIA	**27,136**	**36,569**	**50,996**	**58,678**	**107,646**	**8.45**	**83.45**
China (*)	8,574	10,410	16,573	20,323	51,704	4.06	154.41
Hong Kong, China	1,325	1,824	440	897			
Japan	10,931	14,998	20,951	23,421	33,506	2.63	43.06
Korea, Republic of	3,595	4,318	5,965	6,133	11,700	0.92	90.77
Taiwan, Province of China	2,711	5,019	7,067	7,904	10,736	0.84	35.83
SOUTH-EAST ASIA	**20,512**	**31,978**	**36,389**	**63,438**	**68,163**	**5.35**	**7.45**
Indonesia	1,039	1,281	2,011	2,812	11,161	0.88	296.91
Malaysia	6,878	13,101	15,915	29,181	20,914	1.64	-28.33
Philippines	1,421	1,369	2,394	4,761	11,745	0.92	146.69
Singapore	7,976	12,514	10,666	15,453	15,020	1.18	-2.80
Thailand	3,198	3,713	5,403	11,231	9,323	0.73	-16.99
AUSTRALASIA	**25,872**	**36,813**	**48,912**	**48,147**	**69,265**	**5.43**	**43.86**
Australia	23,249	33,512	43,737	42,310	62,242	4.88	47.11
New Zealand	2,623	3,301	5,175	5,837	7,023	0.55	20.32
OTHER EAST ASIA AND THE PACIFIC	**1,983**	**5,456**	**5,454**	**5,647**	**10,327**	**0.81**	**82.88**
Other countries of Asia	1,832	5,244	2,955	3,755	7,296	0.57	94.30
Other countries of Oceania	151	212	2,499	1,892	3,031	0.24	60.20
EUROPE	**196,363**	**290,802**	**372,353**	**448,310**	**531,132**	**41.67**	**18.47**
CENTRAL/EASTERN EUROPE	**26,177**	**35,630**	**51,922**	**70,437**	**112,737**	**8.84**	**60.05**
Russian Federation	11,390	13,312	21,291	30,156	47,265	3.71	56.73
Other countries Central/East Europe	14,787	22,318	30,631	40,281	65,472	5.14	62.54
NORTHERN EUROPE	**88,977**	**123,222**	**134,204**	**152,069**	**169,328**	**13.28**	**11.35**
Denmark	1,306	4,301	6,640	9,753	6,746	0.53	-30.83
Finland	742	1,971	3,819	6,230	2,763	0.22	-55.65
Norway	1,669	3,884	5,135	9,093	8,971	0.70	-1.34
Sweden	3,578	7,128	11,715	15,165	15,423	1.21	1.70
United Kingdom	81,682	105,938	106,895	111,828	135,425	10.62	21.10
SOUTHERN EUROPE	**9,597**	**16,001**	**20,061**	**27,370**	**26,712**	**2.10**	**-2.40**
Italy	7,214	11,512	14,182	17,661	17,860	1.40	1.13
Spain	2,383	4,489	5,879	9,709	8,852	0.69	-8.83
WESTERN EUROPE	**68,437**	**113,576**	**161,717**	**191,947**	**213,065**	**16.72**	**11.00**
Austria	2,411	3,963	6,185	6,601	9,394	0.74	42.31
Belgium	2,613	5,371	10,853	13,013	10,432	0.82	-19.83
France	16,205	31,119	50,175	55,473	62,771	4.92	13.16
Germany	29,664	45,981	55,339	69,652	91,150	7.15	30.86
Netherlands	11,297	17,628	26,004	25,564	21,989	1.73	-13.98
Switzerland	6,247	9,514	13,161	21,644	17,329	1.36	-19.94
OTHER EUROPE	**3,175**	**2,373**	**4,449**	**6,487**	**9,290**	**0.73**	**43.21**
Other countries of Europe	3,175	2,373	4,449	6,487	9,290	0.73	43.21
MIDDLE EAST	**23,821**	**37,501**	**36,376**	**58,901**	**62,680**	**4.92**	**6.42**
All countries of Middle East	23,821	37,501	36,376	58,901	62,680	4.92	6.42
SOUTH ASIA	**124,902**	**171,962**	**243,934**	**257,877**	**344,551**	**27.03**	**33.61**
Bangladesh	1,295	1,846	4,934	5,748	10,037	0.79	74.62
India	83,650	125,112	178,359	191,281	229,674	18.02	20.07
Maldives	31,890	35,401	43,926	45,321	78,726	6.18	73.71
Nepal	679	602	858	984	2,019	0.16	105.18
Pakistan	7,388	9,001	15,857	14,543	24,095	1.89	65.68

Yearbook of Tourism Statistics, Data 2009 – 2013, 2015 Edition

SRI LANKA

1. Arrivals of non-resident tourists at national borders, by country of residence

	2009	2010	2011	2012	2013	Market share 2013	% Change 2013-2012
TOTAL (*)	447,820	654,476	855,975	1,005,605	1,274,593	100.00	26.75
AFRICA	1,479	2,308	3,614	5,045	8,081	0.63	60.18
EAST AFRICA	397	539	621	929	1,472	0.12	58.45
Comoros					350	0.03	
Kenya	229	297	394	645	507	0.04	-21.40
Mauritius	117	179	160	284	288	0.02	1.41
Seychelles					327	0.03	
Zambia	51	63	67				
NORTH AFRICA	69	71	64		805	0.06	
Algeria	69	71	64				
Morocco					396	0.03	
Sudan					409	0.03	
SOUTHERN AFRICA	779	1,415	1,962	3,048	3,366	0.26	10.43
South Africa	779	1,415	1,962	3,048	3,366	0.26	10.43
WEST AFRICA	131	212	378	684	550	0.04	-19.59
Nigeria	131	212	378	684	550	0.04	-19.59
OTHER AFRICA	103	71	589	384	1,888	0.15	391.67
Other countries of Africa	103	71	589	384	1,888	0.15	391.67
AMERICAS	25,565	40,836	50,093	60,862	68,782	5.40	13.01
NORTH AMERICA	24,948	40,216	49,057	59,236	66,047	5.18	11.50
Canada	10,707	21,123	24,671	29,329	30,926	2.43	5.45
Mexico					431	0.03	
United States of America	14,241	19,093	24,386	29,907	34,690	2.72	15.99
SOUTH AMERICA	500	512	541	1,092	1,720	0.13	57.51
Argentina	75	133	148	387	400	0.03	3.36
Bolivia	39	76	23	229			
Brazil	157	217	362	476	803	0.06	68.70
Chile					252	0.02	
Colombia					265	0.02	
French Guiana	229	86	8				
OTHER AMERICAS	117	108	495	534	1,015	0.08	90.07
Other countries of the Americas	117	108	495	534	1,015	0.08	90.07
EAST ASIA AND THE PACIFIC	74,397	105,720	142,661	190,506	243,933	19.14	28.04
NORTH-EAST ASIA	27,216	35,715	51,785	74,253	101,931	8.00	37.28
China	8,550	10,430	16,308	25,781	54,288	4.26	110.57
Hong Kong, China	1,330	1,230	2,199	1,535			
Japan	10,926	14,352	20,586	26,085	31,505	2.47	20.78
Korea, Republic of	3,695	4,426	5,485	7,838	12,207	0.96	55.74
Macao, China			197	311			
Taiwan, Province of China	2,715	5,277	7,010	12,703	3,931	0.31	-69.05
SOUTH-EAST ASIA	20,813	32,362	43,672	57,537	80,837	6.34	40.50
Cambodia					580	0.05	
Indonesia	1,040	1,343	2,049	2,890	17,295	1.36	498.44
Malaysia	6,850	13,367	16,094	21,776	19,181	1.50	-11.92
Myanmar	262	262	914	1,108	2,848	0.22	157.04
Philippines	1,421	1,391	2,047	5,687	14,616	1.15	157.01
Singapore	7,808	11,875	15,953	17,273	15,546	1.22	-10.00
Thailand	3,208	3,684	5,880	7,897	9,608	0.75	21.67
Viet Nam	224	440	735	906	1,163	0.09	28.37
AUSTRALASIA	25,911	36,943	45,940	57,255	60,426	4.74	5.54
Australia	23,239	33,456	41,728	51,614	54,252	4.26	5.11
New Zealand	2,672	3,487	4,212	5,641	6,174	0.48	9.45
OTHER EAST ASIA AND THE PACIFIC	457	700	1,264	1,461	739	0.06	-49.42
Other countries of Asia	300	353	737	940	329	0.03	-65.00
Other countries of Oceania	157	347	527	521	410	0.03	-21.31

Yearbook of Tourism Statistics, Data 2009 – 2013, 2015 Edition

SRI LANKA

1. Arrivals of non-resident tourists at national borders, by country of residence

	2009	2010	2011	2012	2013	Market share 2013	% Change 2013-2012
EUROPE	198,897	296,961	371,794	452,676	556,351	43.65	22.90
CENTRAL/EASTERN EUROPE	26,310	35,517	49,249	70,941	124,092	9.74	74.92
Azerbaijan					247	0.02	
Belarus					3,809	0.30	
Bulgaria	207	703	375	789			
Czech Republic	2,814	4,204	5,548	5,877	8,881	0.70	51.11
Estonia					1,753	0.14	
Georgia					280	0.02	
Hungary	418	836	911	1,418	1,653	0.13	16.57
Kazakhstan			240	996	2,362	0.19	137.15
Lithuania	546	636	673	1,078	1,405	0.11	30.33
Poland	5,138	6,613	5,817	5,806	9,688	0.76	66.86
Romania	272	710	726	1,029	1,687	0.13	63.95
Russian Federation	11,834	13,278	21,385	28,402	51,235	4.02	80.39
Slovakia	1,164	1,716	1,314	2,040	1,731	0.14	-15.15
Ukraine	2,577	5,703	9,967	22,348	38,607	3.03	72.75
Uzbekistan					269	0.02	
Other countries Central/East Europe	1,340	1,118	2,293	1,158	485	0.04	-58.12
NORTHERN EUROPE	90,286	124,648	133,679	150,810	175,414	13.76	16.31
Denmark	1,362	4,393	6,582	8,323	9,845	0.77	18.29
Finland	738	1,950	3,649	4,840	2,471	0.19	-48.95
Ireland	1,366	1,758	1,452	1,951	4,512	0.35	131.27
Norway	1,666	3,955	4,977	7,703	8,573	0.67	11.29
Sweden	3,560	7,096	10,937	13,775	12,597	0.99	-8.55
United Kingdom	81,594	105,496	106,082	114,218	137,416	10.78	20.31
SOUTHERN EUROPE	11,372	18,333	21,685	26,889	33,168	2.60	23.35
Croatia					679	0.05	
Greece	906	1,599	1,240	1,415	4,010	0.31	183.39
Italy	7,514	11,423	13,527	15,871	17,982	1.41	13.30
Malta					217	0.02	
Portugal	565	850	1,032	1,284	2,097	0.16	63.32
Spain	2,387	4,461	5,886	8,319	8,183	0.64	-1.63
WESTERN EUROPE	68,188	113,623	159,037	194,627	211,718	16.61	8.78
Austria	2,409	3,925	6,262	7,991	11,300	0.89	41.41
Belgium	2,617	5,398	10,122	11,323	9,138	0.72	-19.30
France	15,886	31,285	48,695	56,863	64,388	5.05	13.23
Germany	29,654	45,727	55,882	71,642	85,470	6.71	19.30
Netherlands	11,291	17,861	23,966	26,754	22,281	1.75	-16.72
Switzerland	6,331	9,427	14,110	20,054	19,141	1.50	-4.55
EAST MEDITERRANEAN EUROPE	2,464	4,583	7,335	8,672	11,222	0.88	29.40
Cyprus					278	0.02	
Israel	1,901	3,919	6,164	7,212	8,545	0.67	18.48
Turkey	563	664	1,171	1,460	2,399	0.19	64.32
OTHER EUROPE	277	257	809	737	737	0.06	
Other countries of Europe	277	257	809	737	737	0.06	
MIDDLE EAST	20,007	31,057	47,943	47,142	68,832	5.40	46.01
Bahrain	943	1,459	1,819	2,016	2,743	0.22	36.06
Egypt	510	849	767	800	1,806	0.14	125.75
Iraq					565	0.04	
Jordan	1,108	1,708	1,478	1,852	2,976	0.23	60.69
Kuwait	1,123	2,303	2,812	3,245	7,427	0.58	128.88
Lebanon	940	1,816	1,960	2,116	3,371	0.26	59.31
Oman	727	1,359	2,177	2,602	7,634	0.60	193.39
Palestine					625	0.05	
Qatar	1,158	1,574	2,788	2,271	1,073	0.08	-52.75
Saudi Arabia	6,685	9,301	15,081	19,423	23,753	1.86	22.29
United Arab Emirates	5,974	9,825	17,664	11,083	8,471	0.66	-23.57
Yemen					618	0.05	
Other countries of Middle East	839	863	1,397	1,734	7,770	0.61	348.10

692

SRI LANKA

1. Arrivals of non-resident tourists at national borders, by country of residence

	2009	2010	2011	2012	2013	Market share 2013	% Change 2013-2012
SOUTH ASIA	**127,475**	**177,594**	**239,870**	**249,374**	**328,614**	**25.78**	**31.78**
Afghanistan	200	176	363	649	559	0.04	-13.87
Bangladesh	1,294	1,954	4,726	4,646	10,037	0.79	116.04
Bhutan	668	530	824	831	266	0.02	-67.99
India	83,634	126,882	171,374	176,340	208,795	16.38	18.40
Iran, Islamic Republic of	1,270	1,900	2,223	1,815	2,058	0.16	13.39
Maldives	31,916	35,791	44,018	47,572	79,474	6.24	67.06
Nepal	676	753	826	1,038	2,019	0.16	94.51
Pakistan	7,373	9,148	14,724	16,056	25,336	1.99	57.80
Other countries of South Asia	444	460	792	427	70	0.01	-83.61

Yearbook of Tourism Statistics, Data 2009 – 2013, 2015 Edition

SRI LANKA

6. Overnight stays of non-resident tourists in all types of accommodation establishments, by nationality

	2009	2010	2011	2012	2013	Market share 2013	% Change 2013-2012
TOTAL	4,075,799	6,544,760	8,559,753	10,056,053			
AFRICA	12,569	22,265	64,666	65,940			
OTHER AFRICA	12,569	22,265	64,666	65,940			
All countries of Africa	12,569	22,265	64,666	65,940			
AMERICAS	272,480	430,627	570,943	598,547			
NORTH AMERICA	265,887	424,628	559,471	588,677			
Canada	121,871	231,418	280,207	305,132			
United States of America	144,016	193,210	279,264	283,545			
OTHER AMERICAS	6,593	5,999	11,472	9,870			
Other countries of the Americas	6,593	5,999	11,472	9,870			
EAST ASIA AND THE PACIFIC	692,400	1,137,681	1,497,005	1,827,563			
NORTH-EAST ASIA	213,271	345,705	488,344	562,966			
China	68,592	103,059	161,421	198,352			
Hong Kong, China	9,540	17,328	4,092	8,190			
Japan	83,076	137,982	201,130	224,842			
Korea, Republic of	30,917	40,157	54,282	56,178			
Taiwan, Province of China	21,146	47,179	67,419	75,404			
SOUTH-EAST ASIA	155,091	295,878	342,837	599,645			
Indonesia	7,585	11,785	18,903	25,870			
Malaysia	53,648	125,770	154,853	284,223			
Philippines	11,652	12,184	21,642	43,135			
Singapore	59,820	110,123	95,354	138,150			
Thailand	22,386	36,016	52,085	108,267			
AUSTRALASIA	292,992	419,388	550,005	537,028			
Australia	266,500	385,388	495,978	475,564			
New Zealand	26,492	34,000	54,027	61,464			
OTHER EAST ASIA AND THE PACIFIC	31,046	76,710	115,819	127,924			
Other countries of Asia	29,687	74,612	90,685	108,436			
Other countries of Oceania	1,359	2,098	25,134	19,488			
EUROPE	1,914,137	3,049,358	3,901,289	4,700,719			
CENTRAL/EASTERN EUROPE	200,674	365,657	525,555	715,140			
Russian Federation	96,815	135,782	218,020	304,274			
Other countries Central/East Europe	103,859	229,875	307,535	410,866			
NORTHERN EUROPE	905,446	1,316,932	1,418,104	1,615,543			
Denmark	13,321	43,010	67,861	99,676			
Finland	6,826	20,104	38,343	62,612			
Norway	18,025	40,782	53,404	95,113			
Sweden	37,569	74,844	121,133	157,109			
United Kingdom	829,705	1,138,192	1,137,363	1,201,033			
SOUTHERN EUROPE	95,004	159,308	199,126	272,931			
Italy	70,697	113,969	138,984	173,608			
Spain	24,307	45,339	60,142	99,323			
WESTERN EUROPE	683,803	1,184,917	1,712,260	2,032,624			
Austria	22,422	37,649	59,623	63,634			
Belgium	27,175	54,247	110,049	132,342			
France	155,568	326,750	548,915	604,656			
Germany	302,573	491,997	588,807	741,794			
Netherlands	112,970	176,280	266,281	262,287			
Switzerland	63,095	97,994	138,585	227,911			
OTHER EUROPE	29,210	22,544	46,244	64,481			
Other countries of Europe	29,210	22,544	46,244	64,481			
MIDDLE EAST	178,658	382,510	371,035	591,366			
All countries of Middle East	178,658	382,510	371,035	591,366			
SOUTH ASIA	1,005,555	1,522,319	2,154,815	2,271,918			
India	657,835	1,105,900	1,558,858	1,671,796			
Maldives	292,310	336,310	454,195	469,526			
Pakistan	55,410	80,109	141,762	130,596			

Yearbook of Tourism Statistics, Data 2009 – 2013, 2015 Edition

SUDAN

1. Arrivals of non-resident tourists at national borders, by nationality

	2009	2010	2011	2012	2013	Market share 2013	% Change 2013-2012
TOTAL (*)	420,370	495,158	536,400	574,624	591,348	100.00	2.91
AFRICA	59,802	49,516	53,640	103,818	108,167	18.29	4.19
OTHER AFRICA	59,802	49,516	53,640	103,818	108,167	18.29	4.19
All countries of Africa	59,802	49,516	53,640	103,818	108,167	18.29	4.19
AMERICAS	21,000	19,806	21,456	24,179	26,443	4.47	9.36
OTHER AMERICAS	21,000	19,806	21,456	24,179	26,443	4.47	9.36
All countries of the Americas	21,000	19,806	21,456	24,179	26,443	4.47	9.36
EAST ASIA AND THE PACIFIC	239,920	29,709	32,184	35,557	38,760	6.55	9.01
OTHER EAST ASIA AND THE PACIFIC	239,920	29,709	32,184	35,557	38,760	6.55	9.01
All countries of Asia	239,920	29,709	32,184	35,557	38,760	6.55	9.01
EUROPE	99,648	74,274	80,460	50,849	51,174	8.65	0.64
OTHER EUROPE	99,648	74,274	80,460	50,849	51,174	8.65	0.64
All countries of Europe	99,648	74,274	80,460	50,849	51,174	8.65	0.64
MIDDLE EAST		272,338	295,020	297,432	302,220	51.11	1.61
All countries of Middle East		272,338	295,020	297,432	302,220	51.11	1.61
SOUTH ASIA		39,612	42,912	47,134	48,729	8.24	3.38
All countries of South Asia		39,612	42,912	47,134	48,729	8.24	3.38
NOT SPECIFIED		9,903	10,728	15,655	15,855	2.68	1.28
Other countries of the World		9,903	10,728	15,655	15,855	2.68	1.28

Yearbook of Tourism Statistics, Data 2009 – 2013, 2015 Edition

SURINAME

1. Arrivals of non-resident tourists at national borders, by country of residence

	2009	2010	2011	2012	2013	Market share 2013	% Change 2013-2012
TOTAL	150,628	204,519	220,475	240,041	249,102	100.00	3.77
AFRICA	171	246	290	525	280	0.11	-46.67
OTHER AFRICA	171	246	290	525	280	0.11	-46.67
All countries of Africa	171	246	290	525	280	0.11	-46.67
AMERICAS	59,175	88,680	103,709	123,731	138,048	55.42	11.57
CARIBBEAN	10,497	13,417	14,448	14,329	15,840	6.36	10.55
Dominican Republic	77	71	48	76	62	0.02	-18.42
Haiti	127	202	216	272	435	0.17	59.93
Trinidad and Tobago	2,567	3,972	4,862	4,370	5,060	2.03	15.79
Other countries of the Caribbean	7,726	9,172	9,322	9,611	10,283	4.13	6.99
CENTRAL AMERICA	397	504	568	472	513	0.21	8.69
All countries of Central America	397	504	568	472	513	0.21	8.69
NORTH AMERICA	6,284	8,320	9,726	10,380	9,230	3.71	-11.08
Canada	1,320	1,720	1,972	2,206	1,763	0.71	-20.08
United States of America	4,964	6,600	7,754	8,174	7,467	3.00	-8.65
SOUTH AMERICA	41,997	66,439	78,967	98,550	112,465	45.15	14.12
Brazil	7,840	11,158	14,427	19,452	23,084	9.27	18.67
Colombia	178	173	286	290	523	0.21	80.34
Guyana	18,753	30,446	33,010	43,846	42,816	17.19	-2.35
Venezuela	287	430	474	435	1,841	0.74	323.22
Other countries of South America	14,939	24,232	30,770	34,527	44,201	17.74	28.02
EAST ASIA AND THE PACIFIC	1,940	3,382	4,838	4,714	4,670	1.87	-0.93
NORTH-EAST ASIA	1,241	2,220	2,713	2,681	2,606	1.05	-2.80
China	1,069	1,980	2,470	2,491	2,356	0.95	-5.42
Japan	124	206	214	154	184	0.07	19.48
Korea, Republic of	48	34	29	36	66	0.03	83.33
SOUTH-EAST ASIA	144	252	526	262	278	0.11	6.11
Indonesia	144	252	526	262	278	0.11	6.11
OTHER EAST ASIA AND THE PACIFIC	555	910	1,599	1,771	1,786	0.72	0.85
Other countries of Asia	542	824	1,441	1,530	1,554	0.62	1.57
All countries of Oceania	13	86	158	241	232	0.09	-3.73
EUROPE	87,817	110,255	108,188	107,655	103,341	41.49	-4.01
NORTHERN EUROPE	471	775	1,010	1,487	955	0.38	-35.78
United Kingdom	471	775	1,010	1,487	955	0.38	-35.78
WESTERN EUROPE	86,344	108,106	105,479	104,639	101,255	40.65	-3.23
Belgium	1,013	1,464	1,640	2,009	2,057	0.83	2.39
France	3,794	4,455	5,222	6,983	10,464	4.20	49.85
Germany	420	609	563	556	732	0.29	31.65
Netherlands	81,117	101,578	98,054	95,091	88,002	35.33	-7.45
OTHER EUROPE	1,002	1,374	1,699	1,529	1,131	0.45	-26.03
Other countries of Europe	1,002	1,374	1,699	1,529	1,131	0.45	-26.03
MIDDLE EAST	19	47	42	56	10	0.00	-82.14
All countries of Middle East	19	47	42	56	10	0.00	-82.14
SOUTH ASIA	454	556	585	504	581	0.23	15.28
India	454	556	585	504	581	0.23	15.28
NOT SPECIFIED	1,052	1,353	2,823	2,856	2,172	0.87	-23.95
Other countries of the World	1,052	1,353	2,823	2,856	2,172	0.87	-23.95

Yearbook of Tourism Statistics, Data 2009 – 2013, 2015 Edition

SWAZILAND

2. Arrivals of non-resident visitors at national borders, by country of residence

	2009	2010	2011	2012	2013	Market share 2013	% Change 2013-2012
TOTAL	1,343,967	1,342,531	1,328,363	1,278,528	1,298,744	100.00	1.58
AFRICA	1,191,259	1,218,054	1,225,220	1,165,225	1,169,763	90.07	0.39
EAST AFRICA	302,780	283,808	280,437	272,268	271,742	20.92	-0.19
Kenya	2,343	2,709	2,069	2,072	1,945	0.15	-6.13
Malawi	3,109	3,017	3,183	3,313	3,689	0.28	11.35
Mozambique	266,560	241,334	236,507	222,989	213,827	16.46	-4.11
United Republic of Tanzania	4,802	4,677	5,522	6,242	6,493	0.50	4.02
Zambia	6,086	7,128	6,915	7,004	6,535	0.50	-6.70
Zimbabwe	19,880	24,943	26,241	30,648	39,253	3.02	28.08
SOUTHERN AFRICA	875,379	920,153	931,624	880,095	883,557	68.03	0.39
Botswana	3,931	4,053	3,710	4,328	4,293	0.33	-0.81
Lesotho	4,864	4,906	3,348	4,308	3,632	0.28	-15.69
South Africa	866,584	911,194	924,566	871,459	875,632	67.42	0.48
WEST AFRICA	3,202	2,744	2,768	2,785	3,567	0.27	28.08
Nigeria	3,202	2,744	2,768	2,785	3,567	0.27	28.08
OTHER AFRICA	9,898	11,349	10,391	10,077	10,897	0.84	8.14
Other countries of Africa	9,898	11,349	10,391	10,077	10,897	0.84	8.14
AMERICAS	20,187	20,499	18,826	20,259	20,784	1.60	2.59
NORTH AMERICA	18,242	18,333	16,914	18,161	19,041	1.47	4.85
Canada	3,317	3,192	2,696	3,489	3,225	0.25	-7.57
United States of America	14,925	15,141	14,218	14,672	15,816	1.22	7.80
SOUTH AMERICA	1,234	1,085	1,041	1,076	1,048	0.08	-2.60
Brazil	1,234	1,085	1,041	1,076	1,048	0.08	-2.60
OTHER AMERICAS	711	1,081	871	1,022	695	0.05	-32.00
Other countries of the Americas	711	1,081	871	1,022	695	0.05	-32.00
EAST ASIA AND THE PACIFIC	10,945	11,061	9,826	11,263	12,321	0.95	9.39
NORTH-EAST ASIA	4,656	4,299	4,674	4,670	4,893	0.38	4.78
China	2,137	1,980	2,344	2,531	2,184	0.17	-13.71
Korea, Republic of	1,133	1,137	1,260	988	1,616	0.12	63.56
Taiwan, Province of China	1,386	1,182	1,070	1,151	1,093	0.08	-5.04
SOUTH-EAST ASIA	569	497	339	455	563	0.04	23.74
Philippines	569	497	339	455	563	0.04	23.74
AUSTRALASIA	2,810	2,874	2,191	2,777	3,529	0.27	27.08
Australia	2,810	2,874	2,191	2,777	3,529	0.27	27.08
OTHER EAST ASIA AND THE PACIFIC	2,910	3,391	2,622	3,361	3,336	0.26	-0.74
Other countries of Asia	2,910	3,391	2,622	3,361	3,336	0.26	-0.74
EUROPE	114,047	85,195	66,930	73,807	86,875	6.69	17.71
NORTHERN EUROPE	28,050	24,729	18,355	17,390	19,136	1.47	10.04
Norway	1,056	891	725	774	941	0.07	21.58
Sweden	2,894	2,107	1,271	1,334	1,767	0.14	32.46
United Kingdom	24,100	21,731	16,359	15,282	16,428	1.26	7.50
SOUTHERN EUROPE	11,647	11,398	9,140	10,157	9,695	0.75	-4.55
Italy	3,478	3,104	2,225	2,858	3,054	0.24	6.86
Portugal	8,169	8,294	6,915	7,299	6,641	0.51	-9.01
WESTERN EUROPE	62,334	39,797	31,494	38,903	49,019	3.77	26.00
Belgium	7,892	3,205	3,015	3,158	3,637	0.28	15.17
France	16,638	12,737	8,273	9,776	10,445	0.80	6.84
Germany	15,639	11,294	10,406	14,911	18,933	1.46	26.97
Netherlands	19,604	10,788	8,161	9,011	13,032	1.00	44.62
Switzerland	2,561	1,773	1,639	2,047	2,972	0.23	45.19
EAST MEDITERRANEAN EUROPE	877	713	1,058	682	970	0.07	42.23
Israel	877	713	1,058	682	970	0.07	42.23
OTHER EUROPE	11,139	8,558	6,883	6,675	8,055	0.62	20.67
Other countries of Europe	11,139	8,558	6,883	6,675	8,055	0.62	20.67
MIDDLE EAST	218	213	91	143	206	0.02	44.06
Kuwait	122	63	21	32	31	0.00	-3.13
Saudi Arabia	18	4	13	2	10	0.00	400.00
United Arab Emirates	11	30	6	3	3	0.00	
Other countries of Middle East	67	116	51	106	162	0.01	52.83

697

SWAZILAND

2. Arrivals of non-resident visitors at national borders, by country of residence

	2009	2010	2011	2012	2013	Market share 2013	% Change 2013-2012
SOUTH ASIA	**7,311**	**7,509**	**7,470**	**7,831**	**8,795**	**0.68**	**12.31**
India	4,339	3,970	4,103	3,972	4,613	0.36	16.14
Iran, Islamic Republic of	43	46	67	84	57	0.00	-32.14
Pakistan	2,929	3,493	3,300	3,775	4,125	0.32	9.27

Yearbook of Tourism Statistics, Data 2009 – 2013, 2015 Edition

SWAZILAND

3. Arrivals of non-resident tourists in hotels and similar establishments, by country of residence

	2009	2010	2011	2012	2013	Market share 2013	% Change 2013-2012
TOTAL	334,391	338,032	308,389	304,594	302,897	100.00	-0.56
AFRICA	201,585	257,997	235,377	232,231	187,484	61.90	-19.27
EAST AFRICA	9,613	15,326	14,000	13,835	13,017	4.30	-5.91
Mozambique	9,613	15,326	14,000	13,835	13,017	4.30	-5.91
SOUTHERN AFRICA	170,468	230,768	219,269	216,298	168,490	55.63	-22.10
South Africa	167,520	227,986	207,981	205,059	158,442	52.31	-22.73
Other countries of Southern Africa	2,948	2,782	11,288	11,239	10,048	3.32	-10.60
OTHER AFRICA	21,504	11,903	2,108	2,098	5,977	1.97	184.89
Other countries of Africa	21,504	11,903	2,108	2,098	5,977	1.97	184.89
AMERICAS	14,105	19,557	17,114	16,974	21,600	7.13	27.25
OTHER AMERICAS	14,105	19,557	17,114	16,974	21,600	7.13	27.25
All countries of the Americas	14,105	19,557	17,114	16,974	21,600	7.13	27.25
EAST ASIA AND THE PACIFIC	13,196	6,158	5,618	5,800	33,233	10.97	472.98
AUSTRALASIA	2,423	1,717	1,566	1,560	2,270	0.75	45.51
Australia	2,423	1,717	1,566	1,560	2,270	0.75	45.51
OTHER EAST ASIA AND THE PACIFIC	10,773	4,441	4,052	4,240	30,963	10.22	630.26
Other countries of Asia	10,773	4,441	4,052	4,240	30,963	10.22	630.26
EUROPE	105,505	54,320	49,553	49,589	60,580	20.00	22.16
NORTHERN EUROPE	13,351	10,780	9,834	10,794	5,377	1.78	-50.19
United Kingdom	13,351	10,780	9,834	10,794	5,377	1.78	-50.19
OTHER EUROPE	92,154	43,540	39,719	38,795	55,203	18.23	42.29
Other countries of Europe	92,154	43,540	39,719	38,795	55,203	18.23	42.29
NOT SPECIFIED			727				
Other countries of the World			727				

Yearbook of Tourism Statistics, Data 2009 – 2013, 2015 Edition

SWEDEN

2. Arrivals of non-resident visitors at national borders, by country of residence

	2009	2010	2011	2012	2013	Market share 2013	% Change 2013-2012
TOTAL			19,404,572	20,011,205	18,813,709	100.00	-5.98
AFRICA			39,458	34,768	73,581	0.39	111.63
OTHER AFRICA			39,458	34,768	73,581	0.39	111.63
All countries of Africa			39,458	34,768	73,581	0.39	111.63
AMERICAS			672,243	651,965	740,205	3.93	13.53
NORTH AMERICA			559,786	559,988	592,261	3.15	5.76
Canada			67,731	81,436	74,659	0.40	-8.32
United States of America			492,055	478,552	517,602	2.75	8.16
OTHER AMERICAS			112,457	91,977	147,944	0.79	60.85
Other countries of the Americas			112,457	91,977	147,944	0.79	60.85
EAST ASIA AND THE PACIFIC			355,994	313,626	422,022	2.24	34.56
OTHER EAST ASIA AND THE PACIFIC			355,994	313,626	422,022	2.24	34.56
All countries of Asia			246,238	198,990	262,043	1.39	31.69
All countries of Oceania			109,756	114,636	159,979	0.85	39.55
EUROPE			18,242,022	18,910,126	17,448,706	92.74	-7.73
CENTRAL/EASTERN EUROPE			2,079,582	2,258,374	2,221,878	11.81	-1.62
All countries Central/East Europe			2,079,582	2,258,374	2,221,878	11.81	-1.62
NORTHERN EUROPE			13,238,468	13,570,102	12,364,288	65.72	-8.89
Denmark			3,954,524	3,818,185	3,355,633	17.84	-12.11
Finland			3,600,624	3,891,586	3,757,126	19.97	-3.46
Norway			5,052,583	5,129,596	4,614,196	24.53	-10.05
United Kingdom			630,737	730,735	637,333	3.39	-12.78
WESTERN EUROPE			2,197,967	2,459,333	2,138,794	11.37	-13.03
France			266,448	289,806	343,166	1.82	18.41
Germany			1,576,110	1,721,290	1,455,097	7.73	-15.46
Netherlands			355,409	448,237	340,531	1.81	-24.03
OTHER EUROPE			726,005	622,317	723,746	3.85	16.30
Other countries of Europe			726,005	622,317	723,746	3.85	16.30
MIDDLE EAST			48,961	60,012	62,679	0.33	4.44
All countries of Middle East			48,961	60,012	62,679	0.33	4.44
SOUTH ASIA			45,894	40,708	66,516	0.35	63.40
All countries of South Asia			45,894	40,708	66,516	0.35	63.40

700

SWEDEN

3. Arrivals of non-resident tourists in hotels and similar establishments, by country of residence

	2009	2010	2011	2012	2013	Market share 2013	% Change 2013-2012
TOTAL	3,042,926	3,281,502	3,367,288	3,357,562	3,469,062	100.00	3.32
AFRICA	15,650	13,031	18,909	17,930	19,847	0.57	10.69
SOUTHERN AFRICA	5,003	3,202	5,362	4,202	3,818	0.11	-9.14
South Africa	5,003	3,202	5,362	4,202	3,818	0.11	-9.14
OTHER AFRICA	10,647	9,829	13,547	13,728	16,029	0.46	16.76
Other countries of Africa	10,647	9,829	13,547	13,728	16,029	0.46	16.76
AMERICAS	200,876	244,812	259,294	267,831	271,357	7.82	1.32
NORTH AMERICA	185,812	223,162	231,890	239,617	241,405	6.96	0.75
Canada	16,853	20,347	21,399	21,128	25,586	0.74	21.10
United States of America	167,062	200,179	205,912	214,325	212,449	6.12	-0.88
Other countries of North America	1,897	2,636	4,579	4,164	3,370	0.10	-19.07
SOUTH AMERICA	6,867	11,593	13,614	17,581	18,996	0.55	8.05
Brazil	6,867	11,593	13,614	17,581	18,996	0.55	8.05
OTHER AMERICAS	8,197	10,057	13,790	10,633	10,956	0.32	3.04
Other countries of the Americas	8,197	10,057	13,790	10,633	10,956	0.32	3.04
EAST ASIA AND THE PACIFIC	150,235	181,189	209,124	221,323	230,886	6.66	4.32
NORTH-EAST ASIA	93,959	109,934	126,528	135,876	141,478	4.08	4.12
China	42,739	52,201	69,226	74,199	86,801	2.50	16.98
Japan	43,039	46,286	44,416	48,507	40,813	1.18	-15.86
Korea, Republic of	8,181	11,447	12,886	13,170	13,864	0.40	5.27
AUSTRALASIA	18,456	21,944	22,941	24,902	27,228	0.78	9.34
Australia	16,332	19,878	20,763	22,650	24,669	0.71	8.91
New Zealand	2,124	2,066	2,178	2,252	2,559	0.07	13.63
OTHER EAST ASIA AND THE PACIFIC	37,820	49,311	59,655	60,545	62,180	1.79	2.70
Other countries of Asia	37,820	49,311	59,655	60,545	62,180	1.79	2.70
EUROPE	2,420,120	2,517,918	2,456,954	2,423,440	2,493,587	71.88	2.89
CENTRAL/EASTERN EUROPE	198,855	190,971	194,435	220,559	228,184	6.58	3.46
Bulgaria	1,829	2,321	2,478	1,804	2,039	0.06	13.03
Czech Republic	9,897	11,314	11,618	13,688	13,735	0.40	0.34
Estonia	9,608	11,969	11,271	12,602	12,161	0.35	-3.50
Hungary	9,582	8,274	9,811	9,582	10,353	0.30	8.05
Latvia	10,574	6,877	7,468	9,469	8,540	0.25	-9.81
Lithuania	13,456	7,677	8,140	10,820	10,170	0.29	-6.01
Poland	51,701	36,894	43,873	53,778	55,230	1.59	2.70
Romania	4,016	5,738	6,832	9,587	8,592	0.25	-10.38
Russian Federation	77,655	92,395	83,604	90,456	95,990	2.77	6.12
Slovakia	6,673	4,159	4,048	4,254	5,832	0.17	37.09
Ukraine	3,864	3,353	5,292	4,519	5,542	0.16	22.64
NORTHERN EUROPE	1,263,558	1,308,856	1,254,600	1,281,551	1,307,631	37.69	2.04
Denmark	285,185	273,437	247,121	230,969	223,968	6.46	-3.03
Finland	173,405	185,440	171,935	182,661	189,408	5.46	3.69
Iceland	6,060	7,923	7,159	8,401	9,118	0.26	8.53
Ireland	13,488	11,918	14,563	16,144	15,501	0.45	-3.98
Norway	528,083	566,916	552,421	587,487	604,024	17.41	2.81
United Kingdom	257,337	263,222	261,401	255,889	265,612	7.66	3.80
SOUTHERN EUROPE	229,540	231,119	218,641	174,419	193,389	5.57	10.88
Croatia					3,484	0.10	
Greece	12,230	11,389	10,352	8,437	9,483	0.27	12.40
Italy	130,668	127,241	120,853	95,269	96,922	2.79	1.74
Malta	969	852	1,110	1,156	1,522	0.04	31.66
Portugal	9,134	9,627	9,555	8,779	10,594	0.31	20.67
Slovenia	3,002	1,914	2,021	1,887	14,850	0.43	686.96
Spain	73,537	80,096	74,750	58,891	56,534	1.63	-4.00
WESTERN EUROPE	684,771	755,932	758,930	717,336	730,885	21.07	1.89
Austria	31,219	35,835	42,322	31,159	34,526	1.00	10.81
Belgium	35,719	40,554	42,877	42,873	42,541	1.23	-0.77
France	97,857	107,588	104,211	99,650	100,213	2.89	0.56
Germany	373,038	407,418	404,026	385,735	386,815	11.15	0.28

701

SWEDEN

3. Arrivals of non-resident tourists in hotels and similar establishments, by country of residence

	2009	2010	2011	2012	2013	Market share 2013	% Change 2013-2012
Luxembourg	3,346	3,496	3,675	3,191	3,428	0.10	7.43
Netherlands	87,303	95,210	95,055	85,969	88,001	2.54	2.36
Switzerland	56,289	65,831	66,764	68,759	75,361	2.17	9.60
EAST MEDITERRANEAN EUROPE	**8,917**	**10,350**	**11,335**	**12,830**	**15,242**	**0.44**	**18.80**
Cyprus	979	751	1,254	1,240	1,154	0.03	-6.94
Turkey	7,938	9,599	10,081	11,590	14,088	0.41	21.55
OTHER EUROPE	**34,479**	**20,690**	**19,013**	**16,745**	**18,256**	**0.53**	**9.02**
Other countries of Europe	34,479	20,690	19,013	16,745	18,256	0.53	9.02
SOUTH ASIA	**18,552**	**23,219**	**33,064**	**49,410**	**59,839**	**1.72**	**21.11**
India	18,552	23,219	33,064	49,410	59,839	1.72	21.11
NOT SPECIFIED	**237,493**	**301,333**	**389,943**	**377,628**	**393,546**	**11.34**	**4.22**
Other countries of the World	237,493	301,333	389,943	377,628	393,546	11.34	4.22

702

SWEDEN

4. Arrivals of non-resident tourists in all types of accommodation establishments, by country of residence

	2009	2010	2011	2012	2013	Market share 2013	% Change 2013-2012
TOTAL	4,899,411	5,183,013	5,222,346	5,145,922	5,229,281	100.00	1.62
AFRICA	16,481	13,439	17,923	17,822	19,977	0.38	12.09
SOUTHERN AFRICA	4,969	3,234	4,781	3,940	3,646	0.07	-7.46
South Africa	4,969	3,234	4,781	3,940	3,646	0.07	-7.46
OTHER AFRICA	11,512	10,205	13,142	13,882	16,331	0.31	17.64
Other countries of Africa	11,512	10,205	13,142	13,882	16,331	0.31	17.64
AMERICAS	190,467	226,378	239,538	251,151	258,596	4.95	2.96
NORTH AMERICA	174,634	204,195	211,507	222,890	227,921	4.36	2.26
Canada	17,287	20,410	20,874	21,326	25,616	0.49	20.12
United States of America	155,168	181,097	186,092	197,273	198,800	3.80	0.77
Other countries of North America	2,179	2,688	4,541	4,291	3,505	0.07	-18.32
SOUTH AMERICA	7,445	12,282	14,906	17,460	19,347	0.37	10.81
Brazil	7,445	12,282	14,906	17,460	19,347	0.37	10.81
OTHER AMERICAS	8,388	9,901	13,125	10,801	11,328	0.22	4.88
Other countries of the Americas	8,388	9,901	13,125	10,801	11,328	0.22	4.88
EAST ASIA AND THE PACIFIC	149,799	173,682	198,692	216,946	227,231	4.35	4.74
NORTH-EAST ASIA	91,159	102,728	117,568	129,985	137,275	2.63	5.61
China	42,486	49,096	64,559	71,379	83,554	1.60	17.06
Japan	40,543	42,377	40,978	45,725	39,762	0.76	-13.04
Korea, Republic of	8,130	11,255	12,031	12,881	13,959	0.27	8.37
AUSTRALASIA	21,354	24,515	25,034	28,550	31,383	0.60	9.92
Australia	18,801	22,058	22,564	25,972	28,410	0.54	9.39
New Zealand	2,553	2,457	2,470	2,578	2,973	0.06	15.32
OTHER EAST ASIA AND THE PACIFIC	37,286	46,439	56,090	58,411	58,573	1.12	0.28
Other countries of Asia	37,286	46,439	56,090	58,411	58,573	1.12	0.28
EUROPE	4,293,971	4,469,577	4,380,768	4,273,508	4,308,273	82.39	0.81
CENTRAL/EASTERN EUROPE	256,752	244,802	264,238	303,687	298,411	5.71	-1.74
Bulgaria	2,167	2,860	3,159	2,708	3,298	0.06	21.79
Czech Republic	15,808	15,747	17,511	18,816	19,698	0.38	4.69
Estonia	15,490	19,255	18,637	19,658	20,191	0.39	2.71
Hungary	10,840	9,140	10,027	10,883	10,747	0.21	-1.25
Latvia	14,779	12,986	12,769	15,336	14,354	0.27	-6.40
Lithuania	16,901	13,419	15,799	16,985	15,462	0.30	-8.97
Poland	82,207	63,007	82,792	99,755	90,105	1.72	-9.67
Romania	5,425	6,828	8,385	14,521	11,431	0.22	-21.28
Russian Federation	77,964	92,080	84,521	93,941	98,513	1.88	4.87
Slovakia	10,891	5,796	5,350	5,416	7,714	0.15	42.43
Ukraine	4,280	3,684	5,288	5,668	6,898	0.13	21.70
NORTHERN EUROPE	2,298,179	2,431,874	2,339,956	2,330,248	2,305,880	44.10	-1.05
Denmark	591,979	565,148	470,160	435,132	402,480	7.70	-7.50
Finland	206,103	217,969	205,637	214,837	225,068	4.30	4.76
Iceland	6,214	7,981	7,117	8,114	8,843	0.17	8.98
Ireland	14,626	14,480	17,106	17,097	16,330	0.31	-4.49
Norway	1,225,959	1,365,923	1,381,937	1,402,752	1,392,740	26.63	-0.71
United Kingdom	253,298	260,373	257,999	252,316	260,419	4.98	3.21
SOUTHERN EUROPE	241,045	237,959	227,349	183,559	198,654	3.80	8.22
Croatia	1,458	2,927	3,141	2,776	3,505	0.07	26.26
Greece	11,454	10,614	9,793	8,151	8,967	0.17	10.01
Italy	136,321	130,523	123,709	99,033	102,135	1.95	3.13
Malta	893	832	1,173	1,130	1,528	0.03	35.22
Portugal	11,750	10,675	10,594	9,249	11,289	0.22	22.06
Slovenia	4,050	2,168	2,436	2,137	13,710	0.26	541.55
Spain	75,119	80,220	76,503	61,083	57,520	1.10	-5.83
WESTERN EUROPE	1,443,766	1,511,978	1,507,908	1,411,540	1,457,065	27.86	3.23
Austria	40,616	45,550	51,679	39,293	43,076	0.82	9.63
Belgium	40,538	48,488	49,601	49,240	50,492	0.97	2.54
France	121,160	130,262	129,823	123,206	123,661	2.36	0.37
Germany	879,543	904,950	916,322	869,204	896,455	17.14	3.14

703

SWEDEN

4. Arrivals of non-resident tourists in all types of accommodation establishments, by country of residence

	2009	2010	2011	2012	2013	Market share 2013	% Change 2013-2012
Luxembourg	3,509	3,622	3,723	3,242	3,611	0.07	11.38
Netherlands	272,686	278,565	252,735	222,460	224,469	4.29	0.90
Switzerland	85,714	100,541	104,025	104,895	115,301	2.20	9.92
EAST MEDITERRANEAN EUROPE	**8,993**	**10,147**	**10,670**	**12,341**	**14,695**	**0.28**	**19.07**
Cyprus	946	713	1,116	1,104	1,218	0.02	10.33
Turkey	8,047	9,434	9,554	11,237	13,477	0.26	19.93
OTHER EUROPE	**45,236**	**32,817**	**30,647**	**32,133**	**33,568**	**0.64**	**4.47**
Other countries of Europe	45,236	32,817	30,647	32,133	33,568	0.64	4.47
SOUTH ASIA	**21,905**	**25,577**	**33,974**	**47,166**	**55,753**	**1.07**	**18.21**
India	21,905	25,577	33,974	47,166	55,753	1.07	18.21
NOT SPECIFIED	**226,788**	**274,360**	**351,451**	**339,329**	**359,451**	**6.87**	**5.93**
Other countries of the World	226,788	274,360	351,451	339,329	359,451	6.87	5.93

Yearbook of Tourism Statistics, Data 2009 – 2013, 2015 Edition

SWEDEN

5. Overnight stays of non-resident tourists in hotels and similar establishments, by country of residence

	2009	2010	2011	2012	2013	Market share 2013	% Change 2013-2012
TOTAL	6,087,096	6,363,074	6,532,078	6,650,445	6,874,759	100.00	3.37
AFRICA	30,994	24,852	36,334	35,171	38,991	0.57	10.86
SOUTHERN AFRICA	10,003	6,203	10,393	8,317	7,567	0.11	-9.02
South Africa	10,003	6,203	10,393	8,317	7,567	0.11	-9.02
OTHER AFRICA	20,991	18,649	25,941	26,854	31,424	0.46	17.02
Other countries of Africa	20,991	18,649	25,941	26,854	31,424	0.46	17.02
AMERICAS	401,648	474,260	502,542	530,098	537,758	7.82	1.45
NORTH AMERICA	371,528	432,318	449,430	474,256	478,401	6.96	0.87
Canada	33,698	39,417	41,474	41,817	50,704	0.74	21.25
United States of America	334,037	387,794	399,082	424,197	421,018	6.12	-0.75
Other countries of North America	3,793	5,107	8,874	8,242	6,679	0.10	-18.96
SOUTH AMERICA	13,730	22,459	26,386	34,796	37,645	0.55	8.19
Brazil	13,730	22,459	26,386	34,796	37,645	0.55	8.19
OTHER AMERICAS	16,390	19,483	26,726	21,046	21,712	0.32	3.16
Other countries of the Americas	16,390	19,483	26,726	21,046	21,712	0.32	3.16
EAST ASIA AND THE PACIFIC	327,518	384,066	460,646	535,415	575,224	8.37	7.44
NORTH-EAST ASIA	187,869	212,967	245,228	268,929	280,372	4.08	4.26
China	85,456	101,125	134,169	146,856	172,017	2.50	17.13
Japan	86,055	89,667	86,084	96,006	80,881	1.18	-15.75
Korea, Republic of	16,358	22,175	24,975	26,067	27,474	0.40	5.40
AUSTRALASIA	36,902	42,512	44,464	49,287	53,958	0.78	9.48
Australia	32,656	38,509	40,242	44,830	48,887	0.71	9.05
New Zealand	4,246	4,003	4,222	4,457	5,071	0.07	13.78
OTHER EAST ASIA AND THE PACIFIC	102,747	128,587	170,954	217,199	240,894	3.50	10.91
Other countries of Asia	102,747	128,587	170,954	217,199	240,894	3.50	10.91
EUROPE	4,841,808	4,883,830	4,767,737	4,801,607	4,941,625	71.88	2.92
CENTRAL/EASTERN EUROPE	397,602	369,955	376,842	436,537	452,201	6.58	3.59
Bulgaria	3,657	4,496	4,803	3,570	4,041	0.06	13.19
Czech Republic	19,788	21,918	22,518	27,092	27,220	0.40	0.47
Estonia	19,210	23,186	21,844	24,942	24,099	0.35	-3.38
Hungary	19,159	16,029	19,015	18,964	20,517	0.30	8.19
Latvia	21,143	13,323	14,474	18,742	16,925	0.25	-9.69
Lithuania	26,905	14,872	15,777	21,416	20,155	0.29	-5.89
Poland	103,375	71,472	85,031	106,438	109,452	1.59	2.83
Romania	8,029	11,116	13,242	18,975	17,027	0.25	-10.27
Russian Federation	155,269	178,991	162,035	179,033	190,226	2.77	6.25
Slovakia	13,342	8,057	7,846	8,420	11,557	0.17	37.26
Ukraine	7,725	6,495	10,257	8,945	10,982	0.16	22.77
NORTHERN EUROPE	2,526,451	2,535,563	2,431,572	2,536,474	2,591,378	37.69	2.16
Denmark	570,220	529,712	478,952	457,140	443,846	6.46	-2.91
Finland	346,719	359,242	333,232	361,526	375,356	5.46	3.83
Iceland	12,116	15,348	13,875	16,627	18,070	0.26	8.68
Ireland	26,969	23,088	28,225	31,952	30,719	0.45	-3.86
Norway	1,055,889	1,098,250	1,070,661	1,162,768	1,197,015	17.41	2.95
United Kingdom	514,538	509,923	506,627	506,461	526,372	7.66	3.93
SOUTHERN EUROPE	458,961	447,732	423,750	345,213	383,245	5.57	11.02
Croatia					6,905	0.10	
Greece	24,454	22,064	20,063	16,698	18,792	0.27	12.54
Italy	261,268	246,496	234,228	188,559	192,073	2.79	1.86
Malta	1,937	1,650	2,151	2,288	3,016	0.04	31.82
Portugal	18,264	18,650	18,518	17,375	20,995	0.31	20.83
Slovenia	6,003	3,708	3,916	3,735	29,429	0.43	687.93
Spain	147,035	155,164	144,874	116,558	112,035	1.63	-3.88
WESTERN EUROPE	1,369,182	1,464,420	1,470,899	1,420,449	1,449,135	21.08	2.02
Austria	62,421	69,421	82,025	61,671	68,421	1.00	10.95
Belgium	71,419	78,563	83,101	84,856	84,304	1.23	-0.65
France	195,663	208,424	201,973	197,230	198,596	2.89	0.69
Germany	745,879	789,265	783,052	763,455	766,564	11.15	0.41

705

Yearbook of Tourism Statistics, Data 2009 – 2013, 2015 Edition

SWEDEN

5. Overnight stays of non-resident tourists in hotels and similar establishments, by country of residence

	2009	2010	2011	2012	2013	Market share 2013	% Change 2013-2012
Luxembourg	6,691	6,773	7,122	6,316	6,793	0.10	7.55
Netherlands	174,560	184,444	184,229	170,152	174,394	2.54	2.49
Switzerland	112,549	127,530	129,397	136,769	150,063	2.18	9.72
EAST MEDITERRANEAN EUROPE	**17,829**	**20,051**	**21,968**	**25,394**	**30,205**	**0.44**	**18.95**
Cyprus	1,958	1,455	2,430	2,454	2,286	0.03	-6.85
Turkey	15,871	18,596	19,538	22,940	27,919	0.41	21.70
OTHER EUROPE	**71,783**	**46,109**	**42,706**	**37,540**	**35,461**	**0.52**	**-5.54**
Other countries of Europe	71,783	46,109	42,706	37,540	35,461	0.52	-5.54
SOUTH ASIA	**37,095**	**44,981**	**64,082**	**97,794**			
India	37,095	44,981	64,082	97,794			
NOT SPECIFIED	**448,033**	**551,085**	**700,737**	**650,360**	**781,161**	**11.36**	**20.11**
Other countries of the World	448,033	551,085	700,737	650,360	781,161	11.36	20.11

Yearbook of Tourism Statistics, Data 2009 – 2013, 2015 Edition

SWEDEN

6. Overnight stays of non-resident tourists in all types of accommodation establishments, by country of residence

	2009	2010	2011	2012	2013	Market share 2013	% Change 2013-2012
TOTAL	12,329,657	12,802,832	12,880,617	12,774,599	12,890,245	100.00	0.91
AFRICA	38,189	30,486	40,752	40,738	45,488	0.35	11.66
SOUTHERN AFRICA	11,444	7,325	10,834	9,009	8,312	0.06	-7.74
South Africa	11,444	7,325	10,834	9,009	8,312	0.06	-7.74
OTHER AFRICA	26,745	23,161	29,918	31,729	37,176	0.29	17.17
Other countries of Africa	26,745	23,161	29,918	31,729	37,176	0.29	17.17
AMERICAS	439,581	512,699	544,031	575,365	592,198	4.59	2.93
NORTH AMERICA	403,094	462,432	480,402	510,772	522,257	4.05	2.25
Canada	39,952	46,579	47,351	48,828	58,381	0.45	19.56
United States of America	357,957	409,781	422,759	452,136	455,903	3.54	0.83
Other countries of North America	5,185	6,072	10,292	9,808	7,973	0.06	-18.71
SOUTH AMERICA	17,147	27,746	33,833	39,907	44,158	0.34	10.65
Brazil	17,147	27,746	33,833	39,907	44,158	0.34	10.65
OTHER AMERICAS	19,340	22,521	29,796	24,686	25,783	0.20	4.44
Other countries of the Americas	19,340	22,521	29,796	24,686	25,783	0.20	4.44
EAST ASIA AND THE PACIFIC	345,768	392,822	450,910	496,357	517,703	4.02	4.30
NORTH-EAST ASIA	210,225	232,317	266,589	297,339	312,554	2.42	5.12
China	98,009	111,126	146,432	163,377	190,286	1.48	16.47
Japan	93,493	95,764	92,891	104,519	90,510	0.70	-13.40
Korea, Republic of	18,723	25,427	27,266	29,443	31,758	0.25	7.86
AUSTRALASIA	49,544	55,499	56,929	65,450	71,535	0.55	9.30
Australia	43,664	49,947	51,331	59,509	64,771	0.50	8.84
New Zealand	5,880	5,552	5,598	5,941	6,764	0.05	13.85
OTHER EAST ASIA AND THE PACIFIC	85,999	105,006	127,392	133,568	133,614	1.04	0.03
Other countries of Asia	85,999	105,006	127,392	133,568	133,614	1.04	0.03
EUROPE	10,926,452	11,182,645	10,966,570	10,775,168	10,784,267	83.66	0.08
CENTRAL/EASTERN EUROPE	632,073	597,096	642,223	740,413	721,505	5.60	-2.55
Bulgaria	5,042	6,482	7,159	6,189	7,503	0.06	21.23
Czech Republic	37,394	37,528	42,163	46,817	47,378	0.37	1.20
Estonia	48,974	54,609	49,506	55,452	54,234	0.42	-2.20
Hungary	25,400	20,781	22,844	24,913	24,450	0.19	-1.86
Latvia	37,465	33,086	31,672	35,928	34,442	0.27	-4.14
Lithuania	39,483	31,226	36,952	38,906	35,537	0.28	-8.66
Poland	195,559	151,466	201,409	239,854	216,674	1.68	-9.66
Romania	12,542	15,455	19,015	33,203	26,005	0.20	-21.68
Russian Federation	195,107	225,015	207,306	232,565	241,952	1.88	4.04
Slovakia	25,169	13,094	12,160	13,592	17,606	0.14	29.53
Ukraine	9,938	8,354	12,037	12,994	15,724	0.12	21.01
NORTHERN EUROPE	5,674,756	5,896,321	5,654,279	5,651,356	5,558,625	43.12	-1.64
Denmark	1,610,249	1,538,968	1,279,661	1,187,530	1,098,167	8.52	-7.53
Finland	503,290	527,349	502,313	523,312	541,964	4.20	3.56
Iceland	14,469	18,225	16,302	18,664	20,201	0.16	8.24
Ireland	33,856	32,862	39,009	39,302	37,292	0.29	-5.11
Norway	2,918,025	3,176,610	3,219,249	3,294,129	3,260,831	25.30	-1.01
United Kingdom	594,867	602,307	597,745	588,419	600,170	4.66	2.00
SOUTHERN EUROPE	557,479	540,289	518,581	421,599	456,077	3.54	8.18
Croatia	3,393	6,622	7,118	6,349	7,973	0.06	25.58
Greece	26,446	24,035	22,218	18,637	20,403	0.16	9.48
Italy	315,351	296,578	282,609	227,832	235,686	1.83	3.45
Malta	2,094	1,879	2,681	2,583	3,510	0.03	35.89
Portugal	27,135	24,132	24,009	21,202	25,715	0.20	21.29
Slovenia	9,389	4,915	5,848	4,925	31,190	0.24	533.30
Spain	173,671	182,128	174,098	140,071	131,600	1.02	-6.05
WESTERN EUROPE	3,935,463	4,050,886	4,057,515	3,859,749	3,937,929	30.55	2.03
Austria	97,870	106,959	121,685	94,745	103,466	0.80	9.20
Belgium	95,367	113,525	116,752	115,644	117,124	0.91	1.28
France	280,702	297,748	296,988	283,738	283,243	2.20	-0.17
Germany	2,564,252	2,598,505	2,649,661	2,553,629	2,599,236	20.16	1.79

Yearbook of Tourism Statistics, Data 2009 – 2013, 2015 Edition

SWEDEN

6. Overnight stays of non-resident tourists in all types of accommodation establishments, by country of residence

	2009	2010	2011	2012	2013	Market share 2013	% Change 2013-2012
Luxembourg	8,517	8,441	8,538	7,725	8,380	0.07	8.48
Netherlands	682,103	685,834	619,614	551,697	552,611	4.29	0.17
Switzerland	206,652	239,874	244,277	252,571	273,869	2.12	8.43
EAST MEDITERRANEAN EUROPE	**20,711**	**22,923**	**24,181**	**28,223**	**33,433**	**0.26**	**18.46**
Cyprus	2,178	1,610	2,529	2,523	2,773	0.02	9.91
Turkey	18,533	21,313	21,652	25,700	30,660	0.24	19.30
OTHER EUROPE	**105,970**	**75,130**	**69,791**	**73,828**	**76,698**	**0.60**	**3.89**
Other countries of Europe	105,970	75,130	69,791	73,828	76,698	0.60	3.89
SOUTH ASIA	**50,482**	**57,789**	**76,993**	**107,801**	**126,840**	**0.98**	**17.66**
India	50,482	57,789	76,993	107,801	126,840	0.98	17.66
NOT SPECIFIED	**529,185**	**626,391**	**801,361**	**779,170**	**823,749**	**6.39**	**5.72**
Other countries of the World	529,185	626,391	801,361	779,170	823,749	6.39	5.72

Yearbook of Tourism Statistics, Data 2009 – 2013, 2015 Edition

SWITZERLAND

3. Arrivals of non-resident tourists in hotels and similar establishments, by country of residence

		2009	2010	2011	2012	2013	Market share 2013	% Change 2013-2012
TOTAL	(*)	8,293,918	8,628,284	8,534,305	8,566,037	8,967,432	100.00	4.69
AFRICA		79,919	77,745	74,107	81,655	79,070	0.88	-3.17
NORTH AFRICA		17,881	15,931	15,931	20,176	20,098	0.22	-0.39
All countries of North Africa	(*)	17,881	15,931	15,931	20,176	20,098	0.22	-0.39
SOUTHERN AFRICA		20,263	22,695	23,457	23,028	22,291	0.25	-3.20
South Africa		20,263	22,695	23,457	23,028	22,291	0.25	-3.20
OTHER AFRICA		41,775	39,119	34,719	38,451	36,681	0.41	-4.60
Other countries of Africa		41,775	39,119	34,719	38,451	36,681	0.41	-4.60
AMERICAS		820,495	916,493	924,383	952,018	1,004,083	11.20	5.47
NORTH AMERICA		701,100	778,988	787,365	808,271	850,221	9.48	5.19
Canada		91,222	98,772	99,509	101,350	103,289	1.15	1.91
Mexico				18,895	19,879	20,897	0.23	5.12
United States of America		609,878	680,216	668,961	687,042	726,035	8.10	5.68
SOUTH AMERICA		91,213	105,286	120,704	127,156	134,508	1.50	5.78
Argentina		11,359	12,957	14,634	15,313	17,348	0.19	13.29
Brazil		55,991	66,845	79,080	84,167	86,529	0.96	2.81
Chile		4,299	4,655	5,472	5,660	6,506	0.07	14.95
Other countries of South America		19,564	20,829	21,518	22,016	24,125	0.27	9.58
OTHER AMERICAS		28,182	32,219	16,314	16,591	19,354	0.22	16.65
Other countries of the Americas		28,182	32,219	16,314	16,591	19,354	0.22	16.65
EAST ASIA AND THE PACIFIC		873,877	1,073,702	1,300,226	1,490,662	1,695,646	18.91	13.75
NORTH-EAST ASIA		600,652	761,743	951,757	1,107,025	1,251,076	13.95	13.01
China		187,138	286,420	452,724	575,326	704,945	7.86	22.53
Hong Kong, China		37,125	46,051	50,610	59,683	64,833	0.72	8.63
Japan		275,505	297,562	275,923	295,991	286,681	3.20	-3.15
Korea, Republic of		71,517	94,110	115,733	122,772	133,184	1.49	8.48
Taiwan, Province of China		29,367	37,600	56,767	53,253	61,433	0.69	15.36
SOUTH-EAST ASIA		173,649	196,967	226,663	253,071	299,458	3.34	18.33
Indonesia		15,930	19,660	30,691	35,695	42,154	0.47	18.09
Malaysia		15,429	21,618	25,557	29,278	35,413	0.39	20.95
Philippines		4,736	6,214	7,499	8,172	8,334	0.09	1.98
Singapore		52,171	51,431	55,310	70,565	87,444	0.98	23.92
Thailand		44,680	51,907	56,919	60,107	77,341	0.86	28.67
Other countries of South-East Asia		40,703	46,137	50,687	49,254	48,772	0.54	-0.98
AUSTRALASIA			98,374	106,439	113,783	127,955	1.43	12.46
Australia			98,374	106,439	113,783	127,955	1.43	12.46
OTHER EAST ASIA AND THE PACIFIC		99,576	16,618	15,367	16,783	17,157	0.19	2.23
Other countries of Oceania			16,618	15,367	16,783	17,157	0.19	2.23
All countries of Oceania		99,576						
EUROPE		6,249,760	6,237,359	5,867,915	5,612,190	5,720,209	63.79	1.92
CENTRAL/EASTERN EUROPE		367,959	389,001	412,380	434,806	474,156	5.29	9.05
Belarus		5,236	6,254	5,932	5,476	6,868	0.08	25.42
Bulgaria		15,632	14,970	14,449	13,820	15,419	0.17	11.57
Czech Republic		40,060	42,106	42,803	43,291	45,974	0.51	6.20
Estonia			7,568	7,185	7,503	11,662	0.13	55.43
Hungary		34,351	35,030	33,746	33,219	37,617	0.42	13.24
Latvia			4,053	5,726	5,338	5,031	0.06	-5.75
Lithuania			5,382	6,072	6,272	6,271	0.07	-0.02
Poland		46,920	51,020	49,148	48,060	54,222	0.60	12.82
Romania		30,153	30,561	30,523	30,079	30,880	0.34	2.66
Russian Federation		145,751	157,085	179,168	201,488	215,603	2.40	7.01
Slovakia		12,128	11,634	12,323	12,549	14,222	0.16	13.33
Ukraine		21,125	23,338	25,305	27,711	30,387	0.34	9.66
Baltic countries		16,603						
NORTHERN EUROPE		950,924	997,306	942,073	907,705	950,684	10.60	4.73
Denmark		59,504	59,916	57,611	52,815	57,566	0.64	9.00
Finland		38,736	40,149	38,342	36,353	33,799	0.38	-7.03
Iceland		5,531	4,689	5,020	4,940	4,861	0.05	-1.60
Ireland		32,018	30,499	28,805	29,064	29,853	0.33	2.71

709

SWITZERLAND

3. Arrivals of non-resident tourists in hotels and similar establishments, by country of residence

	2009	2010	2011	2012	2013	Market share 2013	% Change 2013-2012
Norway	39,427	44,873	43,975	43,638	44,866	0.50	2.81
Sweden	84,299	85,130	86,203	81,605	81,364	0.91	-0.30
United Kingdom	691,409	732,050	682,117	659,290	698,375	7.79	5.93
SOUTHERN EUROPE	**885,438**	**867,142**	**840,908**	**819,444**	**831,864**	**9.28**	**1.52**
Croatia	11,183	10,369	9,717	10,714	11,703	0.13	9.23
Greece	51,162	44,591	41,097	33,426	34,439	0.38	3.03
Italy	546,564	520,542	489,182	482,940	493,839	5.51	2.26
Malta		3,266	3,395	2,875	3,838	0.04	33.50
Portugal	43,061	44,723	46,284	46,765	53,882	0.60	15.22
Serbia		10,179	11,025	12,656	14,474	0.16	14.36
Serbia and Montenegro	9,944						
Slovenia	10,902	12,161	11,105	10,524	11,655	0.13	10.75
Spain	212,622	221,311	229,103	219,544	208,034	2.32	-5.24
WESTERN EUROPE	**3,861,998**	**3,815,056**	**3,515,558**	**3,284,685**	**3,295,119**	**36.75**	**0.32**
Austria	187,528	195,190	190,153	187,368	187,210	2.09	-0.08
Belgium	241,830	240,784	215,240	203,768	212,484	2.37	4.28
France	685,842	700,578	680,932	669,344	692,288	7.72	3.43
Germany	2,294,411	2,237,941	2,038,680	1,871,498	1,854,263	20.68	-0.92
Liechtenstein	12,180	13,044	12,398	12,278	12,874	0.14	4.85
Luxembourg	43,254	44,480	40,563	37,875	39,377	0.44	3.97
Netherlands	396,953	383,039	337,592	302,554	296,623	3.31	-1.96
EAST MEDITERRANEAN EUROPE	**93,046**	**100,333**	**104,291**	**109,951**	**116,092**	**1.29**	**5.59**
Cyprus		3,322	3,342	3,791	5,590	0.06	47.45
Israel	61,915	61,183	64,756	68,474	66,707	0.74	-2.58
Turkey	31,131	35,828	36,193	37,686	43,795	0.49	16.21
OTHER EUROPE	**90,395**	**68,521**	**52,705**	**55,599**	**52,294**	**0.58**	**-5.94**
Other countries of Europe	90,395	68,521	52,705	55,599	52,294	0.58	-5.94
MIDDLE EAST	**133,545**	**156,986**	**167,050**	**211,649**	**255,464**	**2.85**	**20.70**
Bahrain			5,044	7,281	7,612	0.08	4.55
Egypt	11,548	11,430	11,423	11,851	12,323	0.14	3.98
Kuwait			15,368	17,779	25,702	0.29	44.56
Oman			3,815	7,436	7,735	0.09	4.02
Qatar			13,876	17,238	19,219	0.21	11.49
Saudi Arabia			47,672	65,472	83,371	0.93	27.34
United Arab Emirates			47,267	59,998	72,702	0.81	21.17
Other countries of Middle East	121,997	145,556	22,585	24,594	26,800	0.30	8.97
SOUTH ASIA	**136,322**	**165,999**	**200,624**	**217,863**	**212,960**	**2.37**	**-2.25**
India	136,322	165,999	200,624	217,863	212,960	2.37	-2.25

710

Yearbook of Tourism Statistics, Data 2009 – 2013, 2015 Edition

SWITZERLAND

5. Overnight stays of non-resident tourists in hotels and similar establishments, by country of residence

		2009	2010	2011	2012	2013	Market share 2013	% Change 2013-2012
TOTAL	(*)	20,164,425	20,442,508	19,733,889	19,076,238	19,734,657	100.00	3.45
AFRICA		232,588	228,776	243,150	265,533	254,653	1.29	-4.10
NORTH AFRICA		52,474	46,627	51,124	66,259	69,353	0.35	4.67
All countries of North Africa	(*)	52,474	46,627	51,124	66,259	69,353	0.35	4.67
SOUTHERN AFRICA		60,549	63,678	67,438	69,934	67,478	0.34	-3.51
South Africa		60,549	63,678	67,438	69,934	67,478	0.34	-3.51
OTHER AFRICA		119,565	118,471	124,588	129,340	117,822	0.60	-8.91
Other countries of Africa		119,565	118,471	124,588	129,340	117,822	0.60	-8.91
AMERICAS		1,908,158	2,086,735	2,115,099	2,159,916	2,238,949	11.35	3.66
NORTH AMERICA		1,590,209	1,731,575	1,765,488	1,805,045	1,864,542	9.45	3.30
Canada		207,353	225,140	228,137	231,642	230,189	1.17	-0.63
Mexico				45,220	48,225	48,886	0.25	1.37
United States of America		1,382,856	1,506,435	1,492,131	1,525,178	1,585,467	8.03	3.95
SOUTH AMERICA		240,950	269,240	305,527	310,449	322,869	1.64	4.00
Argentina		31,573	33,417	37,851	37,274	40,609	0.21	8.95
Brazil		144,977	168,771	194,492	201,298	206,378	1.05	2.52
Chile		12,063	11,737	13,898	14,472	15,556	0.08	7.49
Other countries of South America		52,337	55,315	59,286	57,405	60,326	0.31	5.09
OTHER AMERICAS		76,999	85,920	44,084	44,422	51,538	0.26	16.02
Other countries of the Americas		76,999	85,920	44,084	44,422	51,538	0.26	16.02
EAST ASIA AND THE PACIFIC		1,535,073	1,824,939	2,115,976	2,359,424	2,617,318	13.26	10.93
NORTH-EAST ASIA		958,220	1,174,915	1,399,029	1,589,737	1,757,410	8.91	10.55
China		271,717	404,218	595,264	743,656	894,316	4.53	20.26
Hong Kong, China		61,506	73,207	81,956	92,043	100,230	0.51	8.89
Japan		474,720	507,138	479,743	509,757	491,651	2.49	-3.55
Korea, Republic of		106,700	135,377	167,866	172,467	187,966	0.95	8.99
Taiwan, Province of China		43,577	54,975	74,200	71,814	83,247	0.42	15.92
SOUTH-EAST ASIA		359,533	396,998	446,297	484,977	551,429	2.79	13.70
Indonesia		32,546	38,327	55,797	64,347	76,671	0.39	19.15
Malaysia		35,348	44,590	50,573	57,018	65,969	0.33	15.70
Philippines		14,877	17,138	18,651	20,508	21,454	0.11	4.61
Singapore		106,260	104,563	109,974	129,970	153,625	0.78	18.20
Thailand		73,278	85,851	93,402	101,281	124,477	0.63	22.90
Other countries of South-East Asia		97,224	106,529	117,900	111,853	109,233	0.55	-2.34
AUSTRALASIA			217,688	235,603	247,930	271,304	1.37	9.43
Australia			217,688	235,603	247,930	271,304	1.37	9.43
OTHER EAST ASIA AND THE PACIFIC		217,320	35,338	35,047	36,780	37,175	0.19	1.07
Other countries of Oceania			35,338	35,047	36,780	37,175	0.19	1.07
All countries of Oceania		217,320						
EUROPE		15,694,888	15,381,336	14,272,892	13,189,024	13,418,244	67.99	1.74
CENTRAL/EASTERN EUROPE		1,046,029	1,077,998	1,148,374	1,191,385	1,283,212	6.50	7.71
Belarus		14,978	17,161	15,010	15,101	15,748	0.08	4.28
Bulgaria		37,741	38,124	38,356	39,422	42,784	0.22	8.53
Czech Republic		101,882	104,170	105,436	107,324	111,569	0.57	3.96
Estonia			20,244	16,349	17,046	29,719	0.15	74.35
Hungary		82,413	83,597	84,364	86,876	103,602	0.52	19.25
Latvia			11,585	15,057	14,633	13,046	0.07	-10.85
Lithuania			12,736	14,275	15,748	16,415	0.08	4.24
Poland		134,546	143,288	150,097	140,502	166,400	0.84	18.43
Romania		78,822	83,536	86,785	80,182	80,163	0.41	-0.02
Russian Federation		454,525	467,884	513,754	561,490	578,656	2.93	3.06
Slovakia		33,433	29,822	36,284	35,498	44,572	0.23	25.56
Ukraine		64,044	65,851	72,607	77,563	80,538	0.41	3.84
Baltic countries		43,645						
NORTHERN EUROPE		2,480,438	2,480,756	2,313,644	2,114,638	2,218,327	11.24	4.90
Denmark		134,697	137,162	133,762	120,158	124,197	0.63	3.36
Finland		96,478	97,015	95,284	85,410	79,688	0.40	-6.70
Iceland		11,983	10,966	11,494	10,504	10,475	0.05	-0.28
Ireland		82,296	72,489	65,265	63,722	68,827	0.35	8.01

711

SWITZERLAND

5. Overnight stays of non-resident tourists in hotels and similar establishments, by country of residence

	2009	2010	2011	2012	2013	Market share 2013	% Change 2013-2012
Norway	93,270	108,990	104,576	102,690	108,058	0.55	5.23
Sweden	205,494	200,577	203,516	187,918	186,991	0.95	-0.49
United Kingdom	1,856,220	1,853,557	1,699,747	1,544,236	1,640,091	8.31	6.21
SOUTHERN EUROPE	**1,893,828**	**1,836,482**	**1,760,959**	**1,692,792**	**1,731,414**	**8.77**	**2.28**
Croatia	29,599	26,664	26,760	30,219	30,387	0.15	0.56
Greece	125,956	115,528	101,562	81,523	82,856	0.42	1.64
Italy	1,137,588	1,074,447	1,007,519	971,776	980,646	4.97	0.91
Malta		11,521	10,228	7,784	11,215	0.06	44.08
Portugal	104,800	107,642	110,019	109,833	132,255	0.67	20.41
Serbia		24,706	27,696	29,059	34,430	0.17	18.48
Serbia and Montenegro	24,387						
Slovenia	24,317	26,150	25,712	27,929	32,315	0.16	15.70
Spain	447,181	449,824	451,463	434,669	427,310	2.17	-1.69
WESTERN EUROPE	**9,830,381**	**9,571,896**	**8,669,586**	**7,794,023**	**7,794,093**	**39.49**	**0.00**
Austria	403,871	413,575	400,266	378,277	387,467	1.96	2.43
Belgium	775,090	742,277	678,517	620,658	643,365	3.26	3.66
France	1,433,452	1,449,278	1,394,166	1,318,460	1,350,164	6.84	2.40
Germany	6,031,325	5,816,520	5,207,892	4,625,384	4,573,496	23.17	-1.12
Liechtenstein	26,092	26,379	26,286	24,638	25,184	0.13	2.22
Luxembourg	134,243	134,324	115,021	99,970	104,480	0.53	4.51
Netherlands	1,026,308	989,543	847,438	726,636	709,937	3.60	-2.30
EAST MEDITERRANEAN EUROPE	**238,768**	**254,090**	**262,197**	**272,681**	**275,514**	**1.40**	**1.04**
Cyprus		9,622	9,234	9,493	13,119	0.07	38.20
Israel	161,799	155,512	163,041	168,392	160,575	0.81	-4.64
Turkey	76,969	88,956	89,922	94,796	101,820	0.52	7.41
OTHER EUROPE	**205,444**	**160,114**	**118,132**	**123,505**	**115,684**	**0.59**	**-6.33**
Other countries of Europe	205,444	160,114	118,132	123,505	115,684	0.59	-6.33
MIDDLE EAST	**469,438**	**527,870**	**526,332**	**627,459**	**737,526**	**3.74**	**17.54**
Bahrain			13,510	25,253	27,678	0.14	9.60
Egypt	37,958	38,801	37,097	38,001	38,996	0.20	2.62
Kuwait			47,769	50,219	74,234	0.38	47.82
Oman			12,631	19,625	20,921	0.11	6.60
Qatar			40,154	53,952	61,989	0.31	14.90
Saudi Arabia			163,968	201,061	242,828	1.23	20.77
United Arab Emirates			140,577	168,732	195,555	0.99	15.90
Other countries of Middle East	431,480	489,069	70,626	70,616	75,325	0.38	6.67
SOUTH ASIA	**324,280**	**392,852**	**460,440**	**474,882**	**467,967**	**2.37**	**-1.46**
India	324,280	392,852	460,440	474,882	467,967	2.37	-1.46

712

SYRIAN ARAB REPUBLIC

2. Arrivals of non-resident visitors at national borders, by nationality

	2009	2010	2011	2012	2013	Market share 2013	% Change 2013-2012
TOTAL (*)	7,720,795	10,969,682	6,476,408				
AFRICA	76,245	89,670	46,654				
NORTH AFRICA	76,245	89,670	46,654				
Algeria	31,238	37,664	22,463				
Morocco	8,610	10,009	5,385				
Sudan	20,378	23,636	9,359				
Tunisia	16,019	18,361	9,447				
AMERICAS	84,293	96,601	36,817				
NORTH AMERICA	71,523	81,839	28,909				
Canada	22,869	26,068	10,972				
United States of America	48,654	55,771	17,937				
SOUTH AMERICA	12,770	14,762	7,908				
Argentina	1,419	2,149	544				
Brazil	3,518	4,979	1,715				
Venezuela	7,833	7,634	5,649				
EAST ASIA AND THE PACIFIC	60,349	78,102	31,442				
NORTH-EAST ASIA	17,203	25,887	9,254				
China	8,296	12,526	6,080				
Japan	8,907	13,361	3,174				
SOUTH-EAST ASIA	24,511	29,723	14,201				
Indonesia	19,134	21,802	10,227				
Malaysia	5,377	7,921	3,974				
AUSTRALASIA	18,635	22,492	7,987				
Australia	16,867	20,349	7,378				
New Zealand	1,768	2,143	609				
EUROPE	1,141,584	1,959,035	1,467,615				
CENTRAL/EASTERN EUROPE	94,001	99,657	41,753				
Bulgaria	4,611	5,090	2,571				
Czech Republic/Slovakia	4,476	5,190	1,639				
Hungary	4,204	4,237	2,159				
Poland	8,123	8,736	2,196				
Romania	5,469	6,131	2,945				
Ukraine	4,720	6,201	3,713				
USSR (former)	62,398	64,072	26,530				
NORTHERN EUROPE	86,172	105,065	46,033				
Denmark	14,489	17,899	7,331				
Norway	5,513	7,709	3,952				
Sweden	27,137	31,412	13,538				
United Kingdom	39,033	48,045	21,212				
SOUTHERN EUROPE	67,943	83,529	19,153				
Greece	8,091	7,415	2,696				
Italy	33,331	44,608	9,393				
Spain	21,661	25,763	4,866				
Yugoslavia, SFR (former)	4,860	5,743	2,198				
WESTERN EUROPE	150,393	201,223	67,112				
Austria	7,878	10,970	4,379				
Belgium	8,440	10,621	3,489				
France	51,086	68,515	19,697				
Germany	60,146	80,804	29,303				
Netherlands	15,936	21,206	7,794				
Switzerland	6,907	9,107	2,450				
EAST MEDITERRANEAN EUROPE	743,075	1,469,561	1,293,564				
Cyprus	9,943	9,981	3,194				
Turkey	733,132	1,459,580	1,290,370				
MIDDLE EAST	4,711,686	6,191,855	3,112,533				
Bahrain	75,695	80,382	23,215				
Egypt	49,092	56,771	22,643				
Iraq	894,477	1,006,434	1,000,895				
Jordan	1,062,990	1,949,551	560,132				

713

SYRIAN ARAB REPUBLIC

2. Arrivals of non-resident visitors at national borders, by nationality

	2009	2010	2011	2012	2013	Market share 2013	% Change 2013-2012
Kuwait	146,724	134,255	33,161				
Lebanon	1,815,003	2,291,802	1,262,398				
Libya	30,433	35,967	8,133				
Oman	11,592	13,822	3,009				
Palestine	51,687	35,520	37,360				
Qatar	19,267	17,357	3,901				
Saudi Arabia	476,346	484,087	134,397				
United Arab Emirates	52,536	57,064	11,077				
Yemen	21,747	24,570	10,206				
Other countries of Middle East	4,097	4,273	2,006				
SOUTH ASIA	**499,183**	**961,342**	**700,723**				
Afghanistan	1,432	4,229	15,928				
India	20,984	31,056	30,343				
Iran, Islamic Republic of	455,012	891,807	614,529				
Pakistan	21,755	34,250	39,923				
NOT SPECIFIED	**1,147,455**	**1,593,077**	**1,080,624**				
Other countries of the World	82,518	80,017	37,412				
Nationals Residing Abroad	1,064,937	1,513,060	1,043,212				

Yearbook of Tourism Statistics, Data 2009 – 2013, 2015 Edition

SYRIAN ARAB REPUBLIC

3. Arrivals of non-resident tourists in hotels and similar establishments, by nationality

		2009	2010	2011	2012	2013	Market share 2013	% Change 2013-2012
TOTAL	(*)	**2,068,935**	**2,756,635**	**1,503,766**				
AFRICA		**42,409**	**50,167**	**17,913**				
NORTH AFRICA		**42,409**	**50,167**	**17,913**				
Algeria		21,762	24,108	6,073				
Morocco		3,822	5,619	2,577				
Sudan		8,132	10,575	4,187				
Tunisia		8,693	9,865	5,076				
AMERICAS		**38,723**	**50,849**	**18,671**				
NORTH AMERICA		**28,790**	**41,994**	**14,594**				
Canada		11,516	10,960	4,613				
United States of America		17,274	31,034	9,981				
SOUTH AMERICA		**9,933**	**8,855**	**4,077**				
Argentina		1,150	1,335	314				
Brazil		3,002	3,219	1,021				
Venezuela		5,781	4,301	2,742				
EAST ASIA AND THE PACIFIC		**43,456**	**49,473**	**19,421**				
NORTH-EAST ASIA		**13,669**	**17,535**	**6,281**				
China		6,243	8,521	4,140				
Japan		7,426	9,014	2,141				
SOUTH-EAST ASIA		**19,451**	**18,180**	**8,254**				
Indonesia		15,451	13,182	5,619				
Malaysia		4,000	4,998	2,635				
AUSTRALASIA		**10,336**	**13,758**	**4,886**				
Australia		9,132	12,413	4,501				
New Zealand		1,204	1,345	385				
EUROPE		**397,613**	**538,926**	**301,682**				
CENTRAL/EASTERN EUROPE		**66,636**	**68,407**	**22,226**				
Bulgaria		3,481	3,416	1,562				
Czech Republic/Slovakia		3,870	3,613	1,092				
Hungary		3,185	2,757	973				
Poland		5,869	6,049	1,521				
Romania		3,509	4,393	1,721				
Ukraine		3,560	4,148	2,098				
USSR (former)		43,162	44,031	13,259				
NORTHERN EUROPE		**57,772**	**58,553**	**25,660**				
Denmark		10,555	9,996	4,094				
Norway		4,204	4,336	2,223				
Sweden		16,884	17,155	7,393				
United Kingdom		26,129	27,066	11,950				
SOUTHERN EUROPE		**49,893**	**51,478**	**11,568**				
Greece		5,116	4,160	1,512				
Italy		24,160	27,686	5,830				
Spain		16,807	15,572	2,941				
Yugoslavia, SFR (former)		3,810	4,060	1,285				
WESTERN EUROPE		**95,504**	**105,312**	**35,334**				
Austria		5,931	5,981	2,387				
Belgium		6,449	5,986	2,133				
France		29,605	34,637	9,958				
Germany		39,253	41,968	15,219				
Netherlands		9,318	11,516	4,232				
Switzerland		4,948	5,224	1,405				
EAST MEDITERRANEAN EUROPE		**127,808**	**255,176**	**206,894**				
Cyprus		5,343	5,623	1,800				
Turkey		122,465	249,553	205,094				
MIDDLE EAST		**1,101,986**	**1,164,219**	**539,598**				
Bahrain		19,640	22,376	6,462				
Egypt		21,591	30,980	12,356				
Iraq		239,075	253,496	211,843				
Jordan		375,338	461,406	132,568				

715

SYRIAN ARAB REPUBLIC

3. Arrivals of non-resident tourists in hotels and similar establishments, by nationality

	2009	2010	2011	2012	2013	Market share 2013	% Change 2013-2012
Kuwait	22,378	25,827	6,379				
Lebanon	265,905	235,194	129,552				
Libya	17,106	16,734	3,784				
Oman	3,453	4,185	911				
Palestine	11,171	5,475	5,759				
Qatar	3,756	3,651	821				
Saudi Arabia	100,407	83,027	23,051				
United Arab Emirates	12,517	11,541	2,240				
Yemen	8,514	8,548	3,551				
Other countries of Middle East	1,135	1,779	321				
SOUTH ASIA	**343,596**	**781,743**	**522,090**				
Afghanistan	1,127	2,799	9,324				
India	10,018	16,326	15,951				
Iran, Islamic Republic of	321,725	748,986	480,925				
Pakistan	10,726	13,632	15,890				
NOT SPECIFIED	**101,152**	**121,258**	**84,391**				
Other countries of the World	45,247	41,828	19,557				
Nationals Residing Abroad	55,905	79,430	64,834				

Yearbook of Tourism Statistics, Data 2009 – 2013, 2015 Edition

SYRIAN ARAB REPUBLIC

4. Arrivals of non-resident tourists in all types of accommodation establishments, by nationality

	2009	2010	2011	2012	2013	Market share 2013	% Change 2013-2012
TOTAL (*)	**6,091,889**	**8,545,848**	**5,070,380**				
AFRICA	**68,159**	**79,745**	**41,519**				
NORTH AFRICA	**68,159**	**79,745**	**41,519**				
Algeria	28,882	34,149	20,367				
Morocco	7,742	8,756	4,711				
Sudan	18,486	21,206	8,397				
Tunisia	13,049	15,634	8,044				
AMERICAS	**77,621**	**84,195**	**32,019**				
NORTH AMERICA	**64,851**	**71,382**	**25,166**				
Canada	22,380	22,235	9,359				
United States of America	42,471	49,147	15,807				
SOUTH AMERICA	**12,770**	**12,813**	**6,853**				
Argentina	1,419	1,841	466				
Brazil	3,518	4,380	1,509				
Venezuela	7,833	6,592	4,878				
EAST ASIA AND THE PACIFIC	**56,937**	**66,696**	**26,800**				
NORTH-EAST ASIA	**16,517**	**22,560**	**8,076**				
China	7,753	10,960	5,320				
Japan	8,764	11,600	2,756				
SOUTH-EAST ASIA	**24,449**	**24,896**	**11,896**				
Indonesia	19,072	18,254	8,563				
Malaysia	5,377	6,642	3,333				
AUSTRALASIA	**15,971**	**19,240**	**6,828**				
Australia	14,203	17,357	6,293				
New Zealand	1,768	1,883	535				
EUROPE	**772,031**	**1,305,301**	**920,736**				
CENTRAL/EASTERN EUROPE	**91,604**	**86,936**	**36,413**				
Bulgaria	4,611	4,437	2,241				
Czech Republic/Slovakia	4,476	4,692	1,482				
Hungary	4,204	3,789	1,931				
Poland	8,123	7,633	1,919				
Romania	5,469	5,379	2,584				
Ukraine	4,720	5,387	3,226				
USSR (former)	60,001	55,619	23,030				
NORTHERN EUROPE	**82,233**	**92,455**	**40,516**				
Denmark	14,489	15,805	6,473				
Norway	5,513	6,855	3,514				
Sweden	27,137	27,122	11,689				
United Kingdom	35,094	42,673	18,840				
SOUTHERN EUROPE	**65,310**	**74,688**	**17,152**				
Greece	8,040	6,575	2,391				
Italy	31,115	40,302	8,486				
Spain	21,295	22,538	4,257				
Yugoslavia, SFR (former)	4,860	5,273	2,018				
WESTERN EUROPE	**141,264**	**177,343**	**59,101**				
Austria	7,878	9,455	3,774				
Belgium	8,440	9,464	3,109				
France	46,906	60,527	17,401				
Germany	56,690	71,430	25,903				
Netherlands	14,443	18,207	6,692				
Switzerland	6,907	8,260	2,222				
EAST MEDITERRANEAN EUROPE	**391,620**	**873,879**	**767,554**				
Cyprus	9,943	8,891	2,845				
Turkey	381,677	864,988	764,709				
MIDDLE EAST	**3,522,115**	**4,574,783**	**2,352,504**				
Bahrain	75,059	70,169	20,265				
Egypt	45,154	50,171	20,011				
Iraq	806,118	897,975	893,033				
Jordan	882,750	1,363,644	391,793				

717

SYRIAN ARAB REPUBLIC

4. Arrivals of non-resident tourists in all types of accommodation establishments, by nationality

	2009	2010	2011	2012	2013	Market share 2013	% Change 2013-2012
Kuwait	140,716	120,977	29,881				
Lebanon	921,762	1,467,701	808,457				
Libya	28,337	31,841	7,200				
Oman	11,592	12,299	2,677				
Palestine	47,943	32,502	34,185				
Qatar	19,053	15,173	3,410				
Saudi Arabia	467,095	435,663	120,953				
United Arab Emirates	50,794	51,521	10,001				
Yemen	21,747	21,585	8,966				
Other countries of Middle East	3,995	3,562	1,672				
SOUTH ASIA	**467,012**	**853,065**	**621,327**				
Afghanistan	1,432	3,719	14,008				
India	16,980	27,346	26,719				
Iran, Islamic Republic of	430,880	792,258	545,932				
Pakistan	17,720	29,742	34,668				
NOT SPECIFIED	**1,128,014**	**1,582,063**	**1,075,475**				
Other countries of the World	63,077	69,003	32,263				
Nationals Residing Abroad	1,064,937	1,513,060	1,043,212				

SYRIAN ARAB REPUBLIC

5. Overnight stays of non-resident tourists in hotels and similar establishments, by nationality

	2009	2010	2011	2012	2013	Market share 2013	% Change 2013-2012
TOTAL (*)	**11,530,321**	**12,869,132**	**5,471,525**				
AFRICA	**315,672**	**346,318**	**50,546**				
NORTH AFRICA	**315,672**	**346,318**	**50,546**				
Algeria	135,173	151,845	11,826				
Morocco	35,182	32,670	7,731				
Sudan	88,349	90,271	13,818				
Tunisia	56,968	71,532	17,171				
AMERICAS	**286,050**	**312,612**	**59,267**				
NORTH AMERICA	**238,008**	**265,883**	**47,135**				
Canada	92,379	43,059	13,535				
United States of America	145,629	222,824	33,600				
SOUTH AMERICA	**48,042**	**46,729**	**12,132**				
Argentina	8,743	7,509	1,142				
Brazil	9,923	14,486	2,311				
Venezuela	29,376	24,734	8,679				
EAST ASIA AND THE PACIFIC	**282,720**	**354,791**	**76,983**				
NORTH-EAST ASIA	**95,368**	**120,549**	**30,843**				
China	55,557	64,974	25,420				
Japan	39,811	55,575	5,423				
SOUTH-EAST ASIA	**96,500**	**129,471**	**34,352**				
Indonesia	66,469	96,982	23,531				
Malaysia	30,031	32,489	10,821				
AUSTRALASIA	**90,852**	**104,771**	**11,788**				
Australia	86,229	94,345	10,858				
New Zealand	4,623	10,426	930				
EUROPE	**2,517,393**	**2,876,047**	**805,497**				
CENTRAL/EASTERN EUROPE	**646,934**	**615,671**	**74,727**				
Bulgaria	27,628	26,477	3,866				
Czech Republic/Slovakia	33,660	27,999	2,899				
Hungary	23,256	22,283	2,691				
Poland	83,739	40,831	2,797				
Romania	37,246	27,821	5,941				
Ukraine	25,506	32,148	5,590				
USSR (former)	415,899	438,112	50,943				
NORTHERN EUROPE	**511,639**	**380,203**	**82,120**				
Denmark	108,567	64,977	13,892				
Norway	29,040	28,184	7,261				
Sweden	116,687	111,507	27,644				
United Kingdom	257,345	175,535	33,323				
SOUTHERN EUROPE	**325,657**	**379,635**	**33,167**				
Greece	32,048	24,257	4,351				
Italy	163,353	212,372	16,585				
Spain	105,440	111,541	8,806				
Yugoslavia, SFR (former)	24,816	31,465	3,425				
WESTERN EUROPE	**653,571**	**706,883**	**97,710**				
Austria	35,758	38,874	6,445				
Belgium	39,312	38,908	5,825				
France	249,341	242,494	26,523				
Germany	239,813	277,798	43,492				
Netherlands	63,965	74,852	11,042				
Switzerland	25,382	33,957	4,383				
EAST MEDITERRANEAN EUROPE	**379,592**	**793,655**	**517,773**				
Cyprus	29,380	36,552	5,606				
Turkey	350,212	757,103	512,167				
MIDDLE EAST	**5,454,032**	**3,593,764**	**1,932,302**				
Bahrain	217,890	134,933	42,640				
Egypt	148,474	205,331	45,209				
Iraq	1,310,543	807,296	805,003				
Jordan	1,714,380	1,178,750	461,740				

719

SYRIAN ARAB REPUBLIC

5. Overnight stays of non-resident tourists in hotels and similar establishments, by nationality

	2009	2010	2011	2012	2013	Market share 2013	% Change 2013-2012
Kuwait	129,934	128,760	32,497				
Lebanon	754,041	491,109	349,792				
Libya	130,139	123,616	12,487				
Oman	23,098	22,039	3,871				
Palestine	40,969	29,105	18,726				
Qatar	37,625	19,318	4,078				
Saudi Arabia	742,792	334,917	133,248				
United Arab Emirates	97,896	53,787	11,558				
Yemen	99,200	53,183	10,652				
Other countries of Middle East	7,051	11,620	801				
SOUTH ASIA	**2,067,934**	**4,621,581**	**2,155,678**				
Afghanistan	5,259	18,192	42,957				
India	83,094	114,183	72,230				
Iran, Islamic Republic of	1,903,989	4,362,885	1,971,794				
Pakistan	75,592	126,321	68,697				
NOT SPECIFIED	**606,520**	**764,019**	**391,252**				
Other countries of the World	226,522	224,119	55,355				
Nationals Residing Abroad	379,998	539,900	335,897				

Yearbook of Tourism Statistics, Data 2009 – 2013, 2015 Edition

SYRIAN ARAB REPUBLIC

6. Overnight stays of non-resident tourists in all types of accommodation establishments, by nationality

	2009	2010	2011	2012	2013	Market share 2013	% Change 2013-2012
TOTAL (*)	**77,128,427**	**84,775,969**	**47,618,777**				
AFRICA	**557,453**	**577,805**	**272,681**				
NORTH AFRICA	**557,453**	**577,805**	**272,681**				
Algeria	190,135	223,172	158,999				
Morocco	66,572	61,037	25,975				
Sudan	203,132	183,835	50,866				
Tunisia	97,614	109,761	36,841				
AMERICAS	**641,010**	**638,403**	**184,279**				
NORTH AMERICA	**575,466**	**568,469**	**156,127**				
Canada	175,687	160,662	63,033				
United States of America	399,779	407,807	93,094				
SOUTH AMERICA	**65,544**	**69,934**	**28,152**				
Argentina	13,800	12,210	2,579				
Brazil	12,056	20,453	4,950				
Venezuela	39,688	37,271	20,623				
EAST ASIA AND THE PACIFIC	**349,445**	**515,698**	**137,930**				
NORTH-EAST ASIA	**106,821**	**156,687**	**41,305**				
China	61,829	92,175	33,759				
Japan	44,992	64,512	7,546				
SOUTH-EAST ASIA	**111,654**	**205,733**	**67,648**				
Indonesia	74,117	154,240	52,063				
Malaysia	37,537	51,493	15,585				
AUSTRALASIA	**130,970**	**153,278**	**28,977**				
Australia	124,211	138,104	26,723				
New Zealand	6,759	15,174	2,254				
EUROPE	**6,552,963**	**7,841,108**	**4,535,014**				
CENTRAL/EASTERN EUROPE	**963,078**	**969,868**	**360,228**				
Bulgaria	32,391	39,959	12,759				
Czech Republic/Slovakia	36,962	42,256	8,065				
Hungary	26,616	33,438	13,249				
Poland	86,897	45,414	3,949				
Romania	44,728	42,070	18,047				
Ukraine	32,901	48,518	20,457				
USSR (former)	702,583	718,213	283,702				
NORTHERN EUROPE	**806,310**	**709,244**	**226,514**				
Denmark	120,931	110,995	32,740				
Norway	37,046	48,144	17,494				
Sweden	278,004	190,479	61,680				
United Kingdom	370,329	359,626	114,600				
SOUTHERN EUROPE	**452,260**	**558,428**	**79,054**				
Greece	45,860	46,090	12,290				
Italy	250,671	289,004	32,722				
Spain	126,951	175,846	20,952				
Yugoslavia, SFR (former)	28,778	47,488	13,090				
WESTERN EUROPE	**1,192,710**	**1,339,266**	**302,988**				
Austria	46,847	66,406	17,435				
Belgium	55,571	66,464	13,960				
France	423,885	524,644	107,636				
Germany	527,104	495,880	122,578				
Netherlands	104,078	127,865	30,526				
Switzerland	35,225	58,007	10,853				
EAST MEDITERRANEAN EUROPE	**3,138,605**	**4,264,302**	**3,566,230**				
Cyprus	79,000	62,440	13,890				
Turkey	3,059,605	4,201,862	3,552,340				
MIDDLE EAST	**35,915,459**	**26,497,001**	**15,369,581**				
Bahrain	938,829	636,653	187,541				
Egypt	763,315	343,228	100,209				
Iraq	11,669,785	7,200,257	7,793,504				
Jordan	6,054,940	5,873,743	1,810,674				

721

SYRIAN ARAB REPUBLIC

6. Overnight stays of non-resident tourists in all types of accommodation establishments, by nationality

	2009	2010	2011	2012	2013	Market share 2013	% Change 2013-2012
Kuwait	2,221,736	1,064,245	263,561				
Lebanon	6,935,404	6,430,478	3,621,387				
Libya	250,733	253,144	41,776				
Oman	111,914	77,069	15,851				
Palestine	497,498	328,655	333,794				
Qatar	296,611	114,806	25,539				
Saudi Arabia	5,105,003	3,485,226	1,007,868				
United Arab Emirates	665,615	493,833	96,977				
Yemen	324,652	165,983	57,508				
Other countries of Middle East	79,424	29,681	13,392				
SOUTH ASIA	**2,517,819**	**5,209,221**	**2,957,846**				
Afghanistan	6,158	27,330	86,080				
India	123,582	352,138	304,722				
Iran, Islamic Republic of	2,273,867	4,624,482	2,406,320				
Pakistan	114,212	205,271	160,724				
NOT SPECIFIED	**30,594,278**	**43,496,733**	**24,161,446**				
Other countries of the World	305,159	462,049	166,598				
Nationals Residing Abroad	30,289,119	43,034,684	23,994,848				

Yearbook of Tourism Statistics, Data 2009 – 2013, 2015 Edition

TAIWAN, PROVINCE OF CHINA

2. Arrivals of non-resident visitors at national borders, by country of residence

	2009	2010	2011	2012	2013	Market share 2013	% Change 2013-2012
TOTAL	4,395,004	5,567,277	6,087,484	7,311,470	8,016,280	100.00	9.64
AFRICA	7,735	8,254	8,938	8,865	8,795	0.11	-0.79
SOUTHERN AFRICA	4,009	4,066	4,709	4,222	4,164	0.05	-1.37
South Africa	4,009	4,066	4,709	4,222	4,164	0.05	-1.37
OTHER AFRICA	3,726	4,188	4,229	4,643	4,631	0.06	-0.26
Other countries of Africa	3,726	4,188	4,229	4,643	4,631	0.06	-0.26
AMERICAS	442,036	474,709	495,136	497,597	502,446	6.27	0.97
NORTH AMERICA	431,183	462,610	482,172	484,353	489,048	6.10	0.97
Canada	60,138	64,739	67,545	70,614	72,693	0.91	2.94
Mexico	1,787	2,142	2,010	2,323	2,295	0.03	-1.21
United States of America	369,258	395,729	412,617	411,416	414,060	5.17	0.64
SOUTH AMERICA	4,491	5,090	5,163	5,142	5,064	0.06	-1.52
Argentina	873	984	968	1,045	1,124	0.01	7.56
Brazil	3,618	4,106	4,195	4,097	3,940	0.05	-3.83
OTHER AMERICAS	6,362	7,009	7,801	8,102	8,334	0.10	2.86
Other countries of the Americas	6,362	7,009	7,801	8,102	8,334	0.10	2.86
EAST ASIA AND THE PACIFIC	3,690,485	4,817,622	5,297,032	6,512,815	7,179,272	89.56	10.23
NORTH-EAST ASIA	2,859,231	3,722,151	4,139,789	5,294,188	5,830,894	72.74	10.14
China	972,123	1,630,735	1,784,185	2,586,428	2,874,702	35.86	11.15
Hong Kong, China	718,806	794,362	817,944	1,016,356	1,183,341	14.76	16.43
Japan	1,000,661	1,080,153	1,294,758	1,432,315	1,421,550	17.73	-0.75
Korea, Republic of	167,641	216,901	242,902	259,089	351,301	4.38	35.59
SOUTH-EAST ASIA	689,027	911,174	1,071,975	1,132,592	1,261,596	15.74	11.39
Indonesia	106,612	123,834	156,281	163,598	171,299	2.14	4.71
Malaysia	166,987	285,734	307,898	341,032	394,326	4.92	15.63
Philippines	77,206	87,944	101,539	105,130	99,698	1.24	-5.17
Singapore	194,523	241,334	299,599	327,253	364,733	4.55	11.45
Thailand	78,405	92,949	102,902	97,712	104,138	1.30	6.58
Viet Nam				89,354	118,467	1.48	32.58
Other countries of South-East Asia	65,294	79,379	103,756	8,513	8,935	0.11	4.96
AUSTRALASIA	65,158	70,898	69,503	74,331	76,471	0.95	2.88
Australia	57,147	62,254	60,067	63,597	65,777	0.82	3.43
New Zealand	8,011	8,644	9,436	10,734	10,694	0.13	-0.37
OTHER EAST ASIA AND THE PACIFIC	77,069	113,399	15,765	11,704	10,311	0.13	-11.90
Other countries of Asia	76,054	112,344	14,728	10,621	9,060	0.11	-14.70
Other countries of Oceania	1,015	1,055	1,037	1,083	1,251	0.02	15.51
EUROPE	197,070	203,301	212,148	218,045	223,062	2.78	2.30
CENTRAL/EASTERN EUROPE		5,457	6,667	7,066	7,226	0.09	2.26
Russian Federation		5,457	6,667	7,066	7,226	0.09	2.26
NORTHERN EUROPE	50,822	50,949	50,402	49,904	49,574	0.62	-0.66
Sweden	6,007	6,519	6,983	7,128	7,136	0.09	0.11
United Kingdom	44,815	44,430	43,419	42,776	42,438	0.53	-0.79
SOUTHERN EUROPE	19,237	19,274	19,732	20,287	21,958	0.27	8.24
Greece	1,348	1,258	1,129	1,192	1,167	0.01	-2.10
Italy	12,237	12,246	12,407	12,932	13,663	0.17	5.65
Spain	5,652	5,770	6,196	6,163	7,128	0.09	15.66
WESTERN EUROPE	91,917	98,894	105,801	110,262	113,496	1.42	2.93
Austria	4,968	5,806	6,368	5,609	5,350	0.07	-4.62
Belgium	4,492	4,435	4,348	4,781	4,756	0.06	-0.52
France	25,245	26,455	29,082	31,452	32,384	0.40	2.96
Germany	39,533	42,446	44,644	45,054	46,533	0.58	3.28
Netherlands	11,230	13,158	14,401	15,797	16,443	0.21	4.09
Switzerland	6,449	6,594	6,958	7,569	8,030	0.10	6.09
OTHER EUROPE	35,094	28,727	29,546	30,526	30,808	0.38	0.92
Other countries of Europe	35,094	28,727	29,546	30,526	30,808	0.38	0.92
MIDDLE EAST	12,217	13,542	13,791	13,032	13,918	0.17	6.80
All countries of Middle East	12,217	13,542	13,791	13,032	13,918	0.17	6.80
SOUTH ASIA	18,555	23,849	23,927	23,251	23,318	0.29	0.29
India	18,555	23,849	23,927	23,251	23,318	0.29	0.29
NOT SPECIFIED	26,906	26,000	36,512	37,865	65,469	0.82	72.90
Other countries of the World	26,906	26,000	36,512	37,865	65,469	0.82	72.90

Yearbook of Tourism Statistics, Data 2009 – 2013, 2015 Edition

TAIWAN, PROVINCE OF CHINA

4. Arrivals of non-resident tourists in all types of accommodation establishments, by country of residence

	2009	2010	2011	2012	2013	Market share 2013	% Change 2013-2012
TOTAL	3,899,831	5,061,513	5,519,231	6,735,639	7,384,271	100.00	9.63
AFRICA	6,277	6,645	6,634	6,932	6,724	0.09	-3.00
SOUTHERN AFRICA	3,086	3,066	3,246	3,079	2,992	0.04	-2.83
South Africa	3,086	3,066	3,246	3,079	2,992	0.04	-2.83
OTHER AFRICA	3,191	3,579	3,388	3,853	3,732	0.05	-3.14
Other countries of Africa	3,191	3,579	3,388	3,853	3,732	0.05	-3.14
AMERICAS	403,374	435,573	447,827	458,296	463,569	6.28	1.15
NORTH AMERICA	394,748	425,735	437,624	447,409	452,720	6.13	1.19
Canada	52,611	57,285	60,033	64,840	66,730	0.90	2.91
Mexico	1,291	1,816	1,716	2,032	2,032	0.03	
United States of America	340,846	366,634	375,875	380,537	383,958	5.20	0.90
SOUTH AMERICA	3,696	4,337	4,542	4,645	4,563	0.06	-1.77
Argentina	728	814	836	875	1,013	0.01	15.77
Brazil	2,968	3,523	3,706	3,770	3,550	0.05	-5.84
OTHER AMERICAS	4,930	5,501	5,661	6,242	6,286	0.09	0.70
Other countries of the Americas	4,930	5,501	5,661	6,242	6,286	0.09	0.70
EAST ASIA AND THE PACIFIC	3,270,919	4,389,655	4,819,702	6,018,906	6,642,190	89.95	10.36
NORTH-EAST ASIA	2,684,917	3,577,379	3,929,895	5,084,050	5,606,989	75.93	10.29
China	860,075	1,548,139	1,666,562	2,456,742	2,750,662	37.25	11.96
Hong Kong, China	690,933	768,217	789,520	988,231	1,138,572	15.42	15.21
Japan	975,832	1,052,541	1,242,652	1,392,557	1,381,142	18.70	-0.82
Korea, Republic of	158,077	208,482	231,161	246,520	336,613	4.56	36.55
SOUTH-EAST ASIA	488,637	689,941	783,390	858,359	956,641	12.96	11.45
Indonesia	43,472	54,229	70,444	75,161	76,402	1.03	1.65
Malaysia	153,344	271,956	287,318	317,937	368,959	5.00	16.05
Philippines	36,422	42,704	47,245	52,852	47,220	0.64	-10.66
Singapore	189,115	235,754	290,029	317,568	355,050	4.81	11.80
Thailand	42,156	53,751	53,794	55,561	64,467	0.87	16.03
Other countries of South-East Asia	24,128	31,547	34,560	39,280	44,543	0.60	13.40
AUSTRALASIA	55,994	60,684	60,783	66,770	69,835	0.95	4.59
Australia	48,726	52,864	52,483	57,007	60,305	0.82	5.79
New Zealand	7,268	7,820	8,300	9,763	9,530	0.13	-2.39
OTHER EAST ASIA AND THE PACIFIC	41,371	61,651	45,634	9,727	8,725	0.12	-10.30
Other countries of Asia	40,441	60,728	44,716	8,788	7,691	0.10	-12.48
Other countries of Oceania	930	923	918	939	1,034	0.01	10.12
EUROPE	170,053	179,090	186,429	194,470	200,037	2.71	2.86
CENTRAL/EASTERN EUROPE		4,479	5,700	6,212	6,449	0.09	3.82
Russian Federation		4,479	5,700	6,212	6,449	0.09	3.82
NORTHERN EUROPE	43,004	44,231	44,541	45,263	45,731	0.62	1.03
Sweden	5,705	6,046	6,405	6,643	6,728	0.09	1.28
United Kingdom	37,299	38,185	38,136	38,620	39,003	0.53	0.99
SOUTHERN EUROPE	15,884	17,500	18,043	18,567	20,167	0.27	8.62
Greece	1,056	985	886	930	949	0.01	2.04
Italy	10,231	11,270	11,602	12,045	12,818	0.17	6.42
Spain	4,597	5,245	5,555	5,592	6,400	0.09	14.45
WESTERN EUROPE	80,401	87,815	92,622	97,975	100,517	1.36	2.59
Austria	4,145	4,733	5,269	4,879	4,740	0.06	-2.85
Belgium	3,870	3,850	3,916	4,326	4,380	0.06	1.25
France	22,332	23,716	25,644	28,070	29,399	0.40	4.73
Germany	34,231	38,358	39,566	40,360	40,651	0.55	0.72
Netherlands	9,966	11,044	11,853	13,316	13,733	0.19	3.13
Switzerland	5,857	6,114	6,374	7,024	7,614	0.10	8.40
OTHER EUROPE	30,764	25,065	25,523	26,453	27,173	0.37	2.72
Other countries of Europe	30,764	25,065	25,523	26,453	27,173	0.37	2.72
MIDDLE EAST	11,349	12,630	12,709	12,021	12,771	0.17	6.24
All countries of Middle East	11,349	12,630	12,709	12,021	12,771	0.17	6.24
SOUTH ASIA	15,841	19,702	20,192	19,560	19,375	0.26	-0.95
India	15,841	19,702	20,192	19,560	19,375	0.26	-0.95
NOT SPECIFIED	22,018	18,218	25,738	25,454	39,605	0.54	55.59
Other countries of the World	22,018	18,218	25,738	25,454	39,605	0.54	55.59

Yearbook of Tourism Statistics, Data 2009 – 2013, 2015 Edition

TAIWAN, PROVINCE OF CHINA

6. Overnight stays of non-resident tourists in all types of accommodation establishments, by country of residence

	2009	2010	2011	2012	2013	Market share 2013	% Change 2013-2012
TOTAL	27,948,655	35,754,330	38,934,884	46,297,554	50,634,179	100.00	9.37
AFRICA	75,930	78,195	80,527	88,656	91,917	0.18	3.68
SOUTHERN AFRICA	43,869	38,613	43,382	44,400	46,929	0.09	5.70
South Africa	43,869	38,613	43,382	44,400	46,929	0.09	5.70
OTHER AFRICA	32,061	39,582	37,145	44,256	44,988	0.09	1.65
Other countries of Africa	32,061	39,582	37,145	44,256	44,988	0.09	1.65
AMERICAS	4,434,211	4,585,544	4,751,009	4,980,712	5,317,101	10.50	6.75
NORTH AMERICA	4,323,272	4,468,060	4,624,435	4,837,156	5,173,335	10.22	6.95
Canada	521,194	536,943	604,594	692,612	729,451	1.44	5.32
Mexico	12,617	17,031	17,611	19,101	22,424	0.04	17.40
United States of America	3,789,461	3,914,086	4,002,230	4,125,443	4,421,460	8.73	7.18
SOUTH AMERICA	43,478	47,356	51,043	55,637	52,890	0.10	-4.94
Argentina	10,396	11,430	13,021	12,097	13,042	0.03	7.81
Brazil	33,082	35,926	38,022	43,540	39,848	0.08	-8.48
OTHER AMERICAS	67,461	70,128	75,531	87,919	90,876	0.18	3.36
Other countries of the Americas	67,461	70,128	75,531	87,919	90,876	0.18	3.36
EAST ASIA AND THE PACIFIC	21,552,207	29,053,026	31,740,080	38,555,010	42,360,220	83.66	9.87
NORTH-EAST ASIA	15,570,102	21,360,551	23,423,166	30,553,443	33,504,562	66.17	9.66
China	6,832,027	11,902,626	13,162,258	18,477,125	20,390,168	40.27	10.35
Hong Kong, China	2,995,864	3,305,994	3,463,681	4,329,675	4,942,345	9.76	14.15
Japan	4,925,098	5,178,283	5,751,580	6,566,496	6,661,683	13.16	1.45
Korea, Republic of	817,113	973,648	1,045,647	1,180,147	1,510,366	2.98	27.98
SOUTH-EAST ASIA	4,480,228	5,703,915	6,425,003	7,239,102	8,073,639	15.95	11.53
Indonesia	640,284	691,853	823,093	864,958	862,539	1.70	-0.28
Malaysia	1,173,741	1,896,448	2,045,601	2,367,082	2,781,852	5.49	17.52
Philippines	433,040	449,484	475,826	563,575	510,800	1.01	-9.36
Singapore	1,320,923	1,592,265	1,877,456	2,077,679	2,336,503	4.61	12.46
Thailand	411,026	469,501	511,492	528,641	540,925	1.07	2.32
Other countries of South-East Asia	501,214	604,364	691,535	837,167	1,041,020	2.06	24.35
AUSTRALASIA	442,571	490,904	540,125	604,918	640,600	1.27	5.90
Australia	365,122	402,031	433,424	479,424	515,753	1.02	7.58
New Zealand	77,449	88,873	106,701	125,494	124,847	0.25	-0.52
OTHER EAST ASIA AND THE PACIFIC	1,059,306	1,497,656	1,351,786	157,547	141,419	0.28	-10.24
Other countries of Asia	1,049,739	1,487,441	1,340,780	145,243	129,412	0.26	-10.90
Other countries of Oceania	9,567	10,215	11,006	12,304	12,007	0.02	-2.41
EUROPE	1,548,243	1,572,059	1,773,600	2,020,577	2,174,122	4.29	7.60
CENTRAL/EASTERN EUROPE		53,825	63,643	68,612	70,523	0.14	2.79
Russian Federation		53,825	63,643	68,612	70,523	0.14	2.79
NORTHERN EUROPE	355,294	362,450	397,677	439,223	467,856	0.92	6.52
Sweden	55,755	56,026	62,597	72,393	72,178	0.14	-0.30
United Kingdom	299,539	306,424	335,080	366,830	395,678	0.78	7.86
SOUTHERN EUROPE	124,658	140,488	149,958	176,970	204,036	0.40	15.29
Greece	7,611	5,489	5,596	6,806	7,502	0.01	10.23
Italy	75,003	85,206	90,127	103,344	117,312	0.23	13.52
Spain	42,044	49,793	54,235	66,820	79,222	0.16	18.56
WESTERN EUROPE	801,080	809,994	925,038	1,070,040	1,138,911	2.25	6.44
Austria	44,478	44,963	52,033	55,001	54,978	0.11	-0.04
Belgium	34,721	32,004	34,896	41,753	47,066	0.09	12.72
France	245,079	247,128	293,062	357,413	393,132	0.78	9.99
Germany	336,545	344,795	375,832	405,408	417,826	0.83	3.06
Netherlands	85,530	86,415	109,376	137,816	146,240	0.29	6.11
Switzerland	54,727	54,689	59,839	72,649	79,669	0.16	9.66
OTHER EUROPE	267,211	205,302	237,284	265,732	292,796	0.58	10.18
Other countries of Europe	267,211	205,302	237,284	265,732	292,796	0.58	10.18
MIDDLE EAST	85,839	92,117	101,194	90,554	100,955	0.20	11.49
All countries of Middle East	85,839	92,117	101,194	90,554	100,955	0.20	11.49
SOUTH ASIA	165,749	189,515	199,597	234,762	216,761	0.43	-7.67
India	165,749	189,515	199,597	234,762	216,761	0.43	-7.67
NOT SPECIFIED	86,476	183,874	288,877	327,283	373,103	0.74	14.00
Other countries of the World	86,476	183,874	288,877	327,283	373,103	0.74	14.00

Yearbook of Tourism Statistics, Data 2009 – 2013, 2015 Edition

TAJIKISTAN

2. Arrivals of non-resident visitors at national borders, by country of residence

	2009	2010	2011	2012	2013	Market share 2013	% Change 2013-2012
TOTAL	207,439	159,680	183,154	244,275	207,911	100.00	-14.89
AFRICA	129	188		32	1	0.00	-96.88
EAST AFRICA				7			
Kenya				7			
NORTH AFRICA				9			
Algeria				9			
SOUTHERN AFRICA	129	188		16	1	0.00	-93.75
South Africa	129	188		16	1	0.00	-93.75
AMERICAS	1,334	1,465	587	1,085	764	0.37	-29.59
NORTH AMERICA	1,321	1,415	573	1,047	748	0.36	-28.56
Canada	203	221	161	178	161	0.08	-9.55
Mexico	4	6		21			
United States of America	1,114	1,188	412	848	587	0.28	-30.78
SOUTH AMERICA	13	50	14	38	16	0.01	-57.89
Argentina	13	24	13	13	4	0.00	-69.23
Brazil			1	15	10	0.00	-33.33
Colombia		26		10	2	0.00	-80.00
EAST ASIA AND THE PACIFIC	3,384	3,546	4,280	4,616	1,397	0.67	-69.74
NORTH-EAST ASIA	3,130	3,208	4,196	4,411	1,245	0.60	-71.78
China	2,437	2,694	3,788	4,105	970	0.47	-76.37
Japan	369	294	90	109	198	0.10	81.65
Korea, Dem. People's Republic of	311	200	318	182	72	0.03	-60.44
Mongolia	13	20		15	5	0.00	-66.67
SOUTH-EAST ASIA	84	128	43	51	27	0.01	-47.06
Indonesia	21	36	31	9	1	0.00	-88.89
Malaysia	19	33	3	24	2	0.00	-91.67
Philippines	12	8		9	11	0.01	22.22
Singapore	5	8	5	4	2	0.00	-50.00
Thailand	27	43	4		11	0.01	
Viet Nam				5			
AUSTRALASIA	170	210	41	154	125	0.06	-18.83
Australia	136	128	36	130	119	0.06	-8.46
New Zealand	34	82	5	24	6	0.00	-75.00
EUROPE	188,760	139,902	167,069	222,816	198,921	95.68	-10.72
CENTRAL/EASTERN EUROPE	182,883	134,795	164,184	217,578	196,458	94.49	-9.71
Armenia	283	328	343	345	484	0.23	40.29
Azerbaijan	328	315	708	698	435	0.21	-37.68
Belarus	342	796	785	1,675	393	0.19	-76.54
Bulgaria	17	23	5	13	36	0.02	176.92
Czech Republic	70	74	77	109	95	0.05	-12.84
Estonia	30	39	58	3			
Georgia	136	184	669	444	104	0.05	-76.58
Hungary	35	46	1	36	32	0.02	-11.11
Kazakhstan	3,956	3,464	3,694	5,792	7,231	3.48	24.84
Kyrgyzstan	29,675	24,079	7,799	53,437	57,732	27.77	8.04
Latvia	103	138	112	83	11	0.01	-86.75
Lithuania	55			48	16	0.01	-66.67
Poland	137	152	154	87	93	0.04	6.90
Republic of Moldova	176	171	971	1,644	612	0.29	-62.77
Romania	14	17	22	41	8	0.00	-80.49
Russian Federation	22,556	21,138	18,490	38,461	19,248	9.26	-49.95
Slovakia	49	52	36	32	10	0.00	-68.75
Turkmenistan	832	756	727	497	419	0.20	-15.69
Ukraine	607	773	3,035	5,968	1,306	0.63	-78.12
Uzbekistan	123,482	82,250	126,498	108,165	108,193	52.04	0.03
NORTHERN EUROPE	847	955	513	1,208	637	0.31	-47.27
Denmark	76	99	55	40	17	0.01	-57.50
Finland	57	65	22	28	2	0.00	-92.86
Iceland				20			

726

Yearbook of Tourism Statistics, Data 2009 – 2013, 2015 Edition

TAJIKISTAN

2. Arrivals of non-resident visitors at national borders, by country of residence

	2009	2010	2011	2012	2013	Market share 2013	% Change 2013-2012
Ireland	70	57	22	2	9	0.00	350.00
Norway	47	53	27	29	45	0.02	55.17
Sweden	235	300	60	31	82	0.04	164.52
United Kingdom	362	381	327	1,058	482	0.23	-54.44
SOUTHERN EUROPE	**515**	**551**	**246**	**364**	**146**	**0.07**	**-59.89**
Bosnia and Herzegovina				25			
Croatia		3		11			
Greece	13			20			
Italy	346	372	189	124	102	0.05	-17.74
Portugal	5			9			
Serbia	41	28	2	10			
Slovenia				1			
Spain	95	111	43	164	38	0.02	-76.83
TFYR of Macedonia	15	37	12		6	0.00	
WESTERN EUROPE	**2,582**	**2,117**	**1,465**	**2,009**	**1,036**	**0.50**	**-48.43**
Austria	103	120	135	79	40	0.02	-49.37
Belgium	179	234	76	149	36	0.02	-75.84
France	1,067	542	448	409	247	0.12	-39.61
Germany	985	975	570	1,067	609	0.29	-42.92
Netherlands	107	118	95	71	7	0.00	-90.14
Switzerland	141	128	141	234	97	0.05	-58.55
EAST MEDITERRANEAN EUROPE	**1,933**	**1,484**	**661**	**1,657**	**644**	**0.31**	**-61.13**
Israel	76	43	41	84	37	0.02	-55.95
Turkey	1,857	1,441	620	1,573	607	0.29	-61.41
MIDDLE EAST	**202**	**170**	**56**	**1,001**	**309**	**0.15**	**-69.13**
Egypt	63	27		35			
Iraq	36			16			
Jordan	8	19			26	0.01	
Lebanon	13	22		1	34	0.02	3,300.00
Saudi Arabia	30	19	17	893	247	0.12	-72.34
Syrian Arab Republic	16	24	10	55	2	0.00	-96.36
United Arab Emirates	36	59	29				
Yemen				1			
SOUTH ASIA	**13,630**	**14,409**	**11,162**	**14,725**	**6,519**	**3.14**	**-55.73**
Afghanistan	10,536	11,456	5,790	8,476	4,566	2.20	-46.13
Bangladesh	27	48	1	18	30	0.01	66.67
India	227	254	121	128	119	0.06	-7.03
Iran, Islamic Republic of	2,437	2,387	5,199	5,853	1,438	0.69	-75.43
Nepal	18	40	3	3	29	0.01	866.67
Pakistan	385	224	46	245	337	0.16	37.55
Sri Lanka			2	2			

727

THAILAND

1. Arrivals of non-resident tourists at national borders, by nationality

	2009	2010	2011	2012	2013	Market share 2013	% Change 2013-2012
TOTAL	14,149,841	15,936,400	19,230,470	22,353,903	26,546,725	100.00	18.76
AFRICA	112,403	127,930	137,907	155,544	163,008	0.61	4.80
SOUTHERN AFRICA	43,277	57,100	68,496	76,326	75,748	0.29	-0.76
South Africa	43,277	57,100	68,496	76,326	75,748	0.29	-0.76
OTHER AFRICA	69,126	70,830	69,411	79,218	87,260	0.33	10.15
Other countries of Africa	69,126	70,830	69,411	79,218	87,260	0.33	10.15
AMERICAS	853,380	844,644	952,519	1,083,433	1,166,633	4.39	7.68
NORTH AMERICA	796,556	780,185	876,104	987,992	1,053,383	3.97	6.62
Canada	169,482	168,393	194,356	219,354	229,897	0.87	4.81
United States of America	627,074	611,792	681,748	768,638	823,486	3.10	7.14
SOUTH AMERICA	25,108	30,682	37,530	48,240	58,298	0.22	20.85
Argentina	7,458	10,292	12,970	17,853	21,035	0.08	17.82
Brazil	17,650	20,390	24,560	30,387	37,263	0.14	22.63
OTHER AMERICAS	31,716	33,777	38,885	47,201	54,952	0.21	16.42
Other countries of the Americas	31,716	33,777	38,885	47,201	54,952	0.21	16.42
EAST ASIA AND THE PACIFIC	7,813,650	8,956,796	11,279,400	13,571,969	16,933,311	63.79	24.77
NORTH-EAST ASIA	3,081,733	3,607,034	4,714,867	6,192,086	8,559,613	32.24	38.23
China	777,508	1,122,219	1,721,247	2,786,860	4,637,335	17.47	66.40
Hong Kong, China	318,762	316,476	411,834	473,666	588,335	2.22	24.21
Japan	1,004,453	993,674	1,127,893	1,373,716	1,536,425	5.79	11.84
Korea, Republic of	618,227	805,445	1,006,283	1,163,619	1,295,342	4.88	11.32
Taiwan, Province of China	362,783	369,220	447,610	394,225	502,176	1.89	27.38
SOUTH-EAST ASIA	3,968,579	4,534,235	5,594,577	6,281,153	7,282,266	27.43	15.94
Brunei Darussalam	8,353	7,073	7,471	10,459	14,205	0.05	35.82
Cambodia	96,586	146,274	265,903	423,642	481,595	1.81	13.68
Indonesia	227,205	286,072	370,795	447,820	594,251	2.24	32.70
Lao People's Democratic Republic	655,034	715,345	891,950	975,999	976,639	3.68	0.07
Malaysia	1,757,813	2,058,956	2,500,280	2,554,397	3,041,097	11.46	19.05
Myanmar	79,279	90,179	110,671	129,385	172,383	0.65	33.23
Philippines	217,705	246,430	268,375	289,566	321,571	1.21	11.05
Singapore	563,575	603,538	682,364	831,215	955,468	3.60	14.95
Viet Nam	363,029	380,368	496,768	618,670	725,057	2.73	17.20
AUSTRALASIA	735,103	787,410	930,947	1,044,112	1,018,855	3.84	-2.42
Australia	646,705	698,046	829,855	930,241	900,460	3.39	-3.20
New Zealand	88,398	89,364	101,092	113,871	118,395	0.45	3.97
OTHER EAST ASIA AND THE PACIFIC	28,235	28,117	39,009	54,618	72,577	0.27	32.88
Other countries of Asia	25,878	25,895	36,422	51,975	69,496	0.26	33.71
Other countries of Oceania	2,357	2,222	2,587	2,643	3,081	0.01	16.57
EUROPE	4,170,872	4,558,425	5,226,499	5,780,170	6,440,819	24.26	11.43
CENTRAL/EASTERN EUROPE	518,212	856,350	1,295,073	1,597,540	2,092,795	7.88	31.00
Russian Federation	336,965	644,678	1,054,187	1,316,564	1,746,565	6.58	32.66
Other countries Central/East Europe	181,247	211,672	240,886	280,976	346,230	1.30	23.22
NORTHERN EUROPE	1,680,183	1,654,908	1,735,846	1,769,253	1,768,871	6.66	-0.02
Denmark	144,834	152,398	164,096	167,499	163,186	0.61	-2.57
Finland	156,000	146,946	157,046	154,919	141,692	0.53	-8.54
Ireland	65,530	57,515	58,945	60,305	63,522	0.24	5.33
Norway	121,575	132,108	136,931	148,796	154,049	0.58	3.53
Sweden	350,819	355,214	373,856	364,681	341,398	1.29	-6.38
United Kingdom	841,425	810,727	844,972	873,053	905,024	3.41	3.66
SOUTHERN EUROPE	245,467	235,445	281,252	313,844	330,276	1.24	5.24
Italy	170,105	168,203	185,869	200,703	207,192	0.78	3.23
Spain	75,362	67,242	95,383	113,141	123,084	0.46	8.79
WESTERN EUROPE	1,520,427	1,591,325	1,675,492	1,847,357	1,975,315	7.44	6.93
Austria	85,786	90,026	89,242	94,667	106,278	0.40	12.27
Belgium	80,420	80,000	82,610	94,896	101,109	0.38	6.55
France	427,067	461,670	515,572	576,106	611,582	2.30	6.16
Germany	573,473	606,874	619,133	682,419	737,658	2.78	8.09
Netherlands	205,412	196,994	198,891	208,122	218,765	0.82	5.11
Switzerland	148,269	155,761	170,044	191,147	199,923	0.75	4.59

728

THAILAND

1. Arrivals of non-resident tourists at national borders, by nationality

	2009	2010	2011	2012	2013	Market share 2013	% Change 2013-2012
EAST MEDITERRANEAN EUROPE	**110,884**	**116,050**	**125,093**	**129,551**	**134,874**	**0.51**	**4.11**
Israel	110,884	116,050	125,093	129,551	134,874	0.51	4.11
OTHER EUROPE	**95,699**	**104,347**	**113,743**	**122,625**	**138,688**	**0.52**	**13.10**
Other countries of Europe	95,699	104,347	113,743	122,625	138,688	0.52	13.10
MIDDLE EAST	**373,099**	**453,284**	**476,053**	**475,926**	**495,369**	**1.87**	**4.09**
Egypt	15,733	16,729	16,703	19,918	28,175	0.11	41.45
Kuwait	44,500	41,224	55,788	64,611	71,173	0.27	10.16
Saudi Arabia	10,911	8,463	12,521	17,084	21,452	0.08	25.57
United Arab Emirates	83,625	105,162	108,608	113,547	123,926	0.47	9.14
Other countries of Middle East	218,330	281,706	282,433	260,766	250,643	0.94	-3.88
SOUTH ASIA	**826,437**	**995,321**	**1,158,092**	**1,286,861**	**1,347,585**	**5.08**	**4.72**
Bangladesh	53,420	68,081	65,150	72,657	82,418	0.31	13.43
India	614,566	760,371	914,971	1,013,308	1,050,889	3.96	3.71
Nepal	25,499	28,621	25,382	26,277	25,455	0.10	-3.13
Pakistan	63,260	65,171	73,727	71,982	78,986	0.30	9.73
Sri Lanka	47,138	49,738	53,636	73,346	76,260	0.29	3.97
Other countries of South Asia	22,554	23,339	25,226	29,291	33,577	0.13	14.63

Yearbook of Tourism Statistics, Data 2009 – 2013, 2015 Edition

THAILAND

1. Arrivals of non-resident tourists at national borders, by country of residence

	2009	2010	2011	2012	2013	Market share 2013	% Change 2013-2012
TOTAL	14,149,841	15,936,400	19,230,470	22,353,903	26,546,725	100.00	18.76
AFRICA	107,837	121,816	141,255	157,309	162,647	0.61	3.39
EAST AFRICA	35,140	36,599	42,447				
Burundi	152	127	142				
Comoros	49	188	470				
Djibouti	151	164	192				
Eritrea	47	79	124				
Ethiopia	5,204	5,875	6,234				
Kenya	6,303	5,860	6,134				
Madagascar	5,362	5,229	5,622				
Malawi	399	284	315				
Mauritius	3,689	3,938	4,752				
Mozambique	824	1,018	1,182				
Reunion	3,446	4,054	6,955				
Rwanda	136	211	243				
Seychelles	1,323	1,570	1,597				
Somalia	149	223	309				
Uganda	2,168	2,160	2,474				
United Republic of Tanzania	3,623	3,460	3,434				
Zambia	1,611	1,624	1,521				
Zimbabwe	504	535	747				
CENTRAL AFRICA	5,930	4,575	5,617				
Angola	2,445	1,669	1,941				
Cameroon	2,048	1,436	1,866				
Central African Republic	73	41	31				
Chad	22	36	70				
Congo	1,185	1,117	1,022				
Democratic Republic of the Congo	20		277				
Equatorial Guinea	5	33	45				
Gabon	114	219	327				
Sao Tome and Principe	18	24	38				
NORTH AFRICA	8,226	7,802	9,379				
Algeria	1,592	1,383	1,433				
Morocco	3,443	3,075	4,039				
Sudan	1,910	2,034	2,645				
Tunisia	1,281	1,310	1,262				
SOUTHERN AFRICA	41,937	56,985	68,275	73,530	73,657	0.28	0.17
Botswana	589	649	681				
Lesotho	476	215	101				
Namibia	331	506	626				
South Africa	40,465	55,467	66,705	73,530	73,657	0.28	0.17
Swaziland	76	148	162				
WEST AFRICA	16,104	15,319	15,184				
Benin	477	497	531				
Burkina Faso	202	305	250				
Cabo Verde	59	46	134				
Côte d'Ivoire	695	816	693				
Gambia	368	366	361				
Ghana	2,303	1,877	2,378				
Guinea	2,739	2,592	2,417				
Liberia	1,371	1,019	793				
Mali	2,027	1,734	1,995				
Mauritania	487	275	151				
Niger	74	150	215				
Nigeria	3,099	3,334	3,606				
Senegal	1,486	1,648	931				
Sierra Leone	182	198	229				
Togo	535	462	500				
OTHER AFRICA	500	536	353	83,779	88,990	0.34	6.22

Yearbook of Tourism Statistics, Data 2009 – 2013, 2015 Edition

THAILAND

1. Arrivals of non-resident tourists at national borders, by country of residence

	2009	2010	2011	2012	2013	Market share 2013	% Change 2013-2012
Other countries of Africa	500	536	353	83,779	88,990	0.34	6.22
AMERICAS	**795,110**	**792,190**	**885,598**	**1,006,911**	**1,103,963**	**4.16**	**9.64**
CARIBBEAN	**1,645**	**2,160**	**2,392**				
Antigua and Barbuda	24	21	19				
Bahamas	60	115	131				
Barbados	141	166	154				
Bermuda	95	164	235				
Cayman Islands	22	67	60				
Cuba	181	222	239				
Curaçao	4	36	74				
Dominica	41	40	91				
Dominican Republic	255	210	200				
Grenada	15	8	17				
Guadeloupe	8	29	79				
Haiti	20	52	67				
Jamaica	158	229	284				
Martinique	80	75	86				
Puerto Rico	86	153	119				
Saint Kitts and Nevis	19	52	56				
Saint Lucia	10	37	27				
Saint Vincent and the Grenadines	13	20	21				
Trinidad and Tobago	405	448	421				
United States Virgin Islands	8	16	12				
CENTRAL AMERICA	**2,204**	**2,507**	**2,773**				
Belize	58	134	100				
Costa Rica	731	915	952				
El Salvador	121	115	176				
Guatemala	644	439	437				
Honduras	211	343	417				
Nicaragua	85	109	117				
Panama	354	452	574				
NORTH AMERICA	**755,664**	**744,744**	**826,817**	**919,092**	**997,878**	**3.76**	**8.57**
Canada	147,191	148,287	170,981	192,602	209,059	0.79	8.54
Greenland	66	188	274				
Mexico	8,932	9,761	10,835				
United States of America	599,475	586,508	644,727	726,490	788,819	2.97	8.58
SOUTH AMERICA	**35,096**	**41,591**	**52,636**	**43,892**	**54,258**	**0.20**	**23.62**
Argentina	6,452	9,336	12,005	16,895	20,082	0.08	18.86
Bolivia	269	254	317				
Brazil	13,890	16,753	21,231	26,997	34,176	0.13	26.59
Chile	5,607	5,989	7,748				
Colombia	3,922	3,838	4,601				
Ecuador	550	529	966				
Guyana	46	56	77				
Paraguay	93	150	158				
Peru	1,671	2,058	2,314				
Suriname	95	137	172				
Uruguay	689	1,025	1,311				
Venezuela	1,812	1,466	1,736				
OTHER AMERICAS	**501**	**1,188**	**980**	**43,927**	**51,827**	**0.20**	**17.98**
Other countries of the Americas	501	1,188	980	43,927	51,827	0.20	17.98
EAST ASIA AND THE PACIFIC	**7,994,238**	**9,091,305**	**11,480,750**	**13,810,993**	**17,116,842**	**64.48**	**23.94**
NORTH-EAST ASIA	**3,189,936**	**3,706,326**	**4,829,983**	**6,312,354**	**8,687,027**	**32.72**	**37.62**
China	815,708	1,132,267	1,704,800	2,761,213	4,609,717	17.36	66.95
Hong Kong, China	378,948	391,067	531,192	604,900	694,084	2.61	14.74
Japan	982,607	980,424	1,103,073	1,341,063	1,515,718	5.71	13.02
Korea, Republic of	620,700	805,179	1,001,105	1,153,457	1,292,335	4.87	12.04
Macao, China	21,077	21,457	32,889				
Mongolia	4,179	4,647	6,347				

731

THAILAND

1. Arrivals of non-resident tourists at national borders, by country of residence

	2009	2010	2011	2012	2013	Market share 2013	% Change 2013-2012
Taiwan, Province of China	366,717	371,285	449,346	393,335	503,894	1.90	28.11
Other countries of North-East Asia			1,231	58,386	71,279	0.27	22.08
SOUTH-EAST ASIA	**4,075,459**	**4,596,750**	**5,718,982**	**6,462,647**	**7,410,441**	**27.91**	**14.67**
Brunei Darussalam	10,517	8,906	10,142	13,319	16,181	0.06	21.49
Cambodia	103,168	150,011	271,265	430,538	487,001	1.83	13.11
Indonesia	226,506	285,666	370,681	449,360	595,015	2.24	32.41
Lao People's Democratic Republic	657,658	718,377	895,359	981,081	984,886	3.71	0.39
Malaysia	1,748,341	2,047,175	2,492,034	2,546,072	3,031,072	11.42	19.05
Myanmar	80,068	91,111	111,545	129,714	173,272	0.65	33.58
Philippines	215,150	242,859	262,839	280,585	315,040	1.19	12.28
Singapore	651,454	654,342	789,339	994,631	1,067,286	4.02	7.30
Timor-Leste	791	857	977				
Viet Nam	381,806	397,446	514,801	637,347	740,688	2.79	16.21
AUSTRALASIA	**723,791**	**782,581**	**925,152**	**1,029,393**	**1,012,740**	**3.81**	**-1.62**
Australia	645,534	702,921	835,719	929,962	906,004	3.41	-2.58
New Zealand	78,257	79,660	89,433	99,431	106,736	0.40	7.35
MELANESIA	**3,307**	**4,223**	**5,104**				
Fiji	801	794	876				
New Caledonia	1,391	2,071	2,442				
Papua New Guinea	914	1,041	1,027				
Solomon Islands	84	113	371				
Vanuatu	117	204	388				
MICRONESIA	**688**	**660**	**672**				
Guam	316	341	382				
Kiribati	40	40	38				
Marshall Islands	9	44	33				
Micronesia, Federated States of	19	15	31				
Nauru	266	174	143				
Northern Mariana Islands	23	10	4				
Palau	15	36	41				
POLYNESIA	**600**	**740**	**816**				
Cook Islands	37	41	43				
French Polynesia	202	448	557				
Samoa	99	115	89				
Tonga	92	131	116				
Tuvalu	170	5	11				
OTHER EAST ASIA AND THE PACIFIC	**457**	**25**	**41**	**6,599**	**6,634**	**0.02**	**0.53**
Other countries of Asia	442						
Other countries of Oceania	15	25	41	6,599	6,634	0.02	0.53
EUROPE	**4,031,256**	**4,445,544**	**5,058,583**	**5,580,160**	**6,289,020**	**23.69**	**12.70**
CENTRAL/EASTERN EUROPE	**502,040**	**844,587**	**1,278,080**	**1,578,057**	**2,078,234**	**7.83**	**31.70**
Armenia	551	819	933				
Azerbaijan	695	906	1,230				
Belarus	3,447	5,177	6,037				
Bulgaria	2,809	3,419	4,339				
Czech Republic	25,507	27,370	28,764				
Estonia	6,811	8,357	9,448				
Georgia	460	631	530				
Hungary	14,374	16,757	16,163				
Kazakhstan	24,994	28,922	35,345				
Kyrgyzstan	938	1,243	1,491				
Latvia	3,278	4,233	5,079				
Lithuania	4,867	5,298	6,215				
Poland	30,074	34,832	36,546				
Republic of Moldova	425	660	799				
Romania	5,624	6,670	8,400				
Russian Federation	334,915	643,839	1,052,361	1,311,358	1,745,779	6.58	33.13
Slovakia	7,544	8,426	9,124				
Tajikistan	175	295	299				

732

Yearbook of Tourism Statistics, Data 2009 – 2013, 2015 Edition

THAILAND

1. Arrivals of non-resident tourists at national borders, by country of residence

	2009	2010	2011	2012	2013	Market share 2013	% Change 2013-2012
Turkmenistan	2,207	3,811	4,808				
Ukraine	28,005	36,886	41,233				
Uzbekistan	3,971	5,858	8,720				
Other countries Central/East Europe	369	178	216	266,699	332,455	1.25	24.66
NORTHERN EUROPE	**1,603,566**	**1,595,573**	**1,649,950**	**1,619,090**	**1,638,838**	**6.17**	**1.22**
Denmark	143,326	150,300	159,620	162,022	159,629	0.60	-1.48
Finland	155,574	145,510	154,002	151,516	138,829	0.52	-8.37
Iceland	2,549	3,276	3,614				
Ireland	63,755	54,733	55,038				
Norway	120,668	132,865	137,066	148,689	154,398	0.58	3.84
Sweden	340,381	348,640	369,144	356,791	338,304	1.27	-5.18
United Kingdom	777,313	760,249	771,466	800,072	847,678	3.19	5.95
SOUTHERN EUROPE	**287,075**	**276,659**	**320,211**	**301,430**	**321,217**	**1.21**	**6.56**
Albania	291	289	316				
Andorra	200	227	231				
Bosnia and Herzegovina	314	381	597				
Croatia	2,807	2,828	3,437				
Greece	18,483	17,529	15,231				
Italy	164,341	161,086	174,902	187,552	197,232	0.74	5.16
Malta	1,243	1,565	1,926				
Montenegro	69	164	226				
Portugal	13,418	14,463	16,259				
San Marino	119	174	209				
Serbia	2,441	2,628	3,224				
Slovenia	5,863	5,732	6,062				
Spain	77,160	69,223	97,149	113,878	123,985	0.47	8.88
TFYR of Macedonia	326	370	442				
WESTERN EUROPE	**1,492,771**	**1,567,854**	**1,635,111**	**1,789,101**	**1,928,994**	**7.27**	**7.82**
Austria	87,469	88,788	86,987	92,550	104,359	0.39	12.76
Belgium	81,514	80,246	82,699	94,134	101,147	0.38	7.45
France	401,293	439,773	484,602	538,327	580,062	2.19	7.75
Germany	556,852	596,960	603,979	663,611	723,711	2.73	9.06
Liechtenstein	514	610	676				
Luxembourg	4,011	4,713	4,962				
Monaco	526	643	759				
Netherlands	203,675	190,539	189,727	197,721	209,659	0.79	6.04
Switzerland	156,917	165,582	180,720	202,758	210,056	0.79	3.60
EAST MEDITERRANEAN EUROPE	**145,281**	**159,373**	**173,969**	**125,666**	**133,438**	**0.50**	**6.18**
Cyprus	3,426	3,472	3,704				
Israel	111,243	115,961	125,149	125,666	133,438	0.50	6.18
Turkey	30,612	39,940	45,116				
OTHER EUROPE	**523**	**1,498**	**1,262**	**166,816**	**188,299**	**0.71**	**12.88**
Other countries of Europe	523	1,498	1,262	166,816	188,299	0.71	12.88
MIDDLE EAST	**298,079**	**331,253**	**379,382**	**538,267**	**547,735**	**2.06**	**1.76**
Bahrain	18,545	20,527	23,167				
Egypt	13,394	15,215	15,094	17,918	26,650	0.10	48.73
Iraq	1,973	2,173	2,096				
Jordan	8,913	7,459	8,348				
Kuwait	47,115	45,223	60,425	69,223	75,388	0.28	8.91
Lebanon	6,036	5,666	6,494				
Libya	1,439	2,164	866				
Oman	42,451	47,787	57,876				
Palestine	718	1,037	1,427				
Qatar	15,913	22,341	27,788				
Saudi Arabia	14,636	13,031	17,535	23,007	26,121	0.10	13.54
Syrian Arab Republic	4,503	4,315	4,850				
United Arab Emirates	119,450	140,884	149,873	163,604	164,710	0.62	0.68
Yemen	2,993	3,431	3,543				
Other countries of Middle East				264,515	254,866	0.96	-3.65

733

THAILAND

1. Arrivals of non-resident tourists at national borders, by country of residence

	2009	2010	2011	2012	2013	Market share 2013	% Change 2013-2012
SOUTH ASIA	923,321	1,152,890	1,284,902	1,260,263	1,326,518	5.00	5.26
Afghanistan	1,533	1,511	2,127				
Bangladesh	55,818	70,598	68,024	75,354	84,902	0.32	12.67
Bhutan	12,993	13,664	15,227				
India	596,529	746,214	891,748	985,883	1,028,414	3.87	4.31
Iran, Islamic Republic of	114,021	167,792	147,381				
Maldives	7,784	9,197	8,672				
Nepal	26,683	29,994	26,237	26,326	25,802	0.10	-1.99
Pakistan	62,517	64,091	71,704	69,419	76,935	0.29	10.83
Sri Lanka	45,443	49,827	53,782	73,249	76,484	0.29	4.42
Other countries of South Asia		2		30,032	33,981	0.13	13.15
NOT SPECIFIED		**1,402**					
Other countries of the World		1,402					

Yearbook of Tourism Statistics, Data 2009 – 2013, 2015 Edition

THAILAND

3. Arrivals of non-resident tourists in hotels and similar establishments, by country of residence

	2009	2010	2011	2012	2013	Market share 2013	% Change 2013-2012
TOTAL (*)	11,809,657	13,394,911	16,678,985	19,694,995	23,952,270	100.00	21.62
AFRICA	94,090	107,364	125,341	140,976	144,105	0.60	2.22
SOUTHERN AFRICA	35,708	49,161	59,381	66,322	65,600	0.27	-1.09
South Africa	35,708	49,161	59,381	66,322	65,600	0.27	-1.09
OTHER AFRICA	58,382	58,203	65,960	74,654	78,505	0.33	5.16
Other countries of Africa	58,382	58,203	65,960	74,654	78,505	0.33	5.16
AMERICAS	600,320	593,219	678,010	791,689	884,388	3.69	11.71
NORTH AMERICA	560,343	545,037	617,599	715,600	790,819	3.30	10.51
Canada	113,047	112,121	139,435	153,134	170,690	0.71	11.46
United States of America	447,296	432,916	478,164	562,466	620,129	2.59	10.25
SOUTH AMERICA	16,908	21,998	28,796	38,419	47,902	0.20	24.68
Argentina	4,989	7,727	10,203	14,175	17,123	0.07	20.80
Brazil	11,919	14,271	18,593	24,244	30,779	0.13	26.96
OTHER AMERICAS	23,069	26,184	31,615	37,670	45,667	0.19	21.23
Other countries of the Americas	23,069	26,184	31,615	37,670	45,667	0.19	21.23
EAST ASIA AND THE PACIFIC	6,812,307	7,703,950	10,072,456	12,417,755	15,790,239	65.92	27.16
NORTH-EAST ASIA	2,811,051	3,290,272	4,359,712	5,747,913	8,117,914	33.89	41.23
China	737,552	1,034,585	1,585,394	2,596,113	4,419,852	18.45	70.25
Hong Kong, China	354,285	366,216	504,231	578,021	666,499	2.78	15.31
Japan	834,661	823,694	928,510	1,158,414	1,355,899	5.66	17.05
Korea, Republic of	558,166	742,905	940,368	1,069,631	1,216,785	5.08	13.76
Taiwan, Province of China	326,387	322,872	401,209	345,734	458,879	1.92	32.73
SOUTH-EAST ASIA	3,365,480	3,741,320	4,885,978	5,710,204	6,707,195	28.00	17.46
Brunei Darussalam	9,413	7,899	9,327	12,325	14,918	0.06	21.04
Cambodia	82,425	114,203	213,047	368,631	407,786	1.70	10.62
Indonesia	200,466	255,480	343,688	421,029	563,311	2.35	33.79
Lao People's Democratic Republic	439,080	448,412	599,791	672,312	704,989	2.94	4.86
Malaysia	1,514,040	1,771,632	2,278,863	2,415,119	2,915,820	12.17	20.73
Myanmar	56,665	63,434	80,684	98,062	136,718	0.57	39.42
Philippines	165,915	180,341	206,581	232,626	266,565	1.11	14.59
Singapore	569,176	564,058	698,750	916,828	1,011,827	4.22	10.36
Viet Nam	328,300	335,861	455,247	573,272	685,261	2.86	19.54
AUSTRALASIA	607,971	641,929	782,190	899,142	891,533	3.72	-0.85
Australia	545,001	577,413	706,856	815,239	799,746	3.34	-1.90
New Zealand	62,970	64,516	75,334	83,903	91,787	0.38	9.40
OTHER EAST ASIA AND THE PACIFIC	27,805	30,429	44,576	60,496	73,597	0.31	21.66
Other countries of Asia	24,018	25,663	38,944	55,091	67,843	0.28	23.15
Other countries of Oceania	3,787	4,766	5,632	5,405	5,754	0.02	6.46
EUROPE	3,192,749	3,629,839	4,258,422	4,667,934	5,381,054	22.47	15.28
CENTRAL/EASTERN EUROPE	442,463	775,368	1,191,791	1,456,038	1,932,598	8.07	32.73
Russian Federation	300,739	599,780	988,463	1,224,061	1,636,980	6.83	33.73
Other countries Central/East Europe	141,724	175,588	203,328	231,977	295,618	1.23	27.43
NORTHERN EUROPE	1,185,544	1,181,229	1,230,800	1,274,851	1,321,492	5.52	3.66
Denmark	113,462	122,325	132,702	135,901	136,088	0.57	0.14
Finland	126,718	115,461	121,881	121,911	115,540	0.48	-5.23
Norway	88,528	95,734	99,739	111,617	122,013	0.51	9.31
Sweden	264,074	267,304	281,746	279,020	275,837	1.15	-1.14
United Kingdom	592,762	580,405	594,732	626,402	672,014	2.81	7.28
SOUTHERN EUROPE	198,624	192,329	235,630	253,632	274,468	1.15	8.22
Italy	134,454	133,869	150,302	156,481	167,555	0.70	7.08
Spain	64,170	58,460	85,328	97,151	106,913	0.45	10.05
WESTERN EUROPE	1,148,975	1,249,964	1,344,446	1,427,241	1,566,539	6.54	9.76
Austria	70,104	73,136	74,001	78,218	88,781	0.37	13.50
Belgium	60,572	62,511	66,966	73,781	80,735	0.34	9.43
France	302,883	350,595	403,593	425,544	461,551	1.93	8.46
Germany	435,050	478,332	494,598	523,301	587,659	2.45	12.30
Netherlands	158,499	151,030	154,122	157,624	169,903	0.71	7.79
Switzerland	121,867	134,360	151,166	168,773	177,910	0.74	5.41
EAST MEDITERRANEAN EUROPE	92,728	103,208	117,430	111,888	120,420	0.50	7.63

735

THAILAND

3. Arrivals of non-resident tourists in hotels and similar establishments, by country of residence

	2009	2010	2011	2012	2013	Market share 2013	% Change 2013-2012
Israel	92,728	103,208	117,430	111,888	120,420	0.50	7.63
OTHER EUROPE	**124,415**	**127,741**	**138,325**	**144,284**	**165,537**	**0.69**	**14.73**
Other countries of Europe	124,415	127,741	138,325	144,284	165,537	0.69	14.73
MIDDLE EAST	**381,935**	**466,625**	**494,620**	**508,452**	**519,652**	**2.17**	**2.20**
Egypt	12,305	14,032	14,007	17,164	25,245	0.11	47.08
Kuwait	43,408	43,172	57,806	66,567	72,637	0.30	9.12
Saudi Arabia	13,139	11,297	15,914	21,397	24,415	0.10	14.10
United Arab Emirates	108,940	130,195	138,852	153,481	156,232	0.65	1.79
Other countries of Middle East	204,143	267,929	268,041	249,843	241,123	1.01	-3.49
SOUTH ASIA	**728,256**	**893,914**	**1,050,136**	**1,168,189**	**1,232,832**	**5.15**	**5.53**
Bangladesh	50,269	63,891	61,921	69,210	77,783	0.32	12.39
India	540,141	682,264	829,328	918,825	963,399	4.02	4.85
Nepal	23,021	25,049	22,324	22,439	21,606	0.09	-3.71
Pakistan	55,805	57,605	66,422	64,460	71,502	0.30	10.92
Sri Lanka	40,771	46,102	49,926	69,756	71,652	0.30	2.72
Other countries of South Asia	18,249	19,003	20,215	23,499	26,890	0.11	14.43

736

Yearbook of Tourism Statistics, Data 2009 – 2013, 2015 Edition

THE FORMER YUGOSLAV REP OF MACEDONIA

3. Arrivals of non-resident tourists in hotels and similar establishments, by nationality

	2009	2010	2011	2012	2013	Market share 2013	% Change 2013-2012
TOTAL	219,803	231,485	301,304	324,372	372,732	100.00	14.91
AFRICA		214	390	314	720	0.19	129.30
SOUTHERN AFRICA		31	48	52	87	0.02	67.31
South Africa		31	48	52	87	0.02	67.31
OTHER AFRICA		183	342	262	633	0.17	141.60
Other countries of Africa		183	342	262	633	0.17	141.60
AMERICAS	8,165	9,014	10,150	9,930	12,310	3.30	23.97
NORTH AMERICA	8,165	8,657	9,554	8,920	11,004	2.95	23.36
Canada	1,132	1,155	1,268	1,319	1,457	0.39	10.46
United States of America	7,033	7,056	7,655	7,319	8,853	2.38	20.96
Other countries of North America		446	631	282	694	0.19	146.10
SOUTH AMERICA		132	236	395	580	0.16	46.84
Brazil		132	236	395	580	0.16	46.84
OTHER AMERICAS		225	360	615	726	0.19	18.05
Other countries of the Americas		225	360	615	726	0.19	18.05
EAST ASIA AND THE PACIFIC	3,755	9,612	11,637	14,512	16,903	4.53	16.48
NORTH-EAST ASIA	1,152	3,034	4,823	6,321	8,081	2.17	27.84
China		818	1,616	2,754	4,004	1.07	45.39
Japan	1,152	1,538	2,142	2,396	2,366	0.63	-1.25
Korea, Republic of		678	1,065	1,171	1,711	0.46	46.11
AUSTRALASIA	2,603	3,677	3,852	5,137	5,473	1.47	6.54
Australia	2,446	3,524	3,642	4,955	5,114	1.37	3.21
New Zealand	157	153	210	182	359	0.10	97.25
OTHER EAST ASIA AND THE PACIFIC		2,901	2,962	3,054	3,349	0.90	9.66
Other countries of Asia		1,941	2,723	2,640	3,145	0.84	19.13
Other countries of Oceania		960	239	414	204	0.05	-50.72
EUROPE	202,839	212,645	279,127	299,616	342,799	91.97	14.41
CENTRAL/EASTERN EUROPE	34,262	31,731	37,943	40,798	52,294	14.03	28.18
Belarus	156	86	1,146	225	296	0.08	31.56
Bulgaria	19,479	13,109	16,163	17,419	18,499	4.96	6.20
Czech Republic	1,984	1,986	2,390	2,212	2,099	0.56	-5.11
Estonia		144	248	339	310	0.08	-8.55
Hungary	3,014	3,100	3,083	2,459	2,917	0.78	18.63
Latvia		219	246	556	669	0.18	20.32
Lithuania		201	257	541	576	0.15	6.47
Poland	4,445	5,736	5,895	6,516	11,746	3.15	80.26
Romania	2,143	3,007	3,559	4,493	5,998	1.61	33.50
Russian Federation	1,605	2,493	3,131	3,327	4,105	1.10	23.38
Slovakia	867	889	887	1,104	2,332	0.63	111.23
Ukraine	569	761	938	1,607	2,747	0.74	70.94
NORTHERN EUROPE	11,083	12,142	15,204	13,975	14,780	3.97	5.76
Denmark	1,178	1,188	1,198	1,233	1,751	0.47	42.01
Finland	1,048	1,137	3,083	2,302	932	0.25	-59.51
Iceland	147	154	122	96	88	0.02	-8.33
Ireland	521	694	1,424	675	709	0.19	5.04
Norway	1,473	1,423	1,127	1,405	1,556	0.42	10.75
Sweden	2,089	2,300	2,496	2,469	3,223	0.86	30.54
United Kingdom	4,627	5,246	5,754	5,795	6,521	1.75	12.53
SOUTHERN EUROPE	103,318	114,626	136,034	135,466	144,733	38.83	6.84
Albania	16,232	14,226	11,022	10,798	14,214	3.81	31.64
Bosnia and Herzegovina	3,961	4,856	4,308	4,350	4,197	1.13	-3.52
Croatia	11,285	11,715	12,724	13,058	11,999	3.22	-8.11
Greece	19,379	24,109	44,007	42,652	45,171	12.12	5.91
Italy	4,899	5,650	6,522	7,293	7,223	1.94	-0.96
Malta		21	57	271	61	0.02	-77.49
Montenegro	2,205	3,407	3,149	2,923	3,168	0.85	8.38
Portugal	482	622	593	733	687	0.18	-6.28
Serbia	30,671	29,324	30,587	31,240	33,740	9.05	8.00
Slovenia	12,375	11,511	13,169	12,347	12,235	3.28	-0.91

737

Yearbook of Tourism Statistics, Data 2009 – 2013, 2015 Edition

THE FORMER YUGOSLAV REP OF MACEDONIA

3. Arrivals of non-resident tourists in hotels and similar establishments, by nationality

	2009	2010	2011	2012	2013	Market share 2013	% Change 2013-2012
Spain	1,829	1,547	1,641	1,668	1,760	0.47	5.52
Other countries of Southern Europe		7,638	8,255	8,133	10,278	2.76	26.37
WESTERN EUROPE	**25,873**	**28,481**	**45,457**	**53,804**	**56,578**	**15.18**	**5.16**
Austria	5,758	5,723	5,347	5,781	7,944	2.13	37.42
Belgium	1,596	1,643	2,335	3,513	4,675	1.25	33.08
France	4,344	4,573	4,627	5,279	4,843	1.30	-8.26
Germany	8,326	8,700	9,070	10,331	11,679	3.13	13.05
Luxembourg		52	74	68	131	0.04	92.65
Netherlands	4,275	5,867	21,553	26,160	24,644	6.61	-5.80
Switzerland	1,574	1,923	2,451	2,672	2,662	0.71	-0.37
EAST MEDITERRANEAN EUROPE	**21,796**	**21,872**	**41,867**	**53,274**	**71,352**	**19.14**	**33.93**
Cyprus		193	631	543	791	0.21	45.67
Israel	5,928	2,799	3,212	3,215	3,380	0.91	5.13
Turkey	15,868	18,880	38,024	49,516	67,181	18.02	35.68
OTHER EUROPE	**6,507**	**3,793**	**2,622**	**2,299**	**3,062**	**0.82**	**33.19**
Other countries of Europe	6,507	3,793	2,622	2,299	3,062	0.82	33.19
NOT SPECIFIED	**5,044**						
Other countries of the World	5,044						

738

Yearbook of Tourism Statistics, Data 2009 – 2013, 2015 Edition

THE FORMER YUGOSLAV REP OF MACEDONIA

4. Arrivals of non-resident tourists in all types of accommodation establishments, by nationality

	2009	2010	2011	2012	2013	Market share 2013	% Change 2013-2012
TOTAL	259,204	261,696	327,471	351,359	399,680	100.00	13.75
AFRICA		228	408	333	739	0.18	121.92
SOUTHERN AFRICA		32	52	61	89	0.02	45.90
South Africa		32	52	61	89	0.02	45.90
OTHER AFRICA		196	356	272	650	0.16	138.97
Other countries of Africa		196	356	272	650	0.16	138.97
AMERICAS	9,083	9,724	10,744	10,612	12,858	3.22	21.16
NORTH AMERICA	9,083	9,353	10,084	9,525	11,497	2.88	20.70
Canada	1,257	1,247	1,366	1,465	1,532	0.38	4.57
United States of America	7,826	7,655	8,082	7,773	9,258	2.32	19.10
Other countries of North America		451	636	287	707	0.18	146.34
SOUTH AMERICA		142	252	411	626	0.16	52.31
Brazil		142	252	411	626	0.16	52.31
OTHER AMERICAS		229	408	676	735	0.18	8.73
Other countries of the Americas		229	408	676	735	0.18	8.73
EAST ASIA AND THE PACIFIC	4,255	10,331	12,153	15,531	17,804	4.45	14.64
NORTH-EAST ASIA	1,268	3,160	4,928	6,495	8,255	2.07	27.10
China		853	1,664	2,828	4,075	1.02	44.09
Japan	1,268	1,621	2,194	2,488	2,458	0.61	-1.21
Korea, Republic of		686	1,070	1,179	1,722	0.43	46.06
AUSTRALASIA	2,987	4,174	4,227	5,941	6,134	1.53	3.25
Australia	2,784	3,967	3,974	5,668	5,687	1.42	0.34
New Zealand	203	207	253	273	447	0.11	63.74
OTHER EAST ASIA AND THE PACIFIC		2,997	2,998	3,095	3,415	0.85	10.34
Other countries of Asia		2,015	2,755	2,676	3,194	0.80	19.36
Other countries of Oceania		982	243	419	221	0.06	-47.26
EUROPE	240,333	241,413	304,166	324,883	368,279	92.14	13.36
CENTRAL/EASTERN EUROPE	42,033	36,639	42,903	46,552	58,790	14.71	26.29
Belarus	178	101	1,151	329	314	0.08	-4.56
Bulgaria	23,619	15,513	18,541	19,815	20,914	5.23	5.55
Czech Republic	2,583	2,423	2,695	2,830	2,875	0.72	1.59
Estonia		176	260	390	336	0.08	-13.85
Hungary	3,365	3,492	3,342	2,829	3,361	0.84	18.81
Latvia		239	308	587	738	0.18	25.72
Lithuania		251	280	729	722	0.18	-0.96
Poland	5,827	6,182	6,758	7,490	12,980	3.25	73.30
Romania	2,677	3,351	3,882	4,964	6,444	1.61	29.81
Russian Federation	1,872	2,848	3,545	3,613	4,538	1.14	25.60
Slovakia	1,140	1,082	1,099	1,277	2,551	0.64	99.77
Ukraine	772	981	1,042	1,699	3,017	0.75	77.58
NORTHERN EUROPE	12,611	13,095	16,373	14,931	15,668	3.92	4.94
Denmark	1,338	1,273	1,251	1,307	1,811	0.45	38.56
Finland	1,220	1,233	3,432	2,379	1,018	0.25	-57.21
Iceland	161	164	137	99	107	0.03	8.08
Ireland	610	745	1,500	715	738	0.18	3.22
Norway	1,618	1,503	1,212	1,499	1,638	0.41	9.27
Sweden	2,355	2,530	2,702	2,654	3,421	0.86	28.90
United Kingdom	5,309	5,647	6,139	6,278	6,935	1.74	10.47
SOUTHERN EUROPE	123,310	133,039	150,726	149,495	158,007	39.53	5.69
Albania	19,757	17,110	13,614	13,412	16,982	4.25	26.62
Bosnia and Herzegovina	4,672	5,619	4,959	4,740	4,540	1.14	-4.22
Croatia	12,519	12,791	13,885	13,939	12,722	3.18	-8.73
Greece	22,253	26,843	45,509	43,976	46,184	11.56	5.02
Italy	6,050	6,181	7,140	7,926	7,894	1.98	-0.40
Malta		23	60	274	61	0.02	-77.74
Montenegro	2,653	4,180	3,522	3,197	3,498	0.88	9.42
Portugal	601	655	727	835	736	0.18	-11.86
Serbia	38,744	35,840	35,692	36,530	38,127	9.54	4.37
Slovenia	13,970	12,606	14,063	13,252	13,404	3.35	1.15

739

THE FORMER YUGOSLAV REP OF MACEDONIA

4. Arrivals of non-resident tourists in all types of accommodation establishments, by nationality

	2009	2010	2011	2012	2013	Market share 2013	% Change 2013-2012
Spain	2,091	1,711	1,726	1,801	1,972	0.49	9.49
Other countries of Southern Europe		9,480	9,829	9,613	11,887	2.97	23.66
WESTERN EUROPE	**29,821**	**31,240**	**47,982**	**57,193**	**60,262**	**15.08**	**5.37**
Austria	6,437	6,143	5,681	6,275	8,376	2.10	33.48
Belgium	1,839	1,848	2,519	3,716	5,104	1.28	37.35
France	4,914	4,858	4,901	5,663	5,180	1.30	-8.53
Germany	9,795	9,573	9,822	11,306	13,065	3.27	15.56
Luxembourg		53	107	71	134	0.03	88.73
Netherlands	4,988	6,612	22,219	27,121	25,542	6.39	-5.82
Switzerland	1,848	2,153	2,733	3,041	2,861	0.72	-5.92
EAST MEDITERRANEAN EUROPE	**23,072**	**23,126**	**43,235**	**54,254**	**72,377**	**18.11**	**33.40**
Cyprus		194	675	570	792	0.20	38.95
Israel	6,110	2,885	3,309	3,278	3,461	0.87	5.58
Turkey	16,962	20,047	39,251	50,406	68,124	17.04	35.15
OTHER EUROPE	**9,486**	**4,274**	**2,947**	**2,458**	**3,175**	**0.79**	**29.17**
Other countries of Europe	9,486	4,274	2,947	2,458	3,175	0.79	29.17
NOT SPECIFIED	**5,533**						
Other countries of the World	5,533						

Yearbook of Tourism Statistics, Data 2009 – 2013, 2015 Edition

THE FORMER YUGOSLAV REP OF MACEDONIA

5. Overnight stays of non-resident tourists in hotels and similar establishments, by nationality

	2009	2010	2011	2012	2013	Market share 2013	% Change 2013-2012
TOTAL	468,706	468,822	667,430	727,246	795,566	100.00	9.39
AFRICA		537	1,114	835	1,438	0.18	72.22
SOUTHERN AFRICA		72	238	136	223	0.03	63.97
South Africa		72	238	136	223	0.03	63.97
OTHER AFRICA		465	876	699	1,215	0.15	73.82
Other countries of Africa		465	876	699	1,215	0.15	73.82
AMERICAS	21,647	23,864	24,948	22,447	26,852	3.38	19.62
NORTH AMERICA	21,647	23,185	23,799	20,782	24,625	3.10	18.49
Canada	2,592	2,274	3,171	2,632	2,766	0.35	5.09
United States of America	19,055	19,939	19,309	17,518	20,542	2.58	17.26
Other countries of North America		972	1,319	632	1,317	0.17	108.39
SOUTH AMERICA		268	472	679	975	0.12	43.59
Brazil		268	472	679	975	0.12	43.59
OTHER AMERICAS		411	677	986	1,252	0.16	26.98
Other countries of the Americas		411	677	986	1,252	0.16	26.98
EAST ASIA AND THE PACIFIC	7,036	18,719	22,222	25,816	29,203	3.67	13.12
NORTH-EAST ASIA	2,057	5,354	8,279	9,116	10,605	1.33	16.33
China		1,735	3,929	4,325	5,619	0.71	29.92
Japan	2,057	2,776	3,114	3,460	3,148	0.40	-9.02
Korea, Republic of		843	1,236	1,331	1,838	0.23	38.09
AUSTRALASIA	4,979	7,293	8,252	11,050	11,716	1.47	6.03
Australia	4,745	7,060	7,836	10,747	10,830	1.36	0.77
New Zealand	234	233	416	303	886	0.11	192.41
OTHER EAST ASIA AND THE PACIFIC		6,072	5,691	5,650	6,882	0.87	21.81
Other countries of Asia		4,117	5,031	4,648	6,546	0.82	40.83
Other countries of Oceania		1,955	660	1,002	336	0.04	-66.47
EUROPE	427,495	425,702	619,146	678,148	738,073	92.77	8.84
CENTRAL/EASTERN EUROPE	71,841	65,681	78,318	89,593	115,326	14.50	28.72
Belarus	379	216	2,702	730	1,232	0.15	68.77
Bulgaria	37,823	23,573	29,903	32,798	34,796	4.37	6.09
Czech Republic	4,034	3,921	5,006	4,844	4,675	0.59	-3.49
Estonia		350	902	693	845	0.11	21.93
Hungary	5,227	5,333	5,694	4,743	5,721	0.72	20.62
Latvia		541	718	1,174	1,446	0.18	23.17
Lithuania		503	960	1,676	1,152	0.14	-31.26
Poland	10,998	12,008	11,397	15,132	26,913	3.38	77.85
Romania	4,780	6,888	7,622	9,841	14,952	1.88	51.94
Russian Federation	4,543	7,963	8,952	10,807	12,459	1.57	15.29
Slovakia	2,301	2,279	2,083	2,642	5,837	0.73	120.93
Ukraine	1,756	2,106	2,379	4,513	5,298	0.67	17.39
NORTHERN EUROPE	26,012	28,839	38,442	36,418	34,078	4.28	-6.43
Denmark	2,638	2,412	2,766	3,072	4,048	0.51	31.77
Finland	2,093	2,398	9,731	7,765	2,042	0.26	-73.70
Iceland	483	293	217	215	181	0.02	-15.81
Ireland	1,246	1,992	3,523	1,765	1,545	0.19	-12.46
Norway	3,793	3,399	2,418	3,687	3,406	0.43	-7.62
Sweden	4,850	5,010	5,780	5,766	7,100	0.89	23.14
United Kingdom	10,909	13,335	14,007	14,148	15,756	1.98	11.37
SOUTHERN EUROPE	205,111	219,982	259,689	255,928	271,255	34.10	5.99
Albania	28,698	25,716	19,508	18,039	23,225	2.92	28.75
Bosnia and Herzegovina	8,947	11,813	9,638	10,284	9,204	1.16	-10.50
Croatia	23,104	23,116	25,051	25,976	24,320	3.06	-6.38
Greece	32,158	38,845	74,697	70,442	78,468	9.86	11.39
Italy	10,939	12,042	15,081	15,578	14,705	1.85	-5.60
Malta		62	148	1,027	198	0.02	-80.72
Montenegro	4,492	6,413	6,448	6,274	6,886	0.87	9.75
Portugal	1,233	1,332	1,770	1,621	1,932	0.24	19.19
Serbia	66,906	59,971	60,243	60,469	63,522	7.98	5.05
Slovenia	24,720	23,654	28,343	27,292	25,888	3.25	-5.14

741

THE FORMER YUGOSLAV REP OF MACEDONIA

5. Overnight stays of non-resident tourists in hotels and similar establishments, by nationality

	2009	2010	2011	2012	2013	Market share 2013	% Change 2013-2012
Spain	3,914	3,413	3,278	4,315	3,448	0.43	-20.09
Other countries of Southern Europe		13,605	15,484	14,611	19,459	2.45	33.18
WESTERN EUROPE	**56,660**	**62,120**	**162,044**	**204,922**	**199,104**	**25.03**	**-2.84**
Austria	10,945	10,196	9,959	10,430	12,823	1.61	22.94
Belgium	3,662	3,401	6,923	13,131	18,313	2.30	39.46
France	8,346	9,183	8,849	9,595	9,462	1.19	-1.39
Germany	20,011	20,334	19,980	23,621	27,539	3.46	16.59
Luxembourg		152	271	145	494	0.06	240.69
Netherlands	10,434	15,117	110,061	142,707	124,965	15.71	-12.43
Switzerland	3,262	3,737	6,001	5,293	5,508	0.69	4.06
EAST MEDITERRANEAN EUROPE	**53,603**	**40,935**	**72,794**	**85,788**	**110,613**	**13.90**	**28.94**
Cyprus		305	1,426	1,138	1,312	0.16	15.29
Israel	22,440	7,645	10,252	6,749	7,639	0.96	13.19
Turkey	31,163	32,985	61,116	77,901	101,662	12.78	30.50
OTHER EUROPE	**14,268**	**8,145**	**7,859**	**5,499**	**7,697**	**0.97**	**39.97**
Other countries of Europe	14,268	8,145	7,859	5,499	7,697	0.97	39.97
NOT SPECIFIED	**12,528**						
Other countries of the World	12,528						

Yearbook of Tourism Statistics, Data 2009 – 2013, 2015 Edition

THE FORMER YUGOSLAV REP OF MACEDONIA

6. Overnight stays of non-resident tourists in all types of accommodation establishments, by nationality

	2009	2010	2011	2012	2013	Market share 2013	% Change 2013-2012
TOTAL	**583,796**	**559,032**	**755,166**	**811,746**	**881,375**	**100.00**	**8.58**
AFRICA		**589**	**1,219**	**906**	**1,494**	**0.17**	**64.90**
SOUTHERN AFRICA		**74**	**251**	**165**	**225**	**0.03**	**36.36**
South Africa		74	251	165	225	0.03	36.36
OTHER AFRICA		**515**	**968**	**741**	**1,269**	**0.14**	**71.26**
Other countries of Africa		515	968	741	1,269	0.14	71.26
AMERICAS	**24,564**	**25,614**	**27,078**	**24,290**	**28,466**	**3.23**	**17.19**
NORTH AMERICA	**24,564**	**24,899**	**25,588**	**22,308**	**26,158**	**2.97**	**17.26**
Canada	2,889	2,458	3,630	2,968	3,061	0.35	3.13
United States of America	21,675	21,456	20,632	18,700	21,742	2.47	16.27
Other countries of North America		985	1,326	640	1,355	0.15	111.72
SOUTH AMERICA		**292**	**520**	**741**	**1,047**	**0.12**	**41.30**
Brazil		292	520	741	1,047	0.12	41.30
OTHER AMERICAS		**423**	**970**	**1,241**	**1,261**	**0.14**	**1.61**
Other countries of the Americas		423	970	1,241	1,261	0.14	1.61
EAST ASIA AND THE PACIFIC	**8,070**	**20,978**	**24,252**	**28,187**	**32,793**	**3.72**	**16.34**
NORTH-EAST ASIA	**2,274**	**5,630**	**8,467**	**9,500**	**10,922**	**1.24**	**14.97**
China		1,842	4,027	4,478	5,745	0.65	28.29
Japan	2,274	2,905	3,196	3,634	3,301	0.37	-9.16
Korea, Republic of		883	1,244	1,388	1,876	0.21	35.16
AUSTRALASIA	**5,796**	**8,835**	**9,908**	**12,885**	**14,731**	**1.67**	**14.33**
Australia	5,488	8,523	9,397	12,434	13,666	1.55	9.91
New Zealand	308	312	511	451	1,065	0.12	136.14
OTHER EAST ASIA AND THE PACIFIC		**6,513**	**5,877**	**5,802**	**7,140**	**0.81**	**23.06**
Other countries of Asia		4,472	5,213	4,788	6,762	0.77	41.23
Other countries of Oceania		2,041	664	1,014	378	0.04	-62.72
EUROPE	**536,748**	**511,851**	**702,617**	**758,363**	**818,622**	**92.88**	**7.95**
CENTRAL/EASTERN EUROPE	**90,111**	**77,966**	**92,372**	**106,248**	**132,877**	**15.08**	**25.06**
Belarus	466	290	2,715	1,185	1,274	0.14	7.51
Bulgaria	46,656	29,098	35,152	38,551	40,473	4.59	4.99
Czech Republic	5,074	4,978	5,807	6,421	6,171	0.70	-3.89
Estonia		517	938	859	893	0.10	3.96
Hungary	6,310	6,333	6,458	5,837	6,846	0.78	17.29
Latvia		663	982	1,328	1,774	0.20	33.58
Lithuania		743	1,051	2,526	1,796	0.20	-28.90
Poland	14,099	13,140	13,730	18,119	29,990	3.40	65.52
Romania	6,393	7,940	8,757	11,490	16,488	1.87	43.50
Russian Federation	6,001	9,035	11,082	11,987	14,221	1.61	18.64
Slovakia	2,836	2,794	2,783	2,995	6,612	0.75	120.77
Ukraine	2,276	2,435	2,917	4,950	6,339	0.72	28.06
NORTHERN EUROPE	**29,787**	**31,608**	**41,819**	**39,141**	**36,934**	**4.19**	**-5.64**
Denmark	3,088	2,680	2,899	3,254	4,143	0.47	27.32
Finland	2,391	2,710	10,459	8,099	2,298	0.26	-71.63
Iceland	522	321	257	220	252	0.03	14.55
Ireland	1,488	2,109	3,771	1,861	1,623	0.18	-12.79
Norway	4,056	3,596	2,717	3,935	3,647	0.41	-7.32
Sweden	5,442	5,786	6,488	6,314	8,080	0.92	27.97
United Kingdom	12,800	14,406	15,228	15,458	16,891	1.92	9.27
SOUTHERN EUROPE	**266,210**	**278,647**	**313,521**	**303,394**	**318,413**	**36.13**	**4.95**
Albania	47,711	43,269	35,916	34,707	40,671	4.61	17.18
Bosnia and Herzegovina	10,861	13,985	14,317	11,625	10,276	1.17	-11.60
Croatia	26,061	26,111	28,531	28,574	26,169	2.97	-8.42
Greece	37,478	43,043	77,651	73,018	80,650	9.15	10.45
Italy	15,233	13,381	16,509	17,295	16,131	1.83	-6.73
Malta		68	156	1,045	198	0.02	-81.05
Montenegro	5,412	7,825	7,366	6,943	7,728	0.88	11.31
Portugal	1,619	1,385	2,038	1,960	2,080	0.24	6.12
Serbia	88,882	74,959	72,601	71,153	74,076	8.40	4.11
Slovenia	28,048	26,200	30,681	29,595	28,261	3.21	-4.51

743

THE FORMER YUGOSLAV REP OF MACEDONIA

6. Overnight stays of non-resident tourists in all types of accommodation establishments, by nationality

	2009	2010	2011	2012	2013	Market share 2013	% Change 2013-2012
Spain	4,905	3,905	3,490	4,752	4,060	0.46	-14.56
Other countries of Southern Europe		24,516	24,265	22,727	28,113	3.19	23.70
WESTERN EUROPE	**66,682**	**70,459**	**169,672**	**214,599**	**208,022**	**23.60**	**-3.06**
Austria	12,253	11,506	10,754	11,976	14,248	1.62	18.97
Belgium	4,353	4,097	7,418	13,907	19,747	2.24	41.99
France	9,963	9,909	9,665	10,627	9,993	1.13	-5.97
Germany	23,845	22,767	22,222	26,120	30,335	3.44	16.14
Luxembourg		165	472	149	500	0.06	235.57
Netherlands	12,502	17,417	112,309	145,280	126,972	14.41	-12.60
Switzerland	3,766	4,598	6,832	6,540	6,227	0.71	-4.79
EAST MEDITERRANEAN EUROPE	**56,036**	**44,142**	**76,523**	**89,065**	**114,286**	**12.97**	**28.32**
Cyprus		306	1,597	1,167	1,313	0.15	12.51
Israel	22,823	7,821	10,459	6,907	8,047	0.91	16.50
Turkey	33,213	36,015	64,467	80,991	104,926	11.90	29.55
OTHER EUROPE	**27,922**	**9,029**	**8,710**	**5,916**	**8,090**	**0.92**	**36.75**
Other countries of Europe	27,922	9,029	8,710	5,916	8,090	0.92	36.75
NOT SPECIFIED	**14,414**						
Other countries of the World	14,414						

744

Yearbook of Tourism Statistics, Data 2009 – 2013, 2015 Edition

TIMOR-LESTE

1. Arrivals of non-resident tourists at national borders, by country of residence

	2009	2010	2011	2012	2013	Market share 2013	% Change 2013-2012
TOTAL (*)	44,131	39,825	50,590	57,517			
AMERICAS	3,402	2,523	3,185	3,933			
CARIBBEAN	279						
Cuba	279						
NORTH AMERICA	2,274	1,720	2,207	2,211			
Canada	472						
United States of America	1,802	1,720	2,207	2,211			
SOUTH AMERICA	849	803	978	1,722			
Brazil	849	803	978	1,722			
EAST ASIA AND THE PACIFIC	26,269	28,101	34,766	41,606			
NORTH-EAST ASIA	3,739	3,867	4,696	6,183			
China	1,991	2,659	3,464	4,972			
Japan	1,106	1,208	1,232	1,211			
Korea, Republic of	642						
SOUTH-EAST ASIA	10,501	12,172	16,940	22,470			
Indonesia	5,443	6,744	11,179	15,303			
Malaysia	1,956	1,756	1,829	1,944			
Philippines	1,709	2,177	2,413	3,842			
Singapore	1,393	1,495	1,519	1,381			
AUSTRALASIA	12,029	12,062	13,130	12,953			
Australia	11,207	11,262	12,419	12,138			
New Zealand	822	800	711	815			
EUROPE	6,066	1,925	6,918	7,045			
NORTHERN EUROPE	806	929	1,002	915			
United Kingdom	806	929	1,002	915			
SOUTHERN EUROPE	4,795	996	5,916	6,130			
Italy	294						
Portugal	4,501	996	5,916	6,130			
WESTERN EUROPE	465						
Germany	465						
SOUTH ASIA	2,351	2,426	1,900	1,175			
Bangladesh	459						
India	1,464	2,027	1,451	862			
Pakistan	428	399	449	313			
NOT SPECIFIED	6,043	4,850	3,821	3,758			
Other countries of the World	6,043	4,850	3,821	3,758			

Yearbook of Tourism Statistics, Data 2009 – 2013, 2015 Edition

TOGO

3. Arrivals of non-resident tourists in hotels and similar establishments, by country of residence

		2009	2010	2011	2012	2013	Market share 2013	% Change 2013-2012
TOTAL		149,945	202,044	300,479	234,762	326,826	100.00	39.22
AFRICA		76,496	110,821	135,683	127,254	149,499	45.74	17.48
WEST AFRICA		40,231	48,737	65,158	51,350	61,587	18.84	19.94
Benin		12,520	13,788	16,850	14,627	17,729	5.42	21.21
Burkina Faso	(*)	10,258	13,618	18,620	13,818	16,628	5.09	20.34
Côte d'Ivoire		6,780	8,933	11,624	7,219	9,751	2.98	35.07
Ghana		3,800	4,553	7,961	6,521	6,847	2.09	5.00
Nigeria		6,873	7,845	10,103	9,165	10,632	3.25	16.01
OTHER AFRICA		36,265	62,084	70,525	75,904	87,912	26.90	15.82
Other countries of Africa		36,265	62,084	70,525	75,904	87,912	26.90	15.82
AMERICAS		5,727	5,921	7,959	7,679	8,305	2.54	8.15
NORTH AMERICA		5,448	5,571	6,764	7,265	7,674	2.35	5.63
Canada		946	1,111	1,039	1,028	1,059	0.32	3.02
United States of America		4,502	4,460	5,725	6,237	6,615	2.02	6.06
OTHER AMERICAS		279	350	1,195	414	631	0.19	52.42
Other countries of the Americas		279	350	1,195	414	631	0.19	52.42
EAST ASIA AND THE PACIFIC		6,002	9,578	11,075	10,942	11,341	3.47	3.65
NORTH-EAST ASIA		326	714	860	1,298	686	0.21	-47.15
Japan		326	714	860	1,298	686	0.21	-47.15
OTHER EAST ASIA AND THE PACIFIC		5,676	8,864	10,215	9,644	10,655	3.26	10.48
Other countries of Asia		5,676	8,864	10,215	9,644	10,655	3.26	10.48
EUROPE		61,385	75,136	144,043	87,536	98,462	30.13	12.48
CENTRAL/EASTERN EUROPE		19	458	3,562	245	239	0.07	-2.45
Russian Federation		19	458	3,562	245	239	0.07	-2.45
NORTHERN EUROPE		1,145	2,528	1,138	1,566	2,203	0.67	40.68
United Kingdom		1,073	1,545	1,032	1,073	2,060	0.63	91.99
Scandinavia		72	983	106	493	143	0.04	-70.99
SOUTHERN EUROPE		2,286	2,655	2,779	3,705	3,717	1.14	0.32
Italy		2,286	2,655	2,779	3,705	3,717	1.14	0.32
WESTERN EUROPE		33,456	44,504	50,710	49,762	60,297	18.45	21.17
France		28,229	37,911	44,552	42,502	52,280	16.00	23.01
Germany		3,034	3,029	3,009	4,076	4,513	1.38	10.72
Switzerland		678	868	930	1,078	1,009	0.31	-6.40
Benelux		1,515	2,696	2,219	2,106	2,495	0.76	18.47
OTHER EUROPE		24,479	24,991	85,854	32,258	32,006	9.79	-0.78
Other countries of Europe		24,479	24,991	85,854	32,258	32,006	9.79	-0.78
MIDDLE EAST		166	374	1,224	1,084	1,285	0.39	18.54
All countries of Middle East		166	374	1,224	1,084	1,285	0.39	18.54
NOT SPECIFIED		169	214	495	267	57,934	17.73	21,598.13
Other countries of the World		169	214	495	267	312	0.10	16.85
Nationals Residing Abroad						57,622	17.63	

746

Yearbook of Tourism Statistics, Data 2009 – 2013, 2015 Edition

TOGO

5. Overnight stays of non-resident tourists in hotels and similar establishments, by country of residence

		2009	2010	2011	2012	2013	Market share 2013	% Change 2013-2012
TOTAL		**317,644**	**420,516**	**673,219**	**515,248**	**794,615**	**100.00**	**54.22**
AFRICA		**170,482**	**197,335**	**275,346**	**243,559**	**319,916**	**40.26**	**31.35**
WEST AFRICA		**103,801**	**85,287**	**129,699**	**101,551**	**149,144**	**18.77**	**46.87**
Benin		21,532	16,050	25,044	20,171	34,499	4.34	71.03
Burkina Faso	(*)	38,443	28,904	42,353	34,506	43,513	5.48	26.10
Côte d'Ivoire		17,984	18,902	29,564	17,974	29,071	3.66	61.74
Ghana		6,892	6,851	12,620	9,423	12,350	1.55	31.06
Nigeria		18,950	14,580	20,118	19,477	29,711	3.74	52.54
OTHER AFRICA		**66,681**	**112,048**	**145,647**	**142,008**	**170,772**	**21.49**	**20.26**
Other countries of Africa		66,681	112,048	145,647	142,008	170,772	21.49	20.26
AMERICAS		**13,198**	**18,045**	**25,940**	**28,498**	**23,205**	**2.92**	**-18.57**
NORTH AMERICA		**12,852**	**17,424**	**22,425**	**27,062**	**21,401**	**2.69**	**-20.92**
Canada		1,562	2,322	4,085	3,432	4,861	0.61	41.64
United States of America		11,290	15,102	18,340	23,630	16,540	2.08	-30.00
OTHER AMERICAS		**346**	**621**	**3,515**	**1,436**	**1,804**	**0.23**	**25.63**
Other countries of the Americas		346	621	3,515	1,436	1,804	0.23	25.63
EAST ASIA AND THE PACIFIC		**15,840**	**17,561**	**27,840**	**21,998**	**4,396**	**0.55**	**-80.02**
NORTH-EAST ASIA		**481**	**912**	**2,421**	**4,615**	**2,592**	**0.33**	**-43.84**
Japan		481	912	2,421	4,615	2,592	0.33	-43.84
OTHER EAST ASIA AND THE PACIFIC		**15,359**	**16,649**	**25,419**	**17,383**	**1,804**	**0.23**	**-89.62**
Other countries of Asia		15,359	16,649	25,419	17,383	1,804	0.23	-89.62
EUROPE		**117,244**	**186,984**	**340,344**	**219,202**	**231,789**	**29.17**	**5.74**
CENTRAL/EASTERN EUROPE		**14**	**649**	**1,523**	**255**	**507**	**0.06**	**98.82**
Russian Federation		14	649	1,523	255	507	0.06	98.82
NORTHERN EUROPE		**1,907**	**6,377**	**2,040**	**4,800**	**5,943**	**0.75**	**23.81**
United Kingdom		1,831	5,230	1,921	4,237	5,597	0.70	32.10
Scandinavia		76	1,147	119	563	346	0.04	-38.54
SOUTHERN EUROPE		**3,290**	**4,742**	**4,414**	**14,989**	**10,970**	**1.38**	**-26.81**
Italy		3,290	4,742	4,414	14,989	10,970	1.38	-26.81
WESTERN EUROPE		**62,041**	**85,197**	**100,562**	**123,318**	**153,097**	**19.27**	**24.15**
France		51,546	72,725	86,397	102,953	133,278	16.77	29.46
Germany		6,465	4,626	6,447	12,460	11,791	1.48	-5.37
Switzerland		1,234	3,200	1,684	2,440	2,142	0.27	-12.21
Benelux		2,796	4,646	6,034	5,465	5,886	0.74	7.70
OTHER EUROPE		**49,992**	**90,019**	**231,805**	**75,840**	**61,272**	**7.71**	**-19.21**
Other countries of Europe		49,992	90,019	231,805	75,840	61,272	7.71	-19.21
MIDDLE EAST		**343**	**350**	**3,130**	**1,647**	**2,622**	**0.33**	**59.20**
All countries of Middle East		343	350	3,130	1,647	2,622	0.33	59.20
NOT SPECIFIED		**537**	**241**	**619**	**344**	**212,687**	**26.77**	**61,727.62**
Other countries of the World		537	241	619	344	687	0.09	99.71
Nationals Residing Abroad						212,000	26.68	

747

Yearbook of Tourism Statistics, Data 2009 – 2013, 2015 Edition

TONGA

1. Arrivals of non-resident tourists at national borders, by country of residence

	2009	2010	2011	2012	2013	Market share 2013	% Change 2013-2012
TOTAL (*)	45,711	47,081	46,005	47,736	45,241	100.00	-5.23
AFRICA	203	50	42	94	27	0.06	-71.28
OTHER AFRICA	203	50	42	94	27	0.06	-71.28
All countries of Africa	203	50	42	94	27	0.06	-71.28
AMERICAS	6,137	6,837	5,942	6,069	5,833	12.89	-3.89
NORTH AMERICA	5,884	6,766	5,779	5,938	5,693	12.58	-4.13
Canada	459	394	271	244	225	0.50	-7.79
United States of America	5,425	6,372	5,508	5,694	5,468	12.09	-3.97
OTHER AMERICAS	253	71	163	131	140	0.31	6.87
Other countries of the Americas	253	71	163	131	140	0.31	6.87
EAST ASIA AND THE PACIFIC	28,887	36,810	36,814	38,345	36,431	80.53	-4.99
NORTH-EAST ASIA	1,659	1,558	1,380	1,360	1,248	2.76	-8.24
China	807	850	671	550	542	1.20	-1.45
Japan	709	607	541	687	600	1.33	-12.66
Korea, Republic of	143	101	168	123	106	0.23	-13.82
AUSTRALASIA	24,420	32,022	32,573	33,901	32,397	71.61	-4.44
Australia	9,370	10,392	10,320	10,828	9,527	21.06	-12.02
New Zealand	15,050	21,630	22,253	23,073	22,870	50.55	-0.88
MELANESIA	1,497	1,502	1,535	1,559	1,462	3.23	-6.22
Fiji	1,497	1,502	1,535	1,559	1,462	3.23	-6.22
POLYNESIA	369	648	416	430	242	0.53	-43.72
American Samoa	33	213	130	124	8	0.02	-93.55
Samoa	336	435	286	306	234	0.52	-23.53
OTHER EAST ASIA AND THE PACIFIC	942	1,080	910	1,095	1,082	2.39	-1.19
Other countries of Asia	538	396	356	404	419	0.93	3.71
Other countries of Oceania	404	684	554	691	663	1.47	-4.05
EUROPE	4,844	3,325	3,176	2,882	2,909	6.43	0.94
NORTHERN EUROPE	1,705	819	696	634	669	1.48	5.52
United Kingdom	1,705	819	696	634	669	1.48	5.52
SOUTHERN EUROPE	282	187	175	107	136	0.30	27.10
Italy	282	187	175	107	136	0.30	27.10
WESTERN EUROPE	1,494	1,085	1,085	989	1,050	2.32	6.17
France	553	300	305	247	305	0.67	23.48
Germany	941	785	780	742	745	1.65	0.40
OTHER EUROPE	1,363	1,234	1,220	1,152	1,054	2.33	-8.51
Other countries of Europe	1,363	1,234	1,220	1,152	1,054	2.33	-8.51
SOUTH ASIA	90	33	31	43	41	0.09	-4.65
India	90	33	31	43	41	0.09	-4.65
NOT SPECIFIED	5,550	26		303			
Other countries of the World	5,550	26		303			

748

Yearbook of Tourism Statistics, Data 2009 – 2013, 2015 Edition

TRINIDAD AND TOBAGO

1. Arrivals of non-resident tourists at national borders, by country of residence

		2009	2010	2011	2012	2013	Market share 2013	% Change 2013-2012
TOTAL	(*)	418,864	385,510	430,922	454,683	434,044	100.00	-4.54
AFRICA		1,823	1,159	2,895	2,983	1,327	0.31	-55.51
EAST AFRICA		415	122	491	545			
British Indian Ocean Territory		3	4		2			
Burundi				1				
Comoros			1		2			
Ethiopia		6	5	25	11			
Kenya		114	35	76	112			
Madagascar			1	11	7			
Malawi		28	2	13	20			
Mauritius		23	10	32	30			
Mozambique		9		6	5			
Reunion		3	2					
Rwanda		12	5	10	11			
Seychelles		6	5	7	9			
Somalia				4	7			
Uganda		74	11	189	260			
United Republic of Tanzania		89	13					
Zambia		35	13	49	18			
Zimbabwe		13	15	68	51			
CENTRAL AFRICA		52	52	100	118			
Angola		1	31	27	43			
Cameroon		41	6	60	58			
Central African Republic			4					
Chad			5	1	1			
Congo		5	3	11	4			
Democratic Republic of the Congo		4						
Equatorial Guinea			2		4			
Gabon		1	1	1	8			
NORTH AFRICA		23	14	70	70			
Algeria		3	2	42	45			
Morocco		2	1	19	14			
Sudan		4	2	9	11			
Tunisia		14	9					
SOUTHERN AFRICA		555	469	620	665			
Botswana		130	89	134	107			
Lesotho		4						
Namibia		4	4	9	22			
South Africa		406	370	473	531			
Swaziland		11	6	4	5			
WEST AFRICA		778	502	1,614	1,585	1,327	0.31	-16.28
Benin		3	1	7	5			
Burkina Faso		1		9	5			
Cabo Verde				1	7			
Côte d'Ivoire		6		10	56			
Gambia		11	4	9	11			
Ghana		94	123	276	231			
Guinea		7	3	8	3			
Guinea-Bissau				3	2			
Liberia		5	7	6	14			
Mali		1	1	4				
Mauritania		6	1	3				
Niger		3		7	4			
Nigeria		612	348	1,189	1,188	1,327	0.31	11.70
Saint Helena				3	1			
Senegal		6	5	21	11			
Sierra Leone		22	9	53	38			
Togo		1		5	9			

749

TRINIDAD AND TOBAGO

1. Arrivals of non-resident tourists at national borders, by country of residence

	2009	2010	2011	2012	2013	Market share 2013	% Change 2013-2012
AMERICAS	351,216	325,384	338,957	333,167	337,679	77.80	1.35
CARIBBEAN	58,752	54,713	67,625	65,732	68,894	15.87	4.81
Anguilla	245	228					
Antigua and Barbuda	2,283	2,158	3,990	3,482			
Aruba	355	351					
Bahamas	1,244	1,076	1,178	1,034			
Barbados	15,672	13,576	16,763	14,860			
Bermuda	694	556	322	307			
British Virgin Islands	646	579					
Cayman Islands	579	538					
Cuba	439	467	1,016	1,192			
Curaçao	730	692					
Dominica	1,239	1,154	1,953	1,800			
Dominican Republic	1,115	1,196	1,525	1,564	1,791	0.41	14.51
Grenada	7,339	7,269	10,665	10,954			
Guadeloupe	451	525					
Haiti	188	216	330	301			
Jamaica	7,776	7,548	13,314	13,350			
Martinique	912	950					
Montserrat	147	134	106	96			
Netherlands Antilles	495	522					
Puerto Rico	1,824	1,809					
Saint Kitts and Nevis	1,132	936	1,286	1,049			
Saint Lucia	4,429	4,187	5,359	5,274			
Saint Vincent and the Grenadines	7,421	6,726	9,818	10,469			
Turks and Caicos Islands	138	94					
United States Virgin Islands	1,259	1,226					
Other countries of the Caribbean					67,103	15.46	
CENTRAL AMERICA	4,034	3,206	3,832	4,098	4,347	1.00	6.08
Belize	508	442	634	620	638	0.15	2.90
Costa Rica	1,091	859	792	759			
El Salvador	245	134	248	350			
Guatemala	390	400	565	587			
Honduras	521	173	338	368			
Nicaragua	65	64	139	135			
Panama	1,214	1,134	1,116	1,279			
Other countries of Central America					3,709	0.85	
NORTH AMERICA	246,531	230,910	206,778	192,823	204,795	47.18	6.21
Canada	49,514	46,390	48,710	42,472	61,681	14.21	45.23
Mexico	1,573	1,347	1,959	2,039	2,120	0.49	3.97
Saint Pierre and Miquelon	6	2					
United States of America	195,438	183,171	156,109	148,312	140,994	32.48	-4.93
SOUTH AMERICA	41,899	36,555	60,722	70,514	59,643	13.74	-15.42
Argentina	1,106	730	1,133	1,137			
Bolivia	117	90	183	169			
Brazil	1,481	1,524	2,404	2,644	2,450	0.56	-7.34
Chile	511	351	426	502			
Colombia	2,431	2,313	3,012	3,402	3,454	0.80	1.53
Ecuador	220	219	418	482			
Falkland Islands, Malvinas	1	3		3			
French Guiana	220	289		5			
Guyana	20,679	18,339	31,727	37,568	32,355	7.45	-13.88
Paraguay	40	19	40	32			
Peru	349	290	706	1,010			
Suriname	3,085	2,791	3,073	4,191	3,625	0.84	-13.51
Uruguay	138	54					
Venezuela	11,521	9,543	14,460	16,415	15,008	3.46	-8.57
Other countries of South America			3,140	2,954	2,751	0.63	-6.87

Yearbook of Tourism Statistics, Data 2009 – 2013, 2015 Edition

TRINIDAD AND TOBAGO

1. Arrivals of non-resident tourists at national borders, by country of residence

	2009	2010	2011	2012	2013	Market share 2013	% Change 2013-2012
EAST ASIA AND THE PACIFIC	**5,394**	**4,582**	**9,248**	**10,863**	**8,073**	**1.86**	**-25.68**
NORTH-EAST ASIA	**3,039**	**2,452**	**3,625**	**3,533**	**4,657**	**1.07**	**31.81**
China	2,057	1,548	2,864	2,533	3,657	0.84	44.37
Hong Kong, China	109	125	1	3			
Japan	372	374	640	805	1,000	0.23	24.22
Korea, Dem. People's Republic of	272	266					
Korea, Republic of	189	75					
Macao, China		4					
Mongolia	2		2	9			
Taiwan, Province of China	38	60	118	183			
SOUTH-EAST ASIA	**1,140**	**1,100**	**3,990**	**5,272**	**2,057**	**0.47**	**-60.98**
Brunei Darussalam	13	4		1			
Cambodia	3	1	1	3			
Indonesia	55	39	762	1,383	330	0.08	-76.14
Malaysia	338	369	292	398			
Myanmar	12	12	72	143			
Philippines	431	474	2,567	2,991	1,727	0.40	-42.26
Singapore	209	139	210	209			
Thailand	70	55	23	75			
Timor-Leste			2	2			
Viet Nam	9	7	61	67			
AUSTRALASIA	**1,130**	**1,004**	**1,601**	**2,023**	**1,359**	**0.31**	**-32.82**
Australia	950	819	1,340	1,706	1,359	0.31	-20.34
New Zealand	180	185	261	317			
MELANESIA	**46**	**14**	**17**	**8**			
Fiji	5	9	12	5			
New Caledonia	1	1					
Norfolk Island			1				
Papua New Guinea	26	1	4	2			
Solomon Islands	6	2		1			
Vanuatu	8	1					
MICRONESIA	**11**	**2**	**3**	**6**			
Cocos (Keeling) Islands			2	1			
Marshall Islands	1						
Micronesia, Federated States of	1		1				
Nauru	2			5			
Northern Mariana Islands	7	1					
Wake Island		1 *					
POLYNESIA	**28**	**10**	**12**	**21**			
American Samoa	1		5	14			
Cook Islands	4		2	1			
French Polynesia	4	3					
Pitcairn		1					
Samoa	9	1	3	5			
Tonga	5	5	2	1			
Tuvalu	4						
Wallis and Futuna Islands	1						
EUROPE	**57,667**	**52,364**	**74,429**	**67,686**	**64,868**	**14.95**	**-4.16**
CENTRAL/EASTERN EUROPE	**894**	**920**	**1,790**	**1,871**	**726**	**0.17**	**-61.20**
Armenia			5	1			
Azerbaijan	25	13	22	19			
Belarus	1	4	6	11			
Bulgaria	32	23	138	150			
Czech Republic	105	111					
Estonia	28	78	266	39			
Georgia		1	13	14			
Hungary	72	71	105	123			
Kazakhstan	13	8	36	40			

751

Yearbook of Tourism Statistics, Data 2009 – 2013, 2015 Edition

TRINIDAD AND TOBAGO

1. Arrivals of non-resident tourists at national borders, by country of residence

	2009	2010	2011	2012	2013	Market share 2013	% Change 2013-2012
Kyrgyzstan		1		6			
Latvia	47	63	126	165			
Lithuania	35	19	64	86			
Poland	256	256	931	1,122	726	0.17	-35.29
Republic of Moldova		1					
Romania	115	88					
Russian Federation	84	79					
Slovakia	35	39	68	79			
Tajikistan	4	2		2			
Ukraine	32	60					
Uzbekistan	10	3	10	14			
NORTHERN EUROPE	**42,965**	**38,264**	**46,763**	**42,461**	**48,607**	**11.20**	**14.47**
Denmark	1,193	963	1,042	769			
Faeroe Islands	1	3					
Finland	226	206	372	313			
Iceland	17	20	22	50			
Ireland	722	783	1,492	1,431			
Isle of Man	13	8					
Norway	1,107	993	1,386	1,155			
Sweden	1,286	1,109	1,558	1,343			
United Kingdom	38,400	34,179	40,891	37,400	43,224	9.96	15.57
Scandinavia					5,383	1.24	
SOUTHERN EUROPE	**2,226**	**2,335**	**7,171**	**4,933**	**3,368**	**0.78**	**-31.73**
Albania	4	1	19	35			
Andorra	10	7	5	5			
Bosnia and Herzegovina	7	8	12	14			
Croatia	29	67	321	417			
Gibraltar	6	7	1				
Greece	108	135	293	293			
Holy See	1						
Italy	1,062	966	1,994	1,781	1,769	0.41	-0.67
Malta	36	28	28	38			
Montenegro		2					
Portugal	98	188	457	512			
San Marino	1						
Serbia and Montenegro	8	6	56	66			
Slovenia	48	41	68	60			
Spain	808	879	3,917	1,712	1,599	0.37	-6.60
WESTERN EUROPE	**11,288**	**10,567**	**18,194**	**17,664**	**12,167**	**2.80**	**-31.12**
Austria	437	533	751	625			
Belgium	453	409	505	506			
France	2,177	1,829	5,449	4,934	5,364	1.24	8.72
Germany	4,895	4,657	5,686	6,023	5,836	1.34	-3.10
Liechtenstein			4	2			
Luxembourg	14	15	41	23			
Monaco	4	2					
Netherlands	2,409	2,202	4,694	4,648			
Switzerland	899	920	1,064	903	967	0.22	7.09
EAST MEDITERRANEAN EUROPE	**294**	**278**	**511**	**757**			
Cyprus	33	20	19	23			
Israel	203	168	273	324			
Turkey	58	90	219	410			
MIDDLE EAST	**468**	**390**	**310**	**345**			
Bahrain	4	21	3	2			
Democratic Yemen (former)			7	10			
Egypt	70	63	71	83			
Iraq	2	4	11	16			
Jordan	2	1	14	10			
Kuwait	14	12	4	3			

752

TRINIDAD AND TOBAGO

1. Arrivals of non-resident tourists at national borders, by country of residence

	2009	2010	2011	2012	2013	Market share 2013	% Change 2013-2012
Lebanon	31	14	54	46			
Libya	2	8	17	3			
Oman	9	6	2	7			
Qatar	32	40	1	36			
Saudi Arabia	82	63	10	14			
Syrian Arab Republic	29	25	116	115			
United Arab Emirates	188	133					
Yemen	3						
SOUTH ASIA	**2,267**	**1,620**	**5,083**	**5,116**	**4,489**	**1.03**	**-12.26**
Afghanistan	96	40	3	32			
Bangladesh	134	72	154	183			
Bhutan				3			
India	1,894	1,344	4,498	4,495	4,489	1.03	-0.13
Iran, Islamic Republic of	7	2	13	25			
Nepal	10	14	28	29			
Pakistan	76	115	287	232			
Sri Lanka	50	33	100	117			
NOT SPECIFIED	**29**	**11**		**34,523**	**17,608**	**4.06**	**-49.00**
Other countries of the World	29	11		34,523	17,608	4.06	-49.00

753

TUNISIA

1. Arrivals of non-resident tourists at national borders, by nationality

	2009	2010	2011	2012	2013	Market share 2013	% Change 2013-2012
TOTAL (*)	6,901,406	6,902,749	4,785,119	5,950,464	6,268,582	100.00	5.35
AFRICA	1,036,070	1,136,066	829,254	996,044	1,042,868	16.64	4.70
NORTH AFRICA	991,827	1,090,339	746,276	937,598	987,691	15.76	5.34
Algeria	961,343	1,060,043	693,732	901,677	954,908	15.23	5.90
Morocco	29,458	29,104	34,748	34,875	31,936	0.51	-8.43
Sudan	1,026	1,192	17,796	1,046	847	0.01	-19.02
WEST AFRICA	13,063	13,279	13,100	18,977	17,085	0.27	-9.97
Mauritania	13,063	13,279	13,100	18,977	17,085	0.27	-9.97
OTHER AFRICA	31,180	32,448	69,878	39,469	38,092	0.61	-3.49
Other countries of Africa	31,180	32,448	69,878	39,469	38,092	0.61	-3.49
AMERICAS	39,369	39,195	24,098	30,711	25,955	0.41	-15.49
NORTH AMERICA	36,275	36,203	22,722	28,540	23,601	0.38	-17.31
Canada	16,969	16,910	8,385	11,237	9,705	0.15	-13.63
United States of America	19,306	19,293	14,337	17,303	13,896	0.22	-19.69
SOUTH AMERICA	3,094	2,992	1,376	2,171	2,354	0.04	8.43
Brazil	3,094	2,992	1,376	2,171	2,354	0.04	8.43
EAST ASIA AND THE PACIFIC	17,016	20,997	16,344	13,415	12,523	0.20	-6.65
NORTH-EAST ASIA	14,582	17,997	14,992	11,773	10,768	0.17	-8.54
China	3,509	4,612	11,872	3,771	4,308	0.07	14.24
Japan	11,073	13,385	3,120	8,002	6,460	0.10	-19.27
AUSTRALASIA	2,434	3,000	1,352	1,642	1,755	0.03	6.88
Australia	2,434	3,000	1,352	1,642	1,755	0.03	6.88
EUROPE	3,743,509	3,814,402	2,133,916	2,965,111	2,896,743	46.21	-2.31
CENTRAL/EASTERN EUROPE	480,784	494,435	359,697	503,758	543,253	8.67	7.84
Bulgaria	6,125	6,720	1,334	2,613	2,650	0.04	1.42
Czech Republic	92,713	76,678	67,362	84,895	96,707	1.54	13.91
Hungary	30,148	30,331	17,233	21,028	21,396	0.34	1.75
Poland	175,319	151,372	97,457	109,554	87,936	1.40	-19.73
Romania	14,256	10,494	4,893	8,634	9,358	0.15	8.39
Russian Federation	126,516	188,261	151,911	250,732	296,963	4.74	18.44
Slovakia	35,707	30,579	19,507	26,302	28,243	0.45	7.38
NORTHERN EUROPE	397,519	499,754	254,258	386,544	470,959	7.51	21.84
Denmark	23,386	31,565	6,453	14,575	25,682	0.41	76.21
Finland	15,992	15,822	2,165	7,420	4,417	0.07	-40.47
Ireland	17,250	14,821	4,479	6,620	5,674	0.09	-14.29
Norway	18,636	21,467	4,397	6,749	7,143	0.11	5.84
Sweden	46,603	62,797	9,267	21,561	19,388	0.31	-10.08
United Kingdom	275,652	353,282	227,497	329,619	408,655	6.52	23.98
SOUTHERN EUROPE	545,042	507,857	162,784	282,908	289,028	4.61	2.16
Greece	7,887	5,436	1,966	2,771	1,990	0.03	-28.18
Italy	383,851	354,127	120,933	216,633	231,831	3.70	7.02
Malta	2,985	2,962	1,897	1,998	1,461	0.02	-26.88
Portugal	36,567	40,097	9,786	15,990	16,513	0.26	3.27
Serbia	23,522	21,364	9,635	14,711	12,632	0.20	-14.13
Spain	90,230	83,871	18,567	30,805	24,601	0.39	-20.14
WESTERN EUROPE	2,247,450	2,238,370	1,316,123	1,726,666	1,507,473	24.05	-12.69
Austria	60,654	53,558	23,946	35,132	36,465	0.58	3.79
Belgium	168,108	163,124	138,426	168,532	156,134	2.49	-7.36
France	1,344,697	1,385,293	808,548	985,217	767,138	12.24	-22.14
Germany	484,154	458,631	270,668	411,828	424,455	6.77	3.07
Luxembourg	7,111	6,201	3,484	5,201	4,920	0.08	-5.40
Netherlands	82,904	75,244	28,571	61,178	64,602	1.03	5.60
Switzerland	99,822	96,319	42,480	59,578	53,759	0.86	-9.77
EAST MEDITERRANEAN EUROPE	14,438	18,252	10,716	14,525	15,967	0.25	9.93
Turkey	14,438	18,252	10,716	14,525	15,967	0.25	9.93
OTHER EUROPE	58,276	55,734	30,338	50,710	70,063	1.12	38.16
Other countries of Europe	58,276	55,734	30,338	50,710	70,063	1.12	38.16
MIDDLE EAST	2,034,494	1,862,630	1,730,832	1,925,760	2,270,789	36.22	17.92
Bahrain	663	823	376	657	533	0.01	-18.87

754

TUNISIA

1. Arrivals of non-resident tourists at national borders, by nationality

	2009	2010	2011	2012	2013	Market share 2013	% Change 2013-2012
Egypt	11,151	9,135	67,282	10,999	10,723	0.17	-2.51
Iraq	1,180	1,598	2,022	1,833	1,960	0.03	6.93
Jordan	2,571	2,546	2,226	3,190	2,683	0.04	-15.89
Kuwait	1,689	1,825	801	1,602	1,279	0.02	-20.16
Lebanon	5,097	4,539	3,399	4,342	3,969	0.06	-8.59
Libya	1,995,236	1,825,542	1,642,620	1,887,740	2,236,135	35.67	18.46
Oman	1,074	1,072	514	1,095	1,145	0.02	4.57
Palestine	1,624	1,691	1,591	2,235	2,019	0.03	-9.66
Qatar	1,051	897	992	1,255	983	0.02	-21.67
Saudi Arabia	6,633	6,550	3,068	6,259	6,015	0.10	-3.90
Syrian Arab Republic	3,819	3,597	3,448	2,323	1,588	0.03	-31.64
United Arab Emirates	1,980	1,692	2,093	1,319	1,100	0.02	-16.60
Yemen	726	1,123	400	911	657	0.01	-27.88
NOT SPECIFIED	**30,948**	**29,459**	**50,675**	**19,423**	**19,704**	**0.31**	**1.45**
Other countries of the World	30,948	29,459	50,675	19,423	19,704	0.31	1.45

Yearbook of Tourism Statistics, Data 2009 – 2013, 2015 Edition

TUNISIA

3. Arrivals of non-resident tourists in hotels and similar establishments, by nationality

	2009	2010	2011	2012	2013	Market share 2013	% Change 2013-2012
TOTAL	5,041,840	5,149,048	2,622,578	4,086,320	3,951,509	100.00	-3.30
AFRICA	338,012	394,026	185,406	294,949	276,881	7.01	-6.13
NORTH AFRICA	301,877	353,215	155,381	258,711	243,116	6.15	-6.03
Algeria	288,109	336,768	143,672	240,715	227,601	5.76	-5.45
Morocco	13,768	16,447	11,709	17,996	15,515	0.39	-13.79
OTHER AFRICA	36,135	40,811	30,025	36,238	33,765	0.85	-6.82
Other countries of Africa	36,135	40,811	30,025	36,238	33,765	0.85	-6.82
AMERICAS	80,719	80,270	26,169	36,594	30,959	0.78	-15.40
NORTH AMERICA	79,105	78,396	23,965	34,986	29,285	0.74	-16.30
Canada	40,469	45,927	9,588	18,958	17,706	0.45	-6.60
United States of America	38,636	32,469	14,377	16,028	11,579	0.29	-27.76
SOUTH AMERICA	1,614	1,874	2,204	1,608	1,674	0.04	4.10
Brazil	1,614	1,874	2,204	1,608	1,674	0.04	4.10
EAST ASIA AND THE PACIFIC	50,943	66,817	15,593	52,868	50,355	1.27	-4.75
NORTH-EAST ASIA	48,187	63,181	14,055	51,075	48,564	1.23	-4.92
China	4,663	9,572	4,556	12,427	21,814	0.55	75.54
Japan	43,524	53,609	9,499	38,648	26,750	0.68	-30.79
AUSTRALASIA	2,756	3,636	1,538	1,793	1,791	0.05	-0.11
Australia	2,756	3,636	1,538	1,793	1,791	0.05	-0.11
EUROPE	4,217,298	4,191,497	1,967,865	3,104,373	2,970,693	75.18	-4.31
CENTRAL/EASTERN EUROPE	545,389	552,134	394,668	579,020	645,424	16.33	11.47
Bulgaria	5,729	4,562	1,197	3,042	2,142	0.05	-29.59
Czech Republic	101,953	89,086	71,565	85,215	92,215	2.33	8.21
Hungary	36,764	33,347	18,011	22,938	23,319	0.59	1.66
Poland	188,509	165,150	95,955	117,023	97,747	2.47	-16.47
Romania	12,916	9,723	2,089	5,971	6,949	0.18	16.38
Russian Federation	166,387	220,557	189,567	323,048	403,749	10.22	24.98
Slovakia	33,131	29,709	16,284	21,783	19,303	0.49	-11.39
NORTHERN EUROPE	459,474	549,488	258,974	402,506	503,930	12.75	25.20
Ireland	9,039	8,108	2,077	3,319	2,400	0.06	-27.69
United Kingdom	327,631	412,581	235,960	353,557	446,853	11.31	26.39
Scandinavia	122,804	128,799	20,937	45,630	54,677	1.38	19.83
SOUTHERN EUROPE	785,824	658,807	142,768	319,289	312,171	7.90	-2.23
Greece	17,857	12,445	2,732	5,198	4,274	0.11	-17.78
Italy	473,022	360,571	93,501	204,486	217,386	5.50	6.31
Malta	2,741	2,782	1,625	2,360	1,465	0.04	-37.92
Portugal	23,660	28,146	5,301	10,026	12,424	0.31	23.92
Serbia	16,082	13,856	5,604	14,215	12,646	0.32	-11.04
Spain	252,462	241,007	34,005	83,004	63,976	1.62	-22.92
WESTERN EUROPE	2,357,807	2,365,398	1,136,539	1,740,339	1,444,393	36.55	-17.01
Austria	41,549	39,925	15,605	23,669	21,066	0.53	-11.00
Belgium	181,458	178,201	116,848	170,043	154,395	3.91	-9.20
France	1,374,242	1,418,234	653,082	906,432	618,080	15.64	-31.81
Germany	563,536	552,683	286,146	507,057	531,538	13.45	4.83
Luxembourg	35,473	31,955	14,011	26,145	21,378	0.54	-18.23
Netherlands	78,014	68,384	22,361	63,097	59,724	1.51	-5.35
Switzerland	83,535	76,016	28,486	43,896	38,212	0.97	-12.95
EAST MEDITERRANEAN EUROPE	11,576	12,315	6,476	11,048	9,739	0.25	-11.85
Turkey	11,576	12,315	6,476	11,048	9,739	0.25	-11.85
OTHER EUROPE	57,228	53,355	28,440	52,171	55,036	1.39	5.49
Other countries of Europe	57,228	53,355	28,440	52,171	55,036	1.39	5.49
MIDDLE EAST	207,645	242,515	320,080	428,953	458,142	11.59	6.80
Libya	169,741	202,987	299,904	394,510	424,128	10.73	7.51
Other countries of Middle East	37,904	39,528	20,176	34,443	34,014	0.86	-1.25
NOT SPECIFIED	147,223	173,923	107,465	168,583	164,479	4.16	-2.43
Other countries of the World	128,640	150,146	88,536	130,300	130,660	3.31	0.28
Nationals Residing Abroad	18,583	23,777	18,929	38,283	33,819	0.86	-11.66

Yearbook of Tourism Statistics, Data 2009 – 2013, 2015 Edition

TUNISIA

5. Overnight stays of non-resident tourists in hotels and similar establishments, by nationality

	2009	2010	2011	2012	2013	Market share 2013	% Change 2013-2012
TOTAL	31,556,910	32,136,191	17,207,634	25,920,529	25,761,750	100.00	-0.61
AFRICA	997,642	1,144,741	551,477	858,629	831,669	3.23	-3.14
NORTH AFRICA	868,249	996,312	437,051	725,473	710,442	2.76	-2.07
Algeria	821,824	945,553	401,765	673,684	664,133	2.58	-1.42
Morocco	46,425	50,759	35,286	51,789	46,309	0.18	-10.58
OTHER AFRICA	129,393	148,429	114,426	133,156	121,227	0.47	-8.96
Other countries of Africa	129,393	148,429	114,426	133,156	121,227	0.47	-8.96
AMERICAS	259,458	251,585	129,607	131,850	116,447	0.45	-11.68
NORTH AMERICA	255,228	248,579	127,224	126,906	110,023	0.43	-13.30
Canada	164,801	169,754	47,236	71,940	63,342	0.25	-11.95
United States of America	90,427	78,825	79,988	54,966	46,681	0.18	-15.07
SOUTH AMERICA	4,230	3,006	2,383	4,944	6,424	0.02	29.94
Brazil	4,230	3,006	2,383	4,944	6,424	0.02	29.94
EAST ASIA AND THE PACIFIC	84,053	115,008	35,930	92,719	88,971	0.35	-4.04
NORTH-EAST ASIA	76,334	103,356	32,061	86,920	82,662	0.32	-4.90
China	8,272	18,017	14,093	28,558	37,983	0.15	33.00
Japan	68,062	85,339	17,968	58,362	44,679	0.17	-23.45
AUSTRALASIA	7,719	11,652	3,869	5,799	6,309	0.02	8.79
Australia	7,719	11,652	3,869	5,799	6,309	0.02	8.79
EUROPE	29,157,852	29,403,758	15,125,247	23,171,488	22,848,621	88.69	-1.39
CENTRAL/EASTERN EUROPE	4,311,470	4,493,330	3,210,712	4,508,393	5,033,654	19.54	11.65
Bulgaria	29,170	26,384	10,880	20,605	7,649	0.03	-62.88
Czech Republic	831,093	763,478	576,037	703,075	752,585	2.92	7.04
Hungary	218,581	199,423	118,187	156,333	152,568	0.59	-2.41
Poland	1,508,855	1,328,247	800,813	910,827	717,020	2.78	-21.28
Romania	71,180	44,902	6,324	28,948	29,816	0.12	3.00
Russian Federation	1,407,781	1,902,077	1,582,276	2,532,645	3,224,786	12.52	27.33
Slovakia	244,810	228,819	116,195	155,960	149,230	0.58	-4.32
NORTHERN EUROPE	3,606,448	4,281,921	2,132,066	3,302,101	4,134,692	16.05	25.21
Denmark	151,044	148,373	29,615	45,298	119,027	0.46	162.76
Finland	154,063	160,627	21,551	54,291	38,030	0.15	-29.95
Ireland	69,280	57,959	11,708	16,440	11,321	0.04	-31.14
Norway	87,975	101,930	19,557	30,438	32,494	0.13	6.75
Sweden	414,058	454,243	66,640	159,706	163,735	0.64	2.52
United Kingdom	2,730,028	3,358,789	1,982,995	2,995,928	3,770,085	14.63	25.84
SOUTHERN EUROPE	3,410,170	3,194,606	693,436	1,694,428	1,736,574	6.74	2.49
Greece	43,179	27,182	11,524	18,641	26,373	0.10	41.48
Italy	2,397,247	2,216,105	472,386	1,226,047	1,328,603	5.16	8.36
Malta	14,314	16,759	6,832	12,110	6,771	0.03	-44.09
Portugal	113,910	155,792	31,663	55,623	68,208	0.26	22.63
Serbia	122,718	109,028	52,534	120,511	112,925	0.44	-6.29
Spain	718,802	669,740	118,497	261,496	193,694	0.75	-25.93
WESTERN EUROPE	17,435,009	17,089,975	8,914,555	13,328,996	11,565,686	44.89	-13.23
Austria	317,173	288,858	124,451	191,709	176,226	0.68	-8.08
Belgium	1,553,429	1,503,313	1,084,538	1,482,931	1,378,685	5.35	-7.03
France	8,451,002	8,700,649	4,417,827	5,887,340	4,059,971	15.76	-31.04
Germany	5,655,768	5,336,495	2,768,191	4,780,952	5,035,839	19.55	5.33
Luxembourg	304,744	268,263	124,703	230,824	185,128	0.72	-19.80
Netherlands	541,781	491,312	192,260	454,052	461,187	1.79	1.57
Switzerland	611,112	501,085	202,585	301,188	268,650	1.04	-10.80
EAST MEDITERRANEAN EUROPE	50,222	45,659	20,129	39,732	27,934	0.11	-29.69
Turkey	50,222	45,659	20,129	39,732	27,934	0.11	-29.69
OTHER EUROPE	344,533	298,267	154,349	297,838	350,081	1.36	17.54
Other countries of Europe	344,533	298,267	154,349	297,838	350,081	1.36	17.54
MIDDLE EAST	512,952	566,020	958,383	1,089,323	1,269,117	4.93	16.51
Libya	371,985	427,399	881,939	976,670	1,159,507	4.50	18.72
Other countries of Middle East	140,967	138,621	76,444	112,653	109,610	0.43	-2.70
NOT SPECIFIED	544,953	655,079	406,990	576,520	606,925	2.36	5.27
Other countries of the World	498,141	593,672	354,203	477,636	516,788	2.01	8.20
Nationals Residing Abroad	46,812	61,407	52,787	98,884	90,137	0.35	-8.85

Yearbook of Tourism Statistics, Data 2009 – 2013, 2015 Edition

TURKEY

1. Arrivals of non-resident tourists at national borders, by nationality

	2009	2010	2011	2012	2013	Market share 2013	% Change 2013-2012
TOTAL	30,186,614	31,364,004	34,653,876	35,697,900	37,794,908	100.00	5.87
AFRICA	286,493	246,790	300,712	371,997	419,993	1.11	12.90
NORTH AFRICA	222,205	186,653	220,419	271,526	296,253	0.78	9.11
Algeria	89,776	66,089	82,615	102,358	116,047	0.31	13.37
Morocco	65,398	56,838	67,660	75,966	80,170	0.21	5.53
Sudan	10,578	6,621	7,441	8,158	9,285	0.02	13.81
Tunisia	56,453	57,105	62,703	85,044	90,751	0.24	6.71
SOUTHERN AFRICA	19,982	23,097	27,851	33,445	36,307	0.10	8.56
South Africa	19,982	23,097	27,851	33,445	36,307	0.10	8.56
OTHER AFRICA	44,306	37,040	52,442	67,026	87,433	0.23	30.45
Other countries of Africa	44,306	37,040	52,442	67,026	87,433	0.23	30.45
AMERICAS	559,017	550,380	660,300	713,981	790,002	2.09	10.65
CENTRAL AMERICA	6,649	6,396	8,788	8,983	9,761	0.03	8.66
All countries of Central America	6,649	6,396	8,788	8,983	5,135	0.01	-42.84
NORTH AMERICA	477,577	457,112	545,698	587,152	618,556	1.64	5.35
Canada	81,976	79,427	94,723	97,916	106,966	0.28	9.24
Mexico	10,253	11,175	12,584	15,221	17,828	0.05	17.13
United States of America	385,348	366,510	438,391	474,015	493,762	1.31	4.17
SOUTH AMERICA	74,791	86,872	105,814	117,846	161,685	0.43	37.20
Argentina	12,776	14,943	16,358	18,245	32,619	0.09	78.78
Brazil	39,368	51,545	63,974	70,204	86,239	0.23	22.84
Chile	4,875	4,931	6,609	7,085	8,854	0.02	24.97
Colombia	3,859	4,430	5,444	8,070	16,105	0.04	99.57
Venezuela	5,462	4,061	4,811	5,131	6,032	0.02	17.56
Other countries of South America	8,451	6,962	8,618	9,111	11,836	0.03	29.91
EAST ASIA AND THE PACIFIC	544,858	627,896	720,949	784,130	847,587	2.24	8.09
NORTH-EAST ASIA	292,109	379,789	412,616	457,080	474,867	1.26	3.89
China	67,471	74,763	92,820	109,533	131,369	0.35	19.94
Japan	137,843	184,410	173,672	191,318	159,675	0.42	-16.54
Korea, Republic of	86,795	120,616	146,124	156,229	183,823	0.49	17.66
SOUTH-EAST ASIA	100,165	104,438	124,598	151,130	178,155	0.47	17.88
Indonesia	18,765	22,404	33,199	47,538	49,489	0.13	4.10
Malaysia	28,778	31,381	34,453	39,053	53,075	0.14	35.91
Philippines	23,330	24,416	27,149	32,399	34,939	0.09	7.84
Singapore	19,656	17,759	19,402	20,661	20,821	0.06	0.77
Thailand	9,636	8,478	10,395	11,479	19,831	0.05	72.76
AUSTRALASIA	122,030	110,802	127,623	131,497	141,755	0.38	7.80
Australia	104,927	93,106	108,779	111,683	120,747	0.32	8.12
New Zealand	17,103	17,696	18,844	19,814	21,008	0.06	6.03
OTHER EAST ASIA AND THE PACIFIC	30,554	32,867	56,112	44,423	52,810	0.14	18.88
Other countries of Asia	30,413	30,031	55,788	42,581	52,504	0.14	23.30
Other countries of Oceania	141	2,836	324	1,842	306	0.00	-83.39
EUROPE	21,142,283	21,665,925	23,500,920	24,166,936	26,156,581	69.21	8.23
CENTRAL/EASTERN EUROPE	8,086,131	8,735,805	9,582,745	10,052,939	11,553,419	30.57	14.93
Armenia	64,899	69,268	72,349	70,835	73,224	0.19	3.37
Azerbaijan	422,606	484,850	576,187	591,727	629,552	1.67	6.39
Belarus	141,197	152,176	123,334	137,607	200,096	0.53	45.41
Bulgaria	1,402,195	1,432,416	1,488,384	1,488,398	1,578,647	4.18	6.06
Czech Republic	156,420	168,434	215,323	215,608	210,665	0.56	-2.29
Czech Republic/Slovakia					48,047	0.13	
Estonia	36,044	34,855	34,512	35,028	48,047	0.13	37.17
Georgia	992,886	1,109,614	1,149,360	1,402,018	1,766,268	4.67	25.98
Hungary	79,082	88,100	100,362	89,347	93,263	0.25	4.38
Kazakhstan	219,060	247,690	315,644	379,650	425,199	1.13	12.00
Kyrgyzstan	40,879	35,618	41,186	42,800	64,884	0.17	51.60
Latvia	40,451	38,079	43,918	45,041	54,370	0.14	20.71
Lithuania	76,018	71,255	73,629	67,426	88,138	0.23	30.72

758

Yearbook of Tourism Statistics, Data 2009 – 2013, 2015 Edition

TURKEY

1. Arrivals of non-resident tourists at national borders, by nationality

	2009	2010	2011	2012	2013	Market share 2013	% Change 2013-2012
Poland	408,137	419,094	469,314	413,888	405,893	1.07	-1.93
Republic of Moldova	115,948	96,047	100,852	107,771	111,639	0.30	3.59
Romania	362,830	350,679	383,837	378,560	387,062	1.02	2.25
Russian Federation	2,682,332	3,091,930	3,446,907	3,579,957	4,245,990	11.23	18.60
Slovakia	78,109	90,032	120,029	124,899	125,937	0.33	0.83
Tajikistan	19,814	17,737	16,820	22,823	27,171	0.07	19.05
Turkmenistan	112,356	114,388	137,472	135,165	148,705	0.39	10.02
Ukraine	561,055	555,477	588,364	618,453	739,454	1.96	19.57
USSR (former)					129,215	0.34	
Uzbekistan	73,813	68,066	84,962	105,938	129,215	0.34	21.97
NORTHERN EUROPE	**3,403,380**	**3,706,888**	**3,841,929**	**3,818,163**	**4,020,928**	**10.64**	**5.31**
Denmark	289,496	308,927	361,299	381,767	393,030	1.04	2.95
Finland	129,052	137,607	174,865	187,931	211,267	0.56	12.42
Iceland	7,353	6,250	5,905	5,562	4,602	0.01	-17.26
Ireland	110,050	103,930	106,602	99,188	100,436	0.27	1.26
Norway	251,191	288,044	359,437	388,886	392,723	1.04	0.99
Sweden	389,773	435,634	555,061	599,536	672,677	1.78	12.20
United Kingdom	2,226,465	2,426,496	2,278,760	2,155,293	2,246,193	5.94	4.22
SOUTHERN EUROPE	**1,630,674**	**1,682,132**	**1,770,299**	**1,790,102**	**1,844,692**	**4.88**	**3.05**
Albania	58,961	49,075	51,499	58,033	63,379	0.17	9.21
Bosnia and Herzegovina	52,021	47,107	56,068	61,213	71,468	0.19	16.75
Croatia	28,328	30,567	38,072	43,121	40,769	0.11	-5.45
Greece	560,998	633,458	644,566	627,160	659,608	1.75	5.17
Italy	373,674	376,559	415,378	421,216	416,376	1.10	-1.15
Malta	2,819	2,603	2,977	3,214	4,349	0.01	35.31
Montenegro	11,705	11,051	13,427	15,916	18,177	0.05	14.21
Portugal	36,408	43,519	42,614	36,761	35,162	0.09	-4.35
Serbia	101,529	112,548	136,749	155,858	168,487	0.45	8.10
Slovenia	32,975	34,378	37,825	35,630	32,719	0.09	-8.17
Spain	263,942	225,769	200,718	194,609	193,610	0.51	-0.51
TFYR of Macedonia	107,314	115,498	130,406	137,371	140,588	0.37	2.34
WESTERN EUROPE	**7,692,064**	**7,377,379**	**8,162,679**	**8,345,617**	**8,494,467**	**22.48**	**1.78**
Austria	530,703	479,501	503,118	476,732	492,916	1.30	3.39
Belgium	575,876	528,108	565,196	585,711	627,881	1.66	7.20
France	862,382	858,503	1,033,647	940,106	942,952	2.49	0.30
Germany	4,354,164	4,207,162	4,568,619	4,773,423	4,811,873	12.73	0.81
Luxembourg	8,335	10,386	11,658	12,734	11,954	0.03	-6.13
Netherlands	1,094,332	1,042,712	1,180,504	1,233,678	1,262,857	3.34	2.37
Switzerland	266,272	251,007	299,937	323,233	344,034	0.91	6.44
EAST MEDITERRANEAN EUROPE	**299,407**	**115,430**	**84,527**	**87,636**	**161,656**	**0.43**	**84.46**
Cyprus	9,637	10,441	9,196	8,110	8,407	0.02	3.66
Israel	289,770	104,989	75,331	79,526	153,249	0.41	92.70
OTHER EUROPE	**30,627**	**48,291**	**58,741**	**72,479**	**81,419**	**0.22**	**12.33**
Other countries of Europe	30,627	48,291	58,741	72,479	81,419	0.22	12.33
MIDDLE EAST	**1,424,470**	**1,895,836**	**2,133,169**	**2,376,988**	**3,244,061**	**8.58**	**36.48**
Bahrain	9,034	9,294	9,571	13,083	15,877	0.04	21.36
Egypt	65,733	60,452	77,570	109,526	105,350	0.28	-3.81
Iraq	285,203	280,317	368,974	533,096	730,473	1.93	37.02
Jordan	87,285	96,454	94,530	101,912	102,399	0.27	0.48
Kuwait	26,730	27,207	41,328	64,854	87,834	0.23	35.43
Lebanon	70,839	133,725	135,608	139,011	133,783	0.35	-3.76
Libya	64,702	60,892	53,560	213,651	264,180	0.70	23.65
Oman	5,185	5,394	5,973	7,899	8,867	0.02	12.25
Qatar	4,845	6,024	7,600	13,820	18,489	0.05	33.78
Saudi Arabia	66,625	84,549	116,051	174,981	233,245	0.62	33.30
Syrian Arab Republic	508,385	898,123	970,147	727,319	1,249,454	3.31	71.79
United Arab Emirates	21,965	30,432	35,492	47,962	52,214	0.14	8.87
Yemen	6,174	6,343	8,065	11,825	17,329	0.05	46.55
Other countries of Middle East	201,765	196,630	208,700	218,049	224,567	0.59	2.99

759

Yearbook of Tourism Statistics, Data 2009 – 2013, 2015 Edition

TURKEY

1. Arrivals of non-resident tourists at national borders, by nationality

	2009	2010	2011	2012	2013	Market share 2013	% Change 2013-2012
SOUTH ASIA	1,461,908	1,967,804	1,973,643	1,300,052	1,324,218	3.50	1.86
Bangladesh	3,573	2,172	4,786	6,542	8,785	0.02	34.29
India	51,369	58,367	63,613	79,799	84,885	0.22	6.37
Iran, Islamic Republic of	1,383,057	1,884,897	1,879,033	1,185,864	1,196,482	3.17	0.90
Pakistan	23,909	22,368	26,211	27,847	34,066	0.09	22.33
NOT SPECIFIED	4,767,585	4,409,373	5,364,183	5,983,816	5,012,466	13.26	-16.23
Other countries of the World	86,755	45,178	53,503	55,302	64,118	0.17	15.94
Nationals Residing Abroad	4,680,830	4,364,195	5,310,680	5,928,514	4,948,348	13.09	-16.53

760

TURKEY

2. Arrivals of non-resident visitors at national borders, by nationality

	2009	2010	2011	2012	2013	Market share 2013	% Change 2013-2012
TOTAL (*)	31,759,816	32,997,308	36,769,039	37,715,225	39,860,771	100.00	5.69
AFRICA	294,486	254,823	312,260	387,484	435,781	1.09	12.46
EAST AFRICA	4,991	4,319	4,541	5,510	6,226	0.02	12.99
Kenya	4,991	4,319	4,541	5,510	6 226	0.02	12.99
NORTH AFRICA	224,385	189,890	224,123	277,129	301,770	0.76	8.89
Algeria	91,222	67,954	84,844	104,489	118 189	0.30	13.11
Morocco	65,875	57,447	68,645	77,884	82 579	0.21	6.03
Sudan	10,581	6,634	7,458	8,161	9 319	0.02	14.19
Tunisia	56,707	57,855	63,176	86,595	91 683	0.23	5.88
SOUTHERN AFRICA	24,402	27,177	34,394	40,771	44,798	0.11	9.88
South Africa	24,402	27,177	34,394	40,771	44 798	0.11	9.88
WEST AFRICA	13,497	13,927	20,143	25,547	27,680	0.07	8.35
Nigeria	9,420	9,172	14,564	19,897	22 869	0.06	14.94
Senegal	4,077	4,755	5,579	5,650	4 811	0.01	-14.85
OTHER AFRICA	27,211	19,510	29,059	38,527	55,307	0.14	43.55
Other countries of Africa	27,211	19,510	29,059	38,527	55 307	0.14	43.55
AMERICAS	964,103	946,114	1,151,666	1,165,693	1,262,426	3.17	8.30
CARIBBEAN	913	1,467	2,924	2,073	727	0.00	-64.93
Dominican Republic	913	1,467	2,924	2,073	727	0.00	-64.93
CENTRAL AMERICA	6,399	4,289	7,121	7,654	8,555	0.02	11.77
Panama	1,398	776	1,347	1,529	1 670	0.00	9.22
Other countries of Central America	5,001	3,513	5,774	6,125	6 885	0.02	12.41
NORTH AMERICA	844,341	818,232	978,652	985,665	1,022,085	2.56	3.69
Canada	155,270	152,556	191,903	182,252	199 497	0.50	9.46
Mexico	21,912	22,908	29,606	31,576	36 617	0.09	15.96
United States of America	667,159	642,768	757,143	771,837	785 971	1.97	1.83
SOUTH AMERICA	107,331	117,636	157,862	164,491	224,261	0.56	36.34
Argentina	20,578	22,255	27,136	28,559	46 729	0.12	63.62
Brazil	53,574	65,246	89,442	88,903	113 433	0.28	27.59
Chile	7,612	8,183	11,964	12,765	15 905	0.04	24.60
Colombia	7,248	7,129	9,853	12,987	21 979	0.06	69.24
Ecuador	2,478	2,704	3,892	4,433	4 780	0.01	7.83
Paraguay	385	431	586	700	937	0.00	33.86
Peru	1,926	2,016	2,697	2,952	4 393	0.01	48.81
Uruguay	4,246	2,903	3,735	3,592	4 834	0.01	34.58
Venezuela	9,284	6,769	8,557	9,600	11 271	0.03	17.41
OTHER AMERICAS	5,119	4,490	5,107	5,810	6,798	0.02	17.01
Other countries of the Americas	5,119	4,490	5,107	5,810	6 798	0.02	17.01
EAST ASIA AND THE PACIFIC	612,084	705,357	839,723	921,152	998,526	2.51	8.40
NORTH-EAST ASIA	312,685	402,303	445,622	490,396	512,716	1.29	4.55
China	69,336	77,142	96,701	114,582	138 876	0.35	21.20
Hong Kong, China	6,560	6,442	10,666	13,138	12 650	0.03	-3.71
Japan	147,641	195,404	188,312	203,592	174 150	0.44	-14.46
Korea, Republic of	89,148	123,315	149,943	159,084	187 040	0.47	17.57
SOUTH-EAST ASIA	119,175	116,741	160,138	196,971	215,444	0.54	9.38
Indonesia	23,361	24,349	40,282	56,113	57 385	0.14	2.27
Malaysia	29,557	32,458	36,222	41,169	55 139	0.14	33.93
Philippines	35,814	31,658	51,610	65,272	59 734	0.15	-8.48
Singapore	20,451	18,994	20,957	22,206	22 403	0.06	0.89
Thailand	9,992	9,282	11,067	12,211	20 783	0.05	70.20
AUSTRALASIA	153,540	156,321	182,718	193,177	221,124	0.55	14.47
Australia	129,642	131,685	156,009	164,899	190 457	0.48	15.50
New Zealand	23,898	24,636	26,709	28,278	30 667	0.08	8.45
OTHER EAST ASIA AND THE PACIFIC	26,684	29,992	51,245	40,608	49,242	0.12	21.26
Other countries of Asia	26,493	27,116	50,886	35,918	48 767	0.12	35.77
Other countries of Oceania	191	2,876	359	4,690	475	0.00	-89.87
EUROPE	22,222,671	22,807,259	24,970,083	25,550,426	27,550,675	69.12	7.83
CENTRAL/EASTERN EUROPE	8,155,350	8,796,238	9,669,035	10,138,223	11,644,299	29.21	14.86
Armenia	64,982	69,323	72,393	70,956	73 365	0.18	3.40

761

Yearbook of Tourism Statistics, Data 2009 – 2013, 2015 Edition

TURKEY

2. Arrivals of non-resident visitors at national borders, by nationality

	2009	2010	2011	2012	2013	Market share 2013	% Change 2013-2012
Azerbaijan	424,155	486,381	578,685	593,238	630 754	1.58	6.32
Belarus	142,422	152,421	123,607	138,007	200 659	0.50	45.40
Bulgaria	1,406,604	1,433,970	1,491,561	1,492,073	1 582 912	3.97	6.09
Czech Republic	164,733	174,426	223,369	223,986	217 254	0.55	-3.01
Estonia	36,413	35,136	34,921	35,459	48 537	0.12	36.88
Georgia	995,381	1,112,193	1,152,661	1,404,882	1 769 447	4.44	25.95
Hungary	82,684	90,944	103,918	94,409	97 074	0.24	2.82
Kazakhstan	219,445	247,784	315,907	380,046	425 773	1.07	12.03
Kyrgyzstan	40,882	35,665	41,197	42,866	64 905	0.16	51.41
Latvia	40,686	39,102	45,074	45,725	55 058	0.14	20.41
Lithuania	76,730	71,992	76,036	69,520	90 180	0.23	29.72
Poland	419,475	428,275	486,319	428,440	423 129	1.06	-1.24
Republic of Moldova	117,856	96,196	101,124	108,032	111 915	0.28	3.59
Romania	366,698	355,144	390,248	385,055	395 214	0.99	2.64
Russian Federation	2,694,733	3,107,043	3,468,214	3,599,925	4 269 306	10.71	18.59
Slovakia	80,687	91,765	122,088	126,974	127 455	0.32	0.38
Tajikistan	19,816	17,737	16,822	22,823	27 174	0.07	19.06
Turkmenistan	112,358	114,390	137,476	135,168	148 709	0.37	10.02
Ukraine	574,700	568,227	602,404	634,663	756 187	1.90	19.15
Uzbekistan	73,910	68,124	85,011	105,976	129 292	0.32	22.00
NORTHERN EUROPE	**3,648,575**	**3,995,471**	**4,210,678**	**4,184,264**	**4,353,849**	**10.92**	**4.05**
Denmark	296,085	314,446	369,867	391,312	402 818	1.01	2.94
Finland	136,489	143,204	186,562	195,083	219 044	0.55	12.28
Iceland	7,838	6,476	6,156	5,797	4 909	0.01	-15.32
Ireland	117,360	111,065	118,620	110,863	112 665	0.28	1.63
Norway	262,314	299,405	375,502	406,879	412 870	1.04	1.47
Sweden	401,740	447,270	571,917	617,811	692 186	1.74	12.04
United Kingdom	2,426,749	2,673,605	2,582,054	2,456,519	2 509 357	6.30	2.15
SOUTHERN EUROPE	**2,081,304**	**2,129,507**	**2,288,499**	**2,235,196**	**2,326,639**	**5.84**	**4.09**
Albania	59,958	49,954	53,141	59,565	65 113	0.16	9.31
Bosnia and Herzegovina	52,271	47,361	56,522	61,851	72 086	0.18	16.55
Croatia	31,407	33,563	41,959	47,144	44 058	0.11	-6.55
Greece	616,489	670,297	702,017	669,823	703 168	1.76	4.98
Italy	634,886	671,060	752,238	714,041	731 784	1.84	2.48
Malta	3,616	3,361	5,974	6,397	6 769	0.02	5.82
Montenegro	11,837	11,610	13,793	16,559	18 838	0.05	13.76
Portugal	46,900	53,373	52,319	46,606	45 928	0.12	-1.45
Serbia	102,202	113,465	137,934	157,568	169 988	0.43	7.88
Slovenia	38,134	38,597	41,870	39,899	37 692	0.09	-5.53
Spain	376,215	321,325	300,084	278,164	290 422	0.73	4.41
TFYR of Macedonia	107,389	115,541	130,648	137,579	140 793	0.35	2.34
WESTERN EUROPE	**7,981,251**	**7,712,428**	**8,646,534**	**8,817,029**	**8,964,745**	**22.49**	**1.68**
Austria	548,117	500,321	528,966	505,560	518 273	1.30	2.51
Belgium	592,078	543,003	585,860	608,071	651 596	1.63	7.16
France	932,809	928,376	1,140,459	1,032,565	1 046 010	2.62	1.30
Germany	4,488,350	4,385,263	4,826,315	5,028,745	5 041 323	12.65	0.25
Luxembourg	9,687	11,262	13,286	14,034	15 733	0.04	12.11
Netherlands	1,127,150	1,073,064	1,222,823	1,273,593	1 312 466	3.29	3.05
Switzerland	283,060	271,139	328,825	354,461	379 344	0.95	7.02
EAST MEDITERRANEAN EUROPE	**325,156**	**124,980**	**95,889**	**102,664**	**179,182**	**0.45**	**74.53**
Cyprus	13,574	15,421	16,749	18,924	14 265	0.04	-24.62
Israel	311,582	109,559	79,140	83,740	164 917	0.41	96.94
OTHER EUROPE	**31,035**	**48,635**	**59,448**	**73,050**	**81,961**	**0.21**	**12.20**
Other countries of Europe	31,035	48,635	59,448	73,050	81 961	0.21	12.20
MIDDLE EAST	**1,430,016**	**1,899,958**	**2,142,401**	**2,389,706**	**3,262,572**	**8.18**	**36.53**
Bahrain	9,090	9,375	9,712	13,342	16 230	0.04	21.65
Egypt	66,912	61,560	79,665	112,025	107 437	0.27	-4.10
Iraq	285,229	280,328	369,033	533,149	730 639	1.83	37.04
Jordan	87,694	96,562	94,914	102,154	102 871	0.26	0.70

762

TURKEY

2. Arrivals of non-resident visitors at national borders, by nationality

	2009	2010	2011	2012	2013	Market share 2013	% Change 2013-2012
Kuwait	26,801	27,281	41,617	65,167	88 238	0.22	35.40
Lebanon	71,771	134,554	137,110	144,491	143 629	0.36	-0.60
Libya	64,721	60,917	53,562	213,890	264 266	0.66	23.55
Oman	5,203	5,408	5,998	7,959	8 956	0.02	12.53
Palestine	5,402	4,685	5,447	6,327	7 971	0.02	25.98
Qatar	4,902	6,043	7,661	13,971	18 630	0.05	33.35
Saudi Arabia	66,938	84,934	116,711	175,467	234 220	0.59	33.48
Syrian Arab Republic	509,679	899,494	974,054	730,039	1 252 826	3.14	71.61
United Arab Emirates	22,051	30,480	35,579	48,071	52 424	0.13	9.06
Yemen	6,181	6,344	8,066	11,826	17 354	0.04	46.74
Other countries of Middle East	197,442	191,993	203,272	211,828	216 881	0.54	2.39
SOUTH ASIA	**1,490,181**	**1,987,969**	**2,005,224**	**1,331,712**	**1,359,412**	**3.41**	**2.08**
Afghanistan	21,508	12,511	16,395	15,373	19 704	0.05	28.17
Bangladesh	3,599	2,190	6,168	6,652	8 856	0.02	33.13
India	55,114	63,406	73,731	90,934	95 014	0.24	4.49
Iran, Islamic Republic of	1,383,261	1,885,097	1,879,304	1,186,343	1 196 801	3.00	0.88
Pakistan	24,004	22,540	26,735	28,394	34 170	0.09	20.34
Other countries of South Asia	2,695	2,225	2,891	4,016	4 867	0.01	21.19
NOT SPECIFIED	**4,746,275**	**4,395,828**	**5,347,682**	**5,969,052**	**4,991,379**	**12.52**	**-16.38**
Other countries of the World	63,573	30,724	34,719	36,659	40 706	0.10	11.04
Nationals Residing Abroad	4,682,702	4,365,104	5,312,963	5,932,393	4,950,673	12.42	-16.55

Yearbook of Tourism Statistics, Data 2009 – 2013, 2015 Edition

TURKEY

3. Arrivals of non-resident tourists in hotels and similar establishments, by nationality

	2009	2010	2011	2012	2013	Market share 2013	% Change 2013-2012
TOTAL (*)	14,362,491	17,111,736	18,790,691	19,998,885	20,678,206	100.00	3.40
AFRICA	85,379	180,168	148,587	168,576	198,480	0.96	17.74
NORTH AFRICA	58,173	71,638	96,698	119,978	133,758	0.65	11.49
Algeria	16,313	18,905	31,313	41,310	43,932	0.21	6.35
Morocco	21,335	23,619	35,449	33,488	38,493	0.19	14.95
Sudan	3,531	3,148	5,549	4,885	4,888	0.02	0.06
Tunisia	16,994	25,966	24,387	40,295	46,445	0.22	15.26
SOUTHERN AFRICA	14,036	17,922	25,245	24,165	26,381	0.13	9.17
South Africa	14,036	17,922	25,245	24,165	26,381	0.13	9.17
OTHER AFRICA	13,170	90,608	26,644	24,433	38,341	0.19	56.92
Other countries of Africa	13,170	90,608	26,644	24,433	38,341	0.19	56.92
AMERICAS	529,404	639,657	809,563	858,352	871,433	4.21	1.52
CENTRAL AMERICA	4,375	6,916	5,555	7,473	8,348	0.04	11.71
All countries of Central America	4,375	6,916	5,555	7,473	8,348	0.04	11.71
NORTH AMERICA	457,673	536,910	670,600	692,027	636,626	3.08	-8.01
Canada	44,492	57,509	87,039	90,718	88,030	0.43	-2.96
Mexico	10,925	9,150	11,136	14,288	18,113	0.09	26.77
United States of America	402,239	470,243	572,421	587,003	530,417	2.57	-9.64
Other countries of North America	17	8	4	18	66	0.00	266.67
SOUTH AMERICA	67,356	95,831	133,408	158,852	226,459	1.10	42.56
Argentina	13,636	21,966	33,439	33,299	49,358	0.24	48.23
Brazil	40,846	60,742	79,711	100,218	145,703	0.70	45.39
Chile	5,261	3,357	4,680	6,177	8,405	0.04	36.07
Colombia	1,937	3,513	4,750	6,955	10,670	0.05	53.41
Venezuela	2,174	2,659	2,723	6,250	3,291	0.02	-47.34
Other countries of South America	3,502	3,594	8,105	5,953	9,032	0.04	51.72
EAST ASIA AND THE PACIFIC	802,853	887,307	1,121,244	1,237,605	1,220,840	5.90	-1.35
NORTH-EAST ASIA	580,121	631,461	786,304	875,912	811,388	3.92	-7.37
China	47,714	63,560	113,444	161,373	175,027	0.85	8.46
Japan	430,706	413,508	412,388	418,867	323,820	1.57	-22.69
Korea, Republic of	101,701	154,393	260,472	295,672	312,541	1.51	5.71
SOUTH-EAST ASIA	85,475	90,876	113,794	143,066	154,166	0.75	7.76
Indonesia	8,262	10,453	19,078	36,367	41,594	0.20	14.37
Malaysia	31,342	37,088	38,070	41,496	54,977	0.27	32.49
Philippines	5,178	4,902	6,977	8,606	11,219	0.05	30.36
Singapore	31,465	31,110	34,571	41,594	30,117	0.15	-27.59
Thailand	9,228	7,323	15,098	15,003	16,259	0.08	8.37
AUSTRALASIA	108,056	127,068	145,178	157,556	192,690	0.93	22.30
Australia	99,164	112,065	132,395	143,288	175,666	0.85	22.60
New Zealand	8,892	15,003	12,783	14,268	17,024	0.08	19.32
OTHER EAST ASIA AND THE PACIFIC	29,201	37,902	75,968	61,071	62,596	0.30	2.50
Other countries of Asia	28,122	34,404	65,351	58,591	60,373	0.29	3.04
All countries of Oceania	1,079	3,498	10,617	2,480	2,223	0.01	-10.36
EUROPE	11,921,431	14,066,151	15,267,394	15,804,091	16,415,693	79.39	3.87
CENTRAL/EASTERN EUROPE	3,541,263	4,006,528	4,450,274	4,665,072	5,678,081	27.46	21.71
Armenia	21,262	16,943	14,062	18,217	14,158	0.07	-22.28
Azerbaijan	78,758	85,532	111,442	128,488	147,926	0.72	15.13
Belarus	39,249	44,619	47,161	47,591	72,761	0.35	52.89
Bulgaria	128,412	149,420	135,651	158,414	146,800	0.71	-7.33
Czech Republic	114,066	122,884	174,899	159,878	149,498	0.72	-6.49
Estonia	17,329	26,186	24,236	26,865	47,101	0.23	75.32
Georgia	45,051	47,867	43,623	37,023	42,055	0.20	13.59
Hungary	49,441	64,320	59,323	70,772	58,638	0.28	-17.15
Kazakhstan	127,596	145,637	172,148	255,009	262,295	1.27	2.86
Kyrgyzstan	10,911	10,986	14,035	12,820	15,480	0.07	20.75
Latvia	12,708	18,928	20,352	30,049	34,353	0.17	14.32
Lithuania	45,666	53,493	57,214	67,075	99,022	0.48	47.63

Yearbook of Tourism Statistics, Data 2009 – 2013, 2015 Edition

TURKEY

3. Arrivals of non-resident tourists in hotels and similar establishments, by nationality

	2009	2010	2011	2012	2013	Market share 2013	% Change 2013-2012
Poland	212,989	270,327	311,361	260,920	287,715	1.39	10.27
Republic of Moldova	32,863	39,444	44,427	75,507	68,044	0.33	-9.88
Romania	201,619	212,955	208,741	205,289	183,856	0.89	-10.44
Russian Federation	2,045,159	2,344,193	2,549,215	2,619,041	3,470,777	16.78	32.52
Slovakia	42,780	59,553	86,327	81,564	85,577	0.41	4.92
Tajikistan	4,721	3,985	13,571	8,352	6,543	0.03	-21.66
Turkmenistan	15,740	21,820	22,525	28,236	30,814	0.15	9.13
Ukraine	275,305	247,723	314,751	343,289	414,222	2.00	20.66
Uzbekistan	19,638	19,713	25,210	30,673	40,446	0.20	31.86
NORTHERN EUROPE	**1,650,995**	**2,109,166**	**2,314,032**	**2,271,219**	**2,402,243**	**11.62**	**5.77**
Denmark	82,964	94,358	135,164	160,823	182,550	0.88	13.51
Finland	61,242	71,357	82,751	103,601	127,269	0.62	22.85
Iceland	5,779	6,392	5,210	7,559	6,492	0.03	-14.12
Ireland	70,886	65,476	85,486	72,368	67,721	0.33	-6.42
Norway	97,334	149,087	229,215	248,002	233,094	1.13	-6.01
Sweden	153,068	234,312	348,455	352,684	400,548	1.94	13.57
United Kingdom	1,179,722	1,488,184	1,427,751	1,326,182	1,384,569	6.70	4.40
SOUTHERN EUROPE	**1,226,180**	**1,199,618**	**1,141,344**	**1,159,624**	**1,015,089**	**4.91**	**-12.46**
Albania	30,505	28,890	23,609	28,204	33,774	0.16	19.75
Bosnia and Herzegovina	24,575	27,783	34,192	38,140	31,680	0.15	-16.94
Croatia	17,028	19,966	35,698	43,764	29,287	0.14	-33.08
Greece	201,220	243,232	224,117	197,278	150,717	0.73	-23.60
Italy	428,935	349,605	411,653	413,106	363,825	1.76	-11.93
Malta	1,562	1,579	1,533	1,521	2,035	0.01	33.79
Montenegro	8	72	158	119	383	0.00	221.85
Portugal	50,946	64,667	38,971	37,030	33,682	0.16	-9.04
Serbia	46,711	57,816	59,110	74,032	89,951	0.44	21.50
Slovenia	18,365	20,687	45,273	31,673	22,446	0.11	-29.13
Spain	376,837	353,195	236,552	260,952	224,720	1.09	-13.88
TFYR of Macedonia	29,488	32,126	30,478	33,805	32,589	0.16	-3.60
WESTERN EUROPE	**5,265,506**	**6,642,861**	**7,265,100**	**7,637,822**	**7,202,768**	**34.83**	**-5.70**
Austria	263,973	246,480	271,668	243,563	222,196	1.07	-8.77
Belgium	474,758	454,774	466,602	479,148	501,934	2.43	4.76
France	627,269	762,928	935,719	751,436	656,295	3.17	-12.66
Germany	3,142,293	4,328,235	4,571,741	4,996,223	4,655,207	22.51	-6.83
Luxembourg	11,556	13,214	17,148	16,167	18,783	0.09	16.18
Netherlands	607,770	681,948	795,739	912,816	914,281	4.42	0.16
Switzerland	137,887	155,282	206,483	238,469	234,072	1.13	-1.84
EAST MEDITERRANEAN EUROPE	**230,906**	**101,681**	**89,048**	**61,242**	**104,806**	**0.51**	**71.13**
Cyprus	4,902	13,706	38,809	14,180	12,526	0.06	-11.66
Israel	226,004	87,975	50,239	47,062	92,280	0.45	96.08
OTHER EUROPE	**6,581**	**6,297**	**7,596**	**9,112**	**12,706**	**0.06**	**39.44**
Other countries of Europe	6,581	6,297	7,596	9,112	12,706	0.06	39.44
MIDDLE EAST	**613,018**	**768,447**	**829,125**	**1,282,483**	**1,343,642**	**6.50**	**4.77**
Bahrain	7,353	7,386	9,844	13,168	16,902	0.08	28.36
Egypt	43,559	51,039	63,762	92,981	70,325	0.34	-24.37
Iraq	105,817	129,815	165,889	273,072	285,644	1.38	4.60
Jordan	76,663	57,835	55,580	81,253	70,788	0.34	-12.88
Kuwait	23,081	26,914	38,991	62,819	82,428	0.40	31.22
Lebanon	47,729	84,934	81,192	101,375	101,539	0.49	0.16
Libya	16,832	26,834	32,433	193,411	145,162	0.70	-24.95
Oman	3,258	4,103	3,328	4,964	8,902	0.04	79.33
Qatar	3,968	6,524	7,015	17,111	22,335	0.11	30.53
Saudi Arabia	89,463	134,463	172,789	241,411	266,732	1.29	10.49
Syrian Arab Republic	76,370	121,355	71,777	64,491	109,097	0.53	69.17
United Arab Emirates	37,402	47,509	49,101	65,285	73,153	0.35	12.05
Yemen	3,631	4,532	4,572	7,744	13,524	0.07	74.64
Other countries of Middle East	77,892	65,204	72,852	63,398	77,111	0.37	21.63

Yearbook of Tourism Statistics, Data 2009 – 2013, 2015 Edition

TURKEY

3. Arrivals of non-resident tourists in hotels and similar establishments, by nationality

	2009	2010	2011	2012	2013	Market share 2013	% Change 2013-2012
SOUTH ASIA	312,878	447,938	501,883	529,692	484,486	2.34	-8.53
Bangladesh	1,709	1,545	2,941	2,867	3,928	0.02	37.01
India	36,212	45,516	67,084	78,240	83,809	0.41	7.12
Iran, Islamic Republic of	259,500	383,312	410,040	431,827	373,613	1.81	-13.48
Pakistan	15,457	17,565	21,818	16,758	23,136	0.11	38.06
NOT SPECIFIED	97,528	122,068	112,895	118,086	143,632	0.69	21.63
Other countries of the World	97,528	122,068	112,895	118,086	143,632	0.69	21.63

Yearbook of Tourism Statistics, Data 2009 – 2013, 2015 Edition

TURKEY

4. Arrivals of non-resident tourists in all types of accommodation establishments, by nationality

	2009	2010	2011	2012	2013	Market share 2013	% Change 2013-2012
TOTAL (*)	14,388,998	17,415,364	19,264,058	20,481,308	21,181,668	100.00	3.42
AFRICA	85,583	180,409	149,448	170,236	199,397	0.94	17.13
NORTH AFRICA	58,263	71,793	97,213	120,365	134,199	0.63	11.49
Algeria	16,326	18,917	31,404	41,446	44,063	0.21	6.31
Morocco	21,367	23,668	35,569	33,598	38,602	0.18	14.89
Sudan	3,534	3,166	5,750	4,910	4,982	0.02	1.47
Tunisia	17,036	26,042	24,490	40,411	46,552	0.22	15.20
SOUTHERN AFRICA	14,039	17,942	25,342	25,247	26,641	0.13	5.52
South Africa	14,039	17,942	25,342	25,247	26,641	0.13	5.52
OTHER AFRICA	13,281	90,674	26,893	24,624	38,557	0.18	56.58
Other countries of Africa	13,281	90,674	26,893	24,624	38,557	0.18	56.58
AMERICAS	530,008	663,999	842,432	893,752	915,369	4.32	2.42
CENTRAL AMERICA	4,387	6,984	5,583	7,505	8,435	0.04	12.39
All countries of Central America	4,387	6,984	5,583	7,505	8,435	0.04	12.39
NORTH AMERICA	458,238	558,090	699,486	724,579	672,713	3.18	-7.16
Canada	44,561	58,176	88,394	93,401	90,708	0.43	-2.88
Mexico	10,951	9,267	11,348	14,601	18,525	0.09	26.87
United States of America	402,709	490,639	599,740	616,559	563,414	2.66	-8.62
Other countries of North America	17	8	4	18	66	0.00	266.67
SOUTH AMERICA	67,383	98,925	137,363	161,668	234,221	1.11	44.88
Argentina	13,645	22,528	33,586	33,565	49,756	0.23	48.24
Brazil	40,856	62,961	83,153	102,455	152,649	0.72	48.99
Chile	5,261	3,390	4,691	6,257	8,468	0.04	35.34
Colombia	1,937	3,514	4,818	7,016	10,797	0.05	53.89
Venezuela	2,174	2,659	2,727	6,300	3,333	0.02	-47.10
Other countries of South America	3,510	3,873	8,388	6,075	9,218	0.04	51.74
EAST ASIA AND THE PACIFIC	803,739	996,822	1,241,879	1,430,342	1,442,647	6.81	0.86
NORTH-EAST ASIA	580,691	735,566	897,382	1,049,413	1,005,675	4.75	-4.17
China	47,941	68,569	124,986	179,495	203,105	0.96	13.15
Japan	430,985	500,873	489,160	530,552	434,933	2.05	-18.02
Korea, Republic of	101,765	166,124	283,236	339,366	367,637	1.74	8.33
SOUTH-EAST ASIA	85,530	92,499	115,425	155,827	165,896	0.78	6.46
Indonesia	8,276	10,780	19,487	37,198	43,446	0.21	16.80
Malaysia	31,362	37,383	38,406	50,171	59,739	0.28	19.07
Philippines	5,194	4,972	7,052	8,765	11,541	0.05	31.67
Singapore	31,469	31,772	35,283	43,915	31,851	0.15	-27.47
Thailand	9,229	7,592	15,197	15,778	19,319	0.09	22.44
AUSTRALASIA	108,308	128,324	147,307	159,838	197,077	0.93	23.30
Australia	99,393	113,310	134,433	145,308	179,774	0.85	23.72
New Zealand	8,915	15,014	12,874	14,530	17,303	0.08	19.08
OTHER EAST ASIA AND THE PACIFIC	29,210	40,433	81,765	65,264	73,999	0.35	13.38
Other countries of Asia	28,128	36,904	71,120	62,780	71,767	0.34	14.32
All countries of Oceania	1,082	3,529	10,645	2,484	2,232	0.01	-10.14
EUROPE	11,936,444	14,217,939	15,565,736	16,027,373	16,631,325	78.52	3.77
CENTRAL/EASTERN EUROPE	3,544,735	4,021,775	4,481,312	4,698,290	5,700,076	26.91	21.32
Armenia	21,267	16,949	14,062	18,267	14,173	0.07	-22.41
Azerbaijan	78,953	85,829	111,835	129,481	149,007	0.70	15.08
Belarus	39,279	44,640	47,253	48,473	74,060	0.35	52.79
Bulgaria	128,594	150,170	137,663	159,310	147,247	0.70	-7.57
Czech Republic	114,182	124,979	190,104	161,877	152,881	0.72	-5.56
Estonia	17,335	26,358	24,429	27,144	47,875	0.23	76.37
Georgia	45,165	47,941	43,752	37,592	42,257	0.20	12.41
Hungary	49,443	64,920	60,151	75,610	60,694	0.29	-19.73
Kazakhstan	127,748	145,863	172,460	255,250	262,638	1.24	2.89
Kyrgyzstan	11,000	10,994	14,056	12,873	15,599	0.07	21.18
Latvia	12,710	18,928	20,352	30,070	34,370	0.16	14.30
Lithuania	45,666	53,722	57,496	67,390	99,185	0.47	47.18

Yearbook of Tourism Statistics, Data 2009 – 2013, 2015 Edition

TURKEY

4. Arrivals of non-resident tourists in all types of accommodation establishments, by nationality

	2009	2010	2011	2012	2013	Market share 2013	% Change 2013-2012
Poland	213,249	270,892	312,286	263,565	290,574	1.37	10.25
Republic of Moldova	33,204	39,453	44,565	75,572	68,087	0.32	-9.90
Romania	201,822	213,907	209,220	208,273	185,504	0.88	-10.93
Russian Federation	2,046,457	2,352,400	2,557,505	2,629,697	3,474,000	16.40	32.11
Slovakia	42,780	60,252	87,070	82,560	86,176	0.41	4.38
Tajikistan	4,759	4,014	13,635	8,457	6,587	0.03	-22.11
Turkmenistan	15,850	21,931	22,712	28,760	30,913	0.15	7.49
Ukraine	275,492	247,900	315,441	346,737	417,697	1.97	20.47
Uzbekistan	19,780	19,733	25,265	31,332	40,552	0.19	29.43
NORTHERN EUROPE	**1,655,058**	**2,119,469**	**2,331,365**	**2,293,194**	**2,437,153**	**11.51**	**6.28**
Denmark	83,047	94,696	135,755	161,906	187,981	0.89	16.11
Finland	61,270	71,602	83,417	104,517	127,960	0.60	22.43
Iceland	5,886	6,457	5,260	7,575	7,070	0.03	-6.67
Ireland	70,933	65,570	86,098	72,734	68,181	0.32	-6.26
Norway	99,946	151,991	234,798	255,330	240,624	1.14	-5.76
Sweden	153,257	235,140	349,825	357,358	406,416	1.92	13.73
United Kingdom	1,180,719	1,494,013	1,436,212	1,333,774	1,398,921	6.60	4.88
SOUTHERN EUROPE	**1,228,386**	**1,245,370**	**1,197,890**	**1,203,053**	**1,057,569**	**4.99**	**-12.09**
Albania	30,541	28,896	23,654	28,274	33,862	0.16	19.76
Bosnia and Herzegovina	24,600	27,818	34,256	38,351	31,749	0.15	-17.21
Croatia	17,028	19,968	35,837	45,012	29,899	0.14	-33.58
Greece	202,289	245,473	230,514	200,760	153,736	0.73	-23.42
Italy	429,688	360,830	429,276	425,727	377,651	1.78	-11.29
Malta	1,562	1,586	1,541	1,574	2,046	0.01	29.99
Montenegro	8	72	158	119	383	0.00	221.85
Portugal	50,971	69,908	44,329	41,391	42,932	0.20	3.72
Serbia	46,752	57,869	59,185	74,315	89,980	0.42	21.08
Slovenia	18,373	20,707	45,463	32,669	25,210	0.12	-22.83
Spain	377,053	380,081	263,132	280,697	237,274	1.12	-15.47
TFYR of Macedonia	29,521	32,162	30,545	34,164	32,847	0.16	-3.85
WESTERN EUROPE	**5,270,735**	**6,723,216**	**7,457,986**	**7,762,255**	**7,318,414**	**34.55**	**-5.72**
Austria	264,163	248,559	274,668	244,726	223,565	1.06	-8.65
Belgium	474,845	455,798	468,468	480,482	507,684	2.40	5.66
France	627,822	786,450	995,943	783,252	692,427	3.27	-11.60
Germany	3,145,853	4,379,380	4,694,645	5,078,937	4,720,927	22.29	-7.05
Luxembourg	11,556	13,217	17,202	16,220	18,870	0.09	16.34
Netherlands	608,528	684,089	799,403	917,541	918,017	4.33	0.05
Switzerland	137,968	155,723	207,657	241,097	236,924	1.12	-1.73
EAST MEDITERRANEAN EUROPE	**230,946**	**101,806**	**89,581**	**61,438**	**105,377**	**0.50**	**71.52**
Cyprus	4,904	13,721	39,061	14,217	12,736	0.06	-10.42
Israel	226,042	88,085	50,520	47,221	92,641	0.44	96.19
OTHER EUROPE	**6,584**	**6,303**	**7,602**	**9,143**	**12,736**	**0.06**	**39.30**
Other countries of Europe	6,584	6,303	7,602	9,143	12,736	0.06	39.30
MIDDLE EAST	**616,430**	**784,240**	**845,149**	**1,307,598**	**1,356,986**	**6.41**	**3.78**
Bahrain	7,358	8,632	9,921	13,311	17,282	0.08	29.83
Egypt	43,586	51,100	64,019	93,328	70,628	0.33	-24.32
Iraq	106,061	130,081	166,398	274,159	286,501	1.35	4.50
Jordan	76,667	58,040	58,109	81,658	71,030	0.34	-13.02
Kuwait	23,097	27,492	39,552	63,763	83,566	0.39	31.06
Lebanon	47,736	85,888	81,600	102,309	102,278	0.48	-0.03
Libya	16,847	26,896	32,537	203,845	145,783	0.69	-28.48
Oman	3,259	4,151	3,386	5,005	9,038	0.04	80.58
Qatar	3,968	6,703	7,196	17,591	22,815	0.11	29.70
Saudi Arabia	89,621	136,810	175,356	248,060	271,855	1.28	9.59
Syrian Arab Republic	79,091	129,205	75,187	65,476	110,221	0.52	68.34
United Arab Emirates	37,417	48,331	49,604	67,210	74,453	0.35	10.78
Yemen	3,631	4,582	4,638	7,863	13,708	0.06	74.34
Other countries of Middle East	78,091	66,329	77,646	64,020	77,828	0.37	21.57

768

TURKEY

4. Arrivals of non-resident tourists in all types of accommodation establishments, by nationality

	2009	2010	2011	2012	2013	Market share 2013	% Change 2013-2012
SOUTH ASIA	**313,101**	**448,820**	**504,456**	**532,763**	**487,828**	**2.30**	**-8.43**
Bangladesh	1,709	1,560	2,949	2,887	3,995	0.02	38.38
India	36,221	45,942	67,901	79,516	85,553	0.40	7.59
Iran, Islamic Republic of	259,698	383,660	411,647	433,254	374,783	1.77	-13.50
Pakistan	15,473	17,658	21,959	17,106	23,497	0.11	37.36
NOT SPECIFIED	**103,693**	**123,135**	**114,958**	**119,244**	**148,116**	**0.70**	**24.21**
Other countries of the World	103,693	123,135	114,958	119,244	148,116	0.70	24.21

Yearbook of Tourism Statistics, Data 2009 – 2013, 2015 Edition

TURKEY

5. Overnight stays of non-resident tourists in hotels and similar establishments, by nationality

	2009	2010	2011	2012	2013	Market share 2013	% Change 2013-2012
TOTAL (*)	59,873,570	73,924,293	78,257,238	90,099,501	88,862,049	100.00	-1.37
AFRICA	239,091	759,662	442,085	523,204	599,332	0.67	14.55
NORTH AFRICA	166,387	224,150	296,287	393,359	429,254	0.48	9.13
Algeria	46,119	62,174	110,427	148,363	171,633	0.19	15.68
Morocco	62,616	73,780	103,892	107,133	112,682	0.13	5.18
Sudan	8,051	9,222	12,713	13,035	12,551	0.01	-3.71
Tunisia	49,601	78,974	69,255	124,828	132,388	0.15	6.06
SOUTHERN AFRICA	30,543	38,231	58,995	63,911	73,075	0.08	14.34
South Africa	30,543	38,231	58,995	63,911	73,075	0.08	14.34
OTHER AFRICA	42,161	497,281	86,803	65,934	97,003	0.11	47.12
Other countries of Africa	42,161	497,281	86,803	65,934	97,003	0.11	47.12
AMERICAS	1,140,453	1,387,177	2,070,670	1,997,060	1,989,324	2.24	-0.39
CENTRAL AMERICA	8,768	12,558	14,543	26,965	22,494	0.03	-16.58
All countries of Central America	8,768	12,558	14,543	26,965	22,494	0.03	-16.58
NORTH AMERICA	978,686	1,152,195	1,776,364	1,622,288	1,435,333	1.62	-11.52
Canada	95,639	122,030	186,418	203,599	200,715	0.23	-1.42
Mexico	21,517	19,464	26,532	31,258	40,227	0.05	28.69
United States of America	861,460	1,010,691	1,563,398	1,387,292	1,194,257	1.34	-13.91
Other countries of North America	70	10	16	139	134	0.00	-3.60
SOUTH AMERICA	152,999	222,424	279,763	347,807	531,497	0.60	52.81
Argentina	27,761	60,839	75,402	76,671	158,739	0.18	107.04
Brazil	78,374	129,608	162,069	206,356	287,681	0.32	39.41
Chile	24,487	8,400	10,447	13,971	32,075	0.04	129.58
Colombia	4,612	7,585	10,440	14,686	23,903	0.03	62.76
Venezuela	4,953	6,255	6,397	21,023	8,120	0.01	-61.38
Other countries of South America	12,812	9,737	15,008	15,100	20,979	0.02	38.93
EAST ASIA AND THE PACIFIC	1,316,967	1,439,411	1,844,814	2,047,741	2,042,778	2.30	-0.24
NORTH-EAST ASIA	805,105	922,909	1,150,270	1,350,641	1,242,321	1.40	-8.02
China	94,634	129,901	206,148	357,812	324,641	0.37	-9.27
Japan	564,617	576,610	606,808	598,066	482,340	0.54	-19.35
Korea, Republic of	145,854	216,398	337,314	394,763	435,340	0.49	10.28
SOUTH-EAST ASIA	140,536	146,608	194,652	225,014	260,518	0.29	15.78
Indonesia	14,728	18,875	31,949	55,064	68,051	0.08	23.59
Malaysia	51,739	53,519	64,074	70,426	92,874	0.10	31.87
Philippines	11,796	11,190	15,257	15,648	22,054	0.02	40.94
Singapore	48,392	49,965	62,071	60,148	47,729	0.05	-20.65
Thailand	13,881	13,059	21,301	23,728	29,810	0.03	25.63
AUSTRALASIA	324,915	285,884	341,457	364,640	431,209	0.49	18.26
Australia	306,865	256,750	317,065	336,415	397,116	0.45	18.04
New Zealand	18,050	29,134	24,392	28,225	34,093	0.04	20.79
OTHER EAST ASIA AND THE PACIFIC	46,411	84,010	158,435	107,446	108,730	0.12	1.20
Other countries of Asia	42,522	74,509	108,904	92,077	101,197	0.11	9.90
All countries of Oceania	3,889	9,501	49,531	15,369	7,533	0.01	-50.99
EUROPE	54,630,674	66,808,767	69,892,338	79,858,154	78,778,191	88.65	-1.35
CENTRAL/EASTERN EUROPE	17,032,704	19,153,341	20,207,385	24,166,205	25,886,890	29.13	7.12
Armenia	72,281	59,401	47,101	68,248	49,280	0.06	-27.79
Azerbaijan	265,305	304,033	351,877	467,013	512,504	0.58	9.74
Belarus	240,075	252,010	243,280	311,987	481,634	0.54	54.38
Bulgaria	387,122	428,868	373,211	438,180	453,620	0.51	3.52
Czech Republic	579,391	614,268	713,512	762,373	749,073	0.84	-1.74
Estonia	93,731	143,767	127,224	141,307	249,977	0.28	76.90
Georgia	131,301	119,365	105,320	96,510	118,090	0.13	22.36
Hungary	209,527	316,227	281,164	316,914	240,724	0.27	-24.04
Kazakhstan	598,343	725,185	820,144	1,184,056	1,291,165	1.45	9.05
Kyrgyzstan	25,808	26,851	31,893	37,149	43,155	0.05	16.17
Latvia	68,539	99,093	101,856	135,535	158,824	0.18	17.18
Lithuania	205,498	275,576	268,688	337,597	506,117	0.57	49.92

TURKEY

5. Overnight stays of non-resident tourists in hotels and similar establishments, by nationality

	2009	2010	2011	2012	2013	Market share 2013	% Change 2013-2012
Poland	1,023,017	1,455,787	1,353,244	1,272,024	1,381,048	1.55	8.57
Republic of Moldova	140,742	181,778	181,468	324,501	347,179	0.39	6.99
Romania	754,973	900,166	818,250	774,939	776,814	0.87	0.24
Russian Federation	10,594,606	11,540,679	12,504,898	15,118,830	15,743,497	17.72	4.13
Slovakia	239,148	390,416	373,526	490,913	482,777	0.54	-1.66
Tajikistan	11,945	11,700	53,889	23,036	21,616	0.02	-6.16
Turkmenistan	35,781	44,390	56,145	69,127	80,933	0.09	17.08
Ukraine	1,277,169	1,176,919	1,313,844	1,680,827	2,053,266	2.31	22.16
Uzbekistan	78,402	86,862	86,851	115,139	145,597	0.16	26.45
NORTHERN EUROPE	**7,915,450**	**10,295,216**	**11,162,624**	**11,889,279**	**12,147,177**	**13.67**	**2.17**
Denmark	424,949	447,875	667,373	723,148	850,936	0.96	17.67
Finland	314,509	335,372	410,695	520,382	664,450	0.75	27.69
Iceland	30,956	21,417	22,497	28,391	17,706	0.02	-37.64
Ireland	324,930	296,304	392,913	332,447	334,191	0.38	0.52
Norway	480,635	821,156	924,423	1,161,686	977,977	1.10	-15.81
Sweden	712,347	1,017,083	1,516,503	1,699,339	1,829,068	2.06	7.63
United Kingdom	5,627,124	7,356,009	7,228,220	7,423,886	7,472,849	8.41	0.66
SOUTHERN EUROPE	**2,888,676**	**3,071,508**	**2,899,345**	**2,981,748**	**2,785,208**	**3.13**	**-6.59**
Albania	126,948	118,909	73,730	94,732	131,067	0.15	38.36
Bosnia and Herzegovina	76,943	113,457	109,308	127,652	123,867	0.14	-2.97
Croatia	45,973	55,183	96,854	110,188	80,136	0.09	-27.27
Greece	434,905	549,864	479,398	416,931	315,213	0.35	-24.40
Italy	946,224	851,921	1,038,782	1,010,674	978,345	1.10	-3.20
Malta	4,293	3,696	4,148	4,088	5,426	0.01	32.73
Montenegro	65	125	288	485	1,092	0.00	125.15
Portugal	111,211	155,417	113,688	93,284	101,474	0.11	8.78
Serbia	169,436	227,249	241,089	325,689	357,948	0.40	9.90
Slovenia	77,364	87,120	122,562	80,575	75,554	0.09	-6.23
Spain	800,952	809,997	532,169	614,288	518,612	0.58	-15.58
TFYR of Macedonia	94,362	98,570	87,329	103,162	96,474	0.11	-6.48
WESTERN EUROPE	**26,160,413**	**33,951,969**	**35,318,089**	**40,582,077**	**37,594,140**	**42.31**	**-7.36**
Austria	1,235,296	1,272,529	1,411,417	1,175,934	1,200,886	1.35	2.12
Belgium	2,426,030	2,458,136	2,253,374	2,338,358	2,489,897	2.80	6.48
France	2,155,145	2,511,518	3,139,182	2,557,436	2,425,275	2.73	-5.17
Germany	16,453,952	23,116,350	23,516,104	28,477,289	25,089,982	28.23	-11.89
Luxembourg	60,958	76,375	92,191	82,035	119,652	0.13	45.85
Netherlands	3,172,840	3,721,425	3,964,994	4,731,613	5,037,214	5.67	6.46
Switzerland	656,192	795,636	940,827	1,219,412	1,231,234	1.39	0.97
EAST MEDITERRANEAN EUROPE	**597,791**	**312,128**	**266,773**	**193,132**	**313,184**	**0.35**	**62.16**
Cyprus	12,308	59,973	119,138	47,673	23,868	0.03	-49.93
Israel	585,483	252,155	147,635	145,459	289,316	0.33	98.90
OTHER EUROPE	**35,640**	**24,605**	**38,122**	**45,713**	**51,592**	**0.06**	**12.86**
Other countries of Europe	35,640	24,605	38,122	45,713	51,592	0.06	12.86
MIDDLE EAST	**1,439,671**	**1,940,036**	**2,213,042**	**3,711,264**	**3,639,286**	**4.10**	**-1.94**
Bahrain	17,920	20,936	28,564	33,825	48,839	0.05	44.39
Egypt	111,004	139,242	183,168	308,476	191,102	0.22	-38.05
Iraq	257,193	310,869	404,696	622,974	689,378	0.78	10.66
Jordan	167,641	156,654	146,505	230,708	201,771	0.23	-12.54
Kuwait	61,374	78,473	117,581	205,394	261,259	0.29	27.20
Lebanon	121,396	210,549	228,156	316,418	301,804	0.34	-4.62
Libya	43,935	75,073	94,077	749,816	497,739	0.56	-33.62
Oman	7,795	14,970	9,306	14,108	22,302	0.03	58.08
Qatar	10,375	20,850	25,705	62,989	64,651	0.07	2.64
Saudi Arabia	216,813	358,747	495,531	686,311	733,213	0.83	6.83
Syrian Arab Republic	170,987	254,731	181,053	150,662	233,418	0.26	54.93
United Arab Emirates	92,732	134,156	136,530	175,760	199,343	0.22	13.42
Yemen	9,433	12,789	12,062	21,761	32,631	0.04	49.95
Other countries of Middle East	151,073	151,997	150,108	132,062	161,836	0.18	22.55

771

TURKEY

5. Overnight stays of non-resident tourists in hotels and similar establishments, by nationality

	2009	2010	2011	2012	2013	Market share 2013	% Change 2013-2012
SOUTH ASIA	912,636	1,311,944	1,544,555	1,683,261	1,505,256	1.69	-10.58
Bangladesh	3,859	3,642	6,977	10,375	9,334	0.01	-10.03
India	96,602	120,979	171,817	180,415	219,080	0.25	21.43
Iran, Islamic Republic of	776,692	1,147,783	1,311,620	1,446,438	1,213,884	1.37	-16.08
Pakistan	35,483	39,540	54,141	46,033	62,958	0.07	36.77
NOT SPECIFIED	194,078	277,296	249,734	278,817	307,882	0.35	10.42
Other countries of the World	194,078	277,296	249,734	278,817	307,882	0.35	10.42

772

TURKEY

6. Overnight stays of non-resident tourists in all types of accommodation establishments, by nationality

	2009	2010	2011	2012	2013	Market share 2013	% Change 2013-2012
TOTAL (*)	59,986,967	74,325,670	78,888,865	90,822,045	89,594,261	100.00	-1.35
AFRICA	239,633	760,093	443,980	526,070	601,805	0.67	14.40
NORTH AFRICA	166,561	224,407	297,229	394,547	430,606	0.48	9.14
Algeria	46,132	62,203	110,634	148,818	172,015	0.19	15.59
Morocco	62,684	73,843	104,165	107,420	113,131	0.13	5.32
Sudan	8,057	9,259	13,017	13,129	12,854	0.01	-2.09
Tunisia	49,688	79,102	69,413	125,180	132,606	0.15	5.93
SOUTHERN AFRICA	30,546	38,263	59,221	65,300	73,631	0.08	12.76
South Africa	30,546	38,263	59,221	65,300	73,631	0.08	12.76
OTHER AFRICA	42,526	497,423	87,530	66,223	97,568	0.11	47.33
Other countries of Africa	42,526	497,423	87,530	66,223	97,568	0.11	47.33
AMERICAS	1,142,026	1,414,045	2,115,535	2,043,964	2,048,803	2.29	0.24
CENTRAL AMERICA	8,840	12,790	14,609	27,031	22,641	0.03	-16.24
All countries of Central America	8,840	12,790	14,609	27,031	22,641	0.03	-16.24
NORTH AMERICA	980,116	1,175,575	1,815,595	1,664,858	1,485,408	1.66	-10.78
Canada	95,749	122,855	189,000	207,221	204,859	0.23	-1.14
Mexico	21,562	19,603	26,919	31,694	40,875	0.05	28.97
United States of America	862,735	1,033,107	1,599,660	1,425,804	1,239,540	1.38	-13.06
Other countries of North America	70	10	16	139	134	0.00	-3.60
SOUTH AMERICA	153,070	225,680	285,331	352,075	540,754	0.60	53.59
Argentina	27,794	61,457	75,697	77,347	159,303	0.18	105.96
Brazil	78,404	131,872	166,922	209,392	295,611	0.33	41.18
Chile	24,487	8,478	10,464	14,094	32,251	0.04	128.83
Colombia	4,612	7,587	10,535	14,794	24,093	0.03	62.86
Venezuela	4,953	6,255	6,401	21,108	8,178	0.01	-61.26
Other countries of South America	12,820	10,031	15,312	15,340	21,318	0.02	38.97
EAST ASIA AND THE PACIFIC	1,318,491	1,550,223	1,972,048	2,252,974	2,279,045	2.54	1.16
NORTH-EAST ASIA	805,975	1,027,664	1,265,824	1,533,970	1,447,380	1.62	-5.64
China	94,980	135,052	218,223	376,978	353,792	0.39	-6.15
Japan	565,034	664,353	687,219	715,696	600,228	0.67	-16.13
Korea, Republic of	145,961	228,259	360,382	441,296	493,360	0.55	11.80
SOUTH-EAST ASIA	140,633	148,551	196,761	238,425	273,746	0.31	14.81
Indonesia	14,742	19,254	32,410	56,010	69,997	0.08	24.97
Malaysia	51,763	53,832	64,520	79,228	97,752	0.11	23.38
Philippines	11,847	11,319	15,432	15,858	22,478	0.03	41.75
Singapore	48,399	50,776	62,867	62,821	49,721	0.06	-20.85
Thailand	13,882	13,370	21,532	24,508	33,798	0.04	37.91
AUSTRALASIA	325,427	287,429	344,527	368,874	437,466	0.49	18.59
Australia	307,350	258,263	319,914	340,141	402,956	0.45	18.47
New Zealand	18,077	29,166	24,613	28,733	34,510	0.04	20.11
OTHER EAST ASIA AND THE PACIFIC	46,456	86,579	164,936	111,705	120,453	0.13	7.83
Other countries of Asia	42,534	77,016	115,235	96,327	112,911	0.13	17.22
All countries of Oceania	3,922	9,563	49,701	15,378	7,542	0.01	-50.96
EUROPE	54,713,782	67,033,714	70,304,422	80,257,603	79,166,419	88.36	-1.36
CENTRAL/EASTERN EUROPE	17,040,896	19,173,876	20,246,957	24,213,329	25,922,304	28.93	7.06
Armenia	72,293	59,414	47,101	68,367	49,307	0.06	-27.88
Azerbaijan	265,804	305,304	352,927	470,471	515,768	0.58	9.63
Belarus	240,163	252,067	243,420	312,918	483,037	0.54	54.37
Bulgaria	387,482	430,122	377,536	440,043	455,132	0.51	3.43
Czech Republic	579,646	616,487	728,868	764,873	752,921	0.84	-1.56
Estonia	93,746	143,955	127,423	141,682	250,872	0.28	77.07
Georgia	131,573	119,497	105,533	97,154	118,438	0.13	21.91
Hungary	209,529	316,898	282,251	321,982	243,172	0.27	-24.48
Kazakhstan	598,700	725,788	820,855	1,184,750	1,292,055	1.44	9.06
Kyrgyzstan	26,026	26,876	31,934	37,262	43,344	0.05	16.32
Latvia	68,541	99,093	101,856	135,595	158,876	0.18	17.17
Lithuania	205,498	275,826	269,068	338,058	506,413	0.57	49.80

Yearbook of Tourism Statistics, Data 2009 – 2013, 2015 Edition

TURKEY

6. Overnight stays of non-resident tourists in all types of accommodation establishments, by nationality

	2009	2010	2011	2012	2013	Market share 2013	% Change 2013-2012
Poland	1,023,361	1,456,762	1,354,592	1,275,603	1,385,122	1.55	8.59
Republic of Moldova	141,392	181,791	181,809	324,600	347,268	0.39	6.98
Romania	755,333	901,401	819,130	779,020	779,451	0.87	0.06
Russian Federation	10,598,132	11,550,617	12,515,472	15,134,166	15,751,214	17.58	4.08
Slovakia	239,148	391,174	374,352	492,048	483,617	0.54	-1.71
Tajikistan	12,020	11,757	54,066	23,282	21,731	0.02	-6.66
Turkmenistan	36,025	44,769	56,623	70,354	81,233	0.09	15.46
Ukraine	1,277,592	1,177,377	1,315,090	1,684,909	2,057,546	2.30	22.12
Uzbekistan	78,892	86,901	87,051	116,192	145,787	0.16	25.47
NORTHERN EUROPE	**7,955,652**	**10,339,025**	**11,208,792**	**11,949,571**	**12,225,354**	**13.65**	**2.31**
Denmark	425,480	448,974	669,073	725,377	860,009	0.96	18.56
Finland	314,622	335,723	412,142	521,388	665,315	0.74	27.60
Iceland	31,322	21,513	22,558	28,439	18,365	0.02	-35.42
Ireland	324,981	296,520	394,576	333,287	335,130	0.37	0.55
Norway	515,450	853,600	949,040	1,198,009	1,012,957	1.13	-15.45
Sweden	713,702	1,019,359	1,519,418	1,707,740	1,842,028	2.06	7.86
United Kingdom	5,630,095	7,363,336	7,241,985	7,435,331	7,491,550	8.36	0.76
SOUTHERN EUROPE	**2,894,934**	**3,121,575**	**2,969,147**	**3,042,900**	**2,842,276**	**3.17**	**-6.59**
Albania	127,080	118,962	73,836	94,918	131,233	0.15	38.26
Bosnia and Herzegovina	77,093	113,581	109,389	128,086	124,112	0.14	-3.10
Croatia	45,973	55,188	97,129	111,516	80,903	0.09	-27.45
Greece	437,943	554,235	491,098	426,466	323,601	0.36	-24.12
Italy	948,587	864,644	1,061,724	1,030,235	996,537	1.11	-3.27
Malta	4,293	3,743	4,161	4,153	5,460	0.01	31.47
Montenegro	65	125	288	485	1,092	0.00	125.15
Portugal	111,281	160,730	119,441	98,105	111,672	0.12	13.83
Serbia	169,505	227,354	241,192	326,434	358,038	0.40	9.68
Slovenia	77,378	87,171	123,011	81,636	78,875	0.09	-3.38
Spain	801,320	837,163	560,413	636,069	532,554	0.59	-16.27
TFYR of Macedonia	94,416	98,679	87,465	104,797	98,199	0.11	-6.30
WESTERN EUROPE	**26,188,754**	**34,062,125**	**35,573,689**	**40,812,445**	**37,810,661**	**42.20**	**-7.36**
Austria	1,235,901	1,275,012	1,415,987	1,178,126	1,203,822	1.34	2.18
Belgium	2,426,247	2,459,627	2,256,942	2,341,267	2,496,837	2.79	6.64
France	2,156,631	2,538,021	3,207,763	2,596,094	2,468,440	2.76	-4.92
Germany	16,474,891	23,190,309	23,684,650	28,642,258	25,237,662	28.17	-11.89
Luxembourg	60,958	76,382	92,348	82,149	119,749	0.13	45.77
Netherlands	3,177,548	3,725,732	3,971,501	4,748,224	5,047,058	5.63	6.29
Switzerland	656,578	797,042	944,498	1,224,327	1,237,093	1.38	1.04
EAST MEDITERRANEAN EUROPE	**597,892**	**312,470**	**267,708**	**193,576**	**314,154**	**0.35**	**62.29**
Cyprus	12,334	60,021	119,618	47,772	24,270	0.03	-49.20
Israel	585,558	252,449	148,090	145,804	289,884	0.32	98.82
OTHER EUROPE	**35,654**	**24,643**	**38,129**	**45,782**	**51,670**	**0.06**	**12.86**
Other countries of Europe	35,654	24,643	38,129	45,782	51,670	0.06	12.86
MIDDLE EAST	**1,446,457**	**1,974,936**	**2,241,479**	**3,769,049**	**3,671,232**	**4.10**	**-2.60**
Bahrain	17,927	24,651	28,687	34,239	49,654	0.06	45.02
Egypt	111,058	139,471	183,601	309,317	191,928	0.21	-37.95
Iraq	257,647	311,566	405,828	625,683	690,895	0.77	10.42
Jordan	167,654	157,164	149,990	231,975	202,568	0.23	-12.68
Kuwait	61,421	80,875	119,202	207,534	264,050	0.29	27.23
Lebanon	121,410	212,176	228,863	318,748	303,220	0.34	-4.87
Libya	43,980	75,222	94,236	771,593	500,730	0.56	-35.10
Oman	7,796	15,091	9,406	14,203	22,566	0.03	58.88
Qatar	10,375	21,305	26,124	64,142	65,880	0.07	2.71
Saudi Arabia	217,118	364,700	502,198	701,846	744,500	0.83	6.08
Syrian Arab Republic	176,097	267,585	186,472	153,280	235,919	0.26	53.91
United Arab Emirates	92,767	136,902	137,733	180,469	202,452	0.23	12.18
Yemen	9,433	12,890	12,219	22,015	33,035	0.04	50.06
Other countries of Middle East	151,774	155,338	156,920	134,005	163,835	0.18	22.26

774

TURKEY

6. Overnight stays of non-resident tourists in all types of accommodation establishments, by nationality

	2009	2010	2011	2012	2013	Market share 2013	% Change 2013-2012
SOUTH ASIA	**913,204**	**1,313,594**	**1,550,249**	**1,690,618**	**1,511,227**	**1.69**	**-10.61**
Bangladesh	3,859	3,685	7,001	10,413	9,416	0.01	-9.57
India	96,618	121,560	173,954	183,170	221,545	0.25	20.95
Iran, Islamic Republic of	777,220	1,148,675	1,314,890	1,450,417	1,216,733	1.36	-16.11
Pakistan	35,507	39,674	54,404	46,618	63,533	0.07	36.28
NOT SPECIFIED	**213,374**	**279,065**	**261,152**	**281,767**	**315,730**	**0.35**	**12.05**
Other countries of the World	213,374	279,065	261,152	281,767	315,730	0.35	12.05

Yearbook of Tourism Statistics, Data 2009 – 2013, 2015 Edition

TURKS AND CAICOS ISLANDS

1. Arrivals of non-resident tourists at national borders, by country of residence

	2009	2010	2011	2012	2013	Market share 2013	% Change 2013-2012
TOTAL			354,223	291,723	290,587	100.00	-0.39
AMERICAS			344,337	282,078	280,747	96.61	-0.47
CARIBBEAN			39,913	15,325	16,114	5.55	5.15
All countries of the Caribbean			39,913	15,325	16,114	5.55	5.15
NORTH AMERICA			304,424	266,148	263,448	90.66	-1.01
Canada			42,282	37,877	31,797	10.94	-16.05
United States of America			262,142	228,271	231,651	79.72	1.48
SOUTH AMERICA				605	1,185	0.41	95.87
Brazil				605	1,185	0.41	95.87
EUROPE			6,902	6,955	6,671	2.30	-4.08
NORTHERN EUROPE				4,170	3,267	1.12	-21.65
United Kingdom				4,170	3,267	1.12	-21.65
SOUTHERN EUROPE				608	1,804	0.62	196.71
Italy				608	1,804	0.62	196.71
WESTERN EUROPE				613	727	0.25	18.60
France				613	727	0.25	18.60
OTHER EUROPE			6,902	1,564	873	0.30	-44.18
Other countries of Europe				1,564	873	0.30	-44.18
All countries of Europe			6,902				
NOT SPECIFIED			2,984	2,690	3,169	1.09	17.81
Other countries of the World			2,984	2,690	3,169	1.09	17.81

Yearbook of Tourism Statistics, Data 2009 – 2013, 2015 Edition

TUVALU

1. Arrivals of non-resident tourists at national borders, by nationality

	2009	2010	2011	2012	2013	Market share 2013	% Change 2013-2012
TOTAL	1,580	1,657	1,232				
AMERICAS	83	97	94				
NORTH AMERICA	83	97	94				
Canada	13	26	9				
United States of America	70	71	85				
EAST ASIA AND THE PACIFIC	1,267	1,288	909				
NORTH-EAST ASIA	471	418	190				
China	74	41	9				
Japan	397	377	150				
Taiwan, Province of China			31				
AUSTRALASIA	382	350	249				
Australia	194	166	116				
New Zealand	188	184	133				
MELANESIA	251	285	311				
Fiji	251	285	311				
MICRONESIA	51	34	22				
Kiribati	51	34	22				
OTHER EAST ASIA AND THE PACIFIC	112	201	137				
Other countries of Asia	54	133	48				
All countries of Oceania	58	68	89				
EUROPE	143	134	81				
NORTHERN EUROPE	54	42	22				
United Kingdom	54	42	22				
WESTERN EUROPE	45	45	24				
France	15	17	8				
Germany	30	28	16				
OTHER EUROPE	44	47	35				
Other countries of Europe	44	47	35				
NOT SPECIFIED	87	138	148				
Other countries of the World	87	138	148				

Yearbook of Tourism Statistics, Data 2009 – 2013, 2015 Edition

UGANDA

1. Arrivals of non-resident tourists at national borders, by country of residence

	2009	2010	2011	2012	2013	Market share 2013	% Change 2013-2012
TOTAL	806,655	945,899	1,151,356	1,196,765	1,206,334	100.00	0.80
AFRICA	630,014	675,931	873,348	929,569	933,489	77.38	0.42
EAST AFRICA	515,714	520,159	675,592	735,532	740,962	61.42	0.74
Ethiopia	5,907	6,657	6,148	6,364	5,432	0.45	-14.64
Kenya	261,329	294,170	344,210	393,369	380,614	31.55	-3.24
Rwanda	199,530	177,043	266,221	256,004	280,431	23.25	9.54
United Republic of Tanzania	48,948	42,289	59,013	79,795	74,485	6.17	-6.65
CENTRAL AFRICA	11,664	20,306	42,147	42,604	49,925	4.14	17.18
Democratic Republic of the Congo	11,664	20,306	42,147	42,604	49,925	4.14	17.18
NORTH AFRICA	15,088	22,909	39,333	2,397	1,529	0.13	-36.21
Sudan	15,088	22,909	39,333	2,397	1,529	0.13	-36.21
SOUTHERN AFRICA	14,034	15,115	16,152	19,292	21,184	1.76	9.81
South Africa	14,034	15,115	16,152	19,292	21,184	1.76	9.81
OTHER AFRICA	73,514	97,442	100,124	129,744	119,889	9.94	-7.60
Other countries of Africa	73,514	97,442	100,124	129,744	119,889	9.94	-7.60
AMERICAS	47,065	65,175	59,477	70,749	73,075	6.06	3.29
NORTH AMERICA	44,970	54,209	56,419	66,098	66,495	5.51	0.60
Canada	6,999	8,353	8,550	10,186	9,729	0.81	-4.49
United States of America	37,971	45,856	47,869	55,912	56,766	4.71	1.53
OTHER AMERICAS	2,095	10,966	3,058	4,651	6,580	0.55	41.47
Other countries of the Americas	2,095	10,966	3,058	4,651	6,580	0.55	41.47
EAST ASIA AND THE PACIFIC	19,357	28,163	29,899	34,081	45,503	3.77	33.51
NORTH-EAST ASIA	6,814	8,002	10,633	12,831	14,681	1.22	14.42
China	4,629	5,692	6,971	8,645	10,792	0.89	24.84
Japan	2,185	2,310	3,662	4,186	3,889	0.32	-7.10
AUSTRALASIA	4,638	5,534	5,250	7,855	8,440	0.70	7.45
Australia	4,087	4,870	4,827	7,165	7,842	0.65	9.45
New Zealand	551	664	423	690	598	0.05	-13.33
OTHER EAST ASIA AND THE PACIFIC	7,905	14,627	14,016	13,395	22,382	1.86	67.09
Other countries of Asia	7,905	14,300	12,778	11,031	20,401	1.69	84.94
Other countries of Oceania		327	1,238	2,364	1,981	0.16	-16.20
EUROPE	79,710	112,870	154,542	108,707	108,641	9.01	-0.06
CENTRAL/EASTERN EUROPE	1,038	1,104	5,018	4,633	4,163	0.35	-10.14
Czech Republic/Slovakia	425	371	483	383	621	0.05	62.14
Russian Federation	613	733	4,535	4,250	3,542	0.29	-16.66
NORTHERN EUROPE	47,827	52,374	50,222	58,025	56,832	4.71	-2.06
Denmark	3,000	3,145	4,159	3,890	3,426	0.28	-11.93
Finland	730	577	513	642	490	0.04	-23.68
Ireland	1,820	2,143	1,663	2,414	1,694	0.14	-29.83
Norway	2,827	2,874	1,877	2,705	2,543	0.21	-5.99
Sweden	3,734	4,464	4,308	5,866	5,670	0.47	-3.34
United Kingdom	35,716	39,171	37,702	42,508	43,009	3.57	1.18
SOUTHERN EUROPE	4,595	5,622	5,348	7,101	7,422	0.62	4.52
Italy	4,567	5,505	5,335	6,732	7,128	0.59	5.88
Serbia and Montenegro	28	117	13	369	294	0.02	-20.33
WESTERN EUROPE	21,669	46,203	81,809	34,502	32,844	2.72	-4.81
Austria	897	20,304	53,820	2,132	1,724	0.14	-19.14
Belgium	2,787	3,629	5,156	5,094	5,050	0.42	-0.86
France	3,467	3,893	4,437	4,938	4,594	0.38	-6.97
Germany	6,778	8,650	8,960	11,701	11,070	0.92	-5.39
Netherlands	6,017	7,651	8,380	8,275	7,510	0.62	-9.24
Switzerland	1,723	2,076	1,056	2,362	2,896	0.24	22.61
OTHER EUROPE	4,581	7,567	12,145	4,446	7,380	0.61	65.99
Other countries of Europe	4,581	7,567	12,145	4,446	7,380	0.61	65.99
MIDDLE EAST	8,942	15,538	8,652	8,105	12,918	1.07	59.38
Egypt	1,244	1,843	1,409	2,080	2,494	0.21	19.90
Other countries of Middle East	7,698	13,695	7,243	6,025	10,424	0.86	73.01

Yearbook of Tourism Statistics, Data 2009 – 2013, 2015 Edition

UGANDA

1. Arrivals of non-resident tourists at national borders, by country of residence

	2009	2010	2011	2012	2013	Market share 2013	% Change 2013-2012
SOUTH ASIA	**14,937**	**18,898**	**21,755**	**27,799**	**31,732**	**2.63**	**14.15**
India	12,946	16,747	19,419	24,849	28,647	2.37	15.28
Pakistan	1,991	2,151	2,336	2,950	3,085	0.26	4.58
NOT SPECIFIED	**6,630**	**29,324**	**3,683**	**17,755**	**976**	**0.08**	**-94.50**
Other countries of the World	6,630	29,324	3,683	17,755	976	0.08	-94.50

Yearbook of Tourism Statistics, Data 2009 – 2013, 2015 Edition

UKRAINE

1. Arrivals of non-resident tourists at national borders, by country of residence

	2009	2010	2011	2012	2013	Market share 2013	% Change 2013-2012
TOTAL	20,798,342	21,203,327	21,415,296	23,012,823	24,671,227	100.00	7.21
AFRICA	10,252	12,219	14,977	14,769	16,593	0.07	12.35
EAST AFRICA	748	1,052	1,730	1,315	1,402	0.01	6.62
British Indian Ocean Territory			21	20	3	0.00	-85.00
Burundi		4	4	7	11	0.00	57.14
Comoros		4	21	23	16	0.00	-30.43
Djibouti		8	3	6	3	0.00	-50.00
Eritrea		19	24	29	27	0.00	-6.90
Ethiopia	128	104	207	163	148	0.00	-9.20
Kenya	244	223	320	230	256	0.00	11.30
Madagascar		20	35	28	29	0.00	3.57
Malawi		14	5	8	4	0.00	-50.00
Mauritius		87	90	118	104	0.00	-11.86
Mozambique		21	39	40	56	0.00	40.00
Reunion					1	0.00	
Rwanda		48	158	48	77	0.00	60.42
Seychelles		5	9	12	29	0.00	141.67
Somalia	110	119	84	53	37	0.00	-30.19
Uganda	126	125	73	116	66	0.00	-43.10
United Republic of Tanzania	140	126	490	178	193	0.00	8.43
Zambia		44	62	99	120	0.00	21.21
Zimbabwe		81	85	137	222	0.00	62.04
CENTRAL AFRICA	863	1,213	1,381	1,414	1,279	0.01	-9.55
Angola	151	160	293	340	433	0.00	27.35
Cameroon	417	504	457	435	371	0.00	-14.71
Central African Republic		4	36	3	8	0.00	166.67
Chad		22	17	30	54	0.00	80.00
Congo	155	286	343	439	310	0.00	-29.38
Democratic Republic of the Congo	140	176	170	29	27	0.00	-6.90
Equatorial Guinea		19	26	124	49	0.00	-60.48
Gabon		42	30	11	21	0.00	90.91
Sao Tome and Principe			9	3	6	0.00	100.00
NORTH AFRICA	4,720	4,771	5,269	5,908	6,896	0.03	16.72
Algeria	675	677	837	989	1,019	0.00	3.03
Morocco	1,956	1,925	2,297	2,767	3,622	0.01	30.90
Sudan	538	758	719	690	693	0.00	0.43
Tunisia	1,551	1,411	1,416	1,462	1,562	0.01	6.84
SOUTHERN AFRICA	1,085	1,345	2,099	1,628	1,757	0.01	7.92
Botswana		13	8	45	27	0.00	-40.00
Lesotho		3	828	27	2	0.00	-92.59
Namibia		29	61	218	322	0.00	47.71
South Africa	1,085	1,297	1,196	1,330	1,388	0.01	4.36
Swaziland		3	6	8	18	0.00	125.00
WEST AFRICA	2,836	3,838	4,498	4,504	5,259	0.02	16.76
Benin		14	54	15	25	0.00	66.67
Burkina Faso		46	17	22	19	0.00	-13.64
Cabo Verde		12	12	69	5	0.00	-92.75
Côte d'Ivoire		77	82	73	90	0.00	23.29
Gambia		2	2	3	18	0.00	500.00
Ghana	261	312	417	582	905	0.00	55.50
Guinea	160	99	97	77	101	0.00	31.17
Guinea-Bissau		3	11	4	3	0.00	-25.00
Liberia		48	68	16	19	0.00	18.75
Mali		46	60	52	38	0.00	-26.92
Mauritania		16	11	21	10	0.00	-52.38
Niger		15	20	27	147	0.00	444.44
Nigeria	2,415	2,997	3,518	3,338	3,596	0.01	7.73
Senegal		109	72	121	108	0.00	-10.74
Sierra Leone		20	31	53	145	0.00	173.58

780

UKRAINE

1. Arrivals of non-resident tourists at national borders, by country of residence

	2009	2010	2011	2012	2013	Market share 2013	% Change 2013-2012
Togo		22	26	31	30	0.00	-3.23
AMERICAS	**161,412**	**162,853**	**165,068**	**176,315**	**177,806**	**0.72**	**0.85**
CARIBBEAN	**786**	**842**	**745**	**830**	**913**	**0.00**	**10.00**
Anguilla		10	7	4	1	0.00	-75.00
Antigua and Barbuda		9			2	0.00	
Aruba					1	0.00	
Bahamas		11	18	4	31	0.00	675.00
Barbados		5	27	11	9	0.00	-18.18
Bermuda		4		2	10	0.00	400.00
British Virgin Islands		5	3	9	7	0.00	-22.22
Cayman Islands				1			
Cuba	786	702	564	599	644	0.00	7.51
Dominica		1	12	23	17	0.00	-26.09
Dominican Republic		34	43	35	55	0.00	57.14
Grenada		3	2	2	8	0.00	300.00
Guadeloupe				1			
Haiti		1	5	11	4	0.00	-63.64
Jamaica		12	21	77	46	0.00	-40.26
Montserrat		10	4				
Netherlands Antilles		2	1				
Puerto Rico		1	1				
Saint Kitts and Nevis		7	14	29	18	0.00	-37.93
Saint Lucia		1	1		5	0.00	
Saint Vincent and the Grenadines		2		3	4	0.00	33.33
Trinidad and Tobago		20	21	16	41	0.00	156.25
Turks and Caicos Islands				1	1	0.00	
United States Virgin Islands		2	1	2	9	0.00	350.00
CENTRAL AMERICA	**135**	**277**	**400**	**241**	**282**	**0.00**	**17.01**
Belize		14	4	3	10	0.00	233.33
Costa Rica		74	70	87	91	0.00	4.60
El Salvador		11	237	37	31	0.00	-16.22
Guatemala		56	16	35	58	0.00	65.71
Honduras	135	28	10	16	10	0.00	-37.50
Nicaragua		21	19	20	23	0.00	15.00
Panama		73	44	43	59	0.00	37.21
NORTH AMERICA	**155,488**	**155,539**	**157,462**	**166,755**	**166,867**	**0.68**	**0.07**
Canada	31,372	28,349	28,409	30,945	30,499	0.12	-1.44
Greenland			2	1			
Mexico	1,115	1,337	1,127	1,681	1,696	0.01	0.89
United States of America	123,001	125,853	127,924	134,128	134,672	0.55	0.41
SOUTH AMERICA	**5,003**	**6,195**	**6,461**	**8,489**	**9,744**	**0.04**	**14.78**
Argentina	1,465	1,716	1,710	1,986	2,259	0.01	13.75
Bolivia		173	151	74	42	0.00	-43.24
Brazil	2,290	2,427	2,740	4,494	4,893	0.02	8.88
Chile	211	382	255	347	469	0.00	35.16
Colombia	217	278	224	244	275	0.00	12.70
Ecuador	235	270	264	411	572	0.00	39.17
French Guiana			20	3			
Guyana		3		3	3	0.00	
Paraguay		29	30	57	99	0.00	73.68
Peru	384	397	350	420	528	0.00	25.71
Suriname		2	7	8	23	0.00	187.50
Uruguay		84	108	111	65	0.00	-41.44
Venezuela	201	434	579	300	493	0.00	64.33
Other countries of South America			23	31	23	0.00	-25.81
EAST ASIA AND THE PACIFIC	**43,750**	**45,652**	**49,785**	**52,537**	**49,967**	**0.20**	**-4.89**
NORTH-EAST ASIA	**28,839**	**30,111**	**34,830**	**37,518**	**35,470**	**0.14**	**-5.46**
China	16,137	16,794	19,057	19,718	18,128	0.07	-8.06
Hong Kong, China		134	240	432	532	0.00	23.15

781

UKRAINE

1. Arrivals of non-resident tourists at national borders, by country of residence

	2009	2010	2011	2012	2013	Market share 2013	% Change 2013-2012
Japan	5,439	6,206	7,585	8,528	8,252	0.03	-3.24
Korea, Dem. People's Republic of	333	299	220	502	20	0.00	-96.02
Korea, Republic of	5,374	5,645	6,322	6,912	7,269	0.03	5.16
Macao, China		4	2	1			
Mongolia	483	651	858	1,053	775	0.00	-26.40
Taiwan, Province of China	1,073	378	546	372	494	0.00	32.80
SOUTH-EAST ASIA	**8,817**	**8,759**	**8,305**	**8,228**	**7,306**	**0.03**	**-11.21**
Brunei Darussalam		24	3	15	3	0.00	-80.00
Cambodia		14	48	28	29	0.00	3.57
Indonesia	612	583	569	659	713	0.00	8.19
Lao People's Democratic Republic		22	36	27	32	0.00	18.52
Malaysia	2,452	1,651	1,106	736	445	0.00	-39.54
Myanmar		167	12	23	26	0.00	13.04
Philippines	1,371	1,236	480	486	735	0.00	51.23
Singapore	208	357	1,159	733	420	0.00	-42.70
Thailand	480	354	447	665	617	0.00	-7.22
Viet Nam	3,694	4,351	4,445	4,856	4,286	0.02	-11.74
AUSTRALASIA	**6,094**	**6,742**	**6,638**	**6,774**	**7,148**	**0.03**	**5.52**
Australia	5,224	5,769	5,706	5,880	6,161	0.02	4.78
New Zealand	870	973	932	894	987	0.00	10.40
MELANESIA		**7**	**8**	**8**	**22**	**0.00**	**175.00**
Fiji		1	4	4	10	0.00	150.00
New Caledonia		2	3	4	7	0.00	75.00
Papua New Guinea					2	0.00	
Solomon Islands		3					
Vanuatu		1	1		3	0.00	
MICRONESIA		**30**		**3**	**17**	**0.00**	**466.67**
Guam				1	2	0.00	100.00
Kiribati		12		2	12	0.00	500.00
Marshall Islands		17					
Micronesia, Federated States of					2	0.00	
Nauru					1	0.00	
Palau		1					
POLYNESIA		**3**	**1**	**6**	**4**	**0.00**	**-33.33**
American Samoa		2	1	4			
Samoa				2			
Tonga		1			3	0.00	
Tuvalu					1	0.00	
OTHER EAST ASIA AND THE PACIFIC			**3**				
Other countries East Asia/Pacific			3				
EUROPE	**20,514,394**	**20,911,215**	**21,117,959**	**22,706,004**	**24,368,010**	**98.77**	**7.32**
CENTRAL/EASTERN EUROPE	**19,784,002**	**20,130,512**	**20,243,653**	**21,642,522**	**23,309,903**	**94.48**	**7.70**
Armenia	53,373	52,492	53,627	68,087	83,459	0.34	22.58
Azerbaijan	66,996	77,123	85,482	101,229	111,897	0.45	10.54
Belarus	2,984,672	3,058,023	2,643,988	3,091,780	3,353,652	13.59	8.47
Bulgaria	25,102	27,099	31,661	45,964	56,082	0.23	22.01
Czech Republic	46,646	46,461	51,858	51,955	52,707	0.21	1.45
Estonia	16,016	16,712	17,867	19,812	19,456	0.08	-1.80
Georgia	40,544	36,039	35,861	40,799	52,221	0.21	28.00
Hungary	814,790	944,777	862,051	742,445	771,038	3.13	3.85
Kazakhstan	43,524	50,787	61,826	70,784	84,864	0.34	19.89
Kyrgyzstan	10,520	18,102	21,501	19,441	22,380	0.09	15.12
Latvia	35,555	36,602	36,936	39,840	37,478	0.15	-5.93
Lithuania	48,314	48,907	48,677	54,636	83,355	0.34	52.56
Poland	2,546,132	2,089,647	1,720,104	1,404,086	1,259,209	5.10	-10.32
Republic of Moldova	4,339,138	4,063,459	4,071,785	4,849,115	5,417,966	21.96	11.73
Romania	1,077,299	910,450	735,233	791,281	877,234	3.56	10.86
Russian Federation	6,964,435	7,900,436	9,018,487	9,526,695	10,284,782	41.69	7.96
Slovakia	537,511	609,994	564,337	476,574	424,306	1.72	-10.97

Yearbook of Tourism Statistics, Data 2009 – 2013, 2015 Edition

UKRAINE

1. Arrivals of non-resident tourists at national borders, by country of residence

	2009	2010	2011	2012	2013	Market share 2013	% Change 2013-2012
Tajikistan	29,463	27,851	27,149	42,834	60,336	0.24	40.86
Turkmenistan	7,631	10,082	14,060	19,647	22,120	0.09	12.59
Uzbekistan	96,341	105,469	141,163	185,518	235,361	0.95	26.87
NORTHERN EUROPE	**119,819**	**117,530**	**127,844**	**173,805**	**140,848**	**0.57**	**-18.96**
Denmark	12,697	12,051	12,601	20,498	11,461	0.05	-44.09
Faeroe Islands				1	8	0.00	700.00
Finland	7,992	8,020	9,764	10,832	10,308	0.04	-4.84
Iceland	566	532	674	708	741	0.00	4.66
Ireland	4,951	4,945	6,117	6,318	6,955	0.03	10.08
Isle of Man				1	1	0.00	
Norway	10,712	10,848	12,022	13,486	12,505	0.05	-7.27
Sweden	16,050	16,544	19,491	40,777	17,542	0.07	-56.98
United Kingdom	66,851	64,590	67,175	81,183	81,324	0.33	0.17
Other countries of Northern Europe				1	3	0.00	200.00
SOUTHERN EUROPE	**128,763**	**137,629**	**155,643**	**203,988**	**215,932**	**0.88**	**5.86**
Albania	567	427	493	528	575	0.00	8.90
Andorra		23	39	30	35	0.00	16.67
Bosnia and Herzegovina	999	997	1,014	2,976	4,987	0.02	67.57
Croatia	3,172	3,575	3,432	4,957	5,987	0.02	20.78
Greece	16,377	16,926	17,364	22,760	26,017	0.11	14.31
Holy See		14	21	22	26	0.00	18.18
Italy	73,737	79,174	86,964	89,081	90,819	0.37	1.95
Malta	408	447	479	599	580	0.00	-3.17
Montenegro	1,643	2,037	1,239	1,197	855	0.00	-28.57
Portugal	3,909	4,857	6,783	18,883	11,041	0.04	-41.53
San Marino		61	64	94	107	0.00	13.83
Serbia	5,065	6,340	12,135	29,607	43,680	0.18	47.53
Slovenia	5,499	5,885	6,980	9,160	9,034	0.04	-1.38
Spain	13,453	14,021	16,441	20,628	18,156	0.07	-11.98
TFYR of Macedonia	3,934	2,845	2,195	3,466	4,033	0.02	16.36
WESTERN EUROPE	**349,953**	**373,552**	**389,847**	**457,404**	**424,980**	**1.72**	**-7.09**
Austria	27,218	27,512	28,094	30,032	30,368	0.12	1.12
Belgium	13,455	13,796	14,998	16,407	18,013	0.07	9.79
France	49,810	56,268	62,088	64,804	64,510	0.26	-0.45
Germany	213,995	227,725	231,718	274,073	253,318	1.03	-7.57
Liechtenstein		92	91	107	66	0.00	-38.32
Luxembourg	661	865	825	858	850	0.00	-0.93
Monaco		26	15	29	18	0.00	-37.93
Netherlands	31,548	31,965	33,216	52,417	38,261	0.16	-27.01
Switzerland	13,266	15,303	18,802	18,677	19,576	0.08	4.81
EAST MEDITERRANEAN EUROPE	**131,857**	**151,992**	**200,972**	**228,285**	**276,347**	**1.12**	**21.05**
Cyprus	3,476	3,913	4,428	3,992	3,728	0.02	-6.61
Israel	68,303	81,969	120,181	107,141	120,913	0.49	12.85
Turkey	60,078	66,110	76,363	117,152	151,706	0.61	29.50
MIDDLE EAST	**27,856**	**29,059**	**28,572**	**28,794**	**28,770**	**0.12**	**-0.08**
Bahrain	563	425	364	313	307	0.00	-1.92
Egypt	2,684	2,572	2,649	3,015	3,167	0.01	5.04
Iraq	2,633	4,337	5,201	5,266	6,180	0.03	17.36
Jordan	5,221	5,243	5,728	5,254	5,250	0.02	-0.08
Kuwait	1,188	928	978	946	1,099	0.00	16.17
Lebanon	4,693	4,730	4,696	4,180	3,950	0.02	-5.50
Libya	3,198	2,924	998	2,085	2,159	0.01	3.55
Oman		87	125	153	200	0.00	30.72
Palestine	753	668	591	1,596	888	0.00	-44.36
Qatar		171	174	183	217	0.00	18.58
Saudi Arabia	792	1,140	1,362	1,375	1,054	0.00	-23.35
Syrian Arab Republic	5,290	4,919	4,333	3,528	3,104	0.01	-12.02
United Arab Emirates	573	681	1,169	689	944	0.00	37.01
Yemen	268	234	204	211	251	0.00	18.96

Yearbook of Tourism Statistics, Data 2009 – 2013, 2015 Edition

UKRAINE

1. Arrivals of non-resident tourists at national borders, by country of residence

	2009	2010	2011	2012	2013	Market share 2013	% Change 2013-2012
SOUTH ASIA	**19,871**	**23,012**	**21,819**	**20,037**	**18,439**	**0.07**	**-7.98**
Afghanistan	943	991	1,056	953	1,047	0.00	9.86
Bangladesh	184	245	342	352	324	0.00	-7.95
Bhutan			6	13	5	0.00	-61.54
India	8,183	10,152	9,254	10,264	10,332	0.04	0.66
Iran, Islamic Republic of	8,863	9,677	8,289	6,816	5,085	0.02	-25.40
Maldives		36	45	55	89	0.00	61.82
Nepal	172	183	1,180	159	127	0.00	-20.13
Pakistan	1,227	1,297	1,230	1,103	1,065	0.00	-3.45
Sri Lanka	299	431	417	322	365	0.00	13.35
NOT SPECIFIED	**20,807**	**19,317**	**17,116**	**14,367**	**11,642**	**0.05**	**-18.97**
Other countries of the World	20,807	19,317	17,116	14,367	11,642	0.05	-18.97

Yearbook of Tourism Statistics, Data 2009 – 2013, 2015 Edition

UNITED KINGDOM

2. Arrivals of non-resident visitors at national borders, by country of residence

	2009	2010	2011	2012	2013	Market share 2013	% Change 2013-2012
TOTAL	29,889,075	29,803,000	30,797,000	31,084,000	32,813,000	100.00	5.56
AFRICA	596,415	571,000	527,000	571,200	592,000	1.80	3.64
EAST AFRICA	11,451	8,000	6,000	58,400	32,000	0.10	-45.21
Kenya				32,000	32,000	0.10	
Mauritius				19,500			
Zimbabwe	11,451	8,000	6,000	6,900			
NORTH AFRICA				25,900			
Morocco				25,900			
SOUTHERN AFRICA	244,544	208,000	193,000	210,700	252,000	0.77	19.60
South Africa	244,544	208,000	193,000	210,700	226,000	0.69	7.26
Other countries of Southern Africa					26,000	0.08	
WEST AFRICA	145,113	168,000	142,000	175,000	154,000	0.47	-12.00
Ghana				21,000			
Nigeria	145,113	168,000	142,000	154,000	154,000	0.47	
OTHER AFRICA	195,307	187,000	186,000	101,200	154,000	0.47	52.17
Other countries of Africa	195,307	187,000	186,000	101,200	154,000	0.47	52.17
AMERICAS	4,020,126	3,839,000	4,177,000	4,134,200	4,245,000	12.94	2.68
CARIBBEAN	89,784	71,000	76,000	59,500			
All countries of the Caribbean	89,784	71,000	76,000	59,500			
NORTH AMERICA	3,644,923	3,464,000	3,664,000	3,627,500	3,643,000	11.10	0.43
Canada	686,872	686,000	740,000	704,000	744,000	2.27	5.68
Mexico	80,839	67,000	78,000	83,700	108,000	0.33	29.03
United States of America	2,877,212	2,711,000	2,846,000	2,839,800	2,791,000	8.51	-1.72
SOUTH AMERICA	250,724	275,000	411,000	417,700	415,000	1.26	-0.65
Argentina	69,113	63,000	80,000	103,500	116,000	0.35	12.08
Brazil	151,087	177,000	276,000	259,500	257,000	0.78	-0.96
Chile	13,688	13,000	23,000	26,400	42,000	0.13	59.09
Colombia	6,845	18,000	13,000	14,200			
Venezuela	9,991	4,000	19,000	14,100			
OTHER AMERICAS	34,695	29,000	26,000	29,500	187,000	0.57	533.90
Other countries of the Americas	34,695	29,000	26,000	29,500	187,000	0.57	533.90
EAST ASIA AND THE PACIFIC	2,065,639	2,202,000	2,433,000	2,339,300	2,597,000	7.91	11.02
NORTH-EAST ASIA	581,599	609,000	708,000	751,300	819,000	2.50	9.01
China	89,187	109,000	149,000	178,700	196,000	0.60	9.68
Hong Kong, China	143,472	131,000	149,000	135,200	163,000	0.50	20.56
Japan	235,471	223,000	237,000	242,700	221,000	0.67	-8.94
Korea, Republic of	74,635	115,000	140,000	158,300	202,000	0.62	27.61
Taiwan, Province of China	38,834	31,000	33,000	36,400	37,000	0.11	1.65
SOUTH-EAST ASIA	301,288	323,000	329,000	395,300	439,000	1.34	11.05
Indonesia				27,300	26,000	0.08	-4.76
Malaysia	120,970	133,000	130,000	115,600	171,000	0.52	47.92
Philippines				23,700	22,000	0.07	-7.17
Singapore	111,108	123,000	134,000	153,700	145,000	0.44	-5.66
Thailand	69,210	67,000	65,000	75,000	75,000	0.23	
AUSTRALASIA	1,099,471	1,173,000	1,281,000	1,168,400	1,236,000	3.77	5.79
Australia	912,259	986,000	1,093,000	993,000	1,070,000	3.26	7.75
New Zealand	187,212	187,000	188,000	175,400	166,000	0.51	-5.36
OTHER EAST ASIA AND THE PACIFIC	83,281	97,000	115,000	24,300	103,000	0.31	323.87
Other countries of Asia	83,281	97,000	115,000	22,300	103,000	0.31	361.88
Other countries of Oceania				2,000			
EUROPE	22,241,150	22,203,000	22,604,000	22,934,100	24,253,000	73.91	5.75
CENTRAL/EASTERN EUROPE	2,594,122	2,547,000	2,645,000	2,942,200	3,339,000	10.18	13.49
Bulgaria				138,200	126,000	0.38	-8.83
Czech Republic	389,074	278,000	287,000	325,400	358,000	1.09	10.02
Estonia				35,700	55,000	0.17	54.06
Hungary	260,340	214,000	211,000	261,600	281,000	0.86	7.42
Kazakhstan				21,600			
Latvia				74,500	95,000	0.29	27.52
Lithuania				171,300	205,000	0.62	19.67
Poland	1,040,553	1,101,000	1,058,000	1,222,500	1,357,000	4.14	11.00
Romania				267,100	386,000	1.18	44.52

785

UNITED KINGDOM

2. Arrivals of non-resident visitors at national borders, by country of residence

	2009	2010	2011	2012	2013	Market share 2013	% Change 2013-2012
Russian Federation	137,287	170,000	211,000	227,400	214,000	0.65	-5.89
Slovakia				120,400	148,000	0.45	22.92
Ukraine				38,200	40,000	0.12	4.71
Other countries Central/East Europe	766,868	784,000	878,000	38,300	74,000	0.23	93.21
NORTHERN EUROPE	**4,949,677**	**4,798,000**	**5,004,000**	**4,896,000**	**5,015,000**	**15.28**	**2.43**
Denmark	618,804	558,000	622,000	639,100	703,000	2.14	10.00
Finland	167,331	170,000	233,000	208,100	215,000	0.66	3.32
Iceland	38,500	34,000	41,000	47,300	58,000	0.18	22.62
Ireland	2,947,552	2,629,000	2,574,000	2,452,900	2,395,000	7.30	-2.36
Norway	573,163	649,000	739,000	771,300	850,000	2.59	10.20
Sweden	604,327	758,000	795,000	777,300	794,000	2.42	2.15
SOUTHERN EUROPE	**4,077,714**	**3,981,000**	**4,078,000**	**3,906,100**	**4,049,000**	**12.34**	**3.66**
Croatia				39,800	52,000	0.16	30.65
Gibraltar	28,207	27,000	28,000	28,700			
Greece	192,529	174,000	225,000	159,000	178,000	0.54	11.95
Italy	1,220,907	1,472,000	1,526,000	1,520,500	1,666,000	5.08	9.57
Malta	74,990	66,000	64,000	65,200	84,000	0.26	28.83
Portugal	255,096	316,000	283,000	291,700	286,000	0.87	-1.95
Serbia				31,900	28,000	0.09	-12.23
Slovenia				53,300	51,000	0.16	-4.32
Spain	2,163,809	1,809,000	1,836,000	1,716,000	1,704,000	5.19	-0.70
Yugoslavia, SFR (former)	142,176	117,000	116,000				
WESTERN EUROPE	**10,230,223**	**10,480,000**	**10,464,000**	**10,784,200**	**11,421,000**	**34.81**	**5.90**
Austria	286,148	288,000	271,000	267,700	275,000	0.84	2.73
Belgium	903,127	1,136,000	984,000	1,112,600	1,188,000	3.62	6.78
France	3,784,473	3,618,000	3,633,000	3,786,900	3,930,000	11.98	3.78
Germany	2,779,754	3,004,000	2,947,000	2,967,200	3,162,000	9.64	6.57
Luxembourg	60,171	53,000	73,000	82,800	92,000	0.28	11.11
Netherlands	1,715,460	1,758,000	1,788,000	1,734,900	1,922,000	5.86	10.78
Switzerland	701,090	623,000	768,000	832,100	816,000	2.49	-1.93
Other countries of Western Europe					36,000	0.11	
EAST MEDITERRANEAN EUROPE	**389,414**	**397,000**	**413,000**	**387,300**	**429,000**	**1.31**	**10.77**
Cyprus	133,704	110,000	124,000	103,900	117,000	0.36	12.61
Israel	157,994	158,000	164,000	137,900	158,000	0.48	14.58
Turkey	97,716	129,000	125,000	145,500	154,000	0.47	5.84
OTHER EUROPE				**18,300**			
Other countries of Europe				18,300			
MIDDLE EAST	**596,237**	**529,000**	**589,000**	**630,100**	**687,000**	**2.09**	**9.03**
Bahrain				30,400	30,000	0.09	-1.32
Egypt	47,936	42,000	41,000	50,000	48,000	0.15	-4.00
Jordan				15,300			
Kuwait				66,400	110,000	0.34	65.66
Lebanon				24,400			
Oman				20,200	18,000	0.05	-10.89
Qatar				45,700	61,000	0.19	33.48
Saudi Arabia	88,605	79,000	105,000	110,600	107,000	0.33	-3.25
United Arab Emirates	246,260	213,000	241,000	256,400	262,000	0.80	2.18
Other countries of Middle East	213,436	195,000	202,000	10,700	51,000	0.16	376.64
SOUTH ASIA	**369,508**	**456,000**	**467,000**	**475,100**	**438,000**	**1.33**	**-7.81**
Bangladesh	10,365	13,000	19,000	13,500			
India	272,754	371,000	356,000	339,400	375,000	1.14	10.49
Iran, Islamic Republic of	25,958	15,000	27,000	16,800			
Pakistan	60,431	57,000	65,000	72,500	63,000	0.19	-13.10
Sri Lanka				20,000			
Other countries of South Asia				12,900			
NOT SPECIFIED		**3,000**			**1,000**	**0.00**	
Other countries of the World		3,000			1,000	0.00	

Yearbook of Tourism Statistics, Data 2009 – 2013, 2015 Edition

UNITED KINGDOM

6. Overnight stays of non-resident tourists in all types of accommodation establishments, by country of residence

	2009	2010	2011	2012	2013	Market share 2013	% Change 2013-2012
TOTAL	229,387,112	227,846,000	235,196,000	230,190,600	245,295,000	100.00	6.56
AFRICA	10,982,197	8,343,000	8,754,000	8,485,000	7,943,000	3.24	-6.39
EAST AFRICA	208,776	269,000	134,000	958,800	461,000	0.19	-51.92
Kenya				483,700	461,000	0.19	-4.69
Mauritius				357,300			
Zimbabwe	208,776	269,000	134,000	117,800			
NORTH AFRICA				243,800			
Morocco				243,800			
SOUTHERN AFRICA	4,745,254	2,564,000	2,316,000	2,633,200	3,338,000	1.36	26.77
South Africa	4,745,254	2,564,000	2,316,000	2,633,200	2,899,000	1.18	10.09
Other countries of Southern Africa					439,000	0.18	
WEST AFRICA	2,216,268	2,428,000	2,292,000	2,802,800	1,891,000	0.77	-32.53
Ghana				363,200			
Nigeria	2,216,268	2,428,000	2,292,000	2,439,600	1,891,000	0.77	-22.49
OTHER AFRICA	3,811,899	3,082,000	4,012,000	1,846,400	2,253,000	0.92	22.02
Other countries of Africa	3,811,899	3,082,000	4,012,000	1,846,400	2,253,000	0.92	22.02
AMERICAS	36,647,738	35,589,000	36,452,000	36,604,900	36,137,000	14.73	-1.28
CARIBBEAN	1,533,973	1,108,000	1,022,000	1,092,800			
All countries of the Caribbean	1,533,973	1,108,000	1,022,000	1,092,800			
NORTH AMERICA	31,362,700	30,659,000	31,088,000	31,153,500	30,128,000	12.28	-3.29
Canada	6,802,042	7,413,000	7,061,000	7,035,800	7,350,000	3.00	4.47
Mexico	789,409	507,000	694,000	549,400	744,000	0.30	35.42
United States of America	23,771,249	22,739,000	23,333,000	23,568,300	22,034,000	8.98	-6.51
SOUTH AMERICA	3,300,866	3,368,000	4,033,000	3,900,000	3,175,000	1.29	-18.59
Argentina	676,202	649,000	580,000	1,065,500	649,000	0.26	-39.09
Brazil	2,248,968	1,764,000	2,652,000	2,400,500	2,281,000	0.93	-4.98
Chile	96,517	215,000	252,000	184,200	245,000	0.10	33.01
Colombia	181,067	627,000	430,000	147,600			
Venezuela	98,112	113,000	119,000	102,200			
OTHER AMERICAS	450,199	454,000	309,000	458,600	2,834,000	1.16	517.97
Other countries of the Americas	450,199	454,000	309,000	458,600	2,834,000	1.16	517.97
EAST ASIA AND THE PACIFIC	30,005,010	32,306,000	32,601,000	32,576,400	35,896,000	14.63	10.19
NORTH-EAST ASIA	6,817,481	8,395,000	8,137,000	10,056,800	10,963,000	4.47	9.01
China	1,166,119	2,303,000	2,906,000	4,000,000	4,819,000	1.96	20.48
Hong Kong, China	1,648,135	1,497,000	1,759,000	1,325,900	1,831,000	0.75	38.09
Japan	2,591,520	1,905,000	1,949,000	2,806,200	2,191,000	0.89	-21.92
Korea, Republic of	1,028,912	1,853,000	1,262,000	1,302,400	1,739,000	0.71	33.52
Taiwan, Province of China	382,795	837,000	261,000	622,300	383,000	0.16	-38.45
SOUTH-EAST ASIA	4,605,929	4,683,000	4,491,000	5,941,800	5,919,000	2.41	-0.38
Indonesia				872,800	243,000	0.10	-72.16
Malaysia	2,415,213	1,899,000	2,073,000	1,536,900	2,570,000	1.05	67.22
Philippines				574,100	673,000	0.27	17.23
Singapore	1,053,611	1,226,000	1,255,000	1,555,800	1,319,000	0.54	-15.22
Thailand	1,137,105	1,558,000	1,163,000	1,402,200	1,114,000	0.45	-20.55
AUSTRALASIA	16,534,306	16,788,000	17,132,000	16,209,200	17,355,000	7.08	7.07
Australia	13,309,858	13,929,000	13,601,000	13,365,700	14,963,000	6.10	11.95
New Zealand	3,224,448	2,859,000	3,531,000	2,843,500	2,392,000	0.98	-15.88
OTHER EAST ASIA AND THE PACIFIC	2,047,294	2,440,000	2,841,000	368,600	1,659,000	0.68	350.08
Other countries of Asia	2,047,294	2,440,000	2,841,000	361,200	1,659,000	0.68	359.30
Other countries of Oceania				7,400			
EUROPE	132,954,907	132,140,000	137,466,000	132,911,800	143,462,000	58.49	7.94
CENTRAL/EASTERN EUROPE	26,355,757	23,997,000	26,444,000	26,581,500	29,199,000	11.90	9.85
Bulgaria				1,289,300	1071000	0.44	-16.93
Czech Republic	2,301,997	1,831,000	1,865,000	2,296,800	2,946,000	1.20	28.27
Estonia				336,200	294,000	0.12	-12.55
Hungary	1,909,268	1,536,000	1,762,000	1,493,500	1,758,000	0.72	17.71
Kazakhstan				281,500			
Latvia				712,700	1,538,000	0.63	115.80
Lithuania				2,286,500	1,541,000	0.63	-32.60

787

Yearbook of Tourism Statistics, Data 2009 – 2013, 2015 Edition

UNITED KINGDOM

6. Overnight stays of non-resident tourists in all types of accommodation establishments, by country of residence

	2009	2010	2011	2012	2013	Market share 2013	% Change 2013-2012
Poland	12,028,477	10,731,000	10,141,000	11,751,500	11,915,000	4.86	1.39
Romania				2,481,100	3,746,000	1.53	50.98
Russian Federation	1,307,573	1,683,000	2,240,000	2,055,700	1,987,000	0.81	-3.34
Slovakia				831,100	1,095,000	0.45	31.75
Ukraine				303,300	415,000	0.17	36.83
Other countries Central/East Europe	8,808,442	8,216,000	10,436,000	462,300	893,000	0.36	93.16
NORTHERN EUROPE	**19,615,071**	**19,935,000**	**22,383,000**	**20,348,700**	**22,250,000**	**9.07**	**9.34**
Denmark	2,943,301	2,923,000	2,864,000	2,835,400	3,142,000	1.28	10.81
Finland	775,290	805,000	1,262,000	1,254,700	1,347,000	0.55	7.36
Iceland	170,247	138,000	272,000	183,500	251,000	0.10	36.78
Ireland	9,874,615	9,519,000	10,225,000	9,030,100	9,492,000	3.87	5.12
Norway	2,573,138	2,807,000	3,442,000	3,392,900	3,763,000	1.53	10.91
Sweden	3,278,480	3,743,000	4,318,000	3,652,100	4,255,000	1.73	16.51
SOUTHERN EUROPE	**29,826,772**	**29,334,000**	**28,838,000**	**29,323,100**	**31,586,000**	**12.88**	**7.72**
Croatia				239,300	479,000	0.20	100.17
Gibraltar			150,000	144,700			
Greece	2,041,851	1,408,000	1,566,000	1,326,700	1,597,000	0.65	20.37
Italy	8,293,632	10,330,000	9,676,000	10,020,600	11,469,000	4.68	14.45
Malta			583,000	667,400	712,000	0.29	6.68
Portugal	1,575,699	2,353,000	1,917,000	2,567,500	2,073,000	0.85	-19.26
Serbia				422,000	201,000	0.08	-52.37
Slovenia				253,700	525,000	0.21	106.94
Spain	17,115,037	14,367,000	13,719,000	13,681,200	14,530,000	5.92	6.20
Yugoslavia, SFR (former)	800,553	876,000	1,227,000				
WESTERN EUROPE	**52,250,184**	**54,143,000**	**55,437,000**	**52,406,400**	**56,629,000**	**23.09**	**8.06**
Austria	1,643,383	1,569,000	1,759,000	1,659,300	1,453,000	0.59	-12.43
Belgium	2,925,268	4,002,000	3,101,000	3,551,000	3,714,000	1.51	4.59
France	19,007,830	18,614,000	18,705,000	18,876,500	19,055,000	7.77	0.95
Germany	17,300,078	18,143,000	18,822,000	16,306,100	18,897,000	7.70	15.89
Luxembourg	177,002	259,000	319,000	325,600	352,000	0.14	8.11
Netherlands	7,255,632	7,870,000	8,413,000	7,593,800	8,831,000	3.60	16.29
Switzerland	3,940,991	3,686,000	4,318,000	4,094,100	4,070,000	1.66	-0.59
Other countries of Western Europe					257,000	0.10	
EAST MEDITERRANEAN EUROPE	**2,464,037**	**2,525,000**	**4,364,000**	**3,876,500**	**3,798,000**	**1.55**	**-2.03**
Cyprus			1,368,000	1,206,100	1,372,000	0.56	13.76
Israel	1,067,238	1,155,000	1,160,000	935,800	977,000	0.40	4.40
Turkey	1,396,799	1,370,000	1,836,000	1,734,600	1,449,000	0.59	-16.46
OTHER EUROPE	**2,443,086**	**2,206,000**		**375,600**			
Other countries of Europe	2,443,086	2,206,000		375,600			
MIDDLE EAST	**8,701,807**	**7,217,000**	**8,263,000**	**7,715,100**	**10,439,000**	**4.26**	**35.31**
Bahrain				259,500	316,000	0.13	21.77
Egypt	734,685	559,000	472,000	616,500	533,000	0.22	-13.54
Jordan				155,100			
Kuwait				955,200	2,022,000	0.82	111.68
Lebanon				178,300			
Oman				364,700	390,000	0.16	6.94
Qatar				479,500	884,000	0.36	84.36
Saudi Arabia	1,549,915	923,000	1,890,000	1,462,500	1,979,000	0.81	35.32
United Arab Emirates	2,862,588	2,872,000	2,831,000	2,897,200	3,384,000	1.38	16.80
Other countries of Middle East	3,554,619	2,863,000	3,070,000	346,600	931,000	0.38	168.61
SOUTH ASIA	**10,095,453**	**12,251,000**	**11,660,000**	**11,897,400**	**11,418,000**	**4.65**	**-4.03**
Bangladesh	343,966	391,000	399,000	644,200			
India	7,293,377	9,720,000	8,341,000	7,381,300	9,582,000	3.91	29.81
Iran, Islamic Republic of	487,212	492,000	515,000	598,300			
Pakistan	1,970,898	1,648,000	2,405,000	2,520,000	1,836,000	0.75	-27.14
Sri Lanka				423,300			
Other countries of South Asia				330,300			

Yearbook of Tourism Statistics, Data 2009 – 2013, 2015 Edition

UNITED REPUBLIC OF TANZANIA

2. Arrivals of non-resident visitors at national borders, by country of residence

	2009	2010	2011	2012	2013	Market share 2013	% Change 2013-2012
TOTAL	714,367	782,699	867,994	1,078,178	1,095,884	100.00	1.64
AFRICA	348,765	392,137	445,750	489,864	521,876	47.62	6.53
EAST AFRICA	304,856	334,986	354,635	411,065	456,552	41.66	11.07
Burundi	14,581	17,440	34,341	43,194	34,873	3.18	-19.26
Comoros	3,206	2,657	3,835	1,634	8,123	0.74	397.12
Djibouti	40	193	413	881	412	0.04	-53.23
Eritrea	90	113	137	365	102	0.01	-72.05
Ethiopia	1,349	1,575	1,675	2,983	1,983	0.18	-33.52
Kenya	177,929	193,474	171,473	183,269	193,078	17.62	5.35
Madagascar	78	222	211	4,064	715	0.07	-82.41
Malawi	19,851	22,233	6,523	14,715	18,197	1.66	23.66
Mauritius	366	292	475	484	754	0.07	55.79
Mozambique	6,253	6,151	11,301	16,292	15,225	1.39	-6.55
Rwanda	14,331	14,754	17,676	25,199	46,637	4.26	85.07
Seychelles	171	180	375	292	506	0.05	73.29
Somalia	784	1,326	8,569	1,139	869	0.08	-23.71
Uganda	32,826	31,869	32,634	36,583	39,488	3.60	7.94
Zambia	26,999	34,983	47,898	51,880	64,825	5.92	24.95
Zimbabwe	6,002	7,524	17,099	28,091	30,765	2.81	9.52
CENTRAL AFRICA	7,968	14,465	22,511	18,824	16,015	1.46	-14.92
Angola	270	517	656	609	811	0.07	33.17
Cameroon	817	710	593	1,634	988	0.09	-39.53
Central African Republic	219	186	701	135	165	0.02	22.22
Chad	36	48	94	83	110	0.01	32.53
Congo	605	416	146	728	919	0.08	26.24
Democratic Republic of the Congo	5,879	11,836	19,043	10,264	12,573	1.15	22.50
Equatorial Guinea				1,120			
Gabon	133	664	1,149	4,232	420	0.04	-90.08
Sao Tome and Principe	9	88	129	19	29	0.00	52.63
NORTH AFRICA	1,907	3,899	3,886	2,462	3,244	0.30	31.76
Algeria	86	105	249	390	403	0.04	3.33
Morocco	118	3,039	465	279	791	0.07	183.51
Sudan	1,574	612	328	1,383	1,571	0.14	13.59
Tunisia	129	143	2,844	410	479	0.04	16.83
SOUTHERN AFRICA	27,510	32,442	39,069	35,716	34,974	3.19	-2.08
Botswana	639	741	944	1,107	1,152	0.11	4.07
Lesotho	296	261	493	395	589	0.05	49.11
Namibia	663	895	1,210	924	1,203	0.11	30.19
South Africa	25,586	29,823	33,543	32,701	31,144	2.84	-4.76
Swaziland	326	722	2,879	589	886	0.08	50.42
WEST AFRICA	6,524	6,345	25,649	21,797	11,091	1.01	-49.12
Benin	155	143	125	244	505	0.05	106.97
Burkina Faso	508	179	345	338	787	0.07	132.84
Cabo Verde	21	52	716	1,916	112	0.01	-94.15
Côte d'Ivoire	189	414	9,630	5,530	577	0.05	-89.57
Gambia	221	222	427	483	417	0.04	-13.66
Ghana	1,340	1,750	4,242	7,127	1,871	0.17	-73.75
Guinea	586	304	110	386	470	0.04	21.76
Guinea-Bissau	8	59	1,082	13	26	0.00	100.00
Liberia	82	165	182	293	404	0.04	37.88
Mali	148	97	2,065	383	292	0.03	-23.76
Mauritania	147	254	304	446	312	0.03	-30.04
Niger	108	147	165	169	175	0.02	3.55
Nigeria	2,397	1,982	5,027	3,390	3,963	0.36	16.90
Senegal	364	267	389	553	479	0.04	-13.38
Sierra Leone	150	156	665	281	365	0.03	29.89
Togo	100	154	175	245	336	0.03	37.14
AMERICAS	68,289	70,558	95,503	100,982	100,647	9.18	-0.33
CARIBBEAN	1,168	1,667	2,226	3,923	2,341	0.21	-40.33

789

Yearbook of Tourism Statistics, Data 2009 – 2013, 2015 Edition

UNITED REPUBLIC OF TANZANIA

2. Arrivals of non-resident visitors at national borders, by country of residence

	2009	2010	2011	2012	2013	Market share 2013	% Change 2013-2012
Antigua and Barbuda	206	64	408	81	40	0.00	-50.62
Bahamas	22	12	27	31	24	0.00	-22.58
Barbados	55	21	11	14	28	0.00	100.00
Bermuda	14	12	873	9			
Cuba	59	74	123	99	247	0.02	149.49
Dominica	266	713	102	598	263	0.02	-56.02
Grenada	7	15	21	18	4	0.00	-77.78
Haiti	12	24	24	21	75	0.01	257.14
Jamaica	199	155	152	403	244	0.02	-39.45
Saint Kitts and Nevis	4	4	7	7	139	0.01	1,885.71
Saint Lucia	8	17	5	6	30	0.00	400.00
Saint Vincent and the Grenadines	1	104	14	6			
Trinidad and Tobago	55	93	196	149	205	0.02	37.58
Other countries of the Caribbean	260	359	263	2,481	1,042	0.10	-58.00
CENTRAL AMERICA	**204**	**600**	**696**	**4,944**	**771**	**0.07**	**-84.41**
Belize	5	3	314	4	2	0.00	-50.00
Costa Rica	36	411	195	3,349	178	0.02	-94.68
El Salvador	33	20	20	264	41	0.00	-84.47
Guatemala	59	46	68	62	106	0.01	70.97
Honduras	24	46	31	394	93	0.01	-76.40
Nicaragua	17	50	21	787	285	0.03	-63.79
Panama	30	24	47	84	66	0.01	-21.43
NORTH AMERICA	**63,179**	**64,800**	**65,426**	**84,639**	**90,819**	**8.29**	**7.30**
Canada	14,642	14,819	16,839	18,777	20,188	1.84	7.51
Mexico	594	766	821	752	960	0.09	27.66
United States of America	47,943	49,215	47,766	65,110	69,671	6.36	7.01
SOUTH AMERICA	**3,738**	**3,491**	**27,155**	**7,476**	**6,716**	**0.61**	**-10.17**
Argentina	293	331	588	653	990	0.09	51.61
Bolivia	102	70	131	108	128	0.01	18.52
Brazil	1,138	1,482	1,308	2,400	2,926	0.27	21.92
Chile	660	312	873	1,262	604	0.06	-52.14
Colombia	411	337	376	973	767	0.07	-21.17
Ecuador	44	398	1,216	339	265	0.02	-21.83
Guyana	18	56	19	73	31	0.00	-57.53
Paraguay	88	36	122	108	42	0.00	-61.11
Peru	148	125	1,102	103	215	0.02	108.74
Suriname	4	37	4,620	110	88	0.01	-20.00
Uruguay	698	189	16,609	1,115	437	0.04	-60.81
Venezuela	134	118	191	232	223	0.02	-3.88
EAST ASIA AND THE PACIFIC	**31,013**	**42,520**	**39,619**	**79,179**	**57,218**	**5.22**	**-27.74**
NORTH-EAST ASIA	**15,437**	**19,915**	**16,683**	**33,280**	**30,703**	**2.80**	**-7.74**
China	7,883	10,997	9,018	13,760	17,336	1.58	25.99
Hong Kong, China	92	46	233	250	170	0.02	-32.00
Japan	4,168	4,130	3,984	5,522	7,058	0.64	27.82
Korea, Dem. People's Republic of	197	115	251	10,717	387	0.04	-96.39
Korea, Republic of	2,687	4,309	3,025	2,649	4,815	0.44	81.77
Mongolia	40	41	37	15	56	0.01	273.33
Taiwan, Province of China	370	277	135	367	881	0.08	140.05
SOUTH-EAST ASIA	**2,982**	**8,601**	**5,548**	**19,742**	**6,263**	**0.57**	**-68.28**
Brunei Darussalam	11	312	905	3,776	28	0.00	-99.26
Cambodia	45	24	354	485	224	0.02	-53.81
Indonesia	321	614	792	8,556	843	0.08	-90.15
Malaysia	540	4,531	844	3,177	1,189	0.11	-62.57
Myanmar	94	334	456	927	82	0.01	-91.15
Philippines	912	1,470	1,226	921	2,109	0.19	128.99
Singapore	307	441	400	1,212	958	0.09	-20.96
Thailand	672	721	433	547	687	0.06	25.59
Viet Nam	80	154	138	141	143	0.01	1.42
AUSTRALASIA	**12,443**	**13,694**	**15,704**	**25,751**	**20,034**	**1.83**	**-22.20**

790

UNITED REPUBLIC OF TANZANIA

2. Arrivals of non-resident visitors at national borders, by country of residence

	2009	2010	2011	2012	2013	Market share 2013	% Change 2013-2012
Australia	10,389	11,644	13,394	15,838	17,001	1.55	7.34
New Zealand	2,054	2,050	2,310	9,913	3,033	0.28	-69.40
MELANESIA	**146**	**310**	**1,681**	**406**	**218**	**0.02**	**-46.31**
Fiji	83	252	157	270	135	0.01	-50.00
Papua New Guinea	18	5	5	68	47	0.00	-30.88
Solomon Islands	45	53	1,519	68	36	0.00	-47.06
POLYNESIA	**5**		**3**				
Samoa	5		3				
EUROPE	**233,559**	**242,828**	**249,910**	**330,207**	**361,706**	**33.01**	**9.54**
CENTRAL/EASTERN EUROPE	**12,819**	**17,616**	**12,881**	**40,834**	**26,393**	**2.41**	**-35.37**
Armenia	573	80	49	282	155	0.01	-45.04
Azerbaijan	173	54	249	69	117	0.01	69.57
Belarus	86	44	750	244	518	0.05	112.30
Bulgaria	532	470	256	567	627	0.06	10.58
Czech Republic	1,942	1,639	780	3,674	3,660	0.33	-0.38
Estonia	129	191	210	306	634	0.06	107.19
Hungary	1,262	933	605	3,241	843	0.08	-73.99
Kazakhstan	119	417	299	6,430	1,509	0.14	-76.53
Latvia	125	102	172	206	314	0.03	52.43
Lithuania	131	102	211	279	498	0.05	78.49
Poland	2,241	2,206	2,933	4,863	4,334	0.40	-10.88
Republic of Moldova	24	47	53	126	141	0.01	11.90
Romania	1,708	1,176	2,123	1,208	1,560	0.14	29.14
Russian Federation	2,794	5,204	2,585	4,021	5,699	0.52	41.73
Slovakia	307	251	449	713	759	0.07	6.45
Tajikistan	18	14	19	98	104	0.01	6.12
Ukraine	369	4,263	377	3,974	2,901	0.26	-27.00
Uzbekistan	13	93	533	4,935	1,160	0.11	-76.49
Other countries Central/East Europe	273	330	228	5,598	860	0.08	-84.64
NORTHERN EUROPE	**80,369**	**78,224**	**81,832**	**108,496**	**114,456**	**10.44**	**5.49**
Denmark	5,856	7,898	2,178	7,909	9,982	0.91	26.21
Finland	2,594	2,719	2,625	3,601	4,590	0.42	27.46
Iceland	229	410	549	1,160	714	0.07	-38.45
Ireland	3,322	3,096	5,642	4,422	3,902	0.36	-11.76
Norway	5,818	6,492	5,915	9,380	12,386	1.13	32.05
Sweden	8,797	9,022	6,554	12,344	12,503	1.14	1.29
United Kingdom	53,753	48,587	58,369	69,680	70,379	6.42	1.00
SOUTHERN EUROPE	**59,899**	**71,553**	**59,234**	**71,443**	**77,320**	**7.06**	**8.23**
Albania	29	25	38	132	269	0.02	103.79
Andorra	19	18	54	14	29	0.00	107.14
Bosnia and Herzegovina	36	42	29	102	218	0.02	113.73
Croatia	233	244	445	1,586	606	0.06	-61.79
Greece	798	710	583	1,173	757	0.07	-35.46
Italy	47,804	59,603	45,590	50,187	57,372	5.24	14.32
Malta	57	177	102	202	148	0.01	-26.73
Montenegro	1		791	26			
Portugal	1,201	1,239	1,022	2,450	2,049	0.19	-16.37
San Marino	67	248	2,143	680	678	0.06	-0.29
Serbia	158	156	1,153	2,372	470	0.04	-80.19
Serbia and Montenegro	40	83					
Slovenia	334	496	236	1,366	1,382	0.13	1.17
Spain	9,053	8,478	6,826	10,650	13,144	1.20	23.42
TFYR of Macedonia	69	34	222	503	198	0.02	-60.64
WESTERN EUROPE	**76,937**	**70,558**	**91,304**	**101,891**	**133,115**	**12.15**	**30.64**
Austria	2,735	3,809	4,126	7,195	6,834	0.62	-5.02
Belgium	5,799	5,510	7,323	7,057	9,157	0.84	29.76
France	20,127	15,650	21,919	28,003	33,335	3.04	19.04
Germany	25,508	25,246	36,010	36,626	53,951	4.92	47.30
Liechtenstein	13	32	16	86	36	0.00	-58.14

Yearbook of Tourism Statistics, Data 2009 – 2013, 2015 Edition

UNITED REPUBLIC OF TANZANIA

2. Arrivals of non-resident visitors at national borders, by country of residence

	2009	2010	2011	2012	2013	Market share 2013	% Change 2013-2012
Luxembourg	170	206	276	355	319	0.03	-10.14
Monaco	29	59	19	10	23	0.00	130.00
Netherlands	16,507	14,598	15,500	12,203	20,633	1.88	69.08
Switzerland	6,049	5,448	6,115	10,356	8,827	0.81	-14.76
EAST MEDITERRANEAN EUROPE	**3,535**	**4,877**	**4,659**	**7,543**	**10,422**	**0.95**	**38.17**
Cyprus	182	221	182	231	163	0.01	-29.44
Israel	2,334	2,805	3,007	4,635	5,344	0.49	15.30
Turkey	1,019	1,851	1,470	2,677	4,915	0.45	83.60
MIDDLE EAST	**11,121**	**10,521**	**15,281**	**21,348**	**18,142**	**1.66**	**-15.02**
Bahrain	43	56	64	75	165	0.02	120.00
Egypt	1,170	1,186	1,138	1,715	2,053	0.19	19.71
Iraq	86	61	118	316	101	0.01	-68.04
Jordan	285	295	1,799	2,587	837	0.08	-67.65
Kuwait	71	57	103	599	255	0.02	-57.43
Lebanon	381	303	281	437	483	0.04	10.53
Libya	238	220	139	147	214	0.02	45.58
Oman	5,520	5,440	3,288	9,371	8,697	0.79	-7.19
Palestine	63	32	98	893	393	0.04	-55.99
Qatar	57	190	1,416	152	84	0.01	-44.74
Saudi Arabia	356	299	284	584	791	0.07	35.45
Syrian Arab Republic	157	189	897	536	1,238	0.11	130.97
United Arab Emirates	1,917	1,199	4,931	2,970	1,812	0.17	-38.99
Yemen	777	994	725	966	1,019	0.09	5.49
SOUTH ASIA	**21,620**	**24,135**	**21,931**	**56,598**	**36,295**	**3.31**	**-35.87**
Afghanistan	32	17	36	100	860	0.08	760.00
Bangladesh	661	397	725	597	583	0.05	-2.35
Bhutan	6	5	4	4	3	0.00	-25.00
India	17,002	19,101	17,731	22,862	27,334	2.49	19.56
Iran, Islamic Republic of	503	636	524	1,054	769	0.07	-27.04
Nepal	288	504	1,792	804	1,056	0.10	31.34
Pakistan	2,657	2,659	471	4,189	3,714	0.34	-11.34
Sri Lanka	471	816	648	26,988	1,976	0.18	-92.68

Yearbook of Tourism Statistics, Data 2009 – 2013, 2015 Edition

UNITED STATES OF AMERICA

1. Arrivals of non-resident tourists at national borders, by country of residence

	2009	2010	2011	2012	2013	Market share 2013	% Change 2013-2012
TOTAL	55,102,743	60,010,361	62,820,943	66,657,028	69,768,455	100.00	4.67
AFRICA	290,861	311,205	325,989	371,016	436,413	0.63	17.63
EAST AFRICA	49,707	50,749	51,634	58,761	60,671	0.09	3.25
Burundi	479	671	677	846	1,268	0.00	49.88
Comoros	30	19	21	23	74	0.00	221.74
Djibouti	354	363	340	319	194	0.00	-39.18
Eritrea	248	263	231	244	998	0.00	309.02
Ethiopia	8,629	8,630	9,979	11,189	13,065	0.02	16.77
Kenya	15,833	15,173	13,422	14,954	16,373	0.02	9.49
Madagascar	780	703	729	787	840	0.00	6.73
Malawi	1,210	1,331	1,347	1,519	1,377	0.00	-9.35
Mauritius	2,005	2,523	2,669	3,133	3,348	0.00	6.86
Mozambique	1,151	1,132	1,210	1,473	2,239	0.00	52.00
Reunion	513	533	566	742	677	0.00	-8.76
Rwanda	1,649	1,840	2,139	2,691	2,675	0.00	-0.59
Seychelles	186	217	186	185	248	0.00	34.05
Somalia	72	98	107	42	129	0.00	207.14
Uganda	5,404	5,115	5,611	6,645	6,670	0.01	0.38
United Republic of Tanzania	5,000	4,986	5,013	5,589	1,923	0.00	-65.59
Zambia	2,310	2,994	3,052	3,541	3,558	0.01	0.48
Zimbabwe	3,854	4,158	4,335	4,839	5,015	0.01	3.64
CENTRAL AFRICA	17,008	18,213	19,352	22,206	26,606	0.04	19.81
Angola	6,446	6,610	7,726	9,964	11,647	0.02	16.89
Cameroon	5,072	5,517	5,359	5,064	5,722	0.01	12.99
Central African Republic	166	234	225	205	292	0.00	42.44
Chad	424	265	245	258	421	0.00	63.18
Congo	1,841	2,077	2,310	2,689	1,645	0.00	-38.82
Democratic Republic of the Congo	1,058	1,189	920	1,316	3,601	0.01	173.63
Equatorial Guinea	397	368	460	509	1,043	0.00	104.91
Gabon	1,584	1,793	1,927	2,095	2,190	0.00	4.53
Sao Tome and Principe	20	160	180	106	45	0.00	-57.55
NORTH AFRICA	27,770	30,428	33,578	35,260	39,566	0.06	12.21
Algeria	4,592	4,116	5,054	5,339	6,692	0.01	25.34
Morocco	16,919	18,657	20,230	21,135	22,616	0.03	7.01
Sudan	1,547	2,006	2,499	1,909	1,988	0.00	4.14
Tunisia	4,711	5,622	5,654	6,786	8,175	0.01	20.47
Western Sahara	1	27	141	91	95	0.00	4.40
SOUTHERN AFRICA	83,243	85,019	92,020	100,923	110,371	0.16	9.36
Botswana	2,300	2,279	2,163	2,186	1,700	0.00	-22.23
Lesotho	259	298	339	367	286	0.00	-22.07
Namibia	1,251	1,430	1,732	1,878	1,807	0.00	-3.78
South Africa	78,934	80,174	86,597	95,086	105,009	0.15	10.44
Swaziland	499	838	1,189	1,406	1,569	0.00	11.59
WEST AFRICA	113,133	126,796	129,405	153,866	199,199	0.29	29.46
Benin	1,582	1,876	1,804	1,852	1,728	0.00	-6.70
Burkina Faso	1,882	1,771	1,934	2,237	2,862	0.00	27.94
Cabo Verde	2,708	2,517	1,773	1,695	3,901	0.01	130.15
Côte d'Ivoire	2,892	2,422	1,584	2,166	4,762	0.01	119.85
Gambia	1,859	2,341	2,288	1,807	1,874	0.00	3.71
Ghana	17,069	18,554	19,127	20,775	21,663	0.03	4.27
Guinea	1,827	1,536	1,604	1,795	1,601	0.00	-10.81
Guinea-Bissau	24	37	45	31	115	0.00	270.97
Liberia	1,086	1,543	1,877	2,984	3,155	0.00	5.73
Mali	3,115	3,106	2,832	2,188	2,838	0.00	29.71
Mauritania	496	636	525	562	922	0.00	64.06
Niger	1,039	978	894	1,046	993	0.00	-5.07
Nigeria	68,505	79,427	82,945	104,682	141,618	0.20	35.28
Senegal	6,536	7,176	6,967	6,821	7,446	0.01	9.16
Sierra Leone	1,474	1,734	1,929	1,954	2,276	0.00	16.48

Yearbook of Tourism Statistics, Data 2009 – 2013, 2015 Edition

UNITED STATES OF AMERICA

1. Arrivals of non-resident tourists at national borders, by country of residence

		2009	2010	2011	2012	2013	Market share 2013	% Change 2013-2012
Togo		1,039	1,142	1,277	1,271	1,445	0.00	13.69
AMERICAS		**36,051,508**	**38,859,224**	**40,533,062**	**43,246,601**	**44,860,939**	**64.30**	**3.73**
CARIBBEAN		**1,206,068**	**1,200,740**	**1,091,419**	**1,131,480**	**1,155,088**	**1.66**	**2.09**
Anguilla		5,020	3,362	2,518	2,075	1,367	0.00	-34.12
Antigua and Barbuda		17,213	16,719	15,639	14,893	13,427	0.02	-9.84
Aruba		22,368	16,074	14,752	17,324	16,890	0.02	-2.51
Bahamas		224,812	243,204	222,741	224,997	206,206	0.30	-8.35
Barbados		52,010	54,486	51,323	50,944	46,074	0.07	-9.56
Bermuda		20,743	17,378	10,822	14,559	51,426	0.07	253.22
British Virgin Islands		23,961	20,262	15,113	14,873	21,896	0.03	47.22
Cayman Islands		51,085	46,558	42,402	43,456	39,083	0.06	-10.06
Cuba		32,666	37,871	36,964	36,655	67,488	0.10	84.12
Dominica		6,857	7,379	5,911	6,329	6,182	0.01	-2.32
Dominican Republic		227,948	239,972	230,188	244,417	238,134	0.34	-2.57
Grenada		8,202	8,507	7,928	7,627	7,724	0.01	1.27
Guadeloupe		9,964	8,205	6,221	6,116	3,221	0.00	-47.33
Haiti		80,572	87,334	79,461	83,312	89,101	0.13	6.95
Jamaica		185,526	178,791	159,235	166,984	168,283	0.24	0.78
Martinique		8,014	7,706	7,015	6,245	3,708	0.01	-40.62
Montserrat		593	344	191	207	257	0.00	24.15
Netherlands Antilles		43,114	26,615	10,755	9,044	4,813	0.01	-46.78
Saint Kitts and Nevis		10,222	10,328	9,496	8,646	9,062	0.01	4.81
Saint Lucia		13,397	15,072	13,111	11,811	11,462	0.02	-2.95
Saint Vincent and the Grenadines		6,002	6,221	6,057	5,693	6,911	0.01	21.39
Trinidad and Tobago		141,406	136,628	132,931	144,535	134,567	0.19	-6.90
Turks and Caicos Islands		14,373	11,724	10,645	10,738	7,806	0.01	-27.30
CENTRAL AMERICA		**757,905**	**760,441**	**747,168**	**802,956**	**833,867**	**1.20**	**3.85**
Belize		20,227	18,641	17,319	18,672	17,818	0.03	-4.57
Costa Rica		157,471	165,594	168,722	179,755	182,063	0.26	1.28
El Salvador		123,185	112,346	97,967	100,978	104,735	0.15	3.72
Guatemala		189,455	188,218	183,671	194,373	202,179	0.29	4.02
Honduras		115,405	115,616	119,671	130,386	138,719	0.20	6.39
Nicaragua		42,194	41,050	40,276	45,524	46,775	0.07	2.75
Panama		109,968	118,976	119,542	133,268	141,578	0.20	6.24
NORTH AMERICA		**31,346,000**	**33,647,745**	**34,937,786**	**36,895,990**	**37,729,997**	**54.08**	**2.26**
Canada	(*)	17,973,000	20,175,617	21,336,761	22,697,345	23,387,275	33.52	3.04
Mexico	(*)	13,373,000	13,472,128	13,601,025	14,198,645	14,342,722	20.56	1.01
SOUTH AMERICA		**2,741,535**	**3,250,298**	**3,756,689**	**4,416,175**	**5,141,987**	**7.37**	**16.44**
Argentina		356,428	436,192	512,258	614,504	686,098	0.98	11.65
Bolivia		31,966	32,504	34,467	35,732	41,542	0.06	16.26
Brazil		892,611	1,197,866	1,508,279	1,791,103	2,060,291	2.95	15.03
Chile		126,609	146,736	171,459	187,603	212,199	0.30	13.11
Colombia		424,526	494,739	496,814	602,338	748,116	1.07	24.20
Ecuador		168,432	195,546	210,910	209,828	254,737	0.37	21.40
Falkland Islands, Malvinas		110	51	60	78	90	0.00	15.38
French Guiana		536	612	760	1,063	976	0.00	-8.18
Guyana		14,774	15,601	16,427	24,222	28,662	0.04	18.33
Paraguay		12,564	14,657	16,567	19,354	25,239	0.04	30.41
Peru		160,474	173,269	171,870	190,205	217,967	0.31	14.60
Suriname		8,630	8,941	9,043	10,711	11,840	0.02	10.54
Uruguay		36,690	41,980	46,695	54,680	66,161	0.09	21.00
Venezuela		507,185	491,604	561,080	674,754	788,069	1.13	16.79
EAST ASIA AND THE PACIFIC		**5,905,954**	**7,369,149**	**7,728,449**	**8,796,667**	**9,517,567**	**13.64**	**8.20**
NORTH-EAST ASIA		**4,545,697**	**5,721,747**	**5,906,523**	**6,851,051**	**7,406,803**	**10.62**	**8.11**
China		524,817	801,738	1,089,405	1,474,408	1,806,553	2.59	22.53
Hong Kong, China		116,023	131,712	128,512	133,104	122,134	0.18	-8.24
Japan		2,918,268	3,386,076	3,249,569	3,698,073	3,730,287	5.35	0.87

Yearbook of Tourism Statistics, Data 2009 – 2013, 2015 Edition

UNITED STATES OF AMERICA

1. Arrivals of non-resident tourists at national borders, by country of residence

	2009	2010	2011	2012	2013	Market share 2013	% Change 2013-2012
Korea, Dem. People's Republic of	27	127	132	160	221	0.00	38.13
Korea, Republic of	743,846	1,107,518	1,145,216	1,251,432	1,359,924	1.95	8.67
Macao, China	3,171	3,469	3,376	3,711	3,103	0.00	-16.38
Taiwan, Province of China	239,545	291,107	290,313	290,163	384,581	0.55	32.54
SOUTH-EAST ASIA	**488,275**	**552,150**	**578,493**	**623,715**	**681,268**	**0.98**	**9.23**
Brunei Darussalam	1,080	1,095	1,332	1,420	1,494	0.00	5.21
Cambodia	2,314	2,611	2,380	2,906	3,895	0.01	34.03
Indonesia	50,243	54,539	66,069	73,579	88,652	0.13	20.49
Lao People's Democratic Republic	1,103	808	685	857	2,164	0.00	152.51
Malaysia	43,292	54,080	59,857	67,464	76,247	0.11	13.02
Myanmar	1,536	1,960	1,891	2,285	3,400	0.00	48.80
Philippines	171,680	177,525	166,829	176,218	200,521	0.29	13.79
Singapore	107,400	139,319	159,302	162,077	152,823	0.22	-5.71
Thailand	69,204	74,293	73,318	81,802	88,163	0.13	7.78
Timor-Leste		6	4	6	17	0.00	183.33
Viet Nam	40,423	45,914	46,826	55,101	63,892	0.09	15.95
AUSTRALASIA	**854,588**	**1,078,866**	**1,226,826**	**1,307,886**	**1,414,196**	**2.03**	**8.13**
Australia	723,576	904,247	1,037,852	1,122,180	1,205,060	1.73	7.39
New Zealand	131,012	174,619	188,974	185,706	209,136	0.30	12.62
MELANESIA	**7,152**	**8,140**	**8,233**	**8,412**	**9,262**	**0.01**	**10.10**
Fiji	4,588	6,456	6,888	7,027	7,172	0.01	2.06
New Caledonia	1,459	782	481	453	735	0.00	62.25
Papua New Guinea	778	649	599	620	901	0.00	45.32
Solomon Islands	138	88	106	117	260	0.00	122.22
Vanuatu	189	165	159	195	194	0.00	-0.51
MICRONESIA	**308**	**349**	**393**	**322**	**413**	**0.00**	**28.26**
Christmas Island, Australia	5	7	12	2	26	0.00	1,200.00
Cocos (Keeling) Islands	6	4	10	7	24	0.00	242.86
Kiribati	282	258	279	228	244	0.00	7.02
Nauru	15	80	92	85	119	0.00	40.00
POLYNESIA	**9,934**	**7,897**	**7,981**	**5,281**	**5,625**	**0.01**	**6.51**
Cook Islands	227	66	45	38	55	0.00	44.74
French Polynesia	7,027	5,237	5,677	3,189	2,939	0.00	-7.84
Niue	7	6	17	7	12	0.00	71.43
Pitcairn	1	2	5	11	49	0.00	345.45
Samoa	1,264	1,192	1,020	888	1,184	0.00	33.33
Tonga	1,353	1,316	1,133	1,072	1,298	0.00	21.08
Tuvalu	15	57	72	11	29	0.00	163.64
Wallis and Futuna Islands	40	21	12	65	59	0.00	-9.23
EUROPE	**11,978,394**	**12,436,645**	**13,115,324**	**12,953,856**	**13,423,940**	**19.24**	**3.63**
CENTRAL/EASTERN EUROPE	**581,807**	**620,111**	**689,554**	**747,896**	**884,497**	**1.27**	**18.26**
Armenia	3,546	3,183	3,032	4,451	5,322	0.01	19.57
Azerbaijan	3,121	3,518	3,841	4,799	5,254	0.01	9.48
Belarus	5,764	6,693	7,710	9,331	9,844	0.01	5.50
Bulgaria	20,000	20,200	20,444	20,570	21,850	0.03	6.22
Czech Republic	65,060	63,909	75,618	76,317	80,523	0.12	5.51
Czech Republic/Slovakia	7,397	4,206	1,935	2,000	890	0.00	-55.50
Estonia	15,677	10,753	11,997	13,989	15,773	0.02	12.75
Georgia	2,966	3,496	3,492	3,985	4,875	0.01	22.33
Hungary	48,806	51,333	58,313	57,416	60,128	0.09	4.72
Kazakhstan	8,459	10,852	12,836	15,384	17,119	0.02	11.28
Kyrgyzstan	1,279	1,716	1,851	1,963	2,976	0.00	51.60
Latvia	11,270	11,529	12,568	14,929	14,885	0.02	-0.29
Lithuania	14,264	8,846	4,081	3,746	14,684	0.02	291.99
Poland	115,327	114,702	111,158	111,157	130,420	0.19	17.33
Republic of Moldova	3,976	4,828	5,220	6,345	7,193	0.01	13.36
Romania	41,411	45,444	45,776	47,753	53,056	0.08	11.11
Russian Federation	142,650	174,511	221,888	259,699	335,279	0.48	29.10
Slovakia	27,711	30,911	33,540	33,655	35,026	0.05	4.07

795

UNITED STATES OF AMERICA

1. Arrivals of non-resident tourists at national borders, by country of residence

	2009	2010	2011	2012	2013	Market share 2013	% Change 2013-2012
Tajikistan	1,010	1,047	1,246	1,292	1,048	0.00	-18.89
Turkmenistan	504	596	560	678	1,029	0.00	51.77
Ukraine	37,157	42,591	47,417	51,986	59,204	0.08	13.88
USSR (former)	265	289	300	298	170	0.00	-42.95
Uzbekistan	4,187	4,958	4,731	6,153	7,949	0.01	29.19
NORTHERN EUROPE	**5,216,618**	**5,214,135**	**5,315,486**	**5,243,001**	**5,406,605**	**7.75**	**3.12**
Denmark	245,623	258,788	274,420	271,363	269,496	0.39	-0.69
Finland	114,364	111,840	121,059	125,475	127,978	0.18	1.99
Iceland	28,526	39,153	49,689	46,097	45,831	0.07	-0.58
Ireland	411,203	360,492	346,879	331,850	367,110	0.53	10.63
Norway	193,318	221,145	249,167	262,822	284,311	0.41	8.18
Sweden	324,417	371,853	438,972	442,013	476,571	0.68	7.82
United Kingdom	3,899,167	3,850,864	3,835,300	3,763,381	3,835,308	5.50	1.91
SOUTHERN EUROPE	**1,538,052**	**1,693,265**	**1,807,548**	**1,645,745**	**1,673,578**	**2.40**	**1.69**
Albania	5,230	5,480	4,775	4,847	5,685	0.01	17.29
Andorra	1,449	1,453	1,266	1,184	1,140	0.00	-3.72
Bosnia and Herzegovina	3,897	4,233	4,386	4,523	4,863	0.01	7.52
Croatia	15,407	15,105	15,241	14,484	15,692	0.02	8.34
Gibraltar	1,656	1,304	984	1,131	1,298	0.00	14.77
Greece	56,748	64,581	62,948	58,212	60,801	0.09	4.45
Holy See	15	32	59	53	102	0.00	92.45
Italy	753,310	838,225	891,571	831,343	838,883	1.20	0.91
Malta	4,902	5,380	4,961	5,277	5,367	0.01	1.71
Portugal	74,457	93,584	96,434	93,346	96,678	0.14	3.57
San Marino	694	674	767	598	574	0.00	-4.01
Serbia and Montenegro	723	656	271	146	141	0.00	-3.42
Slovenia	19,213	18,845	19,307	18,608	17,682	0.03	-4.98
Spain	596,766	639,654	700,183	607,273	619,860	0.89	2.07
TFYR of Macedonia	3,585	4,059	4,395	4,720	4,812	0.01	1.95
WESTERN EUROPE	**4,229,228**	**4,476,847**	**4,868,536**	**4,867,319**	**4,959,724**	**7.11**	**1.90**
Austria	162,569	168,403	179,482	183,276	186,010	0.27	1.49
Belgium	245,710	254,892	259,490	260,267	265,875	0.38	2.15
France	1,204,490	1,342,207	1,504,182	1,455,720	1,504,564	2.16	3.36
Germany	1,686,825	1,726,193	1,823,797	1,875,952	1,916,471	2.75	2.16
Liechtenstein	1,877	1,909	2,273	2,145	2,128	0.00	-0.79
Luxembourg	18,084	17,748	17,856	17,457	18,426	0.03	5.55
Monaco	6,156	4,725	3,941	4,119	3,890	0.01	-5.56
Netherlands	547,790	570,179	601,013	591,746	589,296	0.84	-0.41
Switzerland	355,727	390,591	476,502	476,637	473,064	0.68	-0.75
EAST MEDITERRANEAN EUROPE	**412,689**	**432,287**	**434,200**	**449,895**	**499,536**	**0.72**	**11.03**
Cyprus	10,174	10,136	9,505	8,904	7,760	0.01	-12.85
Israel	308,213	306,914	302,673	303,629	331,359	0.47	9.13
Turkey	94,302	115,237	122,022	137,362	160,417	0.23	16.78
MIDDLE EAST	**246,018**	**296,242**	**363,024**	**463,230**	**543,216**	**0.78**	**17.27**
Bahrain	6,566	7,733	7,299	8,702	8,269	0.01	-4.98
Egypt	36,044	41,949	46,346	62,342	66,262	0.09	6.29
Iraq	1,263	2,207	3,786	6,504	10,641	0.02	63.61
Jordan	15,559	16,459	17,246	19,450	23,343	0.03	20.02
Kuwait	29,888	33,296	39,420	46,872	51,240	0.07	9.32
Lebanon	17,969	18,847	20,346	23,055	29,950	0.04	29.91
Libya	2,904	4,440	1,095	2,425	2,948	0.00	21.57
Oman	4,727	4,812	5,629	7,567	8,753	0.01	15.67
Qatar	11,523	14,931	19,101	24,043	26,007	0.04	8.17
Saudi Arabia	62,030	89,409	132,920	182,225	221,230	0.32	21.40
Syrian Arab Republic	5,105	5,625	5,509	5,823	9,074	0.01	55.83
United Arab Emirates	51,472	55,425	63,415	72,949	83,565	0.12	14.55
Yemen	936	1,072	857	1,206	1,934	0.00	60.36
Other countries of Middle East	32	37	55	67			

796

UNITED STATES OF AMERICA

1. Arrivals of non-resident tourists at national borders, by country of residence

	2009	2010	2011	2012	2013	Market share 2013	% Change 2013-2012
SOUTH ASIA	**629,449**	**737,896**	**755,095**	**825,658**	**983,005**	**1.41**	**19.06**
Afghanistan	1,138	1,261	1,722	1,371	1,737	0.00	26.70
Bangladesh	10,175	11,561	12,596	15,794	23,958	0.03	51.69
Bhutan	230	210	225	228	410	0.00	79.82
India	549,474	650,935	663,465	724,433	859,156	1.23	18.60
Iran, Islamic Republic of	10,139	11,460	14,559	14,698	17,858	0.03	21.50
Maldives	181	149	158	184	245	0.00	33.15
Nepal	11,908	12,513	12,089	12,311	12,952	0.02	5.21
Pakistan	36,426	38,954	38,156	43,976	52,291	0.07	18.91
Sri Lanka	9,778	10,853	12,125	12,663	14,398	0.02	13.70
NOT SPECIFIED	**559**				**3,375**	**0.00**	
Other countries of the World	559				3,375	0.00	

Yearbook of Tourism Statistics, Data 2009 – 2013, 2015 Edition

UNITED STATES VIRGIN ISLANDS

3. Arrivals of non-resident tourists in hotels and similar establishments, by nationality

	2009	2010	2011	2012	2013	Market share 2013	% Change 2013-2012
TOTAL	787,153	748,996	680,324	681,107	758,627	100.00	11.38
AFRICA	69	62	229	98	101	0.01	3.06
OTHER AFRICA	69	62	229	98	101	0.01	3.06
All countries of Africa	69	62	229	98	101	0.01	3.06
AMERICAS	766,929	731,749	653,065	633,629	720,883	95.02	13.77
CARIBBEAN	30,069	27,030	27,739	27,093	24,478	3.23	-9.65
Bahamas	250	66	146	168	94	0.01	-44.05
Barbados	222	130	203	526	188	0.02	-64.26
British Virgin Islands	7,859	6,792	6,136	5,643	6,736	0.89	19.37
Dominican Republic	41	45	82	63	126	0.02	100.00
Jamaica	503	230	258	218	149	0.02	-31.65
Puerto Rico	19,776	19,019	18,855	19,201	16,302	2.15	-15.10
Trinidad and Tobago	115	68	146	236	131	0.02	-44.49
Other countries of the Caribbean	1,303	680	1,913	1,038	752	0.10	-27.55
CENTRAL AMERICA	146	169	274	376	226	0.03	-39.89
Costa Rica	63	51	60	102	93	0.01	-8.82
El Salvador	2	2		1	18	0.00	1,700.00
Guatemala	6	1	20	20	6	0.00	-70.00
Honduras	6	35	8	7	8	0.00	14.29
Nicaragua	7	3	5		9	0.00	
Panama	56	75	177	246	87	0.01	-64.63
Other countries of Central America	6	2	4		5	0.00	
NORTH AMERICA	735,717	703,643	623,336	603,540	694,209	91.51	15.02
Canada	10,412	6,601	6,899	7,345	7,208	0.95	-1.87
Mexico	395	154	306	286	486	0.06	69.93
United States of America	724,910	696,888	616,131	595,909	686,515	90.49	15.20
SOUTH AMERICA	997	907	1,716	2,620	1,970	0.26	-24.81
Argentina	219	229	493	647	700	0.09	8.19
Bolivia	22	59	55	1	15	0.00	1,400.00
Brazil	257	244	338	491	366	0.05	-25.46
Chile	347	216	450	548	389	0.05	-29.01
Colombia	70	20	86	299	119	0.02	-60.20
Ecuador	7	4	2	7	3	0.00	-57.14
Guyana	1	6			2	0.00	
Paraguay			1				
Peru	1	20	115	22	46	0.01	109.09
Uruguay	2				6	0.00	
Venezuela	70	89	118	527	89	0.01	-83.11
Other countries of South America	1	20	58	78	235	0.03	201.28
EAST ASIA AND THE PACIFIC	318	367	458	539	563	0.07	4.45
NORTH-EAST ASIA	118	137	93	124	77	0.01	-37.90
Japan	118	136	92	124	77	0.01	-37.90
Taiwan, Province of China		1	1				
AUSTRALASIA	200	230	365	415	486	0.06	17.11
Australia	188	213	298	346	465	0.06	34.39
New Zealand	12	17	67	69	21	0.00	-69.57
EUROPE	16,434	14,393	22,560	31,035	22,735	3.00	-26.74
NORTHERN EUROPE	11,040	9,841	17,245	26,259	18,972	2.50	-27.75
Denmark	9,012	8,191	15,390	24,454	16,413	2.16	-32.88
Finland	53	41	57	59	117	0.02	98.31
Norway	405	174	341	282	370	0.05	31.21
Sweden	133	179	274	319	589	0.08	84.64
United Kingdom	1,437	1,256	1,183	1,145	1,483	0.20	29.52
SOUTHERN EUROPE	3,275	2,569	2,072	1,854	1,041	0.14	-43.85
Greece	112	89	388	16	13	0.00	-18.75
Italy	2,861	1,908	1,306	1,606	890	0.12	-44.58
Portugal	1	20	13	27	8	0.00	-70.37
Spain	301	552	365	205	130	0.02	-36.59

UNITED STATES VIRGIN ISLANDS

3. Arrivals of non-resident tourists in hotels and similar establishments, by nationality

	2009	2010	2011	2012	2013	Market share 2013	% Change 2013-2012
WESTERN EUROPE	**1,484**	**1,360**	**2,345**	**1,807**	**1,977**	**0.26**	**9.41**
Austria	119	48	120	110	61	0.01	-44.55
France	317	280	308	437	362	0.05	-17.16
Germany	477	724	1,134	830	950	0.13	14.46
Netherlands	241	159	329	259	259	0.03	
Switzerland	330	149	454	171	345	0.05	101.75
OTHER EUROPE	**635**	**623**	**898**	**1,115**	**745**	**0.10**	**-33.18**
Other countries of Europe	635	623	898	1,115	745	0.10	-33.18
NOT SPECIFIED	**3,403**	**2,425**	**4,012**	**15,806**	**14,345**	**1.89**	**-9.24**
Other countries of the World	3,403	2,425	4,012	15,806	14,345	1.89	-9.24

Yearbook of Tourism Statistics, Data 2009 – 2013, 2015 Edition

URUGUAY

2. Arrivals of non-resident visitors at national borders, by nationality

		2009	2010	2011	2012	2013	Market share 2013	% Change 2013-2012
TOTAL	(*)	**2,098,780**	**2,407,676**	**2,960,155**	**2,845,989**	**2,815,322**	**100.00**	**-1.08**
AMERICAS		**1,643,319**	**1,888,374**	**2,401,187**	**2,416,628**	**2,308,315**	**81.99**	**-4.48**
NORTH AMERICA		**90,660**	**87,010**	**87,264**	**80,912**	**77,562**	**2.75**	**-4.14**
Canada		10,411	10,212	10,361	9,589	8,271	0.29	-13.74
Mexico		13,026	14,370	16,327	13,771	15,290	0.54	11.03
United States of America		67,223	62,428	60,576	57,552	54,001	1.92	-6.17
SOUTH AMERICA		**1,515,944**	**1,759,347**	**2,286,025**	**2,289,651**	**2,179,476**	**77.41**	**-4.81**
Argentina		1,150,492	1,261,516	1,723,005	1,763,518	1,648,343	58.55	-6.53
Bolivia		3,209	3,959	4,468	4,635	5,807	0.21	25.29
Brazil		263,414	376,894	426,315	396,828	392,992	13.96	-0.97
Chile		41,106	53,194	57,283	53,385	54,474	1.93	2.04
Paraguay		34,347	36,672	42,980	39,321	43,636	1.55	10.97
Peru		11,722	13,673	15,623	13,806	14,837	0.53	7.47
Venezuela		11,654	13,439	16,351	18,158	19,387	0.69	6.77
OTHER AMERICAS		**36,715**	**42,017**	**27,898**	**46,065**	**51,277**	**1.82**	**11.31**
Other countries of the Americas		36,715	42,017	27,898	46,065	51,277	1.82	11.31
EAST ASIA AND THE PACIFIC		**17,193**	**17,327**	**18,516**	**19,223**	**18,343**	**0.65**	**-4.58**
NORTH-EAST ASIA		**5,359**	**6,482**	**7,100**	**8,093**	**9,606**	**0.34**	**18.70**
Japan		2,673	3,046	3,177	3,232	3,840	0.14	18.81
Other countries of North-East Asia		2,686	3,436	3,923	4,861	5,766	0.20	18.62
AUSTRALASIA		**10,985**	**10,077**	**9,593**	**9,340**	**7,346**	**0.26**	**-21.35**
Australia		8,198	7,512	7,571	7,466	5,875	0.21	-21.31
New Zealand		2,787	2,565	2,022	1,874	1,471	0.05	-21.50
OTHER EAST ASIA AND THE PACIFIC		**849**	**768**	**1,823**	**1,790**	**1,391**	**0.05**	**-22.29**
Other countries East Asia/Pacific		849	768	1,823	1,790	1,391	0.05	-22.29
EUROPE		**140,398**	**146,774**	**151,049**	**130,004**	**139,448**	**4.95**	**7.26**
NORTHERN EUROPE		**26,709**	**28,064**	**30,854**	**27,677**	**27,258**	**0.97**	**-1.51**
Denmark		1,742	1,893	2,187	2,021	1,658	0.06	-17.96
Finland		1,767	1,757	2,270	3,305	4,043	0.14	22.33
Ireland		2,489	2,374	2,136	1,897	1,903	0.07	0.32
Norway		1,998	2,429	2,158	2,117	2,319	0.08	9.54
Sweden		3,750	3,874	4,683	4,582	4,073	0.14	-11.11
United Kingdom		14,963	15,737	17,420	13,755	13,262	0.47	-3.58
SOUTHERN EUROPE		**50,683**	**52,529**	**53,889**	**40,446**	**42,070**	**1.49**	**4.02**
Greece		1,033	1,362	912	723	709	0.03	-1.94
Italy		16,098	16,603	17,518	15,423	16,305	0.58	5.72
Portugal		2,470	3,033	3,152	3,116	3,730	0.13	19.70
Spain		31,082	31,531	32,307	21,184	21,326	0.76	0.67
WESTERN EUROPE		**51,563**	**53,632**	**56,045**	**52,711**	**52,711**	**1.87**	
Austria		2,511	2,867	2,794	2,878	2,402	0.09	-16.54
Belgium		2,461	2,190	2,742	2,713	2,924	0.10	7.78
France		17,573	18,505	19,250	17,606	18,163	0.65	3.16
Germany		18,450	19,102	20,267	18,017	17,602	0.63	-2.30
Luxembourg		56	103	78	84	72	0.00	-14.29
Netherlands		5,296	5,018	4,834	5,060	5,064	0.18	0.08
Switzerland		5,216	5,847	6,080	6,353	6,484	0.23	2.06
EAST MEDITERRANEAN EUROPE		**3,601**	**3,680**	**3,601**	**2,376**	**2,858**	**0.10**	**20.29**
Israel		3,601	3,680	3,601	2,376	2,858	0.10	20.29
OTHER EUROPE		**7,842**	**8,869**	**6,660**	**6,794**	**14,551**	**0.52**	**114.17**
Other countries of Europe		7,842	8,869	6,660	6,794	14,551	0.52	114.17
MIDDLE EAST		**226**	**567**	**349**	**304**	**434**	**0.02**	**42.76**
All countries of Middle East		226	567	349	304	434	0.02	42.76
NOT SPECIFIED		**297,644**	**354,634**	**389,054**	**279,830**	**348,782**	**12.39**	**24.64**
Other countries of the World		769	1,656	50,705	2,006	33,669	1.20	1,578.41
Nationals Residing Abroad		296,875	352,978	338,349	277,824	315,113	11.19	13.42

Yearbook of Tourism Statistics, Data 2009 – 2013, 2015 Edition

UZBEKISTAN

1. Arrivals of non-resident tourists at national borders, by country of residence

	2009	2010	2011	2012	2013	Market share 2013	% Change 2013-2012
TOTAL	1,214,700	974,573			1,968,650	100.00	
AFRICA	100	35			7	0.00	
NORTH AFRICA					7	0.00	
Tunisia					7	0.00	
OTHER AFRICA	100	35					
All countries of Africa	100	35					
AMERICAS	6,500	1,189			1,349	0.07	
NORTH AMERICA					1,347	0.07	
United States of America					1,347	0.07	
SOUTH AMERICA					2	0.00	
Brazil					2	0.00	
OTHER AMERICAS	6,500	1,189					
All countries of the Americas	6,500	1,189					
EAST ASIA AND THE PACIFIC	649,300	768,160			43,734	2.22	
NORTH-EAST ASIA					39,323	2.00	
China					11,251	0.57	
Japan					2,184	0.11	
Korea, Dem. People's Republic of					6	0.00	
Korea, Republic of					25,866	1.31	
Mongolia					16	0.00	
SOUTH-EAST ASIA					4,342	0.22	
Malaysia					3,053	0.16	
Singapore					6	0.00	
Thailand					1,278	0.06	
Viet Nam					5	0.00	
AUSTRALASIA					69	0.00	
Australia					69	0.00	
OTHER EAST ASIA AND THE PACIFIC	649,300	768,160					
All countries of Asia	649,300	768,160					
EUROPE	333,200	156,766			1,872,963	95.14	
CENTRAL/EASTERN EUROPE					1,808,622	91.87	
Armenia					25	0.00	
Azerbaijan					3,211	0.16	
Belarus					1,212	0.06	
Bulgaria					89	0.00	
Czech Republic					2,345	0.12	
Estonia					10	0.00	
Georgia					126	0.01	
Hungary					88	0.00	
Kazakhstan					1,090,727	55.40	
Kyrgyzstan					194,550	9.88	
Latvia					3,988	0.20	
Lithuania					284	0.01	
Poland					340	0.02	
Republic of Moldova					60	0.00	
Romania					37	0.00	
Russian Federation					115,142	5.85	
Slovakia					52	0.00	
Tajikistan					284,519	14.45	
Turkmenistan					104,879	5.33	
Ukraine					6,938	0.35	
NORTHERN EUROPE					2,259	0.11	
Denmark					8	0.00	
Finland					5	0.00	
Ireland					31	0.00	
Norway					2	0.00	
Sweden					11	0.00	
United Kingdom					2,202	0.11	

Yearbook of Tourism Statistics, Data 2009 – 2013, 2015 Edition

UZBEKISTAN

1. Arrivals of non-resident tourists at national borders, by country of residence

	2009	2010	2011	2012	2013	Market share 2013	% Change 2013-2012
SOUTHERN EUROPE					6,768	0.34	
Croatia					3	0.00	
Greece					24	0.00	
Italy					4,683	0.24	
Serbia					2	0.00	
Slovenia					73	0.00	
Spain					1,983	0.10	
WESTERN EUROPE					17,303	0.88	
Austria					31	0.00	
Belgium					26	0.00	
France					7,499	0.38	
Germany					9,618	0.49	
Luxembourg					5	0.00	
Netherlands					71	0.00	
Switzerland					53	0.00	
EAST MEDITERRANEAN EUROPE					38,011	1.93	
Cyprus					1	0.00	
Israel					3,187	0.16	
Turkey					34,823	1.77	
OTHER EUROPE	333,200	156,766					
All countries of Europe	333,200	156,766					
MIDDLE EAST	66,800	36,839			3,955	0.20	
Bahrain					10	0.00	
Jordan					38	0.00	
Kuwait					6	0.00	
Lebanon					77	0.00	
Oman					8	0.00	
Qatar					59	0.00	
Saudi Arabia					10	0.00	
United Arab Emirates					3,747	0.19	
All countries of Middle East	66,800	36,839					
SOUTH ASIA	158,800	11,584			46,563	2.37	
Afghanistan					17,186	0.87	
Bangladesh					9	0.00	
India					18,236	0.93	
Iran, Islamic Republic of					7,255	0.37	
Pakistan					3,877	0.20	
All countries of South Asia	158,800	11,584					
NOT SPECIFIED					79	0.00	
Other countries of the World					79	0.00	

Yearbook of Tourism Statistics, Data 2009 – 2013, 2015 Edition

VANUATU

1. Arrivals of non-resident tourists at national borders, by country of residence

	2009	2010	2011	2012	2013	Market share 2013	% Change 2013-2012
TOTAL	**100,676**	**97,180**	**93,960**	**108,161**	**110,109**	**100.00**	**1.80**
AMERICAS	**2,549**	**2,395**	**1,922**	**2,094**	**2,614**	**2.37**	**24.83**
NORTH AMERICA	**2,549**	**2,395**	**1,922**	**2,094**	**2,614**	**2.37**	**24.83**
All countries of North America	2,549	2,395	1,922	2,094	2,614	2.37	24.83
EAST ASIA AND THE PACIFIC	**91,021**	**87,333**	**84,645**	**97,991**	**98,892**	**89.81**	**0.92**
NORTH-EAST ASIA	**642**	**517**	**630**	**705**	**659**	**0.60**	**-6.52**
Japan	642	517	630	705	659	0.60	-6.52
AUSTRALASIA	**77,516**	**70,687**	**69,242**	**79,835**	**80,844**	**73.42**	**1.26**
Australia	64,909	58,760	57,843	65,405	65,776	59.74	0.57
New Zealand	12,607	11,927	11,399	14,430	15,068	13.68	4.42
MELANESIA	**9,155**	**11,410**	**11,376**	**13,138**	**12,515**	**11.37**	**-4.74**
New Caledonia	9,155	11,410	11,376	13,138	12,515	11.37	-4.74
OTHER EAST ASIA AND THE PACIFIC	**3,708**	**4,719**	**3,397**	**4,313**	**4,874**	**4.43**	**13.01**
Other countries of Oceania	3,708	4,719	3,397	4,313	4,874	4.43	13.01
EUROPE	**4,890**	**4,888**	**5,265**	**5,491**	**5,544**	**5.04**	**0.97**
OTHER EUROPE	**4,890**	**4,888**	**5,265**	**5,491**	**5,544**	**5.04**	**0.97**
All countries of Europe	4,890	4,888	5,265	5,491	5,544	5.04	0.97
NOT SPECIFIED	**2,216**	**2,564**	**2,128**	**2,585**	**3,059**	**2.78**	**18.34**
Other countries of the World	2,216	2,564	2,128	2,585	3,059	2.78	18.34

Yearbook of Tourism Statistics, Data 2009 – 2013, 2015 Edition

VENEZUELA

1. Arrivals of non-resident tourists at national borders, by nationality

	2009	2010	2011	2012	2013	Market share 2013	% Change 2013-2012
TOTAL	561,539	526,255	594,681	987,919	985,679	100.00	-0.23
AFRICA	672	311	711	2,587	3,755	0.38	45.15
NORTH AFRICA		23	117	1,561	2,648	0.27	69.63
Algeria		5	1	107	207	0.02	93.46
Morocco		18	116	1,454	2,441	0.25	67.88
SOUTHERN AFRICA	416	198	365	537	568	0.06	5.77
South Africa	416	198	365	537	568	0.06	5.77
WEST AFRICA	256	90	229	489	539	0.05	10.22
Nigeria	256	90	229	489	539	0.05	10.22
AMERICAS	314,432	313,029	373,176	687,957	676,019	68.58	-1.74
CARIBBEAN	31,019	36,257	40,424	51,029	55,628	5.64	9.01
Barbados	445	227	431	384	412	0.04	7.29
Cuba	10,159	8,318	8,344	15,835	22,598	2.29	42.71
Dominica		110	47	75	118	0.01	57.33
Dominican Republic	7,287	7,038	8,413	10,755	13,047	1.32	21.31
Grenada	455	123	300	298	171	0.02	-42.62
Haiti	759	269	651	1,554	2,762	0.28	77.73
Jamaica	267	244	255	282	326	0.03	15.60
Puerto Rico	150	159	143	256	310	0.03	21.09
Saint Lucia	340	312	504	339	115	0.01	-66.08
Saint Vincent and the Grenadines		78	34	90	106	0.01	17.78
Trinidad and Tobago	11,157	19,379	21,302	21,161	15,663	1.59	-25.98
CENTRAL AMERICA	9,822	8,119	9,505	13,540	14,132	1.43	4.37
Costa Rica	2,629	2,300	2,633	3,059	2,663	0.27	-12.95
El Salvador	686	255	692	937	1,113	0.11	18.78
Guatemala	1,383	1,160	1,287	1,745	1,548	0.16	-11.29
Honduras	682	608	546	1,008	595	0.06	-40.97
Nicaragua	836	777	876	1,203	1,604	0.16	33.33
Panama	3,606	3,019	3,471	5,588	6,609	0.67	18.27
NORTH AMERICA	97,385	97,249	106,197	116,614	97,342	9.88	-16.53
Canada	16,581	21,151	24,712	18,919	11,594	1.18	-38.72
Mexico	14,261	12,934	13,636	18,447	16,085	1.63	-12.80
United States of America	66,543	63,164	67,849	79,248	69,663	7.07	-12.09
SOUTH AMERICA	176,206	171,404	217,050	506,774	508,917	51.63	0.42
Argentina	24,361	24,585	35,286	49,840	53,601	5.44	7.55
Bolivia	1,683	1,554	2,083	2,999	4,340	0.44	44.71
Brazil	42,396	48,099	58,550	69,255	79,182	8.03	14.33
Chile	12,026	10,656	10,645	17,942	21,714	2.20	21.02
Colombia	56,282	52,599	74,989	304,581	273,976	27.80	-10.05
Ecuador	12,513	10,319	12,707	22,166	27,755	2.82	25.21
Guyana	562	327	643	737	929	0.09	26.05
Paraguay	562	558	602	1,025	1,042	0.11	1.66
Peru	21,970	19,545	18,413	32,207	38,605	3.92	19.87
Uruguay	3,851	3,162	3,132	6,022	7,773	0.79	29.08
EAST ASIA AND THE PACIFIC	13,598	11,145	12,541	31,764	44,285	4.49	39.42
NORTH-EAST ASIA	11,945	10,381	10,954	29,275	41,433	4.20	41.53
China	6,768	6,006	6,271	22,809	33,784	3.43	48.12
Japan	3,505	3,258	3,278	4,147	4,176	0.42	0.70
Korea, Dem. People's Republic of	256	229	227	219	234	0.02	6.85
Korea, Republic of	997	733	849	1,788	2,931	0.30	63.93
Taiwan, Province of China	419	155	329	312	308	0.03	-1.28
SOUTH-EAST ASIA		21	45	824	1,485	0.15	80.22
Philippines		21	45	824	1,485	0.15	80.22
AUSTRALASIA	1,653	743	1,542	1,665	1,367	0.14	-17.90
Australia	1,295	608	1,249	1,348	1,129	0.11	-16.25
New Zealand	358	135	293	317	238	0.02	-24.92
EUROPE	220,374	193,397	194,148	239,674	230,366	23.37	-3.88
CENTRAL/EASTERN EUROPE	8,970	8,507	11,772	15,193	19,266	1.95	26.81
Belarus		1	10	1,004	1,504	0.15	49.80

804

VENEZUELA

1. Arrivals of non-resident tourists at national borders, by nationality

	2009	2010	2011	2012	2013	Market share 2013	% Change 2013-2012
Bulgaria	342	309	301	350	375	0.04	7.14
Czech Republic	2,627	3,588	3,568	2,538	1,512	0.15	-40.43
Estonia		156	211	65	254	0.03	290.77
Hungary	638	251	465	714	1,042	0.11	45.94
Kazakhstan		9	1	8	16	0.00	100.00
Lithuania	362	214	320	376	317	0.03	-15.69
Poland	2,558	2,177	4,426	3,959	3,254	0.33	-17.81
Romania	772	363	662	1,103	1,386	0.14	25.66
Russian Federation	1,485	1,308	1,591	4,455	8,841	0.90	98.45
Ukraine	186	131	217	621	765	0.08	23.19
NORTHERN EUROPE	**30,520**	**18,807**	**20,392**	**18,711**	**14,051**	**1.43**	**-24.91**
Denmark	3,662	2,354	2,376	1,900	1,235	0.13	-35.00
Finland	2,247	240	682	534	324	0.03	-39.33
Ireland	581	221	474	479	508	0.05	6.05
Norway	1,899	373	1,254	1,016	802	0.08	-21.06
Sweden	6,505	4,138	3,775	3,678	2,810	0.29	-23.60
United Kingdom	15,626	11,481	11,831	11,104	8,372	0.85	-24.60
SOUTHERN EUROPE	**116,121**	**99,672**	**95,673**	**140,597**	**142,704**	**14.48**	**1.50**
Bosnia and Herzegovina		2	1	8	3	0.00	-62.50
Croatia	211	171	180	340	412	0.04	21.18
Greece	860	310	736	1,312	1,449	0.15	10.44
Italy	41,921	37,382	36,384	52,793	49,707	5.04	-5.85
Portugal	15,762	13,906	13,347	23,447	31,433	3.19	34.06
Slovenia		61	34	153	271	0.03	77.12
Spain	57,367	47,840	44,991	62,544	59,429	6.03	-4.98
WESTERN EUROPE	**62,932**	**65,604**	**64,832**	**62,627**	**50,702**	**5.14**	**-19.04**
Austria	3,236	3,058	2,850	2,788	2,054	0.21	-26.33
Belgium	2,349	2,055	2,014	2,160	1,811	0.18	-16.16
France	18,018	22,600	22,645	21,231	15,759	1.60	-25.77
Germany	24,682	21,985	18,488	15,750	12,783	1.30	-18.84
Luxembourg		34	10	41	62	0.01	51.22
Netherlands	9,610	10,889	14,269	15,588	14,111	1.43	-9.48
Switzerland	5,037	4,983	4,556	5,069	4,122	0.42	-18.68
EAST MEDITERRANEAN EUROPE	**1,831**	**807**	**1,479**	**2,546**	**3,643**	**0.37**	**43.09**
Israel	1,493	484	1,135	1,521	1,709	0.17	12.36
Turkey	338	323	344	1,025	1,934	0.20	88.68
MIDDLE EAST	**8,188**	**6,946**	**7,657**	**13,756**	**16,666**	**1.69**	**21.15**
Egypt	277	114	234	486	889	0.09	82.92
Jordan	454	86	353	572	658	0.07	15.03
Lebanon	4,084	3,657	3,698	7,555	8,873	0.90	17.45
Libya	302	285	284	160	49	0.00	-69.38
Saudi Arabia		1	3	78	162	0.02	107.69
Syrian Arab Republic	3,071	2,803	3,085	4,905	6,035	0.61	23.04
SOUTH ASIA	**1,550**	**620**	**1,307**	**3,498**	**4,053**	**0.41**	**15.87**
India	1,032	150	809	1,471	1,660	0.17	12.85
Iran, Islamic Republic of	518	470	498	2,027	2,393	0.24	18.06
NOT SPECIFIED	**2,725**	**807**	**5,141**	**8,683**	**10,535**	**1.07**	**21.33**
Other countries of the World	2,725	807	5,141	8,683	10,535	1.07	21.33

Yearbook of Tourism Statistics, Data 2009 – 2013, 2015 Edition

VENEZUELA

2. Arrivals of non-resident visitors at national borders, by nationality

	2009	2010	2011	2012	2013	Market share 2013	% Change 2013-2012
TOTAL	567,067	535,270	625,224	1,061,020	1,084,776	100.00	2.24
AFRICA	678	294	598	2,600	3,770	0.35	45.00
NORTH AFRICA				1,563	2,651	0.24	69.61
Algeria				108	207	0.02	91.67
Morocco				1,455	2,444	0.23	67.97
SOUTHERN AFRICA	420	204	368	547	578	0.05	5.67
South Africa	420	204	368	547	578	0.05	5.67
WEST AFRICA	258	90	230	490	541	0.05	10.41
Nigeria	258	90	230	490	541	0.05	10.41
AMERICAS	317,526	320,077	400,313	706,641	734,362	67.70	3.92
CARIBBEAN	31,323	36,163	40,444	51,186	55,865	5.15	9.14
Barbados	450	230	431	468	518	0.05	10.68
Cuba	10,259	8,323	8,366	15,839	22,613	2.08	42.77
Dominican Republic	7,359	7,096	8,470	10,790	13,130	1.21	21.69
Grenada	459	123	308	307	174	0.02	-43.32
Haiti	766	269	651	1,558	2,762	0.25	77.28
Jamaica	269	245	256	285	334	0.03	17.19
Puerto Rico	151	159	143	258	310	0.03	20.16
Saint Lucia	343	312	505	341	117	0.01	-65.69
Saint Vincent and the Grenadines				92	107	0.01	16.30
Trinidad and Tobago	11,267	19,406	21,314	21,172	15,682	1.45	-25.93
Other countries of the Caribbean				76	118	0.01	55.26
CENTRAL AMERICA	9,918	8,542	11,586	15,047	18,643	1.72	23.90
Costa Rica	2,655	2,366	3,085	3,522	4,003	0.37	13.66
El Salvador	692	283	749	967	1,320	0.12	36.50
Guatemala	1,396	1,269	1,415	1,922	2,073	0.19	7.86
Honduras	689	610	598	1,047	790	0.07	-24.55
Nicaragua	844	783	909	1,209	1,645	0.15	36.06
Panama	3,642	3,231	4,830	6,380	8,812	0.81	38.12
NORTH AMERICA	98,344	97,667	106,970	117,505	101,563	9.36	-13.57
Canada	16,744	21,196	24,748	19,009	11,778	1.09	-38.04
Mexico	14,402	13,211	14,143	18,759	19,328	1.78	3.03
United States of America	67,198	63,260	68,079	79,737	70,457	6.50	-11.64
SOUTH AMERICA	177,941	177,705	241,313	522,903	558,291	51.47	6.77
Argentina	24,601	25,407	37,916	51,391	58,434	5.39	13.70
Bolivia	1,700	1,566	2,137	3,056	4,512	0.42	47.64
Brazil	42,813	48,293	58,921	69,591	81,520	7.51	17.14
Chile	12,144	10,833	11,297	18,210	24,110	2.22	32.40
Colombia	56,836	57,414	94,279	317,678	308,474	28.44	-2.90
Ecuador	12,636	10,451	13,090	22,297	30,866	2.85	38.43
Guyana	568	328	643	738	941	0.09	27.51
Paraguay	568	558	607	1,053	1,155	0.11	9.69
Peru	22,186	19,608	19,123	32,719	40,128	3.70	22.64
Uruguay	3,889	3,247	3,300	6,170	8,151	0.75	32.11
EAST ASIA AND THE PACIFIC	13,732	10,767	13,215	33,151	45,236	4.17	36.45
NORTH-EAST ASIA	12,063	10,019	11,647	30,198	42,158	3.89	39.61
China	6,835	6,023	6,315	22,850	33,855	3.12	48.16
Japan	3,540	3,261	4,089	5,019	4,808	0.44	-4.20
Korea, Dem. People's Republic of	258		229	219	234	0.02	6.85
Korea, Republic of	1,007	735	859	1,797	2,947	0.27	64.00
Taiwan, Province of China	423		155	313	314	0.03	0.32
SOUTH-EAST ASIA				922	1,638	0.15	77.66
Philippines				922	1,638	0.15	77.66
AUSTRALASIA	1,669	748	1,568	2,031	1,440	0.13	-29.10
Australia	1,308	611	1,266	1,689	1,192	0.11	-29.43
New Zealand	361	137	302	342	248	0.02	-27.49
EUROPE	222,543	194,530	196,033	291,305	267,919	24.70	-8.03
CENTRAL/EASTERN EUROPE	9,060	8,500	11,804	14,713	18,517	1.71	25.85
Bulgaria	346	312	313	370	405	0.04	9.46

806

Yearbook of Tourism Statistics, Data 2009 – 2013, 2015 Edition

VENEZUELA

2. Arrivals of non-resident visitors at national borders, by nationality

	2009	2010	2011	2012	2013	Market share 2013	% Change 2013-2012
Czech Republic	2,653	3,593	3,575	2,565	1,545	0.14	-39.77
Estonia				72	258	0.02	258.33
Hungary	644	253	465	740	1,055	0.10	42.57
Latvia				140	264	0.02	88.57
Lithuania	366	223	338	394	323	0.03	-18.02
Poland	2,583	2,200	4,517	4,064	3,343	0.31	-17.74
Romania	780	376	682	1,157	1,480	0.14	27.92
Russian Federation	1,500	1,363	1,646	4,540	9,035	0.83	99.01
Ukraine	188	180	268	671	809	0.07	20.57
NORTHERN EUROPE	**30,820**	**18,883**	**20,487**	**34,899**	**27,397**	**2.53**	**-21.50**
Denmark	3,698	2,369	2,389	1,918	1,249	0.12	-34.88
Finland	2,269	241	683	549	985	0.09	79.42
Ireland	586	221	476	574	564	0.05	-1.74
Norway	1,917	379	1,261	1,030	834	0.08	-19.03
Sweden	6,570	4,173	3,798	3,707	2,928	0.27	-21.01
United Kingdom	15,780	11,500	11,880	27,121	20,837	1.92	-23.17
SOUTHERN EUROPE	**117,264**	**99,916**	**96,246**	**143,789**	**144,533**	**13.32**	**0.52**
Bosnia and Herzegovina				9	4	0.00	-55.56
Croatia	213	174	185	363	425	0.04	17.08
Greece	868	325	772	1,367	1,496	0.14	9.44
Italy	42,334	37,497	36,482	55,833	49,917	4.60	-10.60
Portugal	15,917	13,972	13,533	23,471	31,534	2.91	34.35
Spain	57,932	47,948	45,274	62,746	61,157	5.64	-2.53
WESTERN EUROPE	**63,550**	**66,416**	**66,011**	**95,344**	**73,798**	**6.80**	**-22.60**
Austria	3,268	3,078	2,858	4,168	2,729	0.25	-34.52
Belgium	2,372	2,066	2,026	2,341	1,975	0.18	-15.63
France	18,195	22,766	22,858	27,175	16,615	1.53	-38.86
Germany	24,925	22,067	18,545	39,284	28,363	2.61	-27.80
Luxembourg				257	160	0.01	-37.74
Netherlands	9,704	11,442	15,148	16,409	19,443	1.79	18.49
Switzerland	5,086	4,997	4,576	5,710	4,513	0.42	-20.96
EAST MEDITERRANEAN EUROPE	**1,849**	**815**	**1,485**	**2,560**	**3,674**	**0.34**	**43.52**
Israel	1,508	484	1,137	1,526	1,718	0.16	12.58
Turkey	341	331	348	1,034	1,956	0.18	89.17
MIDDLE EAST	**8,268**	**6,946**	**7,654**	**13,756**	**16,667**	**1.54**	**21.16**
Egypt	280	114	234	486	890	0.08	83.13
Jordan	458	86	353	572	658	0.06	15.03
Lebanon	4,124	3,658	3,698	7,555	8,873	0.82	17.45
Libya	305	285	284	160	49	0.00	-69.38
Saudi Arabia				78	162	0.01	107.69
Syrian Arab Republic	3,101	2,803	3,085	4,905	6,035	0.56	23.04
SOUTH ASIA	**1,566**	**694**	**1,382**	**3,570**	**4,121**	**0.38**	**15.43**
India	1,043	224	875	1,540	1,728	0.16	12.21
Iran, Islamic Republic of	523	470	507	2,030	2,393	0.22	17.88
NOT SPECIFIED	**2,754**	**1,962**	**6,029**	**9,997**	**12,701**	**1.17**	**27.05**
Other countries of the World	2,754	1,962	6,029	9,997	12,701	1.17	27.05

Yearbook of Tourism Statistics, Data 2009 – 2013, 2015 Edition

VIET NAM

2. Arrivals of non-resident visitors at national borders, by country of residence

	2009	2010	2011	2012	2013	Market share 2013	% Change 2013-2012
TOTAL	3,747,400	5,049,800	6,014,000	6,847,680	7,572,352	100.00	10.58
AMERICAS	487,600	533,200	546,300	557,389	537,201	7.09	-3.62
NORTH AMERICA	487,600	533,200	546,300	557,389	537,201	7.09	-3.62
Canada	84,600	102,200	106,400	113,563	104,973	1.39	-7.56
United States of America	403,000	431,000	439,900	443,826	432,228	5.71	-2.61
EAST ASIA AND THE PACIFIC	2,422,300	3,497,700	4,383,600	4,809,027	5,460,685	72.11	13.55
NORTH-EAST ASIA	1,505,700	2,177,400	2,795,800	3,128,764	3,669,793	48.46	17.29
China	518,900	905,400	1,416,800	1,428,693	1,907,794	25.19	33.53
Hong Kong, China				13,383	10,232	0.14	-23.54
Japan	356,700	442,100	481,500	576,386	604,050	7.98	4.80
Korea, Republic of	360,100	495,900	536,400	700,917	748,727	9.89	6.82
Taiwan, Province of China	270,000	334,000	361,100	409,385	398,990	5.27	-2.54
SOUTH-EAST ASIA	681,000	1,017,500	1,271,500	1,363,798	1,440,299	19.02	5.61
Cambodia	118,300	254,600	423,400	331,939	342,347	4.52	3.14
Indonesia	27,300	51,500	55,400	60,857	70,390	0.93	15.66
Lao People's Democratic Republic	26,100	37,400	118,500	150,678	122,823	1.62	-18.49
Malaysia	165,600	211,300	233,100	299,041	339,510	4.48	13.53
Philippines	45,700	69,200	86,800	99,192	100,501	1.33	1.32
Singapore	138,400	170,700	172,500	196,225	195,760	2.59	-0.24
Thailand	159,600	222,800	181,800	225,866	268,968	3.55	19.08
AUSTRALASIA	235,600	302,800	316,300	316,465	350,593	4.63	10.78
Australia	217,200	278,200	289,800	289,844	319,636	4.22	10.28
New Zealand	18,400	24,600	26,500	26,621	30,957	0.41	16.29
EUROPE	617,900	757,000	811,600	926,957	1,046,101	13.81	12.85
CENTRAL/EASTERN EUROPE	55,200	82,800	101,600	174,287	298,126	3.94	71.05
Russian Federation	55,200	82,800	101,600	174,287	298,126	3.94	71.05
NORTHERN EUROPE	176,500	207,900	231,500	270,183	277,622	3.67	2.75
Denmark	19,600	24,400	25,700	27,970	25,649	0.34	-8.30
Finland				16,204	14,660	0.19	-9.53
Norway	13,300	16,800	19,500	19,928	21,157	0.28	6.17
Sweden	28,100	27,500	30,000	35,735	31,493	0.42	-11.87
United Kingdom	115,500	139,200	156,300	170,346	184,663	2.44	8.40
SOUTHERN EUROPE	41,100	54,300	60,800	62,642	65,326	0.86	4.28
Italy	20,000	24,700	28,300	31,337	32,143	0.42	2.57
Spain	21,100	29,600	32,500	31,305	33,183	0.44	6.00
WESTERN EUROPE	345,100	412,000	417,700	419,845	405,027	5.35	-3.53
Belgium	16,000	20,400	21,900	18,914	21,572	0.28	14.05
France	173,000	199,400	211,400	219,721	209,946	2.77	-4.45
Germany	101,800	123,200	113,900	106,608	97,673	1.29	-8.38
Netherlands	34,700	43,700	45,000	45,862	47,413	0.63	3.38
Switzerland	19,600	25,300	25,500	28,740	28,423	0.38	-1.10
NOT SPECIFIED	219,600	261,900	272,500	554,307	528,365	6.98	-4.68
Other countries of the World	219,600	261,900	272,500	554,307	528,365	6.98	-4.68

Yearbook of Tourism Statistics, Data 2009 – 2013, 2015 Edition

YEMEN

1. Arrivals of non-resident tourists at national borders, by nationality

	2009	2010	2011	2012	2013	Market share 2013	% Change 2013-2012
TOTAL (*)	**1,028,127**	**1,024,762**	**829,190**	**874,425**	**989,566**	**100.00**	**13.17**
AFRICA	**23,587**	**33,387**	**27,835**	**32,542**	**36,673**	**3.71**	**12.69**
EAST AFRICA	**18,920**	**26,961**	**24,138**	**28,201**	**32,305**	**3.26**	**14.55**
Comoros			3,715	3,161	3,013	0.30	-4.68
Djibouti	7,169	8,636	3,852	4,547	5,638	0.57	23.99
Eritrea	2,487	5,361	4,182	2,293	5,777	0.58	151.94
Ethiopia	6,711	9,359	8,134	12,557	11,463	1.16	-8.71
Kenya	1,382	1,998	1,634	2,229	2,007	0.20	-9.96
Somalia			1,697	2,330	3,011	0.30	29.23
United Republic of Tanzania	1,171	1,607	924	1,084	1,396	0.14	28.78
NORTH AFRICA	**3,190**	**4,494**	**2,852**	**3,294**	**3,252**	**0.33**	**-1.28**
Sudan	3,190	4,494	2,852	3,294	3,252	0.33	-1.28
SOUTHERN AFRICA	**425**	**391**	**182**	**219**	**190**	**0.02**	**-13.24**
South Africa	425	391	182	219	190	0.02	-13.24
OTHER AFRICA	**1,052**	**1,541**	**663**	**828**	**926**	**0.09**	**11.84**
Other countries of Africa	1,052	1,541	663	828	926	0.09	11.84
AMERICAS	**25,493**	**28,006**	**18,275**	**27,894**	**30,022**	**3.03**	**7.63**
NORTH AMERICA	**23,441**	**25,784**	**16,968**	**24,195**	**24,259**	**2.45**	**0.26**
Canada	3,914	3,321	1,434	1,624	1,602	0.16	-1.35
United States of America	19,527	22,463	15,534	22,571	22,657	2.29	0.38
OTHER AMERICAS	**2,052**	**2,222**	**1,307**	**3,699**	**5,763**	**0.58**	**55.80**
Other countries of the Americas	2,052	2,222	1,307	3,699	5,763	0.58	55.80
EAST ASIA AND THE PACIFIC	**26,004**	**26,222**	**13,306**	**13,981**	**17,047**	**1.72**	**21.93**
NORTH-EAST ASIA	**8,331**	**7,261**	**2,638**	**2,364**	**4,123**	**0.42**	**74.41**
China	5,843	5,331	1,824	1,831	3,466	0.35	89.30
Japan	1,465	987	343	161	178	0.02	10.56
Korea, Republic of	1,023	943	316	241	282	0.03	17.01
Taiwan, Province of China			155	131	197	0.02	50.38
SOUTH-EAST ASIA	**12,192**	**12,553**	**8,981**	**9,554**	**11,034**	**1.12**	**15.49**
Indonesia	6,799	6,832	5,389	5,150	5,391	0.54	4.68
Malaysia	2,560	2,427	1,657	1,998	2,550	0.26	27.63
Philippines	2,833	3,294	1,340	1,552	2,211	0.22	42.46
Singapore			126	225	300	0.03	33.33
Thailand			202	241	226	0.02	-6.22
Viet Nam			267	388	356	0.04	-8.25
AUSTRALASIA	**1,440**	**1,296**	**425**	**567**	**502**	**0.05**	**-11.46**
Australia	1,440	1,296	425	567	502	0.05	-11.46
OTHER EAST ASIA AND THE PACIFIC	**4,041**	**5,112**	**1,262**	**1,496**	**1,388**	**0.14**	**-7.22**
Other countries of Asia	4,041	5,112	1,262	1,496	1,388	0.14	-7.22
EUROPE	**43,493**	**37,730**	**18,507**	**22,113**	**24,514**	**2.48**	**10.86**
CENTRAL/EASTERN EUROPE	**1,615**	**1,501**	**770**	**882**	**889**	**0.09**	**0.79**
Russian Federation	1,615	1,501	770	882	889	0.09	0.79
NORTHERN EUROPE	**13,844**	**10,949**	**5,174**	**8,058**	**6,384**	**0.65**	**-20.77**
Denmark			91	129	177	0.02	37.21
Ireland			99	101	127	0.01	25.74
Norway			104	198	241	0.02	21.72
Sweden			176	299	338	0.03	13.04
United Kingdom	13,844	10,949	4,704	7,331	5,501	0.56	-24.96
SOUTHERN EUROPE	**2,749**	**2,003**	**1,017**	**844**	**1,020**	**0.10**	**20.85**
Italy	2,749	2,003	791	562	805	0.08	43.24
Spain			226	282	215	0.02	-23.76
WESTERN EUROPE	**13,555**	**12,412**	**4,963**	**5,073**	**6,189**	**0.63**	**22.00**
Austria	532	331	164	102	165	0.02	61.76
Belgium			129	196	236	0.02	20.41
France	6,141	5,567	2,724	2,101	2,620	0.26	24.70
Germany	4,257	4,559	1,235	1,504	1,908	0.19	26.86
Netherlands	2,058	1,565	532	931	1,083	0.11	16.33
Switzerland	567	390	179	239	177	0.02	-25.94
EAST MEDITERRANEAN EUROPE	**4,619**	**5,673**	**5,127**	**5,759**	**7,972**	**0.81**	**38.43**

809

YEMEN

1. Arrivals of non-resident tourists at national borders, by nationality

	2009	2010	2011	2012	2013	Market share 2013	% Change 2013-2012
Turkey	4,619	5,673	5,127	5,759	7,972	0.81	38.43
OTHER EUROPE	**7,111**	**5,192**	**1,456**	**1,497**	**2,060**	**0.21**	**37.61**
Other countries of Europe	7,111	5,192	1,456	1,497	2,060	0.21	37.61
MIDDLE EAST	**289,737**	**376,882**	**289,515**	**335,607**	**353,665**	**35.74**	**5.38**
Bahrain	4,205	4,568	2,255	5,861	9,039	0.91	54.22
Egypt	14,293	18,204	8,855	10,029	11,155	1.13	11.23
Iraq	3,447	3,271	2,669	2,322	2,204	0.22	-5.08
Jordan	7,880	9,069	7,600	4,972	6,549	0.66	31.72
Kuwait		1,518	527	960	1,261	0.13	31.35
Lebanon	3,142	2,795	1,243	1,712	1,322	0.13	-22.78
Oman	46,098	49,559	38,497	49,597	55,431	5.60	11.76
Palestine		3,228	2,228	2,217	2,136	0.22	-3.65
Qatar	4,964	3,643	1,713	3,147	3,937	0.40	25.10
Saudi Arabia	163,000	235,412	198,823	217,287	237,361	23.99	9.24
Syrian Arab Republic	10,792	14,668	12,876	17,657	4,170	0.42	-76.38
United Arab Emirates	22,438	21,681	10,904	17,994	17,071	1.73	-5.13
Other countries of Middle East	9,478	9,266	1,325	1,852	2,029	0.21	9.56
SOUTH ASIA	**25,607**	**33,793**	**20,060**	**27,192**	**31,925**	**3.23**	**17.41**
Bangladesh			680	933	661	0.07	-29.15
India	19,608	26,112	13,251	16,407	19,896	2.01	21.27
Nepal			432	399	486	0.05	21.80
Pakistan	5,999	7,681	5,350	8,953	10,289	1.04	14.92
Sri Lanka			347	500	593	0.06	18.60
NOT SPECIFIED	**594,206**	**488,742**	**441,692**	**415,096**	**495,720**	**50.09**	**19.42**
Nationals Residing Abroad	594,206	488,742	441,692	415,096	495,720	50.09	19.42

Yearbook of Tourism Statistics, Data 2009 – 2013, 2015 Edition

YEMEN

5. Overnight stays of non-resident tourists in hotels and similar establishments, by nationality

	2009	2010	2011	2012	2013	Market share 2013	% Change 2013-2012
TOTAL (*)	11,790,252	16,506,710	9,283,672	9,485,976	10,890,848	100.00	14.81
AFRICA	188,696	267,096	222,680	260,336	293,384	2.69	12.69
EAST AFRICA	151,360	215,688	193,104	225,608	258,440	2.37	14.55
Comoros			29,720	25,288	24,104	0.22	-4.68
Djibouti	57,352	69,088	30,816	36,376	45,104	0.41	23.99
Eritrea	19,896	42,888	33,456	18,344	46,216	0.42	151.94
Ethiopia	53,688	74,872	65,072	100,456	91,704	0.84	-8.71
Kenya	11,056	15,984	13,072	17,832	16,056	0.15	-9.96
Somalia			13,576	18,640	24,088	0.22	29.23
United Republic of Tanzania	9,368	12,856	7,392	8,672	11,168	0.10	28.78
NORTH AFRICA	25,520	35,952	22,816	26,352	26,016	0.24	-1.28
Sudan	25,520	35,952	22,816	26,352	26,016	0.24	-1.28
SOUTHERN AFRICA	3,400	3,128	1,456	1,752	1,520	0.01	-13.24
South Africa	3,400	3,128	1,456	1,752	1,520	0.01	-13.24
OTHER AFRICA	8,416	12,328	5,304	6,624	7,408	0.07	11.84
Other countries of Africa	8,416	12,328	5,304	6,624	7,408	0.07	11.84
AMERICAS	203,944	224,048	146,200	223,152	240,176	2.21	7.63
NORTH AMERICA	187,528	206,272	135,744	193,560	194,072	1.78	0.26
Canada	31,312	26,568	11,472	12,992	12,816	0.12	-1.35
United States of America	156,216	179,704	124,272	180,568	181,256	1.66	0.38
OTHER AMERICAS	16,416	17,776	10,456	29,592	46,104	0.42	55.80
Other countries of the Americas	16,416	17,776	10,456	29,592	46,104	0.42	55.80
EAST ASIA AND THE PACIFIC	208,032	208,976	106,448	111,848	136,376	1.25	21.93
NORTH-EAST ASIA	66,656	57,288	21,104	18,912	32,984	0.30	74.41
China	46,752	42,648	14,592	14,648	27,728	0.25	89.30
Japan	11,720	7,896	2,744	1,288	1,424	0.01	10.56
Korea, Republic of	8,184	6,744	2,528	1,928	2,256	0.02	17.01
Taiwan, Province of China			1,240	1,048	1,576	0.01	50.38
SOUTH-EAST ASIA	97,536	100,424	71,848	76,432	88,272	0.81	15.49
Indonesia	54,392	54,656	43,112	41,200	43,128	0.40	4.68
Malaysia	20,480	19,416	13,256	15,984	20,400	0.19	27.63
Philippines	22,664	26,352	10,720	12,416	17,688	0.16	42.46
Singapore			1,008	1,800	2,400	0.02	33.33
Thailand			1,616	1,928	1,808	0.02	-6.22
Viet Nam			2,136	3,104	2,848	0.03	-8.25
AUSTRALASIA	11,520	10,368	3,400	4,536	4,016	0.04	-11.46
Australia	11,520	10,368	3,400	4,536	4,016	0.04	-11.46
OTHER EAST ASIA AND THE PACIFIC	32,320	40,896	10,096	11,968	11,104	0.10	-7.22
Other countries of Asia	32,320	40,896	10,096	11,968	11,104	0.10	-7.22
EUROPE	347,944	301,840	148,056	176,904	196,112	1.80	10.86
CENTRAL/EASTERN EUROPE	12,920	12,008	6,160	7,056	7,112	0.07	0.79
Russian Federation	12,920	12,008	6,160	7,056	7,112	0.07	0.79
NORTHERN EUROPE	110,752	87,592	41,392	64,464	51,072	0.47	-20.77
Denmark			728	1,032	1,416	0.01	37.21
Ireland			792	808	1,016	0.01	25.74
Norway			832	1,584	1,928	0.02	21.72
Sweden			1,408	2,392	2,704	0.02	13.04
United Kingdom	110,752	87,592	37,632	58,648	44,008	0.40	-24.96
SOUTHERN EUROPE	21,992	16,024	8,136	11,944	15,104	0.14	26.46
Italy	21,992	16,024	6,328	4,496	6,440	0.06	43.24
Spain			1,808	7,448	8,664	0.08	16.33
WESTERN EUROPE	108,440	99,296	39,704	35,392	42,568	0.39	20.28
Austria	4,256	2,648	1,312	816	1,320	0.01	61.76
Belgium			1,032	1,568	1,888	0.02	20.41
France	49,128	44,536	21,792	16,808	20,960	0.19	24.70
Germany	34,056	36,472	9,880	12,032	15,264	0.14	26.86
Netherlands	16,464	12,520	4,256	2,256	1,720	0.02	-23.76
Switzerland	4,536	3,120	1,432	1,912	1,416	0.01	-25.94
EAST MEDITERRANEAN EUROPE	36,952	45,384	41,016	46,072	63,776	0.59	38.43

811

Yearbook of Tourism Statistics, Data 2009 – 2013, 2015 Edition

YEMEN

5. Overnight stays of non-resident tourists in hotels and similar establishments, by nationality

	2009	2010	2011	2012	2013	Market share 2013	% Change 2013-2012
Turkey	36,952	45,384	41,016	46,072	63,776	0.59	38.43
OTHER EUROPE	**56,888**	**41,536**	**11,648**	**11,976**	**16,480**	**0.15**	**37.61**
Other countries of Europe	56,888	41,536	11,648	11,976	16,480	0.15	37.61
MIDDLE EAST	**2,317,896**	**3,015,856**	**2,316,120**	**2,684,856**	**2,829,320**	**25.98**	**5.38**
Bahrain	33,640	36,544	18,040	46,888	72,312	0.66	54.22
Egypt	114,344	145,632	70,840	80,232	89,240	0.82	11.23
Iraq	27,576	26,168	21,352	18,576	17,632	0.16	-5.08
Jordan	63,040	72,552	60,800	39,776	52,392	0.48	31.72
Kuwait			4,216	7,680	10,088	0.09	31.35
Lebanon	25,136	22,360	9,944	13,696	10,576	0.10	-22.78
Oman	368,784	397,272	307,976	396,776	443,448	4.07	11.76
Palestine			17,824	17,736	17,088	0.16	-3.65
Qatar	39,712	29,144	13,704	25,176	31,496	0.29	25.10
Saudi Arabia	1,304,000	1,883,296	1,590,584	1,738,296	1,898,888	17.44	9.24
Syrian Arab Republic	86,336	117,344	103,008	141,256	33,360	0.31	-76.38
United Arab Emirates	179,504	173,448	87,232	143,952	136,568	1.25	-5.13
Other countries of Middle East	75,824	112,096	10,600	14,816	16,232	0.15	9.56
SOUTH ASIA	**204,856**	**270,344**	**160,480**	**217,536**	**255,400**	**2.35**	**17.41**
Bangladesh			5,440	7,464	5,288	0.05	-29.15
India	156,864	208,896	106,008	131,256	159,168	1.46	21.27
Nepal			3,456	3,192	3,888	0.04	21.80
Pakistan	47,992	61,448	42,800	71,624	82,312	0.76	14.92
Sri Lanka			2,776	4,000	4,744	0.04	18.60
NOT SPECIFIED	**8,318,884**	**12,218,550**	**6,183,688**	**5,811,344**	**6,940,080**	**63.72**	**19.42**
Nationals Residing Abroad	8,318,884	12,218,550	6,183,688	5,811,344	6,940,080	63.72	19.42

Yearbook of Tourism Statistics, Data 2009 – 2013, 2015 Edition

ZAMBIA

1. Arrivals of non-resident tourists at national borders, by country of residence

	2009	2010	2011	2012	2013	Market share 2013	% Change 2013-2012
TOTAL	**709,948**	**815,140**	**920,299**	**859,088**	**914,576**	**100.00**	**6.46**
AFRICA	**467,045**	**583,357**	**652,276**	**654,114**	**720,465**	**78.78**	**10.14**
EAST AFRICA	**276,338**	**316,600**	**378,072**	**368,660**	**404,690**	**44.25**	**9.77**
Kenya	10,378	12,785	14,698	10,643	14,515	1.59	36.38
United Republic of Tanzania	81,288	121,275	116,280	214,820	184,187	20.14	-14.26
Zimbabwe	171,232	171,806	227,733	119,100	191,048	20.89	60.41
Other countries of East Africa	13,440	10,734	19,361	24,097	14,940	1.63	-38.00
CENTRAL AFRICA	**57,955**	**80,314**	**71,332**	**65,194**	**121,441**	**13.28**	**86.28**
All countries of Central Africa	57,955	80,314	71,332	65,194	121,441	13.28	86.28
NORTH AFRICA	**1,397**	**2,671**	**2,817**	**1,474**	**2,136**	**0.23**	**44.91**
All countries of North Africa	1,397	2,671	2,817	1,474	2,136	0.23	44.91
SOUTHERN AFRICA	**125,604**	**178,623**	**194,607**	**209,232**	**186,815**	**20.43**	**-10.71**
South Africa	84,413	144,960	134,556	134,602	87,048	9.52	-35.33
Other countries of Southern Africa	41,191	33,663	60,051	74,630	99,767	10.91	33.68
WEST AFRICA	**5,751**	**5,149**	**5,448**	**9,554**	**5,383**	**0.59**	**-43.66**
All countries of West Africa	5,751	5,149	5,448	9,554	5,383	0.59	-43.66
AMERICAS	**63,089**	**41,703**	**51,668**	**31,559**	**41,171**	**4.50**	**30.46**
NORTH AMERICA	**58,939**	**36,899**	**45,537**	**29,344**	**37,398**	**4.09**	**27.45**
Canada	9,488	7,378	10,441	5,517	5,572	0.61	1.00
United States of America	49,451	29,521	35,096	23,827	31,826	3.48	33.57
OTHER AMERICAS	**4,150**	**4,804**	**6,131**	**2,215**	**3,773**	**0.41**	**70.34**
Other countries of the Americas	4,150	4,804	6,131	2,215	3,773	0.41	70.34
EAST ASIA AND THE PACIFIC	**38,542**	**64,271**	**80,429**	**92,256**	**57,326**	**6.27**	**-37.86**
NORTH-EAST ASIA	**5,373**	**26,660**	**41,422**	**67,427**	**33,197**	**3.63**	**-50.77**
China		18,319	30,076	63,892	27,666	3.03	-56.70
Japan	5,373	8,341	11,346	3,535	5,531	0.60	56.46
AUSTRALASIA	**20,308**	**13,880**	**27,982**	**12,397**	**12,076**	**1.32**	**-2.59**
Australia	16,316	10,430	12,599	10,814	10,136	1.11	-6.27
New Zealand	3,992	3,450	15,383	1,583	1,940	0.21	22.55
OTHER EAST ASIA AND THE PACIFIC	**12,861**	**23,731**	**11,025**	**12,432**	**12,053**	**1.32**	**-3.05**
Other countries of Asia	12,861	23,731	11,025	12,432	12,053	1.32	-3.05
EUROPE	**128,340**	**104,395**	**113,831**	**65,826**	**78,542**	**8.59**	**19.32**
NORTHERN EUROPE	**72,190**	**65,403**	**71,268**	**36,636**	**44,311**	**4.84**	**20.95**
Denmark	2,665	3,752	2,377	1,861	2,339	0.26	25.69
Sweden	3,166	3,640	3,625	2,057	2,820	0.31	37.09
United Kingdom	53,370	50,956	59,084	25,446	32,309	3.53	26.97
Scandinavia	12,989	7,055	6,182	7,272	6,843	0.75	-5.90
SOUTHERN EUROPE	**8,238**	**5,515**	**6,883**	**2,972**	**3,797**	**0.42**	**27.76**
Italy	8,238	5,515	6,883	2,972	3,797	0.42	27.76
WESTERN EUROPE	**19,368**	**16,187**	**16,360**	**9,642**	**11,010**	**1.20**	**14.19**
France	6,701	6,416	6,049	3,023	3,859	0.42	27.65
Germany	12,667	9,771	10,311	6,619	7,151	0.78	8.04
OTHER EUROPE	**28,544**	**17,290**	**19,320**	**16,576**	**19,424**	**2.12**	**17.18**
Other countries of Europe	28,544	17,290	19,320	16,576	19,424	2.12	17.18
SOUTH ASIA	**12,932**	**21,414**	**22,095**	**15,333**	**17,072**	**1.87**	**11.34**
India	12,932	21,414	22,095	15,333	17,072	1.87	11.34

813

ZIMBABWE

2. Arrivals of non-resident visitors at national borders, by country of residence

	2009	2010	2011	2012	2013	Market share 2013	% Change 2013-2012
TOTAL	2,017,264	2,239,165	2,423,280	1,794,230	1,832,570	100.00	2.14
AFRICA	1,678,884	1,951,330	2,041,291	1,562,194	1,569,766	85.66	0.48
EAST AFRICA	493,791	389,022	508,728	696,592	737,824	40.26	5.92
Kenya	25,808	8,509	6,514	7,273	8,230	0.45	13.16
Malawi	108,103	67,291	138,676	241,344	286,510	15.63	18.71
Mauritius	967	1,066	2,779	1,191	2,960	0.16	148.53
Mozambique	110,058	131,653	148,857	146,922	174,137	9.50	18.52
Seychelles	360	434	1,321	2,352	383	0.02	-83.72
Uganda	6,906	2,893	11,555	3,914	4,598	0.25	17.48
United Republic of Tanzania	11,391	8,454	14,038	14,740	27,285	1.49	85.11
Zambia	230,198	168,722	184,988	278,856	233,721	12.75	-16.19
CENTRAL AFRICA	27,580	18,036	17,137	25,021	24,960	1.36	-0.24
Angola	8,131	2,285	3,297	1,437	1,796	0.10	24.98
Democratic Republic of the Congo	19,449	15,751	13,840	23,584	23,164	1.26	-1.78
SOUTHERN AFRICA	1,137,761	1,522,208	1,471,791	825,439	795,797	43.43	-3.59
Botswana	183,212	114,718	119,098	64,926	59,441	3.24	-8.45
Lesotho	5,367	4,957	6,655	20,051	4,942	0.27	-75.35
Namibia	33,806	19,917	23,322	11,487	11,037	0.60	-3.92
South Africa	912,244	1,368,238	1,309,463	719,637	715,260	39.03	-0.61
Swaziland	3,132	14,378	13,253	9,338	5,117	0.28	-45.20
WEST AFRICA	4,656	3,290	5,126	2,135	1,893	0.10	-11.33
Ghana	1,258	1,428	3,857	1,274	1,426	0.08	11.93
Nigeria	3,398	1,862	1,269	861	467	0.03	-45.76
OTHER AFRICA	15,096	18,774	38,509	13,007	9,292	0.51	-28.56
Other countries of Africa	15,096	18,774	38,509	13,007	9,292	0.51	-28.56
AMERICAS	57,842	69,008	89,756	58,873	54,157	2.96	-8.01
CARIBBEAN	2,513	804	892	450	293	0.02	-34.89
Cuba					50	0.00	
Jamaica					132	0.01	
Other countries of the Caribbean					111	0.01	
All countries of the Caribbean	2,513	804	892	450			
NORTH AMERICA	49,355	63,343	80,596	54,960	50,278	2.74	-8.52
Canada	5,538	4,098	6,999	3,890	4,324	0.24	11.16
Mexico	546	2,829	992	1,010	458	0.02	-54.65
United States of America	43,271	56,416	72,605	50,060	45,496	2.48	-9.12
SOUTH AMERICA	2,643	2,986	5,778	2,819	2,765	0.15	-1.92
Argentina	1,058	1,027	1,682	858	812	0.04	-5.36
Brazil	1,585	1,959	4,096	1,961	1,953	0.11	-0.41
OTHER AMERICAS	3,331	1,875	2,490	644	821	0.04	27.48
Other countries of the Americas	3,331	1,875	2,490	644	821	0.04	27.48
EAST ASIA AND THE PACIFIC	104,366	84,092	125,257	55,560	72,855	3.98	31.13
NORTH-EAST ASIA	61,534	37,385	75,591	30,765	45,362	2.48	47.45
Hong Kong, China	30,102	12,343	30,549	4,937	16,525	0.90	234.72
Japan	18,389	18,593	32,784	18,032	20,374	1.11	12.99
Korea, Republic of	13,043	6,449	12,258	7,796	8,463	0.46	8.56
SOUTH-EAST ASIA	4,016	5,537	7,114	2,722	4,002	0.22	47.02
Malaysia	2,416	3,497	3,452	1,115	2,030	0.11	82.06
Singapore	1,600	2,040	3,662	1,607	1,972	0.11	22.71
AUSTRALASIA	33,041	37,708	38,841	20,966	22,524	1.23	7.43
Australia	22,612	25,240	26,833	13,355	16,255	0.89	21.71
New Zealand	10,429	12,468	12,008	7,611	6,269	0.34	-17.63
OTHER EAST ASIA AND THE PACIFIC	5,775	3,462	3,711	1,107	967	0.05	-12.65
Other countries of Asia	2,363	2,155	1,333	580	802	0.04	38.28
Other countries of Oceania	3,412	1,307	2,378	527	165	0.01	-68.69
EUROPE	160,316	128,082	158,141	113,956	131,497	7.18	15.39
NORTHERN EUROPE	42,165	35,169	47,627	38,503	51,225	2.80	33.04
United Kingdom	27,580	24,192	35,913	27,587	41,763	2.28	51.39
Scandinavia	14,585	10,977	11,714	10,916	9,462	0.52	-13.32
SOUTHERN EUROPE	29,446	23,342	27,432	20,220	18,444	1.01	-8.78

814

ZIMBABWE

2. Arrivals of non-resident visitors at national borders, by country of residence

	2009	2010	2011	2012	2013	Market share 2013	% Change 2013-2012
Italy	14,161	9,221	13,806	9,127	7,664	0.42	-16.03
Portugal	9,883	4,951	5,482	3,791	3,275	0.18	-13.61
Spain	5,402	9,170	8,144	7,302	7,505	0.41	2.78
WESTERN EUROPE	**77,430**	**57,997**	**69,629**	**47,365**	**52,924**	**2.89**	**11.74**
Austria	5,520	6,475	6,245	4,228	4,251	0.23	0.54
France	27,193	13,687	16,232	11,149	12,956	0.71	16.21
Germany	22,936	16,910	24,300	17,126	18,768	1.02	9.59
Netherlands	16,967	14,088	15,927	9,362	11,333	0.62	21.05
Switzerland	4,814	6,837	6,925	5,500	5,616	0.31	2.11
EAST MEDITERRANEAN EUROPE	**4,451**	**2,851**	**3,838**	**2,427**	**2,596**	**0.14**	**6.96**
Israel	4,451	2,851	3,838	2,427	2,596	0.14	6.96
OTHER EUROPE	**6,824**	**8,723**	**9,615**	**5,441**	**6,308**	**0.34**	**15.93**
Other countries of Europe	6,824	8,723	9,615	5,441	6,308	0.34	15.93
MIDDLE EAST	**5,456**	**1,758**	**2,863**	**1,160**	**1,451**	**0.08**	**25.09**
Egypt	1,198	641	728	428	1,033	0.06	141.36
Kuwait					32	0.00	
Saudi Arabia	116	62	60	12	4	0.00	-66.67
United Arab Emirates	208	101	503	120	212	0.01	76.67
Other countries of Middle East	3,934	954	1,572	600	170	0.01	-71.67
SOUTH ASIA	**10,400**	**4,895**	**5,972**	**2,487**	**2,844**	**0.16**	**14.35**
India	5,446	3,571	3,499	1,809	2,334	0.13	29.02
Iran, Islamic Republic of	1,368	758	1,228	55	51	0.00	-7.27
Pakistan	3,586	566	1,245	623	459	0.03	-26.32

Yearbook of Tourism Statistics, Data 2009 – 2013, 2015 Edition

NOTES 2009 - 2013

1. Arrivals of non-resident tourists at national borders, by nationality

Belarus	**Total**	Organized tourism.
Bhutan	**Total**	Total arrivals 2010: 40,873; 2011: 65,756; 2012: 105,407; 2013: 116,209. The huge margin of difference in 2010-2013 as compared to the previous years is because starting from 2010 the regional high end tourists are included in the total figures.
Brunei Darussalam	**Total**	Arrivals by air.
Burundi	**Total**	Including nationals residing abroad. From 2010: break in the series due to implementation of improved methodology for distinguishing visitors (tourists) from other travellers.
Central African Republic	**Total**	Arrivals by air to Bangui only.
Chile	**Total**	Including nationals residing abroad.
Comoros	**Total**	Arrivals by air.
Democratic Republic of the Congo	**Total**	2009, 2010: arrivals by air only; 2011-2013: the arrivals data relate only to three border posts (N'Djili airport in Kinshasa, the Luano airport in Lubumbashi, and the land border-crossing of Kasumbalesa in Katanga province).
Gambia	**Total**	Charter tourists only.
Guinea	**Total**	Arrivals by air at Conakry airport.
Honduras	**Total**	Excluding tourists arrivals by sea.
Iceland	**Total**	Source: Icelandic Tourist Board. 2012, 2013: arrivals at Keflavik airport only.
India	**Total**	Excluding nationals residing abroad.
Italy	**Total**	Excluding seasonal and border workers.
Kiribati	**Total**	Arrivals by air. Tarawa and Christmas Island.
Lebanon	**Total**	Excluding nationals residing abroad, Syrian nationals and Palestinians.
Maldives	**Total**	Arrivals by air.
Mali	**Total**	2012: arrivals by air only (Bamako-Sénou airport).
Malta	**Total**	Data based on departures by air and by sea. Source: National Statistics Office
Marshall Islands	**Total**	Arrivals by air. 2009: air and sea arrivals.
Mexico	**United States of America**	Including tourists arrivals by air and land, border tourists and nationals tourists residing in the United States of America.
	Other countries of the World	Including border tourists from the southern zone.
Nepal	**Greece**	Including Cyprus.
Norway	**Total**	2009-2011: figures are based on "The Guest survey" carried out by "Institute of Transport Economics". The survey has been discontinued since 2012.
Paraguay	**Total**	Excluding nationals residing abroad and crew members. E/d cards in the "Silvio Petirossi" airport and passenger counts at the national border crossings - National Police and SENATUR.
Sint Maarten	**Total**	Arrivals at Princess Juliana International Airport. Including visitors to St. Maarten (the French side of the island).
	France	Including residents of the French West Indies.
Sri Lanka	**Total**	Excluding nationals residing abroad.
	China	2013: including Hong Kong, China, and Macao, China.
Sudan	**Total**	Including nationals residing abroad.
Tunisia	**Total**	Excluding nationals residing abroad.
Turkey	**Total**	Including Turkish citizens resident abroad.
Yemen	**Total**	Including nationals residing abroad.

817

NOTES 2009 - 2013

1. Arrivals of non-resident tourists at national borders, by country of residence

Andorra	**Total**	In 2009 and 2011 there were changes in the methodology for calculating the number of visitors of the country. In this regard, it is not possible to have comparability for data obtained using different methodologies because the variations reflect not only the variation in the number of visitors but also variations caused by the methodological changes.
Anguilla	**Total**	Excluding nationals residing abroad.
Antigua and Barbuda	**Total**	Arrivals by air. Excluding nationals residing abroad.
Bermuda	**Total**	Arrivals by air.
Canada	**Total**	Source: Canadian Tourism Commission and Statistics Canada
	Other countries of Africa	Including Chagos Archipelago, Ascension Island and Tristan da Cunha.
	Panama	Including Panama Canal Zone.
	Other countries of Oceania	Including Bismarck Archipelago, Marquesas Islands, Pitcairn Island and Tuamotu Archipelago.
Cayman Islands	**Total**	Arrivals by air.
Colombia	**Total**	Source: Administrative Department of Security (DAS) / "Migración Colombia". Provisional data. Excluding cruise passengers. 2010-2013: arrivals of non-resident tourists by immigration checkpoints. 2011-2013: including nationals residing abroad. 2009: data by nationality.
Cook Islands	**Total**	Arrivals by air and sea.
Curaçao	**Total**	Arrivals by air.
Dominican Republic	**Total**	Arrivals by air.
Ethiopia	**Total**	Arrivals through all ports of entry.
Fiji	**Total**	Excluding nationals residing abroad.
France	**Total**	Source: "Dge", "Banque de France". Non resident visitor survey ("EVE") - results 2012 revised, results 2013 provisional.
	All countries of North Africa	Algeria, Egypt, Libya, Morocco and Tunisia.
	China	Including Hong Kong, China, and Macao, China.
	Switzerland	Including Liechtenstein.
French Polynesia	**Total**	Arrivals by air. Excluding nationals residing abroad.
	Samoa	Including American Samoa.
Greece	**Total**	Information based on the border survey conducted by the Bank of Greece.
	Egypt	Including Sudan.
	Lebanon	Including Syrian Arab Republic.
Guadeloupe	**Total**	Arrivals by air. 2013: including residents and non-residents. Source: OAG Aviation software.
Guinea	**Total**	Arrivals by air at Conakry airport.
Guyana	**Total**	Arrivals to Timehri Airport only.
Haiti	**Total**	Arrivals by air. Including nationals residing abroad.
Ireland	**United Kingdom**	Including Northern Ireland resident arrivals. Change in methodology in estimating Northern Ireland tourists in 2010; as a result figures prior to 2010 not directly comparable.
Israel	**Total**	Excluding nationals residing abroad.
Jamaica	**Total**	Arrivals by air. Including nationals residing abroad.

818

NOTES 2009 - 2013

1. Arrivals of non-resident tourists at national borders, by country of residence

Malawi	Total	Departures.
Malaysia	Total	Including Singapore residents crossing the frontier by road through Johore Causeway.
Mali	Total	2013: arrivals by air only (Bamako-Sénou airport).
Marshall Islands	Total	Arrivals by air. 2009: air and sea arrivals.
Martinique	Total	Including French overseas departments and territories.
Mexico	Total	Including nationals residing abroad.
Micronesia, Federated States of	Total	Arrivals in the States of Kosrae, Chuuk, Pohnpei and Yap.
Nepal	Greece	Including Cyprus.
New Caledonia	Total	Including nationals residing abroad.
	All countries of the Caribbean	Martinique, Guadeloupe and Guyana.
Niue	Total	Including Niuans residing usually in New Zealand.
Palau	Total	Arrivals by air (Palau International Airport).
Peru	Total	Including nationals residing abroad. Preliminary data.
Philippines	Nationals Residing Abroad	Philippine passport holders permanently residing abroad; excludes overseas Filipino workers.
Puerto Rico	Total	Arrivals by air. Fiscal year July to June. Source: "Junta de Planificación de Puerto Rico".
Reunion	Total	Source: INSEE: Survey on Tourism Flows
	All countries of Africa	Indian Ocean.
Saint Kitts and Nevis	Total	Arrivals by air.
Saint Lucia	Total	Excluding nationals residing abroad.
Saint Vincent and the Grenadines	Total	Arrivals by air.
Sierra Leone	Total	Arrivals by air.
Sint Eustatius	Total	Excluding Netherlands Antillean residents.
South Africa	Total	Since 2009 a new methodology has been applied and therefore, the information is not comparable to previous years.
Spain	Total	2012: provisional data.
Sri Lanka	Total	Excluding nationals residing abroad.
Timor-Leste	Total	Arrivals by air at Dili Airport.
Tonga	Total	Arrivals by air.
Trinidad and Tobago	Total	Arrivals by air. 2011-2013: data by nationality.
United States of America	Canada	Historical data may reflect revisions made by "Statistics Canada".
	Mexico	Historical data may reflect revisions made by "Banco de México".

NOTES 2009 - 2013

2. Arrivals of non-resident visitors at national borders, by nationality

Albania	Total	Excluding nationals residing abroad.
Algeria	Total	Including nationals residing abroad.
Bahrain	Total	Excluding nationals residing abroad.
Belize	Total	Including transit passengers and border permits.
Brunei Darussalam	Total	Arrivals by air, cruise and borders.
Ecuador	Total	Excluding nationals residing abroad.
Egypt	Total	Excluding nationals residing abroad.
Italy	Total	Border survey. Excluding seasonal and border workers.
Japan	Total	Excluding nationals residing abroad.
Korea, Republic of	Total	Including nationals residing abroad and crew members.
Macao, China	Total	Source of data: Public Security Police
Nigeria	Total	Source: Nigerian Tourism Development Corporation (NTDC)
Poland	Total	Since Poland joined the Schengen area, precise counting of incoming traffic is not possible. Data presented here are based on surveys by the Institute of Tourism. Only approximate results for main countries can be given.
Republic of Moldova	Total	Visitors who have benefited from tourism services provided by the tourism agencies and tour operators (titulars of tourism licences). Excluding the left side of the river Nistru and the municipality of Bender.
Singapore	Total	Excluding Malaysian citizens arrivals by land.
	Hong Kong, China	From 2013 included in China.
	Macao, China	From 2013 included in China.
Syrian Arab Republic	Total	Survey of the incoming tourism.
Turkey	Total	Including Turkish citizens resident abroad.
Uruguay	Total	Excluding cruise passengers arrivals.

NOTES 2009 - 2013

2. Arrivals of non-resident visitors at national borders, by country of residence

Australia	**Total**	Excluding nationals residing abroad and crew members. Source: Australian Bureau of Statistics
Canada	**Total**	Source: Canadian Tourism Commission and Statistics Canada
	China	Including Mongolia and Tibet.
	Estonia	Including Latvia and Lithuania.
	Hungary	Including Slovenia, Bulgaria and Romania.
	Denmark	Including Faeroe Islands.
	United Kingdom	Including Gibraltar.
	Italy	Including San Marino, the Holy See and Malta.
	Yugoslavia, SFR (former)	Including Croatia, Bosnia and Herzegovina, The Former Yugoslav Republic of Macedonia and Albania.
	France	Including Andorra and Monaco.
	Switzerland	Including Liechtenstein.
Congo	**Total**	Source: "Direction Générale du Tourisme et de l'Hôtellerie", surveys 2011-2013
Finland	**Total**	Border survey. Note: the survey was cancelled at the end of 2012
Hong Kong, China	**United States of America**	Including Guam.
	New Zealand	Including Cook Islands.
	France	Including New Caledonia and French Polynesia.
Israel	**Total**	Excluding nationals residing abroad.
Latvia	**Total**	Non-resident departures. Survey of persons crossing the state border.
Macao, China	**Total**	Source of data: Public Security Police
Mozambique	**Total**	Arrivals at all border posts of the country.
New Zealand	**Total**	Data regarding to short term movements are compiled from a random sample of passenger declarations. Including nationals residing abroad. Source: Statistics New Zealand (International Travel and Migration).
Panama	**Total**	Total number of visitors broken down by permanent residence who arrived in Panama at Tocumen International Airport.
Saint Vincent and the Grenadines	**Total**	Arrivals by air.
Singapore	**Total**	Excluding Malaysian citizens arrivals by land.
South Africa	**Total**	Since 2009 a new methodology has been applied and therefore, the information is not comparable to previous years.
Sweden	**Total**	Data for 2011 and 2012 according to new national border survey (IBIS, Incoming Visitors to Sweden). No data collected in 2009 and 2010. The new border survey (IBIS) started in 2011. Source: Swedish Agency for Economic and Regional Growth.

NOTES 2009 - 2013

3. Arrivals of non-resident tourists in hotels and similar establishments, by nationality

Bolivia	**Total**	Preliminary data. Arrivals in hotels in the regional capitals.
Chad	**Total**	2010: Partial data.
Italy	**Total**	Arrivals at hotels only.
Montenegro	**Serbia**	Including arrivals from Kosovo.
Morocco	**Total**	Arrivals in classified hotels, holiday villages, tourist residences and Riad.
Palestine	**Total**	Source: Palestinian Central Bureau of Statistics, 2014. Hotel Activity Survey 2013. Ramallah - Palestine. The data on hotel activity for 2012 and 2013 represent the West Bank only.
Syrian Arab Republic	**Total**	Survey of the incoming tourism.
Turkey	**Total**	Arrivals at licensed establishments including: hotels, motels, boarding houses, inns, apartment hotels, holiday villages and special hotels. Results of a monthly survey carried out among accommodation establishments licensed by the Ministry of Tourism.

822

NOTES 2009 - 2013

3. Arrivals of non-resident tourists in hotels and similar establishments, by country of residence

Austria	Total	Hotels only.
Cabo Verde	Belgium	Including Netherlands.
Congo	Total	Source: "Direction Générale du Tourisme et de l'Hôtellerie", surveys 2009 to 2013.
Croatia	Total	According to the Regulation on Classification, Minimum Standards and Categorization of Accommodation Facilities, data for hotels and similar establishments do not include Inns and Bed and Breakfast since 2006.
Curaçao	Total	Large and small hotels, guest houses, apartments and bungalows.
Denmark	Total	Hotels only. 2011: change of methodology.
France	Total	Source: "Insee", "Dge", regional partners. Hotel occupancy survey ("EFH").
Germany	China	Including Hong Kong, China.
	Other countries East Asia/Pacific	Including India.
Guinea	Total	Arrivals by air at Conakry airport.
Israel	Total	Arrivals at tourist hotels and not yet listed hotels.
	All countries of South America	Including Central America.
Luxembourg	Total	NACE Rev2 55.100
Macao, China	Total	Source of data: Monthly Survey of Travel Agencies
Netherlands	Total	2013: break in the series because of methodological changes in determining the population.
New Caledonia	Total	It refers to hotels in Noumea.
Poland	Total	Excluding hostels.
	Total	Fiscal year July to June. Hotels registered by the "Compañía de Turismo de Puerto Rico".
	Other countries of the Caribbean	Aggregated data of tourists coming from minor Antilles who did not specify their country of origin are included.
	Other countries of the World	Including crew members.
Romania	Other countries of Africa	Including Egypt and Libya.
Spain	Total	Arrivals at hotels and "hostales" (accommodation establishments providing limited services).
Switzerland	Total	Including health establishments.
	All countries of North Africa	Algeria, Libya, Morocco and Tunisia.
Thailand	Total	2012, 2013: hotels only.
Togo	Burkina Faso	Including Mali and Niger.

Yearbook of Tourism Statistics, Data 2009 – 2013, 2015 Edition

NOTES 2009 - 2013

4. Arrivals of non-resident tourists in all types of accommodation establishments, by nationality

Hungary	**Total**	Collective accommodation establishments.
Montenegro	**Serbia**	Including arrivals from Kosovo.
Republic of Moldova	**Total**	Excluding the left side of the river Nistru and the municipality of Bender.
Syrian Arab Republic	**Total**	Excluding private accommodation. Survey of the incoming tourism.
Turkey	**Total**	Results of a monthly survey carried out among accommodation establishments licensed by the Ministry of Tourism.

NOTES 2009 - 2013

4. Arrivals of non-resident tourists in all types of accommodation establishments, by country of residence

Austria	**Total**	Only paid accommodation; excluding stays at friends and relatives and second homes.
Belgium	**Total**	Hotel establishments, campings, holiday centres, holiday villages and specific categories of accommodation. From 2012 including bed and breakfast.
Croatia	**Total**	Excluding arrivals in ports of nautical tourism.
Denmark	**Total**	Including non-commercial tourism. 2011: change of methodology.
Germany	**China**	Including Hong Kong, China.
	Other countries East Asia/Pacific	Including India.
Malta	**Total**	Data based on departures by air and by sea. Source: National Statistics Office
Netherlands	**Total**	2013: break in the series because of methodological changes in determining the population.
Philippines	**Total**	Arrivals by air.
	Nationals Residing Abroad	Philippine passport holders permanently residing abroad; excludes overseas Filipino workers.
Romania	**Other countries of Africa**	Including Egypt and Libya.
Spain	**Total**	Arrivals at hotels, "hostales", camping, tourism apartments and rural dwellings.

5. Overnight stays of non-resident tourists in hotels and similar establishments, by nationality

Bolivia	**Total**	Preliminary data. Overnights in the regional capitals.
Chad	**Total**	2010: Partial data.
Italy	**Total**	Overnights in hotels only.
Madagascar	**Total**	All star-establishments (registered and non-registered).
Montenegro	**Serbia**	Including arrivals from Kosovo.
Morocco	**Total**	Overnight stays in classified hotels, holiday villages, tourist residences and Riad.
Norway	**Total**	Overnights in registered establishments. Figures relate to establishments with 20 or more beds.
Palestine	**Total**	Source: Palestinian Central Bureau of Statistics, 2014. Hotel Activity Survey 2013. Ramallah - Palestine. The data on hotel activity for 2012 and 2013 represent the West Bank only.
Syrian Arab Republic	**Total**	Survey of the incoming tourism.
Turkey	**Total**	Classified hotels, motels, boarding houses, inns, apartment hotels, holiday villages and special hotels. Results of a monthly survey carried out among accommodation establishments licensed by the Ministry of Tourism.
Yemen	**Total**	Including nationals residing abroad.

NOTES 2009 - 2013

5. Overnight stays of non-resident tourists in hotels and similar establishments, by country of residence

Austria	Total	Hotels only.
Cabo Verde	Belgium	Including Netherlands.
Congo	Total	Source: "Direction Générale du Tourisme et de l'Hôtellerie", surveys 2009 to 2013.
Croatia	Total	According to the Regulation on Classification, Minimum Standards and Categorization of Accommodation Facilities, data for hotels and similar establishments do not include Inns and Bed and Breakfast since 2006.
Denmark	Total	Hotels only. 2011: change of methodology.
France	Total	Source: "Insee", "Dge", regional partners. Hotel occupancy survey ("EFH").
Germany	China	Including Hong Kong, China.
	Other countries East Asia/Pacific	Including India.
Israel	Total	Overnights in tourist hotels and apartment hotels.
	All countries of South America	Including Central America.
Luxembourg	Total	NACE Rev2 55.100
Macao, China	Total	Source of data: Monthly Survey of Hotels and Similar Establishments
Netherlands	Total	2013: break in the series because of methodological changes in determining the population.
New Caledonia	Total	It refers to hotels in Noumea.
Poland	Total	Excluding hostels.
Romania	Other countries of Africa	Including Egypt and Libya.
Spain	Total	Overnights in hotels and "hostales" (accommodation establishments providing limited services).
Switzerland	Total	Including health establishments.
	All countries of North Africa	Algeria, Libya, Morocco and Tunisia.
Togo	Burkina Faso	Including Mali and Niger.

6. Overnight stays of non-resident tourists in all types of accommodation establishments, by nationality

Hungary	**Total**	Collective accommodation establishments.
Montenegro	**Serbia**	Including arrivals from Kosovo.
Republic of Moldova	**Total**	Excluding the left side of the river Nistru and the municipality of Bender.
Syrian Arab Republic	**Total**	Survey of the incoming tourism.
Turkey	**Total**	Results of a monthly survey carried out among accommodation establishments licensed by the Ministry of Tourism.

NOTES 2009 - 2013

6. Overnight stays of non-resident tourists in all types of accommodation establishments, by country of residence

Austria	**Total**	Only paid accommodation; excluding stays at friends and relatives and second homes.
Bahamas	**Total**	Overnights in all forms of commercial accommodation.
Belgium	**Total**	Hotel establishments, campings, holiday centres, holiday villages and specific categories of accommodation. From 2012 including bed and breakfast.
Canada	**Total**	Source: Canadian Tourism Commission and Statistics Canada
	China	Including Mongolia and Tibet.
	Estonia	Including Latvia and Lithuania.
	Hungary	Including Slovenia, Bulgaria and Romania.
	Denmark	Including Faeroe Islands.
	United Kingdom	Including Gibraltar.
	Italy	Including San Marino, the Holy See and Malta.
	Yugoslavia, SFR (former)	Including Croatia, Bosnia and Herzegovina, The Former Yugoslav Republic of Macedonia and Albania.
	France	Including Andorra and Monaco.
	Switzerland	Including Liechtenstein.
Croatia	**Total**	Excluding overnight stays at ports of nautical tourism.
Denmark	**Total**	Including non-commercial tourism. 2011: change of methodology.
France	**Total**	Source: "Dge", "Banque de France". Non resident visitor survey ("EVE") - results 2012 revised, results 2013 provisional.
	All countries of North Africa	Algeria, Egypt, Libya, Morocco and Tunisia.
	China	Including Hong Kong, China, and Macao, China.
	Switzerland	Including Liechtenstein.
Germany	**China**	Including Hong Kong, China.
	Other countries East Asia/Pacific	Including India.
Ireland	**Total**	Including overnights in private homes and holiday homes where no payment is made.
	United Kingdom	Including Northern Ireland residents.
Jamaica	**Total**	Information obtained by multiplying the average length of stay by the number of stop-overs of each country origin. Excluding nationals residing abroad.
	Other countries of the Americas	Latin America.
	All countries of Europe	United Kingdom and rest of Europe.
Malta	**Total**	Data based on overnights spent by departing tourists (by air and by sea). Source: National Statistics Office
Netherlands	**Total**	Excluding overnight stays at fixed pitches (hired on a yearly or seasonal basis). 2013: break in the series because of methodological changes in determining the population.
Romania	**Other countries of Africa**	Including Egypt and Libya.
Spain	**Total**	Overnights in hotels, "hostales", camping, tourism apartments and rural dwellings.

NOTES 2009 - 2013

1. Arrivées de touristes non résidents aux frontières nationales, par nationalité

Bélarus	**Total**	Tourisme organisé.
Bhoutan	**Total**	Total des arrivées 2010: 40.873; 2011: 65.756; 2012: 105.407; 2013: 116.209. L'écart important que l'on peut observer en 2010-2013 par rapport aux années précédentes tient au fait que l'on a inclus les touristes régionaux haut de gamme dans les totaux à partir de 2010.
Brunéi Darussalam	**Total**	Arrivées par voie aérienne.
Burundi	**Total**	Y compris les nationaux résidant à l'étranger. À partir de 2010: rupture de série due à la mise en œuvre d'une méthodologie améliorée qui distingue les visiteurs (touristes) des autres voyageurs.
Chili	**Total**	Y compris les nationaux résidant à l'étranger.
Comores	**Total**	Arrivées par voie aérienne.
Gambie	**Total**	Arrivées en vols à la demande seulement.
Guinée	**Total**	Arrivées par voie aérienne à l'aéroport de Conakry.
Honduras	**Total**	À l'exclusion des arrivées de touristes par voie maritime.
Îles Marshall	**Total**	Arrivées par voie aérienne. 2009: arrivées par voies aérienne et maritime.
Inde	**Total**	À l'exclusion des nationaux résidant à l'étranger.
Islande	**Total**	Source: "Icelandic Tourist Board". 2012, 2013: arrivées à l'aéroport Keflavik seulement.
Italie	**Total**	À l'exclusion des travailleurs saisonniers et frontaliers.
Kiribati	**Total**	Arrivées par voie aérienne. Tarawa et Île Christmas.
Liban	**Total**	À l'exclusion des nationaux résidant à l'étranger, Syriens et Palestiniens.
Maldives	**Total**	Arrivées par voie aérienne.
Mali	**Total**	2012: arrivées par voie aérienne uniquement (aéroport de Bamako-Sénou).
Malte	**Total**	Données tirées des départs par voies aérienne et maritime. Source: "National Statistics Office"
Mexique	**États-Unis d'Amérique**	Y compris les arrivées de touristes par voie aérienne et terrestre, les touristes frontaliers et les touristes nationaux résidant aux États-Unis d'Amérique.
	Autres pays du monde	Y compris les touristes frontaliers de la zone méridionale.
Népal	**Grèce**	Y compris Chypre.
Norvège	**Total**	2009-2011 : les chiffres se fondent sur l'enquête auprès des visiteurs de "Institute of Transport Economics". À partir de 2012, l'enquête a été interrompue.
Paraguay	**Total**	À l'exclusion des nationaux résidant à l'étranger et des membres des équipages. Cartes d'embarquement et de débarquement à l'aéroport Silvio Petirossi et comptages des passagers lors du franchissement des frontières nationales – Police nationale et SENATUR.
République centrafricaine	**Total**	Arrivées par voie aérienne à Bangui uniquement.
République démocratique du Congo	**Total**	2009, 2010 : arrivées par voie aérienne uniquement ; 2011-2013 : les données des entrées ne concernent que 3 postes frontaliers (aéroport de N'Djili à Kinshasa ; aéroport de la Luano à Lubumbashi et le poste terrestre de Kasumbalesa de la province du Katanga).
Saint-Martin	**Total**	Arrivées à l'aéroport international "Princess Juliana". Y compris les visiteurs à St. Martin (partie française de l'île).
	France	Y compris les résidents des Antilles françaises.
Soudan	**Total**	Y compris les nationaux résidant à l'étranger.
Sri Lanka	**Total**	À l'exclusion des nationaux résidant à l'étranger.
	Chine	2013: y compris Hong-Kong (Chine) et Macao (Chine).

NOTES 2009 - 2013

1. Arrivées de touristes non résidents aux frontières nationales, par nationalité

Tunisie	**Total**	À l'exclusion des nationaux résidant à l'étranger.
Turquie	**Total**	Y compris les citoyens turcs résidant à l'étranger.
Yémen	**Total**	Y compris les nationaux résidant à l'étranger.

Yearbook of Tourism Statistics, Data 2009 – 2013, 2015 Edition

NOTES 2009 - 2013

1. Arrivées de touristes non résidents aux frontières nationales, par pays de résidence

Afrique du Sud	**Total**	À partir de 2009, une nouvelle méthodologie a été appliquée. L'information n'est donc pas comparable à celle des années précédentes.
Andorre	**Total**	En 2009 et 2011, des changements ont été apportés à la méthodologie de calcul du nombre de visiteurs du pays. De ce fait, la comparabilité des données obtenues à l'aide des différentes méthodologies n'est pas possible, car les variations reflètent les variations du nombre de visiteurs mais également les variations induites par les changements méthodologiques.
Anguilla	**Total**	À l'exclusion des nationaux résidant à l'étranger.
Antigua-et-Barbuda	**Total**	Arrivées par voie aérienne. À l'exclusion des nationaux résidant à l'étranger.
Bermudes	**Total**	Arrivées par voie aérienne.
Canada	**Total**	Source: "Canadian Tourism Commission" et "Statistics Canada"
	Autres pays d'Afrique	Y compris Archipel des Chagos, Île de l'Ascension et Tristan da Cunha.
	Panama	Y compris la Zone du Canal de Panama.
	Autres pays d'Océanie	Y compris Archipel Bismarck, Îles Marquises, Île Pitcairn et Archipel des Tuamotu.
Colombie	**Total**	Source : Département administratif de sécurité (DAS) / « Migración Colombia ». Données provisoires. À l'exclusion des croisiéristes. 2010-2013 : arrivées de touristes non-résidents par des contrôles d'immigration. 2011-2013 : y compris les nationaux résidant à l'étranger. 2009 : données par nationalité.
Curaçao	**Total**	Arrivées par voie aérienne.
Espagne	**Total**	2012: données provisoires.
États-Unis d'Amérique	**Canada**	Les données historiques peuvent refléter les révisions apportées par "Statistics Canada".
	Mexique	Les données historiques peuvent refléter les révisions apportées par "Banco de México".
Éthiopie	**Total**	Arrivées à travers tous les ports d'entrée.
Fidji	**Total**	À l'exclusion des nationaux résidant à l'étranger.
France	**Total**	Source: Dge, Banque de France. Enquête auprès des visiteurs venant de l'étranger (EVE) – résultats 2012 révisés, résultats 2013 provisoires.
	Toutes pays Afrique du Nord	Algérie, Égypte, Libye, Maroc et Tunisie.
	Chine	Y compris Hong-Kong (Chine) et Macao (Chine).
	Suisse	Y compris Liechtenstein.
Grèce	**Total**	L'information est basée sur l'enquête aux frontières réalisée par la Banque de Grèce.
	Égypte	Y compris Soudan.
	Liban	Y compris République arabe syrienne.
Guadeloupe	**Total**	Arrivées par voie aérienne. 2013: y compris résidents et non résidents. Source: Logiciel OAG Aviation.
Guinée	**Total**	Arrivées par voie aérienne à l'aéroport de Conakry.
Guyane	**Total**	Arrivées à l'aéroport de Timehri seulement.
Haïti	**Total**	Arrivées par voie aérienne. Les nationaux résidant à l'étranger sont inclus.
Îles Caïmanes	**Total**	Arrivées par voie aérienne.
Îles Cook	**Total**	Arrivées par voies aérienne et maritime.
Îles Marshall	**Total**	Arrivées par voie aérienne. 2009: arrivées par voies aérienne et maritime.

NOTES 2009 - 2013

1. Arrivées de touristes non résidents aux frontières nationales, par pays de résidence

Irlande	**Royaume-Uni**	Y compris les arrivées des résidents de l'Irlande du nord. Changement de méthodologie de l'estimation des touristes d'Irlande du Nord en 2010; par conséquent les chiffres antérieurs à 2010 ne sont pas directement comparables.
Israël	**Total**	À l'exclusion des nationaux résidant à l'étranger.
Jamaïque	**Total**	Arrivées par voie aérienne. Y compris les nationaux résidants à l'étranger.
Malaisie	**Total**	Y compris les résidents de Singapour traversant la frontière par voie terrestre à travers le Johore Causeway.
Malawi	**Total**	Départs.
Mali	**Total**	2013: arrivées par voie aérienne uniquement (aéroport de Bamako-Sénou).
Martinique	**Total**	Y compris les départements et territoires français d'outremer.
Mexique	**Total**	Y compris les nationaux résidant à l'étranger.
Micronésie (États fédérés de)	**Total**	Arrivées dans les États de Kosrae, Chuuk, Pohnpei et Yap.
Népal	**Grèce**	Y compris Chypre.
Nioué	**Total**	Y compris les nationaux de Niue résidant habituellement en Nouvelle-Zélande.
Nouvelle-Calédonie	**Total**	Y compris les nationaux résidant à l'étranger.
	Toutes pays Caraïbes	Martinique, Guadeloupe et Guyane.
Palaos	**Total**	Arrivées par voie aérienne (aéroport international de Palaos).
Pérou	**Total**	Y compris les nationaux résidant à l'étranger. Données préliminaires.
Philippines	**Nationaux résidents à l'étranger**	Titulaires d'un passeport philippin résidant en permanence à l'étranger; travailleurs philippins exclus.
Polynésie française	**Total**	Arrivées par voie aérienne. À l'exclusion des nationaux résidant à l'étranger.
	Samoa	Y compris les Samoa américaines.
Porto Rico	**Total**	Arrivées par voie aérienne. Année fiscale de juillet à juin. Source: "Junta de Planificación de Puerto Rico".
République dominicaine	**Total**	Arrivées par voie aérienne.
Réunion	**Total**	Source: INSEE - Enquête flux touristiques
	Toutes les pays d'Afrique	Océan Indien.
Sainte-Lucie	**Total**	À l'exclusion des nationaux résidant à l'étranger.
Saint-Eustache	**Total**	À l'exclusion des résidents des Antilles néerlandaises.
Saint-Kitts-et-Nevis	**Total**	Arrivées par voie aérienne.
Saint-Vincent-et-les Grenadines	**Total**	Arrivées par voie aérienne.
Sierra Leone	**Total**	Arrivées par voie aérienne.
Sri Lanka	**Total**	À l'exclusion des nationaux résidant à l'étranger.
Timor-Leste	**Total**	Arrivées par voie aérienne à l'aéroport de Dili.
Tonga	**Total**	Arrivées par voie aérienne.
Trinité-et-Tobago	**Total**	Arrivées par voie aérienne. 2011-2013: données par nationalité.

Yearbook of Tourism Statistics, Data 2009 – 2013, 2015 Edition

NOTES 2009 - 2013

2. Arrivées de visiteurs non résidents aux frontières nationales, par nationalité

Albanie	Total	À l'exclusion des nationaux résidant à l'étranger.
Algérie	Total	Y compris les nationaux résidant à l'étranger.
Bahreïn	Total	À l'exclusion des nationaux résidant à l'étranger.
Belize	Total	Y compris passagers en transit et passagers à la frontière.
Brunéi Darussalam	Total	Arrivées par voie aérienne, par croisière et aux frontières.
Corée (République de)	Total	Y compris les nationaux résidant à l'étranger et les membres des équipages.
Égypte	Total	À l'exclusion des nationaux résidant à l'étranger.
Équateur	Total	À l'exclusion des nationaux résidant à l'étranger.
Italie	Total	Enquête aux frontières. À l'exclusion des travailleurs saisonniers et frontaliers.
Japon	Total	À l'exclusion des nationaux résidant à l'étranger.
Macao (Chine)	Total	Source des données: Police de sécurité publique
Nigéria	Total	Source: "Nigerian Tourism Development Corporation (NTDC)"
Pologne	Total	Depuis que la Pologne est entrée dans l'espace Schengen, le comptage précis du trafic entrant n'est pas possible. Les données présentées ici sont basées sur les enquêtes de l'Institut du Tourisme. Seuls des résultats approximatifs des principaux pays peuvent être fournis.
République arabe syrienne	Total	Enquête du tourisme récepteur.
République de Moldova	Total	Visiteurs qui ont bénéficié des services touristiques des agences de tourisme et des voyagistes (titulaires d'une licence touristique). À l'exception de la rive gauche de la rivière Nistru et de la municipalité de Bender.
Singapour	Total	À l'exclusion des arrivées de Malaisiens par voie terrestre.
	Hong-Kong (Chine)	Depuis 2013 est inclus en Chine.
	Macao (Chine)	Depuis 2013 est inclus en Chine.
Turquie	Total	Y compris les citoyens turcs résidant à l'étranger.
Uruguay	Total	À l'exclusion des arrivées des croisiéristes.

Yearbook of Tourism Statistics, Data 2009 – 2013, 2015 Edition

NOTES 2009 - 2013

2. Arrivées de visiteurs non résidents aux frontières nationales, par pays de résidence

Afrique du Sud	**Total**	À partir de 2009, une nouvelle méthodologie a été appliquée. L'information n'est donc pas comparable à celle des années précédentes.
Australie	**Total**	À l'exclusion des nationaux résidant à l'étranger et les membres des équipages. Source: "Australian Bureau of Statistics"
Canada	**Total**	Source: "Canadian Tourism Commission" et "Statistics Canada"
	Chine	Y compris Mongolie et Tibet.
	Estonie	Y compris Lettonie et Lituanie.
	Hongrie	Y compris Slovénie, Bulgarie et Roumanie.
	Danemark	Y compris Îles Féroé.
	Royaume-Uni	Y compris Gibraltar.
	Italie	Y compris Saint-Marin, Saint Siège et Malte.
	Yougoslavie, SFR (ancienne)	Y compris Croatie, Bosnie-Herzégovine, Ex-République yougoslave de Macédoine et Albanie.
	France	Y compris Andorre et Monaco.
	Suisse	Y compris Liechtenstein.
Congo	**Total**	Source: Direction Générale du Tourisme et de l'Hôtellerie, enquêtes 2011-2013
Finlande	**Total**	Enquête aux frontières. Note: l'enquête a été annulée à la fin de 2012
Hong-Kong (Chine)	**États-Unis d'Amérique**	Y compris Guam.
	Nouvelle-Zélande	Y compris Îles Cook.
	France	Y compris Nouvelle-Calédonie et Polynésie française.
Israël	**Total**	À l'exclusion des nationaux résidant à l'étranger.
Lettonie	**Total**	Départs des non-résidents. Enquête auprès des personnes qui traversent les frontières du pays.
Macao (Chine)	**Total**	Source des données: Police de sécurité publique
Mozambique	**Total**	Arrivées à tous les postes frontaliers du pays.
Nouvelle-Zélande	**Total**	Les données relatives aux mouvements de courte durée sont obtenues à partir d'un échantillon aléatoire de déclarations des passagers. Y compris les nationaux résidant à l'étranger. Source: Statistiques de la Nouvelle Zélande ("International Travel and Migration").
Panama	**Total**	Nombre total de visiteurs arrivés au Panama par l'aéroport international de Tocumen, classés selon leur résidence permanente.
Saint-Vincent-et-les Grenadines	**Total**	Arrivées par voie aérienne.
Singapour	**Total**	À l'exclusion des arrivées de Malaisiens par voie terrestre.
Suède	**Total**	Données pour 2011 et 2012 d'après la nouvelle enquête aux frontières nationales (IBIS, visiteurs entrant en Suède). Pas de données recueillies en 2009 et 2010. La nouvelle enquête à la frontière (IBIS) a commencé en 2011. Source : "Swedish Agency for Economic and Regional Growth".

835

NOTES 2009 - 2013

3. Arrivées de touristes non résidents dans les hôtels et établissements assimilés, par nationalité

Bolivie	**Total**	Données préliminaires. Mouvement hôtelier dans les capitales de département.
Italie	**Total**	Arrivées dans les hôtels uniquement.
Maroc	**Total**	Arrivées dans les hôtels homologués, villages de vacances, résidences touristiques et Riad.
Monténégro	**Serbie**	Y compris les arrivées en provenance du Kosovo.
Palestine	**Total**	Source: "Palestinian Central Bureau of Statistics, 2014. Hotel Activity Survey 2013. Ramallah - Palestine". Les données sur l'activité hôtelière pour 2012 et 2013 répresentent la Cisjordanie seulement.
République arabe syrienne	**Total**	Enquête du tourisme récepteur.
Tchad	**Total**	2010: Données partielles.
Turquie	**Total**	Arrivées dans les établissements avec licence y compris: hôtels, motels, pensions, auberges, hôtels-appartements, villages de vacances et hôtels spéciaux. Résultats de l'enquête mensuelle réalisée auprès des établissements d'hébergement autorisés par le Ministère du Tourisme.

NOTES 2009 - 2013

3. Arrivées de touristes non résidents dans les hôtels et établissements assimilés, par pays de résidence

Allemagne	Chine	Y compris Hong-Kong (Chine).
	Autres pays Asie Est/Pacifique	Y compris l'Inde.
Autriche	Total	Hôtels uniquement.
Cabo Verde	Belgique	Y compris les Pays-Bas.
Congo	Total	Source: Direction Générale du Tourisme et de l'Hôtellerie, enquêtes 2009 à 2013.
Croatie	Total	Conformément au Règlement sur la classification, les normes minimales et la catégorisation des structures d'hébergement, les données relatives aux hôtels et établissements assimilés ne comprennent pas les auberges et chambres d'hôtes depuis 2006.
Curaçao	Total	Grands et petits hôtels, pensions de famille, appartements et bungalows.
Danemark	Total	Hôtels uniquement. 2011: changement de méthodologie.
Espagne	Total	Arrivées dans les hôtels et les "hostales" (établissements d'hébergement offrant des services limités).
France	Total	Source: Insee, Dge, partenaires régionaux. Enquête de fréquentation hôtelière (EFH).
Guinée	Total	Arrivées par voie aérienne à l'aéroport de Conakry.
Israël	Total	Arrivées dans les hôtels de tourisme et hôtels encore non répertoriés.
	Toutes pays Amérique du Sud	Y compris Amérique centrale.
Luxembourg	Total	NACE Rev2 55.100
Macao (Chine)	Total	Source des données: Enquête mensuelle auprès des agences de voyage
Nouvelle-Calédonie	Total	Il s'agit des hôtels de Nouméa.
Pays-Bas	Total	2013: rupture de série due aux changements méthodologiques dans la détermination de la population.
Pologne	Total	À l'exclusion des hôtelleries.
Porto Rico	Total	Année fiscale de juillet à juin. Hôtels enregistrés par la "Compañía de Turismo de Puerto Rico".
	Autres pays Caraïbes	Les données agrégées des touristes en provenance des petites Antilles qui n'ont pas spécifié leur pays d'origine sont incluses.
	Autres pays du monde	Y compris les membres des équipages.
Roumanie	Autres pays d'Afrique	Y compris Égypte et Libye.
Suisse	Total	Y compris les établissements de cure.
	Toutes pays Afrique du Nord	Algérie, Libye, Maroc et Tunisie.
Thaïlande	Total	2012, 2013: hôtels uniquement.
Togo	Burkina Faso	Y compris Mali et Niger.

NOTES 2009 - 2013

4. Arrivées de touristes non résidents dans tous les types d'établissements d'hébergement, par nationalité

Hongrie	**Total**	Établissements d'hébergement collectif.
Monténégro	**Serbie**	Y compris les arrivées en provenance du Kosovo.
République arabe syrienne	**Total**	À l'exclusion de l'hébergement chez des particuliers. Enquête du tourisme récepteur.
République de Moldova	**Total**	À l'exception de la rive gauche de la rivière Nistru et de la municipalité de Bender.
Turquie	**Total**	Résultats de l'enquête mensuelle réalisée auprès des établissements d'hébergement autorisés par le Ministère du Tourisme.

NOTES 2009 - 2013

4. Arrivées de touristes non résidents dans tous les types d'établissements d'hébergement, par pays de résidence

Allemagne	**Chine**	Y compris Hong-Kong (Chine).
	Autres pays Asie Est/Pacifique	Y compris l'Inde.
Autriche	**Total**	Seulement logement commercial; sont exclus les séjours chez des parents et amis, et les résidences secondaires.
Belgique	**Total**	Établissements hôteliers, terrains de camping, centres de vacances, villages de vacances et catégories spécifiques d'hébergement. À partir de 2012 les chambres d'hôtes sont incluses.
Croatie	**Total**	À l'exclusion des arrivées dans des ports à tourisme nautique.
Danemark	**Total**	Y compris le tourisme non commercial. 2011: changement de méthodologie.
Espagne	**Total**	Arrivées dans hôtels, "hostales", camping, appartements touristiques et logements ruraux.
Malte	**Total**	Données tirées des départs par voies aérienne et maritime. Source: "National Statistics Office"
Pays-Bas	**Total**	2013: rupture de série due aux changements méthodologiques dans la détermination de la population.
Philippines	**Total**	Arrivées par voie aérienne.
	Nationaux résidents à l'étranger	Titulaires d'un passeport philippin résidant en permanence à l'étranger; travailleurs philippins exclus.
Roumanie	**Autres pays d'Afrique**	Y compris Égypte et Libye.

NOTES 2009 - 2013

5. Nuitées de touristes non résidents dans les hôtels et établissements assimilés, par nationalité

Bolivie	**Total**	Données préliminaires. Nuitées dans les capitales de département.
Italie	**Total**	Nuitées dans les hôtels uniquement.
Madagascar	**Total**	Établissements de classe étoile (classés et non classés).
Maroc	**Total**	Nuitées dans les hôtels homologués, villages de vacances, résidences touristiques et Riad.
Monténégro	**Serbie**	Y compris les arrivées en provenance du Kosovo.
Norvège	**Total**	Nuitées dans les établissements enregistrés. Les données ne couvrent que les établissements avec une capacité d'au moins 20 lits.
Palestine	**Total**	Source: "Palestinian Central Bureau of Statistics, 2014. Hotel Activity Survey 2013. Ramallah - Palestine". Les données sur l'activité hôtelière pour 2012 et 2013 répresentent la Cisjordanie seulement.
République arabe syrienne	**Total**	Enquête du tourisme récepteur.
Tchad	**Total**	2010: Données partielles.
Turquie	**Total**	Hôtels classés, motels, pensions de familles, auberges, aparthôtels, villages de vacances et hôtels spéciaux. Résultats de l'enquête mensuelle réalisée auprès des établissements d'hébergement autorisés par le Ministère du Tourisme.
Yémen	**Total**	Y compris les nationaux résidant à l'étranger.

5. Nuitées de touristes non résidents dans les hôtels et établissements assimilés, par pays de résidence

Allemagne	Chine	Y compris Hong-Kong (Chine).
	Autres pays Asie Est/Pacifique	Y compris l'Inde.
Autriche	Total	Hôtels uniquement.
Cabo Verde	Belgique	Y compris les Pays-Bas.
Congo	Total	Source: Direction Générale du Tourisme et de l'Hôtellerie, enquêtes 2009 à 2013.
Croatie	Total	Conformément au Règlement sur la classification, les normes minimales et la catégorisation des structures d'hébergement, les données relatives aux hôtels et établissements assimilés ne comprennent pas les auberges et chambres d'hôtes depuis 2006.
Danemark	Total	Hôtels uniquement. 2011: changement de méthodologie.
Espagne	Total	Nuitées dans les hôtels et les "hostales" (établissements d'hébergement offrant des services limités).
France	Total	Source: Insee, Dge, partenaires régionaux. Enquête de fréquentation hôtelière (EFH).
Israël	Total	Nuitées dans les hôtels de tourisme et aparthôtels.
	Toutes pays Amérique du Sud	Y compris Amérique centrale.
Luxembourg	Total	NACE Rev2 55.100
Macao (Chine)	Total	Source des données: Enquête mensuelle auprès des hôtels et établissements assimilés
Nouvelle-Calédonie	Total	Il s'agit des hôtels de Nouméa.
Pays-Bas	Total	2013: rupture de série due aux changements méthodologiques dans la détermination de la population.
Pologne	Total	À l'exclusion des hôtelleries.
Roumanie	Autres pays d'Afrique	Y compris Égypte et Libye.
Suisse	Total	Y compris les établissements de cure.
	Toutes pays Afrique du Nord	Algérie, Libye, Maroc et Tunisie.
Togo	Burkina Faso	Y compris Mali et Niger.

6. Nuitées de touristes non résidents dans tous les types d'établissements d'hébergement, par nationalité

Hongrie	**Total**	Établissements d'hébergement collectif.
Monténégro	**Serbie**	Y compris les arrivées en provenance du Kosovo.
République arabe syrienne	**Total**	Enquête du tourisme récepteur.
République de Moldova	**Total**	À l'exception de la rive gauche de la rivière Nistru et de la municipalité de Bender.
Turquie	**Total**	Résultats de l'enquête mensuelle réalisée auprès des établissements d'hébergement autorisés par le Ministère du Tourisme.

NOTES 2009 - 2013

6. Nuitées de touristes non résidents dans tous les types d'établissements d'hébergement, par pays de résidence

Allemagne	**Chine**	Y compris Hong-Kong (Chine).
	Autres pays Asie Est/Pacifique	Y compris l'Inde.
Autriche	**Total**	Seulement logement commercial; sont exclus les séjours chez des parents et amis, et les résidences secondaires.
Bahamas	**Total**	Nuitées dans tout moyen d'hébergement commercial.
Belgique	**Total**	Établissements hôteliers, terrains de camping, centres de vacances, villages de vacances et catégories spécifiques d'hébergement. À partir de 2012 les chambres d'hôtes sont incluses.
Canada	**Total**	Source: "Canadian Tourism Commission" et "Statistics Canada"
	Chine	Y compris Mongolie et Tibet.
	Estonie	Y compris Lettonie et Lituanie.
	Hongrie	Y compris Slovénie, Bulgarie et Roumanie.
	Danemark	Y compris Îles Féroé.
	Royaume-Uni	Y compris Gibraltar.
	Italie	Y compris Saint-Marin, Saint Siège et Malte.
	Yougoslavie, SFR (ancienne)	Y compris Croatie, Bosnie-Herzégovine, Ex-République yougoslave de Macédoine et Albanie.
	France	Y compris Andorre et Monaco.
	Suisse	Y compris Liechtenstein.
Croatie	**Total**	À l'exclusion des nuitées dans des ports à tourisme nautique.
Danemark	**Total**	Y compris le tourisme non commercial. 2011: changement de méthodologie.
Espagne	**Total**	Nuitées dans hôtels, "hostales", camping, appartements touristiques et logements ruraux.
France	**Total**	Source: Dge, Banque de France. Enquête auprès des visiteurs venant de l'étranger (EVE) – résultats 2012 révisés, résultats 2013 provisoires.
	Toutes pays Afrique du Nord	Algérie, Égypte, Libye, Maroc et Tunisie.
	Chine	Y compris Hong-Kong (Chine) et Macao (Chine).
	Suisse	Y compris Liechtenstein.
Irlande	**Total**	Y compris nuitées dans hébergement privé non payant (maisons privées et maisons de vacances).
	Royaume-Uni	Y compris les résidents de l'Irlande du Nord.
Jamaïque	**Total**	L'information à été obtenue en multipliant la durée moyenne de séjour par le nombre de touristes (stop-over) provenant de chaque pays d'origine. À l'exclusion des nationaux résidant à l'étranger.
	Autres pays Amériques	Amérique latine.
	Toutes pays d'Europe	Royaume-Uni et le reste de l'Europe.
Malte	**Total**	Données basées sur les nuitées passées par les touristes sortants (par voie aérienne et voie maritime). Source: "National Statistics Office"
Pays-Bas	**Total**	À l'exclusion des nuitées dans des installations fixes (louées sur une base annuelle ou saisonnière). 2013: rupture de série due aux changements méthodologiques dans la détermination de la population.
Roumanie	**Autres pays d'Afrique**	Y compris Égypte et Libye.

Yearbook of Tourism Statistics, Data 2009 – 2013, 2015 Edition

NOTAS 2009 - 2013

1. Llegadas de turistas no residentes en las fronteras nacionales, por nacionalidad

Belarús	**Total**	Turismo organizado.
Bhután	**Total**	Total de llegadas 2010: 40.873; 2011: 65.756; 2012: 105.407; 2013: 116.209. El gran margen de diferencia en 2010-2013 en comparación con los años anteriores se debe a que a partir de 2010 se incluyen en las cifras totales los turistas regionales de alto nivel de renta.
Brunei Darussalam	**Total**	Llegadas por vía aérea.
Burundi	**Total**	Incluidos los nacionales residentes en el extranjero. A partir de 2010: ruptura en la serie debido a la implementación de una mejora en la metodología que distingue a los visitantes (turistas) de otros viajeros.
Chile	**Total**	Incluidos los nacionales residentes en el extranjero.
Comoras	**Total**	Llegadas por vía aérea.
Gambia	**Total**	Llegadas en vuelos fletados únicamente.
Guinea	**Total**	Llegadas por vía aérea al aeropuerto de Conakry.
Honduras	**Total**	Excluidas las llegadas de turistas por vía marítima.
India	**Total**	Excluidos los nacionales residentes en el extranjero.
Islandia	**Total**	Fuente: "Icelandic Tourist Board". 2012, 2013: llegadas al aeropuerto Keflavik únicamente.
Islas Marshall	**Total**	Llegadas por vía aérea. 2009: llegadas por vías aérea y marítima.
Italia	**Total**	Excluidos los trabajadores estacionales y fronterizos.
Kiribati	**Total**	Llegadas por vía aérea. Tarawa e Isla Christmas.
Líbano	**Total**	Excluidos los nacionales residentes en el extranjero, Sirios y Palestinos.
Maldivas	**Total**	Llegadas por vía aérea.
Malí	**Total**	2012: llegadas por vía aérea únicamente (aeropuerto de Bamako-Sénou).
Malta	**Total**	Datos procedentes de las salidas por vías aérea y marítima. Fuente: "National Statistics Office"
México	**Estados Unidos de América**	Incluidas las llegadas de turistas de internación por vía aérea y terrestre, de turistas fronterizos y de turistas nacionales residentes en los Estados Unidos de América.
	Otros países del Mundo	Incluidos los turistas fronterizos de la zona sur.
Nepal	**Grecia**	Incluido Chipre.
Noruega	**Total**	2009-2011: las cifras se basan en la encuesta de los visitantes, un estudio realizado por el "Institute of Transport Economics". A partir de 2012 la encuesta ha sido suspendida.
Paraguay	**Total**	Excluidos los nacionales residentes en el extranjero y los miembros de tripulaciones. Tarjetas E/D en el aeropuerto Silvio Petirossi y planillas de pasajeros en los puestos terrestres - Policía Nacional y SENATUR.
República Centroafricana	**Total**	Llegadas por vía aérea a Bangui únicamente.
República Democrática del Congo	**Total**	2009, 2010: llegadas por vía aérea únicamente; 2011-2013: los datos de entradas se refieren sólo a 3 puestos fronterizos (aeropuerto de N'Djili, en Kinshasa; aeropuerto de Luano, en Lubumbashi, y puesto terrestre de Kasumbalesa, en la provincia de Katanga).
San Martín	**Total**	Llegadas al aeropuerto internacional "Princess Juliana". Incluidos los visitantes a San Martín (parte francesa de la isla).
	Francia	Incluidos los residentes de las Antillas Francesas.
Sri Lanka	**Total**	Excluidos los nacionales residentes en el extranjero.
	China	2013: incluidos Hong-Kong (China) y Macao (China).
Sudán	**Total**	Incluidos los nacionales residentes en el extranjero.

Yearbook of Tourism Statistics, Data 2009 – 2013, 2015 Edition

NOTAS 2009 - 2013

1. Llegadas de turistas no residentes en las fronteras nacionales, por nacionalidad

Túnez	**Total**	Excluidos los nacionales residentes en el extranjero.
Turquía	**Total**	Incluidos los ciudadanos turcos residentes en el extranjero.
Yemen	**Total**	Incluidos los nacionales residentes en el extranjero.

Yearbook of Tourism Statistics, Data 2009 – 2013, 2015 Edition

NOTAS 2009 - 2013

1. Llegadas de turistas no residentes en las fronteras nacionales, por país de residencia

Andorra	**Total**	En 2009 y 2011 se produjeron cambios en la metodología de cálculo del número de visitantes del país. En éste sentido, la comparabilidad de los datos obtenidos con diferentes metodologías no es posible porque las variaciones recogen la variación del número de visitantes, pero también las variaciones motivadas por los cambios metodológicos.
Anguila	**Total**	Excluidos los nacionales residentes en el extranjero.
Antigua y Barbuda	**Total**	Llegadas por vía aérea. Excluidos los nacionales residentes en el extranjero.
Bermuda	**Total**	Llegadas por vía aérea.
Canadá	**Total**	Fuente: "Canadian Tourism Commission" y "Statistics Canada"
	Otros países de África	Incluidos Archipiélago de Chagos , Isla Ascención y Tristán de Acuña.
	Panamá	Incluida la Zona del Canal de Panamá.
	Otros países de Oceanía	Incluidos Archipiélago Bismarck, Islas Marquesas, Isla Pitcairn y Archipiélago Tuamotu.
Colombia	**Total**	Fuente: Departamento Administrativo de Seguridad (DAS) / Migración Colombia. Datos provisionales. Excluidos los pasajeros en crucero. 2010-2013: llegadas de turistas no residentes por puntos de control migratorio. 2011-2013: incluidos los nacionales residentes en el extranjero. 2009: datos por nacionalidad.
Curaçao	**Total**	Llegadas por vía aérea.
España	**Total**	2012: datos provisionales.
Estados Unidos de América	**Canadá**	Los datos históricos pueden reflejar revisiones hechas por "Statistics Canada".
	México	Los datos históricos pueden reflejar revisiones hechas por "Banco de México".
Etiopía	**Total**	Llegadas a todos los puestos fronterizos.
Fiji	**Total**	Excluidos los nacionales residentes en el extranjero.
Filipinas	**Nacionales residentes en el extranjero**	Titulares de pasaportes filipinos que residen permanentemente en el extranjero; están excluidos los trabajadores filipinos.
Francia	**Total**	Fuente: "Dge", "Banque de France". Encuesta a los visitantes que vienen del extranjero ("EVE") - resultados 2012 revisados, resultados 2013 provisionales.
	Todos los países de África del Norte	Argelia, Egipto, Libia, Marruecos y Túnez.
	China	Incluidos Hong-Kong (China) y Macao (China).
	Suiza	Incluido Liechtentein.
Grecia	**Total**	La información se basa en la encuesta en fronteras realizada por el Banco de Grecia.
	Egipto	Incluido Sudán.
	Líbano	Incluida República Árabe Siria.
Guadalupe	**Total**	Llegadas por vía aérea. 2013: incluye residentes y no residentes. Fuente: Software Aviación OAG.
Guinea	**Total**	Llegadas por vía aérea al aeropuerto de Conakry.
Guyana	**Total**	Llegadas al aeropuerto de Timehri únicamente.
Haití	**Total**	Llegadas por vía aérea. Se incluye a los nacionales residentes en el extranjero.
Irlanda	**Reino Unido**	Incluidas las llegadas de los residentes de Irlanda del Norte. Cambio en la metodología de estimación de turistas del norte de Irlanda en 2010; como resultado las cifras anteriores a 2010 no son directamente comparables.
Islas Caimán	**Total**	Llegadas por vía aérea.

NOTAS 2009 - 2013

1. Llegadas de turistas no residentes en las fronteras nacionales, por país de residencia

Islas Cook	**Total**	Llegadas por vías aérea y marítima.
Islas Marshall	**Total**	Llegadas por vía aérea. 2009: llegadas por vías aérea y marítima.
Israel	**Total**	Excluidos los nacionales residentes en el extranjero.
Jamaica	**Total**	Llegadas por vía aérea. Incluidos los nacionales residentes en el extranjero.
Malasia	**Total**	Incluidos residentes de Singapur que atraviesan la frontera por vía terrestre a través de Johore Causeway.
Malawi	**Total**	Salidas.
Malí	**Total**	2013: llegadas por vía aérea únicamente (aeropuerto de Bamako-Sénou).
Martinica	**Total**	Incluidos los departamentos y territorios franceses de ultramar.
México	**Total**	Incluidos los nacionales residentes en el extranjero.
Micronesia (Estados Federados de)	**Total**	Llegadas en los Estados de Kosrae, Chuuk, Pohnpei y Yap.
Nepal	**Grecia**	Incluido Chipre.
Niue	**Total**	Incluidos los nacionales de Niue que residen habitualmente en Nueva Zelandia.
Nueva Caledonia	**Total**	Incluidos los nacionales residentes en el extranjero.
	Todos los países del Caribe	Martinica, Guadalupe y Guyana.
Palau	**Total**	Llegadas por vía aérea (aeropuerto internacional de Palau).
Perú	**Total**	Incluidos los nacionales residentes en el extranjero. Datos preliminares.
Polinesia Francesa	**Total**	Llegadas por vía aérea. Excluidos los nacionales residentes en el extranjero.
	Samoa	Incluida Samoa americana.
Puerto Rico	**Total**	Llegadas por vía aérea. Año fiscal de julio a junio. Fuente: Junta de Planificación de Puerto Rico.
República Dominicana	**Total**	Llegadas por vía aérea.
Reunión	**Total**	Fuente: INSEE, encuesta de flujos turísticos
	Todos los países de África	Océano Índico.
Saint Kitts y Nevis	**Total**	Llegadas por vía aérea.
San Eustaquio	**Total**	Excluidos los residentes de las Antillas neerlandesas.
San Vicente y las Granadinas	**Total**	Llegadas por vía aérea.
Santa Lucía	**Total**	Excluidos los nacionales residentes en el extranjero.
Sierra Leona	**Total**	Llegadas por vía aérea.
Sri Lanka	**Total**	Excluidos los nacionales residentes en el extranjero.
Sudáfrica	**Total**	A partir de 2009 se aplicó una nueva metodología y por lo tanto la información no es comparable con años anteriores.
Timor-Leste	**Total**	Llegadas por vía aérea al aeropuerto de Dili.
Tonga	**Total**	Llegadas por vía aérea.
Trinidad y Tabago	**Total**	Llegadas por vía aérea. 2011-2013: datos por nacionalidad.

NOTAS 2009 - 2013

2. Llegadas de visitantes no residentes en las fronteras nacionales, por nacionalidad

Albania	**Total**	Excluidos los nacionales residentes en el extranjero.
Argelia	**Total**	Incluidos los nacionales residentes en el extranjero.
Bahrein	**Total**	Excluidos los nacionales residentes en el extranjero.
Belice	**Total**	Incluidos pasajeros en tránsito y cruce de fronteras.
Brunei Darussalam	**Total**	Llegadas por vía aérea, en crucero y en las fronteras.
Corea (República de)	**Total**	Incluidos los nacionales residentes en el extranjero y los miembros de las tripulaciones.
Ecuador	**Total**	Excluidos los nacionales residentes en el extranjero.
Egipto	**Total**	Excluidos los nacionales residentes en el extranjero.
Italia	**Total**	Encuesta en fronteras. Excluidos los trabajadores estacionales y fronterizos.
Japón	**Total**	Excluidos los nacionales residentes en el extranjero.
Macao (China)	**Total**	Fuente de los datos: Policía de seguridad pública
Nigeria	**Total**	Fuente: "Nigerian Tourism Development Corporation (NTDC)"
Polonia	**Total**	Dado que Polonia se unió al espacio Schengen, el recuento preciso de tráfico entrante no es posible. Los datos presentados aquí se basan en encuestas realizadas por el Instituto de Turismo. Únicamente se cuenta con resultados aproximados de los principales países.
República Árabe Siria	**Total**	Encuesta del turismo receptor.
República de Moldova	**Total**	Visitantes que se beneficiaron de los servicios turísticos de las agencias de turismo y operadores turísticos (titulares de licencias turísticas). Excluido el margen izquierdo del río Nistru y la municipalidad de Bender.
Singapur	**Total**	Excluidas llegadas de los malasios por vía terrestre.
	Hong Kong (China)	Desde 2013 se incluye en China.
	Macao (China)	Desde 2013 se incluye en China.
Turquía	**Total**	Incluidos los ciudadanos turcos residentes en el extranjero.
Uruguay	**Total**	Excluidas las llegadas de pasajeros en crucero.

NOTAS 2009 - 2013

2. Llegadas de visitantes no residentes en las fronteras nacionales, por país de residencia

Australia	**Total**	Excluidos los nacionales residentes en el extranjero y los miembros de tripulaciones. Fuente: "Australian Bureau of Statistics"
Canadá	**Total**	Fuente: "Canadian Tourism Commission" y "Statistics Canada"
	China	Incluidos Mongolia y Tibet.
	Estonia	Incluidos Letonia y Lituania.
	Hungría	Incluidos Eslovenia, Bulgaria y Rumania.
	Dinamarca	Incluidas Islas Feroe.
	Reino Unido	Incluido Gibraltar.
	Italia	Incluidos San Marino, Santa Sede y Malta.
	Yugoslavia, RSF (antigua)	Incluidos Croacia, Bosnia y Herzegovina, Ex República Yugoslava de Macedonia y Albania.
	Francia	Incluidos Andorra y Mónaco.
	Suiza	Incluido Liechtenstein.
Congo	**Total**	Fuente: "Direction Générale du Tourisme et de l'Hôtellerie", encuestas 2011-2013
Finlandia	**Total**	Encuesta en las fronteras. Nota: la encuesta fue cancelada a finales de 2012
Hong Kong (China)	**Estados Unidos de América**	Incluido Guam.
	Nueva Zelandia	Incluidas Islas Cook.
	Francia	Incluidas Nueva Caledonia y Polinesia Francesa.
Israel	**Total**	Excluidos los nacionales residentes en el extranjero.
Letonia	**Total**	Salidas de no residentes. Encuesta realizada en los puestos fronterizos del país.
Macao (China)	**Total**	Fuente de los datos: Policía de seguridad pública
Mozambique	**Total**	Llegadas a todos los puestos fronterizos del país.
Nueva Zelandia	**Total**	Los datos relativos a los movimientos de corta duración se obtienen de una muestra aleatoria de declaraciones de los pasajeros. Incluidos los nacionales residentes en el extranjero. Fuente: Estadísticas Nueva Zelanda ("International Travel and Migration").
Panamá	**Total**	Total de visitantes ingresados a Panamá por el aeropuerto internacional de Tocumen según residencia permanente.
San Vicente y las Granadinas	**Total**	Llegadas por vía aérea.
Singapur	**Total**	Excluidas llegadas de los malasios por vía terrestre.
Sudáfrica	**Total**	A partir de 2009 se aplicó una nueva metodología y por lo tanto la información no es comparable con años anteriores.
Suecia	**Total**	Datos para 2011 y 2012 según una nueva encuesta nacional de fronteras (IBIS, visitantes que entran en Suecia). En 2009 y 2010 no se recopilaron datos. La nueva encuesta de fronteras (IBIS) se empezó a realizar en 2011. Fuente: "Swedish Agency for Economic and Regional Growth".

NOTAS 2009 - 2013

3. Llegadas de turistas no residentes a los hoteles y establecimientos asimilados, por nacionalidad

Bolivia	**Total**	Datos preliminares. Movimiento hotelero en las capitales de departamento.
Chad	**Total**	2010: Datos parciales.
Italia	**Total**	Llegadas a los hoteles únicamente.
Marruecos	**Total**	Llegadas en hoteles clasificados, ciudades de vacaciones, residencias turísticas y Riad.
Montenegro	**Serbia**	Incluidas las llegadas de Kosovo.
Palestina	**Total**	Fuente: "Palestinian Central Bureau of Statistics, 2014. Hotel Activity Survey 2013. Ramallah - Palestine". Los datos sobre la industria hotelera para 2012 y 2013 representan a Cisjordania únicamente.
República Árabe Siria	**Total**	Encuesta del turismo receptor.
Turquía	**Total**	Llegadas a los establecimientos con licencia incluidos: hoteles, moteles, pensiones, albergues, apartahoteles, ciudades de vacaciones y hoteles especiales. Resultados de la encuesta mensual realizada en ciertos establecimientos de alojamiento autorizados por el Ministerio de Turismo.

NOTAS 2009 - 2013

3. Llegadas de turistas no residentes a los hoteles y establecimientos asimilados, por país de residencia

Alemania	**China**	Incluido Hong Kong (China).
	Otros países Asia Oriental/Pacífico	Incluida India.
Austria	**Total**	Hoteles únicamente.
Cabo Verde	**Bélgica**	Incluido los Países Bajos.
Congo	**Total**	Fuente: "Direction Générale du Tourisme et de l'Hôtellerie", encuestas 2009 a 2013.
Croacia	**Total**	Según el Reglamento sobre clasificación, normas mínimas y categorización de las instalaciones de alojamiento, los datos para los hoteles y establecimientos asimilados no incluyen posadas ni "Bed and Breakfast" (habitación con desayuno) desde 2006.
Curaçao	**Total**	Grandes y pequeños hoteles, casas de huéspedes, apartamentos y bungalows.
Dinamarca	**Total**	Hoteles únicamente. 2011: cambio de metodología.
España	**Total**	Llegadas a hoteles y hostales.
Francia	**Total**	Fuente: "Insee", "Dge", socios regionales. Encuesta de ocupación hotelera ("EFH").
Guinea	**Total**	Llegadas por vía aérea al aeropuerto de Conakry.
Israel	**Total**	Llegadas a los hoteles de turismo y hoteles aún no registrados.
	Todos los países de América del Sur	Incluida América Central.
Luxemburgo	**Total**	NACE Rev2 55.100
Macao (China)	**Total**	Fuente de los datos: Encuesta mensual de agencias de viajes
Nueva Caledonia	**Total**	Corresponde a los hoteles de Noumea.
Países Bajos	**Total**	2013: ruptura en la serie debido a los cambios metodológicos en la determinación de la población.
Polonia	**Total**	Excluidos los hostales.
Puerto Rico	**Total**	Año fiscal de julio a junio. Hoteles endosados por la Compañía de Turismo de Puerto Rico.
	Otros países del Caribe	Se incluyen cifras agregadas de los turistas procedentes de las Antillas menores que no especificaron su país de procedencia.
	Otros países del Mundo	Incluidos los miembros de las tripulaciones.
Rumania	**Otros países de África**	Incluidos Egipto y Libia.
Suiza	**Total**	Incluidos los establecimientos de cura.
	Todos los países de África del Norte	Argelia, Libia, Marruecos y Túnez.
Tailandia	**Total**	2012, 2013: hoteles únicamente
Togo	**Burkina Faso**	Incluidos Malí y Níger.

NOTAS 2009 - 2013

4. Llegadas de turistas no residentes en todo tipo de establecimientos de alojamiento, por nacionalidad

Hungría	**Total**	Establecimientos de alojamiento colectivo.
Montenegro	**Serbia**	Incluidas las llegadas de Kosovo.
República Árabe Siria	**Total**	Excluido el alojamiento privado. Encuesta del turismo receptor.
República de Moldova	**Total**	Excluido el margen izquierdo del río Nistru y la municipalidad de Bender.
Turquía	**Total**	Resultados de la encuesta mensual realizada en ciertos establecimientos de alojamiento autorizados por el Ministerio de Turismo.

NOTAS 2009 - 2013

4. Llegadas de turistas no residentes en todo tipo de establecimientos de alojamiento, por país de residencia

Alemania	**China**	Incluido Hong Kong (China).
	Otros países Asia Oriental/Pacífico	Incluida India.
Austria	**Total**	Únicamente alojamiento de pago; excluidas las estancias con amigos y familiares y las viviendas secundarias.
Bélgica	**Total**	Establecimientos hoteleros, terrenos de camping, centros vacacionales, ciudades de vacaciones y categorías específicas de alojamiento. A partir de 2012 se incluye "bed and breakfast".
Croacia	**Total**	Excluidas las llegadas a puertos de turismo náutico.
Dinamarca	**Total**	Incluido el turismo no comercial. 2011: cambio de metodología.
España	**Total**	Llegadas en hoteles, hostales, camping, apartamentos turísticos y alojamientos/casas rurales.
Filipinas	**Total**	Llegadas por vía aérea.
	Nacionales residentes en el extranjero	Titulares de pasaportes filipinos que residen permanentemente en el extranjero; están excluidos los trabajadores filipinos.
Malta	**Total**	Datos procedentes de las salidas por vías aérea y marítima. Fuente: "National Statistics Office"
Países Bajos	**Total**	2013: ruptura en la serie debido a los cambios metodológicos en la determinación de la población.
Rumania	**Otros países de África**	Incluidos Egipto y Libia.

NOTAS 2009 - 2013

5. Pernoctaciones de turistas no residentes en hoteles y establecimientos asimilados, por nacionalidad

Bolivia	**Total**	Datos preliminares. Pernoctaciones en las capitales de departamento.
Chad	**Total**	2010: Datos parciales.
Italia	**Total**	Pernoctaciones en los hoteles únicamente.
Madagascar	**Total**	Todos los establecimientos categorizados por estrellas (clasificados y no clasificados).
Marruecos	**Total**	Pernoctaciones en hoteles clasificados, ciudades de vacaciones, residencias turísticas y Riad.
Montenegro	**Serbia**	Incluidas las llegadas de Kosovo.
Noruega	**Total**	Pernoctaciones en los establecimientos registrados. Los datos cubren solamente los establecimientos con una capacidad de 20 o más camas.
Palestina	**Total**	Fuente: "Palestinian Central Bureau of Statistics, 2014. Hotel Activity Survey 2013. Ramallah - Palestine". Los datos sobre la industria hotelera para 2012 y 2013 representan a Cisjordania únicamente.
República Árabe Siria	**Total**	Encuesta del turismo receptor.
Turquía	**Total**	Hoteles homologados, moteles, pensiones, albergues, apartahoteles, ciudades de vacaciones y hoteles especiales. Resultados de la encuesta mensual realizada en ciertos establecimientos de alojamiento autorizados por el Ministerio de Turismo.
Yemen	**Total**	Incluidos los nacionales residentes en el extranjero.

NOTAS 2009 - 2013

5. Pernoctaciones de turistas no residentes en hoteles y establecimientos asimilados, por país de residencia

Alemania	**China**	Incluido Hong Kong (China).
	Otros países Asia Oriental/Pacífico	Incluida India.
Austria	**Total**	Hoteles únicamente.
Cabo Verde	**Bélgica**	Incluido los Países Bajos.
Congo	**Total**	Fuente: "Direction Générale du Tourisme et de l'Hôtellerie", encuestas 2009 a 2013.
Croacia	**Total**	Según el Reglamento sobre clasificación, normas mínimas y categorización de las instalaciones de alojamiento, los datos para los hoteles y establecimientos asimilados no incluyen posadas ni "Bed and Breakfast" (habitación con desayuno) desde 2006.
Dinamarca	**Total**	Hoteles únicamente. 2011: cambio de metodología.
España	**Total**	Pernoctaciones en hoteles y hostales.
Francia	**Total**	Fuente: "Insee", "Dge", socios regionales. Encuesta de ocupación hotelera ("EFH").
Israel	**Total**	Pernoctaciones en hoteles de turismo y apartahoteles.
	Todos los países de América del Sur	Incluida América Central.
Luxemburgo	**Total**	NACE Rev2 55.100
Macao (China)	**Total**	Fuente de los datos: Encuesta mensual de hoteles y establecimientos asimilados
Nueva Caledonia	**Total**	Corresponde a los hoteles de Noumea.
Países Bajos	**Total**	2013: ruptura en la serie debido a los cambios metodológicos en la determinación de la población.
Polonia	**Total**	Excluidos los hostales.
Rumania	**Otros países de África**	Incluidos Egipto y Libia.
Suiza	**Total**	Incluidos los establecimientos de cura.
	Todos los países de África del Norte	Argelia, Libia, Marruecos y Túnez.
Togo	**Burkina Faso**	Incluidos Malí y Níger.

855

NOTAS 2009 - 2013

6. Pernoctaciones de turistas no residentes en todo tipo de establecimientos de alojamiento, por nacionalidad

Hungría	**Total**	Establecimientos de alojamiento colectivo.
Montenegro	**Serbia**	Incluidas las llegadas de Kosovo.
República Árabe Siria	**Total**	Encuesta del turismo receptor.
República de Moldova	**Total**	Excluido el margen izquierdo del río Nistru y la municipalidad de Bender.
Turquía	**Total**	Resultados de la encuesta mensual realizada en ciertos establecimientos de alojamiento autorizados por el Ministerio de Turismo.

NOTAS 2009 - 2013

6. Pernoctaciones de turistas no residentes en todo tipo de establecimientos de alojamiento, por país de residencia

Alemania	**China**	Incluido Hong Kong (China).
	Otros países Asia Oriental/Pacífico	Incluida India.
Austria	**Total**	Únicamente alojamiento de pago; excluidas las estancias con amigos y familiares y las viviendas secundarias.
Bahamas	**Total**	Pernoctaciones en todo tipo de alojamiento comercial.
Bélgica	**Total**	Establecimientos hoteleros, terrenos de camping, centros vacacionales, ciudades de vacaciones y categorías específicas de alojamiento. A partir de 2012 se incluye "bed and breakfast".
Canadá	**Total**	Fuente: "Canadian Tourism Commission" y "Statistics Canada"
	China	Incluidos Mongolia y Tibet.
	Estonia	Incluidos Letonia y Lituania.
	Hungría	Incluidos Eslovenia, Bulgaria y Rumania.
	Dinamarca	Incluidas Islas Feroe.
	Reino Unido	Incluido Gibraltar.
	Italia	Incluidos San Marino, Santa Sede y Malta.
	Yugoslavia, RSF (antigua)	Incluidos Croacia, Bosnia y Herzegovina, Ex República Yugoslava de Macedonia y Albania.
	Francia	Incluidos Andorra y Mónaco.
	Suiza	Incluido Liechtenstein.
Croacia	**Total**	Excluidas las pernoctaciones en puertos de turismo náutico.
Dinamarca	**Total**	Incluido el turismo no comercial. 2011: cambio de metodología.
España	**Total**	Pernoctaciones en hoteles, hostales, camping, apartamentos turísticos y alojamientos/casas rurales.
Francia	**Total**	Fuente: "Dge", "Banque de France". Encuesta a los visitantes que vienen del extranjero ("EVE") - resultados 2012 revisados, resultados 2013 provisionales.
	Todos los países de África del Norte	Argelia, Egipto, Libia, Marruecos y Túnez.
	China	Incluidos Hong-Kong (China) y Macao (China).
	Suiza	Incluido Liechtentein.
Irlanda	**Total**	Incluidas pernoctaciones en alojamiento privado gratuito (casas de huéspedes y casas particulares).
	Reino Unido	Incluidos los residentes de Irlanda del Norte.
Jamaica	**Total**	Se ha obtenido la información multiplicando la duración media de estancia por el número de turistas (stop-overs) procedentes de cada país de origen. Excluidos los nacionales residentes en el extranjero.
	Otros países de las Américas	América Latina.
	Todos los países de Europa	Reino unido y resto de Europa.
Malta	**Total**	Datos basados en las pernoctaciones de los turistas que salen (por vía aérea y vía marítima). Fuente: "National Statistics Office"
Países Bajos	**Total**	Excluidas las pernoctaciones en instalaciones fijas (alquiladas anualmente o por temporada). 2013: ruptura en la serie debido a los cambios metodológicos en la determinación de la población.
Rumania	**Otros países de África**	Incluidos Egipto y Libia.

Yearbook of Tourism Statistics, Data 2009 – 2013, 2015 Edition

DATA SOURCES

Albania	Institute of Statistics – INSTAT
	http://www.instat.gov.al/
Algeria	Ministère du Tourisme et de l'Artisanat
	Office National des Statistiques
	http://www.mta.gov.dz
American Samoa	Department of Commerce - Statistics Division
	http://www.spc.int/prism/americansamoa/
Andorra	Ministerio de Turismo y Medio Ambiente
	Ministerio de Finanzas
	http://www.estadistica.ad/serveiestudis/web/index.asp?lang=2
Angola	Ministério de Hotelaria e Turismo - Gabinete de Estudos, Planeamento e Estatística
Anguilla	Anguilla Statistics Department - Ministry of Finance, Economic Development, Investment, Commerce and Tourism
	http://www.gov.ai/statistics/cab_external.htm
Antigua and Barbuda	Ministry of Tourism
	http://www.visitantiguabarbuda.com/
Argentina	Dirección de Estudios de Mercado y Estadística - Secretaría de Turismo de la Nación
	http://www.turismo.gov.ar/
	http://desarrolloturistico.gob.ar/estadistica/ultimas-cifras
Armenia	Tourism Department - Ministry of Economy of the Republic of Armenia
	http://www.armstat.am/en/
Aruba	Aruba Tourism Authority
	http://www.cbs.aw/index.php/statistics/tables-statistics/68-tables/tourism
Australia	Australian Bureau of Statistics
	http://www.abs.gov.au/
Austria	Statistics Austria
	http://www.statistik.at/web_en/statistics/tourism/accommodation/index.html
Azerbaijan	Ministry of Culture and Tourism
	Sate Statistical Committee
	http://www.stat.gov.az
Bahamas	Bahamas Ministry of Tourism
	http://www.tourismtoday.com/home/statistics/
Bahrain	Tourism Sector - Ministry of Culture and Information
	Central Informatics Organization (CIO)
Bangladesh	Bangladesh Bureau of Statistics (BBS)
Barbados	Barbados Tourism Marketing Inc
	http://www.tourism.gov.bb/tourism-publications.html
Belarus	State Border Committee
	National Statistical Committee of the Republic of Belarus
Belgium	Institut National de Statistique
Belize	Belize Tourist Board
Benin	Direction du développement et de promotion touristiques - Ministère de la culture, de l'alphabétisation, de l'artisanat et du tourisme
Bermuda	Bermuda Department of Tourism
	http://www.gov.bm/portal/server.pt?space=CommunityPage&control=SetCommunity&CommunityID=227
Bhutan	Department of Tourism - Royal Government of Bhutan
	http://www.nsb.gov.bt/index.php?id=13
	http://www.tourism.gov.bt/annual-reports/bhutan-tourism-monitor
Bolivia	Instituto Nacional de Estadística
	http://www.ine.gov.bo/default.aspx
Bosnia and Herzegovina	Agency for Statistics of Bosnia and Herzegovina
	http://www.bhas.ba

DATA SOURCES

Brazil	Ministério do Turismo
	http://www.dadosefatos.turismo.gov.br/dadosefatos/home.html
British Virgin Islands	Central Statistics Office
Brunei Darussalam	Brunei Tourism - Ministry of Industry and Primary Resources
Bulgaria	Ministry of Economy, Energy and Tourism
	National Statistical Institute
	Bulgarian National Bank
	http://www.nsi.bg/otrasalen.php?otr=57
Burkina Faso	Service de l'analyse statistique et de la Coopération touristique - Ministère de la Culture, des Arts et du Tourisme
	http://www.insd.bf/
Cabo Verde	Instituto Nacional de Estatística
	Ministério da Economia, Crescimento e Competitividade
	http://www.ine.cv/dadostats/dados.aspx?d=2
Cambodia	Ministry of Tourism
	http://www.tourismcambodia.org/mot/index.php?view=statistic_report#comp
Canada	Canadian Tourism Commission
	Statistics Canada
	http://en-corporate.canada.travel/research/statistics-figures
Cayman Islands	Cayman Islands Department of Tourism
	http://www.caymanislands.ky/statistics/
	http://www.eso.ky
Central African Republic	Ministère de l'Economie forestière, de l'environnement et du Tourisme
Chad	Ministère du Tourisme et de l'Artisanat - Direction de la Planification et des Études Prospectives
Chile	Servicio Nacional de Turismo - SERNATUR
	http://www.sernatur.cl/estadisticas-sernatur
China	National Tourism Administration
	http://en.cnta.gov.cn/
Colombia	Departamento Administrativo de Seguridad (DAS) / Migración Colombia / Puertos Marítimos
	Ministerio de Comercio, Industria y Turismo
	http://www.mincomercio.gov.co
Comoros	Direction Nationale de la Promotion du Tourisme et de l'Hôtellerie - Ministère du Transport, Tourisme, Postes et Télécommunications
	Banque centrale des Comores
Congo	Direction Générale du Tourisme et de l'Hôtellerie - Ministère du tourisme et de l'environnement
Cook Islands	Cook Islands Tourism Corporation
	Cook Islands Statistics Office
Costa Rica	Banco Central de Costa Rica (BCCR)
	Instituto Costarricense de Turismo (ICT)
	Instituto Nacional de Estadística y Censos (INEC)
	http://www.visitcostarica.com/ict/paginas/modEst/estudios_demanda_turistica.asp?ididioma=1
Croatia	Croatian Bureau of Statistics
	http://www.dzs.hr/default_e.htm
	http://www.mint.hr/default.aspx?id=363
Cuba	Oficina Nacional de Estadística e Información
	http://www.one.cu/sitioone2006.asp
Curaçao	Curaçao Tourist Board
	http://www.curacao.com/en/directory/corporate/statistics-and-downloads/
Cyprus	Statistical Service of Cyprus
	Cyprus Tourism Organization
	http://www.mof.gov.cy/mof/cystat/statistics.nsf/index_en/index_en?OpenDocument
Czech Republic	Czech Statistical Office, TSA
	Ministry for Regional Development
	http://www.czso.cz/eng/redakce.nsf/i/home

859

DATA SOURCES

Democratic Republic of the Congo	Office National du Tourisme
Denmark	VisitDenmark Statistics Denmark http://www.dst.dk/HomeUK.aspx
Dominica	Discover Dominica Authority http://tourism.gov.dm/statistics
Dominican Republic	Ministerio de Turismo http://www.bancentral.gov.do/estadisticas_economicas/turismo/
Ecuador	Ministerio de Turismo http://servicios.turismo.gob.ec/index.php/?option=com_content&view=article&id=30#comp-i
Egypt	Ministry of Tourism
El Salvador	Corporación Salvadoreña de Turismo (CORSATUR) - Ministerio de Turismo
Eritrea	Ministry of Tourism
Estonia	Estonian Tourist Board / Enterprise Estonia http://pub.stat.ee/px-web.2001/I_Databas/Economy/databasetree.asp http://visitestonia.com/en/additional-navigation/press-room/eas-views-on-tourism/estonian-tourism-statistics
Ethiopia	Ministry of Culture and Tourism
Fiji	Fiji Islands Bureau of Statistics http://www.statsfiji.gov.fj/
Finland	Tourism Statistics - Statistics Finland http://www.mek.fi/w5/mekfi/index.nsf/(pages)/Tutkimukset_ja_tilastot
France	DGE (Direction générale des entreprises) INSEE (Institut national de la statistique et des études économiques) http://www.entreprises.gouv.fr/etudes-et-statistiques/statistiques-du-tourisme/accueil http://www.insee.fr/fr/default.asp
French Polynesia	Institut de la Statistique - ISPF http://www.ispf.pf/Home.aspx
Gambia	Gambia Tourism Authority http://www.visitthegambia.gm
Georgia	Georgian National Tourism Agency - Ministry of Economy and Sustainable Development National Statistics Office of Georgia http://www.gnta.ge/?61/statistics/&lan=en
Germany	Statistiches Bundesamt http://www.destatis.de
Greece	Hellenic Statistical Authority (EL.STAT.) http://www.statistics.gr/portal/page/portal/ESYE
Grenada	Grenada Board of Tourism
Guadeloupe	Comité du Tourisme des Îles de la Guadeloupe
Guam	Guam Visitors Bureau http://www.bsp.guam.gov http://www.visitguam.org
Guatemala	Instituto Guatemalteco de Turismo - INGUAT http://www.inguat.gob.gt/estadisticas.php
Guinea	Division Observatoire du Tourisme - Ministère du Tourisme, de l'Hôtellerie et de l'Artisanat
Guyana	Guyana Tourism Authority
Haiti	Ministère du Tourisme
Honduras	Instituto Hondureño de Turismo http://www.iht.hn
Hong Kong, China	Hong Kong Tourism Board http://partnernet.hktb.com/en/research_statistics/index.html http://www.censtatd.gov.hk/hong_kong_statistics/index.jsp

DATA SOURCES

Hungary	Hungarian Central statistical Office
	http://www.ksh.hu/tourism_catering
Iceland	Hagstofa Íslands Statistics Iceland
	http://www.statice.is/Statistics/Tourism,-transport-and-informati
India	Ministry of Tourism - Government of India
	http://tourism.gov.in/
Indonesia	Ministry of Tourism and Creative Economy BPS Statistics Indonesia
	http://www.bps.go.id/eng/menutab.php?tabel=1&kat=2&id_subyek=16 http://www.parekraf.go.id
Iran, Islamic Republic of	Iran Cultural Heritage and Tourism Organization (ICHTO)
Iraq	Ministry of Tourism and Antiquities
Ireland	Fáilte Ireland
	http://www.failteireland.ie/
Israel	Ministry of Tourism
	http://www1.cbs.gov.il/reader/?MIval=cw_usr_view_SHTML&ID=432
Italy	Banca d'Italia Istituto Nazionale di Statistica (ISTAT)
	http://www.bancaditalia.it http://www.istat.it
Jamaica	Jamaica Tourist Board
	http://www.jtbonline.org/statistics/Annual%20Travel/Forms/AllItems.aspx
Japan	Japan Tourism Agency Japan National Tourism Organization
	http://www.mlit.go.jp/kankocho/en/siryou/toukei/index.html http://www.tourism.jp/en/statistics/
Jordan	Ministry of Tourism and Antiquities
	http://www.tourism.jo
Kazakhstan	Agency of Statistics of the Republic of Kazakhstan
Kenya	Kenya Tourist Board
Kiribati	Kiribati National Tourism Office Ministry of Communication, Transport and Tourism Development PATA
Korea, Republic of	Ministry of Culture, Sports and Tourism
	http://kto.visitkorea.or.kr/eng/tourismStatics/keyFacts/visitorArrivals.kto
Kuwait	Central Statistical Bureau
	http://www.csb.gov.kw/Socan_Statistic_EN.aspx?ID=19
Kyrgyzstan	National Statistical Committee
Lao People's Democratic Republic	Lao National Tourism Administration Ministry of Information, Culture and Tourism - Tourism Development Department
	http://www.tourismlaos.org/show.php?Cont_ID=43
Latvia	Transport and Tourism Statistics Section - Central Statistical Bureau
	http://www.csb.gov.lv/en/statistikas-temas/tourism-key-indicators-30715.html
Lebanon	Ministère du Tourisme
Lesotho	Lesotho Tourism Development Corporation
	http://www.ltdc.org.ls/researchArrivalStats.php
Liechtenstein	Office of Statistics Liechtenstein. Tourism Statistics
	http://www.llv.li/#/11961/tourismusstatistik
Lithuania	Lithuanian State Department of Tourism
	http://www.stat.gov.lt/
Luxembourg	STATEC
	http://www.statistiques.public.lu

DATA SOURCES

Macao, China	Statistics and Census Service Macau Government Tourist Office http://www.dsec.gov.mo/Statistic/TourismAndServices/VisitorArrivals.aspx http://industry.macautourism.gov.mo/en/index.php
Madagascar	Ministère des Transports et du Tourisme
Malawi	Ministry of Tourism, Wildlife and Culture
Malaysia	Department of Statistics Malaysia Tourism Malaysia http://corporate.tourism.gov.my/research.asp?page=facts_figures
Maldives	Ministry of Tourism http://www.tourism.gov.mv
Mali	Office malien du tourisme et de l'hôtellerie (O.MA.T.HO)
Malta	Malta Tourism Authority National Statistics Office http://www.mta.com.mt/research http://www.nso.gov.mt
Marshall Islands	Marshall Islands Visitors Authority
Martinique	Comité Martiniquais du Tourisme
Mauritius	Ministry of Tourism and Leisure http://tourism.govmu.org/English/Pages/default.aspx
Mexico	Secretaría de Turismo de México (SECTUR) Instituto Nacional de Estadística y Geografía (INEGI) http://www.datatur.beta.sectur.gob.mx/SitePages/Inicio.aspx http://www.inegi.org.mx
Micronesia, Federated States of	Office of Staistics, Budget and Economic Management, Overseas Development Assistance, and Compact Management http://www.sboc.fm
Monaco	Direction du Tourisme et des Congrès http://www.imsee.mc
Mongolia	National Tourism Center - Ministry of Nature, Environment and Tourism
Montenegro	Ministry of Sustainable Development and Tourism http://www.monstat.org/eng/page.php?id=43&pageid=43
Montserrat	Statistics Department Montserrat
Morocco	Ministère du tourisme http://www.tourisme.gov.ma/
Mozambique	Ministry of Tourism Instituto Nacional de Estatística http://www.ine.gov.mz
Myanmar	Ministry of Hotels and Tourism http://www.myanmartourism.org/
Namibia	Ministry of Environment and Tourism Namibian Tourism Board http://www.namibiatourism.com.na/research-center/
Nepal	Nepal Tourism Board Ministry of Culture, Tourism and Civil Aviation http://www.tourism.gov.np
Netherlands	Statistics Netherlands http://www.cbs.nl/en-GB/menu/themas/vrije-tijd-cultuur/nieuws/default.htm
New Caledonia	Institut de la Statistique et des Études Économiques (ISEE) http://www.isee.nc/
New Zealand	Statistics New Zealand (SNZ) Ministry of Business, Innovation & Employment (MBIE) http://www.stats.govt.nz/ http://www.med.govt.nz/sectors-industries/tourism/tourism-research-data

DATA SOURCES

Nicaragua	Instituto Nicaragüense de Turismo (INTUR)
	http://www.intur.gob.ni/index.php?option=com_content&view=article&id=27&Itemid=14
Niger	Ministère du Tourisme et de l'Artisanat
	Institut National de la Statistique
	http://www.stat-niger.org/statistique/
Nigeria	Nigerian Tourism Development Corporation
Niue	Statistics Niue
Northern Mariana Islands	Marianas Visitors Authority
Norway	Statistics Norway
	Institute of Transport Economics
	http://www.ssb.no/english/subjects/
Oman	Ministry of Tourism
	Ministry of National Economy
	http://www.omantourism.gov.om
Pakistan	Pakistan Tourism Development Corporation - Ministry of Tourism
Palau	Office of Planning and Statistics, Bureau of Budget and Planning - Ministry of Finance
	Palau Visitors Authority
	http://www.visit-palau.com/
Palestine	Palestinian Central Bureau of Statistics
	http://www.pcbs.gov.ps
Panama	Autoridad de Turismo de Panamá
	http://www.atp.gob.pa
Papua New Guinea	Papua New Guinea Tourism Promotion Authority
	http://www.tpa.papuanewguinea.travel/
Paraguay	Secretaría Nacional de Turismo - SENATUR
	http://www.senatur.gov.py
Peru	Superintendencia Nacional de Migraciones
	Banco Central de Reserva del Perú
	Ministerio de Comercio Exterior y Turismo
	http://www.mincetur.gob.pe/newweb/Default.aspx?tabid=141
Philippines	Department of Tourism
	http://www.tourism.gov.ph/Pages/TourismResearch.aspx
Poland	Institute of Tourism
	http://www.intur.com.pl/itenglish/institute_en.htm
Portugal	Turismo de Portugal, I.P.
	http://www.ine.pt/xportal/xmain?xpid=INE&xpgid=ine_main
Puerto Rico	Junta de Planificación de Puerto Rico
	Compañía de Turismo de Puerto Rico
	http://www.jp.gobierno.pr/
Qatar	Qatar Statistics Authority
	www.qatartourism.gov.qa
Republic of Moldova	National Bureau of Statistics
	http://www.statistica.md/category.php?l=en&idc=293&
Reunion	Institut National de la Statistique et des Études Économique - INSEE
	Comité du Tourisme de la Réunion
	http://observatoire.reunion.fr/les-chiffres-cles.html
Romania	National Institute of Statistics
	http://www.insse.ro/cms/en
Russian Federation	Russian Federal Agency for Tourism
Rwanda	Rwanda Development Board
	http://www.rdb.rw/welcome-to-rwanda/tourism-research-and-statistics.html

863

DATA SOURCES

Saint Kitts and Nevis	Ministry of Sustainable Development Eastern Caribbean Central Bank http://www.eccb-centralbank.org/Statistics/index.asp#tourismdata
Saint Lucia	Saint Lucia Tourist Board http://investstlucia.com/sectors/view/tourism.html
Saint Vincent and the Grenadines	St. Vincent and the Grenadines Tourism Authority http://www.discoversvg.com/index.php/es/about-svg/tourism-statistics
Samoa	Samoa Tourism Authority Statistical Services Division (Ministry of Finance) http://www.sbs.gov.ws http://www.mof.gov.ws
San Marino	Segreteria di Stato per il Turismo ed i Rapporti con l'AASS http://www.statistica.sm/on-line/home/dati-statistici/attivita-economiche-e-turismo.html
Sao Tome and Principe	Direcçao do Turismo e Hotelaria
Saudi Arabia	The Saudi Commission for Tourism and Antiquities (SCTA) http://www.mas.gov.sa/
Serbia	Statistical Office of the Republic of Serbia National Bank of Serbia http://webrzs.stat.gov.rs/WebSite/
Seychelles	National Bureau of Statistics Seychelles Tourism Board http://www.nbs.gov.sc/
Sierra Leone	National Tourist Board Statistics Sierra Leone http://www.statistics.sl/
Singapore	Singapore Tourism Board http://www.singstat.gov.sg https://app.stb.gov.sg/asp/tou/tou02.asp#VS
Sint Maarten	St. Maarten Tourist Bureau Department of Statistics Sint Maarten http://stat.gov.sx/
Slovakia	Statistical Office of the Slovak Republic National Bank of Slovakia www.statistics.sk www.nbs.sk www.mindop.sk
Slovenia	Statistical Office - Tourism Statistics, Structual Business Statistics, Statistical register of employment Bank of Slovenia http://www.stat.si/eng/tema_ekonomsko_turizem.asp
Solomon Islands	Solomon Islands National Statistics Office
South Africa	Statistics South Africa South African Tourism http://www.statssa.gov.za/default.asp
Spain	Instituto de Estudios Turísticos Instituto Nacional de Estadística http://www.iet.tourspain.es/paginas/home.aspx?idioma=es-ES http://www.ine.es/inebmenu/mnu_hosteleria.htm
Sri Lanka	Sri Lanka Tourist Board http://www.sltda.lk/statistics
Sudan	Ministry of Tourism and Wildlife
Suriname	Suriname Tourism Foundation
Swaziland	Swaziland Tourism Authority Ministry of Tourism and Environmental Affairs http://www.thekingdomofswaziland.com/pages/content/index.asp?PageID=57

DATA SOURCES

Sweden	Swedish Agency for Economic and Regional Growth - Tillväxtverket
	http://www.tillvaxtverket.se/english http://www.scb.se/Pages/Product____11830.aspx
Switzerland	Swiss Federal Statistical Office
	http://www.bfs.admin.ch/bfs/portal/fr/index/themen/10.html
Syrian Arab Republic	Ministry of Tourism - Survey of the incoming tourism
Taiwan (Province of China)	Planning Division Tourism Bureau - Ministry of Transportation and Communication
	http://admin.taiwan.net.tw/statistics/release_en.aspx?no=7
Tajikistan	Committee of Youth Affairs, Sports and Tourism under the Government of the Republic of Tajikistan
Thailand	Ministry of Tourism and Sports
	http://www.tourism.go.th/home
The Former Yugoslav Republic of Macedonia	State Statistical Office
	http://www.stat.gov.mk/OblastOpsto_en.aspx?id=25
Timor-Leste	Direcçao Nacional de Estatística
	http://dne.mof.gov.tl/publications/index.htm
Togo	Ministère du Tourisme
Tonga	Ministry of Commerce, Tourism and Labour
Trinidad and Tobago	Tourism Development Company Limited
	http://www.tdc.co.tt/stopover_statistics.htm
Tunisia	Ministère du Tourisme - Office National du Tourisme Institut National de la Statistique
	http://www.ins.nat.tn/indexfr.php
Turkey	Ministry of Culture and Tourism
	http://sgb.kulturturizm.gov.tr/belge/1-90750/turizm-istatistikleri.html http://www.turkstat.gov.tr/PreTablo.do?tb_id=51&ust_id=14
Turks and Caicos Islands	Turks and Caicos Tourist Board
Tuvalu	Ministry of Foreign Affairs, Trade, Tourism, Environment and Labour
	http://www.spc.int/prism/tuvalu/index.php/migration-and-tourism
Uganda	Ministry of Tourism, Trade and Industry Uganda Bureau of Statistics
	http://www.ubos.org/?st=pagerelations2&id=19&p=related%20pages%202:Migration%20and%20Tourism%20Statistics
Ukraine	State Statistics Committee of Ukraine
	http://www.ukrstat.gov.ua/operativ/operativ2007/tyr/tyr_e/arh_vig_e.html
United Kingdom	VisitBritain Office for National Statistics
	http://www.visitbritain.org/insightsandstatistics/ http://www.ons.gov.uk/ons/index.html
United Republic of Tanzania	Tourism Division - Ministry of Natural Resources and Tourism National Bureau of Statistics
United States of America	U.S. Department of Commerce - National Travel and Tourism Office
	http://travel.trade.gov http://www.ahla.com/content.aspx?id=3448
United States Virgin Islands	Bureau of Economic Research
	http://www.usviber.org/publications.htm
Uruguay	Ministerio de Turismo y Deporte
	http://www.turismo.gub.uy/index.php/es/estadistica
Uzbekistan	National Company "Uzbektourism"
Vanuatu	Vanuatu National Statistics Office
	http://www.vnso.gov.vu/
Venezuela	Ministerio del Poder Popular para el Turismo
	http://www.mintur.gob.ve/mintur/turismo-en-cifras-2/

Yearbook of Tourism Statistics, Data 2009 – 2013, 2015 Edition

DATA SOURCES

Viet Nam	Viet Nam National Administration of Tourism General Statistics Office http://www.vietnamtourism.com/e_pages/news/index.asp?loai=1&chucnang=07 http://www.gso.gov.vn/default_en.aspx?tabid=491
Yemen	Ministry of Tourism Central Statistical Organization http://www.yementourism.com/statistics/ http://www.cso-yemen.org/content.php?lng=english&pcat=131
Zambia	Ministry of Tourism and Arts
Zimbabwe	Zimbabwe Tourism Authority – ZTA http://www.zimbabwetourism.net/directory/index.php/downloads/category/tourism-trends

Other UNWTO publications of interest!

**Compendium
of Tourism Statistics
Data 2009 – 2013
2015 Edition**

trilingual version

**Measuring Employment in the
Tourism Industry –
Guide and Best Practices**

published in English

**International
Recommendations for
Tourism Statistics 2008**

published in
English, Spanish, French, Russian
Arabic and Chinese

**Tourism Satellite Account –
Recommended
Methodological Framework
2008**

published in
English, Spanish, French, Russian
Arabic and Chinese

**UNWTO
World Tourism Barometer**

Six numbers per year
published in English, Spanish,
French and Russian

**Statistical Data in Excel™
Format**
 – Data from 2009 – 2013
 – Data from 1995 onwards

Seperate country tables
in Excel™ format,
updated three times per year

**Statistics and TSA
Issue Paper Series** (2013)

– Governance for the Tourism
  Sector and its Measurement

– Regional Tourism Satellite
  Account

– The Economic Impact
  of Tourism – Overview and
  Examples of Macroeconomic
  Analysis

**Sources and Methods: Labour
Statistics – Employment in the
Tourism Industries
(Special Edition)**

published in English

For UNWTO publications in printed version visit the UNWTO Infoshop: www.unwto.org/infoshop …
… and for the electronic versions visit the UNWTO Elibrary: www.e-unwto.org